Vietnam

Nick Ray
Peter Dragicevich, Regis St Louis

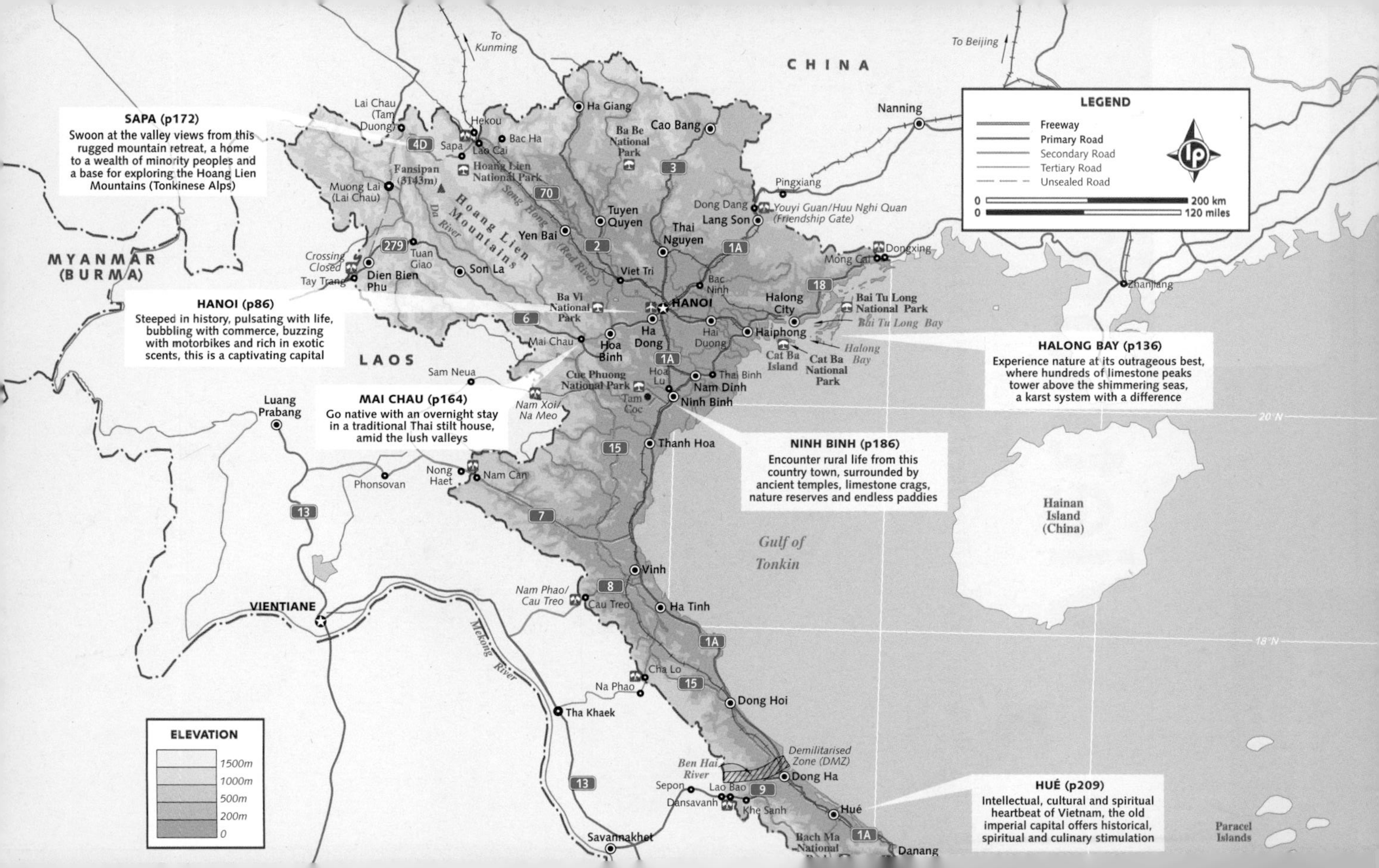

CHINA
MYANMAR (BURMA)
LAOS
SAPA (p172)
Swoon at the valley views from this rugged mountain retreat, a home to a wealth of minority peoples and a base for exploring the Hoang Lien Mountains (Tonkinese Alps)
HANOI (p86)
Steeped in history, pulsating with life, bubbling with commerce, buzzing with motorbikes and rich in exotic scents, this is a captivating capital
MAI CHAU (p164)
Go native with an overnight stay in a traditional Thai stilt house, amid the lush valleys
NINH BINH (p186)
Encounter rural life from this country town, surrounded by ancient temples, limestone crags, nature reserves and endless paddies
HALONG BAY (p136)
Experience nature at its outrageous best, where hundreds of limestone peaks tower above the shimmering seas, a karst system with a difference
HUÉ (p209)
Intellectual, cultural and spiritual heartbeat of Vietnam, the old imperial capital offers historical, spiritual and culinary stimulation
LEGEND
Freeway
Primary Road
Secondary Road
Tertiary Road
Unsealed Road
0 200 km
0 120 miles
ELEVATION
1500m
1000m
500m
200m
0
To Kunming
To Beijing
Nanning
Pingxiang
Youyi Guan/Huu Nghi Quan (Friendship Gate)
Dong Dang
Lang Son
Cao Bang
Ba Be National Park
Ha Giang
Tuyen Quyen
Thai Nguyen
Lai Chau (Tam Duong)
Hekou
Bac Ha
Sapa
Lao Cai
Hoang Lien National Park
Fansipan (3143m)
Muong Lai (Lai Chau)
Hoang Lien Mountains
Song Hong (Red River)
Da River
Yen Bai
Viet Tri
Bac Ninh
HANOI
Ha Dong
Hai Duong
Haiphong
Halong City
Mong Cai
Dongxing
Zhanjiang
Bai Tu Long National Park
Bai Tu Long Bay
Halong Bay
Cat Ba Island
Cat Ba National Park
Crossing Closed
Tay Trang
Dien Bien Phu
Tuan Giao
Son La
Ba Vi National Park
Mai Chau
Hoa Binh
Hoa Lu
Thai Binh
Nam Dinh
Ninh Binh
Cuc Phuong National Park
Tam Coc
Sam Neua
Nam Xoi/ Na Meo
Luang Prabang
Thanh Hoa
Nong Haet
Nam Can
Phonsovan
Hainan Island (China)
Gulf of Tonkin
20°N
18°N
Vinh
Nam Phao/ Cau Treo
Cau Treo
Ha Tinh
VIENTIANE
Mekong River
Cha Lo
Na Phao
Tha Khaek
Dong Hoi
Demilitarised Zone (DMZ)
Ben Hai River
Sepon
Lao Bao
Dong Ha
Dansavanh
Khe Sanh
Hué
Savannakhet
Bach Ma National
Danang
Paracel Islands
4D
70
3
2
1A
18
279
6
15
7
13
8
9

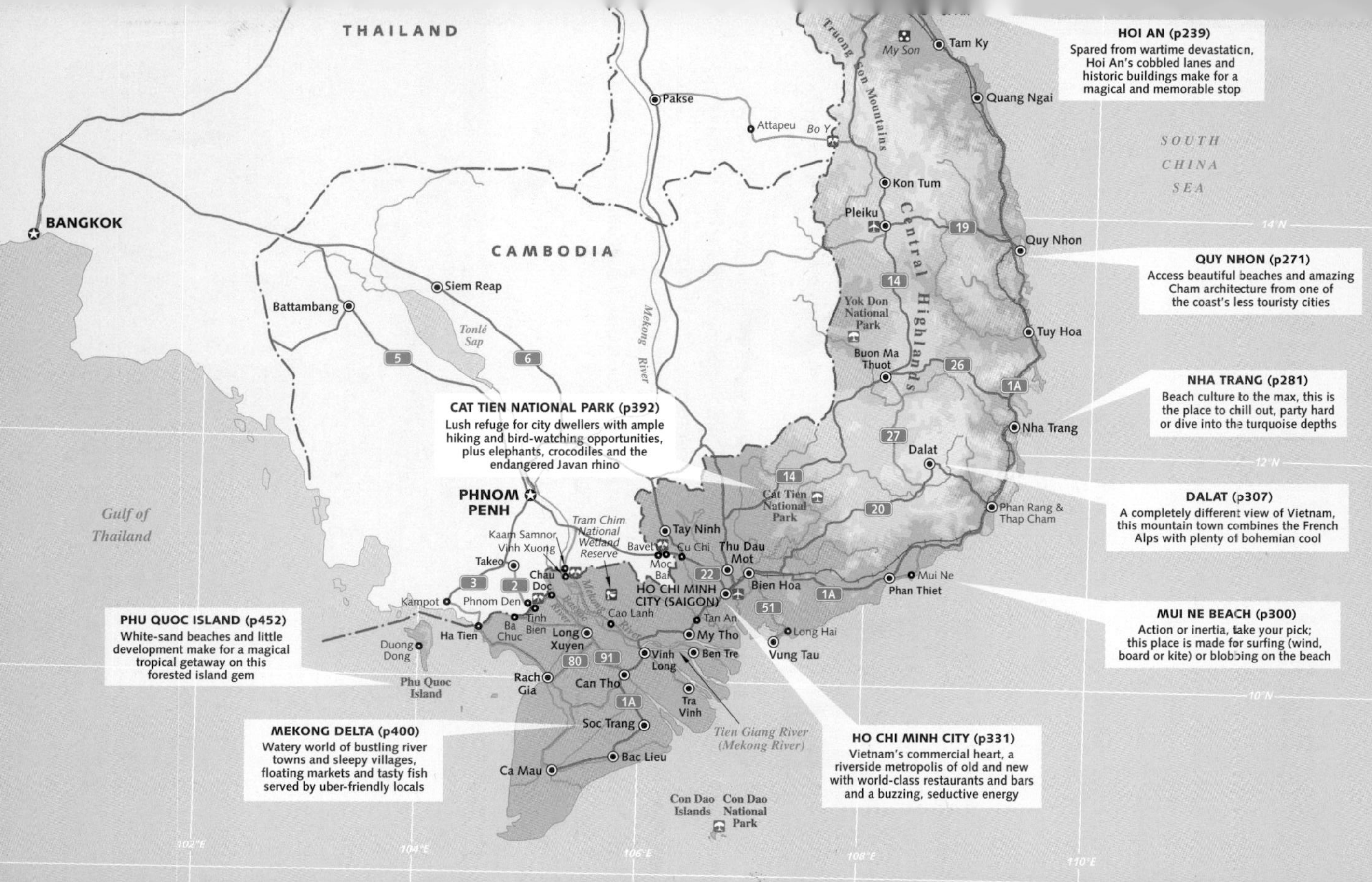
HOI AN (p239)
Spared from wartime devastation, Hoi An's cobbled lanes and historic buildings make for a magical and memorable stop
QUY NHON (p271)
Access beautiful beaches and amazing Cham architecture from one of the coast's less touristy cities
NHA TRANG (p281)
Beach culture to the max, this is the place to chill out, party hard or dive into the turquoise depths
DALAT (p307)
A completely different view of Vietnam, this mountain town combines the French Alps with plenty of bohemian cool
MUI NE BEACH (p300)
Action or inertia, take your pick; this place is made for surfing (wind, board or kite) or blobbing on the beach
HO CHI MINH CITY (p331)
Vietnam's commercial heart, a riverside metropolis of old and new with world-class restaurants and bars and a buzzing, seductive energy
MEKONG DELTA (p400)
Watery world of bustling river towns and sleepy villages, floating markets and tasty fish served by uber-friendly locals
PHU QUOC ISLAND (p452)
White-sand beaches and little development make for a magical tropical getaway on this forested island gem
CAT TIEN NATIONAL PARK (p392)
Lush refuge for city dwellers with ample hiking and bird-watching opportunities, plus elephants, crocodiles and the endangered Javan rhino
THAILAND
CAMBODIA
SOUTH CHINA SEA
Gulf of Thailand
BANGKOK
PHNOM PENH
HO CHI MINH CITY (SAIGON)
Tam Ky
My Son
Quang Ngai
Pakse
Attapeu
Bo Y
Truong Son Mountains
Central Highlands
Kon Tum
Pleiku
Quy Nhon
Yok Don National Park
Tuy Hoa
Buon Ma Thuot
Nha Trang
Dalat
Cat Tien National Park
Phan Rang & Thap Cham
Siem Reap
Battambang
Tonlé Sap
Mekong River
Tay Ninh
Tram Chim National Wetland Reserve
Kaam Samnor
Vinh Xuong
Takeo
Bavet
Cu Chi
Moc Bai
Thu Dau Mot
Bien Hoa
Chau Doc
Phnom Den
Tinh Bien
Ba Chuc
Kampot
Ha Tien
Duong Dong
Phu Quoc Island
Long Xuyen
Cao Lanh
Bassac River
Mekong River
Tan An
My Tho
Vinh Long
Ben Tre
Tra Vinh
Rach Gia
Can Tho
Soc Trang
Bac Lieu
Ca Mau
Tien Giang River (Mekong River)
Vung Tau
Long Hai
Phan Thiet
Mui Ne
Con Dao Islands
Con Dao National Park
1A
5
6
3
2
14
19
20
22
26
27
51
80
91
14°N
12°N
10°N
102°E
104°E
106°E
108°E
110°E

Destination Vietnam

Welcome to another world, a world where the colours are more vivid, the culture is richer, and the history more compelling. This is the world of Vietnam, the latest Asian dragon to awake from its slumber.

Nature has blessed Vietnam with a bountiful harvest. Soaring mountains, a killer coastline and radiant rice fields, Vietnam is simply stunning. Blanketed from head to toe with a patchwork of emerald-green rice paddies, timelessly tended by peasant women in conical hats, this time the brochures don't lie.

The rumble of a million motorbikes, the cries of hawkers and the buzz of business transactions are as ever-present as the tinkle of the past in the pagodas, and the swish of the scythe. Modern Asia meets medieval Asia and, in the Old Quarter of Hanoi, the two become one.

For culinary adventurers, Vietnam is a treasure trove of more than 500 different dishes. It's a wonderful world of pungent herbs and secret spices. Dip delicate spring rolls in *nuoc mam,* a fish sauce that is as compulsory as ketchup for the Vietnamese. Or play 'down-in-one' with *xeo* (rice wine), the whisky of the mountains.

'Nam to a generation, the sorrow of war weighs heavily on the consciousness of all who can remember it, but here the Viet side of the story is told at poignant sites across the country. Fiercely protective of their independence and sovereignty, the Vietnamese are graciously welcoming of foreigners who come as guests not conquerors.

Don't believe the hype. Or the propagandist party billboards that are as common as statues of 'Uncle Ho'. Believe your senses, as you discover one of the most enriching, enlivening and exotic countries on earth.

STU SMUC

STU SMUCKER

Pay a visit to the Black H'mong in Sapa (p172)

Shop till you drop in bustling downtown Ho Chi Minh City (p370)

STU SMUCKER

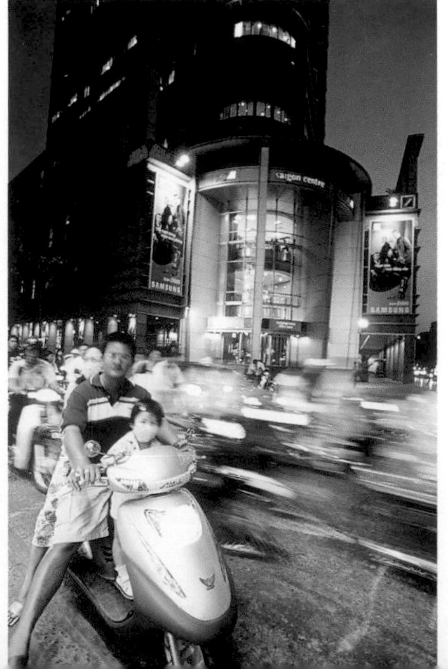

JOHN BANAGAN

Book a boat tour (p287) amid the fishing boats in Nha Trang Harbour, Nha Trang

JOHN BANAGAN

Try a drink with a bit of a bite: snake wine (p49)

Be enchanted by the limestone formations of Hang Thien Cung (p138), Halong Bay

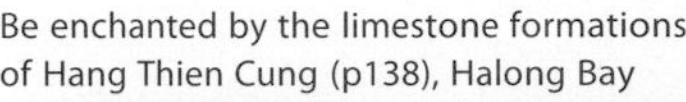

MARK DAFFEY

Opposite:
Have an encounter with the Flower H'mong during a trek to a local village (p181)
STU SMUCKER

Savour the peacefulness of Hoan Kiem Lake (p103), Hanoi

CAROLE MARTIN

STU SMU

Lose yourself in the tranquility of Lang Co (p227), central Vietnam

Enjoy the seafood bounty (p47) of Vietnam's coastline

OLIVER STREWE

SIMON FOALE

Wander the enigmatic Cham ruins at My Son (p262)

DOMINIC BONUCCELLI

Greet some friendly locals in the backpacker district of Pham Ngu Lao (p356), Ho Chi Minh City

Witness the start of the life of a rice noodle (p46)

PATRICK SYDER

Choose from a wealth of Chinese lanterns in Hoi An (p252)

JOHN BANAGAN

MARK DAFFEY

Marvel at the impressive Cham architecture, Po Nagar Cham towers (p283), Nha Trang

Walk past old houses on the Thu Bon River, Hoi An (p239)

MARK DAFFEY

Wonder where your next meal is coming from (p47)

KEREN

MARK DAFFEY

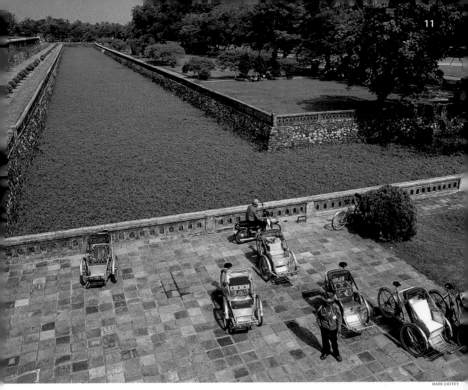

Explore the fascinating Imperial Enclosure (p211), Hué

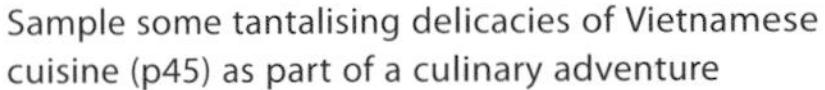

Sample some tantalising delicacies of Vietnamese cuisine (p45) as part of a culinary adventure

GREG ELMS

MICHAEL GEBICKI

Go shopping, Montagnard-style (p157)

PETER SOL

Check out some roadside food stalls in Hanoi (p111)

ANTONY GIBLIN

Light some incense inside Quan Am Pagoda during Tet Festival (p64)

Row your boat all the way to the floating markets (p426) of the Mekong Delta

JOHN BANAGAN

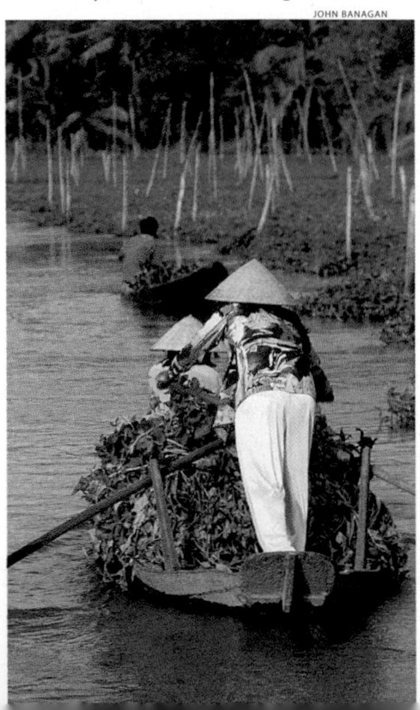

Contents

Regional Map Contents

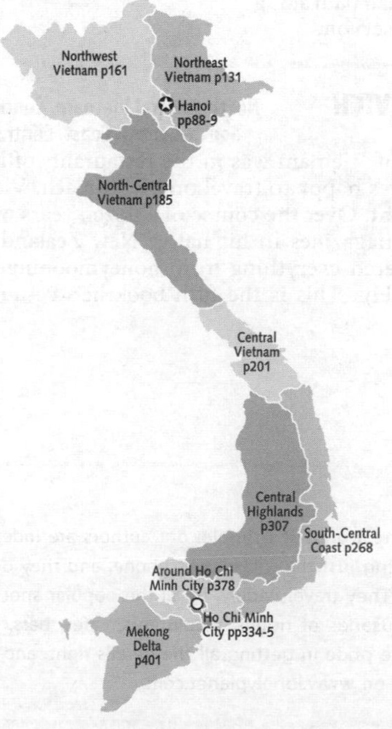

Northwest Vietnam p161
Northeast Vietnam p131
Hanoi pp88-9
North-Central Vietnam p185
Central Vietnam p201
Central Highlands p307
South-Central Coast p268
Around Ho Chi Minh City p378
Ho Chi Minh City pp334-5
Mekong Delta p401

The Authors

NICK RAY

Coordinating Author, Hanoi, Northeast Vietnam, Northwest Vietnam

Nick comes from Watford, the sort of town that makes you want to travel. He has been visiting Vietnam for more than a decade, as a traveller and later leading people astray as an adventure-travel tour leader. Living in Phnom Penh, Vietnam is his backyard of sorts and he has co-authored *Cycling Vietnam, Laos & Cambodia* as well as the *Cambodia* and the new *Vietnam, Cambodia, Laos & the Greater Mekong* books. Nick has been to almost every province from north to south, but he is most at home in the mountains of the north.

Coordinating Author's Favourite Trip

Taking on the northwest mountains on a Minsk is one of the most memorable road trips in Asia. It's hard to leave Hanoi (p86), but the scenery around Mai Chau (p164) makes it easier. The hairpins dropping into the Muong Thanh Valley around Dien Bien Phu (p168) are hard to forget, but the most beautiful road has to be the Tram Ton Pass (p175) into Sapa (p172). It keeps getting better as you go east to Ha Giang (p182) and the incredible road from Dong Van (p183) to Meo Vac (p183). Cross-country to Ba Be National Park (p157) is a rollercoaster, especially in the dark, though 'the road of certain death', a small path along a cliffside, has been submerged by a new reservoir.

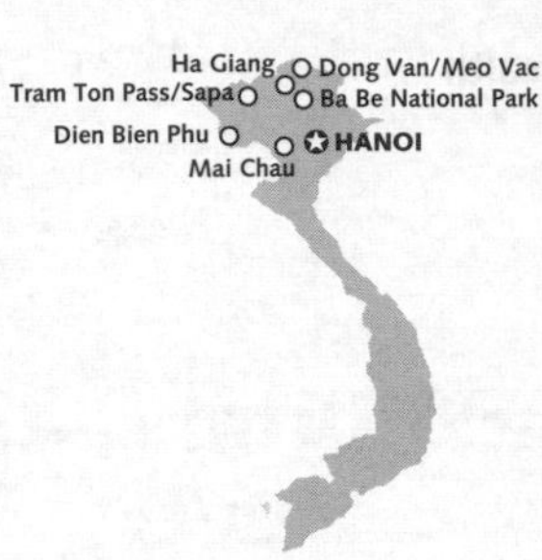

PETER DRAGICEVICH

North-Central Vietnam, Central Vietnam, South-Central Coast, Central Highlands

Peter's first taste of Vietnam was in the restaurants of Melbourne and Sydney. Always happy to travel on his stomach, Vietnam was a dream assignment. Over the course of a dozen years working for newspapers and magazines in his native New Zealand and Australia, Peter's covered everything from honeymooning in Verona to gay resorts in Fiji. This is the fifth book he's co-authored for Lonely Planet.

LONELY PLANET AUTHORS

Why is our travel information the best in the world? It's simple: our authors are independent, dedicated travellers. They don't research using just the internet or phone, and they don't take freebies in exchange for positive coverage. They travel widely, to all the popular spots and off the beaten track. They personally visit thousands of hotels, restaurants, cafés, bars, galleries, palaces, museums and more – and they take pride in getting all the details right, and telling it how it is. For more, see the authors section on www.lonelyplanet.com.

REGIS ST LOUIS

Ho Chi Minh City, Around Ho Chi Minh City, Mekong Delta

Regis first caught the Vietnam buzz when he researched the country for a social studies class at St Benedict Elementary School. Since then he's delved deeply into Vietnam, reading extensively about its rich cultures and tumultuous history and travelling countless dusty roads in search in search of hidden pagodas and the perfect bowl of *pho*. Regis has worked on numerous Lonely Planet guidebooks, and his travel essays have appeared in the *Los Angeles Times* and the *Chicago Tribune*, among other publications. He lives in New York City.

CONTRIBUTING AUTHOR

Dr Trish Batchelor wrote the Health chapter (p494). Trish is a general practitioner and travel-medicine specialist who works at the CIWEC Clinic in Kathmandu, Nepal, as well as being a Medical Advisor to the Travel Doctor New Zealand clinics.

Getting Started

There's a buzz about Vietnam and we're not just talking motorbike engines. Vietnam is hot and the word is travelling far and wide. The country offers an intoxicating blend: vibrant yet traditional cities, unashamedly idyllic coastline, incredible scenery, pulsating history and culture, and a kaleidoscope of people. Vietnam has it all, but it's also raw in places, so pack some flexibility, humour and patience. Come expecting the unexpected, be ready for an adventure as much as a holiday, and Vietnam will deliver.

WHEN TO GO

When it comes to weather, it's a tough call, as Vietnam's climate is so diverse. Think frosts and occasional snow in the mountains of the north, and temperatures soaring to 40°C in the south during the dry season.

Vietnam's weather is dictated by two monsoons. The winter monsoon comes from the northeast between October and March, bringing damp and chilly winters to all areas north of Nha Trang, and dry and warm temperatures to the south. From April or May to October, the summer monsoon brings hot, humid weather to the whole country except for those areas sheltered by mountains. For the best balance, try the months of April, May or October. For those sticking to the south, November to February is dry and a touch cooler. From July to November, violent and unpredictable typhoons hit central and northern Vietnam, which can dampen the spirits of even the most enthusiastic traveller.

It gets pretty crowded from November to March and in July and August. Prices tend to peak over the Christmas and New Year period, and if you don't fancy sharing the sites with the masses, try to avoid these busy times.

See Climate Charts (p464) for more information.

Some travellers like to time a visit with Tet (Vietnamese New Year; see p64), which is the biggest festival in the calendar in late January or early February; a nice idea, but not ideal, as the whole country is on the move. High season in Vietnam runs from November to March, with a summer surge in July and August, particularly for domestic tourists. May, June and September are usually the quietest months.

COSTS & MONEY

The cost of travel in Vietnam varies from pocket change to the platinum card, depending on taste and comfort. Ascetics could just about get by on

DON'T LEAVE HOME WITHOUT...

Bring as little as possible, as Vietnam has pretty much anything you can find back home but at lower prices. All the soaps and smellies are cheap and plentiful, and clothing, shoes and backpacks are all manufactured in Vietnam and available at a snip. Tampons are available in all major towns and cities, but not in more remote areas.

A Swiss army knife or equivalent comes in handy, but you don't need 27 separate functions, just one blade and an opener. A torch (flashlight) and compass are also useful.

Other handy things to bring are business cards, as Vietnamese deal them out like a deck of cards; ear plugs to block the ever-present soundtrack that is Vietnam; a universal plug adaptor; a rain cover for the backpack; a sweater for the highlands and air-con bus trips; and mosquito repellent to keep the bugs at bay.

Finally, the secret of successful packing: plastic bags, as not only do they keep things separate and clean, but also dry. That means a lot at the end of a long, wet day.

US$10 a day, while a conventional budget traveller can live it up from US$20 to US$25. Midrange travellers can have a ball from US$50 to US$100 a day, staying comfortably, eating well and travelling comfortably. At the top end, spending US$200 or more a day, anything is possible.

Foreigners are frequently overcharged, particularly when buying souvenirs and occasionally in restaurants. Rapacious bus and taxi drivers will often bump up their rates to several times the Vietnamese price. However, don't assume that everyone is trying to rip you off. Despite widespread poverty, many Vietnamese will only ask the local price for many goods and services.

The official currency may be Vietnam dong (d), but the US dollar is pretty widely accepted. In tourist centres, most hotels will accept either, while other businesses may prefer dong. As you venture off the trail, make sure you are packing plenty of local currency. Rooms start from as little as US$3 to US$5 in busy tourist centres. Spending US$10 to US$20 will boost the comforts quickly, and rooms will generally include air-con, satellite TV, fridge and hot water. Make the step up to US$50 and three-star frills are available. At US$100 and above, it's five-star territory. Don't be afraid to negotiate for a discount if it is low season or if numbers are down.

Dining out is where Vietnam comes into its own. Surfing the street stalls and markets, meals can be found for between US$0.50 and US$1. Local restaurants are more comfortable and you can eat well for between US$1 and US$3.50. Then there are the Vietnamese gourmet restaurants, where you can still only spend around US$10 with drinks; with the right wines you could easily spend US$50.

Domestic flights are relatively expensive compared with some countries in the region. A one-way ticket from Hanoi to Ho Chi Minh City (HCMC) is around US$110. Trains are great value and overnight sleepers are a good way to cover long distances like Hanoi to Hué or HCMC to Nha Trang.

Bus travel is a bargain by Western standards. Public buses between major destinations have fixed fares, but when travelling by bus in remote areas, overcharging is the rule. For maximum flexibility, many travellers prefer to rent a car or 4WD and go exploring with a guide. Costs run from about US$25 around town to as much as US$100 a day upcountry (including the driver's food and lodging). A guide costs from US$20 to US$40, depending on the destination.

HOW MUCH?

Restaurant meal US$3-10

Hotel room with air-con US$10-20

Internet access US$0.20-0.50 per hour

Short *cyclo* ride US$0.50

Two-kilometre taxi ride US$1-2

TRAVEL LITERATURE

Vietnam: A Traveller's Literary Companion (1996), edited by Nguyen Qui Doc, is an engaging collection of stories by various Vietnamese writers, ranging from folklore and the tragedy of war to love and family ties, all set against evocative backdrops from Hanoi to Dalat.

Vietnam: Journeys of Body, Mind and Spirit (2003), edited by Nguyen Van Huy, is a beautifully shot photographic journey that gets to the heart of Vietnam. It's put together by locals and residents of Vietnam and offers an intimate portrait of the country today.

Fragrant Palm Leaves (1998) is a remarkable, poetic collection of journal entries by Zen monk and peace crusader Thich Nhat Hanh, written in Vietnam and the USA during the 1960s. As the American War in Vietnam rages on, he tries to make sense of it all, and there are some vivid scenes from South Vietnam in the 1960s.

Sparring with Charlie: Motorbiking down the Ho Chi Minh Trail (1996), by Christopher Hunt, is a light-hearted travelogue about modern Vietnam that takes the reader off the tourist trail and into some less-travelled parts of the country.

TOP 10

VIETNAM EXPERIENCES

Travel is not just about visiting, it's about experiencing. It's not enough to tick off the sights and charge down the coast between Hanoi and Ho Chi Minh City (HCMC). Try to get beneath the skin of the country: this can take many shapes or forms. It might be a culinary adventure or a walk on the wild side. It could be a cultural encounter or perhaps spiritual enlightenment. It could be you.

1 Count the number of locals crammed on to one motorbike in the countryside
2 Get the measure of a tailor, the only time you want to be stitched up in Vietnam
3 Haggle with a cyclo driver about the price before enjoying the ride
4 Cross the road like a local in a busy city
5 Meet the minorities, a multicoloured mosaic of mountain people
6 Play *tram phan tram* (100%) or bottoms up with the locals in a backstreet bar
7 See the sunrise over the South China Sea from a beautiful beach
8 Slurp a steaming bowl of *pho* at a street stall
9 Take some time out in a temple, the spiritual sanctuary of the Vietnamese
10 Turn down the volume and drift down a river by sampan

MUST-SEE MOVIES

Filmmakers have found a rich vein of material in the tales of Vietnamese history, and foreign and local directors have tapped it well. There are some moody, atmospheric movies set in a time before the torment, a whole host of films dealing with the American experience in Vietnam, and some that deal with both Americans and Vietnamese coming to terms with life after so much death.

1 *Apocalypse Now* (1979) Director: Francis Ford Coppola
2 *Born on the Fourth of July* (1989) Director: Oliver Stone
3 *Cyclo* (1995) Director: Tran Anh Hung
4 *The Deer Hunter* (1978) Director: Michael Cimino
5 *Heaven and Earth* (1993) Director: Oliver Stone
6 *The Lover* (1992) Director: Jean-Jacques Annaud
7 *Platoon* (1986) Director: Oliver Stone
8 *The Quiet American* (2002) Director: Phillip Noyce
9 *The Scent of Green Papaya* (1992) Director: Tran Anh Hung
10 *We Were Soldiers* (2002) Director: Randall Wallace

TOP EATS, TOP DRINKS

Vietnam's cuisine is full of sensual flavours, subtle aromas and super-fresh ingredients. *Bia hoi* (beer) is the new tea, but in the mountains it is all about *xeo* (rice wine), medicine to the minorities.

1 **Bia hoi** The world's cheapest draught beer keeps on flowing
2 **Ca phe** Caffeine cravers unite, Vietnam's coffee has a real kick
3 **Cao lau** Hoi An's answer to fried noodles, made with water from a well
4 **Nem** Spring rolls are the country's most famous export, fried or fresh
5 **Nuoc mam** Fermented fish sauce, the stinky secret of Vietnamese cuisine
6 **Pho bo** Rice-noodle soup with beef, the meal that built a nation
7 **Rau muong** Just the thing on a glorious morning, with a dash of garlic and chilli
8 **Thit cho** Dog lover has a whole different meaning in this part of the world
9 **333** *Ba ba ba,* learn to count with the leading local beer in the south
10 **Xeo** The local firewater, particularly potent is the 'five times a night' variety

In a similar vein is *Ten Years After* (1987) by Tim Page. This impressive book boasts '12-months' worth of photos taken 10 years after the war'. The author also returned to Vietnam to write *Derailed in Uncle Ho's Victory Garden* (1995), the story of his quest to erect a war memorial in the Demilitarised Zone (DMZ) to honour the fallen war correspondents on all sides.

A Dragon Apparent (1952) is Norman Lewis' fascinating account of his journeys through Vietnam, Laos and Cambodia in 1950, and is a good insight into the last days of French rule.

Karin Muller's *Hitchhiking Vietnam* (1998) is a travelogue detailing one woman's tumultuous seven-month journey through Vietnam.

Part memoir and part travel narrative, *Catfish and Mandala* (1999) is Vietnamese-American Andrew X Pham's fascinating account of his escape from the war-torn Vietnam of 1977 and his subsequent return two decades later, equipped with a bicycle and a need to work out his mixed-up cultural identity.

The ultimate spoof guidebook, *Phaic Tan: Sunstroke on a Shoestring* (2004) makes fun of us all. No-one is spared, not the locals, not the travellers, not even hallowed guidebook authors. An absolute must for anyone travelling through Vietnam and the region beyond.

INTERNET RESOURCES

Jewels of the Mekong Delta (www.travelmedia.com/mekong) Features travel information and news about countries along the Mekong River.

Living in Vietnam (www.livinginvietnam.com) One of the most popular expat websites on Vietnam and a good source of information on settling down here, including job adverts.

Lonely Planet (lonelyplanet.com) Provides summaries on travelling to Vietnam, the Thorn Tree forum travel news and loads of links to other useful travel resources.

Things Asian (www.thingsasian.com) Bubbling with information on the culture of Vietnam, this site has everything, including architecture, literature and fashion.

Vietnam Adventures Online (www.vietnamadventures.com) Another fine site full of practical travel information that features monthly adventures and special travel deals.

Vietnam Online (www.vietnamonline.com) Loaded with useful travel lore and handy coverage of employment and business opportunities in Vietnam.

Itineraries

CLASSIC ROUTES

THE GREAT OCEAN ROAD **Three to Four Weeks / Hanoi to HCMC**

Acclimatise in the capital, **Hanoi** (p86); see the sights, wine and dine and prepare for the long ride south. Head to nearby **Ninh Binh** (p186), gateway to the striking scenery of **Tam Coc** (p187) and **Hoa Lu** (p188), and the funky gibbons of **Cuc Phuong National Park** (p190).

Experience **Hué** (p209), imperial capital of old, then head up and over (or under) the mighty Hai Van Pass to **Danang** (p229), gateway to **China Beach** (p237). **Hoi An** (p239) is the place for some time out – sightseeing, shopping and sunning yourself on the beach.

Head to the golden sands of **Quy Nhon** (p277) for some relaxation. Enter **Nha Trang** (p281), the biggest, and brashest, beach resort in Vietnam, and try a hedonistic boat trip to nearby islands. If it's all too much, carry on south to **Mui Ne Beach** (p300), a tropical idyll with smart resorts, blissed-out budget options, towering dunes and crazy kitesurfing.

Finish up in **Ho Chi Minh City** (HCMC, p331), where you can indulge in sophisticated shopping, delectable dining and the liveliest night scene in the country.

Many tour companies offer this trip in a two-week timeframe, but this barely allows enough time to unpack your bags in each place. Train, bus or opt for a car and driver for this 1710km epic.

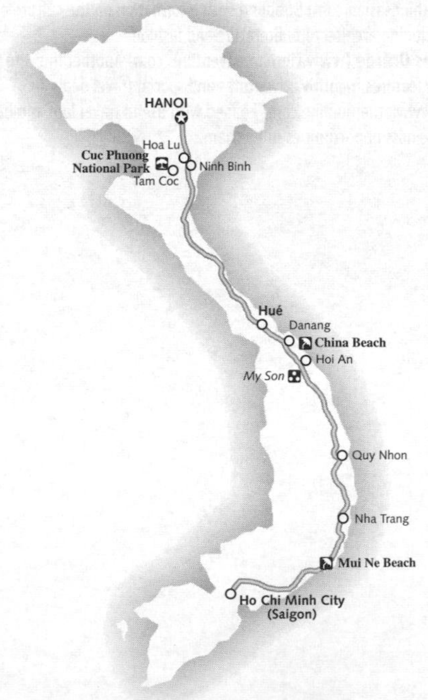

THE WORKS

One Month or More / HCMC to Sapa

Run this one in reverse, start out in the cauldron of commerce that is **Ho Chi Minh City** (p331). Hit the markets, browse a couple of museums and go underground into the alternate world that is the **Cu Chi Tunnels** (p378). Carry on to **Tay Ninh** (p381), headquarters of the Cao Dai sect and its rococo temple, for a morning service.

Dip into the Mekong Delta for a day or two. Try an overnight or two at **Can Tho** (p421), the social and commercial heart of the region, and take to the water to cruise through the watery world of the floating markets.

Head up into the central highlands to the romantic hill station of **Dalat** (p307). Back down on the coast, take in the stops from the Great Ocean Road itinerary (see opposite), including the beach resort of **Nha Trang** (p281), the cultured charmer that is **Hoi An** (p239) and the old imperial capital of **Hué** (p209). North of Hué is the former Demilitarised Zone (DMZ) that divided North and South Vietnam. All around this area are famous sites from the American War, including **Khe Sanh Combat Base** (p206) and the **Vinh Moc Tunnels** (p203). All aboard the night train to **Hanoi** (p86), gateway to the north, or cruise up the coast checking out the up and coming beach destination of **Dong Hoi** (p197).

To the east of the capital lies **Halong Bay** (p136), with more than 3000 limestone outcrops dotting the scenic bay. Cruise through the bay to the rugged, foreboding **Cat Ba Island** (p143) before looping back to the capital through **Haiphong** (p132), for the feel of old Hanoi.

Take a night train to **Sapa** (p172), unofficial capital of the northwest hill-tribe region and a beautiful base for hiking and biking.

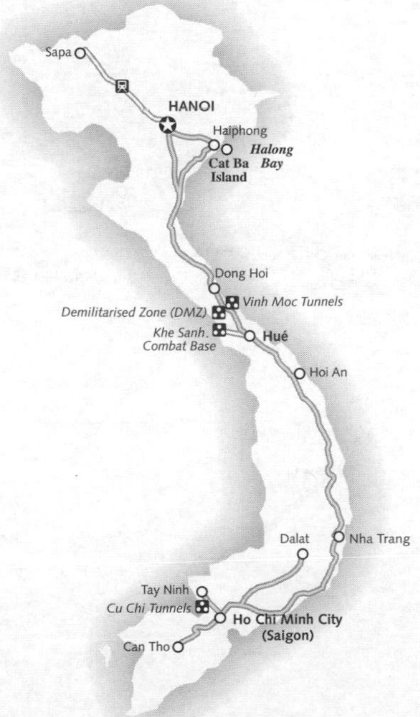

Trains and buses stop at most destinations, but to cover this huge distance a Hué–Hanoi flight could save time. Travel by boat around the Halong Bay area – the only way to get a good look at the crazy karsts.

ROADS LESS TRAVELLED

MINORITY REPORT

One to Three Weeks / Hanoi to Cao Bang

Northern Vietnam is a world unto itself, a land of brooding mountains, a mosaic of ethnic minorities, a region of overwhelming beauty. Hit the road by 4WD or motorbike for an adventure more than a holiday.

Leaving the capital, head west to the villages of **Mai Chau** (p164), which are home to the White Thai people and a perfect introduction to the life of the minorities. Northwest of here, where the road begins to climb into the Hoang Lien Mountains (Tonkinese Alps), a logical stop is **Son La** (p165).

Dien Bien Phu (p168) is a name that resonates with history; it was here that the French colonial story ended with their overwhelming defeat at the hands of the Viet Minh in one of the most celebrated military victories in Vietnamese history.

Climb over the mighty **Tram Ton Pass** (p175) to **Sapa** (p172). This is the premier destination in the northwest, thanks to the infinite views (on a clear day!), an amazing array of minority peoples and some of the region's most colourful markets. Bail out here by train from **Lao Cai** (p179), or continue east to **Bac Ha** (p180), home to the Flower H'mong. Motorbikers can continue on to **Ha Giang** (p182), a realm of mythical landscapes and unchartered territory. From here head to the lovely lakes of **Ba Be National Park** (p157) before heading north east to **Cao Bang** (p154), a province peppered with karsts, caves and beautiful waterfalls.

The snaking roads on this journey are some of the most treacherous in Vietnam, and landslips and floods are common. The motorbiking here is pure heaven for seasoned two-wheelers, but for the majority a 4WD is the sanest way to go.

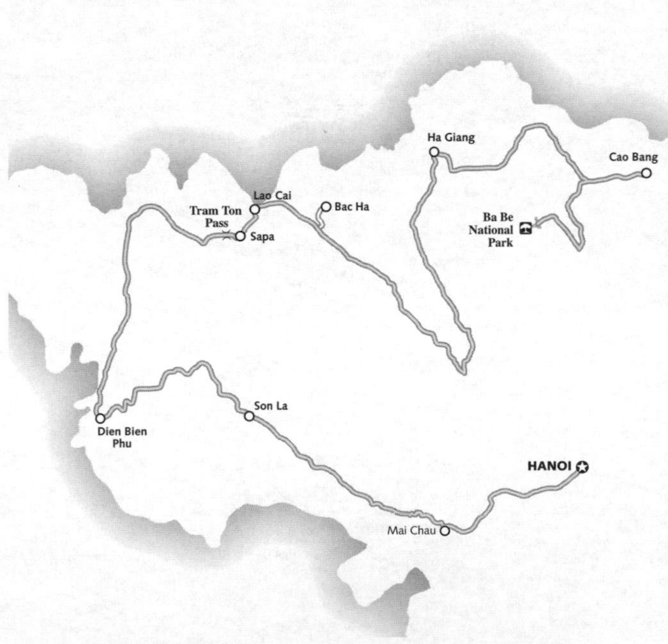

MEKONG MEANDERS

Two Weeks / Ben Tre to Phu Quoc Island

With their own wheels, travellers can tear up the three-day tourist trail through the Mekong byways and delve deeper into the delta to be rewarded with its rhythms, fragrances and colours. For anyone battling the insane highways of the delta by motorbike, a helmet is a wise accessory (and required by law)!

Beginning in **Ben Tre** (p407), take a boat trip to the islands around Vinh Long for an overnight in a bungalow set in a small longan orchard. From Ben Tre, a trek to **Can Tho** (p421) takes you to the home of the famous Ho Chi Minh 'Tin Man' statue and the delta's most cosmopolitan and commercial city. Take a detour to **Soc Trang** (p427), home to a sizeable Cambodian community and its wonderful *wats* (temples).

Float by boat through the local floating markets before moving on to charming **Chau Doc** (p436), a border-crossing town for those pushing westward into Cambodia via river or road. Check out the views of the pancake delta from the heights of **Sam Mountain** (p440).

The departure from the road more travelled starts here, heading southwest to **Ba Chuc** (p443) and its bone pagoda, and then through **Ha Tien** (p443), another border town with a beach to boot. Even more bucolic a beach can be found at **Hon Chong** (p447), where the sunset meets the sea and the rocky coastal geography contrasts sharply with the sandy beaches east of Ho Chi Minh City.

From here, travellers can take the highway along the southern edge of the delta region to **Rach Gia** (p448), the jumping-off point for those bound for **An Thoi** (p452) on serene **Phu Quoc Island** (p452). Phu Quoc affords rest and relaxation, *nuoc mam* (fish sauce) and forest reserves – a spectacular end to the Mekong Delta experience.

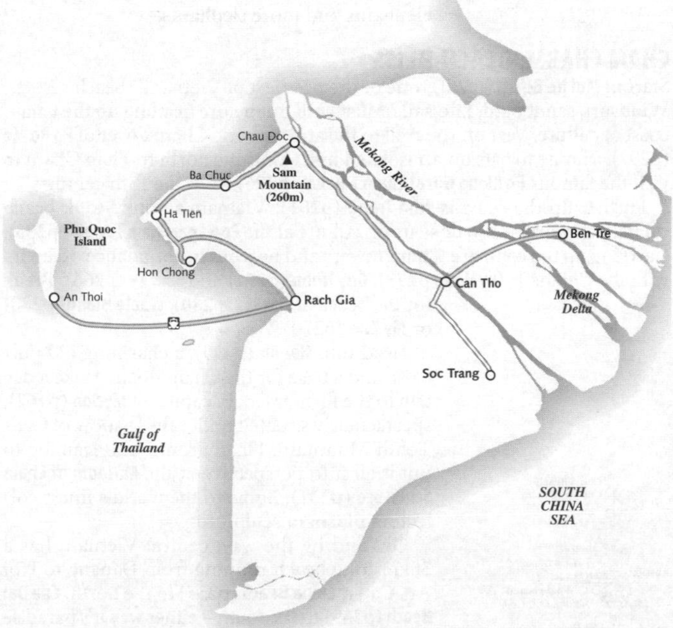

Down to Chau Doc, public transport is a breeze; after that, it's sparse and requires flexibility. Flights from Phu Quoc Island to HCMC run daily; if flying back to HCMC, book return flights well before hitting the delta to guarantee a quick getaway.

TAILORED TRIPS

NATURAL HIGHS

For adrenaline junkies or nature lovers, Vietnam has plenty to offer. Start out with a visit to **Halong Bay** (p136) for some sea kayaking among the karsts. Experienced climbers with their own gear might leave the water far below, as these limestone outcrops offer some excellent ascents, plus there is organised climbing around **Cat Ba Island** (p143).

Further northeast in **Bai Tu Long Bay** (p148), take to the water by local boat to see the 'new' Halong Bay without the tourists. Boating, kayaking, even surfing, are possibilities here and there are some beautiful beaches on Quan Lan's east coast.

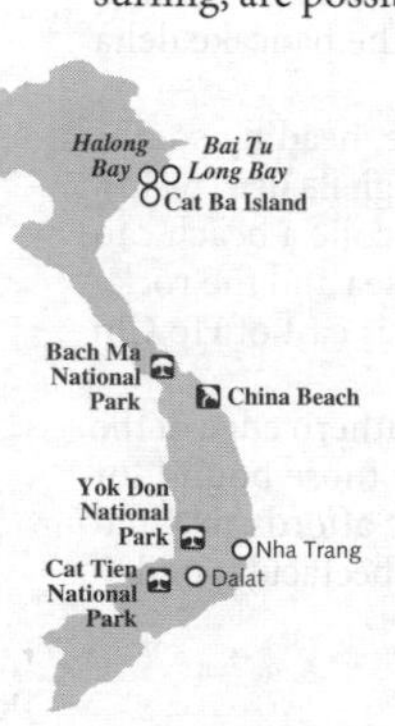

Heading south to central Vietnam, **Bach Ma National Park** (p225) is well geared up for walkers and has a series of lush trails to secluded waterfalls. Down on the coast below Bach Ma is **China Beach** (p237).

Go under the waves at **Nha Trang** (p281), dive capital of Vietnam, before heading up towards the hills of the central highlands. Wind up, or down, in **Dalat** (p307), a base for abseiling, cycling or rock climbing. Don't forget two of Vietnam's best-known national parks: the birding hot spot of **Cat Tien** (p392), with a population of rare Javan rhinos, and **Yok Don** (p323), home to elephants, elephants and more elephants.

CHAM CHARM, BEACH BLISS

Start in **Mui Ne Beach** (p300), one of the prettiest of Vietnam's beach resorts. Windsurf, sandboard, kite sail or just chill out before heading up the Cham coast of culture. Veer off the trail to the atmospheric Cham tower of **Po Ro Me** (p297), a home to bats on an isolated hill. Continue north to Thap Cham to visit the famous **Po Klong Garai Cham Towers** (p296) from the 13th century.

Further up the coast is **Nha Trang** (p281), Vietnam's honky-tonk beach capital, but you can also dose up on culture at the **Po Nagar Cham Towers** (p283). Carrying up the coast are Cham towers and beaches in abundance. Keep up with the Chams at **Tuy Hoa** (p279), **Quy Nhon** (p271) and **Tam Ky** (p266). Break for the beach at **Doc Let** (p280), **Whale Island** (p280) or **My Khe** (p270).

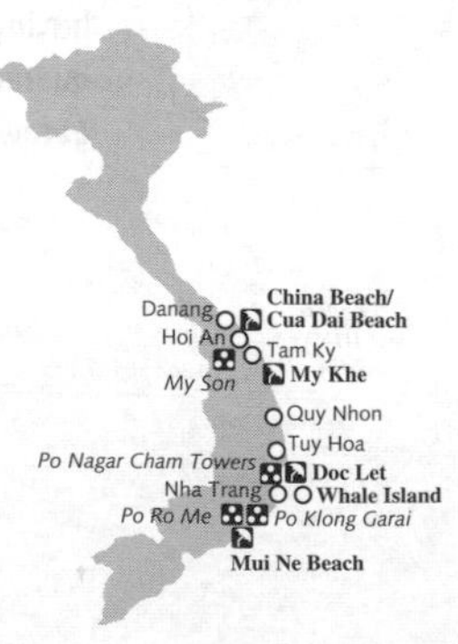

Head into **Hoi An** (p239), a charming old port town and a base for the Cham finalé. Make a day trip to the former Cham capital of **My Son** (p262), spectacularly situated under the shadow of Cat's Tooth Mountain. Finally romp into Danang to put it all into perspective at the **Museum of Cham Sculpture** (p231), home to the world's finest collection of Cham sculpture.

Oh, and by the way, central Vietnam has a 30km-long beach running from Danang to Hoi An. Call it **China Beach** (p237) to the north, **Cua Dai Beach** (p239) to the south – either way it's paradise and the perfect end to this trip.

Snapshot

Vietnamese society has undergone a profound transition in the past decade, even if the politics hasn't come along for the ride. Communism, the mantra for a generation, has taken a back seat to capitalism and the rush to embrace the market. Following the Chinese road to riches espoused by Deng Xiaoping, the Vietnamese have taken the brakes off the economy while keeping a firm hand on the steering wheel. The result is a contradictory blend of ultraliberal economics and ultraconservative politics that has left many Vietnamese confused about the country in which they live. They have the freedom to make money but not the basic freedom to voice a political opinion. And the more the average Vietnamese person engages with the outside world – through business, tourism, the internet – the harder this paradox is to swallow.

For now, the economy keeps the communist circus on the road. It's one of the new generation of Asian tigers, growing at more than 8% a year, one of the few countries capable of keeping the Chinese juggernaut in their sights. Political power may be held by a small elite, but economic power is firmly in the hands of the middle classes. The government is buying the popularity it hasn't tested at the ballot box by embarking on a building spree of immense proportions. Roads, bridges, tunnels, civic buildings – the scale is enormous, but it has to be, otherwise questions could be asked.

It is not only the government that is spending, not to mention *making* money like there is no tomorrow. International investors can't get enough of the place and joint ventures are springing up all over the country. The Socialist Republic of Vietnam (Vietnam's official name) was welcomed back to the world stage in 2006. The country played host to the APEC summit in November and became a fully fledged member of the World Trade Organisation (WTO). It's a world away from collectivisation and Communist International.

The minorities are revolting, or that is what the central government seems to think. Vietnamisation is in full swing in the central highlands and the northwest; when the central highlanders said enough is enough, their protests provoked a repressive reaction. Engaging the minority people on equal terms is something the party has yet to grapple with. As a growing population seeks pastures new, there is a chance some of these cultures will be swamped, quite literally, as the power-hungry Vietnamese are damming the rivers like eager beavers.

Marx and Lenin may have been laid to rest in their homeland, but they are alive and well in Vietnam. Just how tenable this is as Vietnam engages with its neighbours and plugs into the world economy is anyone's guess. Whatever the Vietnamese may make of communism in private, Ho Chi Minh remains a man for all seasons. Politics aside, he was a nationalist and patriot who delivered Vietnam its independence. Come what may to the party, Ho's place in history as a hero is assured.

FAST FACTS

Population: 84 million

Life expectancy: 68 for men, 73 for women

Infant mortality: 30 per 1000 births

GDP: US$53.1 billion

Adult literacy rate: 94%

Annual rice production: 32.3 million tonnes

Tonnage of bombs dropped on Vietnam: 15 million

Number of motorbikes: 10 million and counting

Litres of *nuoc mam* (fish sauce) produced per year: 200 million

Members of Communist Party: 2 million

History

Vietnam has a history as rich and evocative as anywhere on the planet. Sure, the American War in Vietnam captured the attention of the West, but centuries before that Vietnam was scrapping with the Chinese, the Khmers, the Chams and the Mongols. Vietnamese civilisation is as sophisticated as that of its mighty northern neighbour China, from where it drew many of its influences under a thousand-year occupation. Later came the French and the humbling period of colonialism from which Vietnam was not to emerge until the second half of the 20th century. The Americans were simply the last in a long line of invaders who had come and gone through the centuries and, no matter what was required or how long it took, they too would be vanquished. If only the planners back in Washington had paid just a little more attention to the history of this very proud nation, then Vietnam might have avoided the trauma and tragedy of a horribly brutal war.

The people of the Dong Son period were major traders in the region and bronze drums from northern Vietnam have been found as far afield as the island of Alor, in eastern Indonesia.

Visitors to Vietnam can't help but notice that the same names pop up again and again on the streets of every city and town. These are Vietnam's national heroes who, over the last 2000 years, have led the country in its repeated expulsions of foreign invaders and whose exploits have inspired subsequent generations of patriots.

THE EARLY DAYS

Recent archaeological finds suggest that the earliest human habitation of northern Vietnam was about 500,000 years ago. Neolithic cultures were romping around the same area just 10,000 years ago and engaged in primitive agriculture as early as 7000 BC. The sophisticated Bronze Age Dong Son culture, which is famous for its drums, emerged sometime around the 3rd century BC.

Archaeologists conducting excavations at Oc-Eo discovered a Roman medallion dating from AD 152, bearing the likeness of Antoninus Pius.

From the 1st to 6th centuries AD, southern Vietnam was part of the Indianised Cambodian kingdom of Funan – famous for its refined art and architecture. Known as Nokor Phnom to the Khmers, this kingdom was centred on the walled city of Angkor Borei, near modern-day Takeo. The Funanese constructed an elaborate system of canals both for transportation and the irrigation of rice. The principal port city of Funan was Oc-Eo in the Mekong Delta and archaeological excavations here tell us of contact between Funan and China, Indonesia, Persia and even the Mediterranean.

The Hindu kingdom of Champa emerged around present-day Danang in the late 2nd century AD (see p264 for more information). Like Funan, it adopted Sanskrit as a sacred language and borrowed heavily from Indian art and culture. By the 8th century Champa had expanded southward to include what is now Nha Trang and Phan Rang. The Cham were a feisty bunch who conducted raids along the entire coast of Indochina, and thus found themselves in a perpetual state of war with the Vietnamese to the north and the Khmers to the south. Ultimately this cost them their kingdom, as they found themselves squeezed between two great powers. Check out some brilliant sculptures in the Museum of Cham Sculpture in Danang (p231).

TIMELINE

2000 BC

The Bronze Age Dong Son culture emerges in the Red River Delta around Hanoi

AD 40

The Trung Sisters (Hai Ba Trung) lead a rebellion against the Chinese occupiers

1000 YEARS OF CHINESE DOMINATION

The Chinese conquered the Red River Delta in the 2nd century BC. In the following centuries, large numbers of Chinese settlers, officials and scholars moved south to impose a centralised state system on the Vietnamese.

Needless to say, local rulers weren't very happy about this and in the most famous act of resistance, in AD 40, the Trung Sisters (Hai Ba Trung) rallied the people, raised an army and led a revolt that sent the Chinese governor fleeing. The sisters proclaimed themselves queens of an independent Vietnam. In AD 43 the Chinese counterattacked and, rather than suffer the ignominy of surrender, the Trung Sisters threw themselves into the Hat Giang River. There were numerous small-scale rebellions against Chinese rule – which was characterised by tyranny, forced labour and insatiable demands for tribute – from the 3rd to 6th centuries, but all were crushed.

For a closer look at China's thousand-year occupation of Vietnam, which was instrumental in shaping the country's outlook and attitude today, try *The Birth of Vietnam* by Keith Weller Taylor.

During this era, Vietnam was a key port of call on the sea route between China and India. The Chinese introduced Confucianism, Taoism and Mahayana Buddhism to Vietnam, while the Indians brought Theravada Buddhism. Monks carried with them the scientific and medical knowledge of these two great civilisations and Vietnam was soon producing its own great doctors, botanists and scholars.

The early Vietnamese learned much from the Chinese, including the construction of dikes and irrigation works. These innovations helped make rice the 'staff of life', and paddy agriculture remains the foundation of the Vietnamese way of life to this day. As food became more plentiful the population expanded, forcing the Vietnamese to seek new lands. The ominous Truong Son Mountains prevented westward expansion, so the Vietnamese headed south.

LIBERATION FROM CHINA

In the early 10th century the Tang dynasty in China collapsed. The Vietnamese seized the initiative and launched a long overdue revolt against Chinese rule in Vietnam. In 938 AD popular patriot Ngo Quyen finally vanquished the Chinese armies at a battle on the Bach Dang River, ending 1000 years of Chinese rule. However, it was not the last time the Vietnamese would tussle with their mighty northern neighbour.

In AD 679 the Chinese changed the name of Vietnam to Annam, which means the 'Pacified South'. Ever since this era, the collective memory of Chinese domination has played an important role in shaping Vietnamese identity and attitudes towards their northern neighbour.

From the 11th to 13th centuries, Vietnamese independence was consolidated under the enlightened emperors of the Ly dynasty, founded by Ly Thai To. During the Ly dynasty, many enemies launched attacks on Vietnam, among them the Chinese, the Khmer and the Cham but all were repelled. Meanwhile, the Vietnamese continued their expansion southwards and slowly but surely began to consolidate control of the Cham kingdom.

Mongol warrior Kublai Khan completed his conquest of China in the mid-13th century. For his next trick, he planned to attack Champa and demanded the right to cross Vietnamese territory. The Vietnamese refused, but the Mongol hordes – all 500,000 of them – pushed ahead, seemingly invulnerable. However, they met their match in the legendary general Tran Hung Dao; he defeated them in the battle of Bach Dang River, one of the most celebrated scalps among many the Vietnamese have taken. See the boxed text 'Playing for High Stakes' (p138) for more on this big win or soak up some of the story in Halong Bay (p136).

938

The Chinese are kicked out of Vietnam after more than a thousand years of occupation

1010

Thanh Long (City of the Soaring Dragon) known today as Hanoi, becomes Vietnam's capital

CHINA BITES BACK

The Chinese seized control of Vietnam again in the early 15th century, carting off the national archives and some of the country's intellectuals to China – an irreparable loss to Vietnamese civilisation. The Chinese controlled much of the country from 1407, imposing a regime of heavy taxation and slave labour. The poet Nguyen Trai (1380–1442) wrote of this period:

> Were the water of the Eastern Sea to be exhausted, the stain of their ignominy could not be washed away; all the bamboo of the Southern Mountains would not suffice to provide the paper for recording all their crimes.

LE LOI ENTERS THE SCENE

In 1418 wealthy philanthropist Le Loi sparked the Lam Son Uprising, travelling the countryside to rally the people against the Chinese. Upon victory in 1428, Le Loi declared himself Emperor Le Thai To, the first in the long line of the Le dynasty. To this day, Le Loi is riding high in the Top Ten of the country's all-time national heroes.

Following Le Loi's victory over the Chinese, Nguyen Trai, a scholar and Le Loi's companion in arms, wrote his infamous *Great Proclamation* (Binh Ngo Dai Cao). Guaranteed to fan the flames of nationalism almost six centuries later, it articulated Vietnam's fierce spirit of independence:

> Our people long ago established Vietnam as an independent nation with its own civilisation. We have our own mountains and our own rivers, our own customs and traditions, and these are different from those of the foreign country to the north…We have sometimes been weak and sometimes powerful, but at no time have we suffered from a lack of heroes.

Le Loi and his successors launched a campaign to take over Cham lands to the south, wiping the kingdom of Champa from the map, and parts of eastern Laos were forced to kowtow to the might of the Vietnamese.

THE COMING OF THE EUROPEANS

The first Portuguese sailors came ashore at Danang in 1516 and were soon followed by a proselytising party of Dominican missionaries. During the following decades the Portuguese began to trade with Vietnam, setting up a commercial colony alongside those of the Japanese and Chinese at Faifo (present-day Hoi An, p239). The Catholic Church eventually had a greater impact on Vietnam than on any country in Asia except the Philippines (which was ruled by the Spanish for 400 years).

Ho Chi Minh City (Saigon) began life as humble Prey Nokor in the 16th century, a backwater of a Khmer village in what was then the eastern edge of Cambodia.

LORDING IT OVER THE PEOPLE

In a dress rehearsal for the tumultuous events of the 20th century, Vietnam found itself divided in half through much of the 17th and 18th centuries. The powerful Trinh Lords were later Le kings who ruled the North. To the south were the Nguyen Lords, who feigned tribute to the kings of the north but carried on like an independent kingdom. The powerful Trinh failed in their persistent efforts to subdue the Nguyen, in part because their Portuguese weaponry was far inferior to the Dutch armaments supplied to the Nguyen.

1076
Vietnam's first university, the Temple of Literature in Hanoi, opens its doors to scholars

1428
Le Loi's uprising brings victory over the Chinese

For their part, the Nguyen expanded southwards again, absorbing the Khmer territories of the Mekong Delta.

TAY SON REBELLION

In 1765 a rebellion erupted in the town of Tay Son near Qui Nhon. The Tay Son Rebels, as they soon became known, were led by the brothers Nguyen. In less than a decade they controlled the whole of central Vietnam. In 1783 they captured Saigon from the Nguyen Lords as well as the rest of the South, killing the reigning prince and his family. Nguyen Lu became king of the South, while Nguyen Nhac was crowned king of central Vietnam.

Buddhism flourished during the 17th and 18th centuries and many pagodas were erected across the country. However, it was not pure Buddhism, but a peculiarly Vietnamese blend mixed with ancestor worship, animism and Taoism.

Continuing their conquests, the Tay Son Rebels overthrew the Trinh Lords in the North. Ever the opportunists, the Chinese moved in to take advantage of the power vacuum. In response, the third brother, Nguyen Hue, proclaimed himself Emperor Quang Trung. In 1789 Nguyen Hue's armed forces overwhelmingly defeated the Chinese army at Dong Da in another of the greatest hits of Vietnamese history.

In the South, Nguyen Anh, a rare survivor from the original Nguyen Lords – yes, know your Nguyens if you hope to understand Vietnamese history – gradually overcame the rebels. In 1802 Nguyen Anh proclaimed himself Emperor Gia Long, thus beginning the Nguyen dynasty. When he captured Hanoi, his victory was complete and, for the first time in two centuries, Vietnam was united, with Hué as its new capital city.

THE LAST OF THE NGUYENS

Emperor Gia Long returned to Confucian values in an effort to consolidate his precarious position. Conservative elements of the elite appreciated the familiar sense of order, which had evaporated in the dizzying atmosphere of reform stirred up by the Tay Son Rebels.

One of the most illustrious of the early missionaries was the brilliant French Jesuit Alexandre de Rhodes (1591–1660), widely lauded for his work in devising *quoc ngu,* the Latin-based phonetic alphabet in which Vietnamese is written to this day.

Gia Long's son, Emperor Minh Mang, worked to strengthen the state. He was profoundly hostile to Catholicism, which he saw as a threat to Confucian traditions, and extended this antipathy to all Western influences.

The early Nguyen emperors continued the expansionist policies of the preceding dynasties, pushing into Cambodia and westward into the mountains along a wide front. They seized huge areas of Lao territory and clashed with Thailand to pick apart the skeleton of the fractured Khmer empire.

THE FRENCH TAKEOVER

France's military activity in Vietnam began in 1847, when the French Navy attacked Danang harbour in response to Emperor Thieu Tri's suppression of Catholic missionaries. Saigon was seized in early 1859 and, in 1862, Emperor Tu Duc signed a treaty that gave the French the three eastern provinces of Cochinchina. However, over the next four decades the French colonial venture in Indochina was carried out haphazardly and without any preconceived plan. It repeatedly faltered and, at times, only the reckless adventures of a few mavericks kept it going.

The next saga in French colonisation began in 1872, when Jean Dupuis, a merchant seeking to supply salt and weapons to a Yunnanese general via the Red River, seized the Hanoi Citadel. Captain Francis Garnier, ostensibly dispatched to rein in Dupuis, instead took over where Dupuis left off and began a conquest of the North.

1516
Portuguese traders land at Danang, sparking the start of European interest in Vietnam

1765
Tay Son Rebellion erupts, led by the brothers Nguyen

A few weeks after the death of Tu Duc in 1883, the French attacked Hué and imposed the Treaty of Protectorate on the imperial court. There then began a tragi-comic struggle for royal succession that was notable for its palace coups, mysteriously dead emperors and heavy-handed French diplomacy.

The Indochinese Union proclaimed by the French in 1887 may have ended the existence of an independent Vietnamese state, but active resistance continued in various parts of the country for the duration of French rule. The expansionist era came to a close and the Vietnamese were forced to return territory seized from Cambodia and Laos.

The French colonial authorities carried out ambitious public works, such as the construction of the Saigon–Hanoi railway, the government taxed the peasants heavily to fund these activities, devastating the rural economy. Colonialism was supposed to be a profitable proposition, so operations became notorious for the low wages paid by the French and the poor treatment of Vietnamese workers. Shades of King Leopold's Congo.

INDEPENDENCE ASPIRATIONS

Throughout the colonial period, a desire for independence simmered under the surface. Seething nationalist aspirations often erupted into open defiance of the French. This ranged from the publishing of patriotic periodicals to a dramatic attempt to poison the French garrison in Hanoi.

The imperial court in Hué, although quite corrupt, was a centre of nationalist sentiment and the French orchestrated a game of musical thrones, as one emperor after another turned against their patronage. This comical caper culminated in the accession of Emperor Bao Dai in 1925, who was just 12 years old at the time and studying in France.

Ultimately, the most successful of the anticolonialists were the communists, who were able to tune into the frustrations and aspirations of the population – especially the peasants – and effectively channel their demands for fairer land distribution.

The story of Vietnamese communism, which in many ways is also the political biography of Ho Chi Minh (see p34), is complicated. Keeping it simple, the first Marxist grouping in Indochina was the Vietnam Revolutionary Youth League, founded by Ho Chi Minh in Canton, China, in 1925. This was succeeded in February 1930 by the Vietnamese Communist Party. In 1941 Ho formed the League for the Independence of Vietnam, much better known as the Viet Minh, which resisted the Japanese and carried out extensive political activities during WWII. Despite its nationalist programme, the Viet Minh was, from its inception, dominated by Ho's communists. But Ho was pragmatic, patriotic and populist and understood the need for national unity.

WWII BREAKS OUT

When France fell to Nazi Germany in 1940, the Indochinese government of Vichy France collaborators acquiesced to the presence of Japanese troops in Vietnam. For their own convenience the Japanese left the French administration in charge of the day-to-day running of the country. For a time, Vietnam was spared the ravages of Japanese occupation and things

1802
Emperor Gia Long takes the throne and the Nguyen dynasty is born; it rules until 1945

1883
The French impose the Treaty of Protectorate on the Vietnamese, marking the start of 70 years of colonial control

continued much as normal. However, as WWII drew to a close, Japanese rice requisitions, in combination with floods and breaches in the dikes, caused a horrific famine in which two million of North Vietnam's 10 million people starved to death. The only forces opposed to both the French and Japanese presence in Vietnam were the Viet Minh and Ho Chi Minh received assistance from the US government during this period. As events unfolded in Europe, the French and Japanese fell out and the Viet Minh saw its opportunity to strike.

A FALSE DAWN

By the spring of 1945 the Viet Minh controlled large parts of the country, particularly in the north. In mid-August, Ho Chi Minh formed the National Liberation Committee and called for a general uprising, later known as the August Revolution, to take advantage of the power vacuum. In central Vietnam, Bao Dai abdicated in favour of the new government, and in the South the Viet Minh soon held power in a shaky coalition with noncommunist groups. On 2 September 1945 Ho Chi Minh declared independence at a rally in Hanoi's Ba Dinh Square. Throughout this period, Ho wrote no fewer than eight letters to US president Harry Truman and the US State Department asking for US aid, but received no replies.

A footnote on the agenda of the Potsdam Conference of 1945 was the disarming of Japanese occupation forces in Vietnam. It was decided that the Chinese Kuomintang would accept the Japanese surrender north of the 16th Parallel and that the British would do the same to the south.

When the British arrived in Saigon, chaos reigned. The Japanese were defeated, the French were vulnerable, the Viet Minh was looking to assert itself, plus private militias were causing trouble. In order to help the Brits restore order, defeated Japanese troops were turned loose. Then 1400 armed French paratroopers were released from prison and, most likely looking for vengeance after Ho Chi Minh's declaration of independence, immediately went on a rampage around the city, breaking into the homes and shops of the Vietnamese and indiscriminately clubbing men, women and children. The Viet Minh responded by calling a general strike and by launching a guerrilla campaign against the French. On 24 September French general Jacques Philippe Leclerc arrived in Saigon, pompously declaring 'We have come to reclaim our inheritance'. The end of the war had brought liberation for France, but not, it seemed, for its colonies.

In the north, Chinese Kuomintang troops were fleeing the Chinese communists and pillaging their way southward towards Hanoi. Ho tried to placate them, but as the months of Chinese occupation dragged on, he decided 'better the devil you know' and accepted a temporary return of the French. For the Vietnamese, even the French colonisers were better than the Chinese. The French were to stay for five years in return for recognising Vietnam as a free state within the French Union.

Between 1944 and 1945, the Viet Minh received funding and arms from the US Office of Strategic Services (OSS, the CIA today). When Ho Chi Minh declared independence in 1945, he had OSS agents at his side and borrowed liberally from the American Declaration of Independence. Such irony.

WAR WITH THE FRENCH

The French had managed to regain control of Vietnam, at least in name. But when the French shelled Haiphong in November 1946, killing hundreds of civilians, the patience of the Viet Minh snapped. Only a few weeks later fighting broke out in Hanoi, marking the start of the Franco–Viet Minh War.

1887
The French proclaim the Indochinese Union, which sees active resistance by some Vietnamese

1911
Ho Chi Minh leaves Vietnam to work in Europe where his political consciousness evolves

UNCLE OF THE PEOPLE

Ho Chi Minh (Bringer of Light) is the best known of some 50 aliases assumed by Nguyen Tat Thanh (1890–1969) over the course of his long career. He was founder of the Vietnamese Communist Party and president of the Democratic Republic of Vietnam from 1946 until his death. Born the son of a fiercely nationalistic scholar-official of humble means, he was educated in the Quoc Hoc Secondary School in Hué.

In 1911 he signed up as a cook's apprentice on a French ship, sailing the seas to North America, Africa and Europe. He stopped off in Europe where, while odd-jobbing as a gardener, snow sweeper, waiter, photo retoucher and stoker, his political consciousness began to develop.

Ho Chi Minh moved to Paris, where he adopted the name Nguyen Ai Quoc (Nguyen the Patriot). During this period he mastered a number of languages (including English, French, German and Mandarin) and began to promote the issue of Indochinese independence. During the 1919 Versailles Peace Conference, he tried to present an independence plan for Vietnam to US President Woodrow Wilson.

Ho Chi Minh was a founding member of the French Communist Party, which was established in 1920. In 1923 he was summoned to Moscow for training by Communist International and from there to Guangzhou (Canton), China, where he founded the Revolutionary Youth League of Vietnam.

During the early 1930s the English rulers of Hong Kong obliged the French government by imprisoning Ho for his revolutionary activities. After his release he travelled to the USSR and China. In 1941 Ho Chi Minh returned to Vietnam for the first time in 30 years. That same year, at the age of 51, he helped found the Viet Minh, the goal of which was the independence of Vietnam from French colonial rule and Japanese occupation. In 1942 he was arrested and held for a year by the Nationalist Chinese. As Japan prepared to surrender in August 1945, Ho Chi Minh led the August Revolution, and his forces then established control throughout much of Vietnam.

The return of the French shortly thereafter forced Ho Chi Minh and the Viet Minh to flee Hanoi and take up armed resistance. Ho spent eight years conducting a guerrilla war until the Viet Minh's victory against the French at Dien Bien Phu in 1954. He led North Vietnam until his death in September 1969 – he never lived to see the North's victory over the South. Ho is affectionately referred to as 'Uncle Ho' (Bac Ho) by his admirers.

The party has worked hard to preserve the image of Bac Ho who, like his erstwhile nemesis South Vietnamese president Ngo Dinh Diem, never married. His image dominates contemporary Vietnam more than three decades after his death and no town is complete without a statue of Ho, no city complete without a museum in his name. This cult of personality is in stark contrast to the simplicity with which Ho lived his life.

However, a surprise spate of sensationalist stories published in Vietnamese newspapers during the early 1990s alleged that Ho had had numerous lovers, two wives – one French – and a son born to a Tay minority woman. She later died in mysterious circumstances. Perhaps time will reveal the true story. For the fullest picture of Ho's legendary life, check out *Ho Chi Minh,* the excellent biography by William J Duiker.

The Vietnamese government has so far refused anyone permission to capitalise on Ho Chi Minh's name. A proposed American joint venture called 'Uncle Ho's Hamburgers' floated like a lead balloon, although Kentucky Fried Chicken successfully entered Vietnam. The Vietnamese joint-venture partner, however, was not amused when the American business rep pointed out that Ho Chi Minh does vaguely resemble Colonel Sanders. 'No' said the frowning Vietnamese, 'Ho Chi Minh was a general.'

1925
Ho Chi Minh establishes the Vietnam Revolutionary Youth League in Canton, later to morph into the Vietnamese Communist Party

1941
Ho Chi Minh forms the Viet Minh

Ho Chi Minh and his forces fled to the mountains, where they would remain for the next eight years.

In the face of determined Vietnamese nationalism, the French proved unable to reassert their control. Despite massive US aid (an effort to halt the communist domino effect throughout Asia)and the existence of significant indigenous anticommunist elements, it was an unwinnable war. As Ho said to the French at the time, 'You can kill 10 of my men for every one I kill of yours, but even at those odds you will lose and I will win.'

After eight years of fighting, the Viet Minh controlled much of Vietnam and neighbouring Laos. On 7 May 1954, after a 57-day siege, more than 10,000 starving French troops surrendered to the Viet Minh at Dien Bien Phu (p168). This was a catastrophic defeat that brought an end to the French colonial adventure in Indochina. The following day, the Geneva Conference opened to negotiate an end to the conflict. Resolutions included an exchange of prisoners; the temporary division of Vietnam into two zones at the Ben Hai River (near the 17th Parallel) until nationwide elections could be held; the free passage of people across the 17th Parallel for a period of 300 days; and the holding of nationwide elections on 20 July 1956. In the course of the Franco–Viet Minh War, more than 35,000 French fighters had been killed and 48,000 wounded; there are no exact numbers for Vietnamese casualties, but they were certainly far higher.

In May 1954 the Viet Minh dug a tunnel network under the French defences on Hill A1 and rigged it with explosives. Comrade Sapper Nguyen Van Bach volunteered himself as a human fuse in case the detonator failed. Luckily for him it didn't and he is honoured as a national hero.

A SEPARATE SOUTH VIETNAM

After the Geneva Accords were signed and sealed, the South was ruled by a government led by Ngo Dinh Diem, a fiercely anticommunist Catholic. His power base was significantly strengthened by 900,000 refugees, many of them Catholics, who had fled the communist North during the 300-day free-passage period.

Nationwide elections were never held, as the Americans rightly feared that Ho Chi Minh would win with a massive majority. During the first few years of his rule, Diem consolidated power fairly effectively, defeating the Binh Xuyen crime syndicate and the private armies of the Hoa Hao and Cao Dai religious sects. During Diem's 1957 official visit to the USA, President Eisenhower called him the 'miracle man' of Asia. As time went on Diem became increasingly tyrannical in dealing with dissent. Running the government became a family affair.

In the early 1960s the South was rocked by anti-Diem unrest led by university students and Buddhist clergy, which included several highly publicised self-immolations by monks that shocked the world (see p222). The US decided Diem was a liability and threw its support behind a military coup. A group of young generals led the operation in November 1963. Diem was to go into exile, but the generals got over-excited and both Diem and his brother were killed. He was followed by a succession of military rulers who continued his erratic policies.

The USA closed its consulate in Hanoi on 12 December 1955 and would not officially re-open an embassy in the Vietnamese capital for more than 40 years.

A NEW NORTH VIETNAM

The Geneva Accords allowed the leadership of the Democratic Republic of Vietnam to return to Hanoi and assert control of all territory north of the 17th Parallel. The new government immediately set out to eliminate those elements of the population that threatened its power. Tens of thousands of 'landlords', some with only tiny holdings, were denounced to 'security committees' by envious neighbours and arrested. Hasty 'trials' resulted in between 10,000 and 15,000 executions and the imprisonment of thousands more. In 1956, the party, faced with widespread rural unrest, recognised that things had got out of control and began a Campaign for the Rectification of Errors.

In Hanoi and the North, Ho Chi Minh created a very effective police state. The regime was characterised by ruthless police power; denunciations by a huge network of secret informers; and the blacklisting of dissidents, their children and their children's children.

THE NORTH–SOUTH WAR

The campaign to 'liberate' the South began in 1959. The Ho Chi Minh Trail, which had been in existence for several years, was expanded. In April 1960 universal military conscription was implemented in the North. Eight months later, Hanoi announced the formation of the National Liberation Front (NLF), which came to be known, derogatorily, as the Viet Cong or the VC. Both are abbreviations for Viet Nam Cong San, which means Vietnamese communist. American soldiers nicknamed the VC 'Charlie'.

As the NLF launched its campaign, the Diem government rapidly lost control of the countryside. To stem the tide, the Strategic Hamlets Program was implemented in 1962, based on British tactics in Malaya. This involved forcibly moving peasants into fortified 'strategic hamlets' in order to deny the VC bases of support. This programme was abandoned with the death of Diem, but years later the VC admitted that it had caused them major problems.

The 2002 remake of *The Quiet American*, starring Michael Caine, is a must. Beautifully shot, it is a classic introduction to Vietnam in the 1950s, as the French disengaged and the Americans moved in to take their place.

And for the South it was no longer just a battle with the VC. In 1964 Hanoi began sending regular North Vietnamese Army (NVA) units down the Ho Chi Minh Trail. By early 1965 the Saigon government was on its last legs. Desertions from the Army of the Republic of Vietnam (ARVN), whose command was notorious for corruption and incompetence, had reached 2000 per month. The South was losing a district capital each week, yet in 10 years only one senior South Vietnamese army officer had been wounded. The army was getting ready to evacuate Hué and Danang, and the central highlands seemed about to fall. It was clearly time for the Americans to 'clean up the mess'.

ENTER THE CAVALRY

The Americans saw France's colonial war in Indochina as an important part of a worldwide struggle against communist expansion. Vietnam was the next domino and could not topple. In 1950, the US Military Assistance Advisory Group (MAAG) rocked into Vietnam, ostensibly to instruct local troops in the efficiency of US firepower; there would be American soldiers on Vietnamese soil for the next 25 years, first as advisers, and then the main force. By 1954 US military aid to the French topped US$2 billion.

A decisive turning point in US strategy came with the August 1964 Gulf of Tonkin Incident. Two US destroyers, the *Maddox* and the *Turner Joy*, claimed to have come under 'unprovoked' attack while sailing off the North Vietnamese coast. Subsequent research indicates that there was plenty of provocation; the first attack took place while the *Maddox* was in North Vietnamese waters assisting a secret South Vietnamese commando raid and the second one never happened.

However, on US President Johnson's orders, 64 sorties rained bombs on the North – the first of thousands of such missions that would hit every single

1954
French forces surrender en masse to Viet Minh fighters at Dien Bien Phu on 7 May, marking the end of colonial rule in Indochina

1956
Vietnam remains divided at the 17th Parallel into communist North Vietnam and 'free' South Vietnam

TRACKING THE AMERICAN WAR

The American War in Vietnam was *the story* for a generation. Follow in the footsteps of soldiers, journalists and politicians on all sides with a visit to the sites where the story unfolded.

- **China Beach** (p237) The strip of sand near Danang where US soldiers dropped in for some rest and relaxation.
- **Cu Chi Tunnels** (p378) The Vietnamese dug an incredible and elaborate tunnel network to evade American forces, just 30km from Saigon and right under the noses of a US base.
- **Demilitarised Zone** (DMZ; p202) The no-man's land at the 17th Parallel, dividing North and South Vietnam after 1954, became one of the most heavily militarised zones in the world.
- **Dien Bien Phu** (p168) The ultimate historic battle site, where the French colonial story came to a close in May 1954.
- **Ho Chi Minh Trail** (p329) The supply route for the South; the North Vietnamese moved men and munitions down this incredible trail through the Truong Son Mountains in an almost unparalleled logistical feat.
- **Hué Citadel** (p211) The ancient citadel was razed to the ground in street-to-street fighting in early 1968 when the Americans retook the city from the communists after a three-week occupation.
- **Khe Sanh** (p207) This was the biggest smokescreen of the war, as the North Vietnamese massed forces around this US base in 1968 to draw attention away from the coming Tet Offensive.
- **Long Tan Memorial** The Australian contingent who fought in Vietnam, mostly based near Vung Tau in the south, is remembered here. The Long Tan Memorial Cross was erected by Australian survivors of a fierce 1967 battle. The original is now in Bien Hoa Military Museum. The Vietnamese erected a memorial cross in 2002, but you need to arrange a permit to visit (for more details see www.diggerhistory.info/pages-memorials/longtan.htm).
- **My Lai** (p269) The village of My Lai is infamous as the site of one of the worst atrocities in the war, when American GIs massacred hundreds of villagers in March 1968.
- **Vinh Moc Tunnels** (p203) The real deal, these tunnels haven't been surgically enlarged for tourists and they mark yet another feat of infrastructural ingenuity.

road and rail bridge in the country, as well as 4000 of North Vietnam's 5788 villages. Two US aircraft were lost and Lieutenant Everett Alvarez became the first American prisoner of war (POW) of the conflict; he would remain in captivity for eight years.

A few days later, an indignant (and misled) US Congress overwhelmingly passed the Tonkin Gulf Resolution, which gave the president the power to 'take all necessary measures' to 'repel any armed attack against the forces of the United States and to prevent further aggression'. Until its repeal in 1970, the resolution was treated by US presidents as carte blanche to do whatever they chose in Vietnam without any congressional control.

As the military situation of the Saigon government reached a new nadir, the first US combat troops splashed ashore at Danang in March 1965. By December 1965 there were 184,300 US military personnel in Vietnam and 636 Americans had died. By December 1967 the figures had risen to 485,600 US soldiers in country and 16,021 dead. There were 1.3 million

1960

Civil war erupts in the South and the Ho Chi Minh Trail re-opens for business

1962

The Strategic Hamlets Program is initiated in order to deny the Viet Cong support systems men fighting for the Saigon government, including the South Vietnamese and other allies.

By 1966 the buzz words in Washington were 'pacification', 'search and destroy' and 'free-fire zones'. Pacification involved developing a pro-government civilian infrastructure in each village, and providing the soldiers to guard it. To protect the villages from VC raids, mobile search-and-destroy units of soldiers moved around the country hunting VC guerrillas. In some cases, villagers were evacuated so the Americans could use heavy weaponry such as napalm and tanks in areas that were declared free-fire zones.

These strategies were only partially successful: US forces could control the countryside by day, while the VC usually controlled it by night. Even without heavy weapons, VC guerrillas continued to inflict heavy casualties in ambushes and by using mines and booby traps. Although free-fire zones were supposed to prevent civilian casualties, plenty of villagers were nevertheless shelled, bombed, strafed or napalmed to death – their surviving relatives soon signed up to join the VC.

Neil Sheehan's account of the life of Colonel John Paul Vann, *Bright Shining Lie,* won the Pulitzer Prize and is the portrayal of one man's disenchantment with the war, mirroring America's realisation it could not be won.

THE TURNING POINT

In January 1968 North Vietnamese troops launched a major attack at Khe Sanh (p207) in the Demilitarised Zone. This battle, the single largest of the war, was in part a massive diversion to draw attention away from the Tet Offensive.

The Tet Offensive marked a decisive turning point in the war. On the evening of 31 January, as the country celebrated the Lunar New Year, the VC launched a series of strikes in more than 100 cities and towns, including Saigon. As the TV cameras rolled, a VC commando team took over the courtyard of the US embassy in central Saigon.

US forces had long been itching to engage the VC in open battle and the Tet Offensive delivered. Although utterly surprised – a major failure of US military intelligence – the South Vietnamese and Americans immediately counterattacked with massive firepower, bombing and shelling heavily populated cities as they had the open jungle. The counterattack devastated the VC, but also traumatised the civilian population. In Ben Tre, a US officer bitterly remarked that they 'had to destroy the town in order to save it'.

The Tet Offensive killed about 1000 US soldiers and 2000 ARVN troops, but VC losses were more than 10 times higher, at around 32,000 deaths. In addition, some 500 American and 10,000 North Vietnamese troops had died at the battle of Khe Sanh the preceding week.

Hitch a ride with Michael Herr and his seminal work *Dispatches*. A correspondent for *Rolling Stone* magazine, Herr tells it how it is, as some of the darkest events of the American War unfold around him, including the siege of Khe Sanh.

The VC may have lost the battle, but this was the critical turning point on the road to winning the war. The military had long been boasting that victory was just a matter for time. Watching the killing and chaos in Saigon beamed into their living rooms, many Americans stopped believing the hype. While US generals were proclaiming a great victory, public tolerance of the war and its casualties reached breaking point. For the VC the Tet Offensive ultimately proved a success: it made the cost of fighting the war unbearable for the Americans.

Simultaneously, stories began leaking out of Vietnam about atrocities and massacres carried out against unarmed Vietnamese civilians, including the infamous My Lai Massacre (see p271 for more information). This helped turn the tide and a coalition of the concerned emerged that threatened the

1963
South Vietnam's president Ngo Dinh Diem is overthrown and killed in a coup backed by the USA

1964
The US bombs North Vietnam for the first time

establishment. Antiwar demonstrations rocked American university campuses and spilled onto the streets.

NIXON & HIS DOCTRINE

Richard Nixon was elected president in part because of a promise that he had a 'secret plan' to end the war. The Nixon Doctrine, as it was called, was unveiled in July 1969 and it called on Asian nations to be more 'self-reliant' in defence matters. Nixon's strategy called for 'Vietnamisation', which meant making the South Vietnamese fight the war without US troops. More recently, it's been dusted off for Iraq, but no-one has yet referred to it as the Bush Doctrine.

Even with the election of 'Tricky Dicky', the first half of 1969 saw yet greater escalation of the conflict. In April the number of US soldiers in Vietnam reached an all-time high of 543,400. While the fighting raged, Nixon's chief negotiator, Henry Kissinger, pursued peace talks in Paris with his North Vietnamese counterpart Le Duc Tho.

The American War in Vietnam claimed the lives of countless journalists. For a look at the finest photographic work from the battlefront, *Requiem* is an anthology of work from fallen correspondents on all sides of the conflict and a fitting tribute to their trade.

In 1969 the Americans began secretly bombing Cambodia in an attempt to flush out Vietnamese communist sanctuaries across the border. Given the choice between facing US troops and pushing deeper into Cambodia, they fled west. In 1970 US ground forces were sent into Cambodia to extricate ARVN units, whose combat ability was still unable to match the enemy's. The North Vietnamese moved deeper into Cambodian territory and together with their Khmer Rouge allies controlled half of the country by the summer of 1970, including the world-famous temples of Angkor.

This new escalation provoked yet more bitter antiwar protests. A peace demonstration at Kent State University in Ohio resulted in four protesters being shot dead by National Guard troops. The rise of organisations such as Vietnam Veterans Against the War demonstrated that it wasn't just 'cowardly students fearing military conscription' who wanted the USA out of Vietnam. It was clear that the war was tearing America apart.

In the spring of 1972 the North Vietnamese launched an offensive across the 17th Parallel; the USA responded with increased bombing of the North and by laying mines in North Vietnam's harbours. The 'Christmas bombing' of Haiphong and Hanoi at the end of 1972 was meant to wrest concessions from North Vietnam at the negotiating table. Eventually, the Paris Peace Accords were signed by the USA, North Vietnam, South Vietnam and the VC on 27 January 1973, which provided for a cease-fire, the total withdrawal of US combat forces and the release of 590 American POWs. The agreement failed to mention the 200,000 North Vietnamese troops still in South Vietnam.

The definitive American War movie has to be *Apocalypse Now*. Marlon Brando plays renegade Colonel Kurtz who has gone AWOL, and native, in the wilds of northeast Cambodia. Martin Sheen is sent to bring him back and the psychotic world into which he is drawn is one of the most savage indictments of war ever seen on screen.

In total, 3.14 million Americans (including 7200 women) served in the US armed forces in Vietnam during the war. Officially, 58,183Americans were killed in action or are listed as missing in action (MIA). Pentagon figures indicate that by 1972, 3689 fixed-wing aircraft and 4857 helicopters had been lost and 15 million tonnes of ammunition had been expended. The direct cost of the war was officially put at US$165 billion, though its real cost to the economy was double that or more.

By the end of 1973, 223,748 South Vietnamese soldiers had been killed in action; North Vietnamese and VC fatalities have been estimated at one million. Approximately four million civilians (or 10% of the Vietnamese population) were injured or killed during the war, many of them as a direct

1965
The first US marines wade ashore at Danang

1967
By December there are 1.3 million soldiers fighting for the South; nearly half a million of these are US soldiers

result of US bombing in the North. At least 300,000 Vietnamese and 2200 Americans are still listed as MIA or 'Missing in Action'. US teams continue to search Vietnam, Laos and Cambodia for the remains of their fallen comrades. In more recent years, the Vietnamese have been searching for their own MIAs in Cambodia and Laos. Individual family members often use mediums to try and locate the remains of their loved ones.

For a human perspective on the North Vietnamese experience during the war, read *The Sorrow of War* by Bao Ninh, a poignant tale of love and loss that shows the soldiers from the North had the same fears and desires as most American GIs.

OTHER FOREIGN INVOLVEMENT

Australia, New Zealand, South Korea, the Philippines and Thailand also sent military personnel to South Vietnam as part of what the Americans called the 'Free World Military Forces', whose purpose was to help internationalise the American war effort and thus confer upon it some legitimacy. Sound familiar?

Australia's participation in the conflict constituted the most significant commitment of its military forces since WWII. There were `46,852 Australian military personnel that served in the war; the Australian casualties totalled 496 dead and 2398 wounded.

Most of New Zealand's contingent, which numbered 548 at its high point in 1968, operated as an integral part of the Australian Task Force, which was stationed near Baria, just north of Vung Tau.

Mostly neglected by writers is the painful experience of the fatherless Amerasian children left behind in Vietnam after 1975. The sordid tale is recounted in unforgettable detail in *Vietnamerica* by Thomas Bass.

THE FALL OF THE SOUTH

All US military personnel departed Vietnam in 1973, leaving behind a small contingent of technicians and CIA agents. The bombing of North Vietnam ceased and the US POWs were released. Still the war raged on, only now the South Vietnamese were fighting alone.

In January 1975 the North Vietnamese launched a massive ground attack across the 17th Parallel using tanks and heavy artillery. The invasion provoked panic in the South Vietnamese army, which had always depended on the Americans. In March, the NVA occupied a strategic section of the central highlands at Buon Ma Thuot. South Vietnam's president, Nguyen Van Thieu, decided on a strategy of tactical withdrawal to more defensible positions. This proved to be a spectacular military blunder.

Whole brigades of ARVN soldiers disintegrated and fled southward, joining hundreds of thousands of civilians clogging Hwy 1. City after city – Hué, Danang, Quy Nhon, Nha Trang – were simply abandoned with hardly a shot fired. The ARVN troops were fleeing so quickly that the North Vietnamese army could barely keep up.

The concept of 'embedded' journalists was a direct result of bad press coverage during the war in Vietnam. Journalists were allowed to travel anywhere and everywhere during the conflict and told both sides of the story. Some American military commanders maintain it was the press that lost the US the war.

Nguyen Van Thieu, in power since 1967, resigned on 21 April 1975 and fled the country, allegedly carting off millions of dollars in ill-gotten wealth. The North Vietnamese pushed on to Saigon and on the morning of 30 April 1975 their tanks smashed through the gates of Saigon's Independence Palace (now called Reunification Palace). General Duong Van Minh, president for just 42 hours, formally surrendered, marking the end of the war.

Just a few hours before the surrender, the last Americans were evacuated by helicopter from the US embassy roof to ships stationed just offshore. Iconic images of US Marines booting Vietnamese people off their helicopters were beamed around the world. And so more than a quarter of a century of American military involvement came to a close. Throughout the entire conflict, the USA never actually declared war on North Vietnam.

1968

The Viet Cong launches the Tet Offensive, an attack on towns and cities throughout the South that catches the Americans unaware

1973

All sides put pen to paper to sign the Paris Peace Accords on 27 January 1973

The Americans weren't the only ones who left. As the South collapsed, 135,000 Vietnamese also fled the country; in the next five years, at least half a million of their compatriots would do the same. Those who left by sea would become known to the world as 'boat people'. These refugees risked everything to undertake perilous journeys on the South China Sea. Pirates raped and pillaged, storms raged, but eventually these hardy souls found a new life in places as diverse as Australia and France.

REUNIFICATION OF VIETNAM

On the first day of their victory, the communists changed Saigon's name to Ho Chi Minh City (HCMC). This was just the first of many changes.

The sudden success of the 1975 North Vietnamese offensive surprised the North almost as much as it did the South. Consequently, Hanoi had no specific plans to deal with the reintegration of the North and South, which had totally different social and economic systems.

The North was faced with the legacy of a cruel and protracted war that had literally fractured the country. There was bitterness on both sides, and a mind-boggling array of problems. Damage from the fighting extended from unmarked minefields to war-focused, dysfunctional economies; from a chemically poisoned countryside to a population who had been physically or mentally battered. Peace may have arrived, but in many ways the war was far from over.

Until the formal reunification of Vietnam in July 1976, the South was ruled by the Provisional Revolutionary Government. The Communist Party did not trust the Southern urban intelligentsia, so large numbers of Northern cadres were sent southward to manage the transition. This fuelled resentment among Southerners who had worked against the Thieu government and then, after its overthrow, found themselves frozen out.

The party decided on a rapid transition to socialism in the South, but it proved disastrous for the economy. Reunification was accompanied by

Oliver Stone has never been one to shy away from political point-scoring and in the first of his famous trilogy about Vietnam, *Platoon*, he earns dix points. A brutal and cynical look at the conflict through the eyes of rookie Charlie Sheen, with great performances from Tom Berenger and Willem Dafoe.

INNOCENT VICTIMS OF THE WAR

One tragic legacy of the American War was the plight of thousands of Amerasians. Marriages, relationships and commercial encounters between Americans and Vietnamese were common during the war. But when the Americans headed home, many abandoned their 'wives' and mistresses, leaving them to raise children who were half-American or half-Vietnamese in a society not particularly tolerant of such racial intermingling.

After reunification, the Amerasians – living reminders of the American presence – were often mistreated by Vietnamese and even abandoned, forcing them to live on the streets. They were also denied educational and vocational opportunities, and were sadly referred to as 'children of the dust'.

At the end of the 1980s, the Orderly Departure Program (ODP) was designed to allow Amerasians and political refugees who otherwise might have tried to flee the country by land or sea to resettle in the West (mostly in the USA).

Unfortunately, many Amerasian children were adopted by Vietnamese eager to emigrate, but were then dumped after the family's arrival in the USA. **Asian American LEAD** (☎ 202-518 6737; www.aalead.org; 1323 Girard St NW, Washington, DC 20009, USA) is an organisation that has done some fine work training and mentoring Amerasian kids as they adapt to life in the USA.

1975

On 30th April 1975 Saigon falls to the North Vietnamese and is renamed Ho Chi Minh City

1978

Vietnam invades Cambodia on Christmas Day, overthrowing the Khmer Rouge government in 1979 widespread political repression. Despite repeated promises to the contrary, hundreds of thousands of people who had ties to the previous regime had their property confiscated and were rounded up and imprisoned without trial in forced-labour camps, euphemistically known as re-education camps. Tens of thousands of businesspeople, intellectuals, artists, journalists, writers, union leaders and religious leaders – some of whom had opposed both Thieu and the war – were held in horrendous conditions.

Contrary to its economic policy, Vietnam sought some sort of *rapprochement* with the USA and by 1978 Washington was close to establishing relations with Hanoi. But the China card was ultimately played: Vietnam was sacrificed for the prize of US relations with Beijing and Hanoi was pushed into the arms of the Soviet Union, on whom it was to rely for the next decade.

Relations with China to the north and its Khmer Rouge allies to the west were rapidly deteriorating and war-weary Vietnam seemed beset by enemies. An anticapitalist campaign was launched in March 1978, seizing private property and businesses. Most of the victims were ethnic-Chinese – hundreds of thousands soon became refugees or 'boat people', and relations with China soured further.

Author and documentary filmmaker John Pilger was ripping into the establishment long before Michael Moore rode into town. Get to grips with his hard-hitting views on the American War at http://pilger.carlton.com/vietnam.

Meanwhile, repeated attacks on Vietnamese border villages by the Khmer Rouge forced Vietnam to respond. Vietnamese forces entered Cambodia on Christmas Day 1978. They succeeded in driving the Khmer Rouge from power on 7th January 1979 and set up a pro-Hanoi regime in Phnom Penh. China viewed the attack on the Khmer Rouge as a serious provocation. In February 1979 Chinese forces invaded Vietnam and fought a brief, 17-day war before withdrawing (see the boxed text Neighbouring Tensions, p152).

Liberation of Cambodia from the Khmer Rouge soon turned to occupation and a long civil war. The command economy was strangling the commercial instincts of Vietnamese rice farmers. Today, the world's leading rice exporter, by the early 1980s Vietnam was a rice importer. War and revolution had brought the country to its knees and a radical change in direction was required.

OPENING THE DOOR

In 1985 President Mikhael Gorbachev came to power in the Soviet Union. *Glasnost* (openness) and *perestroika* (restructuring) were in, radical revolutionaries were out. Vietnam followed suit in 1986 by choosing reform-minded Nguyen Van Linh to lead the Vietnamese Communist Party. *Doi moi* (economic reform) was experimented with in Cambodia and introduced to Vietnam. As the USSR scaled back its commitments to the communist world, the far-flung outposts were the first to feel the pinch. The Vietnamese decided to unilaterally withdraw from Cambodia in 1989, as they could no longer afford the occupation. The party in Vietnam was on its own and needed to reform to survive.

The majority of 'Vietnamese boat people' who fled the country in the late 1970s were not in fact Vietnamese, but ethnic-Chinese whose wealth and business acumen, to say nothing of their ethnicity, made them an obvious target for the revolution.

However, dramatic changes in Eastern Europe in 1989 and the collapse of the Soviet Union in 1991 were not viewed with favour in Hanoi. The party denounced the participation of noncommunists in Eastern Bloc governments, calling the democratic revolutions 'a counterattack from imperialist circles' against socialism. Politically things were moving at a glacial pace, but economically the Vietnamese decided to embrace the market. It has taken

1979

China invades northern Vietnam in February to 'punish' the Vietnamese for attacking Cambodia

1986

Doi moi (economic reform), the first step towards re-engaging with the West, is launched

THE NORTH–SOUTH DIVIDE

Sound familiar? It's how George Bush won two elections. It keeps England divided at the Watford Gap. It sometimes threatens to snap Italy in two. Vietnam knows more about north-south divides than most, as the country spent 21 years partitioned along the 17th Parallel á la Korea.

War and politics are not the only explanation for two Vietnams. Climatically, the two regions are very different and this has an impact on productivity, the Mekong Delta yielding three rice harvests a year and the Red River just two. There are two dialects with very different pronunciation. There is different food. And, some say, a different persona.

The war amplified the differences. The north experienced communist austerity and US bombing. The south experienced the rollercoaster ride that was the American presence in 'Nam. As the war came to a close and southerners began to flee, thousands settled abroad, known as the *Viet Kieu*. Many have returned, confident thanks to an overseas education and savvy in the ways of the world. Their initiative and investment has helped to drive the economy forward.

This meant that is was the south that benefited most from the economic reforms of *doi moi*, self-confident Saigon the dynamo driving the rest of the country forward. The economy has grown by more than 7% for a whole decade, but this is heavily skewed to the south. Much of this is down to the attitude of government officials and the fact that many northern cadres were far more suspicious of reform than their southern cousins.

The government is aware of these divisions and tries to ensure a fair balance of the offices of state. It wasn't always so and many southern communists found themselves frozen out after reunification, but these days the party ensures that if the prime minister is from the south, the head of the Communist Party is from the north.

When it comes to the older generation, the south has never forgiven the north for bulldozing their war cemeteries, imposing communism and blackballing whole families. The north has never forgiven the south for siding with the Americans against their own people. Luckily for Vietnam, the new generation seems to have less interest in their harrowing history and more interest in making money. Today there is only one Vietnam and its mantra is business.

time, but capitalism has taken root and it's unlikely Ho Chi Minh would recognise the dynamic Vietnam of today.

VIETNAM TODAY

Relations with Vietnam's old nemesis, the USA, have improved in recent years. In early 1994 the USA finally lifted its economic embargo, which had been in place since the 1960s. Full diplomatic relations with the USA have been restored and Bill Clinton, who didn't fight in the war (and didn't inhale!), became the first US president to visit northern Vietnam in 2000. George W Bush followed suit in 2006, as Vietnam was welcomed into the World Trade Organization (WTO).

Relations have also improved with the historic enemy China. Vietnam is still overshadowed by its northern neighbour and China still secretly thinks of Vietnam as a renegade province. But Vietnam's economic boom has caught Beijing's attention and it sees northern Vietnam as the fastest route from Yunnan and Sichuan to the South China Sea. Cooperation towards the future is more important than the conflict of the past.

Vietnam is an active member of Asean, an organisation originally established as a bulwark against communism, and this is all adding up to a rosy economic picture. Vietnam's economy is growing at more than 8% a year and

1989
Vietnamese forces pull out of Cambodia and Vietnam is at peace for the first time in decades

1995
Vietnam joins the Association of South-East Asian Nations (Asean)

tourists just can't get enough of the place. The future is bright, but ultimate success depends on how well the Vietnamese can follow the Chinese road to development: economic liberalisation without political liberalisation. With only two million paid-up members of the Communist Party and 80 million Vietnamese, it is a road they must tread carefully.

2000

Bill Clinton visits Vietnam and becomes the first American president to set foot in Hanoi

2006

Vietnam's rehabilitation is complete as it plays host to the glitzy APEC summit and formally joins the WTO

Food & Drink

Table set up with the northern dish of *bun cha* (grilled pork served with fresh herbs and a dipping sauce), Hanoi
AUSTIN BUSH

One of the delights of visiting Vietnam is the cuisine, and there are said to be about 500 traditional dishes. Eating is such an integral part of the culture that a time-honoured Vietnamese proverb, '*hoc an, hoc noi*', dictates that people should 'learn to eat before learning to speak'.

Vietnamese cuisine is the sum of many parts. Vietnam has an enviable natural prosperity, and the cooking techniques showcase the bounty from land and sea to great advantage. Colonialism and foreign influences led to a marrying of techniques and ingredients. The result? The Vietnamese table.

Famous dishes such as *pho* (rice-noodle soup) and fresh spring rolls are but the tip of a gastronomic iceberg. In addition to a myriad of foods and preparations, there are a staggering number of sauces and dips limited only by the imagination of the cook. If cooking were painting, Vietnam would have one of the world's most colourful palettes. The Vietnamese have no culinary inhibitions and are always willing to try something new. When you combine these two tendancies, nothing is ruled out.

A steaming dish of *pho bo*
AUSTIN BUSH

STAPLES & SPECIALITIES

From the land comes rice, and from the sea and waterways fresh fish for *nuoc mam* (fish sauce; see the boxed text p46). Together they form the bedrock of Vietnamese cuisine. In supporting roles are the myriad pungent roots, leafy herbs and aromatic tubers, which give Vietnamese salads, snacks, soups and stews their distinctive fragrance and kick. But there are constants: for the Vietnamese cook, freshness and a balanced combination of flavours and textures are paramount.

Pho

You can have *pho* everywhere in Vietnam, but it is almost a cult in Hanoi. This full and balanced meal in a bowl will cost you less than US$1. In the north the people eat it at any time of day or night, while in the south (the southern variety comes with a lot more DIY herbs and sauces) it's popular for breakfast. It is artistry, practicality and economy. Pho comes in two varieties: chicken *(pho ga)* or beef *(pho bo)*.

THERE'S SOMETHING FISHY AROUND HERE...

Nuoc mam (fish sauce) is the one ingredient that is quintessentially Vietnamese and it lends a distinctive character to Vietnamese cooking. The sauce is made by fermenting highly salted fish in large ceramic vats for four to 12 months. Connoisseurs insist the high-grade rocket fuel has a much milder aroma than the cheaper variety. Dissenters insist it is a chemical weapon. It is very often used as a dipping sauce, and takes the place of salt on a Western table. Insist on the real thing (rather than the lighter stuff) – you will not have been to Vietnam otherwise.

If *nuoc mam* isn't strong enough for you, try *mam tom,* a powerful shrimp paste that American soldiers sometimes called 'Viet Cong tear gas'. It's often served with dog meat, a popular dish in the north – foreigners generally find it far more revolting than the dog itself.

Banh goi (Vietnamese-style turnovers) served with fresh veggies and herbs and a sweet dipping sauce
AUSTIN BUSH

Com

Vietnamese have a reverence for *com* (rice). It is the 'staff of life', not only at the table but in the economy and culture. Rice can be made into almost anything – wrappers, wine and noodles. *Banh trang* (rice paper) is something of a misnomer: this stuff is not very good for writing on, but is very good for eating. People use it to wrap Vietnamese spring rolls.

Nem

One of the most popular dishes is *nem* (fried Vietnamese spring rolls), which are known as *cha gio* in the south and *nem Sai Gon* or *nem ran* in the north. They are made of rice paper, and are filled with minced pork, crab, vermicelli, onion, mushroom and eggs. *Nem rau* are vegetable spring rolls.

A variation on the theme are the delicious larger 'fresh' spring rolls called *banh trang* in the south and *banh da* in the north. Put the ingredients (rice paper, lettuce, onions, herbs, cucumber and meat or fish or shrimp) together yourself and roll your own in restaurants. You can also try *goi cuon chay* (vegetarian rice-paper rolls).

Herbs & Spices

While rice and *nuoc mam* define Vietnamese 'food', it is spices that define Vietnamese 'cuisine' – the study, practice and development of the kitchen arts. There could be no *pho bo* without them, just plain beef noodle soup, and nothing to wax lyrical about. Mint brings coolness, chillies bring

Street vendor, Hanoi
AUSTIN BUSH

Fresh herbs and vegetables: an essential and colourful part of Vietnamese cooking
AUSTIN BUSH

heat, ginger offsets aromas, coriander is king and crowns every dish, while lemongrass has a citrus tang.

Fruits & Vegetables

After rice, fruits and vegetables make up the bulk of the Vietnamese diet. If given the choice of abandoning vegetables or abandoning meat, virtually all Vietnamese would eschew flesh and keep the vegies. *Rau muong* (water spinach) is a staple. Considered a weed in many countries, it tastes divine with garlic and oyster sauce *(rau muong xao)* . Other constants include succulent eggplant (aubergine) and meaty mushrooms, as well as bamboo shoots and bean sprouts. The Vietnamese would not be the inveterate snackers and grazers that they are were it not for the gift of fruit. For more on the flourishing fruits of Vietnam, see p425.

Fish, Meat & Fowl

Thanks to Vietnam's long coastline, seafood has always been a major source of protein. Crabs, prawns, shrimps, cuttlefish, clams, eel, shellfish and many species of fin fish can be found up and down the coast. For seafood lovers a coastal culinary cruise is a highlight of a trip to Vietnam.

In Vietnam, chickens, as well as other fowl, are produced in barnyards. Beef tends to be expensive as there is not much suitable land for cattle to graze. Pork is one of the favourite meats. Frogs' legs are popular but lamb and mutton are rarely seen. Then there are those, shall we say, 'unusual' meats (see the boxed text Travel Your Tastebuds, p48).

Dining streetside, Hanoi
AUSTIN BUSH

Desserts

Do ngot (Vietnamese sweets) and *do trang mieng* (desserts) are popular everywhere, and are especially prevalent during festivals, when *banh* (traditional cakes) come in a wide variety of shapes and flavours. Believe it or not given the bright colours, rice flour is the base for most desserts, sweetened with sugar palm, coconut milk and other goodies. Yellow and green beans turn up in many desserts, as do crisp lotus seeds. The French influence is evident in crème caramel–style custards. *Sua chua* is a healthy option, Vietnam's answer to frozen yoghurt.

Regional Specialities

For such a long country, the way that the people treat their produce is bound to differ according to where they are. Northern food displays a Chinese heritage, but in the south, where the weather is more tropical, the dishes have a more aromatic, spicy nose. In the middle lies Hué, the home

All the ingredients for a grilled seafood feast
AUSTIN BUSH

of Vietnamese imperial cooking, which features a range of sophisticated, refined dishes designed to tempt jaded royal appetites of yore.

THE NORTH

We are forever thankful to the capital for *pho*, but there are other tasty teasers in the north. *Banh cuon* (rice crepe rolls; wafer thin rice-paper sheets that contain chopped pork, fried garlic, chopped mushrooms and a side of herbs and salad) are produced everywhere in Vietnam, but those that are made in Hanoi have special characteristics, with wrappings as thin as a sheet of paper.

In Hanoi there is an *oc* (snail) living in ponds and lakes that grows to the size of a golf ball, has a streaked colour and, while chewy, is very tasty.

THE CENTRE

Emperor Tu Duc (1848–83) was a demanding diner who expected 50 dishes to be prepared by 50 cooks to be served by 50 servants at every meal, but Hué should be thankful as his legacy is some of the best food in Vietnam.

Preparing silkworms for sale
AUSTIN BUSH

TRAVEL YOUR TASTEBUDS

No matter what part of the world you come from, if you travel much in Vietnam you are going to encounter food that to you might seem unusual. The fiercely omnivorous Vietnamese find nothing strange in eating insects, algae, offal or fish bladders. They'll feast on the flesh of dogs, they'll eat a crocodile, or a dish of cock's testicles. They'll kill a venomous snake before your eyes, cut out its still-beating heart, feed it to you with a cup of the serpent's blood to wash it down, and say it increases your potency. They'll slay a monkey and then barbecue it at your tableside.

To the Vietnamese there is nothing 'strange' about anything that will sustain the body. They'll try anything once, even KFC.

During your travels, avoid eating endangered species, as this will only further endanger them. If you are keen for some canine chow, or keen to avoid it, look out for the words *thit cho* in the north, *thit cay* in the south.

We Dare You!

- crickets
- dog
- duck embryo
- field mouse

Appearance is very important, not only in the use of colour and presentation, but also in the style of serving. The menu for an imperial-style banquet today, whether in a fine restaurant or hotel banquet room or even a private home, might include up to a dozen dishes.

Hoi An is best known for *cao lau* (doughy flat noodles mixed with croutons, bean sprouts and greens and topped off with pork slices). True *cao lau* can only be made from water drawn from the Ba Le Well (p247), and (honest) you can taste the difference if someone tries to sneak a bastardised version by you.

Freshly squeezed sugarcane: one of the most refreshing drinks on a hot Vietnamese day
AUSTIN BUSH

THE SOUTH

With the cultivation of a greater range of tropical and temperate fruits and vegetables, and more varieties of spice, the south favours spicy dishes. Curries have been around since earliest times, although – unlike the Indian originals – they are not hot but aromatic, influenced by Cambodia. Almost anything cooked in coconut milk is a typical southern dish.

DRINKS

Vietnam has a healthy drinking culture, and the heat and humidity will ensure that you hunt out anything on offer to slake your thirst.

You will never be more than a few minutes from beer. There is no national brand, but a rip-roaring selection of regional beers, some of them distributed countrywide. Memorise the words *bia hoi,* which mean 'draught beer'. There are signs advertising it everywhere and most cafés have it on the menu. See the boxed text on p118 for the full picture on this Vietnam institution.

Xeo (rice wine) is as old as the hills. Formerly seen as a sort of cider for country bumpkins, it is gaining new kudos in the cities as a cheap and cheerful route to oblivion.

Another Vietnamese speciality is *ruou ran* (snake wine). This is basically rice wine with a pickled snake floating in it. This elixir is considered a tonic and allegedly cures everything from night blindness to impotence.

The preparation, serving and drinking of tea has a social importance seldom appreciated by Western visitors. Serving tea in the home or office is more than a gesture of hospitality, it is a ritual.

Vietnamese coffee is fine stuff. There is, however, one qualifier: most drinkers need to dilute it with hot water. The Vietnamese prefer their coffee so strong and sweet that it will strip the enamel from your teeth. Ordering 'iced coffee with milk' *(ca phe sua da)* usually results in coffee

Open-air bar serving *bia hoi* (draught beer), Hanoi
AUSTIN BUSH

Eating *nem chua* (fermented pork) served with fresh herbs and rice paper, Hanoi
AUSTIN BUSH

with about 30% to 40% sweetened condensed milk. Hot coffee with milk *(ca phe sua nong)* is available in big cities and tourist places, but not in more remote areas where they might not keep fresh milk.

CELEBRATIONS

Vietnam, for all its poverty, is a land rich with abundant natural resources and potential. There are many holidays and festivals accompanied by special food, as well as weddings and other family celebrations.

For a festival, the family coffers are broken open and no matter how much they hold, it is deemed insufficient. They will go towards the Vietnamese version of Peking duck, sliced into juicy slabs, drizzled with a piquant sauce. The more highly prized species of fish will be steamed or braised whole, and the cooks will give themselves over to the Chinese penchant for elaborate decoration.

In the highly structured Vietnamese society, the standard meal is knocked askew for the feast, symbolising the fact that during the festival the world is a different, better, place. Attendance at a festive meal in Vietnam will convince you, should you even need convincing, that the Vietnamese do not eat to live, but live to eat.

Dining in Vietnam, typically an informal affair
AUSTIN BUSH

WHERE TO EAT & DRINK

Whatever your taste, one eatery or another in Vietnam is almost certain to offer it, be it the humble peddler with his yoke, a roadside stall, a simple *pho* shop or a fancy-pants restaurant.

Barbecue is a speciality and many such restaurants are easy to locate by the aroma wafting through the streets. Also popular is the dish known as *bo bay mon,* which is beef prepared in seven different ways – a good feed when you're feeling protein-impaired.

Don't neglect the remaining French and Chinese restaurants. They are not as common as they used to be, but they are an important part of Vietnam's culinary and cultural legacy. And they have now been supplemented by Indian, Italian, Turkish and Thai restaurants, as the cities of Vietnam boast truly international cuisine.

There are often no set hours for places to eat, but as a general rule of thumb, cafés are open most of the day and into the night. Street stalls are open from very early in the morning until late at night. Restaurants usually open for lunch (between 11am and 2pm) and dinner (between 5pm or 6pm and 10pm or 11pm).

A mobile rambutan stall
AUSTIN BUSH

Quick Eats

Street food is an important part of everyday life. Like much of Southeast Asia, the Vietnamese people are inveterate snackers. They can be found in impromptu stalls at any time of day or night, delving into a range of snacky things. Streetfood is cheap, cheerful and it's a cool way to get up close and personal with Vietnamese cuisine.

VEGETARIANS & VEGANS

The good news is that there is now more choice than ever before when it comes to vegetarian dining. The bad news is that you have not landed in Veg Heaven, for the Vietnamese are voracious omnivores. While they dearly love their vegies, they also dearly love anything that crawls on the ground, swims in the sea or flies in the air.

In keeping with Buddhist precepts, many restaurants go vegie on the 1st and 15th of each lunar month, and this is a great time to scour the markets. Otherwise, be wary. Any dish of vegetables is likely to have been cooked with fish sauce or shrimp paste. If you're vegan, you've got a bigger challenge.

'Mock meat' restaurants are an exquisite experience for those who want to remain true to their vegetarian principles, but secretly miss their bacon sandwiches. Found all throughout Vietnam, these restuarants use tofu and pulses to cook up magic meat-like dishes that even the most hardened carnivores enjoy. These restaurants are known as *com chay* (vegetarian restaurant) and serve such dishes as *dau phu/tau hu kho* (braised tofu – North/South).

HABITS & CUSTOMS

Enter the Vietnamese kitchen and you will be convinced that good food comes from simplicity. Essentials consist of a strong flame, basic cutting utensils, a mortar and pestle, and a well-blackened pot or two. The kitchen is so sacred that it is inhabited by its own deities. The spiritual guardian of the hearth must have its due and the most important object in the kitchen is its altar.

The Vietnamese like to eat three meals a day. Breakfast is simple and may be *pho* or *congee* (rice porridge). Baguettes are available at any time of day or night, and go down well with coffee.

Betel leaves, often accompanied by betel nuts
AUSTIN BUSH

DOS & DON'TS

- Do wait for your host to sit first.
- Don't turn down food placed in your bowl by your host.
- Do learn to use chopsticks.
- Don't leave chopsticks in a V-shape in the bowl (a symbol of death).
- Do use the cold towel that is usually provided.
- Don't jump out of your seat when somebody pops open the cold towel.
- Do tip directly to the staff and not with the bill, as this will ensure the staff get the gratuity.
- Don't tip if there is already a service charge on the bill.
- Do drink every time someone offers a toast.
- Don't be sick or pass out face down on the table if festivities go on all night.

A speciality of northern Vietnam: *banh cuon* (steamed rice noodles with a savoury filling)
AUSTIN BUSH

Lunch starts early, around 11am. People traditionally went home to eat with their families, but many locals now eat at nearby street cafés, washing the food down with lashings of *bia hoi*.

Dinner is a time for family bonding. The dishes are arranged around the central rice bowl and diners each have a small eating bowl.

When ordering from a restaurant menu don't worry about the proper succession of courses. All dishes are placed in the centre of the table as soon as they are ready. It may seem like gastronomic Russian roulette, but just spin the cylinder, pull the trigger and take your chance. The worst blast you can get will come from the spices.

Table Etiquette

Sit at the table with your bowl on a small plate, chopsticks and a soup spoon at the ready. Each place setting will include a small dipping bowl at the top right-hand side of the bowl for the *nuoc mam, nuoc cham* (dipping sauce made from *nuoc mam,* with oil, sugar, garlic, rice wine vinegar, lime juice and onions) or other dipping sauces.

When serving yourself from the central bowls, use the communal serving spoon so as not to dip your chopsticks into it. To begin eating, just pick up your bowl with the left hand, bring it close to your mouth and use the chopsticks to manoeuvre in the food.

It is polite for the host to offer more food than the guests can eat, and it is polite for the guests not to eat everything in sight. If you are invited out, bringing something that links back to your home country will always be a winner.

COOKING COURSES

The best way to tackle Vietnamese cuisine head on is to sign up for a cooking course during your stay. For those who fall in love with the food, there is no better experience than re-creating the real recipes back home. It's also a great way to introduce your Vietnam experience to friends; they may not want to hear the stories or see the photos, but offer them a mouthwatering meal and they will all come running!

Cooking courses have really taken off in the last few years as more and more travellers combine the twin passions of eating and exploring. Courses range from budget classes in the local specialities of Hoi An (p248) to gastronomic gallops through the country's classic cuisine at some of the luxury hotels in Hanoi (p106) and Ho Chi Minh City (HCMC; p355). If you are set on serious studies, try a short course in Hoi An and negotiate for something longer once you've tasted the experience.

Dishing up steamed crabs
AUSTIN BUSH

EAT YOUR WORDS

Speaking some of the local lingo always helps and never more than when it's time for a meal. Locals will appreciate your efforts, even if your pronunciation is off the mark, and might just introduce you to some regional specialities you would otherwise never have discovered.

Useful Phrases

restaurant
nhà hàng — nyaà haàng

Do you have a menu in English?
Bạn có thực đơn bằng tiếng Anh không? — baạn káw tụhrk đern bùhng díng aang kawm

I'm a vegetarian.
Tôi ăn chay. — doy uhn jay

I'd like ...
Xin cho tôi ... — sin jo doy ...

What's the speciality here?
Ở đây có món gì đặc biệt? — ẻr đay kó món zeè dụhk bee·ụht

Not too spicy please.
Xin đừng cho cay quá. — sin đùrng jo ğay gwaá

No sugar.
Không đường. — kawm dur-èrng

No salt.
Không muối. — kawm moo-eé

Can I get this without the meat?
Cho tôi món này không thịt được không? — jo doi món này kawm tịt đuhr-ẹrk kawm

I'm allergic to ....
Tôi bị dị ứng với ... — doy beẹ zeẹ úhrng ver-eé ...

I don't eat ...
Tôi không được ăn ... — doy kawm đuhr-ẹrk uhn ...

- **beef** — *thịt bò* — tịt bò
- **chicken** — *thịt gà* — tịt gaà
- **fish** — *cá* — kaá
- **fish sauce** — *nước mắm* — nuhr-érk múhm
- **pork** — *thịt heo* — tịt hay-o
- **peanuts** — *lạc/đậu phộng (N/S)* — lak/dọh fọm

Can you please bring me ...?
Xin mang cho tôi...? — sin maang jo doy ...

- **a spoon** — *cái thìa* — ğaí tee-ùh
- **a knife** — *con dao* — ğon zow
- **a fork** — *cái dĩa/cái nĩa (N/S)* — ğaí deẽ-uh/ğaí neẽ-uh

chopsticks
đôi đũa đoy-ee đoõ-uh
a glass
cái cốc/cái ly (N/S) ğaí káwp/ğaí lee

Can I have a (beer) please?
Xin cho tôi (chai bia)? sin jo doy (jai bee-uh)
Thank you, that was delicious.
Cám ơn, ngon lắm. ğaám ern, ngon lúhm
The bill, please.
Xin tính tiền. sin díng dee-ùhn

Menu Decoder

TYPICAL DISHES

bánh bao (baáng bow) – **sweet, doughy Chinese pastry filled with meat and vegetables and dunked in soy sauce**
bánh chưng (baáng juhrng) – **square cakes made from sticky rice and filled with beans, onion and pork, boiled in leaves for 10 hours**
bánh cuốn (baáng ğoo-úhn) – **steamed rice-paper rolls with minced and pressed pork, dried shrimp**
bò bảy món (bò bảy món) – **seven beef dishes**
bún bò huế (bún bò hwé) – **spicy beef noodle soup**
bún chả (bún jaả) – **rice vermicelli with pork and vegetables**
bún thịt nướng (bún tịt nuhr-érng) – **rice vermicelli with char-grilled pork**
canh khổ qua (ğaáng kảw gwaa) – **a bitter soup**
chả (jaả) – **pressed pork, a cold meat/cold cut**
chả cá lã vọng (jaả ğaá laã vọm) – **grilled fish cooked with noodles, dill, turmeric and spring onions in a charcoal brazier**
chả cá (jaả ğaá) – **filleted fish slices grilled over charcoal**
chả quế (jaả gwé) – **pressed pork prepared with cinnamon**
chạo tôm (jọw dawm) – **grilled sugar cane rolled in spiced shrimp paste**
ếch tẩm bột rán (ék dủhm bạwt zaán) – **frog meat soaked in a thin batter and fried in oil**
gỏi ngó sen (gỏy ngó san) – **lotus stem salad**
khoai tây rán/chiên (N/S) (kwai day zaán/jee-uhn) – **french fries**
lẩu (lỏh) – **Vietnamese hotpot, with fish** *(lẩu cá)*, **goat** *(lẩu dê)* **or vegetables only** *(lẩu rau)*
ốc nhồi (áwp nyòy) – **snail meat, pork, chopped green onion, fish sauce and pepper rolled up in ginger leaves and cooked in snail shells**
rau muống xào (zoh moo-úhng sòw) – **stir-fried water spinach with garlic and oyster sauce**

NOODLES

bún bò (bún bò) – **braised beef with rice vermicelli**
hủ tiếu bò kho (hoả dee-oó bò ko) – **beef stew with flat rice noodles**
mì gà (meè gaà) – **chicken soup with thin egg noodles**
miến cua (mee-úhn ğoo-uh) – **cellophane-noodle soup with crab**
phở gà/bò (fẻr gaà/bò) – **rice-noodle soup with chicken/beef**

VEGETARIAN

đậu phụ/tàu hũ (N/S) kho (đọw fụ/tòw hoõ ko) – **braised tofu**
đậu phụ/tàu hũ (N/S) xào xả ớt (đọw fụ/tòw hoõ sòw saả ért) – **tofu fried with lemon grass and chilli**
gỏi cuốn chay (gỏy ğoo-úhn jay) – **vegetarian rice-paper rolls**
nấm rơm kho (núhm zerm ko) – **braised straw mushrooms**
rau cải xào thập cẩm (zoh ğai sòw tụhp ğảhm) – **stir-fried mixed vegetables**
súp rau (súp zoh) – **vegetable soup**

DESSERTS

bánh đậu xanh (baáng đọh saang) – mung-bean cake
bánh ít nhân đậu (baáng ít nyuhn đọh) – pastry made of sticky rice, beans and sugar that's steamed in a banana leaf folded into a triangular pyramid
chè (jà) – served in a tall ice-cream sundae glass containing beans, fruit, coconut and sugar
kem dừa (ğam zuhr-ùh) – mix of ice cream, candied fruit and the jellylike flesh of young coconut
mứt (mút) – candied fruit or vegetables, made with carrot, coconut, kumquat, gourd, ginger root, lotus seeds or tomato
sữa chua (sũhr-uh joo-uh) – sweetened yoghurt

Food Glossary

RICE

mixed fried rice	*cơm rang thập cẩm* (N)	ğerm zaang tụhp ğủhm
	cơm chiên (S)	ğerm jee-uhn
rice	*cơm*	ğerm
rice porridge	*cháo*	jów
steamed rice	*cơm trắng*	ğerm chaáng

MEAT & SEAFOOD

beef	*thịt bò*	tịt bò
chicken	*thịt gà*	tịt gaà
crab	*cua*	ğoo-uh
eel	*lươn*	luhr-ern
fish	*cá*	ğaá
frog	*ếch*	ék
goat	*thịt dê*	tịt ze
offal	*thịt lòng*	tịt lòm
pork	*thịt lợn/heo* (N/S)	tịt lẹrn/hay-o
shrimp/prawns	*tôm*	dawm
snail	*ốc*	áwp
squid	*mực*	mụhrk

FRUIT

apple	*táo/bơm* (N/S)	dów/berm
banana	*chuối*	joo-eé
coconut	*dừa*	zuhr-ùh
grapes	*nho*	nyo
lemon	*chanh*	chaang
lychee	*vải*	vaỉ

FURTHER CULINARY ADVENTURES

- For the lowdown on great eating in HCMC, visit www.noodlepie.com, an excellent foodie insider's guide to Saigon written by a *bun cha*-loving expat.
- *Pleasures of the Vietnamese Table* (2001), by Mai Pham, owner of the renowned Lemon Grass Restaurant in Sacramento, California, sees the author returning to Vietnam to reconnect with her family and food.
- Sticky Rice (http://stickyrice.typepad.com) the website for foodies in Hanoi, and has the lowdown on dozens of places to dine and drink in the city.
- For the full take on Vietnamese cuisine, check out *Authentic Vietnamese Cooking: Food from a Family Table* (1999) by Corinne Trang. Illustrated with captivating black and white images, this is an entertaining way to learn the art of cooking.

mandarin	*quýt*	gweét
mango	*xoài*	swaì
orange	*cam*	ğaam
papaya	*đu đủ*	đoo đỏo
pineapple	*dứa*	zuhr-úh
strawberry	*dâu*	zoh
watermelon	*dưa hấu*	zuhr-uh hóh

VEGETABLES

cabbage	*bắp cải*	búhp ğaỉ
carrot	*cà rốt*	ğaà záwt
corn	*ngô/bắp* (N/S)	ngow/búp
cucumber	*dưa leo*	zuhr-uh lay-o
eggplant	*cà tím*	ğaà dím
green beans	*đậu xanh*	đọh saang
green pepper	*ớt xanh*	ért saang
lettuce	*rau diếp*	zoh zee-úhp
mushrooms	*nấm*	núhm
peas	*đậu bi*	đọh bee
potato	*khoai tây*	kwai day
pumpkin	*bí ngô*	beé ngaw
sweet potato	*khoai lang*	kwai laang
tomato	*cà chua*	ğaà joo-uh

DRINKS

beer	*bia*	bi-a
coffee	*cà phê*	ğaà fe
fruit shake	*sinh tố*	sing dáw
hot black coffee	*cà phê đen nóng*	ğaà fe đen nóm
hot black tea	*trà nóng*	chaà nóm
hot milk	*sữa nóng*	sũhr-uh nóm
hot milk black tea	*trà sữa nóng*	chaà sũhr-uh nóm
hot milk coffee	*nâu nóng* (N)	noh nóm
	cà phê sữa nóng (S)	ğaà fe sũhr-uh nóm
ice	*đá*	đaá
iced black coffee	*cà phê đá*	ğaà fe đaá
iced chocolate	*cacao đá*	ğa-ğow đaá
iced lemon juice	*chanh đá*	jaang đaá
iced milk	*sữa đá*	sũhr-uh đaá
iced milk coffee	*nâu đá* (N)	noh đaá
	cà phê sữa đá (S)	ğaà fe sũhr-uh đaá
milk	*sữa*	sũhr-uh
mineral water	*nước khoáng* (N)	nuhr-érk kwaáng
	nước suối (S)	nuhr-érk soo-eé
no ice	*không đá*	kawm đaá
orange juice	*cam vắt*	ğaam vúht
soda water & lemon	*soda chanh*	so-daa jaang
soy milk	*sữa đậu nành*	sũhr-uh đọh naàng
tea	*chè/trà* (N/S)	jà/chaà

The Culture

THE NATIONAL PSYCHE

The Vietnamese have been shaped by their history, which is littered with the scars of battles against enemies old and new. The Chinese have been the traditional threat and the proximity of this northern giant has cast a long shadow over Vietnam and its people. They respect but fear China, and in the context of 2000 years of history, the French and the Americans are but a niggling annoyance that were duly dispatched. The Vietnamese are battle-hardened, proud and nationalistic, as they have earned their stripes in successive skirmishes with the world's mightiest powers.

But that's the older generation, who remember every inch of the territory for which they fought and every bomb and bullet that rained upon them during the long, hard years. For the new generation, Vietnam is a different place: a place to succeed, a place to ignore the staid structures set in stone by the communists, and a place to go out and have some fun. While Uncle Ho (Chi Minh) is respected and revered down the generations for his dedication to the national cause, the young are more into Manchester United's latest signings than the party's latest pronouncements.

It's not only young and old who are living a life apart, but also the urban and rural populations, and the rich and poor. Communism is dead; long live the one-party capitalist dictatorship, where survival of the fittest is the name of the game. Some have survived the transition better than others, and this has created strains in the shape of rural revolts and political backlash. One of the great ironies of the Vietnamese revolution is that it strove to impose a communist system on a people born with a commercial gene, a competitive instinct to do business and to do it at any hour of the dayor night. To the Vietnamese, business, work, commerce – call it what you like – is life.

The north-south divide lingers on. The war may be history, but prejudice is alive and well. Ask a southerner what they think of northerners and they'll say they have a 'hard face', that they take themselves too seriously and don't know how to have fun. Ask a northerner what they think of southerners and they will say they are too superficial, obsessed by business and, well, bling. Caricatures they may be, but they shed light on the very real differences between north and south that go beyond the language. Climate plays its part too; just think of the differences between northern and southern Europe and you have a snapshot of how one people can become two. Not forgetting that the north has lived with communism for more than half a century, while the south had more than two decades of freewheelin' free-for-all with the Americans. For more on this, see The North-South Divide, p43.

Shadows and Wind (1999) by journalist Robert Templer is a snappily written exploration of contemporary Vietnam, from Ho Chi Minh personality cults to Vietnam's rock-and-roll youth.

Finally, don't forget 'face' – or more importantly the art of not making the locals lose face. Face is all in Asia, and in Vietnam it is above all. Having 'big face' is synonymous with prestige, and prestige is particularly important in Vietnam. All families, even poor ones, are expected to have big wedding parties and throw their money around like it is water in order to gain face. This is often ruinously expensive but far less important than 'losing face'. And it is for this reason that foreigners should never lose their tempers with the Vietnamese; this will bring unacceptable 'loss of face' to the individual involved and end any chance of a sensible solution to the dispute.

LIFESTYLE

Traditionally, Vietnamese life has revolved around family, fields and faith, the rhythm of rural existence continuing for centuries at the same pace. For the majority of the population still living in the countryside, these constants have remained unchanged, with several generations sharing the same roof, the same rice and the same religion. But in recent decades these rhythms have been jarred by war and ideology, as the peasants were dragged from all they held dear to defend their motherland, and later herded into cooperatives as the party tried to take over as the moral and social beacon in the lives of the people.

The Communist Party failed to move the masses in the post-war period. Communism only converted a few, just as the French and Americans had only corrupted a few before it, and, for the majority, it was to the familiar they looked to define their lives. But this is beginning to change and it's not due to Uncle Ho or Tricky Dicky (Nixon), but to a combination of a population shift from the countryside to the cities and a demographic shift from old to young.

For an in-depth insight into the culture of Vietnam, including fashion, film and music, check out www.thingsasian.com.

Like China and Thailand before it, Vietnam is experiencing its very own '60s swing, as the younger generation stand up for a different lifestyle to that of their parents. This is creating plenty of feisty friction in the cities, as sons and daughters dress as they like, date who they want and hit the town until all hours. But few live on their own and they still come home to mum and dad at the end of the day, where arguments might arise, particularly when it comes to marriage and settling down.

Extended family is important to the Vietnamese and that includes second or third cousins, the sort of family that many Westerners may not even realise they have. The extended family comes together during times of trouble and times of joy, celebrating festivals and successes, mourning deaths or disappointments. This is a source of strength for many of the older generation,

DISPATCHES FROM THE NORTH

How has Vietnam changed in your lifetime?

Life was very hard before *doi mo* (economic reform; 1986) as many people lived on subsidies. *Doi moi* was not only an economic awakening, but a social awakening, as people had a better understanding of the shortages and the misery of the past. Now we have access to information and news from all over the world and this has raised our national expectations.

The government has begun to look after the cultural history of the country. Monuments and buildings have been restored, artists like me have more freedom to express our vision and the media is more free to discuss the bad as well as the good.

How has Hanoi changed?

Life is changing every day in Hanoi. Hanoi is no longer poor like it was in the 1980s. There is lots of construction and it sometimes seems the buildings sprout like mushrooms after the rain.

Many people in Hanoi are earning high salaries working for foreign companies, but they soon start to live a foreign lifestyle. They forget who they are and lose touch with their traditions and this is also changing the face of Hanoi. Hanoi is growing, but growth is not always for the best.

How has your life changed?

When I came back to Vietnam from the Soviet Union 20 years ago, life was difficult. I had to cycle daily from Hanoi to Bat Trang to work as a painter to earn money to attend the Fine Arts University.

In 1993, I graduated but it was not an easy climate to find a job. I had to take a job in advertising to make money to follow my dream to be a painter. In 1996, the tourism industry started to grow and I started work as a painter for a tourist company, which allowed me to travel all over the country.

while for the younger generation it's likely to be friends, girlfriends or gangs who play the role of anchor.

With so many family members under one roof, the Vietnamese don't share Western concepts of privacy and personal space. Don't be surprised if people walk into your hotel room without knocking. You may be sitting starkers in your hotel room when the maid unlocks the door and walks in unannounced.

One tradition that remains central to Vietnamese life is geomancy, or feng shui as most of us know it today. Known as *phong thuy* to the locals, this is the art (or science) of living in tune with the environment. The orientation of houses, tombs, *dinh* (communal meeting halls) and pagodas is determined by geomancers. The location of an ancestor's grave is an especially serious matter: if the grave is in the wrong spot or facing the wrong way, there's no telling what trouble the spirits might cause. The same goes for the location of the family altar, which can be found in nearly every Vietnamese home. Westerners planning to go into business with a Vietnamese partner will need to budget for a geomancer to ensure the venture is successful.

Failing businesses often call in a geomancer (feng shui expert). Sometimes the solution is to move a door or a window. If this doesn't do the trick, it might be necessary to move an ancestor's grave. Distraught spirits may have to be placated with payments of cash.

GOVERNMENT & ECONOMY

Vietnam is a paradox. It's a communist government with a capitalist economy. Telling it how it is, communism, socialism, call it what you will, is dead. This is a one-party capitalist bureaucracy that doesn't need to sweat about bothersome elections and democratic rights. Officially, communism is still king, but there can be few party hacks that really believe Vietnam is a Marxist utopia. Market-oriented socialism is the new mantra, although socially-responsible capitalism might be nearer the mark.

My real love is painting and my work is quite popular. My living is stable, my family is happy, and we like to visit new areas of Vietnam for our holidays. I like to wander around the desolate and natural places that will soon disappear when life moves on.

How has tourism affected Vietnam?

As tourism grows, many people are trying to study foreign languages. Tourists are coming not only to enjoy, but also to learn about the culture and tradition of our country. Tourism has re-invigorated our traditional culture, such as water puppets, hand-made silk and folk songs.

Nowadays the young Vietnamese like travelling. They are exploring the beauty of the country, the spirit of the Vietnamese nation. They are also learning about foreign cultures and traditions. It has opened their mind and reinforced their pride to be Vietnamese.

What about the north-south divide?

The southerners are generous and free. They live for today, and don't worry about tomorrow. Southerners are not good at saving up for rainy days. They work hard by day but play hard by night. They are quick-learners. They are as sharp as a needle in business and dare to take risks. This means service in the South is of a higher standard than in the north.

Southerners respect northerners, because they see them as polite and courteous. When southerners meet Hanoi people for the first time, they often don't like them. Yet the more they get to know each other, the more the Saigonese really treasure their brothers from Hanoi.

Your favourite place in Vietnam?

I like Hoi An very much. Everybody is very kind. Hoi An has ancient streets, an old village atmosphere and a beautiful beach.

Conversations in Hanoi with artist Mr Tran Do Nghia

It's full steam ahead, China style, with Vietnam becoming Asia's second-fastest growing economy in 2005, posting growth of 8.4%. Ho Chi Minh may be a hero, but it is Deng Xiaoping's school of economics that has prevailed, not the austere collectivism once espoused by Ho. And it's working well. Vietnam has become the new darling among international investors, challenging Thailand's ambition to become the 'Detroit' of Asia, churning out garments galore for Western fashion houses and sucking in hi-tech investors such as Intel, with multimillion dollar plans for chip plants. Let the good times roll, Vietnam's economy is in top gear. It's not only the big ticket industries that are doing well; Vietnam recently overtook Thailand as the world's largest rice exporter, proving that the rural economy is roaring.

Vietnam now produces and uses more cement each year than its former colonial ruler France.

Vietnam joined the World Trade Organization in late 2006. It remains to be seen how this will impact on the economy, but even more interesting will be to see how the government deals with the issues of piracy and intellectual property rights. Vietnam, like China, has long been a nation where copy-catting is a national pastime. Not just software, music, books and the usual suspects, but even hotels, restaurants and travel agents. It will be interesting to see if the government has the teeth to tackle this issue.

Doi moi or economic reform began in 1986. Collectivisation had almost bankrupted the country and turned the rice bowl of the region into a rice importer. As Soviet aid was scaled back, the Communist Party realised it had to reform to survive. Free market reforms were slowly introduced and Vietnam's economy began to take off.

POPULATION

Vietnam's population hovers at around 84 million, making it the 13th most populous country in the world, and with its population growth rate it might soon hit the top 10. Vietnam is a young country, with an incredible 65% of the population under the age of 30, and after years of revolutionary initiatives encouraging large families, a two-child policy is now enforced in urban areas.

Traditionally a rural agrarian society, the race is on for the move to the cities. Like Thailand and Malaysia before it, Vietnam is experiencing a tremendous shift in the balance of population, as increasing numbers of young

DISPATCHES FROM THE SOUTH

How has Vietnam changed in your lifetime?

Vietnam has changed in so many ways. It is not so long ago that Vietnam had food shortages and now we are one of the largest exporting rice countries in the world. More freedom to study overseas, plus increasing access to information from the internet, is contributing to more open-mindedness in Vietnam. Vietnamese people have more choices in what they want for their lives: what they want to study, what they want to buy, what they want to do, where they want to go. Life is just not as difficult as it was in my parents time days before *doi moi* (1986).

How has Saigon changed?

Saigon has changed so much. As a local, I can feel the changes in every little corner. People have more liberty and freedom in their lives. Saigon is a young dynamic city where people can have fun. We have learned to be more relaxed and live life to the full. Physically, the city has changed a lot, with new buildings altering the skyline every year. It's not as crazy as Bangkok yet, but it is getting there.

How has your life changed?

I am 30 years old now, so I didn't really experience the difficulties of my parents' generation. But I have heard a lot of stories and often compare my life to that of my father. I have been a lot more lucky than him. I am living without the war. I am living very comfortably. I can choose to study at university. I can choose any job or career. I can choose where I want to go for holiday. When my father was this age, he just didn't have any real choices.

people desert the fields in search of those mythical streets paved with gold in Hanoi or Ho Chi Minh City (HCMC). The population of HCMC and its suburbs is already approaching seven million, Hanoi has more than three million, and both Danang and Haiphong are millionaires. As economic migrants continue to seek their fortune, these numbers look set to soar.

THE PEOPLE OF VIETNAM

Vietnamese culture and civilisation have been profoundly influenced by the Chinese, and to many observers of Vietnamese history, China has long treated Vietnam as some sort of renegade province rather than an independent entity. However, the Vietnamese existed as a people in the Red River Delta region long before the first waves of Chinese arrived more than 2000 years ago.

Vietnamese who have emigrated are called Viet Kieu. They have traditionally been maligned by locals as cowardly, arrogant and privileged. In the '90s, returning Viet Kieu were often followed by police but now official policy is to welcome them, and their money, back to the motherland.

History has, however, influenced the mix of Vietnamese minorities. The steady expansion southwards in search of cultivable lands absorbed first the Kingdom of Champa and later the eastern extent of the Khmer empire, and both the Chams and the Khmers are sizeable minorities today. There are perhaps one million Khmers inhabiting the Mekong Delta, or what they refer to as Kampuchea Krom (lower Cambodia), and almost as many Chams living along the coastal regions between Phan Rang and Danang.

Traffic was not only one way. Many of the 50 or more ethno-linguistic minority groups that inhabit the far northwest only migrated to these areas from Yunnan (China) and Tibet in the last few centuries. They moved into the mountains that the lowland Vietnamese considered uncultivable and help make up the most colourful part of the ethnic mosaic that is Vietnam today. For more on the minorities who inhabit the mountains of Vietnam, see Hill Tribes, p72.

While the invasions and occupations of old may be over, the largest minority group in Vietnam has always been the ethnic-Chinese community, which

How has tourism affected Vietnam?

People over the world know more about Vietnam, because the media coverage has changed. No more wars, no more soldiers, just a beautiful country with smiling people. More and more tourists are coming to Vietnam. This brings more money into the economy, more knowledge to the local people, and promotes cultural exchange. This is good for everyone, the locals and the tourists.

What about the north-south divide?

I think northern people are still very traditional when compared with Saigon. They are more discreet than the more open southerners, but can be a bit self-righteous. They are a little more frugal than southerners when it comes to spending money, but they seem more industrious than Saigon people. But I think Saigon people are friendly, open-minded, easy-going, simple… of course, I'm from the south!

Your favourite place in Vietnam?

In Vietnam, it has to be Saigon. In my heart, the name 'Saigon' is so spiritual and so dear… Even though I travel a lot, I can't wait to get back to Saigon. I love that feeling when the plane is landing at Tan Son Nhat Airport in Saigon, I can imagine the heat of the weather, the haste of the people and the buzz of traffic… Everything seems so familiar and so friendly… I whisper to myself, 'home'.

Conversations in Saigon with office manager Miss Nhu Ly Thu

WHEN IN NAM… DO AS THE VIETS

Take your time to learn a little about the local culture in Vietnam. Not only will this ensure you don't inadvertently cause offence or, worse, spark an international incident, but it will also ingratiate you to your hosts. Here are a few top tips to help you go native.

Dress Code

Respect local dress standards: shorts to the knees, women's tops covering the shoulder, particularly at religious sites. Always remove your shoes before entering a temple. Nude sunbathing is considered *totally* inappropriate, even on beaches.

Meet & Greet

The traditional Vietnamese form of greeting is to press your hands together in front of your body and bow slightly. These days, the Western custom of shaking hands has almost completely taken over.

It's on the Cards

Exchanging business cards is an important part of even the smallest transaction or business contact. Get some printed before you arrive in Vietnam and hand them out like confetti.

Deadly Chopsticks

Leaving a pair of chopsticks sitting vertically in a rice bowl looks very much like the incense sticks that are burned for the dead. This is a powerful sign and is not appreciated anywhere in Asia.

Mean Feet

Like the Chinese and Japanese, Vietnamese strictly maintain clean floors and it's usual to remove shoes when entering somebody's home. It's rude to point the bottom of your feet towards other people. Never, ever point your feet towards anything sacred, such as a Buddha image.

Hats Off to Them

As a form of respect to elderly or other esteemed people, such as monks, take off your hat and bow your head politely when addressing them. In Asia, the head is the symbolic highest point – never pat or touch an adult on the head.

makes up much of the commercial class in the cities. While the government has traditionally viewed them with suspicion, and drove many of them out of the country as 'boat people' in the late 1970s, many are now comfortably resettled and play a major part in driving economic development.

In the past, the term *lien xo!* (Soviet Union) was often shouted at Westerners, all of whom were assumed to be the legendary and very unpopular Russians residing in Vietnam. These days, depending on your dress, a more common name is *tay balo!* (literally, 'Westerner backpack'), a contemporary term for scruffy-looking backpackers.

RELIGION

Four great philosophies and religions have shaped the spiritual life of the Vietnamese: Buddhism, Confucianism, Taoism and, later, Christianity. Over the centuries, Confucianism, Taoism and Buddhism have fused with popular Chinese beliefs and ancient Vietnamese animism to create the Tam Giao (Triple Religion). When discussing religion, most Vietnamese people are likely to say that they are Buddhist, but when it comes to family or civic duties they are likely to follow the moral and social code of Confucianism, and turn to Taoist concepts to understand the nature of the cosmos.

Although the majority of the population has only a vague notion of Buddhist doctrines, they invite monks to participate in life-cycle ceremonies, such as funerals. Buddhist pagodas are seen by many Vietnamese as a physical and spiritual refuge from an uncertain world.

Buddhism

Buddhism, like all great religions, has been through a messy divorce, and arrived in Vietnam in two flavours: Mahayana Buddhism (the Northern school) proceeded north into Nepal, Tibet, China, Korea, Mongolia, Vietnam and Japan, while Theravada Buddhism (the Southern school) took the southern route from India, Sri Lanka, Myanmar and Cambodia.

The Theravada school of Buddhism is an earlier and, according to its followers, less corrupted form of Buddhism than the Mahayana schools found around East Asia and the Himalayan regions. As Therevada followers tried to preserve and limit the Buddhist doctrines to only those canons codified in the early Buddhist era, the Mahayana school gave Theravada Buddhism the pejorative name 'Hinayana' (meaning 'Lesser Vehicle'). They considered themselves 'Greater Vehicle' because they built upon the earlier teachings.

Mahayana Buddhists believe in Boddhisatvas (Quan Am in Vietnam) or Buddhas that attain nirvana but postpone their enlightenment to stay on earth to save their fellow beings.

The predominant school of Buddhism, and indeed religion, in Vietnam is Mahayana Buddhism (Dai Thua, or Bac Tong, meaning 'From the North'). The largest Mahayana sect in the country is Zen (Dhyana or Thien), also known as the school of meditation. Dao Trang (the Pure Land school), another important sect, is practised mainly in the south.

Theravada Buddhism (Tieu Thua, or Nam Tong) is found mainly in the Mekong Delta region, and is mostly practised by ethnic-Khmers.

Vietnamese Buddhist monks *(bonze)* minister to the spiritual needs of the peasantry, but it is largely up to the monks whether they follow the lore of Taoism or the philosophy of Buddhism.

Taoism

Taoism (Lao Giao, or Dao Giao) originated in China and is based on the philosophy of Laotse (The Old One), who lived in the 6th century BC. Little is known about Laotse and there is some debate as to whether or not he actually existed. He is believed to have been the custodian of the imperial archives for the Chinese government, and Confucius is supposed to have consulted him.

To learn more about Buddhism in Vietnam, check out the website www.quangduc.com. The official website of the Quang Duc Monastery in Melbourne, Australia, it is a gateway to all things Buddhist.

Understanding Taoism is not easy. The philosophy emphasises contemplation and simplicity. Its ideal is returning to the Tao (The Way, or the essence of which all things are made), and it emphasises *am* and *duong*, the Vietnamese equivalents of Yin and Yang. Much of Taoist ritualism has been absorbed into Chinese and Vietnamese Buddhism, including, most commonly, the use of dragons and demons to decorate temple rooftops.

Confucianism

More a philosophy than an organised religion, Confucianism (Nho Giao, or Khong Giao) has been an important force in shaping Vietnam's social system and the lives and beliefs of its people.

Confucius (Khong Tu) was born in China around 550 BC. He saw people as social beings formed by society yet also capable of shaping their society.

PAGODA OR TEMPLE?

Travelling around Vietnam, there are a lot of pagodas and temples, but how does the average person know which is which? The Vietnamese regard a *chua* (pagoda) as a place of worship where they make offerings or pray. A Vietnamese *den* (temple) is not really a place of worship, but rather a structure built to honour some great historical figure (Confucius, Tran Hung Dao, even Ho Chi Minh).

The Cao Dai temple seems to somehow fall between the cracks. Given the mixture of ideas that is part and parcel of Cao Daism, it's hard to say if it's a temple, pagoda, church or mosque.

TET: THE BIG ONE

Tet is Christmas, New Year and birthdays all rolled into one. Tet Nguyen Dan (Festival of the First Day) ushers in the Lunar New Year and is the most significant date in the Vietnamese calendar. It's a time when families reunite in the hope of good fortune for the coming year, and ancestral spirits are welcomed back into the family home. And the whole of Vietnam celebrates a birthday; everyone becomes one year older.

The festival falls some time between 19 January and 20 February, the same dates as Chinese New Year. The first three days after New Year's Day are the official holidays but many people take the whole week off, particularly in the south.

Tet rites begin seven days before New Year's Day. This is when the Tao Quan – the three Spirits of the Hearth, found in the kitchen of every home – ascend to the heavens to report on the past year's events to the Jade Emperor. Altars, laden with offerings, are assembled in preparation for the gods' departure, all in the hope of receiving a favourable report and ensuring good luck for the family in the coming year.

Other rituals as Tet approaches include visiting cemeteries and inviting the spirits of dead relatives home for the celebrations. Absent family members return home so that the whole family can celebrate Tet under the same roof. All loose ends are tied up so that the new year can be started with a clean slate; debts are paid and cleaning becomes the national sport.

A New Year's tree *(cay neu)* is constructed to ward off evil spirits. Kumquat trees are popular throughout the country, while branches of pink peach blossoms *(dao)* grace houses in the north, and yellow apricot blossoms *(mai)* can be found in homes further south.

For a spectacular sight, go to ĐL Nguyen Hue in Ho Chi Minh City, much of which is taken over by the annual Tet flower market. In Hanoi, the area around Pho Hang Dau and Pho Hang Ma is transformed into a massive peach-blossom and kumquat-tree market.

On New Year's Eve the Tao Quan return to earth. At the stroke of midnight all problems from the previous year are left behind and mayhem ensues. The goal is to make as much noise as possible. Drums and percussion are popular, as were firecrackers until they were banned in 1995.

The events of New Year's Day are crucial as it's believed they affect the course of life in the year ahead. People take extra care not to be rude or show anger. Other activities that are believed to attract bad spirits include sewing, sweeping, swearing and breaking things.

It's crucial that the first visitor of the year to each household is suitable. They're usually male – best of all is a wealthy married man with several children. Foreigners are sometimes welcomed as the first to enter the house, although not always, so it's unwise to visit any Vietnamese house on the first day of Tet, unless explicitly invited.

Apart from New Year's Eve itself, Tet is not a particularly boisterous celebration. It's like Christmas Day, a quiet family affair. Difficulty in booking transport and accommodation aside, this is an excellent time to visit the country, especially to witness the contrasting frenzied activity before the New Year and the calm (and quiet streets!) that follows. Wherever you're staying, you're sure to be invited to join in the celebrations.

If you are visiting Vietnam during Tet, be sure you learn this phrase: *chúc mùng nam mói* – Happy New Year!

He believed that the individual exists in and for society and drew up a code of ethics to guide the individual in social interaction. This code laid down a person's obligations to family, society and the state, which remain the pillars of Vietnamese society today.

Ancestor Worship

Vietnamese ancestor worship dates from before the arrival of Confucianism or Buddhism. Ancestor worship is based on the belief that the soul lives on after death and becomes the protector of its descendants. Because of the influence the spirits of one's ancestors exert on the living, it is considered not only shameful for the spirits to be upset or restless, but downright dangerous.

Traditionally, the Vietnamese worship and honour the spirits of their ancestors regularly, especially on the anniversary of their death. To request help for success in business or on behalf of a sick child, sacrifices and prayers are given to the ancestral spirits. Important worship elements are the family altar and a plot of land whose income is set aside for the support of the ancestors.

Cao Daism is a cocktail of the world's faiths and philosophies. Its prophets include Buddha, Confucius, Jesus Christ, Moses and Mohammed, and some wacky choices, such as Joan of Arc, William Shakespeare and Victor Hugo.

Cao Daism

Cao Daism is a Vietnamese sect that seeks to create the ideal religion by fusing the secular and religious philosophies of both East and West. It was founded in the early 1920s based on messages revealed in seances to Ngo Minh Chieu, the group's founder. At present there are about two million followers of Cao Daism in Vietnam. The sect's colourful headquarters is in Tay Ninh (p381), 96km northwest of HCMC.

LUNAR CALENDAR

The Vietnamese lunar calendar closely resembles that of the Chinese. Year one of the Vietnamese lunar calendar corresponds to 2637 BC and each lunar month has 29 or 30 days, resulting in years with 355 days.

Approximately every third year is a leap year; an extra month is added between the third and fourth months to keep the lunar year in time with the solar year. If this was not done, the seasons would shift around the lunar year, playing havoc with all elements of life linked to the agricultural seasons. To check the Gregorian (solar) date corresponding to a lunar date, pick up any Vietnamese or Chinese calendar.

The Vietnamese have 12 zodiacal animals, each of which represents one year in a 12-year cycle. If you want to know your sign in the Vietnamese zodiac, look up your year of birth in the following chart. Don't forget that the Vietnamese New Year falls in late January or mid February. If your birthday is in the first half of January it will be included in the zodiac year before the calendar year of your birth.

Rat *(tý)*: generous, social, insecure, idle

1924	1936	1948	1960	1972	1984	1996	2008

Buffalo *(suu)*: stubborn, conservative, patient

1925	1937	1949	1961	1973	1985	1997	2009

Tiger *(dan)*: creative, brave, overbearing

1926	1938	1950	1962	1974	1986	1998	2010

Cat *(mao)*: timid, affectionate, amicable

1927	1939	1951	1963	1975	1987	1999	2011

Dragon *(thin)*: egotistical, strong, intelligent

1928	1940	1952	1964	1976	1988	2000	2012

Snake *(ty)*: luxury seeking, secretive, friendly

1929	1941	1953	1965	1977	1989	2001	2013

Horse *(ngo)*: emotional, clever, quick thinker

1930	1942	1954	1966	1978	1990	2002	2014

Goat *(mui)*: charming, good with money, indecisive

1931	1943	1955	1967	1979	1991	2003	2015

Monkey *(than)*: confident, humorous, fickle

1932	1944	1956	1968	1980	1992	2004	2016

Rooster *(dau)*: diligent, imaginative, needs attention

1933	1945	1957	1969	1981	1993	2005	2017

Dog *(tuat)*: humble, responsible, patient

1934	1946	1958	1970	1982	1994	2006	2018

Pig *(hoi)*: materialistic, loyal, honest

1935	1947	1959	1971	1983	1995	2007	2019

Hoa Hao Buddhism

The Hoa Hao Buddhist sect (Phat Giao Hoa Hao) was founded in the Mekong Delta in 1939 by Huynh Phu So. After he was miraculously cured of an illness, So began preaching a reformed Buddhism based on the common people and embodied in personal faith rather than elaborate rituals. His Buddhist philosophies involve simplicity in worship and no intermediaries between humans and the Supreme Being. Hoa Hao Buddhists are thought to number approximately 1.5 million.

Christianity

Catholicism was introduced in the 16th century by missionaries. Today, Vietnam has the highest percentage of Catholics (8% to 10% of the population) in Asia outside the Philippines. Under the communist government Catholics faced severe restrictions on their religious activities. As in the USSR, churches were viewed as a capitalist institution and a rival centre of power that could subvert the government. Since 1990, the government has taken a more liberal line and Catholicism is making a comeback.

Protestantism was introduced to Vietnam in 1911 and most of the 200,000 today are Montagnards living in the central highlands. Protestants were doubly unfortunate in that they were persecuted first by the pro-Catholic regime of Diem and later by the communists.

Islam

Muslims, mostly ethnic-Chams, make up about 0.5% of the population. The Chams consider themselves Muslims, but in practice they follow a localised adaptation of Islamic theology and law. Though Muslims usually pray five times a day, the Chams pray only on Fridays and celebrate Ramadan (a month of dawn-to-dusk fasting) for only three days. In addition, their Islam-based religious rituals co-exist with animism and the worship of Hindu deities. Circumcision is symbolically performed on boys at age 15, when a religious leader makes the gestures of circumcision with a wooden knife.

Hinduism

Champa was profoundly influenced by Hinduism and many of the Cham towers, built as Hindu sanctuaries, contain *lingas* that are still worshipped by ethnic-Vietnamese and ethnic-Chinese alike. After the fall of Champa in the 15th century, most Chams who remained in Vietnam became Muslims (Arab traders brought Islam to Indonesia and Malaysia; these merchants then brought it to Champa) but continued to practise various Hindu rituals and customs. Hundreds of thousands more migrated southwest to Cambodia, where they make up an important minority today.

WOMEN IN VIETNAM

As in many parts of Asia, Vietnamese women take a lot of pain for little gain, with plenty of hard work to do and little authority at the decision-making level. Vietnamese women were highly successful as guerrillas in the American War and brought plenty of grief to US soldiers. After the war, their contributions were given much fanfare, but all the government posts were given to men. In the countryside, you'll see women doing backbreaking jobs, such as crushing rocks at construction sites and carrying heavy baskets. It's doubtful that many Western men would be capable of such strenuous activity.

For a look at the impact of *doi moi* (economic reform) on some Vietnamese women, Vu Xuan Hung's film *Misfortune's End* (1996) tells the tale of a silk weaver deserted by her husband for an upwardly mobile businesswoman.

The country's two-children-per-family policy is boosting the independence of Vietnamese women, and more are delaying marriage to get an education. Around 50% of university students are female, but they're not always given the same opportunity as males to shine after graduation.

One of the sadder realities of the recent opening up to the West has been the influx of pimps posing as 'talent scouts'. Promises of lucrative jobs in developed countries are dangled in front of naive Vietnamese women who later find themselves enslaved as prostitutes. The trafficking of poor, rural women into the sex industry in Cambodia has been a huge problem and in many cases this involves the connivance of family members sacrificing one of their daughters for the rest to survive.

The Vietnamese consider pale skin to be beautiful. On sunny days, trendy Vietnamese women can often be seen strolling under the shade of an umbrella in order to keep from tanning. Women who work in the fields will go to great lengths to preserve their pale skin by wrapping their faces in towels and wearing long-sleeved shirts, elbow-length silk gloves and conical hats. To tell a Vietnamese woman that she has white skin is a great compliment; telling her that she has a 'lovely suntan' is a grave insult.

MEDIA

To the untrained eye, Vietnam looks like it has a flourishing free press, with plenty of newspapers and glossy magazines. However, in reality it is not possible to get a publishing licence unless you are affiliated to the communist party. As many in media say, there is no censorship in Vietnam, only self-censorship. Newspapers and magazines that cross the line are periodically closed down, sometimes for good. TV is even more tightly controlled, although the advent of satellite TV and the internet have made it much easier to get unbiased information from overseas. Vietnam uses the same technology as China to block access to (politically) undesirable websites.

ARTS

Music

TRADITIONAL

Heavily influenced by the Chinese to the north and Indian-influenced Khmer and Cham musical traditions to the south, this blend has produced an original style and instrumentation for Vietnamese music. Written music and the five note (pentatonic) scale may be of Chinese origin, but Vietnamese choral music is unique, as the melody and the tones must move as one; the melody cannot rise during a verse that has a falling tone.

Founded in 1981, Tieng Hat Que Huong's mission is to preserve, develop and promote Vietnamese traditional music, building a bridge between artists, old and new. Visit them at www.tienghatquehuong.com and look up details of forthcoming performances in HCMC.

Vietnamese folk music is usually sung without any instrumental accompaniment and was adapted by the Communist Party for many a patriotic marching song.

Classical, or 'learned music', is rather formal and frigid. It was performed at the imperial court for the entertainment of the mandarin elite. There are two main types of classical chamber music: *hat a dao* from the north and *ca Hue* from central Vietnam.

Traditional music is played on a wide array of indigenous instruments, dating back to the ancient *do son* drums that are sought-after works of art. The best known traditional instrument in use is the *dan bau,* a single-stringed zither that generates an astounding array of tones. Also common at performances of traditional music is the *dan tranh,* a 16-string zither with a haunting melody, and the *to rung,* a large bamboo xylophone.

Each of Vietnam's ethno-linguistic minorities has its own musical traditions that often include distinctive costumes and instruments, such as reed flutes, lithophones (similar to xylophones), bamboo whistles, gongs and stringed instruments made from gourds.

The easiest way to catch a performance of Vietnamese music is to dine at one of the many local restaurants offering traditional performances. Several museums offer short performances.

CONTEMPORARY/POP

Like the rest of Southeast Asia, Vietnam has a thriving domestic pop scene. The most celebrated artist is Khanh Ly, who left Vietnam in 1975 for the USA. She is massive both in Vietnam and abroad. Her music is widely available in Vietnam, but the government frowns on her recently composed lyrics that recall the trials of her life as a refugee.

Vietnam's number one domestic heart-throb is Hué-born Quang Linh, whose early popularity among Saigonese shot him up the local pop charts. He is adored by Vietnamese of all ages for his radiant love songs.

Other celebrated local pop singers include sex symbol Phuong Thanh, Vietnam's answer to Madonna or Britney Spears, only with more clothes. Vietnamese girls are seriously into heart-throb Lam Truong.

Of the legion of legendary Vietnamese contemporary-music composers, the leader of the pack was Trinh Cong Son, who died in HCMC in 2001. A former literature student from Hué, he wrote more than 500 songs, making him perhaps the most prolific Vietnamese composer in history.

Dance

Traditionally reserved for ceremonies and festivals, tourism has brought Vietnamese folk dance back to the mainstream. The Conical Hat Dance is one of the most visually stunning dances. A group of women wearing *ao dai* (the national dress of Vietnam) shake their stuff and spin around, whirling their classic conical hats like Fred Astaire with his cane.

Vietnam's ethnic minorities have their own dancing traditions, which are distinctly different from the Vietnamese majority. A great deal of anthropological research has been carried out in recent years in order to preserve and revive important indigenous traditions.

Some upmarket restaurants host dance performances at the weekend. Minority dances are organised in some of the more popular tourist stops in northwest Vietnam.

Theatre & Puppetry

Vietnamese theatre fuses music, singing, recitation, dance and mime into an artistic whole. These days, the various forms of Vietnamese theatre are performed by dozens of state-funded troupes and companies around the country.

TOP OF THE POPS

Pop music in Vietnam is a fickle beast and artists go in and out of fashion like David Beckham's haircuts. At the time of writing, the music currently doing the rounds on DJ turntables includes this Top 10 of albums.

genre	artist/band	album
Pop Diva	Hong Nhung	*Khu Vuon Yen Tinh*
R&B Diva	My Linh	*Made in Vietnam*
Pop Diva	Phuong Thanh	*Tim Lai Loi The*
Pop Diva	My Tam	*Yesterday and Now*
Male Pop	Dam Vinh Hung	*Hung*
Male Pop	Dan Truong	*Di Ve Noi Xa*
Girl Band	5DK (Nam Dong Ke)	*Em*
Boy Band	MTV	*Rock Show Thoi Gian*
Boy Band	AC&M	*Xin Chao*
Rock Band	The Wall	*Bong Hong Thuy Tinh*

Classical theatre is known as *hat tuong* in the north and *hat boi* in the south and is based on Chinese opera. Classical theatre is very formal, employing fixed gestures and scenery similar to the Chinese classics. The accompanying orchestra, which is dominated by the drum, usually has six musicians. Often, the audience also has a drum so it can pass judgement on the onstage action. It has a limited cast of characters, each of whom is easily identifiable through their make-up and costume. Red face-paint represents courage, loyalty and faithfulness, while traitors and cruel people have white faces. A male character expresses emotions (pensiveness, worry, anger) by fingering his beard in different ways.

To learn more about the unique art of water puppetry or 'Punch and Judy in a pool', visit www.thanglongwaterpuppet.org

Popular theatre *(hat cheo)* expresses social protest through satire, although there has been less protest and more satire since 1975. The singing and verse are in everyday language and include many proverbs and sayings, accompanied by folk melodies.

Modern theatre *(cai luong)* originated in the South in the early 20th century and shows strong Western influences. Spoken drama *(kich noi* or *kich)*, with its Western roots, appeared in the 1920s and is popular among students and intellectuals.

Conventional puppetry *(roi can)* and the uniquely Vietnamese art form of water puppetry *(roi nuoc)*, draw their plots from the same legendary and historical sources as other forms of traditional theatre. It is believed that water puppetry developed when determined puppeteers in the Red River Delta managed to continue performances despite annual flooding (see the boxed text Punch & Judy in a Pool, p121).

Cinema

One of Vietnam's earliest cinematographic efforts was a newsreel of Ho Chi Minh's 1945 Proclamation of Independence. Later, parts of the battle of Dien Bien Phu (p169) were restaged for the benefit of movie cameras.

Returning to Ngo Thuy (1977), directed by Le Manh Thich and Do Khanh Toan, pays homage to the women of Ngo Thuy village. In 1971, these women were the subject of a propaganda film to encourage people to sign up for the war effort.

Prior to reunification, the South Vietnamese movie industry produced a string of sensational, low-budget flicks. Conversely, North Vietnamese film-making efforts were dedicated to 'the mobilisation of the masses for economic reconstruction, the building of socialism and the struggle for national reunification'. Yawn.

In recent years, Vietnamese cinema has evolved from the realm of propaganda to a world that more closely reflects the lives of modern Vietnamese people and the issues they face. Contemporary films span a wide range of themes, from warfare to modern romance.

In Nguyen Khac's *The Retired General* (1988), the central character copes with adjusting from his life as a soldier during the American War to life as a civilian family man, symbolising Vietnam's difficult transition to the post-war era.

Dang Nhat Minh is perhaps Vietnam's most prolific film-maker. In *The Return* (1993), Minh hones in on the complexities of modern relationships, while *The Girl on the River* (1987) tells the stirring tale of a female journalist who joins an ex-prostitute in search of her former lover, a Viet Cong soldier whose life she had saved and whose heart she'd been promised.

Dancing Girl, directed by Le Hoang, caused a major splash with its release in 2003. Telling the story of two HIV-positive prostitutes, Hoa (played by My Duyen) is seen mainlining heroin.

Young overseas-Vietnamese film directors are steadily carving a niche for themselves in the international film industry and snapping up awards at film festivals worldwide.

Tran Anh Hung's touching *The Scent of Green Papaya* (1992), filmed in France, celebrates the coming of age of a young girl working as a servant for an affluent Saigon family during the 1950s. *Cyclo* (1995), Tran Anh Hung's visually stunning masterpiece, charges to the core of HCMC's gritty underworld and its violent existence.

Vietnamese-American Tony Bui made a splash in 1999 with his exquisite feature debut *Three Seasons* (1999). Set in present-day HCMC, this beautifully made film weaves together the lives of four unlikely characters with a US war veteran, played by Harvey Keitel, who comes to Vietnam in search of his long-lost daughter.

Literature

There are three veins of Vietnamese literature. Traditional oral literature *(truyen khau)* began long before recorded history and includes legends, folk songs and proverbs. Sino-Vietnamese literature was written in Chinese characters *(chu nho)*. Dominated by Confucian and Buddhist texts, it was governed by strict rules of metre and verse. Modern Vietnamese literature *(quoc am)* includes anything recorded in *nom* characters. The earliest text written in *nom* was the late-13th-century *Van Te Ca Sau* (Ode to an Alligator).

One of Vietnam's literary masterpieces, *Kim Van Kieu* (The Tale of Kieu) was written during the first half of the 19th century by Nguyen Du (1765–1820), a poet, scholar, mandarin and diplomat.

Paradise of the Blind, by Duong Thu Huong, the first Vietnamese novel to be published in the USA, is set in a northern village and a Hanoi slum and recalls the lives of three women and the hardships they faced over some 40 years.

Architecture

The Vietnamese have not been prolific builders like their Khmer neighbours, who erected the monuments of Angkor in Cambodia, and the Chams, whose graceful brick towers adorn many parts of the southern half of the country. For more on the Chams, check out the boxed text on p264 or follow in their footsteps (p26).

Traditionally, most Vietnamese constructions were made of wood and other materials that decayed in the tropical climate. This, coupled with the fact that almost all stone structures erected by the Vietnamese have been destroyed in countless feudal wars and invasions, means that very little premodern Vietnamese architecture remains.

Plenty of pagodas and temples founded hundreds of years ago are still functioning, but they have usually been rebuilt many times with little concern for the original. As a result, many modern elements have been casually introduced into pagoda architecture – those garish neon haloes for statues of Buddha are a shining example.

Thanks to the custom of ancestor worship, many graves from previous centuries survive today. These include temples erected in memory of high-ranking mandarins, royal-family members and emperors.

Memorials for Vietnamese who died in the wars against the Chinese, French and Americans usually contain cement obelisks inscribed with the words *to quoc ghi cong* ('the country will remember their exploits').

The Sacred Willow (2000), by Duong Van Mai Elliot, spans four tumultuous generations of an upper-class Vietnamese family. This enlightening historical memoir traces French colonisation, WWII and the wars with the French and Americans.

Painting & Sculpture

Painting on frame-mounted silk dates from the 13th century and was at one time the preserve of scholar-calligraphers, who painted grand scenes from nature. Before the advent of photography, realistic portraits for use in ancestor worship were produced. Some of these – usually of former head monks – can still be seen in certain Buddhist pagodas.

During the past century, Vietnamese painting has been influenced by Western trends. Much recent work has had political rather than aesthetic or artistic motives. These propagandist pieces are easy to spot at the Fine Arts Museum (p102) in Hanoi.

The recent economic liberalisation has convinced many young artists to abandon the revolutionary themes and concentrate on producing commercial paintings. Some have gone back to the traditional-style silk or lacquer paintings, while others are experimenting with contemporary subjects.

Vietnamese Painting – From Tradition to Modernity, by Corinne de Ménonville, is a lush look at Vietnamese contemporary painting. For the contributions of women to the art scene, check out *Vietnamese Women Artists* (2004).

The Chams produced spectacular carved sandstone figures for their Hindu and Buddhist sanctuaries. Cham sculpture was profoundly influenced by Indian art but over the centuries it managed to also incorporate Indonesian and Vietnamese elements. The largest single collection of Cham sculpture in the world is found at the Museum of Cham Sculpture (p231) in Danang. For the lowdown on Cham architecture, see the Po Klong Garai Cham Towers, p296.

Lacquerware & Ceramics

The art of making lacquerware was brought to Vietnam from China in the mid-15th century. During the 1930s, the Fine Arts School in Hanoi had several Japanese teachers who introduced new styles and production methods.

Lacquer *(son mai)* is made from resin extracted from the rhus tree. It is creamy white in raw form, but is darkened with pigments in an iron container for 40 hours. After the object has been treated with glue, the requisite 10 coats of lacquer are applied. Each coat must be dried for a week and then thoroughly sanded with pumice and cuttlebone before the next layer can be applied. A specially refined lacquer is used for the 11th and final coat, which is sanded with a fine coal powder and lime wash before the object is decorated. Designs include engraving in low relief, or inlaying mother-of-pearl, egg shell or precious metals.

If you're crazy about your china, or pots about your pottery, try to find a copy of *Viet Nam Ceramics,* an illustrated insight into Vietnamese pottery over the centuries.

The production of ceramics *(gom)* has a long history in Vietnam. In ancient times, ceramic objects were made by coating a wicker mould with clay and baking it. Later, ceramic production became very refined, and each dynastic period is known for its particular techniques and motifs.

It's possible to view ancient ceramics in museums throughout Vietnam. Excavations of archaeological sites are still revealing ancient examples, as are the ongoing discoveries of shipwreck treasures.

Bat Trang (p125), located near Hanoi, is famous for its contemporary ceramic industry.

SPORT

Football (soccer) is Vietnam's number-one spectator sport and the country is mad for it. During the World Cup, the European Champions League or other major clashes, half the country stays up all night to watch live games in different time zones around the world. Post-game fun includes hazardous high-speed motorbike cruising in the streets of Hanoi and HCMC, horns blaring, flags waving. Sadly the national team has not kept pace with this obsession and although one of the stronger teams in Southeast Asia, they remain minnows on the international stage. Think World Cup 2030 or beyond. Their FIFA world ranking is a lowly 172, only one place above Tahiti.

Tennis has considerable snob appeal these days and trendy Vietnamese like to both watch and play. Similarly, golf has taken off as a way to earn brownie points with international investors or local movers and shakers. Golf courses have been developed all over the country, although membership fees ensure it remains a game for the elite.

The Vietnamese are a nation of badminton players and every street is a potential court. Other favourite sports include volleyball and table tennis.

The Hill Tribes

Commonly known as 'hill tribes', a mosaic of ethnic minorities inhabits the mountainous regions of Vietnam. Encountering these hardy people in their mystical mountain homeland is undoubtedly one of the highlights of a visit to Vietnam. Many of the minorities wear incredible costumes and this isn't just a day job. So elaborate are some that it's easy to believe minority girls learn to embroider before they can walk. Even the architecture is individual and most minority houses are raised on stilts and finished in natural materials, in tune with their environment.

To get up close and personal with the north-eastern hill tribes, Tim Doling's *Mountains and Ethnic Minorities: North East Vietnam,* available in most Hanoi bookshops, is an essential companion for a tour of the region.

The French called these ethnic minorities Montagnards (highlanders or mountain people) and this term is still used today. The Vietnamese traditionally referred to them as *moi,* a derogatory term meaning savages, which reflects all too common attitudes among lowland majority Vietnamese. The current government prefers the term 'national minorities'. There are more than 15 separate groups.

The most colourful of these minorities live in the northwest of Vietnam, carving an existence out of the lush mountain landscapes along the Chinese and Lao borders. Many of the minorities in the central highlands and the south can be difficult to distinguish, at least by dress alone, from other Vietnamese.

While some of these minorities number as many as a million people, it is feared that other groups have dwindled to as few as 100. Some hill-tribe groups have lived in Vietnam for thousands of years, others only migrated south in the past few hundred years from China. In some ways they are 'fourth world' people in that they belong neither to the first-world powers nor to the developing nations. Rather, they have crossed and continue to cross national borders, often fleeing oppression by other cultures, without regard for recent nationhood. They inhabit a world that falls beyond the boundaries of modern nation states. The areas inhabited by each group are often delineated by altitude, with more recent arrivals settling at a higher altitude. First come, first served even applies to the remote mountains of the north.

Each hill tribe has its own language, customs, mode of dress and spiritual beliefs. Language and culture constitute the borders of their world. Some groups are caught between medieval and modern worlds, while others have already assimilated into modern life.

Most groups share a rural, agricultural lifestyle with similar village architecture and traditional rituals, coupled with a long history of intertribal warfare. Most hill-tribe communities are seminomadic, cultivating crops such as rice and using slash-and-burn methods, which have taken a heavy toll on the environment. The government has been trying to encourage the hill tribes to adopt standard agriculture at lower altitudes, including wet rice agriculture and cash crops such as tea and coffee. Despite incentives such as subsidised irrigation, better education and health care, the long history of independence and a general distrust of the ethnic-Vietnamese majority keep many away from the lowlands.

As in other parts of Asia, the traditional culture of so many of Vietnam's ethnic minorities is gradually giving way to a variety of outside influences. Many no longer dress in traditional clothing and those who do are often found only in the remote villages of the far north. Often it is the women of the community who keep the costume alive, weaving the traditional clothes and passing the knowledge on to their daughters. While factors such as the introduction of electricity, modern medicine and education improve the standard of living, they have also contributed to the abandonment of many age-old traditions.

A more recent, and equally threatening, outside influence is tourism. With growing numbers of people travelling to see the different ethnic minorities, increased exposure to business-savvy lowlanders and ever greater commercialism, it is a situation that could get worse before it gets better. It has resulted in some children, particularly in Sapa, expecting hand-outs of money or sweets. Worse, domestic tourism has created a market for karaoke, massage and sex, and in some areas unscrupulous ethnic-Vietnamese are luring minority women into this trade (see Prostitution, p465). See Tread Lightly in the Hills, (p76) for tips on minimising impact.

Vietnam's hill-tribe minorities have substantial autonomy and, though the official national language is Vietnamese, children still learn their local languages, though this can vary from group to group (see Hill Tribe Languages, p515, for useful phrases). Taxes are supposed to be paid, but Hanoi is far away and it seems that if the Montagnards don't interfere with the political agenda, they can live as they please. But if they choose to interfere it's a different story, as shown by the harsh suppression of demonstrations in the central highlands during 2001 and 2002 over language rights in schools and against the Vietnamisation of their culture.

Traditionally highland areas were allowed to remain independent as long as their leaders recognised Vietnamese sovereignty and paid tribute and taxes. Two autonomous regions were established in the northwest in 1959 and only abolished in 1980.

While there may be no official discrimination system, cultural prejudice against hill-tribe people helps ensure they remain at the bottom of the educational and economic ladder. Despite improvements in rural schooling and regional healthcare, many minority people marry young, have large families and die young. Put simply, life is a struggle for most of the minority people.

Here we profile some of the better known minority groups in Vietnam, including those that many visitors will encounter on a journey into the mountains.

BAHNAR

Pop: 135,000
Origin: China
Area: Kon Tum, Binh Dinh, Phu Yen
Economy: rice, corn
Belief system: animism
Cultural characteristics: The Bahnar are believed to have migrated long ago to the Central Highlands (p306) from the coast. They are animists and worship trees such as the banyan and ficus. The Bahnar keep their own traditional calendar, which calls for 10 months of cultivation, with the remaining two months set aside for social and personal duties, such as marriage, weaving, ceremonies and festivals. Traditionally when babies reached one month of age, a ceremony was held in which their lobes were pierced to make them a member of the village. Those who died without such holes were believed to be taken to a land of monkeys by a black-eared goddess called Dudyai. The Bahnar are skilled woodcarvers and wear similar dress to the Jarai.

Many of the hill tribes in the northwest find their spouse at regional love markets. Speed-dating minority style, this is where youngsters find new love and old flames fan the embers of a by-gone passion. For more, see the box, p183.

DZAO

Pop: 470,000
Origin: China
Area: Chinese and Lao border areas, including Sapa
Economy: rice, corn
Belief system: animism
Cultural characteristics: The Dzao (or Zao/Dao) are one of the largest and most colourful of Vietnam's ethnic groups and live in the northwestern provinces (p172) near China and Laos. The Dzao practise ancestor worship of spirits or 'Ban Ho' (no relation to Uncle Ho) and hold elaborate rituals with

sacrifices of pigs and chickens. The Dzao's close proximity to China explains the common use of traditional medicine and the similarity of the Nom Dao script to Chinese characters.

The Dzao are famous for their elaborate dress. Women's clothing typically features intricate weaving and silver-coloured beads and coins – the wealth of a woman is said to be in the weight of coins she carries. Their long flowing hair, shaved above the forehead, is tied up into a large red or embroidered turban. A curious blend of skinhead and Sikh.

EDE

Pop: 25,000
Origin: China
Area: Gia Lai, Kon Tum, Dac Lac
Economy: livestock, forest products
Belief system: animism
Cultural characteristics: The polytheistic Ede live communally in beamless boat-shaped longhouses on stilts. About one-third of these homes, which often accommodate large extended families, are reserved for communal use, with the rest partitioned into smaller sections to give some privacy to married couples. Speaking of which, like the Jarai, the Ede girls must propose to the men and after marriage the couple resides with the wife's family and bears the mother's name. Inheritance is also the preserve of women, in particular the youngest daughter of the family. Ede women generally wear colourfully embroidered vests with copper and silver jewellery.

H'MONG

Pop: 550,000
Origin: China
Area: Cao Bang, Ha Giang, Lai Chau, Lao Cai, Son La, Yen Bai
Economy: medicinal plants, opium, livestock
Belief system: animism
Cultural characteristics: Since migrating from China in the 19th century, the H'mong have grown to become one of the largest ethnic groups in Vietnam. Numbering around half a million, they are spread across the far north, but most visitors will run into them in Sapa (p172) or Bac Ha (p180). The H'mong are animist, and worship spirits.

For more on the H'mong people, their culture and their music, head to www.learnabouthmong.com, a US-based website with lots of information about this dispersed minority.

The H'mong live at high altitudes and cultivate dry rice and medicinal plants (including opium), and raise animals. There are several groups within the H'mong, including Black, White, Red, Green and Flower, each of which has its own subtle dress code. One of the most recognisable are the Black H'mong, who wear indigo-dyed linen clothing, with women typically wearing skirts, aprons, retro leggings and cylindrical hats. The Flower H'mong women wear extrovert outfits, with bright rainbow banding and '70s-style sequins from head to toe. Many H'mong women wear large silver necklaces, earrings and clusters of silver bracelets.

The H'mong are also found in neighbouring Laos and Thailand and many have fled to Western countries as refugees. Their cultivation of opium has made them the target of much government suspicion over the years.

JARAI

Pop: 200,000+
Origin: China
Area: Dac Lac, Gia Lai, Khanh Hoa, Phu Yen
Economy: rice, corn
Belief system: animism

Cultural characteristics: The Jarai are the most populous minority in the central highlands, many living around Pleiku (p325), as well as northeast Cambodia and southern Laos. Villages are often named for a nearby river, stream or tribal chief, and a *nha-rong* (communal house) is usually found in the centre. Jarai women typically propose marriage to men through a matchmaker, who delivers the prospective groom a copper bracelet. Animistic beliefs and rituals still abound, and the Jarai pay respect to their ancestors and nature through a host or *yang* (genie). Popular spirits include the King of Fire (Po Teo Pui) and the King of Water (Po Teo La) who are summoned to bring forth the rain.

The Jarai construct elaborate cemeteries for their dead, which include carved effigies of the deceased. These totems can be found in the forests around villages, but sadly many are being snapped up by culturally insensitive collectors.

Perhaps more than any of Vietnam's other hill tribes, the Jarai are renowned for their indigenous musical instruments, from bronze gongs to bamboo tubes, which act as wind flutes and percussion. Jarai women typically wear sleeveless indigo blouses and long skirts.

During the war, many of the Montagnards in the central highlands were enrolled in the Civil Irregular Defense Program (CIDG), part of the US Army Special Forces, and were highly regarded by the Green Berets.

MUONG

Pop: 900,000
Origin: China
Area: Hoa Binh, Thanh Hoa
Economy: rice, corn
Belief system: animism
Cultural characteristics: Mainly concentrated in Hoa Binh province (p162), the male-dominated Muong live in small stilt-house hamlets. Though their origins lie close to the ethnic-Vietnamese, the Muong have a culture similar to the Thai.

They are known for producing folk literature, poems and songs, much of which have been translated into Vietnamese. Musical instruments such as the gong, drums, pan pipes, flutes and two-stringed violin are popular. Muong women wear long skirts and short blouses, while the men traditionally wear indigo tops and trousers.

NUNG

Pop: 700,000
Origin: China
Area: Bac Thai, Cao Bang, Ha Bac, Lang Son
Economy: fruit, vegetables, spices, bamboo
Belief system: ancestor worship
Cultural characteristics: The Nung inhabit the far northeastern provinces near the Chinese border. Concentrated into small villages, Nung homes are typically divided into two areas, one to serve as living quarters and the other for work and worship.

From ardent ancestral worship to traditional festivities, the Nung are spiritually and socially similar to the Tay people. Nung brides traditionally command high dowries from their prospective grooms and tradition dictates inheritance from father to son, which is a sure sign of Chinese influence.

Most Nung villages still have medicine men who are called upon to help get rid of evil spirits and cure the ill. The Nung are also known for their handicrafts, such as bamboo furniture, basketry, silverwork and paper making. The Nung primarily wear black and indigo clothing, and the women have elaborate headdresses.

SEDANG

Pop: 95,000
Origin: China
Area: Kon Tum, Quang Ngai, Quang Ngam
Economy: rice, corn
Belief system: animism
Cultural characteristics: Native to the central highlands, the Sedang extend as far west as Cambodia. Like many of their neighbours, the Sedang have been adversely affected by centuries of war and outside invasion and may have been raided by both the Cham and the Khmer to become slaves. They do not carry family names, and there is said to be complete equality between the sexes. The children of one's siblings are also given the same treatment as one's own, creating a strong fraternal tradition. The Sedang practise unique customs, such as grave abandonment (unlike the other hill-tribe groups who return to graves annually for ceremonies), sharing of property with the deceased and giving birth at the forest's edge. Sedang women traditionally wear long skirts and a sarong-like top wrap.

TREAD LIGHTLY IN THE HILLS

For the world's indigenous people, tourism is both a blessing and a curse.

Studies show indigenous cultures are a major drawcard for travellers and attract substantial revenue. However, little of it directly benefits these minority groups, who are often among their country's poorest and most disadvantaged.

Hill-tribe communities in Vietnam aren't usually involved in initiating tourist activities, often they aren't the major economic beneficiaries from these activities, are powerless to stop the tide and have little say in its development.

Tourism can bring many benefits to highland communities. These include cross-cultural understanding; improved infrastructure, such as roads; cheaper market goods; and tourist dollars supporting handicraft industries and providing employment opportunities.

However, there are also negative side-effects. Tourism creates or contributes to overtaxing of natural resources; increased litter and pollutants; dependency on tourist dollars; proliferation of drug use and prostitution; and erosion of local values and practices.

If you travel to these regions, the good news is that you can make a positive contribution and ensure that the benefits of your stay outweigh the costs.

Interaction

- Be polite and respectful.
- Dress modestly.
- Minimise litter.
- Do not urinate or defecate near villagers' households; bury faeces.
- Do not take drugs – young children tend to imitate tourists' behaviour.
- Do not engage in sexual relationships with local people, including prostitutes.
- Try to learn something about the community's culture and language and teach something good about yours.

Gifts

- Do not give children sweets or money; it encourages begging and paves the way for prostitution for 'gifts' and money. Sweets also contribute to tooth decay.
- Do not give clothes – communities are self-sufficient.

TAY

Pop: 1.2 million
Origin: China
Area: Bac Kan, Cao Bang, Lang Son, Thai Nguyen
Economy: rice, tobacco, herbs, spices
Belief system: Tam Giao, animism
Cultural characteristics: The Tay are the largest group among the hill tribes and live at low elevations and in valleys between Hanoi and the Chinese border. They traditionally live in wooden stilt houses, although a long history of interaction with the Vietnamese has seen a gradual shift to brick structures. They adhere closely to Vietnamese beliefs in Buddhism, Confucianism and Taoism, but also worship genies and local spirits. Since they developed their own script in the 16th century, Tay literature and arts have become famous throughout Vietnam. Tay people wear distinctive indigo-blue and black clothes. They often wear head wraps of the same colours and can sometimes be seen carrying machete-like farming tools in belt sheaths.

- Don't give medicines – it erodes traditional healing practices and the medicine may not be correctly administered.
- Individual gifts create jealousy and create expectations. Instead make donations to the local school, medical centre or community fund.
- No matter how poor they are, villagers are extremely hospitable; however, feeding a guest can result in food shortages. If you accept an invitation to share a meal, be sure to bring a generous contribution. Usually it is possible to chip in with a chicken or something similar in a remote village. However, most guides will be able to offer help on what is appropriate.

Shopping

- Haggle politely and always pay the agreed (and fair) price for goods and services.
- Do not ask to buy a villager's personal household items or the jewellery or clothes they are wearing.
- Don't buy village treasures, such as altar pieces or totems.

Photographs

- Do not photograph without first asking permission – this includes children. Some hill tribes (particularly the Dzao people) believe the camera will capture their spirit. Don't photograph altars.
- If you take a picture, do it quickly and avoid using a flash. It is polite to send copies (if possible) – if you promise to do so, keep your word.

Travel

- Travel in small, less disruptive groups.
- Stay, eat and travel with local businesses.
- Try to book tours with responsible tourism outlets who employ hill-tribe people or contribute to community welfare.

Note, www.hilltribe.org is aimed at visiting the hill tribes of northern Thailand, but it's still a useful resource on how to behave yourself in hill-tribe villages.

Compiled with assistance from Oxfam Community Aid Abroad

THAI

Pop: 1 million
Origin: China
Area: Dien Bien Phu, Hoa Binh, Lai Chau, Son La
Economy: rice, corn
Belief system: animism
Cultural characteristics: Like the Tay, the Thai originated in southern China before settling along the fertile riverbeds of the northwest from Hoa Binh (p162) to Muong Lay (p170). Villagers typically consist of 40 or 50 thatched houses built on bamboo stilts. The Thai minority are usually categorised by colour, including the Red, Black and White Thai. Black Thai women wear vibrantly coloured blouses and headgear, while the White Thai tend to dress in contemporary clothing. Theories vary on the relationship with the Thais of Thailand, as they do when it comes to the many colour groupings. Some suggest it corresponds to colours on the women's skirts, while others believe it comes from the nearby Red and Black Rivers.

For a lavish introduction to the landscapes of the northwest, check out *The Colours of Sapa*, a photographic portrait of the incredible people and breathtaking scenery around this old French hill station.

The Thai, using a script developed in the 5th century, have produced literature ranging from poetry and love songs to folk tales. Travellers staying overnight in Mai Chau (p164) can usually catch a performance of the Thai's renowned music and dance.

WHERE TO VISIT THE HILL TRIBES

The ethnic minorities of Vietnam are spread throughout the highland areas in the north and centre of the country. The old French hill station of Sapa (p172) is the gateway to the northwest and the most popular place in the country to encounter the Montagnards. Most famous for Black H'mong and Red Dzao villages, it is also within striking distance of the colourful Flower H'mong markets around Bac Ha (p180).

Homestays with minority families are a rewarding experience and Mai Chau (p164) is famous for the warm welcome of the White Thai people. Other centres in the northwest also offer opportunities for ethnic minority encounters, including Ha Giang (p182) and Lai Chau (p172).

Further east, the province of Cao Bang (p154) is a less travelled region with several minorities, including the H'mong, the Nung and the Tay. Lang Son (p153) also provides a home to these minority groups, but sees fewer tourists still.

Down in the Central Highlands, Buon Ma Thuot (p319), Dalat (p307), Kon Tum (p327) and Pleiku (p325) are useful bases to meet the Bahnar, Jarai and Sedang. However, most families here have forsaken their traditional costume, so meet-the-minorities tourism has less pulling power than in the north.

Environment

THE LAND

Vietnam is a land shaped by its history. Dominated by the Chinese for a thousand years, the Vietnamese pushed southwards seeking new lands for cultivation and to put a bit of distance between them and their northern neighbour. Hemmed in by the Truong Son Mountains to the west, they had little choice but to head on down the coast, eating up the Kingdom of Champa and taking a bite-sized chunk out of Cambodia.

The result is the map of Vietnam today. As the Vietnamese are quick to point out, it resembles a *don ganh,* the ubiquitous bamboo pole with a basket of rice slung from each end. The baskets represent the main rice-growing regions of the Red River Delta in the north, and the Mekong Delta in the south. The country is S-shaped, broad in the north and south and very narrow in the centre, where at one point it is only 50km wide.

Vietnam stretches more than 1600km along the eastern coast of the Indochinese peninsula. The country's land area is 326,797 sq km, making it a bit bigger than Italy and slightly smaller than Japan. Vietnam has 3451km of coastline and 3818km of land borders.

The coastline is one of the big drawcards for tourists and it doesn't disappoint, with sweeping beaches, towering cliffs, undulating dunes and countless uninhabited islands along its length. The largest of these islands is Phu Quoc (p452), off the coast of Cambodia in the Gulf of Thailand. Other major islands include Cat Ba (p143) and Van Don (p148) in the Halong Bay area and a splattering of dots off Nha Trang (p281).

The Red River Delta and the Mekong Delta are pancake flat and prone to flooding. Silt carried by the Red River and its tributaries, confined to their paths by 3000km of dikes, has raised the level of the river beds above the surrounding plains. Breaches in the dikes result in disastrous flooding. The Mekong Delta has no such protection and when *cuu long* (the nine dragons – the nickname for the nine tributaries of the Mekong where it splits in the delta) burst their banks it creates havoc for communities and crops. The Mekong Delta expands at a rate of about 100m per year, though global warming and the consequent rise of sea levels around the world could one day submerge it.

Three-quarters of the country consists of rolling hills and mighty mountains, the highest of which is 3143m-high Fansipan (p175) in the far northwest. The Truong Son Mountains, which form the central highlands, run almost the full length of Vietnam along its borders with Laos and Cambodia.

The most striking geological features in Vietnam are the karst formations. Karst consists of limestone in which erosion has produced fissures, sinkholes, caves and underground rivers. Northern Vietnam is a showcase for these outcrops, with stunning examples at Halong Bay (p136) and Bai Tu Long Bay (p148), and around Ninh Binh (p186) and the Perfume Pagoda (p125). At Halong and Bai Tu Long Bays, an enormous limestone plateau has steadily sunk into the ocean and the old mountain tops stick out of the sea like bony vertical fingers pointing towards the sky.

Not all of Vietnam's mountains are limestone. The coastal ranges near Nha Trang and those at Hai Van Pass (Danang) are composed of granite, and the giant boulders littering the hillsides are a surreal sight.

The western part of the central highlands, near Buon Ma Thuot and Pleiku, is well known for its red volcanic soil, which is incredibly fertile. The highlands are, of course, high above sea level, but are mostly undulating and not as scenic as the north.

The Vietnamese are starting to take environmental protection seriously, particularly as the popularity of national parks soars. The Vietnam Environment Protection Agency has the tough task of environmental watchdog; see its website at www.nea.gov.vn/english.

TRAVEL WIDELY, TREAD LIGHTLY, GIVE SUSTAINABLY – THE LONELY PLANET FOUNDATION

The Lonely Planet Foundation proudly supports nimble nonprofit institutions working for change in the world. Each year the foundation donates 5% of Lonely Planet company profits to projects selected by staff and authors. Our partners range from Kabissa, which provides small nonprofits across Africa with access to technology, to the Foundation for Developing Cambodian Orphans, which supports girls at risk of falling victim to sex traffickers.

Our nonprofit partners are linked by a grass-roots approach to the areas of health, education or sustainable tourism. Many – such as Louis Sarno who works with BaAka (Pygmy) children in the forested areas of Central African Republic – choose to focus on women and children as one of the most effective ways to support the whole community. Louis is determined to give options to children who are discriminated against by the majority Bantu population.

Sometimes foundation assistance is as simple as restoring a local ruin like the Minaret of Jam in Afghanistan; this incredible monument now draws intrepid tourists to the area and its restoration has greatly improved options for local people.

Just as travel is often about learning to see with new eyes, so many of the groups we work with aim to change the way people see themselves and the future for their children and communities.

WILDLIFE

Despite some disastrous bouts of deforestation, Vietnam's flora and fauna is as exotic, abundant and varied as any tropical country. Scientists are only just beginning to effectively catalogue the country's plant and animal life, and the government is showing some determined enthusiasm for ecological conservation.

Animals

On paper, Vietnam has plenty to offer to those who are wild about wildlife, but in reality many of the animals live in remote forested areas and an encounter is extremely unlikely. A lot of the wildlife is rapidly disappearing, thanks to population pressures and the destruction of habitats. Hunting, poaching and pollution have taken their toll, too.

With a wide range of habitats – from equatorial lowlands to high, temperate plateaus and even alpine peaks – the wildlife of Vietnam is enormously diverse. It is home to 275 species of mammal, more than 800 species of bird, 180 species of reptile, 80 species of amphibian, hundreds of species of fish and thousands of species of invertebrates.

Every now and then Vietnam throws up a new creature that manages to elude scientific classification. Since Vietnam reopened for business around 1990, zoologists have discovered several previously unknown species of large mammal in Vietnam, including a new breed of muntjac deer in 1998. The scientific and conservation value of these recent discoveries has not been lost on authorities, and the Vietnamese government has been expanding the size of national parks and nature reserves, and banning logging within these areas. As research and conservation efforts gather pace, Vietnam may turn out to be a treasure chest of undiscovered species.

Twitchers with a serious interest in the birdlife of Vietnam should seek out a copy of *A Field Guide to the Birds of South-East Asia* (1982) by Ben King, Martin Woodcock and Edward Dickinson, which has thorough coverage of Vietnam.

Rare and little-known birds previously thought to be extinct have been spotted and no doubt there are more in the extensive forests along the Lao border. Edwards' pheasant, previously believed to be extinct, was found on a scientific expedition, and other excursions have yielded the white-winged wood duck and white-shouldered ibis.

Even casual visitors will spot a few bird species: swallows and swifts flying over fields and along watercourses; flocks of finches at roadsides and in paddies; and bulbuls and mynahs in gardens and patches of forest. Vietnam is on the east-Asian flyway and is an important stopover for migratory waders en route from Siberian breeding grounds to their Australian winter quarters.

ENDANGERED SPECIES

Tragically, Vietnam's wildlife has been in deadly decline as forest habitats are destroyed and waterways polluted. In addition, widespread illegal hunting has exterminated local animal populations, in some cases wiping out entire species. Continued deforestation and poaching means that many endangered species are on a one-way ticket to extinction. Captive-breeding programmes may be the only hope for some.

Officially, the government has recognised 54 species of mammal and 60 species of bird as endangered. The tapir and Sumatran rhinoceros are already extinct in Vietnam. In the early 1990s a small population of Javan rhinos (the world's rarest rhinoceros) was discovered in Cat Tien National Park (p392), northeast of Ho Chi Minh City (HCMC), but there are probably just 10 to 20 left in the entire country.

Larger animals crucial to the country's conservation efforts include the elephant, tiger, leopard, black bear, honey bear, snub-nosed monkey, flying squirrel, crocodile and turtle.

In a positive sign, some wildlife populations are re-establishing themselves in reforested areas. Birds, fish and crustaceans have reappeared in replanted mangrove forests. Areas in which large animals were thought to have been wiped out by war are now hot spots of biodiversity and abundance. The extensive forests of the central highlands and far north remain a home to some of nature's most noble creatures, such as the tiger, Asian elephant, clouded leopard and sun bear. Their chance of survival rests in the balance, as Vietnam's population continues to expand, eating up more and more of the remaining wilderness areas. Only when the population learns to live in harmony with nature rather than live off the environment will the situation improve.

Vietnam: A Natural History is well worth tracking down for those who want to learn more about the country's extraordinary flora and fauna. A collaboration between American and Vietnamese biodiversity scientists, it is exquisitely illustrated.

Plants

Years ago Vietnam was blanketed in forest, from vast mangrove fringing the coast to dense rainforest in the mountainous regions. Over the centuries the forests have progressively been pushed back: first by the clearing of land for cultivation, and later by a booming population and the ravages of war.

Although the scars of war are still visible and much of the damage is long-term, reforestation programmes have been implemented and today some of the landscape is showing signs of recovery. Natural forests at higher elevations, such as those in the northwest, feature wild rhododendrons, dwarf bamboo and many varieties of orchid; the central coast is drier and features stands of pine; while the river deltas support mangrove forests, which are valuable nurseries for fish and crustaceans, as well as feeding sites for many bird species.

The remaining forests of Vietnam are estimated to contain more than 12,000 plant species, only around 7000 of which have been identified and 2300 of which are known to be valuable to humanity. Recently the islands and caves of Halong Bay yielded seven previously unknown plants – the largest and most conspicuous of the new flora has been christened the Halong Fan Palm.

The Vietnamese make good use of the plants around them for medicines and remedies. Locals forage in the forests for barks, roots, herbs and flowers, which go into making cures for all sorts of ailments.

NATIONAL PARKS

Vietnam has been rapidly expanding the number of national parks in the country and there are now almost 30. There is also an expanding array of nature reserves, numbering more than 30 today. There are plans to increase and improve existing parks and nature reserves, as all too many of them remain lines on maps and are not properly protected.

Most of Vietnam's national parks are seldom visited by travellers, who tend to get stuck on the 'must-see' tourist trail, without the time or wanderlust to explore the parks. Access can be problematic with some parks hidden in remote areas, but others are easy to reach. For those who make the effort to seek them out, national parks reveal a whole different face to Vietnam. They also have the added appeal of being among the few places in Vietnam where tourists are unlikely to be hassled to buy anything. However, if you are wanting a bit of peace and quiet to soak up the serenity and splendour, it is better to visit parks during the week, as hordes of Vietnamese descend during the weekend.

The most interesting and accessible parks are Cat Ba National Park (p144), Bai Tu Long National Park (p148), Ba Be National Park (p157), Hoang Lien National Park (p174) and Cuc Phuong National Park (p190) in the north; Bach Ma National Park (p225) in the centre; and Cat Tien National Park (p392) and Yok Don National Park (p323) in the south. All of the parks levy some sort of admission charge, but it is usually very reasonable at around 10,000d or less than US$1. Most of the parks have accommodation available, most often a mix of rooms and bungalows, and camping is sometimes possible if you have your own gear.

Cat Ba National Park is on a beautiful island and during the summer months it attracts a steady stream of foreign travellers willing to make the boat journey. In 2000, Vietnam also created Bai Tu Long National Park, a protected reserve situated to the northeast of Halong Bay, which includes

NATIONAL PARKS: THE TOP 10

park (size in hectares)	features	activities	best time to visit	page
Ba Be (7610)	lakes, rainforest, waterfalls, towering peaks, caves, bears, langurs	hiking, boating, birding	Apr-Nov	p157
Bai Tu Long (15,000)	karst peaks, hidden beaches, caves	boating, kayaking, swimming, surfing, hiking	Apr-Nov	p148
Bach Ma (22,000)	waterfalls, tigers, primates	hiking, birding	Feb-Aug	p225
Cat Ba (15,200)	jungle, caves, langurs, boars, deer, waterfowl	hiking, swimming, birding	Apr-Aug	p144
Cat Tien (73,878)	primates, elephants, birdlife, rhinos, tigers	hiking, birding jungle exploration	Nov-Jun	p392
Con Dao (19,998)	dugongs, turtles, beaches	birding, snorkelling	Nov-Jun	p397
Cuc Phuong (22,200)	jungle, grottoes, primates, birding centre, caves	hiking, endangered-primate viewing	Sep-Apr	p190
Hoang Lien (24,658)	mountains, minority people, birdlife	hiking, cycling, birding, mountain climbing	Sep-Nov, Apr-May	p174
Phong Nha-Ke Bang (85,800)	caves, karsts, birdlife	boat trips, caving, birding	Apr-Sep	p195
Yok Don (115,545)	minority people, stilt houses	elephant rides, hiking	Nov-Feb	p323

more than 15,000 hectares of tropical evergreen forest, plenty of hidden beaches and a spot of surf.

Ba Be National Park features spectacular waterfalls and is accessible by hired 4WD or motorbike from Hanoi. Hoang Lien National Park was recently created to protect the landscape and peoples around Sapa. Cuc Phuong National Park is less visited, but easily reached from Hanoi and offers great hiking, plus an amazing array of rescued primates that are being rehabilitated. Bach Ma National Park, near Hué, receives far fewer visitors than its attractions deserve, but is demonstrating good potential for responsible ecotourism.

Cat Tien National Park, in the southern part of the central highlands, is relatively easy to reach from HCMC or Dalat, and very popular with birdwatchers. Also in the central highlands is Yok Don National Park, which is home to many elephants and local minority tribes.

One other park in the south that is a must for any serious birder is Tram Chim Nature Reserve (p420), east of Chau Doc in Dong Thap province. This is home to the magnificent rare eastern sarus crane and one of only two nesting sites in the world, the other at Ang Trapeng Thmor in northwest Cambodia.

ENVIRONMENTAL ISSUES

Vietnam's environment is not teetering on the brink, but there are some worrying signs. Vietnam is a poor, densely populated, agricultural country, so humans are competing with native plants and animals over the same limited resources.

Deforestation is the most serious problem facing the country today. Since the arrival of human beings many millennia ago, Vietnam has been progressively denuded of forest cover. While 44% of the original forest cover was extant in 1943, by 1983 only 24% was left and in 1995 it was down to 20%. In a positive turnaround, recent reforestation projects by the Ministry of Agriculture and Rural Development, including the banning of unprocessed timber exports in 1992, have seen a slight rise in the amount of forest cover. However, it's bad news for the neighbours, as it simply means the Vietnamese have been sourcing their timber from Laos and Cambodia.

Flora and Fauna International produces an excellent *Nature Tourism Map of Vietnam,* which includes detailed coverage of all the national parks in Vietnam. As well as 1:1,000,000 scale map, there are breakout boxes on most of the popular parks. All proceeds from sales of the map go towards supporting primate conservation in Vietnam.

The Ministry of Education and Training has made the planting and taking care of trees part of the school curriculum. However, even at this rate, reforestation cannot keep up with forest losses. Each hectare of land stripped of vegetation contributes to a multitude of environmental problems, including the flooding of areas downstream from catchment areas; irreversible soil erosion; the silting up of rivers, streams, lakes and reservoirs; the loss of wildlife habitat; and unpredictable climatic changes. This could get worse again before it gets better, as more and more lowland Vietnamese are resettling the mountainous areas of the central highlands and the far north, putting new pressures on land for plantations and farmland.

Vietnam has so far suffered little industrial pollution largely because there has been little industry. However, the nation's rapid economic and population growth indicate environmental trouble ahead. The dramatic increase in the number of noisy, smoke-spewing motorbikes in recent years should be taken as a sign of abominations to come.

Ecotourism

Ecotourism is increasingly on the rise, with trekking and other outdoor activities becoming more and more popular with travellers. The government has set aside tens of thousands of square kilometres of forest land with plans to create around 100 protected areas in the form of national parks and

Ecotourism is increasingly popular in Vietnam and more and more companies are launching environmentally friendly biking and hiking tours. Vietnam Ecotours (www.ecotourisminvietnam.com) is dedicated to promoting ecotourism.

nature reserves. Local ecologists hope that as tropical ecosystems have highly diverse species but low densities of individual species, reserve areas will be large enough to contain viable populations of each species. However, there are development interests that are not particularly amenable to boosting the size of Vietnam's national parks and nature reserves. As in the West, even the best-laid plans can sometimes go awry. Massive infrastructure projects such as new highways are threatening protected areas, as it is cheaper for the government to use park land than compensate villagers for farm land. A case in point is the Ho Chi Minh road, Hwy 15, which cuts through Cuc Phuong National Park.

That said, ecotourism will continue to be a growth industry, as more and more international visitors demand environmentally friendly activities. As well as trekking in national parks and mountain areas, cycling is increasingly popular and kayaking has taken off in Halong Bay. However, the fact is that ecotourism remains a much used-and-abused phrase and many of the so-called 'ecotourism' products in Vietnam are more about marketing than the environment.

War on the Environment

Some 13 million tonnes of bombs – equivalent to 450 times the energy of the atomic bomb used on Hiroshima – were dropped on the Indochina region. This equates to 265kg for every man, woman and child in Vietnam, Cambodia and Laos.

Much has been written about the human and economic devastation wrought by the USA during the American War, but there was also ecocide – the war saw the most intensive attempt to destroy a country's natural environment the world has ever seen. American forces sprayed 72 million litres of herbicides (named Agents Orange, White and Blue after the colour of their canisters) over 16% of South Vietnam to destroy the Viet Cong's natural cover.

Another environmentally disastrous method of defoliation employed during the war involved the use of huge bulldozers called 'Rome ploughs' to rip up the jungle floor. Large tracts of forest, agricultural land, villages and even cemeteries were bulldozed, removing the vegetation and topsoil. Flammable melaleuca forests were ignited with napalm. In mountain areas, landslides were deliberately created by bombing and spraying acid on limestone hillsides. Elephants, useful for transport, were attacked from the air with bombs and napalm. By the war's end, extensive areas had been taken over by tough weeds (known

DOING YOUR BIT

- Vietnam has a low level of environmental awareness and responsibility, and many people remain unaware of the implications of littering. Try and raise awareness of these issues by example, and dispose of your litter as responsibly as possible.
- Vietnam's faunal populations are under considerable threat from domestic consumption and the illegal international trade in animal products. Though it may be 'exotic' to try wild meat such as muntjac, bats, deer, sea horses, shark fins and so on – or to buy products made from endangered plants and animals – doing so will indicate your support or acceptance of such practices and add to the demand for them.
- When visiting coral reefs and snorkelling or diving, or simply boating, be careful not to touch live coral or anchor boats on it, as these hinder the coral's growth. If it's possible to anchor in a sandy area, try to convince the operator to do so and indicate your willingness to swim to the coral. Don't buy coral souvenirs.
- When visiting limestone caves, be aware that touching the formations hinders growth and turns the limestone black. Don't break off the stalactites or stalagmites as they take lifetimes to regrow. Don't carve graffiti onto limestone formations, cave walls or other rock.
- Do not remove or buy 'souvenirs' that have been taken from historical sites and natural areas.

locally as 'American grass'). The government estimates that 20,000 sq km of forest and farmland were lost as a direct result of the American War.

Scientists have yet to conclusively prove a link between the residues of chemicals used by the USA and spontaneous abortions, stillbirths, birth defects and other human health problems. However, the circumstantial evidence is certainly compelling. In 2002, on the heels of a landmark Agent Orange conference in Hanoi, the USA and Vietnam initiated a joint investigation into the health effects of this damaging herbicide. Delegates from Vietnam's Environment Protection Agency and the US National Institute of Environmental Health Sciences co-signed a directive for scientists to explore possible links between Agent Orange and various physical illnesses, such as cancers in adults and leukaemia in children.

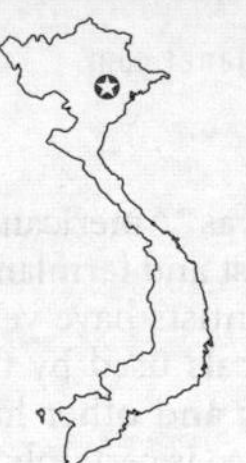

Hanoi

Imagine a city where the exotic chic of old Asia blends with the dynamic face of new Asia. Where the medieval and modern co-exist. A city with a blend of Parisian grace and Asian pace, an architectural museum piece evolving in harmony with its history, rather than bulldozing through like many of the region's capitals. Hanoi is where imagination becomes reality.

A mass of motorbikes swarms through the tangled web of streets that is the Old Quarter, a cauldron of commerce for almost 1000 years and still the best place to check the pulse of this resurgent city. Hawkers in conical hats ply their wares, locals sip coffee and *bia hoi* (beer) watching life (and plenty of tourists) pass them by. Witness synchronised t'ai chi at dawn on the shores of Hoan Kiem Lake while goateed grandfathers tug at their wisps over the next chess move. See the bold and beautiful dine at designer restaurants and cut the latest moves on the dance floor. Hanoi has it all: the ancient history, a colonial legacy and a modern outlook. There is no better place to untangle the paradox that is modern Vietnam.

The grand old dame of Asia, Hanoi lay in a deep slumber after Vietnam's partition in 1954 until the effects of economic reforms kicked in four decades later. The city survived American bombs and Russian planners to emerge relatively unscathed in the early 1990s as an example of a French-conceived colonial city. Huge mansions line grand boulevards, and lakes and parks dot the city, providing a romantic backdrop to the nonstop soundtrack. There are still moments of Paris, as the smell of baguettes and *café au lait* permeates street corners.

Known by many names down the centuries, Thanh Long (City of the Soaring Dragon) is the most evocative, and let there be no doubt that this dragon is on the up once more.

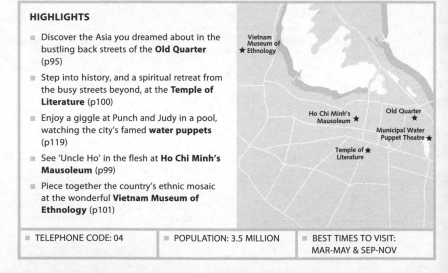

HIGHLIGHTS

- Discover the Asia you dreamed about in the bustling back streets of the **Old Quarter** (p95)
- Step into history, and a spiritual retreat from the busy streets beyond, at the **Temple of Literature** (p100)
- Enjoy a giggle at Punch and Judy in a pool, watching the city's famed **water puppets** (p119)
- See 'Uncle Ho' in the flesh at **Ho Chi Minh's Mausoleum** (p99)
- Piece together the country's ethnic mosaic at the wonderful **Vietnam Museum of Ethnology** (p101)

Vietnam Museum of Ethnology ★
Ho Chi Minh's Mausoleum ★
Old Quarter ★
Municipal Water Puppet Theatre ★
Temple of Literature ★

- TELEPHONE CODE: 04
- POPULATION: 3.5 MILLION
- BEST TIMES TO VISIT: MAR-MAY & SEP-NOV

HISTORY

The site where Hanoi stands today has been inhabited since the Neolithic period. Emperor Ly Thai To moved his capital here in AD 1010, naming it Thang Long (City of the Soaring Dragon). There should be some spectacular celebrations in honour of the 1000th birthday of the city in 2010. The decision by Emperor Gia Long, founder of the Nguyen dynasty in 1802, to rule from Hué relegated Hanoi to the status of a regional capital for a century.

Down the centuries, Hanoi has been called many names, including Dong Kinh (Eastern Capital), from which the Europeans derived the name they eventually applied to all of northern Vietnam – Tonkin. The city was named Hanoi (The City in a Bend of the River) by Emperor Tu Duc in 1831. From 1902 to 1953, Hanoi served as the capital of French Indochina.

Hanoi was proclaimed the capital of Vietnam after the August Revolution of 1945, but it was not until the Geneva Accords of 1954 that the Viet Minh, driven from the city by the French in 1946, were able to return.

During the American War, US bombing destroyed parts of Hanoi and killed hundreds of civilians; almost all the damage has since been repaired. One of the prime targets was the 1682m-long Long Bien Bridge, originally built between 1888 and 1902 under the direction of the same architect who designed the Eiffel Tower in Paris. US aircraft repeatedly bombed the strategic bridge, yet after each attack the Vietnamese managed to improvise replacement spans and return it to road and rail services. It is said that the US military ended the attacks when US prisoners of war (POWs) were put to work repairing the bridge.

ORIENTATION

Hanoi sprawls along the banks of Song Hong (Red River), which is spanned by two bridges – the Long Bien Bridge (now used only by nonmotorised vehicles and pedestrians) and, 600m to the south, the newer Chuong Duong Bridge.

The elegant heart of Hanoi is centred on the Hoan Kiem Lake. Just north of this lake is the Old Quarter (known to the French as the Cité Indigène), which is characterised by narrow streets with names that change every one or two blocks. Most visitors prefer to base themselves in this part of town thanks to the incredible energy of the area.

Along the western periphery of the Old Quarter is the ancient Hanoi Citadel, which was originally constructed by Emperor Gia Long. Unfortunately, the citadel is now a military base and also the residence of high-ranking officers and their families – in other words, closed to the public. Most of the ancient buildings were tragically destroyed by French troops in 1894, and US bombing during the American War took care of the rest. There are persistent rumours that this area will soon be opened up to development, but the military remain a powerful force in Vietnam, more than three decades after the war.

Further west is Ho Chi Minh's Mausoleum. Most of the foreign embassies, which are housed in classical architectural masterpieces from the French-colonial era, are found in this neighbourhood and posh joint-venture hotels have also sprung up here. Ho Tay (West Lake), Hanoi's largest lake, is north of Ho Chi Minh's Mausoleum and is emerging as a new front on the drinking and dining scenes.

Taxis, an airport minibus and local buses link Hanoi's Noi Bai International Airport with the city centre. From bus and train stations, there are metered taxis, *xe om* (motorbike taxis) or *cyclos* to ferry you to your destination.

Maps

Hanoi city maps come in every size and scale. Some are freebies subsidised by advertising and others precise works of cartography.

Leading maps include detailed ones at a scale of 1:10,000 or 1:17,500. Covit produces a couple of hand-drawn 3D maps of Hanoi, including a detailed Old Town map, which make nice souvenirs. These maps are available at leading bookshops in Hanoi.

There is also an excellent bus map available. *Xe Buyt Ha Noi* (5000d) is an essential companion for anyone planning to get about on the improved bus network and is easy to use.

INFORMATION

Bookshops

If you're running low on reading material, Hanoi is a good place to stock up. Many of the budget hotels and travellers cafés in the Old Quarter have small book exchanges.

Bookworm (Map pp92-3; ☎ 943 7226; bookworm@fpt.vn; 15a Ngo Van So; 🕒 10am-7pm Tue-Sun) Definitely the place for bookworms, this place has the best selection of English-language books in Hanoi. New and secondhand books, plus plenty of fiction and some good travel stock.

AROUND HANOI

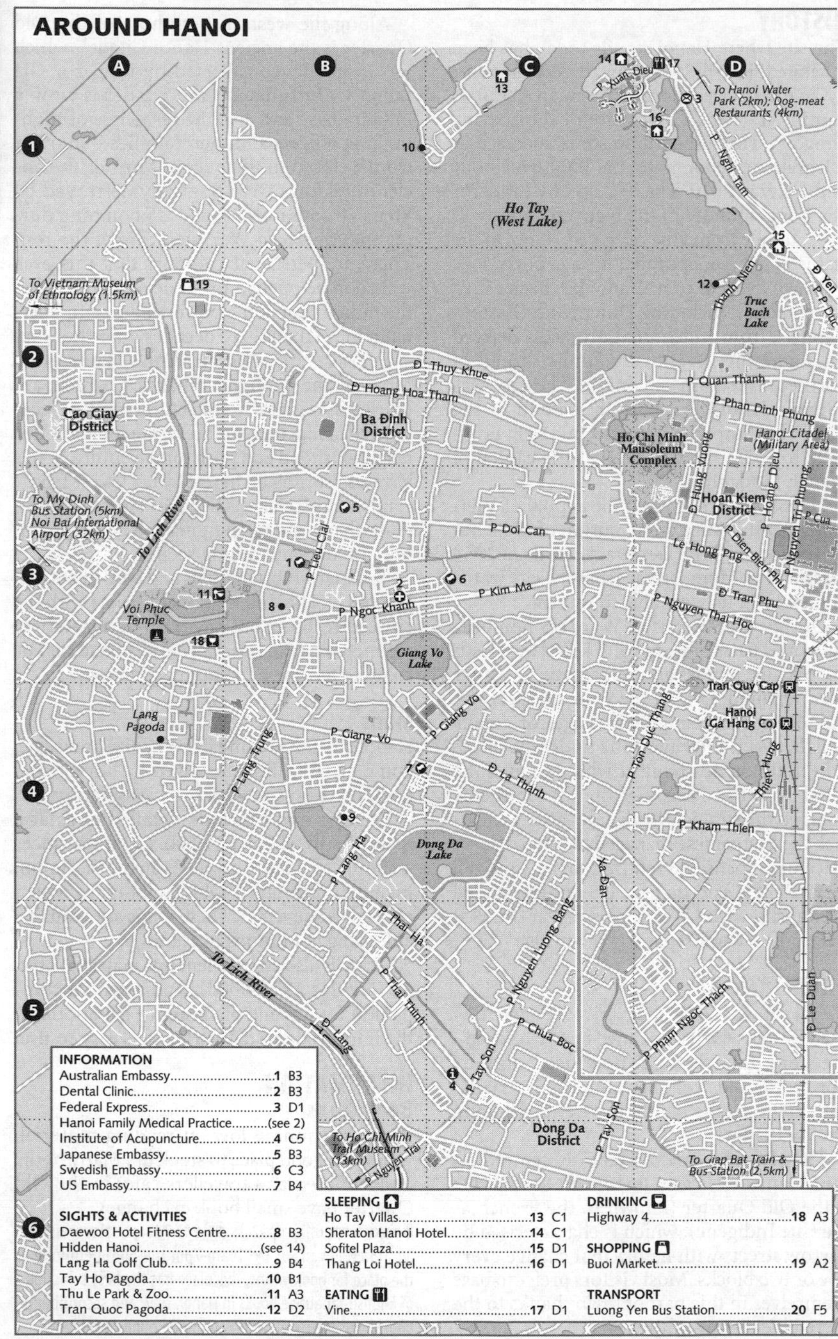

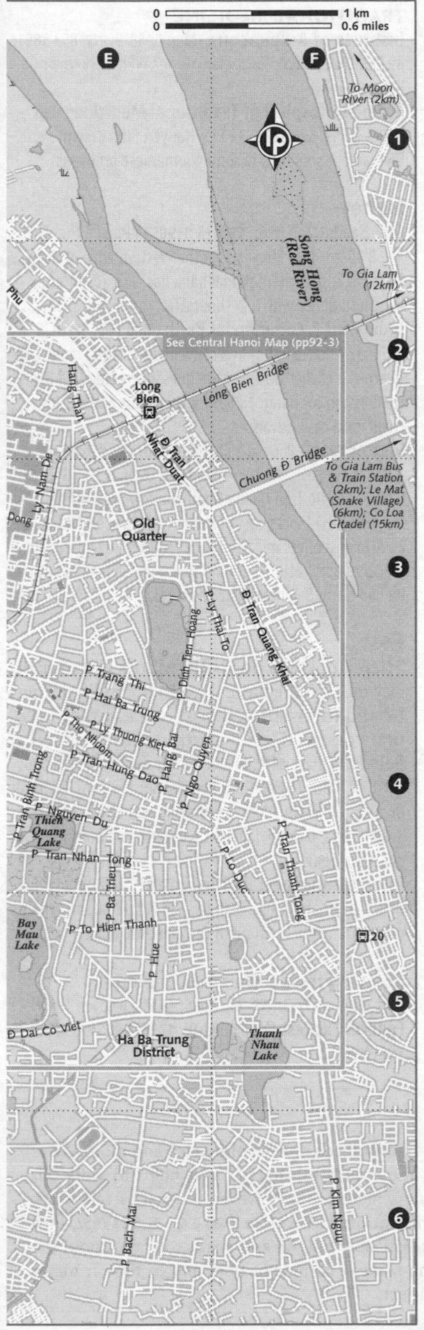

Foreign Language Bookshop (Map p96; ☎ 825 7376; 64 Pho Trang Tien) It sells just what it says it sells…a healthy selection of foreign-language titles, particularly in French.

Love Planet (Map p96; ☎ 828 4864; 25 Pho Hang Bac) An exchange as well as a shop, this Old Quarter place has lots of secondhand books.

Thang Long Bookshop (Map p96; ☎ 825 7043; 53-55 Pho Trang Tien) One of the biggest bookshops in town with English and French titles, plus some international newspapers and magazines.

Cultural Centres

For periodicals and newspapers from home, head to the following places:

American Club (Map p96; ☎ 824 1850; amclub@fpt.vn; 19-21 Pho Hai Ba Trung)

British Council (Map pp92-3; ☎ 843 6780; www.britishcouncil.org.vn; 40 Pho Cat Linh) Right next to the Hanoi Horison Hotel.

Centre Culturel Française de Hanoi (Map p96; ☎ 936 2164; 24 Pho Trang Tien) In the L'Espace building, a modernist venue near the Opera House.

Emergency

Hanoi is organised enough that the emergency services should be able to transfer you to an English-speaker.

Ambulance (☎ 115)

Fire (☎ 114)

Police (☎ 113)

Internet Access

It's hard to go more than a few hundred metres anywhere in the city without stumbling across an internet café, in particular those at backpacker cafés and travel agents along Pho Hang Bac and Pho Hang Be in the Old Quarter. Many places do not display prices, so check before you notch up a couple of hours online: overcharging isn't unheard of in some places. Rates start as low as 3000d. Most budget and midrange hotels offer free internet access as standard: the fancier places in the room, the cheaper places in the lobby.

Wi-fi has come to Hanoi with a vengeance and lots of hotels, cafés and bars offer free access for laptop users. Some places require a password, some don't. In the claustrophobic Old Quarter, it's not uncommon to have a choice of several networks. Try and sign into a secure network to ensure no-one is dabbling with your data.

Internet Resources

There are several good websites to help get the most out of Hanoi.

New Hanoian (www.newhanoian.com) This is the place to get the rub on what Hanoi expats get up to in the city. Places to see, dining out, special events, even jobs – it's all here.
Shivaaa! (www.shiva.com.vn) Shiva is an internet search site for Hanoi, an online gateway to lots of small restaurants, bars and shops in the city. The site includes detailed maps and customer reviews.
Sticky Rice (http://stickyrice.typepad.com) The website for foodies in Hanoi, this has the lowdown on dozens of places to dine and drink in the city.

Libraries

National Library and Archives (Map p96; ☎ 825 3357; 31 Pho Trang Thi) This grand old building has some English and French material available, but it's mostly Vietnamese.

Medical Services

Dental Clinic (Map pp88-9; ☎ 846 2864; thedental@netnam.vn; Van Phuc Diplomatic Compound, 1 Pho Kim Ma) The tooth hurts? Deal with it here, part of the Hanoi Family Medical Practice.
French Embassy Clinic (Map pp92-3; ☎ 825 2719; 49 Pho Ba Trieu) A 24-hour clinic for French nationals.
Hanoi Family Medical Practice (Map pp88-9; ☎ 843 0748, 24hr emergency service 090-340 1919; www.vietnammedicalpractice.com; Van Phuc Diplomatic Compound, 1 Pho Kim Ma) Includes a team of well-respected international physicians. Prices are high, so check your medical insurance is in order.
SOS International Clinic (Map p96; ☎ 934 0555; fax 934 0556; 31 Pho Hai Ba Trung; 🕑 8am-7pm Mon-Fri, 8am-2pm Sat, emergency 24hr) International chain of clinics with annual policies for expats living in Vietnam. English, French and Japanese are spoken.
Viet Duc Hospital (Benh Vien Viet Duc; Map p96; ☎ 825 3531; 40 Pho Trang Thi; 🕑 24hr) Old Quarter unit for emergency surgery; the doctors here speak English, French and German.
Vietnam-Korea Friendship Clinic (Map pp92-3; ☎ 843 7231; 12 Chu Van An; 🕑 9am-noon & 2-5pm Mon-Fri) Anyone crazy enough to travel without insurance should head here. This nonprofit clinic is the cheapest in town.

TRADITIONAL MEDICINE

Institute of Acupuncture (Map pp88-9; ☎ 853 3881; 49 Pho Thai Thinh) Holistic medicine? Well, very small holes anyway.
National Hospital of Traditional Medicine (Map pp92-3; ☎ 826 3616; 29 Pho Nguyen Binh Khiem) Vietnamese solutions to some Vietnamese problems.

Money

ANZ Bank (Map p96; ☎ 825 8190; 14 Pho Le Thai To; 🕑 8.30am-4pm Mon-Fri) On the western edge of Hoan Kiem Lake, this international bank has cash advances in dong and dollar with a 24-hour ATM.
Industrial & Commercial Bank (Map p96; ☎ 825 4276; 37 Pho Hang Bo) In a convenient location in the Old Quarter, it cashes travellers cheques at the standard 0.5% commission for dong, 1.25% for US dollars and 3% for credit-card cash advances.
Vietcombank Pho Hang Bai (Map p96; ☎ 826 8031; 2 Pho Hang Bai); Pho Tran Quang Khai (Map p96; ☎ 826 8045; 198 Pho Tran Quang Khai) The towering HQ is located a few blocks east of Hoan Kiem Lake and it has an ATM and offers most currency services. Several smaller branches are scattered around town, including a handy one on Pho Hang Bai, near Hoan Kiem Lake.

Post

There are small post-office kiosks all over the city that do the basics. Go to the main domestic and international post offices in the event that you need to do anything complicated.
Domestic post office (Buu Dien Trung Vong; Map p96; ☎ 825 7036; 75 Pho Dinh Tien Hoang; 🕑 7am-9.30pm) Occupies a full city block overlooking Hoan Kiem Lake. Send letters, pick up domestic packages and purchase philatelic items.
International postal office (☎ 825 2030; cnr Pho Dinh Tien Hoang & Pho Dinh Le; 🕑 7am-8.30pm) With its own entrance to the right of the domestic office.

Some courier companies in Hanoi:
DHL (Map pp92-3; ☎ 733 2086; 49 Pho Nguyen Thai Hoc)
Federal Express (Map pp88-9; ☎ 824 9054; 63 Pho Yen Phu)

MAKE THAT COMPLAINT COUNT...

We get a lot of letters complaining about hotels, guesthouses, travel companies and more. We're not complaining. It's great to give us feedback about all these things, as it helps to work out which businesses care about their customers and which don't. However, as well as telling us, make sure you tell the **Vietnam National Administration of Tourism** (Map p96; ☎ 824 7652; www.hanoitourism.gov.vn; 3 Pho Le Lai); its Hanoi office is reasonably helpful and needs to know about the problems before it can do anything about them. Make a complaint here and in time it might well pressure the cowboys into cleaning up their act.

HANOI IN...

A Day

Begin with breakfast in an Old Quarter café before jumping on a *cyclo* to **Ho Chi Minh's Mausoleum** (p99), where you might be lucky enough to catch a changing of the guard. Check out the surreal **museum** (p99) and the balancing act that is the **One Pillar Pagoda** (p100) before moving on to the **Temple of Literature** (p100). This is a great escape from the hustle and bustle of Hanoi and just opposite is **KOTO** (p111) on Van Mieu, an essential lunch stop as all proceeds from this great restaurant go towards helping street children. In the afternoon, it is time to take a serious look at the **Old Quarter** (p95), browsing its buildings, shops or bars to soak up the unique atmosphere. If you haven't already been tempted, stop for a *bia hoi* (draught beer) around sunset and watch Hanoi shift from work to play. Catch a performance of the wonderful **water puppets** (p119) before enjoying a local meal and some beers on nearby Pho Bao Khanh.

Two Days

After the fun of day one, it is time to immerse yourself in some museums. Head into the suburbs to the excellent **Vietnam Museum of Ethnology** (p101) to discover the ethnic mosaic that makes up Vietnam today. Have a local lunch in **Nha Hang Lan Chin** (p118), tucked away next to the **Museum of Vietnamese Revolution** (p102) and hop across the road to the **History Museum** (p101). The building is stunning and the contents a fine introduction to 2000 years of highs and lows. Head back to the Old Quarter for a look at **Memorial House** (p102) and then kick back in a café and contemplate the next part of your journey.

Telephone

For domestic telephone calls, the post offices throughout town are as good as anywhere. Guesthouses and internet cafés are also a convenient option for local calls within Hanoi. For international telephone calls, the cheapest option are guesthouses or internet cafés as they offer cheaper internet services. Even the post office is getting in on this game, so essentially calls are good value everywhere now.

Tourist Information

The new **Tourist Information Center** (☎ 926 3366; www.vntourists.com; 4G Đ Le Loi) is a pretty slick operation with free information and plenty of handouts on hotels, restaurants and activities. However, it's privately-run and it also sells tours and the like.

Even though this is the capital of the country, forget anything really useful like a helpful government-run tourism office that dishes out free information. There is a tourist information office at Noi Bai International Airport these days, but beyond a few handouts it doesn't have much to offer.

The best source of tourism information in Hanoi, as in the rest of Vietnam, is asking around at different guesthouses, travel agencies and bars, and talking to your fellow travellers. See Internet Resources (p89) earlier for some recommended websites covering Hanoi.

Travel Agencies

There are lots of travel agencies in Hanoi, both government-run and privately owned, that can book tours, provide cars and guides, issue air tickets and arrange visa extensions.

Several budget agencies also double as restaurant-cafés, which offer cheap eats, rooms for rent and internet access. However, there are so many clones these days that it is sometimes difficult to differentiate the good from the bad. In the old days, it was only Sinh Café that was copied, but these days most of the main operators have experienced the problem. Some places are blatant, some more subtle, but you should be able to gain some clues from the set-up of the office and the knowledge of the staff. The harder the sell, the more likely they are fly-by-night operators trying to make a quick buck. Check the address and website carefully to make sure you are buying the authentic product.

The majority of Hanoi's hotels also peddle tours, but it is not advisable to book trips through hotels: although the prices are roughly the same, booking directly with the tour operators will give a much better idea of what you'll get for your money.

There has been a torrent of complaints about various budget tour operators in Hanoi. The biggest issue seems to be the gap between what they promise and what they actually

CENTRAL HANOI
500 m
0.3 miles
Ho Tay (West Lake)
Truc Bach Lake
Song Hong (Red River)
Long Bien Bridge
Chuong Đ Bridge
Long Bien
See Old Quarter Map (p96)
Ho Chi Minh Mausoleum Complex
Hoan Kiem District
Hanoi Citadel (Military Area)
Old Quarter
Hoan Kiem Lake
Hanoi Horison Hotel
Tran Quy Cap
Đ Thanh Nien
P Quan Thanh
Đ Thuy Khue
P Phan Dinh Phung
Dang Tat
Ng Canh Chan
P Nguyen Bieu
P Dang Dung
P Cua Bac
P Chau Long
Pham Hong Thai
Nguyen Truong
P Hang Bun
Hang Than
P Hang Dau
Nguyen Thiep
P Gam Cau
Cao Thang
Nguyen Thien Thuat
Đ Tran Nhat Duat
P Hang Chieu
P Hang Ma
P Hang Buom
P Lan Ong
P Hang Bo
P Hang Bac
P Hang Gai
P Cau Go
Hoang Van Thu
P Ngoc Ha
Đ Hung Vuong
Đ Bac Son
P Nguyen Tri Phuong
P Cua Dong
Ly Nam De
P Ly Nam De
P Đ Thanh
P Doi Can
Le Hong Png
P Dien Bien Phu
Đ Hoang Dieu
Chu Van An
Khuc Hao
Đ Tran Phu
P Giang Vo
P Nguyen Thai Hoc
Cao Ba Quat
P Van Mieu
P Quoc Tu Giam
P Cam Chi
P Phung Hung
Hang Ga
P Hang Bong
P Quan Su
P Phu Doan
P Trang Thi
P Le Thai To
P Dinh Tien Hoang
P Hang Dau
P Ly Thai To
Tran Nguyen Han
Le Lai
P Tong Dan
Nam Ngu
Phan Boi Chau

Đ Tran Quang Khai
P Pham Ngu Lao
Đ Thai Than Lao
P Le Thanh Tong
P Tran Thanh Tong
P Kim Nguu
Phan Huy Chu
P Han Thuyen
P Hang Chuoi
P Lo Duc
Phan Chu Trinh
P Trang Tien
P Ngo Quyen
P Ngo Thi Nham
P Dong Nhan
P Hang Bai
P Le Van Huu
P Tran Xuan Soan
P Hoa Ma
P Hue
Đ Dai Co Viet
Ha Ba Trung District
P Bach Mai
P Ham Long
P Ba Trieu
P Ly Thuong Kiet
P Hai Ba Trung
P Trieu Viet Vuong
P Bui Thi Xuan
P Doan Tran Nghiep
Thai Phien
P Ba Trieu
P Tran Hung Dao
P Nguyen Du
Nguyen Binh Khiem
P To Hien Thanh
P le Dai Hanh
P Quang Trung
Nguyen Dinh Chieu
Thien Quang Lake
P Tran Nhan Tong
P Quan Su
Friendship Cultural Hall
P Tran Quoc Toan
P Tran Binh Trong
P Yet Kieu
Lenin Park
Bay Mau Lake
Thanh Nhau Lake
Đ Le Duan
Ba Man Lake
Hanoi (Ga Hang Co)
Thien Hung
Ngo Cho Kham Thien
P Pham Ngoc Thach
P Kham Thien
Đ La Thanh
Chu Van An
Xa Dan
Đ La Thanh
P Nguyen Luong Bang
Dong Da District
P Chua Boc
5
6
7
8

INFORMATION
Bookworm 1 D6
British Council 2 A4
Cambodian Embassy 3 D5
Canadian Embassy 4 B3
Chinese Embassy 5 B3
DHL 6 C4
French Embassy 7 D5
French Embassy Clinic (see 7)
German Embassy 8 C4
Immigration Police 9 E5
Lao Embassy 10 C6
National Institute of Traditional Medicine 11 D6
Philippines Embassy 12 E6
Singapore Embassy 13 B3
Thailand Embassy 14 B4
Vietnam-Korea Friendship Clinic 15 B3

SIGHTS & ACTIVITIES
Ambassadors' Pagoda 16 C5
Army Museum 17 C3
Ba Dinh Square 18 B2
Botanical Gardens 19 A2
Cua Bac (Northern Gate of Old Citadel) 20 C2
Cua Bac Church 21 C1
Cua Nam Market 22 C4
Fine Arts Museum 23 B4
Flag Tower 24 B3
Hai Ba Trung Temple 25 E7
Ham Long Church 26 E6
Hanoi Foreign Language College (see 28)
Hanoi University 27 C8
History Museum 28 F5
Ho Chi Minh Mausoleum Complex Entrance 29 B3
Ho Chi Minh Museum 30 A3
Ho Chi Minh's Mausoleum 31 B2
Ho Chi Minh's Stilt House 32 A2
Hoa Binh Hotel 33 E5
Hoa Sua (see 52)
Lenin Park Main Gate 34 C6
Museum of Vietnamese Revolution 35 F5
One Pillar Pagoda 36 A2
Presidential Palace 37 A2
Quan Thanh Temple 38 B1
Revolutionary Museum 39 F5
Temple of Literature (Van Mieu) 40 B4
Vu Doo Salon 41 B4

SLEEPING
Army Hotel 42 F5
De Syloia Hotel 43 E6
Galaxy Hotel 44 D2
Guoman Hotel 45 C5
Hotel 30/4 46 C5
Hotel Nikko 47 C6

EATING
Benkay Restaurant (see 47)
Brothers Café 48 C4
Com Chay Nang Tam 49 D5
Duong Thuy Khue (Specialty Food Street) 50 A1
Emperor 51 F6
Hoa Sua 52 D5
Kinh Do Café 53 C4
KOTO on Van Mieu 54 B4
Luna d'Autumno 55 C4
Maison Vanille 56 E6
Nam Phuong 57 E5
P Cam Chi (Speciality Food Street) 58 C4
P To Hien Thanh (Speciality Food Street) 59 D7
Quan An Ngon 60 C4
Restaurant 1,2,3 61 E6
San Ho Restaurant 62 C5
Seasons of Hanoi 63 C1
Van Anh (see 58)
Wild Lotus 64 D6
Wild Rice 65 E6

DRINKING
Luna Lounge (see 55)
Nha Hang Lan Chin (see 35)

ENTERTAINMENT
Apocalypse Now 66 A8
Cay Cau (see 43)
Central Circus 67 C6
Megastar Cineplex 68 D7
Nam Phuong (see 57)
Seventeen Saloon 69 C5

SHOPPING
Antique Shops 70 C6
Craft Link 71 B4
Hom Market 72 E6
Ipa-Nima 73 E6
Viet Art Centre 74 C5

TRANSPORT
Kim Ma Bus Station 75 A3
Long Bien Bus Station 76 E1
Pacific Airlines 77 C4

deliver. Competition is fierce and price-cutting among various tour operators has driven the cost of tours so low that in some cases it has become difficult to deliver.

You can buy a two-day/one-night, all-inclusive excursion to Halong Bay for less than US$20, but do you really want to travel on a 45-seat bus and be herded en masse onto a boat to tour the bay and grottoes? Plus, you can't expect gourmet meals at this price. In the long run, the dollars saved will probably not be remembered as much as the experience itself. Each to their own, but if you buy the cheapest trip available it probably won't live up to expectations.

We suggest that you take time to seek out tour operators who stick to small groups and use their own vehicles and guides. New places open all the time, and existing places change, so the suggestions here are not exhaustive. Shop around and consider the following companies:

A to Z Queen Café (Map p96; ☎ 826 0860; www.queencafe.com.vn; 65 Hang Be) One of the original budget companies offering tours to Halong Bay and the far north. Cheap trips at budget standards.

ET Pumpkin (Map p96; ☎ 926 0739; www.et-pumpkin.com; 89 Pho Ma May) Strange name, but there's nothing wrong with the service at this company. It offers tours throughout the north, and operates its own private carriage on the night train to Sapa.

Ethnic Travel (Map p96; ☎ 926 1951; www.ethnictravel.com.vn; 35 Pho Hang Giay) One of the newer companies in the north, offering an innovative selection of adventures that also involve some public transport to meet the real Vietnamese. Plus Bai Tu Long Bay.

Explorer Tours (Map p96; ☎ 923 0713; www.explorer.com.vn; 85 Pho Hang Bo) This company has steadily moved upmarket and offers a good selection of tailored trips around the north.

Free Wheelin Tours (Map p96; ☎ 747 0545; www.freewheelin-tours.com; Pho Luong Ngoc Quyen) Best known for its adventurous motorbike tours (p491), this company also offers 4WD tours, local homestays and boat trips to Bai Tu Long Bay.

Handspan Adventure Travel (Map p96; ☎ 926 0581; www.handspan.com; 80 Pho Ma May) A deservedly popular company offering Halong Bay tours with some kayaking, cruises into Bai Tu Long Bay and jeep tours in the northeast. This outfit also operates an office in Sapa for biking and hiking. The walk-in office is in the Tamarind Café.

Ocean Tours (Map p96; ☎ 926 1294; www.oceantours vietnam.com; 7 Pho Dinh Liet) This operator has been earning a good name for itself by specialising in Halong Bay. Also operates the backpacker retreat Ocean Beach Resort (p147) at Cat Ba.

ODC Travel (Map p96; ☎ 824 3024; www.odctravel .com; Camellia Hotel, 13 Pho Luong Ngoc Quyen) Formerly Old Darling Café, this is one of the most established names in the business. It forsook the café business to concentrate on travel and it seems to have paid off, with very positive reviews for all its budget tours of the north.

Sinh Café (Map p96; ☎ 926 0646; www.sinhcafevn.com; 52 Pho Luong Ngoc Quyen) The original open tour bus operator, it remains one of the better options for travellers taking the long road south.

Vega Travel (Map p96; ☎ 926 2092; www.vega-travel .com; 24a Pho Hang Bac) Formerly known as Fansipan Tours, the company decided to change its name after as many as 10 copycats sprung up. Let's hope it sticks with Vega, as it has a good range of budget trips throughout the north.

For an extensive list of nationwide operators that also offer tours of Hanoi and northern Vietnam, see p490. For more on specialist companies offering motorbike tours of the north, see p491.

DANGERS & ANNOYANCES

Back in the bad old days, Hanoi used to be the hardest place to travel in Vietnam, then in the late 1990s things improved massively. More recently it has become the capital of hotel and tour scams in Vietnam, so be sure to keep your antennae up. We have heard several substantiated reports of verbal aggression and physical violence towards tourists when deciding against a hotel room or tour. Stay calm and back away slowly or things could quickly flare up. Some Western women have been hassled by young men around town who follow them home, so it pays to hit the town in larger numbers. Walking alone in well-lit areas of the Old Quarter is usually safe, but stay alert in the darker streets, particularly in the early hours of the morning. When getting from one part of town to the other at night, particularly from late-night spots, it is more sensible for solo women, and even men, to take a metered taxi or *xe om*.

Scams

The biggest scams in town are inextricably linked. The taxi and minibus mafia at the airport shuttle unwitting tourists to the wrong hotel. Invariably, the hotel has appropriated the name of another popular property and will then attempt to appropriate as much of your money as possible. For more on the airport–hotel scam and how to avoid it, see the boxed texts on p109 and p124.

Gay men should be aware of a scam going on around the Hoan Kiem Lake. It starts with a friendly stranger approaching a foreigner and suggesting a night out. This leads to a karaoke bar and a private room for a few drinks and some songs. The bill arrives and it's miraculously US$100 or more. The situation deteriorates from here and ends in extortion. Be careful and follow your instincts. Subtle variations on this theme involving Western men and local women have been going on for years, and few 'victims' think of it as a scam.

SIGHTS

Old Quarter

This is the Asia we dreamed of from afar. Steeped in history, pulsating with life, bubbling with commerce, buzzing with motorbikes and rich in exotic scents, the Old Quarter is Hanoi's historic heart. The streets are narrow and congested, and crossing the road is an art form, but remember to look up as well as down, as there is some elegant old architecture in and among the chaos. Hawkers pound the streets, sizzling and smoking baskets hiding a cheap meal for the locals. *Pho* stalls and *bia hoi* dens hug every corner, resonant with the sound of gossip and laughter. Modern yet medieval, there is no better way to spend time in Hanoi than walking the streets, soaking up the sights, sounds and smells.

Home to a thousand years of history, the commercial quarter of the city evolved alongside the Red River and the smaller To Lich River, which once flowed through the city centre in an intricate network of canals and waterways, teeming with boats. Waters could rise as high as 8m during the monsoon. Dikes were constructed to protect the city and these can still be seen along Tran Quang Khai.

In the 13th century Hanoi's 36 guilds established themselves here, each taking a different street – hence the original name '36 Streets'. Today, there are more than 50 streets in today's Old Quarter. *Hang* means

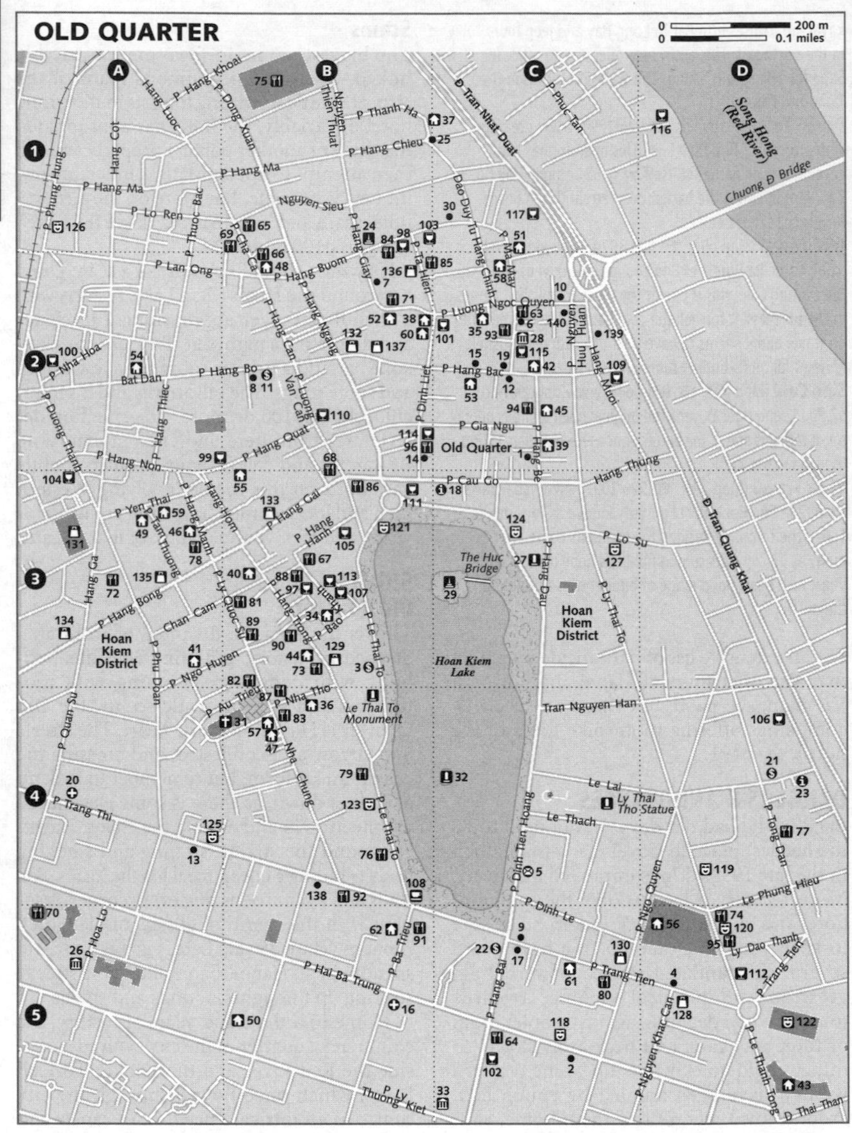

'merchandise' and is usually followed by the name of the product that was traditionally sold in that street. Thus, Pho Hang Gai translates as 'Silk Street' (see the boxed text, p98, for the rest); these days the street name may not indicate what's sold there, otherwise there would be lots of Pho Hang Du Lich (Tourism Streets).

Exploring the maze of back streets is fascinating: some streets open up while others narrow into a warren of alleys. The area is known for its tunnel (or tube) houses – so called because of their narrow frontages and long rooms. These tunnel houses were developed to avoid taxes based on the width of their street frontage. By feudal law, houses were

INFORMATION

A to Z Queen Café 1 C2
American Club 2 C5
ANZ Bank 3 B3
British Embassy (see 16)
Centre Culturel Française de Hanoi 4 D5
Domestic Post Office 5 C4
ET Pumpkin 6 C2
Ethnic Travel 7 B2
Explorer Tours 8 B2
Foreign Language Bookshop 9 C5
Free Wheelin' Tours 10 C2
Handspan Adventure Travel (see 93)
Industrial & Commercial Bank 11 B2
International Post Office (see 5)
Love Planet 12 C2
National Library & Archives 13 A4
New Zealand Embassy (see 74)
ODC Travel (see 35)
Ocean Tours 14 B2
Sinh Café 15 C2
SOS International Clinic 16 B5
Thang Long Bookshop 17 C5
Tourist Information Center 18 C3
Vega Travel 19 C2
Viet Duc Hospital 20 A4
Vietcombank 21 D4
Vietcombank 22 C5
Vietnam National Administration of Tourism 23 D4

SIGHTS & ACTIVITIES

Bach Ma Temple 24 B1
Cua O Quan Chuong (Old East Gate) 25 C1
Dong Xuan Market (see 75)
Hoa Lo Prison Museum 26 A5
Martyrs' Monument 27 C3
Memorial House 28 C2
Ngoc Son Temple 29 C3
QT Salon (see 79)
SF Salon & Spa 30 C1
St Joseph Cathedral 31 B4
Thap Rua (Tortoise Tower) 32 C4
Women's Museum 33 C5

SLEEPING

Artist Hotel (see 118)
Bao Khanh Hotel 34 B3
Camellia Hotel 35 C2
Church Hotel 36 B4
City Gate Hotel 37 B1
Classic Hotel 38 B2
Classic Street Hotel 39 C2
Golden Lotus Hotel 40 B3
Hanoi Backpackers Hostel 41 A3
Hanoi Elegance Hotel 42 C2
Heart Hotel (see 105)
Hilton Hanoi Opera 43 D5
Ho Guom Hotel 44 B3
Hoa Binh Palace Hotel 45 C2
Hong Ngoc Hotel 1 46 A3
Hotel Thien Trang 47 B4
Majestic Salute Hotel 48 B2
Manh Dung Guesthouse 49 A3
Melia Hotel 50 B5
Old Street Hotel 51 C1
Prince Hotel 52 B2
Queen Hotel 53 C2
Quoc Hoa Hotel 54 A2
Real Darling Café 55 B3
Sofitel Metropole Hotel 56 D5
Spring Hotel 57 B4
Sunshine Hotel 58 C2
Thu Giang Guesthouse 59 A3
Thuy Nga Guesthouse 60 B2
Trang Tien Hotel 61 C5
Viet Fun Hotel (see 58)
Zephyr Hotel 62 B5

EATING

69 Bar-Restaurant 63 C2
Al Fresco's 64 C5
Ba Mien (see 43)
Baan Thai Restaurant 65 B1
Baguette & Chocolat 66 B2
Café des Arts 67 B3
Café Pho Co 68 B2
Cha Ca La Vong 69 B1
Citimart 70 A5
Club Opera (see 95)
Culi Café 71 B2
Cyclo Bar & Restaurant 72 A3
Dakshin 73 B3
Diva 74 D5
Dong Xuan Market 75 B1
Fanny Ice Cream 76 B4
Fivimart 77 D4
Golden Land Restaurant (see 66)
Green Tangerine (see 1)
Hanoi Garden 78 A3
Intimex 79 B4
Kem Trang Tien 80 C5
La 81 B3
La Place 82 B3
La Salsa 83 B4
Ladybird Restaurant 84 B1
Le Beaulieu Restaurant (see 56)
Little Hanoi 1 85 B2
Little Hanoi 2 86 B3
Mediterraneo (see 83)
Moca Café 87 B4
Old Hanoi (see 19)
Pane E Vino (see 73)
Pepperoni's Pizza & Café 88 B3
Pepperoni's Pizza & Café 89 B3
Pho 24 (see 22)
Puku 90 B3
Restaurant Bobby Chinn 91 B5
Saigon Sakura 92 B4
Spices Garden (see 56)
Stop Café (see 67)
Tamarind Café 93 C2
Tandoor 94 C2
The Restaurant 95 D5
Whole Earth Restaurant 96 B2

DRINKING

Amazon Bar 97 B3
Bar Le Maquis 98 B1
Bia Hoi 68 Hang Quat 99 A2
Bia Hoi Ha Noi 100 A2
Bia Hoi Junction 101 C2
Bia Hoi Viet Ha 102 C5
Dragonfly 103 B1
Finnegan's Irish Pub 104 A3
Funky Monkey 105 B3
Gambrinus 106 D4
GC Pub 107 B3
Hapro 108 B4
Highway 4 109 C2
Jazz Club By Quyen Van Minh 110 B2
Le Pub (see 45)
Legends Beer 111 B3
Met Pub (see 56)
My Way 112 D5
Polite Pub 113 B3
Quan Bia Minh 114 B2
Red Beer 115 C2
Solace 116 D1
Thuy Ta Café (see 121)
Toilet Pub 117 C1

ENTERTAINMENT

Centre Culturel Française de Hanoi (see 4)
Cinematheque 118 C5
Club 51 119 D4
Club Opera 120 D5
Dinh Lang Restaurant 121 B3
Hanoi Opera House 122 D5
I-Box 123 B4
Municipal Water Puppet Theatre 124 C3
New Century Nightclub 125 A4
Piano Bar 126 A1
R&R Tavern 127 C3
Terrace Bar (see 95)

SHOPPING

A Gallery (see 130)
Chi Vang 128 D5
Dome 129 B3
Gallery Huong Xuyen 130 C5
Hadong Silk (see 133)
Hang Da Market 131 A3
Hanoi Contemporary Art Gallery (see 130)
Hanoi Gallery 132 B2
Khai Silk 133 B3
Mai Gallery 134 A3
Pearl Ha 135 A3
Shoe Market (see 27)
Things of Substance (see 36)
Viet Hien 136 B2
Vietnamese House 137 B2

TRANSPORT

Airport Minibus 138 B4
Buffalo Tours 139 C2
Cuong's Motorbike Adventure 140 C2
Vietnam Airlines (see 138)

OLD QUARTER STREET NAMES

street name	description	street name	description
Bat Dan	wooden bowls	Hang Giay	paper or shoes
Bat Su	china bowls	Hang Hanh	onions
Cha Ca	roasted fish	Hang Hom	cases
Chan Cam	string instruments	Hang Huong	incense
Cho Gao	rice market	Hang Khay	trays
Gia Ngu	fishermen	Hang Khoai	sweet potatoes
Hai Tuong	sandals	Hang Luoc	combs
Hang Bac	silversmiths	Hang Ma	votive papers
Hang Be	rafts	Hang Mam	pickled fish
Hang Bo	baskets	Hang Manh	bamboo screens
Hang Bong	cotton	Hang Muoi	salt
Hang Buom	sails	Hang Ngang	transversal street
Hang But	brushes	Hang Non	hats
Hang Ca	fish	Hang Phen	alum
Hang Can	scales	Hang Quat	fans
Hang Chai	bottles	Hang Ruoi	clam worms
Hang Chi	threads	Hang Than	charcoal
Hang Chieu	mats	Hang Thiec	tin
Hang Chinh	jars	Hang Thung	barrels
Hang Cot	bamboo lattices	Hang Tre	bamboo
Hang Da	leather	Hang Trong	drums
Hang Dao	(silk) dyers	Hang Vai	cloth
Hang Dau	beans or oils	Lo Ren	blacksmiths
Hang Dieu	pipes	Lo Su	coffins
Hang Dong	copper	Ma May	rattan
Hang Duong	sugar	Ngo Gach	bricks
Hang Ga	chicken	Thuoc Bac	herbal medicines
Hang Gai	silk		

also limited to two storeys and, out of respect for the king, could not be taller than the Royal Palace. These days there are taller buildings, but no real high-rise buildings.

Opportunities to dispense with your dong are endless. As you wander around you'll find clothes, cosmetics, fake sunglasses, luxury food, T-shirts, musical instruments, plumbing supplies, herbal medicines, jewellery, religious offerings, spices, woven mats and much, much more (see Shopping, p119 for details).

Some of the specialised streets include Pho Hang Quat, with its red candlesticks, funeral boxes, flags and temple items; and the more glamorous Pho Hang Gai, with its silk, embroidery, lacquerware, paintings and water puppets – silk sleeping-bag liners and elegant *ao dai* (the national dress of Vietnam) are popular here. Finally, no trip to the Old Quarter would be complete without a visit to the **Dong Xuan Market** (Map p96; cnr Pho Hang Khoai & Pho Dong Xuan), rebuilt after a fire in 1994.

A stroll through the historic Old Quarter can last anywhere from an hour to the better part of a day, depending on your pace. However long, or whatever detours you might take, the Walking Tour (p105) will provide you with a heady dose of Vietnamese culture, lots of shopping opportunities and some insight into the city's long history.

Ho Chi Minh Mausoleum Complex

This is the holiest of the holies for many Vietnamese. To the west of the Old Quarter, the **Ho Chi Minh mausoleum complex** (Map pp92-3; entrance cnr Pho Ngoc Ha & Pho Doi Can) is an important place of pilgrimage for many Vietnamese, combining the secular and the spiritual. A traffic-free area of parks, monuments, memorials and pagodas, it's usually crowded with groups of all ages who have come to pay their respects.

HO CHI MINH'S MAUSOLEUM

In the tradition of Lenin and Stalin before him and Mao afterwards **Ho Chi Minh's Mausoleum** (Map pp92-3; admission free; 8-11am Tue-Thu, Sat & Sun Dec-Sep, last entry usually 10.15am) is a monumental marble edifice that is a mecca for many Vietnamese. Contrary to his desire for a simple cremation, the mausoleum was constructed of native materials gathered from all over Vietnam between 1973 and 1975. The roof and peristyle are said to evoke either a traditional communal house or a lotus flower, though to many tourists it looks like a concrete cubicle with columns. Set deep in the bowels of the building in a glass sarcophagus is the body of Ho Chi Minh. The mausoleum is closed for about three months each year while Ho Chi Minh's embalmed corpse goes to Russia for maintenance. Some sceptics have suggested Madame Tussaud's has the contract these days.

The queue, which moves quite quickly, usually snakes for several hundred metres to the mausoleum entrance itself. Inside, more guards, regaled in snowy-white military uniforms, are posted at intervals of five paces, giving an eerily authoritarian aspect to the slightly macabre spectacle of the embalmed body with its wispy white hair.

The following rules are strictly applied to all visitors to the mausoleum:

- People wearing shorts, tank tops and so on will not be admitted.
- Nothing (including day packs, cameras and mobiles) can be taken inside.
- Maintain a respectful demeanour at all times: no talking or sniggering.
- For obvious reasons of decorum, photography is absolutely prohibited inside the mausoleum.
- It is forbidden to put your hands in your pockets.
- Hats must be taken off inside the mausoleum building.

Most of the visitors are Vietnamese and it's interesting to watch their reactions. Most show deep respect and admiration for Ho Chi Minh, who is honoured for his role as the liberator of the Vietnamese people from colonialism, as much as for his communist ideology. This view is reinforced by Vietnam's educational system, which emphasises Ho's deeds and accomplishments.

If you're lucky, you'll catch the changing of the guard outside Ho's mausoleum – the pomp and ceremony displayed here rivals the British equivalent at Buckingham Palace.

Photography is permitted outside the building but not inside and visitors must leave their bags and mobile phones at a counter just inside the entrance.

HO CHI MINH'S STILT HOUSE & THE PRESIDENTIAL PALACE

Behind Ho Chi Minh's Mausoleum is a **stilt house** (Nha San Bac Ho; Map pp92-3; admission 5000d; 8-11am & 2-4pm), where Ho lived on and off from 1958 to 1969. The house is an upmarket interpretation of traditional rural dwelling, and has been preserved just as Ho left it. It's set in a well-tended garden next to a carp-filled pond. Just how much time he actually spent here is questionable – the house would have been a tempting target for US bombers had it been suspected that Ho was hanging out here.

In stark contrast to the understated stilt house is the imposing **Presidential Palace** (Map pp92–3), a beautifully restored colonial building constructed in 1906 as the Palace of the Governor General of Indochina. It is now used for official receptions and isn't open to the public. There is a combined entrance gate to the stilt house and Presidential Palace grounds on Pho Ong Ich Kiem, inside the mausoleum complex; when the main mausoleum entrance is closed, enter from Đ Hung Vuong near the palace building.

HO CHI MINH MUSEUM

The two separate sections of the **Ho Chi Minh Museum** (Bao Tang Ho Chi Minh; Map pp92-3; admission 5000d; 8-11am & 1.30-4.30pm Tue-Thu, Sat & Sun) relate to the past and future. Start in the past and move to the future by walking in a clockwise direction downwards through the museum, starting from the right-hand side of the top of the stairs. The modern displays all have messages, such as 'peace', 'happiness' and 'freedom'.

It's probably worth taking an English-speaking guide, since some of the symbolism is hard to interpret. The 1958 Ford Edsel bursting through the wall – a US commercial failure to symbolise its military failure – is a knockout. All in all, it's slightly surreal, but worth a visit if time allows.

The museum is the huge cement structure next to Ho Chi Minh's Mausoleum. Photography is forbidden and, upon entry, you must leave bags and cameras at reception.

ONE PILLAR PAGODA

A Hanoi landmark, the **One Pillar Pagoda** (Chua Mot Cot; Map pp92-3; Pho Ong Ich Kiem) was built by the Emperor Ly Thai Tong, who ruled from 1028 to 1054. According to the annals, the heirless emperor dreamed that he had met Quan The Am Bo Tat, the Goddess of Mercy, who, while seated on a lotus flower, handed him a male child. Ly Thai Tong then married a young peasant girl and had a son and heir by her. As a way of expressing his gratitude for this event, he constructed this pagoda in 1049.

The delicate One Pillar Pagoda, built of wood on a single stone pillar, is designed to resemble a lotus blossom, the symbol of purity, rising out of a sea of sorrow. One of the last (malicious and pointless) acts of the French before quitting Hanoi in 1954 was to destroy the original One Pillar Pagoda; the structure was rebuilt by the new government. The pagoda is between the mausoleum and the museum.

Temples & Pagodas

TEMPLE OF LITERATURE

A rare example of well-preserved traditional Vietnamese architecture, the **Temple of Literature** (Van Mieu; Map pp92-3; ☎ 845 2917; Pho Quoc Tu Giam; admission 5000d; 🕑 8am-5pm) is a relaxing retreat from the noisy streets of Hanoi. If you only plan to visit one temple in Hanoi, be sure to make it this one.

It was founded in 1070 by Emperor Ly Thanh Tong, who dedicated it to Confucius (Khong Tu) in order to honour scholars and men of literary accomplishment. Vietnam's first university was established here in 1076 to educate the sons of mandarins. In 1484 Emperor Le Thanh Tong ordered that stelae be erected to record the names, places of birth and achievements of men who received doctorates in triennial examinations held from 1442. Although 116 examinations were held between 1442 and 1778, when the practice was discontinued, only 82 stelae are extant. In 1802 Emperor Gia Long transferred the National University to his new capital, Hué. Major renovations were carried out here in 1920 and 1956.

The Temple of Literature is made up of five separate courtyards. The central pathways and gates between them were reserved for the king. The walkways on one side were for the use of administrative mandarins, while those on the other side were for military mandarins.

The main entrance is preceded by a gate, on which there's an inscription requesting that visitors dismount their horses before entering. Make sure you do. Khué Van Pavilion, at the far side of the second courtyard, was constructed in 1802 and is a fine example of Vietnamese architecture. The 82 stelae, considered to be the most precious artefacts in the temple, are arrayed to either side of the third enclosure; each one sits on a stone tortoise.

The secular intrudes on the spiritual these days, with a host of souvenir shops flanking the Thai Hoc courtyard. Everything from postcards to retired water puppets are available but bargain hard as prices are high.

The Temple of Literature is about 2km west of Hoan Kiem Lake.

NGOC SON TEMPLE

Founded in the 18th century, **Ngoc Son Temple** (Jade Mountain Temple; Map p96; admission 2000d; 🕑 8am-5pm) is on an island in the northern part of Hoan Kiem Lake. Surrounded by water and shaded by trees, it is a delightfully quiet place to escape the bustle of Hanoi. The temple is dedicated to the scholar Van Xuong, General Tran Hung Dao, who defeated the Mongols in the 13th century, and La To, the patron saint of physicians.

Ngoc Son Temple is reached via the red The Huc (Rising Sun) Bridge, constructed in 1885. The nearby **Martyrs' Monument** was erected to those who died fighting for Vietnam's independence.

AMBASSADORS' PAGODA

The official centre of Buddhism in Hanoi, the **Ambassadors' Pagoda** (Chua Quan Su; Map pp92-3; ☎ 825 2427; 73 Pho Quan Su) attracts quite a crowd on holidays. During the 17th century there was a guesthouse here for the ambassadors of Buddhist countries. Today there are about a dozen monks and nuns based at the Ambassadors' Pagoda. Next to the pagoda is a shop selling Buddhist ritual objects.

The Ambassadors' Pagoda is located between Pho Ly Thuong Kiet and Pho Tran Hung Dao.

BACH MA TEMPLE

Nestled in a corner of the Old Quarter, the small **Bach Ma Temple** (Map p96; cnr Pho Hang Buom & Pho Hang Giay) is the oldest temple in the city. It was built by King Ly Thai To to honour a white horse that guided him to the site to construct his city walls. The pagoda includes a statue of the legendary white horse, as well as a beautiful red-lacquered funeral palanquin.

HAI BA TRUNG TEMPLE

Two kilometres south of Hoan Kiem Lake, this **temple** (Map pp92-3; Pho Tho Lao) was founded in 1142. A statue shows the two Trung sisters (who lived in the 1st century AD) kneeling with their arms raised in the air, as if they are addressing a crowd. Some say the statue shows the sisters, who had been proclaimed the queens of the Vietnamese, about to dive into a river. They are said to have drowned themselves rather than surrender following their defeat at the hands of the Chinese.

QUAN THANH TEMPLE

Shaded by huge trees, **Quan Thanh Temple** (Map pp92–3) was established during the Ly dynasty (1010–1225) and was dedicated to Tran Vo (God of the North), whose symbols of power were the tortoise and the snake. A bronze statue and bell date from 1677. The temple is on the shores of Truc Bach Lake, near the intersection of Đ Thanh Nien and Pho Quan Thanh.

TAY HO PAGODA

The most popular spot for worship in Hanoi is at **Tay Ho Pagoda** (Map pp88-9; Pho Tay Ho). Throngs of people come here on the first and 15th day of each lunar month in the hope of receiving good fortune. The entrance includes a colourful lane of stalls selling temple offerings and food, while a line of good fresh seafood restaurants fronts the lake. It's a great place to watch the world go by.

TRAN QUOC PAGODA

One of the oldest in Vietnam, **Tran Quoc Pagoda** (Map pp88–9) is on the eastern shore of Ho Tay, just off Đ Thanh Nien, which divides Ho Tay from Truc Bach Lake. A stele here, dating from 1639, tells the history of this site. The pagoda was rebuilt in the 15th century and again in 1842. There are a number of monks' funerary monuments in the garden.

Museums

It's worth noting that in addition to the usual two-hour lunch break, most of the museums in Hanoi are closed on Monday.

VIETNAM MUSEUM OF ETHNOLOGY

The Musée de l'Homme in Paris helped design the wonderful **Vietnam Museum of Ethnology** (Map p126; ☎ 756 2193; Đ Nguyen Van Huyen; admission 20,000d; ⏰ 8.30am-5.30pm Tue-Sun). It features a fascinating collection of art and everyday objects gathered from Vietnam and its diverse tribal people.

The museum has excellent maps and the displays are well labelled in Vietnamese, French and English. Interesting sections portray a typical village market, the making of conical hats, and a Tay shamanic ceremony, while videos show the real-life contexts. There are fabulous displays of weaving and fabric motifs. Visitors can also enter a traditional Black Thai house reconstructed within the museum, and there are outdoor exhibits in the landscaped grounds. Ede, H'mong and Jarai houses are popular places to pose for wedding photos: quite a surreal sight. There are often special exhibitions, including the current display on life in the early 1980s under the coupon system. This could become a permanent feature, as it is so well presented and surprisingly honest about the hardships of life at the time.

A craft shop – affiliated with Craft Link, which is a fair-trade organisation – sells books, beautiful postcards, and arts and crafts from ethnic communities.

The museum is quite a way from central Hanoi, but it shouldn't be missed.

Getting There & Away

The museum is in the Cau Giay district, about 7km from the city centre. A good way to get here is by rented bicycle (30 minutes). If you're short of time or energy, an air-con metered taxi costs around 40,000d each way. The cheapest way to get here is to take local bus 14 (3500d) from Hoan Kiem Lake and get off at the junction between Đ Hoang Quoc Viet and Đ Nguyen Van Huyen.

HISTORY MUSEUM

A must for the architecture more than the collection, the **History Museum** (Bao Tang Lich Su; Map pp92-3; 1 Pho Trang Tien; admission 15,000d; ⏰ 8-11.30am & 1.30-4.30pm Tue-Sun) was formerly home to the École Française d'Extrême Orient in Vietnam. It is an elegant, ochre-coloured structure built between 1925 and 1932. French architect Ernest Hebrard was among the first in Vietnam to incorporate a blend of Chinese and French design elements in his creations, and this particular building remains one of Hanoi's most stunning architectural showpieces.

Collections here cover the ups more than the downs of Vietnamese history. Highlights include some excellent bronzes from the Dong Son culture (3rd century BC to 3rd century AD) and some striking Hindu statuary from the Khmer and Champa kingdoms. More recent history is a little one-sided and includes the struggle against the French and the story of the Communist Party.

MUSEUM OF VIETNAMESE REVOLUTION

A must for all budding revolutionaries, the history of the Vietnamese Revolution is enthusiastically presented in this **museum** (Bao Tang Cach Mang; Map pp92-3; 216 Pho Tran Quang Khai; admission 10,000d; 8-11.45am & 1.30-4.15pm Tue-Sun). It's diagonally across the road from the History Museum.

MEMORIAL HOUSE

It is worth making a detour to this delightful **house** (Map p96; 87 Pho Ma May; admission 5000d; 9-11.30am & 2-5pm), north of Hoan Kiem Lake in the Old Quarter. This thoughtfully restored traditional Chinese-style dwelling is sparsely but beautifully decorated, and offers a bygone glimpse into the lives of local merchants in the Old Quarter. The restoration of the house was carried out in 1999 in cooperation with the city of Toulouse, France. While there are many such living museums in Hoi An, there is nothing else like this in Hanoi.

FINE ARTS MUSEUM

The former French Ministry of Information is home to Hanoi's **Fine Arts Museum** (Bao Tang My Thuat; Map pp92-3; 66 Pho Nguyen Thai Hoc; admission 10,000d; 9.15am-5pm Tue-Sun). The collection here includes some very intricate sculptures, paintings, lacquerware, ceramics and other traditional Vietnamese fine arts. It's a good starting point for anyone seriously considering investing in Vietnamese art. Reproductions of antiques are on sale here, but be sure to ask for a certificate to clear these goods through customs when you leave Vietnam.

The Fine Arts Museum is on the corner of Pho Cao Ba Quat, across the street from the northern wall of the Temple of Literature.

WOMEN'S MUSEUM

There are some engaging displays in the worthy **Women's Museum** (Bao Tang Phu Nu; Map p96; 36 Pho Ly Thuong Kiet; admission 20,000d; 8am-4pm). The inevitable tribute to women soldiers is balanced by some great exhibits from the international women's movement protesting the American War. And there's much more in terms of cultural and political information. The 4th floor includes different costumes worn by the women of the ethnic-minority groups, and examples of tribal basketware and fabric motifs. This is one place where many of the exhibits have multilingual explanations.

ARMY MUSEUM

Easy to spot thanks to a large collection of weaponry out front, the **Army Museum** (Bao Tang Quan Doi; Map pp92-3; Pho Dien Bien Phu; admission 20,000d; 8-11.30am & 1.30-4.30pm Tue-Sun) displays Soviet and Chinese equipment alongside French- and US-made weapons captured during years of warfare. The centrepiece is a Soviet-built MiG-21 jet fighter, triumphant amid the wreckage of French aircraft downed at Dien Bien Phu, and a US F-111. The displays include scale models of various epic battles from the long military history of Vietnam, including Dien Bien Phu and the capture of Saigon.

Next to the Army Museum is the hexagonal Flag Tower, which has become one of the symbols of Hanoi. Some museum guards may offer to show you this tower, but will then ask for US$10 to pay for the privilege.

HOA LO PRISON MUSEUM

This thought-provoking site is all that remains of the former **Hoa Lo Prison** (Map p96; ☎ 824 6358; 1 Pho Hoa Lo, cnr Pho Hai Ba Trung; admission 5000d; 8-11.30am & 1.30-4.30pm Tue-Sun), ironically nicknamed the 'Hanoi Hilton' by US POWs during the American War. Those incarcerated at Hoa Lo included Pete Peterson, who later became the first US Ambassador to a unified Vietnam in 1995, and Senator John McCain.

The vast prison complex was built by the French in 1896. Originally intended to house around 450 inmates, records indicate that by the 1930s there were close to 2000 prisoners. Much of the prison was razed to make room for the Hanoi Towers skyscraper, though the section at the front of the site has been thoughtfully preserved and restored as a museum – look for the sign over the gate reading 'Maison Centrale'. There are some English and French labels corresponding with the displays, and it is possible to find an English-speaking guide on site.

The bulk of the exhibits here relate to the prison's use up to the mid-1950s, focusing on the Vietnamese struggle for independence from France. Notable gruesome exhibits in the dark chambers include an ominous French guillotine that was used to behead Vietnamese revolutionaries during the colonial period, and the fetters with which prisoners were chained to the bunks. Even allowing for the propaganda, it looks like the treatment of Americans by the Vietnamese was infinitely better than that of Vietnamese nationalists by the French.

There are also mug shots on display of Americans and Vietnamese who served time at Hoa Lo. Missing in Action (MIA) teams continue to search for remains of missing US air personnel all over Vietnam.

Lakes

HOAN KIEM LAKE

The epicentre of old Hanoi, **Hoan Kiem Lake** (Map p96) is an enchanting body of water. Legend has it that, in the mid-15th century, Heaven sent Emperor Le Thai To (formerly Le Loi) a magical sword, which he used to drive the Chinese out of Vietnam. One day after the war he happened upon a giant golden tortoise swimming on the surface of the water; the creature grabbed the sword and disappeared into the depths of the lake. Since that time, the lake has been known as Ho Hoan Kiem (Lake of the Restored Sword) because the tortoise restored the sword to its divine owners.

Ngoc Son Temple (p100) sits on an island near the northern end of Hoan Kiem Lake. The ramshackle **Thap Rua** (Tortoise Tower), on an islet near the southern end of the lake, is topped with a red star and is often used as an emblem of Hanoi. Early risers should make for the lake, as every morning around 6am local residents can be seen doing their traditional t'ai chi on the shore. It's a graceful sight, plus there are joggers and games of badminton.

HO TAY (WEST LAKE)

The largest lake in Hanoi – about 13km in circumference– the shores of **Ho Tay** (Map pp88–9) are fast developing a reputation as a desirable place to live for those that can afford the luxury villas. To the south of the lake, along Đ Thuy Khue, there's a string of popular seafood restaurants (p116) that are *de rigeur* for a local night out. To the east are some luxury hotels and an emerging enclave of restaurants, bars and boutiques. The rest is mainly residential.

Two legends explain the origins of Ho Tay, which is also known as the Lake of Mist and the Big Lake. According to one legend, Ho Tay was created when the Dragon King drowned an evil nine-tailed fox in his lair, which was in a forest on this site. Another legend relates that in the 11th century a Vietnamese Buddhist monk, Khong Lo, rendered a great service to the emperor of China, who rewarded him with a vast quantity of bronze from which he cast into a huge bell. The sound of the bell could be heard all the way to China, where the Golden Buffalo Calf, mistaking the ringing for its mother's call, ran southward, trampling on the site of Ho Tay and turning it into a lake.

The geological explanation is that the lake was created when Song Hong (Red River) overflowed its banks. The flood problem has been partially controlled by building dikes,

THE TORTOISES OF HOAN KIEM LAKE: FACT OR FICTION?

Unbelievably, there *are* tortoises in the mysterious and murky waters of Hoan Kiem Lake.

Surfacing on rare occasions, and bringing luck to anyone fortunate enough to see one, the Sword Lake tortoise (*Rafetus leloii*) is not just your common garden-variety tortoise: it is a huge beast. A specimen that died in 1968 weighed in at 250kg and was 2.1m long! Its preserved remains are on show in the Ngoc Son Temple complex (p100), together with a photo taken of a tortoise that appeared in the lake in 2000. No-one is sure how many there still are, or how they have survived in this urban setting.

Rumours abound. Are these really the lake-dwelling descendants of the golden tortoise of Le Thai To? Or are they safeguarded in enclosures elsewhere and transported to the lake from time to time, where their occasional appearance is simply an orchestrated ploy to keep the legend of the lake alive?

Those ripples on the lake surface will never seem so innocent again.

and the highway along the eastern side of Ho Tay is built upon one.

TRUC BACH LAKE

This **lake** (Ho Truc Bach; Map pp88–9) is separated from Ho Tay by Đ Thanh Nien, which is lined with flame trees. During the 18th century the Trinh lords built a palace on the lakeside; it was later transformed into a reformatory for wayward royal concubines, who were condemned to spend their days weaving a pure white silk.

St Joseph Cathedral

Stepping inside the Old Quarter's neo-Gothic **St Joseph Cathedral** (Map p96; Pho Nha Tho; main gate 5-7am & 5-7pm) is a journey to medieval Europe. The cathedral, inaugurated in 1886, is noteworthy for its square towers, elaborate altar and stained-glass windows. Unfortunately, it is in dire need of a paint job these days. The cathedral stands facing the western end of Pho Nha Tho, which is a fashionable strip of restaurants, cafés and boutiques.

The main gate to St Joseph Cathedral is open when Mass is held. Guests are welcome at other times of the day, but must enter the cathedral via the compound of the Diocese of Hanoi, the entrance to which is a block away at 40 Pho Nha Chung. Walking through the main gate, go straight and then turn right. When you reach the side door to the cathedral, ring the small bell high up to the right-hand side of the door and someone should let you in.

Thu Le Park & Zoo

With its vast expanses of shaded grass and ponds, **Thu Le Park & Zoo** (Bach Thu Le; Map pp88-9; admission 2000d; 4am-10pm) is about 4km west of Hoan Kiem Lake. While it's not Singapore Zoo, it is not one of Asia's horror shows either, and children will enjoy the fun park and swan pedal boats. The easiest way to get here is by metered taxi. From Hoan Kiem Lake, bus 9 runs right past the park.

ACTIVITIES

Fitness Clubs

A number of international hotels open their exercise centres to the public for a fee. Among these is the top-of-the-market **Clark Hatch Fitness Centres** (826 6919) in the Sofitel Metropole Hotel (p110) and Sofitel Plaza (p110), which each has a day-use fee of US$15 for the gym, including pool access. Similar is the **Daewoo Hotel Fitness Centre** (Map pp88-9; 835 1000; 360 Đ Kim Ma) which has a day-use fee of US$20 for all facilities including the pool.

Golf

King's Island (772 3160; www.kingsislandgolf.com), 45km west of Hanoi, close to the base of Ba Vi Mountain, is north Vietnam's first 36-hole golf course. Offering a lakeside or mountain view course, membership starts at a whopping US$14,000, but the club is open to visitors from US$70 during the week.

On the western side of Hanoi, but still within the city limits, is the **Lang Ha Golf Club** (Map pp88-9; 835 0909; 16A Pho Lang Ha; nonmember fee US$20; 6am-10pm), opposite the TV tower. Basically, this is just a driving range – you'll have to go to King's Island if you want to pursue a white ball over hills and fields.

There is a popular new course at Tam Dao Hill Station; see p128 for more details.

Hash House Harriers

For the uninitiated, these are the drinkers with a running problem. The 'hash', as all expats refer to it, meets at Finnegan's Irish Pub (p117) at 2pm on Saturdays. It costs around US$5 and includes a lot of drinks.

Massage & Spa

The government has severely restricted the number of places licensed to give massages because of the concern that naughty 'extra services' might be offered (as indeed they are at many places). At present, you can get a good legitimate massage at the **Hoa Binh Hotel** (Map pp92-3; 825 3315; 27 Ly Thuong Kiet; per hr US$8). Other places include the upmarket Guoman Hotel (p110), charging US$18 per hour, and the Sofitel Metropole Hotel (p110), at US$32.

For a spa splurge on facials or body treatments, head to **QT Salon** (Map p96; 928 6116; 28 Pho Le Thai To; 10am-8pm), overlooking Hoan Kiem Lake.

A newer spa, **SF Salon & Spa** (Map p96; 926 2032; 16 Pho Hang Buom; 8.30am-11pm) offers Swedish and Thai massage (US$10), plus the full range of spa treatments, including wraps, scrubs and polishes.

If you feel in need of sprucing, **Vu Doo Salon** (Map pp92-3; 823 3439; 32c Pho Cao Ba Quat) is a reliable hairdresser. Cuts start from US$10; manicures and pedicures from about US$5.

Swimming

Hotels that open their swimming pools to the public include the Army Hotel (p110), near the History Museum. It charges US$3.50 for day use of its pool, which is big enough to do laps and is open all year.

Just about big enough to do laps – but a much nicer place to lounge around afterwards – is the pool at the Melia Hotel (p110), where 'walk-in-members' pay US$6 to swim, or US$10 to swim and use the gym. Some other hotels charge a US$10 day-use fee.

Out by Ho Tay, the Thang Loi Hotel (Map p110) has a swimming pool in a fine lakeside location that's just 30,000d for nonguests, but it is only open from about May to October.

Hanoi Water Park (Map p126; ☎ 753 2757; 9am-9pm Wed-Mon Apr 15-Nov) is about 5km north of the city centre and offers a fun selection of pools, slides and splashing opportunities. Entry costs 50,000d for those over 110cm tall, and 30,000d for shorter people, translating roughly as adults and children.

WALKING TOUR

If the Old Quarter is the heart of Hanoi, there is no better way to check its beat than pounding the narrow streets on foot. Start by paying your respects at the **Ngoc Son Temple** (**1**; p100) at the northern end of Hoan Kiem Lake. Cross back over bright-red **Huc Bridge (2)**, stop for a quick look at the **Martyrs' Monument** (**3**; p100). Follow the lake around on Pho Dinh Tien Hoang and pick up some tickets for an evening performance at the **Water Puppet Theatre** (**4**; p119) on So Lau. Head north on Pho Hang Dau and you'll soon be swimming in **shoe shops (5)** selling every shape, size and style – demonstrating how serious Hanoians are about their footwear. Cross over Pho Cau Go to Pho Hang Be, and browse the colourful **market (6)**, which occupies the narrow eastern terminus of Pho Gia Ngu.

Back on Pho Hang Be, continue north to the T-junction with Pho Hang Bac. Near here are several shops where artisans hand-carve intricate **gravestones (7)**, most bearing an image of the deceased. A short detour north on Pho Ma May leads you to the **Memorial House** (**8**; p102) at No 87, an exquisite Chinese merchant's home that has been restored as a museum.

Return to Pho Hang Bac and head west past a strip of snazzy **jewellery shops (9)**. Don't miss the small entry to **house 102 (10)**, which includes a fully functioning temple where most people would have a lounge room. Exit and turn right onto Pho Hang Ngang past a row of **clothing shops (11)**, and right again onto Pho Hang Buom. This will take you past the small **Bach Ma Temple** (**12**; p100). As you pass the pagoda, with its red funeral palanquin, look for its white-bearded guards, who spend their days sipping tea.

Legend has it that Ly Thai To used the pagoda to pray for assistance in building the city walls because they persistently collapsed, no matter how many times he rebuilt them. His prayers were finally answered when a white horse appeared out of the temple and guided him to the site where he could safely build his walls. Evidence of his success is still visible at **Cua O Quan Chuong (13)**, the quarter's well-preserved Old East Gate at the eastern end of Pho Hang Chieu, near the intersection with Pho Tran Nhat Duat.

Continue north along the narrow Pho Thanh Ha, which has a **traditional street market (14)**, with squirming fish, chunky frogs and heaped produce. Follow this round to the left and emerge near **Dong Xuan Market** (**15**; p120), one of the most important in the city. Venture in, but bookmark any serious shopping for later as there is still plenty to experience.

Backtrack south on Nguyen Thien Thuat and turn right on to Pho Hang Chieu, past a handful of **shops (16)** selling straw mats and rope. This becomes one of Hanoi's most interesting streets, **Pho Hang Ma (17)** – the name translates as Counterfeit Street – where imitation 'ghost money' is sold for burning in Buddhist ceremonies – there are even US$5000 bills! Loop around and follow your ears to the sounds of **blacksmiths (18)** pounding away on metal on the corner of Pho Lo Ren and Pho Thuoc Bac. Moving south on Pho Thuoc Bac, turn onto Pho Lan Ong, where a fantastic row of **herb sellers (19)** fills the street with pungent aromas. Continue to the end and take a breather at the **Baguette et Chocolat** (**20**; p111), a café with cold drinks and exquisite pastries.

Double back to Pho Thuoc Bac and head south past the **tin-box makers (21)**, opposite the **mirror shops (22)** on Pho Hang Thiec, then turn left towards the interesting shops selling **Buddhist altars and statues (23)** along Pho Hang Quat.

From here, head south on Pho Luong Van Can past all the **toy shops (24)**, which could save the day if you are following this walk with flagging children. Then wander west along

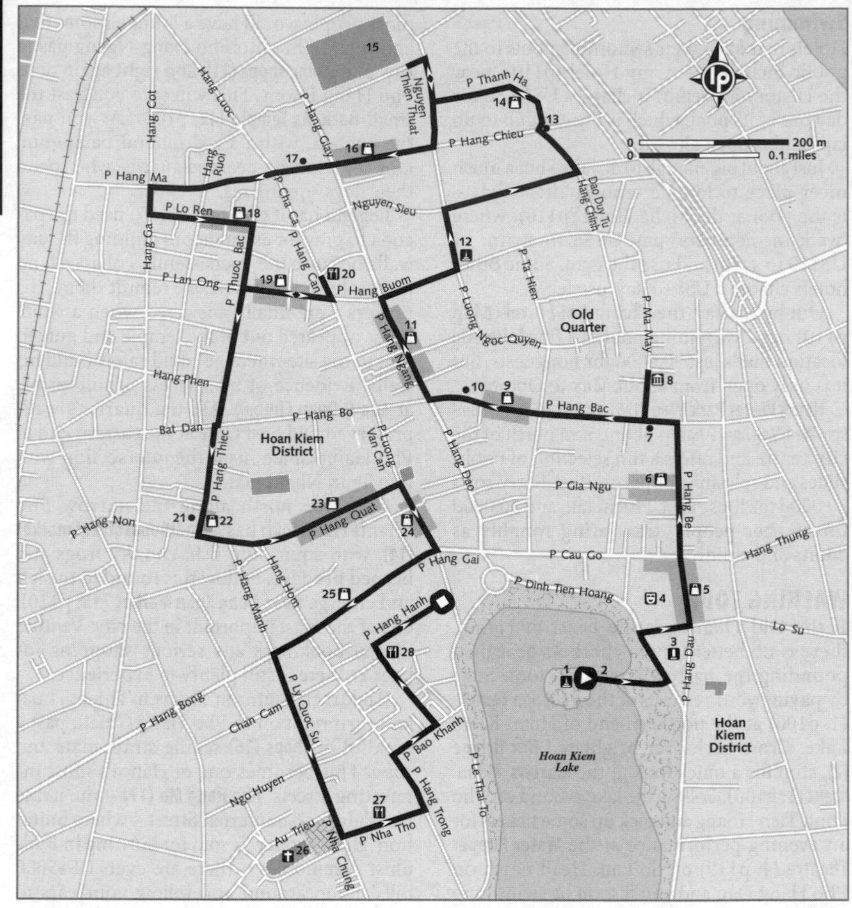

> **WALK FACTS**
>
> **Distance** 3.5km
> **Duration** Minimum two hours; more with sights and stops
> **Start** Ngoc Son Temple, Hoan Kiem Lake
> **Finish** Pho Bao Khanh bar strip

Pho Hang Gai, window shopping as you pass the elegant designer **silk shops** (**25**; p119). Head south on Pho Ly Quoc Su to the superb neo-Gothic **St Joseph Cathedral** (**26**; p104). If the exercise is taking its toll on a hot day, just a few steps from the church, along Pho Nha Tho, there's a cluster of stylish **restaurants and cafés** (**27**).

If you're looking for something a bit more local in flavour, turn left at the end of Pho Nha Tho onto Pho Hang Trong, right onto Pho Bao Khanh and left at Pho Hang Hanh. This street is chock-a-block with Vietnamese **cafés and bars** (**28**) and is a good place to stop, rest your weary legs and watch the world go by.

COURSES

Cooking

Cooking classes are really taking off all over Vietnam and Hanoi is no exception.

Hidden Hanoi (Map pp88-9; ☎ 091-225-4045; www.hiddenhanoi.com) offers cooking classes for US$30 per person in its hidden garden out near the Sheraton Hanoi Hotel on Ho Tay. It also offers language classes.

Hoa Sua (p111) offers classes for a cause to raise funds for its training programme for disadvantaged youth. Costs vary from US$7 to US$10 for soups and salads, to US$10 to US$15 for main courses.

Popular restaurant-bar Highway 4 (p112) also has cooking classes. Prices range from US$19 to US$32 depending on numbers and include a trip to Hom Market, three dishes and, of course, a feed. It starts at 8am.

Language

Hanoi Foreign Language College (Map pp92-3; ☎ 826 2468; 1 Pho Pham Ngu Lao), housed in the History Museum compound, is a branch of Hanoi National University where foreigners can study Vietnamese for about US$7 per lesson.

HANOI FOR CHILDREN

Hanoi is a fun city for children thanks to the all-action Old Quarter (p95) and the city's many parks and lakes. Wandering the Old Quarter can be tiring for young ones, but there are enough diversions to keep them entertained, and plenty of ice-cream shops and fruit markets for those little treats along the way.

Boating is a fun family activity and there is the choice of bigger boats on Ho Tay (p103) or pedal-powered boats in Thu Le Park (p104). Hanoi Water Park (p105) is a great place to take children to cool off, but it is only open half the year. Come the evening, there is only one place for any self-respecting child to be, and that is at the water puppets (p119), a Punch and Judy pantomime on the water.

TOURS

Anyone arriving in Hanoi on an organised trip will have a city tour included. If you're travelling independently, Hanoi is a city best enjoyed at your own pace without the timetable of a tour. If you really want an organised city tour, contact one of the travel agencies recommended on p91. Prices start from US$12 for a group tour, including guide, transport and entrance fees. For a private tour by car, expect to pay more in the region of US$50.

Motorbike Tours

If you're a competent motorbiker, it's easy to organise a trip on your own. For general information about motorbike rental in Hanoi, see p122.

There is a handful of motorbike tour companies based in Hanoi that know secret roads in the mountains and can open doors that you would never imagine from a cursory scan of the map. For more on a motorbike tour through the hidden north, see p491.

FESTIVALS & EVENTS

Tet (Tet Nguyen Dan/Vietnamese Lunar New Year; late January or early February) During the week preceding Tet, there is a flower market on Pho Hang Luoc. There's also a colourful, two-week flower exhibition and competition, beginning on the first day of the new year, that takes place in Lenin Park near Bay Mau Lake. For much, much more on Tet, see the boxed text, p64).

Quang Trung Festival (February/March) Wrestling competitions, lion dances and human chess take place on the 15th day of the first lunar month at Dong Da Mound, site of the uprising against Chinese invaders led by Emperor Quang Trung (Nguyen Hué) in 1788.

Vietnam's National Day (2 September) Celebrated with a rally and fireworks at Ba Dinh Sq, in front of Ho Chi Minh's Mausoleum. There are also boat races on Hoan Kiem Lake.

SLEEPING

The majority of Hanoi's budget accommodation is within walking distance of Hoan Kiem Lake. Unlike Ho Chi Minh City's (HCMC) Pham Ngu Lao district, where the cheapies are lined up wall-to-wall, lodgings here are more scattered, though they're mostly in and around the Old Quarter.

There are several budget places around with both dorm beds and cheap rooms (under US$10), but for between US$10 and US$20 the choice includes a wide selection of minihotels, which offer clean, air-con rooms, satellite TV and hot water.

In the US$25 to US$75 range, there is usually a step up in service, and the rooms may be larger than those in the minihotels or guesthouses.

Above and beyond US$75, it is possible to stay in plush four- and five-star hotels that would cost double in cities, such as Hong Kong or Bangkok. Keep an eye out in the *Guide* and *Time Out* for the latest deals, and always ask about current 'promotions' at reception.

Most of the budget and midrange hotels include free internet access. Most of the top-end hotels levy a charge. Always check whether tax and service is included. It should be at cheaper places, but staff will sometimes spring a surprise at the last minute.

Old Quarter

BUDGET

Thu Giang Guesthouse (Map p96; ☎ 828 5734; www.tgguesthouse.com; 5A Pho Tam Thuong; r US$5-10) This is a flashback to old Hanoi, a small, friendly, family-run place with cheap yet cheerful rooms. You'll find it tucked away down a narrow alley between Pho Yen Thai and Pho Hang Gai. This guesthouse now has a second branch for overspills at 35A Pho Hang Dieu.

Manh Dung Guesthouse (Map p96; ☎ 826 7201; tranmanhdungvn@yahoo.com; 2 Pho Tam Thuong; r US$5-10) Opposite the Thu Giang, this place was under wraps for a renovation during our last visit, but is well worth seeking out as the family really look after its guests. Prices may rise.

our pick **City Gate Hotel** (Map p96; ☎ 828 0817; www.citygatehotel.com.vn; 10 Pho Thanh Ha; r US$8-18) Hidden away down a small lane near the old East Gate, this smart minihotel offers a warm welcome and friendly service. Rooms are super clean, bathrooms include a bath, there's free internet downstairs and even a lift.

Spring Hotel (Map p96; ☎ 826 8500; spring.hotel@fpt.vn; 8A Pho Nha Chung; r US$10-30) Close to the Thien Trang, the friendly family here ensures a warm welcome to all. The cheaper rooms are a little small, but good value for this upwardly mobile part of town.

Thuy Nga Guesthouse (Map p96; ☎ 826 6053; thuyngahotel@hotmail.com; 24C Pho Ta Hien; s/d/t US$10/12/15) The area may be rapidly gentrifying but this place is staying loyal to its roots. Consisting of just six rooms, it's a family affair with smallish but smart rooms including extras, such as TV, fridge and IDD telephone.

Viet Fun Hotel (Map p96; ☎ 926 2353; vietfunhotels@yahoo.com; 48 Pho Ma May; r US$8-15) This place should appeal to those for whom size matters almost as much as money. Rooms this big usually come at a higher price, and the enthusiastic service and helpful advice ensure it is, well, fun.

Hanoi Backpackers Hostel (Map p96; ☎ 828 5372; www.hanoibackpackershostel.com; 48 Pho Ngo Huyen; dm/r around US$6/20) This Aussie-style backpackers' pad offers smart and secure dorms and a couple of dedicated rooms. The price includes breakfast, lockers, internet access, and tea and coffee, not forgetting fun and frolics on the rooftop bar.

Hotel Thien Trang (Map p96; ☎ 826 9823; thientranghotel24@hotmail.com; 24 Pho Nha Chung; r US$10-20) Close enough to the trendy Nha Tho to live the dream, but cheap enough not to break the budget, the Thien Trang is a popular place. The spacious rooms are great value given the location.

our pick **Artist Hotel** (Map p96; ☎ 825 3044; vietcultour@hn.vnn.vn; 22A Pho Hai Ba Trung; s/d US$18/21) The rooms might be more appropriate to the struggling artiste, but the atmosphere will appeal to anyone wanting to meet locals and expats with a creative bent. Set around a lovely leafy courtyard, rooms include satellite TV, but who needs it when there is the Cinematheque (p118) downstairs?

Camellia Hotel (Map p96; ☎ 828 3583; www.camellia-hotels.com; 13 Pho Luong Ngoc Quyen; r US$15-24) The Camellia family now includes six properties. The original remains top value for money, as the rates include satellite TV, a buffet breakfast and free internet access.

Prince Hotel (Map p96; ☎ 828 0155; www.hanoiprincehotel.com; 51 Pho Luong Ngoc Quyen; r US$15-25) Barely scraping into the budget category these days, this is the original Prince, a name now borrowed by countless impostors. The big rooms include chunky Chinese-style furnishings and are well tended. Breakfast and internet access are included.

A couple more options among the 999 other minihotels:

Old Street Hotel (Map p96; ☎ 828 0195; www.oldstreethotel.com; 23 Pho Ma May; r US$10-15) Clean rooms, smart touches and a good location make this worth the walk.

Real Darling Café (Map p96; ☎ 826 9386; darling_cafe@hotmail.com; 33 Pho Hang Quat; r US$5-12) Almost as old as the Old Quarter, it's still one of the cheapest in town.

MIDRANGE

Hanoi Elegance Hotel (Map p96; ☎ 825 3740; www.hanoielegancehotel.com; 8 Pho Hang Bac; r US$18-30) The friendly staff here make it feel like a home from home. Rooms are large and each includes a computer for personal internet access. The only drawback is the lack of a lift, as the best rooms are on the upper floors.

Sunshine Hotel (Map p96; ☎ 926 1559; www.hanoisunshinehotel.com; 42 Pho Ma May; r US$25-30) The rooms are indeed bright at the Sunshine. Nicely proportioned and well finished, some have balconies with a perfect view of the mighty Ma May strip below.

Bao Khanh Hotel (Map p96; ☎ 928 7702; www.baokhanhhotel.com.vn; 22 Pho Bao Khanh; r US$20-55;) In stumbling distance of the popular Bao Khanh bar strip, this rambling complex has 50 rooms. The US$20 rooms are a little pokey, but they get bigger as the price rises, as do the views.

Classic Street Hotel (Map p96; ☎ 825 2421; www.classicstreet-phocohotel.com; 41 Pho Hang Be; r US$25-30;) Hang Be is one of the liveliest streets in the Old Quarter and this hotel is a stylish base to explore. All rooms have air-con and satellite TV, and some have fantastic views of the quarter's higgledy-piggledy rooftops. Also known as the Pho Co Hotel.

Heart Hotel (Map p96; ☎ 928 6682; www.heart-hotel.com; 11B Pho Hang Hanh; r US$25-35;) A smart little hotel in the centre of the action near Hoan Kiem Lake. The rooms show real attention to detail at this price, with hairdryers and even slippers. The lobby is an art gallery: still it's a welcome change from being peddled tours.

our pick **Queen Hotel** (Map p96; ☎ 826 0860; www.azqueentravel.com; 65 Pho Hang Bac; r US$35-65;) The Zen lobby sets the standard for one of Hanoi's most atmospheric little properties. The rooms are thoughtfully decorated with wooden furnishings and silk lamps, and include a personal DVD player. Book ahead as there are just 10 rooms.

our pick **Golden Lotus Hotel** (Map p96; ☎ 928 8583; www.goldenlotushotel.com.vn; 32 Pho Hang Trong; r US$40-50;) A rich blend of Eastern flavours and Western chic, the Golden Lotus is a touch more expensive than its neighbours, but it's money well spent. Rooms have wooden floors, silk trim, art aplenty and broadband internet connections. Breakfast is included.

Church Hotel (Map p96; ☎ 928 8118; churchhotel@vnn.vn; 9 Pho Nha Tho; r US$40-70;) Looking for a hotel with a holistic touch? Look no further, the Church has elegant rooms with decorative flair, plus the functional extras like in-room internet. On the happening Nha Tho strip, this is a fine base, particularly if you indulge in the US$70 suite.

Hong Ngoc Hotel 1 (Map p96; ☎ 828 5053; hongngochotel@hn.vnn.vn; 34 Pho Hang Manh; r US$45-55;) The Hong Ngoc group has four properties scattered across the Old Quarter. This is a smart business-like hotel with spacious and well-appointed rooms. Breakfast is included in the popular downstairs restaurant.

Hoa Binh Palace Hotel (Map p96; ☎ 926 3646; www.hoabinhpalacehotel.com.vn; 27 Pho Hang Be; s/d US$50/60;) An unlikely intruder in the heart of backpackersville, this smart new property brings new-world comforts to old-world Hanoi. All rooms include extra touches like safety deposit boxes and hairdryers, plus the suites include Jacuzzis.

Majestic Salute Hotel (Map p96; ☎ 923 0036; www.majesticsalutehotel.com; 19 Pho Cha Ca; r US$69-89;) Continuing the upward trend in the Old Quarter, in height as much as comfort, this hotel offers genuine three-star comfort. Facilities include Jacuzzi, sauna and steam bath.

Still want more? Try these wholesome hotels:

Classic Hotel (Map p96; ☎ 826 6224; www.hanoiclassichotel.com; 22A Pho Ta Hien; r US$16-30;)

DO THE HUSTLE

Hanoi is not only the political capital of Vietnam, it is also the capital of hotel hustles. Copycat hotels and fly-by-night hotels abound. These sharks rent a building, appropriate the name of another hotel, and then work with touts to bring unwitting tourists to their 'chosen' accommodation. Visitors who question the alternative location are told the hotel has moved and it is not until they check the next day that they realise they have been had. These hotels overcharge on anything they can, often giving a price for the room on check-in and a price per person on check-out. The best way to avoid this is to pre-book a room by phone or via email. This way, you know the hotel is still open, still in the same location and not full. Airport taxis and minibuses often work in partnership with these copycat hotels, as they give the biggest commissions.

Worse still, some of these hotels are working in partnership with unscrupulous Westerners who help to steer backpackers their way. In return for free board and lodging, these backpackers will latch onto tourists wandering the Old Quarter and tell them about the 'great hotel' they have found. It's sad but true: friendly advice might not be as friendly as it seems. For more on scams and how to avoid them, see p95 and the boxed text, p124.

Clean, comfortable, friendly and secure, just the adjectives to ensure a hassle-free stay.

Ho Guom Hotel (Map p96; ☎ 825 2225; hoguomtjc@hn.vnn.vn; 76 Pho Hang Trong; r $US20-30;) A rare government-run hotel that's clean and quiet, with friendly staff and a good location.

Trang Tien Hotel (Map p96; ☎ 825 6115; fax 825 1416; 35 Pho Trang Tien; r US$15-30;) It's overdue a facelift some time soon, but the location is perfect: between Hoan Kiem Lake and the Opera House.

TOP END

Melia Hotel (Map p96; ☎ 934 3343; www.meliahanoi.com.vn; 44B Pho Ly Thuong Kiet; r from US$90;) An ugly duckling on the outside, things get a bit more swan-like on the inside, with all the five-star features anyone could need. Ask for an upper floor for some big, big views over Hanoi.

Hilton Hanoi Opera (Map p96; ☎ 933 0500; www.hanoi.hilton.com; 1 Pho Le Thanh Tong; r from US$110;) Rubbing shoulders with the grand old dame that is Hanoi Opera House, this striking property is an indulgent base to discover the city. The rooms are Hilton through and through, and at these rates it is the best all-rounder for location and comfort at this end of the scale. Treat yourself to day-use of the luxurious health club and swimming pool for US$15.

our pick **Sofitel Metropole Hotel** (Map p96; ☎ 826 6919; sofitelhanoi@hn.vnn.vn; 15 Pho Ngo Quyen; r from US$169;) Whispered in the same breath as Raffles in Singapore and the Oriental in Bangkok, this is one of Asia's great luxury hotels. The property has undergone an extensive renovation in the past few years and the rooms in the old wing are to be savoured. Wide-screen TVs, Jacuzzi-like bathtubs: you won't want to leave. The modern Opera Wing has also been beautifully renovated, but doesn't have the history. This place has a French motif that just won't quit – close the curtains and you'll think you're in Paris.

There are also a couple of business-like 'boutique' hotels, although they are not that boutique:

Quoc Hoa Hotel (Map p96; ☎ 828 4528; www.quochoahotel.com; 10 Pho Bat Dan; s/d from US$110/120;) Smart and sophisticated, this is a sound option, but the rates are a little ambitious.

Zephyr Hotel (Map p96; ☎ 934 1256; www.zephyrhotel.com.vn; 4 Pho Ba Trieu; s/d from US$88/98;) Pitching itself as a boutique hotel, the rooms feature sharp lines and subtle trim. Great location.

Central Hanoi

Hotel 30/4 (Map pp92-3; ☎ 942 0807; 115 Pho Tran Hung Dao; r US$10-20;) Right opposite Hanoi train station and named in honour of Saigon's liberation on 30 April 1975, it is, unsurprisingly, state-owned. This Art Deco–style place retains a certain olde worlde charm even if the staff are, on the whole, charmless.

Army Hotel (Khach San Quan Doi; Map pp92-3; ☎ 825 2896; armyhotel@fpt.vn; 33C Pho Pham Ngu Lao; r US$30-40;) Owned by the army and operated by the army, but it's a world away from boot camp. The uninspiring décor may owe something to its military mentors, but it's the cheapest place with a pool, which is a pretty impressive saltwater number.

Galaxy Hotel (Map pp92-3; ☎ 828 2888; galaxyhtl@netnam.org.vn; 1 Pho Phan Dinh Phung; s/d US$40/45;) The long-running Galaxy is based around an original 1918 building and includes a business centre and a popular café-restaurant. All rooms feature satellite TV and a safe.

De Syloia Hotel (Map pp92-3; ☎ 824 5346; www.desyloia.com; 17A Pho Tran Hung Dao; s/d US$65/75;) This place must be feeling the competition, as it is one of the few properties to have lowered its rates. The theme is decidedly French and the rooms are finished to European levels of comfort. Plus, there's a fitness centre and sauna.

Guoman Hotel (Map pp92-3; ☎ 822 2800; guomanhn@hn.vnn.vn; 83A Pho Ly Thuong Kiet; r US$90-115;) This grandiose building is home to a friendly, four-star standard hotel with staff who remember your name. It is often possible to get discounts here so inquire ahead. Facilities include a sleek health club, fine dining and two bars.

Greater Hanoi

Ho Tay Villas (Map pp88-9; ☎ 804 7772; hotayvillas@fmail.vnn.vn; Đ Dang Thai Mai; r US$45-120;) Once the Communist Party guesthouse and the exclusive preserve of top party officials, these spacious villas even played host to Ho Chi Minh – room 505 for history buffs. These days, dollar-toting tourists are welcome to use the once-splendid facilities. The hotel is 5.5km north of central Hanoi, overlooking Ho Tay.

Thang Loi Hotel (Cuban Hotel; Map pp88-9; ☎ 829 4211; thangloihtl@hn.vnn.vn; Đ Yen Phu; r from US$80;) Unique and not always for the right reasons, the 'Cuban Hotel' was constructed in the 1970s with Castro's assistance. Built over the water, it feels like an oversized beach house. The hotel also has a swimming pool and tennis courts.

Check the rates, as the list prices are a little unrealistic for such dated kitsch. It is 3.5km from the city centre on the shores of Ho Tay.

Moon River (Map pp88-9; ☎ 871 1658; wildrice@fpt.vn; Bac Cau, Gia Lam; r US$90-120;) This little gem of a hideaway feels like an ancient temple in a secret garden. Hard to find and harder to leave, the rooms here are exquisitely decorated with antiques and drapes, and the larger suites include Balinese-style sunken baths. It is way out in the Gia Lam suburb on the east bank of the Song Hong, 3km north of the Chuong Duong Bridge.

Some of the biggest names in the hotel industry are also found in the Hanoi suburbs:

Sheraton Hanoi Hotel (Map pp88-9; ☎ 719 9000; www.sheraton.com/hanoi; 11 Pho Xuan Dieu; r from US$130;) George Bush took over three floors of this place during the APEC summit. Most guests opt for just one room. Luxurious indeed.

Sofitel Plaza (Map pp88-9; ☎ 823 8888; www.sofitelplazahn.com.vn; 1 Đ Thanh Nien; r from US$135;) Sofitel's not-so-historic other half, it boasts the region's first indoor-outdoor swimming pool with a retractable roof.

EATING

In recent years Hanoi has undergone a miraculous transformation from a culinary wasteland to a world-class city for drinking and dining. The city boasts everything from cheap backpacker joints (yes, *more* banana pancakes) to exquisite Vietnamese restaurants and a growing legion of chic cafés.

Restaurants, bars and cafés have a strong tendency to change names, location, management and just about everything else, so ask around or check out the current listings in the *Guide* and *Time Out*.

Dining for a Cause

Combine food for the body with food for the soul at restaurants and cafés that run vocational training programmes for street kids. Good cause, good food, good idea.

KOTO on Van Mieu (Map pp92-3; ☎ 747 0338; www.streetvoices.com.au; 59 Pho Van Mieu; mains 30,000-50,000d; closed dinner Mon;) Recently relocated into a much larger property, KOTO has a cracking menu of local specialities, home comforts, delicious sandwiches and cakes, real coffees, fruit shakes and other wholesome dishes. With five floors, there is something for everyone, including an expanded bar with cocktails. KOTO is a not-for-profit grassroots project providing career training and guidance to former street kids. KOTO stands for 'Know One, Teach One'. The restaurant overlooks the Temple of Literature, making it the perfect place to recharge the batteries before or after some sightseeing. Want more? Free wi-fi it is.

Hoa Sua (Map pp92-3; ☎ 824 0448; www.hoasuaschool.com; 28A Pho Ha Hoi; Vietnamese/French set lunch 35,000/75,000d; lunch & dinner) A shady retreat by day, a dignified diner by night, this restaurant offers the perfect blend of East and West. The set menus are a good deal, or go à la carte for some DIY fusion. Menu highlights include Argentinean steaks and a pistachio crème brûlée. Hoa Sua is a successful goodwill project that trains a steady stream of disadvantaged kids for culinary careers. It also offers cooking classes (p106) at its training school.

Baguette & Chocolat (Map p96; ☎ 923 1500; 11 Pho Cha Ca; cakes around 10,000d; breakfast, lunch & dinner) Another member of the extended Hoa Sua family, this is a bewitching bakery with divine (or devilish) cakes and pastries, depending on your calorie count. Remember those patisseries in Paris, with artistic creations at €4 a go? Try them here for less than US$1.

Vietnamese

For some of the tastiest, and certainly cheapest Vietnamese food, stroll up to some of the street stalls around town. The food is as fresh as it comes and the kitchen is right there in front of you. Most of Vietnam's greatest hits are available if you shop around, and it's a great way to plug the hole after a long night on the town. Almost every corner and alley in the Old Quarter has street stalls. Check out how many locals are eating there: the more, the merrier, as the food must be good. Overcharging is the norm rather than the exception at many of these places, so it is worth checking the price before you order a spread.

Another excellent and inexpensive fast track to a feed is to visit one of the innumerable *bia hoi* joints around the city. All of them have minimenus to help hold off the hangover. For more on the national institution that is the *bia hoi* scene, see the boxed text, p118.

For other Vietnamese options, consider the speciality food streets (p115).

OLD QUARTER

There is an incredible array of Vietnamese restaurants to choose from in the Old Quarter.

Little Hanoi 1 (Map p96; ☎ 926 0168; 9 Pho Ta Hien; meals from 20,000d; ⏲ breakfast, lunch & dinner) Blink and you'll miss it, this tiny little restaurant recently moved up the road. This small place has a big personality and the popular speciality is do-it-yourself fish spring rolls, a delicious dish.

Pho 24 (Map p96; 1 Pho Hang Khay; meals 25,000d; ⏲ breakfast, lunch & dinner) Fast *pho*, Vietnamese-style, this may be part of an expanding chain, but it's growing for a reason: heavenly noodle soups. *Pho* is cheaper on the street, but rarely better. Choose by the cut.

our pick **69 Bar-Restaurant** (Map p96; ☎ 926 0452; 69 Pho Ma May; meals 20,000-60,000d; ⏲ lunch & dinner) Located in a beautifully restored old Vietnamese house, this is an atmospheric escape from the bustle of the Old Quarter. The predominantly Vietnamese menu includes succulent tuna steaks and a large vegetarian selection.

Ladybird Restaurant (Map p96; ☎ 926 1863; 57 Pho Hang Buom; meals 25,000-35,000d; ⏲ breakfast, lunch & dinner) Hidden away in the northern section of the Old Quarter, this little restaurant has been earning rave reviews for its affordable eats. Whether it is Vietnamese or Western, it's all tasty.

Hanoi Garden (Map p96; ☎ 824 3402; 36 Pho Hang Manh; à la carte/set menus from 40,000d/80,000d; ⏲ lunch & dinner) This restaurant is very popular with Vietnamese diners: always a positive sign. Hanoi Garden serves southern Vietnamese and spicy Chinese dishes in a relaxed setting with an open-air courtyard for steamy summer nights.

One of Hanoi's most famous food specialities is *cha ca* (filleted fish slices grilled over charcoal), your very own fresh fish barbecue. **Cha Ca La Vong** (Map p96; ☎ 825 3929; 14 Pho Cha Ca; cha ca 70,000d; ⏲ lunch & dinner), the *cha ca* capital of the Old Quarter, has been family-run for five generations. It cracks out the condiments, fire up the hot coals and so begins a free cooking class in the art of *cha ca*. The succulent fish is all that's on the menu, so it's great for indecisive types.

Other places to seek out:

Golden Land Restaurant (Map p96; ☎ 828 1056; 15 Pho Cha Ca; meals 20,000-60,000d; ⏲ breakfast, lunch & dinner) Elegant décor, efficient air-con and a hearty mixed menu add up to a good place.

Old Hanoi (Map p96; ☎ 824 5251; 106 Pho Ma May; meals 25,000-75,000d; ⏲ lunch & dinner) A sophisticated little eatery with tasty Vietnamese specialities.

CENTRAL HANOI

Restaurant 1,2,3 (Map pp92-3; ☎ 822 9100; 55 Pho Hué; meals 30,000d; ⏲ breakfast, lunch & dinner) Need a quick fix? This place delivers a range of Vietnamese favourites in double-quick time. The barbecued fish and 'fish porridge' *(chao)* are smart selections.

our pick **Quan An Ngan** (Map pp92-3; ☎ 942 8162; 15 Pho Phan Boi Chau; dishes 30,000-60,000d) Fancy that street food experience, but afraid to take the plunge? Build your courage with a meal here; it brings street and market food to the middle-class masses. Minikitchens turn out terrific food, including *banh cuon* (rice-paper rolls with minced pork) and *chao tom* (grilled sugar cane rolled in spiced shrimp paste).

GREATER HANOI

Highway 4 (Map pp88-9; ☎ 212 8998; 575 Pho Kim Ma; meals 30,000-80,000d; ⏲ lunch & dinner) Bringing the fabled food of the mountains to lowland Vietnam, this is the latest in a growing family. Specialities include the catfish spring rolls with *wasabi* dip and the Son La smoked pork. Wash it down with its smooth signature Son Tinh rice wine. There's another **Highway 4** (Map pp92-3; ☎ 976 2647; 5 Pho Mai Hac De; ⏲ lunch & dinner) that's very popular with the Vietnamese.

Gourmet Vietnamese

OLD QUARTER

Club Opera (Map p96; ☎ 824 6950; 59 Pho Ly Thai To; mains from US$6; ⏲ lunch & dinner) Tucked away beneath the Press Club, the Opera has delectable Vietnamese dining with a refined European atmosphere. The menu changes, but always includes an impressive array of seafood.

Club 51 Ly Thai To (☎ 936 3069; 51 Pho Ly Thai To; meals 50,000-200,000d; ⏲ lunch & dinner) Set in an elegant old residence, entering Club 51 is like gaining membership to the Groucho, a hidden world of lounge chairs, long drapes and fine food. Drop by for a drink or some fusion flavours.

CENTRAL HANOI

Wild Rice (Map pp92-3; ☎ 943 8896; 6 Pho Ngo Thi Nham; mains 40,000-120,000d; ⏲ lunch & dinner) Deceptively simple from outside, the elegant interior is a fine backdrop for the contemporary Vietnamese cuisine. Start with a spring roll selection, as there is a unique take on this most traditional of foods.

Emperor (Map pp92-3; ☎ 826 8801; 18B Pho Le Thanh Tong; mains 50,000-100,000d; ⏲ lunch & dinner) Long considered one of the best Vietnamese restaurants in town, try to get a table overlooking the lively courtyard. Experience live traditional music (7.30pm to 9.30pm) on Wednesday and Saturday, and good food at any time.

our pick **Wild Lotus** (Map pp92-3; ☎ 943 9342; 55A Pho Nguyen Du; mains 50,000-150,000d; lunch & dinner) The ultimate designer restaurant, this is an art gallery as much as an eatery. The menu includes three spice journeys: set menus that guide you through the highlights of the Vietnam table. The seafood is superb, including scallops and king crab.

Brothers Café (Map pp92-3; ☎ 733 3866; 26 Pho Nguyen Thai Hoc; lunch/dinner buffet US$6.50/12) Located in the courtyard of a beautifully restored 250-year-old Buddhist temple, this brings a touch of Zen to the buffet experience. Yes, it's buffet only and the lunch is a snip. For those who like choice, try the wine list as it's extensive.

And the style goes on:

Nam Phuong (Map pp92-3; ☎ 824 0926; 19 Pho Phan Chu Trinh; mains from 50,000d; lunch & dinner) A chic place in a charming villa with authentic and delicious Vietnamese food.

Seasons of Hanoi (Map pp92-3; ☎ 843 5444; 95B Pho Quan Thanh; dishes 40,000-100,000d; lunch & dinner) This classic French villa is decorated with Vietnamese and colonial-era antiques. The food is equally impressive.

There are also some good Vietnamese restaurants at the leading hotels in town. **Ba Mien** (Map p96; ☎ 933 0624; Hilton Hanoi Opera, 1 Pho Le Thanh Tong; US$12 set lunch; breakfast, lunch & dinner) is causing a stir thanks to its authentic regional cuisine. **Spices Garden** (Map p96; ☎ 826 6919; Sofitel Metropole Hotel, 15 Pho Ngo Quyen; mains around US$7-15; breakfast, lunch & dinner) offers a serious spread from around the region.

Other Asian

OLD QUARTER

Baan Thai Restaurant (Map p96; ☎ 828 1120; 3B Pho Cha Ca; mains 30,000-100,000d; lunch & dinner) An established Thai restaurant with a loyal following among the growing Thai community in Hanoi. For anyone that has been in Vietnam long enough to have forgotten their Thai favourites, there is a handy photo-illustrated menu at the door.

Tandoor (Map p96; ☎ 824 5359; 24 Pho Hang Be; mains 40,000-80,000d; lunch & dinner) Right in the thick of things in the Old Quarter, this is a place to spice up your life. Not surprisingly, the tandoori is tops here, plus there are good value thalis if you feeling indecisive. Halal food.

Saigon Sakura (Map p96; ☎ 825 7565; 17 Pho Trang Thi; lunch & dinner) There are lots of Japanese restaurants in Hanoi these days, but this one remains a firm favourite thanks to fresh sashimi and beautifully presented sushi. Expect to pay around US$15 for a set.

CENTRAL HANOI

Benkay Restaurant (Map pp92-3; ☎ 822 3535; 84 Tran Nhan Tong; set lunches around US$10; lunch & dinner) Talk to Hanoi's resident Japanese, and they'll tell you that it is hard to beat Benkay for a taste of the motherland. Location is another matter, as it's on the 2nd floor of the sprawling Hotel Nikko.

Van Anh (Map pp92-3; ☎ 928 5163; 5A Pho Tong Duy Tan; meals 30,000-100,000d; lunch & dinner) This was the first non-Vietnamese restaurant to dare to take on the mass of Vietnamese restaurants in speciality food street Pho Cam Chi (p116). The taste of Thailand.

International

OLD QUARTER

Cyclo Bar & Restaurant (Map p96; ☎ 828 6844; 38 Pho Duong Thanh; mains from 60,000d; lunch & dinner) No-one ever forgets this place…no, it's not down to the tasty Vietnamese and French food, but the *cyclos* that have been creatively transformed into tables. The set lunch is a good deal at 80,000d.

Al Fresco's (Map p96; ☎ 826 7782; 23L Pho Hai Ba Trung; meals from 80,000d; lunch & dinner) The original location of this expanding empire, this place has been turning out juicy Tex-Mex ribs, fish fajitas and pastas for a decade now. Al Fresco's is also well known for its margaritas, but beware as they are seriously strong.

Café des Arts (Map p96; ☎ 828 7207; 11B Pho Bao Khanh; mains from US$5; 9am-late) Part Parisian brasserie, part art gallery, this gastronomic grill has an impressive menu of French flavours. The steaks are particularly good, but rare really means rare here.

Stop Café (Map p96; ☎ 828 7207; 11A Pho Bao Khanh; steaks 60,000d; 9am-late) The phone number sort of gives it away: this is the place to sample Café des Arts cuisine at cheaper prices.

La (Map p96; ☎ 928 8933; 49 Pho Ly Quoc Su; mains 135,000-210,000d; lunch & dinner) A loveable little bistro with an inviting menu of international fare. Fresh sea bass, chunky tenderloins and desserts to die for…chocolate espresso brownie tart anyone?

our pick **Green Tangerine** (Map p96; ☎ 825 1286; 48 Pho Hang Be; mains around US$15; lunch & dinner) A beautifully restored 1928 house is the backdrop for this renowned French restaurant. Salmon steak in tamarind sauce and delicate cuts of duck headline the menu. The wine list is impressive for those who appreciate a liquid accompaniment to their meal.

La Salsa (Map p96; ☎ 828 9052; 25 Pho Nha Tho; meals 25,000-150,000d; 10.30am-midnight) Specialising in paella, slabs of steak and tapas, this bar-restaurant has a prime position on the hip strip opposite St Joseph Cathedral.

our pick **Restaurant Bobby Chinn** (Map p96; ☎ 934 8577; www.bobbychinn.com; 1 Pho Ba Trieu; mains US$10-20; 10am-late) Owner-chef Bobby Chinn is part Chinese and Egyptian, and draws on his roots to offer the liveliest of menus. It changes monthly, but includes rich tastes and textures. For an aperitif or a coffee, move through the silk drapes to the chill-out cushions at the back where smokers can stoke up a *sheesha* (water pipe) with fruit-flavoured tobacco.

Restaurant (Press Club; Map p96; ☎ 934 0888; 59A Pho Ly Thai To; mains US$15-25; lunch & dinner) *The* restaurant to see and be seen for a business lunch or dinner, it is drawing more tourists who come in search of innovative international flavours. Specials include imported salmon and lamb, plus a smattering of seafood.

Le Beaulieu Restaurant (Map p96; ☎ 826 6919 ext 8028; Sofitel Metropole Hotel, 15 Pho Ngo Quyen; mains from US$20; breakfast, lunch & dinner) At the refined Sofitel Metropole Hotel, Le Beaulieu is the home of fine French food. This is the place for authentic French cooking, regular regional specialities and a professional wine list.

GREATER HANOI

Vine (Map pp88-9; ☎ 719 8000; 1A Xuan Dieu; mains US$10-20; lunch & dinner) Home of the grape, this restaurant, on the shores of Ho Tay, has one of the best wine lists in the world according to *Wine Spectator* magazine. Sink a bottle with a rib eye steak with blue cheese and you will sleep well. The Xuan Dieu strip is taking off, with plenty of restaurants and shops in this area.

Italian

OLD QUARTER

Pepperoni's Pizza & Café (Map p96; ☎ 928 5246; 29 Pho Ly Quoc Su; mains from 40,000d; lunch & dinner) This is a laudable lunch stop, thanks to the US$2 all-you-can-eat weekday lunchtime pasta and salad bar. It also has authentic pizzas and takeaway. Try the busy **branch** (Map p96; ☎ 928 7030; 31 Pho Bao Khanh) on the popular Bao Khanh strip.

Mediterraneo (Map p96; ☎ 826 6288; 23 Pho Nha Tho; mains US$5-7; lunch & dinner) This small Italian restaurant is in the heart of happening Nha Tho. The pasta sauces are rich and filling, including gorgonzola ravioli, and perfect with a crisp salad.

Pane e Vino (Map p96; ☎ 826 9080; 98 Pho Hang Trong; meals US$5-15; lunch & dinner) This trattoria-wine bar is a great place to take a break from commercial blitz of Hang Trong. Memorable moments include chestnut and almond ravioli, and rice Italian style, such as porcini mushroom with truffle oil.

CENTRAL HANOI

our pick **Luna d'Autunno** (Map pp92-3; ☎ 823 7338; 11B Pho Dien Bien Phu; pizza from 60,000d, fresh pasta from 90,000d) It doesn't get more popular than Luna, one of the best-known and best-loved Italian restaurants in Hanoi. The menu includes a superb selection of homemade antipasto and some of the only fresh pasta in town. Upstairs is the Luna Lounge, a lively drinking den for the after-dinner crowd.

Seafood

Sam Son Seafood Market (☎ 825 0780; 77 Pho Doc Bac) This huge restaurant doubles up as a giant fish market. On the banks of Song Hong (Red River), this is fish heaven, or fish hell if you happen to be a fish. Survey the scene, choose your fish and it will be at your table in minutes.

San Ho Restaurant (Map pp92-3; ☎ 934 9184; 58 Pho Ly Thuong Kiet; meals around 200,000d) Set in an attractive French-era villa, San Ho is considered one of the best seafood restaurants in Hanoi. Crustaceans and molluscs come in every shape and size, bathed in delicious sauces. Most prices are by the kilo.

Vegetarian

Dakshin (Map p96; ☎ 928 6872; 94 Pho Hang Trong; meals 25,000-60,000d) Under the same ownership as Tandoor, Dakshin is all-vegetarian and enjoys legendary status among the curry crew in Hanoi. The menu features speciality southern Indian food, including delicious *dosas* (paper-thin lentil-flour pancakes).

Whole Earth Restaurant (Map p96; ☎ 926 0696; 7 Pho Dinh Liet; set menus from 30,000d; 8am-11pm) In the middle of the lively Dinh Liet strip, this is the place to come and be healthy before moving on to the less healthy pursuits in nearby bars. It specialises in mock meat dishes.

Com Chay Nang Tam (Map pp92-3; ☎ 826 6140; 79A Pho Tran Hung Dao; meals from 30,000d) It is a mystery how this place can make simple vegetables and pulses look and even taste like meat. Hardcore vegetarians may find this a contradiction, but it is actually an ancient Buddhist tradition that is designed to make meat-eating guests feel at home. Yes, it really is down that unlikely looking alley behind those buildings. It's smoke free, so it's healthier still.

our pick **Tamarind Café** (Map p96; ☎ 926 0580; 80 Pho Ma May; meals US$2-4; 6am-midnight) Vegetarian heaven: there are some wonderful creations here blending together Asian and European elements. Impressive shakes and smoothies include some healthy anti-oxidants for the morning after. Free wi-fi too.

Cafés

OLD QUARTER

Café Pho Co (Map p96; ☎ 928 8153; 11 Pho Hang Gai; shakes 15,000d) One of Hanoi's best-kept secrets, this old house has a historic courtyard and plum views over Hoan Kiem Lake. Enter through the Feeling Gallery, which sells paintings, and continue up to the top floor for the monumental vista.

Moca Café (Map p96; ☎ 825 6334; 14-16 Pho Nha Tho; espresso 20,000d; 7.30am-11pm) One of the most popular cafés in Hanoi, this the perfect spot for people-watching thanks to its huge windows. See which boutiques are in fashion this month by the names on the shopping bags while tucking into excellent Vietnamese, Western and Indian food.

Little Hanoi 2 (Map p96; ☎ 928 5333; 21 Pho Hang Gai; sandwiches from 25,000d; 7.30am-11pm) Unrelated to Little Hanoi 1, this is a likeable little café with a tempting selection of baguettes, pastas and salads. On a busy corner near Hoan Kiem Lake, the French breakfast is a steal at around US$2.

Puku (Map p96; ☎ 928 5244; upstairs 60 Pho Hang Trong; snacks 25,000-35,000d; 7am-10pm) A funky little café on fashionable Hang Trong, this place has a fun vibe, tasty food and two floors. It also has regular art exhibitions showcasing emerging artists.

our pick **La Place** (Map p96; ☎ 928 5859; 4 Pho Au Trieu; meals from 30,000d) Readers have been raving about this place so we checked it out. We're joining the rave. The menu is small but includes iced shakes with bite and delicious savoury crepes. After dark, it morphs into a café-bar and drinking is the name of the game.

Diva (Map p96; ☎ 934 4088; 57 Pho Ly Thai To; light meals from 35,000d; 7am-midnight) You don't have to be a diva to come here for a leisurely lunch or a sneaky sundowner. Diva is set in a charming French-period villa with a big outdoor terrace.

Culi Café (Map p96; ☎ 926 2241; 40 Pho Luong Ngoc Quyen; meals around 50,000d; 7.30am-11pm) Sangers, pies, burgers and more, this Australian-run café-bar is a popular stop for tasty tucker. There are also pizzas and all-day breakfasts, plus plenty of beer. Good travel information too, as the owners run Wide Eyed Tours (p484), plus free wi-fi.

CENTRAL HANOI

Maison Vanille (Map pp92-3; ☎ 933 2355; 49 Pho Phan Chu Trinh; cakes 10,000-20,000d) Caffeine addicts suggest that this is home to the best coffee in town. The pastries could in the running too, as they are almost too beautiful to eat.

Kinh Do Café (Map pp92-3; ☎ 825 0216; 252 Pho Hang Bong; light meals 20,000d; 7am-10pm) Fans of Catherine Deneuve will want to make a pilgrimage here, as this was the simple setting where she had her morning cuppa during the making of the film *Indochine*. It serves healthy yoghurt, plus tasty French pastries and feisty coffee. Le patron speaks French.

Ice Cream

OLD QUARTER

Fanny Ice Cream (Map p96; ☎ 828 5656; 48 Pho Le Thai To; ice creams from 10,000d) The place for French-style ice cream in Hanoi. During the right season try the *com*, a delightful local flavour extracted from young sticky rice; otherwise taste the ginger for the flavour of Asia.

Kem Trang Tien (Map p96; 54 Pho Trang Tien; ice creams from 5000d) There is always a scrum outside this place, as locals struggle to get their hands on the popular ice cream. Located between the Opera House and Hoan Kiem Lake, you'll spot the crowd long before you see the café.

Speciality Food Streets

If you would like to combine eating with exploration, most of the following food streets are in central Hanoi.

PHO CAM CHI

A super-small street – more of an alley – Pho Cam Chi (Map pp92–3) is crammed full of lively street stalls turning out cheap and tasty food. Forget about English menus and don't expect comfortable seating. But there's little room for complaint when you get a small banquet for a few dollars. Cam Chi translates as 'Forbidden to Point' and dates from centuries ago. It is said that the street was named as a reminder for the local residents to keep their curious fingers in their pockets when the king and his entourage went through the neighbourhood. Cam Chi is about 500m northeast of Hanoi train station.

DUONG THUY KHUE

On the southern bank of Ho Tay, Đ Thuy Khue (Map pp92–3) features dozens of outdoor seafood restaurants. The peaceful lakeside setting is popular with locals. The level of competition is evident by the daredevil touts who literally throw themselves in front of oncoming traffic to steer people to their tables. You can eat well here for about 100,000d a head.

PHO NGHI TAM

About 10km north of central Hanoi, Pho Nghi Tam has a 1km-long stretch of about 60 **dog-meat restaurants** (Map p126; meals from 75,000d). The street runs along the embankment between West Lake and Song Hong (Red River) and the restaurants are on the right as you leave town: look for the words *thit cho*. Even if you have no interest in eating dog meat, it's interesting to cruise this stretch of road on the last evening of the lunar month. Hanoians believe that eating dog meat in the first-half of the month brings bad luck, so the restaurants are deserted. Business picks up in the second-half of the month and the last day is particularly auspicious with the restaurants packed. Now we know why dogs howl at the moon! Cruise by in the evening and you'll see thousands of motorbikes parked here.

Self-Catering

OLD QUARTER

Fivimart (Map p96; 210 Tran Quang Khai) One of the best stocked supermarkets in the centre of town.

Citimart (Map p96; Hanoi Towers, 49 Hai Ba Trung) A supermarket with a teasing range of treats for the many expats that live in the skyscraper above.

Intimex (Map p96; Pho Le Thai Tho) This is another option for any creature comforts you might need. It's on the western side of Hoan Kiem Lake, tucked down a driveway behind the Clinique beauty shop.

DRINKING

Bars

There is a drink for all seasons in Hanoi, with sophisticated bars, congenial pubs and grungy clubs. Don't forget to warm up with some quality time drinking *bia hoi*, the world's cheapest beer (see the boxed text, p118 for more). Busy Bao Khanh has a cool choice of bars and is a good starting or finishing point for a bar crawl.

Bear in mind that the fun police supervise a fairly strict curfew of midnight during the week and 1am at the weekend, which takes the edge off the nightlife. However, there are some late-night lock-ins; read on for the inside story.

our pick **Le Pub** (Map p96; ☎ 926 2104; 25 Pho Hang Be) The name says it all: the attitude of a British pub with the atmosphere of a continental bar. It's rapidly earning a name for itself as a friendly place to drink and draws both expats and tourists. Late-night lock-ins have been known.

GAY & LESBIAN HANOI

By Vietnam's standards there's a lively gay scene in Hanoi, but there are few, if any, gay venues: just some places that are more gay-friendly than others. There is a bustling cruising area along Pho Bao Khanh, plus nearby Hoan Kiem Lake, although gay males should watch out for an extortion scam linked to the latter (see p95).

Official attitudes are still fairly conservative and Hanoi is home to these official attitudes. Police raids in the name of 'social reform' aren't unknown and that tends to ensure gays and lesbians keep a low profile. **Funky Monkey** (opposite) is a lively bar-cum-club that turns up the volume at weekends, while late-night bars **Apocalypse Now** (p118) and **Solace** (opposite) both attract a small gay crowd.

Quan Bia Minh (Map p96; ☎ 934 5233; 7A Pho Dinh Liet) Bottled beer doesn't come much cheaper than this, a buzzing backpacker favourite with a blissful balcony terrace overlooking Dinh Liet.

Red Beer (Map p96; ☎ 8260247; 97 Pho Ma May) Microbreweries, sort of upmarket *bia hoi* places, are taking off in Hanoi and this was one of the first. There are several flavours of home brew for those who like to experiment.

our pick **Gambrinus** (Map p96; ☎ 935 1114; 198 Pho Tran Quang Khai) Czech beer lovers will be rubbing their hands in glee. Gambrinus, that shy and retiring Czech beer, even has a home here. It's a vast, impressive brauhaus with shiny vats of freshly brewed Czech beer. Very popular with the Vietnamese.

Legends Beer (Map p96; ☎ 557 1277; 109 Pho Nguyen Tuan) Every beer comes with free views of Hoan Kiem Lake. The 2nd-floor balcony is a good place to watch the traffic below and homebrews include an excellent *weiss* (white) beer.

our pick **Highway 4** (Map p96; ☎ 926 0639; 5 Pho Hang Tre) Head here to discover the mystical, medicinal, not to mention intoxicating qualities of Vietnamese rice wine *(xeo)*. Take it straight, fruity or 'five times a night' – the possibilities are endless. A popular rallying point for members of Hanoi's infamous Minsk Club (p123), the bar downstairs is for drinkers and there's a rooftop terrace for diners. For more on its food, see p112.

Bar Le Maquis (Map p96; ☎ 928 2618; 2A Pho Ta Hien) Small but perfectly formed, this little bar doesn't need a crowd to make it feel busy. Like many of the bars around Ta Hien, it stays open later than most.

Dragonfly (Map p96; 15 Pho Hang Buom) Just around the corner from Le Maquis, Dragonfly has an inviting upstairs lounge and DJs rumble on into the night. One of the latest spots in the Old Quarter.

Finnegan's Irish Pub (Map p96; ☎ 828 9065; 16A Pho Duong Thanh) Every city has an Irish pub these days and Hanoi is not to be left out. It's a popular sports bar for the weekend games.

Polite Pub (Map p96; ☎ 825 0959; 5 Pho Bao Khanh) Don't forget your manners at this place, unless your favourite English Premier League team is 3-0 down at half-time. There is always a crowd here and the drinks are pretty reasonable.

GC Pub (Map p96; ☎ 825 0499; 7 Pho Bao Khanh) Bars come in and out of fashion in Hanoi, and GC has swung right back into favour with Hanoi residents. There's a popular pool table and very friendly staff.

Amazon Bar (Map p96; ☎ 928 7338; 10 Pho Bao Khanh) Just over the road and reinforcing Bao Khanh's reputation as a drinkers' den, Amazon has Russian (vodka and Red Bull 25,000d), London (gin and tonic 25,000d) and other promo nights that keep pulling the crowds.

Funky Monkey (Map p96; ☎ 928 6113; 15B Pho Hang Hanh) An extension of the Bao Khanh beat, the action regularly spills over on to the dance floor at this hip bar-club. Not the place to come for a quiet conversation.

Toilet Pub (Map p96; ☎ 928 7338; 10 Pho Bao Khanh) If you're squeamish about bathroom talk, avoid this place. Spirits are displayed in urinals and toilets are everywhere. Trendy as hell with rich Vietnamese, drinks are expensive (50,000d a beer).

Solace (Map p96; ☎ 932 3244; Song Hong, Phuc Tan district) Floating in the Song Hong, many a drinker has found their night floats by here as well. A late-night spot, it doesn't really warm up until after midnight and bobs along until daybreak.

Met Pub (Map p96; ☎ 826 6919; Sofitel Metropole Hotel, 15 Pho Ngo Quyen) For a more refined atmosphere, check out the bar at the Sofitel Metropole Hotel. The Met is an atmospheric pub with fine food and a good beer selection, but it's also expensive unless you hit the happy hour (5pm to 7pm).

My Way (☎ 936 5917; www.myway.com.vn; 60 P Ly Thai To) This trendy new lounge bar offers a grand tour of world beers, including the best of Belgian, German and, of course, Vietnamese. Some come by the keg, but aren't cheap.

Coffee Shops

Thuy Ta Café (Map p96; ☎ 828 8148; 1 Pho Le Thai To; pastries 10,000d; 🕒 6am-11pm) One of the most memorable settings in all of Hanoi for a morning coffee, Thuy Ta's shady garden is smack-bang on the northern shore of Hoan Kiem Lake.

Hapro (Map p96; Pho Le Thai Tho) At the opposite end of Hoan Kiem Lake, this café has a prime patio for drinks and is an ideal place to watch the world go by on a warm day.

There is a lively, packed and chaotic cluster of coffee shops on the Old Quarter's Pho Hang Hanh; relax on one of the upstairs balconies and watch the bustle below on one of Hanoi's most happening streets.

BIA AHOY!

'Tram phan tram!' Remember these words well as all over Vietnam, glasses of *bia hoi* are raised and emptied, cries of '100%' or 'bottoms up' echo around the table.

Bia hoi (beer) is Vietnam's very own draught beer or microbrew. This refreshing, light-bodied Pilsener was first introduced to Vietnam by the Czechs. Decades later *bia hoi* is still brewed and delivered daily to drinking establishments throughout Ho Chi Minh City (HCMC), Hanoi and all points between. Brewed without preservatives, it is meant to be enjoyed immediately. And enjoyed it is! Many tourists and expats have never heard of this nectar, but that's their loss, especially given it costs as little as 2000d a glass.

If you think you're ready to try *bia hoi,* be prepared – drinking with the pros is not for the meek. A Western face is a bit unusual at any *bia hoi* establishment and inevitably attracts curious attention from fellow patrons. Raising your glass in toast more often than not results in an invitation to join a group.

Hanoi is the *bia hoi* capital of Vietnam and there are microbars on almost every street corner. Hitting the Old Quarter for a *bia hoi* crawl is a brilliant way to get beneath the skin of the capital. Put US$10 in your pocket and you will be able to afford nearly 100 beers, so you'll soon make lots of friends. One of the best places to sample this bargain beer is 'bia hoi junction' (Map p96) in the heart of the Old Quarter where Pho Ta Hien meets Pho Luong Ngoc Quyen. Here are three bustling *bia hoi* places occupying different corners, all packed with backpackers and locals every night and knocking out the ale. Don't forget that most *bia hoi* also serve delicious and inexpensive food.

An alternative *bia hoi* junction that is more local in flavour is where Pho Nha Hoa meets Pho Duong Thanh on the western edge of the Old Quarter. **Bia Hoi Ha Noi** (Map p96; 2 Pho Duong Thanh), does the best spare ribs in town for a little something to go with the beer.

For the best quality *bia hoi,* try **Bia Hoi Viet Ha** (Map p96; Pho Hang Bai), which is well loved by Hanoi insiders, as it has the biggest chillers in town. It recently relocated to a much bigger premises on Hang Bai, but it's still hard to get a table.

Other good spots to sample the brew include **Bia Hoi 68 Hang Quat** (Map p96; Pho Hang Quat), which we have been drinking at for a decade now, and **Nha Hang Lan Chin** (Map pp92-3; 2 Pho Trang Tien), one of the most popular local lunch spots in town.

ENTERTAINMENT

Cinemas

Megastar Cineplex (Map pp92-3; ☎ 974 3333; 6th fl, Vincom Tower, 191 Ba Trieu) The international multiplex cinema arrives in Hanoi. This is a serious place, complete with the latest international films.

Cinematheque (Map p96; 22A Hai Ba Trung; ☎ 936 2648) The Cinematheque is popular with the Hanoi expat community thanks to its adventurous choice of films – from shorts to a mixed selection of arthouse films.

Centre Culturel Française de Hanoi (Map p96; ☎ 936 2164; 24 Trang Tien) Set in the sublime L'Espace building near the Opera House, it offers a regular programme of French flicks.

Circus Troupes

Central Circus (Rap Xiec Trung Uong; Map pp92-3; admission US$2.50; 🕑 shows 8-10pm Tue-Sun, 9am Sun) The circus is one Russian entertainment tradition that has survived and thrived in Vietnam. Performers – gymnasts, jugglers, animal trainers – were originally trained in Eastern Europe, though today's new recruits learn their skills from their Vietnamese elders.

Performances are held in a huge tent near the northern entrance to Lenin Park. A special show is staged for children on Sunday morning. However, animal lovers won't appreciate the conditions in which the animals are kept.

Nightclubs

If you want to see the beautiful people of Vietnam cutting their moves, there are several local clubs to check out. Many of the aforementioned bars morph into clubs come the weekend. New clubs tend to blow hot and cold, so ask around for what's hot or not before venturing forth.

Apocalypse Now (Map pp92-3; Pho Dong Thac; 🕑 8pm-1am) This place has lost some of its lustre since moving a long way south in town. However, it remains a popular place of pilgrimage for Hanoi's hedonists. Definitely one of the more gay-friendly clubs in town.

New Century Nightclub (Map p96; ☎ 928 5285; 10 Pho Trang Thi) New places come and go, but the New Century remains the place to see and be seen for young Vietnamese ready to flash the cash. Dress sharp, as the beautiful people are out in force.

I-Box (Map p96; ☎ 828 8820; 32 Pho Le Thai Tho) Café-bar by day, with luxurious drapes and free wi-fi, by night it turns club with decent DJs and a throbbing dance floor.

Live Music

CLASSICAL

Hanoi Opera House (Nha Hat Lon; Map p96; ☎ 825 4312; Pho Trang Tien) This magnificent 900-seat venue looks along Pho Trang Tien to Hoan Kiem Lake. It was built in 1911 and has been restored to its former glory. It was from a balcony on this building that the Viet Minh–run Citizens' Committee announced, on 16 August 1945, that it had taken over the city. Performances of classical music are periodically held here in the evenings and the atmosphere is incredible. The theatre's Vietnamese name appropriately translates to 'House Sing Big'.

Check the listings in the *Guide* or *Time Out* to find out if anything is happening here during your stay.

JAZZ & MODERN

Jazz Club By Quyen Van Minh (Cau Lac Bo; Map p96; ☎ 825 7655; 31-33 Pho Luong Van Can; 🕒 performances 9-11.30pm) *The* place in Hanoi to catch live jazz. Owner Minh teaches saxophone at the Hanoi Conservatory and moonlights here, jamming with a variety of musicians from his talented son to top international jazz players.

Piano Bar (Map p96; ☎ 923 2677; 93 Pho Phung Hung) The Piano Bar is reborn after a long absence. There's a grand piano on the 1st floor to serenade couples while they wine and dine, and weekends see a string quartet join the action. Happy hour is from 5pm to 7pm daily.

R&R Tavern (Map p96; ☎ 934 4109; 47 Pho Lo Su) A reliable little venue for live music, the Vietnamese band here knows all the counterculture '60s classics. Drinks are very reasonably priced given the free soundtrack.

Seventeen Saloon (Map pp92-3; ☎ 942 6822; 98 Tran Hung Dao) Yee-haa! Welcome to the wild west. Cowboy bars are curiously popular in Asia and this place has live bands every night.

Terrace Bar (Press Club; Map p96; ☎ 934 0888; 59A Pho Ly Thai To) A popular place to be on Friday, when half of Hanoi's high-flyers seem to descend here for the happy hour (6pm). Drink specials include access to the roving platters of finger food and a soundtrack of live music.

TRADITIONAL

The best places to catch live traditional music are upmarket Vietnamese restaurants in central Hanoi, like **Cay Cau** (Map pp92-3; ☎ 824 5346; De Syloia Hotel, 17A Pho Tran Hung Dao) in De Syloia Hotel, **Club Opera** (Map p96; ☎ 824 6950; 59 Pho Ly Thai To), **Dinh Lang Restaurant** (Map p96; ☎ 828 6290; 1 Pho Le Thai Tho) and **Nam Phuong** (Map pp92-3; ☎ 928 5085; 16 Pho Bao Khanh). It's aimed at tourists, but close your eyes and the music is hauntingly beautiful.

There is also live music performed daily at the Temple of Literature (p100).

Water Puppets

This fascinating art form (see the boxed text, p121) originated in northern Vietnam, and Hanoi is the best place to catch a show.

Performances are held at the **Municipal Water Puppet Theatre** (Roi Nuoc Thang Long; Map p96; ☎ 825 5450; 57B Pho Dinh Tien Hoang; www.thanglongwaterpuppet.org; admission 20,000-40,000d, still-camera fee 10,000d, video fee 50,000d; 🕒 performances 4pm, 5.15pm, 6.30pm, 8pm & 9.15pm). The higher admission price buys the best seats and you can take-home a CD of the music for US$2. Multilingual programmes allow the audience to read up on each vignette as it's performed. Check out the faces of enthralled Vietnamese kids in the audience – they're magic. Try and arrange a ticket in advance, as shows are often sold out, especially during high season.

SHOPPING

Designer Boutiques

Khai Silk (Map p96; ☎ 825 4237; khaisilk@fpt.vn; 96 Pho Hang Gai) Almost a national institution these days, Khai Silk is the place to find funky, fashionable silk clothing, as well as more austere classical creations.

Hadong Silk (Map p96; ☎ 928 5056; 102 Pho Hang Gai) One of the biggest silk shops on (appropriately enough) silk street. Hilary Clinton shopped here during her visit with Bill in 2000.

Pearl Ha (Map p96; ☎ 942 1872; 40 Pho Hang Bong; www.pearlha.com) Home to an eclectic collection of cool clothing, designer jewellery and other titbits, designer Ha Linh Thu has outlets in major hotels including the Hilton and the Melia.

Ipa-Nima (Map pp92-3; ☎ 933 4000; 34 Pho Han Thuyen; www.ipa-nima.com) This boutique promises 'smart humour, bright colours, subtle satire' and it delivers. Designer clothing, bags and jewellery for those in the market for something original.

Things of Substance (Map p96; ☎ 828 6965; 5 Pho Nha Tho) A popular clothes shop on Nha Tho, this offers tailored fashions at affordable prices – a thing of substance indeed.

Chi Vang (Map p96; ☎ 824 0933; 17 Pho Trang Tien) Anyone who has been to Bali and browsed the beautiful Ulu Watu lace shops will know the script here. Exquisite lace creations, including clothing and homewares.

Dome (Map p96; ☎ 843 6036; 71 Pho Hang Trong) One of the best shops for home accessories. Unique designs and the best of Vietnamese materials make the perfect keepsake.

There are several beautiful furnishings shops on Pho Nha Tho if you are in the mood for shipping stuff back home or planning to set up house.

Galleries

Aspiring young artists display their works in Hanoi's private art galleries in the hope of attracting a buyer. The highest concentration of upmarket galleries is on Pho Trang Tien, between Hoan Kiem Lake and the Opera House – just stroll down the strip. Most art galleries have some English-speaking staff, and are open daily until 8pm or 9pm. Prices range from a few dollars to a few thousand and polite bargaining is the norm.

Viet Art Centre (Map pp92-3; 42 Pho Yet Kieu) This new art centre was just opening its doors as we were in town, and promises cutting edge contemporary art and classic paintings. Worth a browse plus there is an excellent little café to contemplate.

Hanoi Gallery (Map p96; 110 Pho Hang Bac) If you are in the market for propaganda posters from the old days, this place has a huge selection. It includes translations of the slogans and mailing tubes for easy carrying or posting.

Mai Gallery (Map p96; ☎ 828 5854; www.maigallery-vietnam.com; 183 Pho Hang Bong) Run by resident artist Mai, this is a good place to learn more about Vietnamese art before making a purchase.

In a cluster around the Old Quarter corner of Pho Trang Tien and Pho Ngo Quyen are Gallery Huong Xuyen (Map p96), which also stocks some beautiful greetings cards; **A Gallery** (Map p96; www.vietnamesepainting.com), with both permanent and visiting exhibitions; and **Hanoi Contemporary Art Gallery** (Map p96; www.hanoiartgallery.com), with some ceramics as well as paintings.

Handicrafts & Antiques

There are quite a few shops in Hanoi offering new and antique Vietnamese handicrafts (lacquerware, mother-of-pearl inlaid furniture, ceramics, sandalwood statuettes and so on), as well as watercolours, oil paintings, prints and assorted antiques (real and fake). Pho Hang Gai, Pho To Tich, Pho Hang Khai and Pho Cau Go are happy hunting grounds.

Viet Hien (Map p96; ☎ 826 9769; 8B Pho Ta Hien) An enormous warehouse of antiques, paintings, furniture and handicrafts, including rattan creations that are a hell of a lot cheaper than at home.

Vietnamese House (Map p96; ☎ 826 2455; 92 Pho Hang Bac) A small but attractive shop dealing in a mix of old and new treasures.

There is a strip of antique shops (Map pp92–3) located on Le Duan, across from Hotel Nikko on Tran Nhan Tong, but most tend to be overpriced.

Markets

Dong Xuan Market (Map p96) is a three-storey market located in the Old Quarter of Hanoi, 900m north of Hoan Kiem Lake. The market burned down in 1994, killing five people, all of whom had entered the building after the fire started, to either rescue goods or steal them. It has now been rebuilt and is a tourist attraction in its own right. There are hundreds of stalls here, employing around 3000 people.

Hang Da Market (Map p96) is a relatively small market, but it is good for imported foods, wine, beer and flowers. The 2nd floor is good for fabric and ready-made clothing. It is very close to the Protestant Church off Pho Hang Ga, 300m west of Hoan Kiem Lake.

Hom Market (Map pp92–3), on the northeast corner of Pho Hué and Pho Tran Xuan Soan, is a good general-purpose market with lots of imported food items. It's a good place to buy fabric if you plan to have clothes made.

Cua Nam Market (Map pp92–3) is a few blocks north of the Hanoi train station. The market is itself of no great interest (except maybe for the flowers), but Đ Le Duan between the market and the train station is a

PUNCH & JUDY IN A POOL

The ancient art of water puppetry *(roi nuoc)* was virtually unknown outside of northern Vietnam until the 1960s. It originated with rice farmers who worked the flooded fields of the Red River Delta. Some say they saw the potential of the water as a dynamic stage, others say they adapted conventional puppetry during a massive flood. Whatever the real story, it is at least 1000 years old.

The farmers carved the puppets from water-resistant fig-tree timber *(sung)* in forms modelled on the villagers themselves, animals from their daily lives and more fanciful mythical creatures such as the dragon, phoenix and unicorn. Performances were usually staged in ponds, lakes or flooded paddy fields.

Contemporary performances use a square tank of waist-deep water for the 'stage'; the water is murky to conceal the mechanisms that operate the puppets. The wooden puppets can be up to 50cm long and weigh as much as 15kg, and are painted with a glossy vegetable-based paint. Each lasts only about three to four months if used continually, so puppet production provides several villages outside Hanoi with a full-time livelihood.

Eleven puppeteers, each one trained for a minimum of three years, are involved in each performance. The puppeteers stand in the water behind a bamboo screen and have traditionally suffered from a host of water-borne diseases – these days they wear waders to avoid this nasty occupational hazard.

Some puppets are simply attached to a long pole, while others are set on a floating base, in turn attached to a pole. Most have articulated limbs and heads, some also have rudders to help guide them. In the darkened auditorium it looks as if they are literally walking on water.

The considerable skills required to operate the puppets were traditionally kept secret and passed only from father to son; never to daughters through fear that they would marry outside the village and take the secrets with them.

The music, which is provided by a band, is as important as the action on stage. The band includes wooden flutes *(sao)*, gongs *(cong)*, cylindrical drums *(trong com)*, bamboo xylophones and the fascinating single-stringed zither (*dan bau*).

The performance consists of a number of vignettes depicting pastoral scenes and legends. One memorable scene tells of the battle between a fisherman and his prey, which is so electric it appears as if a live fish is being used. There are also fire-breathing dragons (complete with fireworks) and a flute-playing boy riding a buffalo.

The performance is a lot of fun. The water puppets are both amusing and graceful, and the water greatly enhances the drama by allowing the puppets to appear and disappear as if by magic. Spectators in the front-row seats can expect a bit of a splash.

treasure-trove of household goods, such as electronics and plasticware.

Buoi Market (Map pp88–9) is located out in the far northwest. Notable for live animals (chickens, ducks, pigs and so on), it also features ornamental plants.

For something completely different, there is now a **night market** (🕑 7pm-midnight) running through the heart of the Old Quarter. It starts near Dong Xuan Market on Pho Hang Giay and runs almost to Hoan Kiem Lake on Pho Hang Dao. It is little more than a spill-over from the many shops that now dot the Old Quarter, but at least the streets are closed to traffic and it's cooler to browse. Watch out for pickpockets, as this has become the new Hanoi hotspot.

Souvenirs & Other Shops

Around Pho Hang Bong and Pho Hang Gai, just northwest of Hoan Kiem Lake, are plenty of souvenir shops selling T-shirts and Viet Cong (VC) headgear. It might be worth noting, however, that neither Ho Chi Minh T-shirts nor VC headgear are very popular apparel with Vietnamese refugees and certain war veterans living in the West. Wearing such souvenirs while walking down a street in Los Angeles or Melbourne might offend someone and result in a costly trip to the dentist.

Pho Hang Gai and its continuation, Pho Hang Bong, are good places to look for embroidered tablecloths, T-shirts and wall hangings. Pho Hang Gai is also a good place to have clothes custom-made. Take a look along Pho Hang Dao, just north of Hoan Kiem Lake, for souvenir Russian-made watches.

If you don't make it up to Sapa (p172), there is a wide selection of ethnic-minority garb and handicrafts available in Hanoi; a stroll along Pho Hang Bac or Pho To Tich will turn up close to a dozen places.

Craft Link (Map pp92-3; ☎ 843 7710; 43 Pho Van Mieu) is a not-for-profit organisation that buys good quality tribal handicrafts and weavings at fair-trade prices, and funds community development initiatives for the artisans.

There is an outstanding **shoe market** (Map p96; Pho Hang Dau) at the northeast corner of Hoan Kiem Lake.

For the best in CDs and DVDs, there are several shops along Pho Hang Bong and Pho Trang Tien. Be aware that they're bootleg, though, so not strictly legal.

On Pho Trang Tien you'll also find many shops willing to make dirt-cheap eyeglasses in a mere 10 minutes, using decent imported lenses from France or Japan.

GETTING THERE & AWAY

Air

Hanoi has fewer direct international flights than HCMC, but with a change of aircraft in Hong Kong or Bangkok you can get to almost anywhere. For further information about international flights, see p477.

Vietnam Airlines (Map p96; ☎ 943 9660; www.vietnamair.com.vn; 25 Pho Trang Thi; 🕑 7am-6.30pm Mon-Fri, 8-11.30am & 1.30-5pm Sat, Sun & holidays) links Hanoi to destinations throughout Vietnam. Popular routes include Hanoi to Danang, Dien Bien Phu, HCMC, Hué and Nha Trang, all served daily.

Pacific Airlines (Map pp92-3; ☎ 974 5555; 193 Đ Ba Trieu) has daily flights to Danang and HCMC.

Bus & Minibus

Hanoi has several main long-distance bus stations and each one serves a particular area. They are fairly well organised, with ticket offices, fixed prices and printed schedules. You should consider buying tickets the day before you plan to travel on the longer-distance routes to ensure a seat.

In central Hanoi, **Kim Ma bus station** (Map pp92-3; cnr Pho Nguyen Thai Hoc & Pho Giang Vo) has buses to the northwestern part of Vietnam, including Hoa Binh (25,000d, two hours) and Dien Bien Phu (120,000d, 16 hours).

Gia Lam bus station (Map p126; ☎ 827 1569; Đ Ngoc Lam) is the place for buses to points northeast of Hanoi. These include Halong Bay (40,000d, 3½ hours), Haiphong (35,000d, two hours), and Lang Son (50,000d, three hours) and Lao Cai (53,000d, nine hours), both near the Chinese border. The bus station is 2km northeast of the centre – cross the Song Hong (Red River) to get there. *Cyclos* can't cross the bridge, so take a taxi (around 30,000d) or motorbike. More convenient is the Loung Yen bus station in the southeast of town, serving the same places, plus Cao Bang (80,000d, eight hours) and Ha Giang (76,000d, seven hours).

Giap Bat bus station (Map p126; ☎ 864 1467; Đ Giai Phong) serves points south of Hanoi, including Ninh Binh (28,000d, two hours) and Hué (80,000d, 12 hours). It is 7km south of the Hanoi train station.

My Dinh bus station (Map p126; ☎ 768 5549, Đ Pham Hung) is another option in the west of town, which serves a range of destinations, including Halong City, Lang Son, Cao Bang, Ha Giang and Dien Bien Phu.

Tourist-style minibuses can be booked through most hotels and cafés. Popular destinations include Halong Bay and Sapa.

Many open-ticket tours through Vietnam start or finish in Hanoi – for more details see p487.

Car & Motorcycle

To hire a car with a driver, contact a hotel, travellers café or travel agency. The main roads in the northeast are generally OK, but in parts of the northwest they can be dire in the wet season and only suitable for a 4WD.

The average cost for a six-day trip in a Russian jeep is about US$300 per person, including the jeep, a driver and petrol. These old jeeps fit only two passengers and are pretty uncomfortable: they're dusty and hot, or damp and cold, depending on the weather. For a smarter Japanese air-con 4WD, double the rate. The price usually includes the driver's expenses, and it's a good idea to clarify this.

If you plan to tour the north by bike, there are several good outfits that can arrange guides and rentals and help with itinerary planning. Check out p491 for more details.

The 125cc Russian-made Minsk is the best overall bike for touring the north – you'll need this kind of power for the mountainous regions, and all mechanics know how to fix them. Quality of rental motorbikes can be extremely variable, so try to find a reputable dealer, especially if you're planning long trips.

For the most reliable Minsk rental in town, make for **Cuong's Motorbike Adventure** (Map p96; ☎ 926 1534; 1 Pho Luong Ngoc Quyen). Cuong rents out bikes for US$5 a day, including a full range of spares and a repair manual.

For more on the mighty Minsk, check out the official website of the **Minsk Club** (www.minskclubvietnam.com). Its motto is 'In Minsk We Trust' and the site is full of useful information on the motorbike and the mountains to explore.

Train

The main **Hanoi train station** (Ga Hang Co; Map pp92-3; ☎ 825 3949; 120 Đ Le Duan; ticket office 7.30am-12.30pm & 1.30-7.30pm) is at the western end of Pho Tran Hung Dao; trains from here go to destinations south. Foreigners can buy tickets for southbound trains at counter 2, where the staff speak English. It's often best to buy tickets at least one day before departure to ensure a seat or sleeper.

To the right of the main entrance of the train station is a separate ticket office for northbound trains to Lao Cai (for Sapa) and China. Tickets to China must be bought from counter 13.

However, the place where you purchase the ticket is not necessarily where the train departs. Just behind the main 'A Station' on Đ Le Duan is **Tran Quy Cap station** (B Station; Pho Tran Qui Cap; ☎ 825 2628) and all northbound trains leave from there.

To make things even more complicated, some northbound (Lao Cai and Lang Son included) and eastbound (Haiphong) trains depart from Gia Lam (Map p126) on the eastern side of the Song Hong (Red River), and **Long Bien** (Map pp92-3; ☎ 826 8280) on the western (city) side of the river. Be sure to ask just where you need to go to catch your train. Tickets can be bought at the main station until about two hours before departure; if it's any closer to the departure time, go to the relevant station and buy tickets there.

Check with **Vietnam Rail** (Duong Sat Viet Nam; www.vr.com.vn) for current timetables. For more information on trains see p492.

GETTING AROUND

To/From the Airport

Hanoi's Noi Bai International Airport (Map p126) is about 35km north of the city and the trip takes 45 minutes to an hour. The airport freeway is one of the most modern roads in Vietnam and terminates in the north of town after crossing the Thang Long bridge.

Vietnam Airlines minibuses between Hanoi and Noi Bai airport charge US$2 a seat. There are few information signs inside the new terminal building; you need to go outside and look for the signs for taxis and minibuses. See the boxed text (p124) for more on avoiding potential problems.

To get to the airport from town, you can take one of the minibuses that depart roughly every half-hour from opposite the same Vietnam Airlines office on Pho Trang Thi. It's best – though not essential – to book the day before.

The cheapest way to get between Noi Bai airport and central Hanoi is to use public buses 7 or 17, which run to/from Kim Ma bus station and Long Bien bus station (Map pp92–3) respectively. Services depart every 15 minutes from around 5am to 9pm and tickets are just 3500d – perhaps the cheapest airport run in the world. It can take more than an hour, however. Arrange an onward metered taxi from the bus station to your chosen hotel.

Airport Taxi (☎ 873 3333) charges US$10 for a taxi ride door-to-door to or from Noi Bai airport. They do *not* require that you pay the toll for the bridge you cross en route. Some other taxi drivers require that you pay the toll, so ask first.

Inside the terminal, touts will offer taxi services. Don't use the meter with a tout, as it may well be rigged. The 'official' taxi rank is outside the concourse and you buy tickets from the seller at the head of the taxi line.

In central Hanoi, there is always a collection of taxi drivers just outside the Vietnam Airlines office or at the northern end of Hoan Kiem Lake.

Bicycle

A good way to get around Hanoi is by bicycle, although the traffic can be daunting at first. Many guesthouses and cafés offer these for rent for about US$1 to US$2 per day.

Bus

There are now more than 60 public bus lines serving routes in and around Hanoi. The buses are clean and comfortable, and the fare is just 3500d: only walking would be cheaper. Pick up a copy of the *Xe Buyt Hanoi* (Hanoi bus

MIND THE MAFIA

It happens all over the world and Hanoi is no exception. Many of the drivers who hang out at Noi Bai airport are working in cahoots with hotels in Hanoi to fill their rooms. They know every trick in the book and usually carry the cards of all the popular budget hotels. 'It's full today' is popular, as is 'they have a new place, much nicer, number two'. Usually it's a bunch of lies. The best defence is to insist you already have a reservation. Even if the place does turn out to be full, you can plot your own course from there. When it comes to the Vietnam Airlines minibus, the best bet is to bail out at the Vietnam Airlines office, usually the first stop in the centre. Otherwise you will be dragged around endless commission-paying hotels in the Old Quarter. Another option to avoid the nonsense is to book a room in advance and arrange an airport pick-up. Someone will be waiting with a nameboard and you can wave to the taxi touts as you exit the airport.

map; 5000d) from recommended bookstores on Pho Trang Tien. It is all in Vietnamese but easy enough to follow with routes and numbers clearly marked.

Car & Motorbike

For travellers well versed in the ways of Asian cities, Hanoi is a lot of fun to explore by motorbike. Most guesthouses and hotels can arrange new motorbikes for around US$5 a day. However, for the uninitiated, it is *not* the easiest place to learn. Traffic conditions are definitely not as orderly as home, and driving at night can be dangerous, particularly crossing the busy junctions with no traffic lights. Then there are the hassles of dealing with parking and possible theft. It's also easy to unknowingly violate road rules, in which case the police will help you part with some cash.

Cyclo

The *cyclos* in Hanoi are wider than the HCMC variety, making it possible for two people to fit in one and share the fare. One common *cyclo* driver's ploy when carrying two passengers is to agree on a price, and then *double* it upon arrival, gesturing 'no, no, no…that was per person'.

Aim to pay around 10,000d per person for a journey in the city centre. Longer rides or night rides are double that or more. It should be cheaper but they won't budge with tourists. Try to negotiate in dong, not dollars. You'll also find that a little bit of Vietnamese goes a long way when talking about prices.

The *cyclo* drivers in Hanoi are even less likely to speak English than in HCMC, so take a map of the city with you. That said, many are now wising up and now have a command of basic English.

Motorbike Taxi

You won't have any trouble finding a *xe om* in Hanoi. Just stroll along any major street and you'll get an offer from a driver almost every 10 seconds.

Like *cyclos*, expect to pay around 5000d to 10,000d for shorter rides and more again for longer rides.

Taxi

There are several companies in Hanoi offering metered taxi services. All charge similar rates. Flag fall is around 10,000d to 15,000d, which takes you one or two kilometres; every kilometre thereafter costs about 8000d. Bear in mind that there are lots of dodgy operators with high-speed meters. Try and use the more reliable companies:

Airport Taxi (☎ 873 3333)
Hanoi Taxi (☎ 853 5353)
Mai Linh Taxi (☎ 822 2666)
Taxi CP (☎ 824 1999)

AROUND HANOI

The rich alluvial soils of the Red River Delta nurture a rich rice crop and many of the communities surrounding Hanoi are still engaged in agriculture. The contrast between the modern face of Hanoi and the medieval lifestyle of the villages is stark. Many of the small tour operators (p91) in Hanoi offer cycling tours to villages near Hanoi, which are a great way to discover a different world. **Onbike Tour** (☎ 732 4788; www.onbikevietnam.com) specialises in cycling tours around Hanoi. Taking a tour also avoids having to survive the suburbs of Hanoi on your own, as a minibus takes the strain.

HO CHI MINH TRAIL MUSEUM

If you're interested in this amazing feat of human determination, the **Ho Chi Minh Trail Museum** (Bao Tang Duong Ho Chi Minh; Map p126; Hwy 6; admission 10,000d; 7.30-11am & 1.30-4pm Tue-Sun) is an introduction to the famous supply route from the communist north to the occupied south of Vietnam. There is a great model of the trail, which shows the nightmarish terrain through which it passed. It is located about 13km southwest of Hanoi and can be combined with a visit to Van Phuc handicraft village (right), or visited on the way to the Perfume Pagoda.

PERFUME PAGODA

North Vietnam's very own Marble Mountains (p236), the **Perfume Pagoda** (Chua Huong; admission 35,000d incl return boat trip) is a striking complex of pagodas and Buddhist shrines built into the karst cliffs of Huong Tich Mountain (Mountain of the Fragrant Traces). Among the better-known sites here are Thien Chu (Pagoda Leading to Heaven); Giai Oan Chu (Purgatorial Pagoda), where the faithful believe deities purify souls, cure sufferings and grant offspring to childless families; and Huong Tich Chu (Pagoda of the Perfumed Vestige). This is a domestic drawcard and it is an interesting experience just to see the Vietnamese tourists at play.

The entertaining boat trip along the scenic waterways between limestone cliffs takes about two hours return; allow a couple more hours return to climb to the top. The path to the summit is steep in places and if it's raining the ground can get *very* slippery. However, the good news is that there is now a cable car to the summit, costing 30,000d one way. A smart combination is to use the cable car to go up and then walk down.

Great numbers of Buddhist pilgrims come here during a festival that begins in the middle of the second lunar month and lasts until the last week of the third lunar month (usually corresponding to March and April). It's *very* busy during this period, especially on the even dates of the lunar month; you'll have a much easier time if you establish the lunar date and plan to go on an odd date. Weekends tend to draw crowds year round, when pilgrims and other visitors spend their time boating, hiking and exploring the caves. Litter and hawkers are part and parcel of the visit, and some hawkers are persistent enough to hassle visitors all the way to the top; you have been warned!

Getting There & Away

The Perfume Pagoda is about 60km southwest of Hanoi by road. Getting there requires a journey first by road, then by river, then on foot or by cable car.

First, travel from Hanoi by car for two hours to the township of My Duc. Vehicles usually drop you about a 15-minute walk from the boat ramp, or you can hop on a *xe om*. Then take a small boat, usually rowed by women, for one hour to the foot of the mountain.

The main pagoda area is about a 4km-steep hike up from where the boat lets you off. Allow yourself at least two hours to make the return trip, longer if it's been raining and is slippery.

Most of the travellers' cafés in Hanoi offer inexpensive tours to the pagoda. You can find day trips as cheap as US$10, inclusive of transport, guide and lunch. For a higher quality small-group tour expect to spend up to US$20. This is one of those places where it is easier to take a tour. Unless you charter a vehicle, it's a real pain trying to do this trip by public transport.

HANDICRAFT VILLAGES

There are numerous villages surrounding Hanoi that specialise in a variety of cottage industries. Visiting these villages can make for a rewarding day trip, though you will need a good guide to make the journey worthwhile.

Bat Trang (Map p126) is known as the 'ceramic village'. Here artisans mass-produce ceramic vases and other pieces in their kilns. It's hot, sweaty work, but the results are superb and very reasonably priced compared with the boutiques in town. There are masses of ceramic shops but poke around down the lanes and behind the shops to find the kilns. Bat Trang is 13km southeast of Hanoi. Public bus 47 runs here from Long Bien bus station (Map pp92–3).

So is known for its delicate noodles. The village even produces the flour from which the noodles are made. The flour is made from yams and cassava (manioc) rather than wheat. So is in Ha Tay province, about 25km southwest of Hanoi.

Van Phuc (Map p126) specialises in silk. Silk cloth is produced here on looms and lots of visitors like to buy or order tailor-made clothes. Many of the fine silk items you see on sale in Hanoi's Pho Hang Gai originate here. There's a small daily fruit-and-vegetable market here in the morning, and a pretty village pagoda with a lily pond. Van Phuc is 8km southwest of Hanoi in Ha Tay province. City bus 1 runs here from Long Bien bus station.

Dong Ky (Map p126) was known as the 'firecracker village' until 1995, when the Vietnamese government banned firecrackers. With that industry now extinguished, the village survives by producing beautiful traditional furniture inlaid with mother-of-pearl. You can have handcrafted furniture custom-made here and exported directly to your door. Dong Ky is 15km northeast of Hanoi.

Le Mat (Map p126), 7km northeast of central Hanoi, is a snake village. The locals raise snakes for upmarket restaurants in Hanoi, as well as spicing up medicinal spirits. Fresh snake cuisine and snake elixir is available at this village, and for around US$10 you can try a set course consisting of snake meat prepared in around 10 different ways. On the 23rd day of the third lunar month is the colourful **Le Mat Festival**, featuring 'snake dances' and other activities.

Other handicraft villages in the region produce conical hats, delicate wooden bird cages, and herbs.

THAY & TAY PHUONG PAGODAS

Stunning limestone outcrops loom up from the emerald green paddy fields and clinging to the cliffs are these two pagodas, about 20 minutes apart from each other by road.

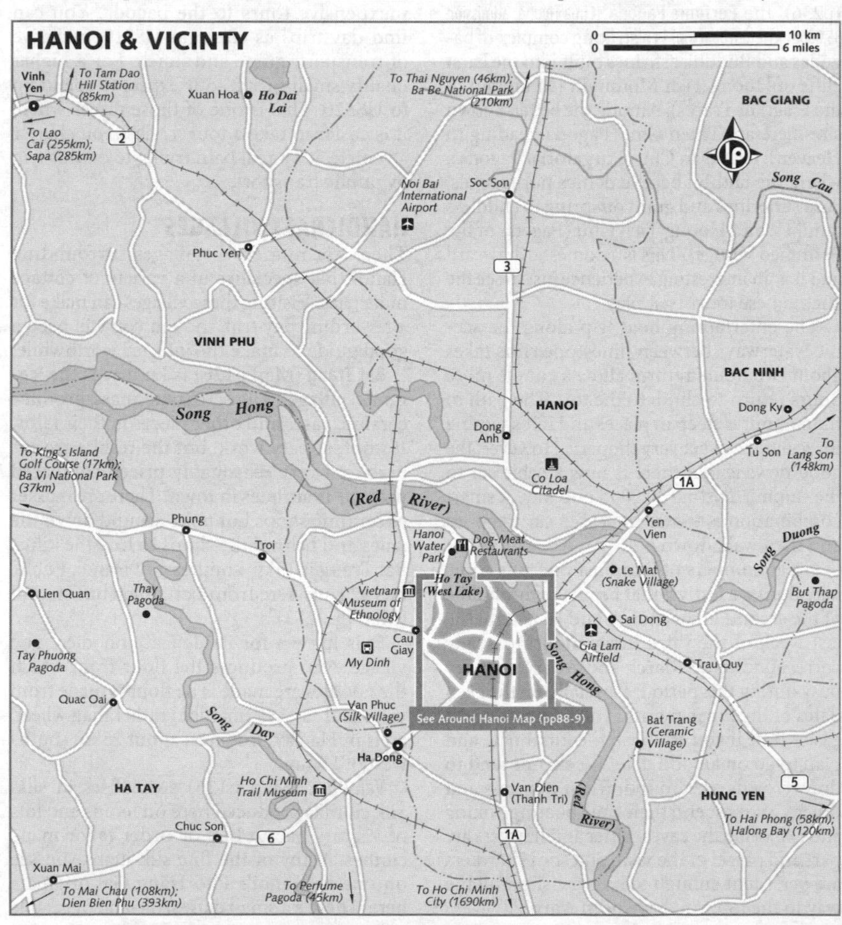

MRS THUYEN, BOAT WOMAN

Anyone who visits the Perfume Pagoda will approach the sacred mountain by rowing boat. Here, one of the rowers tells her story:

'I've rowed tourists to the Perfume Pagoda for about two years now. Our boat group is made up of 27 boats rowed by women who all belong to martyrs' families – our husbands or fathers or children were killed or injured in the war. There are more than 100 of us in the same group, but only 27 of us are allowed to work at one time, so there's an annual lottery to establish which of us will row each year. So I may not work every year, but when I do it's consistent and I get paid 30,000d every day, regardless of how many trips I do, or even if there's no work for a day or two.

'You see our group of martyrs' families has priority for rowing all the foreigners. It's easier because there are fewer people in the boat and if we're lucky we get tips. Other boats have to compete on their own for customers and sometimes might not have any and might not make any money. A boat costs about one million dong, and we all save to buy our own. Every three or four years we have to change the floor of the boat and that costs 300,000d.

'We all also have a plot of land nearby, and we grow and sell things when we're not working on the boats. I grow longan fruit. My husband raises bees; he moves his hives around other people's plantations depending on what's flowering, and pays for the bees' use of the flowers with a litre or two of honey. Honey sells for about 80,000d a litre. Last year was a bad year; my husband only made 50L all year, but in the first three months of this year he's already made 30L.

'I used to be a soldier; that's how I met my husband. Our children are 19, 16 and 14 years old and when they were little I didn't row the boat; I sold jewellery and incense at the pagoda. It's hard work but I think about my children finishing their study and becoming successful and that keeps me going.'

Thay Pagoda (Master's Pagoda; Map p126; admission 5000d), also known as Thien Phuc (Heavenly Blessing), is dedicated to Thich Ca Buddha (Sakyamuni, the historical Buddha). To the left of the main altar is a statue of the 12th-century monk Tu Dao Hanh, the master in whose honour the pagoda is named. To the right is a statue of King Ly Nhan Tong, who is believed to have been a reincarnation of Tu Dao Hanh.

In front of the pagoda is a small stage built on stilts in the middle of a pond; water-puppet shows are staged here during festivals. Follow the path around the outside of the main pagoda building, and take a steep 10-minute climb up to a beautiful smaller pagoda perched high on the rock. Thay Pagoda is a big and confusing complex for non-Buddhists – consider hiring a pagoda guide to get the most from a visit.

The pagoda's **annual festival** is held from the fifth to the seventh days of the third lunar month. Pilgrims and other visitors enjoy watching water-puppet shows, hiking and exploring caves in the area.

Tay Phuong Pagoda (Pagoda of the West; Map p126; admission 5000d), also known as Sung Phuc Pagoda, consists of three single-level structures built in descending order on a hillock said to resemble a buffalo. The figures representing 'the conditions of man' are carved from jackfruit wood, many dating from the 18th century, and are the pagoda's most celebrated feature. The earliest construction here dates from the 8th century. Take the steep steps up to the main pagoda building, then find a path at the back that loops down past the other two pagodas and wanders through the hillside village that surrounds the complex.

Getting There & Away

The pagodas are about 30km west of Hanoi in Ha Tay province. Travel companies in Hanoi offer combined day tours of the Thay and Tay Phuong Pagodas. Alternatively, hire a car and driver for about US$40, and plot a rewarding day trip combining the pagodas and Ba Vi National Park.

BA VI NATIONAL PARK

☎ 034

Centred on scenic Ba Vi Mountain (Nui Ba Vi), **Ba Vi National Park** (☎ 881 205; admission 10,000d, motorbike 5000d) attracts Hanoians looking for a weekend escape from the city. The park has several rare and endangered plants in its protected forest, and its mammals include two species of rare 'flying' squirrel. Human encroachment on the area has made the chances of seeing any of these pretty rare.

There's an orchid garden and a bird garden, and **hiking** opportunities through the forested slopes of the mountain. There's a **temple** to Uncle Ho at the mountain's summit (1276m) – it's a hard but beautiful 30-minute climb up 1229 steps through the forest – with spectacular views of the Red River valley and Hanoi in the distance. At least there are views between April and December when the air is clear; at other times it's damp and misty but eerily atmospheric. The road to the summit car park is seriously steep, slippery and narrow, but road widening is ongoing.

Sleeping & Eating

Ba Vi Guesthouse (☎ 881 197; r 120,000-150,000d) spreads over several blocks in the heart of the park. Prices are an extra 50,000d per room on weekends and there's a big swimming pool that is chaos in the summer months. Go for one of the less-noisy guesthouses away from the pool and restaurant area if you're here on a weekend. You *must* have your passport with you to check into the guesthouse here.

Despite its unpromising appearance, the park restaurant serves good, cheap, fresh-cooked food; a tasty meal for two costs around 50,000d, so make this your lunch stop if you're on a day trip. The toilets are terrible – pee behind a tree.

Getting There & Away

Ba Vi National Park is about 65km west of Hanoi, and the only practical option for visiting is by hired vehicle from Hanoi. Travelling by motorbike, it is possible to visit Ba Vi before taking a beautiful riverside road down to Hoa Binh and onwards into the northwest.

There has been some confusion between attractions near Ba Vi town, which is well away from the park boundaries, and Ba Vi National Park. Make sure your driver knows you want the national park.

CO LOA CITADEL

Dating from the 3rd century BC, **Co Loa Citadel** (Co Loa Thanh; Map p126; admission per person/car 2000/5000d; ⏰ 8am-5pm) was the first fortified citadel in Vietnamese history and became the national capital during the reign of Ngo Quyen (AD 939–44). Only vestiges of the ancient ramparts, which enclosed an area of about 5 sq km, remain.

In the centre of the citadel are temples dedicated to the rule of King An Duong Vuong (257–208 BC), who founded the legendary Thuc dynasty, and his daughter My Nuong (Mi Chau). Legend tells that My Nuong showed her father's magic crossbow trigger, which made him invincible in battle, to her husband, the son of a Chinese general. He stole it and gave it to his father. With this not-so-secret weapon, the Chinese defeated An Duong Vuong, beginning a thousand years of Chinese occupation.

Co Loa Citadel is 16km north of central Hanoi in Dong Anh district, and can be visited as a short detour while on the way to or from Tam Dao Hill Station. Public bus 46 runs here from My Dinh bus station (p122). Buses 15 and 17 run past the access road from Long Bien bus station (Map pp92–3).

TAM DAO HILL STATION

☎ 0211 / elevation 930m

'La Cascade d'Argent' (Silver Waterfall) to the French, and Thac Bac to the Vietnamese, Tam Dao Hill Station was a popular place of escape from the heat of the Red River Delta. Founded in 1907 by the French, most of the grand old colonial villas were destroyed during the Franco–Viet Minh War in the 1950s and the ruins have since been replaced by Soviet-inspired, concrete-box architecture. A somewhat belated effort to restore some of the colonial villas is now under way.

Hanoi residents sometimes call Tam Dao 'the Dalat of the north'. This has more to do with its high elevation and cool climate than any resemblance to Dalat. If you're living in Hanoi and would like to find a summer weekend retreat, it's worth heading up for the cool weather and a change of pace. However, unless you plan to do some serious hiking or bird-watching, there really isn't that much to see and do here.

Tam Dao National Park was designated in 1996 and covers much of the area. Tam Dao means 'Three Islands', and the three summits of Tam Dao Mountain, all about 1400m in height, are sometimes visible to the northeast of the hill station, floating like islands in the mist. The relative dampness and altitude makes the area particularly rich in rainforest and associated animals. There are at least 64 mammal species, including langurs, and 239 bird species in the park, but you'll need a good local guide and be prepared to do some hiking to find them. Illegal hunting remains a big problem.

Remember that it is cool up in Tam Dao and that this part of Vietnam has a distinct winter. Don't be caught unprepared. Hikes vary from half an hour return to the **waterfall**, to eight hours into **primary rainforest**. A guide is essential for the longer treks and can be hired from 50,000d; ask about these at the Mela Hotel (right). The best time to visit is between late April and mid-October, when the mist sometimes lifts and the weather can be fine. As with other popular sites in Vietnam, weekends can be packed with Vietnamese tour groups, so try to make your visit during the week if possible.

The new **Tam Dao Golf and Resort** (☎ 04-736 6457; http://tamdaogolf.com) is causing quite a stir in the capital. Set against the beautiful backdrop of the 'Three Islands', membership starts at a hefty US$13,000 or you can swing your club for just US$30 during the week.

Sleeping & Eating

There's a host of hotels and guesthouses in Tam Dao. The town is easy to navigate, so look around, negotiate and watch out for neighbouring karaoke bars.

Huong Lien Hotel (☎ 824 282; r 150,000d) One of the cheaper hotels amid the misty mountains, it's a family-run place with clean rooms.

Green World Hotel (☎ 824 315; r 180,000-350,000d) The biggest hotel in town, if Tam Dao can be called a town, it has all wood furnishings, sparkling bathrooms and balconies.

Mela Hotel (☎/fax 824 352; r US$45-65) This is a favoured haunt for Hanoi expats looking to escape for the weekend. The most stylish hotel in town, the rooms are seriously smart and the roaring fire downstairs is inviting on a chilly night.

There are hotel restaurants galore and several rows of *com pho* (rice-noodle soup) places in town. Try to avoid eating the local wildlife.

Getting There & Away

Tam Dao is 85km northwest of Hanoi in Vinh Phuc province. Buses run from Kim Ma bus station (p122) in Hanoi to Vinh Yen (20,000d, one hour). From there you can hire a motorbike (about 50,000d one way) to travel the 24km single-lane road that leads to the national park.

Hiring a car and driver for the day from Hanoi will cost about US$50. If you rent a motorbike in Hanoi, the journey time is about two hours, and the last part of the ride into the park is beautiful.

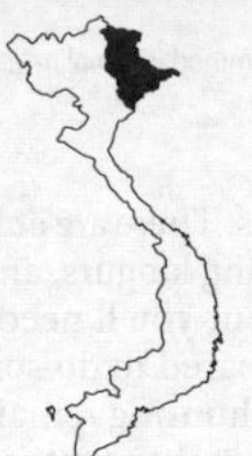

Northeast Vietnam

For most visitors, the northeast is all about Halong Bay. The sublime seascape at this World Heritage site is undoubtedly one of Vietnam's most enchanting experiences. But high up in the rugged mountains of the interior are some of the country's most intriguing destinations and far fewer tourists than in the coastal clusters.

Bizarre but beautiful, Halong Bay is geology gone wild, with hundreds and thousands of limestone pinnacles protruding from the waters. North of Halong Bay is the less-visited Bai Tu Long Bay, where nature's spectacular show continues all the way to the Chinese border. To the south of Halong Bay is Cat Ba Island, a 'lost world' landscape with hiking, biking or just hanging around the order of the day. And just a hydrofoil ride away is Haiphong, the north's major port and a step back in time with wide boulevards and elegant architecture.

Looming above the coast, the brooding mountains of the northeast are another world entirely. The karst connection continues into Cao Bang province, the surreal scenery some of the most stunning in all Vietnam. It is the perfect base for meeting Montagnard minorities and exploring idyllic waterfalls or Ba Be National Park.

Getting back to the basics, this area is a popular route for travelling overland between China and Vietnam. There are two border crossings: one on the coast at Mong Cai that is seldom used, and nother near Lang Son. With all this border traffic, it's looking good for the locals and the northeast is riding on a boom, as the gateway to Hanoi, by land and by sea.

HIGHLIGHTS

- Cruise emerald waters and see where nature has gone wild to create more than 3000 weird and wonderful islands in **Halong Bay** (p136)
- Breach the rugged coast to see the hidden beaches and dense jungle of **Cat Ba Island** (p143)
- Turn the clocks back 10 years to discover the Hanoi of yesteryear in the somnolent port city of **Haiphong** (p132)
- Board a boat to glide through lakes and rivers, and spend the night with a minority family in a homestay at **Ba Be National Park** (p157)
- In a pretty province of waterfalls, caves and superb scenery, check out the crazy karsts of **Cao Bang** (p154)

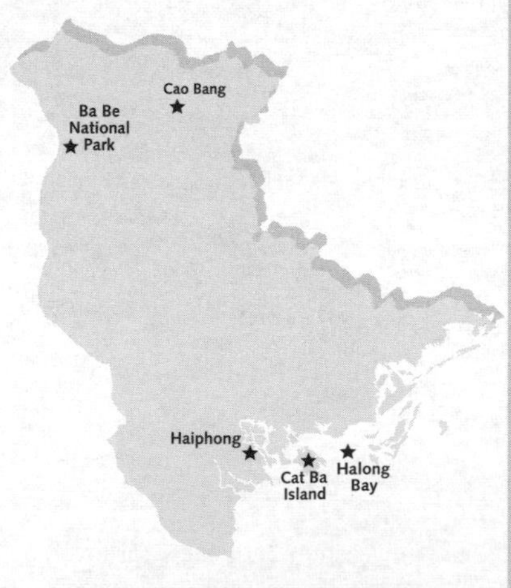

- ELEVATION: 0M-1980M
- BEST TIME TO VISIT: MAR-MAY & SEP-NOV

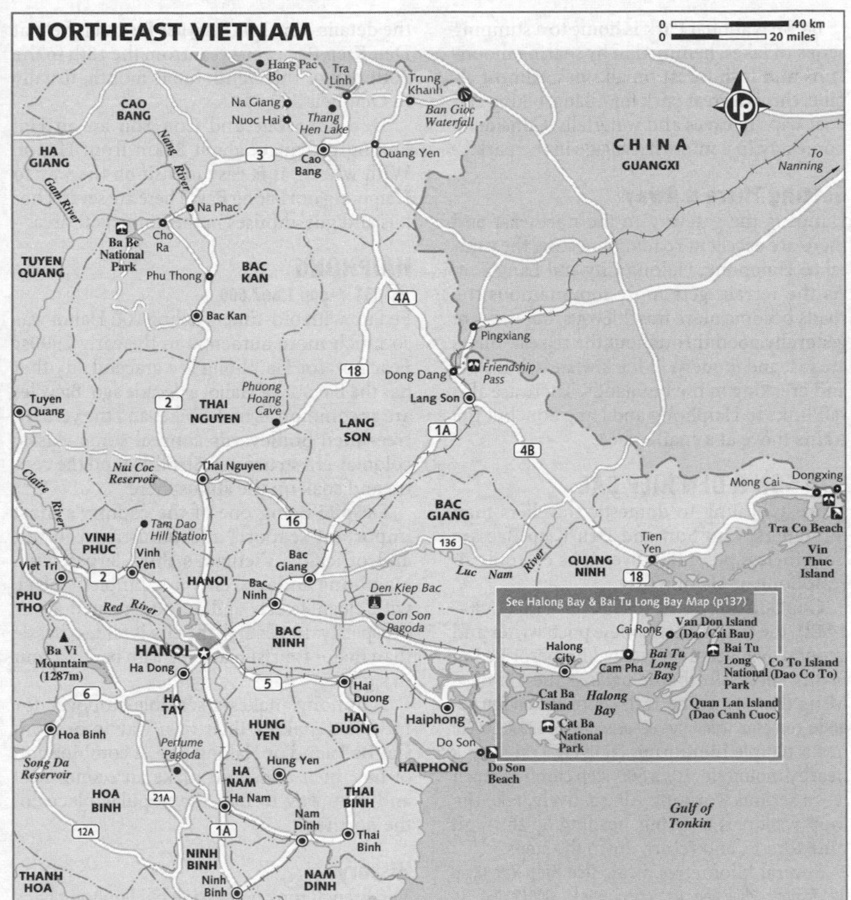

History

Dominated by the Red River basin and the sea, the fertile northeast is the cradle of Vietnamese civilisation. Much of Vietnamese history (and not all of it happy) was made here. Vietnam has had less than cordial relations with the Chinese, who invaded in the 2nd century BC and stuck around for about 1000 years. They were finally vanquished in the 10th century; see the boxed text, p138.

Any time the Chinese wanted to interfere in Vietnam's affairs, it was through the northeast that they approached. The last time was in 1979 to punish the Vietnamese for invading Cambodia (see the boxed text, p152).

As well as invasions, this region has also witnessed an exodus during the late 1970s and early 1980s, as thousands of ethnic-Chinese and later thousands more Vietnamese took to the mountains or the seas to search for a better life in China, Hong Kong and beyond.

National Parks

The beautiful national parks of the northeast all involve a certain amount of water-based activity. Cat Ba National Park, near Halong Bay, is straight out of Lost Valley of the Dinosaurs, a rugged island jutting out of the sea, liberally cloaked in lush jungle.

Further north, Halong Bay becomes Bai Tu Long National Park, a stunning scene of karsts that is every bit the equal of its more illustrious neighbour. Enjoy the beauty without the tourists and explore the hidden beaches.

Ba Be National Park is home to a stunning series of lakes, hemmed in by soaring mountains and lush forest on all sides. Almost alpine, this is a great park for hiking, biking and boat trips to caves and waterfalls. Consider a homestay in a minority village in the park.

Getting There & Away

Hanoi is the gateway to the northeast and there are excellent roads connecting the capital to Haiphong, Halong City and Lang Son. As the terrain gets more mountainous the roads become more mischievous, but they are generally good throughout the region. Buses are fast and modern in the lowlands, but slow and creaking in the highlands. There are also rail links to Haiphong and Lang Son, but the trains move at a snail's pace.

CON SON & DEN KIEP BAC

More appealing to domestic travellers than foreigners, Con Son and Den Kiep Bac are nonetheless potential diversions en route to Haiphong or Halong City.

Con Son was home to Nguyen Trai (1380–1442), the famed Vietnamese poet, writer and general. Nguyen Trai assisted Emperor Le Loi in his successful battle against the Chinese Ming dynasty in the 15th century. **Con Son pagoda complex** (admission per person/vehicle 3000/5000d) has a temple honouring Nguyen Trai atop a nearby mountain. It's a 600-step climb to reach it – a serious workout. Alternatively, take the loop walk past a spring, heading up through pine forests, and return down the steps.

Several kilometres away, **Den Kiep Bac** (Kiep Bac Temple; admission per person/vehicle 2000/5000d) is dedicated to Tran Hung Dao (1228–1300). An outstanding general of renowned bravery, his armies defeated 500,000 Mongol invaders in the mid-1280s. Perhaps second only to Ho Chi Minh in the historic hall of fame, he is a revered Vietnamese folk hero.

This beautiful temple was founded in 1300 and built on the site where Tran Hung Dao is said to have died. The temple was built not only for the general, but also to honour other notable members of his family. One was the general's daughter, Quyen Thanh, who married Tran Nhat Ton, who was credited with founding the Truc Lam sect of Vietnamese Buddhism.

Within the temple complex there's a small exhibition on Tran Hung Dao's exploits, but you'll need a Vietnamese speaker to translate the details. The **Tran Hung Dao Festival** is held at Den Kiep Bac every year from the 18th to the 20th day of the eighth lunar month, usually in October.

Den Kiep Bac and Con Son are in Hai Duong province, about 80km from Hanoi. With wheels, it is easy to visit on the way to Haiphong or Halong Bay. There are several hotels and guesthouses in the immediate area.

HAIPHONG

☎ 031 / pop 1,667,600

Fed up with old-timers telling you Hanoi was so much more authentic in the early 1990s? Fear not, for Haiphong is a graceful city that has the flavour of Hanoi a decade ago. Bicycles are as common as motorbikes and the verdant tree-lined boulevards conceal some classic colonial-era structures. Stroll around the centre and soak up the atmosphere.

Despite being one of the country's most important seaports and industrial centres, and officially Vietnam's third-largest city, Haiphong today seems a somnolent place with clean streets and an understated air of prosperity. In general, the city is far less hassle than major tourist magnets, with barely a tout in sight.

Haiphong makes a sensible stopover for travellers making their own way to or from Cat Ba Island or Halong Bay. A combination of bus, boat and train make an economical and easy way to link the popular places of the northeast.

History

The French took possession of Haiphong back in 1874 when it was just a small market town. The city developed rapidly, becoming a major port. Heavy industry was a natural choice thanks to its proximity to coal supplies.

One of the most immediate causes of the Franco-Viet Minh War was the infamous French bombardment of the 'native quarters' of Haiphong in 1946, in which hundreds of civilians were killed and injured. A contemporary French account estimated civilian deaths at more than 6000.

Haiphong came under US air and naval attack between 1965 and 1972. In May 1972 President Nixon ordered the mining of Haiphong Harbour to cut the flow of Soviet military supplies to North Vietnam. As part of the Paris cease-fire accords of 1973, the USA agreed to help clear the mines from Haiphong

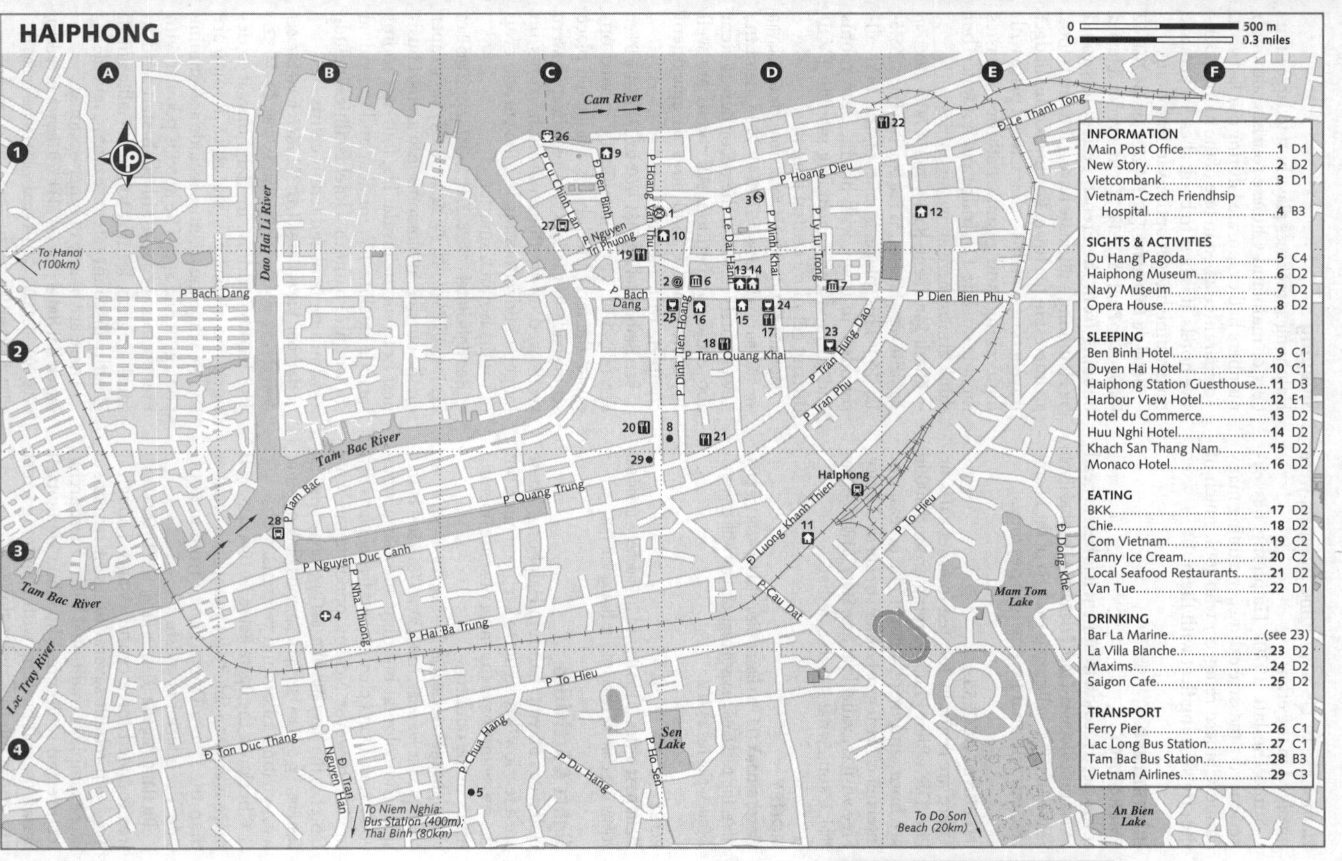
HAIPHONG
0 500 m
0 0.3 miles
INFORMATION
Main Post Office 1 D1
New Story 2 D2
Vietcombank 3 D1
Vietnam-Czech Friendhsip Hospital 4 B3
SIGHTS & ACTIVITIES
Du Hang Pagoda 5 C4
Haiphong Museum 6 D2
Navy Museum 7 D2
Opera House 8 D2
SLEEPING
Ben Binh Hotel 9 C1
Duyen Hai Hotel 10 C1
Haiphong Station Guesthouse 11 D3
Harbour View Hotel 12 E1
Hotel du Commerce 13 D2
Huu Nghi Hotel 14 D2
Khach San Thang Nam 15 D2
Monaco Hotel 16 D2
EATING
BKK 17 D2
Chie 18 D2
Com Vietnam 19 C2
Fanny Ice Cream 20 C2
Local Seafood Restaurants 21 D2
Van Tue 22 D1
DRINKING
Bar La Marine (see 23)
La Villa Blanche 23 D2
Maxims 24 D2
Saigon Cafe 25 D2
TRANSPORT
Ferry Pier 26 C1
Lac Long Bus Station 27 C1
Tam Bac Bus Station 28 B3
Vietnam Airlines 29 C3
Cam River
Dao Hai Li River
Tam Bac River
Loc Tray River
Mam Tom Lake
An Bien Lake
Sen Lake
Haiphong
To Hanoi (100km)
To Do Son Beach (20km)
To Niem Nghia Bus Station (400m); Thai Binh (80km)
Đ Le Thanh Tong
P Dien Bien Phu
P Hoang Dieu
P Ly Tu Trong
P Minh Khai
P Le Dai Hanh
P Hoang Van Thu
Đ Ben Binh
P Cu Chinh Lan
P Nguyen Tri Phuong
P Bach Dang
P Dinh Tien Hoang
P Tran Quang Khai
P Tran Hung Dao
P Tran Phu
Đ Luong Khanh Thien
P Cau Dat
P To Hieu
Đ Dong Khe
P Quang Trung
P Tam Bac
P Nguyen Duc Canh
P Nha Thuong
P Hai Ba Trung
P Ho Sen
P Du Hang
P Chua Hang
Đ Tran Nguyen Han
Đ Ton Duc Thang

Harbour – 10 US navy mine-sweepers were involved in the effort.

Since the late 1970s Haiphong has experienced a massive exodus, including many ethnic-Chinese refugees, who took much of the city's fishing fleet with them.

Information

EMERGENCY

If you need medical treatment it is best to head to Hanoi. **Vietnam-Czech Friendship Hospital** (Benh Vien Viet-Tiep; Pho Nha Thuong) is the best of the hospitals, but rely on it for emergencies only.

INTERNET ACCESS

There are centrally located internet cafés on Pho Dien Bien Phu, charging around 3000d per hour, and there seems to be at least one internet café on most other streets in the city. Free wi-fi is available at **New Story** (84 Pho Dien Bien Phu), a somewhat kitsch café-bar.

MONEY

Vietcombank (11 Pho Hoang Dieu) Not far from the post office, this beautifully housed bank can deal with cash and cheques, plus has an ATM.

POST

Main post office (3 Pho Nguyen Tri Phuong) A grand old yellow dame on the corner of Pho Hoang Van Thu.

Sights & Activities

Half a day on your hands in Haiphong? There are a few low-key sights to keep you busy, but the museums have the most obscure opening times in the country.

Haiphong Museum (Pho Dien Bien Phu; admission free; 8-10.30am Tue & Thu, 7.30-9.30pm Wed & Sun) is in a splendid colonial building and has a small collection. Don't change your travel plans just to visit, however. Nearby, opposite the Navy Hotel, is the **Navy Museum** (Bao Tang Hai Quan; Pho Dien Bien Phu; 8-11am Tue, Thu & Sat), possibly popular with visiting sailors and veterans.

Check out the **Opera House** (Pho Quang Trung) if there is anyone able to let you inside. Smaller than the Hanoi Opera House from the outside, the interior is lavish.

Du Hang Pagoda (Chua Du Hang; 121 Pho Chua Hang) was founded three centuries ago. Though it has been rebuilt several times, it remains a fine example of traditional Vietnamese architecture and sculpture. Pho Chua Hang itself is narrow and bustling with Haiphong street life, and is fun to wander along.

Sleeping

Haiphong sometimes plays host to large numbers of mainland Chinese tourists, although numbers had evaporated during our last visit. To guarantee a bed in one of the more expensive hotels, it is best to book ahead. There are no genuine budget options in Haiphong.

Hotel du Commerce (384 2706; fax 384 2560; 62 Pho Dien Bien Phu; r US$10-18) In a venerable old building from the French period, this could be Haiphong's ultimate retreat if tourists took an interest in the town. Fortunately for budget travellers, it remains a characterful place with high ceilings and gigantic bathrooms. Basics include satellite TV, fridge and hot water, but think atmosphere above amenities.

Khach San Thang Nam (374 7216; vntourism.hp@bdvn.vnmail.vnd.net; 55 Pho Dien Bien Phu; r US$15-18) This place is one of the best all-rounders in town, with bright, clean rooms and all mod cons, including satellite TV. It doesn't get more central than this.

Monaco Hotel (374 6468; monacohotel@hn.vnn.vn; 103 Pho Dien Bien Phu; r US$20-40) One of the newer hotels in town, the décor here is a cut above the competition. All rooms are well appointed, but US$40 buys an apartment complete with a kitchen.

Ben Binh Hotel (384 2260; fax 384 2524; 6 Đ Ben Binh; r US$25-40) Conveniently located opposite the ferry pier, this is a huge old place set in spacious gardens. The old cheapies were swallowed up by the renovation, so it's no longer a budget option, but the current crop of rooms is much smarter.

Huu Nghi Hotel (382 3244; fax 382 3245; 62 Pho Dien Bien Phu; r US$35-45) An ugly skyscraper on the outside, it blossoms into a smart business hotel on the inside. The four-star rooms include satellite TV, minibar and individual shower and bathtub. Hotel facilities include a swimming pool and tennis courts.

Harbour View Hotel (382 7827; www.harbourviewvietnam.com; 4 Pho Tran Phu; s/d US$70/80) The leading address in Haiphong, it is designed in classic colonial style. Rooms are stylish, while the facilities include a swimming pool, gym and spa. The hotel is popular with French tour groups, although staff tend to speak English, leading to much Gallic angst. Healthy discount rates are often available.

There are plenty of other options:

Duyen Hai Hotel (384 2134; 6 Đ Nguyen Tri Phuong; r 200,000-300,000d) A good-value central option if other places are full.

NORTHEAST VIETNAM

Haiphong Station Guesthouse (☎ 385 5391; 75 Đ Luong Khanh Thien; r 150,000-180,000d; ❄) Overpriced given the air of dereliction, but it's literally in the train station for an early ride.

Eating

Haiphong is noted for its sumptuous fresh seafood, which is available at all the popular restaurants in town.

The best options for cheap eats are the glut of eateries on Pho Minh Khai. Another good hunting ground is Pho Quang Trung, with a whole strip of point-and-cook tanks outside. This strip is also brimming with popular *bia hoi* (beer) bars and cafés.

Fanny Ice Cream (☎ 153 0475; 4 Pho Hoang Van Thu; ice cream from 10,000d) Famous in Hanoi, Fanny has expanded to Haiphong. Indulge in fine French ice cream while strolling along the old French boulevards.

Com Vietnam (☎ 384 1698; 4 Pho Hoang Van Thu; mains 20,000-60,000d) A blink-and-you'll-miss-it courtyard restaurant, it's consistently popular with the local crowd, thanks to affordable local seafood and Vietnamese specialities.

Van Tue (☎ 374 6338; 1 Pho Hoang Dieu; mains 20,000-150,000d) This is one of the biggest Vietnamese restaurants in town, with a menu to match. The seafood selection is dizzying, as is the home-brewed Czech beer if you drink too much.

BKK (☎ 382 1018; 22 Pho Minh Khai; mains 30,000-60,000d) The card proclaims 'trendy Thai restaurant' and it's damn right. Set in a thoughtfully restored colonial-era house, this is boutique dining. The menu includes all the Thai favourites, plus a serious amount of seafood. It can double as a bar for those looking for clever cocktails and a sophisticated ambience.

Chie (☎ 382 1018; 18 Pho Tran Quang Khai; mains from US$3-15) Probably the best Japanese restaurant in town – yes, believe it or not, there is more than one. Exquisite presentation and serious sushi and sashimi thanks to an endless supply of fresh fish.

Drinking & Entertainment

It's hardly Hanoi, let alone HCMC, but there is a subtle buzz to the place. Bia Haiphong is the local brew and it gets the thumbs up from aficionados of the amber nectar.

La Villa Blanche (Pho Tran Hung Dao). For a one-size-fits-all night stop, head to this old French mansion. Aptly nicknamed the White House in English, it has a shady garden housing several bargain *bia hoi* shops. It fills up with locals from mid-afternoon and the food is impressive.

Bar la Marine (☎ 382 2934; Pho Ly Tu Trong) In the same compound as La Villa Blanche is this claustrophobic cavern of a place that is a minor institution with Francophone expats. Mind your head, particularly if partaking of the extensive spirit selection.

Saigon Cafe (cnr Pho Dien Bien Phu & Pho Dinh Tien Hoang) One of the trendiest spots in town, it was about to get trendier thanks to an expensive renovation. A loungey café-bar with an extensive food and drinks menu, plus live music most evenings.

Maxims (☎ 3822 934; 51B Pho Dien Bien Phu) A sort of vague relation to the famous Maxims in Saigon, it has live music from classical to jazz most nights.

Getting There & Away

AIR

Vietnam Airlines (☎ 9381 0890; www.vietnamair.com.vn; 30 Pho Hoang Van Thu) serves the Haiphong–Ho Chi Minh City (HCMC) and the Haiphong–Danang routes.

BOAT

All boats leave from the **ferry pier** (Đ Ben Binh), 10 minutes' walk from the centre of town.

Hydrofoils leave for Cat Ba (45 minutes) three times a day in the high summer season and just once a day the rest of the year. Summer season services depart between 7am and 11am. The rest of the year, the services leave at about 9am. **Transtour** (☎ 384 1009) runs the Mekong Express (100,000d), which is the safest and most comfortable option. **Tahaco** (☎ 374 7055) has smaller hydrofoils, which are cheaper at 70,000d. There are no longer hydrofoils operating to Halong City, as the road journey is faster.

Transtour also has a fast boat to Mong Cai (200,000d, four hours) leaving at 7.30am daily. There is also a slow ferry (70,000d, eight hours) departing daily at 6pm. Do the maths, it arrives at an ungodly hour.

BUS

Haiphong has three long-distance bus stations. Buses to Hanoi (35,000d, two hours) leave from **Tam Bac bus station** (Pho Tam Bac) about every 10 minutes throughout the day. Buses to points south such as Ninh Binh leave from **Niem Nghia bus station** (Đ Tran Nguyen Han).

Lac Long bus station (Pho Cu Chinh Lan) has buses to Bai Chay (Halong City; 25,000d, 1½ hours), and from there connections to Mong Cai on the Chinese border by boat or road. Lac Long also has buses to/from Hanoi, convenient for those connecting with the Cat Ba hydrofoil.

CAR & MOTORBIKE

Haiphong is 103km from Hanoi on Hwy 5. This expressway (Vietnam's first) between the two cities was completed in 1999 and is one of the biggest and busiest roads in the country.

TRAIN

Haiphong is not on the main line between Hanoi and HCMC, but there is a spur line connecting it to Hanoi. There's one express train daily to Long Bien station (24,000d, two hours) at 6.10pm and several slower trains (18,000d, 2½ hours).

There are two train stations within the Haiphong city limits. Thuong Li train station is in the western suburbs of the city, while Haiphong train station is right in the city centre.

Getting Around

Haiphong is serviced by several companies that use metered, air-con taxis. Try **Haiphong Taxi** (☎ 383 8383) or **Taxi Mai Linh** (☎ 383 3833). There are also plenty of *cyclos* (pedicabs) and *xe om* (motorbike taxis) cruising around town (between 5000d and 15,000d, depending on distance).

AROUND HAIPHONG

Do Son Beach

Do Son Beach, 21km southeast of central Haiphong, is a honky-tonk seaside resort that is popular with Vietnamese for karaoke and massage, otherwise known as singing and sex. The hilly, 4km-long promontory ends with a string of islets, and the peninsula's nine hills are known as Cuu Long Son (Nine Dragons). There are plenty of colourful fishing boats on the water and a long promenade, but the beaches are disappointingly small and disappear completely at high tide. The resort is not all it's cracked up to be (or should that be: it's more cracked up than it used to be?). Many hotels are looking rather forlorn.

In 1994 the first casino to open in Vietnam since 1975 commenced operation as a joint venture between the government and a Hong Kong company. Foreigners are welcome to win or lose their fortunes at **Doson Resort Hotel** (☎ 031-386 4888; www.dosonresorthotel.com.vn), but your average Vietnamese person is barred from entering the casino.

Do Son town is famous for its ritual **buffalo fights**, the finals of which are held annually on the 10th day of the eighth lunar month, usually late September or October, commemorating the date when the leader of an 18th-century peasant rebellion was killed here.

HALONG BAY

☎ 033

Majestic and mysterious, inspiring and imperious: words alone cannot do justice to the natural wonder that is Halong Bay. Imagine 3000 or more incredible islands rising from the emerald waters of the Gulf of Tonkin and you have a vision of breathtaking beauty. Halong Bay is pure art, a priceless collection of unfinished sculptures hewn from the hand of nature.

In 1994 it was designated a World Heritage site. Visitors can't help but compare the magical, mystical landscape of limestone islets to Guilin in China and Krabi in southern Thailand, but in reality Halong Bay is more spectacular. These tiny islands are dotted with beaches and grottoes created by wind and waves, and have sparsely forested slopes ringing with birdsong.

Beyond the breathtaking vistas on a boat cruise through the bay, visitors to Halong come to explore the caves – some of which are beautifully illuminated for the benefit of tourists – and to hike in Cat Ba National Park. There are few real beaches in Halong Bay, but Lan Ha Bay (off the coast of Cat Ba Island) has more than 100 sandy strips.

Halong City is the gateway to Halong Bay but not the ideal introduction to this incredible World Heritage site. Developers have not been kind to the city and most visitors sensibly opt for tours that include sleeping on a boat in the bay. In short, Halong Bay is the attraction; Halong City is not. For more on tours in and around the bay, see the boxed text (p140).

As the number-one tourist attraction in the northeast, Halong Bay draws a steady stream of visitors year-round. From February to April the weather in this region is often cool and drizzly. The ensuing fog can make visibility low, but this adds an ethereal air to the place and the temperature rarely falls below

NORTHEAST VIETNAM

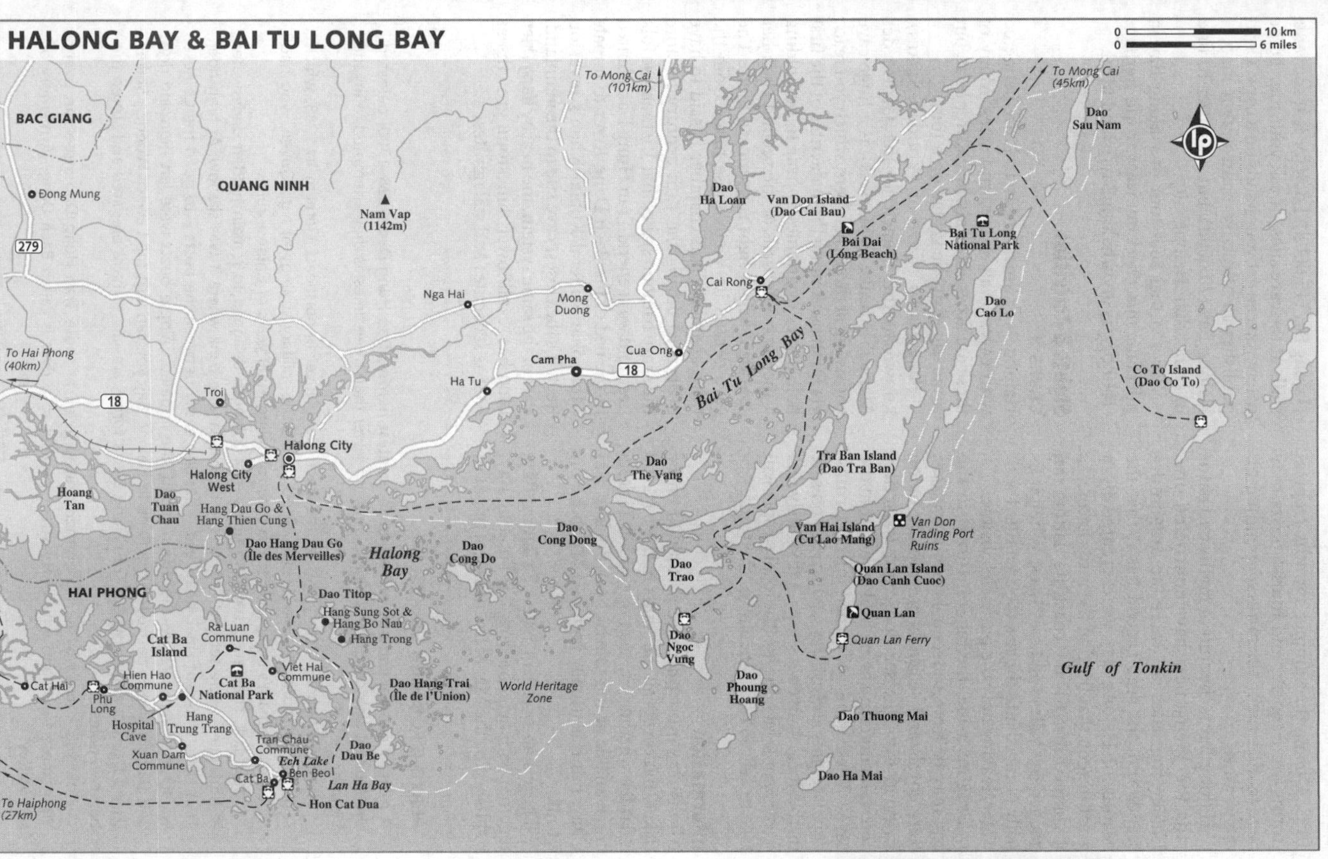

NORTHEAST VIETNAM

10°C. During the summer months tropical storms are frequent, and tourist boats may have to alter their itineraries, depending on the weather.

Halong Bay is the stuff of myths and naturally the Vietnamese have concocted one. *Halong* translates as 'where the dragon descends into the sea'. Legend has it that the islands of Halong Bay were created by a great dragon that lived in the mountains. As it charged towards the coast, its flailing tail gouged out valleys and crevasses. When it finally plunged into the sea, the area filled with water, leaving only the pinnacles visible.

Dragons aside, the biggest threat to the bay may be from souvenir-hunting tourists. Rare corals and seashells are rapidly being stripped from the sea floor, and stalactites and stalagmites are being broken off from the caves. These items get turned into key rings, paperweights and ashtrays, which are on sale in the local souvenir shops. Obviously the fewer people buy, the less the local people will take to sell, so don't encourage the trade.

Information

All visitors must purchase a 30,000d entry ticket that covers all the sights in the bay. It's a flat fee whether you visit one or all. Tickets are available at the tourist boat dock in Bai Chay, but it is usually included for those on a tour.

There's an excellent map of Halong Bay, together with neighbouring Bai Tu Long Bay, published by the Management Department of Halong Bay (15,000d). Look for it at souvenir stalls at the cave sites, or ask your tour guide where you can get your hands on a copy. Covit publishes an attractive hand-drawn map of Halong Bay (20,000d), but it's easier to find in Hanoi than Halong City.

For a virtual 360° tour of Halong Bay in full panorama, check out www.world-heritage-tour.org/asia/vn/halongBay/island.html.

Sights & Activities

CAVES

Halong Bay's limestone islands are peppered with caves of all shapes and sizes. Many of these are accessible only by charter boat, but some can easily be visited on a tour.

Hang Dau Go (Cave of Wooden Stakes), known to the French as the Grotte des Merveilles (Cave of Marvels), is a huge cave consisting of three chambers, which you reach via 90 steps. Among the stalactites of the first hall, scores of gnomes appear to be holding a meeting. The walls of the second chamber sparkle if bright light is shone on them. The cave derives its Vietnamese name from the third chamber. This chamber is said to have been used during the 13th century to store the sharp bamboo stakes that Vietnamese folk hero and war general Tran Hung Dao planted in the bed of the Bach Dang River to impale Mongolian general Kublai Khan's invasion fleet. It's the closest cave site to the mainland. Part of the same system, the nearby **Hang Thien Cung** has 'cauliflower' limestone growths as well as stalactites and stalagmites.

PLAYING FOR HIGH STAKES

A military general and one of Vietnam's greatest heroes, Tran Hung Dao (1228–1300) defeated the Mongol warriors of the Chinese army no fewer than three times as they attempted to invade Vietnam.

His most famous victory was at the Bach Dang River in northeast Vietnam in 1288, which secured the country's sovereignty. He borrowed the military strategy of Ngo Quyen, who had regained Vietnam's independence in 939, following 1000 years of Chinese rule.

After dark, sharpened bamboo poles – of a length designed to remain hidden underwater at high tide – were set vertically in the river, near the bank where it was shallow. At high tide, Tran Hung Dao sent small boats out – passing easily between the posts – to goad the Chinese warships to approach. As the tide receded, the impaled Chinese boats were left high and dry, and flaming arrows destroyed the fleet. In Halong Bay you can visit the Cave of Wooden Stakes (Hang Dau Go; above), where Tran Hung Dao's forces are said to have prepared and stored the bamboo poles.

Now you know why he is commemorated in all of those Tran Hung Dao streets in every Vietnamese town, and why every street parallel to a river is called Bach Dang, in memory of the victory.

HALONG BAY'S VERY OWN LOCH NESS MONSTER

The dragon that gave birth to Halong Bay may be legend, but sailors have often reported sightings of a mysterious marine creature of gargantuan proportions known as the *tarasque*. The more paranoid elements of the military suspect it's an imperialist spy submarine, while eccentric travellers believe they have discovered Vietnam's version of the Loch Ness monster. Meanwhile, the monster – or whatever it is – continues to haunt Halong Bay, unfettered by the marine police, Vietnam Tourism and the immigration authorities. Enterprising Vietnamese boat owners have made a cottage industry out of the creature, offering cash-laden tourists the chance to rent a junk and pursue the *tarasque* before it gets bored and swims away.

Hang Sung Sot is a popular cave to visit. It too has three vast and beautiful chambers, in the second of which there's an astonishing pink-lit rock phallus, which is regarded as a fertility symbol. 'Penis rock' is the only way to describe it. It, too, requires a hike up steps to reach it, and a loop walk through the cool interior takes you back to the bay. **Hang Bo Nau**, another impressive cave, can be visited nearby.

Hang Trong (Drum Grotto) is so named because when the wind blows through its many stalactites and stalagmites, visitors think they can hear the sound of distant drumbeats.

Exactly which of the caves you visit will probably be decided on the day you travel. It depends on several factors, including the weather, number of other boats in the vicinity, and the number of people putting environmental pressure on the caves.

ISLANDS

Dao Tuan Chau (Tuan Chau Island), just 5km west of Bai Chay (western Halong City), is one of the few islands in Halong Bay that has seen any development. For many years the only accommodation was in Ho Chi Minh's former summer residence, an elegant but decaying structure. However, all this changed as the island rebranded itself **Tuan Chau International Recreation Complex** (☎ 842 115; aulaco@hn.vnn.vn; r US$80-110; ❄ 💻 🏊), complete with aquarium, circus, golf course and private villas. There are more than 300 rooms in this vast complex. The beachside rooms are tasteful and the top rate includes steam baths and saunas in the rooms.

Dao Titop (Titop Island) is a small island in the middle of the bay with a small, somewhat scruffy beach. Ignore its dubious charms and make for the summit of the island, which offers one of the best panorama views of Halong Bay. It's cheaper than a chopper.

Cat Ba Island (p143) is the best known and most developed of Halong Bay's islands.

KAYAKING

A leisurely paddle among the karsts is an activity that has taken off in recent years and Halong Bay is now following hard on the heels of Krabi in Thailand as kayaking capital of Southeast Asia. Many of the boat tours to Halong Bay include the option of kayaking into hollow karsts or through a floating village. Specialist operator **Handspan Adventure Travel** (☎ in Hanoi 04-926 0581; www.handspan.com; 80 Pho Ma May) was one of the first to offer kayaking and operates a private island camp near Quan Lan Island.

Getting There & Away

AIR

Northern Airport Flight Service Company (☎ 04-827 4409; fax 827 2780; 173 Pho Truong Chinh, Hanoi) offers a helicopter charter service from Gia Lam in Hanoi to Halong Bay on Saturday from 8am. Free transfers are available from the Sofitel Metropole Hotel (p110). The cost for the charter service is US$175 per person, but it only runs with a minimum of six guests. The same helicopters can be privately chartered for US$3695 round trip.

WATCH THOSE VALUABLES!

Take real care with your valuables when cruising the waters of Halong Bay. Do not leave valuables unattended as they might grow legs and walk. Always try and ensure there is someone you know and trust watching your valuables on a day cruise. When it comes to overnight cruises, most boats have lockable cabins. Also take care with cameras and other items when your tour boat is approached by smaller, nimbler boats, as snatch thefts are not unknown.

BUS & BOAT

For more on tours to Halong Bay, see the boxed text below. It is hard to do it any cheaper on your own, but some travellers prefer to steer their own course. Travelling independently allows you to take more or less time in places, depending on the weather. The downside is that it is hard to arrange an overnight on a boat this way. You can take a bus to Halong City from Hanoi (40,000d, 3½ hours) and book a passage on a Cat Ba tourist boat (130,000d including entry ticket, six hours). This boat takes in the main sites and drops you at Ben Beo harbour. Then chill out on Cat Ba before taking a hydrofoil to Haiphong and a bus to Hanoi. Alternatively, run the route in reverse and try and hook up with a tour boat in Cat Ba.

CRUISING THE KARSTS: TOURS TO HALONG BAY

Don't even think about a day trip to Halong, as the real beauty of the bay is best experienced from the deck of a junk over a gin and tonic as the sun sinks into the horizon. Many travellers to this part of the country book a one- or two-night Halong Bay tour at cafés or hotels in Hanoi. While we don't usually promote the tour option, Halong Bay is hard to explore properly without the services of an experienced tour company. However, for those with a bit more money to spend, there are lots of specialised boat companies offering excursions in the bay. Tourists travelling on inclusive tours through Vietnam have the Halong experience aboard a luxury junk. There are also now some genuine sailing junks operating in the bay and these are able to explore further afield when the wind is up. Finally, there is the option of a luxurious replica paddle ship.

Budget trips sold out of Hanoi are reasonably priced, starting from US$15 per person for a dodgy day trip and rising to as much as US$100 for two nights on the bay with kayaking. Remember, you get what you pay for and the cheaper the tour, the more basic the boat, the meals and the service. We get heaps of complaints about poor service, bad food and rats running around the boats, but these tend to be on the cheapest of the cheap tours. Spend a little more and enjoy the experience a lot more. Most tours include transport, meals, the boat tour and, sometimes, island hikes. Drinks are extra and are generally more expensive than on the mainland.

If you book a tour there is always a small chance that the boat-trip part may be cancelled due to bad weather. This may actually entitle you to a partial refund, but remember that the boat trip is only a small portion of the cost of the journey. Depending on the number of people in the group, you probably won't get back more than a handful of dollars if the boats don't sail.

For a list of reliable operators offering two- and three-day tours of the bay, check out the travel agents in Hanoi (p91) or in the Transport chapter (p490).

Boat Operators

There are hundreds of boats plying the waters these days. The following is just a selection of the most interesting companies. For more on the government-run boats that are available for charter, see opposite.

Emeraude Classic Cruise (☎ 04-934 0888; www.emeraude-cruises.com; s/d US$245/290) The *Emeraude* is a replica paddle steamer that cruises the waters of Halong Bay daily. The smart cabins include hot-water showers, meals are served buffet style and the upper deck and bar offer superb views. The main drawback is that the cruise is relatively short compared with the competition. Plans are afoot to build a second boat, which should make two-nighters a possibility.

Halong Ginger (☎ 04-984 2807; www.cruisehalong.com; d from US$373) This beautiful junk is visible from a distance thanks to its trademark ginger sails. Well finished throughout, it also has a good reputation for its food.

Huong Hai Junks (☎ 033-845 042; www.halongtravels.com; s/d US$125/220) The leading boat company in Halong Bay, Huong Hai has a fleet of traditional junks that are all kitted out to a three-star standard. Most of the boats have about a dozen cabins and include an open-plan restaurant and bar on the upper floor.

Tropical Sails (☎ 04-923 2559; www.tropical-sails.com; s/d from US$127/196) This small outfit operates some of the only junks with working sails, allowing the boats to get up a head of steam on a windy day. Most trips venture further afield to the southern reaches of Bai Tu Long Bay. The company also runs the *Dragon's Pearl*, a larger luxury junk with 12 cabins.

Getting Around

You won't see much unless you take a boat tour of the islands and their grottoes. For those travelling independently, life has gotten much easier under the watch of **Halong Bay Management Department** (☎ 846 592; http://halong.org.vn/; 166 Đ Le Thanh Tong). It regulates pricing for cruises on the bay and has a published list in its office at the Bai Chay tourist dock. Some of the staff speak English and can usually hook you up with other people. Be aware that the tourist boat dock is a bit of a circus, as dozens of boats unload one set of passengers and welcome another. There are usually hundreds of people milling about around midday.

There is no need to rent a whole boat for yourself, as there are plenty of other travellers, Vietnamese and foreign, to share with. The official prices are ridiculously reasonable at 30,000/40,000d for a four-/six-hour cruise. Whole boats can be chartered starting from 100,000/140,000/160,000/220,000d per hour for a no-star/1-star/2-star/3-star boat respectively – an affordable indulgence for those wanting some privacy. Boats to Cat Ba Island cost 100,000d per person or from 1,000,000d for a charter.

HALONG CITY

☎ 033 / pop 149,900

If Halong Bay is heaven, Halong City can be hell. Overdeveloped but underloved, the hideous high-rise hotels come in every shade of pastel and the beaches are definitely not the best in the region. However, the majority of food, accommodation and other life-support systems for Halong Bay are found in Halong City. The capital of Quang Ninh province, it is sin city, with 'massage' heavily promoted at every hotel. The town draws large numbers of domestic tourists and, until recently, was a major magnet for Chinese tourists. Suddenly they stopped coming, giving birth to a million conspiracy theories about bankrupting hotels to buy them out.

Orientation

Halong City is bisected by a bay, and the most important district for travellers is called Bai Chay. Located on the western side, Bai Chay is closer to Hanoi and offers a better choice of hotels and restaurants. It's also where the majority of tourist boats are moored.

A short ferry ride (500d) across the bay takes you to the Hon Gai district. Hon Gai is the main port district for coal exports, which means it's a bit dirty, but at least there is some local flavour.

There is a bridge nearing completion to finally link Bai Chay and Hon Gai, which is good news for everyone (except perhaps the ferry captains). It will have opened by the time you read this.

District names are important: most long-distance buses will be marked 'Bai Chay' or 'Hon Gai' rather than 'Halong City'.

Information

Industrial & Commercial Bank (Đ Le Thanh Tong) Useful ATM for those staying in Hon Gai.

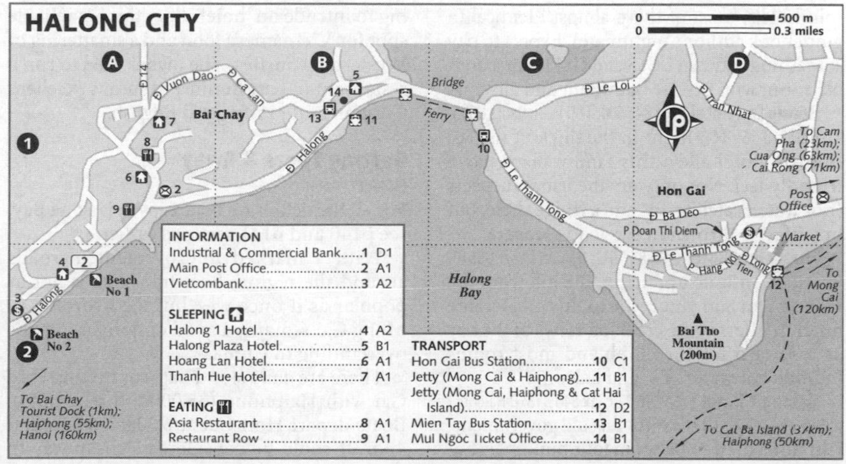

Main post office (Đ Halong) Along with the usual postal services, there's cheap and fast internet access with plenty of webcams.

Vietcombank (Đ Halong) A new and more convenient branch in Bai Chay with the usual exchange facilities and ATM.

Beaches

The 'beaches' around Halong City are basically mud and rock – a problem the authorities have tried to 'correct'. There are two beaches in Bai Chay, both 'built' with imported sand, but they are not great for swimming as the water is pretty murky.

Sleeping

If you have any choice in the matter, stay on a boat in the bay rather than in a hotel in Halong City. The majority of visitors who do stay here opt for Bai Chay. There are hundreds of hotels located here, and keen competition keeps prices down, especially if you can avoid the commission-seeking touts. Prices rise in the peak season (summer) or during the Tet festival. There are also accommodation options in Hon Gai, but it's noisier and dustier across the water…coal dust that is!

The nearby island of Dao Tuan Chau (p139) has been overhauled as a luxury resort retreat, an attempted antidote to the mistakes made in the development of Halong City.

BAI CHAY

The heaviest concentration of hotels is in town, in the aptly named 'hotel alley' of Đ Vuon Dao. This is where you'll find more than 50 minihotels, most of them almost identical (a guidebook author's nightmare). Expect to pay something between US$8 and US$12 for a double room with private bathroom and air-con.

Hoang Lan Hotel (☎ 846 504; 17 Đ Vuon Dao; s US$8-12, d US$10-15; ❄) Right in the thick of the action on hotel alley, this family place has a friendly feel. Not only are the usual suspects (hot water, satellite TV and a fridge) here, but breakfast is thrown in for good measure.

Thanh Hue Hotel (☎ 847 612; Đ Vuon Dao; r US$10-12; ❄) Continue up, up, up the hill from the Hoang Lan and you come to this great-value hotel. It offers some cracking views of the bay as a reward for the climb and most rooms include hot water, TV and balcony.

Halong 1 Hotel (☎ 846 320; fax 846 318; Đ Halong; r US$30-55; ❄ 💻) This rambling old government-run hotel used to be set in four buildings, but the other blocks have recently branched out on their own. Set in a rambling old colonial-era building, this place always had the charm. Splash the extra for the space of a suite. You'll be following in the footsteps of Catherine Deneuve who stayed here during the filming of *Indochine*.

Halong Plaza Hotel (☎ 845 810; www.halongplaza.com; 8 Đ Halong; r from US$140; ❄ 💻 🏊) A huge hotel with about 200 rooms, this place looms large over the car-ferry landing. Rooms are business-like, but are packing four stars. Discounts of at least 30% off the published rates are usually offered, making for a real deal.

Eating

Minihotels aside, most hotels have restaurants. If you're in Halong City as part of a tour, the meals are usually included.

Unsurprisingly, seafood is a serious feature of most menus. There are a couple of seafood strips in the centre of town, just south of the post office along Đ Halong. The strip nearest the post office is on the slide and several places have been converted to souvenir shops in the last couple of years. However, the second strip, a few hundred metres south, is still going strong. Aim for the places with fresh seafood in tanks out the front, or gravitate to where the locals are dining. All have tables inside and spill out onto the pavement at night. These are good places to indulge in a beer in the absence of any real bars in town.

Asia Restaurant (☎ 846 927; Đ Vuon Dao; mains 20,000-40,000d) One of the few restaurants daring to intrude on 'hotel alley', this is a reliable spot for Vietnamese food and a smattering of Western favourites. The owner used to run a restaurant in East Berlin and speaks excellent German and pretty good English.

Getting There & Away

BOAT

For all the details on boat trips in Halong Bay, see p140 and p141 sections earlier.

With a marked improvement in roads around the region, boat transport is not as popular as it once was, but the hydrofoil to Mong Cai remains a good option for anyone overlanding to China.

There are daily slow boats connecting Hon Gai with Haiphong (35,000d, three hours). Boats depart Hon Gai at 6.30am, 11am and 4pm. It could be considered a cheap way to do a Halong Bay tour. There are no longer hydrofoils linking Halong and Haiphong, as travel by road is cheaper and just as fast.

From Bai Chay, **Mui Ngoc** (☎ 847 888; Đ Halong) operates hydrofoils to Mong Cai (US$15, three hours) leaving at 8am and 1pm; the ticket office is almost next door to the Mien Tay bus station. The trip is definitely preferable to the long road journey. Book ahead, as demand often outstrips supply.

The best way to get to Cat Ba Island is to hop onto the regular tourist boats from Bai Chay tourist-boat dock. It costs 100,000d one way, including a leisurely cruise through the most beautiful parts of the bay. An extra 30,000d brings entry to the most important caves and grottoes in the bay. The whole trip takes about five or six hours, but there are no precise departure times, as it depends on numbers.

As always, be prepared for changes to these schedules.

BUS

Buses from Halong City to Hanoi (40,000d, 3½ hours) leave from **Mien Tay bus station** (Đ Ca Lan) in Bai Chay every 15 minutes. Buses to Haiphong (25,000d, 1½ hours) depart every 20 minutes from here.

Most buses to northeastern destinations start from Mien Tay bus station before passing through **Hon Gai bus station** (Đ Le Loi). Buses for Mong Cai (42,000d, five hours) and Cai Rong (20,000d, 1½ hours) for Van Don Island (Dao Cai Bau) depart frequently during daylight hours. There is also one bus a day to Lang Son (45,000d, five hours) at 12.30pm, handy for anyone heading to Nanning.

CAR & MOTORBIKE

Halong City is 160km from Hanoi and 55km from Haiphong. The one-way trip from Hanoi to Halong City takes about three hours by private vehicle.

Getting Around

Bai Chay is fairly spread out, so metered taxis are a good option for moving around. **Mai Linh** (☎ 822 226) is a reliable option. Otherwise, there are usually some taxis hanging around near the bus stations or the post office.

CAT BA ISLAND

☎ 031 / pop 7000

Rugged, craggy and jungle-clad Cat Ba, the largest island in Halong Bay, is straight out of Jurassic Park. **Lan Ha Bay**, off the eastern side of the island, is especially scenic and offers numerous beaches to explore. While the vast majority of Halong Bay's islands are uninhabited vertical rocks, Cat Ba has a few **fishing villages**, as well as a fast-growing town.

Except for a few fertile pockets, the terrain is too rocky for serious agriculture; most residents earn their living from the sea, while others cater to the tourist trade. Life has always been hard here and many Cat Ba residents joined the exodus of Vietnamese boat people in the 1970s and '80s. Although the island lost much of its fishing fleet this way, overseas Vietnamese have sent back large amounts of money to relatives on the island, fuelling the hotel boom of the past decade. Cat Ba is still relatively laid-back, despite about a 20-fold increase in hotel rooms (and karaoke machines!) since 1996.

Almost half of Cat Ba Island (which has a total area of 354 sq km) and 90 sq km of the adjacent waters were declared a national park in 1986 to protect the island's diverse ecosystems. These include subtropical evergreen forests on the hills, freshwater swamp forests at the base of the hills, coastal mangrove forests, small freshwater lakes and coral reefs. Most of the coastline consists of rocky cliffs, but there are a few sandy beaches hidden away in small coves.

There are numerous lakes, waterfalls and grottoes in the spectacular limestone hills, the highest of which rises 331m above sea level. The largest permanent body of water on the island is **Ech Lake**, which covers an area of 3 hectares. Almost all of the surface streams are seasonal; most of the island's rainwater flows into caves and follows underground streams to the sea, which creates a shortage of fresh water during the dry season.

The waters off Cat Ba Island are home to 200 species of fish, 500 species of mollusc and 400 species of arthropod. Larger marine animals in the area include seals and three species of dolphin.

Ho Chi Minh paid a visit to Cat Ba Island on 1 April 1951 and there is a large annual festival on the island to commemorate the event. A **monument** to Uncle Ho stands on Mountain No 1, the hillock opposite the pier in Cat Ba town.

The best weather on Cat Ba Island is from late September to November, particularly the latter, when the air and water temperature is mild and skies are mostly clear. December to February is cooler, but still pleasant. From February to April rain is common, while the summer months, from June through August, are hot and humid. This is also peak season and the island is overrun with Vietnamese tourists from Hanoi and beyond.

Cat Ba National Park

This accessible **national park** (☎ 216 350; admission 15,000d, guide fee per day US$5; 🕐 dawn-dusk) is home to 32 types of mammals – including langurs, wild boar, deer, squirrels and hedgehogs – and more than 70 species of birds have been sighted, including hawks, hornbills and cuckoos. The golden-headed langur is officially the world's most endangered primate with just 60 left in the park. Cat Ba lies on a major migration route for waterfowl, which feed and roost on the beaches in the mangrove forests. There are 745 species of plants recorded on Cat Ba, including 118 timber species and 160 plants with medicinal value. The park is also home to a species of tree called Cay Kim Gao. In ancient days, kings and nobles would eat only with chopsticks made from this timber, as anything poisonous it touches is reputed to turn the light-coloured wood to black.

A guide is not mandatory, but is definitely recommended if you want to go walking; otherwise, all you are likely to see is a canopy of trees.

Two caves in and around the national park are open to visitors. **Hospital Cave** oozes historical significance, as it served as a secret, bomb-proof hospital during the American War. This cave is actually just outside the park and the entrance is located about 2 kilometres along the road to Cat Ba town. **Hang Trung Trang** (Trung Trang Cave) is easily accessible, but you will need to contact a ranger to make sure it is open. Bring a torch (flashlight) as it is gloomy inside.

There is a challenging 18km hike through the park and up to one of the mountain summits. Arrange a guide for this six-hour hike, and organise a bus or boat transport to the trailhead and a boat to get back to town. All of this can be easily organised with rangers at the national park headquarters or at the hotels in Cat Ba if you're travelling independently. Many hikes end at Viet Hai, a remote minority village just outside the park boundary, from where boats shuttle back to Cat Ba town (about 250,000d per boat). Don't get stranded or you'll get stiffed. Take proper hiking shoes, a raincoat and a generous supply of water for this hike. Independent hikers can buy basic snacks at the kiosks in Viet Hai, which is where many hiking groups stop for lunch. This is *not* an easy walk, and is much harder and more slippery after rain. There are shorter hiking options that are less hard core. If you're planning to join an organised tour from Hanoi, check the trekking options before you book, as many of the cheaper trips don't actually hike through the park at all.

To reach the national park headquarters at Trung Trang, take a minibus from one of the hotels in Cat Ba town (15,000d, 30 minutes). Another option is to hire a motorbike (one way 30,000d).

Beaches

The white-sand Cat Co beaches (simply called Cat Co 1, Cat Co 2 and Cat Co 3) used to be great places to lounge around for the day. However, 1 and 3 have been taken over by new resorts, leaving Cat Co 2 as the only sane and safe haven. There is also simple accommodation here. It is accessible via a wooden cliffside walkway around the mountain from Cat Co 1.

On weekends the beaches fill up with Vietnamese tourists and litter becomes a real blight, but during the week the crowds diminish.

The beaches are about 1km southeast from Cat Ba town over a steep headland, and can be reached on foot or by motorbike (about 10,000d).

MONKEY BUSINESS

Monkey Island is also part of Cat Ba National Park and many visitors make a boat trip here. However, we do not recommend this trip as the troop of monkeys on this island is pretty aggressive and many travellers have been bitten. The bite itself can be painful and shocking, but worse are the rabies shots that follow. Save the monkey business for somewhere more interesting like Cuc Phuong National Park (p190).

Other beaches include Cai Vieng, Hong Xoai Be and Hong Xoai Lon.

Cat Ba Town

A sleepy fishing village just a decade ago, it is now the Costa del Cat Ba! Since being 'discovered' by Hanoi residents, Cat Ba has turned into a highly popular summer getaway, filling up on weekends and holidays, when the town is jumping. This has been a boon for the range of amenities available, from hotels to restaurants, but the downside is a boom in karaoke joints and the tuneless wailing they often emit. During the summer the town also fills up with cars, as Hanoi residents use the car ferries to come via Cat Hai. Weekdays are saner, as is just before or just after the peak summer season.

INFORMATION

Internet Access

There are now several internet cafés in Cat Ba. Prices tend to be higher than the mainland, at 15,000d an hour or more, and the connections quite slow. There are a couple of places to the southeast of the boat pier, plus one or two on 'hotel alley'.

Money

Remarkably, there are still no banks on Cat Ba Island, but **Vu Binh Jewellers** (☎ 888 641) can change cheques at 3% commission and does credit card cash advances at 5%. The nearest ATMs are in Haiphong or Halong City.

Post

The **main post office** (Đ 1-4) is a one-stop-shop for postal needs and telephone calls.

Tourist Information

There is now an official **Tourism Information & Development Centre** (☎ 688 215; Đ 1-4), located almost opposite the boat pier in Cat Ba town. The staff here can bring you up to speed on transport options in and around Cat Ba, plus it has *Cat Ba Biosphere Reserve* maps available.

Most guesthouses and hotels can 'help' with tourist information (booking you on their trips, in other words).

SLEEPING

Over the past few years the number of accommodation offerings in Cat Ba has risen

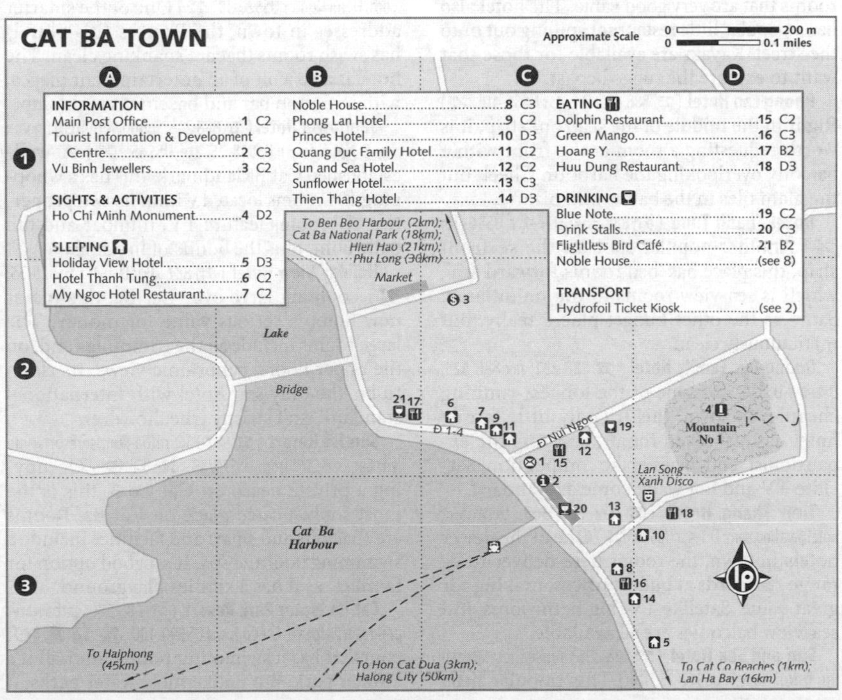

dramatically to keep pace with an ever-expanding tourist market. Look around, as the quality of hotels varies widely. There are now a couple of upmarket resorts in prime beachfront locations for those with the money to spend.

Most hotels are situated on the waterfront in Cat Ba town. The ones to the east, built right up against the hillside, tend to offer better cross-breezes and less of the karaoke call-girl scene. Most hotels have at least one staff member who speaks English.

Room rates fluctuate greatly. In the high-season summer months (May to September) you can expect to pay a minimum of US$15 per room. During the slower winter months (October to April) you can find decent rooms for US$10 or under. The rates given here are for low season, when there's usually the opportunity for negotiation. It is impossible to quote high-season rates, as they tend to pick a number out of their head depending on demand.

Budget

My Ngoc Hotel Restaurant (☎ 888 199; fax 888 422; Đ 1-4; r US$5-8; ❄) This old-timer has simple, clean rooms that are very good value. The hotel also has a popular little restaurant spilling out onto the street. Kayaks are available for those that want to explore the rugged coast.

Phong Lan Hotel (☎ 888 605; Đ 1-4; r US$5-10; ❄) Right in the middle of the seafront strip, it is worth requesting a room at the front with a balcony overlooking the harbour. Check out the glam tiles in the bathroom: bizarre.

Hotel Thanh Tung (☎ 888 364; Đ 1-4; r US$6-10; ❄) Another popular spot on the seafront strip, this place has 'bed rooms forward sea', which is sea-view rooms to the uninitiated. Same as the other budget places really, but meticulously clean.

Quang Duc Family Hotel (☎ 888 231; fax 888 423; Đ 1-4; r US$10; ❄) One of the longest-running cheapies in town, this friendly little family hotel has just seven rooms, resisting the expansionist tendencies of the competition. Satellite TV and hot water come as standard.

Tien Thang Hotel (☎/fax 888 568; tienthanghotel@yahoo.com; Đ 1-4; r US$10; ❄) One of the newer hotels in town, the rooms here deliver midrange standards at budget prices, making for great value. Satellite TV, big bathrooms and sea-view balconies are all available.

Sun and Sea Hotel (☎ 888 315; sunseahotel@mail.ru; Đ Nui Ngoc; r US$12-15; ❄) This popular little hotel is a friendly place to rest a weary head. All rooms include satellite TV, fridge and hot water, plus breakfast is thrown in for good measure…not literally thrown in, you eat it at the table just like normal.

To avoid the hoopla in town, try a night in the rustic **guesthouse** (r 120,000d) over on Cat Co 2. The huts are basic bamboo shelters and the price includes a tent to protect you from the elements.

The small village of Hien Hao offers homestays in local houses. This is quite an authentic experience and what's more the villagers are very friendly. For more details contact **Mr Tuan** (☎ 888 737). Hien Hao is about 20km from Cat Ba town or just 12km from the ferry landing at Phu Long.

Midrange & Top End

Noble House (☎ 888 363; thenoblehousevn@yahoo.com; Đ 1-4; r US$10-30; ❄) Small in size, big in character, this place has thoughtful decoration and elegant bathrooms. It's worth booking ahead, but bear in mind that prices leap to US$30 or more during peak season.

Princes Hotel (☎ 888 899; www.princeshotel-catba.com; Đ Nui Ngoc; r US$20-30; ❄) One of the smarter addresses in town, the Princes (it's plural) has swish rooms that are spanking clean. The hotel is also a bit of an entertainment mecca, with a rooftop bar and basement nightclub.

Sunflower Hotel (☎ 888 215; sunflowerhotel@hn.vnn.vn; Đ Nui Ngoc; r US$18-25, ste US$45; ❄) A well-established Cat Ba landmark, this has a whopping 104 rooms located within its two properties. All rooms feature TV, minibar and full bathroom, plus the bonus of breakfast.

Holiday View Hotel (☎ 887 200; Đ 1-4; r US$25-35; ❄) Looming large over Cat Ba, this major new hotel is serious value for money. The large rooms include all the trimmings and, on the upper floors, panoramic views. Its claim to be 'the only star hotel with international standard' isn't strictly true, however.

Sunrise Resort (☎ 887 366; catba-sunriseresort@vnn.vn; Cat Co 3; s/d from US$79/89; ❄ 💻 🏊) Occupying a private beach on Cat Co 3, this is the most sophisticated place on Cat Ba. Rooms are spacious and smart and facilities include a swimming pool and spa. It's a good option for families, as it has a kiddies playground.

Cat Ba Water Park Resort (☎ 688 686; catbawaterparkresort@fpt.vn; Cat Co 1; s/d US$90-100; ❄ 💻 🏊) Of course it has a swimming pool – after all it's a water park. But unlike most water parks, it also offers smart rooms for those that want to linger at Cat Co 1. It's a better bet during the week or low season, as the water park draws huge crowds on summer weekends.

Ocean Beach Resort (☎ 210 668; www.oceanbeachresort.com.vn; r per person from US$35) Going one better than a private beach, this little retreat boasts its own island about 5km offshore. Accommodation is in traditional but comfortable bungalows set on the beach and all rates include boat transfers and breakfast.

EATING

Sumptuous seafood is the smart choice in Cat Ba town and there are plenty of restaurants to choose from along the seafront strip.

Huu Dung Restaurant (Đ Nui Ngoc; dishes 10,000-50,000d) This place has always served up wholesome food, but it's best to eat early, as the Lan Song Xanh Disco is right across the road and cranks up the volume from 8pm or so. The house special is whole steamed fish with lashings of garlic and soy sauce.

Hoang Y (Đ 1-4; dishes 15,000-50,000d) If you are in the market for fresh grilled shrimp or squid with garlic, this little seafront place is a popular option. As well as a solid selection of seafood dishes, there are also good vegetarian dishes on offer.

Dolphin Restaurant (☎ 888 804; Đ Nui Ngoc; mains 20,000-50,000d) This place is popular with travellers thanks to a selection of Western dishes to complement the reliable Vietnamese fare. Don't worry, definitely no dolphin!

Green Mango (☎ 887 151; Đ 1-4; mains 50,000-100,000d) *The* restaurant of choice in Cat Ba, the chef here learnt his tricks at Bobby Chinn's in Hanoi. The alluring menu includes a selection of smaller appetisers if you just can't settle on one thing. The braised duck is superb but save some space for the delightful desserts. The interior is all drapes and candles, so customers often linger for cocktails.

DRINKING

One of the most enjoyable ways to spend time in the evening is to sit at tables on the waterfront towards the eastern end of the harbour, order a drink from one of the stalls, and watch the world go by.

Noble House (☎ 888 363) As well as a popular restaurant downstairs, this spot has a great 2nd-floor bar. Comfy chairs and inspired décor help people settle in for the evening, plus there's a free pool table, board games and plenty of drinks flowing.

Flightless Bird Café (☎ 888 517; Đ 1-4; from 6.30pm). Little more than a hole in the wall, this small, welcoming place is a good option for those with their drinking boots on and as the night wears on, travellers gravitate . There is a breezy 2nd-floor balcony overlooking the harbour, plus a small book exchange.

Blue Note (Đ Nui Ngoc) The after-hours haunt in town, this is karaoke with kudos. The well-stocked bar stays open until the last person leaves and the song list includes indie anthems from Oasis and Radiohead. Plus there is a stage: perform at your peril.

Getting There & Away

Cat Ba Island is 45km east of Haiphong and 20km south of Halong City. Be aware that there are several piers on Cat Ba Island. Most handy is the jetty directly in front of Cat Ba town from where the hydrofoils to Haiphong depart. A second popular one is at Ben Beo, about 2km from Cat Ba town where most of the tourist boats berth. The other pier is at Phu Long, 30km from Cat Ba, where boats

FLOATING RESTAURANTS

There are numerous 'floating' seafood restaurants just offshore in Cat Ba Harbour. There have been several stories of overcharging, so be sure to work out in advance the price, as well as the cost of a boat to get you out there and back. Locals advise heading around the bay to the couple of floating restaurants in Ben Beo Harbour: the water's cleaner and it's less touristy. A boat ride there and back, including waiting time, should cost around 50,000d. Ask your hotel to recommend a boatman.

One of these restaurants is **Xuan Hong** (☎ 888 485), a fish-farm-cum-restaurant at Ben Beo Pier, just next to the passenger jetty, where you can tread on the edges of the large fish cages and get a close look at the workings of the 'farm'. You will know that the fish is fresh when it is plucked from the cages *after* you've ordered. Prices simply go by weight and type of seafood; you can eat your fill of a selection of fish for around 100,000d.

NORTHEAST VIETNAM

from Cat Hai arrive. At Phu Long, motorbike drivers wait to whisk passengers from the ferries to town (or the 15km to Cat Ba National Park) for about 50,000d. There is also a public bus that meets the boats, but this takes longer to get across the island.

The best option for independent travellers is the hydrofoils linking Cat Ba directly to Haiphong. These air-con rockets reduce the journey to just 45 minutes. There are several companies running the route, with three departures a day in the high summer season and just once a day the rest of the year. Summer season services depart between 10am and 5pm. **Transtour** (☎ 888 314) runs the *Mekong Express* (100,000d, 2.45pm departure), which is the safest and most comfortable option. **Tahaco** (☎ 031-374 7055) has smaller hydrofoils, which are cheaper at 70,000d and depart at 3.15pm. There are no longer hydrofoils operating to Halong City.

The easiest way to get from Halong City to Cat Ba is to hop on the tourist boats (100,000d, five hours) that leave several times a day. This is less organised going in the other direction to Halong City, but your guesthouse or hotel should be able to hook you up with a boat going that way.

There are also plenty of slow, chartered tourist boats making the run from Halong City to Cat Ba Island; check with the cafés and travel agencies in Hanoi about tour options. Such trips generally include all transport, accommodation, food and a guide, but double check to be sure.

An alternative way to reach Cat Ba town is via the island of Cat Hai, which is closer to Haiphong. A boat departs Haiphong and makes a brief stop in Cat Hai on the way to the port of Phu Long on Cat Ba Island. It is also possible to drive a motorbike or car to Haiphong, from where you can get the ferry to Cat Hai, then drive 15 minutes across the island to a pier from where you take a ferry to Phu Long. This accounts for all those surreal traffic jams during the summer season. A bridge is under construction to Cat Hai which will make Cat Ba even easier to reach by vehicle.

There are also direct buses from Hanoi to Cat Ba town. Hoang Long bus operates four services daily to Cat Ba (120,000d, four hours) from the Luong Yen bus station. However, it is just as easy to use the bus-hydrofoil combination via Haiphong.

Getting Around

Rented bicycles are a great way to explore the island and many of the hotels can arrange Chinese mountain bikes (70,000d per day). There are also some tandems available for double the pedal power.

Minibuses with driver are easily arranged. Motorbike rentals (with or without a driver) are available from most of the hotels (from US$5 without a driver). If you are heading out to the beaches or national park, pay the parking fee to ensure that the bike is still there when you return: there have been reports of theft and vandalism.

You'll get plenty of offers to tour Cat Ba Harbour in a rowboat (around 30,000d), or you can hire a kayak from one of the hotels.

Tours of the island and national park, boat trips around Halong Bay and fishing trips are peddled by nearly every hotel and restaurant in Cat Ba. Cost depends on the number of people, but typical prices are US$8 for day trips and US$20 for two-day, one-night trips.

Among the consistently reputable tour operators, take a look at the **My Ngoc Hotel** (☎ 888 199) and **Quang Duc Family Hotel** (☎ 888 231).

BAI TU LONG BAY

☎ 033

There's more to northeastern Vietnam than Halong Bay. The sinking limestone plateau, which gave birth to the bay's spectacular islands, continues for some 100km to the Chinese border. The area immediately northeast of Halong Bay is part of **Bai Tu Long National Park** (☎ 793 365).

Bai Tu Long Bay is every bit as beautiful as its famous neighbour. Indeed, in some ways it's more beautiful, since it has scarcely seen any tourist development. This is good news and bad news. The bay is unpolluted and undeveloped, but there's little tourism infrastructure. It's pretty hard travelling around and staying here, and unless you speak Vietnamese, it's difficult to get information.

Charter boats can be arranged to Bai Tu Long Bay from Halong Bay; boats range from 100,000d to 250,000d per hour depending on size and amenities. See the Halong Bay entry (p141) for more details; the one-way trip takes about five hours. A cheaper alternative is to travel overland to Cai Rong and visit the outlying islands by boat from here. Foreigners are almost always charged double the going rate on the ferries around Bai Tu Long Bay.

Van Don Island (Dao Cai Bau)

Van Don is the largest, most populated and most developed island in the archipelago. However, there remains only very limited tourism development here to date.

Cai Rong (pronounced Cai Zong) is the main town on the island, which is about 30km in length and 15km across at the widest point. **Bai Dai** (Long Beach) runs along much of the southern side of the island and is hard-packed sand with some mangroves. Just offshore, almost touching distance away, there are stunning **rock formations** similar to those in Halong Bay.

SLEEPING & EATING

The only hotels are at Cai Rong pier, about 8km north of the new bridge to the mainland. Cai Rong is a colourful, busy area, with lots of fishing boats and passenger vessels, and a backdrop of limestone mountains in the bay. It's also full of karaoke bars and motorbikes. You might want to get a room with air-con to block out some of the noise. There's no beach.

Hung Toan Hotel (☎ 874 220; r 120,000d; ❄) Head to the top floor for the best rooms, which share a huge balcony. This value-for-money spot is about 100m before the pier.

Viet Linh Hotel (☎ 793 898; r 180,000; ❄) One of the newer hotels in Cai Rong, this is very clean and rooms include satellite TV, fridge and hot-water bathtubs.

Bai Tu Long Ecotourism Resort (☎ 793 156; www.atiresorts.com; bungalows 250,000-450,000d; ❄) This resort is up on Long Beach and is a much nicer alternative to the places in Cai Rong. There are attractive beachside bungalows or more traditional rooms in stilt houses, and the beach has a beautiful backdrop.

GETTING THERE & AWAY

There is a new bridge linking Van Don to the mainland, making it much more accessible from Halong City. Frequent buses run between Hon Gai (Halong City) and Cai Rong bus station (20,000d, 1½ hours). You'll pass plenty of coal mines en route – your face (and lungs) will receive a fine coating of black coal dust before the journey is completed. Just pity the people who live here and have to breathe this in every day.

A good way to get to Van Don is with the **Mui Ngoc hydrofoil** (☎ 793 335) from Halong City (US$8, one hour) departing at 8am. In the other direction, it leaves for Halong City at 4pm. There is also an irregular service to Mong Cai (US$10, two hours), departing Van Don at 8.30am and returning at 2pm.

Note that these boat schedules may change and are dependent on the weather. Be prepared to hang around here a day or so.

Several of the companies offering tours of Halong Bay also offer tours of Bai Tu Long Bay; see p91 for more details. **ATI** (www.atiresorts.com) operates ecolodges on Van Don and Quan Lan Islands and offers a combination of tours to the bay.

Other Islands

Cai Rong Pier (Cai Rong Pha) is just on the edge of Cai Rong town. This is the place for boats to the outlying islands. Chartering a boat from here to Halong City costs around US$10 per hour (the one-way journey takes five hours).

Tourist boats can be chartered at Cai Rong to cruise the nearby islands for a few hours. Ask at the pier. The hourly rate is between 120,000d and 150,000d, but the boats are basic compared with what's on offer at Halong.

QUAN LAN ISLAND (DAO CANH CUOC)

The main attraction here is a beautiful, 1km-long **white-sand beach** shaped like a crescent moon. The water is clear blue and the waves are suitable for surfing. However, there is no shortage of blissful beaches on the eastern seaboard, so take a hike. The best time to play in the water is from about May to October – winter is a bit chilly.

The northeastern part of the island has some battered **ruins** of the old Van Don Trading Port. There is little to show that this was once part of a major trading route between Vietnam and China. Deep-water ports, such as Haiphong and Hon Gai, long ago superseded these islands in importance.

The rowing-boat festival **Hoi Cheo Boi** is held here from the 16th to the 18th day of the sixth lunar month. It's the biggest festival in the bay area, and thousands of people turn out to see it.

There are several cheapies on the island: **Minh Vu Guesthouse** (☎ 877 479) and **Vinh Ly Guesthouse** (☎ 877 354) both have solar-powered hot water and rooms around the 120,000d mark.

Quan Lan Ecotourism Resort (☎ 033-877 417; www.atiresorts.com; bungalows from 150,000-350,000d) has a fine location on the beach, with a choice of comfortable bungalows or a large stilt house for larger groups.

A ferry service between Quan Lan and Van Don runs daily (25,000d, two hours), departing Van Don at 2pm and Quan Lan at 7am; in other words, a trip to the island requires an overnight stay. Foreigners usually get charged 50,000d.

TRA BAN ISLAND (DAO TRA BAN)

One of the largest islands in Bai Tu Long Bay, Tra Ban borders Bai Tu Long National Park and offers some of the most dramatic karst scenery in the bay. The southern part of the island is blanketed in thick jungle like Cat Ba and provides a habitat for many colourful butterflies. There are boats to and from Van Don Island at 7am and 2pm (20,000d, 90 minutes).

NGOC VUNG ISLAND (DAO NGOC VUNG)

This island is one of the most southerly in Bai Tu Long Bay, bordering on Halong Bay, and offers scenery every bit as good as the more famous World Heritage site. There is some accommodation available here in some basic **beach houses** (150,000d). There are daily boats between Cai Rong (1pm) and Ngoc Vung (6am), costing 50,000d for foreigners and taking three hours.

CO TO ISLAND (DAO CO TO)

In the northeast, Co To Island is the furthest inhabited island from the mainland. Its highest peak reaches a respectable 170m. There are numerous other hills, and a large lighthouse atop one of them. The coastline is mostly cliffs and large rocks, but there's at least one fine sandy **beach**. Fishing boats usually anchor just off here, and you can walk to some of the boats during low tide. There is a small and very basic guesthouse on the island.

Ferries bound for Co To Island depart Van Don Island on Monday, Wednesday and Friday at unspecified times – check the schedule in Cai Rong. They return from Co To Island on Tuesday, Thursday and Friday. The one-way fare is 50,000d and the journey takes about five hours, depending on the winds.

MONG CAI & CHINESE BORDER

☎ 033 / pop 48,100

Mong Cai is a revealing place. The Vietnamese are fast developing their side of the border while the Chinese side remains a bit of a backwater. The Vietnamese are making a statement of intent, a show of face that their economy is keeping pace with China. China is making its own statement: 'We don't care, we have bigger fish to fry', sharing as they do borders with India, Russia and several other economic giants.

It would take a real optimist to think Mong Cai is an attractive place. For the Vietnamese, the big draw here is the chance to purchase low-priced (and low-quality) Chinese-made consumer goods. For the Chinese, the attraction is mostly gambling and girls.

Chinese speakers will find plenty of opportunity to practice in Mong Cai. Most of the market stalls are run by Chinese. This explains why the market shuts so early: the Chinese have to head back across the border before it closes at 4.30pm. It also means it's easy to offload any leftover Chinese yuan.

Other than the prospect of crossing the border, Mong Cai is of no interest to tourists. The town is dusty, the buildings are ramshackle, and there's construction-site chaos everywhere. Dongxing (on the Chinese side) is even less appealing.

Information

Vietcombank, in the centre of town, can change travellers cheques and also has a handy ATM. **Internet access** (per hr 3000d) is available in a cluster of places on Pho Hung Vuong near the post office.

Sleeping & Eating

It is possible to spend the night in the nearby beach retreat of Tra Co (opposite). There are masses of hotels in Mong Cai catering to cross-border traders.

There are currently two huge casino resorts under construction to cater to Chinese high rollers. They should be open by the time you read this if you need to flutter away some dong before crossing into China.

BORDER CROSSING: MONG CAI/DONGXING

Mong Cai is located on the Chinese border in the extreme northeastern corner of Vietnam. One of three official international overland border crossings with China, it's open from 7.30am to 4.30pm daily.

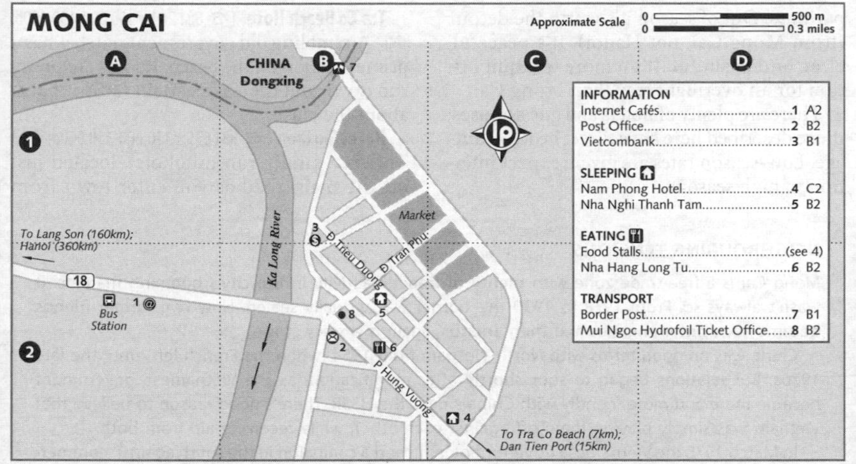

Nha Nghi Thanh Tam (☎ 881 373; Đ Trieu Duong; r 120,000d; ❄) Rooms here are just US$8 for those who have just arrived and can't sort their dongs from their yuan. Clean and comfortable, this is good value and the family are warm and welcoming.

Nam Phong Hotel (☎ 887 775; fax 887 779; Pho Hung Vuong; s/d 220,000/250,000d; ❄) A smart business hotel, this is one of the only places in town where staff speak English. The rooms are well kitted out with satellite TV and water and there is a good Vietnamese restaurant at the rear.

Nha Hang Long Tu (☎ 770 489; Pho Hung Vuong; mains 20,000-50,000d) A long-running restaurant, this eatery offers a plastic-fantastic set-up downstairs and a more refined dining room upstairs. Try a table-top barbecue or steamboat, or indulge in the seafood.

There are plenty of food stalls on Pho Hung Vuong, including several good spots near the Nam Phong Hotel.

Getting There & Away

BOAT

Mui Ngoc (☎ 883 988; Pho Hung Vuong) runs high-speed hydrofoils daily from Mong Cai to Bai Chay (US$15, three hours) in Halong City at 9am and 2pm (8am and 1pm from Halong City). From Mong Cai, shuttle vans leave the hydrofoil ticket offices for the pier at Dan Tien Port, about 15km away. Arriving in Mong Cai, the hydrofoils often berth in the middle of the open sea; don't worry, you haven't broken down! Low tides require a transfer by small boat.

Mui Ngoc has hydrofoils to Cai Rong on Van Don Island. The boat heads south to Van Don (US$10, two hours) at 2pm. In the other direction, it departs Van Don at 8.30am.

Finally, there is also a slow ferry to Haiphong (70,000d, eight hours), departing daily at 6pm. Do the maths, it arrives at an ungodly hour.

BUS

Mong Cai is located 360km from Hanoi. Buses to/from Hanoi (75,000d, nine hours) depart regularly in the morning. Many buses and minibuses connect Mong Cai and Hon Gai (42,000d, five hours) between 5.30am and 4.30pm. Smart folk take the hydrofoil.

For Mong Cai to Lang Son (50,000d, five hours) there is just one bus a day at 12.30pm. Don't miss it, as going your own way involves two changes. Much of the road is unpaved – expect plenty of dust or mud.

AROUND MONG CAI

Tra Co Beach

☎ 033

Tra Co's claim to fame is that it is the northernmost beach resort in Vietnam. The downside is that it's also the closest to China. A fine beach of hard-packed sand with shallow water at 17km in length it's one of the longest stretches of sandy beachfront real estate in Vietnam. Sadly it's succumbing to dodgy developments.

It's still a small-scale resort, but there's a high season between May and August, with many Vietnamese and Chinese tourists and the usual swathe of karaoke bars and massage parlours. Out of season it's worth the detour (from Mong Cai, not Hanoi). It's peaceful, clean and beautiful. It's a more tranquil option for an overnight stay than Mong Cai.

There are plenty of hotels and guesthouses; those described here have direct beach frontage. Low-season rates are given; expect inflation in high season.

Tra Co Beach Hotel (☎ 881 264; r 100,000-150,000d; ❄) A rambling old government hotel, it has a prime location on the beach. Rooms are pretty run down, but there is a certain raffish charm about the place.

Hotel Gio Bien (☎ 881 635; r 120,000-150,000d; ❄) This is a family-run minihotel, located just off the main road as you enter town from

NEIGHBOURING TENSIONS

Mong Cai is a free-trade zone with plenty of frenetic activity in the city's booming markets. It wasn't always so. From 1978 to 1990 the border was virtually sealed. How two former friends became such bitter enemies and then 'friends' again is a spicy story.

China was on good terms with North Vietnam from 1954 (when the French left) until the late 1970s. But relations began to sour shortly after reunification, as the Vietnamese government became more and more friendly with China's rival, the USSR. There's good reason to believe that Vietnam was simply playing them off against each other, while receiving aid from both.

In March 1978 the Vietnamese government launched a campaign in the south against 'commercial opportunists', seizing private property to complete the country's 'socialist transformation'.

The campaign hit the ethnic Chinese particularly hard. It was widely assumed that the Marxist-Leninist rhetoric was a smokescreen for ancient Vietnamese antipathy towards the Chinese.

The anti-capitalist and anti-Chinese campaign caused up to 500,000 of Vietnam's 1.8 million ethnic Chinese citizens to flee the country. Those in the north fled overland to China, while those in the south left by sea. The creation of Chinese refugees in the south proved to be lucrative for the government – to leave, refugees typically had to pay up to US$5000 each in 'exit fees'. Chinese entrepreneurs in Ho Chi Minh City (HCMC) had that kind of money, but refugees in the north were mostly dirt poor.

In response, China cut all aid to Vietnam, cancelled dozens of development projects and withdrew 800 technicians. Vietnam's invasion of Cambodia in late 1978 was the final straw: Beijing – alarmed because the Khmer Rouge was its close ally, and worried by the huge build-up of Soviet military forces on the Chinese–Soviet border – became convinced that Vietnam had fallen into the Russian camp, which was trying to encircle China with hostile forces. Which, ironically enough, was exactly what Vietnam suspected about the Chinese–Khmer Rouge alliance.

In February 1979 China invaded northern Vietnam at Lang Son 'to teach the Vietnamese a lesson'. Just what lesson the Vietnamese learned is not clear, but the Chinese learned that Vietnam's troops, battle-hardened by many years of fighting the USA, were no pushovers. Although China's forces were withdrawn after 17 days, and the operation was officially declared a 'great success', most observers soon realised that China's People's Liberation Army (PLA) had been badly mauled by the Vietnamese. It is believed to have suffered 20,000 casualties in 2½ weeks of fighting. Ironically, China's aid to Vietnam was partially responsible for China's humiliation.

Officially, these 'misunderstandings' are considered ancient history. Trade across the Chinese–Vietnamese border is booming and both countries profess to be 'good neighbours'. In practice, China and Vietnam remain highly suspicious of each other's intentions. Continued conflicts over who owns oil-drilling rights in the South China Sea are exacerbating tensions. The border area remains militarily sensitive, though the most likely future battleground is at sea.

If you visit China and discuss this border war, you will almost certainly be told that China acted in self-defence because the Vietnamese were launching raids across the border and murdering innocent Chinese villagers. Virtually all Western observers, from the US government's Central Intelligence Agency to historians, consider China's version of events to be nonsense. The Chinese also claim they won this war. Nobody outside of China believes that, either.

For the inside story on how the communist comrades fell out, read *Brother Enemy* (1988) by Nayan Chanda, an excellent account of Cold War power plays and the making and breaking of alliances.

Mong Cai. Rooms on the upper floors have shared balconies and a bird's-eye panorama over the beach.

Opposite the Tra Co Beach Hotel, on the edge of the beach, are some great little **restaurants** (dishes 15,000-50,000d) knocking out fresh seafood.

GETTING THERE & AWAY

A one-way metered taxi from Mong Cai will be about 75,000d. A motorbike taxi is cheaper at 30,000d. Inexplicably, the road deteriorates into a pot-holed mess on arrival in Tra Co, before turning into a superhighway after a couple of kilometres.

LANG SON

☎ 025 / pop 62,300 / elevation 270m

Nestled amid a nest of karst peaks, Lang Son is the capital of mountainous Lang Son province. The town of Lang Son is in an area populated largely by Tho, Nung, Man and Dzao Montagnards. You'll see that many of these people continue living their traditional way of life.

Lang Son was partially destroyed in February 1979 by invading Chinese forces (see the boxed text, opposite); the ruins of the town and the devastated frontier village of Dong Dang were frequently shown to foreign journalists as evidence of Chinese aggression. Although the border is still heavily fortified, both towns have been rebuilt and Sino–Vietnamese trade is in full swing again.

Close to Lang Son, there are a couple of impressive caves in the surrounding limestone hills, and remnants of the ruined 16th-century Mac dynasty Citadel. Most travellers come to Lang Son when crossing between Vietnam and China: the border is actually just outside Dong Dang, a village 18km to the north. It's not a town to linger in, but if you find yourself with a few hours to spare there's enough to explore.

Information

Internet access is pretty straightforward in Lang Son these days and almost every street has a little gaming place, including Đ Thanh Tam. You can expect to pay about 3000d an hour.

Check out **Incombank** (51 Đ Le Loi) for all your currency needs, and you can use up the last of your Vietnamese stamps at the **main post office** (Đ Le Loi).

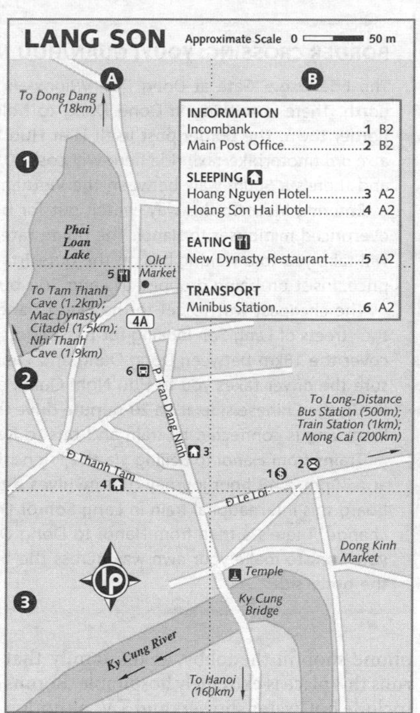

Sights & Activities

There are two large and beautiful **caves** (admission 5000d; 6am-6pm) just a few kilometres from the centre of Lang Son. In fact it's fair to say that they are now in the suburbs. Both are illuminated, which makes for easy exploration, and have Buddhist altars inside. **Tam Thanh Cave** is vast and seductive. There's an internal pool and a viewing point or natural 'window' offering a sweeping view of the surrounding rice fields. Just a few hundred metres up a stone staircase are the ruins of the **Mac Dynasty Citadel**. It's a lovely, deserted spot, with stunning views across the countryside.

The Ngoc Tuyen River flows through **Nhi Thanh Cave**, 700m beyond Tam Thanh. The cave entrance has a series of carved poems written by the cave's discoverer, a soldier called Ngo Thi San, in the 18th century. There's also a carved stone plaque commemorating an early French resident of Lang Son, complete with his silhouette in European clothing.

Sleeping & Eating

Hoang Nguyen Hotel (☎ 870 349; 84 Pho Tran Dang Ninh; s/d US$10/15;) Ignore the unlikely mobile

BORDER CROSSING: YOUYI GUAN/HUU NGHI QUAN

The Friendship Gate at Dong Dang/Pingxiang is the most popular border crossing in the far north. There is nothing in Dong Dang to hold the traveller's interest, except its position as a border town. The border post itself is at Huu Nghi Quan (Friendship Gate), 3km north of town; a *xe om* (motorbike taxi) ride here will cost 20,000d. The border is open from 7am to 5pm daily, and there's a 500m walk between the Vietnamese and Chinese frontiers.

Entering Vietnam this way, watch out for border touts herding unsuspecting travellers on to overpriced minibuses to Hanoi. The going rate from Lang Son to Hanoi is 50,000d, but the touts will take you to a waiting bus on the outskirts of town and try to charge three or four times the price. Insist on being dropped at Lang Son bus station.

The cheapest way to get to the Dong Dang border is to take a minibus (5000d). They cruise the streets of Lang Son looking for passengers and leave throughout the day. The fastest way to cover the 18km between Dong Dang and Lang Son is to hire a motorbike (50,000d). Just make sure the driver takes you to Huu Nghi Quan, as there are other checkpoints for locals only.

On the Chinese side, it's a 20-minute drive from the border to Pingxiang by bus or shared taxi. Pingxiang is connected by train and bus to Nanning, the capital of China's Guangxi province.

Trains from Hanoi to Beijing via the Friendship Gate depart the capital on Tuesday and Friday at 6.30pm, a 48-hour journey that involves a three-hour stop for border formalities. You cannot board this international train in Lang Son or Dong Dang. Check the schedule in Hanoi, as it may change. There's a train from Hanoi to Dong Dang (37,000d), via Lang Son, three times a day, if you want to make your own way across the border and get on a Chinese train when you reach the other side.

phone shop in the lobby, as the family that runs this place is extremely hospitable. Rooms include hot-water showers and TV, although 'satellite' is stretching it.

Hoang Son Hai Hotel (☎ 710 479; 57 Đ Thanh Tam; r US$17; ❄) This tall and thin hotel has some of the smartest rooms in town. There is not a great deal of English spoken, but the universal language of comfort is apparent. There is even a lift, a rarity in these parts.

New Dynasty Restaurant (Phai Loan Lake; mains 15,000-75,000d) By night there is only one place to be in town: the New Dynasty. Set on the shores of the lake, this vast place has a garden restaurant to the right, complete with an extensive Vietnamese menu and a draft beer emporium. To the left is a bar and beer garden with local music. It's heaving.

There are plenty of other hotels and guesthouses in town, of much the same standard. Few have restaurants, but there are some *com pho* places in town and a couple of cheap restaurants near the bus station.

Getting There & Away

Buses heading to Hanoi's Long Bien bus station (50,000d, three hours) depart regularly from the **long-distance bus station** (Đ Le Loi). A daily bus leaves Lang Son for Cao Bang (65,000d, five hours), but it's a rollercoaster ride. Minibuses heading to Cao Bang via That Khe and Dong Khe leave regularly from the **minibus station** (Pho Tran Dang Ninh).

Three daily trains run between Lang Son and Hanoi (33,000d, five hours).

Getting Around

There are plenty of *xe om* (motorbike taxis) around the post office and the market. **Taxi Tam Gia** (☎ 818 181) is a reliable company for metered taxis.

On Pho Tran Dang Ninh there are plenty of minibuses looking for passengers who are heading to the border at Dong Dang.

CAO BANG

☎ 026 / pop 45,500

Cao Bang province is one of the most beautiful places in all of Vietnam. The same cannot be said for the town of Cao Bang, but nobody cares as it is a useful base to explore the surrounding countryside. Cao Bang town is high above sea level and has a gentle climate.

While in Cao Bang town, hit the hill leading up to the **War Memorial**. Head up the second lane off Đ Pac Bo, go under the entrance to a primary school, and you'll see the steps. There are great 360-degree views from the summit, and it's very peaceful, not to mention good exercise.

Information

Internet access has come to Cao Bang and there are several places to get an online fix on Pho Vuon Cam, just north of the Thanh Loan Hotel.

The Bank for Foreign Investment and Development will change US dollars but it's a major exercise, undertaken by sleepy staff. Try to arrive with enough cash to cover your stay. There are still no ATMs in town.

Sleeping & Eating

Nguyet Nga Hotel (☎ 856 445; r 140,000d; ❄) Just over the bridge on the east bank of the river, this is one of the most reliable cheapies. Don't be put off by the drab exterior, as the rooms are on the large side and include TV, fridge and hot water.

Thanh Loan Hotel (☎ 857 026; fax 857 028; 159 Pho Vuon Cam; r US$15; ❄ 💻) The best all-rounder in town, this hotel is clean and friendly. All rooms are the same price, irrespective of size, so check out a couple of options to get a bigger, brighter one. The only drawback is the strange stuffed animal collection adorning the lobby. Rates include breakfast.

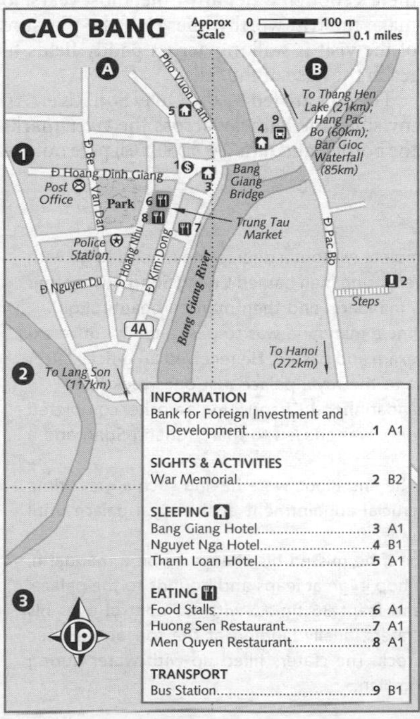

INFORMATION
Bank for Foreign Investment and Development....1 A1

SIGHTS & ACTIVITIES
War Memorial....2 B2

SLEEPING
Bang Giang Hotel....3 A1
Nguyet Nga Hotel....4 B1
Thanh Loan Hotel....5 A1

EATING
Food Stalls....6 A1
Huong Sen Restaurant....7 A1
Men Quyen Restaurant....8 A1

TRANSPORT
Bus Station....9 B1

Bang Giang Hotel (☎ 853 431; fax 855 984; r 240,000-300,000d; ❄) The biggest hotel in town, this government-run place is almost a village, complete with shops, restaurants and massage. The staff are friendly and it's popular with tour groups. Located near the bridge in the north of town, rooms at the back on the upper floors have sweeping views overlooking the river.

Men Quyen Restaurant (☎ 856 433; meals 20,000-40,000d) Tucked away behind the market, this is the most popular diner in town. And diner it is, with all the meals on display in steaming vats. Browse the selection and make your choice. The sheer number of Vietnamese eating here is a good sign.

Huong Sen Restaurant (meals 10,000-30,000d) Formerly the leading restaurant in town, although there wasn't much competition, this *com binh dan* place has a nice location on the riverbank. Basic food but at basic prices.

Besides the hotel restaurants, there are plenty of good **food stalls** (meals from 10,000d) near the market. It is best to eat early, as most eateries are closed by 9pm.

Getting There & Away

Cao Bang is 272km north of Hanoi, along Hwy 3. This is a sealed road, but due to the mountainous terrain, it's a full day's drive. There are several direct buses daily from Hanoi (80,000d, nine hours) and Thai Nguyen. There is also a daily bus to/from Lang Son (62,000d, five hours), departing from the **bus station** (Đ Kim Dong).

AROUND CAO BANG

Thang Hen Lake

This is a large lake that can be visited year-round; however, what you get to see varies according to the seasons. During the rainy season, from about May to September, the 36 lakes in the area are separated by convoluted rock formations. In the dry season, most of the lakes – except Thang Hen itself – are dry. However, during this time of year the lake level drops low enough to reveal a large **cave**, which can be explored by bamboo raft – if you can locate anyone at all in the vicinity to ask. There are opportunities for good day **walks** throughout this area, but you'll need a local guide; try the hotels in Cao Bang for assistance.

There are still no restaurants or hotels at Thang Hen, nor is there any public transport. To get here from Cao Bang, drive 20km to the top of Ma Phuc Pass. From there carry on for 1km to the fork in the highway – take the left branch and continue another 4km.

Hang Pac Bo (Water-Wheel Cave)

Hang Pac Bo (Water-Wheel Cave) is just 3km from the Chinese border. The cave and the surrounding area is sacred ground for Vietnamese revolutionaries. Here, on 28 January 1941, Ho Chi Minh re-entered Vietnam ready to lead the revolution that he had long been planning during 30 years of exile.

Ho Chi Minh lived in this cave, writing poetry while waiting for WWII to end. He stuck close to China so that he would be able to flee across the border if French soldiers discovered his hiding place. He named the stream in front of his cave Lenin Creek and a nearby mountain Karl Marx Peak.

There's an Uncle Ho **museum** (admission free; 7.30-11.30am & 1.30-4.30pm) at the entrance to the Pac Bo area. About 2km beyond this is a parking area. The cave is a 10-minute walk away, and a **jungle hut**, which was another of Ho's hideouts, is about 15 minutes' walk in the opposite direction, across a paddy field and in a patch of forest. On the way to the hut is a rock outcrop used as a 'dead-letter box', where he would leave and pick up messages. It's a lovely, quiet spot and has seen very little development compared with other parts of Vietnam.

Hang Pac Bo is about 60km northwest of Cao Bang; allow three hours to make the return trip by road, plus 1½ hours to poke around. To do this as a return half-day trip by *xe om*, expect to pay around US$10. No permits are currently needed, despite the proximity to the Chinese border.

Ban Gioc Waterfall

One of Vietnam's best-known waterfalls, its image adorns the lobby of many a cheap guesthouse throughout Vietnam. It's a very scenic spot, marking the border with China, but sees very few visitors. The name Ban Gioc is derived from the Montagnard languages spoken in the area, and is sometimes spelt Ban Doc.

The waterfall is the largest, although not the highest, in the country. The vertical drop is 53m, but it has an impressive 300m span; one end of the falls is in China, the other is in Vietnam. The water volume varies considerably between the dry and rainy seasons: the falls are most impressive from May to September, but swimming during this period in the waterholes below may be difficult due to turbulence. The falls have three levels, creating a sort of giant staircase, and there's enough water any time, most years, to make the trip worthwhile. Half the pleasure of the visit is walking across paddy fields to reach the base of the falls.

The falls are fed by the Quay Son River. An invisible line halfway across the river marks the border, and **rafts** (per trip 50,000d) pole out the

THE LEGEND OF THE LAKES

The charming setting of Thang Hen wouldn't be complete without a depressing legend to go with it. It seems that there was a very handsome and clever young man named Chang Sung. His mother adored him and deemed that he should become a mandarin and then marry a beautiful girl.

Under Confucian tradition, the only way to become a mandarin was to pass a competitive examination. Chang Sung, being a clever boy, sat the exam and passed. He received an official letter bearing the good news and ordering him to report to the royal palace just one week later.

With her son virtually guaranteed admission to mandarinhood, Chang Sung's mother completed her plan. A beautiful girl, Biooc Luong (Yellow Flower), was chosen to marry Chang Sung and a big wedding was hastily arranged.

Chang Sung couldn't have been happier. In fact, he and Biooc were having such a great time on their honeymoon that he forgot all about his crucial appointment at the royal palace until the night before the deadline.

Knowing how disappointed his mother would be if he missed his chance to be a mandarin, Chang Sung summoned magical forces to help him hop in great leaps and bounds to the palace. Unfortunately, he messed up the aerodynamics and leapt 36 times, with no control over his direction or velocity, and wound up creating 36 craters, finally landing at the top of Ma Phuc Pass, where he died of exhaustion and became a rock. The craters filled up with water during the rainy season and became the 36 Lakes of Thang Hen.

few metres to exactly the halfway mark – and no further – from each side. There's been some development of tourist facilities on the Chinese side in recent years, including a large resort, but almost nothing except a bamboo footbridge and a couple of bamboo rafts on the Vietnamese side.

There is no official border checkpoint here, but you need a police permit to visit. However, this no longer needs to be arranged in advance and can be picked up at the police office near the falls for just 50,000d.

NGUOM NGAO CAVE

This is one of the most spectacular caves in northeast Vietnam. There are two sections to visit but the main entrance to the **cave** (admission 5000d) is 2km from Ban Gioc Waterfall, just off the road to Cao Bang. Electricity has been installed in the main cave and the lighting is quite beautiful compared with the kitsch colours in most Vietnamese caves. It takes about 45 minutes to explore. Solo travellers will have to pay 30,000d to fire up the lights. There is a second, bigger cave that is simply enormous and one branch reaches almost all the way to the waterfalls, where there is a 'secret' entrance. A full tour takes around two hours and requires the use of a torch (flashlight). Expect to pay about 50,000d for this experience.

SLEEPING & EATING

There are no hotels located on the Vietnamese side of the border. Cao Bang is really the closest option for decent accommodation. There is limited local food available in Ban Gioc. Try the little stall by the car park.

GETTING THERE & AWAY

The road between Cao Bang and Ban Gioc via Quang Yen is in pretty good shape, and is presently fine for cars and minibuses. The 87km trip takes about 2½ hours each way; it's mountainous and winding and very beautiful. If you take the loop route to and from the falls, the section between Tra Linh and Trung Khanh is still a bit bumpy, and 4WD is recommended, especially after rain. There is public transport between Cao Bang and Trung Khanh but nothing beyond that; negotiate for a *xe om* in Trung Khanh to take you to the falls. Hotels and guesthouses in Cao Bang can arrange a motorbike (self-drive) or vehicle (with driver).

Montagnard Markets

In the province of Cao Bang, Kinh (ethnic Vietnamese) are a distinct minority. The largest ethnic groups are the Tay (46%), Nung (32%), H'mong (8%), Dzao (7%) and Lolo (1%). Intermarriage, mass education and 'modern' clothing is gradually eroding tribal and cultural distinctions.

Check out Tim Doling's *Mountains and Ethnic Minorities: North East Vietnam* for detailed accounts of tribal people in the region It's available from the Vietnam Museum of Ethnology (p101) and bookshops in Hanoi.

Most of Cao Bang's Montagnards remain blissfully naive about the ways of the outside world. Cheating in the marketplace, for example, is virtually unknown and even tourists are charged the same price as locals without bargaining. Whether or not this innocence can withstand the onslaught of even limited tourism remains to be seen.

The following big Montagnard markets in Cao Bang province are held every five days, according to lunar calendar dates.

Nuoc Hai 1st, 6th, 11th, 16th, 21st and 26th day of each lunar month

Na Giang 1st, 6th, 11th, 16th, 21st and 26th day of each lunar month. Attracting Tay, Nung and H'mong, this is one of the best and busiest markets in the provinces.

Tra Linh 4th, 9th, 14th, 19th, 24th and 29th day of each lunar month

Trung Khanh 5th, 10th, 15th, 20th, 25th and 30th day of each lunar month

BA BE NATIONAL PARK

☎ 0281 / elevation 145m

Often referred to as Ba Be Lakes, **Ba Be National Park** (☎ 894 014; fax 894 026; admission per person /car 10,000/20,000d) is in Bac Kan province and was established in 1992 as Vietnam's eighth national park. It really is a babe: a beautiful region that covers more than 7000 hectares and boasts mountains high, rivers deep, waterfalls, plunging valleys, lakes and caves set amid towering peaks. The surrounding area is home to members of the Tay minority, who live in stilt homes.

The park is a tropical-rainforest area with over 550 named plant species, and the government subsidises the villagers not to cut down the trees. The 300 or so wildlife species in the forest include 65 (mostly rarely seen) mammals, 214 bird species, butterflies and other insects. Hunting is forbidden, but villagers are permitted to fish.

THE LEGEND OF WIDOW'S ISLAND

A tiny islet in the middle of Ba Be Lakes is the source of a local legend. The Tay people believe that what is a lake today was once farmland, and in the middle was a village called Nam Mau.

One day, the Nam Mau residents found a buffalo wandering in the nearby forest. They caught it, butchered it and shared the meat. However, they didn't share any with a certain lonely old widow.

Unfortunately for the villagers, this wasn't just any old buffalo. It belonged to the river ghost. When the buffalo failed to return home, the ghost went to the village disguised as a beggar. He asked the villagers for something to eat, but they refused to share their buffalo buffet and ran the poor beggar off. Only the widow was kind to him and gave him some food and a place to stay for the night.

That night the beggar told the widow to take some rice husks and sprinkle them on the ground around her house. Later in the evening, it started to rain, and then a flood came. The villagers all drowned, the flood washed away their homes and farms, thus creating Ba Be Lakes. Only the widow's house remained: it's now Po Gia Mai (Widow's Island).

The park is surrounded by steep mountains, up to 1554m in height. The 1939 *Madrolle Guide to Indochina* suggests travelling around Ba Be Lakes 'in a car, on horseback, or, for ladies, in a chair', meaning, of course, a sedan chair.

Ba Be (Three Bays) is in fact three linked lakes, which have a total length of 8km and a width of about 400m. The deepest point in the lakes is 35m, and there are nearly 50 species of freshwater fish.

Two of the lakes are separated by a 100m-wide strip of water called Be Kam, sandwiched between high walls of chalk rock. The **Thac Dau Dang** (Dau Dang or Ta Ken Waterfall) consists of a series of spectacular cascades between sheer walls of rock, and is accessible by boat and on foot during day trips. Just 200m below the rapids is a small Tay village called Hua Tang. It costs 400,000d for a boat here and takes at least four hours.

Hang Puong (Puong Cave) is visited on day tours. It's about 30m high and 300m long, and completely passes through a mountain. A navigable river flows through the cave, making for an interesting boat trip. It costs 300,000d for a boat and takes three hours.

Renting a boat is *de rigueur,* and costs from 150,000d per hour. The boats can carry about 12 people (but it's the same price if there are just two), and you should allow at least seven hours to take in most sights. Enjoy the ride: it's lovely despite the noisy engines. An optional guide, worth considering, costs US$10 per day. The boat dock is about 2km from park headquarters.

The park staff can organise several **tours**. Costs depend on the number of people, but expect to pay at least US$25 per day if you're travelling alone. There's the option of a one-day tour by boat; a one-day tour combining motorboat, a 3km or 4km walk, and a trip by dugout canoe; and there are also combination cycling, boating and walking possibilities. Homestays can be arranged at several of the villages in the park, and longer treks can also be arranged.

The park entrance fee is payable at a checkpoint on the road into the park, about 15km before the park headquarters, just beyond the town of Cho Ra.

Sleeping & Eating

Not far from the park headquarters are two accommodation options. Rooms in the newer **guesthouse** (r 165,000d) are fine, if a bit pricey. There are also comfortable air-con two-room **cottages** (r 275,000d). There's a reasonable **restaurant** (dishes 10,000-30,000d) – note that you'll need to place your order an hour or so before you want to eat.

It's also possible to stay in **stilt houses** (per person 60,000) at Pac Ngoi village on the lakeshore. The park office can help organise this. Food is available at the homestays, which can include fresh fish from the lake, and prices are reasonable.

Take enough cash for your visit – there are no money-exchange facilities, although there are banks in Bac Kan, the provincial capital en route from Hanoi.

Getting There & Away

Ba Be National Park is in Bac Kan province not far from the borders of Cao Bang province and Tuyen Quang province. The lakes are 240km from Hanoi, 61km from Bac Kan and 18km from Cho Ra.

Most visitors to the national park get there by chartered vehicle from Hanoi. Since the 2000 opening of a new road into the park, 4WD is no longer necessary. The one-way journey from Hanoi takes about six hours; most travellers allow three days and two nights for the trip.

Reaching the park by public transport is possible, but not easy. Take a bus from Hanoi to Phu Thong (50,000d, five hours) via Thai Nguyen and/or Bac Kan, and from there take another bus to Cho Ra (15,000d, one hour). In Cho Ra arrange a motorbike (about 40,000d) to cover the last 18km.

THAI NGUYEN

☎ 028 / pop 171,400

It's definitely not northeast Vietnam's most interesting city, but Thai Nguyen is home to the **Museum of the Cultures of Vietnam's Ethnic Groups** (Bao Tang Van Hoa Cac Dan Toc; admission 10,000d; 7-11am & 2-5.30pm Tue-Sun). The largest Montagnard museum in Vietnam, it's worth a stop on the way to or from Ba Be National Park. The giant pastel-pink building houses a wide array of colourful exhibits representing the 50-odd hill tribes residing in Vietnam. There is an interesting English booklet about the displays available for US$2.

Thai Nguyen is 76km north of Hanoi, and the road here is in good shape. Buses and minibuses to Thai Nguyen (15,000d, two hours) depart from Hanoi's Gia Lam station regularly between 5am and 5pm.

AROUND THAI NGUYEN

Phuong Hoang Cave

Phuong Hoang Cave is one of the largest and most accessible caverns in northeastern Vietnam. There are four main chambers, two of which are illuminated by the sun when the angle is correct. Most of the stalactites and stalagmites are still in place, although quite a few have been broken off by thoughtless souvenir hunters. Like many caves in Vietnam, this one served as a hospital and ammunition depot during the American War. If you want to see anything, bring a good torch.

The cave is a 40km motorbike ride over a bumpy road from Thai Nguyen.

Nui Coc Reservoir

A scenic spot popular with locals, **Nui Coc Reservoir** (admission 10,000d; hotel rooms) is 25km west of Thai Nguyen. It's a pretty stretch of water, and is a major drawcard for Hanoi residents looking to get away from it all (hotel rooms 80,000-250,000d). On summer weekends it can get particularly crowded. A one-hour, circular motorboat tour of the lake is *the* thing to do and costs about 250,000d. You can use the water park's swimming pool for 20,000d, and also rent rowboats. It could be worth a visit if you're travelling to Ba Be National Park, with your own wheels, and fancy a dip.

Northwest Vietnam

Welcome to the roof of Vietnam, where the mountains of the Tonkinese Alps (Hoang Lien Mountains) soar skyward, their long shadows concealing some of the country's best-kept secrets. The landscape is a rich palette that provides some of the most spectacular scenery in Vietnam. Forbidding and unforgiving terrain for lowlanders, the mountains have long been a haven for an eclectic mix of hill tribes. Dressed in elaborate costumes, the Montagnards live as they have for generations and extend the hand of friendship to strangers; an encounter with the Montagnards is both a humbling and heart-warming experience.

For many visitors, Sapa is *the* northwest, an atmospheric old hill station set amid stunning scenes of near-vertical rice terraces and towering peaks. But beyond Sapa the voluptuous views continue, and there are many other options to come face to face with the bold landscapes and colourful inhabitants of this region – Bac Ha, Dien Bien Phu and Mai Chau. For the ultimate motorbike adventure head to Ha Giang, the final frontier in northern Vietnam.

Although many of the roads in this region are surfaced, many are dangerous cliffhangers that are regularly wiped out by landslides in the wet season. The stretch from Lai Chau into Sapa offers some of the best mountain vistas in Southeast Asia, as the road climbs more than 1000m over the Tram Ton Pass. The northwestern roads are always improving, but if you suffer from vertigo, backache or (God forbid) haemorrhoids, you might want to stick to the shorter trips. The northwest loop from Hanoi, via Dien Bien Phu and Sapa, is a gruelling but definitive road trip to discover the secrets of the region.

HIGHLIGHTS

- Meet Montagnards, trek through valleys to villages or just drool over the scenery around **Sapa** (p172)
- Learn about local life with a stay in a minority stilt house in the rural villages of **Mai Chau** (p165)
- Make for the minority markets – a blaze of colour when the Flower H'mong are in town – around **Bac Ha** (p181)
- Rise to the challenge of a two-day ascent of Vietnam's highest peak, **Fansipan** (p175)
- Discover how the Viet Minh overcame their French colonial masters in the decisive battle of **Dien Bien Phu** (p169)

- ELEVATION: 100M-3143M
- BEST TIME TO VISIT: MAR-MAY & SEP-NOV

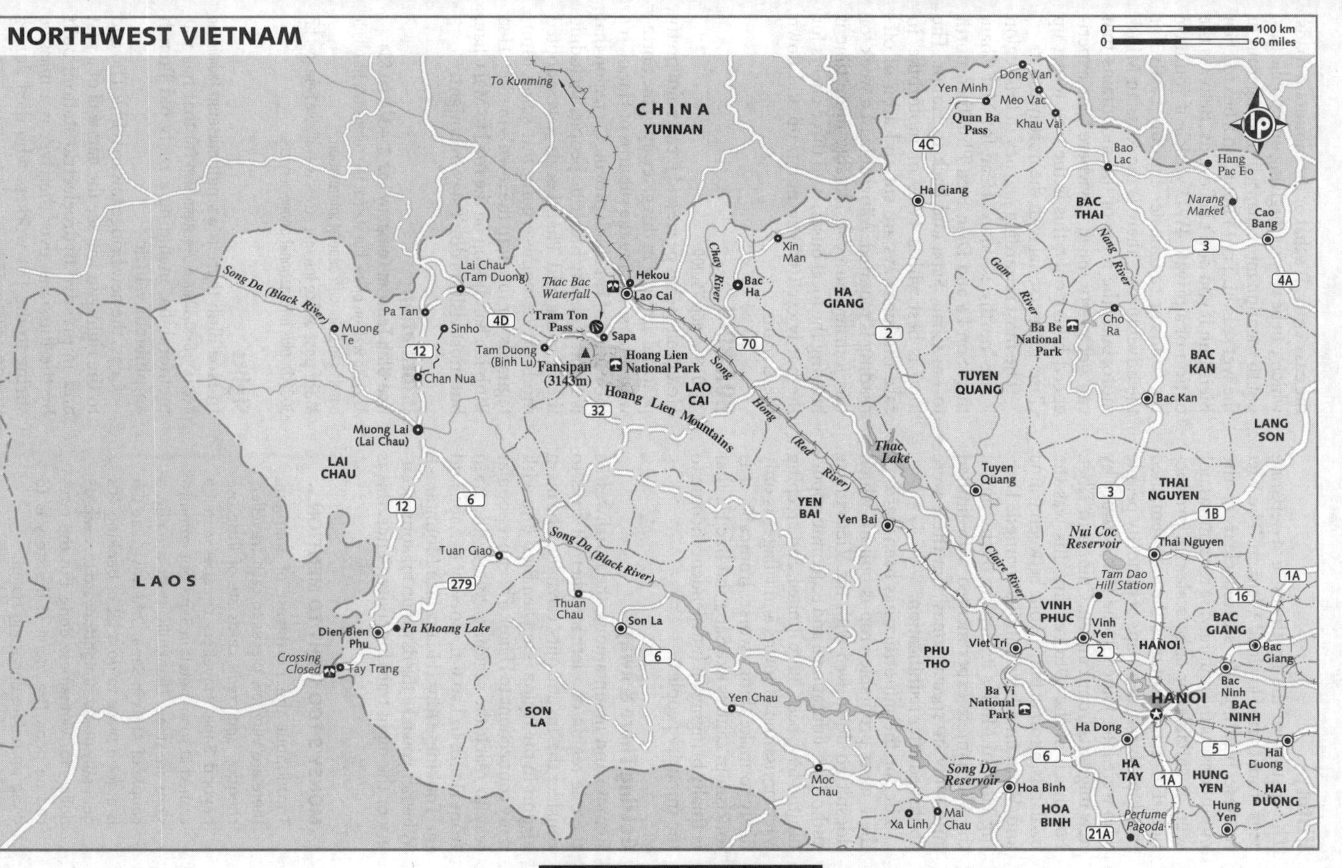
NORTHWEST VIETNAM
0 100 km
0 60 miles
To Kunming
CHINA
YUNNAN
Dong Van
Yen Minh
Meo Vac
Quan Ba Pass
Khau Vai
4C
Bao Lac
Hang Pac Eo
Ha Giang
BAC THAI
Narang Market
Cao Bang
3
Xin Man
Chay River
Bac Ha
Gam River
Nang River
4A
Hekou
Lao Cai
Thac Bac Waterfall
HA GIANG
Cho Ra
Song Da (Black River)
Lai Chau (Tam Duong)
Pa Tan
4D
Tram Ton Pass
Sapa
2
Ba Be National Park
Muong Te
Sinho
70
12
Tam Duong (Binh Lu)
Hoang Lien National Park
Song
BAC KAN
Fansipan (3143m)
Chan Nua
LAO CAI
TUYEN QUANG
Hoang Lien Mountains
Bac Kan
32
Hong
Muong Lai (Lai Chau)
LANG SON
(Red
Thac Lake
LAI CHAU
River)
Tuyen Quang
THAI NGUYEN
3
12
6
YEN BAI
Yen Bai
1B
Nui Coc Reservoir
Song Da (Black River)
Thai Nguyen
Tuan Giao
Claire River
LAOS
Tam Dao Hill Station
1A
279
16
Thuan Chau
VINH PHUC
BAC GIANG
Vinh Yen
Dien Bien Phu
Pa Khoang Lake
Son La
HANOI
Viet Tri
Bac Giang
PHU THO
2
Crossing Closed
Tay Trang
6
Bac Ninh
Ba Vi National Park
HANOI
BAC NINH
Yen Chau
SON LA
Ha Dong
5
Hai Cuong
6
Song Da Reservoir
HA TAY
HUNG YEN
Moc Chau
Hoa Binh
1A
HAI DUONG
Hung Yen
Xa Linh
Mai Chau
HOA BINH
Perfume Pagoda
21A

History

The history of the northwest is a separate saga from that of lowland Vietnam. The Vietnamese traditionally steered clear of the mountains, as the unforgiving terrain was not seen as suitable for large-scale rice production. For many centuries the area remained inhabited by small groups of minority people who were later joined in the 19th century by new migrants from Yunnan, China and Tibet. For much of the 19th century this was the badlands, a sort of buffer zone between China and Vietnam where bandits roamed. During Ho Chi Minh's leadership of the north, the Vietnamese experimented with limited autonomy in 'special zones', but these were abolished after reunification.

Life for the minorities has been hard, as their most profitable crop is opium, which doesn't go down well with the Vietnamese authorities. Educational and economic opportunities have been more limited, and creeping Vietnamisation of towns and villages is only likely to make things worse. Ironically, it is tourism in centres like Sapa and Bac Ha that is finally bringing an independent income to the minority people.

Getting There & Away

Remote and mountainous, the northwest is the one region of Vietnam where it pays to consider the 'ins and outs' carefully. The main airport in the region is at Dien Bien Phu with daily connections to Hanoi. The most popular way to reach the region is to take the train from Hanoi to Lao Cai, gateway to Sapa and the Tonkinese Alps (Hoang Lien Mountains). Whether you take the day train for some scenery or the night train for convenience, this is the easy entry. It's that or the mountain roads, which can be very unforgiving on a public bus, not to mention more than a little dangerous in the wet season. Try 14 hours on a bus to Dien Bien Phu if you don't believe us. Better is the option of a private 4WD vehicle if you have the funds or can muster a group. Lastly, for the adventurous, there is the Russian Minsk motorbike, the mule of the mountains that can get pretty much anywhere. For experienced bikers only, this is the way to get up close and personal with the northwest.

The most rewarding journey in this region is the 'northwest loop'. Head for Mai Chau, then Son La and Dien Bien Phu, then north to Lai Chau, Sapa and back to Hanoi. The loop is best with a 4WD or motorbike, in case the highways are cut and a bit of off-roading is required. Allow at least a week for this journey, and considerably more time if braving the local buses. And three cheers for the hardy cyclists who pump up and down these roads.

MONEY'S TOO TIGHT TO MENTION...

Throughout the northwest of Vietnam, there are very few places to cash travellers cheques, and credit cards are of little use beyond Sapa. Travellers cheques can be cashed at some hotels in Sapa, but commissions are steep. Thankfully, there are now a couple of ATMs in Sapa. Otherwise, Lao Cai is a good place to do a bit of banking. It's generally pretty straightforward to swap US dollars for Vietnamese dong, but the rates can be poor. The moral of the story is to dong up before departing Hanoi.

HOA BINH

☎ 018 / pop 75,000

Hoa Binh means peace and it can seem pretty peaceful arriving in this gateway to the northwest after surviving the suburbs of Hanoi. It's the capital of Hoa Binh province, a region that is home to many hill-tribe people, including the H'mong and Thai. Locals have adopted modern Vietnamese garb, but some Montagnards venture into the town's market. Hoa Binh is a handy stop on the road to Mai Chau, but most visitors don't stay overnight.

Information

Hoa Binh Tourism Company (☎ 854 374; fax 854 372) No walk-in office, but staff at the company's Hoa Binh hotels can help with general information.

Main post office Internet access is available here (per hr 3000d), plus international phone services.

Sights

In Hoa Binh there is a small **museum** (admission free; 8-10.30am & 2-4.30pm Mon-Fri) that has war memorabilia, including a rusty old French amphibious vehicle.

Cross the new bridge towards Phu Tho and to the right you will see the **dam wall** of a vast and impressive hydroelectric station, built by the Russians; over the river is a massive shrine to the 161 workers who died during its construction.

THE ROADS WELL TRAVELLED: CONVERSATIONS WITH JEEP DRIVERS

I didn't plan to be a tourist driver. In the early 1980s I went to Moscow on a scholarship, to take a degree in civil engineering, and hoped to make that my career. Many of us Vietnamese went to study in Russia during that time. I learned to speak Russian, too, of course. That lasted three years, but by the time I came back the political climate here had changed, a Russian education was not highly valued and my degree didn't count for much.

My extended family pooled our money and bought this 4WD. It's a 1993 model and we bought it secondhand in a shipment that came from the US. It registers miles, not kilometres, which was a bit confusing for me at first!

I drive all over the country, but the northwest is the area that tourists want most to see and I go there most often, I suppose at least 30 times a year. Yes, they're long days, but as long as I can have an hour at lunch to eat and rest that's fine. And the tourists usually bring snacks to share during the journey; I really like M&Ms.

Mostly when I drive foreigners there's a guide/interpreter with them, so I don't need to speak another language. You can understand a lot just by gestures and tone of voice and expressions. But I know it would be sensible to learn more English. I can understand some, but I'm not good at speaking it. My last passenger and I had fun learning to say things from the phrasebook; I taught her how to pronounce the Vietnamese and she taught me how to pronounce the English, then we'd test each other on the longer road trips. Foreigners always find it really hard to pronounce Vietnamese, though – too many tones. She left the book with me, so I must keep practising.

I'm usually home in Hanoi for one night and one day a week if I'm lucky. My wife works full-time in an office, but our children are almost teenagers so they can pretty well look after themselves when we're busy. We spend a lot on mobile phone calls though!

Sleeping & Eating

Thap Vang Hotel (☎ 852 864; 213 Đ Cu Chinh Lan; r 150,000d; ❄) Set just off the main street in town, this is a smart minihotel offering hot water, a cold fridge and satellite TV.

Hoa Binh Hotels I & II (☎ 854 374; fax 854 372; s/d US$23/28; ❄) Straddling either side of the road to Mai Chau, rooms here are set in mock Montagnard stilt-houses. These include reassuring nontraditional amenities like hot water and TV. It's well run compared with some of the state-owned places.

Cuisine is not necessarily Hoa Binh's main attraction, but there are many *com pho* places lining Hwy 6 in the centre of town. Locals venture across the new bridge to a string of *bia hoi* (beer) shacks along the riverbank.

Getting There & Away

Hoa Binh is 74km southwest of Hanoi and accessible by public bus (25,000d, two hours). Those with transport can visit Ba Vi National Park (p127) and follow a riverbank road to Hoa Binh.

SONG DA RESERVOIR (HO SONG DA)

Stretching west from Hoa Binh is Song Da Reservoir (Ho Song Da), one of Vietnam's largest. The flooding of the Da River has displaced a large number of farmers for about 200km upstream, and is part of a major hydroelectric scheme generating power for northern Vietnam. In 1994 a 500kV power line was extended to the south, temporarily freeing Ho Chi Minh City (HCMC) from seasonal power shortages.

Easiest access to the reservoir is by taking a spur road that cuts off from Hwy 6 at Dong Bang Junction (60km west of Hoa Binh and just outside Mai Chau). From the junction it's about a 5km drive to Bai San Pier. There's no obvious jetty here – hang around and someone

SLEEPING ON STILTS

If you are anticipating an exotic Indiana Jones encounter – sharing a bowl of eyeball soup, taking part in an ancient fertility ritual or entering a shamanic trance with the local medicine man – think again. Spending a night in one of Mai Chau's minority villages is a very 'civilised' experience: the local authorities have made sure that the villages are up to tourist standards, so electricity flows, modern amenities abound and there are hygienic Western-style toilets. Mattresses and mosquito nets are provided. While this is eminently more comfortable, it may not live up to your rustic hill-tribe trekking expectations. Tour operators are not helping the situation: somehow they cannot seem to resist slapping up their oversized stickers wherever their groups stop to eat or drink, even if that happens to be on these lovely wooden stilt houses.

Despite – or perhaps because of – modern amenities, it's still a memorable experience and many people end up staying longer than planned. The Thai villages are exceedingly friendly and, when it's all said and done, even with TV and the hum of the refrigerator, it *is* a peaceful place and you're still sleeping in a thatched-roof stilt house on split-bamboo floors.

Reservations are not necessary. Just show up, but try and arrive before dark, just to get your bearings as much as anything else. You can book a meal at the house where you're staying for around 30,000d, depending on what you require. The women here have learned to cook everything from fried eggs to French fries, but try to eat the local food – it's more interesting. Try to establish the price of meal before departure, as there have been occasional disagreements over the bill.

will come out from a house and ask where you want to go. You'll need a Vietnamese speaker to help make arrangements.

One of the trips you can take is to the **Ba Khan Islands**. The islands are the tops of submerged mountains. The return trip to the islands takes three hours and costs about 250,000d per boat (each boat can seat 10).

Another possible boat trip is to **Than Nhan village**, home to members of the Dzao tribe. The two-hour return trip costs about 180,000d. The boat leaves you at a pier from where it's a steep 4km uphill walk to the village. If you'd like to stay in the village, take the boat one way for 100,000d and get a return boat to Bai San Pier the next day.

MAI CHAU

☎ 018 / pop 47,500 / elevation 300m

Mai Chau is the heart of a beautiful valley that is a world away from the hustle and bustle of Hanoi. The modern village is an unappealing sprawl, but as you emerge on the rice fields and rural living it is transformed into a real paradise. It's a stunning area, and most people here are ethnic White Thai, distantly related to tribes in Thailand, Laos and China.

Although most locals no longer wear traditional dress, the Thai women are masterful weavers who ensure that there is plenty of traditional-style clothing to buy in the village centre. You will see women weaving on looms under or inside their houses in the village. Much of the silk looks similar to that seen in Laos. The Thai of Mai Chau are less likely to employ strong-arm sales tactics than their H'mong counterparts in Sapa: polite bargaining is the norm rather than endless haggling.

Sights & Activities

This is one of the closest places to Hanoi where you can experience a 'real' **Montagnard village**. Other attractions here include staying overnight in one of the Thai stilt houses (see

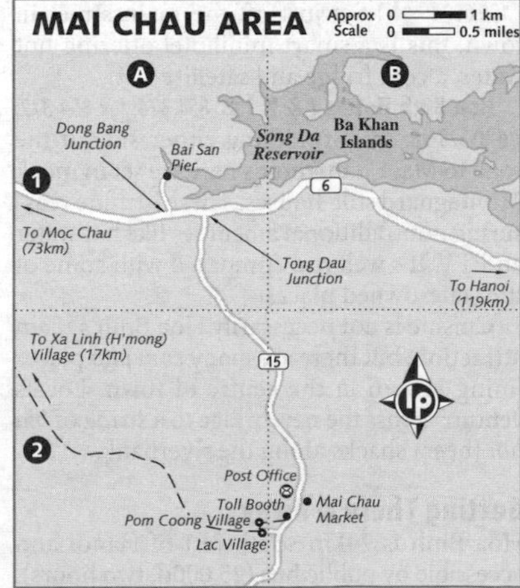

the boxed text, opposite), **walking** through the beautiful valley through the rice fields and **trekking** to minority villages. A typical trek further afield covers 7km to 8km; a local guide can be hired for about US$5.

There is a popular 18km trek from **Lac village** (Ban Lac) in Mai Chau to **Xa Linh village**, near a mountain pass (elevation 1000m) on Hwy 6. Lac village is home to the White Thai people, while the inhabitants of Xa Linh are H'mong. The trek is quite strenuous to undertake in a day, so most people spend the night in a village along the way. Arrange a local guide and a car to meet you at the mountain pass for the journey back to Mai Chau. Be warned that there is a 600m climb in altitude and the trail can be slippery in the rain.

Longer treks of three to seven days are possible. Ask around in the Mai Chau villages of Lac or Pom Coong. Many cafés and travel agencies in Hanoi run inexpensive trips to Mai Chau (see p91). These include all transport, food and accommodation.

Sleeping

There are two accommodation centres in Mai Chau: the village of Lac and the village of Pom Coong. Pom Coong is slightly more rural and less developed than Lac, so opt for it if you have the choice.

Set a few hundred metres back from the 'main' roadside, both villages offer a rustic experience in traditional **Thai stilt houses** (60,000d per person). Villagers will sometimes organise traditional song-and-dance performances in the evenings and anyone is free to join in the fun. A mild word of warning about the showers: the doors may have fairly large gaps between the walls and the occasional opportunist guide or driver has taken the chance to observe the proceedings. Use your towel to good effect.

Getting There & Away

Mai Chau is 135km from Hanoi and just 5km south of Tong Dau junction on Hwy 6. There's no direct public transport to Mai Chau from Hanoi; however, buses to nearby Hoa Binh (25,000d, two hours) are plentiful. From Hoa Binh there are several scheduled buses to Mai Chau (20,000d, two hours) daily. Usually these stop at Tong Dau junction; a *xe om* (motorbike taxi) from there to Mai Chau proper will cost about 15,000d.

Theoretically, foreigners must pay a 5000d entry fee to Mai Chau; there's a toll booth at the state-run guesthouse on the 'main' road. More often than not, there is nobody there to collect the fee.

MOC CHAU

☎ 022 / pop 113,100 / elevation 1500m

This highland town produces some of Vietnam's best tea and is a good place to stock up. The surrounding area is also home to several ethnic minorities, including Green H'mong, Dzao, Thai and Muong.

Moc Chau boasts a pioneering dairy industry that started in the late 1970s with Australian (and, later, UN) assistance. The dairy provides Hanoi with such delectable luxuries as fresh milk, sweetened condensed milk and little tooth-rotting bars called *banh sua*. Not surprisingly, Moc Chau is a good place to sample some fresh milk and yogurt. Indulge yourself at one of the dairy shops that line Hwy 6 as it passes through Moc Chau.

Should you get stuck in Moc Chau, **Duc Dung Guesthouse** (☎ 866 181; r 120,000d; ❄) is a reliable option to rest a weary head. About 300m from the post office on Hwy 6, it's a basic but friendly family-run pad.

Moc Chau is 200km from Hanoi (54,000d), and the journey takes about five hours by private vehicle. It's a further 120km from Moc Chau to Son La (26,000d).

YEN CHAU

☎ 022 / pop 50,800

Predominantly agricultural, this district is known for its abundant fruits. Bananas aside, all fruits grown here are seasonal – mangoes, plums and peaches are harvested from April to June, longans in July and August, and custard apples in August and September.

The mangoes are considered to be some of the tastiest in Vietnam, although travellers may find them disappointing at first, as they are small and green rather than big, yellow and juicy as in the tropical south. However, many Vietnamese prefer the somewhat tart taste and aroma of the green ones, especially dipped in *nuoc mam* (fish sauce) and sugar.

Yen Chau is 260km from Hanoi (67,000d), approximately seven hours by road. A bus from Yen Chau to Son La will cost 15,000d.

SON LA

☎ 022 / pop 61,600

Son La has prospered on the back of its location as a natural transit point between

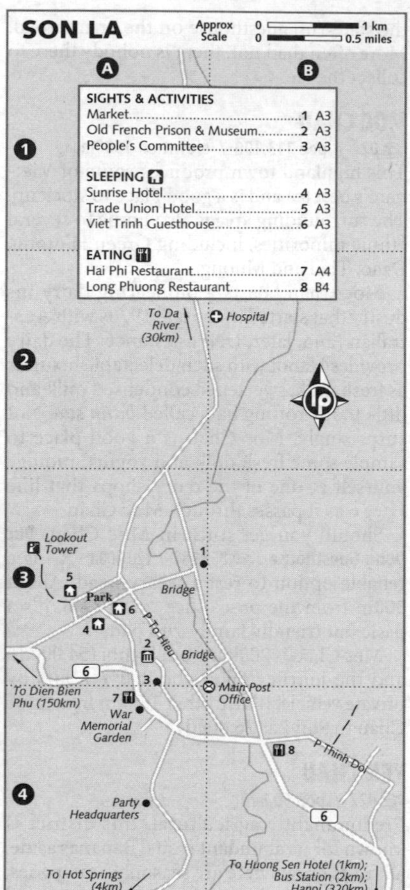

Hanoi and Dien Bien Phu. It may not be one of Vietnam's must-see destinations, but the surrounding scenery is impressive and there are enough diversions to occupy half a day.

The area is populated predominantly by Montagnards, notably the Black Thai, Meo, Muong and White Thai. Vietnamese influence in the area was minimal until the 20th century; from 1959 to 1980 the region was part of the Tay Bac Autonomous Region.

Sights & Activities

The **Old French Prison & Museum** (Nha Tu Cu Cua Phap; admission 5000d; 7.30-11am & 1.30-5pm) in Son La was once the site of a French penal colony where anticolonial revolutionaries were incarcerated. It was destroyed by the infamous 'off-loading' of unused ammunition by US warplanes that were returning to their bases after bombing raids, but it has been partially restored. Rebuilt turrets and watchtowers stand guard over the remains of cells, inner walls and a famous lone surviving peach tree. The tree, which blooms with traditional Tet flowers, was planted in the compound by To Hieu, a former inmate from the 1940s. To Hieu has subsequently been immortalised, with various landmarks now named after him.

A narrow road leads uphill to the prison, off the main highway. Nearby is a People's Committee office with a small **museum** on the top floor, where there are some local hill-tribe displays and a good bird's-eye view of the prison ruins. The prison itself is at the back, the entrance beneath a faded sign marked 'Penitencier'.

Perched above the town, a **lookout tower** offers a sweeping overview of Son La and the surrounding area. The climb is steep and takes about 20 minutes, but the view from the top is worth the effort. The stone steps leading up to the tower are immediately to the left of the Trade Union Hotel.

You can find a small selection of colourful woven shoulder bags, scarves, silver buttons and necklaces, clothing and other Montagnard crafts at Son La's **market**.

A few kilometres south of town are **hot springs** (Suoi Nuoc Nong). There's a rather soupy small communal **pool** (admission free), and several privately run concrete **cubicles** (admission 5000d) where water is pumped into private bathtubs. Unless you particularly like sharing other people's bathwater, you can probably give it a miss. To get here, start opposite the museum road and follow the trail past the party headquarters building.

The township of Thuan Chau is about 35km northwest of Son La. Try and pass through early in the morning when the small daily local **market** is full of incredibly colourful hill-tribe women. Between 9am and 10am, a steady stream of women can be seen walking, cycling and motorbiking home to their villages along the main road.

Sleeping & Eating

Almost all travellers journeying between Hanoi and Dien Bien Phu spend the night in Son La. There are plenty of hotels in town, some of which double as brothels. There is a cluster of welcoming hotels on Đ 26/8 that are the exception to this rule.

Viet Trinh Guesthouse (☎ 852 263; 15 Đ 26/8; r 80,000d;) One of the cheapest options in town, the large rooms include hot showers. It's pretty clean for the price, but English is in short supply.

Sunrise Hotel (☎ 858 798; fax 859 799; 53 Đ 26/8; r US$10-15;) A little further up the road is this smart establishment. The rooms come with all the trimmings like hot water and satellite TV and the tiles are clean enough to double as mirrors, which might be slightly unnerving.

Huong Sen Hotel (☎ 851 980; 228 Đ Truong Chinh; r 150,000-200,000d;) The newest place in town, this is on the superhighway to Hanoi. Rooms are spick 'n' span and also include a smart bathroom.

Trade Union Hotel (Khach San Cong Doan; ☎ 852 804; congdoanhotelsonla@yahoo.com.vn; s/d/t US$10/15/20;) A rare species in the provinces, this is a warm and welcoming government-run hotel. The large rooms come with all the trimmings and include a hearty breakfast. There are also some newer VIP rooms for US$35 if you are feeling very important. There's a reliable restaurant upstairs that fills up in the evening.

Long Phuong Restaurant (☎ 852 339; Pho Thinh Doi; mains 10,000-40,000d) Located at one of the busier junctions in town, this restaurant is the place to sample some of the minority dishes from around the region. Consider the sour *mang dang* (bamboo shoots) soup, a speciality of the Thai minority people, washed down with sticky rice dipped in sesame seed salt.

Hai Phi Restaurant (Hwy 6; mains 15,000-50,000d) Son La is famous for its *lau* (goat meat) and here they serve up Billy in every shape and size. Try the highly prized *tiet canh*, a bowl of goat's-blood curd dressed with a sprinkling of peanuts and veggies. Or go for the more mainstream, but tasty, goat-meat steamboat.

Getting There & Away

Son La's bus station is 2km southwest of town. Buses run from 4am to noon between Son La and Hanoi (78,000d), taking about 10 hours or so, assuming there are no serious breakdowns. Regular morning buses also run to Dien Bien Phu (50,000d, five hours).

Son La lies 320km from Hanoi and 150km from Dien Bien Phu. By 4WD or motorbike, the Hanoi–Son La run typically takes eight hours. Son La to Dien Bien Phu takes another four hours.

TUAN GIAO

☎ 023 / pop 94,900 / elevation 600m

This remote mountain town is at the junction of Hwy 42 to Dien Bien Phu (three hours, 80km) and Hwy 6 to Muong Lay (three hours, 98km). Few people spend the night here unless they are running behind schedule and can't make it to Dien Bien Phu. However, if you are taking your time through the northwest, it is a logical place to bed down for the night.

Tuan Giao Hotel (☎ 862 613; r 150,000-200,000d) has been recently renovated, although you wouldn't necessarily know it when you arrive. The rooms aren't bad, including hot showers, but the beds are pretty hard, even compared with sleeping on the floor in Mai Chau. It's about 150m from the main junction in the direction of Muong Lay.

One of the only real restaurants in town, **Hoang Quat Restaurant** (☎ 862 482; dishes 15,000-40,000d) is a popular lunchtime stop for small groups touring the northwest, but it is almost deserted by night – a telling sign that few people overnight here. It is about 500m from the junction towards Dien Bien Phu and has a small selection of Vietnamese favourites and Western classics.

Most travellers approach Tuan Giao from Son La (two hours, 75km). The government is continuing the new road from Son La this way, carving new cuts into the mountain, but it will be some years before it is ready for use. Few travellers use the direct road from Tuan Giao to Muong Lay, as most are visiting Dien Bien Phu. It's a wild road, and also a wild ride, for experienced motorbikers, but it does offer some of the best scenery in the region.

PA KHOANG LAKE

A beautiful body of water, Pa Khoang Lake is 17km east of Dien Bien Phu, on the road from Son La, and 4km off the highway. About 15km drive around the lake's edge, or an hour's boat ride plus a 3km forest walk, is the **bunker of General Giap**, the Vietnamese commander of the Dien Bien Phu campaign. There is little left to see, but for war junkies it is an essential stop on the trail of Vietnam's legendary military tactician. There is also a remote **Thai village** that can be visited across the lake. Hire a motor boat (US$15 return) to the bunker or villages, and stay for a spot of lunch.

DIEN BIEN PHU

☎ 023 / pop 25,000

Dien Bien Phu is famous as the site of a battle that was truly decisive. The French colonial forces were roundly defeated at the hands of the Viet Minh on 7 May 1954 and the days of their Indochina empire were finally numbered.

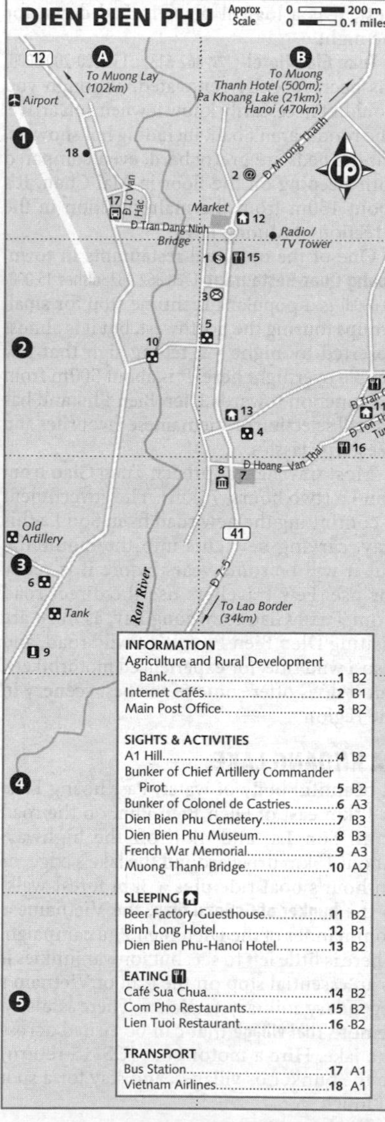

Dien Bien Phu, known as DBP for short, now enjoys the prestigious status of provincial city, like Hanoi and Ho Chi Minh City, although it is not quite in the same league. Set in one of the most remote parts of Vietnam, the town is 34km from the Lao border in the flat, heart-shaped Muong Thanh Valley, surrounded by steep, heavily forested hills. The size and look of the city is surprising considering the remote location, especially if you managed to survive getting here overland.

History is the main attraction here and the scenery is more stunning on the journey to or from Dien Bien Phu than around the town itself. Not surprisingly, the majority of travellers who come here now are French – Dien Bien Phu seems to hold the same sort of fascination for them as the Demilitarised Zone (DMZ) does for Americans.

For centuries Dien Bien Phu was a transit stop on the caravan route from Myanmar and China to northern Vietnam. The town itself was established in 1841 by the Nguyen dynasty to prevent raids on the Red River Delta by bandits.

The area is inhabited by Montagnards, most notably the Thai and H'mong. The government has been encouraging ethnic Vietnamese to settle in the region and they currently make up about half of the Muong Thanh Valley's total population.

Orientation & Information

It may enjoy the same status as metropolises such as HCMC and Danang, but in reality Dien Bien Phu is an overgrown village when it comes to navigating. The Ron River splits the town in half, but most of the accommodation and attractions are on the east bank. To the west is the airport and what might pass as suburbs.

Internet access is available at several little cafés along Đ Muong Thanh.

Agriculture and Rural Development Bank (☎ 825 786; Đ7-5) Represents Western Union and can change cash.

Main post office (Đ7-5) Post and phone services and internet access.

Sights & Activities

The site of the decisive battle is now marked by several monuments, including the **Dien Bien Phu Museum** (☎ 824 971; admission 5000d; ⏰ 7.30-11am & 1.30-4.30pm), an informative if dry look at one of Vietnam's finest hours. Across the river the

bunker headquarters (admission 5000d; 7.30-11am & 1.30-4.30pm) of the French commander, Colonel Christian de Castries, has been re-created, and there are old French tanks and artillery pieces nearby. There is a monument to Viet Minh casualties on the site of the former French position, known to the French as Eliane and to the Vietnamese as **A1 Hill** (admission 5000d; 7.30-11am & 1.30-4.30pm), where bitter fighting took place. The elaborate trenches at the heart of the French defences have recently been re-created.

The old **Muong Thanh Bridge** is preserved and closed to four-wheeled traffic. Near the southern end of the bridge – though not much more than a crater in the ground overgrown with weeds – is the **bunker** where Chief Artillery Commander Pirot committed suicide.

A **memorial** to the 3000 French troops buried under the rice paddies was erected in 1984 on the 30th anniversary of the battle. The stylishly designed **Dien Bien Phu Cemetery** commemorates the Vietnamese dead, and you can catch a good view over it by climbing the stairs inside the main entry gate. Looking over the endless headstones begs the question: are there any victors in war?

Sleeping

Beer Factory Guesthouse (Khach San Cong Ty Bia; ☎ 824 635; r 150,000-180,000d; Đ Tran Can;) A beer drinker's idea of heaven, unfortunately the minibar does not include free draught beer. This brewery-run guesthouse is clean and good value, and the popular rooms include hot water and TV. Just mind your head on the stairs up, particularly if you have taken advantage of the countless *bia hoi* pubs lining the nearby streets.

Binh Long Hotel (☎ 824 345; 429 Đ Muong Thanh; tw US$12;) A small and friendly family-run place, the rooms here are all twins. The rooms aren't exactly huge, but the cleaners take their job very seriously. Rates include breakfast.

Muong Thanh Hotel (☎ 810 043; fax 810 713; Đ Muong Thanh; r US$15-25;) Deservedly the most popular place in town, this is the residence of choice for many tour groups, so book ahead.

THE SIEGE OF DIEN BIEN PHU

In early 1954 General Henri Navarre, commander of the French forces in Indochina, sent 12 battalions to occupy the Muong Thanh Valley to prevent the Viet Minh from crossing into Laos and threatening the former Lao capital of Luang Prabang. The French units, of which about 30% were ethnic Vietnamese, were soon surrounded by a Viet Minh force under General Vo Nguyen Giap that consisted of 33 infantry battalions, six artillery regiments and a regiment of engineers. The Viet Minh force, which outnumbered the French by five to one, was equipped with 105mm artillery pieces and anti-aircraft guns, carried by porters through jungles and across rivers in an unbelievable feat of logistics. The guns were placed in carefully camouflaged positions dug deep into the hills that overlooked the French positions.

When the guns eventually opened up, French Chief Artillery Commander Pirot committed suicide. He had assumed there was no way the Viet Minh could get heavy artillery to the area. Now it was a reality, Dien Bien Phu would only end in defeat. A failed Viet Minh human-wave assault against the French was followed by weeks of intense artillery bombardments. Six battalions of French paratroopers were parachuted into Dien Bien Phu as the situation worsened, but bad weather and the Viet Minh artillery, impervious to French air and artillery attacks, prevented sufficient French reinforcements and supplies from arriving. An elaborate system of trenches and tunnels allowed Viet Minh soldiers to reach French positions without coming under fire. The trenches and bunkers were overrun by the Viet Minh after the French decided against the use of US conventional bombers – and the Pentagon's proposal to use tactical atomic bombs. All 13,000 men in the French garrison were either killed or taken prisoner; Viet Minh casualties were estimated at 25,000.

Just one day before the Geneva Conference on Indochina was set to begin half a world away, Viet Minh forces overran the beleaguered French garrison at Dien Bien Phu after a 57-day siege. This shattered French morale and forced the French government to abandon its attempts to re-establish colonial control of Vietnam. For the full story of this incredible siege, pick up a copy of *Hell in a Small Place – The Siege of Dien Bien Phu* by legendary French reporter Bernard S Fall.

Split into several buildings, try for the newer wing, as the old wing is showing signs of age. Facilities include a swimming pool, plus a huge barn-like restaurant. Throw in karaoke and 'Thai Massage' (honest), and it is *the* place to be in DBP.

Dien Bien Phu-Hanoi Hotel (☎ 825 103; fax 826 290; 279 Đ 7-5; r 250,000-350,000d; ✈ ▣) Possibly the smartest hotel in town right now, it is a bit business-like and somehow lacks the coy charm of the Muong Thanh. All the rooms are well finished, with satellite TV, minibar and snappy bathrooms. Breakfast included.

Eating

Given the size of the town, there are surprisingly few dining options. Some of the better restaurants are located at the bigger hotels, including the Muong Thanh.

Lien Tuoi Restaurant (☎ 824 919; Đ Hoang Van Thai; mains 20,00-50,000d) Long popular for a combination of good Vietnamese and Chinese food, this eating establishment is a good choice after a long day on the road. The menu is in English and French with some imaginative translations. It is about 400m up the road from the cemetery.

There is a superb little Café Sua Chua opposite the Beer Factory Hotel, turning out some of the tastiest *pho* in the northwest and it is always heaving with locals. There are also a few decent local *com pho* joints on Đ 7-5.

Getting There & Away

The overland trip to Dien Bien Phu can be more intriguing than the actual battlefield sites for which the town is so celebrated. Of course, you miss out on this if you fly.

AIR

Vietnam Airlines (☎ 824 948; fax 825 536; ⏲ 7.30-11.30am & 1.30-4.30pm) operates daily flights between Dien Bien Phu and Hanoi. The office is just before the airport, about 1.5km from the town centre, along the road to Muong Lay.

BUS

The bus station is on Hwy 12, at the corner of Đ Tran Dang Ninh. There is a direct bus service that runs from Hanoi to Dien Bien Phu (120,000d, 14 hours) leaving at 6am and 8am.

Buses to Muong Lay (35,000d, three hours) leave in the morning. Daily buses to Son La (50,000d, four hours) start at 4.30am, but for normal people who like to get up at normal times there are regular departures until noon.

Although the bus is cheap, it's not really much fun. Buses are so packed that the only scenery you get to admire is the armpit of the person sitting next to you. If overloaded vehicles, bad roads and bad brakes worry you, definitely fly or travel overland by 4WD or motorbike.

CAR & MOTORBIKE

The 470km drive from Hanoi to Dien Bien Phu on Hwys 6 and 42 takes at least 12 hours (if you're lucky). Conceivably it could be done in a single direct journey, but almost everyone stays overnight in Son La. Speaking from experience, it's no picnic hanging on to the hairpins on a motorbike in the dark!

MUONG LAY

☎ 023 / pop 19,600 / elevation 600m

Formerly known as Lai Chau, this small town is nestled in a pretty valley carved from spectacular mountains by the Da River, and makes a good lunch or overnight stop for people travelling between Dien Bien Phu and Sapa.

Beneath Muong Lay's beauty lies a difficult existence for locals. Despite a marked increase in tourist numbers, for most of the people it's a hard living. Far from busy trade routes,

ALL CHANGE IN THE NORTH

There's been a lot of confusing name changes in the northwest in the past couple of years. A large chunk of old Lai Chau province, including the provincial capital, is due to go under water in a few more years. The government struck first and created the new province of Dien Bien Phu and relocated the province of Lai Chau to the northeast. The old town of Lai Chau is now Moung Lay; the old town of Tam Duong is now Lai Chau, the provincial capital of the new province; and the old town of Binh Lu is now Tam Duong. Confused? So were we. More than a few travellers have been jumping off the bus in the new town of Lai Chau, hunting for the popular Lan Anh Hotel. No, that's in Muong Lay – the old Lai Chau. Aarrgghh!

BORDER CROSSING: TAY TRANG/SOP HUN

The Lao border at Tay Trang, gateway to Phongsali province, is only 34km from Dien Bien Phu. Persistent rumours circulate about this crossing opening to foreign tourists soon, but at the time of writing it was still closed. OK, so we've said it for a few years now, but it really is likely to open during the lifetime of this book. Keep your ear to the ground and do your homework in Hanoi. Check out the motorbiking website *GT Rider* (www.gt-rider.com) for the latest, as these guys are eagerly waiting for it to open.

normal commerce is limited and the town has only been really successful in harvesting cash crops such opium and timber. Needless to say, opium harvesting does not find favour with the central government, which has been trying to discourage the Montagnards from producing poppies.

If the opium business is falling on hard times, the same must be said for the timber industry. In recent years the forest cover has been reduced and flooding has increased dramatically. Around 140 people lost their lives in 1990 in a devastating flood on the Da River that swept through the narrow valley. An even worse flood in 1996 killed 100 people and cut all roads into town for two months; the ruins of the flooded former cultural hall can be seen in the middle of town.

It seems that this kind of flooding will become a permanent feature of Muong Lay. There is a massive dam under construction, just above the current Song Da Reservoir, and this will fill the valley with water. When this comes to pass (not before 2010), this will be the largest hydroelectric station in Southeast Asia. It also could mean that in the future the only way to visit Muong Lay will be by submarine.

Being underwater, however, would at least keep things cooler. Odd as it might seem, in summer Muong Lay is one of the hottest places in Vietnam. June and July temperatures can soar as high as 40°C.

Sleeping & Eating

Lan Anh Hotel (☎ 852 682; fax 852 370; r US$10-20; ❄) These guys run a tight ship, which is pretty fortunate given the town will be under water in the next few years. One of the most switched-on hotels in the northwest, it offers helpful tourism information, good food and a steady stream of cold beer. The main compound has wooden Thai-style stilt houses with wide fan-cooled balconies. The hotel has expanded into a mishmash of buildings dotting the nearby street. More expensive rooms come with air-con and hot water. The hotel also offers an extensive program of tours and boat trips around Lai Chau. It's situated just past the market, to the right before the bridge.

Song Da Hotel (☎ 852 527; r 120,000d; ❄) How to compete with the Lan Anh? Given the town is going under, literally, these folk have given up trying. The rooms are rather run down, but it could be an option for those wanting to avoid other tourists. It's located on the road to Dien Bien Phu.

Getting There & Away

Most travellers arrive from Dien Bien Phu (three hours, 103km), although there's also the rocky road option of Hwy 6 from Tuan Giao (four hours, 96km). The road from Lai Chau to Sapa (six hours, 155km) is one of the most beautiful drives in Vietnam, particularly the final climb up over the Tram Ton Pass.

Public buses make the run to/from Hanoi, as well Dien Bien Phu (35,000d, three hours) and Sapa (53,000d).

MUONG TE

☎ 023 / pop 43,900 / elevation 900m

Muong Te is one of Vietnam's most remote outposts, 98km northwest of Muong Lay along the scenic Da River. The majority of the population is ethnic Thai, although they have assimilated enough to be nearly indistinguishable from the Vietnamese. Other minority groups found in the area include the Lahu (Khau Xung), Si La and Ha Nhi.

Apart from a small Sunday **market** and some nearby **villages**, there is not much to see or do in Muong Te. The only accommodation available in town is the shabby People's Committee Guesthouse, which also has a small restaurant.

SINHO

☎ 023 / pop 8500 / elevation 1054m

Sinho is a scenic mountain village that is home to a large number of ethnic minorities. It should attract more tourists, but the police

GET OFF MY LAND!

Follow the road from the signposted turn-off on Hwy 12 towards Muong Te for about 8km to encounter a peculiar historical relic: an ancient poem carved in stone by 15th-century emperor Le Loi, who had succeeded in expelling the Chinese from the region. The poem was left as a warning for any other potential invaders not to mess with Le Loi. The translation from Chinese reads:

Hey! The humble, coward and frantic rebels, I come here to counter-attack for the sake of the border inhabitants. There existed the betrayed subjects since the beginning of human history. The land is no longer dangerous. The plants' figures, the whisper of the wind, and even the singing of the songbirds startle the mean enemy. The nation is now integrated and this carved poem an amulet for Eastern peace of the country.

An Auspicious Day of December, The Year of the Pigs (1432)

To find this vestige, look for the narrow flight of steps marked by a small stone placard reading 'Di Tich Lich Su – Bia Le Loi' on the roadside overlooking the river.

have a poor reputation here and there is a 'You ain't from around here look' on the faces of many locals. Strange, but true. There is a colourful Sunday **market**, although the dingy People's Committee Guesthouse has the only beds in town and they have to be pressured into accepting foreigners.

Sinho is a 38km climb on a treacherous dirt road that is one of the most spectacular runs in the region. The turn-off is about 1km north of Chan Nua, on the road from Muong Lay, and it takes about 1½ hours each way. The road has been under construction for years, but it is still not complete. However, the road from the new Lai Chau to the north is in pretty reasonable shape and is helping to slowly put Sinho on the map.

LAI CHAU

☎ 023 / pop 94,400

Formerly known as Tam Duong, this remote town lies between Sapa and Moung Lay and is set in a verdant valley of conical peaks that resemble diminutive volcanoes. While the town is nothing special, the countryside around is sublime and it's a handy lunch stop between Muong Lay and Sapa.

The local **market**, about midway through the town on Hwy 12, is worth exploring. The majority of people are Montagnards from nearby villages, although ethnic Vietnamese make up the largest single group. If you're not in a rush to get to Sapa or Muong Lay, you could base yourself in Lai Chau for a day or so and explore the surrounding areas.

The drive from Lai Chau to Sapa along Hwy 4D, threading through the Fansipan Mountain Range near the Chinese border, is a beautiful stretch of road.

Sleeping & Eating

Tay Bac Hotel (☎ 875 879; r 120,000-150,000d; ❄) The most atmospheric beds in town are found here, in an attractive Thai-style wooden house at the rear. Rooms come with air-con and hot water, and they boast a 'safe big car park'.

Tuan Anh Restaurant (meals 10,000-30,000d) offers the best food in town for those on a lunch run. Other nearby *com pho* spots like Phuong Thanh are cheap and cheerful. Be aware that canine fare is popular: dog lover takes on a whole new meaning in Lai Chau.

SAPA

☎ 020 / pop 36,200 / elevation 1650m

The Queen of the Mountains, Sapa sits regally overlooking a beautiful valley, lofty mountains towering over the town on all sides. Welcome to *the* destination in northwest Vietnam, gateway to another world of mysterious minority cultures and luscious landscapes. The spectacular scenery that surrounds Sapa includes cascading rice terraces that spill down the mountains like a patchwork quilt. The mountains are often shrouded in mist that rolls back and forth along the peaks, offering tantalising glimpses of what lies in wait on a clear day. The valleys and villages around Sapa are home to a host of hill-tribe people who wander in to town to buy, sell and trade.

In a beautiful valley close to the Chinese border, Sapa is a former hill station built in 1922. History has not always been kind to Sapa, and the series of conflicts that swept over Vietnam nearly saw it wiped off the map. From WWII, successive wars against the French and the USA, not forgetting the more recent border skirmish with China in 1979, took their toll. The old hotels built by the French were allowed to fall into disrepair and Sapa was forgotten by all but a handful of residents.

With the advent of tourism, Sapa has experienced a renaissance. Bad roads have been upgraded, many streets have been given names, countless new hotels have popped up, the electricity supply is reliable and the food has improved immeasurably. Inherent in all of this prosperity is cultural change for the Montagnards, many of whom are now well versed in the ways of the cash economy and are reaping the financial rewards of the tourism influx. The downside is a building boom that has seen one hotel after another raise the roof in a continual quest for better views. Height restrictions are rarely enforced and the Sapa skyline is changing for the worse.

Another inconvenience that will not change is the weather. If you visit off-season, don't forget your winter woollies. Not only is it cold (like 0°C), but winter brings fog and drizzle. Quite why the French alighted on this spot is difficult to comprehend: it must have been one of those rare clear days when the views are to die for. The chilly climate does have its advantages, however. The area boasts temperate-zone fruit trees bearing peaches and plums, and gardens for raising medicinal herbs.

The dry season in Sapa lasts from around January to June. January and February are the coldest (and foggiest) months. From March to May the weather is often excellent, and the summer is warm despite the rains between June and August. The window from September to mid-December is a rewarding time to be in Sapa, though there is a bit of lingering rain at the start and the temperature dips by December.

Sapa would be of considerably less interest without the H'mong and Dzao people, the largest ethnic groups in the region. The billowing red headdresses of the Red Dzao are visible all over town, a surreal sight amid the accelerating development. The H'mong are more numerous and canny traders. Their

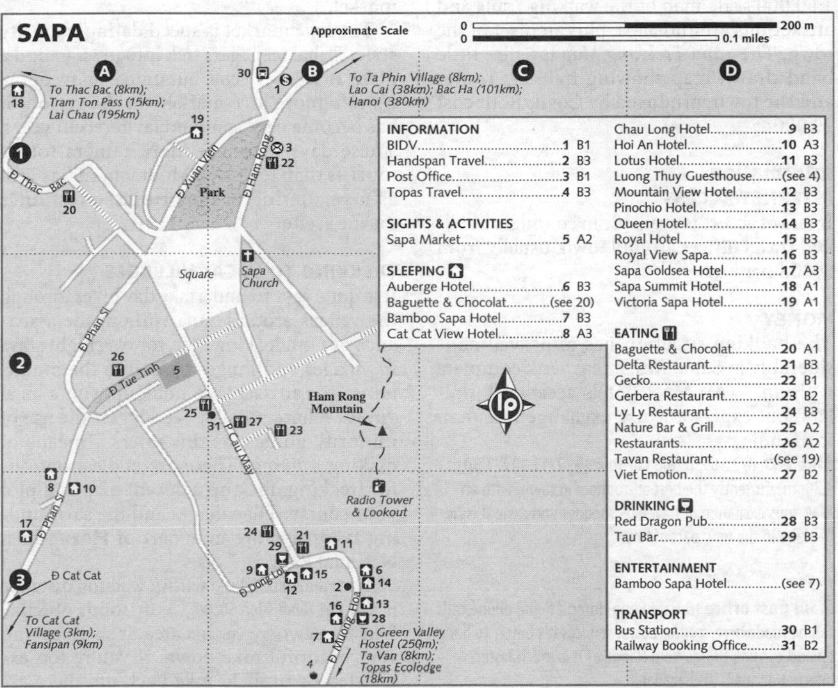

villages may look medieval but most will have a mobile phone and an email address to stay in touch. Traditionally, they were the poorest of the poor, but have rapidly learnt the spirit of free enterprise. Most of the Montagnards have had little formal education and are illiterate, yet all the youngsters have a good command of English, French and a handful of other languages.

If possible, try to visit during the week, when Sapa is less crowded and more intimate. Crowds flock to Sapa for the Saturday market, but a smaller market is held every day. There is plenty to see on weekdays, and there are lots of interesting villages within walking distance of the centre.

Orientation

There is some confusion regarding Pho Cau May and Đ Muong Hoa. Note that places on the western side use Pho Cau May as their address while locations on the eastern side use Đ Muong Hoa.

MAPS

The *Sapa Tourist Map* is an excellent 1:60,000 scale map of the walking trails and attractions around Sapa, plus an inset of the town. The *Sapa Trekking Map* is a nice little hand-drawn map showing trekking routes and the town, produced by Covit. Both cost 20,000d.

Information

INTERNET ACCESS

Internet access is available in countless hotels and travel offices around town, usually from 5000d per hour.

MONEY

The banking situation has improved considerably in Sapa, with a real bank complete with an ATM. Most hotels accept US dollars, but expect a worse exchange rate than in Hanoi.

BIDV (☎ 872 569; Đ Ngu Chi Son; 🕑 7-11.30 & 1.30-4.30pm) Currently the best all-rounder in town, with an ATM, plus exchange of travellers cheques and cash. It is by the lake in the new part of town.

POST

Main post office (Đ Ham Rong) International phone calls can be made here, but for postal services it's better to hang on and consign things from Hanoi, as it is much faster. Internet access is also available.

TRAVEL AGENCIES

There are several reliable travel companies in Sapa for trekking, mountain biking and other adventure activities, as well as those recommended under below.

Handspan Travel (☎/fax 872 110; www.handspan.com; 8 Pho Cau May) A popular outfit for trekking and mountain biking, it offers overnight tours to nearby villages and markets, with a combination of trekking and biking.

Topas Travel (☎ 871 331; www.topas-adventure-vietnam.com; 24 Muong Hoa) A Sapa-based ecotourist operator offering trekking, biking and village encounters, it employs many of its guides from the minority groups in the region. It also operates the Topas Eco Lodge (p177).

Sights & Activities

The easiest trek in town is to follow the steps up to the **Sapa radio tower** (admission 15,000d) for killer views of the valley.

Montagnards from surrounding villages don their best clothes and go to the **Sapa market** most days. Saturday is the busiest day, and the town is choking with tourists as the evening 'love market' is a big magnet for organised tour groups from Hanoi. If you'd rather enjoy Sapa at a more sedate pace, avoid the Saturday market.

The love market is speed dating minority style. Tribal teenagers trek into town to find a mate. It's all very coy, but unlike many of the more remote love markets in the region, it has become very commercial in recent years. These days there are more camera-toting tourists than love-sick Montagnards, as well as a smattering of opportunist prostitutes on the scene.

TREKKING TO LOCAL VILLAGES

It is quite easy to undertake day hikes through the valleys around Sapa without the assistance of a guide. However, for overnight stays in villages and longer treks into the mountains, it is advisable to hook up with a local guide. Where possible we suggest the use of minority guides, as this offers a means of making a living. There are endless options for trekking. Pick up a decent map and plot your course. The villages and the surrounding landscape are now part of Hoang Lien National Park.

The nearest village within walking distance is **Cat Cat** (admission 5000d), 3km south of Sapa. Like everywhere in this area, it's a steep and very beautiful hike down; if you're too exhausted or unfit to hike back up, there are plenty of *xe om* ready and willing to cart you back to your hotel.

Another popular hike is to **Ta Phin village** (admission 5000d), home to Red Dzao and about 10km from Sapa. Most people take a *xe om* to a starting point about 8km from Sapa, and then make a 14km loop through the area, passing through Black H'mong and Red Dzao villages. Most hotels offer guided day and half-day treks; depending on the number of people and what, if any, vehicles are needed, expect to pay somewhere between US$10 and US$30.

There are also community-based tours to the nearby H'mong village of **Sin Chai** with an overnight in the village to learn about textiles or music and dance. Other popular communities to visit include the Giay village of **Ta Van** and the Black H'mong village of **Matra**.

Long-standing (and still recommended) places to ask about guided treks include **Auberge Hotel** (☎ 871 243), **Cat Cat View Hotel** (☎ 871 946) and **Mountain View Hotel** (☎ 871 334). There are also several tour-booking offices on the main street.

FANSIPAN

Surrounding Sapa are the Hoang Lien Mountains, nicknamed the Tonkinese Alps by the French. These mountains include Fansipan, which at 3143m is Vietnam's highest peak. The summit towers above Sapa, although it is often obscured by clouds and is occasionally dusted with snow. The peak is accessible all year to those in good shape and properly equipped, but don't underestimate the challenge. It is very wet, and can be perilously slippery and generally cold, so you must be prepared. Do not attempt an ascent if the weather is terrible in Sapa, as limited visibility on Fansipan could be treacherous.

The summit of Fansipan is 19km from Sapa and can be reached only on foot. The terrain is rough and adverse weather is frequent. Despite the short distance, the round trip usually takes three days; some very fit and experienced hikers do it in two days, but this is rare. After the first morning you won't see any villages: just the forest, striking mountain vistas and perhaps some local wildlife such as monkeys, mountain goats and birds.

No ropes or technical climbing skills are needed, just endurance. There are no mountain huts or other facilities along the way (yet), so you need to be self-sufficient. This means taking a sleeping bag, waterproof tent, food, stove, raincoat or poncho, compass and other miscellaneous survival gear. Hiring a reputable guide is vital and, unless you are a seriously experienced mountaineer, finding porters who will carry your gear is also strongly recommended.

For recommendations on trekking guides, see the earlier sections on Trekking to Local villages (opposite) and Travel Agencies (opposite). If you organise the climb through a local operator, you'll find yourself paying an all-inclusive rate of around US$90 per person for a couple, US$80 per person for a group of four and US$70 per person for the sensible maximum group size of six.

Weather-wise the best time for making the ascent is from mid-October to mid-December, and again in March, when wildflowers are in bloom.

TRAM TON PASS

The incredible road between Sapa and Lai Chau crosses the Tram Ton Pass on the northern side of Fansipan, 15km from Sapa. At 1900m this is the highest mountain pass in Vietnam. Even if you are not planning to carry on around the northwest, it is well worth coming up here to experience the incredible views from the top of this pass. Descend by mountain bike before returning by truck or rent a motorbike to make the short hop to the new Tam Duong (Binh Lu). This is a seriously spectacular ride.

On the Sapa side of the mountain the weather is often cold, foggy and generally miserable. Drop down a few hundred metres below the pass on the Lai Chau side and it will often be sunny and warm. Ferocious winds come ripping over the pass, which is not surprising given the temperature differences – Sapa is the coldest place in Vietnam while Lai Chau is the warmest. Tram Ton Pass is the dividing line between two great weather fronts – who says you can't see air?

Alongside the road, about 5km towards Sapa, is **Thac Bac** (the Silver Waterfall). With a height of 100m, it's a big one, and the **loop track** (admission 3000d) is steep and scenic.

Sleeping

Hotels are popping up like mushrooms around Sapa. Luckily the mushroom mantra of 'keep them in the dark and feed them shit' that applies to the attitude of so many budget hotels in Hanoi is not common here. However, prices can fluctuate wildly according to the volume of tourist traffic and they often double on busy weekends. Look around and negotiate. Needless to say, it's wise to avoid the weekend rush. Accommodation is pre-arranged for travellers on tours booked in Hanoi, although it is worth checking the standard of the hotel in advance so you don't get any unpleasant surprises.

There are now dozens of accommodation options, from a solid string of cheap guesthouses to a luxury resort. The hotels named here generally offer rooms and/or balconies with views – the scenery is, after all, one of the main reasons for visiting Sapa. However, be aware that the building boom can wipe out a view overnight: always check the view before you rent the room. It is a real shame the local government hasn't done more to enforce height restrictions on the valley edge. New hotels can be better value than the older ones, so it is worth taking a look if you hear of somewhere that's just opened. Almost no hotels have air-conditioning as it is never hot enough to warrant it.

This is not an exhaustive list of places to sleep: there are *plenty* of other hotels in town that are also good value, especially in the newer part of town, but they lack the scenic setting.

Beware of hotels using old-style charcoal burners for heat, as the fumes can cause severe breathing problems if the room's not well ventilated. These caused a number of deaths in the early years of tourism, but most hotels have switched over to electric heaters or open fireplaces for the winter.

NORTHWEST VIETNAM

BUDGET

Lotus Hotel (☎ 871 308; 5 Đ Muong Hoa; r US$4-10) Occupying a strategic corner in the centre of town, this place is enticingly good value. Staff are friendly, the rooms are pretty spacious and many include balconies with views across to the valley. All rooms have hot water, TV and a fireplace.

Pinochio Hotel (☎ 871 876; 15 Đ Muong Hoa; r US$4-8) This is a real labyrinth of a place that winds its way up the hillside. Make the effort to climb the stairs to the top, as the rooms here have balconies, views and easy access to the rooftop restaurant.

Queen Hotel (☎ 871 301; fax 871 783; Đ Muong Hoa; r US$5-10) One of the old-timers in town, this place remains popular thanks to the fun and friendly staff. Size matters when it comes to price, but all rooms have hot water and TV. Aim high for views.

Hoi An Hotel (☎ 872 220; Đ Phan Si; r US$10) One of the newer hotels in town, at least at the time of writing, this is consequently great value. The rooms are desirably decorated with sparkling bathrooms and the views should remain uninterrupted for some time.

our pick **Mountain View Hotel** (☎ 871 334; fax 871 690; Đ Cau May; r US$8-18) Location, location, location. This hotel has just that, sitting in the centre of town, but offering 180° views of the valley below. The owner was one of the first female trekking guides in Sapa and has reinvested wisely. Invest the US$18 for doubly dramatic views from corner rooms. All rooms come with hot water and TV.

Other good possibilities that are located a short stroll down the valley:

Green Valley Hostel (☎ 871 449; 45 Đ Muong Hoa; r US$4-8) The Hostelling International choice in town, this place has cheap, comfortable rooms and unobstructed views.

Luong Thuy Guesthouse (☎ 872 310; 28 Đ Muong Hoa; r US$4-8) A little closer to town, this is another bargain with small rooms, but big views from the balconies.

MIDRANGE

our pick **Cat Cat View Hotel** (☎ 871 946; www.catcathotel.com; Đ Phan Si; r US$10-30; 💻) Deservedly popular for its friendly and honest service, this is a sprawling complex draped over the hillside. The small wing across the road has cheaper rooms, while those way above reception, with all the trimmings, are a few dollars more. It's worth the trek, as the views are breathtaking.

Sapa Summit Hotel (☎ 872 967; 10 Đ Thac Bac; r US$10-30; 💻) A new hotel on the road to Thac Bac, this is currently the best deal in town. Rooms include wooden floors, real satellite TV, central heating and sharp bathrooms. The gardens are lovingly laid out and include day facilities for those awaiting the night train.

Baguette & Chocolat (☎ 871 766; www.hoasuaschool.com; Đ Thac Bac; r US$18) Run by the popular Hoa Sua group helping disadvantaged youth, this is a tiny four-bedroom guesthouse above the excellent bakery. The elegant little rooms are thoughtfully decorated, but it's essential to book ahead. Rates include a great breakfast downstairs.

Auberge Hotel (☎ 871 243; auberge@fpt.vn; 7 Đ Muong Hoa; r US$15-28; 💻) Akin to a Sapa institution, this place has been around as long as the mist over the valley. As usual, it pays to wind your way up through the bonsai garden for clear views. The more expensive upper-floor rooms have fireplaces and fine furnishings. It's a good place for travel and trekking information, plus credit cards are accepted.

Topas Eco Lodge (☎ 871 331; www.topas-eco-lodge.com; bungalows US$25) With a striking setting overlooking the voluptuous valley below, Topas Eco Lodge is located in Tan Kim village, about 18km from Sapa and much lower in altitude, so it can be warmer and clearer in the winter months. Featuring solar power, waste-water management and minority staff, let's hope this is first of many such ventures. The Lodge can provide transfers at extra cost for arrival and departure.

Bamboo Sapa Hotel (☎ 871 076; bamboosapa@hn.vnn.vn; Đ Muong Hoa; s/d US$29-39; 💻) One of the first serious midrange hotels to open in town, it is still going strong. Standards are three star with large, airy rooms and breezy balconies with extensive views.

Royal View Sapa (☎ 872 989; www.royalsapa.com; 16 Pho Cau May; r US$30-65; 💻) Brazenly breaching all the height restrictions in town, this consequently has top views of the valley. Smart touches include a well-stocked minibar and ample bathtubs. There is also a lift and a terrace café for dining with a view.

Other places that are worth checking out:

Royal Hotel (☎ 871 313; royalhotel_sapa@yahoo.com; Pho Cau May; r US$12-20; 💻) A well-established hotel that sees a lot of tour business.

Sapa Goldsea Hotel (☎ 871 869; www.sapagoldsea-hotel.com.vn; Đ Phan Si; r US$17-45) Creature comforts on the road to Cat Cat is what you get at this modern hotel.

TOP END

Chau Long Hotel (☎ 871 245; www.chaulonghotel.com; 24 Đ Dong Loi; r US$32-180) The Chau Long was long a smart midrange hotel that famously resembled a castle. When the neighbours started obscuring the views, the owner bought them out and built a smart new four-star hotel. It has big valley views and all the amenities you might expect. If the new wing prices are as steep as the valley walls from US$115, then opt for the old wing, where just US$32 buys a piece of the action.

Victoria Sapa Hotel (☎ 871 522; www.victoriahotels-asia.com; r from US$165; ❄ 💻 🏊) This is the place where Sapa becomes Switzerland: a delightful mountain lodge with stylish service and smart rooms. This hotel has it all: sweeping views from the restaurant, two bars, a heated indoor swimming pool, a fitness centre and a tennis court. Visit the website for the two- or three-day discount packages for a real deal. Hotel guests can travel between Hanoi and Lao Cai in the resort's *Victoria Express* (luxurious train carriages à la the *Orient Express* attached to the regular night train). Return berths start from US$95 without meals during the week to US$280 with all meals at weekends.

Eating

Most of the busier hotels have reasonably priced cafés, which get more popular as the weather worsens. There's a string of popular restaurants worth checking out below the market on Đ Tue Tinh as you head in the direction of Cat Cat village.

our pick **Baguette & Chocolat** (Đ Thac Bac; cakes 6000-15,000d; 🕑 breakfast, lunch & dinner) On a cold and wet day, this place is a welcome retreat for a warm cocoa and delectable gateaux. The menu keeps growing and now includes some Asian greatest hits for around 40,000d. Or indulge in comfort food from home, with pizzas, salads and baguettes. Takeaway picnics are a smart option for trekkers.

Nature Bar & Grill (Pho Cau May; meals 15,000-50,000d; 🕑 breakfast, lunch & dinner) It's easy to sink into the comfy furnishings and while away an afternoon or evening. The extensive menu includes authentic Vietnamese cuisine and a few Western exiles for good measure. Speaking of measures, they also shake up a good cocktail.

Viet Emotion (☎ 872 559; 25 Pho Cau May; mains 20,000-40,000d; 🕑 breakfast, lunch & dinner) A smart new café-restaurant on the main drag, this place has an original menu of specials, including goose. If that sounds too exotic, there are good shakes and more familiar food.

Gerbera Restaurant (☎ 871 064; Pho Cau May; mains from 20,000d; 🕑 breakfast, lunch & dinner) Set just a staircase above the main drag, this restaurant has an unending menu of Vietnamese favourites. From the upstairs panorama room, there are some great views over town and the mountains beyond.

Ly Ly Restaurant (36 Pho Cau May; mains US$1-5; 🕑 breakfast, lunch & dinner) It may not be obvious from the name, but this little eatery has morphed into the town's first and only Indian restaurant. Curries, dhal, nan and lassis, it's possible to indulge in a Mumbai masterclass here.

Gecko (☎ 871 504; Đ Ham Rong; mains around US$5; ⏲ lunch & dinner) The original French restaurant in Sapa, not counting the 1920s of course, this is authentically housed in an old colonial-era property. The set menus are good value at just US$6 for something simple or US$10 for a banquet of Vietnamese cuisine. The bar is a possible retreat on a cold night.

Delta Restaurant (☎ 871 799; Pho Cau May; mains US$5; ⏲ lunch & dinner) The taste of Italy in Sapa, Delta turns out the most authentic pizzas in town. Pastas and home-cooking complete the picture.

Tavan Restaurant (☎ 871 522; US$4-12; ⏲ lunch & dinner) The restaurant at the Victoria Sapa Hotel is one of the best in town, with a full complement of fine European food and the best in Asian fusion. Open to nonresidents, you can finish off with a local liqueur at the bar.

Drinking & Entertainment

Considering the number of travellers to Sapa, organised entertainment is relatively scarce and the bar scene slow. For most, an evening out is the guesthouse balcony, particularly when the fog rolls in.

Red Dragon Pub (☎ 872 085; 23 Đ Muong Hoa) Don't let yourselves be put off by the quaint tearoom downstairs, as upstairs is a little drinking den of a Brit-style pub that fills up most evenings. Befitting a respectable pub, there is a serious range of beers and some good pub grub. The tearoom downstairs is a good stop for bangers and mash or herbal teas during the day.

Tau Bar (☎ 871 322; 42 Pho Cau May) As the night warms up, the only place to be is Tau Bar. Claiming to be 'slightly lounge', Tau brings a different kind of cool to the mountains of the north. There is a DIY jukebox on the computer, the cocktails are mixed by a pro and there is a pool table that always pulls a crowd.

Bamboo Sapa (☎ 871 076; bamboosapa@hn.vnn.vn; Pho Cau May) This popular hotel hosts a free traditional hill-tribe music-and-dance show from 8.30pm Friday and Saturday.

Shopping

Sapa is emerging as the top shopping destination in the mountainous north. Most of the items are clothing, accessories and jewellery produced by the multitude of minority peoples in the area. More recently some Vietnamese designers have also been getting in on the act, producing clothes and household furnishings inspired by tribal motifs and patterns. Check out some of the stores on Pho Cau May for the best selection of designer gear.

Lots of the minority women and young girls have gone into the souvenir business; the older women in particular are known for their strong-armed selling tactics. One frequent Sapa sight is a frenzy of elderly H'mong women clamouring around a hapless traveller to hawk their goods, which range from colourful ethnic garb to little pouches of opium stashed away in matchboxes. When negotiating prices, you do need to hold your ground, but go easy when it comes to bargaining. They may be persistent, but are not nearly as rapacious as Vietnamese vendors.

A word of warning on the clothes: as beautiful and cheap as they are, the dyes used are natural and not set. Much of the stuff sold

PROCLAIMING INDEPENDENCE

When it comes to budget hotels in Hanoi, everyone seems to be trying to sell a tour. While this can be a cheap and convenient way to see Halong Bay, it is really not necessary for Sapa and the surrounding villages. Sapa is easily accessible by a combination of train and bus, finding a good hotel is very straightforward and it's an adventure to hike or bike around the valleys on your own. If you get pressured into a tour, then you have no choice over what you see and do in and around Sapa. Perhaps you want to stay a day longer, perhaps you want a smarter room, perhaps you want a homestay in a Dzao village or perhaps you want to drop off the top of the Tram Ton Pass on a mountain bike? Too late, you've signed on the line. There are lots of good tour operators (some affiliated to the popular hotels) based in Sapa who specialise in the area. Our recommendation would be to travel here independently and make arrangements as you go. This brings choice and flexibility – what travelling independently is meant to be about.

If you are still set on taking a tour, check out the list of recommended agents in the Hanoi chapter (p91).

has the potential to turn anything it touches (including your skin) an unusual blue/green colour – check out the hands and arms of the H'mong for an idea. Wash the fabric separately in cold salt water as it helps to stop the dye from running. Wrap anything you buy in plastic bags before stuffing it in your luggage.

Getting There & Away

BUS, MINIBUS & MOTORBIKE

Sapa's proximity to the border region makes it a possible first or last stop for travellers crossing between Vietnam and China.

The gateway to Sapa is Lao Cai, 38km away on the Chinese border. Buses to points west such as Lai Chau and Dien Bien Phu pass through a few times a day from Lao Cai, the main transport hub. Sapa's bus station (for minibuses in this case) is in the north of town.

Minibuses make the trip from Lao Cai regularly between 5am and 5pm (25,000d, 1½ hours). In Sapa, minibuses wait in front of the church but do not run to any particular schedule. However, in Lao Cai minibuses wait for the train that arrives from Hanoi. If you are arriving from China, you can pick one up at Lao Cai bus station.

The advertised rate of hotel minibus services to Bac Ha (110km) for the Sunday market is around US$10 per person; departure from Sapa is at 6am and from Bac Ha at 1pm. It's cheaper to go to Bac Ha by public minibus, changing buses in Lao Cai.

Driving a motorbike from Hanoi to Sapa is feasible, but it's a very long trip, so start early. The total distance between Hanoi and Sapa is 380km. The last 38km are straight uphill – unless you've been training for the Olympics, it's hell on a bicycle.

TRAIN

The train trip between Lao Cai (gateway station to Sapa) and Hanoi has become much more comfortable with the advent of a soft-sleeper class and private rail carriages hitching a ride on the main train. Currently, a sleeper ticket between Hanoi and Sapa can be booked only through hotels and agencies in Sapa, but in Hanoi you can book at the station. There is an official **Railway Booking Office** (☎ 871 480; 🕓 7.30-11am & 1.30-4pm) on Pho Cau May in Sapa which charges a 7000d service fee for seats, 10,000d for a sleeper.

Ticket prices start at 79,000d for a hard seat (bad choice!) to 223,000d for an air-conditioned soft sleeper, and rise by about 10% at weekends. There are also several companies operating special private carriages with comfortable sleepers, including the affordable **ET Pumpkin** (www.et-pumpkin.com) and the more luxurious and expensive **Victoria Express** (www.victoriahotels-asia.com).

The day train leaves Lao Cai at 10.20am, while two night trains depart 8.35pm and 9.15pm, with the later express service including the private carriages. The journey takes about 10 hours. From Hanoi the all-stations day train departs at 6.15am and the night trains depart at 9.20pm and 10pm respectively.

Getting Around

The best way to get around Sapa is to walk, and almost everywhere it's steep! Anyone training for the Tour de France can rent a bicycle for the day, but you might spend half the time pushing it up steep, steep hills. For excursions further afield you can hire a self-drive motorbike from about US$6 a day, or take one with a driver for about US$10. Cars, 4WDs and minibuses are also available for hire through hotels, guesthouses and travel agents. Rates vary widely depending on the destination and the distance.

LAO CAI

☎ 020 / pop 35,100 / elevation 650m

Lao Cai, the end of the line so to speak, is right on the Vietnam–China border. The town was razed in the Chinese invasion of 1979, so most of the buildings are new. The border crossing here slammed shut during the 1979 war and only reopened in 1993.

Today Lao Cai is a major destination for travellers journeying between Hanoi or Sapa and Kunming in China, but Lao Cai is no place to linger with Sapa just an hour or so away.

The border town on the Chinese side is called Hekou – you would have to be an enthusiast of Chinese border towns to want to hang out there.

MONEY

Be especially wary of black marketeers, especially on the Chinese side – they frequently short-change tourists. If you do black-market dealings, it's best to change only small amounts.

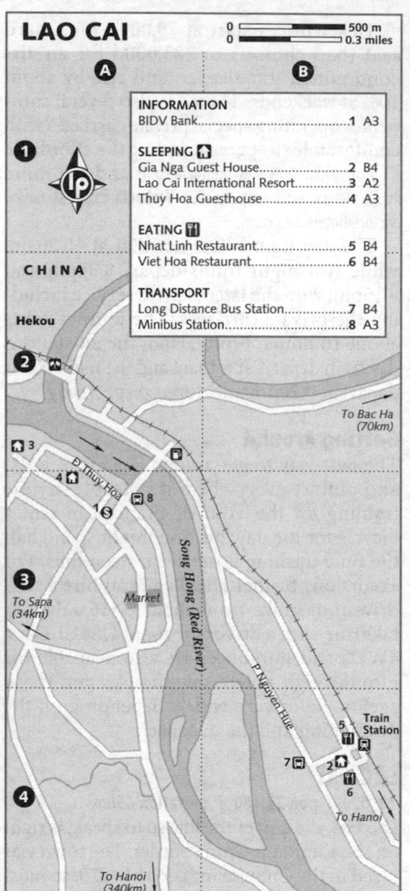

Directly across the bridge on the west bank of the river, the **BIDV Bank** (Đ Thuy Hoa) can exchange cash and travellers cheques, and also has an ATM.

Sleeping & Eating

Gia Nga Guest House (☎ 830 459; Pho Moi; r 100,000-150,000d;) No need to stay here, but the owner pioneered a popular deal to offer a shower (20,000d with towel and soap) to freshen up after the night train.

Thuy Hoa Guesthouse (☎ 826 805; fax 824 689; 118 Đ Thuy Hoa; r 170,000-185,000;) If you happen to be in the market for views across the Red River to China, this is a comfortable guesthouse. All rooms come with hot water and TV.

Lao Cai International Resort (☎ 826 668; laocaihotel@hn.vnn.vn; 88 Đ Thuy Hoa; r US$70-85;) Still claiming to be the 'ultimate choice' – perhaps the management hasn't travelled the 38km to Sapa. The rooms are pretty smart and include safety deposit boxes, which are handy if you happen to land a big win in the casino downstairs. Chinese currency accepted.

Nhat Linh Restaurant (☎ 835 346; Pho Nguyen Hué) A reliable little travellers' café outside Lao Cai station, the friendly staff and extensive menu make this the obvious stop before or after a long train ride.

Viet Hoa Restaurant (☎ 830 082; Đ Phan Dinh Phung; mains 25,000-75,000d) The biggest restaurant in town, this is the place for local luminaries wanting the best of Vietnamese and Chinese cuisine. As well as weddings, they accept 'merry making party'.

Getting There & Away

Minibuses to Sapa (25,000d, 1½ hours) leave regularly until late afternoon from the station next to the Red River bridge. Minibuses to Bac Ha (28,000d, two hours) leave several times daily; the departs last at 1pm.

Lao Cai is about 340km from Hanoi. Buses make the journey (85,000d, nine hours), leaving early in the morning from the **long distance bus station** (Pho Nguyen Hué), but most travellers sensibly prefer taking the train. See Getting There & Away under Sapa (p179) for details on train travel between Hanoi and Lao Cai.

BAC HA

☎ **020 / pop 70,200 / elevation 700m**

Long touted as the weekend alternative to Sapa, this small highland town doesn't have the same dramatic location of its more il-

BORDER CROSSING: LAO CAI/HEKOU

The Lao Cai–Hekou crossing is popular with travellers making their way between Yunnan and northern Vietnam. The border is open daily between 7am and 5pm. China is separated from Vietnam by a road bridge and a separate rail bridge over the Red River. Pedestrians pay a toll of 3000d to cross.

The border is about 3km from Lao Cai train station. This journey is easily done on a *xe om* (15,000d).

lustrious neighbour, but it is calmer when Saturday comes. It fills up to choking point on Sunday morning, when visitors flood in to meet the Flower H'mong at the morning market.

Compared with Sapa, tourism is still in its infancy here and during the week the town has a deserted feel. Bac Ha is a good base to explore the surrounding highlands. Around 900m above sea level, it is noticeably warmer than Sapa. There are 10 Montagnard groups that live around Bac Ha: the colourful Flower H'mong are the most visible, but other groups include Dzao, Giay (Nhang), Han (Hoa), Xa Fang, Lachi, Nung, Phula, Thai and Thulao.

One of Bac Ha's main industries is the manufacture of alcoholic home brews (rice wine, cassava wine and corn liquor). The corn hooch produced by the Flower H'mong is so potent it can ignite! Bac Ha is the only place in Vietnam where you'll find this particular moonshine; there's an entire area devoted to it at the Sunday market. Swill some down before deciding whether to buy a buffalo or cow.

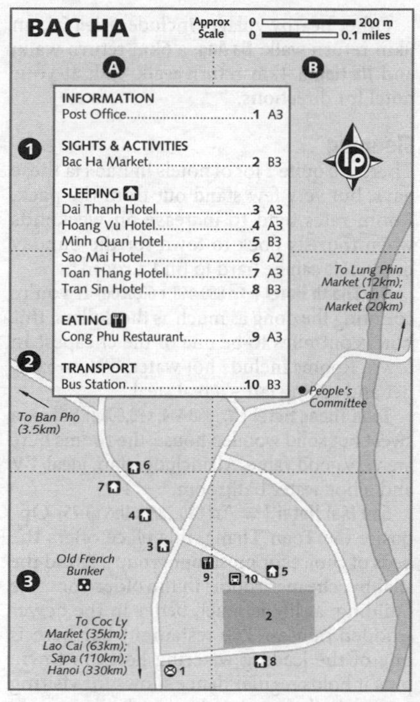

Sights & Activities

MONTAGNARD MARKETS

There are several interesting markets in and around Bac Ha, most within 20km of each other.

Bac Ha Market

This lively and crowded concrete bazaar is the main market in Bac Ha proper. It draws large numbers of Flower H'mong from the surrounding hills. The women embroider elaborate floral motifs on their skirts, making a technicolour dream for photographers. Items on sale include water buffaloes, pigs, horses, dogs and chickens: hardly convenient purchases for most visitors. Tourists stick to buying handicrafts, textiles and the local firewater. The market operates only on a Sunday. Get here early to experience it without the razzamatazz of day-trippers from Sapa.

Can Cau Market

This is one of the biggest open-air markets in the region, specialising in livestock. It's 20km north of Bac Ha and just 9km south of the Chinese border. Can Cau attracts a large number of Chinese traders, evidenced by the booming dog trade here. The market is only open on Saturday.

Lung Phin Market

This small market is between Can Cau market and Bac Ha town, about 12km from the town. It's less busy than other markets, and is open on Sunday. It is a good place to move onto once the tour buses arrive in Bac Ha from Sapa, and has a very real feel.

Coc Ly Market

This Tuesday market is about 35km from Bac Ha. You can get here via a fairly good road, or by road and river; hotels in Sapa and Bac Ha can organise trips.

TREKKING TO LOCAL VILLAGES

Villages around Bac Ha provide an opportunity to see how Montagnard people live. **Ban Pho** is nearest, and the villagers live simply. The Flower H'mong villagers are so hospitable – some of the kindest people you'll meet in Vietnam. Ban Pho is a 7km return trip from Bac Ha. Take a loop route to get there and back.

Other nearby villages include: **Trieu Cai**, an 8km return walk; **Na Ang**, a 6km return walk; and **Na Hoi**, a 4km return walk. Ask at your hotel for directions.

Sleeping

There are quite a lot of hotels in Bac Ha these days, but very few stand out from the pack. Room rates tend to increase on weekends when tourists flock to town for the Sunday market; it can be hard to find a room.

Dai Thanh Hotel (☎ 880 448; r 60,000d) If you're counting the dong as much as the dollars, this hotel continues to be one of the cheapest in town. Rooms include hot water, TV, mozzie net and ceiling fan – a real steal.

Toan Thang Hotel (☎ 880 444; r 80,000d) Set in a sweet but solid wooden house, the rooms here are very good value. All include a fan, local TV and a hot-water bathroom.

Sao Mai Hotel (☎/fax 880 288; r US$10-25) Opposite the Toan Thang, this place offers the beds of choice for most tour groups. Avoid the shabby, cheaper rooms in the older concrete building, as life is much better in the newer wooden houses. The restaurant-bar here is one of the leading watering holes in town, plus it holds regular dance shows for visiting groups in the courtyard car park.

Minh Quan Hotel (☎ 880 222; r 120,000-150,000d) Most people are here for the market, so why not enjoy a bird's-eye view of the Sunday action from this comfortable hotel? Rooms include smart bathrooms and some have immense views of the mountains beyond.

Other places worth a look:

Tran Sin Hotel (☎ 880 240; r 100,000d) Another hotel that overlooks the market; get a balcony to follow the action.

Hoang Vu Hotel (☎ 880 264; r 120,000d) Big rooms with balconies, but small views. Reliable tour information is available.

Eating

Many of the hotels have restaurants, but if you want to break out, make for the **Cong Phu Restaurant** (☎ 880 254; mains 15,000-30,000d). No, the waiters don't look like extras out of a Bruce Lee movie, but they do offer wholesome meals. The menus are large photocopies in English; just tick the boxes and the food will arrive.

Getting There & Away

Minibuses depart from Lao Cai for Bac Ha (28,000d, two hours) around 6.30am and 1pm daily. Buses from Bac Ha leave for Lao Cai between 5.30am and 1pm. The road is well maintained and the rural scenery sublime.

Locals on motorbikes will do the Lao Cai–Bac Ha run for about US$10, or even Sapa–Bac Ha (110km) for US$15, but it's a long way to be on the back of a bike. Sunday minibus tours from Sapa to Bac Ha start at US$10, including transport, guide and trekking to a minority village. On the way back to Sapa you can bail out in Lao Cai and catch the night train back to Hanoi.

Bac Ha is about 330km (10 hours) from Hanoi. Some cafés in Hanoi offer four-day bus trips to Sapa, with a visit to Bac Ha included.

HA GIANG PROVINCE

Ha Giang is the final frontier in northern Vietnam, a lunar landscape of limestone pinnacles and granite outcrops. On a map: it juts up like a boil into southern China, or at least that is how the Chinese seem to view it. The far north of the province has some of the most spectacular scenery in Vietnam and the trip between Dong Van and Meo Vac is a mind-blower for motorbikers, but not much fun on buses. It should be one of the most popular destinations in this region, but is one of those rare provinces that still requires a travel permit and the bureaucratic baloney keeps most at bay.

Ha Giang

☎ 019 / pop 45,000

Ha Giang is somewhere to recharge the batteries on the long road north. The scenery is a good taste of things to come, with limestone outcrops soaring skywards over the town. Those heading further north to explore the districts of Yen Minh, Dong Van, Meo Van and Bac Me need to arrange a permit (per person US$10) here.

INFORMATION

Travel permits can be arranged through the provincial police, with offices on the right bank of the River Mien, or through your hotel or **Ha Giang Tourist Company** (☎ 867 054; Pho Tran Hung Dao). It is easier to avoid the stone-faced police. The tourist company can also provide guides, which are officially required and cost US$15 per day plus board and lodging.

SLEEPING & EATING

There are some great-value hotels in Ha Giang. As there are few foreigners, foreigner pricing doesn't seem to exist.

KHAU VAI LOVE MARKET: SPEED DATING FOR THE MINORITIES

Scenery aside, the other major drawcard in Ha Giang is the annual love market of Khau Vai. Forget the weekly jamboree in Sapa: this love market takes place but once a year and draws H'mong, Dao and Tay from all over the region.

The love market is speed dating minority style. Original swingers, the good folk of Khau Vai have been wife swapping, and husband swapping for that matter, for almost 100 years. Youngsters come to find a mate. Old flames fan the dying embers of a lost passion. It is adult friend finder before the internet made it easy. However, they are not in the market for Westerners.

It takes place on the 27th day of the 3rd lunar month in the Vietnamese calendar. For those of us that don't know our dogs from our dragons, that is usually sometime from late April to mid-May, essentially three months after Tet or Vietnamese New Year. Khau Vai is about 20km southeast of Meo Vac.

Hai Dang Hotel (☎ 866 863; 15 Pho Nguyen Trai; r 100,000d) A real bargain and opposite the bus station. Normally this could be a negative, but for those making the road trip north, the buses pull out early, so convenience is king.

Huy Hoan Hotel (☎ 861 288; 14 Pho Nguyen Trai; r 100,000-250,000d) The smartest place in town with slick rooms, big beds and a lift: not something you'd expect in these parts.

Sao Mai Hotel (☎ 863 019; Pho Nguyen Trai; r US$10) One of the first places when approaching on the road from Hanoi, this is the best all-rounder in town. Enjoy hot water, TV and comfortable beds. There's karaoke at all hours, though.

Thanh Thu Restaurant (Pho Tran Hung Dao) One of the best eateries in town run by a friendly family who look after diners. Bring a Vietnamese phrasebook, as there is no English menu.

Be careful venturing into local *pho* shops for a quiet breakfast. We popped in for some noodles and stumbled out having done 20 shots of *xeo* with the friendly locals. And it was only 8am.

GETTING THERE & AWAY

Ha Giang is 290km north of Hanoi (76,000d, seven hours by bus) on Hwy 2. It is also possible to get here from Bac Ha, but the tough road is only for the strongest 4WD or very experienced bikers. The route passes through the lively towns of Xin Man and Huong Su Phi and is very beautiful. There are daily buses north to scenic towns like Meo Vac, but it's much better to explore the beauty of Ha Giang with your own wheels.

Around Ha Giang

It's all about the motorbike trip north to the districts of Dong Van and Meo Vac, nestled against the border with China. Leaving Ha Giang, the road climbs over the **Quan Ba Pass** (Heaven's Gate). Poetic licence is a national pastime in Vietnam, but this time the romantics have it right. The road winds over a saddle and opens up on to a vista straight out of Lost Valley of the Dinosaurs. Like Halong Bay, it's dizzying to think of the forces of nature that carved out these incredible limestone towers.

Dropping into **Yen Minh** through pine forests, it is worth stopping for a drink before the final leg into the surreal scenery near China. **Dong Van** is just a small, dusty outpost, but don't be disappointed as it is the gateway to the best road trip in Vietnam: the 22km that snakes its way along the mountainside to **Meo Vac**. The road has been cut into the side of a cliff face and far below are the distant waters of the Nho Que River and, towering above, the rock face of this mighty gorge. Take your time and soak it up, as this journey is one to savour.

Meo Vac is a district capital hemmed in by mountains and, like many towns in the northwest, it is steadily being settled by Vietnamese from elsewhere. There are several small faceless guesthouses in town, charging 60,000d for a basic room with shared bathroom. Best is the **Viet Hung Guesthouse** (r 60,000d) with comfy beds and a TV, located on the road to Khau Vai district. You need to show your travel permit when checking in at any guesthouse. There are a couple of *com pho* places around town, plus the market has some food stalls.

Looking at a map it's seems possible to continue from Meo Vac to Bao Lac in Cao Bang province. However, Ha Giang authorities are dead against this and will do their best to stop you. Approaching from Cao Bang Province, there is little they can do but force you to carry on to Ha Giang city. However, be prepared for a hefty fine and a lot of negotiation.

North-Central Vietnam

Most tourists' only experience of north-central Vietnam is a torturous 16-hour bus trip from Hanoi to Hué. While it's true that you'll find more English-speakers and Western-style hotels in the south, this region offers something perhaps more tourist-friendly – the opportunity to potter about, largely left to your own devices. After the clamour of Hanoi and Hué this makes for a nice change.

While the stunning karst-ridden countryside around Ninh Binh can be seen from a tourist bus on a day trip from Hanoi, it doesn't rate with the experience of cycling around the idyllic rice paddies by yourself or on the back of a motorbike, as children leading water buffalo stop to wave and shout hello. Architecture and Graham Greene fans alike won't want to miss Phat Diem, the fascinating cathedral unchanged from its vivid description in *The Quiet American* (albeit without the bodies floating in the canals).

South of Ninh Binh it's likely you won't see another foreigner or meet many English-speakers. While some might find that daunting, for the more intrepid this presents another side of Vietnam – even if at times it can be a grim place in the still-recovering war-devastated cities of the north. The excellent *Reunification Express* train services make it easy to break the journey into comfortable legs, with Vinh and Dong Hoi interesting spots for an overnight stay.

If you're anxious to hit the beaches, you're better off saving it for the south. The popular coastal communes of the north, with their ever-present concrete and litter, don't hold much appeal for foreign travellers.

HIGHLIGHTS

- Marvel at the limestone-sprouting countryside around Hoa Lu's **ancient temples** (p188)
- Zen out on the serene Ngo Dong River at **Tam Coc** (p187) – before the amusing money scramble begins
- Spot the scars of war, ever-present in a regenerating **Dong Hoi** (p197)
- Discover that East-meets-West is about more than just fashionable food, while checking out the fusion architecture of **Phat Diem Cathedral** (p189)
- Trek yourself troppo on the jungle tracks of **Cuc Phuong National Park** (p190)

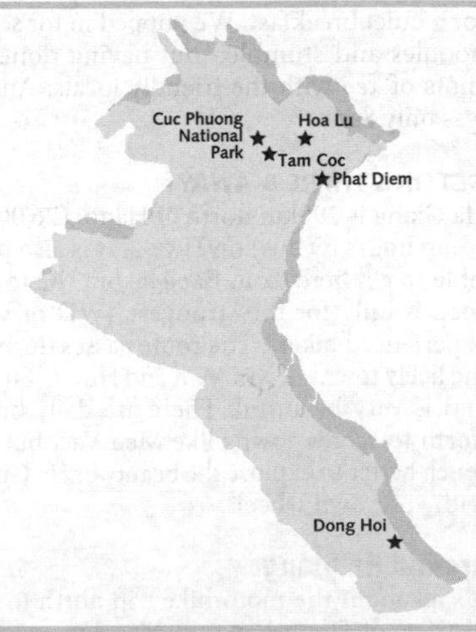

- ELEVATION: 1-2711M
- BEST TIME TO VISIT: APR-OCT

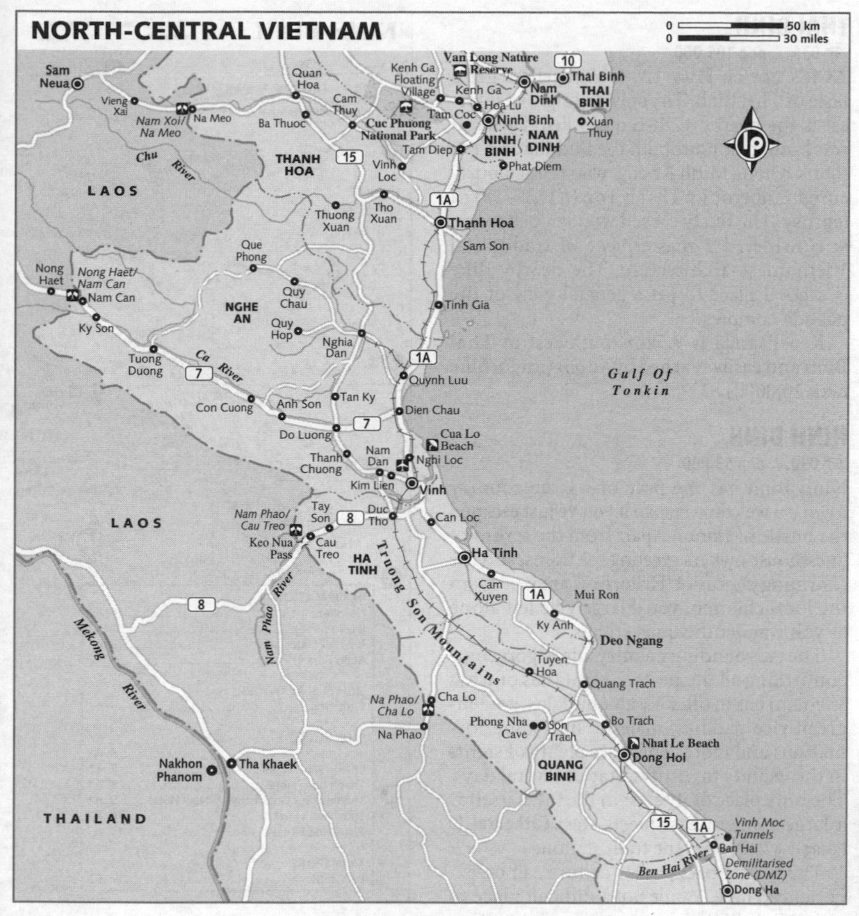

History

This region contains much more historical importance than it might appear at first glance. One of Vietnam's earliest capitals was at Hoa Lu, where magnificent temples are strategically set amid a dramatic landscape of towering limestone cliffs and serene rice paddies.

In the 13th and 14th centuries, Tran dynasty kings ruled from the capital of Thang Long (present-day Hanoi). This was the only period in Vietnamese history when the heirs to the throne partially succeeded their fathers, taking the official role of king, while the older generation shared power in a second unofficial capital in Tuc Mac, about 5km from Nam Dinh. This prevented the succession disputes which had previously been the norm, making the Tran dynasty one of the most politically stable and prosperous periods in Vietnamese history.

During the American War, north-central Vietnam suffered tremendous damage from US bombing. Further south, Vinh marked the start of the Ho Chi Minh Trail, as supplies passed through the docks on the way inland to the Truong Son Mountains.

Getting There & Away

The major north–south rail route cuts a swathe directly through the region, as does Hwy 1A. The only airport is situated at Vinh, and it has only limited flights to Ho Chi Minh City (HCMC).

THAI BINH

☎ 036 / pop 105,000

As it's not on Hwy 1A, few travellers get a taste of Thai Binh. The only real sight of interest is the nearby 12th-century **Keo Pagoda**. It was built to honour both the Buddha and the monk Khong Minh Khong, who miraculously cured Emperor Ly Thanh Ton (r 1128–38) of leprosy. The finely carved wooden bell tower is considered a masterpiece of traditional Vietnamese architecture. The nearby dike is a good place to get a general view of the pagoda complex.

Keo Pagoda is 9.5km southwest of Thai Binh and easily reached by *xe om* (motorbike taxi; 20,000d).

NINH BINH

☎ 030 / pop 53,000

Ninh Binh has the pace of a large country town – a welcome respite if you've just escaped the bustle of Hanoi. Apart from the scrum of guesthouse owners greeting the trains, and the charming chorus of 'Hello, how are you' from the local children, you'll largely be left alone as you wander the quiet streets.

The surrounding countryside is gorgeous, confirming all the postcard fantasies of what Vietnam has to offer – water buffalos, golden-green rice paddies, majestic limestone formations and more. There are plenty of sights in the vicinity to justify a stay of several days. The only place of interest in the town itself is a large modern east-meets-west **Cathedral** (Đ Hoang Hoa Tham) near the train station.

The best of backpacker culture can be experienced here. While not a difficult place to visit, Ninh Binh seems to attract interesting travellers with a zest for new experiences. It's a great place to make travel buddies.

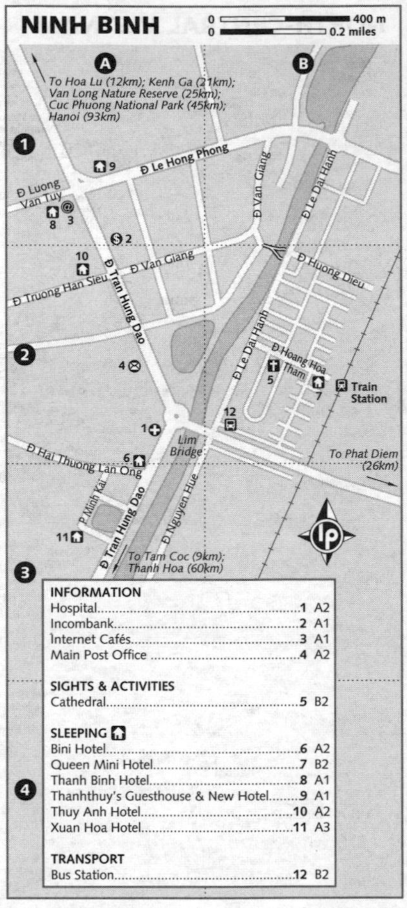

Information

Internet cafés are spread around town, with a cluster on Đ Luong Van Tuy, west of Đ Tran Hung Dao (per hour 5000d).

Incombank (☎ 872 675; Đ Tran Hung Đao) Deals with cash, travellers cheques and most plastic and has an ATM outside.

Hospital (☎ 871 152; So 2 Đ Tran Hung Đao)

Main post office (Đ Tran Hung Dao)

Sleeping & Eating

Ninh Binh hoteliers have a reputation for friendliness and good service, making a stay smoother than you might expect for a town of this size. Most can make tour and transport arrangements. Generally all but the cheapest rooms have air-con, but you can save a few bucks if you forgo it. The town doesn't have much in the way of restaurants and most travellers tend to eat at their hotel, many of which serve excellent food. Goat meat is a local speciality – delicious wrapped with herbs in fresh rice paper.

our pick **Thanhthuy's Guest House & New Hotel** (☎ 871 811; tuc@hn.vnn.vn; 128 Đ Le Hong Phong; r guesthouse US$5-8, hotel US$12; ❄ 💻) The central courtyard is a great place to meet other travellers over a meal (dishes 15,000 ti40,000d) and a drink. The New Hotel is very comfortable, set back from the street, while the guesthouse is basic and clean, with shared bathrooms and no air-con. The owner speaks excellent English and German, and has a crew of safe drivers available for local tours.

Queen Mini Hotel (☎ 871 874; luongvn2001@yahoo.com; 21 Đ Hoang Hoa Tham; r US$3-15;) Right by the station, the tiny fan rooms are the cheapest in town.

Xuan Hoa Hotel (☎ 880 970; xuanhoahotel@hotmail.com; 31D Pho Minh Kai; r US$5-15;) Another social place with charming owners and staff, this is a firm favourite. The rooms are comfortable and clean and the food excellent. Motorbike and bicycle rentals and day trips can be arranged.

Thanh Binh Hotel (☎ 872 439; thaibinhhotel@yahoo.com; 31 Đ Luong Van Tuy; r US$6-18;) Very friendly, nice and new, the lower floors have larger rooms, but there are some cheapies upstairs. Breakfast is included in the price.

Bini Hotel (☎/fax 882 809; 2 Đ Hai Thuong Lan Ong; r US$10;) This is an attractive new family-run hotel with large, clean rooms.

Thuy Anh Hotel (☎ 871 602; www.thuyanhhotel.com; 55A Đ Truong Han Sieu; r US$7-40;) Quite the smartest operation in town. The old wing offers spotless rooms of varying shapes and sizes, while the slick new wing, complete with lift, pulls in the tour groups. There's a good restaurant (dishes 20,000 to 60,000d) downstairs and a rooftop bar for drinkers.

Getting There & Away

The bus station in Ninh Binh is located near the Lim Bridge, just below the overpass to Phat Diem. Regular public buses leave almost hourly for the Giap Bat bus station in Hanoi (28,000d, 2½ hours, 93km). Ninh Binh is also a stop for open-tour buses between Hanoi (US$4, two hours) and Hué (US$6, 10 hours), which drop off and pick up passengers at some of the hotels.

Ninh Binh's **train station** (☎ 673 619; 1 Đ Hoang Hoa Tham) is a scheduled stop for *Reunification Express* trains, with destinations including Hanoi (40,000d, two to 2½ hours, four daily), Thanh Hoa (20,000d, one to 1½ hours, three daily) and Hué (205,000d, 12½ to 13½ hours, three daily).

Travelling distances to the nearest major towns are 93km to Hanoi, 60km to Thanh Hoa and 49km to Thai Binh.

Getting Around

Bikes and motorbikes (with or without drivers) can be hired from most hotels. Bicycle hire usually only costs around US$1 to US$2 per day, while motorbikes are around US$5 to US$6. A driver's rates will depend on distance and time, but for a full day is likely to be around US$10.

AROUND NINH BINH

Tam Coc

Poetically penned 'Halong Bay on the rice paddies', the area around Tam Coc boasts stunning scenery. While Halong Bay (p136) has rugged rock formations jutting out of the sea, here they soar skywards from a sea of green.

Tam Coc (entry fee 30,000d, boat 40,000d) is named after the low caves through which the Ngo Dong River flows. The essential Tam Coc experience is to sit back and be rowed through the caves – a serene and scenic trip, which turns into a surreal dance towards the end (see p188).

The boats carry two people as well as the main rower at the rear and a secondary rower, usually an elderly woman, whose purpose becomes clear at the end of the journey. Hang Ca, the first cave, is 127m long; Hang Giua 70m long; and the third, Hang Cuoi, is only 45m. The boat trip takes about two hours and tickets are sold at the small booking office by the car park. Even on cloudy days, bring sunscreen and a hat or umbrella, as there's no shade in the boats. It pays to arrive early in the morning or late in the afternoon to avoid the day-tripping crowds from Hanoi.

The area behind the Tam Coc restaurants is **Van Lan village**, which is famous for its embroidery. Here local artisans make napkins, tablecloths, pillowcases and T-shirts. A lot of these items wind up being sold on Hanoi's Pho Hang Gai (p121), but it is cheaper to buy them here directly from the artisan. The village has a much better selection and slightly lower prices than those available from the boat vendors.

BICH DONG PAGODA

This charming cave pagoda is just a couple of kilometres north of Tam Coc and worth a visit if you have your own wheels. The scenic road winds through rice fields hemmed in by karsts and ends in a dusty village. Bich Dong (Jade Grotto) is cut into the caves of a karst and is a holy site of pilgrimage for Vietnamese. The smoke of burning incense and the gloom of the caves give this place an unearthy atmosphere.

SLEEPING & EATING

With all the recent development it's possible to stay the night in comfort in this quiet village and get an early start on the river the next day.

The Long (☎ 618 077; luongvn2001@yahoo.com; r 200,000d;) This attractive new building opposite the jetty has big rooms with balconies, and a large restaurant (meals 60,000d) on the ground floor.

GETTING THERE & AWAY

Tam Coc is 9km southwest of Ninh Binh. Follow Hwy 1A south and turn west at the Tam Coc turn-off. Ninh Binh hotels run day tours, but it is more fun to make your own way by bicycle or motorbike. Hotel staff can also advise you on some beautiful back roads that link Tam Coc with Hoa Lu. Budget cafés in Hanoi book day trips to Tam Coc and Hoa Lu; the fast-food version goes for about US$15, but it's closer to US$20 with a smaller group, comfortable vehicle and professional guide.

Hoa Lu

Hoa Lu was the capital of Vietnam during the Dinh (968–80) and early Le (980–1009) dynasties. The site was a smart choice for a capital city because of the natural protection afforded by the region's bizarre landscape, with rocky outcrops as spectacular as Tam Coc's. The **ancient citadel of Hoa Lu** (admission 10,000d), most of which has been destroyed, covered an area of about 3 sq km. The outer ramparts encompassed temples, shrines and the king's palace. The royal family lived in the inner citadel.

Yen Ngua Mountain provides a scenic backdrop for Hoa Lu's two remaining temples. The first, **Dinh Tien Hoang**, was restored in the 17th century and is dedicated to the Dinh dynasty. At the front of the main temple building is the stone pedestal of a royal throne; inside are bronze bells and a statue of Emperor Dinh Tien Hoang with his three sons. In a building to the right a display features photos and some artefacts, while to the left are three Buddhist prayer stones – one supported by a turtle, another with a crab and two rats at the base.

The second temple is dedicated to **Le Dai Hanh**, an early Le monarch. Inside the main hall are an assortment of drums, gongs, incense burners, candle holders and weapons, with a statue of the king in the middle, his queen on the right and their son on the left. In the left-hand section of this complex a modern museum features part of the excavations of the 10th-century citadel wall, unearthed in 1998.

THE TAM COC TANGO

As with many tourist traps in Vietnam, don't attempt the Tam Coc boat trip without a good sense of humour, or at least a modicum of patience.

As you head through the caves you'll notice boats starting to circle, stocked up with snacks and drinks. Usually they wait until you reach the dead end before they lunge. After they've exhausted the refreshment limits of their captive audience, they try their next, extremely effective, gambit: 'Drink for Madame?' Given that you're probably already feeling awkward that the frail-looking octogenarian has had to paddle you all this way, it's a hard line to resist. Many travellers cave in, only to find that 'Madame' sells the drink straight back to the vendor for half the price. A good scheme to appease your conscience without being scammed is to offer Madame some of your own drink – she'll probably refuse.

With this little dance completed, the boats head back and it's Madame's turn to cut in. It seems that all that splashing about wasn't required at all, as she's now suddenly able to put down her oar and start producing an endless stream of embroidered pictures, tablecloths and T-shirts for sale. Some of them are quite lovely, but be warned – even if you buy the entire boxful it won't be enough to satisfy.

As you reach the respite of the shore, laden down with hand-stitched doilies for the great-aunts' Christmas presents, Madame unashamedly reaches out her hand and asks for a $2 tip – more than what most Vietnamese make in a day!

Still, you got off lightly. If this scenario pans out, at least you got to see the caves. Another common scam is for people driving towards Tam Coc to be approached by women offering to lead them to the boats. Instead you're driven to someone's private boat elsewhere on the river where a paddle around random rice paddies may cost 120,000d.

Once you've navigated the hassle of persistent sellers on the way in, it's very peaceful inside the complex, especially in the early morning or late afternoon when the crowds head back to Hanoi. On the hillside above the temples is the **tomb of Dinh Tien Hoang**. It's a good 15-minute climb up 207 steps, but your efforts will be rewarded with great views.

GETTING THERE & AWAY

Hoa Lu is 12km northwest of Ninh Binh; turn left 6km north of town on Hwy 1A. There is no public transport, so most travellers get there by bicycle, motorbike or car. Ask your hotel about the blissful back roads linking Hoa Lu to Tam Coc.

Kenh Ga

The village of Kenh Ga (Chicken Canal) gets its name, apparently, from the number of wild chickens that used to live here. It's a lovely area, and one of the best places outside of the Mekong Delta to see river life – but nowhere in the Delta will you find stunning limestone formations like the ones providing the backdrop here. Another difference: people in Kenh Ga row boats with their feet, leaning back and watching the world go by.

The local people seem to spend most of their lives on or in the water: at their floating fish-breeding pens, harvesting river grass used for fish feed, trawling in the muddy shallows for shellfish or selling veggies boat-to-boat. Even the children commute to school by boat. The river is used for everything from bathing, to washing plucked chickens, to defecating in.

Until recent years this was largely a floating village, with just a few permanent buildings on the riverbanks. You'll still see some tiny wooden shelters on boats where the poorest of the poor live. However, as fortunes improve, people aim to stake their claim on solid ground.

From the pier you can hire a **motorboat** (☎ 868 560; 40,000d) to take you for an hour or so touring around the village.

GETTING THERE & AWAY

Kenh Ga is 21km from Ninh Binh off the road to Cuc Phuong National Park. Follow Hwy 1A north for 11km, then it's a 10km drive west to reach the boat pier. Hotels in Ninh Binh can arrange tours, often through fantastic back roads with wonderful scenery.

Van Long Nature Reserve

Set amid yet more of the limestone pinnacles that characterise this region, **Van Long** (entry 20,000d) is a reedy wetland that attracts the birds. It's become a popular spot for international birdwatchers keen for a sighting of a rare black-faced spoonbill, a cotton pygmy goose, a white-browed crake or other fantastically named feathery fauna. The fee includes a punt through the shallow waters and, with your eyes peeled, you just might see a Delacour's langur monkey lurking in the outcrops. Van Long can be easily combined with a visit to Kenh Ga and, at a stretch, both can be visited en route to Cuc Phuong National Park.

Van Long is 2km east of Tran Me, a small town 23km from Ninh Binh along the road to Cuc Phuong.

PHAT DIEM

The Tay Ninh (p381) of the north, Phat Diem is the home of a celebrated **cathedral** (1891), which is remarkable for its vast dimensions and superb Sino-Vietnamese architecture – with a dash of European dressing for good measure.

During the French era this was an important centre of Catholicism and there was a seminary here. In a throwback to the middle ages, Phat Diem's bishop ruled the area with his own private army until 1951, when they were replaced by French troops. The cathedral featured prominently in Graham Greene's novel *The Quiet American*. The 1954 division of Vietnam caused Catholics to flee south en masse and the cathedral was closed. It is now functional again, along with several dozen other churches in the district, serving the area's estimated 120,000 Catholics.

The cathedral complex comprises a number of buildings fronted by an ornamental lake with a statue of an open-armed Christ rising from an island at its centre. The cathedral itself has a vaulted ceiling supported by massive wooden columns that are almost 1m in diameter and 10m tall. Above the altar made from a single block of granite, Vietnamese-looking cherubs with golden wings swarm, while Chinese-style clouds drift across the blue ceiling. Beneath them are icons of the martyrs slaughtered by Emperor Tu Duc during the anti-Catholic purges of the 1850s. The sides of the building open up to allow the breeze to blow through and the light to flood in. Note the delicate stone carvings at the front.

Opposite the cathedral's main doors is the free-standing bell tower, with stone columns carved to look like bamboo. At its base lie two enormous stone slabs, one atop the other. Their sole purpose was to provide a perch for the mandarins to sit and observe – no doubt with great amusement – the rituals of the Catholic mass.

Atop the tower is such an enormous bell that Quasimodo's famous chimer in Paris pales significantly in comparison. This was pulled to the cathedral's top via an enormous earthern ramp. After construction was completed, the dirt was used to raise the whole site about 1m higher than the surrounding terrain. All the large carved stones were transported from some 200km away with only very rudimentary equipment.

Between the tower and the cathedral is the tomb of the founder, a Vietnamese priest named Six. Behind the main building is a large pile of limestone boulders – Father Six piled them up to test whether the boggy ground would support his plans. The test was a success, and the rock heap has been used to form a Lourdes grotto.

The five other chapels within the compound, built in the same style, are also worth exploring. Unfortunately, as with most Vietnamese churches, these are often locked outside of mass times. However, the windowless stone and wood construction affords plenty of gaps for a good peek at the interiors. There are also large statues of the pietà and nativity within the grounds.

Hordes of Vietnamese tourists come to this place. Few of them are Catholic, but many of them are extremely curious about churches and Christianity in general. Admission to the complex is free, but you may have to negotiate hordes of sellers and aggressive beggars at busy times. Daily mass is celebrated at 5am and 5pm.

Not far from this cathedral is a **covered bridge** dating from the late 19th century. **Dong Huong Pagoda** is the largest in the area, catering to the Buddhist community. Many of its congregation are from the minority Muong people. To find it, turn right at the canal as you're approaching town from the north and follow the small road alongside the water for 3km.

Getting There & Away

Phat Diem, sometimes known by its former name Kim Son, is 121km south of Hanoi and 26km southeast of Ninh Binh. There are direct buses from Ninh Binh to Phat Diem (one hour), or you can go by bicycle or motorbike. Day trips are easily arranged from Ninh Binh – US$7 for a motorcycle and driver, including waiting time.

CUC PHUONG NATIONAL PARK

☎ 030 / elevation 150-656m

Established in 1962, **Cuc Phuong National Park** (☎ 848 006; www.cucphuongtourism.com; admission adult/child 40,000/20,000d) is one of Vietnam's most important protected areas. Ho Chi Minh personally took time off from the war in 1963 to declare this Vietnam's first national park, saying: 'Forest is gold. If we know how to conserve it well, it will be very precious. Destruction of the forest will lead to serious effects on both life and productivity.'

This national park is 70km from the coast and covers an area about 25km long and 11km wide, spanning the provinces of Ninh Binh, Hoa Binh and Thanh Hoa. Its highest peak is Dinh May Bac (Silver Cloud Peak) at 656m.

The park is home to the excellent Endangered Primate Rescue Center (see opposite). The centre is located about 500m before the national park reception centre. You can't wander around the centre alone, so if you're travelling independently you need first to go to the national park reception area and arrange a guide. Entry is free, but you might consider purchasing some postcards or a poster, or making a donation.

Though wildlife has suffered a precipitous decline in Vietnam in recent decades, the park's 222 sq km of primary tropical forest remains home to an amazing variety of animal and plant life. There are 320 species of bird, 97 species of mammal including bats, and 36 species of reptile identified so far. Of the 2000 plant species, 433 have medicinal properties and 299 are food sources. The park is home to a species of tree called Cay Kim Gao *(Podocarpus fleuryi hickel)*. In ancient times, kings and mandarins would only eat with chopsticks made from this lumber – it was said that anything poisonous it touches turns the light-coloured wood to black.

Poaching and habitat destruction are a constant headache for the park rangers. Many native species, such as the Asiatic black bear, Siamese crocodile, wild dog and tiger, have vanished from the area as a result of human impact. Episodes of violence have erupted

SERIOUS MONKEY BUSINESS

A highlight of a visit to Cuc Phuong is the **Endangered Primate Rescue Center** (☎ 848 002; www.primatecenter.org; admission free; 9-11am & 1-4pm). The facility, run by a mixture of German biologists and local Vietnamese, is a laudable endeavour aiming to improve the wellbeing of Vietnam's primates.

What started out as a small-scale operation in 1995 with just a handful of animals has grown into a highly productive centre, where today over 100 creatures are cared for, studied and bred. There are around 14 species of gibbon and langur on site. The langur is a long-tailed, tree-dwelling monkey; the gibbon is a long-armed, fruit-eating ape. There are also lorises (smaller nocturnal primates) at the centre.

There are estimated to be only about 20 species of primate remaining in the wild in Vietnam, most of which are threatened by hunters and/or habitat destruction. Some people attempt to keep these animals as pets, which is almost impossible. Langurs survive exclusively on fresh-cut leaves and their digestive systems will not tolerate anything else. By feeding them incorrectly, people usually discover they've killed their new pet before they can even flaunt it to their friends. All the animals in the centre were either bred here or rescued either from cages or illegal traders, who transport them mostly to China to become medicinal ingredients. Such rare animals can fetch anywhere between US$200 and US$1000 from buyers looking to cash in on their 'medicinal worth', be it for gallstone relief or as an aphrodisiac.

In cooperation with the Vietnamese authorities, the centre has had some major recovery and breeding successes, including the world's first grey-shanked Douc langur bred in captivity. The red-shanked Douc langurs are breeding fantastically and are fascinating animals that look as though they are wearing red shorts (their Vietnamese name translates as 'monkeys wearing shorts'). Some southern species of langur at the centre have heated sleeping quarters in winter, which is more than can be said of the human residents.

One of the larger aims of the centre is to reintroduce these primates into their natural habitat. Currently hunting pressures are still too high, but as a preliminary step, some gibbons and a group of Hatinh langurs have been released into a 2-hectare, semi-wild area adjacent to the centre; and a group of Douc langurs are in a second, 4-hectare, semi-wild enclosure.

between the Muong and park rangers who have tried to stop logging in the park. The government has responded by relocating the villagers further from the park's boundary. Some ecotourism ventures such as village homestays (see p192) provide income to the local people, thereby giving conservation a direct economic benefit to them.

Improved roads have led to increased illegal logging, which in turn is having a huge impact on the growth, movement and conservation of plants and animals.

The best time of year to visit the park is in the dry months from November to February. From April to June it becomes increasingly hot, wet and muddy, and from July to October the rains arrive, bringing lots of leeches. Visitors in April and May should be lucky enough to see some of the literally millions of butterflies that breed here.

There is a low-key, informative **visitor centre** a few hundred metres before the park entrance.

Hiking

Excellent hiking opportunities abound in the park and you could spend several days trekking through the forest here.

Short walks include a large, enclosed **botanic garden** near the park headquarters where some native animals – deer, civets, gibbons and langurs – have been released. Another short trail leads to a steep stairway up to the **Cave of Prehistoric Man**, where in 1966 human graves and tools were found dating back 7500 years, making it one of the oldest sites of human habitation in Vietnam.

Popular day-trails include an 8km-return walk to the massive, 1000-year-old **Big Tree** *(Tetrameles nudiflora)*; and a longer hike to **Silver Cloud Peak**. There's also a strenuous five-hour hike to **Kanh**, a Muong village. You can overnight here with local families (p192) and also raft on the Buoi River.

Park staff can provide you with basic maps to find the well-marked trail heads, but a guide is recommended for day trips and is

LAOS BORDER BLUES 1

All of the border crossings between north-central Vietnam and Laos have a degree of difficulty. If you've got the time, you're much better to head south and cross at Lao Bao. The crossing at **Nam Xoi/Na Meo** (7am-6pm) in Thanh Hoa province is the most remote, in a mountainous area 175km northwest of Thanh Hoa city and 70km east of Xam Nua (Laos). From the Lao side you should be able to get a *saengthaew* (pick-up truck) from Vieng Xai to the border (15,000k). There is not much here but across the border in Vietnam there's a small village with some incredibly basic accommodation – avoid it if you can. Once in Vietnam you're probably best to negotiate a motorbike for the lengthy, bumpy ride to Thanh Hoa. Another option is to take a motorbike to a town such as Ba Thuoc (US$10, 54km) and try to find a minibus. However, we've heard reports of drivers demanding 300,000d for the journey to Thanh Hoa – over six times the going rate. The same is true if you're travelling in the opposite direction, although you're slightly less likely to be scammed if you buy your bus ticket from the Thanh Hoa station. Be aware that Lao visas are not available at this border. All in all, expect a 15-hour ordeal if you take this route.

mandatory for longer treks. A guide will cost a minimum of US$5 per day for up to five people, plus US$1 for each extra person.

Sleeping & Eating

There are two accommodation areas in the park, with a complicated range of prices and options.

The centre of the park, 18km from the gate, is the best place to be for an early morning walk or bird-watching. Here there are basic rooms in a **pillar house** (per person US$6), or a couple of self-contained **bungalows** (s/d US$15/25). There's also an enormous river-fed swimming pool.

At park headquarters there are self-contained **bungalows & guesthouse rooms** (s/d US$15/20), as well as rooms in a **pillar house** (per person US$5). The smartest rooms are those constructed around an artificial lake just inside the park boundary. You can **camp** (per person US$2) at either location, but need to bring your own gear. **Meals** (10,000-25,000d) are available from reception, including a vegetarian option.

If you're looking for an unforgettable experience of tribal life, you might consider the hike to Kanh village (see p191), where it's possible to stay with local families. The dwellings are predictably basic – don't expect anything resembling a toilet as we know it. You'll need to pay US$20 for a guide to lead you and stay overnight, but the accommodation only costs US$5.

It can get very busy here at weekends and during Vietnamese school holidays. Reservations can be made by contacting the national park office.

Getting There & Away

Cuc Phuong National Park is 45km from Ninh Binh. The turn-off from Hwy 1A is north of Ninh Binh and follows the road that goes to Kenh Ga and Van Long Nature Reserve. There is no public transport all the way to the park so you're best to arrange a motorbike or car in Ninh Binh.

VINH

☎ 038 / pop 226,000

Hurriedly rebuilt after its wartime devastation, Vinh is only now lifting off the mantle of concrete ugliness that has been its reputation over the last 30 years. Trees have been planted along its wide boulevards, new parks opened and the lakesides landscaped – injecting a much needed splash of green among the grey Stalinist patina. There's still not a lot to detain a tourist for more than a day, but it's becoming a more attractive option for breaking up the long journey between Hanoi and Hué. The capital of Nghe An province, it has a few almost-attractions nearby, including Ho Chi Minh's birthplace Kim Lien and the beach resort of Cua Lo.

History

While the area has been inhabited for at least 4000 years, it was in the 18th century that Vinh came to prominence. Leaders of the Tay Son rebellion aimed to set up 'Phoenix Capital City' here during their short-lived rule. In 1930 it was the site of a brutally suppressed May Day demonstration, where police fired on marchers, killing seven. Revolutionary fervour spread, with Vinh's various Communist cells, trade unions and farmers' organisations earning it the appellation 'Red-Glorious City'.

From a pleasant citadel city, it was reduced to rubble in the early 1950s as a result of French aerial bombing and the Viet Minh's scorched-earth policy. Later, a huge fire finished off anything that was left standing.

The Ho Chi Minh Trail began in Nghe An province, and many of the war supplies sent south were shipped via the port of Vinh. The US military's response was to once again obliterate the city in hundreds of bombardments from 1964 to 1972, which left only two buildings intact. Casualties were high on both sides – more US aircraft and pilots were shot down over Nghe An and Ha Tinh provinces than over any other part of North Vietnam. The heavy loss of planes and pilots was one reason why the USA later brought in battleships to pound North Vietnam from a distance.

Orientation

As Hwy 1A enters Vinh from the south, it crosses over the mouth of the Lam River (Ca River), also known as the Cua Hoi Estuary. Street numbers are rarely used in Vinh.

Information

The city has an official website (www.vinhcity.gov.vn).

Incombank (☎ 359 5230; Đ 9 Nguyen Sy Sach) Has an ATM and exchange services.

Main post office (☎ 356 1408; Đ Nguyen Thi Minh Khai; 🕓 6.30am-10pm) For phone calls and postal services. Also has an air-conditioned internet café attached.

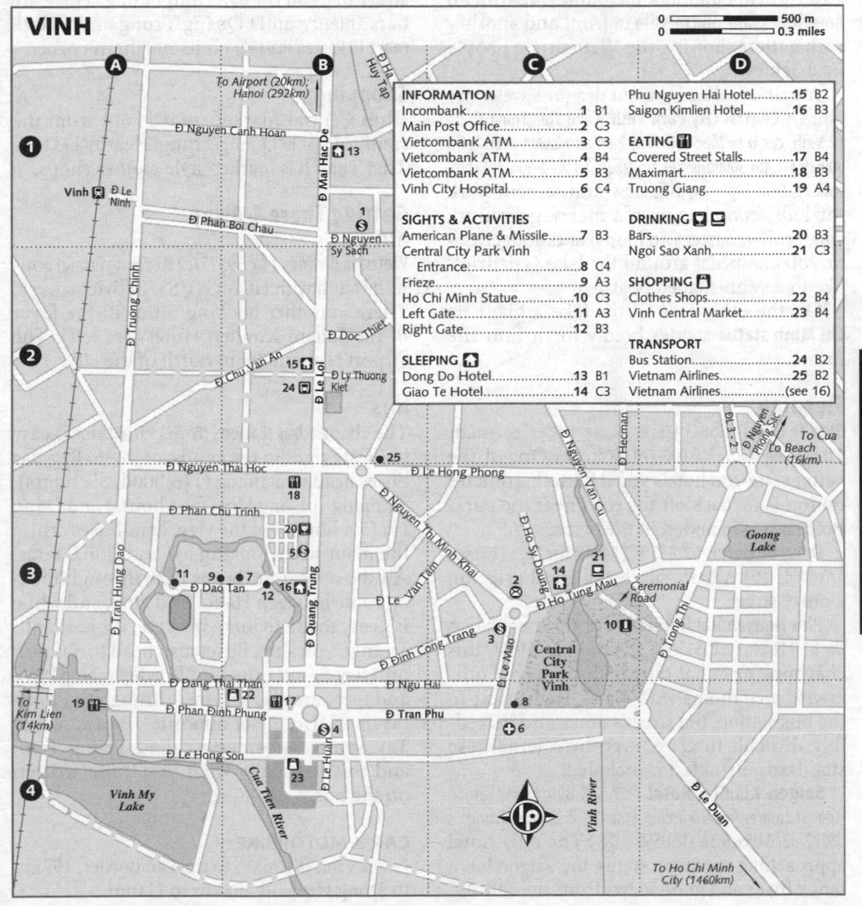

Vietcombank (53 Đ Le Huan) Has an ATM. Further ATMs may be found at 33 Đ Le Mao and Đ Quang Trang, a block north of the Saigon Kimlien Hotel.

Vinh City Hospital (Benh Vien da Khoa; ☎ 835 279; 178 Đ Tran Phu) For medical emergencies.

Sights & Activities

Although the shape of Vinh's **Ancient Citadel** is easy to see on any city map, there's not a lot left that's visible from street level, apart from the moat and the **Left Gate** (Cua Ta; Đ Dao Tan) and **Right Gate** (Cua Huu; Đ Dao Tan). The citadel is not actually all that ancient, having been built in 1831. Its 4.4m-high walls once stretched for 2520m, supported by a 28m-wide, 3.2m-deep moat. The citadel is now home to a sports stadium, homes, shops and government buildings, including one with an **American plane and missile** in front and another with a **frieze** showing the Vietnamese people in shackles.

A pair of colourful giant dragons welcome you to **Central City Park Vinh** (Cong Vien Trung Tham TP Vinh; cnr Đ Le Mao & Đ Tran Phu; admission over 1.4m 5000d/1-1.4m 3000d/under 1m free; ⌚ Wed-Sun 3-11pm, holidays 8am-11pm), a big new amusement park for kids, complete with a merry-go-round, small rollercoaster (no loops) and dodgems – or you can pedal around the lake Galadriel-like in a swan-shaped boat.

On the other side of the lake a giant **Ho Chi Minh statue** strides boldly forth into the future.

Sleeping

Giao Te Hotel (☎ 843 175; ks_giaote_na@yahoo.com.vn; 9 Đ Ho Tung Mau; r 100,000-220,000d; ❄) One of the better state-run hotels you'll find, this quieter option is set back off the road near the park. Breakfast is included in the price.

Dong Do Hotel (☎ 846 989; 14 Mai Hac De; r 110,000-170,000d; ❄) A basic place at a good price on a noisy street.

Phu Nguyen Hai Hotel (☎ 848 429; ctpnh@hn.vnn.vn; 81 Đ Le Loi; s/d US$15/20; ❄) Built in 1928, this charming place has tatty bathrooms but otherwise nice rooms with views. Right next to the bus station, the street's noisy and incredibly difficult to cross even by Vietnamese standards. Breakfast is included.

Saigon Kimlien Hotel (☎ 838 899; www.saigon-tourist.com/en/hotel/kimlien.htm; 25 Đ Quang Trung; s US$22-32, d US$26-36, ste US$60; ❄) The only hotel approaching upmarket status, the Saigon has a fancy foyer and good views from the rooms.

Eating & Drinking

Truong Giang (☎ 838 523; 2 Đ Phan Dinh Phung; meals 40,000d; ⌚ lunch & dinner) When it's all getting too crazy, this pillar house over a lake is a good escape from the hustle and bustle. Its grand entrance past a fountain and over a red-carpeted bridge is at odds with its shabby reception-lounge charm. There's no English menu, but the staff will help you order. The fish is very good.

Ngoi Sao Xanh (☎ 567 878; 17 Đ Ho Tung Mau) This café opposite the park is a charming dive – bamboo walls are complemented by carved wooden Disney figures. The upstairs area has views over the park.

You can get *pho bo* (beef noodle soup) and a drink for less than 20,000d from the covered street stalls on Đ Phan Dinh Phung. There are bars aplenty on Đ Quang Trung and a **Maximart** (Đ Nguyen Thai Hoc) on its northern corner.

Shopping

Vinh Central Market sprawls out from the south end of Đ Quang Trung. Nearby Đ Dang Thai Than has market-style clothes shops.

Getting There & Away

AIR

Vietnam Airlines (☎ 595 777; 2 Đ Le Hong Phong) connects Vinh with HCMC (US$72) twice a week. There's another booking office in the foyer of the Saigon Kimlien Hotel (see left). The airport is about 20km north of the city.

BUS

The chaotic **bus station** (☎ 833 997; Đ Le Loi) is easy to locate right in the centre of town. Regular buses head to Danang (116,000d, 8½ hours), stopping at Dong Hoi (four hours) and Dong Ha (5½ hours) on the way. Minibuses cruise the main street looking for additional fares. All the open-tour buses pass through town en route between Hanoi and Hué, and while it's easy to ask to jump off here, it's harder to arrange a pick up. Buses also head to Tay Son on Hwy 8, near the Lao border (see p196), and there are also services through to Phonsavan on Hwy 7 (see opposite). Be aware that Tay Son was formerly called Trung Tam, and this is usually what you'll see written on the bus.

CAR & MOTORBIKE

From Vinh it's 96km to the Lao border, 197km to Dong Hoi and 292km to Hanoi.

NORTH-CENTRAL VIETNAM

LAOS BORDER BLUES 2

Nong Haet/Nam Can (🕑 7am-6pm) is the northernmost of the two crossings to Laos from Nghe An province. On Tuesdays, Thursdays and Sundays it's possible to catch a bus at 6am from Vinh to Phonsavan (US$12, 11 hours, bookings Mr Lam ☎ 038-383 5782). Otherwise catch a morning bus from Vinh to Muang Xen (29,000d, seven hours), which departs when full. Grab a motorbike for the spectacular 25km uphill run to the border (50,000d) and get ready to wait around on the Lao side. Local transport on to Nong Haet is about 5000k if anything shows up. From Nong Haet, there are several buses a day on to Phonsavan (20,000k, four hours) starting from 7am sharp. It might also be possible to charter a private car from US$30. From Phonsavan it is easy to connect to Luang Prabang or Vientiane.

Heading in the opposite direction, the motorbike drivers on the Vietnamese side of the border may try to demand as much as US$10 for the 25km journey downhill.

TRAIN

The **Vinh train station** (Ga Vinh; ☎ 853 158; Đ Le Ninh) is on the northwestern edge of town. The *Reunification Express* heads to destinations including Hanoi (113,000d, 5½ to eight hours, seven daily), Ninh Binh (73,000d, 3½ to 4½ hours, four daily), Thanh Hoa (50,000d, 2½ to 3½ hours, six daily), Dong Hoi (80,000d, 3½ to 9½ hours, eight daily) and Hué (143,000d, 6½ to 10 hours, seven daily).

AROUND VINH

Cua Lo Beach

This is one of three original state-dominated beach resorts in the northern half of the country – the others being Sam Son and Do Son. The beach here is beautiful, with white sand, clean water and a shady grove of pine trees along the shore. During holiday season it's a popular destination for locals, but the concrete, karaoke, massage parlours and litter won't suit many foreign travellers. Nevertheless, if you're in the area and the weather is warm, Cua Lo is worth a visit for a cooling dip and a good seafood lunch at one of the restaurants on the beach.

There are masses of **guesthouses** (r from US$5) along the waterfront and huge **government hotels** (r US$30). Most offer 'massage' and karaoke, and most have prostitutes hanging around outside, even in low season. Hotel rates drop considerably during the winter months – the name of the game is negotiation if for some reason you really want to stay here.

Cua Lo is 16km northeast of Vinh and can be reached easily by motorbike or taxi.

Kim Lien

Just 14km northwest of Vinh is **Ho Chi Minh's birthplace** in the village of Hoang Tru. The house is maintained as a sacred shrine; it's a popular pilgrimage spot for Vietnamese tourists. Ho Chi Minh's childhood home is a simple farmhouse that's made of bamboo and palm leaves, reflecting his humble beginnings, although what you see today is a 1959 recreation. He was raised in this house until 1895, when the family sold it and moved to Hué so that his father could study.

In 1901 Ho Chi Minh's family returned to a **house** in Kim Lien, about 2km from Hoang Tru. Not far from this house, there is a **museum**, complete with the usual black-and-white photos of Ho's life.

Admission to all the **sites** (🕑 7.30-11am & 1.30-5pm) is free. However you are obliged to buy three bouquets of flowers (10,000d each) from the reception desk and place one by each of the altars. No English-language information is available.

There is no public transport to Kim Lien, but it's easy enough to hire a motorbike or taxi in Vinh.

PHONG NHA CAVE

☎ 052

The complex karst formations stretching throughout the surrounding Ke Bang National Park were formed approximately 400 million years ago, making them the oldest in Asia. Part of this system, **Phong Nha Cave** (☎ 675 110; admission 30,000d, charter boat 100,000d; 🕑 7am-4pm) is the largest and most beautiful cave in Vietnam. Located in the village of Son Trach, 55km northwest of Dong Hoi, it was designated a Unesco World Heritage site in 2003. It's remarkable for its thousands of metres of underground passageways and river caves filled with abundant stalactites and stalagmites. In November and December the river is prone to flooding and the underground cave may be closed.

Phong Nha means Cave of Teeth, but, unfortunately, the 'teeth' (or stalagmites) that were by the entrance are no longer there. Once you get further into the cave, it's mostly unspoiled. In 1990 a British expedition explored 35km of the cave and made the first reliable map of the underground (and underwater) passageways. They discovered that the main cavern is nearly 8km long, with 14 other caves nearby.

Tien Son Cave (☎ 675 110; admission 20,000d; ⏲ 7am-4pm) is a dry cave in the mountainside just above Phong Nha Cave. You can walk to it from the entrance to Phong Nha Cave (10 minutes) – look for the sign at the foot of the stairs.

The Chams used the cave's grottoes as Hindu sanctuaries in the 9th and 10th centuries; the remains of their altars and inscriptions are still here. Vietnamese Buddhists continue to venerate these sanctuaries, as they do other Cham religious sites.

More recently, this cave was used as a hospital and ammunition depot during the American War. The entrance shows evidence of aerial attacks. That US war-planes spent considerable time bombing and strafing the Phong Nha area is hardly surprising: this was one of the key entrance points to the Ho Chi Minh Trail (see p329). Some overgrown remains of the trail are still visible, though you'll need a guide to point them out to you.

You should be aware that Phong Nha is heavily visited by Vietnamese groups. The cave itself is fantastic, the experience less so. That is, unless you like your World Heritage sites to incorporate litter, noise, people climbing on stalagmites and cigarette smoke in confined spaces. Of course these things are prohibited, but enforcement is lax to say the least. Presumably these distractions can be avoided if you arrive early in the morning. The toilets might be less putrid then, too.

The Phong Nha Reception Department, an enormous complex in **Son Trach village**, organises tourist access to the cave. You buy your

LAOS BORDER BLUES 3

The **Nam Phao/Cau Treo border** (⏲ 7am-6pm) is 96km west of Vinh and about 30km east of Lak Sao in Laos. While the most travelled and shortest distance of the four crossings in north-central Vietnam, there are still lots of horror stories from travellers on this route. This area is well known to drug smugglers and other dodgy dealers. Lao Bao, near Dong Ha in Central Vietnam, is a much better option.

30-day Lao visas (US$30) are available on arrival in Nam Phao, but Vietnamese visas still need to be arranged in advance; try the Vietnamese embassy in Vientiane.

Buses from Vinh for Tay Son (formerly Trung Tam; 10,000d) leave 10 times a day between 6am and 2pm. A lot of travellers have reported bad experiences on this local bus, including chronic overcharging and being kicked off in the middle of nowhere. From Tay Son it's a further 26km to the border. Take a minibus or hire a motorbike to cover the last stretch; both cost 50,000d. The last 25km climbs through some spectacular steep and forested country. There is absolutely nothing here except the border post itself, so stock up on water and snacks in Tay Son when passing through.

The Vietnamese border guards have been known to close the country for lunch – any time from 11.30am to 1.30pm. It's also quite common for them to ask for a US$1 fee to stamp your visa. From the Vietnamese side it's a short walk to the Laos border. Once in Laos, *jumbo* (three-wheeled taxis) and *sawngthaew* (pick-up trucks) to Lak Sao leave the border when full or cost about US$10 to charter.

Coming the other way from Laos to Vietnam, *sawngthaew* (US$1.50, 45 minutes) depart regularly from the market. Once in Vietnam the vultures begin circling to arrange transport to Vinh. Many will try to charge US$20 per person to Vinh, but US$5 is more sensible. Try to hook up with as many other people as possible as you cross the border to improve your bargaining position.

A common scam exists with minibuses in Lak Sao offering travellers a ride directly on to Vinh. Once they're in a suitably remote section on the Vietnamese side they stop and demand an extra US$20 on threat of abandonment in the dark. There are four direct buses a day and a ticket should cost no more than US$10.

admission ticket here and organise a boat to take you to the cave. Boats seat up to 10 people and it's cheaper to share. The cave system is electrically lit, but you may want to bring a torch (flashlight).

Sleeping & Eating

There is better accommodation available in Dong Hoi, but staying in Son Trach may help you to beat the crowds.

Saigon Phong Nha (☎ 675 016; sgquangbinhtourist@vnn.vn; r US$13;) This hotel provides rooms with en suites and hot water, and free breakfast.

In Son Trach itself there are plenty of cheap *com pho* places. Don't expect *haute cuisine*. Make sure you bring cash, as there are no banks here.

Getting There & Away

From Dong Hoi head 20km north on Hwy 1A to Bo Trach and then turn west for the 30km to Son Trach. Some hotels in Dong Hoi offer tours, but a cheaper option is by motorbike.

The actual cave entrance is 3km by river from Son Trach. The one-way ride takes about 30 minutes and gives a great glimpse of the life of river people. Overall, it takes about two hours to visit the river cave, or about four hours with a trip to the dry cave too.

DONG HOI

☎ 052 / pop 130,640

Following the 1954 partition, Dong Hoi and its southern neighbour Dong Ha went from being at the centre of the country to frontier towns. Both suffered more than most during the American War – as the ruins and bomb craters throughout the area will attest. The fact that Dong Hoi has bounced back to become an attractive city while Dong Ha still retains a badlands feel surely owes a lot to being on the winning side.

It has a wonderful location with the Nhat Le River dividing the main part of the city from a beautiful sandy spit, with lengthy stretches of beach to the north and south of town. While most tourists head from Hanoi to Hué, Dong Hoi is the best spot to break up the journey. It's also a much nicer base to explore the DMZ sites than Dong Ha – but it's slightly further away, and being on the northern side you won't find as many English-speaking drivers. From Dong Hoi you can easily make a day trip to the Phong Nha Cave (see p195).

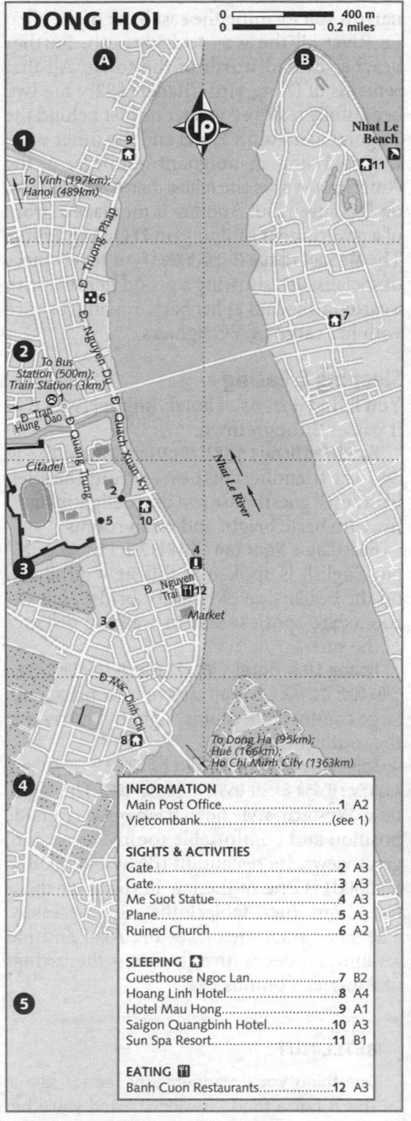

Information

Main post office (☎ 822 560; 1 Đ Tran Hung Dao; 7am-9.30pm)

Vietcombank has an ATM outside the post office.

Sights

A major new bridge links the town with **Nhat Le Beach**, a long stretch of sand lining the narrow spit forming the east bank of the Nhat Le River all the way to its mouth. Further beaches extend north of the town. All that remains of Dong Hoi Citadel (1825) are two beautifully restored **gates**, one just behind the Saigon Quangbinh Hotel and the other on Đ Quang Trung. A poignant reminder of the American War is the **ruined church**, by the river on Đ Nguyen Du. Another is the **plane** in front of a government building on Đ Quang Trung. The **Me Suot statue** (Đ Quach Xuan Ky) is lovely piece of socialist art, showing a proud heroine with a cartoonish wind at her back, rowing forward with her cargo of VC fighters.

Sleeping & Eating

You'll find dozens of hotels lining Hwy 1A as it passes through town.

Hotel Mau Hong (☎ 821 804; Đ Truong Phap; r US$7-10; ❄) The friendliest of the riverfront cheapies, it's a small guesthouse run by a delightful family, with basic bright and clean rooms.

Guesthouse Ngoc Lan (☎ 843 732; r 120,000d; ❄) No English is spoken at this new minihotel on the beach side of Nhat Le bridge, but the rooms are spotless and in walking distance of the surf.

Hoang Linh Hotel (☎ 821 608; Đ Mac Dinh Chi; r 180,000d; ❄ 💻) An attractive new place with large comfortable rooms, right by the river at the south end of town.

Saigon Quangbinh Hotel (☎ 822 276; 20 Đ Quach Xuan Ky; r US$58-81, ste US$127; ❄ 💻 🏊) This flash, new, Western-style hotel has a quiet riverside position and comfortable rooms, some with great views. Its restaurant (dishes 40,000d to 80,000d) is one of the few in town for those for whom linen tablecloths are a necessity. The small pool area faces the road and has an unusual decorative feature – the casings of American bombs.

Sun Spa Resort (☎ 842 999; sunsparesortvietnam.com; r US$86-127, ste US$207; ❄ 💻 🏊) This massive complex on Nhat Le Beach has a large pool, tennis courts and an opulent landscaped garden complete with a waterfall, fountain, swan-shaped boats on a lake and tethered deer. You shouldn't find yourself short of a bed amongst the 234 well-furnished rooms and 50 luxury villas facing on to the beautiful private beach.

There is a cluster of very good **local restaurants** (meals around 15,000d) situated on Đ Nguyen Trai near the market. They specialise in the delicious pancake-like *banh cuon* (rice-crepe rolls).

Getting There & Away

BUS

Buses to all destinations zip up and down Hwy 1A, including open-tour buses between Hanoi and Hué. It's easy to leave an open tour bus in Dong Hoi, but more difficult to arrange to be picked up from here.

From the **bus station** (☎ 822 150; Đ Tran Hung Dao) you can catch services south to Danang (56,000d, five hours, six daily) via Dong Ha (30,000d, two hours), and north to Vinh (50,000d, four hours).

It's possible to get a bus to the busy Lao border at Lao Bao (40,000d, three daily) and directly to the Lao city of Muang Khammouan (190,000d, 11 hours, twice weekly, bookings Mr Thang ☎ 828 939) passing through the little used **Cha Lo/Na Phao border crossing** (🕒 7am-5pm) situated between Don Bai Dinh (Vietnam) and Na Phao (Laos). The buses leave from Dong Hoi at 6am on Mondays and Fridays, with the return journey leaving from Muang Khammouan at 7am on Wednesdays and Sundays. It is not possible to arrange a Lao visa at this border.

BETEL NUT

One thing you'll undoubtedly see for sale at street stalls everywhere in Vietnam is betel nut. This is not a food – swallow it and you'll be sorry! The betel nut is the seed of the betel palm (a beautiful tree, by the way) and is meant to be chewed. The seed usually has a slit in it and is mixed with lime and wrapped in a leaf. Like tobacco, it's strong stuff that you can barely tolerate at first, but eventually you'll be hooked.

The first time you bite into betel nut, your whole face gets hot – chewers say it gives them a buzz. Like chewing tobacco, betel nut causes excessive salivation and betel chewers must constantly spit. The reddish-brown stains you see on footpaths are not blood, but betel-saliva juice. Years of constant chewing cause the teeth to become stained progressively browner, eventually becoming nearly black.

CAR & MOTORBIKE

Dong Hoi is on Hwy 1A, 166km north of Hué, 95km north of Dong Ha and 197km south of Vinh.

TRAIN

The **train station** (Ga Dong Hoi; ☎ 820 558; Đ Thuan Ly) is located 3km from Hwy 1A. Take Đ Tran Hung Dao until it crosses a bridge. A signpost directs you to take the next right, then take another right and then the station is directly ahead.

The *Reunification Express* heads to destinations that include Hanoi (202,000d, nine to 12 hours, six daily), Vinh (80,000d, 3½ to 9½ hours, eight daily), Dong Ha (38,000d, two to 2½ hours, six daily) and Hué (65,000d, 2½ to 5½ hours, eight daily).

Central Vietnam

Home to historical sites, fantastic food and the country's most iconic beach, central Vietnam deserves to rate as a top priority for travellers. Tourists wanting to avoid lengthy bus journeys will find Danang's airport the perfect gateway to a fascinating set of the country's most famous destinations, including three must-see Unesco World Heritage sites – history-seeped Imperial Hué, architecturally impressive Hoi An and the sacred ruins of ancient My Son.

The north of the region continues to attract its share of former servicemen revisiting the Demilitarised Zone (DMZ), the old border between North and South Vietnam, which saw some of the fiercest fighting of the American War. Other GIs have returned permanently to join the ex-pat community in bustling Danang. It's not just veterans that find these locales fascinating – the war's impact on popular culture also attracts legions of younger tourists.

There are plenty of relatively undiscovered spots deserving of exploration, including the beautiful cool heights of Bach Ma National Park and Ba Na Hill Station, and, surprisingly, large tracts of tele-famous China Beach. Other spots, such as the Marble Mountains and Hai Van Pass, are choked with hawkers but still make fascinating stops.

The range of accommodation on offer is extraordinary – from great-value budget places to some of the most luxurious resorts in the country. Hoi An is a shopper's paradise and, along with Hué, a great location for foodies.

Do the maths: it all adds up to make this region a *must* on any trip through Vietnam.

HIGHLIGHTS

- Eat your way around the local specialities in the beautiful buildings and historic streets of **Hoi An** (p239)
- Get imperious, making yourself at home in the Forbidden Purple City in **Hué** (p209)
- Chill out above the clouds in beautiful **Ba Na Hill Station** (p228)
- Savour the atmosphere of the holy places of the Cham people at **My Son** (p262)
- Cruise on the back of a bike along the 30km white sand stretch of **China Beach** (p237)

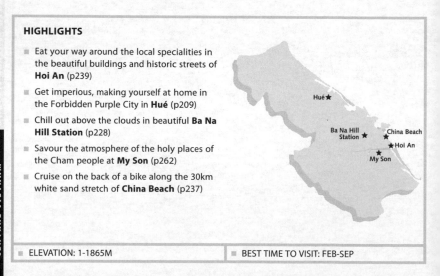

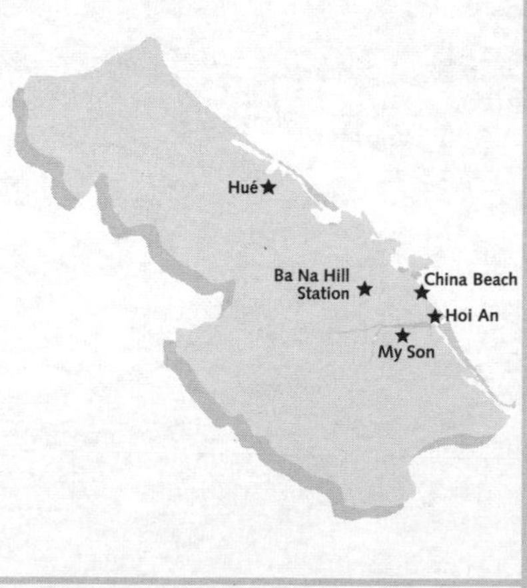

- ELEVATION: 1-1865M
- BEST TIME TO VISIT: FEB-SEP

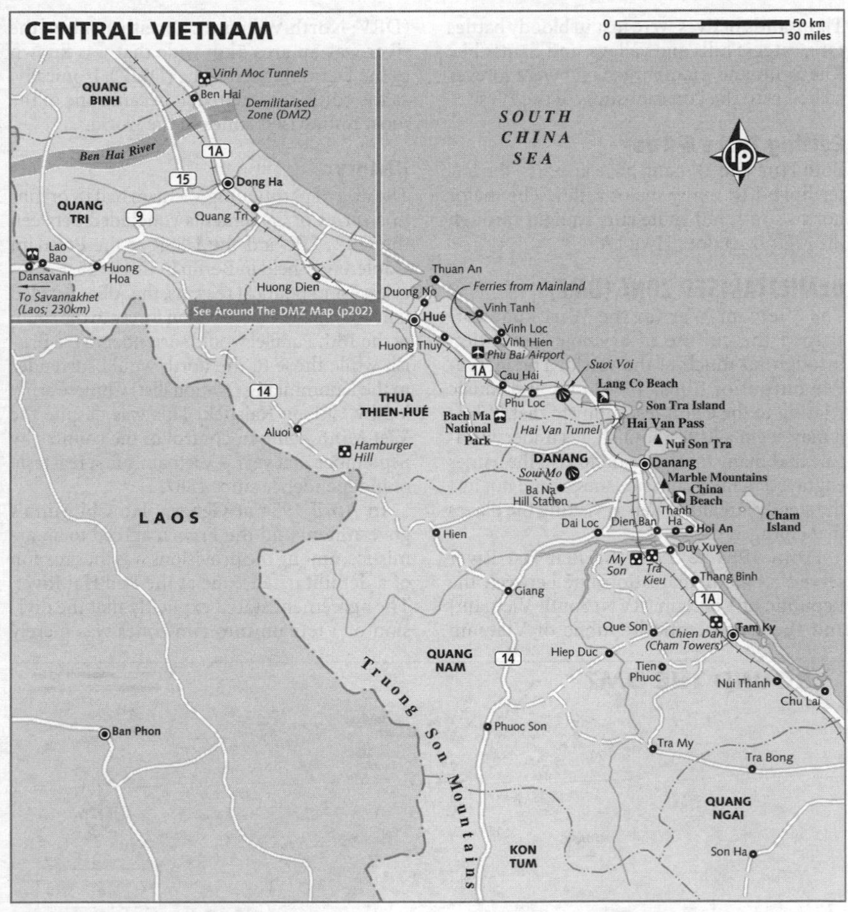

History

History hangs heavily over the central Vietnam region, and the Vietnamese are only one element of the successive stories that have unfolded here. This region was the heartland of the ancient kingdom of Champa (see the boxed text, p264), and the Chams left their mark in the shape of the many towers dotting the landscape, the most renowned of which are at My Son.

As the Vietnamese pushed southwards, pacifying the Chams, the first Europeans set foot in Vietnam: Portuguese traders, who arrived in Danang in the 16th century.

The French would come to dominate Vietnam, but not before the balance of power shifted decisively to central Vietnam under the last royal dynasty, the Nguyens, who ruled from 1802 to 1945. Successive emperors established a lavish imperial court at Hué, which became the centre of political intrigue, intellectual excellence and spiritual guidance in Vietnam. The French broke the will of later emperors and the balance of power shifted back to Hanoi by the time of independence.

History was not to ignore this once-proud region, but this time it was a tale of tragedy. As Vietnam found itself engulfed in the American War, the Demilitarised Zone (DMZ) was the scene of some of the heaviest fighting. The North Vietnamese sought to infiltrate the south along the Ho Chi Minh Trail, while American forces and their South Vietnamese allies tried their best to disrupt supplies.

Thousands of lives were lost in bloody battles for strategic hills and valleys, and names like Khe Sanh and Hamburger Hill were forever etched into the consciousness of the West.

Getting There & Away

Both Hué and Danang have airports, the latter linked to many major cities. The major north–south rail route cuts straight through the region, as does Hwy 1A.

DEMILITARISED ZONE (DMZ)

The Vietnam War (as the West knows it) shaped the culture of a whole generation throughout much of the world. The incredible output of films, TV shows and music relating to the war is testimony to that. While it may seem a little ghoulish, it's understandable that many tourists want to visit the names engraved in their consciousness – and not just the steady stream of Vets revisiting the places that changed their lives.

From 1954 to 1975 the Ben Hai River served as the demarcation line between the Republic of Vietnam (RVN; South Vietnam) and the Democratic Republic of Vietnam (DRV; North Vietnam). On either side of the river was an area 5km wide that was known as the Demilitarised Zone (DMZ). Ironically, as the conflict escalated, it became one of the most militarised zones in the world.

History

The idea of partitioning Vietnam had its origins in a series of agreements concluded between the USA, UK and the USSR at the Potsdam Conference, held in Berlin in July 1945. For logistical and political reasons, the Allies decided that the Japanese occupation forces to the south of the 16th Parallel would surrender to the British while those to the north would surrender to the Kuomintang (Nationalist) Chinese army led by Chiang Kaishek. This was despite the Viet Minh being in control of the country by September that year – Vietnam's first real taste of independence since 1887.

In April 1954 at Geneva, Ho Chi Minh's government and the French agreed to an armistice; among the provisions was the creation of a demilitarised zone at the Ben Hai River. The agreement stated explicitly that the division of Vietnam into two zones was merely

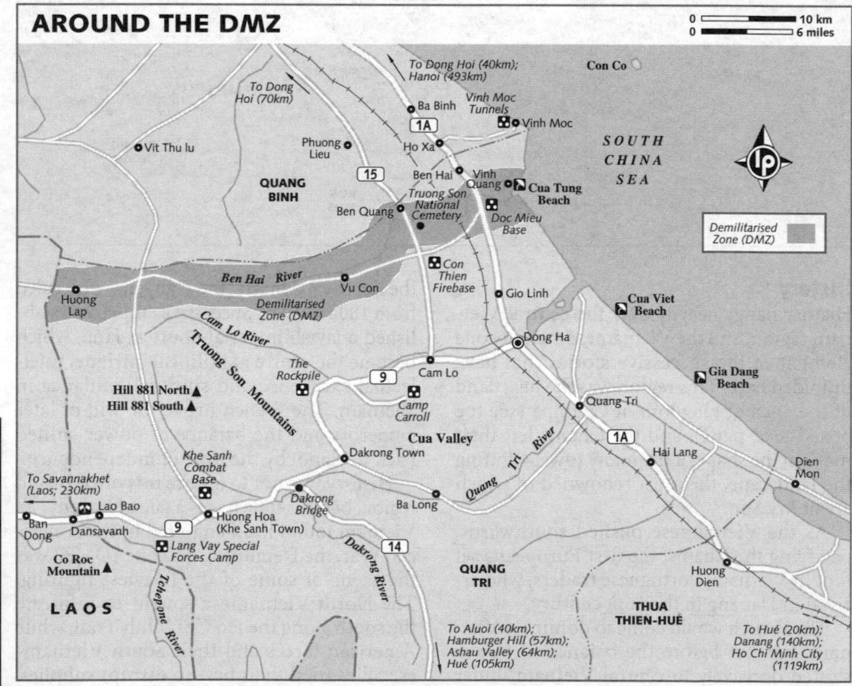

WARNING

The war may be over, but death and injury still come easy in the old DMZ. At many of the places listed in this section there may be live mortar rounds, artillery projectiles and mines strewn about. Watch where you step and don't leave the marked paths. As tempted as you might be to collect souvenirs, *never* touch any left-over ordnance. If the locals have not carted it off for scrap it means that even they are afraid to disturb it. White phosphorus shells – whose contents burn fiercely when exposed to air – are remarkably impervious to the effects of prolonged exposure and are likely to remain extremely dangerous for many more years.

It's not just the DMZ that's affected. It's estimated that as much as 20% of Vietnam remains uncleared, with more than three million mines and 350,000 to 800,000 tonnes of unexploded ordnance (UXO). This represents a staggering 46 tonnes of UXO per sq km or 280kg per person. Between 1975 and 2000 it resulted in the deaths of 38,849 people and 65,852 injuries nationwide. Around 1200 to 3000 people are injured every year.

The People's Army is responsible for most ongoing mine clearance, but they're joined by a number of foreign NGOs. One of the most active is the **Mines Advisory Group** (www.mag.org.uk). Details on how to donate to the cause are available on its website.

temporary and that the demarcation line did not constitute a political boundary. But when nationwide general elections planned for July 1956 were cancelled by the South who predicted a Viet Minh win, Vietnam found itself divided into two states with the Ben Hai River, which is almost exactly at the 17th Parallel, as their de facto border.

During the American War, the area just south of the DMZ was the scene of some of the bloodiest battles of the conflict. Quang Tri, The Rockpile, Khe Sanh, Lang Vay and Hamburger Hill became household names in the USA as, year after year, TV pictures and casualty figures provided Americans with their evening dose of war.

Since 1975, 5000 people have been injured or killed in and around the DMZ by mines and ordnance left over from the war. Despite the risk, impoverished peasants still dig for chunks of leftover metal to sell as scrap, for which they are paid a pittance.

Orientation

The old DMZ extends from the coast westward to the Lao border; Hwy 9 runs basically parallel to the DMZ, about 10km south, and passes beside several US bases.

The road leading southeast from the Dakrong Bridge on Hwy 9 goes to Aluoi and the Ashau Valley (site of the infamous Hamburger Hill).

Information

For an in-depth tour of the DMZ, it is best to link up with a good guide, both to fully appreciate the history and, critically, to physically find some of the sites. Many are unmarked, and it's easy to get lost in the labyrinth of dirt tracks.

Day tours are most readily available in Hué and Dong Ha. Bookings can be made at almost any hotel or café in either town. There are only a few agencies running the tours, so no matter where you sign up you'll probably wind up as part of a group. Expect to pay around US$8 to US$15 for a day-long outing. Most of these tours have English-speaking guides, but some speak French. The main complaint about these bus tours is that they are extremely long and, as they cover quite a distance, there's more time spent driving than sightseeing. A car and guide from Hué may set you back around US$65.

In Dong Ha you can't move for motorcyclists offering tours on the back of their bikes. Many of the older guys speak excellent English as they once worked for the American military or fought alongside them. Unfortunately the one-time defenders of capitalism also demand extortionate fees – US$15 is fair for a day's tour.

Military Sites off Highway 1A

VINH MOC TUNNELS

The incredible tunnels of **Vinh Moc** (admission 15,000d; 7am-4.30pm) are a monument to the perseverance of the North Vietnamese. The 2.8km of tunnels, all of which can be visited, are the real thing and unadulterated for viewing by tourists, unlike the tunnels at Cu Chi (p378). Vinh Moc's underground passageways are larger and taller than those at Cu Chi, which makes for an easier and slightly less claustrophobic visit. There are lights installed inside the tunnels, but you may also want to bring a torch (flashlight). There's an interesting museum on site, housing photos and relics of tunnel life. Outside, American bomb casings are dotted around everywhere, as are the craters that they created.

A visit to the tunnels can be combined with bathing at the beaches that extend for many kilometres to the north and south.

The turn-off to Vinh Moc from Hwy 1A is 6.5km north of the Ben Hai River in the village of Ho Xa. Follow this road east for 13km.

CUA TUNG BEACH

This long, secluded stretch of sand, where Vietnam's last emperor, Bao Dai, used to holiday, is just north of the mouth of the Ben Hai. There are beaches on the southern side of the Ben Hai River as well. Every bit of land in the area not levelled for planting is pockmarked with big bomb craters.

There are no buses to Cua Tung Beach, which can be reached by turning east off Hwy 1A at a point 1.2km north of the Ben Hai River. Cua Tung Beach is about 7km south of Vinh Moc via the dirt road that runs along the coast.

DOC MIEU BASE

Doc Mieu Base, next to Hwy 1A on a low slope 8km south of the Ben Hai River, was once part of an elaborate electronic system (McNamara's Wall, named after the US Secretary of Defense between 1961 and 1968) intended to prevent infiltration across the DMZ. Today it is a lunar landscape of bunkers, craters, shrapnel and live mortar rounds. Bits of cloth and decaying military boots are strewn about on the red earth. This devastation was created not only by the bombs, but also by scrap-metal hunters, who found excavations at this site particularly rewarding.

BEN HAI RIVER

Twenty-two kilometres north of Dong Ha, Hwy 1A crosses the Ben Hai River, once the demarcation line between North and South Vietnam. Check out the old wartime bridge – until 1967, when it was bombed by the Americans, the northern half of the bridge that stood on this site was painted red, while the southern half was yellow. Following the signing of the Paris cease-fire agreements

GOING UNDERGROUND

In 1966 the USA began a massive aerial and artillery bombardment of North Vietnam. Just north of the DMZ, the villagers of Vinh Moc found themselves living in one of the most heavily bombed and shelled strips of land on the planet. Small family shelters could not withstand this onslaught and villagers either fled or began tunnelling by hand into the red-clay earth.

The Viet Cong (VC) found it useful to have a base here and encouraged the villagers to stay. After 18 months of work, during which the excavated earth was camouflaged to prevent its detection from the air, an enormous complex was established underground. Civilians were employed in the digging and were accommodated in new underground homes. Whole families lived here and 17 babies were born in the underground delivery room. Later, the civilians and VC were joined by North Vietnamese soldiers, whose mission was to keep communications and supply lines to nearby Con Co Island open.

Other villages north of the DMZ also built tunnel systems, but none was as elaborate as Vinh Moc. The poorly constructed tunnels of Vinh Quang village (at the mouth of the Ben Hai River) collapsed after repeated bombing, killing everyone inside.

The tunnel network at Vinh Moc remains essentially as it looked in 1966, though some of the 12 entrances – seven of which open onto the palm-lined beach – have been retimbered and others have become overgrown. The tunnels were built on three levels ranging from 12m to 23m below the crest of the bluff.

US warships stationed off the coast consistently bombarded the tunnels, but the only ordnance that posed a real threat was the feared 'drilling bomb'. Only once did such a bomb score a direct hit, but it failed to explode and no-one was injured; the inhabitants adapted the bomb hole for use as an air shaft. Occasionally the mouths of the tunnel complex that faced the sea were struck by naval gunfire.

in 1973, the present bridge and the two flag towers were built.

TRUONG SON NATIONAL CEMETERY

Truong Son National Cemetery is a sobering memorial to the tens of thousands of North Vietnamese soldiers who were killed in the Truong Son Mountain Range along the Ho Chi Minh Trail. Row after row of white tombstones stretch across the hillsides. The cemetery is maintained by disabled war veterans.

The soldiers are buried in five zones according to the part of Vietnam they came from, and each zone is further subdivided into provinces. The gravestones of five colonels and seven decorated heroes, including one woman, are in a separate area. Each headstone bears the inscription 'Liet Si', which means martyr. The remains of soldiers interred here were originally buried near the spot where they were killed and were brought here after reunification. Many graves are empty, simply bearing the names of a small number of Vietnam's 300,000 MIAs.

The site where the cemetery now stands was used as a base by the May 1959 Army Corps from 1972 to 1975. Named after the date on which they were founded, they had the mission of constructing and maintaining a supply line to the South – the legendary Ho Chi Minh Trail. On the hilltop above the sculpture garden is a three sided stele with inscriptions paying tribute to this corps and outlining their history.

The road to Truong Son National Cemetery intersects Hwy 1A 13km north of Dong Ha and 9km south of the Ben Hai River; the distance from the highway to the cemetery is 17km.

A rocky path that is passable by motorbike links Cam Lo (on Hwy 9) with Truong Son National Cemetery (18km). This track passes rubber plantations and also the homes of Bru (Van Kieu) people, who cultivate, among many other crops, black pepper.

CON THIEN FIREBASE

In September 1967 North Vietnamese forces, backed by long-range artillery and rockets, crossed the DMZ and besieged the US Marine Corps base of Con Thien, which was established as part of McNamara's Wall in an attempt to stop infiltrations across the DMZ.

The USA responded with 4000 bombing sorties (including 800 by B-52s), during which more than 40,000 tonnes of bombs were dropped on the North Vietnamese forces around Con Thien, transforming the gently sloping brush-covered hills into a smoking moonscape of craters and ash. The siege was lifted, but the battle had accomplished its real purpose: to divert US attention from South Vietnam's cities in preparation for the Tet Offensive. The area around the base is still considered too dangerous, even for scrap-metal hunters, to approach.

Con Thien Firebase is 10km west of Hwy 1A and 7km south of Truong Son National Cemetery along the road that links the highway with the cemetery. Concrete bunkers mark the spot a few hundred metres to the south of the road where the base once stood.

Military Sites on Highway 9

The legendary Ho Chi Minh Trail – the main artery of supplies for the North's war effort – was not one path but many, leading through the jungles of the country's mountainous western spine. In an effort to cut the line near the border, the Americans established a series of bases along Hwy 9, including (from west to east) Lang Vay, Khe Sanh, Ca Lu (now called Dakrong Town), The Rockpile, Camp Carroll, Cam Lo, Dong Ha, Gio Linh and Cua Viet. Ultimately their efforts were unsuccessful.

LANG VAY SPECIAL FORCES CAMP

In February 1968 Lang Vay Special Forces Camp was attacked and overrun by North Vietnamese infantry backed by nine tanks. Ten of the 24 Americans at the base were killed, along with 316 South Vietnamese, Bru and Montagnard (term meaning highlanders, used to refer to the ethnic minorities) defenders. All that's left of the dog bone–shaped camp are the overgrown remains of numerous concrete bunkers, and a rusty tank memorial.

The base is on a ridge southwest of Hwy 9, between Khe Sanh bus station (9.2km) and Lao Bao (7.3km).

HUONG HOA (KHE SANH TOWN)

This town has now been officially renamed Huong Hoa, but the Western world remembers it as Khe Sanh. Set amid beautiful hills, valleys and fields at an elevation of about 600m, it is a verdant district capital. The town is known for its coffee plantations, which were originally cultivated by the French.

Many of the inhabitants are of the Bru tribe who moved here from the surrounding hills. You'll notice their different clothing, with women wearing sarong-like skirts, and woven baskets taking the place of plastic bags.

About the only reason for staying here is if you're planning to hit the road to Laos the next morning. The **Huong Hoa (Khe Sanh) Guesthouse** (☎ 053-880 740; 64 Khe Sanh; r 120,000d; ❄) offers private bathrooms and hot water.

The bus station is on Hwy 9, about 600m towards the Lao frontier from the triangular intersection where the road to Khe Sanh Combat Base branches off. Buses to Dong Ha (15,000d, 1½ hours) and Lao Bao (10,000d, one hour) depart regularly. Change at Dong Ha for all other destinations.

KHE SANH COMBAT BASE

The site of the most famous siege – and one of the most controversial battles – of the American War, **Khe Sanh Combat Base** (admission 30,000d; 🕑 7am-4.30pm) sits silently on a barren plateau, surrounded by vegetation-covered hills that are often obscured by mist and fog. It is hard to imagine as you stand in this peaceful, verdant land that in early 1968 the bloodiest battle of the war took place here. About 500 Americans (the official figure of 205 was arrived at by statistical sleight of hand), 10,000 North Vietnamese troops and uncounted civilian bystanders died amid the din of machine guns and the fiery explosions of 1000kg bombs, white-phosphorus shells, napalm, mortars and artillery rounds of all sorts.

The site includes the recent addition of a small memorial museum. A couple of bunkers have been recreated and some photos and other memorabilia are on show. Behind the main site, the outline of the airfield remains distinct – to this day nothing will grow on it. Some of the comments in the visitors' book, especially those written by visiting war veterans, can make for emotional reading.

A MIA team still visits the area regularly to search for the bodies of Americans who disappeared during the fierce battles in the surrounding hills. Most remains they find are Vietnamese.

Getting There & Away

To get to Khe Sanh Combat Base from Huong Hoa bus station, head 600m towards Dong Ha then turn northwest at the triangular intersection; there's a small sign. The base is 2.5km further, 500m off the right-hand (east) side of the road.

DAKRONG BRIDGE

Crossing the Dakrong River 13km east of the Khe Sanh bus station, Dakrong Bridge was rebuilt in 2001. The road to Aluoi that heads southeast from the bridge passes by the stilted homes of the Bru people and was once a branch of the Ho Chi Minh Trail.

ALUOI

On Hwy 14 – a route synonymous with the Ho Chi Minh Trail – is Aluoi, approximately 65km southeast of Dakrong Bridge and 60km southwest of Hué. There are several waterfalls and cascades in the surrounding area. Tribes living in this mountainous area include the Ba Co, Ba Hy, Ca Tu and Taoi. US Army Special Forces bases in Aluoi and Ashau were overrun and abandoned in 1966; the area then became an important centre for supplies coming down the Trail.

Among the better-known military sites around Aluoi are **landing zones Cunningham**, **Erskine** and **Razor**, as well as **Hill 1175** (west of the valley) and **Hill 521** (in Laos). Further south, in the Ashau Valley, is **Hamburger Hill** (Apbia Mountain). In May 1969 US forces on a search-and-destroy operation near the Lao border fought in one of the fiercest battles of the war. In less than a week of fighting, 241 US soldiers died at Hamburger Hill – a fact that was very well publicised in the US media. A month later, after the US forces withdrew from the area to continue operations elsewhere, the hill was reoccupied by the North Vietnamese Army.

THE ROCKPILE

Back on Hwy 9, this 230m-high pile of rocks once had a US Marine Corps lookout on top and a base for American long-range artillery nearby.

Today there isn't much left of The Rockpile and you will probably need a guide to point it out to you. It's 26km west of Dong Ha on Hwy 9.

CAMP CARROLL

Established in 1966, Camp Carroll was named after a Marine Corps captain who was killed while trying to seize a nearby ridge. The gargantuan 175m cannons at Camp Carroll were used to shell targets as far away as Khe Sanh.

THE FIGHT FOR NOWHERE

Despite opposition from marine corps brass, the small US Army Special Forces (Green Beret) base at Khe Sanh, built to recruit and train local Montagnards, was turned into a marines' stronghold in late 1966. In April 1967 there began a series of 'hill fights' between US forces and the well-dug-in North Vietnamese infantry, who held the hills 8km to the northwest. In only a few weeks, 155 marines and thousands of North Vietnamese were killed.

In late 1967 American intelligence detected the movement into the hills around Khe Sanh of tens of thousands of North Vietnamese regulars, armed with mortars, rockets and artillery. General Westmoreland became convinced that the North Vietnamese were planning another Dien Bien Phu (the decisive battle in the Franco-Viet Minh War in 1954). This analogy was foolhardy, given American firepower and the proximity of Khe Sanh to supply lines and other US bases. President Johnson himself became obsessed by the spectre of 'Din Bin Foo', as he famously referred to it. To follow the course of the battle, he had a sand-table model of the Khe Sanh plateau constructed in the White House situation room and took the unprecedented step of requiring a written guarantee from the Joint Chiefs of Staff that Khe Sanh could be held.

Westmoreland, determined to avoid another Dien Bien Phu at all costs, assembled an armada of 5000 planes and helicopters and increased the number of troops at Khe Sanh to 6000. He even ordered his staff to study the feasibility of using tactical nuclear weapons.

The 75-day siege of Khe Sanh began on 21 January 1968 with a small-scale assault on the base perimeter. As the marines and the South Vietnamese Rangers braced for a full-scale ground attack, Khe Sanh became the focus of global media attention. It was the cover story for both *Newsweek* and *Life* magazines, and appeared on the front pages of countless newspapers around the world. During the next two months the base was subject to continuous ground attacks and artillery fire. US aircraft dropped 100,000 tonnes of explosives on the immediate vicinity of Khe Sanh Combat Base. The expected attempt to overrun the base never came and, on 7 April 1968 after heavy fighting, US troops reopened Hwy 9 and linked up with the marines to end the siege.

It now seems clear that the siege was merely an enormous diversion intended to draw US forces and the attention of their commanders away from the South Vietnamese population centres in preparation for the Tet Offensive, which began a week after the siege started. However, at the time, Westmoreland considered the entire Tet Offensive to be a 'diversionary effort' to distract attention from Khe Sanh.

After Westmoreland's tour of duty in Vietnam ended in July 1968, US forces in the area were redeployed. Policy had been reassessed and holding Khe Sanh, for which so many men had died, was deemed unnecessary. After everything at Khe Sanh was buried, trucked out or blown up (nothing recognisable that could be used in a North Vietnamese propaganda film was to remain), US forces upped and left Khe Sanh Combat Base under a curtain of secrecy. The American command had finally realised what a marine officer had expressed long before: 'When you're at Khe Sanh, you're not really anywhere. You could lose it and you really haven't lost a damn thing.'

In 1972 the South Vietnamese commander of the camp, Lieutenant Colonel Ton That Dinh, surrendered and joined the North Vietnamese Army.

These days there is not that much to see at Camp Carroll, except for a Vietnamese memorial marker, a few overgrown trenches and the remains of their timber roofs. Bits of military hardware and rusty shell casings can still be found. The concrete bunkers were destroyed by local people seeking to extract the steel reinforcing rods to sell as scrap. Concrete chunks from the bunkers were hauled off for use in construction.

The area around Camp Carroll now belongs to State Pepper Enterprises. On the road in, you'll see pepper plants trained so that they climb up the trunks of jackfruit trees. There are also rubber plantations nearby.

The turn-off to Camp Carroll is 10km west of Cam Lo and 23km northeast of Dakrong Bridge. The base is 3km from Hwy 9.

DONG HA

☎ 053 / pop 80,000

Like Dong Hoi to the north, Dong Ha awoke in 1954 to find that it had moved from the centre of the country to the edge of a heavily militarised border. There's still an element of the Wild West to Dong Ha. It's not a particularly friendly or attractive place, and the scramble for tourist dollars borders on aggressive.

The capital of the reconstituted Quang Tri province, Dong Ha is at the busy intersection of Hwys 1A and 9. Dong Ha served as a US Marine Corps command and logistics centre from 1968 to 1969. In the spring of 1968 a division of North Vietnamese troops crossed the DMZ and attacked the city. Later it was the site of a South Vietnamese army base.

Today there is no conceivable reason to visit, save as a base to explore the DMZ or a stop on the way to the Lao border. Hwy 1A traffic thunders through town, dust blowing and horns blaring, and almost all the hotels are close by. The public loudspeakers start their broadcasting at 5am.

Orientation

Hwy 1A is called Đ Le Duan as it passes through Dong Ha. Hwy 9, with signs reading 'Lao Bao', intersects Hwy 1A next to the bus station.

Information

Dich Vu Internet (☎ 857 177; 177 Đ Le Duan)

Incombank (189 Đ Le Duan) Has an ATM in front of Sepon Travel.

Quang Tri Tourism (☎ 852 927; dmzqtri@dng.vnn.vn; 66 Đ Le Duan) Situated at the Mekong Hotel, this state office runs DMZ tours and arranges car rentals.

Sepon Travel (☎ 855 289; www.sepon.com.vn; 189 Đ Le Duan) Handles bookings for DMZ bus tours, buses to Savannakhet (Laos) and Vietnam Airlines. Can also arrange cars and drivers for private DMZ tours.

Sleeping

Hotel Mai Yen (☎ 551 750; 24 Đ Nguyen Trai; r 120,000-150,000d; ❄) Situated on a leafy street just off the highway near the bus station, this is a friendly place with scrupulously clean rooms.

Melody Hotel (☎ 554 664; www.melodyhotel.net; 62 Đ Le Duan; s/d/tr 120,000/150,000/180,000d; ❄) Although on the noisy highway, the sky-blue Melody Hotel has tidy rooms with all the usual facilities, as well as motorbikes for rent (80,000d per day).

Khach San Duong 9 Xanh (Highway 9 Hotel; ☎ 550 991; 4 Đ Nguyen Trai; r US$9-15; ❄) On the same quiet strip as Mai Yen, the rooms are a little run down but they all have a TV, fridge and hot water.

Mekong Hotel (☎ 852 292; fax 855 234; 66 Đ Le Duan; r 150,000-200,000d; ❄) With what looks like a taxidermied vampire deer in reception (check out the fangs), this larger hotel has clean and well-maintained rooms. Aim for one as far to the rear as possible to escape the highway noise. The hotel's restaurant is the breakfast stop for many DMZ bus tours from Hué.

Eating & Drinking

Trung Tam Lu Hanh (☎ 852 927; 66 Đ Le Duan; dishes 12,000d) One of a number of street-side eateries on the main highway, this one serves a decent *pho ga* (rice noodle soup with chicken).

Quan Chay Vegetarian House (☎ 854 634; 34 Đ Nguyen Trai; meals 20,000d) A small, tidy place on Dong Ha's nicest street.

A good breakfast option is the no-name **bakery** (☎ 859 356; 4 Đ Hung Vuong; pastries 6000d) on Dong Ha's main street, running parallel to the highway. Nearby **Duy Tuong** (14 Đ Hung Vuong) is a local café with an unlikely poster of '80s poodle-haired rockers Cinderella on the wall.

Getting There & Away

BUS

Dong Ha bus station (Ben Xe Khach Dong Ha; ☎ 851 488; 68 Đ Le Duan) is near the intersection of Hwys 1A and 9. Vehicles to Dong Hoi (30,000d, two hours), Hué (25,000d, 1½ hours), Khe Sanh (15,000d, 1½ hours) and Lao Bao (20,000d, two hours) depart regularly.

It is sometimes necessary to change buses in Khe Sanh for Lao Bao. Buses are also advertised to Savannakhet in Laos, but the station won't book a ticket for foreigners. You'll need to cross the road to Sepon Travel (left).

CAR & MOTORBIKE

Road distances from Dong Ha are: Dong Hoi (95km), Hué (77km), Danang (190km), Khe Sanh (65km), Lao Bao (85km) and Vinh Moc (41km).

Motorbike hire tours to the DMZ start from US$10. A one-way car trip to the Lao Bao border will set you back US$25. Motorbikes can be hired from Melody Hotel (left).

TRAIN

Reunification Express trains stop in **Dong Ha Train Station** (Ga Dong Ha; ☎ 850 631; 2 Đ Le Thanh Ton). Destinations include Hanoi (235,000d, 12½ to 15½ hours, four daily), Dong Hoi (38,000d, two to 2½ hours, six daily) and Hué (25,000d, 1½ to 2½ hours, six daily).

To get to the Dong Ha train station from the bus station, head 1km southeast on Hwy 1A to a big guesthouse called Nha Khach 261. Turn right here and the back of the train station is about 150m over the tracks.

LAO BAO (LAOS BORDER)

☎ 053 / pop 33,000

Lao Bao, on the Sepon River (Song Xe Pon), which marks the Vietnam–Laos border, is an important crossing for trade and tourism between the two countries. Towering above Lao Bao on the Laos side of the border is Co Roc Mountain, once a North Vietnamese artillery stronghold.

There is a huge border market on the Vietnamese side, where goods smuggled from Thailand are readily available. Merchants accept either Vietnamese dong or Lao kip. Don't change US dollars at the border unless you have to: the rate can be about 50% lower than the banks.

There's no reason to linger in Lao Bao, but if you miss the border opening hours (see p210) and need a place to stay, **Bao Son Hotel** (☎ 877 848; fax 877 660; r US$12; ❄) is a smart business hotel and good value for the money. There is the inevitable row of *com pho* (rice-noodle soup) places in the centre of town.

Lao Bao town is 18km west of Khe Sanh, 85km from Dong Ha, 152km from Hué, 45km east of Sepon (Laos) and 255km east of Savannakhet (Laos).

QUANG TRI

☎ 053 / pop 15,400

Quang Tri was once an important citadel city. In the spring of 1972 four divisions of North Vietnamese regulars, backed by tanks, artillery and rockets, poured across the DMZ into Quang Tri province in what became known as the Eastertide Offensive. They laid siege to Quang Tri town, shelling it heavily before capturing it along with the rest of the province.

During the next four months the city was almost completely obliterated by South Vietnamese artillery and carpet bombing by US fighter-bombers and B-52s. The South Vietnamese army suffered 5000 casualties in the rubble-to-rubble fighting to retake the city.

Today there is little to see except a few remains of the moat, ramparts and gates of the Citadel, which once served as a South Vietnamese army headquarters. The remnants are 1.6km north from Hwy 1A. Along Hwy 1A, on the Hué side of Quang Tri, is the skeleton of a church chillingly scarred with bullet holes and mortar shells.

The **bus station** (Đ Tran Hung Dao) is about 1km from Hwy 1A, but buses can just as easily be flagged down on the side of the road.

HUÉ

☎ 054 / pop 311,700

If art and architecture matter more to you than beaches and beer, Hué will be high on your Vietnam must-visit list. The capital of the Nguyen emperors, Hué is packed with temples, tombs, palaces and pagodas – or at least the remains of those that successive armies didn't manage to completely destroy. Foodies won't want to miss the fussy degustation-style Imperial cuisine for which this city is rightly famous.

On the banks of the enigmatically named Perfume River, the peculiar light of this historic place imbues photographs with a hazy, purple tinge. It would all be quite idyllic if it weren't for the constant dogging most tourists face as soon as they step off the bus. The touts in Hué are more incessant than most.

While the offshoots of mass tourism may be annoying, it should be remembered that Hué's cultural sites were destined for oblivion without it. After 1975 they were left to decay – Imperialist reminders of the feudal Nguyen dynasty. In 1990 that the local People's Committee recognised the potential of the place and declared these sites 'national treasures'. In 1993 Unesco designated the complex of monuments in Hué a World Heritage site, and restoration and preservation work continues.

The **Festival of Hué** is celebrated biennially in even-numbered years, with local and international cultural performers at locations throughout the city. Hotel accommodation is at a premium at this time, so book ahead if you can.

History

The citadel city of Phu Xuan was built in 1687, 5km northeast of present-day Hué. In 1744 Phu Xuan became the capital of the southern part of Vietnam, which was under the rule of the Nguyen lords. The Tay Son Rebels occupied the city from 1786 until 1802, when it fell to Nguyen Anh. He crowned himself Emperor Gia Long, thus founding the Nguyen dynasty, which ruled the country – at least in name – until 1945.

BORDER CROSSING: LAO BAO/DANSAVANH

The **Lao Bao border** (7am-6pm) is the most popular and least problematic crossing between Laos and Vietnam. You can get a 30-day Lao visa (US$30) on arrival in Dansavanh, but Vietnamese visas still need to be arranged in advance; drop in on the Vietnamese consulate in Savannakhet.

Dong Ha is the junction town for Lao Bao, with regular bus services (see p208). Sepon Travel in Dong Ha (see p208) has buses to Savannakhet (US$12, 7½ hours), continuing on to Vientiane (13 hours); they leave Dong Ha at 8am every second day and return the next day. These buses also pass through Hué (US$14 to US$15, add 1½ hours), and can be booked from the Mandarin and Sinh Cafés (see opposite). If you're travelling across the border by tourist bus, expect a wait while documents are checked. When booking a tourist bus, make sure to confirm (preferably in writing) that the same bus carries on through the border. We've heard plenty of stories of tourists being bundled off nice buses on the Vietnam side and on to overcrowded local buses once they reach Laos.

The border post used to be 2km from Lao Bao town, but the town has expanded so fast it runs almost up to the border. From the bus station the local price for a *xe om* (motorbike taxi) to the border is 5000d (foreigners pay about 10,000d), or walk it in about 20 minutes. Between the Vietnam and Laos border posts is a short walk of a few hundred metres.

Once in Laos there is only one public bus a day direct to Savannakhet, which leaves when full. *Sawngthaew* (pick-up trucks) leave fairly regularly to Sepon, from where you can get a bus or further *sawngthaew* to Savannakhet.

Coming the other way, Route 9 from Savannakhet to the border is now one of the best roads in Laos. From Savannakhet, buses (US$3, 255km, five hours) leave at 7am and noon for the border. Alternatively, take a *sawngthaew* to Sepon (US$3, 210km, four hours) and another from there to the border (US$1.20, 45km, one hour).

Travellers coming from Laos should be aware that no public buses go directly to Hué, despite what drivers may tell you! Some through-buses arrive at the border after it's closed, making for an uncomfortable overnight wait – we've had reports from travellers who have been groped and manhandled while trying to catch some sleep on buses packed with coal and rice.

In 1885, when the advisers of 13-year-old Emperor Ham Nghi objected to French activities in Tonkin, French forces encircled the city. Unwisely, the outnumbered Vietnamese forces launched an attack; the French responded mercilessly. According to a contemporary French account, the French forces took three days to burn the imperial library and remove from the palace every single object of value – everything from gold and silver ornaments to mosquito nets and toothpicks. Ham Nghi fled to Laos, but he was eventually captured and exiled to Algeria. The French replaced him with the more pliable Dong Khanh, thus ending any pretence of genuine independence for Vietnam.

Hué was the site of the bloodiest battles of the 1968 Tet Offensive and was the only city in South Vietnam to be held by the Communists for more than a few days. While the American command was concentrating its energies on Khe Sanh, North Vietnamese and VC troops skirted the American stronghold and walked right into Hué.

Immediately on taking the city, political cadres implemented detailed plans to remove Hué's 'uncooperative' elements. Thousands of people were rounded up in extensive house-to-house searches, conducted according to lists of names meticulously prepared months before.

During the 3½ weeks Hué remained under Northern control, over 2500 people – including wealthy merchants, government workers, monks, priests and intellectuals – were summarily shot, clubbed to death or buried alive. Shallow mass graves were discovered at various spots around the city over the following few years.

When the South Vietnamese army units proved unable to dislodge the occupying North Vietnamese and VC forces, General Westmoreland ordered US troops to recapture the city. Over the next few weeks, whole neighbourhoods were levelled by VC rockets and US bombs.

Over the next month, most of the area inside the Citadel was battered by the South Vietnamese air force, US artillery and brutal house-to-house fighting. Approximately 10,000 people died in Hué, including thousands of VC troops, 400 South Vietnamese soldiers and 150 US marines, but most of those killed were civilians.

Journalist Gavin Young's 1997 memoir *A Wavering Grace* is a moving account of his 30-year relationship with a family from Hué, and with the city itself, during and beyond the American War. It makes a good literary companion for a stay in the city.

Orientation

The city of Hué lies along either side of the Perfume River. The north side of the river is dominated by the Citadel and has a quieter local feel, while the south side has most of the tourist hotels and restaurants. The island on which the Phu Cat and Phu Hiep subdistricts are located can be reached by crossing the Dong Ba Canal near Dong Ba Market.

MAPS

The fold-up *Hué Tourism Map* (5000d) is available in tourist outlets; there's not much detail, but handy to stuff in the pocket.

Information

INTERNET ACCESS

There are lots of internet cafés on the tourist strips of Đ Hung Vuong and Đ Le Loi, and a fast, cheap service can be found at the main post office and at **Huenet 2** (22B Đ Le Loi; per hr 2000d).

MEDICAL SERVICES

Hué Central Hospital (Benh Vien Trung Uong Hué; ☎ 822 325; 16 Đ Le Loi)

MONEY

Vietcombank (☎ 824 572; 78 Đ Hung Vuong) has an ATM and exchanges travellers cheques and foreign currency. There's another **Vietcombank branch** (30 Đ Le Loi; 🕒 7am-10pm Mon-Sat) located at the Hotel Saigon Morin. You can find a **Vietcombank ATM** (Đ Luong The Vinh) outside the Imperial Hotel and another **Vietcombank ATM** (5 Đ Le Loi) located outside La Residence Hotel.

POST

Main post office (☎ 823 468; 8 Đ Hoang Hoa Tham; 🕒 6am-9.30pm); Đ Le Loi (☎ 832 072; 38 Đ Le Loi); Đ Ly Thuong Kiet (☎ 825 850; 14 Đ Ly Thuong Kiet); Đ Bui Thi Xuan (☎ 823 109; 1 Đ Bui Thi Xuan) Postal, internet and telephone services.

TRAVEL AGENCIES

Café on Thu Wheels (☎ 832 241; minhthuhue@yahoo.com; 10/2 Đ Nguyen Tri Phuong) Immensely popular cycling and motorbiking tours around Hué with a large dose of laughs.

Mandarin Café (☎ 821 281; mandarin@dng.vnn.vn; 3 Đ Hung Vuong) Watched over by the eagle eyes of photographer Mr Cu, this place is great for information, transport and tours.

Sinh Café (☎ 823 309; www.sinhcafévn.com; 7 Đ Nguyen Tri Phuong) Books open-tour buses and buses to Laos.

Sights & Activities

CITADEL

Most of Hué's sights and a sizeable chunk of its population reside within the 2m-thick, 10km-long walls of its **Citadel** (Kinh Thanh) on the north bank of the river. Begun in 1804 on a site chosen by Emperor Gia Long's geomancers, it was originally made of earth and later strengthened with brick.

Roughly square shaped, three sides of the Citadel are straight; the fourth is rounded slightly to follow the curve of the river. The ramparts are encircled by a zigzag moat, which is 30m across and about 4m deep. There are 10 fortified gates, each accessed via a bridge. In the northern corner of the Citadel is Mang Ca Fortress, which is still used as a military base.

At the centre of the wall facing the river, the 37m-high **Flag Tower** (Cot Co) is Vietnam's tallest flagpole. Erected in 1809 and extended in 1831, it was knocked down in 1904 by a typhoon that devastated the city. It was rebuilt in 1915 only to be destroyed again in 1947. Two years later it was erected once again, in its present form. During the VC occupation in 1968, the National Liberation Front flag flew defiantly from the tower for 3½ weeks.

Located just inside the Citadel ramparts, near the gates to either side of the Flag Tower, the **Nine Holy Cannons**, symbolic protectors of the palace and kingdom, were cast in 1804 from brass captured from the Tay Son Rebels. Commissioned by Emperor Gia Long, they were never intended to be fired. Each is 5m long, has a bore of 23cm and weighs about 10 tonnes. The four cannons near **Ngan Gate** represent the four seasons, while the five cannons next to **Quang Duc Gate** represent the five elements: metal, wood, water, fire and earth.

IMPERIAL ENCLOSURE

Housing the emperor's residence and the main buildings of state, the **Imperial Enclosure** (admission

HUÉ

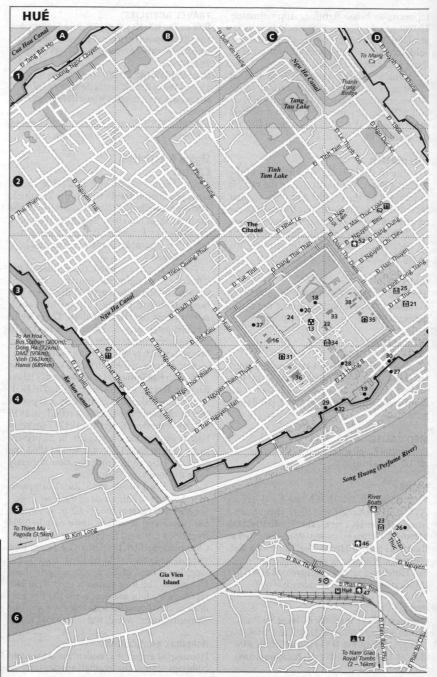

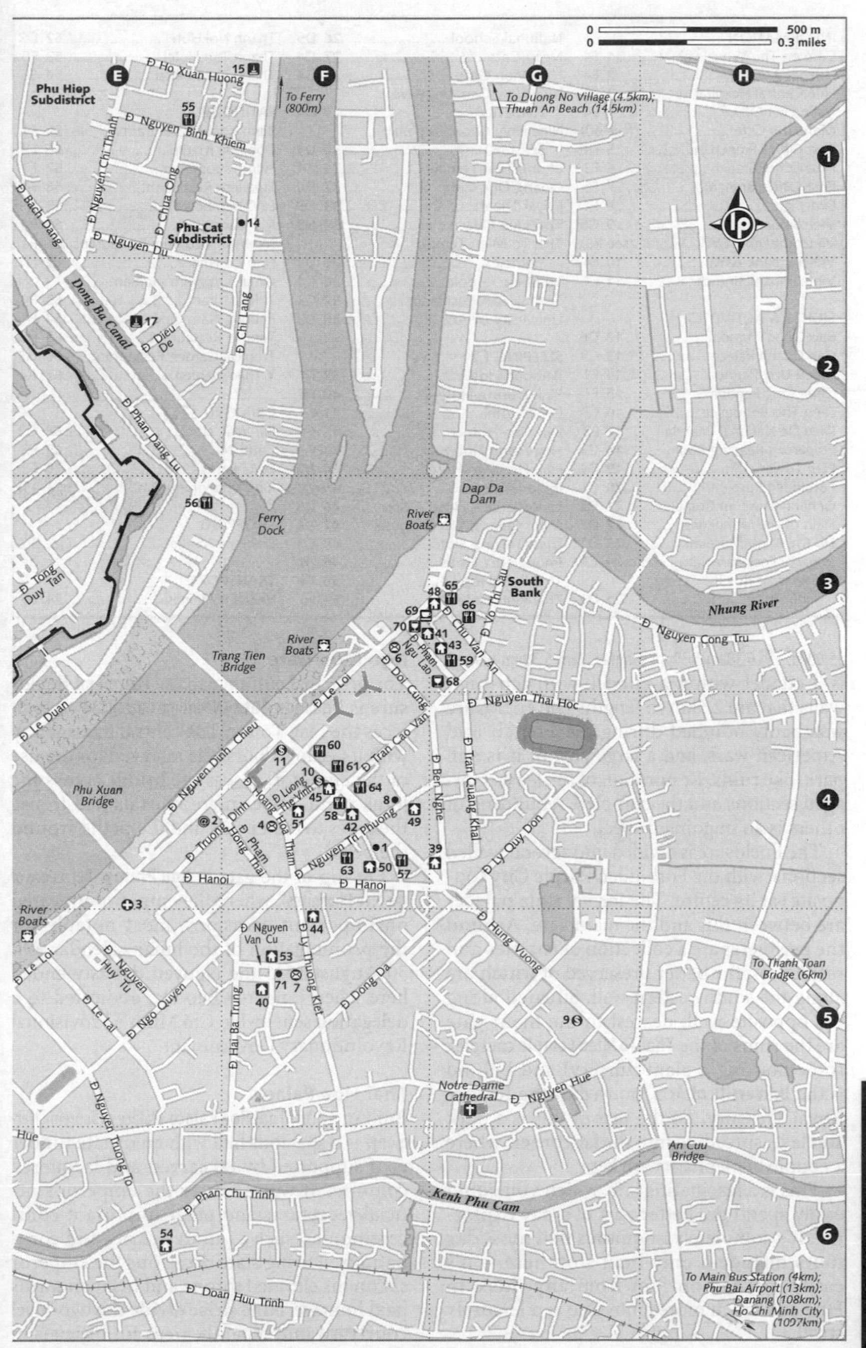

CENTRAL VIETNAM

INFORMATION
Café on Thu Wheels....1 F4
Huenet 2....2 E4
Hué Central Hospital....3 E4
Main Post Office....4 F4
Mandarin Café....(see 60)
Post Office Branch....5 D6
Post Office Branch....6 F3
Post Office Branch....7 F5
Sinh Café....8 F4
Vietcombank....9 G5
Vietcombank ATM....(see 46)
Vietcombank ATM....10 F4
Vietcombank Branch....11 F4

SIGHTS & ACTIVITIES
Bao Quoc Pagoda....12 D6
Can Chanh Palace....13 C3
Chieu Ung Pagoda....14 F1
Chua Ong Pagoda....15 F1
Dien Tho Residence....16 C3
Dieu De National Pagoda....17 E2
Emperor's Reading Room....18 C3
Flag Tower....19 D4
Forbidden Purple City....20 C3
General Museum Complex....21 D3
Halls of the Mandarins....22 D3
Ho Chi Minh Museum....23 D5
Imperial Enclosure....24 C3
Museum of Royal Fine Arts....25 D3
National School....26 D5
Ngan Gate....27 D4
Ngo Mon Gate....28 D4
Nine Holy Cannons (Five Elements)....29 D4
Nine Holy Cannons (Four Seasons)....30 D4
Phung Tien Temple....31 C4
Quang Duc Gate....32 D4
Royal Theatre....33 D3
Thai Hoa Palace....34 D3
Thai To Mieu Temple Complex....35 D3
To Mieu Temple....36 C4
Truong San Residence....37 C3
University of Arts....38 D3

SLEEPING
Bamboo Hotel....39 F4
Binh Duong Hotel 2....40 F5
DMZ Hotel....41 F3
Duy Tan Hotel....42 F4
Hoa Hong Hotel....43 G3
Hue Heritage Hotel....44 F5
Imperial Hotel....45 F4
La Residence Hotel & Spa....46 D5
Minh Quang Guest House....47 D6
Ngoc Huong Hotel....48 G3
Phong Nha Hotel....49 F4
Thai Binh Hotel 1....50 F4
Thai Binh Hotel 2....51 F4
Thanh Noi Hotel....52 D3
Thanh Tan Hotel....53 F5
Thanh Thao Hotel....54 E6

EATING
Banh Khoai Restaurants....55 E1
Dong Ba Market....56 E3
Hung Vuong Inn....57 F4
Japanese Restaurant....58 F4
La Carambole....59 G3
Mandarin Café....60 F4
Minh & Coco Mini Restaurant....61 F4
Ngo Co Nhan....62 D2
Omar Khayyam's Indian Restaurant....63 F4
Phuong Nam Café....64 F4
Temple Restaurant....65 G3
Tropical Garden Restaurant....66 G3
Y Thao Garden....67 A4

DRINKING
Bar Why Not?....68 G3
Cathi 24....69 F3
DMZ Bar & Cafe....70 F3
King's Panorama Bar....(see 45)

SHOPPING
Dong Ba Market....(see 56)

TRANSPORT
Vietnam Airlines....71 F5

55,000d; 6.30am-5.30pm summer, 7am-5.30pm winter) is a citadel-within-a-citadel, with 6m-high walls that are 2.5km in length. The enclosure was badly bombed during the French and American wars, and a large part of it is still park-like ruins. Restoration of the least damaged sections and the complete rebuilding of others is an ongoing project.

The Enclosure is divided into several walled sections, with the Forbidden Purple City (opposite) at its centre. The formal state palaces are between this and the main gate. Around the perimeter are a collection of temples and residences, the better preserved of which are along the southwestern wall. Situated along the opposite wall, nearest to the main gate are the ruins of the **Thai To Mieu temple complex** (now housing a plant nursery) and behind it the **University of Arts**, housed in the former Royal Treasury. To the rear of this is a park and lake, spreading into the far corner, where a couple of elephants are kept.

This is a fascinating site, which you could easily spend the better part of a day exploring. It's completely iniquitous that most day tours include a only brief stop here – it's easily reached on foot from anywhere in Hué and much more enjoyable as a leisurely stroll.

Ngo Mon Gate

The principal entrance to the Imperial Enclosure is **Ngo Mon Gate** (Noontime Gate; 1833), which faces the Flag Tower. The central passageway with its yellow doors was reserved for the use of the emperor, as was the bridge across the lotus pond. Other mere mortals had to use the gates to either side and the paths around the pond.

On top of the gate is **Ngu Phung** (Belvedere of the Five Phoenixes), where the emperor appeared on important occasions, most notably for the promulgation of the lunar calendar. On 30 August 1945 the Nguyen dynasty ended here when Emperor Bao Dai abdicated to a delegation sent by Ho Chi Minh's Provisional Revolutionary Government.

Thai Hoa Palace

Built in 1803, **Thai Hoa Palace** (Palace of Supreme Harmony) is a spacious hall with an ornate timber roof supported by 80 carved and lacquered columns. It was used for the emperor's official receptions and other important court ceremonies, such as anniversaries and coronations. During state occasions the emperor sat on his elevated throne and his mandarins paid homage. Nine stelae divide the two-level courtyard into separate areas for officials in each of the nine ranks of the mandarinate; administrative mandarins stood to one side while the military mandarins stood to the other.

Halls of the Mandarins

The buildings in which the mandarins prepared for court ceremonies were restored in 1977. The structures are located directly behind Thai Hoa Palace on either side of a courtyard, where there are two gargantuan bronze *vac dong* (cauldrons) dating from the 17th century. The hall to the left has been set up for cheesy tourist photos; you can pose in Imperial costume on the throne for 20,000d, while two flunkies will pose with you for 40,000d. The opposite hall houses a collection of gowns and porcelain from the Nguyen era.

Behind the courtyard are the ruins of the **Can Chanh Palace**, a large hall for receptions.

Forbidden Purple City

Behind the palaces, in the very centre of the Imperial Enclosure, the **Forbidden Purple City** (Tu Cam Thanh) is a citadel-within-a-citadel-within-a-citadel. Reserved solely for the personal use of the emperor, the only servants allowed into this compound were eunuchs who would pose no threat to the royal concubines. It was almost entirely destroyed in the wars, and a large part is now draped in green foliage. Take care as you wander around the ruins as there are some gaping holes.

To the right the **Royal Theatre** (Duyen Thi Duong; tickets 20,000d), begun in 1826 and later home to the National Conservatory of Music, has been rebuilt on the former foundations. Cultural performances are held here daily at 9am, 10am, 2.30pm and 3.30pm.

Behind this, the two-storey **Emperor's Reading Room** (Thai Binh Lau), decorated with interesting roof mosaics, was the only part of the Forbidden Purple City to have escaped damage during the French reoccupation of Hué in 1947.

To Mieu Temple Complex

Taking up the south corner of the Imperial Enclosure, this walled complex dedicated to the Nguyen emperors has been beautifully restored.

After entering through the ornate temple gate, you must then pass through the three-tiered **Hien Lam Pavilion**. On the other side of this stand **Nine Dynastic Urns**. These *dinh* (urns) were cast between 1835 and 1836, each dedicated to a different Nguyen sovereign. Engraved into the sides are heavenly bodies and landscapes. About 2m in height and weighing 1900kg to 2600kg each, the urns symbolise the power and stability of the Nguyen throne. The central urn, which is the largest and most ornate, is dedicated to Gia Long.

Also in the courtyard are two dragons, trapped in what look like phone boxes.

On the other side of the courtyard is the long, low, red and gold **To Mieu Temple** itself. Inside are shrines to each of the emperors, topped by their photos. Under the French only the seven liked by the colonial power were thus honoured – Ham Nghi, Thanh Thai and Duy Tan were only added in 1959. The temple is flanked on the right by a small robing house and on the left by a shrine to a soil god.

Behind each of these, a gate leads into the next part of the complex – a Divine Kitchen and Divine Storehouse sit on either side of a small walled enclosure housing the **Hung To Mieu Temple**. This is a restored 1951 reconstruction of the original, built in 1804 to honour Gia Long's parents. Both temples were used by the court on death anniversaries, but women (including the Empress) were strictly forbidden.

Phung Tien Temple

Behind To Mieu, **Phung Tien Temple** still lies in ruins. It once served a similar purpose to the former, although women were permitted to worship here.

Dien Tho Residence

Behind the two temples is the stunning, partially ruined **Dien Tho Residence** (1804). This comprised the apartments and audience hall of the Queen Mothers of the Nguyen dynasty. The audience hall houses an exhibition of photos illustrating its former use, and there is a display of embroidered royal garments. Just outside is their Highnesses' enchanting pleasure pavilion, a carved wooden building set above a lily pond.

Truong San Residence

The rebuilding of this war-devastated compound was near to completion at the time of research. This landscaped flower garden was originally constructed under Emperor Minh

Mang in 1822, comprising a crescent-shaped lake, a rockery, palace and pagoda. In 1844 Emperor Thieu Tri, acting like a latter-day magazine editor, listed it as one of the top 20 beautiful spots in Hué.

TINH TAM LAKE
In the middle of Tinh Tam Lake, which is 500m north of the Imperial Enclosure, are two islands connected by bridges. The emperors used to come here with their retinues to relax. Now the bridge has been appropriated by fisherman.

TANG TAU LAKE
An island on Tang Tau Lake, which is northeast of Tinh Tam Lake, was once the site of a royal library. It is now occupied by a small Theravada Buddhist pagoda, called Ngoc Huong Pagoda.

MUSEUMS
Museum of Royal Fine Arts
The beautiful hall that houses the **Museum of Royal Fine Arts** (3 Đ Le Truc; admission 22,000d; 7am-5pm) was built in 1845 and restored when the museum was founded in 1923. The walls are inscribed with poems written in *nom* (Vietnamese script). The most precious artefacts were lost during the American War, but the ceramics, furniture and royal clothing that remain are well worth the visit. The outside courtyard has interesting ceremonial cannons, stone court sculptures and large brass bells and vats.

General Museum Complex
The equally exquisite building across the street was once a school for princes and the sons of high-ranking mandarins. It's now a gallery, and forms part of the **General Museum Complex** (☎ 522 397; Đ 23 Thang 8; admission free; 7.30-11am & 1.30-5pm Tue-Sun). It combines, in an odd juxtaposition, a pagoda devoted to archaeology, a small Natural History Museum and a building devoted to the 'movement of revolutionary struggle and anti-French colonialism resistance war'. There's a tank collection out front.

Ho Chi Minh Museum
On display at this **museum** (☎ 822 152; 7 Đ Le Loi; admission 10,000d; 7am-2pm Tue-Sun) are photographs, some of Ho Chi Minh's personal effects, and documents relating to his life and accomplishments. All have English captions.

PAGODAS
Bao Quoc Pagoda
Last renovated in 1957, **Bao Quoc Pagoda** (Pagoda Which Serves the Country; ☎ 820 488; Ham Long Hill) was founded in 1670 by Giac Phong, a Buddhist monk from China. It was given its present name in 1824 by Emperor Minh Mang, who celebrated his 40th birthday here in 1830.

To get here, head south from Đ Le Loi on Đ Dien Bien Phu and turn first right after crossing the railway tracks.

Dieu De National Pagoda
The entrance to **Dieu De National Pagoda** (Quoc Tu Dieu De; 102 Đ Bach Dang), built under Emperor Thieu Tri's rule (1841–47), is along Dong Ba Canal. It is one of the city's three 'national pagodas', which were once under the direct patronage of the emperor. Dieu De is famous for its four low towers, one to either side of the gate and two flanking the sanctuary. There are bells in two of the towers; the others contain a drum and a stele dedicated to the emperor.

During the regime of Ngo Dinh Diem (1955–63) and through the mid-1960s, Dieu De National Pagoda was a stronghold of Buddhist and student opposition to the South Vietnamese government and the war. In 1966 the pagoda was stormed by police, who confiscated the opposition movement's radio equipment and arrested many monks, laypeople and students.

The pavilions on either side of the main sanctuary entrance contain the 18 La Ha, whose rank is just below that of Bodhisattva, and the eight Kim Cang, protectors of Buddha. In the back row of the main dais is Thich Ca Buddha flanked by two assistants.

Chieu Ung Pagoda
Founded by the Hainan Chinese Congregation in the mid-19th century, **Chieu Ung Pagoda** (Chieu Ung Tu; opposite 138 Đ Chi Lang) was rebuilt in 1908. The pagoda's sanctuary retains its original ornamentation, which is becoming faded but has been mercifully unaffected by the third-rate modernistic renovations that have marred other such structures. The pagoda was built as a memorial to 108 Hainan merchants, who were mistaken for pirates and killed in Vietnam in 1851.

Chua Ong Pagoda
Founded by Hué's Fujian Chinese Congregation during the reign of Vietnamese emperor

Tu Duc (1848–83), **Chua Ong Pagoda** (opposite 224 Đ Chi Lang) was severely damaged during the Tet Offensive when a nearby ammunition ship blew up. A gold Buddha sits in a glass case opposite the main doors of the sanctuary. The left-hand altar is dedicated to the goddess of the sea, Thien Hau Thanh Mau, who is flanked by her two assistants, 1000-eyed Thien Ly Nhan and red-faced Thuan Phong Nhi, who can hear for 1000 miles.

NATIONAL SCHOOL

One of the most famous secondary schools in Vietnam, the **National School** (Truong Quoc Hoc; 10 Đ Le Loi; ⌚ after 3pm) was founded in 1896 and run by Ngo Dinh Kha, the father of South Vietnamese president Ngo Dinh Diem. Many of the school's pupils later rose to prominence in both North and South Vietnam. One of them was General Vo Nguyen Giap, strategist of the Viet Minh victory at Dien Bien Phu and North Vietnam's long-serving deputy premier, defence minister and commander-in-chief. Pham Van Dong, North Vietnam's prime minister for over a quarter of a century, and the secretary-general and former prime minister Do Muoi also studied here. Even Ho Chi Minh attended the school briefly in 1908.

The school was given a major renovation in 1996 to celebrate its 100th anniversary and a statue of Ho Chi Minh was erected. The National School cannot be visited until after classes finish.

BOAT TRIPS

Many sights in the vicinity of Hué, including Thuan An Beach, Thien Mu Pagoda and several of the Royal Tombs (p221), can be reached by a journey along the Perfume River.

Rates for chartering a boat are around 60,000d for an hour's sightseeing on the river; a half-day charter to one or more sites will cost around 150,000d. Ask directly at any of the four main river-boat moorings on the south side of the river; it's cheaper than chartering through an agency and you can negotiate your own route. Be clear on your requirements, preferably in writing: you may find yourself paying more for lunch at the family's restaurant than for the boat.

Most hotels and travellers' cafés are keen to push shared tours, which typically take in the tombs of Tu Duc, Thieu Tri, Minh Mang and the Thien Mu Pagoda. Prices vary, but are generally implausibly cheap at around US$2 per person (which may include lunch but not entry fees). The journey takes about six hours, and usually runs from 8am to 2pm. Given the time constraints you'll need to catch a motorbike to get from the moorings to the first two tombs. The third tomb's less than a kilometre's walk, but they'll try to get you on a bike for that one as well. Once the various entry fees have been factored in, many travellers wish they had cycled or arranged a motorbike instead.

Sleeping

BUDGET

There are two main clusters of budget accommodation on the south side of the river. One is in the triangle formed by Đ Hung Vuong, Đ Nguyen Tri Phuong and Đ Hanoi. The other is a few blocks north in the little laneways between Đ Le Loi and Đ Vo Thi Sau. The numerous guesthouses offer varying degrees of comfort for invariably cheap rates; given their proximity it's easy to shop around. The trade-off is that this puts you in the heart of tourist town, where the hawkers swoop before your hotel door closes behind you.

Phong Nha Hotel (☎ 827 729; phongnha_hotel@yahoo.com; 10/10 Đ Nguyen Tri Phuong; r US$6-15; ❄ 💻) The facilities in this spotless minihotel differ from room to room, but what doesn't change is the good reports we hear about the friendly and enthusiastic staff.

Binh Duong Hotel 2 (☎ 846 466; 8 Đ Ngo Gia Tu; r US$8-15; ❄ 💻) On a side street a little apart from the main tourist scrum, this hotel has rooms ranging from cheapies with internal windows to larger ones with bathtubs and balconies.

Thai Binh Hotel 1 (☎ 828 058; www.thaibinhhotel-hue.com; 6/34 Đ Nguyen Tri Phuong; r US$8-18; ❄ 💻) An excellent option, Thai Binh offers midrange standards at budget prices.

DMZ Hotel (☎ 826 831; 1A Đ Pham Ngu Lao; s/d US$9-14; ❄ 💻) From the people behind the popular tourist bar, this brand-new minihotel has a range of comfortable rooms of different sizes and facilities.

Minh Quang Guest House (☎ 824 152; 16 Đ Phan Chu Trinh; r US$10; ❄) Located near the railway station, a long way from tourist traps, this friendly family offers new, clean rooms with TVs, fridges and bathtubs. English is not their strong point.

Bamboo Hotel (☎ 828 345; www.bamboohotel.net; 61 Đ Hung Vuong; s/d US$10/12; ❄ 💻) The owners made an effort with the décor, with (unsurprisingly) bamboo decoration downstairs and elaborate green cornices in the rooms. The bedding's nice and all the rooms have TVs, fridges and bathtubs.

our pick **Thai Binh Hotel 2** (☎ 827 561; www.thaibinhhotel-hue.com; 2 Đ Luong The Vinh; r US$12-15;) The recently arrived, more upmarket sister of the longstanding budget favourite, Thai Binh 2 is excellent value for money. The attractive bedrooms have mother-of-pearl inlaid furniture, while the bathrooms have tubs and novelties such as shower curtains. There are stunning views from balconies on the higher floors.

Thanh Tan Hotel (☎ 824 146; thanhtancom@dng.vnn.vn; 12 Đ Nguyen Van Cu; s/d US$12/15;) A similar standard is set at this superb new place, just removed from the main tourist neighbourhood.

Thanh Thao Hotel (☎ 831 358; thanhthaohotel@yahoo.com; 33 Đ Nguyen Truong To; r 250,000d;) On what would be a quiet street near the Catholic cathedral if it weren't for the railway tracks, Thanh Thao has comfortable rooms with good facilities including wi-fi internet access.

MIDRANGE

Duy Tan Hotel (☎ 825 001; nkduytan@dng.vnn.vn; 12 Đ Hung Vuong; r US$10-25;) About as central as it gets, the more expensive rooms are large and bright and have balconies.

Thanh Noi Hotel (Imperial Garden; ☎ 522 478; thanhnoi@dng.vnn.vn; 57 Đ Dang Dung; r US$18-45;) Located in a quiet street in the heart of the Citadel, near the Imperial Enclosure, the residential surroundings offer a very different view of Hué life. The peaceful tree-shaded compound has a restaurant and a fair-sized swimming pool with water jets.

Hoa Hong Hotel (☎ 824 377; hoahonghotel@dng.vnn.vn; 1 Đ Pham Ngu Lao; s US$25-70, d US$30-80;) Although a little older, the rooms are well-appointed – some with views, spa baths and (luxury of luxuries) shower curtains. Breakfast is included in the price.

Ngoc Huong Hotel (☎ 830 111; www.ngochuonghotels.com; 8-10 Đ Chu Van An; r US$30-40, ste US$80;) Located in a popular part of town, this is a smart, friendly hotel. The large rooms include all the creature comforts one might want, plus there's a Jacuzzi and sauna for winding down.

Hue Heritage Hotel (☎ 838 888; www.hueheritagehotel.com; 9 Đ Ly Thuong Kiet; r US$40-80, ste US$90-120;) The mock-classical frontage sets the scene for an upmarket hotel, with a cool roof-top swimming pool. The comfortable rooms have space-age massaging showers and wooden floors.

TOP END

La Residence Hotel & Spa (☎ 837 475; www.la-residence-hue.com; 5 Đ Le Loi; r US$95-135, ste US$150-165;) Housed in the former French Governor's residence, this chic boutique hotel has lovely river views, lush gardens and beautiful rooms. The Colonial suites are ostentatiously themed: *Suite d'Ornithologue, Monuments d'Egypte* and *Voyage en Chine*.

Imperial Hotel (☎ 882 222; www.imperial-hotel.com.vn; 8 Đ Hung Vuong; r US$159, ste US$239-719;) Hello big boy! Critics will surely bemoan the arrival of historic Hue's first hefty hotel tower – but this 16-floor, five-star megalith is actually pretty fab. The grand lobby has a dramatic lotus-shaped chandelier, and a number of excellent bars and restaurants carry on the opulence.

Eating

We have the famed fussy-eater Emperor Tu Duc to thank for the culinary variety of Hué (see p48). While the elaborate decoration of Imperial cuisine may seem a little silly, the *degustation*-style banquets are sublime – well worthy of a splurge. The best restaurants aren't necessarily easy to find, and many tourists sadly settle for the Western-oriented eateries of the budget ghettoes.

A local speciality worth hunting for is the royal rice cakes, the most common of which is *banh khoai*. You'll find these along with other variations *(banh beo, banh loc, banh it* and *banh nam)* in restaurants around Đ Nguyen Binh Khiem, on the island to the northeast of the Citadel. For another gastronomic adventure, explore the noodle stalls set up around the Citadel at night.

Vegetarian food has a long tradition in Hué. Stalls in the **Dong Ba Market** (Đ Tran Hung Dao; dishes 5000-10,000d) serve lots of options on the first and 15th days of the lunar month. You'll find several vegie options on most menus in town, some using soya-bean mock meat.

VIETNAMESE

Ngo Co Nhan (☎ 513 399; 47 Đ Nguyen Bieu; dishes 15,000-35,000d; lunch & dinner) Raised up on stilts in a quiet Citadel street, this open-sided dining platform serves excellent grilled seafood and beer to a mainly Vietnamese clientele.

CENTRAL VIETNAM

Tropical Garden Restaurant (☎ 847 143; 27 Đ Chu Van An; dishes 22,000-85,000d; ⏰ dinner) This popular place offers romantic dining in a lush garden. It specialises in central Vietnamese cuisine, and is the best place in Hué to catch a traditional music performance (from 7pm nightly). While it's a regular stop for tour groups, they don't tend to spoil the atmosphere – although they do slow the service down.

Temple Restaurant (☎ 830 716; 5 Đ Chu Van An; dishes 22,000-85,000d; ⏰ lunch & dinner) A similar option, but this one has a stylish indoor dining room.

our pick **Y Thao Garden** (☎ 523 018; 3 Đ Thach Han; set-course meal US$8; ⏰ lunch & dinner) Tucked in a quiet corner of the Citadel, a seven-course set menu is served among the huge palms on the garden terrace of a traditional Hué home that's brimming with antiques. This is Imperial cuisine at its fiddliest – peacocks with carved carrot heads and pineapple-stalk tails play pin-cushion to spring rolls on toothpicks, and green bean cakes are moulded to look like fruit and served on a branch. The overall experience is enchanting – particularly on a steamy night with the rain battering the tropical garden. It's best to book ahead, as it can get busy.

INTERNATIONAL

Mandarin Café (☎ 821 281; mandarin@dng.vnn.vn; 3 Đ Hung Vuong; dishes 5000-40,000d; ⏰ breakfast, lunch & dinner) A magnet for travellers, the cheerful owner, Mr Cu, speaks English and French and serves big dollops of travel advice along with *pho*, BLTs, salads and pancakes.

Hung Vuong Inn (☎ 821 068; 20 Đ Hung Vuong; pastries/meals 5000/30,000d; ⏰ breakfast, lunch & dinner) Right in the heart of the budget strip, this little guesthouse is a great breakfast option, serving delicious French-style pastries and bread. More expansive meals featuring Hué specialities are also on offer.

Japanese Restaurant (☎ 834 457; 34 Đ Tran Cao Van; dishes US$1-8) There's no prizes for guessing the cuisine on offer. What's more surprising is the heart-warming story behind it (see the boxed text, p220). The food's excellent and the service exceptionally polite.

Minh & Coco Mini Restaurant (☎ 821 822; 1 Đ Hung Vuong; mains 10,000-30,000d) Run by two lively sisters, this humble joint is a fun place to get an inexpensive feed.

Phuong Nam Café (☎ 849 317; 38 Đ Tan Cao Van; mains 10,000-30,000d; ⏰ breakfast, lunch & dinner) This little eatery has good, cheap food and amazing fruit shakes.

La Carambole (☎ 810 491; 19 Đ Pham Ngu Lao; mains 25,000-90,000d; ⏰ breakfast, lunch & dinner) Extravagantly decorated with hanging lanterns and dragon's heads, this place has a good range of French-style dishes, including steaks and grills. There are also Vietnamese dishes and pizza to keep everyone happy, plus a healthy wine list.

Omar Khayyam's Indian Restaurant (☎ 821 616; 10 Đ Nguyen Tri Phuong; curries 30,000-60,000d) This vegetarian-friendly curry house is low on atmosphere but high on flavour.

Drinking

Cathi 24 (☎ 831 210; 64 Đ Le Loi) Based in and around the garden of a French-colonial home, this little café specialises in therapeutic herbal teas – although the less pure will also find caffeine and alcohol on offer. At night it's particularly romantic, lit up with oil lamps. Order a drink and free plates of crackers, bread and fruit keep arriving.

DMZ Bar & Cafe (44 Đ Le Loi) Long the leading late-night spot, the beer flows into the night, the tunes match the mood and there is a popular pool table in the middle of things.

Bar Why Not? (☎ 824 793; 21 Đ Vo Thi Sau) Loud rock music, cheap cocktails and a pool table make for a winning formula. Why not, indeed?

King's Panorama Bar (☎ 882 222; www.imperialhotel.com.vn; 8 Đ Hung Vuong; ⏰ 7am-midnight) Quite the swankiest (and priciest) boozer in town, the rooftop of the Imperial Hotel has tasteful décor and unhindered views.

Shopping

Hué produces the finest conical hats in Vietnam. The city's speciality is 'poem hats', which, when held up to the light, reveal shadowy scenes of daily life. It's also home to one of the largest and most beautiful selections of rice-paper and silk paintings available in Vietnam, but the prices quoted are usually inflated to about four times the real price.

Dong Ba Market (Đ Tran Hung Dao; ⏰ 6.30am-8pm) On the Perfume River north of Trang Tien Bridge, this is Hué's largest market, where anything and everything can be bought.

Getting There & Away

AIR

The main office of **Vietnam Airlines** (☎ 824 709; 23 Đ Nguyen Van Cu; ⏰ 7.15-11.15am & 1.30-4.30pm Mon-Sat) handles reservations. Several flights a day connect Hué to both Hanoi and Ho Chi Minh City (HCMC).

BUS

The main bus station is 4km to the southeast on the continuation of Đ Hung Vuong (it becomes Đ An Duong Vuong and Đ An Thuy Vuong). The first main stop south is Danang (40,000d, three hours, six daily). **An Hoa bus station** (Hwy 1A), northwest of the Citadel, serves northern destinations, including Dong Ha (25,000d, 1½ hours).

Hué is a regular stop on the open-tour bus routes. Most will drop passengers off around the Đ Hung Vuong tourist ghetto and pick up from the hotels. Expect a complete circus when the bus stops, as you're likely to be followed by several persistent touts, all keen to direct your wallet to their hotel.

Mandarin and Sinh Cafés (see p211) can arrange bookings for the bus to Savannakhet, Laos (see p210).

CAR & MOTORBIKE

Some of the principal destinations from Hué include Hanoi (689km), Dong Ha (77km), Lao Bao (152km), Danang (108km) and HCMC (1097km).

TRAIN

The **Hué train station** (☎ 822 175; 2 Đ Phan Chu Trinh) is at the southwestern end of Đ Le Loi. Destinations include Ninh Binh (205,000d, 12½ to 13½ hours, three daily), Vinh (143,000d, 6½ to 10 hours, seven daily), Dong Hoi (65,000d, 2½ to 5½ hours, eight daily), Dong Ha (25,000d, 1½ to 2½ hours, six daily) and Danang (40,000d, 2½ to four hours, seven daily).

Getting Around

TO/FROM THE AIRPORT

Hué is served by Phu Bai Airport, once an important US air base, 14km south of the city centre. Taxi fares are typically around US$8, although share-taxis cost as little as US$2 – inquire at hotels to find these vehicles. **Vietnam Airlines** (☎ 824 709; 23 Đ Nguyen Van Cu; 🕑 7.15-11.15am & 1.30-4.30pm Mon-Sat) runs its own minibus from

THE JASS MAN

Warning: visiting Vietnam can change your life.

Fifteen years ago Mr Michio Koyama was a teacher in Tokyo, working with kids whose biggest concern was where their next Hello Kitty accessory would come from. It was during a visit to Ho Chi Minh City (HCMC) in 1992 that his eyes were opened to the plight of Vietnam's street children. Here were youngsters no older than the ones he was teaching, living in extreme poverty and turning to crime to fill their bellies. Many of them were orphaned or were the abandoned encumbrance of a marriage split, discarded at the insistence of the new husband or wife.

It shocked him so much that the next year he left his life in Tokyo, determined to do something for them. He first got a job teaching Japanese at the university in Hué, earning money to set up a house. Built in 1994, 10 years later 300 children had passed through its doors – having received shelter, food, schooling and vocational guidance.

At present, 66 children aged from five to 22 years live at Streetchildren's Home. Normally they're expected to be self-sufficient by their 18th birthday, but an exception has been made for those who have gone on to university. Mr Koyama bursts with paternal pride as he talks about one of his young charges who is currently completing her medical degree.

This extraordinary man (who speaks fluent Vietnamese, English and French) has brought this about by working with communists and capitalists alike. The first Japanese person to be granted citizenship of Hué, he has the support of the local People's Committee and was recently awarded with a Friendship medal from the Vietnamese government. The funding has largely come from Japanese sources, including government grants and donations from individuals and companies. He has established his own NGO, Japanese Association Supporting Streetchildren (JASS), which now has 14,000 members and donors.

With this added support he's also been able to broaden his program to work with disabled children throughout the province. Another new initiative is Japanese Restaurant, a little like KOTO in Hanoi, where some of his protégés have been given training in Japanese cuisine and employment in the restaurant.

Eating at the restaurant is an inexpensive way to support this worthwhile cause, but if you feel like doing more, information is available on the JASS website (www001.upp.so-net.ne.jp/jass/).

its office to the airport, a couple of hours before flight times (tickets 20,000d).

BICYCLE, MOTORBIKE & CAR HIRE

Pedal power is a fun way to tour Hué and the nearby Royal Tombs. Many hotels rent out bicycles for about US$1 per day. Self-drive motorbikes are available from US$5. A car with driver is available from US$25 per day.

CYCLO & XE OM

While Hué is an easy city to walk around, a typical street scene is a foreigner walking down the street with two *cyclos* (pedicab or bicycle rickshaw) and a motorbike in hot pursuit – the drivers yelling, 'hello *cyclo*' and 'hello motorbike' and the foreigner yelling, 'no, thank you, no!' There's a pretty standard fare for both of 10,000d per kilometre.

TAXI

There are several metered taxi companies in Hué. Try **Co Do Taxi** (☎ 830 830), **Gili** (☎ 828 282), **Mai Linh** (☎ 898 989) or **Phu Xuan** (☎ 87 87 87).

AROUND HUÉ

Thien Mu Pagoda

Built on a hillock overlooking the Perfume River, 4km southwest of the Citadel, this **pagoda** (Linh Mu; admission free) is an icon of Vietnam. The existing 21m-high octagonal tower, Thap Phuoc Duyen, was constructed under the reign of Emperor Thieu Tri in 1844 and has become the unofficial symbol of the city. Each of the seven storeys is dedicated to a *manushi-buddha,* which is a Buddha that appeared in human form.

Thien Mu Pagoda was originally founded in 1601 by Nguyen Hoang, governor of Thuan Hoa province. According to legend, a Fairy Woman (Thien Mu) appeared and told the people that a lord would come to build a pagoda for the country's prosperity. On hearing this, Nguyen Hoang ordered a pagoda to be constructed here. Over the centuries its buildings have been destroyed and rebuilt several times. Since the 1960s it has been a flashpoint of political demonstrations (see p222).

To the right of the tower is a pavilion containing a stele dating from 1715. It is set on the back of a massive marble turtle, a symbol of longevity. To the left of the tower is another six-sided pavilion, this one sheltering an enormous bell, Dai Hong Chung, which was cast in 1710 and weighs 2052kg; it is said to be audible

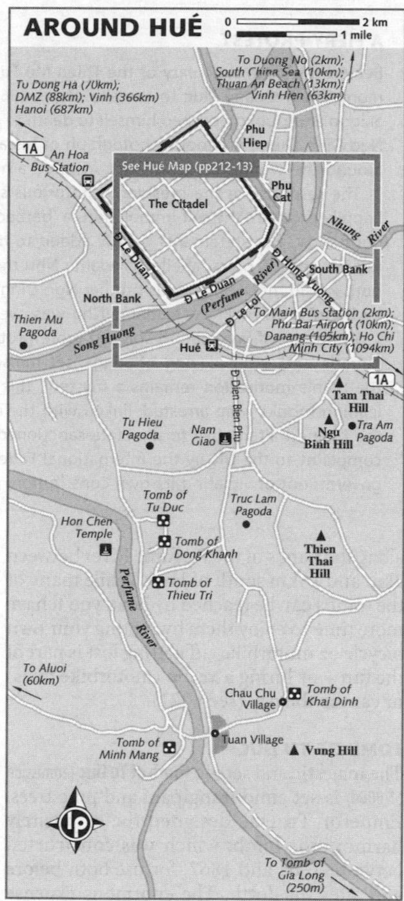

10km away. In the main sanctuary, in a case behind the bronze laughing Buddha, are three statues: A Di Da, the Buddha of the Past; Thich Ca, the historical Buddha (Sakyamuni); and Di Lac Buddha, the Buddha of the Future.

For a nice bicycle ride, head southwest (parallel to the Perfume River) on riverside Đ Tran Hung Dao, which turns into Đ Le Duan after passing Phu Xuan Bridge. Cross the railway tracks and keep going on Đ Kim Long. Thien Mu Pagoda can also be reached by dragon boat and a visit is included in most city tours.

Royal Tombs

The **tombs** (🕒 6.30am-5.30pm, 7am-5pm in winter) of the rulers of the Nguyen dynasty (1802–1945) are extravagant mausoleums, constructed

A FIERY PROTEST

Behind the main sanctuary of the Thien Mu Pagoda is the Austin motorcar that transported the monk Thich Quang Duc to the site of his 1963 self-immolation. Thich Quang Duc travelled to Saigon and publicly burned himself to death to protest the policies of South Vietnamese President Ngo Dinh Diem. A famous photograph of his act was printed on the front pages of newspapers around the world. His death soon inspired a number of other self-immolations.

The response of the president's notorious sister-in-law, Tran Le Xuan (Madame Nhu), was to happily proclaim the self-immolations a 'barbecue party', saying 'Let them burn and we shall clap our hands'. Her statements greatly added to the already substantial public disgust with Diem's regime; the US press labelled Madame Nhu the 'Iron Butterfly' and 'Dragon Lady'. In November both President Diem and his brother Ngo Dinh Nhu (Madame Nhu's husband) were assassinated by Diem's own military. Madame Nhu was overseas at the time.

Another self-immolation sparked more protest in 1993. In this instance a man arrived at the pagoda and, after leaving offerings, set himself alight chanting the word 'Buddha'. Although the man's motivation remains a mystery, this set off a chain of events whereby the pagoda's leading monks were arrested, linked with the independent United Buddhist Church of Vietnam, the banned alternative to the state-sanctioned Vietnam Buddhist Church. This led to an official complaint to the UN by the International Federation of Human Rights accusing the Vietnamese government of violating its own constitution, protecting freedom of religion.

along the banks of the Perfume River between 2km and 16km south of Hué. While many of the tombs can be reached by boat, you'll have more time to enjoy them by renting your own bicycle or motorbike – if getting lost is part of the fun – or hiring a *xe om* (motorbike taxis) or car for the day (see p221).

TOMB OF TU DUC

The majestic and serene **tomb of Tu Duc** (admission 55,000d) is set amid frangipani and pine trees. Emperor Tu Duc designed the exquisitely harmonious tomb, which was constructed between 1864 and 1867, for use both before and after his death. The enormous expense of the tomb and the forced labour used in its construction spawned a coup plot that was discovered and suppressed in 1866.

It is said that Tu Duc, who had the longest reign of any Nguyen monarch (1848–83), lived a life of ultimate imperial luxury. Though he had 104 wives and countless concubines, he had no offspring. One theory has it that he became sterile after contracting smallpox.

His tomb is entered from the southeast via Vu Khiem Gate. A path leads to a boat landing on the shore of a lake. The island to the right is where Tu Duc used to hunt small game. Across the water to the left is Xung Khiem Pavilion, built on piles over the water, where the emperor would sit among the columns with his concubines, composing or reciting poetry.

Across the courtyard from the landing are steps leading to Hoa Khiem Temple, where Tu Duc and Empress Hoang Le Thien Anh (Tu Duc's wife) are worshipped. Before his death, Tu Duc used this as a palace, staying here during his long visits to the complex. It contains a number of interesting items, including two thrones, the larger of which was for the empress (Tu Duc was only 153cm tall).

Minh Khiem Chamber, to the right behind Hoa Khiem Temple, was originally built for use as a theatre. Tu Duc's mother, Tu Du, is worshipped in Luong Khiem Temple, directly behind Hoa Khiem Temple.

At the bottom of the stairway, the path continues along the shore of the lake to the Honour Courtyard. Across the lake are the tombs of Tu Duc's adopted son, Emperor Kien Phuc, who ruled for only seven months (1883–84), and Empress Hoang Le Thien Anh. After walking between the honour guard of elephants, horses and diminutive mandarins (they were made even shorter than the emperor), you reach the Stele Pavilion, which shelters a stone tablet weighing about 20 tonnes. It took four years to transport the stele, the largest in Vietnam, 500km from near Thanh Hoa in the north. Tu Duc drafted the inscriptions himself in order to clarify certain aspects of his reign. He freely admitted that he had made mistakes and chose to name his tomb Khiem, which means 'modest'. The two nearby towers symbolise the emperor's power.

Tu Duc's tomb, enclosed by a wall, is on the other side of a half-moon-shaped lake. He was never actually interred here. The site where his remains were buried (along with great treasure) is not known. Because of the danger of grave robbers, extreme measures were taken to keep the location secret – every one of the 200 servants who buried the king was beheaded.

Tu Duc's tomb is about 5km south of Hué on Van Nien Hill in Duong Xuan Thuong Village.

TOMB OF DONG KHANH

The smallest of the Royal Tombs, **Dong Khanh's mausoleum** (admission 30,000d) was built in 1889. Emperor Dong Khanh was the nephew and adopted son of Tu Duc, and was placed on the throne by the French after they captured his predecessor, Ham Nghi. Predictably, Dong Khanh proved docile; he ruled from 1885 until his death three years later.

Seldom visited, there is a certain serenity here. It is just over 5km from the city, 500m behind the tomb of Tu Duc.

TOMB OF THIEU TRI

Construction of the **tomb of Thieu Tri** (admission 22,000d), who ruled from 1841 to 1847, was completed in 1848. It is the only Royal Tomb not enclosed by a wall. The tomb has a similar floor plan to his father Minh Mang's tomb but is substantially smaller.

During his lifetime, an effort to preserve Vietnamese independence by cracking down on missionaries resulted in a French naval attack in 1847, where Vietnam's coastal forts were destroyed and three junks sunk. The emperor's response was to decree that all Christians be summarily executed. The orders were never followed and Thieu Tri died shortly afterwards.

The tomb is about 7km from Hué, in a peaceful rural landscape, and is off the tour-bus trail. If you're walking, cycling or on a motorbike, there's a pretty 2km or so cross-country track that leads here from the tomb of Dong Khanh.

TOMB OF KHAI DINH

The hillside **tomb of Khai Dinh** (admission 55,000d), who ruled from 1916 to 1925, is perhaps symptomatic of the decline of Vietnamese culture during the colonial era. Begun in 1920 and completed in 1931, the grandiose concrete structure is completely unlike Hué's other tombs, being a synthesis of Vietnamese and European elements. Even the stone faces of the mandarin honour guards are endowed with a mixture of Vietnamese and European features.

After climbing 36 steps between four dragon banisters, you reach the first courtyard, flanked by two pavilions. The Honour Courtyard, with its rows of elephants, horses

REGAL RESTING PLACES

Although all are unique in structure and design, most of the mausoleums consist of five parts:

- A stele pavilion in which the accomplishments, exploits and virtues of the deceased emperor are engraved on a marble tablet, usually written by the dead ruler's successor.
- A temple for the worship of the emperor and empress. In front of each altar, on which the deceased ruler's funerary tablets were placed, is an ornate dais that once held items the emperor used every day, such as his betel-nut trays and cigarette cases.
- A sepulchre, usually inside a square or circular enclosure, where the emperor's remains are buried.
- An honour courtyard paved with dark-brown *bat trang* bricks, along the sides of which stand stone elephants, horses, and civil and military mandarins. The civil mandarins wear square hats and hold an ivory sceptre, the symbol of their authority; the military mandarins wear round hats and hold swords.
- A lotus pond surrounded by frangipani and pine trees.

Almost all of the tombs, which are in walled compounds, were planned by the Nguyen emperors during their lifetimes. Many of the precious ornaments that were once reposited in the tombs disappeared during Vietnam's wars.

and mandarins, is 26 steps further up the hillside. In the centre of the courtyard is an octagonal Stele Pavilion.

Up three more flights of stairs is the main building, Thien Dinh, which is divided into three halls. The walls and ceiling are decorated with murals of the Four Seasons, Eight Precious Objects and Eight Fairies. Under a graceless, one-tonne concrete canopy is a gilt bronze statue of Khai Dinh in regalia. His remains are interred 18m below the statue and he is worshipped in the last hall.

The tomb of Khai Dinh is 10km from Hué, in Chau Chu Village.

TOMB OF MINH MANG

Perhaps the most majestic of all of the Royal Tombs is that of **Minh Mang** (admission 55,000d), who ruled from 1820 to 1840. Renowned for its architecture, which harmoniously blends into the natural surroundings, the tomb was planned during Minh Mang's lifetime and built between 1841 and 1843 by his successor.

The Honour Courtyard is reached via three gates on the eastern side of the wall. Three granite staircases lead from the courtyard to the square Stele Pavilion (Dinh Vuong). Nearby there once stood an altar on which buffaloes, horses and pigs were sacrificed.

Sung An Temple, dedicated to Minh Mang and his empress, is reached via three terraces and Hien Duc Gate. On the other side of the temple, three stone bridges span Trung Minh Ho (Lake of Impeccable Clarity). The central bridge, Cau Trung Dao, constructed of marble, was for the emperor's use only. Minh Lau Pavilion stands on the top of three superimposed terraces that represent the 'three powers': the heavens, the earth and water. Visible to the left is the Fresh Air Pavilion; the Angling Pavilion is to the right.

From a stone bridge across crescent-shaped Tan Nguyet Lake (Lake of the New Moon), a monumental staircase with dragon banisters leads to the sepulchre, which is surrounded by a circular wall symbolising the sun. Behind the bronze door in the middle of the enclosure is the emperor's burial place: a mound of earth covered with mature pine trees and dense shrubbery.

The tomb of Minh Mang, which is on Cam Ke Hill in An Bang Village, is over the bridge on the west bank of the Perfume River, about 12km from Hué.

TOMB OF GIA LONG

Emperor Gia Long, who founded the Nguyen dynasty in 1802 and ruled until 1819, ordered the construction of his tomb in 1814. According to royal annals, the emperor himself chose the site after scouting the area on the back of an elephant. The rarely visited **tomb** (admission free), which is presently in a state of ruin, is around 14km south of Hué and 3km from the west bank of the Perfume River.

Temple of Nam Giao

The **Temple of Nam Giao** (Temple of Heaven; admission free) was once the most important religious site in all of Vietnam. It was here that, every three years, the emperor solemnly offered elaborate sacrifices to the All-Highest Emperor of the August Heaven (Thuong De). The topmost esplanade, which represents heaven, is round, while the middle terrace, representing earth, is square, as is the lowest terrace representing humanity.

After reunification, the provincial government erected an obelisk in memory of soldiers killed in the American War on the site where the sacrificial altar had once stood. There was strong public sentiment in Hué against the obelisk and it was finally torn down in 1993. Nam Giao remains unrestored and crumbling.

To find it, head south on Đ Dien Bien Phu for nearly 2km after the railway tracks.

Thanh Toan Bridge

Situated 7km east of central Hué, the Thanh Toan Bridge is a classic covered Japanese footbridge. Architecturally similar to its cousin in Hoi An, it receives far fewer visitors – it's mostly used by local villagers for naps in the shady walkway.

The bridge is best reached by motorbike or bicycle. Finding it is a bit tricky, but tolerable if you consider getting lost part of the excursion. Head north for a few hundred metres on Đ Ba Trieu until you see a sign to the Citadel Hotel. Turn right here and follow the bumpy dirt road for another 6km past villages, rice paddies and several pagodas until you reach the bridge.

Duong No Village

The peaceful village of Duong No makes for a refreshing trip from Hué. The main attraction here is the well-preserved, modest and beautiful **Ho Chi Minh's House** (Nha Bac Ho; admission free), where Uncle Ho lived from 1898 to 1900. Walk a few metres further along the riverbank to **Ben Da**, the steps down to the water where Ho bathed. Another 300m or so beyond them, over a quaint bridge, is an **Am Ba** ('female spirit' temple). It's in some disrepair, but it's quiet and contemplative, with ceramic mosaic work decorating the walls.

Duong No, 6km northeast of Hué, can easily be reached by bicycle or motorbike. Look for a small wooden sign on the left at a bridge off the main road; cross over the bridge and turn immediately right. Ho Chi Minh's House is a few hundred metres along the riverbank. A loop can be made by following the path beside the house to a road at the end; turn left and continue through a pretty rural village for a couple of kilometres. Turn left again, and the road rejoins the bridge to the main road.

Thuan An to Vinh Hien

Thuan An Beach, 15km northeast of Hué, is on a splendid lagoon near the mouth of the Perfume River, at the tip of a long, thin island. It's lovely for beachcombing, and is quite undeveloped except for a few kiosks, but between September and April the water's often too rough to swim in.

It is joined to the mainland by a short bridge, and beyond the beach a 50km scenic road (actually Hwy 49, though you'd never guess) stretches the length of the undeveloped island (no maps give it a name) from Thuan An to Vinh Hien. This makes a great day trip by motorbike or car from Hué. It also offers an alternative route to or from Hué for travellers making their way on two wheels along the coast road.

Coming from Thuan An, the island is skinny and the road winds along with the lagoon on one side and the ocean on the other. There are several villages on the way with stacks of enormous *nuoc mam* (fish sauce) jars lining the outer walls of many houses, and miles of fertile raised vegetable gardens. But most extraordinary are the vast, colourful and opulent graves and family temples lining the ocean side of the road; there are thousands upon thousands of them. In Vietnam the area is known as the 'city of tombs', with families vying to outdo their neighbours' ancestral monuments. There was a huge outflow of boat people from this area and the overseas Vietnamese now provide the funds to construct these excessive structures.

GETTING THERE & AWAY

There are at least three options for driving this road: two for day-trippers from Hué, and one for through travellers.

Those on day trips can just drive as far as they like and then return to Thuan An. An alternative is to drive to Vinh Tanh and, about halfway along the road, turn right and head to a wharf where a ferry runs back and forth across the lagoon until about 4pm. The 20-minute crossing costs 5000d for motorbikes and 30,000d for cars, and moors 13km from Hwy 1A, a little south of Phu Bai Airport.

An option for through travellers continuing south after visiting Hue – on motorbikes and bicycles only – is to make your way to Vinh Hien and, from there, catch a public boat to Cau Hai on the mainland, close to the Bach Ma National Park access road. The cost for two people and a motorbike is 5000d, and the journey takes an hour or so. Be aware that weather conditions affect the running of the boats, so be prepared to backtrack if necessary.

BACH MA NATIONAL PARK

☎ 054 / elevation 1450m

A French-era hill station, **Bach Ma National Park** (Vuon Quoc Gia Bach Ma; ☎ 871 330; www.bachma.vnn.vn; adult 10,500d/child 5500d/child under 5 free) reaches a peak of 1450m at Bach Ma mountain, only 18km from the coast. The cooler climate attracted the French, who started building villas here in 1930; by 1937 the number of holiday homes had reached 139 and it became known as the 'Dalat of central Vietnam'. Most of the visitors were high-ranking French VIPs. Not surprisingly the Viet Minh tried hard to spoil the holiday – the area saw some heavy fighting in the early 1950s. After independence from the French, Bach Ma was soon forgotten and the villas abandoned; today they are in total ruin and only a few stone walls remain.

Bach Ma has some stunning views across the coastline near Hai Van Pass, which the Americans used to their advantage: during the war, US troops turned the area into a fortified bunker. The VC did their best to harass the Americans, but couldn't dislodge them. Between the eerie remains and memories of the American War, spooky stories abound among locals, who maintain that the park is a realm of ghosts.

In 1991, 22,031 hectares of land were set aside as a nature preserve and designated Bach

Ma National Park. Efforts are now fast under way to regenerate patches of forest that were destroyed by clear-felling and defoliation during the American War.

Forty-three species of mammal have been definitively recorded within the boundaries of the park, with a further 76 species, including tigers and leopards, potentially present. A recent victory in the wildlife stakes came with the discovery in 1992 of evidence of *sao la*, a previously unknown antelope-like creature whose footprints and horns were found. Two other animals were discovered in the late 1990s: the deer-like Truong Son muntjac and the giant muntjac. With enforced protection from poachers, there is hope that wild elephants, now restricted to the Lao side of the border, will return to seek the sanctuary of Bach Ma.

As most of the park's resident mammals are nocturnal, sightings demand a great deal of effort and patience. Bird-watching is fantastic here, but you need to be up at dawn to get the best sightings. Of the 800-odd species of bird known to inhabit Vietnam, the park is home to some 330, including the fabulous crested argus pheasant and the tenacious Edwards' pheasant – unseen and thought to be extinct for 50 years, it was recently discovered in the park's buffer zone.

More than 1400 species of plant have been discovered here, representing a fifth of the flora of Vietnam. Among these, at least 430 species are medicinal plants, 33 produce essential oils, 26 are used for weaving and 22 bear edible fruit.

It was not until March 1998 that Bach Ma National Park began receiving visitors. Despite its tender age, the efforts of the park's staff are laudable and they are hard at work protecting the area, working on community development with the ethnic minorities in the area and promoting sustainable ecotourism. Several young rangers here speak English well and there is an interesting display in the **Visitor Centre**, located at the park entrance. As well as plenty of natural-history information, there's a huge crate of confiscated hunting tools, weaponry and the remains of a crashed helicopter. From here you can book village and bird-watching tours, English or French-speaking guides (150,000d per day), and Russian jeeps (one way/return 200,000/300,000d) or 12-seater minibuses (one way/return 250,000/400,000d) to take you to the summit. Motorcycles and bikes are strictly prohibited.

Bach Ma is the wettest place in Vietnam, with the heaviest of the rain falling in October and November. With the wet weather come plenty of leeches. Still, even these months are not out of the question for visiting. The best time to visit Bach Ma is from February to September, particularly between March and June, for what's likely to be the best weather.

Sleeping & Eating

National Park Guesthouse (☎/fax 871 330; camp sites per person 3000d, 6-person tents 80,000d, entrance r 100,000-120,000d, summit dm 120,000d, r 150,000-300,000d) The park authority has a small camping ground and four guesthouses near the summit and two more guesthouses near the entrance. One of the summit guesthouses has a 12-person dorm with a shared bathroom. The more expensive twin-bed rooms are a better bet for views and facilities. This is a prime spot, rebuilt from the ruins of Emperor Bao Dai's summer retreat. Bookings should be made at the Visitor Centre. Give at least four hours' notice for meal requirements, as fresh food is brought up to the park from the market on demand.

Several private companies have recently built low-key accommodation in the park, under the watchful eye of the park authorities. Near the summit trail, **Morin-Bach Ma Hotel** (☎ 871 199; www.huonggiangtourist.com/huonggiangtourist/hotel/Bachma_Hotel.htm; s/d US$25/30), built in a French style, offers some smart rooms with balconies.

Getting There & Away

Bach Ma is 28km west of Lang Co and 40km southeast of Hué. The turn-off is signposted in the town of Cau Hai on Hwy 1A. The entrance is 3km along the narrow road into the park.

It's another steep and meandering 16km on the sealed road from the gate to the summit and, unless you have your own vehicle or are willing to walk, you'll need to hire private transport from the Visitor Centre. Walking takes about three to four hours down, so carry plenty of water and wear a hat, as there is little canopy protection on the lower part of the road.

There are buses to the park from Danang (US$3, two hours) and Hué (US$2, one hour). Local buses stop at Cau Hai, where *xe om* drivers can ferry you to the entrance. Cau Hai also has a **train station** (☎ 871 362; Loc Dien village), but the one daily service in either direction is slow and arrives/departs at antisocial times.

Getting Around

Your visit will be much easier if you can hire a vehicle for your time in the park, especially if you plan to walk some of the trails, as they are spread along the 16km summit-access road.

SUOI VOI (ELEPHANT SPRINGS)

About 15km north of Lang Co Beach, **Suoi Voi** (admission 10,000d, plus per car 10,000/per motorbike 2000d) is a secluded recreation area, where you can easily spend a half-day traipsing through the forest and swimming in cool, crystal-clear streams. It's a pleasant detour and is recommended for motorbikers and cyclists who are braving their way along Hwy 1A.

The main springs are a short walk from the parking area. The natural pool is ringed by huge boulders – one vaguely in the shape of an elephant's head, and cosmetically enhanced to look more like it. The stream turns into a hydro-slide over the smooth rocks. Further exploration will lead to less-populated swimming holes, including the **Vung Do Pool**, about 200m beyond the main area.

Foreign visitors here are scarce and on weekdays you may have the whole place to yourself. Weekends, however, are jam-packed with Vietnamese, notably young couples exploring the birds and bees.

To reach the springs from Hwy 1A, turn inland at the road marker reading 'Danang 52km' (if coming from the north) or 'Phu Bai 44km' (if heading from the south). You will see the 19th-century Thua Lau Church just ahead of you. Keep the church on your left and follow the dirt road for 5km to the entry gate. Buy a ticket here and hold onto it as you may be asked to show it more than once. From here it's a bumpy 1.5km to the parking area. Along the way you'll pass basic bungalows (no hot water) for rent at **Hoa Thin 1** (☎ 054-891 805; r 150,000d). One suspects they're often used for, ahem, short-term stays on the weekends.

There are some simple food stalls near the springs, but it's better to bring a picnic.

LANG CO BEACH

☎ 054

Lang Co is an attractive, island-like stretch of palm-shaded white sand, with a crystal-clear, turquoise lagoon on one side and 10 kilometres of beachfront on the other. Unfortunately the beach and the edges of the lagoon can turn into litter traps. Many open-tour buses make a lunch stop here and it makes a fine place to hop off for a night or two, depending on the weather.

The beach is best enjoyed between April and July. From late August till November rains are frequent, and from December to March it can get chilly. Lang Co was devastated by a

WALKING TRAILS IN BACH MA NATIONAL PARK

These trails and others are described more fully in the national park's map, which you get with your ticket; further information is found in the *Bach Ma National Park* booklet, available for 12,000d at the park entrance. Check with the rangers for the current condition of each track.

- **Pheasant Trail** is named after the rare and beautiful crested argus pheasant, but you're more likely to hear the birds calling than see them. The 2.5km track starts 5km along the summit-access road, and leads through forest to a series of waterfalls and pools. You can cool off here before the return hike.
- **Five Lakes Cascade Trail** starts 1km beyond the national-park guesthouse. A 2km walk takes you through forest and follows a series of cascades. The cold water is home to a recently discovered species of frog.
- **Rhododendron Trail** can be walked as an extension of the Five Lakes Cascade Trail, or can be reached by a separate track from Km16 on the summit-access road. February and March are the best months to walk this trail, when the rhododendrons are in bloom. At the end of the trail is a spectacular waterfall, and you can get to the bottom if you're prepared to climb back up the 650 steps. The water eventually makes its way down to join up with the Perfume River in Hué.
- **Summit Trail** is a steep but short 500m walk to Hai Vong Dai, the 1450m summit of Bach Ma. Today visitors simply enjoy the stunning views, but in 1968 a helicopter base was maintained at this strategic spot. The streams of cloud *(bach ma)* often seen at the summit are thought to resemble the mane of a white horse, inspiring the park's name.

major typhoon in late 2006, but within a few weeks all of the resorts had reopened and rebuilding was well underway.

There are spectacular views of Lang Co from the Hai Van Pass and from the trains linking Danang and Hué. Most of the accommodation is north of the town along the highway.

Sleeping & Eating

Lang Co Hotel (☎ 874 426; codolangco@dng.vnn.vn; r US$15-20, bungalow US$35;) This beachside pad offers the choice of bungalows set in a shaded garden compound or a block of big, well-priced rooms, although the cheapest don't have hot water.

Thanh Tam Seaside Resort (☎ 874 456; fax 873 762; r 350,000d;) Situated about 1km north of Lang Co Hotel is this collection of beachside bungalows. The terrace restaurant has great views and is a popular seafood stop for tourists making the journey between Hué and Danang.

Lang Co Beach Resort (☎ 873 555; www.langcobeachresort.com.vn; r US$60-70;) Set amid lavishly landscaped gardens, this is the most upmarket option in Lang Co. Rooms have nice linen, and facilities include a large pool, fitness centre and wireless internet in the attractive Chinese-style reception.

New guesthouses have sprung up on the lagoon side of the road, only a short stroll to the beach. Opposite Lang Co Beach Resort, **Chi Na Guesthouse** (☎ 874 597; r US$10;) offers cheap rooms, and the friendly family speak some English.

Getting There & Away

Lang Co is just on the other side of the new Hai Van Tunnel from Danang, which has reduced the distance to 20km. Tourist buses pass through daily, en route for Hué, Danang and Hoi An, with all tickets costing just US$2. However, those on two wheels will still need to take the 35km scenic route over the Hai Van Pass.

Lang Co **train station** (☎ 874 423) is 3km from the beach, towards the lagoon. Finding someone to take you by motorbike from the train station to the beach shouldn't be difficult. The train journey from here to Danang (13,000d, 1½ to two hours, four daily) is one of the most spectacular in Vietnam. Services also head to and from Hué (24,000d, 1½ hours, two daily).

HAI VAN PASS & TUNNEL

The Hai Van (Sea Cloud) Pass crosses over a spur of the Truong Son Mountain Range that juts into the sea. About 30km north of Danang, the road climbs to an elevation of 496m, passing south of the Ai Van Son peak (1172m). It's an incredibly mountainous stretch of highway with spectacular views. The railway track, with its many tunnels, goes around the peninsula, following the beautiful and deserted shoreline to avoid the hills.

In the 15th century this pass formed the boundary between Vietnam and the Kingdom of Champa. Until the American War it was heavily forested. At the summit is a bullet-scarred French fort, later used as a bunker by the South Vietnamese and US armies, with incredible views over Lang Co.

If you cross in winter, the pass serves as something of a visible dividing line between the climates of the north and south. Acting as a virtual wall, it protects Danang from the fierce 'Chinese winds' that sweep in from the northeast. From about November to March the exposed Lang Co side of the pass can be uncomfortably wet and chilly, while just to the south it's warm and dry. When the winter weather is lousy in Hué, it is usually good in Danang.

At the top of the pass you'll have to fight off a rather large crowd of very persistent vendors. You would be wise not to change money with anyone here, as you're more than likely to get short-changed.

In 2005 the 6280m-long Hai Van Tunnel opened, using Austrian technology, bypassing the Pass and shaving an hour off the journey between Danang and Hué. Motorcycles and bikes are not permitted in the tunnel, but most cars and buses now take this route. The diversion of this traffic from the Pass road has made it a much safer and more enjoyable route, although you may still find yourself playing chicken with a suicidal truck driver.

BA NA HILL STATION

☎ 0511 / elevation 1485m

It's easy to see why the French would run to the hills at the first opportunity, and why the Vietnamese were less keen. As you climb the winding road to beautiful **Ba Na** (admission 10,000d, per motorbike/car 5000/10,000d) you can feel the temperature and humidity dropping away. When it's 36°C on the coast, it's likely to be between 15°C and 26°C up the mountain.

Rain often falls in the section between 700m and 1200m above sea level, but around the hill station itself, the sky is usually clear, the view is truly spectacular, and the air is fresh and cool. Mountain tracks lead to a variety of waterfalls and viewpoints.

Founded in 1919, of the 200-odd villas that originally stood, a few tattered, atmospheric ruins remain. Until WWII the French were carried up the last 20km of rough mountain road by sedan chair.

Near the top, the **Linh Ung Pagoda** (1999) is a supremely peaceful spot, with a 24m-high white seated Buddha visible for miles around. Near the pagoda a **cable car** (return ticket 35,000d) whisks visitors up to the hill station. The vistas are huge.

The provincial government has high hopes of once again making Ba Na a magnet for tourists – branding it 'the Dalat of Danang province' and developing the site to suit domestic visitors. This has led to a variety of accommodation and restaurants, but also lots of karaoke, a loud PA and litter.

There are no ATMs up here, but there is a small **post office** (☎ 791 500) near Le Nim restaurant.

Sleeping & Eating

Le Nim (☎ 791 504; r 200,000-400,000d) For sweeping views look no further than Le Nim, situated near the top of the cable car. Many of the rooms have beautiful wood panelling and there are a number of freestanding stone bungalows. The restaurant serves up terrific fresh seafood dishes.

Ba Na By Night Resort (☎ 791 056; bananight@dng.vnn.vn; r 200,000-500,000d) This has probably the best choice of rooms at Ba Na, set in *rong* houses (thatched-roof houses on stilts) or various villas, but you miss out on the views. Facilities include a popular bar and tennis courts. The remnants of a colonial-era wine cellar and French villa are interesting to check out, and from here it's an easy walk down the stairs to the giant Buddha of Linh Ung Pagoda and the bottom of the cable car.

Getting There & Away

Ba Na is 42km west of Danang along a beautiful winding road that can be dangerous on a foggy day. Pay the admission fee at the Reception Centre at the bottom of the access road. From here it's a steep climb uphill, and many motorbikes won't attempt it. Shuttle buses, leaving when full, take passengers up the mountain for 20,000d (30,000d return). Otherwise you can hire a Ba Na local with a high-powered motorcycle for the trip (60,000d).

SUOI MO

A short detour on the way to Ba Na, the waterfall at **Suoi Mo** (Dream Springs, admission 3000d) has some clear swimming holes for a dip. It's a pretty, undeveloped spot, if you can ignore the litter; go on a weekday to avoid the crowds.

Suoi Mo is clearly signposted from the road to Ba Na. Continue up the bumpy track for 2km or so and look for a small arrowed sign on the left. Park here and walk along the track that leads off to the right beside a few houses. A 20-minute climb (slippery when wet) brings you to a waterfall.

DANANG

☎ 0511 / pop 781,000

While most tourists neglect Vietnam's fourth-largest city in favour of nearby Hué and Hoi An, Danang has considerable charm in its own right. The economic powerhouse of central Vietnam, it combines the buzz of a bigger city with beautiful beaches and great restaurants. A lot of money has recently been poured into tree-lined boulevards, bridges and beachside resorts.

Back in the heady days of the American War, Danang was referred to as the 'Saigon of the North'. This held a note of both praise and condemnation: like its big southern sister, Danang was notable for its booming economy, fine restaurants, busy traffic and glittering shops. Entertaining the soldiers from the nearby American base was a profitable business – bars and prostitution were major industries, and that sleazy legacy lingers. Men travelling together or alone may find themselves (or more accurately, their wallets) subjected to unwanted attention in even the ritziest of bars.

Danang marks the northern limits of Vietnam's tropical zone and boasts a pleasant climate all year round.

History

Known during French colonial rule as Tourane, Danang succeeded Hoi An as the most important port in central Vietnam during the 19th century, and it remains the principal one for central Vietnam.

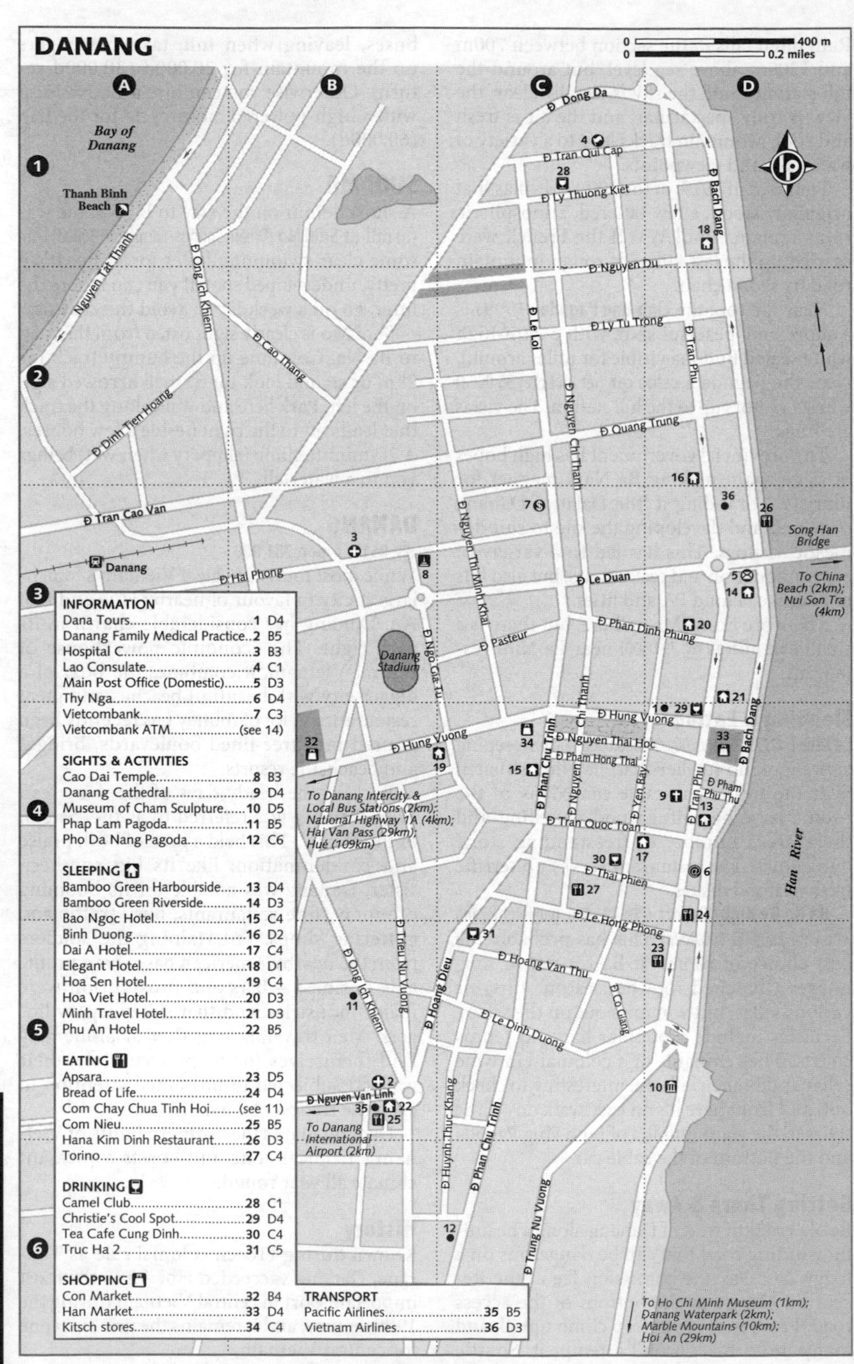

DANANG
0 400 m
0 0.2 miles
A
B
C
D
1
2
3
4
5
6
Bay of Danang
Thanh Binh Beach
Nguyen Tat Thanh
Đ Ong Ich Khiem
Đ Cao Thang
Đ Dinh Tien Hoang
Đ Tran Cao Van
Danang
Đ Hai Phong
Đ Dong Da
Đ Tran Qui Cap
Đ Ly Thuong Kiet
Đ Bach Dang
Đ Nguyen Du
Đ Le Loi
Đ Ly Tu Trong
Đ Tran Phu
Đ Nguyen Chi Thanh
Đ Quang Trung
Đ Nguyen Thi Minh Khai
Song Han Bridge
Đ Le Duan
To China Beach (2km); Nui Son Tra (4km)
Đ Phan Dinh Phung
Đ Pasteur
Danang Stadium
Đ Ngo Gia Tu
Chi Thanh
Đ Hung Vuong
Đ Nguyen Thai Hoc
Đ Pham Hong Thai
Đ Phan Chu Trinh
Đ Yen Bay
Đ Pham Phu Thu
To Danang Intercity & Local Bus Stations (2km); National Highway 1A (4km); Hai Van Pass (29km); Hué (109km)
Đ Tran Quoc Toan
Đ Thai Phien
Han River
Đ Le Hong Phong
Đ Hoang Van Thu
Đ Co Giang
Đ Trieu Nu Vuong
Đ Hoang Dieu
Đ Le Dinh Duong
Đ Nguyen Van Linh
To Danang International Airport (2km)
Đ Huynh Thuc Khang
Đ Trung Nu Vuong
To Ho Chi Minh Museum (1km); Danang Waterpark (2km); Marble Mountains (10km); Hoi An (29km)
INFORMATION
Dana Tours....1 D4
Danang Family Medical Practice..2 B5
Hospital C....3 B3
Lao Consulate....4 C1
Main Post Office (Domestic)....5 D3
Thy Nga....6 D4
Vietcombank....7 C3
Vietcombank ATM....(see 14)
SIGHTS & ACTIVITIES
Cao Dai Temple....8 B3
Danang Cathedral....9 D4
Museum of Cham Sculpture....10 D5
Phap Lam Pagoda....11 B5
Pho Da Nang Pagoda....12 C6
SLEEPING
Bamboo Green Harbourside....13 D4
Bamboo Green Riverside....14 D3
Bao Ngoc Hotel....15 C4
Binh Duong....16 D2
Dai A Hotel....17 C4
Elegant Hotel....18 D1
Hoa Sen Hotel....19 C4
Hoa Viet Hotel....20 D3
Minh Travel Hotel....21 D3
Phu An Hotel....22 B5
EATING
Apsara....23 D5
Bread of Life....24 D4
Com Chay Chua Tinh Hoi....(see 11)
Com Nieu....25 B5
Hana Kim Dinh Restaurant....26 D3
Torino....27 C4
DRINKING
Camel Club....28 C1
Christie's Cool Spot....29 D4
Tea Cafe Cung Dinh....30 C4
Truc Ha 2....31 C5
SHOPPING
Con Market....32 B4
Han Market....33 D4
Kitsch stores....34 C4
TRANSPORT
Pacific Airlines....35 B5
Vietnam Airlines....36 D3

In March 1975 Danang, the second-largest city in South Vietnam, was the scene of utter chaos. Saigon government forces were ordered to abandon Hué, while Quang Ngai had fallen to the communists, cutting South Vietnam in two. Desperate civilians tried to flee the city, as some soldiers of the South Vietnamese army engaged in looting, pillage and rape. On 29 March 1975, two truckloads of communist guerrillas, more than half of them women, drove into what had been the most heavily defended city in South Vietnam and, without firing a shot, declared Danang liberated.

Orientation

Danang is on the western bank of the Han River. The city is part of a long, thin peninsula, at the northern tip of which is Nui Son Tra (called Monkey Mountain by US soldiers). China Beach and the Marble Mountains lie south of the city, and the Hai Van Pass overlooks Danang from the northwest.

MAPS

The *Danang Tourist Map* is a pocket-sized foldout that is available for 8000d in bookshops and hotels in Danang and Hoi An.

Information

INTERNET ACCESS

There are internet cafés scattered all over Danang, including several by the river on Đ Bach Dang. **Thy Nga** (Map p230; 216 Đ Bach Dang; per hr 3000d) has a reasonably fast connection.

MEDICAL SERVICES

Danang Family Medical Practice (Map p230; ☎ 582 700; 50-52 Đ Nguyen Van Linh) Set up like a mini hospital with in-patient facilities, this excellent practice has sister clinics in Hanoi and HCMC. This branch is run by an Australian doctor and the friendly staff speak excellent English.

Hospital C (Map p230; Benh Vien C; ☎ 821 483; 122 Đ Haiphong) The most advanced of the four hospitals in town.

MONEY

Vietcombank (Map p230; ☎ 823 503; 140 Đ Le Loi) The best place to change travellers cheques.

Vietcombank ATM (Map p230; Đ 177 Tran Phu) Outside the Bamboo Green Riverside.

POST

Main post office (Map p230; ☎ 821 327; Đ Bach Dang) Near the Song Han bridge.

TRAVEL AGENCIES

Cuong Easy Ride's Tour (☎ 090-5173 903) A one-man operation offering day trips (around 240,000d) or longer tours on the back of his bike. He's a friendly guy who speaks good English, has a spare helmet and doesn't drive like a maniac.

Dana Tours (Map p230; ☎ 825 653; www.vietnamwelcomes.com; 76 Đ Hung Vuong; 🕓 Mon-Sat) Offers car rentals, boat trips, visa extensions and treks in nearby Ba Na or Bach Ma.

Sights & Activities

MUSEUM OF CHAM SCULPTURE

The leading sight in Danang is the internationally renowned **Museum of Cham Sculpture** (Bao Tang Dieu Khac Champa Da Nang; Map p230; cnr Đ Trung Nu Vuong & Đ Bach Dang; admission 30,000d; 🕓 7am-5pm). Founded in 1915 by the École Française d'Extrême Orient, this collection is the finest of its kind in the world. Many of the sandstone carvings – including altars, *lingas* (see p265), garudas, Ganeshas, and

FIGHTING TO FLEE

Almost the only fighting that took place as Danang fell was between South Vietnamese soldiers and civilians battling for space on flights and ships out of the city. On 27 March 1975 the president of World Airways, Ed Daly, ignored explicit US government orders and sent two 727s from Saigon to Danang to evacuate refugees. When the first plane landed, about a thousand desperate and panicked people mobbed the tarmac. Soldiers fired assault rifles at each other and at the plane as they tried to shove their way through the rear door. As the aircraft taxied down the runway trying to take off, people climbed up into the landing-gear wells and someone threw a hand grenade, damaging the right wing.

Those who managed to fight their way aboard, kicking and punching aside anyone in their way, included over 200 soldiers. The only civilians on board were two women and one baby – and the baby was only there after being thrown aboard by its desperate mother, who was left on the tarmac. Several of the stowaways in the wheel wells couldn't hold on and, as the plane flew southward, TV cameras on the second 727 filmed them falling into the South China Sea.

images of Shiva, Brahma and Vishnu – are exquisitely detailed. Allow yourself at least a good hour to soak it up.

The museum's artefacts, which date from the 7th to 15th centuries, were discovered at Dong Duong (Indrapura), Khuong My, My Son (see p262), Tra Kieu (see p266) and other sites, mostly in Quang Nam and Danang provinces. The museum's rooms are named after the localities in which the objects displayed were found.

A trilingual (Vietnamese, English and French) guidebook about the museum, *Museum of Cham Sculpture – Danang,* was written by its director, Tran Ky Phuong, who is Vietnam's most eminent scholar of Cham civilisation. The book provides excellent background on the art of Champa and details on the museum's exhibits. It's usually on sale at the entrance.

Guides (some better than others) wait at the entrance of the museum to offer their services, but agree on a price before you begin.

HO CHI MINH MUSEUM

There are three sections to the **Ho Chi Minh Museum** (Map p236; ☎ 615 982; 3 Đ Nguyen Van Troi; admission free; 🕑 7-11am & 1.30-4.30pm) – a museum of military history in front of which US, Soviet and Chinese weaponry is displayed; a replica of Ho Chi Minh's house in Hanoi (complete with a small lake); and, across the pond from the house, a museum solely about Uncle Ho.

It's easy to tire of Vietnam's numerous military and Ho Chi Minh museums. This one isn't bad, but don't bother if you're visiting the larger incarnations in Hanoi or HCMC. The museum is 250m west of Đ Nui Thanh.

DANANG WATERPARK

The enormous **water park** (Map p236; adult/child 40,000/30,000d; 🕑 7.30am-6.30pm Wed-Mon) is lots of fun – and not just for kids – with slides, pools and the like. It's on the riverbank, 2km beyond the Ho Chi Minh Museum.

DANANG CATHEDRAL

Known to locals as Con Ga Church (Rooster Church) because of the weathercock on top of the steeple, the candy-pink **Danang Cathedral** (Map p230; Đ Tran Phu) was built for the city's French residents in 1923. Today it serves a Catholic community of 4000 – it's standing room only if you arrive late for Mass.

Mass is usually held from Monday to Saturday at 5am and 5.30pm, and on Sunday at 5am, 6.15am, 7.30am, 3.30pm and 5pm.

CAO DAI TEMPLE

Built in 1956, **Cao Dai Temple** (Map p230; 63 Đ Haiphong) is the largest such structure outside the sect's headquarters in Tay Ninh (p381). There are 50,000 Cao Dai faithful in Quang Nam and Danang provinces – 20,000 in Danang itself. As with all Cao Dai temples, prayers are held four times a day: at 6am, noon, 6pm and midnight.

The left-hand gate to the complex is for women; the right-hand gate for men. The doors to the sanctuary are similarly segregated, although priests of either gender use the central door. Behind the main altar sits an enormous globe with the Cao Dai 'divine eye' symbol on it.

A sign reading *van giao nhat ly* (All religions have the same reason) hangs from the ceiling in front of the altar. Behind the gilded letters is a picture of the founders of five of the world's great religions. From left to right are Mohammed, Laotse (wearing Eastern Orthodox robes), Jesus (portrayed as he is in French icons), a Southeast Asian–looking Buddha and Confucius (looking as Chinese as could be).

Portraits of early Cao Dai leaders, dressed in turbans and white robes, are displayed in the building behind the main sanctuary. Ngo Van Chieu, the founder of Cao Daism, is shown standing, wearing a pointed white turban and a long white robe with blue markings.

PAGODAS

Built in 1936, **Phap Lam Pagoda** (Map p230; ☎ 823 870; 574 Đ Ong Ich Khiem) has in its grounds a brass statue of Dia Tang (the King of Hell), a large yellow Happy Buddha and a giant pink Buddha with a swastika (a common Buddhist symbol) on his chest. A massive new pagoda was being built here at the time of research.

Pho Da Nang Pagoda (Map p230; ☎ 826 094; 340 Đ Phan Chu Trinh) was built in 1923 in a traditional architectural configuration. Local people participate actively in the pagoda's lively religious life.

Sleeping

Compared with the bargains to be found in Hoi An and Hué, rooms are expensive– Danang is more used to catering to business-people than tourists. However, the explosion of hotel construction does hold the promise of falling prices in the future. For information on accommodation just across the river at My Khe Beach, see p238.

BUDGET

Minh Travel Hotel (Map p230; ☎ 812 661; mtjraymond@yahoo.ca; 105 Đ Tran Phu; r US$3-9;) This tiny place is developing a reputation among super-budget travellers for the friendliness and honesty of its owners and its rock-bottom prices. The cheapest rooms are like prison cells (no air-con and a basic shared bathroom), but the others offer more creature comforts.

Hoa Sen Hotel (Map p230; ☎ 829 000; fax 829 001; 119-123 Đ Hung Vuong; r 200,000d;) Close to the train station, this is a tidy budget option, although some rooms are windowless and dark. They're brightened somewhat by large silk flowers.

Phu An Hotel (Map p230; ☎ 825 708; phuan.hotel.dn@gmail.com; 29 Đ Nguyen Van Linh; r US$13-15;) Apart from some bad air-brushed portraits, this spotless new hotel on a busy street is a tasteful and comfortable option.

Bao Ngoc Hotel (Map p230; ☎ 817 711; baongochotel@dng.vnn.vn; 48 Đ Phan Chu Trinh; r US$15-16;) With an inexplicable kiwi logo and excessively floral sheets, this inner-city hotel offers good-value clean rooms.

Hoa Viet Hotel (Map p230; ☎ 840 111; fax 840 242; 8 Đ Phan Dinh Phung; r US$16-17;) This well-priced new joint near the river has attractive, clean rooms.

MIDRANGE

Binh Duong (Map p230; ☎ 821 930; fax 827 666; 32-34 Đ Tran Phu; r US$15-25;) Popular with longer-term stayers, the friendly staff at Binh Duong speak excellent English and some of the ample rooms have large corner bathtubs.

our pick **Dai A Hotel** (Map p230; ☎ 827 532; www.daiahotel.com; 51 Đ Yen Bay; r US$15-30;) The large Jesus painting and papal crown light fixture in the reception leave no doubt as to the religious affiliation of this establishment, close to the Catholic cathedral. The well-appointed rooms have free internet access, the staff are extremely helpful and there are some lovely views from the higher floors.

Bamboo Green Harbourside (Map p230; ☎ 822 722; bamboogreen2@dng.vnn.vn; 177 Đ Tran Phu; r US$25-30, ste US$40;) In a good location opposite Danang Cathedral and near the river, many of the rooms have good views and breakfast is included in the prices.

Bamboo Green Riverside Hotel (Map p230; ☎ 832 591; www.vitours.com.vn; 68 Đ Bach Dang; r US$30-50;) Even the cheaper rooms have views, bathtubs and silk robes in this impressive place conveniently situated right by the Song Han Bridge.

Elegant Hotel (Map p230; ☎ 892 893; elegant@dng.vnn.vn; 22A Đ Bach Dang; s US$25-60, d US$30-65;) While the outside is less elegant than it once was, this riverside hotel has well-maintained, bright rooms and free wi-fi.

Eating

VIETNAMESE

Com Chay Chua Tinh Hoi (Map p230; 574 Đ Ong Ich Khiem; dishes from 3000d) Known for the best vegetarian food in town; it's just inside the entrance gate to the Phap Lam Pagoda.

Com Nieu (Map p230; K254/2 Đ Hoang Dieu; dishes 10,000-40,000d) A local favourite tucked away off a lane, this is the place to try the local speciality *hoanh thanh* – a wonton-like combination of minced pork and shrimp served fried or steamed.

Au Lac (Map p236; ☎ 611 074; 4-6 Đ 2/9; dishes 25,000-70,000d; lunch & dinner) This stylish restaurant serving tasty Vietnamese dishes has an impressive outdoor dining area and a colourful bar.

our pick **Apsara** (Map p230; ☎ 561 409; www.apsara-danang.com; 222 Đ Tran Phu; meals US$15; lunch & dinner) The best dining experience in Danang, Apsara has excellent food, great service, a good wine list and an atmospheric setting – with Cham-influenced décor and live traditional music. The cuisine flirts with Japanese and Chinese, but is mainly Vietnamese, with an emphasis on seafood.

INTERNATIONAL

Bread of Life (Map p230; ☎ 893 456; 215 Đ Tran Phu; cakes/breakfast 10,000/20,000d; breakfast & lunch Mon-Sat) A great spot for a Western-style breakfast or a coffee and cake, this little café employs deaf staff and gives a percentage of profits to charity. They also screen movies in English every Wednesday.

Torino (Map p230; ☎ 565 124; 283 Đ Nguyen Chi Thanh; mains 40,000-90,000d; lunch & dinner Tue-Sun) This new authentically Italian restaurant serves excellent pasta, pizza and proper espresso, as well as more exotic dishes such as frogs and crocodile. The windowless dining room takes on a better vibe at night when it doubles as a jazz club.

Hana Kim Dinh Restaurant (Map p230; ☎ 830 024; 15 Đ Bach Dang; meals 90,000d; ❄) Well located right on the river, this restaurant serves an interesting mix of Japanese, Vietnamese, Chinese and Korean dishes, along with pizza and pasta.

Phi Lu Chinese Restaurant (Map p236; ☎ 611 888; 1-3 Đ 2/9; dishes 30,000-350,000d) A popular Chinese restaurant with three branches in Danang, this one has the most character – festooned with red lanterns at night. The food is excellent.

Drinking & Entertainment

Christie's Cool Spot (Map p230; ☎ 824 040; 112 Đ Tran Phu) The downstairs bar is the place to meet US war veterans and join their debates about whether the Iraq war was even more or less pointless than Vietnam. What brings them back to Vietnam? Without taking a scientific survey, the answer seems to be the women. Christie's also serves Western comfort food, including pizza and roast chicken.

Tea Café Cung Dinh (Map p230; ☎ 562 990; 112 Đ Yen Bay) It's amazing what a little mood lighting can do. This garden café set in a dreary car park becomes a fairyland at night, lit by red Chinese lanterns. It serves a range of exotic teas and delicious cakes.

Truc Ha 2 (Map p230; ☎ 562 498; K121/3 Đ Hoang Van Thu) This lush garden café hidden off a inner city laneway is an oasis of calm during the day – less so at night when the karaoke starts up.

Camel Club (Map p230; ☎ 887 462; 16 Đ Ly Thuong Kiet; admission 20,000d; 🕑 7pm-1am) This is where Danang's beautiful people come for pricy drinks (from 30,000d) and heavy beats.

Shopping

Han Market (Cho Han; Map p230; cnr Đ Hung Vuong & Đ Tran Phu; 🕑 6am-9pm) is a fine place for a casual stroll or to shop in the evenings. The **Con Market** (Cho Con; Map p230; Đ Ong Ich Khiem) is Danang's largest, but is mainly a daytime affair.

If you're looking for a shimmering framed Ho Chi Minh portrait with a clock inset, or a plastic dragon that lights up and sings Old McDonald, check out the collection of kitsch stores (Map p230) near the corner of Đ Hung Vuong and Đ Phan Chu Trinh.

Getting There & Away

AIR

During the American War, Danang had one of the busiest airports in the world. Now it settles for being the third busiest in Vietnam.

Pacific Airlines (Map p230; ☎ 583 583; 35 Đ Nguyen Van Linh) Daily flights from Danang to HCMC and Hanoi.

Vietnam Airlines (Map p230; ☎ 821 130; 35 Đ Tran Phu; 🕑 7-11am & 1.30-5pm Mon-Fri, 7.30-11am & 1.30-4.30pm Sat & Sun) Connects Danang with Hanoi, HCMC, Pleiku, Buon Ma Thuot, Cam Ranh (Nha Trang) and Quy Nhon.

BUS

The large **Danang intercity bus station** (Map p236; ☎ 821 265; 33 Đ Dien Bien Phu; 🕑 ticket office 7-11am & 1-5pm) is 3km west from the city centre. A metered taxi to the riverside will cost 50,000d.

Buses leave for all major centres, including Dong Hoi (56,000d, five hours, six daily), Hué (40,000d, three hours, six daily), Quy Nhon (65,000d, six hours, 11 daily) and Kon Tum (85,000d, five hours, three daily).

There are three weekly services to Savannakhet (240,000d, 14 hours), crossing the border at Lao Bao. Phone Nguyen Phuoc for bookings (☎ 0913-412 442).

Regular buses to Hoi An (8000d, one hour) depart from a local bus station 200m away from the intercity bus station. Foreigners tend to be overcharged, especially if you pick up the bus from street. Check the price before boarding and stand your ground.

With an advance booking, **Sinh Café** (☎ 0510-863 948) open-tour buses will pick up from outside the Cham museum twice a day en route to Hué (US$3, 2½ hours).

CAR & MOTORBIKE

The simplest way to get to Hoi An (30km) is to hire a car for around US$10 from a local travel agency (see p231), or a motorbike for around US$4 to US$6 from one of the guys on the street corners. For a slightly higher fee you can ask the driver to stop off and wait while you visit the Marble Mountains and China Beach.

You can also reach My Son by motorbike (US$12) or car (US$32), with the option of being dropped off in Hoi An on the way back.

Distances to major destinations from Danang include Hanoi (764km), Hué (108km) and HCMC (972km).

TRAIN

Danang's **train station** (☎ 823 810; 202 Đ Haiphong) is served by all *Reunification Express* trains, with stops including Hué (40,000d, 2½ to four hours, seven daily), Lang Co (13,000d, 1½ to two hours, four daily), Quang Ngai

(47,000d, 2½ to four hours, six daily), Tuy Hoa (153,000d, seven to 10 hours, five daily) and Nha Trang (203,000d, 8½ to 12½ hours, seven daily).

The train ride to Hué is one of the best in the country – it's worth taking as an excursion in itself.

Getting Around

TO/FROM THE AIRPORT

Danang's airport is just 2km west of the city centre, close enough to reach by *xe om* in 10 minutes (around 10,000d). A metered taxi to the centre costs about 20,000d.

CYCLO & XE OM

Danang has plenty of motorbike taxis and *cyclo* drivers; take the usual caution and be prepared to bargain the fare. Trips around town shouldn't cost more than 10,000d to 15,000d. Be careful of *xe om* drivers at night offering to take you to bars/girls – you may find yourself heavied into parting with hundreds of dollars.

TAXI

Both **Airport Taxi** (☎ 27 27 27) and **VN Taxis** (☎ 52 52 52) provide modern vehicles with air-con and meters.

AROUND DANANG

Nam O Beach

Nam O Beach (Map p236) is on the Bay of Danang about 15km northwest of the city. The small local community supported itself for years by producing firecrackers. Since the ban on firecrackers by the government in 1995, the resourceful locals have recently gone into making *nuoc mam* instead – and while it's not as profitable as firecrackers, it's better than nothing.

There is another local speciality here called *goi ca,* which is fresh, raw fish fillets marinated in a special sauce and coated in a spicy powder – something like Vietnamese sushi.

At the time of research a massive new complex, Red Beach Resort, was being built at the city end of the beach.

Nui Son Tra (Monkey Mountain)

Jutting out into the sea like a giant pair of Mickey Mouse ears, the Son Tra peninsula is crowned by the mountain that the American soldiers called Monkey. Until recently Monkey had a military base on its back, but gradually the military has been loosening its grip. An excellent new road winds around the southern edge and several resorts have sprung up – mainly catering to Vietnamese tourists (see below). The large foreigner-friendly Nui Son Tra resort on the isolated eastern side was under construction at the time of research, as was a major bridge linking Tien Sa Port (Cang Tien Sa) with the northern tip of Danang.

A memorial near Nui Song Tra's eastern edge commemorates an unfortunate episode of colonial history. Spanish-led Filipino and French troops attacked Danang in August 1858, ostensibly to end Emperor Tu Duc's mistreatment of Catholics. The city quickly fell, but the invaders had to contend with cholera, dysentery, scurvy, typhus and mysterious fevers. By the summer of 1859, the number of invaders who had died of illness was 20 times the number of those who had been killed in combat.

Many of the **tombs** (Map p236; admission free) of the Spanish and French soldiers are below a chapel near Tien Sa Port. The names of the dead are written on the walls. To get here, cross Song Han Bridge and turn left onto Đ Ngo Quyen, continuing north to the port. The ossuary, a small white building, stands on the right on a low hill, about 500m before the gate of the port and below the chapel.

The sheltered **Tien Sa Beach** (Map p236), behind the port and the chapel, is quiet and calm, with clear water. It's good for a swim if you can ignore the litter, and there are great views across to the Hai Van Pass.

SLEEPING & EATING

Bai Rang (Map p236; ☎ 0511-971 904; Son Tra; r 150,000d) This place will only appeal to a certain type of backpacker. Unquestionably the real deal, you'll be sleeping in a thatched roof shack where you may want to check the toilet for frogs before you use it. Take a sleeping mat if you choose to stay. There is a ramshackle restaurant and a boat on poles serving as a bar, all set in a placid bay.

Bien Dong Resort (Map p236; ☎ 0511-990 179; Son Tra; r 300,000d;) Wonderfully isolated, nobody speaks a word of English here. A number of tidy bungalows are dotted around the edge of the jungle. There are two swimming pools for those bored with the idyllic beach, as well as a restaurant and bar. Concrete deer guard the grounds.

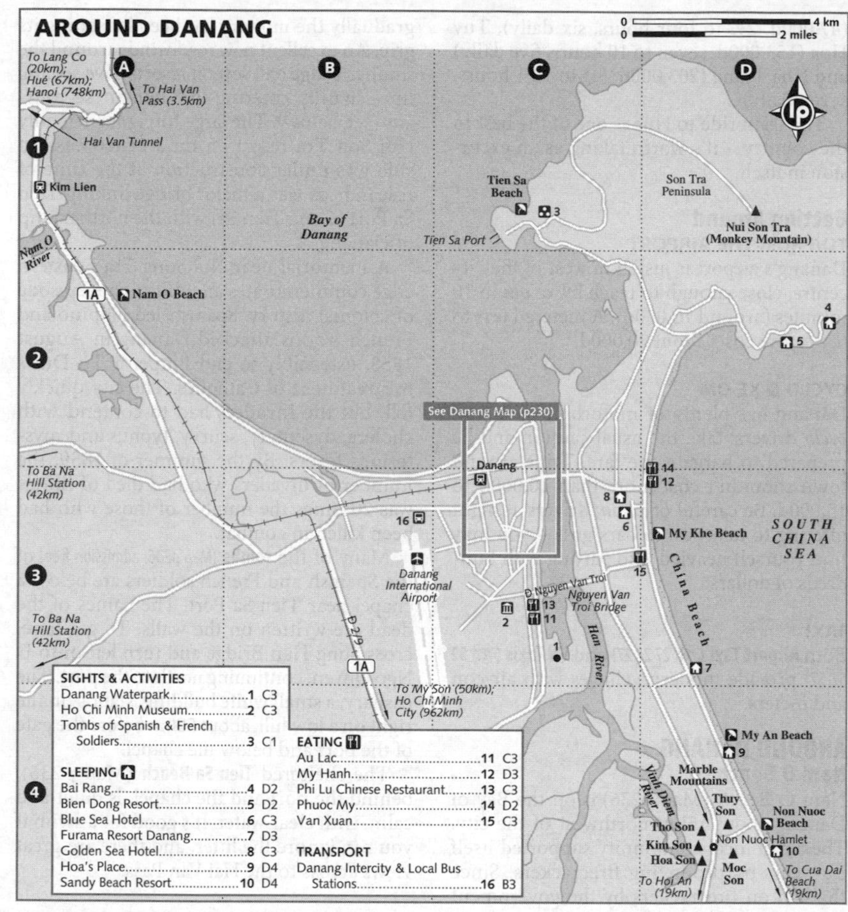

Marble Mountains

A spectacular sight from the new China Beach coastal road, **Marble Mountains** (Map p236; admission 15,000d; 7am-5pm) consist of five craggy marble outcrops topped with delicate pagodas. Ironically, the sculptors based around the mountains now use marble shipped in from China, as locals began to realise that at the rate they were using it, there wouldn't be any marble, or any mountains, left to entice visitors.

Each mountain is said to represent a natural element and is named accordingly: Thuy Son (Water), Moc Son (Wood), Hoa Son (Fire), Kim Son (Metal or Gold) and Tho Son (Earth). The largest and most famous, **Thuy Son**, has a number of natural caves in which first Hindu, and later Buddhist, sanctuaries have been built over the centuries.

Of the two paths leading up Thuy Son, the one closer to the beach (at the end of the village) makes for a better circuit. At the top of the staircase is a gate, **Ong Chon**, which is pockmarked with bullet holes. Behind Ong Chon is **Linh Ong Pagoda**. Entering the sanctuary, look to the left to see a fantastic figure with a huge tongue. To the right of Linh Ong are monks' quarters and a small orchid garden.

Behind Linh Ong, a path leads left through two short tunnels to several caverns known as **Tang Chon Dong**. There are several concrete buddhas and blocks of carved stone of Cham origin in these caves. Near one of the altars is a flight of steps leading up to another cave, partially open to the sky, with two seated Buddhas in it.

Immediately to the left as you enter Ong Chon Gate is the main path to the rest of Thuy Son. Stairs off the main pathway lead to **Vong Hai Da**, a viewpoint for a brilliant panorama of China Beach.

The stone-paved path continues to the right and into a canyon. On the left is **Van Thong Cave**. Opposite the entrance is a cement Buddha, and behind that there is a narrow passage that leads up to a natural chimney open to the sky.

Exit the canyon and pass through a battle-scarred masonry gate. There's a rocky path to the right, which goes to **Linh Nham**, a tall chimney-shaped cave with a small altar inside. Nearby, another path leads to **Hoa Nghiem**, a shallow cave with a Buddha inside. If you go down the passageway to the left of the Buddha, you come to cathedral-like **Huyen Khong Cave**, lit by an opening to the sky. The entrance to this spectacular chamber is guarded by two administrative mandarins (to the left of the doorway) and two military mandarins (to the right).

Scattered about the cave are Buddhist and Confucian shrines; note the inscriptions carved into the stone walls. On the right a door leads to two stalactites, dripping water that comes from heaven, according to local legend. Actually, only one stalactite drips; the other one supposedly ran dry when Emperor Tu Duc touched it. During the American War this chamber was used by the VC as a field hospital. Inside is a plaque dedicated to the Women's Artillery Group, which destroyed 19 US aircraft from a base below the mountains in 1972.

Just to the left of the masonry gate is **Tam Thai Tu**, a pagoda restored by Emperor Minh Mang in 1826. A path heading obliquely to the right goes to the monks' residence, beyond which are two shrines. From there a red dirt path leads to five small pagodas. Before you arrive at the monks' residence, stairs on the left-hand side of the path lead to **Vong Giang Dai**, which offers a fantastic 180-degree view of the other Marble Mountains and the surrounding countryside. To get to the stairway follow the path straight on from the gate.

A torch (flashlight) is handy for exploring the caves. Local children have learned that foreigners buy souvenirs and leave tips for unsolicited guided tours, so you won't begin your visit alone. And watch your wallets! The local government adopted a regulation that the children cannot take tips, but can sell souvenirs. This seems counterproductive; most travellers would rather tip the kids for the guided tours than buy the sorry souvenirs on offer. In general, the kids are good-natured, if extremely persistent, and some of the caves are difficult to find without their assistance.

Local buses between Danang and Hoi An (tickets 8000d) can drop you at Marble Mountains, 19km north of Hoi An.

Non Nuoc Hamlet

Non Nuoc Hamlet is on the southern side of Thuy Son and is a few hundred metres west of Non Nuoc Beach. The marble carvings made here would make great gifts if they didn't weigh so much. It's fun to watch the carvers at work, and there are some tiny carved figures that make nice presents.

The town has been spruced up for tourism. During the war, the Americans referred to the shantytown near here as 'Dogpatch', after a derelict town in the comic strip *L'il Abner*. Most of the residents living here at the time were refugees fleeing the fighting in the surrounding countryside.

China Beach

Thanks to the eponymous 1980s TV series, China Beach will forever be associated with pretty young military nurses complaining about their love lives to the accompaniment of the Rolling Stones' *Paint It Black*. During the war the Americans used the name to refer to the beautiful 30km swoop of fine white sand that starts at Monkey Mountain and finishes near Hoi An, with the Marble Mountains near its centre. The part they were most familiar with was the area close to Danang where soldiers stationed all over the country would be sent for some R&R. For some, a picnic on the beach was their last meal before their return to combat by helicopter.

The Vietnamese call sections of the beach by different names, including My Khe, My An, Non Nuoc and Cua Dai. In the last decade a clever entrepreneur cashing in on the TV series started calling the area in front of his hotel China Beach – although it's considerably south of where the Americans hung out.

While My Khe is now basically a suburb of Danang and Cua Dai is widely considered Hoi An's beach, much of the area in between

WARNING

The best time for swimming at China Beach is from May to July, when the sea is at its calmest. During other times the water can get rough; lifeguards only patrol parts of the beach. The dangerous winter conditions go hand-in-hand with large breakers, which are ideal for surfing – if you know what you're doing.

is gorgeously undeveloped. Not for long, however: a major four-lane dual carriageway has just been built along the entire length, with the beginnings of side roads starting and then abruptly stopping in the sand after a few metres. As you drive through small towns you can see where houses have been cut in half to widen the route.

The beachfront land has been divided into parcels with the government actively encouraging resort development. This could easily turn into another Mui Ne (see p300), with the open sandy vista hidden by the walls of luxury resorts. There are already a number of exclusive resorts at Cua Dai; quite how developers would fill another 30 is anyone's guess. Like Mui Ne, it may result in prices falling in the future.

In December 1992 China Beach was the site of the first international surfing competition in Vietnam. The surf can be very good from around mid-September to December, particularly in the morning when wind conditions are right.

MY KHE BEACH

Just across the Song Han Bridge (10,000d by *xe om*), My Khe is fast becoming Danang's easternmost suburb. In the early morning and evening the beach fills up with city-siders doing Tai Chi. After dark the deckchairs are more in demand than during the day, with young couples escaping crowded family homes for a starlit canoodle. Offshore the lights of the squid boats are a surreal sight – like a floating highway.

The water has a dangerous undertow, especially in winter. However, it is safer than the rest of China Beach; the bulk of Nui Son Tra protects it from winds that whip up rough surf.

This was the part of China Beach well known to American servicemen, and unfortunately a sleazy undertone lingers in parts.

Sleeping

The main beachside hotels are all looking a little shabby, but a couple of new entrants in the surrounding streets offer better value.

Blue Sea Hotel (Map p236; ☎ 0511-942 426; blueseahotel@gmail.com; 235 Đ Nguyen Van Thoai; r US$20-40; ❄) This friendly midsized hotel offers new and spotless rooms with satellite TV, fridges and bathtubs. Take the lane beside the My Khe Hotel and turn left at the end.

Golden Sea Hotel (Map p236; ☎ 0511-936 666; goldenseahotel@vnn.vn; B26-29 Đ Pham Van Dong; r US$25-30, ste US$50; ❄ 💻) Well positioned halfway between the city and beach, the large new Golden Sea Hotel is in walking distance of both. Breakfast and internet access are provided free, and the suites have a steam room attached.

Eating & Drinking

My Khe Beach is rightly known for its excellent seafood restaurants.

My Hanh (Map p236; ☎ 0511-831 494; 18 Đ Du Lich Son Tra; mains 80,000d; 🕑 lunch & dinner) My Khe Beach's most famous restaurant, it serves a wide selection of fish, shrimp, squid, eel and crab dishes on its seaside terrace.

Van Xuan (Map p236; ☎ 0511-941 234; 233A Đ Nguyen Van Thoai; dishes 18,000-100,000d; 🕑 lunch & dinner) An upmarket addition, Van Xuan has large tanks of live fish, lobsters and crocodiles. The owner once lived in Prague, and the restaurant brews its own Czech-style Five Mountains Beer.

Also worth trying is **Phuoc My** (Map p236; ☎ 0511-831 962; Đ Du Lich Son Tra; meals 25,000-100,000d; 🕑 lunch & dinner) – a giggle-inducing name when pronounced correctly.

MY AN & NON NUOC BEACHES

The central section of China Beach is the least developed, with only a few hamlets and isolated resorts. It also offers the best surfing and diving.

Sleeping & Eating

Hoa's Place (Map p236; ☎ 0511-969 216; My An Beach; hoasplace@hotmail.com; r U$6) This joint is small-scale, low key and laid back. Hoa and his wife ensure their home is your home. Good food and cheap beer (6000d) make it a smart lunch stop for passers-by. Take the second turning on the left past Furama heading south.

Sandy Beach Resort (Map p236; ☎ 0511-836 216; www.sandybeachdanang.com; 255 Đ Huyen Tran Cong Chua, Non Nuoc Beach; s US$85-214, d US$90-219, bungalow US$120-231, villa US$160-375; ❄ 💻 🏊) An older resort given a make-over, Sandy Beach has intriguing echoes of 1970s socialist architecture, but it's clean and smart with two swimming pools, three bars and two restaurants. It has a wonderful location – just south of the Marble Mountains – on an isolated stretch of sand patrolled by its own lifeguards. Wi-fi internet is free.

Furama Resort Danang (Map p236; ☎ 0511-847 888; www.furamavietnam.com; 68 Đ Ho Xuan Huong, My An Beach; s US$207-299, d US$230-322, ste US$575-690;) This is Danang's luxury hotel. In fact, for a long time it was Vietnam's luxury hotel. Perched on a private slice of China Beach, this lavish resort features a diving facility, a golf driving range, a gym and two pools, one with a waterfall. Rooms have opulent bathrooms and the finest five-star trim. Day-use of the grounds, pools and fitness centre is US$12 for nonguests. The restaurant is excellent although pricy; expect an extra US$14 charge for breakfast.

CUA DAI BEACH

The fine sands of palm-lined Cua Dai Beach are popular at weekends, but can be deserted at other times. Safe swimming is usually only possible between April and October, but it's nice to walk or just hang out here. During the full moon, people wander around until late at night. Fresh seafood and refreshments are sold at a line of restaurants along the beachfront, all of which have deckchairs for hire.

Cua Dai Beach is 5km east of Hoi An on Đ Cua Dai.

Activities

Cua Dai is a good base for scuba divers exploring the nearby Cu Lao Cham Marine Park, 25 minutes away by speedboat (see p261). Vietnam's longest-standing and best-respected dive company, **Rainbow Divers** (☎ 0510-927 678; www.divevietnam.com) has a base at Cua Dai Beach, at the Hoi An Beach Resort. For certified divers, two dives cost US$75. Training is available for beginners.

Cua Dai Beach is also the home of **Hoian Eco-Tour** (☎ 0510-927 808; www.hoianecotour.com; 7 Đ Cua Dai Beach; tours US$35-50), which offers a range of tours giving an insight into traditional Vietnamese life, including river and sea fishing.

Sleeping

Cua Dai is home to some of the priciest resorts in Vietnam. If you're after a bargain, head for Hoi An.

Victoria Hoi An Resort (☎ 0510-927 040; www.victoriahotels-asia.com; r US$121-202, ste US$242;) Sitting on a huge slice of beach, this resort boasts all the stylish facilities you'd expect for the price, including a large pool, a separate children's pool and free wi-fi. Low-season discounts are usually available.

Palm Garden Resort (☎ 0510-927 927; www.palmgardenresort.com.vn; Đ Lac Long Quan; r US$173-225, bungalow US$248-282, ste US$1380;) Another massive, super-flash new resort taking up a big chunk of beautiful beachfront, this one has an immense pool with a fountain and spouting dolphins, and a huge boat-shaped bar-restaurant. Active types can hire surfboards, windsurfers and jet skis, and there's a beach volleyball court set up.

Luxury junkies should keep an eye out for the **Nam Hai** (☎ 0510-940 000; www.ghmhotels.com; villas US$550-2300;). Not open at the time of research, it promises an exquisitely designed luxury village of villas, each with their own private pool.

HOI AN

☎ 0510 / pop 79,600

A highlight of any trip to Vietnam, Hoi An is a town oozing charm and history, having largely escaped the destruction of successive wars. Once a sleepy riverside village, it's now quite definitely a tourist town – with hotels, restaurants, bars, tailors and souvenir shops dominating the old centre. Despite this air of irreality, Hoi An's charisma pervades.

The local People's Committee periodically clamps down on touts, and while this doesn't mean a completely hassle-free visit, a stroll down the street is usually more relaxed here than in Hué or Nha Trang. Hoi An is pedestrian-friendly: the Old Town is closed to cars and the distances from the hotels to the centre are walkable. It's a great place to hire a bike.

Known as Faifo to Western traders, from the 17th to 19th centuries it was one of Southeast Asia's major international ports. Vietnamese ships and sailors based here sailed all around Vietnam, Thailand and Indonesia.

Perhaps more than any other place in Vietnam, Hoi An retains a sense of history that envelops you as you explore it. This is especially true on 'Hoi An Legendary Night'. Every month on the full moon, motorbikes are banned from the Old Town, which is transformed into a magical land of silk lanterns, traditional food, song and dance, and games in the streets.

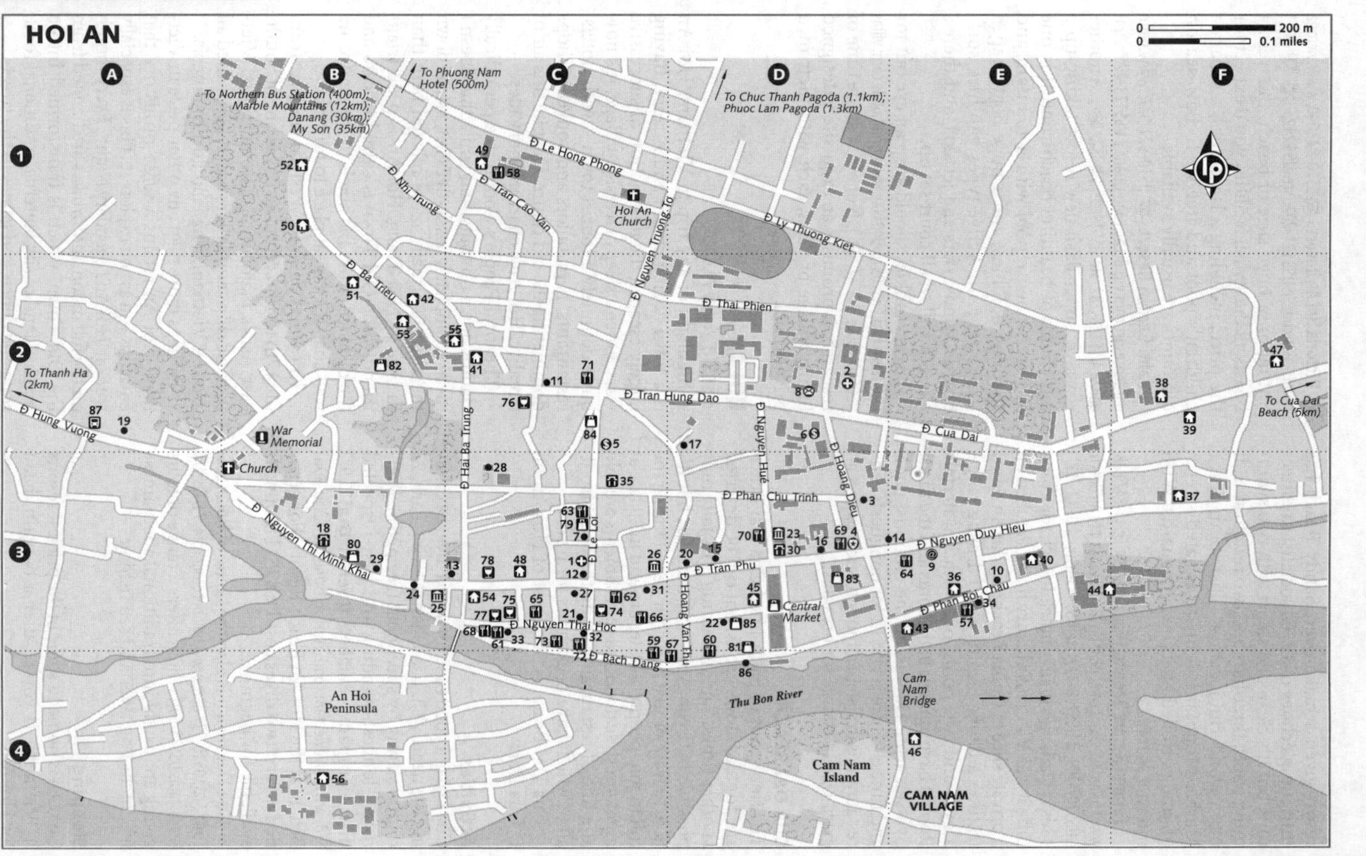
HOI AN
0 200 m
0 0.1 miles
To Northern Bus Station (400m); Marble Mountains (12km); Danang (30km); My Son (35km)
To Phuong Nam Hotel (500m)
To Chuc Thanh Pagoda (1.1km); Phuoc Lam Pagoda (1.3km)
To Thanh Ha (2km)
To Cua Dai Beach (5km)
Đ Le Hong Phong
Đ Nhi Trung
Đ Tran Cao Van
Hoi An Church
Đ Nguyen Truong To
Đ Ly Thuong Kiet
Đ Ba Trieu
Đ Thai Phien
Đ Tran Hung Dao
Đ Hung Vuong
War Memorial
Church
Đ Hai Ba Trung
Đ Cua Dai
Đ Nguyen Hué
Đ Hoang Dieu
Đ Phan Chu Trinh
Đ Le Loi
Đ Nguyen Thi Minh Khai
Đ Nguyen Duy Hieu
Đ Tran Phu
Đ Hoang Van Thu
Đ Phan Boi Chau
Central Market
Đ Nguyen Thai Hoc
Đ Bach Dang
An Hoi Peninsula
Thu Bon River
Cam Nam Bridge
Cam Nam Island
CAM NAM VILLAGE

INFORMATION

Dr Ho Huu Phuoc Practice....1 C3
Hoi An Hospital....2 D2
Hoi An Police Station....3 D3
Incombank....4 C2
Incombank....5 D2
Khai Tri....6 C3
Main Post Office....7 D2
Min's Computer....8 E3
Nga....9 E3
Sinh Café....10 C2
Tourist Service Office....11 C3

SIGHTS & ACTIVITIES

Assembly Hall of the Cantonese Chinese Congregation....12 C3
Assembly Hall of the Chaozhou Chinese Congregation....13 E3
Assembly Hall of the Fujian Chinese Congregation....14 D3
Assembly Hall of the Hainan Chinese Congregation....15 D3
Ba Le Well....16 D2
Cam Pho Temple....17 B3
Cao Dai Pagoda....18 A2
Chinese All-Community Assembly Hall....19 D3
Diep Dong Nguyen House....20 C3
Handicraft Workshop....21 D3
Hoi An Museum of History & Culture....22 D3
Hoi An Old Town Booth....23 D3
Japanese Covered Bridge....24 B3
Museum of Sa Huynh Culture & Museum of the Revolution....25 B3
Museum of Trading Ceramics....26 C3
Old House at 103 Tran Phu....27 C3
Phac Hat Pagoda....28 C3
Phung Hung Old House....29 B3
Quan Cong Temple....30 D3
Quan Thang House....31 C3
Rainbow Divers....32 C3
Tan Ky House....33 C3
Tran Duong House....34 E3
Tran Family Chapel....35 C3

SLEEPING

An Huy Hotel....36 E3
An Phu Hotel....37 F3
Glory Hotel Hoi An....38 F2
Green Field Hotel....39 F2
Ha An Hotel....40 E3
Hoi Pho Hotel....41 C2
Hop Yen Hotel....42 B2
Huy Hoang 1 Hotel....43 E3
Life Resort Hoi An....44 E3
Minh A Ancient Lodging House....45 D3
Pho Hoi Riverside Resort....46 E4
Phu Thinh II Hotel....47 F2
Phu Tinh I Hotel....48 C3
Phuoc An Hotel....49 C1
Thanh Xuan Hotel....50 B1
Thien Nga Hotel....51 B2
Thien Thanh Hotel....52 B1
Thuy Doung 3 Hotel....53 B2
Vinh Hung 1 Hotel....54 C3
Vinh Hung 2 Hotel....55 C2
Vinh Hung Resort....56 B4

EATING

Brothers Café....57 E3
Café 43....58 C1
Café Can....59 C4
Café des Amis....60 D4
Cargo Club....61 C3
Dac San Hoi An....62 C3
Good Morning Vietnam....63 C3
Green Moss....64 E3
Hai Scout Café....65 C3
Hoai River Restaurant....66 C3
Hoi An Hai San....67 D4
Mango Rooms....68 C3
Mermaid Restaurant....69 D3
Miss Ly Cafeteria 22....70 D3
Omar Khayyam's Indian Restaurant....71 C2
Quan Loan....72 C3
Restaurant Café 96....73 C3

DRINKING

Before & Now....74 C3
Lounge Bar x....75 C3
Re-Treat Café....76 C2
Tam Tam Cafe....77 C3
Treat's Café....78 C3

SHOPPING

A Dong Silk....79 C3
Art Galleries....80 B3
Ceramics Shops....81 D4
Faifoo....82 B2
Hoi An Cloth Market....83 D3
Phuoc An....84 C2
Reaching Out....(see 61)
Yaly....85 D3

TRANSPORT

Boat Landing....86 D4
Hoi An Bus Station....87 A2

Every year during the rainy season, particularly in October and November, Hoi An has problems with flooding, especially in areas close to the waterfront. The greatest flood ever recorded in Hoi An took place in 1964, when the water reached all the way up to the roof beams of the houses. In late 2006 the town bore the brunt of the worst typhoon in 50 years, although at the time of research repairs were well in hand.

There's plenty to do in Hoi An. Emphatically the most enchanting place along the coast, this is one spot worth lingering in.

History

Recently excavated ceramic fragments from 2200 years ago constitute the earliest evidence of human habitation in the Hoi An area. They are thought to belong to the late-Iron Age Sa Huynh civilisation, which is related to the Dong Son culture of northern Vietnam.

From the 2nd to the 10th centuries, this was a busy seaport of the Champa kingdom (see p264). Persian and Arab documents from the latter part of the period mention Hoi An as a provisions stop. Archaeologists have uncovered the foundations of numerous Cham towers around Hoi An: the bricks and stones were reused by Vietnamese settlers.

In 1307 the Cham king married the daughter of a monarch of the Tran dynasty and presented Quang Nam province to the Vietnamese as a gift. After his death, his successor refused to recognise the deal and fighting broke out: for the next century chaos reigned. By the 15th century peace had been restored, allowing normal commerce to resume. During the next four centuries Chinese, Japanese, Dutch, Portuguese, Spanish, Indian, Filipino, Indonesian, Thai, French, British and American ships came to Hoi An to purchase high-grade silk (for which the area is famous), fabrics, paper, porcelain, tea, sugar, molasses, areca nuts, pepper, Chinese medicines, elephant tusks, beeswax, mother-of-pearl, lacquer, sulphur and lead.

The Chinese and Japanese traders sailed south in the spring, driven by winds from the northeast. They would stay in Hoi An until the summer, when southerly winds would blow them home. During their four-month sojourn in Hoi An, the merchants rented waterfront houses for use as warehouses and living quarters. Some traders began leaving full-time agents in Hoi An to take care of off-season business affairs. This is how foreign colonies got started, although the Japanese ceased coming to Hoi An after 1637, when the Japanese government forbade all contact with the outside world.

Hoi An was the site of the first Chinese settlement in southern Vietnam. The town's Chinese *hoi quan* (congregational assembly halls) still play a special role among southern Vietnam's ethnic Chinese, some of whom come to Hoi An from all over the region to participate in congregation-wide celebrations. Today 1300 of Hoi An's population of 75,800 are ethnic Chinese. Relations between ethnic Vietnamese and ethnic Chinese in Hoi An are excellent, partly because the Chinese have become assimilated to the point where they even speak Vietnamese among themselves.

This was also the first place in Vietnam to be exposed to Christianity. Among the 17th-century missionary visitors was the French priest Alexandre de Rhodes, who devised the Latin-based *quoc ngu* script for the Vietnamese language.

Hoi An was almost completely destroyed during the Tay Son Rebellion. It was rebuilt and continued to serve as an important port for foreign trade until the late 19th century, when the Thu Bon River (Cai River), which links Hoi An with the sea, silted up and became too shallow for navigation. During this period Danang (Tourane) began to eclipse Hoi An as a port and centre of commerce. In 1916 a rail line linking Danang with Hoi An was destroyed in a terrible storm; it was never rebuilt.

Under French rule Hoi An served as an administrative centre. During the American War the city, with the cooperation of both sides, remained almost completely undamaged.

Orientation

The Thu Bon River forms the southern edge of the Old Town. Bridges link this to the An Hoi Peninsula and Cam Nam Island. The newer part of town stretches to the north. The road to Cua Dai Beach heads east. Many streets have changed names and/or been renumbered. In some cases the old and new numbers sit side by side on buildings.

Information

BOOKSHOPS

Khai Tri (52 Đ Le Loi) Sells secondhand books and dodgy copies.

EMERGENCY

Hoi An Police Station (☎ 861 204; 84 Đ Hoang Dieu)

INTERNET ACCESS

Min's Computer (☎ 914 323; 125 Đ Nguyen Duy Hieu; per hr 4000d) Access is slow throughout Hoi An, but this is as good as any.

MEDICAL SERVICES

Dr Ho Huu Phuoc Practice (☎ 867 419; 74 Đ Le Loi; ⏲ 11am-12.30pm & 5-7.30pm Mon-Fri, 7am-12.30pm Sat & Sun) A local doctor who speaks English.

Hoi An Hospital (☎ 861 364; 4 Đ Tran Hung Dao) If it's anything serious, make for Danang.

MONEY

Incombank (☎ 861 261; 4 Đ Hoang Dieu) This branch and another at 9 Đ Le Loi both change cash and travellers cheques, offer Visa advances and have ATMs.

POST

Main post office (☎ 861 480; 6 Đ Tran Hung Dao)

TRAVEL AGENCIES

Competition is pretty fierce, so for expensive or complicated arrangements it's probably worth checking out a few options and negotiating.

Hoi An Old Town Booth (Đ Hoang Dieu) A handy spot to pick up an Old Town ticket.

Nga (☎ 863 485; lenga22us@yahoo.com; 22 Đ Phan Boi Chau) Handles plane, train and open-tour bus bookings, tours to My Son and Cham Island, boat trips and car rentals.

Sinh Café (☎ 863 948; www.sinhcafévn.com; 18B Đ Phan Dinh Phung) Books reputable open-tour buses.

Tourist Service Office (☎ 862 952; 78 Đ Le Loi) Also books good open-tour buses

Dangers & Annoyances

Generally speaking, Hoi An is one of the safer towns in Vietnam, but there have been stories of late-night bag-snatching in the poorly lit market area of town.

We have also heard accounts of women being followed to their hotels and assaulted on very rare occasions. If you are a lone female, try and make sure you walk home with somebody. In the very unlikely event that something like this happens, shout and scream as Hoi An is a very quiet town by night.

A worrying trend here as in other parts of Vietnam is the use of children to sell trinkets, postcards and newspapers. Don't be fooled into thinking that the kids actually see the money themselves. One can only hope that if tourists stop buying from the children, their controllers will stop using them – perhaps freeing them to pursue an education.

Sights

Now a Unesco World Heritage site, **Hoi An Old Town** (www.hoianworldheritage.org; entrance ticket 75,000d) is governed by preservation laws that are well up to speed. Several buildings of historical and cultural significance are open for public viewing, a number of streets in the centre of town are off-limits to cars, and building alterations and height restrictions are well enforced. If only Hanoi would follow suit in its historic Old Quarter.

The admission fee goes towards funding this conservation work. This ticket gives you a complicated choice of heritage attractions to visit. You can attend a traditional music show at the handicraft workshop, and one each of the four following types of attractions: museums; assembly halls; old houses; and 'other'. If you want to visit additional attractions, then it is necessary to buy another ticket; there are ticket offices dotted around the centre.

But for those who only want to buy one ticket, what are the best options? The most interesting museum is that of Trading Ceramics, mainly for the building it's housed in. Among the assembly halls, the Fujian folk probably have the edge. When it comes to old houses, the Tran Family Chapel offers an interesting and informative tour. Finally there is that obscure 'other' category: the shrine in the Japanese Bridge or Quan Cong Temple. Choose the temple: the Japanese Bridge ticket just gets you into a small shrine that is second-best to the bridge itself, which you can enjoy free.

The system doesn't seem to be too well monitored, but hopefully the fees do get collected and end up as part of the restoration and preservation fund. Not all of Hoi An's old houses and assembly halls require a ticket, and there's certainly nothing to stop anybody from wandering the old streets to admire the houses.

Despite the number of tourists who come to Hoi An, it is still a conservative town, and visitors should dress modestly when visiting the sites.

JAPANESE COVERED BRIDGE

This famed **bridge** (Cau Nhat Ban) connects Đ Tran Phu with Đ Nguyen Thi Minh Khai. The first bridge on this site was constructed in the 1590s. It was built by the Japanese community of Hoi An in order to link them with the Chinese quarters across the stream.

The Japanese Covered Bridge is very solidly constructed; the original builders were concerned about the threat of earthquakes. Over the centuries the ornamentation has remained relatively faithful to the original Japanese design. Its understatement contrasts greatly with the Vietnamese and Chinese penchant for wild decoration. The French flattened out the roadway to make it suitable for their motor vehicles, but the original arched shape was restored during major renovation work in 1986.

Built into the northern side of the bridge is a small **temple** (Chua Cau; admission Hoi An Old Town ticket). The writing over its door is the name given to the bridge in 1719 to replace the name meaning Japanese Covered Bridge. However the new name, Lai Vien Kieu (Bridge for Passers-by from Afar), never quite caught on.

According to legend, there once lived an enormous monster called Cu, who had its head in India, its tail in Japan and its body in Vietnam. Whenever the monster moved, terrible disasters such as floods and earthquakes befell Vietnam. This bridge was built on the monster's weakest point and killed it, but the people of Hoi An took pity on the slain monster and built this temple to pray for its soul.

The entrances of the bridge are guarded by a pair of monkeys on one side and a pair of dogs on the other. According to one story, these animals were popularly revered because many of Japan's emperors were born in years of the dog and monkey. Another tale says that construction of the bridge started in the year of the monkey and was finished in the year of the dog.

The stelae, listing all the Vietnamese and Chinese contributors to a subsequent restoration of the bridge, are written in *chu nho* (Chinese characters) – the *nom* script had not yet become popular in these parts.

MUSEUMS

Showcasing a collection of blue and white ceramics of the Dai Viet period, the **Museum of Trading Ceramics** (80 Đ Tran Phu; admission Hoi An Old Town ticket) occupies a simply restored house made of dark wood. In particular, check out the great ceramic mosaic that's set above the pond in the inner courtyard.

Housed in the Quan Am Pagoda, the **Hoi An Museum of History & Culture** (7 Đ Nguyen Hué; admission Hoi An Old Town ticket; 8am-5pm) has a small collection of bronze temple bells, gongs and Cham artefacts.

Artefacts from the early Dong Son civilisation of Sa Huynh are displayed downstairs at the **Museum of Sa Huynh Culture & Museum of the Revolution** (149 Đ Tran Phu; admission Hoi An Old Town ticket; 8am-5pm). Upstairs, the Revolution museum has the usual collection of local photos and mementos of the last two wars, including a boat used to transport cadres. It would be more accessible if full English captions were provided.

ASSEMBLY HALLS

Assembly Hall of the Fujian Chinese Congregation

Founded as a place to hold community meetings, this **assembly hall** (Phuc Kien; opposite 35 Đ Tran Phu; admission Hoi An Old Town ticket) was later transformed into a temple for the worship of Thien Hau, a deity from Fujian province. The triple gate to the complex was built in 1975.

The mural on the right-hand wall near the entrance to the main hall depicts Thien Hau, her way lit by lantern light as she crosses a stormy sea to rescue a foundering ship. On the wall opposite is a mural of the heads of the six Fujian families who fled from China to Hoi An in the 17th century, following the overthrow of the Ming dynasty.

The penultimate chamber contains a statue of Thien Hau. To either side of the entrance stand red-skinned Thuan Phong Nhi and green-skinned Thien Ly Nhan. When either sees or hears sailors in distress, they inform Thien Hau, who sets off to effect a rescue. The replica of a Chinese boat along the right-hand wall is 1:20 scale.

The central altar in the last chamber contains seated figures of the heads of the six Fujian families. The smaller figures below them represent their successors as clan leaders. Behind the altar on the left is the God of Prosperity. On the right are three fairies and smaller figures representing the 12 *ba mu* (midwives), each of whom teaches newborns a different skill necessary for the first year of life: smiling, sucking, lying on their stomachs and so forth. Childless couples often come here to pray for offspring. The three groups of figures in this chamber represent the elements most central to Chinese life: ancestors, children and financial wellbeing.

The middle altar of the room to the right of the courtyard commemorates deceased leaders of the Fujian congregation. On either side are lists of contributors – women on the left and men on the right. The wall panels represent the four seasons.

The Fujian assembly hall is fairly well lit and can be visited after dark. Shoes should be removed upon mounting the platform just past the naves.

Assembly Hall of the Cantonese Chinese Congregation

Founded in 1786, this **assembly hall** (176 Đ Tran Phu; admission Hoi An Old Town ticket; 8am-5pm) has a main altar that is dedicated to Quan Cong (see p246). Note the long-handled brass fans to either side of the altar. The lintel and door posts of the main entrance and a number of the columns supporting the roof are made of single blocks of granite. The other columns were carved out of the durable wood of the jackfruit tree. There are intricate carvings on the wooden beams that support the roof in front of the main entrance.

Assembly Hall of the Chaozhou Chinese Congregation

The Chaozhou Chinese in Hoi An built their **congregational hall** (Trieu Chau; opposite 157 Đ Nguyen Duy Hieu; admission Hoi An Old Town ticket; 8am-5pm) in 1776. Some outstanding woodcarvings are on the beams, walls and altar. On the doors in front of the altar are carvings of two Chinese girls wearing their hair in a Japanese style.

Chinese All-Community Assembly Hall

Founded in 1773, the **Chinese All-Community Assembly Hall** (Chua Ba; ☎ 861 935; 64 Tran Phu; admission free) was used by Fujian, Cantonese, Hainan, Chaozhou and Hakka congregations in Hoi An. The pavilions off the main courtyard incorporate elements of 19th-century French architecture.

Assembly Hall of the Hainan Chinese Congregation

Built in 1851, this **assembly hall** (10 Đ Tran Phu; admission free; 8am-5pm) is a memorial to 108 merchants from Hainan Island who were mistaken for pirates and killed in Quang Nam province during the reign of Emperor Tu Duc. The elaborate dais contains plaques to their memory. In front of the central altar is a fine gilded woodcarving of Chinese court life.

OLD HOUSES

Tan Ky House

Built two centuries ago as the home of a well-to-do ethnic-Vietnamese merchant, **Tan Ky House** (☎ 861 474; 101 Đ Nguyen Thai Hoc; admission Hoi An Old Town ticket; 8am-noon & 2-4.30pm) has been lovingly preserved and today looks almost exactly as it did in the early 19th century.

The design of Tan Ky House shows some evidence of the Japanese and Chinese influence on local architecture. Japanese elements include the ceiling (in the area immediately before the courtyard), which is supported by three progressively shorter beams, one on top of the other. There are similar beams in the salon. Under the crab-shell ceiling there are carvings of crossed sabres wrapped in silk ribbon. The sabres symbolise force; the silk represents flexibility.

Chinese poems written in inlaid mother-of-pearl are hung from a number of the columns that hold up the roof. The Chinese characters on these 150-year-old panels are formed entirely of birds gracefully portrayed in various positions of flight.

The courtyard here has several functions: to let in light, provide ventilation, bring a glimpse of nature into the home, and collect rainwater and provide drainage. The stone tiles covering the patio floor were brought from Thanh Hoa province in north-central Vietnam. The carved wooden balcony supports around the courtyard are decorated with grape leaves, which are a European import and further evidence of the unique blending of cultures that took place in Hoi An.

The back of the house faces the river. In the past, this section of the building was rented out to foreign merchants. That the house was a place of commerce as well as a residence is indicated by the two pulleys attached to a beam in the storage loft just inside the front door.

The exterior of the roof is made of tiles; inside, the ceiling consists of wood. This design keeps the house cool in summer and warm in winter. The floor tiles were brought from near Hanoi.

Tan Ky House is a private home; the owner, whose family has lived here for seven generations, speaks fluent French and English.

Tran Family Chapel

The Tran family moved from China to Vietnam in around 1700. Built in 1802, the **Tran Family Chapel** (21 Đ Le Loi; admission Hoi An Old Town ticket) is a house for worshipping ancestors. It was built by one of the Tran clan who ascended to the rank of mandarin and once served as an Ambassador to China. His picture is to the right of the chapel.

The architecture of the building reflects the influence of Chinese and Japanese styles. The central door is reserved for the dead – it's opened at Tet and on the anniversary of the main ancestor. Traditionally, women entered from the left and men from the right, although these distinctions are no longer observed in supposedly egalitarian communist Vietnam.

The wooden boxes on the altar contain the Tran ancestors' stone tablets – featuring chiselled Chinese characters setting out the dates of birth and death – along with some small personal effects. On the anniversary of each family member's death, their box is opened, incense is burned and food is offered. Nowadays photographs have replaced the stone tablets.

There's a museum and souvenir shop at the back of the chapel. The small garden behind is where the placentas of newborn family members are buried – the practice is meant to prevent fighting between the children.

Quan Thang House

This private **house** (77 Tran Phu; admission Hoi An Old Town ticket; 7am-5pm) is three centuries old and has been in the family for six generations, having been built by an ancestor who was a Chinese captain. Again, the architecture includes Japanese and Chinese elements. There is some especially fine carving on the teak walls of the rooms around the courtyard, on the roof beams and under the crab-shell roof (in the salon next to the courtyard). Look out for the green ceramic tiles built into the railing around the courtyard balcony.

Phung Hung Old House

In a lane full of beautiful buildings, this old **house** (4 Đ Nguyen Thi Minh Khai; admission Hoi An Old Town ticket; 8am-7pm) stands out. It's still a family home, having housed eight generations over 226 years. At present it showcases hand embroidery and souvenirs; wander through and enjoy the ambience.

Tran Duong House

There's a whole city block of colonnaded French-colonial buildings on Đ Phan Boi Chau, between Nos 22 and 73, among them the 19th-century **Tran Duong House** (25 Đ Phan Boi Chau; admission free, donations welcome; 9am-6pm). Mr Duong, a charming retired mathematics teacher, speaks English and French, and is happy to explain the history of his 62m-long house that has been in his family for six generations. The large wooden table in the front room is the family bed.

Diep Dong Nguyen House

Built for a wealthy Chinese merchant in the late 19th century is **Diep Dong Nguyen House** (58 Đ Nguyen Thai Hoc; admission free; 8am-noon & 2-4.30pm). The front room on the ground floor was once a dispensary for *thuoc bac* (Chinese medicine); the medicines were stored in the glass-enclosed cases lining the walls. The owner's private collection of antiques – which includes photographs, porcelain and furniture – is on display upstairs. Two of the chairs were once lent by the family to Emperor Bao Dai.

Old House at 103 Đ Tran Phu

The wooden frontage and shutters make a good photographic backdrop to this eclectic **shop** (103 Đ Tran Phu; admission free), where women make silk lanterns.

TEMPLES & PAGODAS

Quan Cong Temple

Founded in 1653, **Quan Cong Temple** (Chua Ong; 24 Đ Tran Phu; admission Hoi An Old Town ticket) is dedicated to Quan Cong – a highly esteemed Chinese general who is worshipped as a symbol of loyalty, sincerity, integrity and justice. His partially gilt statue, made of papier-mâché on a wooden frame, is in the central altar at the back of the sanctuary. On the left is a statue of General Chau Xuong, one of Quan Cong's guardians, striking a tough-guy pose. On the right is the rather camp and plump administrative mandarin Quan Binh. The life-size white horse recalls a mount ridden by Quan Cong, until he was given a red horse of extraordinary endurance, representations of which are common in Chinese pagodas.

Check out the carp-shaped rain spouts on the roof surrounding the courtyard. The carp

ARCHITECTURAL SURVIVORS

Given the amount of bombs dropped on Vietnam in the last 70 years, it's hardly surprising that structures less than a century old are often tagged 'ancient' – leaving tourists wondering why they went out of their way to see a plain French colonial building that wouldn't warrant a second glance on the streets of Sydney or Auckland, let alone Paris or London.

Hoi An is the exception. More than 800 structures of historical significance have been officially identified, including a number of wooden buildings dating from the 18th century. Many exhibit features of traditional architecture rarely seen today.

As they have for centuries, some shopfronts are shuttered at night with horizontal planks inserted into grooves that cut into the columns that support the roof. Some of the buildings' roofs are made up of thousands of brick-coloured *am* and *duong* (Yin and Yang) roof tiles – so called because of the way the alternating rows of concave and convex tiles fit snugly together. During the rainy season the lichens and moss that live on the tiles spring to life, turning entire rooftops bright green.

A number of Hoi An's houses have round pieces of wood with an *am-duong* symbol in the middle surrounded by a spiral design over the doorway. These *mat cua* (door eyes) are supposed to protect the residents from harm.

It's not just individual buildings that have survived – it's whole streetscapes. This is particularly true around the Old Town's Đ Tran Phu and the waterside promenade Đ Bach Dang. In the former French quarter to the east of Cam Nam Bridge there's a whole block of colonnaded houses, painted in the mustard yellow typical of French colonial buildings.

Hoi An's historic structures are gradually being restored and there is a sincere effort being made to preserve the unique character of the city. The local government has put some thought into this: old houses must be licensed for restoration work, which must be done in a tasteful manner. One can only hope that at some point money will be found to bury the mesh of drooping powerlines underground.

is a symbol of patience in Chinese mythology and is popular in Hoi An.

Shoes should be removed when mounting the platform in front of the statue of Quan Cong.

Chuc Thanh Pagoda

Founded in 1454 by Minh Hai, a Buddhist monk from China, **Chuc Thanh Pagoda** (Khu Vuc 7, Tan An; 🕒 8am-6pm) is the oldest pagoda in Hoi An. Among the antique ritual objects still in use are several bells, a stone gong that is two centuries old and a carp-shaped wooden gong said to be even older.

In the main sanctuary the gilt Chinese characters inscribed on a red roof beam give details of the pagoda's construction. An A Di Da Buddha flanked by two Thich Ca Buddhas sits under a wooden canopy on the central dais. In front of them is a statue of a boyhood Thich Ca flanked by his servants.

To get to Chuc Thanh Pagoda, go north all the way to the end of Đ Nguyen Truong To and turn left. Follow the sandy path for 500m.

Phuoc Lam Pagoda

Phuoc Lam Pagoda (Thon 2A, Cam Ha; 🕒 8am-5pm) was founded in the mid-17th century. The head monk at the end of that century was An Thiem, a Vietnamese prodigy who became a monk at the age of eight. When he was 18, the king drafted An Thiem's brothers into his army to put down a rebellion. An Thiem volunteered to take the places of the other men in his family and eventually rose to the rank of general. After the war he returned to monkhood, but felt guilty about the many people he had slain. To atone for his sins, he volunteered to clean the Hoi An Market for 20 years. When that time was up, he was asked to come to Phuoc Lam Pagoda as head monk.

To reach the pagoda, continue past Chuc Thanh Pagoda for 400m. The path passes an obelisk that was erected over the tomb of 13 ethnic Chinese, who had been decapitated by the Japanese during WWII for resistance activities.

Other Temples & Pagodas

Serving the local community, the **Cao Dai pagoda** (88 Đ Hung Vuong), near the bus station, is surrounded by peaceful gardens.

The **Phac Hat Pagoda** (673 Hai Ba Trung) has a colourful façade of ceramics and murals and is an active place of worship.

The less ornate and newish **Cam Pho Temple** (52 Đ Nguyen Thi Minh Khai; 🕒 8am-5pm) is notable mainly for its ceramic dragon roof line.

HANDICRAFT WORKSHOP

Housed in the 200-year-old trading house of a Chinese merchant, the **Handicraft Workshop** (☎ 910 216; 9 Đ Nguyen Thai Hoc; admission Hoi An Old Town ticket) delivers what it promises – in the back section you can watch artisans making silk lanterns and taking part in traditional crafts like embroidery. It's a good place to pick up souvenirs. Fascinating cultural performances are held in the front hall twice daily (10.15am and 3.15pm), featuring traditional singers, dancers and musicians.

BA LE WELL

Said to date from Cham times, this well is square in shape. Its claim to fame is that it's the only place you're able to draw water from if you're to make authentic *cao lau*, a Hoi An specialty (see p250). You're likely to see elderly people making their daily pilgrimage to fill metal pails here. To find it, turn down the alley opposite 35 Đ Phan Chu Trinh and take the second laneway to the right.

Hoi An Walking Tour

This tasty little trail takes you past Hoi An's main sights in a half-day amble. If you want to venture inside some of the buildings, call into the Tourist Service Office (p242) to purchase your Hoi An Old Town ticket before you set off.

Start at the **Tran Family Chapel** (**1**; p245). Head south on Đ Le Loi and turn left at the next junction onto Đ Tran Phu. On your right you'll find **Quan Thang House** (**2**; p245) and a little further on the left, the **Museum of Trading Ceramics** (**3**; p243). Continuing along Đ Tran Phu, there is a cluster of interesting buildings on the left side of the road, including the **Chinese All-Community Assembly Hall** (**4**; p244) and the **Assembly Hall of the Fujian Chinese Congregation** (**5**; p244). Keep heading east and at the next junction take a short detour north on Đ Nguyen Hue to the **Hoi An Museum of History & Culture** (**6**; p244). Back on Tran Phu you'll see the **Quan Cong Temple** (**7**; opposite). Still walking east on Đ Tran Phu, the **Assembly Hall of the Hainan Chinese Congregation** (**8**; p244) is on the left. Cross the next junction and the road becomes Đ Nguyen Duy Hieu. On the left is the **Assembly Hall of the Chaozhou Chinese Congregation** (**9**; p244).

Take the second right and turn right again onto Đ Phan Boi Chau. There is a whole city block of colonnaded French buildings here between Nos 22 and 73, among them the 19th-century **Tran Duong House** (**10**; p246). Wander along Đ Phan Boi Chau, turning right just past the market and then left into Đ Nguyen Thai Hoc and soak up the ambience of this street. On the left is the **Handicraft Workshop** (**11**; p247) – if you time it correctly you might be able to catch a cultural performance. Just past the next street is the intriguingly named **Hoi An Department of Managing & Gathering Swallow's Nests** (**12**; 53 Nguyen Thai Hoc). The nests are gathered from Cham Island twice a year; if you're lucky you'll be able to watch worker's sorting their precious harvest here (see p295).

Turn right onto Đ Le Loi, then left onto Đ Tran Phu. Almost immediately on the left is the **Old House at 103 Tran Phu** (**13**; p246). Keep heading west and you'll pass the **Assembly Hall of the Cantonese Chinese Congregation** (**14**; p244). A little further along on the left is the **Museum of Sa Huynh Culture & Museum of the Revolution** (**15**; p244). Beyond the museum is the famed **Japanese Covered Bridge** (**16**; p243), which connects Đ Tran Phu with Đ Nguyen Thi Minh Khai. Continue westward and keep an eye out for **Phung Hung Old House** (**17**; p245). Also check out **Cam Pho Temple** (**18**; p247).

From here either retrace your steps or continue on to the **Cao Dai Pagoda** (**19**; p247). Then, back across the Japanese bridge, turn right and follow the road onto Đ Nguyen Thai Hoc, where you'll see the **Tan Ky House** (**20**; p245). On the left before the next junction is the **Diep Dong Nguyen House** (**21**; p246). Now you can settle down for a long, cool drink at one of the nearby bars.

WALK FACTS

Distance: 2.5km
Duration: one to five hours (depending on how many sights you visit)
Start: Tran Family Chapel
Finish: Diep Dong Nguyen House

Activities

For eco-tours and swimming at Cua Dai Beach to the east, see p239.

COOKING COURSES

For many visitors to Vietnam the food is a highlight and eating it a serious activity in itself. Hoi An is Foodie Heaven, and budding gourmets who want to take a step further into Vietnamese cuisine will find ample opportunity here. Many of the popular eateries offer cooking classes, and the best bit is that you then get to sit down and enjoy the fruits of your labour.

One of the best classes is offered by Hai Scout Café (see p251) at its **Red Bridge Cooking School** (☎ 933 222; www.visithoian.com; bookings Hai Scout Café). Starting out with a trip to the market, you then cruise down the river to this relaxing retreat about 4km from Hoi An. The lesson includes a tour of the herb garden,

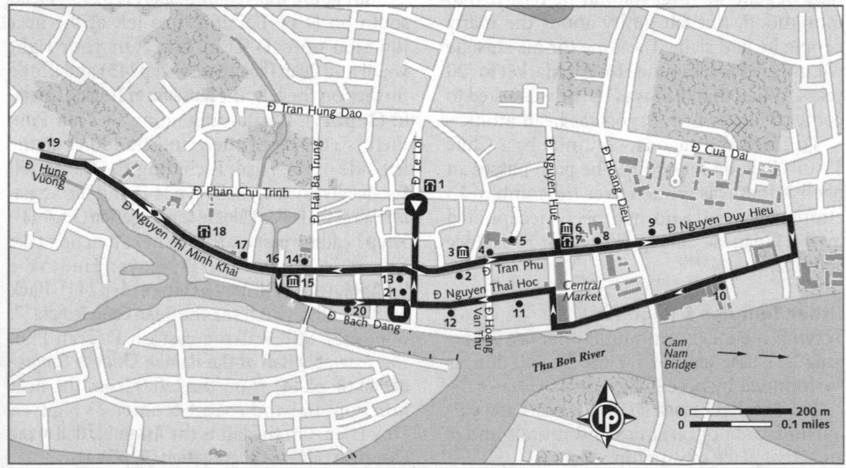

making rice paper, several local specialities and some decorative flourishes – although it's hard to imagine how your dinner party guests back home will react to tomatoes morphed into roses and lotus flowers. The class costs 235,000d per person; it starts at 8.45am and finishes at 1pm. You're given print-outs of the recipes to try at home.

More informal classes can be found at Restaurant Café 96 (50,000d per person; see p251), Green Moss (choose off the menu and pay a US$2 supplement; see p251) and Café des Amis (US$20; see p251).

DIVING

Rainbow Divers (☎ 911 123; www.divevietnam.com; 98 Đ Le Loi) have an office in the Old Town, where you can book dives at Cu Lao Cham Marine Park (p261).

Sleeping

Hoi An has the best-value accommodation in Vietnam, and quite possibly the whole of Asia. Don't be surprised to find a stylish air-conditioned room in a brand-new hotel with free breakfast and a swimming pool for less than US$15. Some places even throw in complimentary bicycles for guests' use.

A building boom has resulted in a glut of options, with 1000 beds added in a six-month period in 2003 alone. Still, if you have your heart set on a particular hotel, you should probably book ahead at busy times.

Considering how small and walkable Hoi An is, there should be no great compulsion to find a place in the heart of the Old Town. In addition, the older hotels in the centre tend to charge the same as the quieter and more spacious ones on the edge, but lack the extras like swimming pools. There's a cluster of new hotels with rear views over rice paddies around Đ Ba Trieu to the north, and several more on the road to the beach (Đ Cua Dai) – although these latter are a good 10-minute walk from the action. Many of the new hotels are second or third incarnations of old favourites, with innovative names like II and III. The most upmarket options are on the riverbank or at nearby Cua Dai Beach (see p239).

Prices listed here are standard rates. Many places advertise two rates for rooms: with or without air-con. It was common for rates to rise during the peak December and January period, but now with such oversupply it is generally no longer the case. Outside of these times you may be able to negotiate a considerable discount.

BUDGET

Hoi Pho Hotel (☎ 916 382; hoiphohotel@yahoo.com; 627 Đ Hai Ba Trung; r US$7-10;) This modest, family-owned minihotel offers straightforward value for money, with clean rooms and attentive service.

Minh A Ancient Lodging House (☎ 861 368; 2 Đ Nguyen Thai Hoc; r US$8-12) Brimming with character, this splendid 180-year-old traditional wooden home is a cross between a B&B and a museum – offering an intriguing insight into Old Town family life. There's an ornate ancestor altar in the front room, a well in the courtyard behind and three guest rooms upstairs.

Huy Hoang I Hotel (☎ 861 453; kshuyhoang1@dng.vnn.vn; 73 Đ Phan Boi Chau; r US$8-20;) While not the cleanest of the budget options, it certainly has the best location – with its terrace restaurant right above the river, next to the Cam Nam Bridge.

Thien Nga Hotel (☎ 916 330; thiennga_hotel@pmail.vnn.vn; 52 Đ Ba Trieu; r US$10-20;) An old favourite that keeps getting better, this little place is terrific value – offering clean, comfortable rooms with views over the rice paddies, an indoor-outdoor swimming pool and free breakfast.

An Phu Hotel (☎ 914 345; anphutourist@hoian.zzn.com; 30 Đ Nguyen Duy Hieu; r US$12-15;) Fans of Asian kitsch need look no further than the temple-like An Phu. Stars twinkle over the reception, dragons hover over the pool and grand staircases curve up to the rooms – where the cheaper ones have ridiculous balconies opening on to a brick wall. Owned by An Phu Tourist, the hotel's a much better proposition than their bus services, which are best avoided.

Thanh Xuan Hotel (☎ 916 696; www.thanhxuanhotel.com; 22-23 Đ Ba Trieu; r US$12-20;) A nifty new place with the best bathtubs you are likely to find for this sort of money. Nice design, nice rooms, nice price.

Green Field Hotel (Dong Xanh Hotel; ☎ 863 484; www.greenfieldhotel.com; 423 Đ Cua Dai; dm US$5, r US$15-40;) Painted a lurid rice-paddy green, the rooms here are comfortable and perks include a free 'happy hour' cocktail, free wi-fi, a pool table and a swimming pool. You'll have to enquire specifically about the basic four-person dorm, as they keep it quiet.

Other budget options:

Hop Yen Hotel (☎ 863 153; hopyenhotel@yahoo.com; Đ Ba Trieu; r US$6-12;) A humble hostel that has helpful staff. The cheapest rate will get you a small room with no air-conditioning up four flights of stairs.

Phu Thinh I Hotel (☎ 861 297; www.phuthinhhotels.com; 144 Đ Tran Phu; r US$8-20;) Some of the rooms are dark and windowless, but the location's great, the price is good and there's a pleasant garden forecourt.

MIDRANGE

Phuong Nam Hotel (☎ 923 401; www.hoianphuongnamhotel.com; 224 Đ Ly Thai To; r US$12-30;) This popular new place with clean, comfy rooms is tied in with the Sinh Café open-tour crowd. The quiet location to the north of town is a blessing and a curse, as there's not much in easy walking distance. Hourly shuttles head to and from the centre and bicycles are provided free of charge.

our pick **Phuoc An Hotel** (☎ 916 757; www.hoianhotels.com.vn; 31/1 Đ Tran Cao Van; r US$12-35;) The staff at this wonderful hotel are exceptionally welcoming, and the rooms attractive and very comfortable – although it can get a little noisy. Bicycles, breakfast and internet access are provided free.

Thien Thanh Hotel (Blue Sky Hotel; ☎ 916 545; www.bluesky-hoian.com; 16 Đ Ba Trieu; r US$15-35;) Most of the rooms have breezy balconies at the back with views over the rice paddies. The hotel is smart, laid-back and friendly. The swimming pool and wireless internet are the icing on the cake.

Vinh Hung 1 Hotel (☎ 861 621; quanghuy.ha@dng.vnn.vn; 143 Đ Tran Phu; r US$15-45;) Set in a classic Chinese trading house, this is an atmospheric hotel. Splash the cash for one of two rooms used as dressing rooms by Michael Caine while filming *The Quiet American*; each is decorated with antiques and a beautiful canopy bed.

Pho Hoi Riverside Resort (☎ 862 628; www.phohoiriversidehoian.com; T1, Cam Nam Village; r US$15-65, bungalow US$60-70;) This sprawling, flash place on the south bank of the river has the best views in town. The cheaper rooms are in the old block behind, but the majority have a picturesque and quiet garden setting.

An Huy Hotel (☎ 862 116; www.anhuyhotel.com; 30 Đ Phan Boi Chau; r US$18-25;) In the French quarter of the Old Town, this new boutique hotel has small but stylish rooms, and offers free breakfast and bicycles.

Vinh Hung 2 Hotel (☎ 863 717; quanghuy.ha@dng.vnn.vn; cnr Đ Hai Ba Trung & Đ Ba Trieu; r US$20-40;) The chic, comfortable, Chinese-themed rooms all face on to the swimming pool in the central courtyard.

Phu Thinh II Hotel (☎ 923 923; www.phuthinhhotels.com; 488 Đ Cua Dai; r US$30-35;) The swimming pool and palm-shaded garden at the rear of this large complex face on to beautiful fields and a lotus lake. The quiet rooms are fitted with dark wooden furniture, and some have power showers.

Ha An Hotel (☎ 863 126; tohuong@fpt.vn; 6-8 Đ Phan Boi Chau; r US$30-50;) A French Quarter hotel, with a dose of decorative flair. This strip of buildings is built in Hoi An style (one French, one Chinese and so on), all set in a lush garden.

Other solid options, both with rooms facing on to central swimming pools, backing on to rice fields:

Thuy Duong 3 Hotel (☎ 916 565; www.thuyduonghotel-hoian.com; 92-94 Đ Ba Trieu; r US$35-45;) The décor has a Chinese feel.

Glory Hotel Hoi An (☎ 914 444; www.gloryhotelhoian.com; 538 Đ Cua Dai; r US$35-80;) A similar standard, further out, on the road to the beach.

TOP END

Vinh Hung Resort (☎ 910 577; vinhhung.ha@dng.vnn.vn; An Hoi Peninsula; r US$70-100, ste US$110;) The latest member of the Vinh Hung family has a lovely quiet location and a lush garden. Rooms are enormous and set around a central swimming pool.

Life Resort Hoi An (☎ 914 555; www.life-resorts.com; 1 Đ Pham Hong Thai; r US$159, ste US$182-308;) The most luxurious option in Hoi An, Life Resort has a prime French Quarter riverside frontage, lush gardens and a stunning infinity pool framed by frangipani trees. The rooms are beautifully designed, and the spa treatments suitably enticing.

Eating

Hoi An's main contribution to Vietnamese cuisine is *cao lau,* doughy flat noodles combined with croutons, bean sprouts and greens and topped off with pork slices. It is mixed with crumbled, crispy rice paper immediately before eating. Other Hoi An specialities are fried won ton, *banh xeo* (crispy savoury pancakes rolled with herbs in fresh rice paper) and the delicate 'white rose' (shrimp encased in rice paper and steamed).

The beauty of Hoi An is that you can find a spectacular cheap meal at the Central Market and in local restaurants in secluded residential laneways – or you can chose an upmarket eatery, lavish even by Western standards, serving excellent fusion cuisine. There are heaps of such restaurants on Đ Nguyen Thai Hoc, Đ Tran Phu and on the waterfront. A newer stretch of eateries and bars is worth exploring, facing the Old Town on the An Hoi riverbank. While a pricy town for Vietnam, it remains a bargain for most visitors.

VIETNAMESE – TRADITIONAL

Green Moss (☎ 863 728; 155 Đ Nguyen Duy Hieu; dishes 10,000-30,000d) Housed in a lovely French-colonial house, Green Moss serves a tasty mix of Vietnamese and Thai dishes with plenty of vegetarian options. Try for the two-person tables under the shade of the trees on the colonnaded balcony.

our pick **Restaurant Café 96** (☎ 910 441; 96 Đ Bach Dang; dishes 10,000-35,000d) With paint peeling to expose the brick beneath and a woven flax ceiling, this riverside restaurant has the perfectly decrepit look Western interior designers would spend a fortune creating. The food is sublime – traditional Vietnamese with all of the Hoi An specialties. Try the set menu (40,000d), or at the very least the grilled fish wrapped in banana leaf.

Café 43 (43 Đ Tran Cao Van; dishes 15,000-40,000d) Stuck away in a quiet laneway, this humble restaurant occupies the doorstep of a delightful family's home. At night it's lit with red silk lanterns. The food's excellent (try the *banh xeo*) and incredibly cheap, and the ice-cold beer's even cheaper.

Dac San Hoi An (☎ 861 533; 89 Đ Tran Phu; dishes 7000-60,000d; lunch & dinner) True to its name (translating as Hoi An specialities), this place does great *banh xeo*, *cao lau* and 'white rose'. The upstairs balcony affords a great view of one of Hoi An's nicest streets.

Mermaid Restaurant (☎ 861 527; 2 Đ Tran Phu; dishes 18,000-68,000d; lunch & dinner) One of the original Hoi An eateries, this is still a favourite for its fried spring rolls with noodles and herbs, and its excellent 'white rose'.

Also worth checking out:

Hoai River Restaurant (☎ 910 809; 44 Đ Nguyen Thai Hoc; dishes 10,000-20,000d) A cheap and friendly traditional family restaurant. Food is bought to order from the nearby market – so expect super-fresh but slow.

Quan Loan (98 Đ Le Loi; dishes 10,000-20,000d) This humble noodle nook serves excellent *pho* and *cao lau*.

Miss Ly Cafeteria 22 (☎ 861 603; 22 Đ Nguyen Hue; dishes 15,000-45,000d) A local institution for local specialities.

VIETNAMESE – UPMARKET

Café des Amis (☎ 861 616; 52 Đ Bach Dang; 5-course set menu 90,000d; dinner) This little riverside eatery has earned a loyal following over the past decade. There's no menu; the set dinner is whatever the chef, Mr Kim, feels like cooking that day. It's always delicious and there's always a vegetarian option.

Mango Rooms (☎ 910 839; 111 Đ Nguyen Thai Hoc; mains 85,000-145,000d) This restaurant's well-justified reputation for interesting modern Vietnamese cuisine has spread far and wide – with even Mick Jagger seeking culinary satisfaction here. Tropical fruits and fresh herbs feature prominently in the food, as well as in the inventive cocktails. Stylishly decorated in bright primary colours, you can choose between the formal dining room at the front or low tables with cushions on the river side. The kitchen in the centre proudly demonstrates that it's got nothing to hide from fussy hygiene-sensitive tourists.

Brothers Café (☎ 914 150; 27-29 Đ Phan Boi Chau; dishes US$6-12; lunch & dinner) Looking like a film set, in one of the finest French-colonial buildings in town, the attention to designer detail is perfect. It is properly pricey by Hoi An standards, so many just drop by for a drink in the gorgeous riverside garden.

INTERNATIONAL

Hai Scout Café (☎ 863 210; 98 Đ Nguyen Thai Hoc; dishes 12,000-55,000d; breakfast, lunch & dinner) Another interesting Old Town building, it stretches into a large garden courtyard which breaks into a bar by night. It serves sandwiches, Western-style breakfasts, Vietnamese and European mains, and real espresso. There's a display on WWF projects in central Vietnam out back, and some traditional minority tribal crafts for sale.

Café Can (☎ 861 525; 74 Đ Bach Dang; dishes 15,000-70,000d) Housed in a grand old French building, this café has a wide sundeck out front for a breezy bite to eat. Choose from Vietnamese and international dishes or just dabble with the drinks.

The Cargo Club (☎ 910 489; 107 Đ Nguyen Thai Hoc; dishes 18,000-70,000d; breakfast, lunch & dinner) If you're chasing an omelette for breakfast or a baguette for lunch, this is your place. It has mouth-watering pastries downstairs and distinguished dining upstairs, plus a balcony terrace overlooking the river. The menu's an eclectic mix of French, Italian, Vietnamese and Thai. After dark it morphs into a groovy bar.

Omar Khayyam's Indian Restaurant (☎ 864 538; 24 Đ Tran Hung Dao; dishes 30,000-80,000d) The place for curry connoisseurs, with plenty of vegetarian options.

Hoi An Hai San (☎ 861 652; 64 Đ Bach Dang; dishes 30,000-110,000d; ⏰ breakfast, lunch & dinner) This seafood restaurant serves innovative Vietnamese concoctions and some Swedish dishes to keep the chef-owner in touch with his roots.

Good Morning Vietnam (☎ 910 227; 34 Đ Le Loi; mains 38,000-105,000d) The real deal with Italian owners and chefs, it serves the best pizzas and pastas in town.

Drinking

For a little place, Hoi An has quite the selection of interesting bars – most offering two for one local cocktails in happy hours that stretch dangerously long. Many of them are open into the early hours, which is quite unusual in itself. If you last the distance, you may have the uniquely Vietnamese experience of stepping over sleeping hotel staff catching their precious few hours of rest on the reception floor.

Avoid *xe om* drivers at night offering to take you to out-of-the-way venues. We've heard reports of extortionate prices for the return trip being demanded, occasionally accompanied by physical threats. Luckily all the best bars are smack in the centre of the Old Town.

Before & Now (☎ 910 599; 51 Đ Le Loi) This swanky bar wouldn't be out of place in London, particularly given the Brit-pop playlist. The walls are plastered in pop-art portraits of everyone from Marx, Lenin, Mao and Che to Marilyn, Gandhi and Bono-as-Superman.

Tam Tam Cafe (☎ 862 212; 110 Đ Nguyen Thai Hoc) Tam Tam has its home in a lovingly restored tea warehouse. There are tables on the street, but the heart and soul of this place remains upstairs, where there is a large lounge and dining area as well as a popular pool table. European and Vietnamese food is on offer here, and there's a fine wine list and bar snacks for those just wanting something to partner a jug of beer.

Lounge Bar (☎ 910 480; 102 Đ Nguyen Thai Hoc) Just along the road from Tam Tam, this is a stylish conversion of an ancient house with a huge drinks menu. Out back are cushions and a chill-out area.

Treat's Café (☎ 861 125; 158 Đ Tran Phu) The backpacker bar of old Hoi An, this place is regularly full to bursting. It is a sprawling place with a restaurant-café upstairs. The oh-so-happy happy hours between 4pm and 9pm include two-for-one spirits and bargain beer.

Re-Treat Café (☎ 910 527; 69 Đ Tran Hung Dao) Recreates Treat's recipe in the newer part of town, 'same same but better'. Not quite, but saves a walk if you're staying here.

Shopping

Hoi An has a long history of flogging goods to international visitors, and while the port's no longer in business, the people of Hoi An haven't lost their commercial edge. It's a common occurrence for travellers not planning to buy anything to leave Hoi An laden down with extra bags – which, by the way, are easily purchased here.

The big lure is the clothes (see p262). The number of tailor shops is just extraordinary – somewhere around 500. For a look at the material available locally, take a peek at the **Hoi An Cloth Market** (Đ Tran Phu). Hoi An has long been known for fabric production.

It is not only clothes that are being turned out in quantity – shoes are now a popular purchase. The cobblers here can copy anything from sneakers (trainers) to the highest heels or the coolest Cubans. Prices are very low, so it's a great place to pick up sandals, copycat Campers or anything else that takes your fancy.

Reaching Out (☎ 862 460; 103 Đ Nguyen Thai Hoc; ⏰ 7.30am-9.30pm) is a great place to spend your dong. It's a fair-trade gift shop with profits going towards assisting disabled artisans.

The presence of numerous tourists has turned the fake-antique business into a major growth industry for Hoi An. Theoretically you could find something here that is really old, but it's hard to believe that all the genuine stuff wasn't scooped up long ago. Proceed with scepticism. On the other hand, there is some really elegant artwork around, even if it was turned out only yesterday. Paintings are generally of the mass-produced kind, but are still hand-painted; for a few US dollars you can't complain. A row of **art galleries** (Đ Nguyen Thi Minh Khai), inside the gorgeous old buildings just across from the Japanese Covered Bridge, are great to browse through.

And now that you've bought that lovely artwork, you need to light it properly. Lighting is a major growth industry here and lanterns lead the way. Popular Chinese lanterns come in various shapes and sizes, all easily foldable.

(Continued on page 261)

PETER SOLNESS

An outdoor street restaurant (p111), Hanoi

JOHN ELK III

Prayer hall of the Temple of Literature (Van Mieu; p100), Hanoi

Motorcyclists, Hanoi (p86)

BRENT WINEBRENNER

Ba Be National Park (p157), northeast Vietnam

STU SMUCKER

SIMON FOALE

Fruit vendor, Halong Bay (p136)

Boats around Cat Ba Island (p143)

SIMON

OLIVER STREWE

Landscape of Vietnam's ancient capital, Hoa Lu (p188)

Old French Prison & Museum (p166), Son La

JOHN BORTHWICK

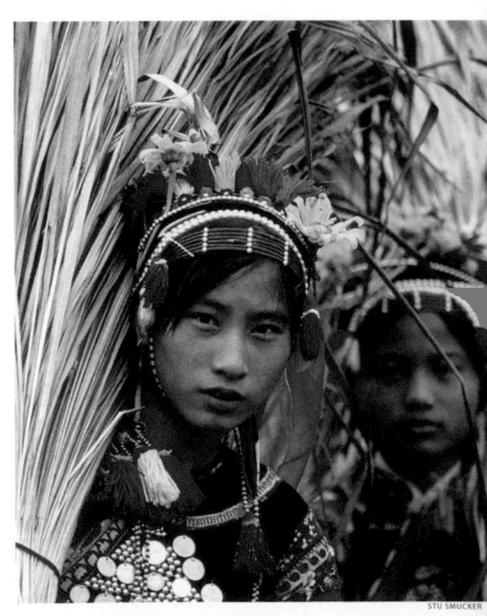

STU SMUCKER

Ethnic Ha Nhi (p171) girls carrying rice stalks, northwest Vietnam

CHRISTOPHER GROEN

Japanese Covered Bridge (p243), Hoi An

Reception hall inside Ngo Mon Gate (p214), entrance to the Citadel's Imperial Enclosure, Hué

MARK DAFFEY

STU SMUCKER

Thien Mu Pagoda (p221), central Vietnam

Man fishing for delicacies (p47) in a lotus pond, south-central Vietnam

STU SMUCKER

STU SMUCKER

Sunset, Mui Ne beach (p300)

Construction of reclining Buddha at Long Son Pagoda (p285), Nha Trang

STU SMUCKER

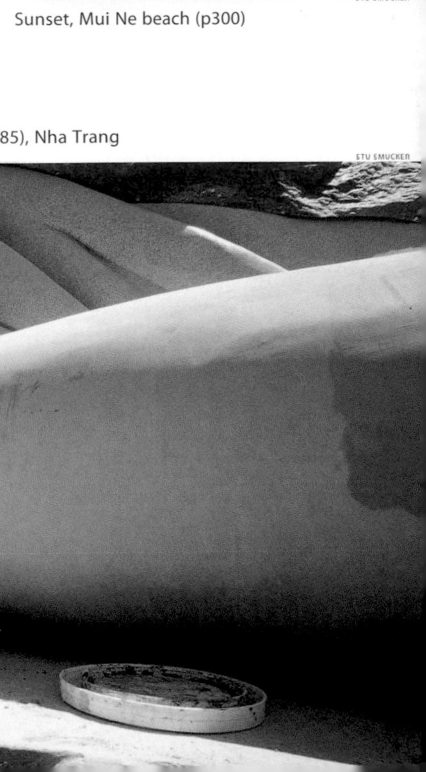

Dray Sap Falls (p322), Central Highlands

DAVID GREEDY

DAVID GREEDY

Montagnards outside Dalat (p307)

Emperor Bao Dai's Summer Palace (p310), Dalat

JOHN

STU SMUCKER

Kite-flying in District 7, Ho Chi Minh City (p331)

Traffic in Ho Chi Minh City (p331)

ANTONY GIBLIN

STU SMUCKER

Reunification Palace (p339), Ho Chi Minh City

Khmer Buddhist monk, Tra Vinh (p413)

STU SMUCKER

DAVID GREEDY

Young child with pineapples, Cai Be Floating Market (p412), Mekong Delta

Rarely seen large pancake hats, My Tho (p402)

STU SM

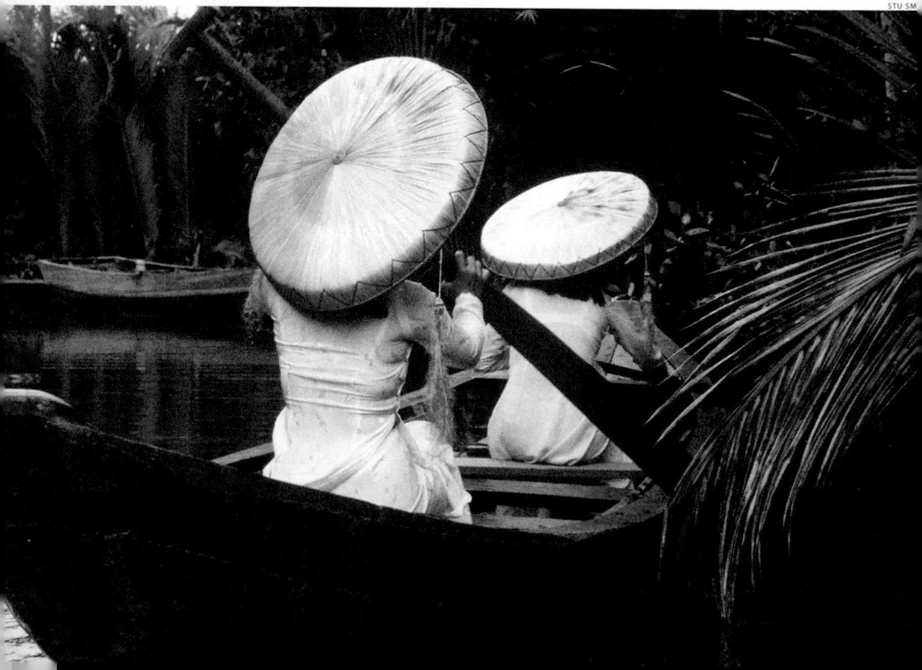

(Continued from page 252)

Woodcarvings are also a local speciality. Cross Cam Nam Bridge to Cam Nam Village, to watch the carvers at work. Woodcarving is a speciality on Cam Kim Island (see right).

Vietnam has a great reputation for its ceramics, and while much of what is on sale here comes from around Hanoi, it is worth stocking up if you are only visiting central Vietnam. The black pottery with a glassy glaze is particularly striking. It's best to browse the strip of small **ceramics shops** (Đ Bach Dang) along the riverfront.

Getting There & Away

AIR

The closest airport is 45 minutes away, in Danang (see p234).

BUS

The main **Hoi An bus station** (☎ 861 284; 96 Đ Hung Vuong) is 1km west of the centre of town. Buses from here go to Danang (8000d, one hour), Quang Ngai and other points. More frequent services to Danang leave from the **northern bus station** (Đ Le Hong Phong) from 5am until the late afternoon.

A regular stop on the open-bus route, it's easy to pick up a service to or from Hué (US$3, four hours) or Nha Trang (US$6 to US$8, 11 to 12 hours).

CAR & MOTORBIKE

To get to Danang (30km) you can either head north out of town and join up with Hwy 1A, or east to Cua Dai Beach and follow the excellent new road along China Beach. The going rate for a motorbike taxi between Danang and Hoi An is US$4 to US$6. A taxi costs around US$10.

Shop around for rates on car hire. A journey to Hué can vary from US$35 to US$70. A day trip around the surrounding area, including My Son, is about for US$15 to US$20. Agree on your itinerary in advance and get a copy in writing.

Getting Around

Anywhere within town can be reached on foot. To go further afield, rent a bicycle from 10,000d per day – check with your hotel as it may provide them free. Cross the An Hoi Footbridge for a pleasant walk or ride through attractive rural countryside. A motorbike without/with a driver will cost around US$6/10 per day. Hire places are located all over town.

A taxi to the beach costs a couple of dollars.

BOAT

A boat trip on the Thu Bon River can be a fascinating experience. A simple rowing boat, complete with rower, costs something like US$2 per hour, and one hour is probably long enough for most travellers. Some My Son tours offer part of the journey by boat – a lovely but lengthy voyage.

Boats that carry up to five people can be hired to visit handicraft and fishing villages in the area; expect to pay around US$4 per hour. Look for the boats near the dock close to the market.

AROUND HOI AN

Cam Kim Island

The master woodcarvers, who in previous centuries produced the fine carvings that graced the homes of Hoi An's merchants and the town's public buildings, came from Kim Bong Village on Cam Kim Island. Most of the woodcarvings on sale in Hoi An are produced here.

To reach the island, catch one of the boats that leave from the boat landing at Đ Hoang Van Thu in Hoi An (10,000d, one hour).

Cham Island

Cham Island is 21km from Hoi An in the South China Sea. The island is famous as a source of swiftlet nests (see p295). It's also part of the Cu Lao Cham Marine Park – comprising eight islands, it's home to 155 species of coral, 202 species of fish, four species of lobster and 84 species of mollusc. Diving trips can be arranged through Rainbow Divers (see p239).

Permits are needed to visit Cham Island, which still houses a naval base. Public boats leave from the landing on Đ Bach Dang in Hoi An between 7am and 8am and the one-way journey takes three hours, but it's difficult for foreigners to organise the paperwork to travel on one of these boats. It's easiest to book with a travel agency – a day trip costs 18,000d, while an overnighter staying in tents on the beach is around 35,000d. These tours are heavily dependent on the weather.

Thanh Ha

Not so long ago there were many pottery factories in this village, 3km west of Hoi An, but

CRAVING THAT PERFECT FIT

Caution – having clothes made in Hoi An is extremely addictive. You may be able to walk past the first few tailor stores without wavering, but given that you're likely to pass dozens every day you spend here, chances are you'll eventually crack. And when you do, watch out. It's not unusual to see even hardened blokes gleefully ploughing through fabric rolls, trying to pick the perfect satin lining for that second new suit.

Hoi An's numerous tailors can make anything and usually within a day. They're master copiers – bring in an item of clothing you want duplicated or a picture in a magazine, pick out your fabric, and the next day your vision will be brought to life. Many have current fashion catalogues to leaf through. They're also extremely skilled in the art of flattering and pampering. A fitting session can do wonders for the ego – 'You look so good in that…why not buy another one?'

Bargaining has a place here, but basically you get what you pay for. The better tailors and better fabrics are more expensive. One of the hundreds of tailors will probably knock out a men's suit for US$20, but a good-quality, lined woollen suit is more likely to cost US$40 to US$70. Shirts, skirts and casual trousers hover around the US$10 mark.

The trick is to pick a shop you're comfortable with, know your fabrics, check in advance on the details (thread colour, linings and buttons) and allow plenty of time for fittings and adjustments.

When buying silk, it's important to ascertain that it's real and not a synthetic imitation. The only real test is with a cigarette or match (synthetic fibres melt and silk burns), but try not to set the shop on fire. If you're concerned about its authenticity ask for a cut-off sample of the material and go outside to test it. Similarly, don't accept on face value that a fabric is 100% cotton or wool without giving it a good feel and ensuring you're happy with the quality.

Remember to check the seams of the finished garment: a single set of stitching along the inside edges will soon cause fraying and, in many cases, big gaping holes. All well-tailored garments have a second set of stitches (known in the trade as blanket stitching), which binds the edge, oversewing the fabric so fraying is impossible. Where possible, also insist on the clothes being lined, as it helps them move and fall in the right direction.

There are so many tailors that it's difficult to single out individual stores for mention, and impossible (although tempting) to test them all out. Most use a range of outsourced workers who can vary in quality. If you're planning on getting a lot of stuff made, consider trying out a couple of shops with small items before taking the plunge on your wedding dress. That said, some places we're heard good things about are **Phuoc An** (☎ 862 615; 6 Đ Le Loi), **Yaly** (☎ 910 474; 47 Đ Nguyen Thai Hoc), **A Dong Silk** (☎ 861 386; www.adongsilk.com; 40 Đ Le Loi) and **Faifoo** (☎ 862 566; Đ Tran Hung Dao).

the industry has been in decline. The remaining artisans employed in this hot and sweaty work don't mind if you stop for a gander, though they're happier if you buy something. Many tours to My Son visit here on the way back to Hoi An. For a more personalised experience, contact **Mr Trung** (☎ 922 695), a villager who arranges day tours, including lunch and transport, for around US$10.

MY SON

Set within the jungle 55km from Hoi An are the enigmatic ruins of **My Son** (☎ 731 309; admission 60,000d; ⏲ 6.30am-4pm), the most important remains of the ancient kingdom of Champa and a Unesco World Heritage site. Although Vietnam has better preserved Cham sites, none are as extensive and few have such beautiful surroundings – in a verdant valley surrounded by hills and overlooked by Cat's Tooth Mountain (Hon Quap). Clear streams run between the structures and past nearby coffee plantations.

During the centuries when Tra Kieu (which was then known as Simhapura) served as the political capital, My Son was the most important intellectual and religious centre, and may also have served as a burial place for Cham monarchs.

My Son is considered to be Champa's smaller version of the grand cities of Southeast Asia's other Indian-influenced civilisations: Angkor (Cambodia), Ayu-thaya (Thailand), Bagan (Myanmar) and Borobudur (Java). American bombs have reduced many of the towers to ruins, but there's still plenty to see.

History

My Son (pronounced 'me sun') became a religious centre under King Bhadravarman in the late 4th century and was constantly occupied until the 13th century – the longest period of development of any monument in Southeast Asia. Most of the temples were dedicated to Cham kings associated with divinities, particularly Shiva, who was regarded as the founder and protector of Champa's dynasties.

Champa's contact with Java was extensive. Cham scholars were sent to Java to study and there was a great deal of commerce between the two empires – Cham pottery has been found on Java and, in the 12th century, the Cham king wed a Javanese woman.

Because some of the ornamentation work at My Son was never finished, archaeologists know that the Chams first built their structures and only then carved decorations into the brickwork. Researchers have yet to figure out for certain how they managed to get the baked bricks to stick together. According to one theory, they used a paste prepared with a botanical oil that is indigenous to central Vietnam. During one period in their history, the summits of some of the towers were completely covered with a layer of gold.

During the American War this region was completely devastated and depopulated in extended bitter fighting. Finding it to be a convenient staging ground, the VC used My Son as a base; in response the Americans

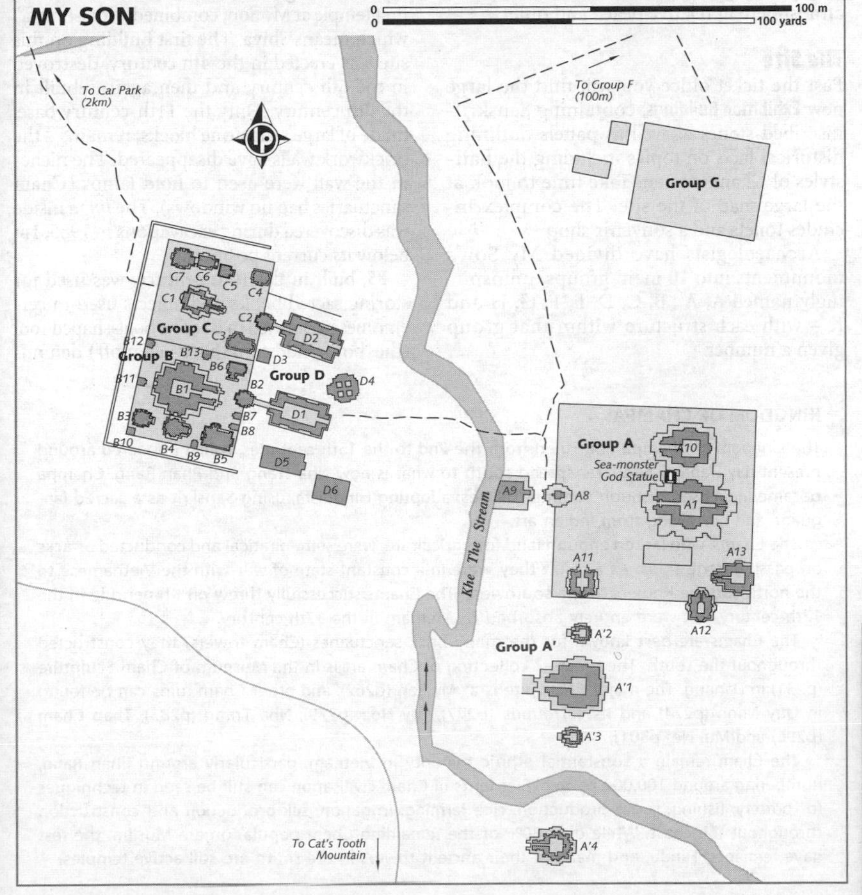

bombed the monuments. Traces of 68 structures have been found, of which 25 survived repeated pillaging in previous centuries by the Chinese, Khmer and Vietnamese. The American bombing failed to destroy about 20 of these, although some sustained extensive damage. Today, Vietnamese authorities are attempting to restore as much as possible of the remaining sites.

Information

The entry fee includes local transport from the parking area to the sites, about 2km away. By departing from Hoi An at about 5am, you will arrive to wake up the gods (and the guards) for sunrise and could be leaving just as the tour groups reach the area. It gets very busy at My Son; go early or late to soak up the atmosphere in relative peace and quiet.

The Site

Past the ticket office you will find the large new **Exhibition Buildings**, containing Sanskrit-inscribed stones as well as panels outlining historical facts on topics including the hairstyles of Cham women. Take time to look at the large map of the site. The complex includes toilets and a souvenir shop.

Archaeologists have divided My Son's monuments into 10 main groups, uninspiringly named A, A', B, C, D, E, F, G, H and K – with each structure within that group given a number.

GROUP C

The 8th-century **C1** was used to worship Shiva, portrayed in human form (rather than in the form of a *linga*, as in B1). Inside is an altar where a statue of Shiva, now in the Museum of Cham Sculpture in Danang, used to stand. On either side of the stone doorway it's possible to see the holes in which two wooden doors once swung. Note the motifs, characteristic of the 8th century, carved into the brickwork of the exterior walls. With the massive bomb crater in front of this group, it's amazing that anything's still standing.

GROUP B

The main *kalan* (sanctuary), **B1**, was dedicated to Bhadresvara, which is a contraction of the name of King Bhadravarman, who built the first temple at My Son, combined with '-esvara', which means Shiva. The first building on this site was erected in the 4th century, destroyed in the 6th century and then again rebuilt in the 7th century. Only the 11th-century base, made of large sandstone blocks, remains – the brickwork walls have disappeared. The niches in the wall were used to hold lamps (Cham sanctuaries had no windows). The *linga* inside was discovered during excavations in 1985, 1m below its current position.

B5, built in the 10th century, was used for storing sacred books and objects used in ceremonies performed in B1. The boat-shaped roof (the 'bow' and 'stern' have fallen off) demon-

KINGDOM OF CHAMPA

The kingdom of Champa flourished from the 2nd to the 15th centuries. It first appeared around present-day Danang and later spread south to what is now Nha Trang and Phan Rang. Champa became Indianised through commercial ties: adopting Hinduism, using Sanskrit as a sacred language and borrowing from Indian art.

The Chams, who lacked enough land for agriculture, were semi-piratical and conducted attacks on passing trade ships. As a result they were in a constant state of war with the Vietnamese to the north and the Khmers to the southwest. The Chams successfully threw off Khmer rule in the 12th century, but were entirely absorbed by Vietnam in the 17th century.

The Chams are best known for the many brick sanctuaries (Cham towers) they constructed throughout the south. The greatest collection of Cham art is in the Museum of Cham Sculpture (p231) in Danang. The major Cham site is at My Son (p262), and other Cham ruins can be found in Quy Nhon (p274) and its surrounds (p277), Tuy Hoa (p279), Nha Trang (p283), Thap Cham (p296) and Mui Ne (p301).

The Cham remain a substantial ethnic minority in Vietnam, particularly around Phan Rang, numbering around 100,000 people. Elements of Cham civilisation can still be seen in techniques for pottery, fishing, sugar production, rice farming, irrigation, silk production and construction throughout the coast. While over 80% of the remaining Cham population are Muslim, the rest have remained Hindu, and many of their ancient towers in the south are still active temples.

strates the influence of Malayo-Polynesian architecture. Unlike the sanctuaries, this building has windows and the Cham masonry inside is original. Over the window on the outside wall facing B4 is a brick bas-relief of two elephants under a tree with two birds in it.

The ornamentation on the exterior walls of **B4** is an excellent example of a Cham decorative style, typical of the 9th century and said to resemble worms. This style is unlike anything found in other Southeast Asian cultures.

B3 has an Indian-influenced pyramidal roof typical of Cham towers. Inside **B6** is a bath-shaped basin for keeping sacred water that was poured over the *linga* in B1; this is the only known example of a Cham basin. **B2** is a gate.

Around the perimeter of Group B are small temples, **B7** to **B13**, dedicated to the gods of the directions of the compass *(dikpalaka)*.

GROUP D

Buildings **D1** and **D2**, which were once meditation halls, now house small displays of Cham sculpture.

GROUP A

The path from Groups B, C and D to Group A leads eastward from near D4.

Group A was almost completely destroyed by US attacks. According to locals, massive **A1**, considered the most important monument at My Son, remained impervious to aerial bombing and was intentionally finished off by a helicopter-borne sapper team. All that remains today is a pile of collapsed brick walls. After the destruction of A1, Philippe Stern, an expert on Cham art and curator of the Guimet Museum in Paris, wrote a letter of protest to the US president Nixon, who ordered US forces to continue killing the VC, but not to do any further damage to Cham monuments.

A1 was the only Cham sanctuary with two doors. One faced east, in the direction of the Hindu gods; the other faced west towards Groups B, C and D and the spirits of the ancestor kings reputedly buried there. Inside A1 is a stone altar. Among the ruins, some of the brilliant brickwork, (typical 10th-century style) is still visible. At the base of A1 on the side facing A10 (decorated in 9th-century style) is a carving of a worshipping figure flanked by round columns, with a Javanese sea-monster god *(kala-makara)* above. There are plans to partially restore A1 and A10 in the future.

> **IS THAT WHAT I THINK IT IS?**
>
> Yes, it's a giant stone penis.
>
> A common sight around Cham temples, these *linga* have an important spiritual value, symbolising the God Shiva. You'll often find them on a square base with a channel cut through it, a *yoni,* which represents female genitalia. An important Cham religious practice at My Son saw priests heading up to Cat's Tooth Mountain (where Shiva was believed to reside) to retrieve water from a sacred stream. This was then ceremonially poured over the head of the *linga,* draining out through the spout of the *yoni.*

OTHER GROUPS

Dating from the 8th century, **Group A'** is at present overgrown and inaccessible. Similarly off-limits, **Group G**, which has been damaged by time rather than war, dates from the 12th century. **Group E** was built from the 8th to 11th centuries, while **Group F** dates from the 8th century. Both were badly bombed and parts are propped up by scaffolding. There are statues scattered around, including a female figure without a head (perfect for those comedy photos), another *linga*, an oxen and several stone tablets scarred by shell holes.

Sleeping & Eating

Hotel Garden (☎ 734 028; thanhphongltd@dng.vnn.vn; s/d 200,000/300,000d) If you're serious about beating the crowds and don't quite believe that 5.30am exists except at the end of a hard night, it's possible to stay right at My Son's gates. This complex offers a number of bungalows scattered around an attractive garden. There's also a large restaurant and a café on site.

Getting There & Away

CAR

A hire car with driver from Hoi An to My Son costs around US$15 to US$20. Going under your own steam gives you the option of arriving before or after the tour groups, and My Son is quite atmospheric when you're one of only a few people there.

BUS/MINIBUS

Numerous hotels in Hoi An can book a day trip to My Son that includes a stop-off at Tra Kieu. At US$2 to US$3 per person, you could hardly do it cheaper unless you walked. The minibuses depart from Hoi An at 8am and return at 1pm. Some agencies offer the option of returning to Hoi An by boat, which adds an extra couple of hours to the trip.

MOTORBIKE

It's possible to get to the sites by rented motorbike. Make sure you park in the official parking area. Otherwise, get somebody else to drive you on their motorbike and then ask them to wait for you.

TRA KIEU (SIMHAPURA)

Formerly called Simhapura (Lion Citadel), Tra Kieu was the first capital city of Champa, serving in that capacity from the 4th to the 8th centuries. Today nothing remains of the ancient city except the rectangular ramparts. A large number of artefacts, including some of the finest carvings in the Museum of Cham Sculpture in Danang (p231), were found here.

Mountain Church

You can get a wonderful view of the city's outlines and the surrounding countryside from the **Mountain Church** (Nha Tho Nui), on the top of Buu Chau Hill. This modern, open-air structure was built in 1970 to replace an earlier church destroyed by an American bomb. A Cham tower once stood on this spot. It's worth visiting the little shop at the bottom of the hill to look at a picture of the site in antiquity and peruse its collection of small artefacts.

The Mountain Church is 6.5km from Hwy 1A and 19.5km from My Son. Within Tra Kieu, it is 200m from the morning **market**, Cho Tra Kieu, and 550m from Tra Kieu Church.

Tra Kieu Church

This **church** (Dia So Tra Kieu), which serves the town's Catholic population of 3000, was built in the late 19th century. There's a fantastic ceramic mosaic dragon on the external stairs. A priest from here, who died in 1988, was interested in the Cham civilisation and amassed a collection of artefacts found by local people. A 2nd-floor room in the building to the right of the church opened as a **museum** in 1990. The round ceramic objects with faces on them, which date from the 8th and 10th centuries, were affixed to the ends of tiled roofs. The face is of Kala, the God of Time.

According to local belief this church was the site of a miracle in 1885, witnessed by 80 people. At that time, when the Catholic villagers were under attack by anti-French forces, a vision of a lady in white, believed to be Mary the mother of Jesus, appeared on the top of the church. At the end of a 21-day siege during which 500 shells were fired on the village, the church and those who had sheltered in it remained unharmed. While not officially recognised by the Catholic Church, this is a popular site for Vietnamese pilgrims. The original Mountain Church (see left) was built to commemorate this event – although it didn't achieve such divine protection itself during the American War.

Tra Kieu Church is 7km from Hwy 1A and 19km from My Son. It is down a street opposite the town's **Clinic of Western Medicine** (Quay Thuoc Tay Y). Expect to stop for directions.

Getting There & Away

Many day trips to My Son from Hoi An include a stop-off at Tra Kieu. Otherwise you'll need to rent a bike or a car and driver (see p261).

TAM KY

Tam Ky, the capital of Quang Nam province, is a nondescript town on the highway between Quang Ngai and Danang. However, the nearby Cham towers of **Chien Dan** (Chien Dan Cham; Hwy 1A; admission 10,000d; 8-11.30am & 1-5.30pm Mon-Fri) are wonderful.

In a pleasant rural setting, few tourists venture here. Chances are you'll be left alone to explore the three towers and small sculpture museum. Although they escaped the bombing that My Son endured, scars from the American War are evident. The eerie feel of the interior of the middle tower is heightened by the numerous bullet holes in the wall – many people died here.

Dating from the 11th or 12th century, each *kalan* (sanctuary) faces east. Many of the decorative friezes remain on the outside walls. The middle tower was dedicated to Shiva; at the front left-hand edge of its base there are carvings of dancing girls and a fight scene. Look for the grinning faces high up between this and the left tower (honouring Brahma) and the two elephants at the rear. The right-hand tower is dedicated to Vishnu.

The site is visible to the right of the road on your approach to Tam Ky, 47km south of Hoi An (5km north of Tam Ky). It will take about 50 minutes to reach by car, and can easily be combined with a trip to My Son.

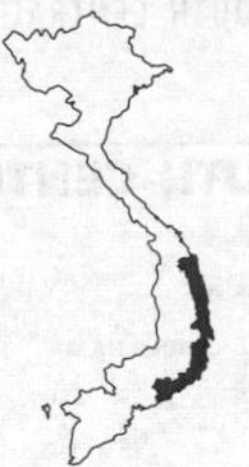

South-Central Coast

Undeniably, the beach is the big attraction in this part of Vietnam. Nha Trang and Mui Ne have become the favoured destinations for those whose idea of paradise is reclining by the water, cocktail in hand, contemplating whether to have a massage or a pedicure before hitting the bars later. These sedentary delights are juxtaposed with an excellent array of outdoor activities – swimming, scuba diving, snorkelling, surfing, windsurfing and kite-surfing – making this simultaneously the action capital of the country.

With most visitors not venturing outside of the two tourist enclaves, the rest of the beautiful coast is wonderfully overlooked – leaving empty beaches to be explored by the more independently minded. The fine art of hassling travellers has not yet spread to the more remote parts, quickly dispelling any negative impressions engendered in the tourist traps.

If you've got the dosh, another way of beating the crowds is to head to one of the exclusive resorts popping up along the coast. Wealthy Western ex-pats from around Asia seem to be doing just that, particularly business-people based in nearby Ho Chi Minh City (HCMC). Those with an eye towards cultural edification will find a wealth of Cham towers and what remains of the Cham population in this region. While not as archeologically important as the My Son site further north, they're much more accessible and, in many ways, more impressive to the untrained eye.

This region is also home to the most poignant reminder of the American War – the Son My Memorial, commemorating the villagers who perished in what the West remembers as the My Lai Massacre.

HIGHLIGHTS

- Explore the tourist-free Cham sites and beautiful beaches around **Quy Nhon** (p277)
- After a hard day lying around the beach, party your way around **Nha Trang's bars** (p292)
- Dodge the bats in the darkness of the sanctuary at remote **Po Ro Me Cham Tower** (p297)
- Catch a wave, touch the wind, or do both at the same time – surfing, windsurfing or kite-surfing at **Mui Ne** (p301)
- Pay your respects at the **Son My Memorial** (p269)

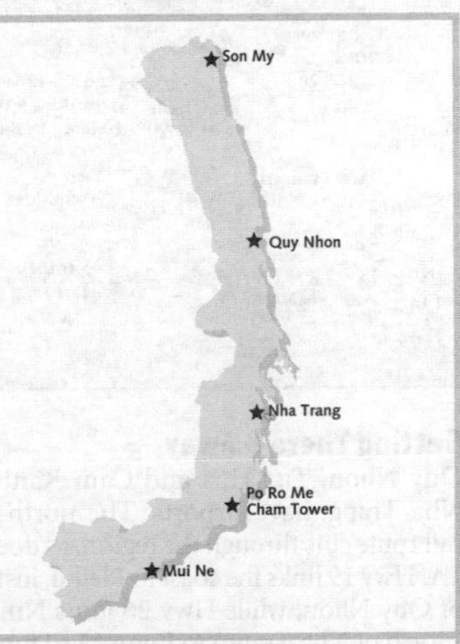

- ELEVATION: 1-1793M
- BEST TIME TO VISIT: FEB OCT

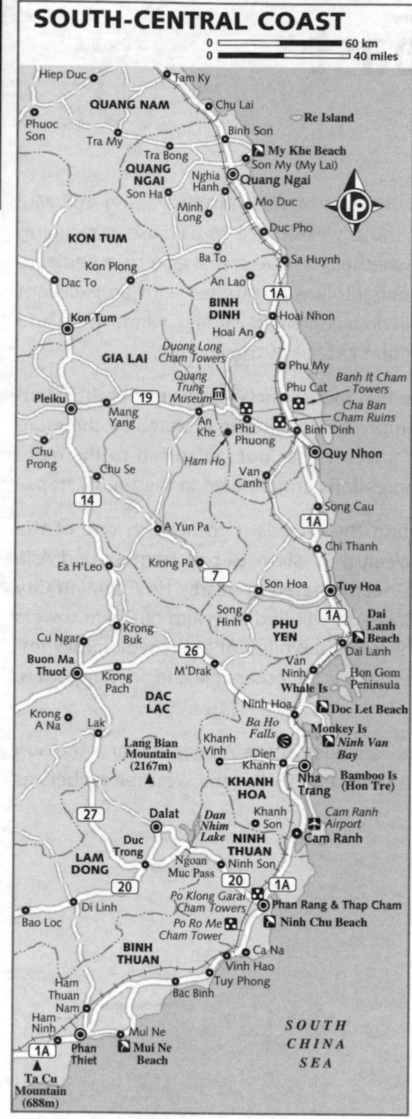

Getting There & Away

Quy Nhon, Tuy Hoa and Cam Ranh, near Nha Trang, have airports. The north–south rail route cuts through the region, as does Hwy 1A. Hwy 19 links the coast to Pleiku, just north of Quy Nhon, while Hwy 26 joins Ninh Hoa (north of Nha Trang) to Buon Ma Thuot, and Hwy 20 connects Phan Rang and Dalat.

QUANG NGAI

☎ 055 / pop 134,000

The capital of the province of the same name, Quang Ngai (aka Quang Nhia or Quangai) was only officially awarded city status in 2005, so the impression of a big country town is justified. The city itself offers no obvious attractions and those few travellers that venture here generally come to pay their respects to the victims of the most famous atrocity of the American War (see p271). Perhaps it's the sombre mood induced by the Memorial that has caused tourists to overlook one of Vietnam's best and least developed beaches, less than 2 kilometres away.

Even before WWII, Quang Ngai was an important centre of resistance to the French. During the Franco-Viet Minh War, the area was a Viet Minh stronghold. In 1962 the South Vietnamese government introduced its ill-fated Strategic Hamlets Program. Villagers were forcibly removed from their homes and resettled in fortified hamlets, infuriating and alienating the local population and increasing popular support for the Viet Cong. Some of the bitterest fighting of the American War took place here.

Orientation

Built on the southern bank of the Tra Khuc River, the city is 15km from the coast. Hwy 1A doubles as the main street Đ Quang Trung as it passes through town. The train station is 1.5km west of the town centre on Đ Hung Vuong.

Information

Deluxe Taxis (☎ 83 83 83)

Main post office (☎ 822 935; 80 Đ Phan Dinh Phung)

Quynh Nhu Internet (☎ 828 851; 65 Đ Tran Hung Dao; per hr 4000d)

Vietcombank (45 Đ Hung Vuong) Branch in the lobby of Hung Vuong Hotel with an ATM outside.

Sleeping

Hung Vuong Hotel (☎ 818 828; 33 Đ Hung Vuong; r 120,000-200,000d; ❄) The friendliness of this family-run minihotel more than makes up for a lack of English. The most expensive rooms can sleep five at a push.

Hung Vuong Hotel (☎ 710 477; www.hungvuong-hotel.com.vn; 45 Đ Hung Vuong; s/d/tr/ste US$25/30/35/45; ❄ 💻) Even by Vietnamese standards this is confusing – two hotels with the same name on the same street. This one's a large multistorey block with spacious rooms, although it's not about to win any prizes for interior design.

Petro Song Tra Hotel (☎ 822 665; pvstc@dng.vnn.vn; 2 Đ Quang Trung; s US$25-30, d US$30-35, ste US$55;) This Soviet-looking place has just been given a make-over. It's still not flash, but it's good value for the price, with ADSL in the rooms, a gym, a beautiful pool, tennis courts and a great location, right by the river and park.

Central Hotel (☎ 829 999; www.vidc.com.vn/centralhotel; 784 Đ Quang Trung; r US$35-95, ste US$149;) It's now looking a little past its prime, but the Central Hotel is still the nicest place in town and probably the cleanest. The cheaper rooms have basic showers, while the suites sport over-sized baths and huge TVs. Extra luxuries include free wi-fi, a tennis court and a pool big enough to swim laps in.

There are several other minihotels on the east side of Đ Quang Trung between Đ Nguyen Nghiem and Đ Tran Hung Dao.

Eating

Quang Ngai province is famous for *com ga*, although it actually originates further north at Tam Ky. It consists of boiled chicken over yellow rice (the colour comes from being steamed with chicken broth) with mint, egg soup and pickled vegies. You'll find *com ga* restaurants all over town. Locals tend to eat it with a spoon, so don't bother struggling with the chopsticks.

An Lac (☎ 822 566; 54 Đ Tran Hung Dao; meals 7000d) For good, cheap vegetarian grub, try this shopfront across from the pink church.

Nhung 1 (☎ 821 797; 474 Đ Quang Trung; meals 10,000d) This friendly eatery is a great place to try *com ga*.

Mimosa (☎ 822 438; 21 Đ Hung Vuong; mains 15,000d) With menus in English and some Western breakfast options, this family-run restaurant bustles with affable service.

Getting There & Away

BUS

The **Quang Ngai bus station** (Ben Xe Khach Quang Ngai; Đ Le Thanh Ton) is situated to the south of the centre, 50m east of Đ Quang Trung. Regular buses head to all the major stops on Hwy 1A, including Sa Huynh (20,000d, 1½ hours) and Quy Nhon (60,000d, 3½ hours). If you're on an open-tour you should be able to leave the bus as it passes through town, but a pick up from here is difficult to arrange.

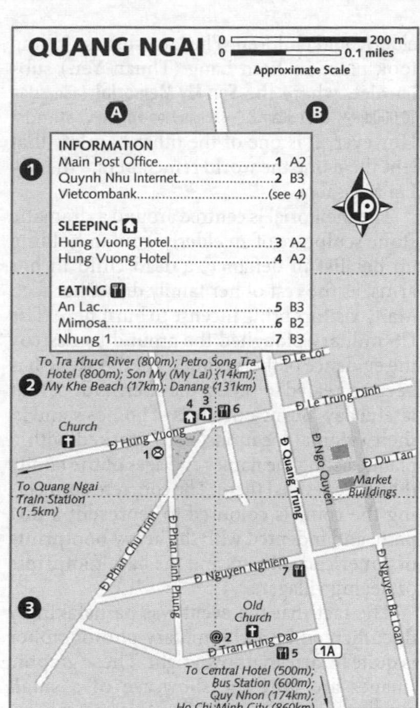

CAR & MOTORBIKE

From Quang Ngai road distances are: 889km to Hanoi, 100km to Hoi An, 174km to Quy Nhon, 412km to Nha Trang and 860km to HCMC.

TRAIN

Reunification Express trains stop at **Quang Ngai Train Station** (Ga Quang Nghia; ☎ 820 280; 204 Đ Nguyen Chi Thanh), 1.5km west of the town centre. Destinations include Hanoi (350,000d, 19½ to 23½ hours, four daily), Danang (47,000d, 2½ to four hours, six daily), Quy Nhon (40,000d, 5½ hours, one local train daily), Nha Trang (146,000d, six to 8½ hours, six daily) and HCMC (300,000d, 13½ to 20 hours, six daily).

AROUND QUANG NGAI

Son My (My Lai)

It's unfathomable that this pleasant rural spot could have been the setting of horrific crimes during the American War. On the morning of 16 March 1968, US troops swept through four hamlets in the Son My subdistrict, systematically killing 504 villagers, many of them elderly and children. The largest mass killing took place in Xom Lang (Thuan Yen) sub-hamlet, where the **Son My Memorial** (admission 10,000d; 8-11.30am & 1-4.30pm Mon-Fri) now stands. However, it is one of the other hamlets that lent the name the world remembers – the My Lai Massacre.

The memorial is centred around a dramatic stone sculpture of an elderly woman holding up her fist in defiance, a dead child in her arms, as the rest of her family die at her feet. Many visitors bring incense to burn here. The US military ploughed the ground to destroy the evidence of their crimes, but the scene has been recreated to reflect the aftermath of that fateful day. Burnt-out shells of homes stand in their original locations, each marked with a plaque listing the names and ages of the family that once resided there. The concrete connecting the ruins is coloured to represent a dirt path, and indented with the heavy bootprints of American soldiers and the bare footprints of fleeing villagers.

The fact that the event was painstakingly documented by a US military photographer is quite bizarre in its own right. These graphic images are now the showcase of a small **museum** on the site. While a distressing experience, the display ends on a hopeful note – chronicling the efforts of the local people to rebuild their lives after liberation. A prominent section honours the GIs who tried to stop the carnage, shielding a group of villagers from certain death, and those responsible for blowing the whistle.

The road to Son My passes through particularly beautiful countryside: rice paddies, cassava patches and vegetable gardens shaded by casuarinas and eucalyptus trees. However, if you look closely you can still make out the odd bomb crater, and the bare tops of hills are testimony to the continuing environmental devastation caused by Agent Orange.

GETTING THERE & AWAY

The best way to get to Son My is by motorbike or regular taxi. The return bike trip, including waiting time, shouldn't cost more than 50,000d. From Quang Ngai head north on Đ Quang Trung (Hwy 1A) and cross the long bridge over the Tra Khuc River. Take the first right (eastward, parallel to the river) where a triangular concrete stele indicates the way and follow the road for 12km. The memorial is just past a small hospital.

My Khe Beach

Only a couple of kilometres from the Son My Memorial, My Khe (not to be confused with the other My Khe Beach near Danang) is a superb beach, with fine white sand and clear water. It stretches for kilometres along a long, thin, casuarina-lined spit of sand, separated from the mainland by Song Kinh Giang, a body of water about 150m inland from the beach. The beach's charm is greatly enhanced by its lack of development, although this means limited accommodation options. Still, if you want an idyllic beach largely to yourself, this is the place to come…for the time being. If tourist numbers increase, the shell of an additional building is already in place to double the size of the resort.

You'll reach the beach after crossing a bridge, 2 kilometres further along the road heading past the Son My memorial.

SLEEPING & EATING

My Khe Restaurant (843 316; Tinh Khe commune; r 100,000d) Hidden from sight behind a large yellow wall to the north of the road is the local commune, with a row of restaurants along the beach. This one, near where the paving broadens out, also has basic stilt houses to rent, each with its own bathroom, fan and TV.

My Khe Resort (686 111; ks_mytra@dng.vnn.vn; Tinh Khe; r/ste US$20/30;) Although not really a resort, this small new hotel is great value with smart, clean rooms looking over the beach. Breakfast is included at the beachfront restaurant across the road. You'll find this attractive green and yellow building 100m to the left once you reach the beach.

SA HUYNH

055

Unfortunately a surfeit of litter means that this beautiful semicircular beach with coarse golden sand is best enjoyed from a distance. The little town is also known for its salt marshes and salt-evaporation ponds. Archaeologists have unearthed remains from the Dong Son civilisation dating from the 1st century AD in the vicinity of Sa Huynh.

Sleeping & Eating

Vinh Hotel (860 385; Hwy 1A; r 120,000d) About 1km to the south of the town, this is a basic collection of rooms behind a popular restaurant with a little bridge linking it to a quiet section of beach. Rooms come with a fan, TV

MY LAI MASSACRE

At about 7.30am on 16 March 1968 – after the area had been bombarded with artillery, and the landing zone raked with rocket and machine-gun fire from helicopter gunships – the US army's Charlie Company (commanded by Captain Ernest Medina) landed by helicopter in the west of Son My, regarded as a Viet Cong stronghold. They encountered no resistance during the 'combat-assault', nor did they come under fire at any time during the entire operation; but as soon as their sweep eastward began, so did the atrocities.

As Lieutenant William Calley's 1st Platoon moved through Xom Lang, they shot and bayoneted fleeing villagers, threw hand grenades into houses and bomb shelters, slaughtered livestock and burned dwellings. Somewhere between 75 and 150 unarmed villagers were rounded up and herded to a ditch, where they were mowed down by machine-gun fire.

In the next few hours, as command helicopters circled overhead and American navy boats patrolled offshore, the 2nd Platoon (under Lieutenant Stephen Brooks), the 3rd Platoon (under Lieutenant Jeffrey La Cross) and the company headquarters group also committed unspeakable crimes. At least half a dozen groups of civilians, including women and children, were assembled and executed. Villagers fleeing towards Quang Ngai were machine-gunned, and wounded civilians (including young children) were summarily shot. As these massacres were taking place, at least four girls and women were raped or gang-raped by groups of soldiers.

By the end of the murderous rampage, 504 people had died including 182 women (17 of them pregnant), 173 children and 37 men over the age of sixty. One soldier is reported to have shot himself in the foot to extricate himself from the slaughter; he was the only American casualty in the entire operation.

Troops who participated were ordered to keep their mouths shut, but several disobeyed orders and went public with the story after returning to the USA. When it broke in the newspapers it had a devastating effect on the military's morale and fuelled further public protests against the war. It did little to persuade the world that the US Army was fighting on behalf of the Vietnamese people. Unlike WWII veterans, who returned home to parades and glory, soldiers coming home from Vietnam often found themselves ostracised and branded as 'baby killers'.

A cover-up of the atrocities was undertaken at all levels of the US army command, eventually leading to several investigations. Lieutenant Calley was made chief ogre and was court-martialled and found guilty of the murders of 22 unarmed civilians. He was sentenced to life imprisonment in 1971 and spent three years under house arrest at Fort Benning, Georgia, while appealing his conviction. Calley was paroled in 1974 after the US Supreme Court refused to hear his case. Calley's case still causes controversy – many claim that he was made a scapegoat because of his low rank, and that officers much higher up ordered the massacres. What is certain is that he didn't act alone.

For the full story of this horrendous event and its aftermath, pick up a copy of *Four Hours in My Lai* by Michael Bilton and Kevin Sim, a stunning piece of journalism.

and private toilet. The seafood restaurant is undoubtedly popular and the food's good, if you can make like a local and ignore the rats.

Getting There & Away

Sa Huynh is on Hwy 1A, about 60km south of Quang Ngai (1½ hours by bus) and 114km north of Quy Nhon (two hours by bus). There is no bus station, but it should be easy enough to pick up a passing bus on the highway in either direction. Make sure to agree on a price before you get on. A ticket bought from the bus station at Quang Ngai to Sa Huynh only costs 20,000d. With this as a guide it should only cost 40,000d to Quy Nhon, although we've heard of people being charged four times as much.

QUY NHON

☎ 056 / pop 260,000

Surrounded by great beaches, ancient Cham temples and other interesting sights, it's inexplicable that Quy Nhon (Qui Nhon, pronounced Wee Ngon) is not firmly on the tourist trail. Yet this is what adds to its appeal. With few foreigners in sight, the peripheral market in hassling tourists is yet to establish itself. You'll find precious few touts, hawkers, beggars, pimps or dealers and it's quite possible to walk down the street without anyone yelling after you 'Hello! Yo! You!'

The capital of Binh Dinh province and one of Vietnam's more active second-string seaports, this is a great spot to sample some fresh local seafood. It's perfectly located to break the long journey from Hoi An to Nha Trang, with plenty to keep you occupied for a week, if lazing around on the beaches isn't enough.

During the American War there was considerable South Vietnamese, US, VC and South Korean military activity in the area. The mayor of Quy Nhon, hoping to cash in on the presence of US troops, turned his official resi-

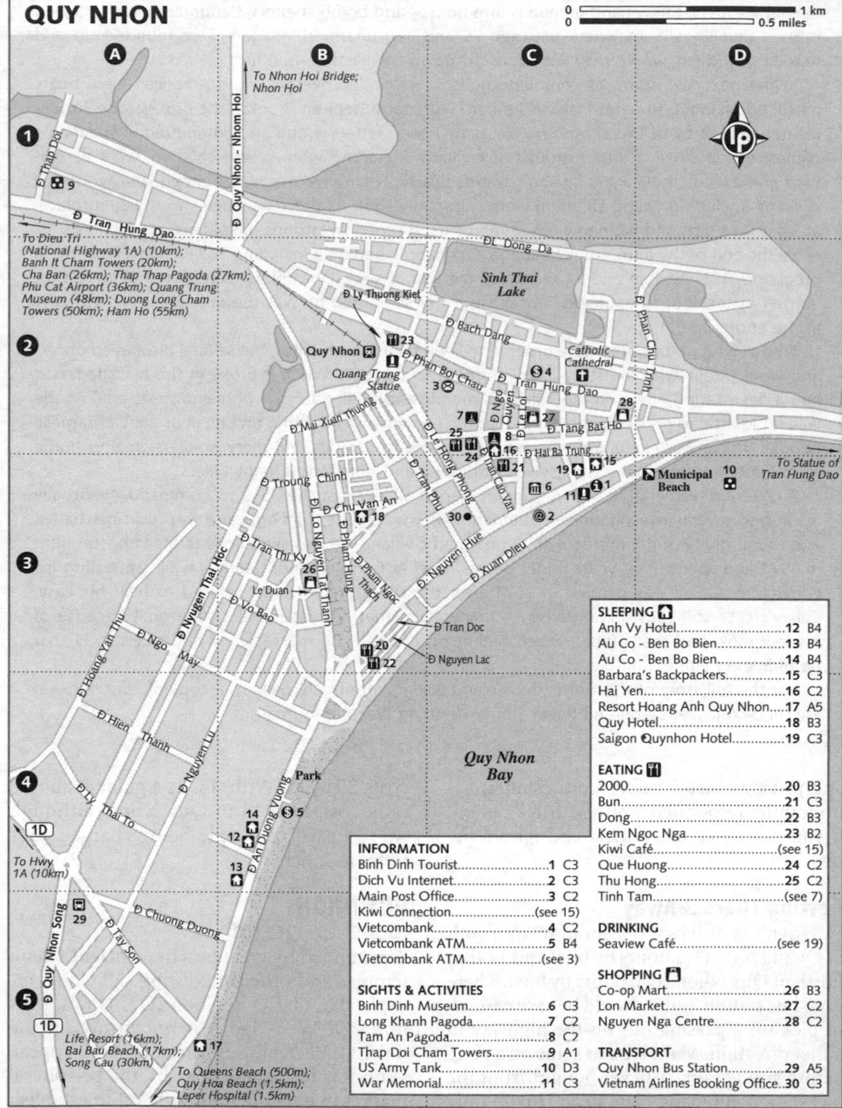

dence into a large massage parlour. The large slums of tin-and-thatch shacks that sprang up around the city, built by refugees dislocated by fighting, have now largely gone.

There's a historical connection between Quy Nhon and New Zealand dating back to the early 1960s, when funds and staff from New Zealand were provided to the provincial hospital and later to aid refugees. The strong links continue today, with New Zealand's Volunteer Service Abroad (VSA) involved in projects in health, fisheries management, agriculture and rural development, and the New Zealand Vietnam Health Trust providing training and specialists for the local hospital. At any one time around half of the small ex-pat community in Quy Nhon are Kiwis.

Orientation

Quy Nhon is on the coast, 10km east of Hwy 1A's Phu Tai junction. The main part of town is on an east–west orientated peninsula, shaped like an anteater's nose. The tip of the nose (the port area) is closed to the public. The municipal beach is on the peninsula's south coast, curving around to face east.

Information

Binh Dinh Tourist (☎ 892 524; fax 891 162; 10 Đ Nguyen Hue) For local tours.

Dich Vu Internet (☎ 811 262; 57 Đ Nguyen Hue; per hr 2000d)

Main post office (☎ 812 700; 197 Đ Phan Boi Chau; 🕓 6.30am-10pm)

Kiwi Connection/Kiwi Café (☎ 892 921; nzbarb@yahoo.com; 18 Đ Nguyen Hue) Free tourist information, bike and motorbike hire, local maps and connections with English-speaking drivers.

Vietcombank (☎ 822 266; 148 Đ Le Loi) On the corner of Đ Tran Hung Dao; has a 24-hour ATM. Further ATMs can be found outside the Hai Au Hotel (489 Đ An Duong Vuong) & the main post office (197 Đ Phan Boi Chau).

Sights

MUNICIPAL BEACH

The long sweep of Quy Nhon's beachfront extends from the port in the northeast to the hills in the south. Beautiful to look at, it's not the cleanest place to swim. In 2006 a fishing village was cleared from the centre of the beach, cleaning up one of the least hygienic areas – a lack of basic sanitation meant you had to watch your step.

At the top end, the nicest section is near Barbara's Backpackers, where a grove of coconuts lines the road. At dawn and in the evenings this area is packed with locals practising Tai Chi. Further up the beach, at low tide one of Quy Nhon's more peculiar sights reveals itself – a **US Army tank**, half submerged in the sand where it was abandoned by its departing owners. In the distance you can see a giant **statue of Tran Hung Dao** giving the Chinese the finger on the far headland (see p138). Heading south, a striking socialist-realist **War Memorial** dominates a small square.

From here, buildings encroach on the waterfront for a kilometre before opening out to a parklike promenade, punctuated by large hotels, stretching to the south end of the bay. At night the bright lights of the squid boats give the illusion of a floating town far out to sea.

BINH DINH MUSEUM

This small **museum** (☎ 822 452; 28 Đ Nguyen Hue; admission free; 🕓 7-11am & 2-5pm summer, 7.30-11am &

SIMPLY BARBARA

Like Kylie or Madonna, Barbara has achieved such a level of renown in Quy Nhon that she needs only one name. She's a one-woman, font-of-all-knowledge on things Quy Nhon, where Barbara's Backpackers (p274) and Kiwi Café (p275) are ex-pat institutions.

Barbara Dawson (she actually does have a last name) first arrived in Quy Nhon in 1995, teaching English in a local high school and administering New Zealand's VSA project. She started her tourist business the Kiwi Connection in 2002, opening Barbara's Backpackers and briefly branching out into a second property, Barbara's on the Beach, before the Vietnamese Army took a shine to it and took it over. When she's not got her tourism hat on, she still acts as a liaison for the New Zealand Vietnam Health Trust.

If you want to find out anything about Quy Nhon, Barbara's trusty tourist folder lists all the major sights, practical information and even listings of rival hotels and restaurants. She has bikes and motorbikes for rent and can introduce you to reliable English-speaking drivers for tours around the area.

1.30-4.30pm winter) features exhibits on regional history. The entry hall focuses on local Communism, including an interesting silk print (Zuy Nhat, 1959) showing a fat French colonist sitting aloft mandarins, in turn supported by bureaucrats, and cruel bosses, with the struggling masses supporting the whole lot. The room to the left has a small Natural History section and some Cham statues, while the rear room has the bulk of the excellent Cham collection. The room to the right of the entrance is devoted to the American War, with local relics such as the 'Spittoon of Heroic Vietnamese Mother Huynh Thi Bon'. A disturbing section captioned in English details various US and South Korean atrocities committed in the area.

THAP DOI CHAM TOWERS

This remarkable pair of **Cham towers** (admission 2000d; 8-11am & 1-6pm) sits within the city confines in a little park. Steep steps lead in to the former temples, which are open to the sky. Atypically for Cham architecture, they have curved pyramidal roofs rather than the usual terracing. The larger tower (20m tall) retains some of its ornate brickwork and remnants of the granite statuary that once graced its summit. The dismembered torsos of *garuda* (griffin-like beings) can be seen at the corners of the roofs.

To get here, take Đ Tran Hung Dao away from the centre and turn right into the lane after number 900 (Đ Thap Doi). The towers are down the first lane on the right, about 100m from the main road.

LONG KHANH PAGODA

It's hard to miss the 17m-high Buddha (built in 1972), heralding Quy Nhon's main pagoda – set back from the road next to 143 Đ Tran Cao Van. Founded in 1715 by a Chinese merchant, the monks who reside here preside over the religious affairs of the city's relatively active Buddhist community.

The pagoda was repaired in 1957 after being damaged during the Franco-Viet Minh War. Mosaic dragons with manes of broken glass lead up to the main building, flanked by towers sheltering a giant drum (on the left) and an enormous bell (right). Inside, in front of the large copper Thich Ca Buddha (with its multicoloured neon halo) is a drawing of multi-armed and multi-eyed Chuan De (the Goddess of Mercy); the numerous arms and eyes symbolise her ability to touch and see all.

TAM AN PAGODA

Quy Nhon's second most active pagoda, **Tam An** (58B Ngo Quyen), is a charming little place that attracts mostly female worshipers, although it's open to all.

Sleeping

BUDGET

Barbara's Backpackers (☎ 892 921; nzbarb@yahoo.com; 18 Đ Nguyen Hue; dm 40,000d, r US$6-10;) An old-school backpackers with considerable charm but less in the way of facilities, Barbara's friendly establishment is Budget Heaven. Directly across from the beach, this slightly rundown but deliciously '70s building has crazy tiles, wood panels and a dramatic curved staircase. The great-value four-person dorm sits atop a large balcony-like rooftop with sea views. It has its own cold-water shower and separate toilet, but no air-con. A private room with a fan and shared bathroom costs US$6, while the US$10 room includes a basic en suite and air-con, but no fridge or TV.

Anh Vy Hotel (☎ 847 763; 8 Đ An Duong Vuong; r 120,000-200,000d;) This new, family-run mini-hotel has clean rooms with tiny en suites and some great sea views.

Quy Hotel (☎ 813 567; fax 812 188; 9 Đ Chu Van An; r 120,000-250,000d;) The décor is wild in this older establishment, where the bathrooms are like little houses inside the rooms and a rickety bamboo bridge leads to a lovely rooftop terrace.

Hai Yen (☎ 822 480; 104 Đ Hai Ba Trung; r 150,000-200,000;) The nicest of the budget accommodation. What the family that runs this place lack in English they more than make up for in friendliness and service. All the rooms are different, so look at a few before deciding. Some are nearly suites, with a sitting area and private balcony.

Au Co – Ben Bo Bien (☎ 747 699; hotel_auco@yahoo.com; 8 & 24 Đ An Duong Vuong; r 160,000-300,000d;) The same family runs these two hotels with the same name a block apart, made even more confusing by one of them sharing the same street address as the Anh Vy Hotel. Number 8 is the slightly nicer of the two, looking like a Vietnamese take on San Francisco's iconic houses. Narrow stairs with carved wooden dragons on the balustrades lead to clean rooms with tiny bathrooms but great sea-views and balconies. Number 24 has the same facilities and prices but is even more kitsch, with fake trees dominating the lobby.

MIDRANGE & TOP END

Saigon Quynhon Hotel (☎ 820 100; www.saigonquynhonhotel.com.vn; 24 Đ Nguyen Hue; s US$35-50, d US$45-60, ste US$100-400;) This flash new hotel, well positioned on the waterfront, has surprisingly reasonable rates. The rooms have all the bells and whistles, including safety boxes, plush carpets, fluffy bathrobes, free wireless internet and seaviews.

Resort Hoang Anh Quy Nhon (☎ 747 100; www.hoanganhhotelgroup.com; 1 Đ Han Mac Tu; s US$80-110, d US$95-140, ste US$200;) Occupying a beautiful stretch of golden sand at the southernmost end of the bay, it's cruel that the water's not clean enough for swimming – although the enticing large swimming pool is just compensation. This stylish resort has a grand reception opening on to the water, a fitness centre, a tennis court and well-appointed rooms with nice linen and seaward balconies.

Life Resort (☎ 840 132; www.life-resorts.com; Ghenh Rang, Bai Dai Beach; r US$152-175, ste US$198;) This Dutch-owned resort, set on a beautiful beach 18km south of the town, seems to have got every detail right. A subtle Cham influence carries through the architecture and interior design. The spacious, bright rooms are unfussily elegant, with stunning open-plan bathrooms. You can indulge in a spa treatment, Tai Chi on the beach, snorkelling or take a boat to the resort's little offshore island. The wonderful staff offer friendly service and speak excellent English – one can only hope they're paid commensurately to the prices. The restaurant's food and wine selection is exceptional.

Eating & Drinking

Kiwi Café (☎ 892 921; nzbarb@yahoo.com; 18 Đ Nguyen Hue; mains 15,000-30,000d; breakfast, lunch & dinner) The choice of ex-pats and tourists alike, this place has a welcoming vibe and serves delicious Western-style food. The smoothies are excellent, and breakfast includes Kiwi favourites such as French toast with bacon, bananas and maple syrup. It's also the best place for a drink in town, with the bar open later than most and interesting conversation easy to come by.

Que Huong (☎ 812 123; 125 Đ Tang Bat Ho; dishes 30,000-40,000d) This friendly eatery spread over two floors has a good down-home vibe, serving everything from seafood and meat to snake and frogs.

Thu Hong (☎ 821 176; 189 Đ Tang Bat Ho; dishes 30,000-40,000d) A small family place, serving a good fish soup.

2000 (☎ 812 787; 1 Đ Tran Doc; dishes 40,000-90,000d; lunch & dinner) There's no denying the freshness of the seafood, as you walk past the large tubs of live crabs and fish downstairs. A table on an upstairs balcony provides a little distance from the rowdy main dining room of this popular boozy joint. Try a seafood hotpot or some of the massive steamed prawns.

Dong (☎ 824 877; 26 Đ Nguyen Lac; dishes US$3-10; lunch & dinner) Another of a cluster of popular seafood restaurants along the tiny lanes of Tran Doc and Nguyen Lac towards the centre of the bay. Keep heading upstairs for a slightly quieter meal.

Tinh Tam (141 Đ Tran Cao Van; mains 5000-10,000d), Right next to Long Khanh Pagoda, this place serves extremely good vegetarian meals in basic surrounds.

Bun (79 Đ Hai Ba Trung; meals 7000d) A humble place which does great *pho*, served with lots of fresh herbs and a pastry stick.

Seaview Café (☎ 820 100; 24 Đ Nguyen Hue) On the 8th-floor rooftop of the Saigon Quyhon Hotel, this is a great place to grab a coffee or a sundowner and enjoy the amazing views. There's also free wi-fi.

Quy Nhon has lots of delicious street food all around the town centre. If you've got a sweet tooth, check out the tasty bakery items and ice cream at **Kem Ngoc Nga** (☎ 821 562; 326 Đ Phan Boi Chau).

Shopping

Lon Market (Cho Lon, Đ Tang Bat Ho) In the dead centre of town, you'll find everything you'd expect from a Vietnamese market – from fruit and meat, to clothes and hardware.

Co-op Mart (☎ 821 321; 7 Đ Le Duan) This huge new development is supposedly a supermarket but, like a traditional market, sells a little bit of everything. The only difference between this and Lon Market is that prices are marked and there are check-outs.

Nguyen Nga Centre (☎ 891 296; nngacenter@dng.vnn.vn; 2 Đ Tang Bat Ho) The shop attached to this centre for disabled children (see p276) sells lovely homemade weavings, handicrafts and clothing, with the money going towards running the centre and giving the students an income. Shedding US$50 here will provide you with a huge bagful of interesting gifts to take home. Don't be put off if the gate's closed – it's kept shut to ensure none of the kids wander off.

THE AMAZING MS NGA

How does a young woman end up responsible for a school for 250 disabled students, 100 of which live on site?

For Ms Nguyen Thi Thanh Nga it all started in 1990 when her younger sister severely injured her leg in an accident. While caring for her sister, the awful plight of disabled people in her poverty-stricken homeland really hit home. In 1993, having just left high school herself, Nga leapt into action – starting vocational handicrafts training (knitting and embroidery) for 10 young people with disabilities. Thirteen years later her school has stretched to two buildings and has programmes in literacy, sign language, Braille, computer skills, dress-making, handicrafts, art and music – for children with impaired hearing, impaired sight, intellectual or physical disabilities. An early intervention programme means that there is residential care for infants ranging from one to six.

Apart from the buildings, the centre gets no financial support from the government. It is completely dependent on donations and the money made by the sale of handicrafts. A contract with Intrepid Travel producing satchels embroidered with the slogan 'Say no to plastic bags' is one way the older kids can earn some money, with a percentage going to the running of the centre.

If you're not financially able to make a donation or buy stacks of goodies in the shop, there are still a number of ways you can contribute. Consider bringing a bagful of old clothes or toys with you. Perhaps someone in the family has a stash of old baby clothes in the attic. How about that old laptop gathering dust since your last upgrade? Look at it this way – you can use the bag you've emptied out to fill up again with new gear in the tailor shops in Hoi An! If you've got experience in working with disabled children, or you're happy to muck in practically, volunteering might be an option. Make sure you email or phone first to see whether you can be of use.

Walking around the centre with Nga, it's obvious how much the kids love her. This beautiful, passionate young woman works here seven days a week. This is her life.

Getting There & Away

AIR

Vietnam Airlines flights link Quy Nhon with HCMC daily (515,000d) and with Danang three times per week (365,000d).

There's a **Vietnam Airlines booking office** (☎ 825 313; 55 Đ Le Hong Phong) offering a minibus transfer (25,000d) for airline passengers between the office and Phu Cat airport, 36km north of the city.

BUS

Quy Nhon bus station (Ben Xe Khach Quy Nhon; ☎ 846 246; Đ Tay Son) is on the south side of town. The next major stop north is Quang Ngai (60,000d, 3½ hours), with 11 daily buses heading on to Danang (65,000d) and one to Hué (110,000d). Heading south there are regular services to Tuy Hoa (50,000d, two hours) and on to Nha Trang (65,000d), with four heading all the way to HCMC (155,000d).

Quy Nhon is a great access point for the central highlands. There are plenty of buses to Pleiku (45,000d, four hours, 18 daily), of which five head on to Kon Tum (50,000d, five hours) and at least one to Buon Ma Thuot (85,000d) and Dalat (110,000d).

It is now possible to get a bus all the way to Pakse in Laos, crossing the new border north of Kon Tum (250,000d, 12 hours, four per week). Lao visas are not available at this border.

CAR & MOTORBIKE

Road distances from Quy Nhon are: 677km to HCMC, 238km to Nha Trang, 186km to Pleiku, 198km to Kon Tum, 174km to Quang Ngai and 303km to Danang.

TRAIN

The nearest the *Reunification Express* trains get to Quy Nhon is Dieu Tri, 10km from the city. **Quy Nhon train station** (Ga Quy Nhon; Đ Le Hong Phong; ☎ 822 036) is at the end of a 10km spur off the main north–south track. Only very slow local trains stop here and they are not worth bothering with. It's better to get to/from Dieu Tri by taxi or *xe om* (motorcycle taxi) for around 50,000d.

Tickets for trains departing from Dieu Tri can be purchased at the Quy Nhon train station, though if you arrive in Dieu Tri by train, your best bet is to purchase an onward ticket before leaving the station. Ticket prices to destinations include: Danang (133,000d, 5½ to 7½ hours, seven daily), Quang Ngai (72,000d, 2½ to four hours, seven daily), Tuy Hoa (44,000d, 1½ to two hours, seven daily), Nha Trang (93,000d, four hours, eight daily) and HCMC (248,000d, 10 to 14 hours, seven daily).

AROUND QUY NHON

Beaches

The water quality of the beaches improves considerably once you round the Ganh Rang hill to the south of the town. Several beaches are easily accessible by bicycle.

QUEEN'S BEACH

Popular with locals, this stony little beach at the foot of Ganh Rang was once a favourite holiday spot of Queen Nam Phuong. There's a café and great views back over Quy Nhon. To get here, take Đ An Duong Vuong to the far south end of Quy Nhon's beachfront and continue as the road starts to climb. After it crosses a small bridge, turn sharply to the left and head through the gates where you will need to pay the entrance fee (5000d). Follow the path up the hill, keeping to the left where it forks. Queen's Beach is signposted to the left.

QUY HOA BEACH & LEPER HOSPITAL

Leprosy may not conjure up images of fun in the sun, but this really is a lovely spot. As leper hospitals go, this one is highly unusual. Rather than being a depressing place, it's a sort of model village near the seafront, where treated patients live together with their families in small, well-kept houses. Depending on their abilities, the patients work in the rice fields, in fishery, and in repair-oriented businesses or small craft shops (one supported by Handicap International produces prosthetic limbs).

The **grounds of the hospital** (☎ 646 343; admission 3000d; 🕑 8-11.30am & 1.30-4pm) are so well maintained that it looks a bit like a resort, complete with a guitar-shaped pavilion and numerous busts of distinguished and historically important doctors (both Vietnamese and foreign). Fronting the village is **Quy Hoa Beach**, one of the nicer stretches of sand around Quy Nhon and a popular weekend hang-out for the city's expat community. Just up from the beach, there's a dirt path to the hillside **Tomb of Han Mac Tu**, a mystical poet who died in 1940.

If travelling by foot or bicycle, continue along the road past Queen's Beach until it descends to the hospital's entrance gates, about 1.5km south of Quy Nhon. It's also accessible from the road to Song Cau by taking a left turn once the water comes back into view after crossing the hills south of town.

BAI BAU BEACH

While the Life Resort charges nonguests an extortionate US$10 to lounge on their beach (whether they've spent a fortune at the restaurant or not), those in the know will head a kilometre to the north for an even better beach at less than a 10th of the price. **Bai Bau** (admission 5000d, deck chair 5000d) is a beautiful white-sand crescent no more than 150m wide, sheltered by rocky headlands, with mountains for a backdrop. It can get busy on the weekend and during Vietnamese holidays, but midweek you'll likely have the place to yourself.

Bai Bau is well signed, just off the road to Song Cau, 19km south of Quy Nhon.

Cham Sites

The former Cham capital of Cha Ban (also known as Vijay and Quy Nhon) was located 26km north of Quy Nhon and 5km from Binh Dinh. While an archaeologically important site, there's not a lot to see. However, there are several interesting Cham structures dotted around the area.

BANH IT CHAM TOWERS

The most interesting and accessible of the area's Cham sites, this group of four towers is clearly visible from Hwy 1A, sitting atop a hill 20km to the north of Quy Nhon. The architecture of each tower is distinctly different, although all were built around the end of the 11th century and the beginning of the 12th. The smaller, barrel-roofed tower has the most intricate carvings, although there's still a wonderfully toothy face looking down on it from the wall of the largest tower. A large Buddhist pagoda sits on the side of the hill under the lowest of the towers. There are great views of the surrounding countryside from the top of the hill.

The **Banh It Cham Towers** (Phuoc Hiep, Tuy Phuoc district; admission free; 🕑 7-11am & 1.30-4.30pm) are easily reached by taking Đ Tran Hung Dao out of town for about 30 minutes, when you'll see the towers in the distance to the right of the road. After the traffic lights joining the main highway, cross the bridge and turn right. Take the left turn heading up the hill to reach the entrance.

DUONG LONG CHAM TOWERS

The **Duong Long Cham towers** (Binh Hoa, Tay Son district; admission free; 7-11am & 1.30-4.30pm) are harder to find, sitting in the countryside about 50km northwest of Quy Nhon. Dating from the late 12th century, the largest of the three brick towers (24m high) is embellished with granite ornamentation representing *naga* (a mythical serpent being with divine powers) and elephants (Duong Long means Towers of Ivory). Over the doors are bas-reliefs of women, dancers, monsters and various animals. The corners of the structure are formed by enormous dragon heads. At the time of research a major dig was taking place, revealing well-preserved carvings about 1m below the present ground level at the base of the towers. A major restoration job was also in progress.

You're best to visit the towers with a driver or a tour, as the site is reached by a succession of pretty country lanes through rice paddies and over rickety bridges.

OTHER TOWERS

Several single towers sprout out of farmland around the area. These are not as well restored as the big sites, and they generally have no gates or admission charges. You'll need an experienced guide (enquire at Barbara's Kiwi Café or Binh Dinh Tourist, see p273) and a couple of days to spare if you want to track them all down.

Thu Thien (Binh Nghi, Tay Son district) is not far off Hwy 19, 35km northwest from Quy Nhon, and can easily be combined with a visit to Duong Long and the Quang Trung Museum. **Phu Loc** (Nhon Thanh village, An Nhon district) translates as the Gold Tower and has beautiful views, while **Canh Tien** (Nhon Hau, An Nhon district), built in the 16th century, is named after upturned leaf shapes at the top which are said to resemble fairy wings. **Binh Lam** (Phuoc Hoa village, Tuy Phuoc district) sits high on a hill, 22km from Quy Nhon.

Quang Trung Museum

Nguyen Hue, the second-oldest of the three brothers who led the Tay Son Rebellion, crowned himself Emperor Quang Trung in 1788. In 1789 Quang Trung led the campaign that overwhelmingly defeated a Chinese invasion of 200,000 troops near Hanoi. This epic battle is still celebrated as one of the greatest triumphs in Vietnamese history.

During his reign, Quang Trung was something of a social reformer. He encouraged land reform, revised the system of taxation, im-

THE LOST CITY OF CHAMPA

Cha Ban, which served as the capital of Champa from the year 1000 (after the loss of Indrapura/Dong Duong) until 1471, was attacked and plundered repeatedly by the Vietnamese, Khmers and Chinese.

In 1044 the Vietnamese Prince Phat Ma occupied the city and carried off a great deal of booty along with the Cham king's wives, harem, female dancers, musicians and singers. Cha Ban was under the control of a Khmer overseer from 1190 to 1220. In 1377 the Vietnamese were defeated and their king was killed in an attempt to capture Cha Ban. The Vietnamese emperor Le Thanh Ton breached the eastern gate of the city in 1471 and captured the Cham king and 50 members of the royal family. During this, the last great battle fought by the Cham, 60,000 Cham were killed and 30,000 more were taken prisoner by the Vietnamese.

During the Tay Son Rebellion, Cha Ban served as the capital of central Vietnam, and was ruled by the eldest of the three Tay Son brothers. It was attacked in 1793 by the forces of Nguyen Anh (later Emperor Gia Long), but the assault failed. In 1799 they laid siege to the city again, under the command of General Vu Tinh, this time capturing it.

The Tay Son soon reoccupied the port of Thi Nai (modern-day Quy Nhon) and then laid siege to Cha Ban themselves. The siege continued for over a year, and by June 1801, Vu Tinh's provisions were gone. Food was in short supply; all the horses and elephants had long since been eaten. Refusing to consider the ignominy of surrender, Vu Tinh had an octagonal wooden tower constructed. He filled it with gunpowder and, arrayed in his ceremonial robes, went inside and blew himself up. Upon hearing the news of the death of his dedicated general, Nguyen Anh wept.

proved the army and emphasised education, opening many schools and encouraging the development of Vietnamese poetry and literature. He died in 1792 at the age of 40. Communist literature portrays him as the leader of a peasant revolution whose progressive policies were crushed by the reactionary Nguyen dynasty, which came to power in 1802 and was overthrown by Ho Chi Minh in 1945.

The **Quang Trung Museum** (Phu Phong; admission 10,000d; ⌚ 8-11.30am & 1-4.30pm Mon-Fri) is built on the site of the brothers' house and encloses the original well and a 200-year-old tamarind tree said to be planted by them. Displays include various statues, costumes, documents and artefacts from the 18th century, most of them labelled in English. Especially notable are the elephant-skin battle drums and gongs from the Bahnar tribe. The museum is also known for its demonstrations of *vo binh dinh,* a traditional martial art that is performed with a bamboo stick.

GETTING THERE & AWAY

The museum is about 50km from Quy Nhon. Take Hwy 19 west for 40km towards Pleiku. The museum is about 5km north of the highway (the turn-off is sign-posted) in Phu Phong, Tay Son district.

Ham Ho

A beautiful nature reserve 55km from Quy Nhon, **Ham Ho** (☎ 880 860; Tay Phu; admission 5,000d; ⌚ 7-11.30am & 1-4.30pm) can easily be combined with a trip to the Quang Trung Museum. Taking up a jungle-lined 3km stretch of clean, fish-filled river, the park is best enjoyed by boat (50,000d). The further up-river you travel, the better the swimming spots are.

The road to Ham Ho is signposted to the south of Hwy 19 at Tay Son.

Thap Thap Pagoda

This peaceful pagoda in the heart of the countryside was built in the 17th century partly from material stripped from neighbouring Cham towers. It's a lovely piece of Buddhist architecture with a deep veranda surrounded by attractive gardens. Take time to wander through the serene cemetery behind.

To find it, take Hwy 1A for 27km northwest of Quy Nhon. Just past Dong Da village turn left before a small bridge labelled Can Van Thuan 2 onto a tiny country lane leading to Nhon Hau village.

SONG CAU

☎ 057

The village of Song Cau is an obscure place that you could easily drive past without ever noticing, but nearby is an immense beautiful bay. It makes a good rest stop for tourists doing the Nha Trang-Hoi An run. Song Cau is along a notorious stretch of Hwy 1A dubbed the 'Happy 16 Kilometres' by long-distance truck drivers, named for the 'taxi girls' who ply their trade by the roadside along this stretch.

Getting There & Away

Song Cau is 170km north of Nha Trang and 30km south of Quy Nhon. Highway buses can drop off and pick up here (with luck). If travelling with your own wheels, consider taking the newly completed coastal road between Song Cau and Quy Nhon; the scenery is stunning, and there are several good beaches en route.

TUY HOA

☎ 057 / pop 165,000

Pronounced Twee Hwa, the capital of Phu Yen province is a friendly little place with a nice wide beach with coarse golden sand – a great overnight stop to break up a longer journey.

The few sights the town has are all on hilltops visible from Hwy 1A. There's a huge **Seated Buddha** which greets you if you're approaching from the north. To the south of town the **Nhan Cham Tower** is an impressive sight, particularly when it's illuminated at night. The climb to the tower takes you through a small **Botanic Garden** and is rewarded by great views. On a side of the same hill a massive white **Monument** was under construction at the time of research, with sails a little like the Sydney Opera House.

Orientation & Information

Hwy 1A forms the western edge of town with the Da Rang River to the south. The main street, Tran Hung Dao, runs several kilometres from the highway to the beach in the east.

Incombank ATM (239 Đ Tran Hung Dao) Opposite the market.

Main post office (cnr Đ Tran Hung Dao & Nguyen Thai)

Phong Thuc Hanh Internet (☎ 836 228; 2 Đ Nguyen Hue)

Sleeping & Eating

Ai Cuc (☎ 819 224; 6 Đ Le Quy Don; r 120,000-300,000d; ❄) This very pink place has a waterfall in the reception and big, bright, clean rooms with balconies. The staff are very welcoming without speaking much English. There are great views from the popular seafood restaurant upstairs (dishes 40,000d to 90,000d). You'll find it on a quiet side street heading north off Tran Hung Dao, a few blocks past the market.

Cong Doan Hotel (☎ 823 187; 53 Đ Doc Lap; r US$15; ❄) Right by the beach, this large blue and peach establishment (they sure love their pastels) has tidy rooms and some amazing sea views.

You'll find more hotels and plenty of humble restaurants and street vendors along the highway and Đ Tran Hung Dao, as well as a stretch of seafood restaurants and *bia hoi* (draught beer) joints along the beach.

Getting there & away

Tuy Hoa has no bus station, but buses tend to stop for fares at the petrol station on Hwy 1A, not far from the Cham Tower. There are regular buses to Quy Nhon (50,000d, two hours, 110km) and Nha Trang (50,000d, 3½ hours, 123km).

A stop on the *Reunification Express*, **Tuy Hoa Train Station** (Ga Tuy Hoa; ☎ 823 672; 149 Le Trung Kien) is on the road parallel to the highway, north of the main street. Destinations include Danang (153,000d, seven to 10 hours, five daily), Quang Ngai (97,000d, five to six hours, four daily) and Nha Trang (44,000d, 2½ hours, five daily).

Vietnam Airlines operates three flights weekly between Tuy Hoa and HCMC (530,000d). There's a **Vietnam Airlines Booking Office** (☎ 826 508; 353 Tran Hung Dao) in the centre of town and the airport is 8km to the south.

BEACHES NORTH OF NHA TRANG

☎ 058

The coastal drive between Tuy Hoa and Nha Trang on Hwy 1A provides tantalising glimpses of a number of beautiful remote spots, while others hide in the jungle along promontories and on islands. Decent accommodation options are limited, but as a day trip there's plenty to discover if you've got your own wheels. Throw away the guidebook for a day and go exploring.

Dai Lanh Beach

While half of semicircular Dai Lanh Beach is eaten up by an unattractive fishing village, the south end is still shaded by casuarina trees, along with the hulk of an abandoned hotel project. About 1km south is a vast sand-dune causeway worth exploring; it connects the mainland to Hon Gom, a mountainous peninsula almost 30km in length. Boats for Whale Island leave from Hom Gom's main village **Dam Mon**, set on a sheltered bay.

It's possible to stay overnight under the trees right on Dai Lanh Beach if you're not fussy about comfort. **Thuy Ta Restaurant** (☎ 842 117; tents 15,000d, r 70,000-120,000d) has tents, as well as some ultra-simple straw-roof beach bungalows, with brick floors and fans. Toilets are shared, and for nonguests there's a charge of 3000d for the use of cold showers. Fresh seafood features prominently on the menu; expect mains to cost about 30,000d. Keep a close eye on your gear; we've had a few reports of theft.

Dai Lanh is situated 40km south of Tuy Hoa and 83km north of Nha Trang on Hwy 1A. Any highway buses can drop you here and there's a local train station.

Whale Island

A 15-minute boat ride from Dam Mon (see above, Whale Island is a tiny speck on the map – home to the lovely and secluded French-run **Whale Island Resort** (☎ 840 501; www.whaleislandresort.com; s/d/tr/q US$110/140/155/180). While single night-rates are expensive for the simple bamboo beachfront bungalows, it discounts substantially depending on length of stay; for example, a five-night stay averages US$52 per night for a single – less than half the rate for one night. Prices include the two-hour car journey from Cam Ranh airport, boat transfers and three meals per day.

Rainbow Divers (see p288) have a permanent base on the island, and the Nha Trang office can take resort bookings and help with transfers. Scuba-diving season ends in mid-October, starting up again in mid-February. Despite the damaging effects of dynamite fishing, environmental protection efforts (including the transplanting of sea coral) around the resort bay have brought about a marked increase in the number of marine species – from 40 to over 170.

Doc Let Beach

This lovely stretch of beachfront is long and wide, with chalk-white sand and shallow water. Doc Let (pronounced 'yop lek') is easily accessible from Nha Trang, and worth considering as a day trip (beach entrance fee

10,000d) or overnight stop. Although there's a small town nearby, the resorts on the beach are fairly isolated. If you're staying here, be prepared to do nothing but lay around.

SLEEPING

Paradise Resort (☎ 670 480; www.vngold.com/doclet/paradise/; bungalows s US$14-16, d US$20-22) Quite separate from the busy part of the beach in the tiny village of Dom Hai, this simple place is run by a Frenchman and his young Vietnamese family. Accommodation is basic, but the flimsy new bamboo huts are atmospheric at least, fitted with mosquito nets and tiny fans. The price would seem hefty if it didn't include three meals, as well as free bottled water, tea, coffee and fruit. Being in the village you can explore the little food market, street stalls and colourful Buddhist pagoda, under the ominous presence of an abandoned American guardtower. Follow the blue signs past the turn-off for Doc Let Resort for 2km, turning right at a petrol station and then right again halfway through the village.

Doc Let Beach Resort (☎ 849 152; docletresort@dng.vnn.vn; bungalows fan/air-con 150,000/250,000d;) Catering mainly to domestic tourists, this large complex with 28 concrete bungalows is nestled in a casuarina grove, right on the beach. Excellent for the price and setting, the rooms are clean, and facilities include a swimming pool, tennis courts, two restaurants, a bar and, of course, karaoke and massage facilities.

White Sand Doclet Resort & Spa (☎ 670 670; www.whitesandresort.com.vn; r US$51, bungalows US$60-88;) Designed with a view to Western tastes, this brand new resort provides an upmarket option, with nice linen, bathrobes, slippers and safes in all the rooms. All the bungalows face the beach, while the more expensive have king-size beds, a large bath, a huge TV and a DVD player. A nicely low-rise hotel looks over the pool, with very similar room facilities to the bungalows, all with a private balcony or terrace.

GETTING THERE & AWAY

Head 35km north of Nha Trang on Hwy 1A, turning right (east) about 4km past Ninh Hoa. Continue for 10km past photogenic salt fields, looking out for the signs to the resorts. Make a left turn to take you through Doc Let village and then a right to the beach. There is no public transport, but tour operators in Nha Trang offer day trips often coupled with Monkey Island. If you're planning on staying here, enquire at your resort regarding transfers.

Ninh Van Bay

This place doesn't really exist – except in an alternate reality populated by European royalty, filmstars and the otherwise rich and secretive. Occupying a secluded beach at the end of a dense jungle-covered peninsula north of Nha Trang, there are no roads to the secure home of **Evason Hideaway & Six Senses Spa at Ana Mandara** (☎ 728 222; www.sixsenses.com/hideaway-anamandara/; villas US$633-2070;). Access is strictly restricted to guests only, via a half-hour ride on the resort's speedboat from a landing point 14km north of Nha Trang. The resort even has its own time zone – setting the clocks an hour ahead in an effort to encourage guests to enjoy the sunrise. The traditionally inspired architecture and the dirt tracks between buildings give the illusion of a jungle village – albeit one where every dwelling is an elegant two-storey villa, each with its own swimming pool and round-the-clock butler service. As you would hope for the price, the facilities and attention to detail are superb, the staff are friendly and helpful, and the setting is simply magical.

NHA TRANG

☎ 058 / pop 315,200

Nha Trang has a split personality. One takes the form of a smaller Danang – a bustling Vietnamese city humming with commerce but blessed with access to a beautiful beach. The other is a Western resort town encompassing several blocks of hotels, tourist shops, bars and international restaurants. Entering this sheltered enclave you could be anywhere in the world, if it weren't for the constant hassling from *xe om* drivers, many of whom seem to moonlight as pimps and dealers.

The city is indisputably beautiful, bordered by mountains, with the beach tracing an impressive long swoop along a bay dotted with islands. Topiary and modern sculpture dot the immaculately manicured foreshore. The only blight on the horizon is the Hollywood-style sign for the Vinpearl complex – an ugly scar dominating nearby Hon Tre Island.

Nha Trang offers plenty to keep tourists occupied – from island-hopping boat trips and scuba diving, to mudbaths and historic sites. But the main attraction for most visitors is

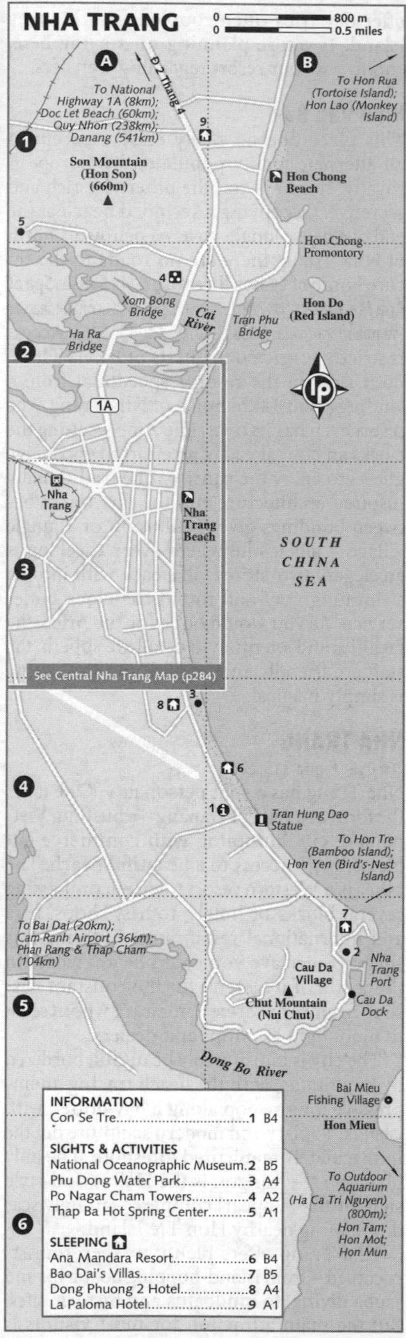

lounging around on deckchairs at a beachfront bar and drinking cocktails in comfort.

Information

BOOKSHOPS

Shorty's Café Bar (Map p284; ☎ 524 057; 1E Đ Biet Thu) Carries secondhand books, mostly in English.

INTERNET ACCESS

Nha Trang has dozens of designated internet cafés all over town, and you can also get online in many hotels and travellers' cafés.

MEDICAL SERVICES

Pasteur Institute (Map p284; ☎ 822 355; 10 Đ Tran Phu) Offers medical consultations and vaccinations. See p286.

MONEY

Vietcombank (Map p284; ☎ 822 720; 17 Đ Quang Trung; ⏲ Mon-Fri) changes travellers cheques and gives cash advances. There's another **Vietcombank branch** (Map p284; ☎ 524 500; 5 Đ Hung Vuong) which has an ATM, and also exchanges cash and travellers cheques. There is a handy **Vietcombank ATM** (Map p284; 4 Đ Le Loi) outside the main post office and another **Vietcombank ATM** (Map p284; 60 Đ Tran Phu) outside the Que Huong Hotel.

POST

Main post office (Map p284; ☎ 823 866; 4 Đ Le Loi; ⏲ 6.30am-10pm)

Post office branches 50 Đ Le Thanh Ton (Map p284; ☎ 652 070; ⏲ 7am-11pm); 1/29 Đ Tran Quang Khai (Map p284; ☎ 522 099)

TRAVEL AGENCIES

Khanh Hoa Tours (Map p284; ☎ 526 753; khtourism@dng.vnn.vn; 1 Đ Tran Hung Dao) Offers various tour programmes, including boat trips.

Mama Linh's Boat Tours (Map p284; ☎ 522 844; fax 522 845; 23C Đ Biet Thu) Known for its boat tours, Mama Linh's can also arrange trips around the province and into the highlands.

Sinh Café (Map p284; ☎ 524 329; sinhcafént@dng.vnn.vn; 10 Đ Biet Thu) Offers bargain basement local tours as well as open-tour buses.

Dangers & Annoyances

In Nha Trang there are many ways for you and your money to part company. We've heard reports of thefts on the beach (pickpockets, and jewellery disappearing during an embrace), during massages (a third person sneaks into the room and removes money from clothes) and from hotel rooms (none of the ones listed in this book, but you should still be cautious). Don't carry too much on you, and consider leaving surplus cash at the hotel reception. That way the hotel is responsible if it goes missing, although even this may not protect you from unscrupulous operators.

At tourist sites unobservant foreigners may be overcharged – check the price on pre-printed tickets, check your change and don't pay more than a 2000 dong for bicycle parking.

A persistent scam exists at the Long Son Pagoda, where you will be approached by children with pre-printed name badges (and occasionally older people) claiming to work for the monks. After showing you around the pagoda, whether invited to or not, they will then demand money 'for the monks' or, if that fails, insist that you buy postcards for 100,000d. The best course of action is to firmly let them know you don't require their services when they first appear. If they persist, tell them that you know they don't work for the monks and you're not about to give them any money – this should ensure a quick disappearance. If you want to give money towards the monks and upkeep of the complex, leave it in the donation boxes as you would in any other pagoda.

Sights

NHA TRANG BEACH

The clear turquoise waters of Nha Trang's 6km beach are best enjoyed during the dry season – from June to early October. During heavy rains, run off from the rivers at each end of the beach flows into the bay, gradually turning it a murky brown. Most of the year, however, the water is as it appears in the tourist brochures. Even in the wettest months, rain usually falls only at night or in the morning. The best beach weather is generally before 1pm; the afternoon sea breezes can make things unpleasant until the wind dies back down around 8pm.

Beach chairs are available for rent where you can sit and enjoy the drinks, light food or massages that the beach vendors have on offer. About the only time you'll need to move is to use the toilet or when the tide comes up. The two most popular lounging spots are the Sailing Club and Louisiane Brewhouse (see p292).

PO NAGAR CHAM TOWERS

The Cham towers of **Po Nagar** (Thap Ba, the Lady of the City; Map p282; admission 4500d; 6am-6pm) were built between the 7th and 12th centuries, although the site was used for worship as early as the 2nd century AD. To this day Cham, ethnic Chinese and Vietnamese Buddhists come to Po Nagar to pray and make offerings, according to their respective traditions. This site has a continuing religious significance, so be sure to remove your shoes before entering.

The towers serve as the Holy See, honouring Yang Ino Po Nagar, the goddess of the Dua (Liu) clan, which ruled over the southern part of the Cham kingdom covering Kauthara and Pan Duranga (present day Khanh Hoa and Thuan Hai provinces). The original wooden structure was razed to the ground by attacking Javanese in AD 774 but was replaced by a stone-and-brick temple (the first of its kind) in 784. There are inscribed stone slabs scattered throughout the complex, most of which relate to history or religion, and provide insight into the spiritual life and social structure of the Cham.

Originally the complex covered an area of 500 sq metres and there were seven or eight towers, four of which remain. All of the temples face east, as did the original entrance to the complex, which is to the right as you ascend the hillock. In centuries past, a person coming to pray passed through the pillared meditation hall, 10 pillars of which can still be seen, before proceeding up the steep staircase to the towers.

The 28m-high **North Tower** (Thap Chinh), with its terraced pyramidal roof, vaulted interior masonry and vestibule, is a superb example of Cham architecture. One of the tallest Cham towers, it was built in AD 817 after the original temples here were sacked and burned. The raiders also carried off a *linga* (see p265) made of precious metal. In AD 918 King Indravarman III placed a gold *mukha-linga* (a carved phallus with a human face painted on it) in the North Tower, but it too was taken, this time by the Khmers. This pattern of statues being destroyed or stolen and then replaced continued until 965, when King Jaya Indravarman I replaced the gold *mukha-linga* with the stone figure, Uma (*shakti*, or a feminine manifestation of Shiva), which remains to this day.

Above the entrance to the North Tower, two musicians flank a dancing four-armed Shiva, one of whose feet is on the head of the bull Nandin. The sandstone doorposts are covered with inscriptions, as are parts of the walls of the vestibule. A gong and a drum stand under the pyramid-shaped ceiling of

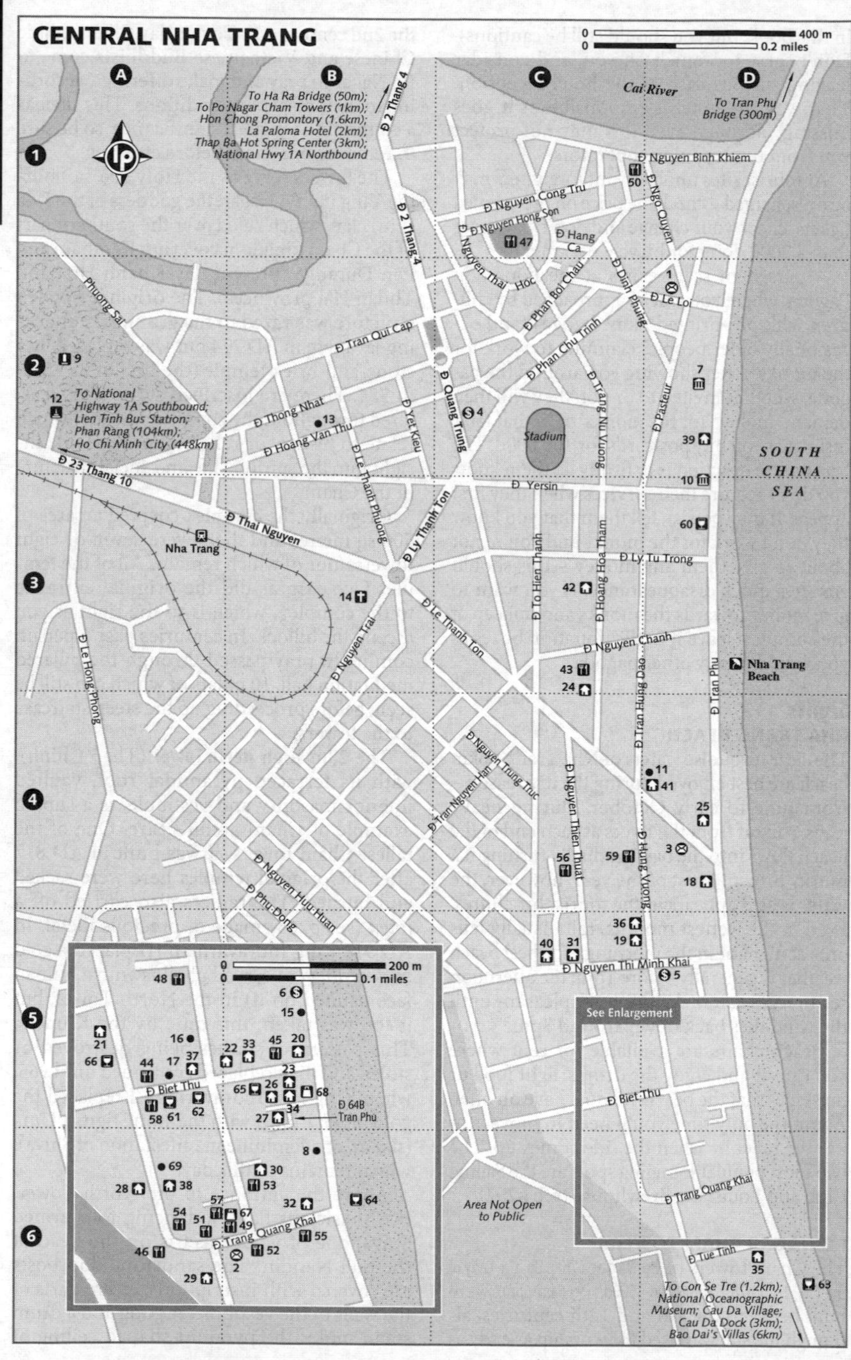
CENTRAL NHA TRANG
0 400 m
0 0.2 miles
A
B
C
D
1
2
3
4
5
6
Cai River
To Ha Ra Bridge (50m); To Po Nagar Cham Towers (1km); Hon Chong Promontory (1.6km); La Paloma Hotel (2km); Thap Ba Hot Spring Center (3km); National Hwy 1A Northbound
To Tran Phu Bridge (300m)
Đ 2 Thang 4
Đ Nguyen Binh Khiem
Đ Nguyen Cong Tru
Đ Nguyen Hong Son
Đ Ngo Quyen
Đ Hang Ca
Đ Nguyen Thai Hoc
Đ Phan Boi Chau
Đ Dinh Phung
Đ Le Loi
Phuong Sai
Đ Tran Qui Cap
Đ Phan Chu Trinh
Đ Quang Trung
Đ Tran Nu Vuong
Đ Pasteur
To National Highway 1A Southbound; Lien Tinh Bus Station; Phan Rang (104km); Ho Chi Minh City (448km)
Đ Thong Nhat
Đ Hoang Van Thu
Đ Yet Kieu
Stadium
Đ 23 Thang 10
Đ Le Thanh Phuong
Đ Yersin
SOUTH CHINA SEA
Đ Ly Thanh Ton
Đ Thai Nguyen
Nha Trang
Đ Ly Tu Trong
Đ To Hien Thanh
Đ Hoang Hoa Tham
Đ Le Thanh Ton
Đ Nguyen Trai
Đ Nguyen Chanh
Nha Trang Beach
Đ Le Hong Phong
Đ Tran Hung Dao
Đ Tran Phu
Đ Nguyen Trung Truc
Đ Tran Nguyen Han
Đ Nguyen Thien Thuat
Đ Hung Vuong
Đ Nguyen Huu Huan
Đ Phu Dong
Đ Nguyen Thi Minh Khai
0 200 m
0 0.1 miles
Đ Biet Thu
Đ 64B Tran Phu
Đ Trang Quang Khai
See Enlargement
Area Not Open to Public
Đ Tue Tinh
To Con Se Tre (1.2km); National Oceanographic Museum; Cau Da Village; Cau Da Dock (3km); Bao Dai's Villas (6km)

the antechamber. In the 28m-high pyramidal main chamber, there is a black stone statue of the goddess Uma with 10 arms, two of which are hidden under her vest; she is seated and leaning back against some sort of monstrous animal.

The **Central Tower** (Thap Nam) was built partly of recycled bricks in the 12th century on the site of a structure dating from the 7th century. It is less finely constructed than the other towers and has little ornamentation; the pyramidal roof lacks terracing or pilasters, although the interior altars were once covered with silver. There is a *linga* inside the main chamber. Note the inscription on the left-hand wall of the vestibule.

The **South Tower** (Mieu Dong Nam), at one time dedicated to Sandhaka (Shiva), still shelters a *linga,* while the richly ornamented **Northwest Tower** (Thap Tay Bac) was originally dedicated to Ganesh. To the rear of the complex is a small **museum** with a few mediocre examples of Cham stonework; the explanatory signs are in Vietnamese only.

The towers of Po Nagar stand on a granite knoll, 2km north of central Nha Trang on the banks of the Cai River. To get here from central Nha Trang, take Đ Quang Trung (which becomes Đ 2 Thang 4) north across the Ha Ra and Xom Bong Bridges. Po Nagar can also be reached via the new Tran Phu Bridge along the beachfront road.

LONG SON PAGODA

This striking **pagoda** (Map p284; 7.30-11.30am & 1.30-8pm) was founded in the late 19th century and has been rebuilt several times over the years. The entrance and roofs are decorated with mosaic dragons constructed of glass and bits of ceramic tile. The main sanctuary is a hall adorned with modern interpretations of traditional motifs. Note the ferocious nose hairs on the colourful dragons wrapped around the pillars on either side of the main altar.

At the top of the hill, behind the pagoda, is a huge white **Buddha** (Kim Than Phat To) seated on a lotus blossom and visible from all over the city. Around the statue's base are fire-ringed relief busts of Thich Quang Duc and six other Buddhist monks who died in self-immolations in 1963 (see p221). The platform around the 14m-high figure has great views of Nha Trang and nearby rural areas. As you approach the pagoda from the street, the 152 stone steps up the hill to the Buddha begin to the right of the

INFORMATION

- Main Post Office 1 D2
- Pasteur Institute (see 7)
- Post Office 2 B6
- Post Office 3 D4
- Vietcombank 4 C2
- Vietcombank 5 D5
- Vietcombank ATM 6 B5
- Vietcombank ATM (see 1)

SIGHTS & ACTIVITIES

- Alexandre Yersin Museum 7 D2
- Blue Diving Club 8 B6
- Buddha 9 A2
- Khanh Hoa Museum 10 D3
- Khanh Hoa Tours 11 D4
- Long Son Pagoda 12 A2
- Long Thanh Gallery 13 B2
- Mama Linh's Boat Tours (see 58)
- Mana Mana Beach Club (see 63)
- Nha Trang Cathedral 14 B3
- Octopus Diving 15 B5
- Rainbow Divers 16 A5
- Sailing Club Divers (see 64)
- Sinh Café 17 A5

SLEEPING

- 44 Tran Phu 18 D4
- 56 Hung Vuong Hotel 19 C5
- 62 Tran Phu Hotel 20 B5
- AP Hotel 21 A5
- Asia Paradise Hotel 22 B5
- Blue Star Hotel 23 B5
- Dong Phuong 1 Hotel (see 38)
- Ha Minh Hotel 24 C3
- Hai Yen Hotel 25 D4
- Hotel An Hoa 26 B5
- Hotel Nhi Hang 27 B5
- Hotel Phuong Ngoc 28 A6
- La Suisse Hotel 29 A6
- Mai Huy 30 B6
- My Long Hotel 31 C5
- Nha Trang Beach Hotel 32 B6
- Perfume Grass Inn 33 B5
- Pho Bien 34 B5
- Phu Quy 2 Hotel 35 D6
- Phu Quy Hotel 36 C5
- Rainbow Hotel 37 A5
- Sao Mai Hotel 38 A6
- Sunrise Beach Resort 39 D2
- Thien Long 40 C5
- Vien Dong Hotel 41 D4
- Yen My Hotel 42 C3

EATING

- Au Lac 43 C3
- Bo De (see 43)
- Bombay 44 A5
- Café des Amis 45 B5
- Cyclo Café 46 A6
- Dam Market 47 C1
- El Coyote 48 A5
- Good Morning Vietnam (see 61)
- Khanh Kat 49 B6
- Lac Canh Restaurant 50 C1
- Le Petit Bistro 51 A6
- Louisiane Brewhouse (see 63)
- Mai Anh 52 B6
- Pho Cali 53 B6
- Sailing Club (see 64)
- Same Same But Different Café 54 A6
- Selene 55 B6
- Thanh Thanh Cafe 56 C4
- Tin Duc 57 A6
- Truc Linh 2 58 A5
- Turkish Cuisine Kebab Restaurant 59 C4

DRINKING

- City View Café 60 D3
- Crazy Kim Bar 61 A5
- Guava 62 A5
- Louisiane Brewhouse 63 D6
- Sailing Club 64 B6
- Shorty's Café Bar 65 B5
- Zippo 66 A5

SHOPPING

- A Mart (see 62)
- My Village 67 B6
- XQ 68 B5

TRANSPORT

- Vietnam Airlines 69 A6

structure. You should take some time to explore off to the left, where there's an entrance to another hall of the pagoda.

Genuinely desperate-seeming beggars congregate within the complex, as do a number of scam-artists (see p282). The pagoda is located about 400m west of the train station, just off Đ 23 Thang 10.

NHA TRANG CATHEDRAL

Built between 1928 and 1933 in the French Gothic style, complete with stained glass windows, **Nha Trang Cathedral** (Map p284; cnr Đ Nguyen Trai & Đ Thai Nguyen) stands on a small hill overlooking the train station. It's a surprisingly elegant building, given that it was constructed of simple cement blocks. A particularly colourful Vietnamese touch is the red neon outlining the crucifix, the pink back-lighting on the tabernacle and the blue neon arch and white neon halo over the statue of St Mary. In 1988 a Catholic cemetery not far from the church was disinterred to make room for a new railway building. The remains were brought to the cathedral and reburied in the cavities behind the wall of plaques that line the ramp up the hill.

LONG THANH GALLERY

Located in the bustling heart of the city, **Long Thanh Gallery** (Map p284; ☎ 824 875; www.elephantguide.com/photographer/longthanh.htm; 126 Đ Hoang Van Thu; ⏰ 8.30-11.30am & 1-6pm Mon-Sat) showcases the work of Vietnam's most prominent photographer. Long Thanh developed his first photo in 1964 and continues to shoot extraordinary black-and-white images of everyday Vietnamese moments.

The powerful images capture the heart and soul of Vietnam. Among his most compelling works, *Under the Rain* is a perfectly timed shot of two young girls caught in a sudden downpour, with a mysterious beam of sunlight streaming down on them. *Afternoon Countryside* is another rare scene – a boy dashing across the backs of a herd of water buffalos submerged in a lake outside Nha Trang.

From the images captured to their processing, there's an honesty to his work. The tactile process of mixing his own chemicals and developing the photos in a makeshift darkroom in his simple kitchen is an integral part of it. 'Colour' and 'digital' are dirty words in his book – let alone 'Photoshop'. His work has been honoured at photographic competitions around the world, showing internationally in nearly 60 group exhibitions, as well as solo exhibitions in Germany, Japan, Australia and the USA.

NATIONAL OCEANOGRAPHIC MUSEUM

Housed in a grand French-colonial building in the port district of Cau Da at the far south end of Nha Trang is the **National Oceanographic Museum** (Map p282; ☎ 590 037; haiduong@dng.vnn.vn; 1 Cau Da; adult/child 15,000/7000d; ⏰ 6am-6pm). Attached to the Oceanographic Institute founded in 1923, signs direct you around the tanks of colourful live marine life and the 60,000 jars of pickled specimens that make up the collection. There are also stuffed birds and sea mammals and displays of local boats and fishing artefacts. Most of the signs have English translations, so a guide is unnecessary.

ALEXANDRE YERSIN MUSEUM

Dr Alexandre Yersin (1863–1943) founded Nha Trang's **Pasteur Institute** in 1895. He was probably the Frenchman most loved by the Vietnamese. Born in Switzerland, he came to Vietnam in 1889 after working under Louis Pasteur in Paris. He learned to speak Vietnamese fluently, and spent the next few years travelling throughout the central highlands and recording his observations. During this period he came upon the site of what is now Dalat and recommended to the government that a hill station be established there. Yersin also introduced rubber and quinine-producing trees to Vietnam. In 1894, while in Hong Kong, he discovered the rat-borne microbe that causes bubonic plague. At his request, Dr Yersin was buried near Nha Trang.

Today, the Pasteur Institute in Nha Trang coordinates vaccination and hygiene programmes for the country's southern coastal region. The institute produces vaccines and carries out medical research and testing to European standards. Physicians at the clinic here offer medical advice to around 70 patients a day. Vietnam's two other Pasteur Institutes are in HCMC and Dalat.

Yersin's library and office are now an interesting **museum** (Map p284; ☎ 822 355; 10 Đ Tran Phu; admission 26,000d; ⏰ 8-11am & 2-4.30pm Mon-Fri, 8-11am Sat). Items on display include laboratory equipment (such as his astronomical instruments), books from his library, a fascinating 3-D photo viewer and some of the thousand or so letters written to his mother! The model boat was given to him by local fishermen with whom he spent a great deal of his time. Tours of the museum are guided in French, English and Vietnamese, and a short film on Yersin's life is also shown.

KHANH HOA MUSEUM

This sleepy local **museum** (Map p284; ☎ 822 227; 16 Đ Tran Phu; admission free; 🕑 8-11am & 2-5pm Mon, Wed, Fri & Sun) features displays of Cham statues and artefacts of the ethnic minorities in the province. The Uncle Ho room features several of Ho Chi Minh's personal effects, such as clothing and the microphone with which he made his famous independence speech in Hanoi on 2 September 1945.

HON CHONG PROMONTORY

The narrow granite promontory of Hon Chong (Map p282) offers views of the mountainous coastline north of Nha Trang and the nearby islands. The beach here has a more local flavour than Nha Trang Beach, but the accompanying refuse makes it a less attractive option for swimming or sunbathing.

There's a gargantuan handprint on the massive boulder balanced at the tip of the promontory. According to legend, a drunken giant male fairy made it when he fell while spying a female fairy bathing nude at Bai Tien (Fairy Beach), the point of land closest to Hon Rua. They fell in love but the gods intervened, sending the male fairy away. The lovesick female fairy waited patiently for him to return, but after a very long time she lay down in sorrow and turned into **Nui Co Tien** (Fairy Mountain). Looking to the northeast from Hon Chong Promontory, the peak on the right is supposed to be her face, gazing up towards the sky; the middle peak is her breasts; and the summit on the left (the highest) forms her crossed legs.

About 300m south of Hon Chong (towards Nha Trang) and a few dozen metres from the beach is tiny **Hon Do** (Red Island), which has a Buddhist temple on top. To the northeast is **Hon Rua** (Tortoise Island), which really does resemble a tortoise. The two islands of **Hon Yen** are off in the distance to the east.

Activities

BOAT TOURS

Khanh Hoa province's 71 offshore islands are renowned for the remarkably clear water surrounding them. A trip to these islands is one of the best reasons for visiting Nha Trang, so try to schedule at least one day for a boat journey. Virtually every hotel and travel company in town books island-hopping boat tours. You can pay more for a less-crowded and more luxurious boat that takes you to more islands. Indeed, you'll have to do this if you want to get in much snorkelling.

Shallow water prevents boats from reaching shore at some of the fishing villages. In this case, you must walk sometimes several hundred metres across floats. The floats were designed for Vietnamese people, and weightier Westerners might get wet – balance carefully and take care with your camera. Nevertheless, it's all good fun and a visit to these villages is highly recommended.

Mama Linh's Boat Tours (Map p284; ☎ 522 844; fax 522 845; 23C Đ Biet Thu) are the hottest ticket for island hopping, guzzling fruit wine at the impromptu 'floating bar', and deck-side dancing. Daily trips last from 8.45am until 4.30pm, and typically include stops on Hon Mun, Hon Mot, Hon Tam and Hon Mieu – see p294. Tickets (US$6) are sold at the office, but you can easily book at your hotel for a dollar or two more.

Of course all of this fun in the sun might not be the best environment for families with children (or for recovering alcoholics). If the cultural fanfare of the Mama Linh experience does not sound up your alley, there are other more orthodox boat tours around.

Con Se Tre (Map p282; ☎ /fax 527 522; 100/16 Đ Tran Phu; 🕑 8am-6pm) offers tours to Hon Tre which include a visit to Vinpearl, a look around the village and lunch (US$15), and snorkelling trips to Hon Mun (one person US$41, two people US$44, group (per person $US12). They also charter speed boats (US$35 to US$50) and wooden boats (US$30 to US$45), including snorkels and a guide.

If you're brave and a good haggler (use the rates above as a benchmark) you can charter a boat directly from Cau Da dock at the south end of Nha Trang. You'll need to get there early – by 10am all the boats are gone. Another attractive alternative is joining up with one of the local dive boats, most of which will take nondivers along for a discounted rate.

The cheapest way to get out on the water is to take the regular local ferry to Vinpearl on Hon Tre (adult/child 40,000/15,000d each way), leaving from Phu Quy harbour just past Cau Da dock. At the time of research, Vinpearl was building a massive cable car to span the 3 kilometres to the island.

In the interests of environmental preservation, when booking a boat tour you might consider asking if the captain anchors his boat to a buoy, as opposed to dropping anchor directly on the coral. Of course, it's hard to know if you'll get a truthful or informed answer to this question.

DIVING

Nha Trang is Vietnam's premier scuba-diving locale. Visibility averages 15m but can be as much as 30m, depending on the season (late October to early January is the worst time of year).

There are around 25 dive sites in the area, both shallow and deep. There are no wrecks to visit, but some sites have good drop-offs and there are a few small underwater caves to explore. The waters support a good variety of soft and hard corals, and a reasonable number of small reef fish.

A full-day outing including boat transport, two dives and lunch typically costs between US$40 and US$70. Most dive operators also offer a range of dive courses, including a 'discover diving' programme for uncertified, first-time divers to experience the thrill under the supervision of a qualified dive master.

There are dozens of dive operators hustling for business on the streets of Nha Trang. The three we've listed below are all long-running operators with environmentally responsible diving practices. There are other reputable operators, but also plenty of cowboys. Remember, the cheapest may not be the safest.

Blue Diving Club (Map p284; ☎ 527 034; www.vietnam-diving.com; 66 Đ Tran Phu)

Rainbow Divers (Map p284; ☎ 524 351; www.divevietnam.com; 90A Hung Vuong) Run by Briton Jeremy Stein, Rainbow Divers is the standard setter for diving in Vietnam, operating out of five centres nationwide. This, its head office, also includes a restaurant and bar.

Sailing Club Diving (Map p284; ☎ 522 788; www.sailingclubvietnam.com; 72-74 Đ Tran Phu) & **Octopus Diving** (Map p284; ☎ 521 629; 62 Đ Tran Phu) These are two names for the same operation operating out of two different locations on the same street.

MORE WATERY FUN

Right on the beach front, **Phu Dong Water Park** (Map p282; Đ Tran Phu; admission 20,000d, lockers 5,000d; 🕑 9am-5pm Sat & Sun) has hydroslides, shallow pools and fountains if salt water is not your thing.

If salt water *is* your thing, check out **Mana Mana Beach Club** (Map p284; ☎ 524 362; www.manamana.com; Louisiane Brewhouse, 29 Đ Tran Phu). Offering windsurfing, sea kayaking, wakeboarding and sailing lessons, Mana Mana uses state-of-the-art equipment and has access to some great surfing spots in Cam Ranh Bay.

Do you think hot muddy water might be your thing? **Thap Ba Hot Spring Center** (☎ 834 939; 25 Ngoc Son; 🕑 8am-8pm) is one of the most fun experiences on offer here. For 180,000d you can sit in a wooden bathtub full of hot thermal mud, or for 60,000d per person you can slop around with a group of friends in a larger pool. The centre also has private mineral baths (50,000d) and a large outdoor heated swimming pool complete with thermal waterfalls (free with a mud or mineral bath, 30,000d otherwise). To get here, follow the signpost on the second road to the left past the Po Nagar Cham Towers and take the twisting, bumpy road for 2.5km.

Sleeping

Nha Trang has over 100 hotels to choose from, from basic to sumptuous, and new ones are sprouting up all the time. Unsurprisingly, the most expensive are on Tran Phu, the waterfront boulevard. Yet a cluster of a dozen brand new minihotels has recently spawned in a laneway at 64 Đ Tran Phu, all offering similar air-conditioned rooms for around US$8 (fan-only, US$5). Most budget rooms offer hot water, private bathrooms, fridges and TVs, although air-con may be extra. In comparison, good-value midrange options are harder to find.

BUDGET

Mai Huy (Map p284; ☎ 527 553; 7H Đ Hung Vuong; r US$5-7; ❄) Pronounced 'may we' (or 'mais oui!' if you're French), it's worth searching out this new family-run minihotel, hidden down a small laneway. At US$5 for a simple clean room with a fan, fridge, satellite TV and private bathroom with hot water, it's unbelievable value for money.

Sao Mai Hotel (Map p284; ☎ 526 412; saomaiht@dng.vnn.vn; 99 Đ Nguyen Thien Thuat; r US$5-8; ❄) With its pretty rooftop terrace adorned with potted plants, this friendly older place is a solid budget option.

56 Hung Vuong Hotel (Map p284; ☎ 524 584; 56hungvuonghotel@dng.vnn.vn; 56 Đ Hung Vuong; r US$6-11; ❄) Although not quite as nice as the Phu Quy next door, this welcoming guesthouse is still a good choice. US$10 will secure you a large room with a balcony and sea view (albeit up several flights of stairs).

Hotel An Hoa (Map p284; ☎ 524 029; anhoahotel@yahoo.com; 64B/6 Đ Tran Phu; r US$6-11; ❄) One of the better options in the new, fabulously located, budget alley, rooms range from cheapies without windows or air-con, to larger pads with bathtubs and decks.

Hotel Nhi Hang (Map p284; ☎ 525 837; www.vngold.com/nt/nhihang; 64B/7 Đ Tran Phu; r US$6-15; ❄) Another great budget alley option, with an almost identical set-up to An Hoa.

Pho Bien (Map p284; ☎ 524 858; phobienhotelint@yahoo.com; 64/1 Đ Tran Phu; r US$8-12; ❄) The best of the budget alley minihotels, some of the cheapest rooms have views and large balconies, if you can handle a few flights of stairs.

Blue Star Hotel (Map p284; ☎ 525 447; quangc@dng.vnn.vn; 1B Đ Biet Thu; r US$8-15; ❄ 💻) This humble hotel offers all the usual facilities and has nice seaviews from the upper floors. Corner rooms have great big balconies.

Thien Long (Map p284; ☎ 524 107; toan034vn@yahoo.com; 50 Đ Nguyen Thi Minh Khai; US$10; ❄) At the nicer end of budget, this new minihotel has comfortable rooms with balconies and good facilities.

Phu Quy Hotel (Map p284; ☎ 521 609; phuquyhotel@dng.vnn.vn; 54 Đ Hung Vuong; r US$6-20; ❄ 💻) Pronounced Foo-Wee, the highlight of this minihotel is its rooftop terrace – it has awesome views and is great for dining, sunning or hanging around in a hammock. All the rooms are quite comfortable, and for US$10 expect a balcony, bathtub and sea view.

Other reliable budget options:

Ha Minh Hotel (Map p284; ☎ 521 048; 30 Đ Hoang Hoa Tham; r US$5-7; ❄) A basic family-run place with small rooms and clean sheets.

Yen My Hotel (Map p284; ☎ 525 064; yenmyhotel@hotmail.com; 22 Đ Hoang Hoa Tham; r US$5-8; ❄ 💻) The rooms are small and basic, but guests enjoy free internet and satellite TV.

Hotel Phuong Ngoc (Map p284; ☎ 526 145; phuongngocsd@dng.vnn.vn; 56B Đ Nguyen Thien Thuat; r US$5-20; ❄) The more expensive rooms are overpriced, but at $5 for a fan room, the cheaper ones are better value.

62 Tran Phu Hotel (Map p284; ☎ 525 095; fax 525 292; 62 Đ Tran Phu; r US$8-20; ❄) This older, state-owned, motel-like facility is set around a large courtyard/car park, right across from the beach. The newer wing

CONSIDERATIONS FOR RESPONSIBLE DIVING

The popularity of diving is placing immense pressure on many sites. Please consider the following tips when diving and help preserve the ecology and beauty of Vietnam's reefs.

- Do not anchor on the reef, and take care not to ground boats on coral. Encourage dive operators and regulatory bodies to establish permanent moorings at popular dive sites.
- Avoid touching living marine organisms with your body or dragging equipment across the reef. Polyps can be damaged by even the gentlest contact. Never stand on corals, even if they look solid and robust. If you must hold on to the reef, touch only exposed rock or dead coral.
- Be conscious of your fins. Even without contact, the surge from heavy fin strokes near the reef can damage delicate organisms. When treading water in shallow reef areas, take care not to kick up clouds of sand. Settling sand can easily smother the delicate organisms of the reef.
- Practise and maintain proper buoyancy control. Major damage can be done by divers descending too fast and colliding with the reef. Make sure you are correctly weighted and that your weight belt is positioned so that you stay horizontal. If you have not dived for a while, have a practice dive in a pool before taking to the reef. Be aware that buoyancy can change over the period of an extended trip: initially you may breathe harder and need more weight; a few days later you may breathe more easily and need less weight.
- Resist the temptation to collect or buy coral or shells. Aside from the ecological damage, taking home marine souvenirs depletes the beauty of a site and spoils the enjoyment of others. The same goes for marine archaeological sites (mainly shipwrecks). Respect their integrity; some sites are protected from looting by law.
- Ensure that you take home all your rubbish and any litter you may find as well. Plastics in particular are a serious threat to marine life. Turtles can mistake plastic for jellyfish and eat it.
- Resist the temptation to feed fish. You may disturb their normal eating habits, encourage aggressive behaviour or feed them food that is detrimental to their health.
- Minimise your disturbance of marine animals.

at the rear has clean, basic rooms, with sheets liberally decorated with cigarette holes.

My Long Hotel (Map p284; ☎ 521 451; mylonghotel@yahoo.com; 26A Đ Nguyen Thien Thuat; r 150,000d;) The rooms have all the usual facilities and are reasonably clean, but it is the lovely staff that are the drawcard here.

MIDRANGE

our pick **Perfume Grass Inn** (Map p284; ☎ 524 286; www.perfume-grass.com; 4A Đ Biet Thu; r US$10-25;) The best rooms at this inviting inn have wooden floors, wood-panelled walls, and bathtubs. Even the bright, comfortable US$10 fan rooms have great sea views. The nice folks running the place offer free internet access and breakfast.

AP Hotel (Map p284; ☎ 527 544; fax 527 268; 34 Đ Nguyen Thien Thuat; r 200,000-400,000d;) This wonderful new minihotel has had an expensive fit-out not in keeping with the cheap rates. The electrical appliances are impressive, especially the computers provided for the free internet service. Cheaper rooms are windowless, but the pricier options have king-size beds, huge bathtubs and balconies with sea glimpses.

Nha Trang Beach Hotel (Map p284; ☎ 524 469; www.nhatrangbeachhotel.com.vn; 4 Đ Tran Quang Khai; r US$13-23;) The multistorey Nha Trang Beach Hotel has a cool granite lobby and friendly, efficient staff. Despite its central location, it's refreshingly quiet in the upper floors, where most of the rooms have great views and internet access.

Rainbow Hotel (Map p284; ☎ 525 480; rainbowhotel@dng.vnn.vn; 10A Đ Biet Thu; r US$15-30;) The Rainbow's been newly renovated, although they've still kept the daggy old linen. It's good value for the price, with some seaviews.

La Paloma Hotel (Map p282; ☎ 831 216; datle@dng.vnn.vn; 1 Đ Hon Chong; r US$15-35;) This is a commendable little family-run oasis, well out of the tourist ghetto, on the northern outskirts of town. Fronting the hotel is a pleasant outdoor dining area in a palm garden, where meals (included in the price) are served family-style. The friendly owner offers guests free jeep rides into town.

Vien Dong Hotel (Map p284; ☎ 821 606; www.nhatrangtourist.com.vn/viendong/viendong_e.htm; 1 Đ Tran Hung Dao; s 275,000-400,000d, d 330,000-440,000d, ste 550,000-650,000d;) Long a travellers' favourite, the biggest drawcard of this large old place is its swimming pool complex, with a pool big enough for laps and a smaller one for splashing about. The rooms aren't flash but they're clean enough.

La Suisse Hotel (Map p284; ☎ 524 353; lasuissehotelnt@vnn.vn; 3/4 Đ Tran Quang Khai; r US$18-30, ste $40;) Down a quiet yet central street, this hotel is friendly and spotless. Room numbers ending in 01 boast gorgeous wrought-iron balconies, but all are pleasingly comfortable.

Bao Dai's Villas (Map p282; ☎ 590 148; www.vngold.com/nt/baodai/; Cau Da village; r US$25-80;) There can't be too many places where the former lodgings of an Emperor fall into the midrange category. Built in the 1920s, Emperor Bao Dai's Villas are set on a hillside close to the south edge of town. The only possible reason to stay here is historical interest, or the peace and quiet afforded by the park-like setting. The prices are quite out of touch with the facilities provided. More austere than opulent, any trace of Imperial grandeur has long disappeared from the massive, high-studded rooms. There's a private beach below and two good restaurants, one with fine bay views.

Phu Quy 2 Hotel (Map p284; ☎ 525 050; www.phuquyhotel.com.vn; 1 Đ Tue Tinh; r US$28-70;) This flash, multistoreyed hotel is the new sister to its popular budget namesake in the centre of town. The attractive, modern design carries into the rooms, with wooden floors, good quality linen and some amazing views.

Also worth checking out:

44 Tran Phu (Map p284; ☎ 523 445; fax 526 395; 44 Đ Tran Phu; r 70,000-800,000d;) In a prime beachfront position and housed in a stately French colonial building, this should be one of the best hotels in town. However, on our visit we encountered surly staff, and the décor is frugal. The upper-end rooms are cavernous but fail to meet their glamorous potential.

Dong Phuong 1 Hotel (Map p284; ☎ 526 986; dongphuongnt@dng.vnn.vn; 101-103 Đ Nguyen Thien Thuat; r in old wing US$6-10, in new wing US$10-30;) There's a shabby charm to some of the rooms here – like the one with the image of a naked woman in the tiles above the bathtub, or the penthouse pad opening on to a massive terrace with sea views.

Dong Phuong 2 Hotel (Map p282; ☎ 522 580; dongphuong2@dng.vnn.vn; 96A Đ Tran Phu; r US$12-20;) Big, blue Dong Phuong 2 has great views, but it's starting to show its age.

Hai Yen Hotel (Map p284; ☎ 822 828; haiyenhotel@dng.vnn.vn; 40 Đ Tran Phu; r 338,000-455,000d, ste 520,000d;) It's getting a bit old, dirty and smelly, but Hai Yen is still notable for its swimming pool (shared with the Vien Dong Hotel), prime location and balcony sea views.

TOP END

Asia Paradise Hotel (Map p284; ☎ 524 686; www.asiaparadisehotel.com; 6 Đ Biet Thu; r US$46-78, ste US$99-124;) This new business-style hotel has elegant décor, comfortable beds and friendly switched-on staff and is scrupulously clean. Extras include a small rooftop pool, gym and spa centre.

Sunrise Beach Resort (Map p284; ☎ 820 999; www.sunrisenhatrang.com.vn; 12-14 Đ Tran Phu; s US$140-200, d US$155-225, ste US$230-550;) The colonnaded balconies make it look like a giant wedding cake, belying the simple elegance of its interiors. The rooms are suitably luxurious, with all the frills – robes, slippers, safes, hairdryers, wi-fi access etc. If you're in a suite you can indulge in a Jacuzzi on a balcony overlooking the beach. Other facilities include a babysitting service, spa and fitness centre and three excellent restaurants (specialising in Japanese, Vietnamese and international cuisine).

Ana Mandara Resort (Map p282; ☎ 522 522; www.evasonresorts.com; Đ Tran Phu; villa US$236-438, ste US$450-513;) A gorgeous complex of open timber-roofed beach villas, this exquisite resort is hands-down Nha Trang's classiest accommodation offering. The décor is simple and elegant, and luxuries include two excellent restaurants, two swimming pools and a serene spa area. Although shut off behind high hedges, special nights bring the food of the street into the resort, with local women invited in as guest cooks. A free weekly cocktail evening on the beach allows guests and hosts to mingle.

Eating

Nha Trang has the widest range of international restaurants of any Vietnamese city outside of the big two. In particular, there are a number of eateries on Đ Tran Quang Khai catering to the significant French ex-pat community. Excellent Vietnamese restaurants dot the tourist area, but for a more authentic experience, head to the local restaurants outside of the ghetto. The street stalls cook a vast array of seafood – don't be surprised to walk past tanks of live lobster and crabs.

VIETNAMESE

Café des Amis (Map p284; ☎ 521 009; 2D Đ Biet Thu; dishes 7,000-40,000d) A popular cheapie focussing on seafood and vegetarian fare, the walls are covered with interesting works by Vietnamese painters.

Lac Canh Restaurant (Map p284; ☎ 821 391; 44 Đ Nguyen Binh Khiem; dishes 10,000-85,000d; lunch & dinner) A Nha Trang institution, Lac Canh is one of the busiest local eateries in town. Here beef, squid, giant prawns, lobsters and the like are grilled at your table.

Cyclo Café (Map p284; ☎ 524 208; khuongthuy@hotmail.com; 5A Đ Tran Quang Khai; mains 12,000-52,000d) Run by a local couple, the Cyclo Café has an intimate atmosphere, great service and excellent Vietnamese and Italian dishes.

our pick **Pho Cali** (Map p284; ☎ 525 885; 7G Đ Hung Vuong; dishes 15,000-25,000d) You can watch the food being cooked at this clean, modern eatery. The meals are absolutely delicious, and the set menu – comprising soup, rice and a hotpot – is outrageously good value at 20,000d.

Truc Linh 2 (Map p284; ☎ 521 089; 21 Đ Biet Thu; dishes 15,000-83,000d; lunch & dinner) With three restaurants dotted around the neighbourhood, popular Truc Linh offers a festive garden setting for diners. In the evening you can choose fresh seafood from a table in front of the restaurant and enjoy a beer while you wait.

Khanh Kat (Map p284; ☎ 826 657; 22 Đ Tran Quang Khai; dishes 15,000-89,000d) The hotpots are excellent at this pleasant little indoor-outdoor restaurant with linen tablecloths. While the cuisine is mainly traditional Vietnamese, you'll find some Chinese and Italian dishes.

Tin Duc (Map p284; 1/30 Đ Tran Quang Khai; dishes 20,000-50,000d) A friendly, family-run place next to a small pagoda, Tin Duc serves a vegetarian-friendly selection of local favourites, as well as pizza and pasta.

Then there's **Dam Market** (Map p284; Đ Trang Nu Vuong), which has a colourful collection of stalls, including vegetarian *(com chay)* in the covered semicircular food pavilion.

VIETNAMESE VEGETARIAN

Two places serving excellent vegetarian food of the I-can't-believe-it's-not-meat variety are **Au Lac** (Map p284; ☎ 813 946; 28C Đ Hoang Hoa Tham; meals 10,000d) and **Bo De** (Map p284; ☎ 810 116; 28A Đ Hoang Hoa Tham; meals 10,000d), neighbouring restaurants near the corner of Đ Nguyen Chanh.

FRENCH

Mai Anh (Map p284; ☎ 815 920; 1/21 Đ Tran Quang Khai; mains 20,000-70,000d; lunch & dinner) Describing its menu as 'French grand cuisine' Mai Anh is the place to go for fillet steak served in a rich cognac or cream-based sauce. For 200,000d you can indulge in a nine-course set menu 'to be shared with darling from a single plate', including a bottle of red wine.

Selene (Map p284; ☎ 526 813; 1/4 Đ Tran Quang Khai; mains 35,000-60,000d; breakfast, lunch & dinner) Run by a French-Canadian, this cute little eatery is adorned with colourful local art and serves a mixture of French and Italian cuisine. The pasta is particularly good.

our pick **Le Petit Bistro** (Map p284; ☎ 527 201; 26D Đ Tran Quang Khai; mains 45,000-180,000d;) The best of the French restaurants, Le Petit Bistro has a fantastic wine selection, as well as sourcing quality cheese and *charcuterie*. A testimony to the great food and wine is the number of French ex-pats who gravitate around this atmospheric little place.

INTERNATIONAL

Same Same But Different Café (Map p284; ☎ 524 079; 111 Đ Nguyen Thien Thuat; mains 12,000-50,000d; breakfast, lunch & dinner) A good travellers' café, this place serves Vietnamese and Western food (including vegie dishes and tasty muesli for breakfast) at reasonable prices.

Thanh Thanh Cafe (Map p284; ☎ 824 413; 10 Đ Nguyen Thien Thuat; meals 15,000-75,000d) Another travellers' café, serving wood-fired pizza, Vietnamese dishes and other standard backpacker fare, Thanh Thanh has a pretty terracotta patio surrounded by plants. It also does deliveries.

Bombay (Map p284; ☎ 524 399; 12 Đ Biet Thu; dishes 22,000-50,000d) This humble Indian restaurant with plastic chairs has plenty of tasty vegetarian and tandoori options.

Turkish Cuisine Kebab Restaurant (Map p284; ☎ 525 328; 24B Đ Hung Vuong; mains 40,000-100,000d; breakfast, lunch & dinner) If you're craving a kebab, this is quite possibly the only Turkish restaurant in Vietnam. It also serves pizza and pasta. Hookah pipes add to the atmosphere.

El Coyote (Map p284; ☎ 526 320; 76 Đ Hung Vuong; mains 40,000-103,000d; breakfast, lunch & dinner) This Coyote does authentic Tex-Mex food including delicious fajitas served on a sizzling plate. The owner has perhaps the most curious ethnic roots in town: he's a mixture of French, Vietnamese, Lao and Cheyenne Indian.

Louisiane Brewhouse (Map p284; ☎ 521 948; 29 Đ Tran Phu; mains 50,000-130,000d; breakfast, lunch & dinner;) Best known for its microbrewery and decadent beachside pool, Louisiane also serves wonderful food and an oddball selection of Moldovan wine. The menu features a mixture of Thai and European favourites, as well as excellent Vietnamese dishes – try the traditional fish salad served with rice paper and herbs. The cakes and pastries (10,000d) are superb.

Sailing Club (Map p284; 72-74 Đ Tran Phu; mains 50,000-185,000d; breakfast, lunch & dinner) One of the most popular hangouts in Nha Trang, the Sailing Club has three distinct restaurants. The wide terrace on the beach serves excellent Vietnamese cuisine. It's also good for people-watching during the day and ocean breezes at night. On the street side, the Indian and Italian restaurants have a garden setting, the latter serving divine desserts.

Good Morning Vietnam (Map p284; ☎ 522 071; 19B Đ Biet Thu; mains 54,000-105,000d) The Nha Trang branch of this Italian-run chain does good pizza, pasta and salads. It also screens DVDs upstairs at 5pm and 8pm daily.

Drinking & Entertainment

Sailing Club (Map p284; ☎ 826 528; 72-74 Đ Tran Phu) The hippest place in town, this popular, Aussie-run, open-air beach bar is where most of the party crowd ends up at some point in the evening. It's best known for thumping music, wild dancing, flowing shots, pool and general mayhem. You can escape the madness (well, sort of) outside on the large beachside terrace.

Louisiane Brewhouse (Map p284; ☎ 521 948; 29 Đ Tran Phu;) True to its name, the shiny copper vats herald good news for beer drinkers at this upmarket restaurant cum microbrewery. However, it's the deckchair-ringed swimming pool and beautiful beachfront that make this one of the best places to laze away the Nha Trang days.

Crazy Kim Bar (Map p284; ☎ 523 072; crazykimbar.com; 19 Đ Biet Thu) Run by the ebullient Kimmy Le, this great party spot is also home base for her commendable 'Hands off the Kids!' campaign, which works to prevent paedophilia. She's now set up a permanent classroom for vulnerable street kids in an upstairs corner of the bar. Part of the proceeds from the food, booze and T-shirt sales go towards the cause. Sign up at the bar if you're interested in volunteering to teach English. Crazy Kim's has regular themed party nights, great music, good pizza and wicked cocktail buckets. Kim's life is about to get crazier – by the time this book hits the streets her new Crazy Kim Spa & Gym should have opened down the road at 1D Đ Biet Thu.

City View Café (Map p284; ☎ 820 090; 18 Đ Tran Phu) A great place to start the evening with a sundowner, the garden bar on the rooftop of the Yasaka Saigon Nhatrang hotel has the best views in town.

Guava (Map p284; ☎ 524 140; www.clubnhatrang.com; 17 Đ Biet Thu) Cool, clean-lined and atmospheric, this lounge bar is super-stylish but never seems particularly busy. Outside is a patio shaded with trees; inside, pillow-laden sofas and a pool table. The substantial 'hangover breakfasts' are conveniently served all day.

Zippo (Map p284; ☎ 521 117; 34F Đ Nguyen Thien Thu) This friendly little bar has a free pool table and happy hours that stretch from 8pm to 11pm.

Shorty's Cafe Bar (Map p284; ☎ 810 985; 1E Đ Biet Thu) If you're looking for an earlier start to the happy hour, Shorty's extends from 6pm to 10pm. There's a free pool table here as well – along with a book exchange if you're after a new read.

Shopping

Nha Trang has emerged as a reasonable place to look for art and local craft. A number of tourist-friendly shops can be found in the blocks surrounding the corner of Đ Tran Quang Khai and Đ Hung Vuong.

XQ (Map p284; ☎ 526 579; www.xqhandembroidery.com; 64 Đ Tran Phu; ⏰ 8am-8pm) You're presented with a glass of green tea as you wander around this peaceful little craft village, where you can watch the artisans at work in the embroidery workshop and gallery. The embroidery 'paintings' may not suit everybody's taste, but the painstaking detail is fascinating.

My Village (Map p284; ☎ 524 825; 4L Đ Hung Vuong) There's some nice lacquer-work, furniture and other souvenir-friendly art and handicraft in this little shop in the heart of the tourist precinct.

A Mart (Map p284; ☎ 523 035; 17A Đ Biet Thu) Everyday supplies available at this handy minimart.

Also worth checking out are the hand-painted T-shirts done by a friendly local painter named **Kim Quang** (☎ 0983-884 5397), who you can find between 2pm and 9pm working from his wheelchair at the Sailing Club (opposite).

Getting There & Away

AIR

Vietnam Airlines (Map p284; ☎ 526 768; 91 Đ Nguyen Thien Thuat) connects Nha Trang with HCMC three times a day, and Hanoi and Danang daily.

BUS

Lien Tinh bus station (Ben Xe Lien Tinh; ☎ 822 192; Đ 23 Thang 10) is Nha Trang's main intercity bus terminal, 500m west of the train station. Seven daily buses head north to Quy Nhon (65,000d, 5½ hours), with at least two continuing to Danang (120,000d). Regular buses head south to Phan Rang (24,000d, 2½ hours), with a dozen continuing on to HCMC (110,000d, 11 hours) and a similar amount heading into the highlands to Dalat (60,000d, seven hours).

Nha Trang is a major stopping point on all of the tourist open-bus tours. These are the best option for accessing Mui Ne, which is not served by local buses. Sinh Café (see p282) runs a comfortable coach at 7.30am, reaching Ca Na before 11am and Mui Ne just after midday. It stops here for lunch before continuing on to HCMC (arriving 5.30pm). It also runs services to Dalat (six hours) and Hoi An (11 hours).

CAR & MOTORBIKE

Road distances from Nha Trang are: 235km to Quy Nhon, 523km to Danang, 104km to Phan Rang, 250km to Mui Ne, 448km to HCMC, 205km to Dalat and 205km to Buon Ma Thuot.

TRAIN

The **Nha Trang train station** (Map p284; ☎ 822 113; Đ Thai Nguyen; ⏰ ticket office 7-11.30am, 1.30-5pm & 6-10pm) is down the hill west of the cathedral. Destinations include Danang (203,000d, 8½ to 12½ hours, seven daily), Tuy Hoa (44,000d, 2½ hours, five daily), Thap Cham (35,000d, 1½ to 2½ hours, eight daily) and HCMC (160,000d, seven to 12½ hours, nine daily).

Getting Around

TO/FROM THE AIRPORT

In the last few years Nha Trang's airport has moved from the centre of town to Cam Ranh Bay, 36km to the south. A shuttle bus runs the route (return/one way 45,000/25,000d), leaving from the site of the old airport (near 86 Đ Tran Phu) two hours before scheduled departure times. The journey takes 40 minutes. If you can't be bothered with waiting around that long, taxis are a speedier option (30 to 40 minutes), but be sure to agree a price in advance. It should cost in the vicinity of 150,000d or US$10, although we've heard of people being scammed for double this.

BICYCLE

It's easy to get around all of the sights, including Thap Ba, by bicycle. Most major hotels have rentals for around 20,000d per day. Watch out for the one-way system around the train station, and the chaotic roundabouts.

TAXI, CYCLO & XE OM

Nha Trang has an excessive amount of all three. The *xe om* drivers are the most consistently annoying, although like taxis all over the world they seem to disappear when you actually want one. A motorcycle ride anywhere in the centre shouldn't cost more than 10,000d. Be careful at night, when some less reputable drivers moonlight as pimps and drug dealers.

AROUND NHA TRANG

Islands

Island tours are a big part of the Nha Trang experience. For details on boat tours and charters see p287.

HON TRE (BAMBOO ISLAND)

The beauty of Nha Trang's largest and closest offshore island is now marred on the city side by a huge Hollywood-style sign advertising Vinpearl Complex International – a new compound of restaurants, nightclubs, shops, kids' rides, hotels and an amphitheatre. The wealthy Ukrainian-Vietnamese owners have now started work on a cable car stretching 3 kilometres from Vinpearl to the mainland.

HON MIEU

All the tourist literature touts Hon Mieu (also called Tri Nguyen Island) as the site of an outdoor aquarium (Ho Ca Tri Nguyen). In fact, the aquarium is an important fish-breeding farm, where over 40 species of fish, crustacean and other marine creatures are raised in three separate compartments. There is also a café built on stilts over the water. Ask around for canoe rentals.

The main village on Hon Mieu is Tri Nguyen. Bai Soai is a gravel beach on the far side of Hon Mieu from Cau Da. There are a few rustic **bungalows** (US$6) on the island.

Most people will take some sort of boat tour booked through a hotel, café or Khanh Hoa Tourist (see p282). Impoverished and less-hurried travellers might catch one of the regular ferries that go to Tri Nguyen village from Cau Da dock.

HON MUN (EBONY ISLAND)

Hon Mun is situated just southeast of Bamboo Island and is well known for its snorkelling.

HON MOT

Sandwiched neatly between Ebony Island and Hon Tam is tiny Hon Mot; it's another great place for snorkelling.

HON YEN (BIRD'S-NEST ISLAND)

Also known as Salangane Island, this is the name applied to two lump-shaped islands visible from Nha Trang Beach. These and other islands off Khanh Hoa province are the source of Vietnam's finest swiftlet *(salangane)* nests (see opposite). There is a small, secluded beach here. The 17km trip out to the islands takes three to four hours by small boat from Nha Trang.

HON LAO (MONKEY ISLAND)

The island is named after its large contingent of resident monkeys and has become a big hit with tourists. Most of the monkeys have grown quite accustomed to receiving food handouts, providing ample photo opportunities. However, these are wild animals and should be treated as such. Bear in mind that monkey bites are a fairly reliable source of rabies.

Aside from being unwilling to participate in a cuddle, the monkeys are materialistic. They'll grab the sunglasses off your face or snatch a pen from your shirt pocket and run off. So far, we haven't heard of monkeys slitting open travellers' handbags with a razor blade, but keep a close eye (and hand) on your possessions.

A word of warning: though the island itself can make for a fun visit, there's also a bear-and-monkey show that you may want to avoid. Travellers have reported seeing the animals beaten by their trainers during performances.

If you're not part of a tour, head 15km north of Nha Trang on Hwy 1A to **Long Phu Tourist** (☎ 839 436; Vinh Luong), easily spotted by the huge colourful dragons forming the entrance, not far from a pagoda. Boats will ferry you to the island for 50,000d (15 minutes). Other destinations reached from here include Hoa Lan Springs on Hon Heo (40,000d, 45 minutes) and Hon Thi (20,000d, 20 minutes).

Thanh Citadel

This citadel dates from the 17th-century Trinh dynasty. It was rebuilt by Prince Nguyen Anh (later Emperor Gia Long) in 1793 during his successful offensive against the Tay Son Rebels. Only a few sections of the walls and gates are extant. Thanh Citadel is 11km west of Nha Trang near Dien Khanh town.

Ba Ho Falls

The three waterfalls and pools at Ba Ho Falls (Suoi Ba Ho) are in a forested area about 20km north of Nha Trang and about 2km west of Phu Huu village. Turn off Hwy 1A just north of Quyen restaurant.

Suoi Tien (Fairy Spring)

The enchanting little spring seems to pop out of nowhere. Like a small oasis, the Fairy Spring is decorated with its own natural garden of tropical vegetation and smooth boulders.

You'll need to rent a motorbike or car to reach the spring. Drive south on Hwy 1A for 27km to Suoi Cat, turning right (west) at the blue and white 'Huong Lo 39' sign. After 5km you'll see a sign directing you to the spring.

Cam Ranh Harbour

The gorgeous natural harbour of **Cam Ranh Bay** is 35km south of Nha Trang and 56km north of Phan Rang. With the opening of the excellent new airport road, beautiful **Bai Dai** (Long Beach), forming the northern head of the harbour, has become much more accessible. Largely unspoilt, the government has been encouraging development – although at the time of research the one major completed resort had long been languishing unopened in search of a buyer.

Driving the beach road, reminders of the American War come in the form of abandoned tanks peering out of the sand. The military still controls access to much of this area but are starting to work with tourist operators. Nha Trang's Mana Mana Beach Club (see p288) has negotiated access to some of the best surf breaks in Vietnam.

To get here you can take the airport shuttle bus (see p293), although you'll need to time your visit around flight times. A one-way journey in a taxi will cost about 150,000d, but you'll be able to negotiate something considerably cheaper, including waiting time, with a motorcycle driver.

PHAN RANG & THAP CHAM

☎ 068 / pop 161,000

If you're travelling Vietnam from north to south you'll notice a big change in the vegetation as you approach the twin cities of Phan Rang and Thap Cham, joint capitals of Ninh Thuan province. The familiar lush green rice paddies are replaced with sandy soil supporting only scrubby plants. Local flora includes poinciana trees and prickly-pear cacti with vicious thorns. Famous for its production of table grapes, many of the houses on the outskirts of town are decorated with vines on trellises.

The area's best-known sight (and a common stop on the Dalat–Nha Trang route) is the group of Cham towers known as Po Klong Garai (p296), from which Thap Cham (Cham Tower) derives its name. There are other towers dotted about the countryside. This province is home to tens of thousands of Cham people, particularly in the vicinity of the twin cities. The Cham, like other ethnic minorities in Vietnam, suffer from discrimination and are usually poorer than their ethnic-Vietnamese neighbours. There are also several thousand Chinese in the area, many of whom come to worship at the 135-year old **Quang Cong Pagoda** (Đ Thong Nhat), a colourful Chinese temple in the town centre.

With both Hwy 1A and Hwy 20 (heading to the central highlands) passing through the towns, this is a good pit stop for either a coastal trip or the journey to Dalat. Nearby Ninh Chu Beach (p299) is another, quieter alternative.

BIRD SPIT SOUP

The nests of the swiftlet *(salangane)* are used in bird's-nest soup as well as in trad itional medicine, and are considered an aphrodisiac. It is said that the extraordinary virility of Emperor Minh Mang, who ruled Vietnam from 1820 to 1840, was derived from the consumption of swiftlet nests.

The nests, which are built out of silk-like salivary secretions, are 5cm to 8cm in diameter. They are usually harvested twice a year. Red nests are the most highly prized. Annual production in Khanh Hoa and Phu Yen provinces is about 1000kg. At present, swiftlet spit fetches US$2000 per kilogram in the international marketplace.

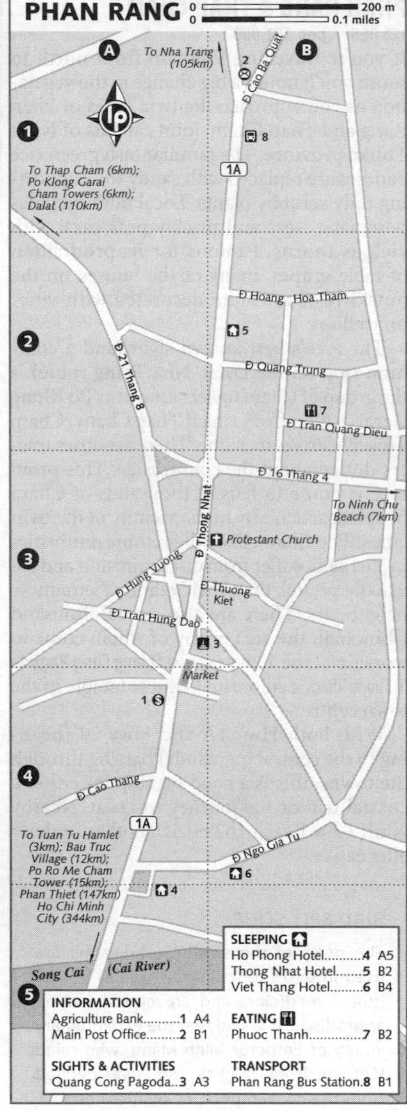

Orientation

Hwy 1A is Phan Rang's main commercial street, and becomes Đ Thong Nhat in town. The main part of town is bordered to the south by the Cai River. Thap Cham, 7km from Phan Rang, is strung out along Hwy 20, which heads northwest from Phan Rang towards Dalat.

Information

Agriculture Bank (☎ 822 714; 540-544 Đ Thong Nhat; Mon-Fri) Exchanges currency.

Main post office (☎ 824 943; 217A Đ Thong Nhat) Also offers internet access.

Sights

PO KLONG GARAI CHAM TOWERS

The four brick towers of **Po Klong Garai** (Thap Cham; admission 5000d; 7.30am-6pm), were constructed at the end of the 13th and beginning of the 14th century. Built as Hindu temples, they stand on a brick platform at the top of Cho'k Hala, a crumbly granite hill covered with some of the most ornery cacti this side of the Rio Grande.

A large modern building in a vaguely Cham style sitting at the base of the hill is dedicated to Cham culture, with separate **galleries** of photographs, paintings and traditional pottery. It's a good reminder that while the Cham kingdom is long gone, the Cham people are alive and kicking (see p264).

Over the entrance to the largest tower (the **kalan**, or sanctuary) is a beautiful carving of a dancing Shiva with six arms. Note the inscriptions in the ancient Cham language on the doorposts. These tell of past restoration efforts and offerings of sacrifices and slaves. If you want to look inside, you'll need to remove your shoes as this is still an active place of worship. Inside the vestibule is a statue of the bull Nandin, symbol of the agricultural productivity of the countryside. To ensure a good crop, farmers would place an offering of fresh greens, herbs and areca nuts in front of Nandin's muzzle. Under the main tower is a *mukha-linga*, a carved phallus with a human face painted on it, sitting under a wooden pyramid.

Inside the **smaller tower** opposite the entrance to the sanctuary, you can get a good look at some of the Cham's sophisticated building technology; the wooden columns that support the lightweight roof are visible. The structure attached to it was originally the **main entrance** to the complex.

On the hill directly south of Cho'k Hala is a concrete water tank built by the Americans in 1965. It is encircled by French pillboxes built during the Franco-Viet Minh War to protect the nearby rail yards. To the north of Cho'k Hala, you can see the concrete revetments of Thanh Son Airbase, used since 1975 by the Vietnamese Air Force.

Po Klong Garai is just north of Hwy 20, at a point 6km west of Phan Rang towards Dalat. The towers are on the opposite side of the tracks to Thap Cham train station. If you're travelling between Dalat and the coast, you will pass the site. Most of the open-tour buses running the route make a requisite pit stop here.

PO RO ME CHAM TOWER

Po Ro Me (Thap Po Ro Me; admission free) is one of the most atmospheric of Vietnam's Cham towers – partly due to its isolated setting on top of a craggy hill with sweeping views over the cactus-strewn landscape. The temple honours the last ruler of an independent Champa, King Po Ro Me (r 1629–51), who died as a prisoner of the Vietnamese. His image and those of his family are to be found on the external decorations. Note the flame motif repeated around the arches.

The temple is still in active use, with ceremonies taking place twice a year. The rest of the time it's locked up, but the caretakers, who are based at the foot of the hill, will open the sanctuary for you. Consider leaving a small donation with them and don't forget to remove your shoes.

The occupants of the temple aren't used to having their rest disturbed, and it can be a little creepy when the bats start chattering and swooping overhead in the confined dark space. Through the gloom you'll be able to make out a blood red and black centrepiece – a bas-relief representing the deified king in the form of Shiva. Behind the main deity and to the left is one of his queens, Thanh Chanh. Look out for the inscriptions on the doorposts and a stone statue of the bull Nandin.

Cham temple architecture has changed considerably if the small concrete hut dated 1962 at the back of the tower is anything to go by. Inside is a statue of the king's first wife – a Muslim woman called Thanh Cat – with an inscription painted on her chest. A statue of the third wife has been removed to a museum, along with other relics from the site. A *linga* (see p265) remains at the front right of the tower. The rubble at the front left is all that remains of a preparation room bombed during the war – revealing how close Po Ro Me came to destruction.

The best way to reach the site is with your own motorbike or a *xe om*. The trip is worthwhile, as long as getting lost is a part of your agenda. Take Hwy 1A south from Phan Rang for 9km. Turn right at the turnoff to Ho Tan Giang, a narrow sealed road just after the petrol station, and continue for a further 6km. Turn left in the middle of a dusty village at a paddock which doubles as a football field and follow the road as it meanders to the right until the tower comes into sight. A sign points the way cross-country for the last 500m. This may be negotiable on a motorbike, but it is deeply rutted, and studded with rocks and cacti. You might like to park and walk the remainder.

BAU TRUC VILLAGE

This Cham village is known for its pottery and you'll see several family shops in front of the mud and bamboo houses. On the way to Po Ro Me turn right off Hwy 1A near the war memorial, into the commune with the banner 'Lang Nghe Gom Bau Truc'. Inside the village take the first left for some of the better pottery stores.

TUAN TU HAMLET

While Cham history is predominately Hindu, significant parts of the remaining population are Islamic. There is a minaret-less mosque

GOODBYE SAILOR

Can Ranh Harbour has long been considered one of Asia's prime deep-water anchorages. The Russian fleet of Admiral Rodjestvenski used it in 1905 at the end of the Russo-Japanese War, as did the Japanese during WWII. At this time the surrounding area was still considered an excellent place for tiger hunting. In the mid-1960s the Americans constructed a vast base here, including an extensive port, ship-repair facilities and an airstrip.

After reunification the Russians and their fleet came back, enjoying far better facilities than they had left seven decades before. For a while this became the largest Soviet naval installation outside the USSR. With the collapse of the Soviet Union in 1991 and the end of the Cold War, economic problems forced the Russians to cut back vastly on their overseas military facilities. Although the initial contract on Cam Ranh Bay was due to expire in 2004, the Russians vacated their position by the end of 2002, the last hurrah for the Russian navy in Asia.

in the Cham hamlet of Tuan Tu (population 1000). This community is governed by elected religious leaders (Thay Mun), who can easily be identified by their traditional costume, which includes a white robe and an elaborate white turban with red tassels. In keeping with Islamic precepts governing modesty, the women here often wear head coverings and long dresses.

To get to Tuan Tu Hamlet, head south from Phan Rang along Hwy 1A. Go 250m south of the large bridge to a small bridge. Cross it and turn left (to the southeast) onto Đ Tran Nhat Duat. The road bends right at a Buddhist pagoda. Turn right at the T-junction after a school and follow the road through the village and over a bridge for about 2km until you reach the hamlet to the right of the road. The mosque is at the centre of the village near the large well. If you continue along the road for a further 2km you'll reach a beach with red sand dunes.

Sleeping

Viet Thang Hotel (☎ 835 899; 430 Đ Ngo Gia Tu; r 120,000-180,000; ❄) Looking a little like a Mondrian painting from the outside, this place will suit backpackers who don't mind the odd cigarette hole or stain on the sheets.

Ho Phong Hotel (☎ 920 333; hophong@yahoo.com; 363 Đ Ngo Gia Tu; r 170,000-250,000d; ❄ 💻) This one's a cross between a castle and a Christmas tree, set behind a little park near the bridge at the bottom of town. It's new, clean and great value – with high ceilings, impressive showers in most rooms (glass walls and two shower heads) and toilets lined with gold trim.

Thong Nhat Hotel (☎ 827 201; thongnhathotel_pr@hcm.vnn.vn; 343 Đ Thong Nhat; r US$15-25; ❄ 💻) This place is starting to show its age, but it's kept clean and breakfast is included in the rates.

Eating

One of the local delicacies here is roasted or baked gecko *(ky nhong)*, served with fresh green mango (see p300). If you prefer self-catering and have quick reflexes, most hotel rooms in Vietnam have a ready supply.

More palatable to tourist tastes is another local speciality, *com ga* – chicken with rice. The local chickens seem to have more meat on them than Vietnam's usual spindly specimens, and people make a point of buying chickens (or at least stopping for a feed) as they pass through. There are a few *com ga* restaurants on Đ Tran Quang Dieu, the best of which is **Phuoc Thanh** (☎ 824 712; 3 Đ Tran Quang Dieu; mains 20,000d).

Phan Rang is the table grape capital of Vietnam. Stalls in the market sell fresh grapes, grape juice and dried grapes (too juicy to be called raisins). Also worth sampling is the green dragon fruit *(thanh long)*. Its mild, kiwifruit-like taste is especially refreshing when chilled. You'll find it in the market, or in grocery shops along Đ Thong Nhat.

Getting There & Away

BUS

Phan Rang bus station (Ben Xe Phan Rang; opposite 64 Đ Thong Nhat) is on the northern outskirts of town. Regular buses head north to Nha Trang (24,000d, 2½ hours), northwest to Dalat (40,000d, 4½ hours), and south to Ca Na (10,000d, one hour) and beyond.

CAR & MOTORBIKE

Phan Rang is 344km from HCMC, 147km from Phan Thiet, 32km from Ca Na, 104km from Nha Trang and 108km from Dalat.

TRAIN

The **Thap Cham Train Station** (Ga Thap Cham; ☎ 888 029; 7 Đ Phan Dinh Phung) is about 6km west of Hwy

CHAMPY NEW YEAR

The Cham New Year *(kate)* is celebrated at Po Klong Garai in the seventh month of the Cham calendar (around October). The festival commemorates ancestors, Cham national heroes and deities such as the farmers' goddess Po Ino Nagar.

On the eve of the festival, a procession guarded by the mountain people of Tay Nguyen carries King Po Klong Garai's clothing, to the accompaniment of traditional music. The procession lasts until midnight. The following morning the garments are carried to the tower, once again accompanied by music, along with banners, flags, singing and dancing. Notables, dignitaries and village elders follow behind. This colourful ceremony continues into the afternoon.

The celebrations then carry on for the rest of the month, as the Cham attend parties and visit friends and relatives. They also use this time to pray for good fortune.

1A, within sight of Po Klong Garai Cham towers. Destinations include Nha Trang (35,000d, 1½ to 2½ hours, eight daily) and HCMC (120,000d, six to 10 hours, eight daily).

NINH CHU BEACH

☎ 068

Southeast of Phan Rang, Ninh Chu Beach is increasingly popular with local tourists. Apart from a bit of litter, the 10km-long beach is quite nice. It makes a quieter alternative to Phan Rang as a base for visiting the Cham ruins.

A bizarre local attraction is the **Hoan Cau Resort** (☎ 890 077; waterpark admission adult/child 10,000/5000d), where Disneyland meets Vietnamese folklore. Hilarious plaster statues adorn the grounds and rooms are shaped like tree stumps. A brief visit is more enjoyable than actually staying here.

Sleeping & Eating

Den Gion Resort (☎ 874 223; www.dengionninhchu.com; r 150,000-500,000d, camping per person 70,000d;) A giant Cham-looking brick building looks set to replace the ugly hospital-like reception that was in use at the time of research. The crimson-brick beach bungalows are surprisingly nice, with crisp new linen, glassed-in showers and wooden ceiling fans. Facilities include an open-air restaurant (mains 30,000d) and tennis courts. Dome-tent camping is possible near the beach.

Saigon Ninhchu Hotel (☎ 876 006; www.saigonninhchuhotel.com.vn; r US$40-55, ste US$80;) Good value for the price, this is easily the best accommodation in the area. Each of the tasteful rooms has a sea view – as well as nice carpets, comfortable beds, quality linen, robes and a safety box. Although the beach is on the doorstep, the swimming pool is hard to resist. Rounding out the picture are a small fitness centre, two restaurants, a bar, a business centre and 24-hour room service.

Getting There & Away

Turn left (southeast) into Đ Ngo Gia Tu, the street immediately before the Cai River bridge in Phan Rang, and continue on, following the signs for 7km. Unless you're driving yourself, it's easiest to take a *xe om* (30,000d).

CA NA

☎ 068

During the 16th century, princes of the Cham royal family would fish and hunt tigers, elephants and rhinoceroses here. Today Ca Na (pronounced *kah nah* – not like the site of the biblical booze-up) is better known for its white-sand beaches which are dotted with huge granite boulders. The best of the beach and accommodation is available right on Hwy 1A, a kilometre north of the fishing village. It's a beautiful spot, but it's tough to ignore the constant honking and rumble of trucks. The payoff, however, is an almost complete lack of hassle from the friendly locals.

The terrain is studded with magnificent prickly-pear cacti. Bright yellow **Lac Son**, a small pagoda on the hillside, makes for an interesting but steep climb. Further afield, **Tra Cang Temple** is about midway between Ca Na and Phan Rang. Unfortunately, you have to sidetrack over an abysmal dirt road in order to reach it. Many ethnic Chinese from Cholon visit the temple.

If you stay here, be aware that there are no banks or ATMs and absolutely no-one accepts credit cards or travellers' cheques.

Sleeping & Eating

Ca Na Hotel (☎/fax 761 320; r 170,000-200,000d;) This place rents crusty rooms in an ancient ferroconcrete hotel near the highway; the quieter beach bungalows are a slightly better choice. Its restaurant is a popular lunch spot for buses on the HCMC–Nha Trang route (dishes 10,000d to 40,000d).

Hon Co Ca Na Motel (☎ 760 998; www.ninhthuantourist.com.vn; r 250,000-300,000d;) Offering attractive bungalows with flowers on trellises and nice, new furniture, it's a shame this place is not better maintained. Giant ants and cobwebs have free reign in the less-than-clean rooms, which can be quite noisy. There's a lovely little beach, tennis courts, a large seafood restaurant (dishes 60,000d) and the ominous combination of karaoke and massage.

Getting There & Away

Ca Na is 114km north of Phan Thiet and 32km south of Phan Rang. Many long-haul buses cruising Hwy 1A can drop you here, including the open-tour buses on the Nha Trang–Mui Ne leg. You can phone to arrange a pick-up from the Sinh Café office in either city. Local buses from Phan Rang (10,000d, one hour) head into Ca Na fishing village – ask to be let out on the highway and catch a *xe om* for the last kilometre.

LIZARD FISHING

When most people think of fishing in the mountains they conjure up images of hooking river trout or lake bass. But in the arid foothills of the south-central coast (notably around places like Ca Na, Phan Rang, Phan Thiet and Mui Ne) there is a whole other kind of angling, and a walk in these hills can yield one of the strangest sights in Vietnam – lizard fishing.

These lizards, called *than lan nui,* are members of the gecko family and good for eating – some say they taste like chicken. The traditional way of catching the lizards is by setting a hook on a long bamboo fishing pole and dangling bait from the top of a boulder until the spunky little reptiles strike.

Lizards are served grilled, roasted or fried, and are often made up into a paté (complete with their finely chopped bones) and used as a dip for rice-paper crackers. Yum.

VINH HAO

☎ 062

Known for its mineral water, which is bottled and sold all over Vietnam, Vinh Hao is an obscure town just off Hwy 1A between Phan Thiet and Phan Rang.

It's also the home of **Vietnam Scuba** (☎ 853 919; www.vietnamscuba.com), an attractive and well-appointed Korean-run dive centre on a private beach about 3.5km south of Ca Na, easy to spot from the highway. This is very much a by-Koreans for-Koreans resort, but serious scuba divers (and *kimchi* [pickled cabbage] lovers) will appreciate the setup and some of the best diving in Vietnam. Marine life includes big fish, manta rays, barracuda and sharks.

Daily dive packages (US$130) include accommodation in nice beachfront villas, boat trips and guides, and three meals a day. A BC and regulator can be rented for an extra US$50 a day. All dive sites are offshore, anywhere from 30 to 90 minutes from the resort's private jetty.

MUI NE BEACH

☎ 062

Mui Ne has quickly been transformed from an isolated stretch of beautiful white sand to one long row of resorts. While there's still a **fishing village** at the east end of the beach, it's tourists that make up most of the population. The boom in top-end resorts hasn't killed the chilled surfie vibe, although it has brought an increasing number of up-market restaurants and souvenir shops. It's an unusual set up, as everything is spread along one 10km stretch of road – the accommodation is on the beach side, and the restaurants and bars mainly on the other.

Mui Ne sees only about half the rainfall of nearby Phan Thiet. The sand dunes help protect its unique microclimate, and even during the wet season (from June to September) rains tend to be fairly light and sporadic.

Mui Ne's developing a reputation as the action capital of the coast. There's no scuba diving or snorkelling to speak of, but when Nha Trang and Hoi An get the rains, Mui Ne gets the waves. Surf's up from August to December. For windsurfers, the gales howl as well, especially from late October to late April, when swells stir over from the Philippine typhoons. Kite-surfing is very popular. If this all sounds too much like hard work you can simply splash about in the clean, clear water.

One major problem the area faces is the steady creep of coastal erosion. Many resorts have almost completely lost their beaches and rely on sandbagging to keep the little they have left.

Orientation

The road follows the curve of the beach, running roughly east to west. Until the explosion of resorts it went by the name of Route 706 with addresses designated by their distance in kilometres from Hwy 1A in Phan Thiet (to the west). Half the properties now follow a new numbering system, with Route 706 given proper street numbers and renamed Đ Nguyen Dinh Chieu on the west half of the beach and Đ Huynh Thuc Khang on the east half. Adding to the confusion, some refer to themselves by the old kilometre marking combined with the new street name.

Information

A great resource for information on Mui Ne is www.muinebeach.net. The main **post office** (☎ 849 799; 348 Huynh Thuc Khang) is in Mui Ne village, but there's a more convenient branch at **Swiss Village** (☎ 847 480; 44 Đ Nguyen Dinh Chieu).

Fami Tour Office (☎ 741 030; 121 Đ Nguyen Dinh Chieu) Local tours, internet access and cheap international internet calls.

Hanh Café/Ha Phuong Tourist (☎ 847 597; 125A Đ Nguyen Dinh Chieu) Local day tours, open tour bookings, fast food and internet access.

Sinh Café (☎ 847 542; 144 Đ Nguyen Dinh Chieu) Operates out of its Mui Ne Resort, booking open-tour buses and offering credit card cash advances.

Tam Nam (☎ 742 457; 49 Nguyen Dinh Chieu) Friendly and cheap laundry service operating out of a small grocery store.

Sights

Mui Ne is famous for its enormous **red and white sand dunes**. These have been a favourite subject matter for many a Vietnamese photographer, including some who sit like camels on the blazing hot sand for hours, waiting for the winds to sculpt the dunes into that perfect Kodak moment. If you visit, be sure to try the sand-sledding.

You'll need a jeep to explore these properly, but be careful to agree on an itinerary for the tour, preferably in writing. We've heard complaints, particularly about 'sunset tours' that cut short with the sun high in the sky and the drivers getting aggressive when challenged.

Also of interest is the **Fairy Spring** (Suoi Tien), which is really a stream that flows through a patch of dunes with interesting sand and rock formations. It's a beautiful trek wading up the stream from the sea to its source, though it might be wise to hire a local guide. You can do the trek barefoot, but if you're heading out into the big sand dunes, you'll need leather soles on your feet; sandals are even questionable during the midday sun.

Heading west, **Po Shanu Cham Towers** (Km5; admission 2000d; ⏲ 7.30-11.30am & 1.30-4.30pm) occupy a hill near Phan Thiet, with sweeping views of the town and a cemetery filled with candy like tombstones. Dating from the 9th century, this complex consists of the ruins of three towers, none of which are in very good shape. There's a small pagoda on the site, as well as a gallery and shop.

Activities

Jibes (☎ 847 405; www.windsurf-vietnam.com; 90 Đ Nguyen Dinh Chieu; ⏲ 7.30am-6pm) is a surfer's heaven, offering lessons and renting state-of-the-art gear

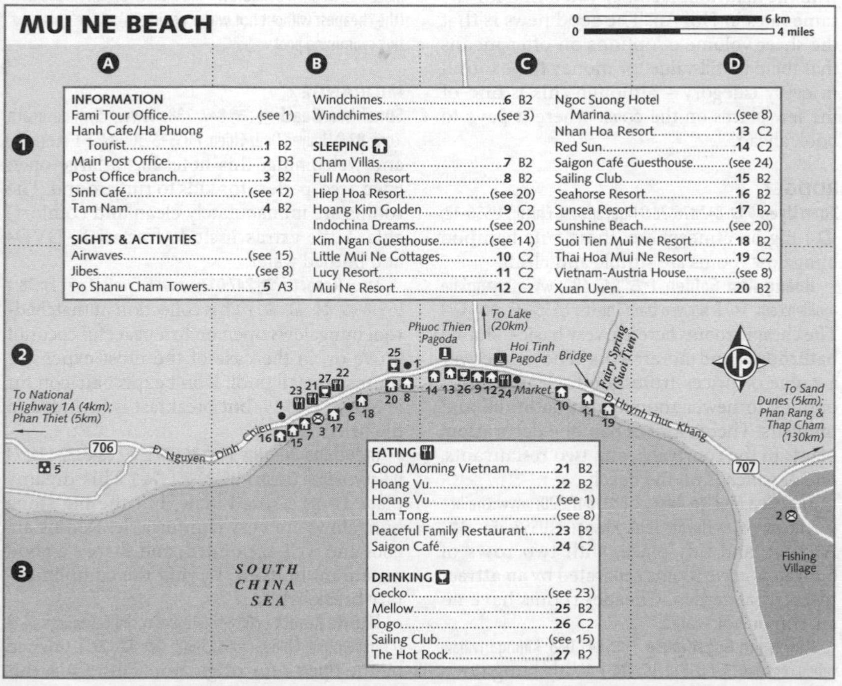

like windsurfers (one hour/half-day/full-day US$12/30/45), surfboards (one hour/half-day/full-day US$10/25/30), kitesurfers (one hour/half-day/full-day US$30/75/95) and kayaks (one hour/half-day/full-day US$5/13/25). Insurance is extra.

Airwaves (☎ 847 440; www.airwaveskitesurfing.com; 24 Đ Nguyen Dinh Chieu), based at the Sailing Club (see opposite), is another outfit offering kite-surfing, windsurfing and sailing lessons and equipment rentals.

Windchimes (☎ 0909-720 017; www.windsurfing-vietnam.com) is a third option, operating out of Saigon Mui Ne Resort (56 Đ Nguyen Dinh Chieu) and Swiss Village (44 Đ Nguyen Dinh Chieu).

Sleeping

Mui Ne has become the escape of choice for ex-pats working in HCMC, meaning that the nicer accommodation can book out during weekends and holiday times. This seems to have encouraged a number of properties with midrange standards to demand top-end prices. At the budget end, prices have also begun to creep up – a rude shock compared with the luxurious facilities you'll find for the same rates in Hoi An. The good news is that the sheer volume of options on offer means that there is still value for money to be found in every category – although this is one of the few places on the coast where it pays to book ahead.

BUDGET

Xuan Uyen (☎ 847 476; 78 Đ Nguyen Dinh Chieu; r US$6-12;) Big on atmosphere, these cute bamboo bungalow rooms are simple and clean.

Hoang Kim Golden (☎ 847 689; www.hoangkim-golden.com; 140 Đ Nguyen Dinh Chieu; r US$6-25;) The cheapie rooms here are very basic – shared bathrooms and no air-con. The rest cover a range of prices from good, clean budget options to newer rooms with bathtubs and minibars. There's a lot of bamboo decoration, plants in the courtyard, and two restaurants, one of which is on the beach.

Thai Hoa Mui Ne Resort (☎ 847 320; www.thaihoaresort.com; 56 Đ Huynh Thuc Khang; r US$8-25;) A cheap and tidy place, with two rows of bungalow-style rooms separated by an attractive central garden. Cheaper rooms have no air-con or hot water.

Kim Ngan Guesthouse (☎ 847 046; kimnganvilla@yahoo.com; km13; r US$10-15;) With bungalows whose tiled balconies jut over the water, this friendly family-run place is a good choice. All the rooms are similar, with a US$5 saving if you forgo air-con.

Hiep Hoa Resort (☎ 847 262; hiephoatourism@yahoo.net; 80 Đ Nguyen Dinh Chieu; r US$12-16;) This is a great spot with a lovely garden and clean, attractive rooms – albeit without frills such as TVs, fridges and phones, or air-con in the US$12 rooms.

Nhan Hoa Resort (☎ /fax 847 371; 128 Đ Nguyen Dinh Chieu; r US$12-26;) The old wing is basic but the newer wing is comfortable enough, and the poolside garden area reaches to the sea.

Back-up budget options:

Saigon Café Guesthouse (☎ 847 091; 168-170 Đ Nguyen Dinh Chieu; r US$5;) These bamboo and thatched-roof bungalows are as cheap and humble as it comes.

Mellow (☎ 743 086; 117C Đ Nguyen Dinh Chieu; r US$6-12) On the wrong (nonbeach) side of the road, the cheaper rooms share bathrooms and toilets. The only treats are hot water and free-standing fans, and a good social vibe in the bar-restaurant.

Vietnam-Austria House (☎ 847 047; ngothikimhong@hotmail.com; km13.5; r US$8-25;) This established place has wooden bungalows and a block of simple rooms (the cheapest without hot water or air-con); there's also a tiny swimming pool.

MIDRANGE

Sunshine Beach (☎ 847 788; www.sunshine-beach.com; 82 Đ Nguyen Dinh Chieu; r US$15-30;) Friendly and welcoming, this hotel has a large open lawn area, perfect for kids to run around. The rooms are immaculately clean and comfortable. Little extras include free wi-fi, DVDs and bottled water.

Lucy Resort (☎ 847 017; www.lucyresort.net; km18; r US$18-45;) This collection of thatched-roof bungalows open on to a peaceful coconut grove or, in the case of the most expensive rooms, a small pool. Don't expect air-con for less than US$25, but breakfast is included in the price.

Indochina Dreams (☎ 847 271; fax 08-8322 174; 74 Đ Nguyen Dinh Chieu; r US$20-25;) This dreamy place is on a small scale, but the big stone bungalows are very comfortable. Rooms are cool and well-appointed, and there's a good restaurant in front, serving the complimentary breakfast.

Mui Ne Resort (☎ 847 542; www.sinhcafevn.com; 144 Đ Nguyen Dinh Chieu; r US$25-30;) Owned by the open-tour originators Sinh Café, this is an incredibly easy option (the buses arrive and depart from here) and an attractive one at that. The rooms are clean, comfortable and reasonably priced, if a little on the small side, and the staff are friendly. The restaurant is huge, to accommodate the bus patrons who swarm into the place several times a day on their compulsory pit stop. Expect a US$5 surcharge on the weekends.

Full Moon Resort (Trang Tron; ☎ 847 008; www.windsurf-vietnam.com; 84 Đ Nguyen Dinh Chieu; r US$35-80;) Most of the bungalows are set around the garden, but the beachfront bungalows have a beautifully traditional feel – with silk hangings, low square tables, wooden ceiling fans, slatted sliding doors and large corner bathtubs. Rooms in the colonial-yellow house have huge bathtubs and sofa beds to accommodate extra guests.

Sunsea Resort (☎ 847 700; www.sunsearesort-muine.com; 50 Đ Nguyen Dinh Chieu; r US$50-70;) The traditionally inspired round bungalows with pointed thatched roofs are dotted around a beautifully maintained large garden under the shade of coconut palms. The oval pool is particularly enticing.

Little Mui Ne Cottages (☎ 847 550; www.littlemuine.com; 10B Huynh Thuc Khang; r US$50-85;) Lots of perks warrant the higher prices: comfortable cottages have lots of space around them, and the pool is big enough for swimming laps. Other special touches are a welcome drink upon arrival and complimentary bottled water, breakfast, internet and bicycles.

Other midrange options:

Red Sun (☎ 847 387; caféloumi@hcm.vnn.vn; km13; r US$15;) Red Sun has six simple clean rooms right by the water and a shady brick courtyard and terrace. The beach disappears at high tide.

Suoi Tien Mui Ne Resort (☎ 847 146; suoitienmuineresort@vnn.vn; 60 Đ Nguyen Dinh Chieu; r US$15-45;) The friendly owners give this place a family feel, although US$15 is a little pricy for a room without air-con or hot water.

Ngoc Suong Hotel Marina (☎ 847 515; ngocsuong@hcm.fpt.vn; 94 Đ Nguyen Dinh Chieu; r US$33-65;) The paintwork could do with some maintenance, but this little place is clean and comfortable.

TOP END

Sailing Club (☎ 847 440; www.sailingclubvietnam.com; 24 Đ Nguyen Dinh Chieu; r US$55, bungalows US$70-100;) Popular for its wide open bar and restaurant overlooking the sea, the Sailing Club has spacious rooms in a lush garden setting. The resort is a stylish blend of Asian and European architecture, and the comfortable, clean rooms are designed with bamboo and dark, matte wood.

Cham Villas (☎ 741 234; www.chamvillas.com; 32 Đ Nguyen Dinh Chieu; r US$95-120;) Set in a beautiful tropical garden with an exquisite swimming pool, this luxury boutique resort only has 14 villas, so it books up quickly. Breakfast and wi-fi internet is included in the price.

Seahorse Resort (☎ 847 507; www.seahorseresortvn.com; km11; r US$110-120, bungalows US$132-190, ste US$253;) Gorgeously designed, the flagstone pathways and narrow pond in the coconut-shaded garden follow the natural contours of the land. Each bungalow has four separate rooms surrounding an interior garden. The rooms themselves are elegantly decorated with Vietnamese art and furnishings, and have exquisite open-air bathrooms.

Eating

Saigon Cafe (☎ 847 091; 168-170 Đ Nguyen Dinh Chieu; dishes 12,000-45,000d) Great Vietnamese BBQ food in a basic setting, with profundities written on the walls in beautiful calligraphy – although we suspect 'It is still very good if you can learn by your mistake to like butter' may have lost something in the translation.

Lam Tong (☎ 847 598; 92 Đ Nguyen Dinh Chieu; dishes 12,000-50,000d) You can watch the food being prepared from your plastic seat in the fairy-light-strewn open-air dining area at the rear of this family house. The tanks of live seafood attest to the freshness of the reasonably priced meals.

Hoang Vu (Double Wheels Restaurant; ☎ 847 525; km12.2 & 121 Đ Nguyen Dinh Chieu; dishes 25,000-52,000d; lunch & dinner) Like most successful businesses in Vietnam this one's cloned itself into two restaurants. The atmosphere's romantically Asian in both and the staff provide casually attentive service and delicious, beautifully presented Vietnamese, Thai and Chinese food with some French influences.

Peaceful Family Restaurant (Yen Gia Quan; ☎ 741 019; 53 Đ Nguyen Dinh Chieu; dishes 30,000-70,000d; lunch & dinner) This friendly family eatery serves wonderful Vietnamese cuisine in a lovely open setting.

Good Morning Vietnam (☎ 847 585; www.goodmorningviet.com; km11.8; mains 60,000-105,000d; lunch & dinner) This is another in the popular chain of Italian eateries. These guys have had the excellent idea of offering free hotel pick-ups to bridge the distance of the strip.

Drinking

No surfie town would be complete without a smattering of beachside bars and Mui Ne doesn't disappoint on this front.

Pogo (☎ 0909-479 346; 138 Đ Nguyen Dinh Chieu) A fun, open-air bar decorated with colourful infantile paintings – it has a pool table, big sound system and bean bags.

Mellow (☎ 743 086; 117C Đ Nguyen Dinh Chieu) Run by an English-Vietnamese couple, this place is popular with the backpacking/kitesurfing fraternity. It also has a pool table, with a cool bicycle/lighting feature.

Jibes (☎ 847 405; 90 Đ Nguyen Dinh Chieu) Decorated with surf boards, this one's an old favourite. There's a pool table here as well.

Hot Rock (☎ 847 608; 12.5km) Another popular place with a pool table, the Hot Rock also serves good food and plays some excellent music.

Gecko (☎ 741 033; 51 Đ Nguyen Dinh Chieu) An upmarket option with lots of fancy cocktails and, yep, there's a pool table

Sailing Club (☎ 847 440; 24 Đ Nguyen Dinh Chieu) Not as raucous as its sister in Nha Trang, the Mui Ne incarnation is a stylish place to hang out.

Getting There & Away

It used to be that Mui Ne was quite isolated and could only be approached by an 11km diversion from Hwy 1A through Phan Thiet. Recently a new road has opened, heading northeast from the eastern end of the beach, connecting back to Hwy 1A halfway to Ca Na. This scenic stretch, past deserted beaches and a beautiful lake ringed with water lilies, greatly reduces the northward journey and allows the open-tour buses to pass through Mui Ne without backtracking.

These buses are the best option for Mui Ne, and Sinh Café and Hanh Café both have daily services to/from HCMC (US$6, four hours), Nha Trang (US$6, five hours) via Ca Na (60,000d, 1½ hours) and Dalat (US$7, 5½ hours). A local bus makes trips between Phan Thiet bus station and Mui Ne, but it is irregular and slow. The best way to reach the beach from the highway in Phan Thiet is by *xe om* (50,000d).

Getting Around

Mui Ne is so spread out that it's difficult to get around on foot. There are plenty of *xe om* drivers to take you up and down the strip; no trip should cost more than 10,000d. Given that the area isn't highly populated and it's not on the main highway, this is not a bad place to hire a bicycle or motorbike (enquire at your hotel or at the travel agencies). However, a German tourist on a motorbike was killed by a bus on this stretch in 2006, so don't be complacent.

PHAN THIET

☎ 062 / pop 168,400

Phan Thiet is traditionally known for its *nuoc mam* (fish sauce), producing 16 to 17 million litres of the stinky stuff per annum. The population includes descendants of the Cham, who controlled this area until 1692. During the colonial period the Europeans lived in their own segregated ghetto stretching along the northern bank of the Phan Thiet River, while the Vietnamese, Cham, Southern Chinese, Malays and Indonesians lived along the southern bank.

The river flowing through the centre of town creates a small **fishing harbour**, which is always chock-a-block with boats, making for interesting photos. To get to Phan Thiet's **beachfront**, turn off Đ Tran Hung Dao (Hwy 1A) into Đ Nguyen Tat Thanh – the road opposite the **Victory Monument**, an arrow-shaped concrete tower with victorious cement people at the base.

The main attraction of Phan Thiet is the **Ocean Dunes Golf Club** (☎ 823 366; odgc@hcm.vnn.vn; 1 Đ Ton Duc Thang, per round US$65), a top-notch 18-hole, par 72 course designed by Nick Faldo, near the beachfront at the Novotel. Very reasonably priced golf package tours are available if you book from HCMC – contact the resort's HCMC **marketing office** (☎ 08-824 3460; www.vietnamgolfresorts.com; New World Hotel, 76 Đ Le Lai).

Orientation & Information

Phan Thiet is built along both banks of the Phan Thiet River (also known as the Ca Ty and the Muong Man River). Hwy 1A becomes Đ Tran Hung Dao as it runs through town.

Binh Thuan Tourist (☎ 816 821; www.binhthuantourist.com; 82 Đ Trung Trac; 🕑 7-11am & 1.30-5pm Mon-Fri, 8-10.30am Sat & Sun) Tourist maps and information.

Sleeping & Eating

Unless you're here for the golf, you're much better off staying in nearby Mui Ne (see p302).

Binh Minh Hotel (☎ 823 344; fax 823 354; Đ Le Loi; r 240,000-300,000d; ❄) It's ugly and the karaoke can be noisy, but this state-owned dinosaur is right by the beach.

Novotel Ocean Dunes & Golf Resort (☎ 822 393; novpht@hcm.vnn.vn; 1 Đ Ton Duc Thang; r US$66-124, ste US$161;) In a beautiful spot between the golf course and a private stretch of beach, the main Novotel building is looking a little tired – although at the time of research new villas had been built near the golf club. The hotel's Seahorse Restaurant is the flashest eatery in town, serving up local seafood (dishes US$5 to US$15).

Getting There & Around

Phan Thiet bus station (Ben Xe Binh Thuan; ☎ 821 361; Đ Tu Van Tu; 5.30am-3.30pm) is on the northern outskirts of town. Phan Thiet is on Hwy 1A, 198km east of HCMC, 250km from Nha Trang and 247km from Dalat. The nearest train station to Phan Thiet is 12km west of town in dusty little Muong Man.

TA CU MOUNTAIN

The highlight here is the **white reclining Buddha** (Tuong Phat Nam). At 49m, it's the largest in Vietnam. The pagoda was constructed in 1861 during the Nguyen dynasty, but the Buddha was only added in 1972. It has become an important pilgrimage centre for Buddhists, who stay overnight in the pagoda's dormitory. Foreigners can't do this without police permission, but there's now a **guesthouse** (☎ 867 484; r 200,000d;) on the mountain.

The mountain is just off Hwy 1A, 28km south from Phan Thiet, from which the Buddha is a beautiful two-hour trek, or a two-minute cable-car ride (55,000d return) and a short, but steep, hike.

Central Highlands

It's easy to get off the beaten track in this wonderfully scenic part of the country. Only Dalat makes it on to most tourists' radars, meaning that the rest of the region still allows an element of adventure. This is a great part of the country to see on the back of a motorbike – stopping at will to admire an amazing mountain view, to explore a wild waterfall or to interact with villagers from the local hill tribes. The cooler climate also makes a good respite for those not used to tropical climes.

However, there's a darker side to this region – large tracts of the highlands around Pleiku and Buon Ma Thuot bear the scars of Agent Orange deforestation from the American War, and children in these areas continue to have a high rate of birth defects.

Also in February 2001 the government forbade travellers from visiting the central highlands because of unrest among the local tribes. In March 2004 a clash in Buon Ma Thuot precipitated another brief closure of the area, so before heading to the hills make local inquiries to confirm that your destinations are accessible. At the time of research, the only restrictions in place likely to affect tourists were around Pleiku.

The upgrading of the historic Ho Chi Minh Trail has made it easier than ever to visit out-of-the-way places like Kon Tum. It remains to be seen whether increased tourism will leave these delightful backwaters unchanged. There's still an openness and friendliness in the highlands that is becoming harder to find in the tourist traps of the coast.

HIGHLIGHTS

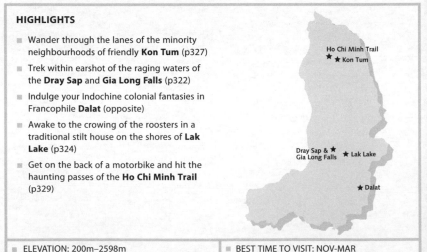

- Wander through the lanes of the minority neighbourhoods of friendly **Kon Tum** (p327)
- Trek within earshot of the raging waters of the **Dray Sap** and **Gia Long Falls** (p322)
- Indulge your Indochine colonial fantasies in Francophile **Dalat** (opposite)
- Awake to the crowing of the roosters in a traditional stilt house on the shores of **Lak Lake** (p324)
- Get on the back of a motorbike and hit the haunting passes of the **Ho Chi Minh Trail** (p329)

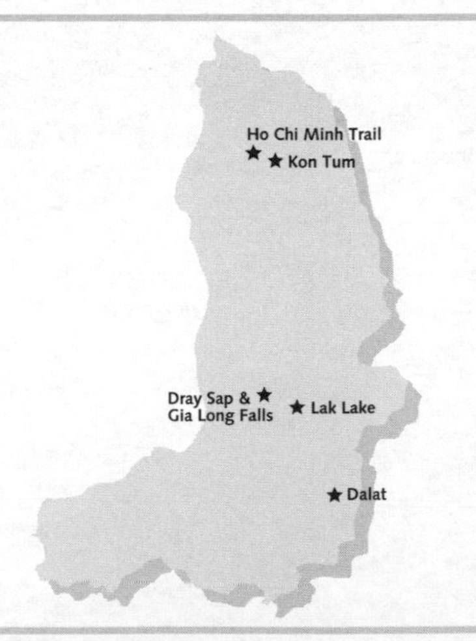

- ELEVATION: 200m–2598m
- BEST TIME TO VISIT: NOV-MAR

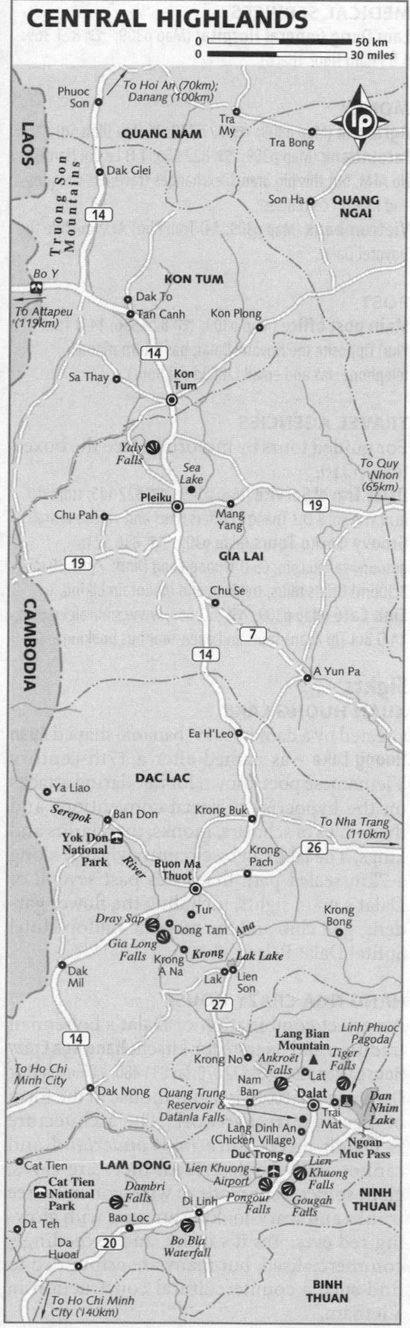

Getting There & Away

The region has three main airports – Dalat, Buon Ma Thuot and Pleiku. You can reach them all from HCMC. From Hanoi you can only fly directly to Dalat; for the other two you'll need to fly through Danang. There are no trains servicing this region.

By road you can access Dalat via Hwy 20 from HCMC or Phan Rang. Hwy 14 is the main north-south route, passing through Buon Ma Thuot, Pleiku and Kon Tum. Pleiku is connected to the coast by Hwy 19, which hits Hwy 1A near Quy Nhon. Similarly, Buon Ma Thuot can be reached from Ninh Hoa, just north of Nha Trang, by Hwy 26. There are frequent buses on all of these routes, although only Dalat is served by open-tour buses.

DALAT

☎ 063 / pop 188,400 / elevation 1475m

Dalat is quite different from anywhere else you'll visit in Vietnam. You would almost be forgiven for thinking you'd stumbled into the French Alps in springtime. This was certainly how the former colonists treated it – escaping to their chalets to enjoy the cooler climate.

The French feel is compounded by a radio mast shaped like the Eiffel Tower and the local bohemian artists' predilection for swanning around in berets. Dalat is small enough to remain charming, and the surrounding countryside is blessed with lakes, waterfalls, evergreen forests and gardens.

Local products include silk, garden vegetables and flowers (especially beautiful hydrangeas), which are sold all over southern Vietnam. But the biggest contribution to the economy is tourism: more than 800,000 domestic tourists and another 80,000 foreigners visit here every year. It's the country's favourite honeymoon spot and still retains the final word in Vietnamese kitsch.

The Dalat area was once famous for hunting and a 1950s brochure boasted that 'a two-hour drive from the town leads to several game-rich areas abounding in deer, roe, peacocks, pheasants, wild boar, black bear, wild caws, panthers, tigers, gaurs and elephants'. So successful were the hunters that all of the big game is now extinct. The closest you'll get to the formerly diverse fauna are the taxidermied specimens about town.

The city's population includes about 5000 members of hill tribes, which make up 33 distinct communities in Lam Dong province.

Traditional dress can occasionally be spotted in the market places. Hill-tribe women of this area carry their infants on their backs in a long piece of cloth worn over one shoulder and tied in the front.

The City of Eternal Spring, Dalat's temperature hovers between a pleasant 15°C (average daily minimum) to 24°C (average daily maximum). Effectively Dalat has two seasons – dry (December to March) and wet (April to November). Despite the mild temperatures, by the end of the dry season the lush green surrounds turn to brown. Even in the wet season, mornings normally remain dry – allowing time for sightseeing before the deluge begins.

History

This area has been home to various Montagnard (hill tribe) groups for centuries. In the local Lat language, 'Da Lat' means 'River of the Lat Tribe'.

The first European to 'discover' Dalat was Dr Alexandre Yersin in 1893 (see p286). The city was established in 1912 and quickly became fashionable with Europeans. At one point during the French colonial period, some 20% of Dalat's population was foreign, as evidenced by the 2500-odd chateau-style villas scattered around the city.

During the American War, Dalat was spared by the tacit agreement of all parties concerned. Indeed, it seems that while South Vietnamese soldiers were being trained at the city's military academy and affluent officials of the Saigon regime were relaxing in their villas, Viet Cong cadres were doing the same thing not far away in *their* villas. Dalat fell to North Vietnamese forces without a fight on 3 April 1975. There is no problem with leftover mines and ordnance in the area.

Orientation

Dalat's sights are spread out and the terrain in and around the city is hilly. Still, trekking or cycling is made easier by the cool temperatures. The Central Market, set in a hollow, marks the middle of the town. To the southeast the 'Eiffel Tower' of the main post office is a useful landmark, rising above the southern shore of Xuan Huong Lake.

Information

INTERNET ACCESS

The main post office (right) has fast, cheap connections.

MEDICAL SERVICES

Lam Dong General Hospital (Map p309; ☎ 821 369; 4 Đ Pham Ngoc Thach)

MONEY

Agribank (Map p309; ☎ 827 740; 36 Hoa Binh Sq)

Incombank (Map p309; ☎ 822 586; 1 Đ Le Dai Hanh) No ATM, but this big branch exchanges travellers cheques and foreign currencies.

Vietcombank (Map p309; 7 Đ Tran Phu) ATM outside the Novotel Dalat.

POST

Main post office (Map p309; ☎ 822 586; 14 Đ Tran Phu) Opposite the Novotel Dalat; has international telephone, fax and email (2000d per hour).

TRAVEL AGENCIES

For guided tours by motorbike, see the boxed text, p310.

Dalat Travel Service (Map p309; ☎ 822 125; ttdhhd@hcm.vnn.vn; 7 Đ 3 Thang 2) Offers tours and vehicle rentals.

Groovy Gecko Tours (Map p309; ☎ 836 521; ggtour@yahoo.com; 65 Đ Truong Cong Dinh; 🕒 7.30am-8.30pm) Offers tours, trekking and mountain biking.

Sinh Café (Map p309; ☎ 822 663; www.sinhcafevn.com; 4A Đ Bui Thi Xuan) Tours and open-tour bus bookings.

Sights

XUAN HUONG LAKE

Created by a dam in 1919, banana-shaped **Xuan Huong Lake** was named after a 17th-century Vietnamese poet known for her daring attacks on the hypocrisy of social conventions and the foibles of scholars, monks, mandarins and kings. The lake can be circumnavigated along a 7km sealed path that leads past several of Dalat's main sights, including the flower gardens, golf club and the majestic hilltop Hotel Sofitel Dalat Palace.

HANG NGA CRAZY HOUSE

A perfect combination of Dalat's bohemian tradition and its taste for kitsch, **Hang Nga Crazy House** (Map p309; ☎ 822 070; fax 831 480; 3 Đ Huynh Thuc Khang; admission 8000d) is a guesthouse in the form of a giant surreal artwork. The architecture is Gaudi-meets-*Alice in Wonderland* and cannot easily be described: there are caves, giant spider webs made of wire, concrete tree trunks and scary-looking animals with glowing red eyes. Yes it's tacky, and exceedingly commercialised, but many are astounded to find such a countercultural construction in Vietnam.

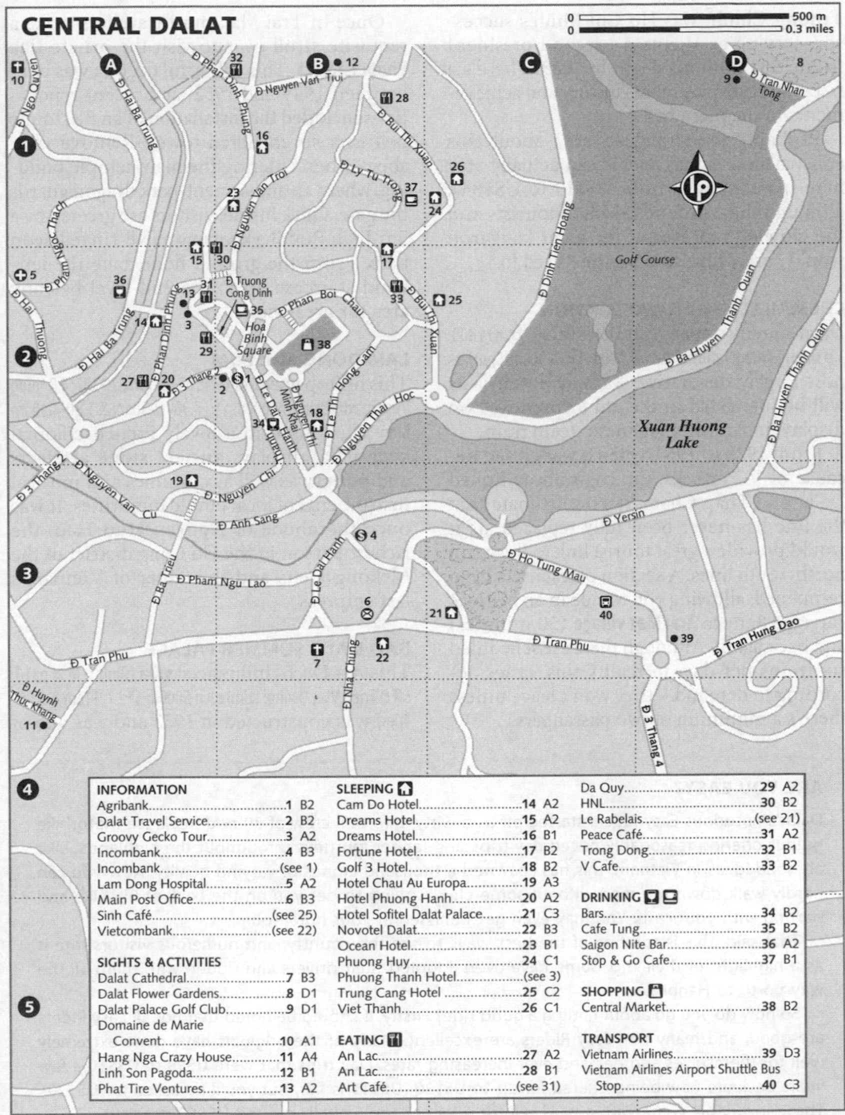

The owner of Hang Nga Crazy House, Mrs Dang Viet Nga, gained a PhD in architecture in Moscow, where she lived for 14 years. Hang Nga, as she's known locally, has designed a number of other buildings that dot the landscape around Dalat, including the Children's Cultural Palace and the Catholic church in Lien Khuong.

The Dalat People's Committee has not always appreciated such innovative designs. An earlier Dalat architectural masterpiece, the 'House with 100 Roofs', was torn down as a fire hazard because the People's Committee thought it looked antisocialist. However, there is little chance that Hang Nga will have such trouble with the authorities. Her father,

Truong Chinh, was Ho Chi Minh's successor, serving as Vietnam's second president from 1981 until his death in 1988. There's a fascinating display on his history and achievements in the main hall.

Probably the strangest thing about this construction is that people can actually stay here (rooms range from US$19 to US$84), although the constant stream of tourists and the glowing red eyes of the giant kangaroo would surely take some getting used to.

CRÉMAILLÈRE RAILWAY STATION

Dalat's pretty **station** (Map p316; Ga Da Lat; ☎ 834 409; 1 Đ Quang Trung; return ticket 70,000d; ⌚ 6.30am-5pm) is now largely decorative. Railway enthusiasts will be interested in the old locomotives on display, including a Japanese steam train.

From 1928 to 1964, when it was closed because of VC attacks, the cog-railway linked Dalat and Thap Cham. It's unfortunate that the line has never been fully replaced, as it would provide a great tourist link to the main north-south lines. A section of track has been re-opened, allowing you to ride in an historic carriage 8km to **Trai Mat village** (30 minutes) and back again. Although there are scheduled six trains per day, in reality this varies according to demand – they won't leave unless there's a minimum of two passengers.

Once in Trai Mat, most travellers make a requisite stroll over to visit the ornate **Linh Phuoc Pagoda**. This colourful pagoda was built between 1949 and 1952, and recent renovations included the installation of an 8½-tonne bell in a seven-tiered tower. Remove your shoes when entering the main temple building, where an amusement-park dragon guards the gate. Once inside, visitors are greeted by a 5m-high Buddha sporting a five-ringed neon halo. From the ground floor, take the left-hand staircase up to the 2nd-level balcony area for great views.

LAM DONG MUSEUM

This hilltop **museum** (Map p316; ☎ 820 387; 4 Đ Hung Vuong; admission 40,000d; ⌚ 7.30-11.30am & 1.30-4.30pm Mon-Sat), housed in a lovely French-colonial style villa, displays ancient stone artefacts and pottery as well as costumes and musical instruments of local ethnic minorities. It was once the abode of Nguyen Huu Hao, the richest person in the Go Cong district of the Mekong Delta and the father of Vietnam's last empress.

BAO DAI'S SUMMER PALACE

This Art Deco–influenced **villa** (Dinh 3; Map p316; off Đ Trieu Viet Vuong; admission 5000d; ⌚ 7-11am & 1.30-4pm) was constructed in 1933 and was one of

ARE YOU EASY?

Dalat's notorious Easy Riders started off as a witty, informal crew of 30-odd freelance motorbike guides offering reasonably priced day trips and longer journeys throughout the highlands. Like all good ideas in Vietnam, this has spawned a thousand clones of varying quality. Now you can hardly walk down the road without some clown trying to get you on the back of his bike and parting with your cash. You may even get harassed in your hotel room.

That said, this is still one of the best ways to see the country, and numerous visitors rate it as a highlight of their trip. Some have even adopted their drivers and ridden with them all the way north to Hanoi.

So how do you go about finding a good ride? Firstly, if should be noted that not all Easy Riders are good, and many non-Easy Riders are excellent. Many of the originals have done extremely well for themselves and demand ever-increasing rates. Day trips that were US$8 to US$10 a few years back are now being offered for up to US$30 (US$15 is fair, but you'll be asked for US$20). These invariably come with a hard sell for a longer trip (usually around US$50 per day).

For those planning a lengthier excursion, it's a good idea to take a day trip first to try to reduce the odds of choosing a suicidal maniac. Make sure you'll be comfortable keeping in close quarters with him for an extended period. Check that the bike is large enough, with a thick padded seat, and that a satisfactory helmet is provided. Most riders can produce portable guestbooks containing raving testimonials from past clients.

Sometimes your hotel can recommend good riders, although less reputable establishments may have vested interests. There should be no problem finding a rider who speaks good English; some speak French or German as well.

three palaces Bao Dai kept in Dalat. The décor has not changed in decades, except for the addition of Ho Chi Minh's portrait over the fireplace, but the palace is filled with artefacts from decades and governments past and is extremely interesting.

In Bao Dai's office, the life-sized white bust above the bookcase is of the man himself; the smaller gold and brown busts are of his father, Emperor Khai Dinh. Note the heavy brass royal seal (on the right) and military seal (on the left). The photographs over the fireplace are of Bao Dai, his eldest son Bao Long (in uniform), and his wife, Empress Nam Phuong.

Upstairs are the living quarters. The room of Bao Long, who now lives in France, is decorated in yellow, the royal colour. The huge semicircular couch was used by the emperor and empress for family meetings, during which their three daughters were seated in the yellow chairs and their two sons in the pink chairs. Check out the ancient tan Rouathermique infrared sauna machine near the top of the stairs.

Bao Dai's Summer Palace is set in a pine grove, 2km southwest of the city centre. Shoes must be removed at the door. There's an extra charge for cameras and videos.

DALAT FLOWER GARDENS

An unusual sight in Vietnam, these **gardens** (Vuon Hoa Thanh Pho; Map p309; ☎ 822 151; Đ Tran Nhan Tong; admission 5000d; 🕑 7.30am-4pm) were established in 1966. Flowers here include hydrangeas, fuchsias and orchids. Most of the latter are in special shaded buildings to the right of the entrance. All in all it's a very nice and well-kept cross section of Dalat foliage, along with some crazy kitsch topiary.

The Dalat Flower Gardens front Xuan Huong Lake, on the road that leads from the lake to Dalat University.

DALAT UNIVERSITY

Dalat's climate has made it something of an education centre; before air-con it was one of the few places in Vietnam where it was possible to study without working up a sweat. **Dalat University** (Map p316; 1 Đ Tran Nhan Tong) was founded as a Catholic university in 1957 by Hué Archbishop Ngo Dinh Thuc (the older brother of unpopular South Vietnamese President Ngo Dinh Diem) with the help of Cardinal Spelman of New York. It was seized from the church in 1975 and reopened two years later as a state-run institution. There are presently more than 13,000 students studying here. Foreign visitors are generally welcome.

DOMAINE DE MARIE CONVENT

The pink tile-roofed structures of this hilltop **convent** (Nha Tho Domaine; Map p309; 6 Đ Ngo Quyen; admission free; 🕑 7-11.30am & 2-5pm), constructed between 1940 and 1942, were once home to 300 nuns. Today the remaining nuns support themselves by making ginger candies and selling the fruit grown in the orchard out the back. The French-speaking nuns are pleased to show visitors around and explain the work they do for orphans, the homeless and children with disabilities. The shop sells handicrafts made by the children and nuns. Mass is celebrated in the large chapel, Sunday to Friday.

LINH SON PAGODA

Built in 1938, this **pagoda** (Chua Linh Son; Map p309; 120 Đ Nguyen Van Troi) is a lovely ochre-coloured building that fuses French and Chinese architecture. The giant bell is said to be made of bronze mixed with gold, its great weight making it too heavy for thieves to carry off.

DALAT CATHEDRAL

This gingerbread-style **cathedral** (Map p309; Đ Tran Phu) was built between 1931 and 1942 for use by French residents and holiday-makers. The cross on the spire is topped by a weathercock, 47m above the ground. The church itself is rarely open outside of mass times.

DU SINH CHURCH

This **church** (Map p316; Đ Huyen Tran Cong Chua) was built in 1955 by Catholic refugees from the north. The four-post, Sino-Vietnamese steeple was constructed at the insistence of a Hué-born priest of royal lineage. The church is on a hilltop with beautiful views in all directions, making this a great place for a picnic.

To get to Du Sinh Church, walk 500m southwest from the **former Couvent des Oiseaux** (Đ Huyen Tran Cong Chua), which is now a teachers' training college.

Activities

ADVENTURE SPORTS

Dalat's cool climate and mountainous surrounds lend themselves to all manner of outdoor activities.

Unlike many operators in Vietnam, who use it as a licence to charge higher prices, **Phat Tire Ventures** (Map p309; ☎ 829 422; www.phattireventures.com; 73 Đ Truong Cong Dinh) takes the term 'ecotourism' seriously. It offers canyoning, abseiling (rappelling), rock climbing, kayaking and treks to minority villages. It also runs a range of kick-arse 'fat tyre' cycling tours of the Dalat area (US$30 to US$38), as well as a two-day ride 120km downhill to the sand dunes at Mui Ne Beach (US$135 including accommodation).

Groovy Gecko Tours (see p308) also offers extended trekking and mountain biking trips, including single-day descents to Mui Ne or Nha Trang for US$60.

CABLE CAR

Dalat's newest attraction, this **cable car** (Cap Treo; Map p316; ☎ 837 938; off Đ 3 Thang 4; adult/child return 50,000/25,000d; 7-11.30am & 1.30-5pm), dangles along a 2.3km wire to Quang Trung Reservoir (p317). Needless to say, the views are stunning but it's not for the faint-hearted.

GOLF

The **Dalat Palace Golf Club** (Map p309; ☎ 821 202; www.vietnamgolfresorts.com; Đ Tran Nhan Tong), established in 1922, was once used by Emperor Bao Dai. Visitors can play 18-hole rounds on this attractive course on the shores of the lake for around US$65 (inquire about its Twilight Specials).

There are some reasonably priced golf-package tours available if you book from **HCMC** (☎ 08-824 3640).

Sleeping

Dalat is one of the few places in Vietnam where you will not need to bother about air-conditioning. Its popularity with local tourists has meant there's a wealth of budget options, while its attractiveness to colonial fantasists has resulted in some extraordinary properties at the top end. While there is not a great amount of accommodation options in between, many of the cheapies offer comfortable midrange standards.

BUDGET

Phuong Huy (Map p309; ☎ 520 243; 5 Đ Bui Thi Xuan; r US$5-8) This clean, new minihotel has good facilities and a wonderfully kitsch *Last Supper* reproduction and mirrored crucifix in reception.

Viet Thanh (Map p309; ☎ 823 369; www.vngold.com/dlt/vthanh/index.html; 16 Đ Bui Thi Xuan; r US$5-9) Further up the same road, this is Buddhist equivalent. Ask for the quiet rooms at the rear facing over the market gardens.

Phuong Thanh Hotel (Map p309; ☎ 825 097; fax 836 521; 65 Đ Truong Cong Dinh; s US$4-5, d US$6-7) You can't beat the prices at this friendly, modest, villa-style home. The cheapest rooms are located in the basement.

Hotel Phuong Hanh (Map p309; ☎ 828 213; fax 838 839; 80-82 Đ 3 Thang 2; r US$7-30) A larger place on the side of a killer hill, the better rooms are spacious and have balconies while the very cheapest are windowless and basic.

our pick **Dreams Hotel** (Map p309; ☎ 833 748; dreams@hcm.vnn.vn; 151 Đ Phan Dinh Phung; r US$10-15; 💻) Sweet dreams are indeed made of this. We get constant fan mail about this super-friendly spot, offering tidy rooms (some with balconies) and a breakfast complete with such rare delicacies as Vegemite, Marmite and peanut butter. There's no hassling over tours – it doesn't sell any and although it will help you make arrangements, it doesn't take any kickbacks.

Ocean Hotel (Dai Duong; Map p309; ☎ 837 793; daiduonghotel@yahoo.com; 130 Đ Phan Dinh Phung; s/d US$8/12) Very much a Vietnamese hotel, with motorbikes (available for hire) in the foyer and a restaurant on the first floor, the staff don't speak much English but try hard to please.

Hotel Chau Au Europa (Map p309; ☎ 822 870; europa@hcm.vnn.vn; 76 Đ Nguyen Chi Thanh; s US$8, d US$10-15, tr US$18; 💻) Another affable family-run place, the Europa has a shared terrace overlooking town and free wi-fi.

Thien An Hotel (Map p316; ☎ 520 607; thienanhotel@vnn.vn; 272A Đ Phan Dinh Phung; r US$12-15; 💻) Carrying on a family tradition of hospitality, this smart new hotel is owned by the brother of the woman who runs Dreams. It follows the same winning formula – great breakfasts, modest rates, sincere friendliness and no hassling for tours. It's a little further out, but free bicycles are provided.

Dreams Hotel (Map p309; ☎ 833 748; dreams@hcm.vnn.vn; 164B Đ Phan Dinh Phung; r US$15-20; 💻) A recurring dream, this is a new, more upmarket companion of the long-standing budget favourite. Rooms are larger, with Jacuzzis and massaging showers.

MIDRANGE

Fortune Hotel (Khach San Dai Loi; Map p309; ☎ 837 333; fax 837 474; 3A Đ Bui Thi Xuan; r US$18-26) Typically

Dalat, the Fortune Hotel is a riot of fairy lights, fake flowers and pink paint. Rooms here are spacious and comfortable; some have balconies overlooking a quiet park-like back lane and corner baths.

Trung Cang Hotel (Map p309; ☎ 822 663; http://www.sinhcafevn.com/Accomodation.asp; 4A Đ Bui Thi Xuan; s/d/tr US$20/25/30; 💻) A new addition to the Sinh Café empire, Trung Cang is an easy option for open-tour ticket holders. The rooms are attractive and clean, and the buses arrive right outside.

Cam Do Hotel (Map p309; ☎ 822 732; www.camdohotel.com.vn; 81 Đ Phan Dinh Phung; s US$30-35, d US$38-45, ste US$40-60; 💻) A one-time backpacker's oasis, Cam Do has been completely transformed into a smart midrange hotel.

Novotel Dalat (Map p309; ☎ 825 777; www.novotel.com; 7 Đ Tran Phu; s US$49-64, d US$55-70, ste US$79-85; 💻) Nearly opposite the Sofitel, the Novotel was constructed in 1932 as the Du Parc Hotel. It retains much of the original French-colonial feel, with an old-fashioned gated lift, sombre wooden corridors and period light fittings. Its simple, smallish rooms are probably more authentic than the sumptuous fit-out across the road.

Golf 3 Hotel (Map p309; ☎ 826 042; golf3hot@hcm.vnn.vn; 4 Đ Nguyen Thi Minh Khai; r US$52-70, ste US$80-100; 💻) This centrally located property has a roof-top café commanding great views of Dalat. The top-end rooms have wood and tile floors, nice linen, sunken bathtubs, views of the lake and DVD players.

TOP END

Hotel Sofitel Dalat Palace (Map p309; ☎ 825 444; www.sofitel.com; 12 Đ Tran Phu; s US$148-178, d US$160-190, ste US$258-310; 💻) This grand old place was built between 1916 and 1922. Major renovation work has perfectly preserved an Indochine fantasy of French-colonial life, right down to claw-foot tubs, working fireplaces, 1920s desk lamps and faux period telephones. Even the reception staff, in their immaculate *ao dai,* have cultivated a whiff of Parisian snobbery. Panoramic views of Xuan Huong Lake can be enjoyed in the expansive ground-floor chandelier-illuminated public areas, where one can sit in a rattan chair and sip iced tea.

Evason Ana Mandara Villas & Spa (Map p316; ☎ 520 558; www.sixsenses.com/evason-dalat/index.php; Đ Le Lai; r US$179-224, ste US$322-460; 💻 🏊) Not quite open at the time of research, this incredible complex is set to be the most desirable location in Dalat. This luxury hillside compound encompasses a collection of unique French villas dating from the 1920s and '30s, nestled among the pine trees. Each unique villa has its own butler, kitchen and outdoor barbecue area. Most have been converted into three to five magnificent rooms or suites, with one being set aside as a spa complex, another as a top-notch restaurant and yet another as the pool house for a heated outdoor pool.

Eating

Making the most of the local produce (see p314), Dalat has an appealing selection of smart eateries scattered throughout the town.

VIETNAMESE

Trong Dong (Map p309; ☎ 821 889; 220 Đ Phan Dinh Phung; mains 24,000-55,000d; 🕑 lunch & dinner) A good place to sample superb Vietnamese food, house specialities include grilled shrimp paste on sugar cane and fish hotpot. It's is a bit outside the centre, but well worth the walk.

Art Café (Map p309; ☎ 510 089; 70 Đ Truong Cong Dinh; dishes 30,000-45,000d; 🕑 lunch & dinner) Owned by an artist whose work adorns the walls, this elegant, bamboo-lined eatery has intimate tables sporting white linen tablecloths. The menu features Vietnamese dishes with a twist, including plenty of vegetarian options.

Da Quy (Wild Sunflower; Map p309; ☎ 510 883; 49 Đ Truong Cong Dinh; dishes 25,000-70,000d) With an upmarket ambience (white linen, fresh roses) and great service, this newcomer has won lots of fans. The traditional clay pots are excellent.

HNL (Map p309; ☎ 835 505; 94 Đ Phan Dinh Phung; dishes 25,000-75,000d) Painted in kooky pastels and with a classic motorbike as its centrepiece, HNL serves interesting Vietnamese dishes – along with pizza to keep the kids happy. There's a fun karaoke lounge upstairs.

VEGETARIAN

There are vegetarian food stalls *(com chay)* in the market area. All serve up delicious 100% vegetarian food, with some meals prepared to resemble and taste like traditional Vietnamese meat dishes.

An Lac (Map p309; ☎ 822 025; 71 Đ Phan Dinh Phung; meals 10,000d) There's an English menu here, and options range from noodle soups to rice and *banh bao* (steamed rice-flour dumplings stuffed with a savoury filling).

An Lac (Map p309; ☎ 833 717; 26 Đ Bui Thi Xuan; meals 10,000d) Yep, it's another one of the same name and incredibly popular with the locals.

INTERNATIONAL

V Cafe (Map p309; ☎ 837 576; 1 Đ Bui Thi Xuan; dishes 25,000-59,000d; breakfast, lunch & dinner) A long-time traveller's favourite, this cute place hung with Chinese lanterns serves a mix of Eastern and Western mains, along with some beautiful desserts (try the chocolate pie).

Le Rabelais (Map p309; ☎ 825 444; 12 Đ Tran Phu; set dinner US$23-33; breakfast, lunch & dinner) For fine French dining, the signature hotel at the Sofitel cannot be beaten – but bring a wheelbarrow full of dong. This impressive dining room is the place to indulge yourself in grand style. If the kids are under 12, they're not welcome in the evenings.

Drinking

Saigon Nite (Map p309; ☎ 820 007; 11A Đ Hai Ba Trung) The best late-night place to shoot pool and share a drink with expats and visitors.

Peace Café (Map p309; ☎ 822 787; 64 Đ Truong Cong Dinh) A popular gathering point for backpackers and Easy Riders, it also serves food.

Stop & Go Cafe (Map p309; ☎ 828 458; 2A Đ Ly Tu Trong) Hidden along a quiet back lane, this little bohemian oasis is run by a poet who always sports a beret and a smile. It's not open at night.

Cafe Tung (Map p309; 6 Hoa Binh Sq) During the 1950s, Cafe Tung was a famous hang-out for Saigonese intellectuals. Old-timers swear that it remains exactly as it was when they were young. As it did then, Cafe Tung serves only tea, coffee, hot cocoa, lemon soda and orange soda to the sound of mellow French music.

There's a lively strip of bars overlooking the market on Đ Le Dai Hanh.

Shopping

In the past few years the Dalat tourist-kitsch market has really come into its own. Without any effort at all you can find that special something for your loved ones – perhaps a battery-powered stuffed koala that sings 'Waltzing Matilda' or a lacquered alligator with a light bulb in its mouth. The **Central Market** (Map p309) is one big buy and sell, and a great place to pick up clothing at a good price.

The hill tribes of Lam Dong province make various handicrafts. Lat products include dyed rush mats and rice baskets that roll up when empty. Koho and Chill people produce the split-bamboo baskets used to carry things on their backs. The Chill also weave cloth, including the dark-blue cotton shawls worn by some of the Montagnard women. If you're interested in Montagnard handicrafts, try Lang Dinh An (Chicken village ; p317) or Lat village (p317).

A fascinating place to visit is **Cuong Hoan Traditional Silk Centre** (☎ 852 338) in Nam Ban village, near the Elephant Falls (see p318). Here you can see every part of the miraculous process, from the live silkworms spinning

DELECTABLE DALAT

For French colonists craving a taste of home, Dalat's climate was perfectly suited for growing fresh garden vegetables. Peas, carrots, radishes, tomatoes, cucumbers, avocados, capsicums, lettuce, beets, green beans, potatoes, garlic, spinach, squash and yams are all grown here, making for meals unavailable elsewhere in the country.

The Dalat area is justly famous for its strawberry jam, dried blackcurrants and candied plums, persimmons and peaches. Apricots are popular, and often served in a heavily salted hot drink. Other local delicacies include avocado ice cream, sweet beans *(mut dao)* and strawberry, blackberry and artichoke extracts (for making drinks). The strawberry extract is great in tea. Artichoke tea, another local speciality, is said to lower blood pressure and benefit the liver and kidneys.

Dalat wine is served all over Vietnam and some of it's quite good. Don't go stressing over grape varietals – your choice is white or red. The reds are pleasantly light in style, while the whites tend to be heavy on the oak.

Dau hu, a type of pudding made from soy milk, sugar and a slice of ginger, is one of Dalat's specialities, as is hot soy milk *(sua dau nanh)*. Both are sold by itinerant female vendors, who walk around carrying a large bowl of the stuff and a small stand suspended from either end of a bamboo pole.

Most vendors in the Central Market will let you sample a bit of something before you buy.

out their precious cacoon, to the vats where they're boiled up and the threads separated, to the loom where the shimmery cloth is woven. You can even sample the cooked grub – they taste kinda nutty. For those of us concerned about fair trade, the women here are paid reasonably well and work only standard government hours. There are some beautiful garments and lengths of fabric for sale, including kimono-style robes for US$10.

Getting There & Away

AIR

Vietnam Airlines (Map p309; ☎ 833 499; 2 Đ Ho Tung Mau) has daily services that connect Dalat to HCMC and Hanoi. Dalat's Lien Khuong Airport is located 30km south of the city.

BUS

Dalat's **long distance bus station** (Map p316; Đ 3 Thang 4) is 1km south of Xuan Huong Lake, although many private services will (if asked) pick up and drop off at the hotel of your choice. Services are available to most of the country, including several to HCMC (60,000d, six to seven hours), Phan Rang (40,000d, 4½ hours), Nha Trang (60,000d, seven hours) and Buon Ma Thuot (65,000d, four hours).

Dalat is a major stop for open-tour buses. Sinh Café (see p308) has a daily bus to Mui Ne (US$7, 5½ hours).

CAR & MOTORBIKE

From HCMC, taking the inland (Hwy 20) route to Dalat via Bao Loc and Di Linh is faster than taking the coastal route (Hwy 1A) via Ngoan Muc Pass.

The following are road distances from Dalat: Di Linh (82km), Nha Trang (205km), Phan Rang (108km), Phan Thiet (247km) and HCMC (308km). There are secondary roads connecting Dalat to Buon Ma Thuot and other parts of the central highlands.

Getting Around

TO/FROM THE AIRPORT

The Vietnam Airlines shuttle bus between Lien Khuong Airport and Dalat (20,000d, 30 minutes) is timed around flights, leaving from the door of the terminal and, in Dalat, from in front of 40 Đ Ho Tung Mau, two hours before each departure.

Private taxis can be hired to make the trip for around US$10, while a motorbike taxi should cost from US$3 to US$5.

BICYCLE

Pedal power is a great way of seeing Dalat, but the hilly terrain and long distances between the sights make it hard work. Several hotels rent out bicycles and sometimes provide them free to guests. It's also well worth looking into the cycling tours on offer (see p311).

MOTORBIKE

Dalat is too hilly for *cyclos*, but a motorbike is a good way of touring the environs. For short trips around town, *xe om* (motorbike taxi) drivers can be flagged down around the Central Market area for 10,000d. Self-drive motorbikes are available for US$6 to US$8 a day.

TAXI & CAR

Taxis are easy to find and a one-way trip to just about anywhere in Dalat costs US$2 or less. Dalat Travel Service (see p308) can arrange daily car rentals (with a driver) for around US$25.

AROUND DALAT

Valley of Love

Named the Valley of Peace by Emperor Bao Dai in a wonderful lack of prescience, this **valley** (Thung Lung Tinh Yeu, or Vallée d'Amour; Map p316; Đ Phu Dong Thien Vuong; adult/child 6000/3000d; 7am-5pm) had its name changed in 1972 by romantically minded students from Dalat University.

Today this ever-tacky place has taken on a surreal atmosphere and cynical locals call it the Valley of Shops. Tourist buses line up to regurgitate visitors and boats line up to accommodate them. Get into the spirit with some aquatic activities: paddle boats, 15-person canoes and obnoxious noise-making motorboats can be hired to tour the lake.

This is a good place to see the 'Dalat cowboys': Vietnamese guides dressed as American cowboys. We've also seen locals dressed as bears. The cowboys rent horses to tourists for a guided tour around the lake. The cowboys and bears expect cash if you take their picture. Refreshments and local delicacies (such as jams and candied fruits) are on sale at the lookout near where the buses disgorge tourists.

The Valley of Love is 5km north of Xuan Huong Lake.

Lake of Sighs

The **Lake of Sighs** (Ho Than Tho; Map p316; admission 5000d) is a natural lake enlarged by a French-built dam. The forests are not Dalat's finest.

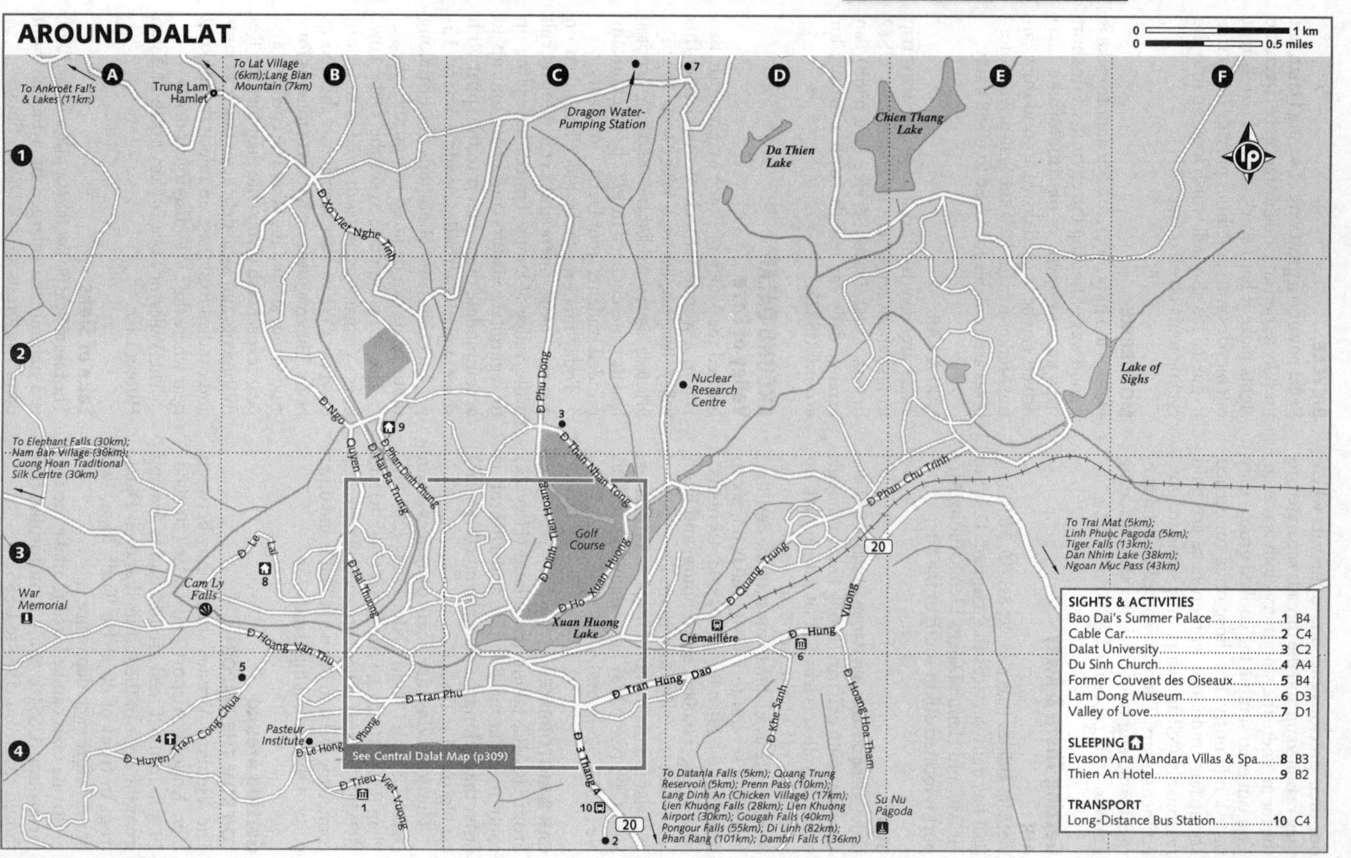
AROUND DALAT
0 1 km
0 0.5 miles
To Ankroët Falls & Lakes (11km)
Trung Lam Hamlet
To Lat Village (6km); Lang Bian Mountain (7km)
Dragon Water-Pumping Station
Da Thien Lake
Chien Thang Lake
Lake of Sighs
Nuclear Research Centre
Đ Xo Viet Nghe Tinh
Đ Ngo Quyen
Đ Phan Dinh Phung
Đ Hai Ba Trung
Đ Phu Dong
Đ Than Nhan Tong
Đ Dinh Tien Hoang
Golf Course
Đ Ho Xuan Huong
Xuan Huong Lake
Đ Hai Thuong
Đ Le Lai
Cam Ly Falls
War Memorial
Đ Hoang Van Thu
Đ Tran Phu
Đ Tran Hung Dao
Đ 3 Thang 4
Đ Huyen Tran Cong Chua
Pasteur Institute
Đ Le Hong Phong
Đ Trieu Viet Vuong
See Central Dalat Map (p309)
To Elephant Falls (30km); Nam Ban Village (30km); Cuong Hoan Traditional Silk Centre (30km)
Đ Phan Chu Trinh
Đ Quang Trung
Crémaillère
Đ Hung Vuong
Đ Khe Sanh
Đ Hoang Hoa Tham
Su Nu Pagoda
20
To Trai Mat (5km); Linh Phuoc Pagoda (5km); Tiger Falls (13km); Dan Nhim Lake (38km); Ngoan Muc Pass (43km)
To Datanla Falls (5km); Quang Trung Reservoir (5km); Prenn Pass (10km); Lang Dinh An (Chicken Village) (17km); Lien Khuong Falls (28km); Lien Khuong Airport (30km); Gougah Falls (40km) Pongour Falls (55km); Di Linh (82km); Phan Rang (101km); Dambri Falls (136km)
SIGHTS & ACTIVITIES
Bao Dai's Summer Palace 1 B4
Cable Car 2 C4
Dalat University 3 C2
Du Sinh Church 4 A4
Former Couvent des Oiseaux 5 B4
Lam Dong Museum 6 D3
Valley of Love 7 D1
SLEEPING
Evason Ana Mandara Villas & Spa 8 B3
Thien An Hotel 9 B2
TRANSPORT
Long-Distance Bus Station 10 C4

The cheery name comes from the story of Mai Nuong and Hoang Tung, who met here in 1788 while he was hunting and she was picking mushrooms. They fell in love and sought their parents' permission to marry. At that time Vietnam was threatened by a Chinese invasion and Hoang Tung, like a macho fool, joined the army without telling Mai Nuong. Mai Nuong sent word for him to meet her at the lake, and when he didn't come she was overcome with sorrow and drowned herself. She clearly wasn't used to being stood up.

There are several small restaurants up the hill from the dam. Horses can be hired for 80,000d an hour, while a ride in a horse-drawn carriage costs 140,000d per hour.

The Lake of Sighs is 6km northeast of the centre of Dalat via Đ Phan Chu Trinh.

Quang Trung Reservoir

Quang Trung Reservoir (Tuyen Lam Lake) is an artificial lake created by a dam in 1980. Paddle boats, rowboats and canoes can be hired nearby. The hills around the reservoir are covered with pine trees, and there's a path up the hill southwest of the water-intake tower. Ethnic-minority farmers live and raise crops in the vicinity.

The fun way to get here is by cable car (see p312). If heights aren't your thing, head out of Dalat on Hwy 20 and turn right at the signpost 5km from town and continue for 2km.

Lat Village

pop 6000

The nine hamlets of **Lat village** (pronounced 'lak') are 12km north of Dalat at the base of Lang Bian Mountain. Only five of the hamlets are actually Lat; the residents of the other four are members of the Chill, Ma and Koho tribes, each of which speaks a different dialect.

Traditionally, Lat houses are built on piles with rough plank walls and a thatched roof. The people here eke out a living on 300 hectares of land, growing rice, coffee, black beans and sweet potatoes. Economics have forced many villagers into producing charcoal, a lowly task often performed by Montagnards. Before 1975 many men from Lat worked with the Americans, as did many Montagnards elsewhere.

Classes in the village's schools are conducted in Vietnamese rather than tribal languages. Lat has one Catholic and one Protestant church. A Koho-language Bible (Sra Goh) was published by Protestants in 1971; a Lat-language Bible, prepared by Catholics, appeared a year later. Both dialects are quite similar and are written in a Latin-based script.

To get to Lat from Dalat, head north on Đ Xo Viet Nghe Tinh. At Trung Lam Hamlet there's a fork in the road marked by a street sign. Continue straight on (northwest) rather than to the left. By bicycle the 12km trip from Dalat to Lat takes about 40 minutes. On foot it's a two-hour walk.

Lang Bian Mountain

Also called Lam Vien Mountain, it has five volcanic peaks ranging in altitude from 2100m to 2400m. Of the two highest peaks, the eastern one is known by the woman's name K'Lang while the western one bears a man's name, K'Biang. Only the upper reaches of the mountain remain forested. Only half a century ago the foothills had lush foliage that sheltered wild oxen, deer, boars, elephants, rhinoceroses and tigers.

The hike up to the top's spectacular views takes three to four hours from Lat village. The path begins due north of Lat and is recognisable as a red gash in the green mountainside.

Dalat Travel Service (p308) offers guided tours which combine the mountain with Lat village.

Lang Dinh An (Chicken Village)

Famous for its giant concrete chicken caught mid-strut in the village centre, **Lang Dinh An** has become very popular with travellers because it's conveniently situated on the highway, 17km from Dalat.

The village is home to about 600 people of the Koho minority, who were enticed down from the hills and have, to a certain extent, been Vietnamised. Most no longer live in stilt houses and they wear Vietnamese-style clothing.

The chicken was an elaborate decorative device for a long-dysfunctional water system, which used to crow as the water was pumped. The symbolism of the chicken probably relates to yet another local legend involving a doomed romance ending in a dead heroine.

Though the residents of Chicken village are extremely poor, we'd suggest that you don't give sweets or money to the children. If you want to help the villagers, there are a couple of shops where you can buy simple things like drinks and biscuits. There are also beautiful weavings for sale near the highway.

Waterfalls

DATANLA FALLS

The nice thing about **Datanla Falls** (admission 5000d) is the short but pleasant walk to get there. The cascade is 350m from Hwy 20 on a path that first passes through a pine forest and then continues steeply down into a rainforest. The other good thing is the wildlife – lots of squirrels, birds and butterflies.

To get to Datanla Falls, turn right off Hwy 20 about 200m past the turn-off to Quang Trung Reservoir. It's well signposted.

TIGER FALLS

These **falls** (Thac Hang Cop; admission 4000d) are named after the local legend of a ferocious tiger living in a nearby cave. There's a huge ceramic tiger statue here, as well as one of a hill-tribe hunter. The falls themselves are set in a quiet pine forest, and are very photogenic. There are good hiking trails in the area.

Tiger Falls is about 14km east of Dalat and can be easily reached by bicycle or motorbike. Follow Đ Hung Vuong to Trai Mat village. From the train station there, continue for another 3.5km to a left-hand turn (signposted). From here it's another 3km along a dirt road to the falls. It is also possible to trek to the falls from Dalat but you'll need to allow a full day.

ANKROËT FALLS & LAKES

The two **Ankroët Lakes** were created as part of a hydroelectric project. The waterfall, **Thac Ankroët**, is about 15m high. The Ankroët Lakes are 18km northwest of Dalat in an area inhabited by hill tribes.

ELEPHANT FALLS

A popular stop on the Easy Rider trail, these imposing curved **falls** (admission 3000d) are best seen from below; a hazardous path heads down to the base – expect to get wet.

Nearby, the **Linh An Pagoda** (2004), has been built to take advantage of the good feng shui of having water in front and a mountain behind. Inside, the large central Buddha is flanked by two multi-armed Buddhas. The one on the right has eyes on his hands, making him all-seeing, while the one of the left has extra arms to help people in need. Around the back is a particularly jolly giant – a Happy Buddha with neon halos and a room built into his ample belly.

The falls are situated near the town of Nam Ban, 30km west of Dalat. You can combine this with a visit to Cuong Hoan Traditional Silk Centre (p314).

PONGOUR, GOUGAH & LIEN KHUONG FALLS

The largest in the area, **Pongour Falls** (admission 6000d) forms a semicircle during the rainy season, but even when it's dry the stepped formation is impressive. Make the most of it, because these falls could dwindle to a trickle when a hydroelectric dam further up the river opens in 2008. A great viewpoint is the pavilion built for Emperor Bao Dai's hunting expeditions. The surrounding area has been badly deforested by slash-and-burn agriculture. The falls are signposted on the right about 50km towards HCMC from Dalat and 6km off the highway.

Gougah Falls (admission 5000d) is 36km from Dalat towards HCMC. It is only 500m from the highway so it's easy to get to.

At **Lien Khuong Falls**, the 100m-wide Dan Nhim River drops 15m over an outcrop of volcanic rock. The best view is from the café, where buying a coffee covers the admission. Sometimes, when the dam upstream is closed, the water disappears completely. The falls are visible from the highway, not far from Lien Khuong Airport, 28km towards HCMC from Dalat.

DI LINH

The town of Di Linh (pronounced zee ling), also known as Djiring, is 1010m above sea level. The area's main product is tea, which is grown on giant plantations founded by the French. Only a few decades ago the region was famous for its tiger hunting, but the hunters were a little too efficient and the tigers now only survive as hideous fur coats and wall-mounted trophies.

The 32m-high **Bo Bla Waterfall** (admission 5000d; 7am-4.30pm) is on the east side of Hwy 20, 16km southwest of Di Linh, near the village of Lien Dam. There's a steep 25-minute walk down to the base of the falls, but you can get a good view from near the top of the path.

Di Linh is 226km northeast of HCMC and 82km southwest of Dalat on Hwy 20. It's a pleasant drive, passing tea and coffee plantations and houses with racks of silk worms.

BAO LOC

pop 136,000

The unassuming town of Bao Loc has a large hill-tribe population. Tea and silk (and the cultivation of the mulberry leaves that make up the silkworms' diet) are the major local industries, and free samples of the local tea can be had at a couple of the roadside rest stops in town. There are also a few guesthouses here, making it a practical place to break the journey between HCMC (180km) and Dalat (118km).

Nearby **Dambri Falls** (admission 10,000d) is one of the highest (90m), most magnificent and easily accessible waterfalls in Vietnam. The views are positively breathtaking – the steep walk up the path to the top of the falls will almost certainly take your breath away (unless you opt to ride the cable car for 5000d).

If you continue walking upstream from the top of the falls you reach Monkey Island, a minizoo filled with monkeys and reindeer living at the usual captive standard (ie poor) of Vietnam. While it's best to avoid the zoo, the Dambri Restaurant, which adjoins the car park, is cheap and good.

To reach Dambri Falls, turn off the main highway north of Bao Loc and follow the road for 18km through tea and mulberry plantations. The high peak to your right is May Bay Mountain.

DAN NHIM LAKE

elevation 1042m

The 9.3 sq km Dan Nhim Lake is often used by movie studios for filming romantic scenes. Created by a dam built between 1962 and 1964 by Japan as part of its war reparations, the huge Dan Nhim hydroelectric project supplies electricity to much of the south. Water drawn from the lake gathers speed as it rushes almost a vertical kilometre down from Ngoan Muc Pass in two enormous pipes.

Dan Nhim Lake is 38km from Dalat as you head towards Phan Rang, about a kilometre to the left of Hwy 20. The power station is at the base of Ngoan Muc Pass near the town of Ninh Son.

NGOAN MUC PASS

Known to the French as Bellevue Pass, **Ngoan Muc Pass** (altitude 980m) is 5km east of Dan Nhim Lake and 64km west of Phan Rang. On a clear day you can see the ocean, 55km away. As the highway winds down the mountain it passes under two gargantuan water pipes – still guarded by armed troops in concrete fortifications – that link Dan Nhim Lake with the hydroelectric power station.

South of the road (to the right as you face the ocean) you can see the steep tracks of the *crémaillère* (cog railway) linking Thap Cham with Dalat (p310). At the top of Ngoan Muc Pass there's a waterfall next to the highway, pine forests and the old Bellevue train station.

BUON MA THUOT

☎ 050 / pop 312,000 / elevation 451m

The caffeine capital of Vietnam, the biggest buzz you'll get in Buon Ma Thuot (also known as Ban Me Thuot) is from the beans. There's not a lot to do here, but it makes for a good base to explore Yok Don National Park and several stunning waterfalls in the vicinity. Before WWII, this was a centre for big-game hunting, but the animals have all but disappeared – along with most of the region's rainforest.

The capital of Dac Lac province, the city has grown exponentially over the last few years, with the coffee industry largely responsible for its improving fortunes. The major approach roads are currently being upgraded to cope with the extra traffic, but it can still be a crawl in and out of town.

A large percentage of the area's population is made up of Montagnards. The government's policy of assimilation has been effective: nearly all of the Montagnards now speak Vietnamese fluently. Not a lot of English is spoken here though, and you won't see too many Western tourists.

The rainy season around Buon Ma Thuot lasts from May to October, though downpours are usually short. Because of its lower elevation, Buon Ma Thuot is warmer and more humid than Dalat; it is also very windy.

Information

MEDICAL SERVICES

Dak Lak General Hospital (☎ 852 665; 2 Đ Mai Hac De)

MONEY

Agriculture & Rural Development Bank (☎ 853 930; 37 Đ Phan Boi Chau) This branch can make foreign-currency exchanges and cash travellers cheques.

Vietcombank (1 Nguyen Tat Thanh) ATM in front of Thang Loi Hotel.

POST & INTERNET ACCESS

Main post office (☎ 852 612; 6 Đ Le Duan; 🕓 6.30am-9pm) Also has internet access.

TRAVEL AGENCIES

Both agencies offer tours of the surrounding villages, waterfalls, Lak Lake and Yok Don National Park.

CENTRAL HIGHLANDS

DakLak Tourist (☎ 852 108; daklaktourist.com.vn; 3 Đ Phan Chu Trinh; 🕑 7.30-11am & 1.30-5pm)

Damsan Tourist (☎ 851 234; damsantour@dng.vnn.vn; 212-214 Đ Nguyen Cong Tru; 🕑 7am-6pm) Attached to the Damsan Hotel.

TRAVEL PERMITS

Permits are still required if you wish to visit certain minority villages in the area surrounding Buon Ma Thuot. Contact DakLak Tourist to get these valuable bits of paper.

Sights

VICTORY MONUMENT

You can hardly miss this monument, as it dominates the square in the centre of town. The **victory monument** commemorates the events of 10 March 1975, when VC and North Vietnamese troops liberated the city. It was this battle that triggered the complete collapse of South Vietnam.

It's one of the most interesting pieces of socialist realist sculpture in the country, consisting of a column supporting a central group of figures holding a flag, with a modernist arch forming a rainbow over a concrete replica tank.

The frieze, starting from the right-hand side of the column, shows hill-tribe people with their traditional gongs and a communal wine vessel. On the rear panel the minority women are shown hugging a proud soldier, while on the left side there's a glimpse into a socialist future, peopled with happy nurses,

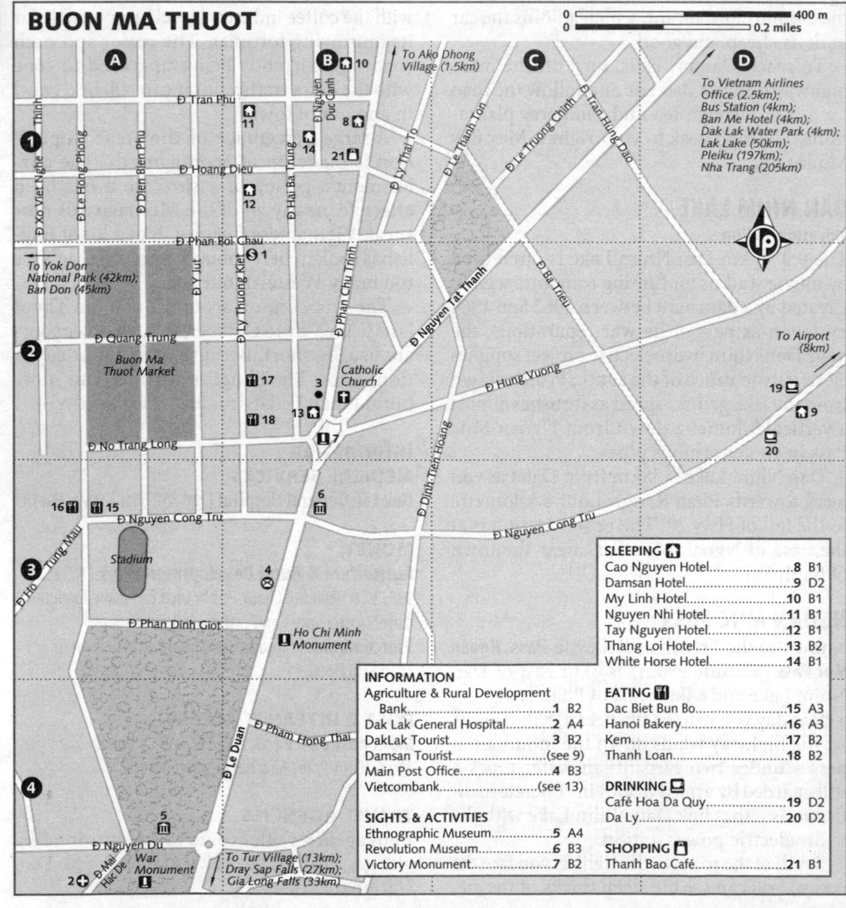

farmers, industrial workers and children carrying a globe. It's a far cry from the reality of the situation in these parts, where many of the hill-tribe people fought with the Americans, and there are continuing allegations of mistreatment at the hands of corrupt officials.

AKO DHONG VILLAGE

Between the northern end of Buon Ma Thuot and outlying coffee plantations, the Ede village of **Ako Dhong** is a neat little community of stilt-house suburbia. Strolling the village makes for a pleasant break from the downtown din (such as it is), and you may be able to find some locals at work weaving traditional fabrics – which might also be for sale.

The village is located about 1.5km from the centre of town and makes an easy walk; take Đ Phan Chu Trinh northward and hang a left on Đ Tran Nhat Duat.

ETHNOGRAPHIC MUSEUM

There are said to be 31 distinct ethnic groups in Dac Lac province, and the **Ethnographic Museum** (☎ 850 426; 4 Đ Nguyen Du; admission 10,000d; 🕑 7.30-11am & 2-5pm) is one place to get some understanding of these disparate groups. Displays at the museum feature traditional costumes, agricultural implements, fishing gear, bows and arrows, weaving looms and musical instruments. There is a photo collection with accompanying explanations about the historical contacts between the Montagnards and the rest of Vietnam – some of the history is plausible, some is pure fiction.

The Ethnographic Museum is housed in the Bao Dai Villa, a grand French-colonial building surrounded by gardens that was one of the former emperor's many residences. A local guide can show you around the exhibits for around 5000d.

REVOLUTION MUSEUM

If you're lucky enough to find it open, this little **museum** (☎ 850 426; 1 Đ Le Duan; admission 10,000d; 🕑 7.30-11am & 2-5pm Wed-Sun) focuses on the city's role during the American War.

DAK LAK WATER PARK

If sampling the local rocket-fuel coffee doesn't raise your heart rate, then perhaps waterslides will at **Dak Lak Water Park** (☎ 950 381; Đ Nguyen Chi Thanh; admission 30,000d; 🕑 9am-6pm). It's about 4km from the centre of town, just before the bus station.

Sleeping

BUDGET

Nguyen Nhi Hotel (☎ 859 868; fax 810 662; 164 Đ Ly Thuong Kiet; s/d/tr/q 160,000/180,000/320,000/350,000d; ❄ 💻) Nobody speaks any English here, but this shiny place has good-value spacious rooms and free wireless internet access.

My Linh Hotel (☎ 815 353; mylinhhotel@yahoo.com; 27-29 Đ Le Dai Hanh; r 150,000-220,000d; ❄ 💻) This chic minihotel borders on the boutique, with modern décor and new computers in the reception. It's a shame about the stains on the sheets.

Tay Nguyen Hotel (☎ 851 009; taynguyenhotel@dng.vnn.vn; 110 Đ Ly Thuong Kiet; s/d US$14/16; ❄) The paint is peeling and it's definitely past its prime, but this decent place has clean rooms and good facilities. The comfortable doubles have terraces and are more spacious than the singles.

Ban Me Hotel (☎ 951 001; fax 954 741; 9 Đ Nguyen Chi Thanh; r US$10-20; ❄) About 4km north of the centre but within walking distance of the bus station is this large, friendly motel with a tidy, garden-like setting. A *xe om* to the centre costs about 10,000d. Air-con rates include breakfast, but fan rooms are more spacious and arguably more comfortable, with bigger terraces upstairs.

MIDRANGE

Cao Nguyen Hotel (☎ 851 913; www.daklaktourist.com/english/hotels/info.html; 65 Đ Phan Chu Trinh; r US$15-45; ❄ 💻) The Cao Nguyen is a few years old but still fairly luxurious and now offers free wi-fi. It's known for its dance hall, karaoke and massage service.

Damsan Hotel (☎ 851 234; www.damsanhotel.com.vn; 212-214 Đ Nguyen Cong Tru; r US$25-40; ❄ 💻 🏊) Although the communal areas are looking a little shabby, the rooms are surprisingly nice, making Damsan the best deal in town. This quiet hotel features clean rooms with wooden floors, bathtubs and satellite TV, plus a raucous restaurant (breakfast is included). Rooms at the back of the building overlook the swimming pool, tennis court and neighbouring coffee plantations.

White Horse Hotel (Khach San Bach Ma; ☎ 851 656; whitehorsehotelvn@yahoo.com; 9-11 Đ Nguyen Duc Canh; r US$25-40; ❄ 💻) Sparkling with varnished surfaces and marble, the White Horse has immaculate, comfortable rooms with satellite TV.

Thang Loi Hotel (☎ 857 615; www.daklaktourist.com/english/hotels/info.html; 1 Đ Phan Chu Trinh; r US$25-40; ❄ 💻) You'll find most amenities at this government-run hotel, including satellite TV and bathtubs. *Thang loi* means 'victory', so it's not surprising that the hotel faces the eponymous monument.

Eating

There aren't a lot of great restaurants in Buon Ma Thuot – unless you're not bothered by rowdy beer halls and the odd rat.

Thanh Loan (☎ 818 464; 14-16 Đ Ly Thuong Kiet; meals 12,000d) It would be tempting to eat at this wonderful roll-your-own rice-paper-roll joint every night. You get a massive plate of green vegies, herbs and edible leaves to roll up in fresh rice paper with fried pork, crunchy rice paper and raw garlic, and then dip in either a meaty broth or a mix of fish sauce and chilli. Delicious.

Dac Biet Bun Bo (☎ 810 135; 10 Đ Le Hong Phong; meals 12,000d) With its big stock pot bubbling on the street, this popular humble eatery serves big hunks of meat in a spicy broth over white noodles, served with a plate of fresh herbs.

Kem (50 Đ Ly Thuong Kiet; ice cream 5000d) After Thanh Loan you can stop here, a few doors down, for a delectable ice cream.

Hanoi Bakery (☎ 853 609; 123-125 Đ Le Hong Phong; pastries 5000d; ⏲ breakfast & lunch) Not only are there shelves of freshly-baked pastries, but it also carries snack foods like cheese and chocolate.

Drinking

Buon Ma Thuot is justifiably famous for its coffee, which is the best in Vietnam. As usual, the Vietnamese serve it so strong and sweet that it will make your hair stand on end, and typically in a very tiny cup that allows no room to water it down. There are dozens of cafés to explore in the streets around Đ Le Thanh Ton. Some also serve alcohol.

Café Hoa Da Quy (☎ 851 304; 173 Đ Nguyen Cong Tru) This stylish open-sided three-storey bar-café is a popular night-time spot and has a good selection of top-shelf spirits.

Da Ly (☎ 812 243; 188 Đ Nguyen Cong Tru) There are great views over a coffee plantation from the garden of this chic café.

Shopping

If you like the coffee enough to take some home, be sure to pick up a bag here because the price is lower and the quality higher than in HCMC or Hanoi. You can buy whole beans or ground coffee at around 15,000d per 500g. Good places to buy the brown gold include **Thanh Bao Café** (☎ 854 164; 32 Hoang Dieu), as well as along the guest-house strip on Đ Ly Thuong Kiet.

Getting There & Around

AIR

There are daily **Vietnam Airlines** (☎ 955 055; fax 956 265; 67 Đ Nguyen Tat Thanh; ⏲ 8am-5pm) flights from both HCMC and Danang. The airport is 8km west of town. A taxi should cost less than 20,000d.

BUS

Buon Ma Thuot's **bus station** (71 Đ Nguyen Chi Thanh) is about 4km from the centre, with plenty of services to Dalat (65,000d, four hours) and Pleiku (46,000d, four hours).

CAR & MOTORBIKE

The road linking the coast with Buon Ma Thuot intersects Hwy 1A at Ninh Hoa (157km), 34km north of Nha Trang. The road is surfaced and in good condition, though fairly steep. Hwy 14 to Pleiku is excellent. There's also a scenic sealed road connecting Buon Ma Thuot with Dalat (via Lak Lake). Though full of twists and turns, it's mainly in good condition.

AROUND BUON MA THUOT

Dray Sap & Gia Long Falls

Both these **waterfalls** (☎ 584 605; admission 8000d), sharing a stretch of the Krong Ana River, are stunning and offer good riverside trekking opportunities. Entering from the main gate, the first turning to the left heads to the spectacular 100m-wide **Dray Sap**. After heading down some slippery steps near the restaurant there's great views from an Indiana Jones–style swinging bridge. Across the bridge there are smaller falls on a fork of the river to the left, past an area where local villagers have cleared the jungle for corn. It's a surreal sight, seeing the spray from the main falls rising over the cornfield. It's this ever-present mist that gave the falls their name, meaning 'smoky falls'.

The **Gia Long Falls** are a further 7km along the road, which cuts through increasingly dense jungle. Less wide or high than Dray Sap, the volume of churning, muddy water still makes for an impressive sight. It's possible to walk a riverside path between the two falls.

To reach them, follow Đ Le Duan until it becomes Nguyen Thi Dinh and eventually Hwy 14 heading south. After 16km you'll pass a major bridge. Cross this and continue for another 5km and turn left about 500m past the Eatling Markets. This road will bring you to the entrance in another 6km.

In Buon Ma Thuot, Damsan Tourist (p320) is the place to inquire about tours to the waterfalls.

Yok Don National Park

☎ 050

The largest of Vietnam's nature preserves, **Yok Don National Park** (Vuon Quoc Gia Yok Don; ☎ 783 049; yokdon@dng.vnn.vn) has been gradually expanded and today encompasses 115,545 hectares of mainly dry deciduous forest, with the beautiful Serepok River flowing through it.

Yok Don is home to 67 mammal species, 38 of which are listed as endangered in Indochina, and 17 of those endangered worldwide. The park habitat accommodates elephants, tigers and leopards, as well as nearly 250 different species of bird – including a pair of critically-endangered giant ibis (*Thaumatibis gigantea*), sighted in 2003. More common wildlife in the park includes deer, monkeys and snakes. In recent years previously unknown animals like the *Canisauvus*, a species of wild dog, have been discovered.

The delicate balance between ecological conservation and the preservation of local cultures is a challenge, considering the poverty of the region [illegible] means of surviva[illegible] the Vietnamese gover[illegible] international agencies, suc[illegible] opment Programme (UNDP), [illegible] ongoing balance, aiming towards [illegible] and community participation in cons[illegible]tion practices.

There are 17 ethnic groups in the region, including a significant number that have migrated from northern Vietnam. The locals are mostly Ede and M'nong, a matrilineal tribe. The family name is passed down through the mother, and children are considered members of their mother's family.

The M'nong are known for their skills in capturing wild elephants, dozens of which live in the area (see below). Traditional elephant-racing festivals are put on from time to time. Visitors can arrange elephant rides or guided treks through beautiful forests. Elephants typically carry three people, but for heavier Westerners two is usually the limit. Elephant rides can be arranged through DakLak Tourist (p319) in Buon Ma Thuot, but you can also just turn up and make arrangements. Booking direct costs from 100,000 to 200,000d per hour.

SIGHTS & ACTIVITIES

Most of the domestic tourist action centres on the village of **Ban Don** in Ea Sup district, 45km

BABY ELEPHANT WALK

Throughout history, kings from Thailand, Vietnam, Cambodia and Laos have come to the area around present-day Yok Don National Park in search of elephants. To this day the tradition of elephant trapping continues, rooted in local culture and traditions.

Typically, hunters use two domesticated elephants in order to catch one wild calf. Only elephants under the age of three are targeted, otherwise they're too hard to train, and run a higher risk of returning to the jungle.

Custom maintains that men must abstain from sex for at least a week before commencing the hunt. The hunts involve a series of quick attacks and retreats, and the hunters' energy needs to be saved in case they are chased down by the angry parents, who are not too keen on their loved offspring being calf-napped. Unlike the elephant poachers in Africa, the hill-tribe hunters never cause physical harm to the parents when capturing their young.

Once the hunting party has returned from the jungle, the village holds a naming ceremony for their new captive. Here's where the niceties cease. The training of these highly intelligent and social creatures initially consists of savage beatings to break the infant's will.

Until recently, a lifetime of heavy toil lay before it – elephants were used as combination bulldozers, fork-lifts and semitrailers. The government has now clamped down on using them to carry wood, and now their main commercial purpose is to ferry tourists. It's an awful dilemma, as there's an undeniable thrill in seeing elephants taking part in village life as they have for centuries. But this delight is tempered by the knowledge of what these beautiful creatures have had to endure in order to spend their years lugging hefty Westerners through the forest.

hwest of Buon Ma Thuot. The village, 5km beyond the turn-off into the national park, often gets overrun with busloads of visitors indulging in traditional activities such as **gong performances** and drinking wine from a **communal jug** – everybody gathers around and drinks at the same time through very long straws.

A good local guide based in Ban Don is **Dang Xuan Vu** (☎ 0905-057 890; xuanvupaulbmt@yahoo.com). He can help with accommodation, treks and elephant rides, as well as information on the park's flora and fauna.

There are the neglected ruins of a 13th-century Cham tower called **Yang Prong** 50km north of Ban Don at Ya Liao, near the Cambodian border. A permit and guide are necessary to visit this spot.

SLEEPING & EATING

At the national park headquarters, **Yok Don Guesthouse** (☎ 853 110; r 150,000d;) has four basic rooms (cold water only), each with two beds.

Camping in the park is possible, but you'll need to have a guide with you. Overnight treks with a guide cost 350,000d, and longer treks can also be arranged. You'll need to bring your own food on all trips.

In Ban Don, contact **Ban Don Tourist** (☎ 798 119) about overnighting in minority **stilt houses** (per person US$5). Another option (also arranged through Ban Don Tourist) is the **bungalows** (US$12) out on nearby Aino Island, reached via a rickety series of bamboo suspension bridges.

Though it can be a bit of a circus, there is a good restaurant in Ban Don. If you're lucky you might catch a local performance of gong music and dancing put on for a group tour.

GETTING THERE & AROUND

Local buses head from Buon Ma Thuot bus station to Yok Don National Park (US$1, 40km, eight daily). Motorbike taxis in Buon Ma Thuot can take you to the park for around US$7/10 one way/return.

Elephants can be hired overnight for 600,000d per day.

Lak Lake

This beautiful spot is awakening to tourism, offering authentic experiences of hill-tribe life, along with increasingly comfortable accommodation choices. Lak Lake (Ho Lak) covers 600 hectares in the rainy season, but shrinks to 400 hectares surrounded by rice paddies in the dry. It was once full of crocodiles, but these have long since found their fate as shoes, handbags and taxidermied monstrosities.

Located on the mountainous road between Dalat (154km southeast) and Buon Ma Thuot (50km north), the surrounding countryside is stunning. Emperor Bao Dai must have thought so, as he built yet another of his palaces (is anyone keeping count?) overlooking the lake (see below).

On the south shores, near the town of Lien Son, **Jun Village** reveals an enigmatic slice of traditional M'nong life. The rattan and wood houses are all built on stilts, which was a way of keeping the animals out. Pigs, cows and chickens wander around at will, and you'll see the odd elephant being ridden around. The villagers go about their daily lives quite uninterested in the tourists in their midst. If you're interested in staying overnight, Mr Duc at **Café Duc Mai** (☎ 586 280; 268 Đ Nguyen Tat Thanh), in the heart of the village, can organise a mattress in one of several traditional stilt longhouses for US$5, as well as gong concerts, elephant rides (US$16), and kayaking or walking tours.

SLEEPING & EATING

Lak Resort (Du Lich Ho Lak; ☎ 586 767; Lien Son; s/d US$8/10, bungalows US$25, shared longhouse US$5;) In a peaceful lake setting, under the shade of jackfruit trees, Lak Resort still offers basic cheap rooms in an old wing or mattresses in a shared M'nong longhouse with an external toilet block, sleeping up to 30 people. At the time of research an upmarket cluster of lakeside bungalows around a central pool was near completion. A romantic restaurant over the lake serves decent food (dishes 25,000d). Tours can be arranged here and bicycles hired. Run by DakLak Tourist, the resort is committed to employing at least 51% M'nong staff.

Bao Dai Villa (☎ 586 767; Lien Son; r US$20-30) DakLak Tourist also owns the former emperor's palace, situated on a hill overlooking the lake. If you can manage to ignore the stuffed crocodiles and ghastly floral bedspreads, the views are lovely and some of the rooms huge. It's clean enough, but it could do with a good coat of paint. There's a restaurant downstairs (meals US$5) and the price includes breakfast.

GETTING THERE & AWAY

Lak Lake is easily and regularly visited as a stop on the Easy Rider trail on the scenic route between Dalat and Buon Ma Thuot. A day-trip on the back of a motorbike from Buon Ma Thuot should only cost around US$12, including waiting time. DakLak Tourist in Buon Ma Thuot offers day or overnight tours (see p319).

Public buses to Lak Lake leave regularly from the Buon Ma Thuot bus station (20,000d) or inquire at DakLak Tourist.

PLEIKU

☎ 059 / pop 141,700 / elevation 785m

Well off the tourist track, Pleiku (or Playcu) makes for little more than a pleasant stopover on Hwy 14. The threat of unrest among the local ethnic minorities means that much of the potential for village tourism has been stymied. You'll need a permit to go anywhere off the highway, and Westerners with their own wheels may find themselves quickly separated from them if they attempt to go it alone. However, you're unlikely to see any aggression on the streets of this sleepy market town.

In February 1965 the VC shelled a US compound in Pleiku, killing eight Americans. Although the USA already had more than 23,000 military advisers in Vietnam, their role was supposed to be noncombative at the time. The attack on Pleiku was used as a justification by US President Johnson to begin a relentless bombing campaign against North Vietnam and the rapid build-up of US troops.

When US troops departed in 1973 the South Vietnamese kept Pleiku as their main combat base in the area. When these troops fled the advancing VC, the whole civilian population of Pleiku and nearby Kon Tum fled with them. The stampede to the coastline involved over 100,000 people and tens of thousands died along the way.

The departing soldiers torched Pleiku, but the city was rebuilt in the 1980s with assistance from the Soviet Union. As a result, it lacks much of the colour and antiquity you find elsewhere in Vietnamese towns.

Information

You need a permit to visit villages in Gia Lai province and you'll also be required to hire a guide. This puts off many travellers, who usually just skip Pleiku entirely and head north to Kon Tum where the authorities are more hospitable. Gia Lai Tourist can arrange the permit and guide as part of one of its packages, for which you're likely to be charged a set fee depending on the length of your tour.

Gia Lai Tourist (☎ 874 571; www.gialaitourist.com; 215 Đ Hung Vuong) Located beside the Hung Vuong Hotel, Gia Lai offers a wide variety of tours, including trekking, elephant riding and programmes catering for war veterans.

Incombank (☎ 871 054; 12 Đ Tran Hung Dao) Branch offering foreign currency and travellers cheque exchanges, and credit-card advances.

Internet 42 (42 Đ Dinh Tien Hoang; per hr 2000d) Cheap and fast.

Main post office (☎ 872 123; 69 Đ Hung Vuong; 6am-9.30pm)

Vietcombank ATM (89 Đ Hung Vuong) In the foyer of the Ialy Hotel.

Sights

MUSEUMS

Pleiku has two museums, neither of them remarkable and both often closed.

The **Ho Chi Minh Museum** (☎ 824 276; 1 Phan Dinh Phuong; admission free; 8-11am & 1-4.30pm Mon-Fri) displays documents and photos to demonstrate Uncle Ho's affinity for hill-tribe people, and their love for Uncle Ho. There are also displays about a Bahnar hero, Anh Hung Nup (1914–98), who led the hill tribes against the French and Americans. There's a **statue of Anh Hung Nup** (cnr Đ Le Loi & Đ Tran Hung Dao) outside the nearby Hoa Lu Theatre.

The **Gia Lai Museum** (☎ 824 520; 28 Đ Quang Trung; admission 10,000d; 8-11am & 1-4.30pm Mon-Fri) features hill-tribe artefacts and photographs that memorialise Pleiku's role during the American War. Check in first at Gia Lai Tourist to get a ticket and an appointment.

LE TU TRONG PARK

This little public **park** (☎ 871 699; 26B Đ Tran Hung Dao) has manicured gardens, a *rong* house (see p328) and a full-length swimming pool.

SEA LAKE

Bien Ho, or Sea Lake, is a deep mountain lake about 7km north of Pleiku, where it's possible to swim in the green water but most visitors prefer to admire it from a dry distance. It is believed to have been formed from a prehistoric volcanic crater. The surrounding area's beautiful and, thankfully, there's little here in the way of development apart from a tiered viewing terrace. This makes a pleasant bike ride and picnic from Pleiku.

Sleeping

Thanh Lich Hotel (☎ 824 674; fax 828 319; 86 Đ Nguyen Van Troi; r US$6-15; ❄) Old and a bit grungy, this place still has clean sheets, hot water and, in the more expensive rooms, air-conditioning. Given Pleiku's comfortable climate you might want to forgo this for the cheaper but quieter rooms at the rear, some with terraces looking across the back-alley roofs.

Ialy Hotel (☎ 824 843; fax 827 619; 89 Đ Hung Vuong; r 220,000-400,000d; ❄) Also aging shabbily, the Ialy still remains a solid choice. The more expensive rooms are large and suite-like, fitted with new furniture including a desk and lounge area.

Duc Long Gia Lai (☎ 876 303; fax 820 784; 95-97 Đ Hai Ba Trung; r US$20-30; ❄ 💻) A crazy yellow coconut tree welcomes you to what is easily the best-value accommodation in town. The staff are friendly and the rooms spotless and new, with good furniture and facilities. The more expensive rooms have balconies and corner tubs.

Tre Xanh Hotel (☎ 715 187; fax 715 788; 18 Đ Le Lai; r US$25-30; ❄ 💻) Next to the fancy plaza of the same name, this new upmarket place has huge rooms with bathtubs. Ask for a room with a view.

Eating & Drinking

Tamba (☎ 826 774; 5-7 Đ Tran Phu) A cross between a bakery and a supermarket, this popular shop serves excellent pastries.

Nem Ninh Hoa (80 Đ Nguyen Van Troi; meals 15,000d; 🕑 lunch & dinner) This simple restaurant does delicious roll-your-own fresh spring rolls.

Hong Ha Café (☎ 824 573; 26 Đ Nguyen Van Troi) This chic, light-strewn café is a good spot for an ice cream, coffee or cocktail.

Tan Tay Nguyen (☎ 874 217; 24 Đ Quang Trung) With a thatched longroom looking on to a garden bar, this is a pleasant place to knock back a beer or a coffee.

Getting There & Away

AIR

The local office of **Vietnam Airlines** (☎ 824 680; fax 825 096; 55 Đ Quang Trung; 🕑 7.30-11am & 1.30-4.30pm) can book tickets on the daily flights to and from HCMC (550,000d) and Danang (400,000d). The airport is very near the town and easily accessible by taxi or *xe om*.

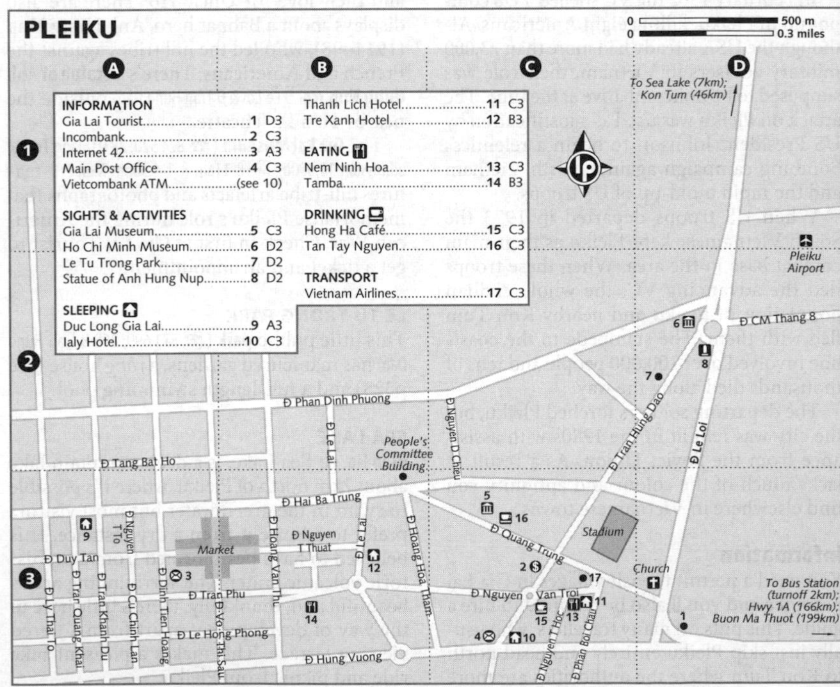

TO DIE JARAI

The Jarai minority of the Pleiku area honour their dead in graveyards set up like miniature villages. Each grave is marked with a shelter or bordered with stakes of bamboo. Simply carved wooden figures are usually placed along the edge, often pictured in a squatting position with their hands over their faces in an attitude of mourning.

For years relatives bring food to the grave and pass the death anniversaries at the gravesite, mourning and celebrating the deceased by feasting and drinking rice wine. After several years the grave is abandoned – the spirit having moved on from the village.

A horrific part of the Jarai funerary tradition was the burial of live babies with their dead mothers, a practice that persisted until the government clamped down on it in the 1990s. This stems back to a time when there were no alternatives to breast milk and the death of the mother would always lead to the baby's death. In order to save on the expense of funerary rites, which involve the slaughter of a water buffalo for a village feast, the two funerals would be combined and the baby buried alive.

BUS

Pleiku's bus station is on the main highway, just over 2km east of town. However, you can usually flag down a minibus circling Đ Le Loi or Đ Hung Vuong without too much trouble. Regular buses head to Buon Ma Thuot (46,000d, four hours), Kon Tum (30,000d, one hour) and Quy Nhon (45,000d, four hours).

There is also an international service linking Pleiku and Attapeu (US$10, 12 hours), departing Pleiku Tuesday, Thursday and Saturday and Attapeu on Monday, Wednesday and Friday.

CAR & MOTORBIKE

The nearest cities to Pleiku are Buon Ma Thuot (199km), Quy Nhon (186km) and Kon Tum (47km). There is a particularly barren stretch of land on the road from Buon Ma Thuot, the result of Agent Orange and overlogging. From Pleiku it's 550km to HCMC and 424km to Nha Trang.

KON TUM

☎ 060 / pop 89,800 / elevation 525m

Quite possibly the friendliest city in Vietnam, when people stop you on the street in Kon Tum to ask where you're from, it's because they're actually interested. In the Bahnar villages, discreetly hidden behind trim rows of Vietnamese houses on the town's outskirts, the kids love to pose for giggly photos and the adults may even invite you into their homes for a chat.

So far Kon Tum remains largely unspoiled and the authorities remain blessedly invisible. There are several sights in the town itself, and this is also a gateway to the historic Ho Chi Minh Trail (see the boxed text, p329).

Like elsewhere in the highlands, Kon Tum saw its share of combat during the American War. A major battle between the South and North Vietnamese took place in and around Kon Tum in the spring of 1972, when the area was devastated by hundreds of American B-52 raids.

Information

BIDV (☎ 862 340; 1 Đ Tran Phu; 🕒 closed Sat) Exchanges US dollars and euros, and gives cash advances on major credit cards.

Incombank (☎ 910 714; 90 Đ Tran Phu)

Internet Café (21 Đ Nguyen Hue)

Kon Tum General Hospital (☎ 862 565; 224A Đ Ba Trieu)

Kon Tum Tourist (☎ 861 626; www.kontumtourist.com.vn; 2 Đ Phan Dinh Phung; 🕒 8-11am & 1-4.30pm) In the Dakbla Hotel, staff can help answer queries and arrange trekking tours, overnight stays in villages and boating trips on Yaly Lake and the Dakbla River.

Main post office (☎ 862 361; 205 Đ Le Hong Phong)

Sights

MONTAGNARD VILLAGES

There are quite a few hill-tribe villages around Kon Tum. Generally the local people welcome tourists, but only if you are not too intrusive. It's fine to wander around the village, but ask permission before pointing a camera into people's faces or homes.

Some small villages (or perhaps we should say neighbourhoods) are on the periphery of Kon Tum. There are two **Bahnar villages**, simply called Lang Bana in Vietnamese: one on the east side and the other on the west side of town. Cows and pigs wander around the dirt lanes, while the kids play naked or in

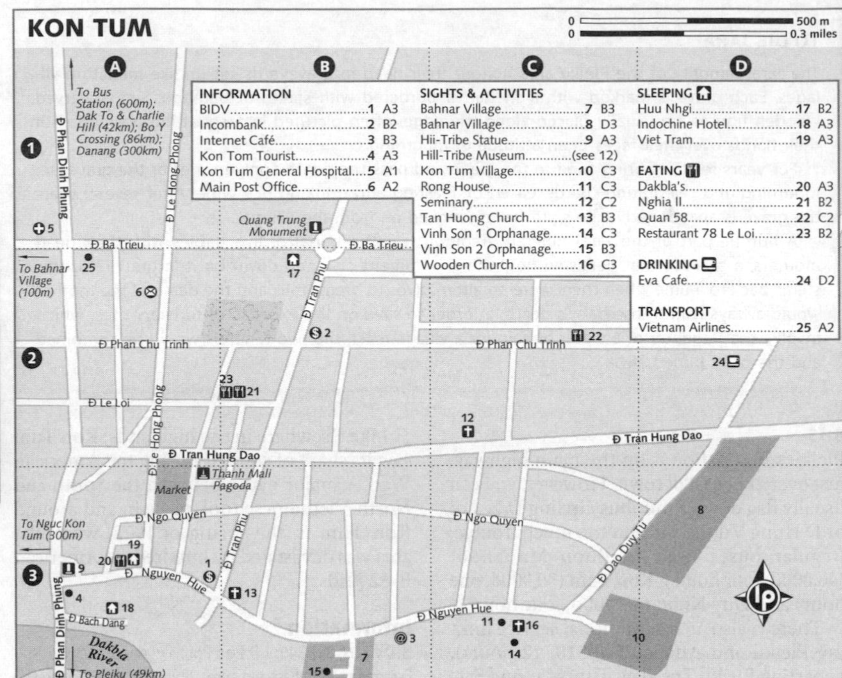

dirty clothes. You're unlikely to see people in traditional garb, unless they're on their way to the Mass in the Bahnar language, held on Sunday nights at the wooden church (right).

Also on the east side of Kon Tum is **Kon Tum village** (Lang Kon Tum). This is, in fact, the original Kon Tum before it grew to become a small city.

If you have time for a multiday trek in the jungle, Kon Tum Tourist (p327) can arrange homestays in villages. Because the guides here are careful not to intrude too frequently on any one village, visitors are always welcomed and traditions remain intact. Email ahead to book a rare and real look at village life.

The Kon Tum police continue to have a relatively open attitude to tourists visiting local minority villages without permits. Check in with Kon Tum Tourist for the latest scoop on the situation.

RONG HOUSE

Kon Tum's **rong house** (Đ Nguyen Hue) is the venue for important local events, such as meetings, weddings, festivals, prayer sessions and so on. *Rong* houses are a type of tall thatched-roof community house built on stilts. The stilts were originally for protection from elephants, tigers and other overly assertive animals.

WOODEN CHURCH

Behind the *rong* house is a beautiful French **wooden church** (Đ Nguyen Hue) with a dark front, sky-blue trim and wide terraces. Inside it's light, airy and elegant. Serving the Bahnar community, the altar is bedecked in traditional woven fabrics.

TAN HUONG CHURCH

Another exquisite Catholic **church** (92 Đ Nguyen Hue), this one's painted in candy pastels and has large, brightly coloured bas-reliefs on its façade, including a wonderfully Vietnamese-looking St Michael stomping on a Chinese dragon. Check out the beautifully carved wooden door. While distinctly European in style, it's blended with Asian curved motifs along the roofline.

HILL-TRIBE STATUE

Welcoming you into town as you cross the bridge on Hwy 14 from Pleiku, this lovely

statue (Đ Phan Dinh Phung) in socialist-realist style is a rarity for Vietnam – nobody's holding a gun. Instead it celebrates the local hill tribes, with its three main figures banging gongs and drums.

SEMINARY & HILL-TRIBE MUSEUM

Kon Tum is home to a lovely old Catholic **seminary** (Đ Tran Hung Dao) that looks as if it was beamed here from a provincial French village. The residents are generally welcoming of visitors, and the **Hill-Tribe Museum** (8-11am & 2-4pm Mon-Sat) on the 2nd floor is worth a look, if it happens to be open, as is the chapel below it.

ORPHANAGES

A short walk from the town centre, these sister orphanages are well worth spending a few hours at: staff at both the **Vinh Son 1** and **Vinh Son 2** orphanages are welcoming of visitors who come to share some time with the adorable multi-ethnic resident children.

If you plan to visit, please make a donation to the orphanage; it is very much in need of support. Canned food, clothing or toys for the kids would be appropriate, and monetary contributions are of course appreciated.

Vinh Son 1 is just behind the wooden church on Đ Nguyen Hue. From here you can continue east to visit nearby minority villages. Vinh Son 2, at the southern edge of town and beyond a small Bahnar village, is less visited and more populous (with around 200 children) so is usually in need of more help. The villagers are used to seeing visitors coming through and will point you in the right direction. You'll find it at the end of the second dirt track on the right after the small paddock.

NGUC KON TUM

This **former prison compound** (7.30-11am & 1-5pm), by the edge of Kon Tum, is now a quiet park on the banks of the Dakbla River. It was once one of the famous prisons run by the South Vietnamese; VC who survived their internment were made into heroes after liberation.

There's a small museum at the prison site, but nothing is left of the original buildings. Outside the museum is a memorial statue; inside, you'll find old photos of prisoners and models of the prison cells, but the explanations are in Vietnamese only.

DAK TO & CHARLIE HILL

The obscure **Dak To** outpost, 42km north of Kon Tum, was a major battlefield during the American War. In 1972 it was the scene of intense fighting and one of the last big battles before American troops pulled out.

Dak To has become popular with visiting groups of US veterans, but you probably won't find much of interest if you're not a war buff. More intriguingly, those few VC veterans with sufficient free time and money also like to come here to stir their memories.

About 5km south of Dak To is **Charlie Hill**. The hill was a fortified South Vietnamese stronghold before the VC tried to overrun it. The South Vietnamese officer in charge, Colonel Ngoc Minh, decided that he would neither surrender nor retreat and the battle became a fierce fight to the death. Unusually for a guerrilla war, this was a prolonged battle. The VC laid siege to the hill for 1½ months before they managed to kill Colonel Minh and 150 South Vietnamese troops, who had made their last stand here. Although largely forgotten in the West, the battle is well known,

THE HO CHI MINH TRAIL

This legendary route was not one but many paths that formed the major supply link for the North Vietnamese and Viet Cong (VC) during the American War. Supplies and troops leaving from the port of Vinh headed inland along inhospitable mountainous jungle paths, crossing in and out of neighbouring Laos, and eventually ending up near Saigon. It's hard to imagine what these soldiers endured – thousands were lost to malaria and American bombs.

While the nature of the trail means that there's no one official route, a widely accepted section follows Hwy 14 north from Kon Tum to Giang, not far from Danang. This exceptionally beautiful track is now served by an excellent road winding along the edge of steep mountains. If you catch a bus between Danang and Kon Tum you'll be following this historic path – albeit in considerably more comfort than the men who first trod it.

For an impression of how the trail once looked, DMZ day tours (see p203) often stop at a branch of the trail near Khe Sanh where the path heads under the jungle canopy.

even now, in Vietnam. The reason for this is largely because the fight was commemorated by a popular song, 'Nguoi O Lai Charlie' (The People Stayed in Charlie).

Not surprisingly, the hill was heavily mined during the war and is still considered unsafe to climb.

There's a **rong house** in Dak To that is worth seeking out.

Sleeping

Viet Tram (☎ 869 269; fax 869 334; 162 Đ Nguyen Hue; r US$8-10;) A friendly minihotel with basic but clean and comfortable rooms.

Huu Nhgi (☎ 911 560; fax 911 556; 69 Đ Ba Trieu; r US$18-30;) There's no English spoken in this new, upmarket and attractive hotel. Rooms at the back look out on a quiet courtyard.

Indochine Hotel (☎ 863 334; kontumtourism.com; 30 Đ Bach Dang; r US$20-40, ste US$70;) This large new place right by the river is downright flash by highlands standards and has great views from the rooftop bar.

Eating & Drinking

Dakbla's (☎ 862 584; 168 Đ Nguyen Hue; dishes 25,000-60,000d) With good food and reasonable prices, Dakbla's tends to draw the most travellers, serving Vietnamese standards plus exotic fare such as wild boar and frog. An impressive collection of hill-tribe artefacts adorns the walls, some of which are for sale.

Quan 58 (☎ 863 814; 58 Đ Phan Chu Trinh; hotpot 50,000d; lunch & dinner) This is an indoor-outdoor goat-meat speciality restaurant. Goat *(de)* can be ordered in over a dozen ways, such as steamed *(de hap)*, grilled *(de nuong)*, sautéed *(de xao lan)*, curried *(de cari)* and the ever-popular hotpot *(lau de)*.

Restaurant 78 Le Loi (☎ 864 404; 78 Đ Le Loi; hotpot 50,000d; lunch & dinner) This place is crowded with locals eating hotpot and drinking beer.

Nghia II (72 Đ Le Loi; mains 10,000d). A few doors down from Restaurant 78 Le Loi, there's good vegetarian food here.

Eva Café (☎ 862 944; 1 Đ Phan Chu Trinh) A pleasant surprise, this is set up like a hill-tribe village, minus the pigs and cows, with thatched buildings scattered throughout the garden. There's a fantastic sculpture of a soldier fashioned from a large bomb, wearing a peace sign on a chain around its neck. This chic café seems a little incongruous in simple Kon Tum, but it's a good place for a coffee, cold beer or a delicious mango smoothie.

Getting There & Around

Kon Tum is easy to traverse on foot, but *xe om* are in ready supply. It shouldn't cost more than 10,000d to get anywhere on the back of a bike.

The local **Vietnam Airlines** (☎ 862 282; 129 Đ Ba Trieu; 7-11am & 1-5pm Mon-Sat) office can handle air-travel bookings; the nearest airport is in Pleiku.

Kon Tum's **bus station** (Đ 279 Phan Dinh Phung) has plenty of services to Pleiku (30,000d, one hour) and Danang (85,000d, five hours). The newly opened Bo Y border crossing into Laos lies 86km northeast of Kon Tum. There are buses that leave Quy Nhon on Mondays, Tuesdays, Thursdays and Sundays, passing through Kon Tum en route to Pakse. These services are new and don't seem to have a fixed stopping point or schedule as yet. The best thing to do is to inquire at the bus station for the latest details. Another option is to catch a bus to Ngoc Hoi (30,000d, two hours, one daily) and then pick up a Lao minivan returning to Attapeu (80,000k, three hours). Note that Lao visas are not available at this border, so you'll have to arrange one in Danang or HCMC.

Hwy 14 north and south of Kon Tum is now in very good repair. Pleiku is 49km south and Danang 300km north.

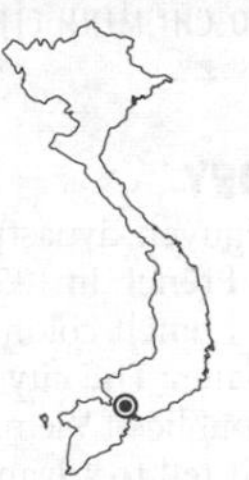

Ho Chi Minh City

Boasting an electric, near palpable energy, Ho Chi Minh City (HCMC) is Vietnam's largest metropolis and its undisputed capital of commerce. For the casual visitor, Saigon – as its still called by all but the city officials who live here – can seem a chaotic mess of traffic-clogged roads and urban bustle, with nary a green space in sight. Yet thousands of expats and Vietnamese immigrants couldn't imagine living anywhere else. They've long since fallen prey to the hidden charms of one of Southeast Asia's liveliest cities.

If every town had a symbol, Saigon's would surely be the motorbike. More than three million of them fly along streets once swarming with bicycles. Cruising along boulevards and back alleys astride a *xe om* (motorbike taxi) is the quickest way to sensory overload – daily fare in this tropical town. Teeming markets, sidewalk cafés, massage and acupuncture clinics, centuries-old pagodas, sleek skyscrapers and ramshackle wooden shops selling silk, spices, baskets and handmade furniture all jockey for attention amid the surreal urban collage.

Saigon is a forward-looking city driving Vietnam's economic boom. Investment has led to new crop of lavish hotels and restaurants, with trendy nightclubs and high-end boutiques dotting tree-lined neighbourhoods. Yet the city hasn't forgotten its past. The ghosts live on in the churches, temples, former GI hotels and government buildings that one generation ago witnessed a city in turmoil. The Saigon experience is about so many things – magical conversations, memorable meals and inevitable frustration – yet it's unlikely to evoke apathy. Stick around this complicated city long enough and you may find yourself smitten by it.

HIGHLIGHTS

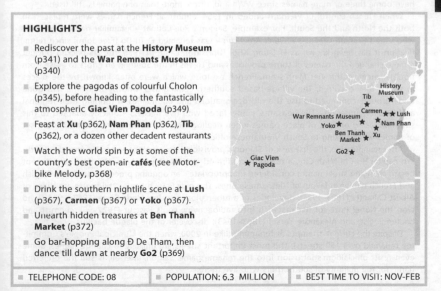

- Rediscover the past at the **History Museum** (p341) and the **War Remnants Museum** (p340)
- Explore the pagodas of colourful Cholon (p345), before heading to the fantastically atmospheric **Giac Vien Pagoda** (p349)
- Feast at **Xu** (p362), **Nam Phan** (p362), **Tib** (p362), or a dozen other decadent restaurants
- Watch the world spin by at some of the country's best open-air **cafés** (see Motorbike Melody, p368)
- Drink the southern nightlife scene at **Lush** (p367), **Carmen** (p367) or **Yoko** (p367).
- Unearth hidden treasures at **Ben Thanh Market** (p372)
- Go bar-hopping along Đ De Tham, then dance till dawn at nearby **Go2** (p369)

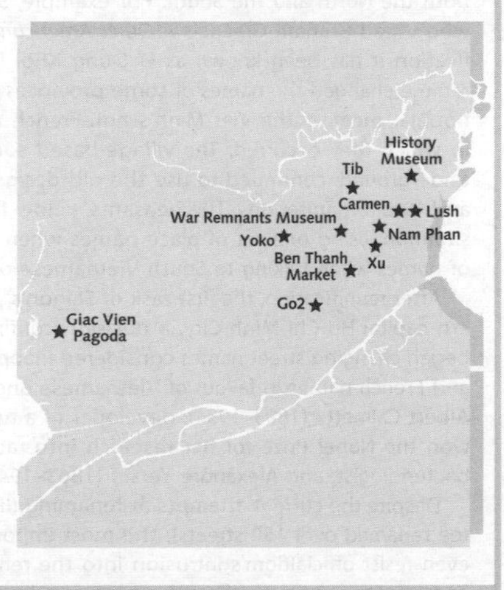

- TELEPHONE CODE: 08
- POPULATION: 6.3 MILLION
- BEST TIME TO VISIT: NOV-FEB

HISTORY

The Nguyen dynasty's Saigon was captured by the French in 1859, becoming the capital of the French colony of Cochinchina a few years later. The city served as the capital of the Republic of Vietnam from 1956 until 1975, when it fell to advancing North Vietnamese forces and was renamed Ho Chi Minh City by the Hanoi government.

Nowadays, the official government census counts only those who have official residence permits, and probably a third of the population lives here illegally. Many of these illegal residents actually lived in the city before 1975, but their residence permits were transferred to rural re-education camps after reunification. Not surprisingly, they and their families have simply sneaked back into the city, although without a residence permit they cannot own property or a business.

Explosive growth, part of the effect of *doi moi* (economic reform) in 1986, is evident in new high-rise buildings, joint-venture hotels and colourful shops. Downsides include the sharp increase in traffic, pollution and other urban ills, but a more open-minded new generation may infuse HCMC's chaotic growth with a more globally conscious attitude.

ORIENTATION

In actuality, HCMC is not so much a city as a small province stretching from the South China Sea almost to the Cambodian border. Rural regions make up about 90% of the land area of HCMC and hold around 25% of the municipality's population; the other 75% is crammed into the remaining 10% of land, which constitutes the urban centre.

HCMC is divided into 16 urban districts (*quan*, derived from the French *quartier*) and five rural districts *(huyen)*.

To the west of Saigon and the city centre is District 5, the huge Chinese neighbourhood called Cholon, which means 'Big Market'. However, it is decidedly less Chinese than it used to be, largely thanks to the anticapitalist and anti-Chinese campaign from 1978 to 1979, when many ethnic Chinese fled the country – taking with them their money and entrepreneurial skills. Many of these refugees have since returned (with foreign passports) to explore investment possibilities, and

RENAMING THE PAST

One of the main battlegrounds for the hearts of Vietnamese during the last four decades has been the naming of Vietnam's provinces, districts, cities, towns, streets and institutions. Some places have borne three or more names since WWII and, often, more than one name is still used.

When French control of Vietnam ended in 1954, almost all French names were replaced in both the North and the South. For example, Saigon's Rue Catinat – a familiar name to anyone who's read Graham Greene's *A Quiet American* – was renamed Đ Tu Do (Freedom); since reunification it has been known as Đ Dong Khoi (Uprising). Later, in 1956, the US-backed puppet regime changed the names of some provinces and towns in the South in an effort to erase from popular memory the Viet Minh's anti-French exploits, which were often known by the places in which they occurred. The village-based southern communists, who by this time had gone underground, continued to use the old designations and boundaries in running their regional and local organisations. The peasants – now faced with two masters – quickly adapted to this situation, using one set of place names when dealing with the communists and a different set of names when talking to South Vietnamese officials.

After reunification, the first task of Saigon's provisional government was to rename the southern capital Ho Chi Minh City, a decision confirmed in Hanoi a year later. The new government began changing street names considered inappropriate – an ongoing process – dropping English and French names in favour of Vietnamese ones. The only French names still in use are those of Albert Calmette (1893–1934), developer of a tuberculosis vaccine; Marie Curie (1867–1934), who won the Nobel Prize for her research into radioactivity; Louis Pasteur (1822–95), chemist and bacteriologist; and Alexandre Yersin (1863–1943), discoverer of the plague bacillus.

Despite the current attempts at renaming (like in 2000, when the Municipal People's Committee renamed over 150 streets), the most important streets are unlikely to change names. Some even resist officialdom's intrusion into the rename game. Saigon, after all, is still the preferred name for the majority of southerners who live there.

HO CHI MINH CITY IN...

One Day

Start your morning with a steaming bowl of *pho* (rice-noodle soup), followed by a stroll among the shops and galleries lining Đ Dong Khoi. Make your way to the **Museum of Ho Chi Minh City** (p341), then have lunch at nearby **Quan An Ngon** (p361), the place to sample a wide variety of Vietnamese delicacies. Continue your journey into the past at the **Reunification Palace** (p339) and the **War Remnants Museum** (p340). In the evening, catch the sunset and stunning views from the rooftop bar of the **Sheraton Saigon** (p360), followed by an elegant meal at either **Temple Club** (p362) or **Nam Phan** (p362). Have a nightcap at **Qing** (p367), a small cosy wine bar.

Two Days

Begin the day at the lively **Ben Thanh Market** (p372), where you can grab a bite while loading up on wooden knick-knacks, sweets and conical hats. Then, grab a taxi to **Cholon** (p345) for a visit to the historic pagodas of HCMC's Chinatown. Have lunch, then pay a final pagoda visit to **Giac Lam** (p348), HCMC's oldest and arguably most impressive pagoda. As the afternoon wanes, treat yourself to a massage or spa treatment at **L'Apothiquaire** (p353), a welcome reward for tired gams. After detoxifying, start the fun all over again with a decadent meal at **Tib** (p362) or **Lemon Grass** (p362). End the night at one of HCMC's stylish bars, such as **Lush** (p367) or **Yoko** (p367).

Cholon's hotels are once again packed with Chinese-speaking businesspeople.

The city's neoclassical and international-style buildings, along with its tree-lined streets set with shops, cafés and restaurants give neighbourhoods such as District 3 an attractive, vaguely French atmosphere. The majority of places and sights described in this chapter are located in District 1, which includes the backpacker district of Pham Ngu Lao, and the tonier area of Dong Khoi, which hosts the city's best assortment of restaurants, bars and boutiques.

The 7km trip into town from the airport should cost around 70,000d in a metered taxi, or about 50,000d by motorbike taxi *(xe om)*. You could also try the airport bus (1000d) that drops you right in central HCMC (see p374). From the train station (Ga Sai Gon; p374), a *xe om* to Pham Ngu Lao costs about 15,000d. Most *xe om* rides from Saigon's intercity bus stations will run between 10,000d to 20,000d; public buses also pass by the central Ben Thanh Market (3000d), but these usually stop running midafternoon. Open-tour buses will unload you directly into Pham Ngu Lao.

Maps

Good, up-to-date maps of HCMC are available at bookstores in Districts 1 and 3; a reliable, central source is Fahasa Bookshop (see right).

INFORMATION

Bookshops

The best area to look for maps, books and stationery is along the north side of ĐL Le Loi, between the Rex Hotel and Đ Nam Ky Khoi Nghia, in the Dong Khoi area (Map p350). There are many small, privately run shops as well as the large government-run ones.

On Đ De Tham, around Pham Ngu Lao (Map p357), there is a handful of shops dealing in used paperbacks (for purchase or trade) and bootleg CDs. Vendors on foot sell pirated paperbacks everywhere in Pham Ngu Lao.

Fahasa Bookshop (Map p350; 🕑 8am-10pm); Đ Dong Khoi (☎ 822 4670; 185 Đ Dong Khoi); ĐL Nguyen Hue (☎ 822 5796; 40 ĐL Nguyen Hue) One of the best government-run bookshops, with good dictionaries, maps and general books in English and French.

Phuong Nam Bookshop (Map p336; ☎ 822 9650; 2A ĐL Le Duan; 🕑 8am-9.30pm) Has imported books and magazines in English, French and Chinese, mostly instructional.

Cultural Centres

British Council (Map p336; ☎ 823 2862; www.britishcouncil.org/vietnam; 25 ĐL Le Duan)

Institute of Cultural Exchange with France (Idecaf; Map p350; ☎ 829 5451; 31 Đ Thai Van Lung)

Emergency

Emergency (☎ 115)
Fire (☎ 114)
Information (☎ 1080)
Police (☎ 113)

HO CHI MINH CITY

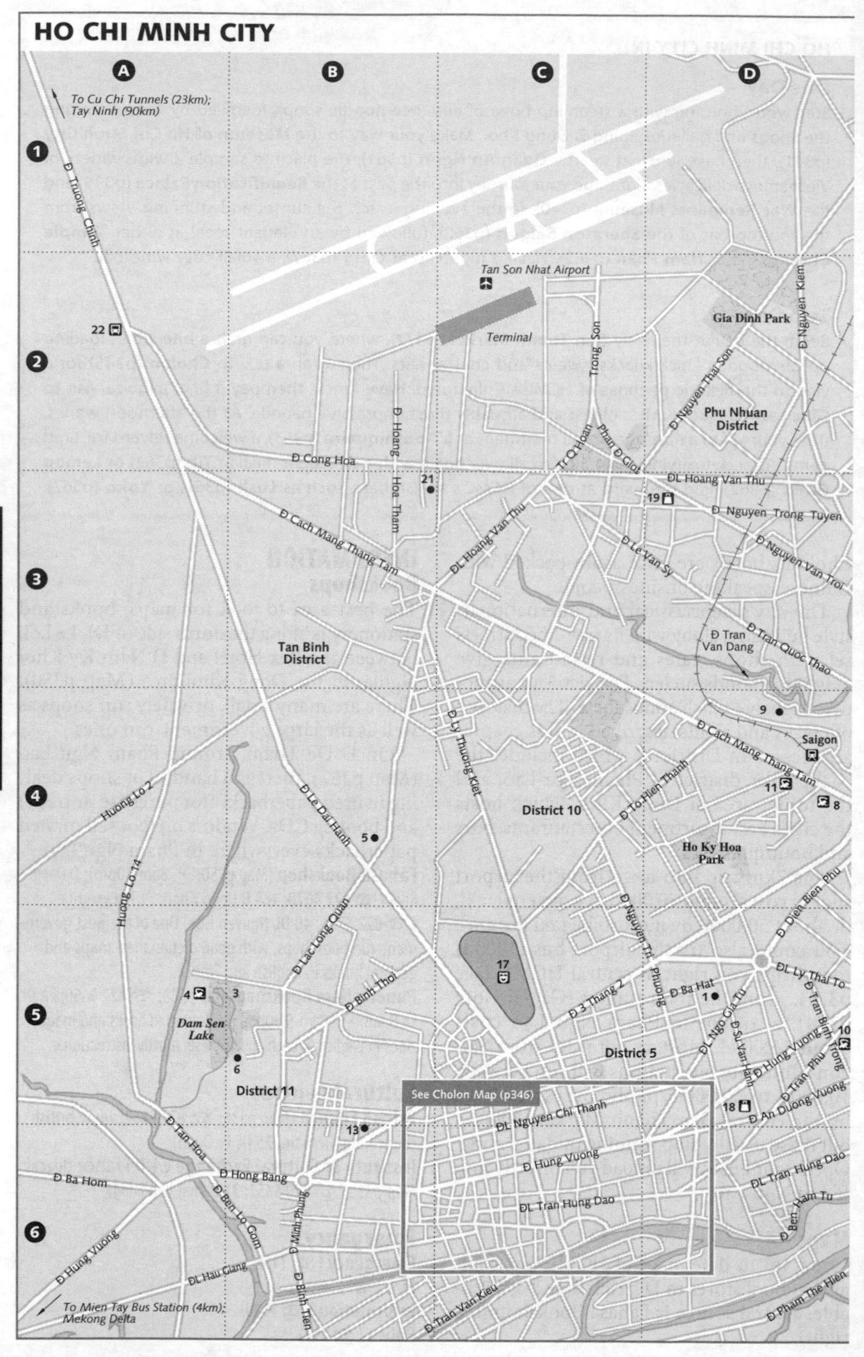

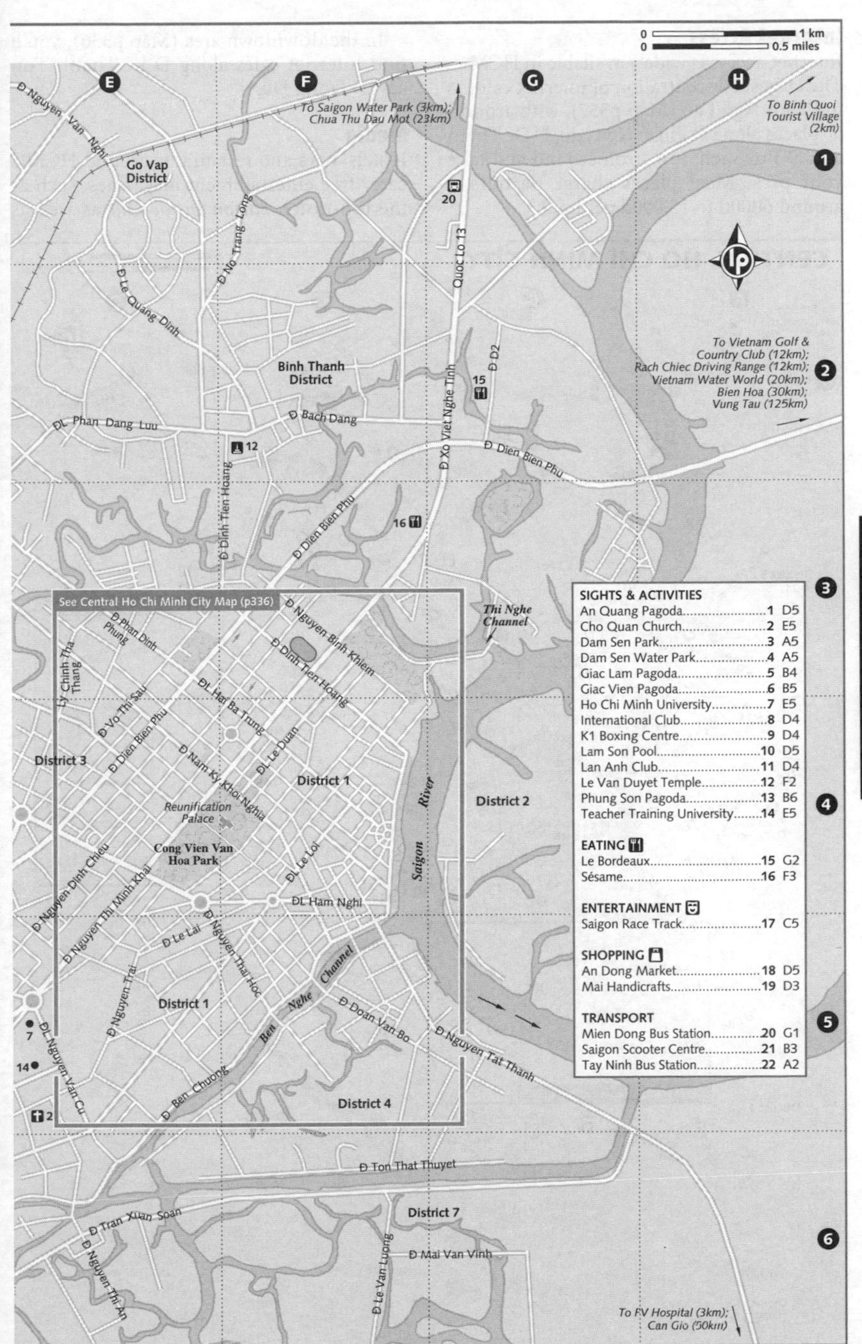
0 1 km
0 0.5 miles
E F G H
1 2 3 4 5 6
To Saigon Water Park (3km); Chua Thu Dau Mot (23km)
To Binh Quoi Tourist Village (2km)
To Vietnam Golf & Country Club (12km); Rach Chiec Driving Range (12km); Vietnam Water World (20km); Bien Hoa (30km); Vung Tau (125km)
To FV Hospital (3km); Can Gio (50km)
Go Vap District
Binh Thanh District
District 1
District 2
District 3
District 4
District 7
Reunification Palace
Cong Vien Van Hoa Park
Thi Nghe Channel
Saigon River
Ben Nghe Channel
Đ Nguyen Van Nghi
Đ No Trang Long
Đ Le Quang Dinh
Quoc Lo 13
Đ D2
ĐL Phan Dang Luu
Đ Bach Dang
Đ XO Viet Nghe Tinh
Đ Dien Bien Phu
Đ Dinh Tien Hoang
Đ Nguyen Binh Khiem
Đ Phan Dinh Phung
Ly Chinh Thang
Đ Vo Thi Sau
ĐL Hai Ba Trung
ĐL Le Duan
Đ Nam Ky Khoi Nghia
Đ Nguyen Dinh Chieu
Đ Nguyen Thi Minh Khai
ĐL Le Loi
ĐL Ham Nghi
Đ Le Lai
Đ Nguyen Thai Hoc
Đ Nguyen Trai
ĐL Nguyen Van Cu
Đ Doan Van Bo
Đ Nguyen Tat Thanh
Đ Ben Chuong
Đ Ton That Thuyet
Đ Tran Xuan Soan
Đ Nguyen Thi An
Đ Le Van Luong
Đ Mai Van Vinh
See Central Ho Chi Minh City Map (p336)
SIGHTS & ACTIVITIES
An Quang Pagoda 1 D5
Cho Quan Church 2 E5
Dam Sen Park 3 A5
Dam Sen Water Park 4 A5
Giac Lam Pagoda 5 B4
Giac Vien Pagoda 6 B5
Ho Chi Minh University 7 E5
International Club 8 D4
K1 Boxing Centre 9 D4
Lam Son Pool 10 D5
Lan Anh Club 11 D4
Le Van Duyet Temple 12 F2
Phung Son Pagoda 13 B6
Teacher Training University 14 E5
EATING
Le Bordeaux 15 G2
Sésame 16 F3
ENTERTAINMENT
Saigon Race Track 17 C5
SHOPPING
An Dong Market 18 D5
Mai Handicrafts 19 D3
TRANSPORT
Mien Dong Bus Station 20 G1
Saigon Scooter Centre 21 B3
Tay Ninh Bus Station 22 A2

Internet Access

Internet access is widely available in HCMC. The largest concentration of internet cafés is in Pham Ngu Lao (Map p357), with around 30 places along Đ Pham Ngu Lao, Đ De Tham and Đ Bui Vien; just stroll around and take your pick. Most places charge peanuts – around 6000d to 15,000d per hour.

In the downtown area (Map p336), you'll find internet cafés along Đ Le Thanh Ton and Đ Dong Du.

Media

Hotels, bars and restaurants around HCMC carry free entertainment magazines, such as the top-notch *Saigon Inside Out* as well as

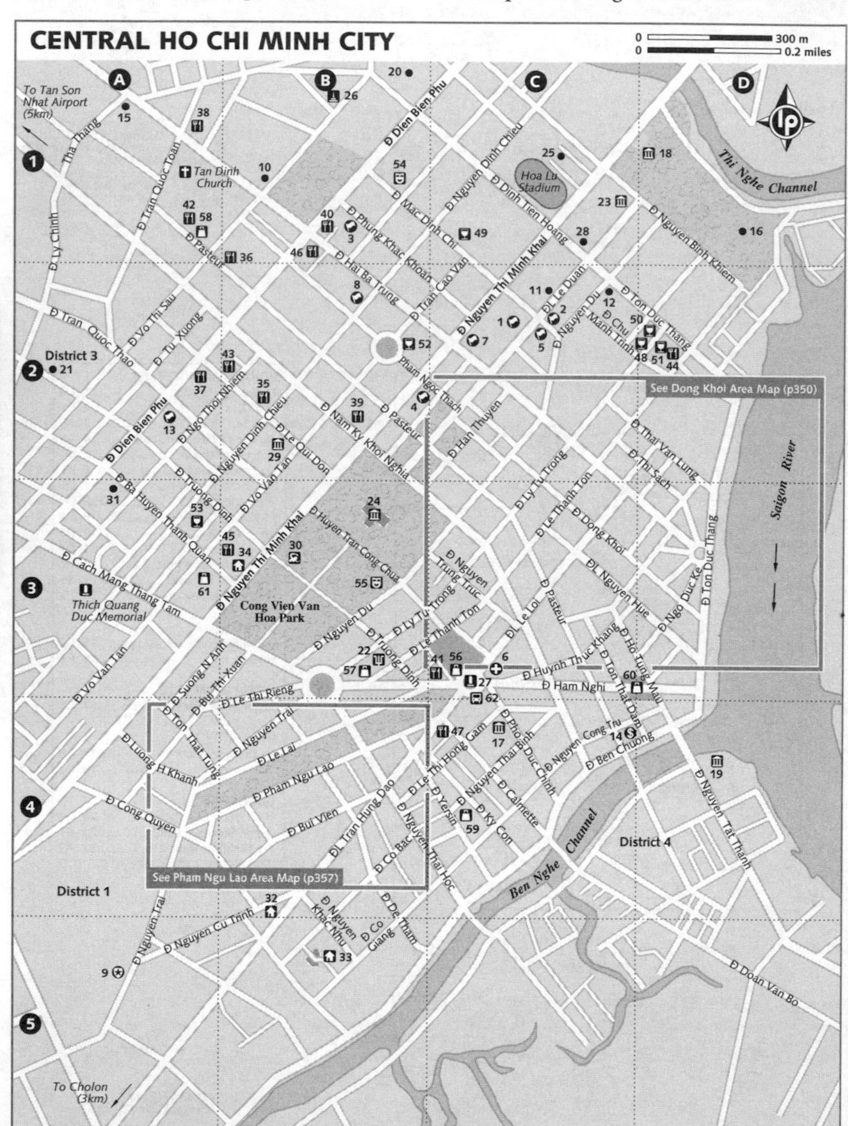

the *Guide* and *Time Out*, weekly supplements published by the *Vietnam Economic Times (VET)* and the *Vietnam Investment Review (VIR)*, respectively.

There is also an eclectic selection of admittedly slightly stale foreign newspapers and magazines – day-old *Le Monde*, or last week's *Newsweek* – for sale (be sure to bargain!) by vendors standing on the corner of Đ Dong Khoi and ĐL Le Loi (Map p350), across from the Continental Hotel.

Medical Services

Cho Ray Hospital (Map p346; ☎ 855 4137; fax 855 7267; 201 ĐL Nguyen Chi Thanh, District 5; consultations from US$4; 🕑 24hr) One of the largest medical facilities in Vietnam, with 1000 beds and a section for foreigners on the 10th floor; about a third of the 200 doctors speak English.

Emergency Centre (Map p336; ☎ 829 2071; 125 ĐL Le Loi; 🕑 24hr) Has doctors that speak English and French.

FV Hospital (Franco-Vietnamese Hospital; Map pp334-5; ☎ 411 3333; www.fvhospital.com; 6 Đ Nguyen Luong Bang, Tan Phu Ward, District 7; 🕑 24hr) French-, Vietnamese- and English-speaking physicians; superb care and equipment.

Grand Dentistry (Map p350; ☎ 821 9446; 24hr emergency ☎ 0903-647 156; Sun Wah Tower, 115 Đ Nguyen Hue) Dental care, emergencies and surgeries.

HCMC Family Medical Practice (Map p350; ☎ 822 7848, 24hr emergency ☎ 0913-234 911; www.vietnammedicalpractice.com; Diamond Plaza, 34 ĐL Le Duan; consultations from US$50; 🕑 24hr) Run by the well-respected Dr Rafi Kot.

International Medical Centre (Map p350; ☎ 827 2366; 24hr emergency ☎ 865 4025; fac@hcm.vnn.vn; 1 Đ Han Thuyen; consultations US$40-80; 🕑 24hr) A nonprofit organisation billing itself as the least expensive Western health-care centre in the country; has English-speaking French doctors.

International SOS (Map p350; ☎ 829 8424, 24hr emergency ☎ 829 8520; www.internationalsos.com; 65 Đ Nguyen Du; consultations US$55-70; 🕑 24hr) Has an international team of doctors speaking English, French, Japanese and Vietnamese.

Maple Dental Clinic (Map p336; ☎ 820 1999; 72 Đ Vo Thi Sau; 🕑 8am-8pm Mon-Fri, 9am-5pm Sat) Dental care (including emergencies) by experienced English-speaking dentists.

Money

Just inside the airport terminal, there's an exchange counter run by **Sasco** (☎ 848 7142), which gives the official exchange rate. Opening hours are irregular, so carry sufficient US dollar notes in small denominations to get into the city in case Sasco's is closed.

Banks with 24-hour ATMs dispense dong only, to a maximum amount of 2,000,000d per day. Visa or MasterCard cash advances for larger amounts of dong, as well as US dollars, can be handled at bank counters during banking hours. All of these banks also

INFORMATION
American Consulate....1 C2
British Consulate....2 C2
British Council....(see 2)
Cambodian Consulate....3 B1
Chinese Consulate....4 B2
Dutch Consulate....5 C2
Emergency Centre....6 C3
Exotissimo....(see 12)
French Consulate....7 C2
German Consulate....8 B2
Immigration Police Office....9 A5
Maple Dental Clinic....10 B1
New Zealand Consulate....(see 4)
Phuong Nam Bookshop....11 C2
Saigon Trade Centre....12 C2
Thai Consulate....13 A2
Vietcombank....14 C4

SIGHTS & ACTIVITIES
Binh Soup Shop....15 A1
Botanic Gardens....16 D1
Fine Arts Museum....17 C4
History Museum....18 D1
Ho Chi Minh Museum....19 D4
Jade Emperor Pagoda....20 B1
L'Apothiquaire....21 A2
Mariamman Hindu Temple....22 B3
Military Museum....23 C1
Reunification Palace....24 B3
Saigon Yoga....25 C1
Spa Tropic....(see 46)
Tran Hung Dao Temple....26 B1
Tran Nguyen Hai Statue....27 C3
University of Social Sciences & Humanities....28 C1
War Remnants Museum....29 B2
Workers' Club....30 B3
Xa Loi Pagoda....31 A3

SLEEPING
Guest House California....(see 33)
Metropole Hotel....32 B4
Miss Loi's Guesthouse....33 B5
Ngoc Son....(see 33)
Saigon Star Hotel....34 B3

EATING
ABC Restaurant....35 B2
Au Lac do Brasil....36 B1
Au Manoir de Khai....37 A2
Banh Xeo 46A....38 A1
DEsignED Café....39 B2
L'Etoile....40 B1
Pho 2000....41 C3
Pho Hoa....42 A1
Serenata....43 B2
Sushi Bar....44 D2
Tandoor....45 B3
Tib Restaurant....46 B1
Tin Nghia....47 C4
Vegetarian Food Stalls....(see 31)

DRINKING
Carmen....48 D2
Hoa Vien....49 C1
Lush....50 D2
No 5 Ly Tu Trong....51 D2
Traffic Circle....52 B2
Yoko....53 A3

ENTERTAINMENT
Ben Thanh....54 B1
Conservatory of Music....55 B3

SHOPPING
Ben Thanh Market....56 C3
Bicycle Shops....57 B3
Blue Space Gallery....(see 17)
Cham Khanh....58 A1
Dan Sinh Market....59 C4
Lacquer & Oil....(see 17)
Old Market....60 D3
Vinh Loi Gallery....61 A3

TRANSPORT
Bus Station....62 C3

exchange traveller's cheques, charging less commission when exchanging for dong. Try the following.

ANZ Bank (Map p350; ☎ 829 9319; 11 Me Linh Sq) Has a 24-hour ATM.

HSBC (Map p350; ☎ 829 2288; 235 Đ Dong Khoi) With secure 24-hour ATM.

Sacombank (Map p357; ☎ 836 4231; www.sacombank.com; 211 Đ Nguyen Thai Hoc) Conveniently located in the budget-traveller zone, with 24-hour ATM.

Vietcombank (Map p336; ☎ 829 7245; 29 Đ Ben Chuong; closed Sun & last day of the month) The eastern building is for foreign exchange only, but is also worth a visit just to see the stunningly ornate interior. There are also branches in **Dong Khoi area** (Map p350; 19 Lam Son Sq).

Post

HCMC's French-style **main post office** (Map p350; ☎ 829 6555; 2 Cong Xa Paris; 7am-9.30pm), with its glass canopy and iron frame, is right next to Notre Dame Cathedral. Built between 1886 and 1891, it is the largest post office in Vietnam and worth visiting just for its architecture.

Customers conduct their post and telecommunications business here under the benevolent gaze of Ho Chi Minh. To your right as you enter the building is the poste restante counter. Pens, envelopes, aerograms, postcards and stamp collections are sold at the counter to the right of the entrance, and outside the post office along Đ Nguyen Du.

Countless other post office branches are scattered around town, see Map p357 and Map p346 for locations. Like the main post office, many of these also keep late hours.

The following private carriers operate near the main post office:

DHL (Map p350; ☎ 823 1525; 2 Cong Xa Paris; 7.30am-5pm Mon-Fri)

Federal Express (Map p350; ☎ 829 0995; www.fedex.com; 146 Đ Pasteur; 7am-8pm Mon-Fri, 7am-2pm Sat)

Saigon Logistics (Map p357; ☎ 837 3435; www.saigonlogistics.com.vn; 293 Đ Pham Ngu Lao; 8am-5.30pm Mon-Sat) Deals in freight forwarding, if you've out-shopped yourself.

Telephone

International and domestic phone calls can be made from post offices and better hotels. At the post office local calls cost 2000d; hotel prices for local calls vary, so be sure to ask the price beforehand.

International calls can also be made over the internet at most internet cafés; rates start at around 5000d per minute, though you can call for free (computer to computer) through Skype (www.skype.com).

Tourist Information

Sasco(☎ 848 7142; www.sascotravel.com.vn; 9am-11pm) Just beyond the baggage carousels, Sasco's Visitors Information & Services counter offers free city maps, tourist literature and an airport timetable, plus transport, accommodation and tour bookings.

Tourist Information Center (Map p350; ☎ 822 6033; www.vntourists.com; 4G Le Loi; 8am-8pm) This sleek, new information centre, which opened in 2006, distributes city maps and brochures and can give limited advice about goings-on in Saigon. There's also a tour operator and currency exchange here.

Travel Agencies

HCMC's official government-run travel agency is **Saigon Tourist** (Map p350; ☎ 829 8914; www.saigontourist.net; 49 Đ Le Thanh Ton; 8-11.30am & 1-5.30pm). The agency owns, or is a joint-venture partner in, more than 70 hotels and numerous restaurants around town, plus a car-rental agency, golf clubs and assorted tourist traps.

There's a plethora of other travel agencies in town, virtually all of them joint ventures between government agencies and private companies. These places can provide cars, book air tickets and extend your visa. Competition is keen and you can often undercut Saigon Tourist's tariffs by 50% if you shop around. Many agencies have multilingual guides who speak English, French, Japanese etc.

Most tour guides and drivers are paid poorly, so if you're happy with their service, consider tipping them. Many travellers on bus tours to Cu Chi or the Mekong Delta, for example, collect a kitty (say US$1 or US$2 per person) and give it to the guide and driver at the end of the trip.

We suggest visiting several tour operators to see what's being offered to suit your taste and budget. Plenty of cheap tours – of varying quality – are sold around Pham Ngu Lao. One excellent appraisal strategy is to grill other travellers who've just returned from a tour.

Another appealing option is to arrange a customised private tour with your own car, driver and guide. Travelling this way provides maximum flexibility and split between a few people can be surprisingly affordable.

For customised tours, **Sinhbalo Adventures** (Map p357; ☎ 837 6766, 836 7682; www.sinhbalo.com; 283/20 Đ Pham Ngu Lao) is one of the best in Vietnam. Sinhbalo specialises in cycling trips, but also arranges innovative special-interest journeys to the Mekong Delta, central highlands and further afield. Its programmes range from remote hill-tribe trekking and bird-watching in national parks to motorbiking the Ho Chi Minh Trail. We've been using them for more than 10 years and have yet to hit a snag.

The well rated Hanoi-based **Handspan Adventure Travel** (Map p350; ☎ 925 7605; www.handspan.com; 7th fl, Titan Bldg, 18A Đ Nam Quoc Cang) recently opened a branch office in Ho Chi Minh City and also deserves special mention for their quality tours.

Although your experience will very much depend on your guide, current favourites among budget agencies listed below are Kim Travel, Sinh Café and TNK Travel; see p490 for more options.

BUDGET AGENCIES

Delta Adventure Tours (Map p357; ☎ 920 2112; www.deltaadventuretours.com; 267 Đ De Tham)
Innoviet (Map p357; ☎ 295 8840; www.innoviet.com; 158 Đ Bui Vien)
Kim Travel (Map p357; ☎ 920 5552; www.kimtravel.com; 270 Đ De Tham)
Linh Cafe (Map p357; ☎ 836 0643; www.linhtravelvn.com; 291 Đ Pham Ngu Lao)
Mekong Tours (Map p357; ☎ 837 6429; mekongtours@hotmail.com; 272 Đ De Tham)
Sinh Café (Map p357; ☎ 836 7338; www.sinhcafévn.com; 246 Đ De Tham; 🕑 6.30am-11pm)
TNK Travel (Map p350; ☎ 920 4766; www.tnktravelvietnam.com; 216 Đ De Tham)

MIDRANGE & TOP-END AGENCIES

Asiana Travel Mate (Map p350; ☎ 825 0615; www.asianatravelmate.com; 4G Đ Le Loi)
Buffalo Tours (Map p350; ☎ 827 9170; www.buffalotours.com; Majestic Hotel, 1 Đ Dong Khoi)
Exotissimo (Map p336; ☎ 825 1723; www.exotissimo.com; Saigon Trade Centre, 37 Ton Duc Thang)

DANGERS & ANNOYANCES

HCMC is the most theft-ridden city in Vietnam; don't become a statistic. See p466 for advice on how to avoid street crime. Be especially careful along the Saigon riverfront, where motorbike 'cowboys' operate.

Scams

One of the more common rip-offs in HCMC involves *cyclo* drivers demanding exorbitant sums at the end of a tour.

Rather than hopping blithely into the seat when the driver smilingly says, 'Price up to you,' clearly negotiate a fair price up front (consider 100,000/200,000d for a half-day/full-day tour). If more than one person is travelling make sure you're negotiating the price for both and not a per-passenger fee. It sometimes pays to sketch out numbers and pictures with pen and paper so all parties agree. Unfortunately, 'misunderstandings' do happen; unless the *cyclo* driver has pedalled you to the 21 districts of HCMC, US$25 is not the going rate.

That said, don't just assume the driver is trying to bamboozle you. It's a tough living, especially as the city government tries to phase out the *cyclos* entirely. If you've had a particularly great guide and ride, tip generously.

SIGHTS

Although HCMC lacks the obvious aesthetic virtues of its rival to the north, the city provides some fascinating sights for the wanderer, from little-visited pagodas hidden down quiet lanes to museums, historic sites and teeming markets all jumbled up in the chaotic urban scene. First-time visitors often focus exclusively on District 1, where many of the sights are found. Those with more than a day in the city can take in central HCMC, the pagodas in Cholon and further afield, leaving enough time to explore the intriguing side of Saigon – like an afternoon at an amusement park or the racctrack.

Central Area

REUNIFICATION PALACE

Striking modern architecture and the eerie feeling you get as you walk through its deserted halls make **Reunification Palace** (Dinh Thong Nhat; Map p336; ☎ 829 4117; 106 Đ Nguyen Du; admission 15,000d; 🕑 7.30-11am & 1-4pm) one of the most fascinating sights in HCMC. The building, once the symbol of the South Vietnamese government, is preserved almost as it was on that day in April 1975 when the Republic of Vietnam, which hundreds of thousands of Vietnamese and 58,183 Americans had died trying to save, ceased to exist. Some recent additions include a statue of Ho Chi Minh and a viewing room where you can watch a video about Vietnamese history in a variety of languages. The national anthem is played at the end of the tape and you are expected to stand up – it would be rude not to.

It was towards this building – then known as Independence Palace or the Presidential Palace – that the first communist tanks to arrive in Saigon charged on the morning of 30 April 1975. After crashing through the wrought-iron gates – in a dramatic scene recorded by photojournalists and shown around the world – a soldier ran into the building and up the stairs to unfurl a VC flag from the 4th-floor balcony. In an ornate 2nd-floor reception chamber, General Minh, who had become head of state only 43 hours before, waited with his improvised cabinet. 'I have been waiting since early this morning to transfer power to you', Minh said to the VC officer who entered the room. 'There is no question of your transferring power', replied the officer. 'You cannot give up what you do not have.'

In 1868 a residence was built on this site for the French governor-general of Cochinchina and gradually it expanded to become Norodom Palace. When the French departed, the palace became home for South Vietnamese President Ngo Dinh Diem. So hated was Diem that his own air force bombed the palace in 1962 in an unsuccessful attempt to kill him. The president ordered a new residence to be built on the same site, this time with a sizeable bomb shelter in the basement. Work was completed in 1966, but Diem did not get to see his dream house because he was murdered by his own troops in 1963. The new building was named Independence Palace and was home to South Vietnamese President Nguyen Van Thieu until his hasty departure in 1975.

Norodom Palace, designed by Paris-trained Vietnamese architect Ngo Viet Thu, is an outstanding example of 1960s architecture. It has an airy and open atmosphere and its spacious chambers are tastefully decorated with the finest modern Vietnamese art and crafts. In its grandeur, the building feels worthy of a head of state.

The ground-floor room with the boat-shaped table was often used for conferences. Upstairs in the **Presidential Receiving Room** (Phu Dau Rong, or Dragon's Head Room) – the one with the red chairs in it – the South Vietnamese president received foreign delegations. He sat behind the desk; the chairs with dragons carved into the arms were used by his assistants. The chair facing the desk was reserved for foreign ambassadors. The room with gold-coloured chairs and curtains was used by the vice president. You can sit in the former president's chair and have your photo taken.

In the back of the structure are the president's living quarters. Check out the model boats, horse tails and severed elephants' feet. The 3rd floor has a card-playing room with a bar and a movie-screening chamber. This floor also boasts a terrace with a heliport – there is still a derelict helicopter parked here. The 4th floor has a dance hall and casino.

Perhaps most interesting of all is the basement with its network of tunnels, telecommunications centre and war room (with the best map of Vietnam you'll ever see pasted on the wall).

Reunification Palace is not open to visitors when official receptions or meetings are taking place. English- and French-speaking guides are on duty during opening hours.

WAR REMNANTS MUSEUM

Once known as the Museum of Chinese and American War Crimes, the **War Remnants Museum** (Bao Tang Chung Tich Chien Tranh; Map p336; ☎ 930 5587; 28 Đ Vo Van Tan; admission 15,000d; 🕓 7.30am-noon & 1.30-5pm) is now the most popular museum in HCMC with Western tourists. Many of the atrocities documented here were well publicised in the West, but rarely do Westerners have the opportunity to hear the victims of US military action tell their own stories.

US armoured vehicles, artillery pieces, bombs and infantry weapons are on display outside. Many photographs illustrating US atrocities are from US sources, including photos of the infamous My Lai Massacre (see p271). There is a model of the notorious tiger cages used by the South Vietnamese military to house Viet Cong (VC) prisoners on Con Son Island and a guillotine used by the French on Viet Minh 'troublemakers'. There are also pictures of deformed babies, their defects attributed to the USA's widespread use of chemical herbicides.

In a final gallery, there's a collection of posters and photographs showing support for the antiwar movement.

There are few museums in the world that drive home so well the point that war is horribly brutal and that many of its victims are civilians. Even those who supported the war would have a difficult time not being horrified by the photos of children mangled by US bombing and napalming. There are also scenes of torture – it takes a strong stomach to look at these. You'll also have the rare chance to see some of the experimental weapons used in the war, which were at one time military secrets, such as the fléchette (an artillery shell filled with thousands of tiny darts).

The War Remnants Museum is in the former US Information Service building, at the intersection with Đ Le Qui Don. Explanations are in Vietnamese, English and Chinese. Though a bit incongruous with the museum's theme, **water-puppet theatre** is staged in a tent on the museum grounds (see p369).

MUSEUM OF HO CHI MINH CITY

Housed in a grey, neoclassical structure built in 1886 and once known as Gia Long Palace (later, the Revolutionary Museum), the **Museum of Ho Chi Minh City** (Bao Tang Thanh Pho Ho Chi Minh; Map p350; ☎ 829 9741; 65 Đ Ly Tu Trong; admission US$1; 8am-4pm) is a singularly beautiful and amazing building.

The museum displays artefacts from the various periods of the communist struggle for power in Vietnam. The photographs of anticolonial activists executed by the French appear out of place in the gilded, 19th-century ballrooms, but then again the contrast gives a sense of the immense power and complacency of the colonial French. There are photos of Vietnamese peace demonstrators in Saigon demanding that US troops get out; and a dramatic photo of Thich Quang Duc, the monk who made headlines worldwide, when he burned himself to death in 1963 to protest against the policies of President Ngo Dinh Diem (see the boxed text, p222).

The information plaques are in Vietnamese only, but some of the exhibits include documents in French or English, and many others are self-explanatory if you know some basic Vietnamese history (but if you don't, see the History chapter, p28). The exhibitions cover the various periods in the city's 300-year history.

Among the most interesting artefacts on display is a long, narrow rowing boat *(ghe)* with a false bottom in which arms were smuggled. Nearby is a small diorama of the Cu Chi Tunnels. The adjoining room has examples of infantry weapons used by the VC and various South Vietnamese and US medals, hats and plaques. A map shows communist advances during the dramatic collapse of South Vietnam in early 1975. There are also photographs of the liberation of Saigon.

Deep beneath the building is a network of reinforced concrete bunkers and fortified corridors. The system, branches of which stretch all the way to Reunification Palace, included living areas, a kitchen and a large meeting hall. In 1963 President Diem and his brother hid here before fleeing to Cha Tam Church (p347). The network is not currently open to the public because most of the tunnels are flooded, but if you want to bring a torch (flashlight), a museum guard might show you around.

In the garden behind the museum is a Soviet tank and a US Huey UH-1 helicopter and anti-aircraft gun. In the garden fronting Đ Nam Ky Khoi Nghia is more military hardware, including the American-built F-5E jet used by a renegade South Vietnamese pilot to bomb the Presidential Palace (now Reunification Palace) on 8 April 1975.

The museum is located a block east of Reunification Palace.

HISTORY MUSEUM

The stunning Sino-French-style building that houses the **History Museum** (Bao Tang Lich Su; Map p336; ☎ 829 8146; Đ Nguyen Binh Khiem; admission 15,000d; 8-11am & 1.30-4.30pm Tue-Sun) was built in 1929 by the Société des Études Indochinoises. It's worth a visit just to view the architecture!

The museum has an excellent collection of artefacts illustrating the evolution of the cultures of Vietnam, from the Bronze Age Dong Son civilisation (13th century BC to 1st century AD) and the Oc-Eo (Funan) civilisation (1st to 6th centuries AD), to the Cham, Khmer and Vietnamese. There are many valuable relics taken from Cambodia's Angkor Wat.

At the back of the building on the 3rd floor is a **research library** (☎ 829 0268; Mon-Sat) with numerous books from the French-colonial period about Indochina.

Across from the entrance to the museum you'll see the elaborate **Temple of King Hung Vuong**. The Hung kings are said to have been the first rulers of the Vietnamese nation, having established their rule in the Red River region before it was invaded by the Chinese.

The museum is just inside the main gate to the city zoo and botanic gardens (p356), where the east end of ĐL Le Duan meets Đ Nguyen Binh Khiem.

Just across Đ Nguyen Binh Khiem is a small **military museum** (Map p336; ☎ 822 9387; 2 ĐL Le Duan) devoted to Ho Chi Minh's campaign to liberate the south. Inside is of minor interest, but some US, Chinese and Soviet war material is on display outdoors, including a Cessna A-37 of the South Vietnamese Air Force and a US-built F-5E Tiger with the 20mm nose gun still loaded. The tank on display is one of the tanks that broke into the grounds of Reunification Palace on 30 April 1975.

JADE EMPEROR PAGODA

Built in 1909 by the Cantonese (Quang Dong) Congregation, the **Jade Emperor Pagoda** (Phuoc Hai Tu or Chua Ngoc Hoang; Map pp334-5; 73 Đ Mai Thi Luu) is truly a gem among Chinese temples. It is one of the most spectacularly colourful pagodas in HCMC, filled with statues of phantasmal divinities and grotesque heroes. The pungent smoke of burning joss sticks fills the air, obscuring the exquisite woodcarvings decorated with gilded Chinese characters. The roof is covered with elaborate tile work. The statues, which represent characters from both the Buddhist and Taoist traditions, are made of reinforced papier-mâché. The pagoda is dedicated to the Emperor of Jade, the supreme Taoist god.

Inside the main building are two especially fierce and menacing figures. On the right (as you face the altar) is a 4m-high statue of the general who defeated the Green Dragon (depicted underfoot). On the left is the general who defeated the White Tiger, which is also being stepped on.

The Taoist Jade Emperor (or King of Heaven, Ngoc Hoang), draped in luxurious robes, presides over the **main sanctuary**. He is flanked by his guardians, the Four Big Diamonds (Tu Dai Kim Cuong), so named because they are said to be as hard as diamonds.

Out the door on the left-hand side of the Jade Emperor's chamber is another room. The semi-enclosed area to the right (as you enter) is presided over by Thanh Hoang, the Chief of Hell; to the left is his red horse. Other figures here represent the gods who dispense punishments for evil acts and rewards for good deeds. The room also contains the famous **Hall of the Ten Hells** – carved wooden panels illustrating the varied torments awaiting evil people in each of the Ten Regions of Hell.

On the other side of the wall is a fascinating little room in which the **ceramic figures** of 12 women, overrun with children and wearing colourful clothes, sit in two rows of six. Each of the women exemplifies a human characteristic, either good or bad (as in the case of the woman drinking alcohol from a jug). Each figure represents one year in the 12-year Chinese calendar. Presiding over the room is Kim Hoa Thanh Mau, the Chief of All Women.

The Jade Emperor Pagoda is in a part of the city known as Da Kao (or Da Cao). To get here, go to 20 Đ Dien Bien Phu and walk half a block to the northwest.

FINE ARTS MUSEUM

A classic yellow-and-white building with a modest Chinese influence, the **Fine Arts Museum** (Bao Tang My Thuat; Map p336; ☎ 829 4441; 97A Đ Pho Duc Chinh; admission 10,000d; 🕑 9am-4.30pm Tue-Sun), houses one of the more interesting collections in Vietnam – ranging from lacquer- and enamelware to contemporary oil paintings by Vietnamese and foreign artists. If that doesn't sound enticing, just go to see the huge hall with its beautifully tiled floors. On the 1st floor is a display of officially accepted contemporary art: most of it is just kitsch or desperate attempts to master abstract art, but occasionally something brilliant is displayed here. Most of the recent art is for sale and prices are fair.

The 2nd floor has older, politically correct art. Some of it is pretty crude: pictures of heroic figures waving red flags, children with rifles, a wounded soldier joining the Communist Party, innumerable tanks and weaponry, grotesque Americans and God-like reverence for Ho Chi Minh. However, it's worth seeing because Vietnamese artists managed not to be as dull and conformist as their counterparts in Eastern Europe sometimes were. Once you've passed several paintings and sculptures of Uncle Ho, you will see that those artists who studied before 1975 managed to somehow transfer their own aesthetics onto the world of their prescribed subjects. Most impressive are some drawings of prison riots in 1973 and some remarkable abstract paintings.

The 3rd floor has a good collection of older art dating back to the 4th century, including Oc-Eo (Funan) sculptures of Vishnu, the Buddha and other revered figures (carved in both wood and stone), which resemble styles of ancient Greece and Egypt. You will also find here the best Cham pieces outside of Danang. Also interesting are the many pieces of Indian art, such as stone elephant heads. Some pieces clearly originated in Angkor culture.

HO CHI MINH MUSEUM

This **museum** (Khu Luu Niem Bac Ho; Map p336; ☎ 840 0647; 1 Đ Nguyen Tat Thanh; admission 5000d; 7.30-11.30am & 1.30-5pm) is in the old customs house in District 4, just across Ben Nghe Channel from the quayside end of ĐL Ham Nghi. Nicknamed the 'Dragon House' (Nha Rong), it was built in 1863. The tie between Ho Chi Minh and the museum building is tenuous: 21-year-old Ho, having signed on as a stoker and galley boy on a French freighter, left Vietnam from here in 1911 and thus began 30 years of exile in France, the Soviet Union, China and elsewhere.

The museum houses many of Ho's personal effects, including some of his clothing (he was a man of informal dress), sandals, his beloved US-made Zenith radio and other memorabilia. The explanatory signs in the museum are in Vietnamese, but if you know something about Uncle Ho (see p34) you should be able to follow most of the photographs and exhibits.

XA LOI PAGODA

Famed as the repository of a sacred relic of the Buddha, **Xa Loi Pagoda** (Map p336; 89 Đ Ba Huyen Thanh Quan) was built in 1956. In August 1963 truckloads of armed men under the command of President Ngo Dinh Diem's brother, Ngo Dinh Nhu, attacked Xa Loi Pagoda, which had become a centre of opposition to the Diem government. The pagoda was ransacked and 400 monks and nuns, including the country's 80-year-old Buddhist patriarch, were arrested. This raid and others elsewhere helped solidify opposition among Buddhists to the Diem regime, a crucial factor in the US decision to support the coup against Diem. This pagoda was also the site of several self-immolations by monks protesting against the Diem regime and the American War.

Women enter the main hall of Xa Loi Pagoda by the staircase on the right as you come in the gate; men use the stairs on the left. The walls of the sanctuary are adorned with paintings depicting the Buddha's life.

Xa Loi Pagoda is in District 3 near Đ Dien Bien Phu. A monk preaches every Sunday from 8am to 10am. On days of the full moon and new moon, special prayers are held from 7am to 9am and 7pm to 8pm.

TRAN HUNG DAO TEMPLE

This small **temple** (Map pp334-5; 36 Đ Vo Thi Sau; 6-11am & 2-6pm Mon-Fri) is dedicated to Tran Hung Dao, a national hero who in 1287 vanquished an invasion force, said to have numbered 300,000 men, that had been dispatched by the Mongol emperor Kublai Khan. The temple is a block northeast of the telecommunication dishes that are between Đ Dien Bien Phu and Đ Vo Thi Sau.

The public park between the dishes and ĐL Hai Ba Trung was built in 1983 on the site of the **Massiges Cemetery**, a burial ground for French soldiers and settlers. The remains of French military personnel were exhumed and repatriated to France. The tomb of the 18th-century French missionary and diplomat Pigneau de Béhaine, Bishop of Adran, which was completely destroyed after reunification, was also here.

NOTRE DAME CATHEDRAL

Built between 1877 and 1883, **Notre Dame Cathedral** (Map p350; Đ Han Thuyen) is set in the heart of HCMC's government quarter. The cathedral faces Đ Dong Khoi. It is neo-Romanesque with two 40m-high square towers tipped with iron spires, which dominate the city's skyline. In front of the cathedral (in the centre of the square bounded by the main post office) is a statue of the Virgin Mary. If the front gates are locked, try the door on the side of the building that faces Reunification Palace.

Unusually, this cathedral has no stained-glass windows: the glass was a casualty of fighting during WWII. A number of foreign travellers worship here and the priests are allowed to add a short sermon in French or English to their longer presentations in Vietnamese. The 9.30am Sunday mass might be the best one for tourists to attend.

MARIAMMAN HINDU TEMPLE

This is the only **Hindu temple** (Chua Ba Mariamman; Map p336; 45 Đ Truong Dinh) still in use in HCMC and is a little piece of southern India in the centre of town. Though there are only 50 to 60 Hindus in HCMC – all of them Tamils – this temple is also considered sacred by many ethnic Vietnamese and ethnic Chinese. Indeed, it is reputed to have miraculous powers. The temple was built at the end of the 19th century and dedicated to the Hindu goddess Mariamman.

The lion to the left of the entrance used to be carried around the city in a street procession every autumn. In the shrine in the middle of the temple is **Mariamman**, flanked by her guardians Maduraiveeran (to her left) and Pechiamman (to her right). In front of the Mariamman figure are two *linga.* Favourite offerings placed nearby often include joss sticks, jasmine, lilies and gladioli. The wooden stairs on the left (as you enter the building) lead to the roof, where you'll find two colourful **towers** covered with innumerable figures of lions, goddesses and guardians.

After reunification, the government took over the temple and turned part of it into a factory for joss sticks. Another section was occupied by a company producing seafood for export – the seafood was dried on the roof in the sun.

Mariamman Hindu Temple is only three blocks west of Ben Thanh Market. Take off your shoes before stepping onto the slightly raised platform.

SAIGON CENTRAL MOSQUE

Built by South Indian Muslims in 1935 on the site of an earlier mosque, the **Saigon Central Mosque** (Map p350; 66 Đ Dong Du) is an immaculately clean and well-kept island of calm in the middle of the bustling Dong Khoi area. In front of the sparkling white-and-blue structure, with its four nonfunctional minarets, is a pool for the ritual ablutions required by Islamic law before prayers. Take off your shoes before entering the sanctuary.

The simplicity of the mosque is in marked contrast to the exuberance of Chinese temple decoration, and the rows of figures facing elaborate ritual objects in Buddhist pagodas. Islamic law strictly forbids using human or animal figures for decoration.

Only half a dozen Indian Muslims remain in HCMC; most of the community fled in 1975. As a result, prayers – held five times a day – are sparsely attended, except on Friday, when several dozen worshippers (mainly non-Indian Muslims) are present.

There are 12 other mosques serving the 5000 or so Muslims in HCMC.

TON DUC THANG MUSEUM

This small, seldom-visited **museum** (Bao Tang Ton Duc Thang; Map p350; ☎ 829 7542; 5 Đ Ton Duc Thang; admission US$1; ⏰ 7.30-11.30am & 1.30-5pm Tue-Fri) is dedicated to Ton Duc Thang, Ho Chi Minh's successor as president of Vietnam, who was born in Long Xuyen, An Giang province, in 1888. He died in office in 1980. Photos and displays illustrate his role in the Vietnamese Revolution, including a couple of very lifelike exhibits representing the time he spent imprisoned on Con Son Island (p397).

The museum is on the waterfront, half a block north of the Tran Hung Dao statue.

PEOPLE'S COMMITTEE BUILDING

HCMC's gingerbread **Hôtel de Ville** (Map p350), one of the city's most prominent landmarks, is now somewhat incongruously the home of the Ho Chi Minh City People's Committee. Built between 1901 and 1908, the Hôtel de Ville is situated at the northwestern end of ĐL Nguyen Hue, facing the river. The former hotel is notable for its gardens, ornate façade and elegant interior lit with crystal chandeliers. It's easily the most photographed building in Vietnam. At night, the exterior is usually covered with thousands of geckos feasting on insects.

Unfortunately, you'll have to content yourself with admiring the exterior only. The building is not open to the public and requests by tourists to visit the interior are rudely rebuffed.

MUNICIPAL THEATRE

A grand colonial building with a sweeping staircase, the **Municipal Theatre** (Nha Hat Thanh Pho; Map p350; ☎ 829 9976; Lam Son Sq) is hard to miss at the intersection of Đ Dong Khoi and ĐL Le Loi. For information on performances held here, see p369.

CONG VIEN VAN HOA PARK

Next to the old Cercle Sportif, which was an elite sporting club during the French-colonial period, the bench-lined walks of **Cong Vien Van Hoa Park** (Map p336) are shaded with avenues of enormous tropical trees.

In the morning, you can often see people here practising the art of *thai cuc quyen,* or slow-motion shadow boxing. Within the park is also a small-scale model of Nha Trang's most famous Cham towers.

This place still has an active **sports club** that is possible to visit. It has 11 tennis courts, a passable swimming pool and a clubhouse, all of which have a faded colonial feel about them. The tennis courts are available for hire at a reasonable fee and hourly tickets are on sale for use of the pool. The antique dressing rooms are quaint, but there are no lockers.

There are also Roman-style baths and a coffee shop overlooking the colonnaded pool.

Other facilities include a gymnasium, table tennis, weights, wrestling mats and ballroom-dancing classes.

Cong Vien Van Hoa Park is adjacent to the Reunification Palace. There are entrances across from 115 Đ Nguyen Du and on Đ Nguyen Thi Minh Khai.

BINH SOUP SHOP

It might seem strange to introduce a noodle-soup restaurant as a sight, but there is more to **Binh Soup Shop** (Map p336; ☎ 848 3775; 7 Đ Ly Chinh Tha Thang, District 3; noodle soup 15,000d) than just the soup. The Binh Soup Shop was the secret headquarters of the VC in Saigon. It was from here that the VC planned its attack on the US embassy and other places in Saigon during the Tet Offensive of 1968. One has to wonder how many US soldiers ate here, completely unaware that the staff were all VC infiltrators. By the way, the *pho* isn't bad here.

Cholon

A jewellery box of interesting Chinese-style temples awaits in Cholon (District 5) – it's well worth heading over to Chinatown for a half-day or more to explore. Aside from the temples and pagodas, you can sample some excellent Chinese and Vietnamese food – or have a swim at one of the water parks, if you get templed out.

While you're roaming, stroll over to the strip of **traditional herb shops** (Map p346; Đ Hai Thuong Lan Ong) between Đ Luong Nhu Hoc and Đ Trieu Quang Phuc for an olfactory experience you won't soon forget. Here the streets are filled with amazing sights, sounds and, most of all, rich herbal smells.

QUAN AM PAGODA

One of Cholon's most active pagodas, **Quan Am Pagoda** (Map p346; 12 Đ Lao Tu) was founded by the Fujian Congregation in the early 19th century and displays obvious Chinese influences. It's named for the Goddess of Mercy, Quan The Am Bo Tat whose statue lies hidden behind a remarkably ornate exterior.

Fantastic ceraminc scenes decorate the roof and depict figures from traditional Chinese plays and stories. The tableaux include ships, village houses and several ferocious dragons. Other unique features of this pagoda are the gold-and-lacquer panels of the entrance doors. Just inside, the walls of the porch are murals, in slight relief, of scenes of China from around the time of Quan Cong. There are elaborate woodcarvings above the porch.

In the courtyard behind the main sanctuary, in the pink-tiled altar, is a figure of A Pho, the Holy Mother Celestial Empress, while Quan The Am Bo Tat, dressed in white embroidered robes, stands nearby.

PHUOC AN HOI QUAN PAGODA

Built in 1902 by the Fujian Congregation, **Phuoc An Hoi Quan Pagoda** (Map p346; 184 Đ Hung Vuong) is one of the most beautifully ornamented pagodas in HCMC. Of special interest are the many small porcelain figures, the elaborate brass ritual objects and the fine woodcarvings on the altars, walls, columns and hanging lanterns. From outside the building you can see the ceramic scenes, each containing innumerable small figurines, which decorate the roof.

To the left of the entrance is a life-size figure of the sacred horse of Quan Cong. Before leaving on a journey, people make offerings to the horse, then stroke its mane and ring the bell around its neck. Behind the main altar, with its stone and brass incense braziers, is Quan Cong, to whom the pagoda is dedicated.

TAM SON HOI QUAN PAGODA

Built by the Fujian Congregation in the 19th century, **Tam Son Hoi Quan Pagoda** (Chua Ba Chua; Map p346; 118 Đ Trieu Quang Phuc) retains most of its original rich ornamentation. The pagoda is dedicated to Me Sanh, the Goddess of Fertility. It's particularly popular among local women who come here to pray for children.

Among the striking figures presented in this pagoda is the deified General Quan Cong with his long black beard. He's found to the right of the covered courtyard. Flanking him are two guardians, the Mandarin General Chau Xuong on the left and the Administrative Mandarin Quan Binh on the right. Next to Chau Xuong is Quan Cong's sacred red horse.

Across the courtyard from Quan Cong is a small room containing ossuary jars and memorials in which the dead are represented by their photographs. Next to this chamber is a small room containing the papier-mâché head of a dragon of the type used by the Fujian Congregation for dragon dancing.

Tam Son Hoi Quan Pagoda is located close to 370 ĐL Tran Hung Dao.

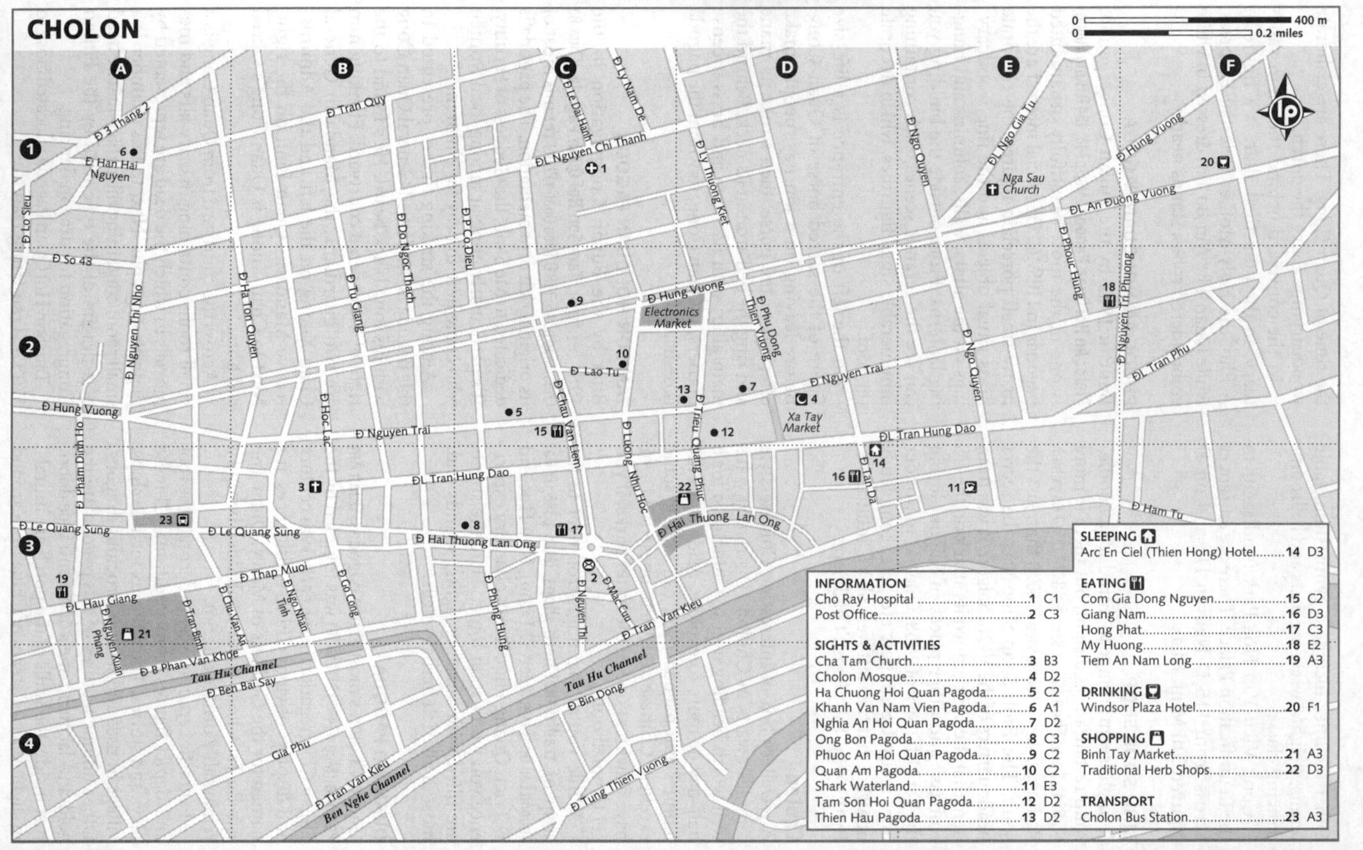
CHOLON
0 400 m
0 0.2 miles
INFORMATION
Cho Ray Hospital 1 C1
Post Office 2 C3
SIGHTS & ACTIVITIES
Cha Tam Church 3 B3
Cholon Mosque 4 D2
Ha Chuong Hoi Quan Pagoda 5 C2
Khanh Van Nam Vien Pagoda 6 A1
Nghia An Hoi Quan Pagoda 7 D2
Ong Bon Pagoda 8 C3
Phuoc An Hoi Quan Pagoda 9 C2
Quan Am Pagoda 10 C2
Shark Waterland 11 E3
Tam Son Hoi Quan Pagoda 12 D2
Thien Hau Pagoda 13 D2
SLEEPING
Arc En Ciel (Thien Hong) Hotel 14 D3
EATING
Com Gia Dong Nguyen 15 C2
Giang Nam 16 D3
Hong Phat 17 C3
My Huong 18 E2
Tiem An Nam Long 19 A3
DRINKING
Windsor Plaza Hotel 20 F1
SHOPPING
Binh Tay Market 21 A3
Traditional Herb Shops 22 D3
TRANSPORT
Cholon Bus Station 23 A3

CHA TAM CHURCH

Cha Tam Church, built around the turn of the 19th century, with its façade of white and lime-green trim has a sleepy, tropical feel to it – a far cry from its role during one of Saigon's more harrowing epochs.

President Ngo Dinh Diem and his brother Ngo Dinh Nhu took refuge in **Cha Tam Church** (Map p346; 25 Đ Hoc Lac) on 2 November 1963, after fleeing the Presidential Palace during a coup attempt. When their efforts to contact loyal military officers (of whom there was almost none) failed, Diem and Nhu agreed to surrender unconditionally and revealed where they were hiding.

The coup leaders sent an M-113 armoured personnel carrier to the church and the two were taken into custody. However, before the vehicle reached central Saigon the soldiers had killed Diem and Nhu by shooting them at point-blank range and then repeatedly stabbing their bodies.

When news of the deaths was broadcast on radio, Saigon exploded with rejoicing. Portraits of the two were torn up and political prisoners, many of whom had been tortured, were set free. The city's nightclubs, which had closed because of the Ngos' conservative Catholic beliefs, were reopened. Three weeks later the US president, John F Kennedy, was assassinated. As his administration had supported the coup against Diem, some conspiracy theorists have speculated that Diem's family orchestrated Kennedy's death in retaliation.

The statue in the tower is of François Xavier Tam Assou (1855–1934), a Chinese-born vicar apostolic (delegate of the pope) of Saigon. Today, the church has a very active congregation of 3000 ethnic Vietnamese and 2000 ethnic Chinese.

Masses are held daily. Cha Tam Church is at the western end of ĐL Tran Hung Dao.

THIEN HAU PAGODA

Built by the Cantonese Congregation in the early 19th century, this large **pagoda** (Ba Mieu, Pho Mieu or Chua Ba; Map p346; 710 Đ Nguyen Trai) is dedicated to Thien Hau and always has a mix of worshippers and visitors, mingling beneath large coils of incense suspended overhead.

Thien Hau (also known as Tuc Goi La Ba) can travel over the oceans on a mat and ride the clouds to wherever she pleases. Her mobility allows her to save people in trouble on the high seas. The Goddess is very popular in Hong Kong and Taiwan, which might explain why this pagoda is included on so many tour-group agendas.

Though there are guardians to each side of the entrance, it is said that the real protectors of the pagoda are the two land turtles that live here. There are intricate ceramic friezes above the roof line of the interior courtyard. Near the huge braziers are two miniature wooden structures in which a small figure of Thien Hau is paraded around the nearby streets on the 23rd day of the third lunar month.

On the main dais are three figures of Thien Hau, one behind the other, all flanked by two servants or guardians. To the left of the dais is a bed for Thien Hau. To the right is a scale-model boat and on the far right is the Goddess Long Mau, Protector of Mothers and Newborns.

NGHIA AN HOI QUAN PAGODA

Built by the Chaozhou Chinese Congregation, **Nghia An Hoi Quan Pagoda** (Map p346; 678 Đ Nguyen Trai) is noteworthy for its gilded woodwork. A large carved wooden boat hangs over the entrance, and, inside to the left of the doorway is an enormous representation of Quan Cong's red horse with its groom. The great general Quan Cong himself occupies a position in a glass case behind the main altar, with his assistants flanking him on both sides. Nghia An Hoi

HO CHI MINH CITY

QUAN AM THI KINH

The legend goes that Quan Am Thi Kinh was a woman unjustly turned out of her home by her husband. She disguised herself as a monk and went to live in a pagoda, where a young woman accused her of fathering her child. She accepted the blame – and the responsibility that went along with it – and again found herself out on the streets, this time with her 'son'. Much later, about to die, she returned to the monastery to confess her secret. When the emperor of China heard of her story, he declared her the Guardian Spirit of Mother and Child.

It is believed that she has the power to bestow male offspring on those who fervently believe in her and as such is extremely popular with childless couples.

Quan lets its hair down on the 14th day of the first lunar month when various dances are staged in front of the pagoda, with offerings made to the spirits.

CHOLON MOSQUE

The clean lines and lack of ornamentation of the **Cholon Mosque** (Map p346; 641 Đ Nguyen Trai) contrast starkly with nearby Chinese and Vietnamese Buddhist pagodas. In the courtyard is a pool for ritual ablutions. Note the tiled niche in the wall *(mihrab)* indicating the direction of prayer, which is towards Mecca. The mosque was built by Tamil Muslims in 1932. Since 1975 it has served the Malaysian and Indonesian Muslim communities.

ONG BON PAGODA

Built by the Fujian Congregation, **Ong Bon Pagoda** (Chua Ong Bon & Nhi Phu Hoi Quan; Map p346; 264 ĐL Hai Thuong Lan Ong) is yet another atmospheric pagoda full of gilded carvings and the ever-present smoke of burning incense. It's dedicated to Ong Bon, the guardian who presides over happiness and wealth. In hope of securing good fortune from the deity, believers burn fake paper money in the pagoda's furnace, located across the courtyard from the pagoda entrance.

Another feature of the pagoda is the intricately carved and gilded wooden altar, which faces Ong Bon. Along the walls of the chamber are rather indistinct murals of five tigers (to the left) and two dragons (to the right).

HA CHUONG HOI QUAN PAGODA

This typical Fujian **pagoda** (Map p346; 802 Đ Nguyen Trai) is dedicated to Thien Hau, who was born in Fujian. The four carved stone pillars, wrapped in painted dragons, were made in China and brought to Vietnam by boat. There are interesting murals to each side of the main altar and impressive ceramic relief scenes on the roof.

The pagoda becomes extremely active during the **Lantern Festival**, a Chinese holiday held on the 15th day of the first lunar month (the first full moon of the new lunar year).

KHANH VAN NAM VIEN PAGODA

Built between 1939 and 1942 by the Cantonese Congregation, **Khanh Van Nam Vien Pagoda** (Map p346; 46/5 Đ Lo Sieu) is said to be the only Taoist pagoda in Vietnam and is unique for its colourful statues of Taoist disciples. The number of true Taoists in HCMC is estimated at no more than 5000, though most Chinese practise a mixture of Taoism and Buddhism.

Features to seek out at this pagoda include the unique 150cm-high statue of Laotse located upstairs. His surreal, mirror-edged halo is one of the more intriguing uses of fluorescent lighting. Off to the left of Laotse are two stone plaques with instructions for inhalation and exhalation exercises. A schematic drawing represents the human organs as a scene from rural China. The diaphragm, agent of inhalation, is at the bottom; the stomach is represented by a peasant ploughing with a water buffalo. The kidney is marked by four Yin-and-Yang symbols, the liver is shown as a grove of trees and the heart is represented by a circle with a peasant standing in it, above which is a constellation. The tall pagoda represents the throat and the broken rainbow is the mouth. At the top are mountains and a seated figure that represent the brain and imagination, respectively.

The pagoda operates a home for several dozen elderly people who have no family. Each of the old folk, most of whom are women, have their own wood stove (made of brick) on which they cook. Next door, which is also run by the pagoda, is a free medical clinic, which offers Chinese herbal medicines and acupuncture treatments to the community. If you would like to support this worthy venture you can leave a donation with the monks.

Prayers are held daily from 8am to 9am. In order to reach the pagoda, turn off Đ Nguyen Thi Nho, which runs perpendicular to Đ Hung Vuong (between Nos 269B and 271B).

Greater HCMC

Although Cholon has a high density of pagodas, there are several particularly striking ones out here, including the peaceful Giac Lam Pagoda with its dazzling architecture and ornamentation.

GIAC LAM PAGODA

Believed to be the oldest pagoda in greater HCMC, **Giac Lam Pagoda** (Map pp334-5; 118 Đ Lac Long Quan) dates from 1744. It's a fantastically atmospheric place full of gilded statues (over 100 in all), colourful wall panels (depicting among other things the path to enlightenment as well as the tortures awaiting those condemned to hell) with one of the country's most impressive stupas (which is 32m tall). For the sick and elderly, the pagoda is a minor pilgrimage sight, as it contains a bronze bell that when rung is believed to answer the prayers posted by petitioners. Home to several monks, the Buddhist pagoda also incorporates aspects of Taoism and Confucianism. It is well worth the trip out here from the city centre and is one of the city's cultural relics.

The pagoda is set in a peaceful, gardenlike setting with the **tombs** of venerated monks to the right of the two-tiered pagoda gate. The looming Bodhi or pipal tree *(bo de)* located in the front garden was the gift of a monk from Sri Lanka in 1953. Next to the tree is a gleaming white statue of Quan The Am Bo Tat standing on a lotus blossom – a symbol of purity.

Inside the reception area of the **main building** is the 18-armed Chuan De, another form of the Goddess of Mercy. Carved hardwood columns bear gilded Vietnamese inscriptions, with the portraits of great monks from previous generations (and dragons hidden in clouds) looking down on the proceedings.

The main **sanctuary** lies in the next room, filled with countless gilded figures. On the dais in the centre of the back row sits A Di Da, the Buddha of the Past (Amitabha), easily spotted by his colourful halo. The fat laughing fellow, seated with five children climbing all over him, is Ameda, the Buddha of enlightenment, compassion and wisdom. On the altars along the side walls of the sanctuary are various Bodhisattvas and two 10-panelled drawings: the first depicts the Judges of the 10 Regions of Hell – and the various gruesome treatments meted out to the unworthy. Next to it are 10 panels showing scenes from Thich Ca Buddha's life from birth to enlightenment.

The red-and-gold Christmas tree–shaped object is a wooden altar bearing 49 lamps and 49 miniature Bodhisattva statues. People pray for sick relatives or ask for happiness by contributing kerosene for use in the lamps. Petitioners' names and those of ill family members are written on slips of paper, which are attached to the branches of the 'tree'.

The frame of the large bronze bell in the corner resembles a bulletin board because petitioners have attached to it lists of names: those of people seeking happiness and those of the sick and the dead, placed there by relatives. It is believed that when the bell is rung, the sound will resonate to the heavens above and the underground heavens, carrying with it the attached supplications.

Prayers here consist of chanting to the accompaniment of drums, bells and gongs, and they follow a traditional rite seldom performed these days. Prayers are held daily from 4am to 5am, 11am to noon, 4pm to 5pm and 7pm to 9pm.

Giac Lam Pagoda is about 3km from Cholon in the Tan Binh district, best reached by taxi or *xe om*.

GIAC VIEN PAGODA

Architecturally similar to Giac Lam, this striking **pagoda** (Map pp334-5; Đ Lac Long Quan; 7-11.30am & 1.30-7pm) shares with it an atmosphere of scholarly serenity, though Giac Vien is less visited and in a more rural setting near Dam Sen Lake in District 11. The pagoda was founded by Hai Tinh Giac Vien in the late 1700s. It is said that Emperor Gia Long, who died in 1819, used to worship at Giac Vien. Today 10 monks live here. The pagoda remains a marvellously preserved artefact from the past, boasting some 100 lavish carvings of various divinities.

Hidden behind a warren of winding streets, the pagoda, like Giac Lam, has several impressive **tombs** on the right leading up to the pagoda itself. Funeral tablets line the first chamber, while the second chamber is dominated by a statue of Hai Tinh Giac Vien holding a horsetail switch. Nearby portraits depict his disciples and successors. Opposite Hai Tinh Giac Vien is a representation of the 18-armed Chuan De, who is flanked by two guardians.

The main **sanctuary** is on the other side of the wall behind the Hai Tinh Giac Vien statue with a dais behind a fantastic brass incense basin with fierce dragon heads emerging from each side. On the altar to the left of the dais is Dai The Chi Bo Tat; on the altar to the right is Quan The Am Bo Tat. The Guardian of the Pagoda is against the wall opposite the dais. Nearby is a 'Christmas tree' similar to the one in Giac Lam Pagoda (opposite). Lining the side walls are the Judges of the 10 Regions of Hell (holding scrolls) and 18 Bodhisattvas.

Giac Vien Pagoda is open during the hours listed, but go before dark as the electricity is often out in the evening. Prayers are held daily from 4am to 5am, 8am to 10am, 2pm to 3pm, 4pm to 5pm and 7pm to 9pm.

PHUNG SON PAGODA

This **pagoda** (Map pp334-5; Phung Son Tu & Chua Go; 1408 ĐL 3/2) is extremely rich in statuary made of bronze, wood, ceramic and hammered copper. It's peopled with a mix of gilded and beautifully carved statues (some painted). This Vietnamese Buddhist pagoda was built between 1802 and 1820 on the site of structures from the Oc-Eo (Funan) period, dating back at least to the early centuries of Christianity. Other foundations of Funanese buildings have also been discovered here.

Once upon a time, it was decided that Phung Son Pagoda should be moved to a different site. The pagoda's ritual objects – bells, drums, statues – were loaded onto the back of a white elephant, but the elephant slipped because of the great weight and all the precious objects fell into a nearby pond. This event was interpreted as an omen that the pagoda should remain at its original location. All the articles were retrieved except for the bell, which locals say was heard ringing, until about a century ago, whenever there was a full or new moon.

The main dais, with its many levels, is dominated by an enormous gilded A Di Da Buddha seated under a canopy flanked by long mobiles resembling human forms without heads. To the left of the main dais is an altar with a statue of Bodhidharma, who brought Buddhism from India to China. The statue, which is made of Chinese ceramic, has a face with Indian features.

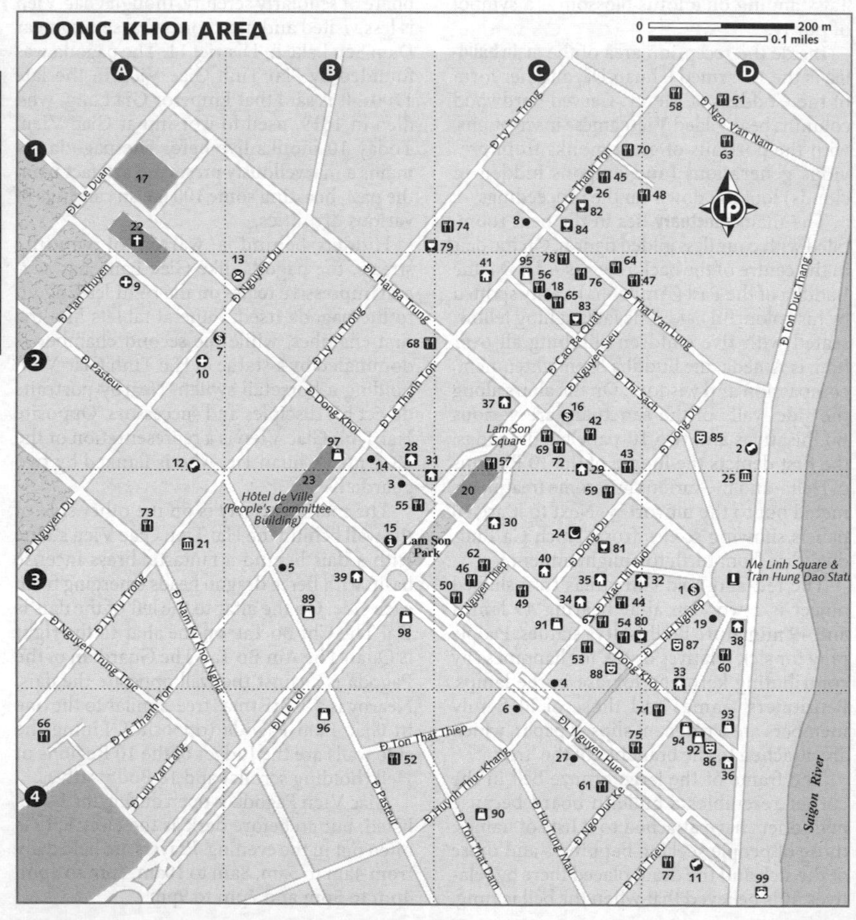

Phung Son Pagoda is in District 11. Prayers are held three times a day, from 4am to 5am, 4pm to 5pm and 6pm to 7pm. The main entrances are locked most of the time because of problems with theft, but the side entrance (to the left as you approach the building) is open during prayer times.

LE VAN DUYET TEMPLE

Dedicated to Marshal Le Van Duyet (1763–1831), this **temple** (Map pp334–5) is also his burial place as well as that of his wife's. The marshal was a South Vietnamese general and viceroy who helped put down the Tay Son Rebellion and reunify Vietnam. When the Nguyen dynasty came to power in 1802, he was elevated by Emperor Gia Long to the rank of marshal. Le Van Duyet fell into disfavour with Gia Long's successor, Minh Mang, who tried him posthumously and desecrated his grave. Emperor Thieu Tri, who succeeded Minh Mang, restored the tomb, thus fulfilling a prophesy of its destruction and restoration. Le Van Duyet was considered a national hero in the South before 1975, but is disliked by the communists because of his involvement in the expansion of French influence.

The temple itself was renovated in 1937 and has a distinctly modern feel to it, though since 1975 the government has done little to keep it from becoming dilapidated. Among the items on display are a portrait of Le Van Duyet, some

INFORMATION

ANZ Bank.........1 D3
Asiana Travel Mate.........(see 15)
Australian Consulate.........2 D2
Buffalo Tours.........(see 36)
Canadian Consulate.........(see 7)
DHL.........(see 13)
Fahasa Bookshop.........3 B3
Fahasa Bookshop.........4 C3
Federal Express.........5 B3
Grand Dentistry.........6 C4
HCMC Family Medical Practice.........(see 17)
HSBC.........7 A2
Institute of Cultural Exchange with France.........8 C1
International Medical Centre.........9 A2
International SOS.........10 A2
Japanese Embassy.........11 D4
Lao Consulate.........12 A2
Main Post Office.........13 B2
New Zealand Consulate.........(see 7)
Saigon Tourist.........14 B2
Tourist Information Center.........15 B3
Vietcombank.........16 C2

SIGHTS & ACTIVITIES

Aqua Day Spa.........(see 40)
Diamond Superbowl.........17 A1
Dong Du Salon.........(see 81)
Golden Lotus Foot Massage.........18 C2
Me Linh Square Point Building.........19 D3
Municipal Theatre.........20 C3
Museum of Ho Chi Minh City.........21 A3
Notre Dame Cathedral.........22 A1
People's Committee Building.........23 B3
Saigon Central Mosque.........24 C3
Ton Duc Thang Museum.........25 D3
Utopia Café.........26 C1
Zanadu Health Club.........27 C4

SLEEPING

Asian Hotel.........28 B2
Bong Sen Annexe.........29 C2
Caravelle Hotel.........30 C3
Continental Hotel.........31 B3
Dong Do Hotel.........32 C3
Grand Hotel.........33 D3
Huong Sen Hotel.........34 C3
Kim Long Hotel.........35 C3
Majestic Hotel.........36 D4
Park Hyatt Saigon.........37 C2
Renaissance Riverside Hotel.........38 D3
Rex Hotel.........39 B3
Sheraton Saigon.........40 C3
Spring Hotel.........41 C2

EATING

Akatonbo.........42 C2
Annam Gourmet Shop.........43 C2
Annie's Pizza.........44 C3
Ashoka.........45 C1
Augustin.........46 C3
Bi Bi.........47 C2
Bia Tuoi Pacific.........48 D1
Brodard Café.........49 C3
Camargue.........(see 83)
Ciao Café.........50 C3
Encore Angkor Plus.........51 D1
Fanny.........52 B4
Gallery Deli.........53 C3
Gardenstadt.........54 C3
Givral.........55 B3
Hakata.........56 C2
Highlands Coffee.........57 C2
Hoi An.........58 D1
Indian Canteen.........(see 24)
Java Coffee Bar.........59 C3
La Fourchette.........60 D3
La Niçoise.........61 C4
Le Jardin.........(see 8)
Lemon Grass.........62 C3
Mandarine.........63 D1
Mi Nhat So 1.........64 C2
Mogambo.........65 C2
Nam Giao.........66 A4
Nam Kha.........67 C3
Nam Phan.........68 B2
Pacharan.........69 C2
Paris Deli.........(see 96)
Pat à Chou.........(see 72)
Pau Hanna.........70 C1
Pho 24.........(see 72)
Pho Oso.........71 D4
Pomodoro.........72 C2
Quan An Ngon.........73 A3
Restaurant 31.........74 C1
Santa Lucia.........75 C4
Skewers.........76 C2
Urvashi.........77 D4
Veggy's.........78 C2
Xu.........(see 69)

DRINKING

Blue Gecko Bar.........79 B1
Heart of Darkness.........(see 82)
Manna.........80 C3
Q Bar.........(see 20)
Qing.........81 C3
Saigon Saigon Bar.........(see 30)
Samsara.........(see 49)
Sheridan's Irish House.........82 C1
Temple Club.........(see 52)
Vasco's.........83 C2
Wild Horse Saloon.........84 C1

ENTERTAINMENT

Apocalypse Now.........85 D2
Diamond Plaza Cinema.........(see 17)
Maxim's Dinner Theatre.........86 D4
Municipal Theatre.........(see 20)
Tropical Rainforest Disco.........87 D3
Underground.........88 C3

SHOPPING

Chi Chi.........89 B3
Huynh Thuc Khang Street Market.........90 C4
Khai Silk.........91 C3
Living & Giving.........(see 60)
Lotus.........92 D4
Nguyen Freres.........93 D4
Precious Qui.........94 D4
Reda.........95 C2
Saigon Centre.........96 B4
Song.........97 B2
Tax Department Store (Russian Market).........98 B3

TRANSPORT

Bach Dang Jetty (Hydrofoils to Vung Tau).........99 D4
Boats for Hire.........(see 99)

of his personal effects (including European-style crystal goblets) and other antiques. There are two wonderful life-size horse statues on either side of the entrance to the third and last chamber, which is kept locked.

During celebrations of Tet and on the 30th day of the seventh lunar month (the anniversary of Le Van Duyet's death), the tomb is thronged with pilgrims. Vietnamese used to come here to take oaths of good faith if they could not afford the services of a court of justice.

There are tropical fish on sale for visitors. The caged birds that are for sale are bought by pilgrims and freed to earn merit. The birds are often recaptured (and liberated again).

The temple is reached by heading north from the city centre on Đ Dinh Tien Hoang, all the way to ĐL Phan Dang Luu; it's easy to spot from the southeast corner.

AN QUANG PAGODA

This **pagoda** (Map pp334-5; Đ Su Van Hanh) gained some notoriety during the American War as the home of Thich Tri Quang, a powerful monk who led protests against the South Vietnamese government in 1963 and 1966. When the war ended you would have expected the communists to be grateful. Instead, he was placed under house arrest and later thrown into solitary confinement for 16 months. Thich Tri Quang was eventually released and is said to be still living at An Quang Pagoda.

An Quang Pagoda is on Đ Su Van Hanh, near the intersection with Đ Ba Hat, in District 10.

CHO QUAN CHURCH

Built by the French about 100 years ago, **Cho Quan Church** (Map pp334-5; 133 Đ Tran Binh Trong; ⌚ 4-7am & 3-6pm Mon-Sat, 4-9am & 1.30-6pm Sun) is one of the largest churches in HCMC. Jesus on the altar has a neon halo, though the best reason to come here is for the view from the belfry (a steep climb). The church is between ĐL Tran Hung Dao and Đ Nguyen Trai. Sunday masses are held at 5am, 6.30am, 8.30am, 4.30pm and 6pm.

ACTIVITIES

Bowling

Diamond Superbowl (Map p350; ☎ 825 7778; Diamond Plaza, 34 ĐL Le Duan; per hr from 120,000d; ⌚ 10-1am) This is a state-of-the-art, 32-lane bowling alley smack dab in the centre of town. It's very popular with locals and is notable for having fluorescent bowling balls and computerised scoring. Attached is a large amusement centre with billiards, a video-game arcade and shops.

Gyms & Pools

Even if you don't make it to one of Saigon's water parks (p355) or to Cong Vien Van Hoa Park (p344), some of HCMC's finer hotels have gyms with attractive swimming pools attached. You needn't stay there to swim, but you'll have to pay an admission fee of US$8 to US$18 per day. Hotels offering access to their pools include the **Legend** (☎ 823 3333; 2A Đ Ton Duc Thang, District 1), Park Hyatt Saigon (p360), Majestic Hotel (p360), Renaissance Riverside Hotel (p360) and Rex Hotel (p360).

There are a number of less-expensive public pools and some of the newer ones are in very good condition. These pools charge by the hour and this works out to be very cheap, if you're staying only a short time.

Lam Son Pool (Map pp334-5; ☎ 835 8028; 342 Đ Tran Binh Trong, District 5; admission per hr 5000d, after 5pm 6000d; ⌚ 8am-8pm) Has an Olympic-sized pool.

Lan Anh Club (Map pp334-5; ☎ 862 7144; 291 Cach Mang Thang Tam, District 10; admission gym/pool 40,000d/25,000d; ⌚ pool 6am-9pm) Good gym here.

Workers' Club (Map p336; ☎ 930 1819; 55B Đ Nguyen Thi Minh Khai, District 3; admission per hr 10,000d)

Golf

If you're serious about golf, there are top-notch courses in both Phan Thiet (p305) and Dalat (p312). Visit www.vietnamgolfresorts.com for more information on the courses and reasonably priced golf package tours.

Vietnam Golf and Country Club (Cau Lac Bo Golf Quoc Te Viet Nam; ☎ 733 0126; www.vietnamgolfcc.com; Long Thanh My Village, District 9; driving range/full round US$10/85), situated about 15km east of central HCMC, was the first in Vietnam to provide night golfing under floodlights. Other facilities include tennis courts and a swimming pool.

Rach Chiec Driving Range (☎ 896 0756; Hwy 1, An Phu Village, District 9; 50 balls 50,000d; ⌚ 6am-10pm) is a good place to practise your swing; clubs, shoes and instructors can be hired. It's a 20-minute drive north from central HCMC.

Massages & Spas

HCMC offers some truly fantastic settings for pampering – the perfect antidote to a frenetic day spent dodging motorbikes. While many midrange and upmarket hotels offer massage service, some are more legitimate than others.

L'Apothiquaire (Map p336; ☎ 932 5181; www.lapothiquaire.com; 64A Đ Truong Dinh; per hr massage US$20; 9am-9pm;), the city's most elegant spa, is housed in a pretty, white mansion tucked down a quiet alley, with numerous services available. Guests enjoy body wraps, massages, facials, foot treatments and herbal baths, and L'Apothiquaire makes its own line of lotions and cosmetics. Those seeking a bit more activity can try yoga, t'ai chi or pilates classes. There's also an excellent meal served during lunchtime, and if you become a member (or book a package), you'll have free use of the pool and sauna.

Vietnamese Traditional Massage Institute (Map p357; ☎ 839 6697; 185 Đ Cong Quynh; per hr 35,000-45,000d, sauna 25,000d; 9am-9pm) is not the cleanest setting, but it does offer inexpensive, no-nonsense massages performed by well-trained blind masseurs from the Ho Chi Minh City Association for the Blind.

Spa Tropic (Map p336; ☎ 822 8895; www.spatropic.com; 187B ĐL Hai Ba Trung, District 3; per hr massage US$25; 10am-8pm) is a good place to spoil yourself with a top-notch 'proper' massage. This Zen-like beauty spa offers an array of aromatherapy facial treatments, body treatments and therapeutic massage, from Swedish and deep-tissue to shiatsu. Spa Tropic is found in the same quiet alley as Tib Restaurant (p362). Call ahead for reservations.

Dong Du Salon (Map p350; ☎ 823 2414; 31 Đ Dong Du; 10am-11pm), above the Qing bar, this well-appointed place offers manicures (US$2), pedicures (US$2) and that all-important foot message (US$10 for 70 minutes).

Aqua Day Spa (Map p350; ☎ 827 2828; www.aquadayspasaigon.com; Sheraton Saigon, 88 Đ Dong Khoi; 10am-11pm) is HCMC's most luxurious spa and is a beautifully set affair offering a range of treatments, including warm stone massage (US$55 for 1½ hours), herbal scrubs (US$45 for one hour), foot pampering (US$35 for 45 minutes) and back massages (US$25 for 30 minutes).

Zanadu Health Club (Map p350; ☎ 822 2999; enquiries@saigon.duxton.com.vn; 63 ĐL Nguyen Hue), the spa at the Duxton Hotel, is a great place to drop in for a massage (US$23 for one hour).

Golden Lotus Foot Massage Club (Map p350; ☎ 829 6400; 20 ĐL Thi Sach) delivers bliss to overworked gams, and also gives general body massage. Lotus' most popular package includes a 90-minute massage followed by ten minutes of 'Lotus tea time' (US$13).

Relax House (Map p357; ☎ 404 2284; 242 Đ Bui Vien; 10am-11pm) offers pedicures (US$2), manicures (US$2) and foot massages (45 minutes US$7).

Yoga & Martial Arts

There are several places in town to take yoga classes, including the calming L'Apothiquaire (left). If you're interested in martial arts, the best place to see (or try) *thai cuc quyen* is at Cong Vien Van Hoa Park (p344) or in the Cholon district, where there is a large ethnic-Chinese population. Ask the staff at the Arc En Ciel Hotel (p360) to point you in the right direction.

Saigon Yoga (Map p336; ☎ 910 5181; www.saigonyoga.com; 10F Đ Nguyen Thi Minh Khai; price per class/month US$12/90; 8am-7pm) is a small yoga studio (tucked down a narrow alley) offering Vikram, Ashtanga, Vinyasa and power yoga as well as pilates classes taught by US and Singaporean instructors. Short-term visitors can take advantage of seven days of unlimited yoga for US$20.

K1 Boxing Centre (Map pp334-5; ☎ 0918 337 111; www.teamminetti.com; 11th fl, 159/52/21B Đ Tran Van Dang; per class 200,000d; 9am-6pm Mon-Fri) is ideal for kick-boxing enthusiasts, and the place to improve your technique. The full-contact dojo is run by Frenchman David 'Serial Striker' Minetti. Private lessons and monthly rates are available.

WALKING TOUR

Although HCMC is a sprawling metropolis – and growing by the day – there is still some splendid exploring you can do on foot. This walking tour covers the city centre, District 1 (or 'Saigon'), and can be done in one, stimulus-filled day.

Begin your excursion bright and early in **Pham Ngu Lao (1)**, a teeming area of colourful shops and backpacker cafés. Skip the greasy eggs and bacon, however, and instead grab a bowl of steaming *pho*, which you can enjoy from a sidewalk vendor (prevalent along Đ Bui Vien) or a few blocks away from **Pho 2000 (2; p365)**, serving tasty noodles to locals, foreigners and the odd dignitary from time to time – including former US president Bill Clinton.

Cross the road and enter the vast indoor **Ben Thanh Market** (**3**; p372), which is at its bustling best in the morning. After exploring the market, cross the massive roundabout (carefully!), where you'll see a statue of **Tran Nguyen Hai (4)** on horseback. One short block south, on Đ Pho Duc Chinh, is the quaint **Fine Arts Museum** (**5**; p342), where you can tour some exhibits, and peek in some excellent galleries behind the museum. Zigzag east to ĐL Ham Nghi and turn north again on Đ Ton That Dam to stroll through the colourful outdoor **street market (6)**. Nearby, on Đ Ton That Dam, you can stop for a snack at **Fanny** (**7**; p365), which serves Saigon's best ice cream. From there, take a left to Đ Pasteur and continue up to ĐL Le Loi, the large boulevard leading towards the grand and thoughtfully restored **Municipal Theatre** (**8**; p344).

One short block before the theatre, turn left at the **Rex Hotel** (**9**; p360) and head up ĐL Nguyen Hue. Just ahead, at the northern end of the boulevard, is the stately French-colonial era **Hôtel de Ville** (**10**; p344). You'll have to admire it from the outside because it's now home to the local People's Commit-

WALK FACTS

Start Pham Ngu Lao
End Sheraton Saigon
Distance 5km
Duration approximately 6 hours

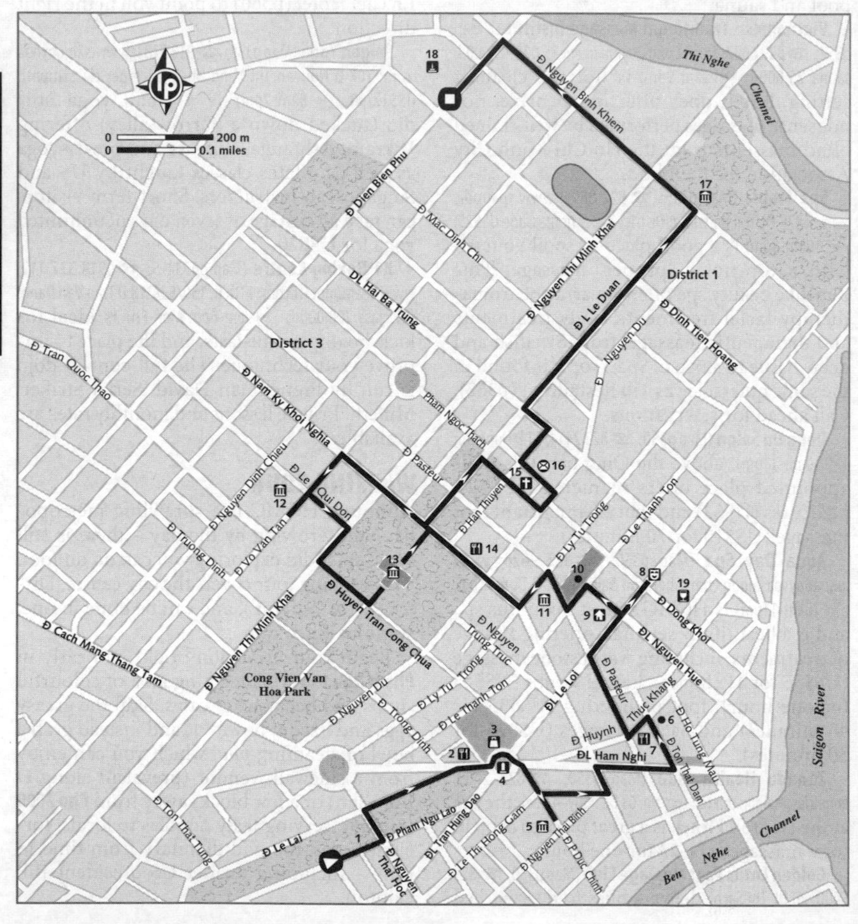

tee – requests to visit the interior are denied. However, a one-block walk south on Đ Le Thanh Ton will bring you to the **Museum of Ho Chi Minh City** (**11**; p341), where visitors are warmly received.

The popular **War Remnants Museum** (**12**; p340) is just a few blocks along Đ Nam Ky Khoi Nghia then left on Đ Vo Van Tan. Nearby is the **Reunification Palace** (**13**; p339). Break up your sightseeing with lunch at one of many excellent restaurants nearby, including **Quan An Ngon** (**14**; p361).

After refuelling, stroll north along ĐL Le Duan, stopping to look at **Notre Dame Cathedral** (**15**; p343) and the impressive French-style **post office** (**16**; p338). There you can buy lovely stamps and post letters to your soon-to-be-jealous friends back home. If your energy is waning, call it a day and skip to No 19, otherwise continue along Đ Le Duan to the end of the boulevard where you'll find one of HCMC's best museums, the excellent **History Museum** (**17**; p341), which is on the grounds of the zoo and botanic gardens.

A few blocks northwest along Đ Nguyen Binh Khiem will bring you to **Jade Emperor Pagoda** (**18**; p342), a remarkably peaceful (and photogenic) refuge just steps from a busy avenue.

As the afternoon wanes, end your walking tour at the rooftop bar of the **Sheraton Saigon** (**19**; p360) – if coming from the Jade Emperor Pagoda, consider hopping on a *xe om* and zipping there for 10,000d. With a refreshing cocktail in hand, you can enjoy fine views over the city – a fair bit of which you've just traversed.

COURSES

Cooking

Several hotels offer cooking classes, including the following:

Caravelle Hotel (Map p350; ☎ 823 4999; 19 Đ Lam Son Sq, District 1; per person US$40) offers a one-day class that includes a visit to the market, followed by in-depth instruction on meal preparation. A minimum of 10 are needed per class.

Bi Saigon (Map p357; ☎ 836 0678; www.bisaigon.com; 185/26 Đ Pham Ngu Lao, District 1; per person per dish US$15). organises private cooking classes on request.

Language

The majority of foreign-language students enrol at **Teacher Training University** (Dai Hoc Su Pham; Map pp334-5; ☎ 835 5100; ciecer@hcm.vnn.vn; 280 An Duong Vuong, District 5; private/group class US$4.50/3), a department of Ho Chi Minh City University.

Classes at the **University of Social Sciences & Humanities** (Dai Hoc Khoa Hoc Xa Hoi Va Nhan Van; Map p336; ☎ 822 5009; 12 Dinh Tien Hoang, District 1; group class per hr US$3) run on a term schedule.

More informal study is available at **Utopia Café** (Map p350; ☎ 824 2487; shop@utopia-café.com; 17/6A Đ Le Thanh Ton, District 1; private lessons per 60/90 min 70,000/90,000d; ⏰ 8.30am-9pm), with one-on-one instruction. Utopia can also arrange visa extensions.

HCMC FOR CHILDREN

See p368 for information about Binh Quoi Tourist Village, a great place for kids.

Dam Sen Park

Probably the single best place in HCMC for kids, the sprawling **Dam Sen Park** (Map pp334-5; ☎ 858 7826; 3 Đ Hoa Binh; www.damsenpark.com.vn; adult/child 18,000/12,000d; ⏰ 7am-9pm) provides a wide variety of amusements, including paddle-boat rides around a lake lined with dragons, games, rides (a monorail courses around the park – a good way to get your bearings; there's also a roller coaster, Ferris wheel and bumper cars) and various parks and theme areas – orchid gardens, an aviary, a dinosaur park and the like. On weekends the bandstand sees a range of shows, featuring singing and dancing warriors, rabbits and hip-hop stars all under the age of 12. Fishing is allowed in the lakes. There's also a water park (p356) on the grounds. Dam Sen Park is located in District 11, northwest of Cholon.

Water Parks

Outside the city centre, a slew of water parks offer cool relief from the heat. Anyone with kids and a half-day to spare will quickly come to appreciate these wet playgrounds on a sweltering day. To avoid the crowds, avoid going on weekends and public holidays.

Saigon Water Park (☎ 897 0456; Đ Kha Van Can, Thu Duc district; adult/child 60,000/35,000d, swim-only ticket 35,000d; ⏰ 9am-5pm Mon-Sat, 9am-6pm Sun & public holidays), a giant oasis in the suburbs, lies on the banks of the Saigon River. It's chock-full of pools and water rides, including loop-the-loop slides, a children's wading pool and even a wave pool. To get here, a meter taxi costs about 60,000d; shuttle buses (every half-hour) from Ben Thanh Market (Map p336) cost 5000d.

Dam Sen Water Park (Map pp334-5; ☎ 858 8418; www.damsenwaterpark.com.vn; 3 Đ Hoa Binh; adult/child 45,000/30,000d; 9am-6pm) is closer to central HCMC than Saigon Water Park. It has water slides, rivers with rapids (or slow currents) and rope swings for flips and fantastic belly flops.

Shark Waterland (Map p346; ☎ 853 7867; 600 Đ Ham Tu, district 5; admission 20,000-45,000d; 8am-9pm Mon-Fri, 10am-9pm Sat & Sun), despite the ominous name, is a good spot if you happen to be in Cholon. On a smaller scale than the larger water parks around HCMC, this place still has pools and slides.

Botanic Gardens

One of the first projects undertaken by the French after they established Cochinchina as a colony was to found the **gardens** (Map p336; Thao Cam Vien; ☎ 829 3901; 2 Đ Nguyen Binh Khiem; adult/child 8000/4000d; 7am-10pm). Though once one of the finest such gardens in Asia, they're now merely a pleasant place for a stroll under giant tropical trees. The emphasis is on the fun fair, with kids' rides, a fun house, miniature train, house of mirrors and such.

We strongly recommend against visiting the poorly kept zoo animals, which live at the usual (ie marginal) Vietnamese standard.

Standing just inside the main zoo gate (Đ Nguyen Binh Khiem on the eastern end of ĐL Le Duan) you'll be flanked by two striking architectural gems, the impressive Temple of King Hung Vuong and the History Museum (p341).

TOURS

There are surprisingly few day tours of HCMC itself available, though any local travel agent can come up with something for a fee. Hiring a *cyclo* for a half-day or full day of sightseeing is an interesting option, but be sure to agree on the price before setting out (most drivers charge around US$1 per hour).

There are heaps of organised tours to the outlying areas such as the Cu Chi Tunnels (p378), Tay Ninh (p381)and the Mekong Delta (p400). Some tours are day trips and other are overnighters. The cheapest tours are available from cafés and agencies in the Pham Ngu Lao area (see p339).

FESTIVALS & EVENTS

Saigon Cyclo Race (mid-March) Professional and amateur *cyclo* drivers find out who's fastest; money raised is donated to local charities.

Festival at Lang Ong (30th day of 7th lunar month) People pray for happiness and the health of the country at the Ong Temple in HCMC's Binh Thanh district; plays and musical performances are staged.

SLEEPING

District 1 is the undisputed lodging capital of HCMC, though the decision whether to go east (fancy) or west (cheap) depends on what you're after. Budget travellers often head straight to the Pham Ngu Lao area (Map p357), where thrifty hotels and backpacker-filled cafés line the streets. Those seeking upscale digs go to Dong Khoi area (Map p350), home to the city's best hotels, restaurants and bars. For an alternative universe, try Cholon (Map p346), home to pagodas, Chinese eateries and which sees many visitors from Hong Kong and Taiwan.

Budget

If you don't know where to stay but are limited by budget, take a taxi into Pham Ngu Lao and proceed on foot. Lugging your bags around makes you a prime target for touts – consider dropping your gear at one of the travellers cafés and walking from there. Most won't mind keeping an eye on your luggage for you and they'll be happy to tell you about their tour programmes. If you book ahead, most hotels will fetch you at the airport for around US$5.

PHAM NGU LAO

Three streets – Đ Pham Ngu Lao, Đ De Tham and Đ Bui Vien – along with intersecting alleys form the heart of this backpacker ghetto, with well over a hundred places to stay. Among the options are countless family-run guesthouses (US$6 to US$12), newer, spiffier hotels (US$10 to US$25) and even a dorm or two.

Yellow House (Map p357; ☎ 836 8830; yellowhousehotel@yahoo.com; 31 Đ Bui Vien; dm/s/d US$5/9/12;) One of the cheapest options in town if you don't mind bunking with strangers, Yellow House has two dormitories (a mixed seven-bed and a three-bed for men or women – whoever arrives first) as well as private rooms. Rooms are basic, but acceptable (some lack windows, some need a scrub) and there's a shared balcony. Breakfast included.

Nga Hoang (Map p357; ☎ 920 3356; www.yellowhousevn.com; 269/19 Đ Pham Ngu Lao; r US$8-20;) Just off Đ De Tham in a small alley, this very clean,

HO CHI MINH CITY

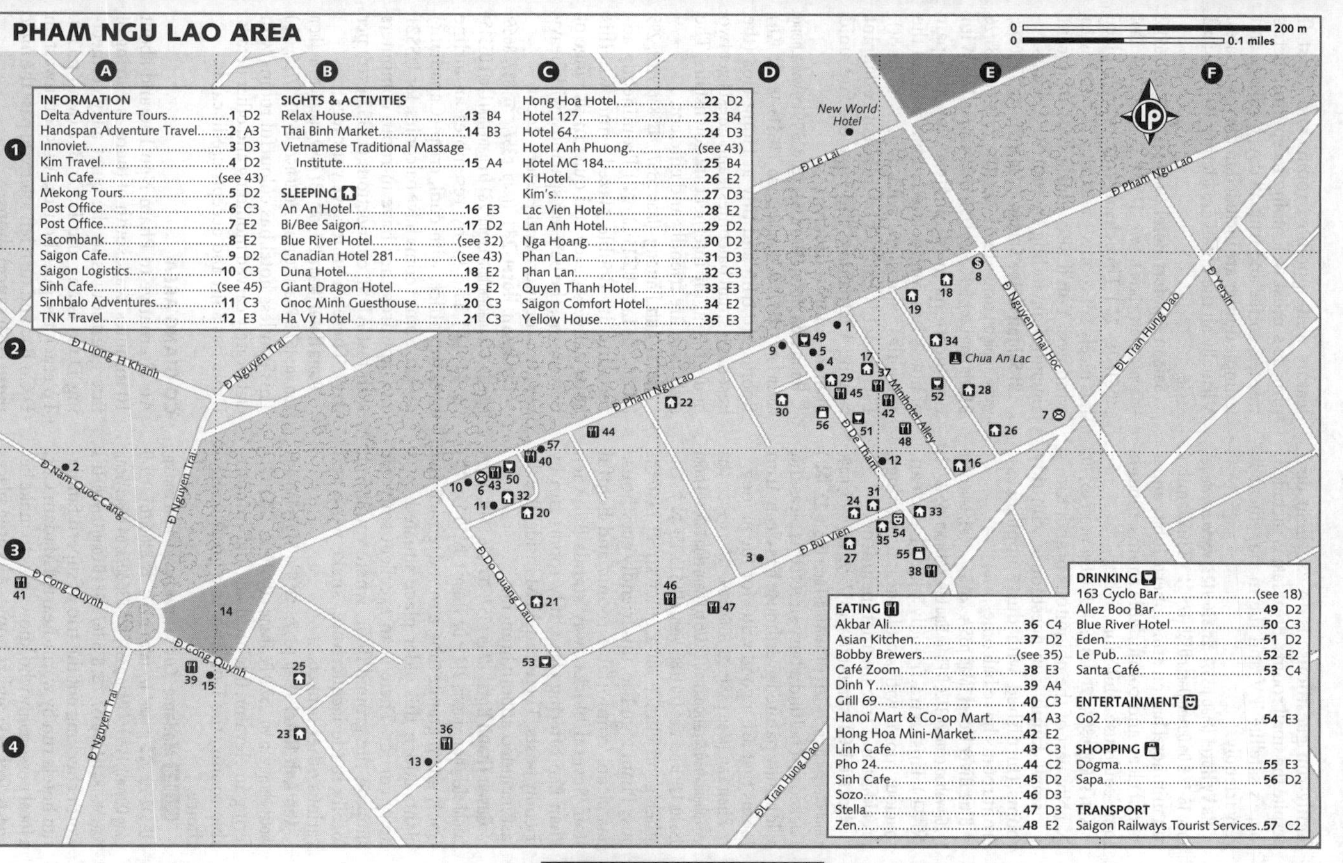
PHAM NGU LAO AREA
0 200 m
0 0.1 miles
INFORMATION
Delta Adventure Tours 1 D2
Handspan Adventure Travel 2 A3
Innoviet 3 D3
Kim Travel 4 D2
Linh Cafe (see 43)
Mekong Tours 5 D2
Post Office 6 C3
Post Office 7 E2
Sacombank 8 E2
Saigon Cafe 9 D2
Saigon Logistics 10 C3
Sinh Cafe (see 45)
Sinhbalo Adventures 11 C3
TNK Travel 12 E3
SIGHTS & ACTIVITIES
Relax House 13 B4
Thai Binh Market 14 B3
Vietnamese Traditional Massage Institute 15 A4
SLEEPING
An An Hotel 16 E3
Bi/Bee Saigon 17 D2
Blue River Hotel (see 32)
Canadian Hotel 281 (see 43)
Duna Hotel 18 E2
Giant Dragon Hotel 19 E2
Gnoc Minh Guesthouse 20 C3
Ha Vy Hotel 21 C3
Hong Hoa Hotel 22 D2
Hotel 127 23 B4
Hotel 64 24 D3
Hotel Anh Phuong (see 43)
Hotel MC 184 25 B4
Ki Hotel 26 E2
Kim's 27 D3
Lac Vien Hotel 28 E2
Lan Anh Hotel 29 D2
Nga Hoang 30 D2
Phan Lan 31 D3
Phan Lan 32 C3
Quyen Thanh Hotel 33 E3
Saigon Comfort Hotel 34 E2
Yellow House 35 E3
EATING
Akbar Ali 36 C4
Asian Kitchen 37 D2
Bobby Brewers (see 35)
Café Zoom 38 E3
Dinh Y 39 A4
Grill 69 40 C3
Hanoi Mart & Co-op Mart 41 A3
Hong Hoa Mini-Market 42 E2
Linh Cafe 43 C3
Pho 24 44 C2
Sinh Cafe 45 D2
Sozo 46 D3
Stella 47 D3
Zen 48 E2
DRINKING
163 Cyclo Bar (see 18)
Allez Boo Bar 49 D2
Blue River Hotel 50 C3
Eden 51 D2
Le Pub 52 E2
Santa Café 53 C4
ENTERTAINMENT
Go2 54 E3
SHOPPING
Dogma 55 E3
Sapa 56 D2
TRANSPORT
Saigon Railways Tourist Services 57 C2
New World Hotel
Đ Le Lai
Đ Pham Ngu Lao
Đ Nguyen Thai Hoc
ĐL Tran Hung Dao
Đ Yersin
Chua An Lac
Minihotel Alley
Đ De Tham
Đ Bui Vien
Đ Do Quang Dau
Đ Luong H Khanh
Đ Nguyen Trai
Đ Nam Quoc Cang
Đ Cong Quynh

family-run guesthouse is an excellent deal despite the small rooms. Breakfast is included, there's satellite TV and the management is very friendly.

Ha Vy Hotel (Map p357; ☎ 836 9123; www.havyhotel.com; 16-18 Đ Do Quang Dau; r US$8-12;) This family-run minihotel has an atmospheric lobby and a mix of clean and comfortable rooms, though some could use a bit more light.

Kim's (Map p357; ☎ 836 8584; 91 Đ Bui Vien; r US$10;) Not part of the ubiquitous brand, Kim's is a small, family-run guesthouse with tidy rooms (furnished with dusty appliances). Front rooms have balconies.

Blue River Hotel (Map p357; ☎ 837 6483; blueriver1126@yahoo.com; 283/2C Đ Pham Ngu Lao; s/d from US$10/12;) This extra-friendly place has clean, spacious rooms with simple, neat furnishings. Breakfast and free internet included.

Ngoc Minh Guesthouse (Map p357; ☎ 837 6407; ngocminhhotel@vnn.vn; 283/11 Đ Pham Ngu Lao; r US$10-12;) Tucked just behind a busy street, this pleasant, colourfully painted guesthouse has clean, trim rooms that are a good value for the money.

Phan Lan (Map p357; ☎ 836 9569;); Đ Pham Ngu Lao (phanlan36@yahoo.com; 283/6 Đ Pham Ngu Lao; s/d from US$10/12); Đ Bui Vien (70 Đ Bui Vien; r US$10-15;) Another good choice on a quiet street just off busy Pham Ngu Lao, this friendly guesthouse has clean, comfortable rooms and helpful staff. Several blocks away stands Bui Vien Phan Lan offering clean, tidy rooms run by friendly hosts. There's an ATM inside. Breakfast included at both branches.

Quyen Thanh Hotel (Map p357; ☎ 836 8570; quyenthanhhotel@hcm.vnn.vn; 212 Đ De Tham; r US$10-15;) Goofy green granite tubs, a round terrace and plants adorn this older place situated on a noisy corner. There is an excellent souvenir shop on the ground floor, where you'll find locally made lacquerware, snake wine and various other trinkets.

Lan Anh Hotel (Map p357; ☎ 836 5197; lan-anh-hotel@hcm.vnn.vn; 252 Đ De Tham; r US$10-18;) Offering an elevator, free breakfast and comfortable rooms, the Lan Anh is a good central choice.

our pick Madame Cuc's (madamcuc@hcm.vnn.vn; r US$12-20;); Hotel 127 (Map p357; ☎ 836 8761; 127 Đ Cong Quynh); Hotel 64 (Map p357; ☎ 836 5073; 64 Đ Bui Vien); Hotel MC 184 (Map p357; ☎ 836 1679; 184 Đ Cong Quynh) It's worth checking out the trio of superb family-run hotels run by warm-hearted Madam Cuc, a local personality who knows how to make her guests feel safe and at home. All three places feature well-appointed rooms and the staff provide a most welcoming reception. There's free tea, coffee and fruit all day; breakfast and a simple dinner are included in the room rates. Virtually all the hotels are identical in size and style.

Saigon Comfort Hotel (Map p357; ☎ 837 6516; saigoncomfort@hcm.fpt.vn; 175/21 Đ Pham Ngu Lao; r US$12-18;) This clean, comfortable place has nicely set rooms – and they all come with windows. You'll also find a host of decent amenities, including en-suite wi-fi access.

Bi Saigon & Bee Saigon (Map p357; ☎ 836 0678; www.bisaigon.com; r US$12-30;); Bi Saigon (185/26 Đ Pham Ngu Lao); Bee Saigon (185/16 Đ Pham Ngu Lao) With two locations in Minihotel Alley, this pair of hotels has comfortable rooms with all the amenities (and some wild designs to boot). Each hotel is fronted by a decent restaurant serving Vietnamese and Japanese fare amid French-colonial décor.

Hong Hoa Hotel (Map p357; ☎ 836 1915; www.honghoavn.com; 185/28 Đ Pham Ngu Lao; r US$13-18;) Rooms are trim and tidy at Hong Hoa (the best have small balconies), and guests get two hours free at the internet café downstairs. The staff here are friendly and efficient.

Hotel Anh Phuong (Map p357; ☎ 836 9248; 295 Đ Pham Ngu Lao; r US$15-20;) Prominently advertising its double-glazed windows, this hotel delivers peace and quiet in its range of tidy rooms; the best are spacious, with heavy wooden furniture and Eastern décor.

Canadian Hotel 281 (Map p357; ☎ 837 8666; hotel@281canadianhotel.com; 281 Đ Pham Ngu Lao; r US$15-28;) The lobby resembles an airline booking office, with cool, crisp (Canadian?) design. Some rooms have balconies; for US$21 and upwards they have in-room computers with fast ADSL connections (US$2 extra per day). There's a lift to save your legs.

Duna Hotel (Map p357; ☎ 837 3699; dunahotelvn@hcm.vnn.vn; 167 Đ Pham Ngu Lao; s/d/tr from US$15/17/25;) This spotless hotel has colourful rooms with elaborately carved moulding and other details. Duna has a lift and accepts credit cards.

CO GIANG AREA

An alternative to Pham Ngu Lao and about 10 minutes' walk south of there, is a string of fine guesthouses in the quiet alley connecting Đ Co Giang and Đ Co Bac (Map p336). To reach the guesthouses, walk southwest on Đ Co Bac and turn left after you pass the *nuoc mam* (fish sauce) shops.

Ngoc Son (Map p336; ☎ 836 4717; ngocsonguesthouse@yahoo.com; 178/32 Đ Co Giang; r US$7-11; ❄) A quiet, eight-room guesthouse, Ngoc Son is a family-style place offering rooms with cable TV and fridge. The friendly, helpful family rents motorbikes and offers breakfast for US$1 extra.

Guest House California (Map p336; ☎ 837 8885; guesthousecalifornia-saigon@yahoo.com; 171A Đ Co Bac; r US$10-18; ❄) Small and intimate, this homey new guesthouse has a relaxed TV area downstairs and a shared kitchen where you can cook your own meals. It's run by a friendly, relaxed couple who also rents bikes and motorbikes.

our pick **Miss Loi's Guesthouse** (Map p336; ☎ 837 9589; missloi@hcm.fpt.vn; 178/20 Đ Co Giang; r US$10-20; ❄) This was the first guesthouse to appear in the neighbourhood and it's still the best. Miss Loi and her especially amiable, helpful staff create a warm, low-key familial environment. The free breakfast is served in the pleasant open-air lobby, where fat, happy fish populate the fish pond and a pool table awaits.

Midrange

PHAM NGU LAO

Giant Dragon Hotel (Map p357; ☎ 836 1935; gd-hotel@hcm.vnn.vn; 173 Đ Pham Ngu Lao; r/ste US$20/25; ❄) Fairly fancy, the immaculate rooms at this lift-equipped place have satellite TV, IDD phones, tubs and hair dryers. Superdeluxe rooms have sitting areas and views of town; all room rates include breakfast.

Lac Vien Hotel (Map p357; ☎ 920 4899; lacvienhotel@hcm.fpt.vn; 28/12 Đ Bui Vien; r US$22-28; ❄) A shiny new hotel, Lac Vien has very clean rooms with attractive furnishings, flat-screen TVs, and modern bathrooms. There's wi-fi access, but the cheapest rooms lack windows.

An An Hotel (Map p357; ☎ 837 8087; www.ananhotel.com; 40 Đ Bui Vien; r US$22-35; ❄ 💻) The usual luxuries such as TV and minibar equip the clean rooms at this slick, newish place. It also offers tours and transport services.

Ki Hotel (Map p357; ☎ 837 5582; www.tamsonco.com; 28/2 Đ Bui Vien; r US$28-38; ❄) This new hotel offers stylish quarters with red and white embroidered bed covers, organic elements (bamboo, paper lanterns), thoughtful extras (robe and slippers) and room enough to stretch out.

Metropole Hotel (Map p336; ☎ 920 1939; fax 920 1960; 148 ĐL Tran Hung Dao; r from US$55; ❄ 🏊) Run by Saigon Tourist, this well-appointed hotel has attractive guestrooms and excellent amenities – pool, workout centre, spa.

DONG KHOI AREA

If you want to base yourself in the city centre, you'll find a good number of well-appointed hotels along Đ Dong Khoi or near the Saigon River. All of them offer amenities such as air-con and satellite TV.

our pick **Spring Hotel** (Map p350; ☎ 829 7362; springhotel@hcm.vnn.vn; 44-46 Đ Le Thanh Ton; s/d with breakfast from US$32/40; ❄ 💻) This trim, nicely designed place has a subtle Japanese feel to it. Rooms are somewhat small and carpeted but offer excellent value for the neighbourhood.

Bong Sen Annexe (Map p350; ☎ 823 5818; bongsen2@hcm.vnn.vn; 61-63 ĐL Hai Ba Trung; s/d with breakfast from US$40/46; ❄ 💻) The BS, as it's affectionately known by business travellers, is an attractive choice, with friendly management and staff. Rooms are clean, carpeted and somewhat uninspiring – but as with the Spring Hotel, it offers fair value for the neighbourhood.

Asian Hotel (Map p350; ☎ 829 6979; asianhotel@hcn.fpt.vn; 150 Đ Dong Khoi; s/d with breakfast from US$45/50; ❄ 💻) In the centre of town, this contemporary hotel has clean, carpeted rooms with a pleasant if simple design and wi-fi access. Book the superior or deluxe for a balcony and decent natural light. There's a good in-house restaurant.

And a few others in the area:

Dong Do Hotel (Map p350; ☎ 827 3637; www.dongdohotel.com; 35 Đ Mac Thi Buoi; r US$25-40; ❄ 💻) Small, simple, quiet rooms here have tile or wood floors; deluxe rooms feel cosy, while standards are a bit barren. Breakfast and in-room ADSL internet connection included.

Huong Sen Hotel (Map p350; ☎ 829 1415; www.vietnamtourism.com/huongsen; 66-70 Đ Dong Khoi; s/d from US$38/52; ❄) Centrally located with tidy carpeted rooms; breakfast is included. Call ahead for promotional rates.

Kim Long Hotel (Map p350; ☎ 822 8558; kimlonghotel@hcm.vnn.vn; 58 Đ Mac Thi Buoi; s/d from US$22/27; 💻) This small, somewhat dour, hotel has worn rooms with tile floors; front rooms have balconies. In-room internet (ADSL) costs an extra US$3 per day.

DISTRICT 3

Saigon Star Hotel (Map p336; ☎ 930 6290; www.saigonstarhotel.com.vn; 204 Đ Nguyen Thi Minh Khai; r US$50-60; ❄ 💻) A decent midrange option, Saigon Star has attentive service and chintzy rooms with floral bedspreads and upholstery. The best rooms have balconies overlooking the Cong Vien Van Hoa Park. Its rooftop restaurant has fine views of the Reunification Palace.

CHOLON

Arc En Ciel Hotel (Thien Hong Hotel or Rainbow Hotel; Map p346; ☎ 855 2550; www.arcenciel-hotel.com; thienhong@hcm.vnn.vn; 52-56 Đ Tan Da; r with breakfast US$35-45;) Featuring modern rooms with tile floors, the Rainbow is a popular venue for tour groups from Hong Kong and Taiwan, with its Rainbow Disco Karaoke. The priciest rooms come with pretty Chinese carved furniture.

Top End

Nearly all of HCMC's top hotels are concentrated in District 1 and most of them are in the Dong Khoi area. Don't be scared off by the published rates; hefty discounts can often be negotiated. Call or email ahead to ask for the current 'promotional' rates.

Continental Hotel (Map p350; ☎ 829 9252; www.continentalvietnam.com; 132-134 Đ Dong Khoi; r US$75-135;) One of the city's most historic lodgings, the Continental was the setting for much of the action that occurred in Graham Greene's novel *The Quiet American*. The hotel dates from the turn of the 19th century and received its last renovation in 1989 (unfortunately, at the hands of its aesthetically challenged owner, Saigon Tourist). Panelled wood ceilings with carved detailing accent the carpeted, cavernous rooms.

Grand Hotel (Map p350; ☎ 823 0163; www.grandhotel.com.vn; 8-24 Đ Dong Khoi; s/d from US$75/85;) Aptly named, the Grand's renovated landmark building is notable for its old-fashioned lift and spacious suites with 4.5m-high ceilings and French windows. Don't bother with modern rooms in the new wing; old-wing rooms are appealing and historic, with parquet wood floors and granite bathrooms. There's also an indoor pool and a gym. Breakfast included.

Rex Hotel (Map p350; ☎ 829 2185; www.rexhotelvietnam.com; 141 ĐL Nguyen Hue; s/d from US$80/90;) The giant Rex is another classic central hotel. Built in 1950, it has an ambience of mellowed kitsch that recalls the time it put up US army officers. Rooms are clean and trim with carpeting; upper-category rooms have views, while standard rooms have only windows opening onto the hall. The Rex has extensive amenities and a rooftop bar, decorated with plaster elephants and birdcages. You can use the swimming pool (open 6am to 9.30pm) for 48,000d.

Renaissance Riverside Hotel (Map p350; ☎ 822 0033; reservations@renaissance-saigon.com; 8-15 Đ Ton Duc Thang; d from US$115;) Not to be confused with the Riverside Hotel nearby, this glitzy riverside skyscraper offers a luxurious atmosphere and exceptionally friendly service. Stunning, spectacular, right-there river views are worth the extra cash.

Majestic Hotel (Map p350; ☎ 829 5517; www.majesticsaigon.com.vn; 1 Đ Dong Khoi; s/d from US$135/150;) Dating back to 1925, the Majestic is right on the Saigon River. Following major renovations it can truly reclaim its title as one of the city's most majestic hotels. Colonial architecture and details like gorgeous wood floors contribute to its charm and unique atmosphere, setting it apart from the more modern behemoths. On hot afternoons take a dip in the courtyard pool; on warm evenings take in the river views with a cocktail in hand at the top-floor bar. Breakfast is included in room rates.

Park Hyatt Saigon (Map p350; ☎ 824 1234; saigon.park.hyatt.com; 2 Lam Son Sq; d from US$210;) New in 2006, the Park Hyatt is easily Saigon's finest hotel. Occupying a fine position in the heart of the city, this 252-room hotel has an elegant white façade and beautifully appointed guest rooms. The common areas – including a classically furnished lounge and a cosy top-floor bar – warrant a visit even if you're not staying here. There's an attractive pool, full spa services and all the other amenities you'd expect from this first-rate hotel.

Sheraton Saigon (Map p350; ☎ 827 2828; www.sheraton.com/saigon; 88 Đ Dong Khoi; r from US$230;) One of the youngest luxury hotels on the block (opened in 2003), the Sheraton boasts lavish rooms with handsome furnishings and all the amenities you'd expect from the big hotel chain – including an excellent spa, an elegant pool and rooftop bar with 360-degree views.

Caravelle Hotel (Map p350; ☎ 823 4999; www.caravellehotel.com; 19 Lam Son Sq; r US$230-1200;) One of the most luxurious options in HCMC, the Caravelle Hotel has plush spacious rooms with all the creature comforts. It sits on the spot once occupied by the Catholic Diocese of Saigon. The rooftop Saigon Saigon Bar (p366) is a spectacular place to have a cocktail in the early evening. Phone ahead for promotional rates.

EATING

Hanoi may have more lakes and colonial charm, but HCMC is the reigning culinary king of Vietnam. Restaurants here range from dirt-cheap sidewalk stalls to atmospheric villas, each serving a unique interpretation of Vietnamese decadence. Besides brilliant regional fare, Saigon offers a smattering of world cuisine, with Indian, Japanese, Thai, French, Italian and East-West fusions well represented.

Good foodie neighbourhoods include the Dong Khoi area, with a high density of top-quality restaurants, as well as nearby District 3. Pham Ngu Lao's eateries, attempting to satisfy every possible culinary whim, are generally less impressive. Chinese fare rules Cholon, though restaurants here can seem sparser than pagodas on a casual stroll through the area.

Local Vietnamese restaurants open from 6am to 9pm; gourmet and international restaurants from 11am to 2pm and 6pm to 11pm; street stalls keep all hours; and markets are open from 6.30am to 5.30pm. English menus are common.

Vietnamese

Nam Giao (Map p350; ☎ 825 0261; 136/15 Đ Le Thanh Ton; mains 10,000-15,000d; ⏰ lunch & dinner) Tucked away in an alley of cosmetic shops near Ben Thanh Market, Nam Giao serves superb Hué-style mains and is always packed with locals. There's a simple photo menu.

our pick **Quan An Ngon** (Map p350; ☎ 825 7179; 138 Đ Nam Ky Khoi Nghia; mains 17,000-60,000d; ⏰ lunch & dinner) This highly recommended place is where to go for an excellent selection of traditional Vietnamese dishes. Surrounding the garden-style patio is a ring of cooks at individual stations, mixing up their nicely spiced creations in the open air. Take a stroll before ordering, and let your instincts be your guide.

Pho Oso (Map p350; ☎ 829 6415; 37 Đ Dong Khoi; mains 18,000-80,000d; ⏰ lunch & dinner) This tiny noodle shop serves delectable bowls of *pho* amid a cosy setting packed with wooden carvings and antique curios. And remember the Oso mantra: 'no delicious, no pay'.

Banh Xeo 46A (Map p336; ☎ 824 1110; 46A Đ Dinh Cong Trang; mains 20,000-30,000; ⏰ breakfast, lunch & dinner) *Banh xeo*, the Vietnamese rice-flour crêpe stuffed with bean sprouts, prawns and pork (there's also a vegetarian version), has been known to induce swoons of gastronomic delight among certain visitors. Come here to try some of the best *banh xeo* in HCMC.

Pho 24 (Map p357; ☎ 821 36 8122; www.pho24.com.vn; 271 Đ Pham Ngu Lao; mains 24,000d; ⏰ breakfast, lunch & dinner) Yeah, it's part of a chain, but this polished noodle shop serves fantastic bowls of high-quality *pho* – along with fresh juices and spring rolls. Visit the website for other Pho 24 locations.

Bia Tuoi Pacific (Map p350; ☎ 825 6802; 15 Đ Le Than Ton; mains 35,000-60,000d; ⏰ lunch & dinner) Tucked

DISH BY DISH: SAIGON'S GREATEST HITS

Restaurant-hopping through Saigon's food-filled streets is one of the great pleasures of the Vietnam experience, but with such an array of temptations – and never enough time – the hardest part of full-time feasting may be knowing where to begin. The following (highly subjective) list includes some of our favourite Vietnamese and foreign bites and where to find them. For more on great eating in HCMC, visit www.noodlepie.com, an excellent foodie insider's guide to Saigon written by a *bun cha* (rice vermicelli with roasted pork and vegetables)–loving expat.

- Best *pho* (rice-noodle soup) – **Pho 24** (above)
- Best *banh xeo* (prawn and pork-filled pancake) – **Banh Xeo 46A** (above)
- Best *bo tung xeo* (grilled beef) – **Restaurant 31** (p362)
- Best vegetarian – **Tin Nghia** (p365)
- Best Hué-style cuisine – **Tib Restaurant** (p362)
- Best Vietnamese haute cuisine – **Temple Club** (p362)
- Best street food – the 50-odd stalls of **Ben Than Market** (p372)
- Best Indian – a tie between **Tandoor** (p363) and **Akbar Ali** (p364)
- Best French – **Le Bordeaux** (p363)
- Best durian ice cream – **Fanny** (p365)
- Best setting for *ca phe sua da* (iced milk coffee) – **Serenata** (p365)

down an alley, this spacious traditional eatery overlooks several other similar restaurants. Snag a table on the terrace and enjoy fresh crab – one of many seafood specialities.

Restaurant 31 (Map p350; ☎ 825 1330; 31 Đ Ly Tu Trong; lunch & dinner) This popular outdoor eatery in the city centre serves tasty Vietnamese barbecue. The house speciality is tender marinated beef (30,000d) that you grill over charcoal right at your table. It's served with salad. There are also good seafood dishes on the menu and the cheerful staff speak English.

Café Zoom (Map p357; 169A Đ De Tham; mains 32,000d; breakfast, lunch & dinner) This buzzy little place has lots of Vespa style and serves Vietnamese and foreign fare to an equally eclectic crowd.

Gourmet Vietnamese

Compared to what you would pay for fine Vietnamese food abroad, HCMC's better Vietnamese restaurants are a bargain. It's possible to eat like royalty in a lavish restaurant for around US$10 for lunch – or US$25 for dinner – per person. Those with a mind for design shouldn't miss the colourful indigenous décor at many of the better places.

Lemon Grass (Map p350; ☎ 822 0496; 4 Đ Nguyen Thiep; mains 50,000-70,000; lunch & dinner) Despite the simple décor, this is one of the best Vietnamese restaurants in the city centre, and you can't go wrong no matter what you order. Reservations essential.

Mandarine (Map p350; ☎ 822 9783; 11A Đ Ngo Van Nam; mains 60,000; lunch & dinner) The fine selection of traditional dishes on offer draws from southern, central and northern cooking styles. The food is superb, and the pleasant décor and traditional music performances make it an all-round good bet. A house speciality worth trying is the Hanoi-style *cha ca (*filleted fish slices grilled over charcoal).

Hoi An (Map p350; ☎ 823 7694; 11 Đ Le Thanh Ton; mains 70,000-120,000d; lunch & dinner) Just down the street from Mandarine – and run by the same people – is this lovely, Chinese-style place decorated in a classical, antique motif. Hoi An specialises in central Vietnamese and imperial Hué-style dishes, and has the heaviest wooden chairs in Vietnam!

our pick **Temple Club** (Map p350; ☎ 829 9244; 29 Đ Ton That Thiep; mains 70,000-130,000d; lunch & dinner) On the second floor of a beautifully restored colonial villa, Temple Club serves delectable Vietnamese plates (such as fish with tamarind or shrimp in coconut milk) and an assortment of fresh salads. Handsome tile floors and elaborate woodwork set the scene. A comfy lounge for drinks adjoins the space.

Nam Phan (Map p350; ☎ 829 2757; 64 Đ Le Than Ton; mains 80,000-140,000d; lunch & dinner) The location in a handsomely restored mansion fronted by an idyllic courtyard sets the scene for excellent traditional fare. Service is sometimes hit or miss.

our pick **Sésame** (Map pp334-5; ☎ 899 3378; triangleghvn@hcmc.netnam.vn; 153 Đ Xo Viet Nghe Tinh, Binh Thanh district; set meals 90,000-120,000d; 11.30am-2pm Tue-Fri & 7-10pm Fri & Sat) A hospitality training school for disadvantaged children, Sésame was set up by the French NGO Triangle Génération Humanitaire. Outside on the flagstone patio, bamboo-strip tables await, adorned with candles and fresh flowers. The butter-yellow walls in the dining room are brightly inviting as well. French-Vietnamese dishes made with fresh local ingredients are delicious and beautifully presented, and the sweet staff are eager to please.

Xu (Map p350; ☎ 824 8469; 1st fl, 75 Đ Hai Ba Trung; mains 90,000-200,000; lunch & dinner) New in 2006, Xu is a stylishly set dining room that serves up imaginative – and highly successful – Vietnamese dishes. The menu features delicately prepared seafood and grilled meats prepared with a rich mixture of spices. The 95,000d three-course lunch is a particularly good value.

Tib Restaurant (Map p336; ☎ 829 7242; 187 ĐL Hai Ba Trung, District 3; mains around 100,000d; lunch & dinner) Housed in a Sino-French villa down a quiet alleyway, Tib does impressive Hué-style dishes and a mean jackfruit salad with grilled sesame. It offers a tasty variety of vegetarian specialities as well.

Nam Kha (Map p350; ☎ 828 8309; 46 Đ Dong Khoi; mains around US$10; lunch & dinner) The unique setting here consists of a reflecting pool in the middle of the restaurant flanked by gold-leaf-covered pillars, with tables scattered around the outside. Savoury Vietnamese dishes match the unique setting.

Other Asian

Indian canteen (Map p350; ☎ 823 2159; 66 Đ Dong Du; dishes 7000d) For really cheap Indian food, seek out this atmospheric, cult-like place behind the Saigon Central Mosque. The fish curry (21,000d) is lovely. Meals come with free iced tea and bananas.

Giang Nam (Map p346; cnr Đ Tan Hang & Tan Da Đ Hai; mains 15,000d; lunch) A hole-in-the-wall diner that's famous for its noodle soups. There's no menu and only one or two dishes a day.

My Huong (Map p346; 856 3586; 131 Đ Nguyen Tri Phuong; mains 20,000-40,000d; lunch & dinner) This is a highly popular indoor-outdoor restaurant serving up all kinds of good food, including superb noodle soup with duck.

Mi Nhat So 1 (Map p350; 930 4839; 8A/5D2 Đ Thai Van Lung; ramen 30,000-42,000d; 11.30-2am) This traditional ramen shop serves tasty bowls of the Japanese noodles. Seating is around the small wooden counter.

Sushi Bar (Map p350; 823 8042; shige@hcm.vnn.vn; 2 Đ Le Thanh Ton; sushi 45,000d; lunch & dinner) Bristling with life, this sushi bar is usually packed with Japanese and has a fun view of a frenzied intersection. The restaurant delivers around HCMC until 10pm.

our pick **Tandoor** (Map p336; 930 4839; 103 Đ Vo Van Tan, District 3; set lunch 58,000d; lunch & dinner) Tandoor serves outstanding North Indian food, and the set lunch is particularly good value. Delivery available.

Tiem An Nam Long (Map p346; 969 4659; 47 Đ Pham Dinh Ho; mains US$2; lunch & dinner) Near the Binh Tay Market, Tiem An Nam Long has earned many fans for its tasty wok-fried dishes. There's open-air seating and an English menu with no prices, but everything is cheap.

Urvashi (Map p350; 821 3102; 27 Đ Hai Trieu; set lunch US$3-4; lunch & dinner) Serving some of the best Indian food in District 1, Urvashi prepares a variety of Indian cooking styles and the *thali* lunch is a guaranteed filler.

Other options:

Akatonbo (Map p350; 824 4928; 36-38 ĐL Hai Ba Trung; mains 60,000d; lunch & dinner) Excellent Japanese food and a picture menu.

Ashoka (Map p350; 823 1372; 17A/10 Đ Le Thanh Ton; mains 25,000d; lunch & dinner) Moderately priced Indian place, with a lunch buffet and halal food.

Com Ga Dong Nguyen (Map p346; 855 7662; 87-91 Đ Chau Van Liem; mains 15,000-30,000d; lunch & dinner) Specialises in tasty roast chicken with rice *(com ga)*.

Encore Angkor Plus (Map p350; 829 8814; 28 Đ Ngo Van Nam; mains 35,000d; lunch & dinner) Excellent Khmer food in a peaceful setting.

Hakata (Map p350; 827 5177; 26 Đ Thi Sach; meals 90,000d; lunch & dinner) Some of the best Japanese fare in town.

Hong Phat (Map p346; 856 7172; 206 Đ Hai Thuong Lan Ong; mains 20,000-30,000d; lunch & dinner) Serves delicious noodle soup with pork.

French

HCMC has a fine selection of French restaurants, from the casual bistro to the exquisite dining room.

L'Etoile (Map p336; 829 7939; 180 ĐL Hai Ba Trung; set meals 15,000d; lunch & dinner) This restaurant serves terrific French food and its all-day 'fast food' menu is good value. A set meal could be roast chicken with a choice of five sauces, a minisalad and baguette.

Le Jardin (Map p350; 825 8465; 31 Đ Thai Van Lung; mains 35,000-55,000d; lunch & dinner) The charming little bistro has a shaded terrace café in the front garden – it's a popular hang-out for local French expats.

La Niçoise (Map p350; 822 8613; 42 Đ Ngo Duc Ke; mains 42,000-90,000d; lunch & dinner Mon-Sat, lunch Sun) This tiny French bistro has just a handful of (mosaic-covered) tables, spilling onto the sidewalk. But it's worth squeezing in for the nicely turned out dishes and changing daily specials (like ravioli with smoked salmon).

Augustin (Map p350; 829 2941; 10 Đ Nguyen Thiep; mains 60,000d; lunch & dinner Mon-Sat) Many consider Augustin the city's best casual French restaurant. It serves tasty bistro-style food.

Bi Bi (Map p350; 829 5783; 8A/8D2 Đ Thai Van Lung; mains 120,000-160,000d; lunch & dinner) The bright Mediterranean décor at Bi Bi creates a pleasant atmosphere for enjoying casual French bistro fare.

La Fourchette (Map p350; 829 8143; 9 Đ Ngo Duc Ke; mains US$7; lunch & dinner) An excellent choice, right in the city centre, La Fourchette serves authentic French food.

Camargue (Map p350; 824 3148; 16 Đ Cao Ba Quat; mains US$15; lunch & dinner) Housed in a beautiful restored villa with an open-air terrace, Camargue is also home to trendy Vasco's bar (p366). The menu includes a variety of gourmet dishes complemented by a well-appointed wine list.

Au Manoir de Khai (Map p336; 930 3394; aumanoir@hcm.vnn.vn; 251 Đ Dien Bien Phu; set lunch/dinner from US$20/45; lunch & dinner) This five-star French restaurant is set in a picturesque villa with a lush courtyard and a lavish interior. It was opened by the Vietnamese fashion guru Khai (the brains behind Khai Silk and a string of other superb restaurants and hotels in Vietnam).

Le Bordeaux (Map pp334-5; 899 9831; 7-8 Đ D2, Binh Than district; mains 150,000-300,000d; lunch & dinner) For a decadent meal with a five-star price tag, Le Bordeaux is the place to go. The city's best French restaurant serves delicate scallops, mouth-watering sea bass and other perfectly prepared dishes. It's a few kilometres north of the centre, so reserve before you taxi out.

International Cuisine

Western backpackers tend to easily outnumber the Vietnamese on Đ Pham Ngu Lao and Đ De Tham, which is the axis of HCMC's budget-eatery haven; indeed, the locals have trouble figuring out the menus (banana muesli does not translate well into Vietnamese).

ABC Restaurant (Map p336; ☎ 823 0388; 172H Đ Nguyen Dinh Chieu, District 3; mains 25,000-50,000d; 🕑 to 3am) A trendy joint for tasty late-night chow, ABC has indoor and outdoor seating and an extensive menu – from noodle soup and fresh seafood to juicy steaks.

Asian Kitchen (Map p357; ☎ 836 7397; 185/22 Đ Pham Ngu Lao; mains 30,000d; 🕑 breakfast, lunch & dinner) This small, bamboo-walled eatery serves tasty dishes of Indian, Japanese and vegetarian provenance. There are a few al-fresco tables on the mosaic patio in front.

Mogambo (Map p350; ☎ 825 1311; 20B Đ Thi Sach; mains 30,000-50,000d; 🕑 lunch & dinner) Noted for its Polynesian décor and juicy burgers, Mogambo is a restaurant, pub and hotel.

Skewers (Map p350; ☎ 829 2216; 8A/1/D2 Đ Thai Van Lung; mains 35,000d; 🕑 lunch & dinner) Skewers specialises in Mediterranean cuisine from Greece to Algeria, notably barbecued skewered meat. There's a nice atmosphere and an open kitchen so you can watch the cooks at work.

Grill 69 (Map p357; ☎ 836 7936; 275H Đ Pham Nu Lao; mains 35,000-80,000d; 🕑 lunch & dinner) Sizzling barbecued meat is the name of the game at this trim and stylish, four-storey restaurant. Grilled kangaroo, ostrich and more pedestrian fare (pork, squid, beef) go nicely with the wine selections. Roof terrace.

Pau Hanna (Map p350; 15/1 Đ Le Thanh Ton; mains 35,000-105,000d; 🕑 8.30am-midnight) This pleasant Hawaiian-owned bistro and bar features eclectic daily specials (pork ribs, quesadillas, bean soup), as well as burgers and vegetarian fare. Head upstairs for a comfier lounge setting – a good place for an evening cocktail.

Annie's Pizza (Map p350; ☎ 823 9044; 45 Đ Mac Thi Buoi; pizzas 40,000-70,000d; 🕑 lunch & dinner) Continuing a yummy pizza tradition, Annie's offers free delivery.

our pick **Akbar Ali** (Map p357; ☎ 836 4205; 240 Đ Bui Vien; mains around 55,000d; 🕑 lunch & dinner) Popular with the Indian expat community, Akbar Ali serves up authentic Indian cuisine to the backdrop of a Bollywood video playing discreetly overhead. You'll also find colourful artwork on the walls and friendly service.

Santa Lucia (Map p350; ☎ 822 6562; 14 ĐL Nguyen Hue; mains 60,000-100,000d; 🕑 lunch & dinner) Santa Lucia dishes up some of the best authentic Italian food in town.

Pacharan (Map p350; ☎ 825 6824; 97 Đ Hai Ba Trung; tapas 75,000-90,000d; 🕑 lunch & dinner) This colourful Spanish tapas restaurant and wine bar is one of Saigon's trendiest spots to meet up over a drink. Tasty bites, excellent wines and a rooftop terrace have earned many expat fans. For heartier meals, try the paella (390,000d), which serves two.

Stella (Map p357; ☎ 836 9220; 121 Đ Bui Vien; mains 75,000-125,000d; 🕑 lunch & dinner) A newcomer to backpacker land, Stella serves delectable risotto, lasagne and gnocchi in a stylish, Zen-like trattoria. Zippy cappuccinos and espressos on hand.

Pomodoro (Map p350; ☎ 823 8998; 79 ĐL Hai Ba Trung; mains 80,000-160,000d; 🕑 10am-10pm) This small Italian restaurant has an arched ceiling and an all-brick interior, a cosy setting for good pizzas, pastas, spinach tart (along with other vegie options) and tiramisu. Delivery available.

Gartenstadt (Map p350; ☎ 822 3623; 34 Đ Dong Khoi; mains 125,000-160,000; 🕑 10.30am-midnight) This cosy little place makes its own bread and German sausages.

Au Lac do Brasil (Map p336; ☎ 820 7157; 238 Đ Pasteur; set dinner 290,000d; 🕑 lunch & dinner) For a taste of Brazil head to Au Lac do Brasil. Decked out with photos of Brazilian cities and colourful Carnaval-themed paintings, this *churrascaria* (barbecue restaurant) serves all-you-can-eat steak (and 11 other cuts of meat), just like you'll find in Rio.

Other popular backpacker cafés:

Kim Cafe (Map p357; ☎ 836 8122; cafékim@hcm.vnn.vn; 268 Đ De Tham; mains 20,000d; 🕑 breakfast, lunch & dinner)

Linh Cafe (Map p357; 291 Đ Pham Ngu Lao; mains 20,000d; 🕑 breakfast, lunch & dinner)

Saigon Cafe (Map p357; 195 Đ Pham Ngu Lao; mains 15,000d; 🕑 breakfast, lunch & dinner)

Vegetarian

The largest concentration of vegetarian restaurants is around the Pham Ngu Lao area.

Dinh Y (Map p357; ☎ 836 7715; 171B Đ Cong Quynh; mains 7000d; 🕑 breakfast, lunch & dinner) Across the road from Thai Binh Market, Dinh Y is run by a friendly Cao Dai family. It serves inexpensive and delicious vegie fare, and has an English menu. The noodle soups are savoury and satisfying.

our pick **Tin Nghia** (Map p357; ☎ 821 2538; 9 ĐL Tran Hung Dao; 7am-8.30pm; mains 8000d) Although you may feel like you're eating in a garage, the owners are strict Buddhists who turn out delicious traditional Vietnamese food, prepared with tofu, mushrooms and other vegetables.

Zen (Map p357; ☎ 837 3713; 185/30 Đ Pham Ngu Lao; mains 10,000-15,000d; breakfast, lunch & dinner) This casual backpackers' favourite serves cheap vegie food with a mellow, family atmosphere.

On the first and 15th days of the lunar month, food stalls around the city, especially in the markets, serve vegetarian versions of meaty Vietnamese dishes. While these stalls are quick to serve, they're usually swamped on these special days. Have a little patience; dinner's worth the wait.

Cafés, Bakeries & Ice Cream

Serenata (Map p336; ☎ 930 7436; 6D Đ Ngo Thoi Thien; 7.30am-10pm Mon-Sat) Down an alley, Serenata is a beautiful setting for coffee. Tables are scattered around a lush, pond-filled courtyard and inside a charming villa. It's a popular drinking spot for couples at night with live music some nights.

Sozo (Map p357; ☎ 095 870 6580; 176 Đ Bui Vien; 3 cookies US$1; 7.30am-10pm Mon-Sat) This lovely, inviting café serves coffees, cinnamon rolls, homemade cookies and sandwiches; it has wi-fi access, and more importantly, trains and employs poor, disadvantaged Vietnamese.

Bobby Brewers (Map p357; ☎ 610 2220; 45 Đ Bui Vien; coffee US$1-2.30; breakfast, lunch & dinner) This multilevel café shows free movies throughout the week. The menu features coffees, fresh juices, sandwiches, burgers and salads. Free delivery in District 1 (US$3 minimum).

Fanny (Map p350; ☎ 821 1633; 29-31 Đ Ton That Thiep; per ice-cream scoop 6000-15,000d; breakfast, lunch & dinner) Set in an attractive French villa with a brick patio, Fanny creates excellent Franco-Vietnamese ice cream of many sublime tropical fruit flavours (try the durian or litchi). Wi-fi access.

Pat à Chou (Map p350; 65 Đ Hai Ba Trung; croissants 7500d; 6.30am-9pm) Popular with locals and expats, this tiny bakery sells delightfully fresh baguettes, *pain au chocolat* (pastry with chocolate) and other Francophile morsels.

Givral (Map p350; ☎ 829 2747; 169 Đ Dong Khoi; breakfast, lunch & dinner) A comfortable, central place to take in views of the Municipal Theatre over pastry (10,000d) and coffee.

Sinh Café (Map p357; ☎ 836 7338; sinhcafévietnam@hcm.vnn.vn; 246-248 Đ De Tham; mains 20,000-40,000d; breakfast, lunch & dinner) Sinh has tasty fresh croissants and *pain au chocolat* as well as sandwiches, juices and Vietnamese fare.

Brodard Café (Map p350; ☎ 822 3966; 131 Đ Dong Khoi; mains 25,000-100,000d; breakfast, lunch & dinner) This Parisian-style oldie but goodie is known for good café food at OK prices.

Paris Deli (Map p350; ☎ 821 6127; 65 Đ Le Loi; cappuccino 28,000d; breakfast, lunch & dinner) This airy café serves excellent pastries in a cosy setting. Fresh flowers adorn the tables, and there's outdoor seating. Heartier European cuisine also served.

Highlands Coffee (Map p350; Lam Son Sq; smoothies 34,000d; breakfast, lunch & dinner) Part of the large chain, this pleasant outdoor café lies behind the Municipal Theatre and serves strong coffee and refreshing smoothies to the backdrop of electronic music and the surrounding traffic.

Java Coffee Bar (Map p350; ☎ 823 0187; 38-42 Đ Dong Du; 7.30am-midnight) With espresso bar, excellent café fare and even smoothies (35,000d) made with silken tofu, Java is chic and relaxed – with the comfiest chairs ever.

Ciao Café (Map p350; ☎ 823 1130; 74 Đ Nguyen Hue; snacks around 50,000; 7.30am-10pm) Set with some lovely tile floors and a lavish wood interior, this is a choice place to sip dark, rich coffee and while away the day with a good book.

DEsignED Café (Map p336; ☎ 930 2600; 180A Đ Nam Ky Khoi Nghia; mains 45,000-90,000d; lunch & dinner) Lunching here on gourmet European and Vietnamese dishes is like dining in a museum café. In fact, upstairs it's an interior design gallery; if you're into Pop Art and sleek Lucite furniture, this is the place for you.

Gallery Deli (Map p350; ☎ 822 2312; 83 Đ Dong Khoi; 7.30am-11pm;) This atmospheric café has colourful artwork lining the walls (all for sale) and prepares tasty snacks and light meals. Internet available (US$2 per hour).

Food Stalls

Noodle soup is available all day long at street stalls everywhere. A large bowl of delicious beef noodle soup usually costs between 7000d and 15,000d. Just look for the signs that say 'pho'.

Pho 2000 (Map p336; ☎ 822 2788; 1-3 Đ Phan Chu Trinh; pho 20,000d; 6am-2am) Near the Ben Thanh Market, Pho 2000 is a good place to sample your first bowl of *pho* – former US president Bill Clinton stopped in for a bowl.

Pho Hoa (Map p336; ☎ 829 7943; 260C Đ Pasteur; soup 15,000d; breakfast, lunch & dinner) This is another popular place with foreigners in District 3.

Markets always have a side selection of food items, often on the ground floor. Clusters of food stalls can be found in Thai Binh, Ben Thanh (Map p336) and An Dong Markets (Map pp334–5).

Sandwiches with a French look and a very Vietnamese taste are sold by street vendors. Fresh baguettes are stuffed with something resembling pâté (don't ask) and cucumbers seasoned with soy sauce. A sandwich costs between 5000d and 15,000d, depending on the fillings. Sandwiches filled with imported French cheese cost a little more. À la carte baguettes usually cost between 500d and 2000d.

Self-Catering

The city's markets and street stalls are a great place to assemble a fresh meal. If you don't feel like going anywhere, **Chez Guido** (☎ 898 3747; www.chezguido.com; mains 20,000-100,000d; 9am-11pm) delivers, fast (even wines and desserts)! The menu offers a mind-boggling cornucopia of international cuisine but specialises in Italian food. Download a menu online.

Two big supermarkets near Pham Ngu Lao are **Hanoi Mart** and **Co-op Mart** (Map p357; Đ Cong Quynh), just down the street from each other.

Other places to try:

Annam Gourmet Shop (Map p350; 16 Đ Hai Ba Trung; 9am-8pm) A small but well-stocked shop with imported cheeses, wines, chocolates and all the other delicacies you won't find elsewhere.

Hong Hoa Mini-Market (Map p357; Hong Hoa Hotel, 185/28 Đ Pham Ngu Lao; 9am-8pm) Small but packed with toiletries, alcohol and Western junk food, such as chocolate bars.

Veggy's (Map p350; ☎ 823 8526; golden-garden@hcm.vnn.vn; 15 Đ Thai Van Lung; 9am-8pm) Carries a quality variety of imported foods, wine and sauces, as well as fresh produce and frozen meats.

DRINKING

Wartime Saigon was known for its riotous nightlife. Liberation in 1975 put a real dampener on evening activities, but the pubs and discos have staged a comeback. However, periodic 'crack-down, clean-up' campaigns – allegedly to control drugs, prostitution and excessive noise – continue to keep the city's nightlife on the quiet side.

Pubs & Bars

HCMC's widest and wildest variety of nightlife choices is in the central area, notably around Đ Dong Khoi. Although places in this area typically close by midnight (owing to pressure from local authorities), you can always depend on the pubs in the Pham Ngu Lao area to stay open till the wee hours.

CENTRAL AREA

Vasco's (Map p350; ☎ 824 3148; 16 Đ Cao Ba Quat; drinks 20,000-70,000d) Much loved by expats, perennially hip Vasco's draws a bigger crowd on weekends when there's live music. There are

DRINKS WITH A VIEW

Although you'll pay more for a cocktail at these rooftop bars than at street level, it's well worth the extra dong – what better way to enjoy the frenetic pace of life on the streets, than at eagles'-nest heights? Among our favourite spots at sunset:

Caravelle Hotel (p360; 11am-late) A bit stylish but staid, Caravelle's Saigon Saigon Bar has great views and space for open-air intrigue. Live entertainment most nights.

Hotel Majestic (p360; 4pm-midnight) Among the best places in Saigon for a relaxing sundowner, the Majestic's top-floor Bellevue Bar offers exquisite views of the river among old-world opulence. If the heady heights make you feel too woozy or blasé, head down to the ground-level Cyclo Bar, with ringside views of motorcycle mayhem.

Rex Hotel (p360; 4-10pm) The Rex wins the kitsch award, featuring plaster animals, empty birdcages and various other…junk, but did we mention the view?

Sheraton Saigon (p360; 4pm-midnight) A fancy-shmancy wine bar on the 23rd floor with live music and a top-notch restaurant attached.

Windsor Plaza Hotel (Map p346; ☎ 833 6688; 18 Đ An Duong Vuong, District 5; 5-11pm) For an alternative view, head to the 24th floor of this looming new hotel in Cholon. Its 360-degree views give a nice perspective of the central business district.

several nice pool tables indoors and out, and inviting tables in the villa courtyard.

Lush (Map p336; ☎ 903 155 461; 2 Đ Ly Tu Trong; drinks 40,000-80,000d) This is an animé-themed bar that gathers an attractive, mixed crowd. The wraparound bar takes centre stage, from which you can enjoy great people-watching and a danceable mix of beats – but there's no dance floor. Pool tables and a 2nd-floor bar are hidden out back.

Carmen (Map p336; ☎ 829 7699; 8 Đ Ly Tu Trong; drinks 20,000-50,000d) One of HCMC's rarer breeds, Carmen has a stone wall exterior and a cosy wine cellarlike interior (duck your head when you enter) with live music nightly (from 7pm-9pm) – often flamenco, hence the name.

Yoko (Map p336; ☎ 933 0577; 22A Đ Nguyen Thi Dieu; drinks 40,000-80,000d) This stylish little spot features live music (from Indie rock to American Country to eclectic world beats) most nights starting around 9pm. It has a tiny stage, comfy chairs and a changing assortment of artwork, plus the photo/shrine to John Lennon.

Manna (Map p350; ☎ 823 3978; 26 Đ HH Nghiep; drinks 40,000-80,000d) This shimmery 2nd-floor bar has a wall of windows, comfy lounge chairs (in purplish hues) and a well-dressed local and expat mix who come for the good-time beats and stylish setting.

Q Bar (Map p350; ☎ 823 3479; 7 Lam Son Sq; drinks 20,000-70,000d) Attracting a sophisticated clientele for cocktails, Q Bar is where HCMC's fashion-conscious, alternative crowd hangs out. The stylish décor is cool and minimalist, and the music is hip. It's on the side of the Municipal Theatre, across from the Caravelle Hotel.

Qing (Map p350; ☎ 823 2414; 31 Đ Dong Du) This slim, nicely designed bar has a classic red finish and atmospheric lighting. Qing gathers an assortment of travellers, expats and locals. There's a good wine and food selection (fusion, Asian tapas) and a decent salon (p353) upstairs.

Hoa Vien (Map p336; ☎ 829 0585; www.hoavener.com; 28 Đ Mac Dinh Chi; half-litre beer 24,000d) Though Hoa Vien is notable for being HCMC's only Czech restaurant, the big drawcard is the draught Czech lager. This is actually a brewery, with shiny copper tanks looming behind the busy bar.

Blue Gecko Bar (Map p350; ☎ 824 3483; 31 Đ Ly Tu Trong) This major Aussie hang-out has the coldest beer in town. The music is good and you can shoot pool or watch sport on the half-dozen or so TVs.

Sheridan's Irish House (Map p350; ☎ 823 0973; 17/13 Đ Le Thanh Ton; 11am-late) This traditional Irish pub seems beamed straight from the back-streets of Dublin; it has live music nightly and good pub grub.

Saigon Saigon Bar (Map p350; ☎ 823 3479; 10th fl, Caravelle Hotel, 19 Lam Son Sq; drinks 25,000-70,000d; 11am-late) For excellent views in the city centre, stop by Saigon Saigon for a drink around dusk. This fancy bar has live music, cool breezes and a casually upscale feel.

No 5 Ly Tu Trong (Map p336; ☎ 825 6300; 5 Đ Ly Tu Trong; drinks 15,000-70,000d) The décor of this restored French-colonial villa is stylish and sleek. Good music, food, beer, pool and friendly staff all contribute to the pleasant atmosphere.

Heart of Darkness (Map p350; ☎ 823 1080; 17B Đ Le Thanh Ton; drinks 25,000-60,000d) This dark, cavernlike bar is a mostly expat affair. There's a DJ presiding over a small dance floor in the back room.

Wild Horse Saloon (Map p350; ☎ 825 1901; 8A/D1 Đ Thai Van Lung) Living up to its name, this saloon has cowboy chic and a decent beer selection.

PHAM NGU LAO

When it comes to nightlife, the Pham Ngu Lao area has several hot spots, in addition to the always jumping travellers-café scene.

Le Pub (Map p357; ☎ 837 7679; www.lepub.org; 175/22 Đ Pham Ngu Lao) New in 2006, this attractive bar is the new expat favourite in Pham Ngu Lao area. It has deep red walls and a small brick patio in front, a fine vantage point for watching the action in backpacker central.

Allez Boo Bar (Map p357; ☎ 837 2505; 187 Đ Pham Ngu Lao; beer from 12,000d) Watch the world scooter by at this bamboo-decked bar that always packs a (foreign) crowd, with a handful of prostitutes thrown in for good measure.

Eden (Map p357; ☎ 836 8154; 185/22 Đ Tham; mains 30,000-60,000d) This multilevel spot has red lanterns over the bar, a cosy, inviting vibe and staff dressed in shimmery red *ao dai* (Vietnamese national dress). Huge menu with all the Asian accents, with tastier fare than neighbouring joints can offer.

163 Cyclo Bar (Map p357; ☎ 920 1567; 163 Đ Pham Ngu Lao) Bar snacks range from tempura to sandwiches to *pho*, and live music (every night except for Sunday) covers the gamut from flamenco to pop.

Santa Café (Map p357; cnr Đ Bui Vien & Đ Do Quang Dau) Divey little place with outdoor seating that's a favourite of the backpacker crowd.

MOTORBIKE MELODY

One of the great embracers of motorbike culture, HCMC has some surreal vantage points to watch the endless procession of passing two-wheelers. Dong Khoi area is a particularly fine place to be on weekend and holiday nights, when the streets fill with cruisers of all ages and styles. Everyone's dressed to impress, with two, three or four packed to a bike, and you can almost taste the electricity in the air (or are those fumes?) as the young and restless check each other out through the handlebars of their matching Honda Futures. The mass of slow-rolling humanity is so thick on Đ Dong Khoi that crossing the street is like moving (cautiously, mind you) through a swarm of honeybees. Despite the apparent chaos of 10 or more lanes of traffic spinning toward each other at each intersection, most of the time, the swarms part and the motorbikes glide smoothly around each other like some strange choreography of vehicular ballet.

Even if you don't want to join the parade, you can still get some great seats to the nightly streetside spectacle. Here are some of our favourite places in town to catch the action (which is far better than TV – and most organised sporting events for that matter).

- **Highlands Coffee** (p365) Hands down, one of the best motorbike vantage points in the country.
- **Traffic circle** (Map p336; cnr Pham Ngoc Thach & Tran Cao Van) Ringed with cafés and restaurants, there's never a dull moment at this attractively landscaped traffic circle (some even call it 'Turtle Circle').
- **Cyclo Bar** (Map p350; 1 Đ Dong Khoi) On the ground floor of the Majestic Hotel, Cyclo Bar is one of the fancier places to watch/hear the engines roar.
- **Café Zoom** (p362) Dedicated to the artfully designed Vespa, this unpretentious café has wondrous views of a city in motion.
- **Allez Boo Bar** (p367) One of the busiest corners in backpackerville; grab a (premium) seat outside and enjoy.
- **Santa Café** (p367) Not so many motorbikes, but still a great spot for people-watching.

ENTERTAINMENT

Pick up the *Guide* or *Time Out* (see p336) to find out what's on during your stay in Saigon. Monthly listings include art shows, live music and theatre performances happening around town. You can also stop by the Municipal Theatre (p344) to see what's on, as it often stages worthwhile plays and musical and dance performances.

Binh Quoi Tourist Village (☎ 899 1831, dinner cruise bookings ☎ 829 8914; www.binhquoiresort.com.vn; 1147 Đ Xo Viet Nghe Tinh, Binh Thanh district; boat rides 20,000-840,000d, dinner adult/child 75,000/45,000d; 🕒 11am-2pm & 5-8pm Sun & holidays, buffet dinner 5-8pm Sat) This 'village' is essentially a resort run by Saigon Tourist, with boat rides, water-puppet shows, tennis courts and amusements for the kids. The weekend buffet dinner, with a dazzling variety of traditional Vietnamese regional specialities, is served along a canal lit with floating lanterns and accompanied by live traditional music. Call for the latest schedule of performances.

The park puts in a plug for Vietnam's ethnic minorities by staging their traditional weddings accompanied by folk music. If you don't mind getting carted around on a tour package, the dinner cruises can be fun and are followed by a traditional music or water-puppet performance at the village.

Binh Quoi Tourist Village is 8km north of central HCMC. You can get here by motorbike or taxi (around 60,000d).

Maxim's Dinner Theatre (Map p350; ☎ 829 6676; 15 Đ Dong Khoi; 🕒 11am-11pm) A Saigon institution next to the Majestic Hotel, this supper club is better recommended for its music performances than for the food. The menu offers Vietnamese, Chinese and Western dishes; though the sea slug may disappoint, the crème caramel definitely won't. The live music goes from Vietnamese folk to show tunes to contemporary pop, and reservations are recommended for dinner.

Cinemas

There are plenty of cinemas *(rap)* in the city centre, but very few films are shown in languages other than Vietnamese.

Foreign-language cinemas:

Diamond Plaza Cinema (Map p350; ☎ 825 7751; Diamond Plaza, 163 Đ Dong Khoi; tickets 30,000-40,000d) English-language films.

Institute of Cultural Exchange with France (Idecaf) (Map p350; ☎ 829 5451; 31 Đ Thai Van Lung) Screens French-language films; videos also available to rent.

Nightclubs

Most of the following dance clubs don't get started until midnight; ask around Pham Ngu Lao bars about the newest hot spots.

Apocalypse Now (Map p350; ☎ 824 1463; 2C Đ Thi Sach) Dance clubs in Vietnam have a tendency to change with the wind, but 'Apo' is one exception to the rule. It's been around forever and gives a good eyeful of the seamier side of international relations. The music is loud, the patrons are from all walks of life and it's apocalyptically rowdy.

Go2 (Map p357; ☎ 836 9575; 187 Đ De Tham) Above an open, airy street-level bar, this popular nightclub gathers a good mix of expats and young Saigon party people. DJs spin a good collection of electronica and Anglo pop, and there are open-air spots where you can retreat when you need a break from dancing.

Tropical Rainforest Disco (Mua Rung; Map p350; ☎ 825 7783; 5-15 Đ Ho Huan Nghiep; cover US$4) This popular nightspot in the city centre attracts a younger crowd. The cover charge entitles you to one free drink.

Underground (Map p350; ☎ 829 9079; 69 Đ Dong Khoi; ⏲ 10am-midnight) Named after the London tube, Underground is located in the basement of the Lucky Plaza building and is a popular gathering spot for expats and travellers alike. There's a good happy hour (15,000d draught beer) and decent pizza.

Theatre

Municipal Theatre (Map p350; Nha Hat Thanh Pho; Map p350; ☎ 829 9976; Đ Dong Khoi) Each week the theatre has a different programme, such as Eastern European–style gymnastics, classical music or traditional Vietnamese theatre. Performances typically begin at 8pm; inquire at the theatre or ask at your hotel. And if there's nothing happening when you're in town, you can at least pop into the stylish Q Bar, around the side of the building, for a drink.

Conservatory of Music (Nhac Vien Thanh Pho Ho Chi Minh; Map p336; ☎ 824 3774; 112 Đ Nguyen Du; ⏲ performances 7.30pm Mon-Fri Mar-May & Oct-Dec) Performances of both traditional Vietnamese and Western classical music are held at the conservatory, near Reunification Palace. Students aged seven to 16 attend the conservatory, which performs all the functions of a public school in addition to providing instruction in music. The music teachers here were trained abroad. The school is free, but most of the students come from well-off families who can afford to purchase the prerequisite musical instruments.

Water Puppets

Although it originates in the north, the art has migrated to HCMC in the last decade – in part because of its popularity with tourists. There are two venues to see water puppets in HCMC: on the grounds of the **War Remnants Museum** (Bao Tang Chung Tich Chien Tranh; Map p336; ☎ 829 8496; 28 Đ Vo Van Tan; admission 30,000d; ⏲ 7.30-11.30am & 1.30-5pm) and at the **History Museum** (Bao Tang Lich

GAY & LESBIAN HO CHI MINH CITY

Though there are few openly gay venues, Saigon's popular bars and clubs are generally gay-friendly. A good mixed bar to check out in Pham Ngu Lao area is **Eden** (p367), which attracts a mostly straight crowd, but is gay-friendly nonetheless. In Dong Khoi area, **Lush** (p367) attracts a good, mixed crowd with danceable music but it doesn't have a dance floor. **Apocalypse Now** (above) attracts a small gay contingent among an otherwise straight crowd, with solid grooves and a spacious dance floor. **Samsara** (Map p350; ☎ 862 2630; 2nd fl, 131 Đ Dong Khoi), above the Brodard Café is a mostly gay affair, with waiters in shirtless vests, good DJs and an action-packed dance floor. Friday and Saturday nights are the time to go. Another popular local spot that gathers mostly gays and a few lesbians is **Ben Thanh** (Orient Club; Map p336; 6 Đ Mac Dinh Chi; cover 45,000d) on Monday nights, with a lively, dance-prone vibe.

A word of warning regarding masseurs: masseurs travel on bicycle through the streets of Pham Ngu Lao area, rattling a small bell to announce their services. They often offer US$2 massages along with other services, but some of them try to extort money afterwards. As things can sometimes get nasty, it's best to avoid them altogether.

Su; Map p336; ☎ 829 8146; Đ Nguyen Binh Khiem; admission 30,000d; 🕑 8-11am & 1.30-4pm Tue-Sun); schedules vary, but shows tend to start when a group of five or more customers has assembled. Expect a 20-minute show, performed by truly skilled and imaginative puppeteers.

Saigon Race Track

Saigon Race Track (Cau Lac Bo The Thao Phu To; Map pp334-5; ☎ 855 1205; 2 Đ Le Dai Hanh, District 11; admission 2000d; 🕑 12.30-7pm Sat & Sun) When South Vietnam was liberated in 1975, one of the Hanoi government's policies was to ban debauched, capitalistic pastimes such as gambling. Horse-racing tracks – mostly found in the Saigon area – were shut down. However, the government's need for hard cash has caused a rethink. Like the state lottery, the track has proved extremely lucrative.

Dating from around 1900, the track reopened in 1989. But grumbling about just where the money is going has been coupled with widespread allegations about the drugging of horses. The minimum legal age for jockeys is 14 years; many look like they're pushing 10.

The overwhelming majority of gamblers are Vietnamese though there is no rule prohibiting foreigners from joining in the fun of risking their dong. The minimum legal bet is 2000d and, for the high rollers hoping to become a dong billionaire, the sky's the limit.

Plans to introduce off-track betting have so far not materialised. However, illegal bookmaking (bets can be placed in gold!) does offer one form of competition to the government-owned monopoly.

SHOPPING

HCMC's teeming streets are like the Elysian Fields for intrepid shopping souls. While there's much junk being peddled to the tourist masses, there are plenty of great discoveries just waiting to be unearthed. Comprising the hunting grounds are sprawling markets, antique stores, silk and fabric boutiques and speciality stores selling ceramics, ethnic fabrics, lacquered bamboo and custom-made clothing. And although the art scene is better up north, HCMC has a growing number of galleries selling everything from lavish oil paintings to photographs to vintage propaganda posters.

There are also the quirkier gems like *cyclos* and helicopters made from beer and soda cans – one place to browse for these is at the War Remnants Museum (p340) gift shop.

The best place to begin any shopping journey is the gallery- and boutique-lined Đ Dong Khoi and the streets that intersect it. This is also the place to look for high-quality souvenirs. Better deals can be found in Pham Ngu Lao, although the selection is poorer. If you're pressed for time, several shopping centres are great one-stop destinations, including the shiny, modern **Saigon Centre** (Map p350; 65 Đ Le Loi); and the inspiringly named (and cheaper) **Tax Department Store** (Russian Market; Map p350; cnr Đ Nguyen Hue & Đ Le Loi), both are great places to browse for electronics, clothing and handicrafts.

Arts & Handicrafts

Dogma (Map p357; ☎ ; www.dogmavietnam.com; 175 Đ De Tham; 🕑 9am-10pm) Proudly advertising the sale of Vietnamese kitsch, this colourful store stocks reproductions of marvellous old propaganda posters emblazoned on coffee mugs, coasters, and T-shirts. There's also men's and women's clothing, purses and assorted other knick-knacks that make for fine browsing.

Living & Giving (Map p350; ☎ 822 3104; www.livinggiving.com; 11 Đ Ngo Duc Ke) Packed with stylish linens and bedding, furniture and unusual home décor in iron, wood and ceramic.

Lotus (Map p350; ☎ 098 908 4449; lotushochiminh@yahoo.com; 25 Đ Dong Khoi) For vintage propaganda

Carved Seals

One item found in every self-respecting bureaucrat's desk is a carved seal. Indeed, no functioning administrator, communist or otherwise, can exist without the official stamps and seals that are the *raison d'être* for legions of clerks. This need is well-catered to by the shops strung out along the street just north of the New World Hotel (opposite side of ĐL Ham Nghi and just west of Ben Thanh Market). In Cholon you can find shops making these seals along Đ Hai Thuong Lan Ong.

Most Vietnamese also own carved seals bearing their name (an old tradition borrowed from China). You can have one made, too, but ask a local to help translate your name into Vietnamese. You might want to get your seal carved in Cholon using Chinese characters; these are certainly more artistic (though less practical) than the Romanised script used by the Vietnamese today.

posters (from the '60s and '70s), this place is a goldmine. Expect to pay upwards of US$85 for an original.

Mai Handicrafts (Map pp334-5; ☎ 844 0988; maivn@hcm.vnn.vn; 298 Đ Nguyen Trong Tuyen, Tan Binh district) Fair-trade shop dealing in ceramics, ethnic fabrics and other gift items, in turn supporting disadvantaged families and street children.

Nguyen Freres (Map p350; ☎ 098 380 3070; nguyenfreres.com; 2 Đ Dong Khoi) Stocks a lovely assortment of antique furnishings and textiles, pillowcases, silks, pottery and lamps.

Precious Qui (Map p350; quasarkhanh@hcm.vnn.vn; ☎ 825 6817; 29A Đ Dong Khoi) Precious Qui specialises in lacquerware and accessories (interesting forks and spoons) fashioned from buffalo horn. It also stocks a limited selection of celadon ceramic ware.

Clothing

Although Saigonese fashion has yet to make a name for itself, there are plenty of places where you can shop for stylish apparel – or even opt for a custom-made *ao dai*, the couture symbol of Vietnam. This quite flattering outfit of silk tunic and trousers is tailored at shops in and around Ben Thanh Market and around the Rex and Continental Hotels. There are also male *ao dai* available – these are a looser fit and come with a silk-covered head wrap to match.

Cham Khanh (Map p336; ☎ 820 6861; 256 Đ Pasteur, District 3) This is one of several *ao dai* shops on this stretch of Đ Pasteur. It sells particularly colourful pieces and is a reliable place for getting an *ao dai* made.

The Dong Khoi neighbourhood is awash with tempting shops selling contemporary clothing. Some will also custom-tailor clothing and shoes, and turnaround usually takes a few days. A survey of the neighbourhood around Đ Pasteur and Đ Le Thanh Ton yields at least a half-dozen boutiques; Đ Dong Khoi and Đ Ngo Duc Ke or Đ Dong Du reveal yet more.

Souvenir T-shirts are prevalent in town, with bargain deals available from vendors along ĐL Le Loi in the city centre, or Đ De Tham in the Pham Ngu Lao area. Prices start at US$2 for a printed T-shirt and US$4 for an embroidered one.

Other clothing stores:

Chi Chi (Map p350; ☎ 824 7812; anhxuanvn@hcm.fpt.vn; 138 Đ Pasteur; 🕑 8am-8pm) Features well-chosen, lovely fabrics and fine designs; custom-tailoring offered here.

Khai Silk (Map p350; ☎ 829 1146; www.khaisilk.org; 107 Đ Dong Khoi) One branch of this well-established silk empire; a reliable choice for tailored suits or *ao dai*.

Reda (Map p350; ☎ 827 2695; reda@hcm.vnn.vn; 29 Đ Le Thanh Ton; 🕑 10am-7.30pm) An assortment of stylish women's apparel, with handmade tailoring available. There's also an adjoining café, for a bite after browsing.

Sapa (Map p357; vudong@hcm.vnn.vn; ☎ 836 5163; 223 Đ De Tham) Incorporates ethnic fabrics and designs with hip style; also sells gifts and jewellery.

Song (Map p350; ☎ 824 6986; songshops@asiasongdesign.com; 76D Đ Le Thanh Ton) A small boutique selling sophisticated, high-end clothing and accessories for both men and women.

Coffee

Vietnamese coffee is prime stuff and is amazingly cheap. The best grades are from Buon Ma Thuot and the beans are roasted in butter. Lovers of weasels and strange things should get their hands on *ca phe chon* ('weasel coffee', No 8 of the signature Trung Nguyen brand). These coffee beans are fed to weasels first, then harvested from their droppings before being sold to you. Brew and enjoy.

The city's major markets, particularly Ben Thanh Market (Map p372), have the best prices and widest selection of both regular and weasel coffee.

Galleries

HCMC is brimming with art galleries. Good places to browse are the handful of galleries around the Fine Arts Museum (p342) and along Đ Dong Khoi. You'll find excellent top-quality works at the following places: **Blue Space Gallery** (Map p336; ☎ 821 3695; 1A Đ Le Thi Hong Gam; 🕑 9am-6pm), **Lacquer & Oil** (Map p336; ☎ 821 2320; 97A Đ Pho Duc Chinh; 🕑 9am-5.30pm) and **Vinh Loi Gallery** (Map p336; ☎ 930 5006; www.galerievinhloi.com; 41 Đ Ba Huyen Thanh Quan, District 3; 🕑 9am-6pm). Any of these places will ship worldwide. For low-quality reproductions of famous paintings, visit the painting shops along Đ Bui Vien (Map p357) in Pham Ngu Lao.

GETTING THERE & AWAY

Air

Tan Son Nhat Airport was one of the three busiest in the world in the late 1960s. The runways are still lined with lichen-covered, mortar-proof aircraft-retaining walls, hangars and other military structures.

For more details on international air travel see p477.

Most domestic flights are operated by Vietnam Airlines. Pacific Airlines also flies the

HCMC-Hanoi and HCMC-Danang route, while Sasco flies between HCMC and the Con Dao Islands. See Map p485 for details on routes and schedules.

Boat

Hydrofoils (adult/child US$10/5, 1¼ hours) depart for Vung Tau (p386) almost hourly from Bach Dang jetty (Map p350) on Đ Ton Duc Thang. For more information contact **Petro Express** (☎ 821 0650) at the jetty.

In Vung Tau you board the hydrofoil at Cau Da pier, opposite the Hai Au Hotel. **Petra Express** (☎ 511 914) has an office in Vung Tau by the pier.

Cargo ferries bound for the Mekong Delta depart from the **dock** (☎ 829 7892) at the river end of ĐL Ham Nghi. Although service is sporadic, travellers with time on their hands can ask about departures to the provinces of An Giang and Vinh Long and to the towns of Ben Tre (eight hours), Ca Mau (30 hours), My Tho (six hours) and Phu Chau (Tan Chau). Buy your tickets on the boat. Simple food may be available on board. Note these ancient vessels lack the most basic safety gear, such as life jackets.

Bus

Intercity buses depart from and arrive at a variety of stations around HCMC. **Cholon bus station** (Map p346; Đ Le Quang Sung) is the most convenient place to get buses to My Tho and other Mekong Delta towns. It's one street north of the sprawling Binh Tay Market.

Less convenient than Cholon, **Mien Tay bus station** (Ben Xe Mien Tay; ☎ 825 5955) nevertheless has even more buses to areas south of HCMC (basically the Mekong Delta). This huge station is about 10km west of HCMC in An Lac, a part of Binh Chanh district (Huyen Binh Chanh). Buses and minibuses from Mien Tay serve most towns in the Mekong Delta.

Buses to points north of HCMC leave from **Mien Dong bus station** (Ben Xe Mien Dong; ☎ 829 4056),

MAGNIFICENT MARKETS

Huynh Thuc Khang Street Market

This **street market** (Map p350; Đ Huynh Thuc Khang & Đ Ton That Dam) in the Dong Khoi area sells everything. The area was known as the 'electronics black market' until early 1989, when it was legalised.

You can still buy electronic goods of all sorts – from mosquito zappers to video cassette recorders – but the market has expanded enormously to include clothing, washing detergent, lacquerware, condoms, pirated cassettes, posters of Ho Chi Minh and Britney Spears, smuggled bottles of Johnny Walker, Chinese-made 'Swiss' army knives and just about everything to satisfy your material needs.

Ben Thanh Market

HCMC has a number of huge indoor markets selling all manner of goods. These are some of the best places to pick up conical hats and *ao dai*. The most central of these is **Ben Thanh Market** (Cho Ben Thanh; Map p336; cnr ĐL Le Loi, ĐL Ham Nghi, ĐL Tran Hung Dao & Đ Le Lai). The market and surrounding streets make up one of the city's liveliest areas. Everything that's commonly eaten, worn or used by the Saigonese is available here: vegetables, meats, spices, sweets, tobacco, clothing, household items, hardware and so forth. There's also a healthy selection of souvenir-worthy items.

Known to the French as Les Halles Centrales, it was built in 1914 from reinforced concrete; the central cupola is 28m in diameter. The main entrance, with its belfry and clock, has become a symbol of HCMC. Opposite the belfry, in the centre of the traffic roundabout, is an equestrian statue of Tran Nguyen Hai, the first person in Vietnam to use carrier pigeons. At the base of it, on a pillar, is a small white bust of Quach Thi Trang, a Buddhist woman killed during antigovernment protests in 1963.

Nearby, food stalls sell inexpensive meals. Ben Thanh Market is located 700m southwest of the Rex Hotel.

The Old Market

Despite the name, the **Old Market** (Map p336) is not the place to go to in order to find antiques. Nor is it the place to look for electronics or machinery (you'll need to go to Dan Sinh Market in Binh Thanh district about 5km from central HCMC on Hwy 13 (Quoc Lo 13), the continuation of Đ Xo Viet Nghe Tinh. The station is just under 2km north of the intersection of Đ Xo Viet Nghe Tinh and Đ Dien Bien Phu.

There are bus services from Mien Dong to Buon Ma Thuot (12 hours, 110,000d), Danang (26 hours, 200,000d), Haiphong (53 hours, 340,000d), Nha Trang (11 hours, 75,000d), Hanoi (49 hours, 320,000d), Hué (24 hours, 220,000d), Pleiku (22 hours, 190,000d), Vinh (42 hours, 260,000d), Quang Ngai (24 hours, 110,000d), Quy Nhon (17 hours, 90,000d), Nam Dinh (47 hours, 300,000d) and Tuy Hoa (12 hours, 80,000d). Most buses leave daily between 5am and 5.30pm.

Buses to Tay Ninh, Cu Chi and points northeast of HCMC depart from the **Tay Ninh bus station** (Ben Xe Tay Ninh; Map pp334-5; ☎ 849 5935), in Tan Binh district west of the centre. To get there, head all the way out on Đ Cach Mang Thang Tam. The station is about 1km past where Đ Cach Mang Thang Tam merges with Đ Le Dai Hanh.

INTERNATIONAL BUS

There are also international bus services connecting HCMC and Phnom Penh, Cambodia. The cheapest tickets are sold at the travellers cafés in HCMC's Pham Ngu Lao area, or try **Capitol Guesthouse** (☎ 023-364104) or **Narin Guesthouse** (☎ 023-982554) in Phnom Penh. There are also direct services with **Phnom Penh Sorya Transport** (HCMC 24; 309 Pham Ngu Lao; Phnom Penh ☎ 023-210359; Psar Thmei). Services depart in either direction five times a day between 6.30am and 1pm, costing US$12. The big advantage with the direct service is that it avoids a change of bus at the border.

Car & Motorbike

Inquire at almost any tourist café, travel agent or your hotel to arrange car rental. Just remember, that your rental will include a driver

for these). Rather, the Old Market is where you can most easily buy imported food, wine, shaving cream, shampoo etc. However, if its Vietnamese name, Cho Cu, is written or pronounced without the correct tones it means 'penis'; your *cyclo* driver will no doubt be much amused if you say that this is what you're looking for. Perhaps directions would be a better bet – the Old Market can be found on the north side of ĐL Ham Nghi between Đ Ton That Dam and Đ Ho Tung Mau.

Dan Sinh Market

Also known as the War Surplus Market, **Dan Sinh Market** (Map p336; 104 Đ Yersin) is the place to shop for a chic pair of combat boots or rusty dog tags. It's also the best market for electronics and other types of imported machinery.

Dan Sinh is next to Phung Son Tu Pagoda. The front part is filled with stalls selling automobiles and motorbikes, but directly behind the pagoda building you can find reproductions of what seems to be secondhand military gear.

Stall after stall sells everything from handy gas masks and field stretchers to rain gear and mosquito nets. You can also find canteens, duffel bags, ponchos and boots. Anyone planning on spending time in Rwanda or New York City should consider picking up a secondhand flak jacket (prices are good).

Binh Tay Market

Cholon's main market is **Binh Tay Market** (Map p346; ĐL Hau Giang), a Chinese-style architectural masterpiece with a great clock tower in the centre. Much of the business here is wholesale.

An Dong Market

Cholon's other indoor market, **An Dong** (Map pp334–5), is very close to the intersection of ĐL Tran Phu and ĐL An Duong Vuong. This market is four storeys high and is crammed with shops. The 1st floor carries nothing but clothing, including imported designer jeans from Hong Kong, the latest pumps from Paris and *ao dai* (Vietnamese national dress). The basement is a gourmet's delight of small restaurants – a perfect place to lunch on the cheap.

as it's illegal for foreigners to drive in Vietnam without a Vietnamese license. The agencies in the Pham Ngu Lao area generally offer the lowest prices. Motorbikes are available (also in Pham Ngu Lao) for around US$10 per day.

Train

Trains from **Saigon train station** (Ga Sai Gon; Map pp334-5; ☎ 823 0105; 1 Đ Nguyen Thong, District 3; ticket office 7.15-11am & 1-3pm) serve cities along the coast north of HCMC.

Train tickets can be purchased from **Saigon Railways Tourist Services** (Map p357; ☎ 836 7640; fax 837 5224; 275C Đ Pham Ngu Lao; 7.30-11.30am & 1-4.30pm) or from most travel agents.

For details on the *Reunification Express* service see p491.

GETTING AROUND

To/From the Airport

Tan Son Nhat Airport is 7km northwest of central HCMC. Metered taxis are your best bet between the airport and the city centre, and cost around 75,000d. You'll be enthusiastically greeted by a group of taxi drivers after you exit the terminal; most are OK, but make sure that the driver agrees to use the meter and it is switched on *after* you get in the car. The airport also has an outfit that provides a reliable taxi into the city. **Sasco Taxi** (☎ 844 6448), just past the baggage carousels, has a counter where you can pre-pay (100,000d) for a taxi.

Be aware that taxi drivers will probably recommend a 'good and cheap' hotel, and deliver you to a hotel for a commission; if you don't know where you're going, this is not a bad system per se. Problems may arise, however, when you ask a taxi driver to take you to a place that doesn't pay commission. The driver may tell you the hotel is closed, burned down, is dirty and dangerous, or anything to steer you somewhere else.

If you're travelling solo and without much baggage, a motorbike taxi is an option for getting to/from the airport. Drivers hang out near the airport car park and typically ask around 50,000d to go to the city centre. If you take a motorbike taxi to Tan Son Nhat, you may have to walk the short distance from the airport gate to the terminal.

To get to the airport you can call a taxi (see p376). Some cafés in the Pham Ngu Lao area do runs to the airport – these places even have sign-up sheets where you can book share-taxis for US$2 per person.

Most economical is the air-conditioned airport bus 152 (1000d), going to and from the airport. Buses leave the airport approximately every 15 minutes, stopping briefly at both the international and domestic terminals before heading downtown. They then make regular stops along Đ De Tham (Pham Ngu Lao area) and international hotels along Đ Dong Khoi, such as the Caravelle and the Majestic. Buses are labelled in English, but you might also look for the words 'Xe Buyt San Bay'.

Bicycle

For brave, pedal-loving souls, a bicycle can be a great, if slow, way to get around the city. Bikes can be rented from a number of places – many hotels, cafés and travel agencies can help you.

A good place to buy a decent (ie imported) bicycle is at the shops near the New World Hotel on Đ Le Thanh Ton (Map p357), a short walk from the Pham Ngu Lao area.

Bicycle parking lots are usually just roped-off sections of pavement. For about 2000d you can safely leave your bicycle (theft is a big problem). Your bicycle will have a number written on the seat in chalk or stapled to the handlebars and you'll be given a reclaim chit – don't lose it! If you come back and your bicycle is gone, the parking lot is supposedly required to replace it.

Boat

It's easy to hire a motorised 5m-long boat to tour the Saigon River. There's always someone hanging around looking to charter a boat. Ask them to bring it to you (they can easily do this), rather than you going to the boat.

The price should be around US$6 per hour for a small boat or US$10 to US$20 for a larger, faster craft. Interesting destinations for short trips include Cholon (along Ben Nghe Channel) and the zoo (along Thi Nghe Channel). Note that both channels are fascinating, but filthy – raw sewage is discharged into the water. Tourists regard the channels as a major attraction, but the government considers them an eyesore and has attempted to move residents out. The channels will eventually be filled in and the water diverted into underground sewerage pipes.

For longer trips up the Saigon River, it is worth chartering a fast speedboat from Saigon Tourist. Although these cost at least US$20 per hour, you'll save money, as a cheap boat takes at least five times longer for the same journey. Although cruising the Saigon River can be interesting, it pales in comparison with the splendour of the canals in the Mekong Delta.

Since you hire boats by the hour, some will go slowly because they know the meter is running. You might want to set a time limit at the start.

Ferries across the Saigon River leave from the dock at the foot of ĐL Ham Nghi and run every half-hour or so between 4.30am and 10.30pm.

Bus

Few tourists make use of the city buses; they are safer than *cyclos,* though less aesthetic. Now that HCMC's People's Committee has resolved to phase out *cyclos,* some money is finally being put into the badly neglected public-transport system.

At present, there are only a few bus routes, though more undoubtedly will be added. No decent bus map is available and bus stops are mostly unmarked, so it's worth summarising the main bus lines.

Saigon-Cholon buses depart from Me Linh Sq (by the Saigon River) and continue along ĐL Tran Hung Dao to Binh Tay Market in Cholon, then return along the same route. The buses running this route have air-con and video movies and the driver is well dressed! All this for 3000d. Buy your ticket on board from the attendant.

Mien Dong–Mien Tay buses (5000d) depart from Mien Dong bus station (northeast HCMC), pass through Cholon and terminate at Mien Tay bus station on the western edge of town.

Car & Motorbike

Travel agencies, hotels and cafés are all in the car-rental business. Most vehicles are relatively recent Japanese- or Korean-made machines – everything from subcompacts to minibuses. Not long ago, classic American cars (complete with tail-fins and impressive chrome fenders) were popular as 'wedding taxis'. Prestige these days, however, means a white Toyota. Nevertheless, some of the old vehicles can be hired for excursions in and around HCMC. You'll also see the occasional French-built Renault or Citroën. The former Soviet Union chips in with Ladas, Moskviches and Volgas.

If you're brave you can rent a motorbike and really earn your 'I Survived Saigon' T-shirt. Many say this is the fastest and easiest way to get around the city – and to the hospital, if you don't know what you're doing. Even if you're an experienced biker, make sure you've spent some time observing traffic patterns before putting yourself in it.

Motorbike rentals are ubiquitous in places where tourists tend to congregate – the Pham Ngu Lao area is as good as any. Ask at the cafés. A 100cc motorbike can be rented for US$6 to US$10 per day and your passport may be kept as collateral. Before renting one make sure it's rideable, and if you're wise you'll also rent a helmet (about US$1 per day).

Saigon Scooter Centre (☎ 848 7816; www.saigonscootercentre.com; 25/7 Đ Cuu Long, Tan Binh district; ⏲ 10am-5pm Mon-Sat) is a reliable source for restored classic Vespa and Lambretta scooters, which are also rented out (as well as a range of other well-maintained bikes). Daily rental rates start from US$10 and discounts are offered for longer rentals. For an extra fee it'll provide a one-way service, with a pick-up of the bikes anywhere in Vietnam.

Cyclo

No longer the icon that it once was, the *cyclo* still makes its appearance along certain streets, particularly along Đ Pham Ngu Lao and around Đ Dong Khoi. Although some Vietnamese still enjoy them, use has declined significantly in the day of the motorbike, and tourists are largely the beneficiaries of this poorly paid trade. In HCMC, many of the drivers are former South Vietnamese army soldiers and quite a few know at least basic English, while others are quite fluent. Some drivers have stories of war, 're-education', persecution and poverty to tell (and will often gladly regale you with tales over a bowl of *pho* or a beer at the end of the day).

In an effort to control HCMC's traffic problems, there are dozens of streets on which *cyclos* are prohibited. As a result, your driver must often take a circuitous route to avoid these trouble spots (and possible fines levied by the police) and may not be able to drop you at the exact address. Try to have some sympathy as it is not the driver's fault.

Short hops around the city centre should cost around 8000d to 12,000d; District 1 to central Cholon costs about 20,000d. Overcharging tourists is the norm, so negotiate a price beforehand and have the exact change ready. You can rent a *cyclo* for around 20,000d per hour, a fine idea if you will be doing a lot of touring; most *cyclo* drivers around the Pham Ngu Lao area can produce a sample tour programme.

You should enjoy *cyclos* while you can, as the municipal government plans to phase them out, and it won't be too long before the cyclo disappears entirely from the city's streets.

Motorbike Taxi

Far more prevalent and much faster than a traditional taxi is the *xe om* (sometimes called a *Honda om*), or motorbike taxi. *Xe om* drivers usually hang out on their parked bikes on street corners, looking for passengers, and will usually wave you down first. When looking for one, it's highly unlikely that you'll have to walk more than 10 steps before being offered a ride. The accepted rate is 10,000d to 15,000d for short rides (Pham Ngu Lao to Dong Khoi area for instance) or you can hire one for around US$2 per hour.

Taxi

Metered taxis cruise the streets, but it's often easier to phone for one. Several companies in HCMC offer metered taxis and charge almost exactly the same rates. The flagfall is around 12,000d to 15,000d for the first kilometre. Most rides in the city centre cost less than 30,000d. Note that faulty meters are much less common here than in Hanoi.

The following contact details are for HCMC's main taxi companies.

Ben Thanh Taxi (☎ 842 2422)
Mai Linh Taxi (☎ 822 6666)
Red Taxi (☎ 844 6677)
Saigon Taxi (☎ 842 4242)
Vina Taxi (☎ 811 1111)
Vinasum Taxi (☎ 827 7178)

Around Ho Chi Minh City

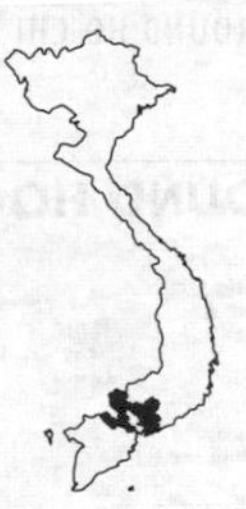

As the geographic footprint of Ho Chi Minh City continues to expand, finding a respite from urban life has become a somewhat complicated undertaking. Thankfully, there are still some refreshing escapes – to wild forests, inviting beaches and fascinating historical and cultural sights – just a short journey from town.

One of the region's top attractions is the Cat Tien National Park, a 70,000-hectare Unesco-rated biosphere boasting a startling variety of flora and fauna. Visitors can go bird-watching, take to hiking trails, overnight in a crocodile swamp and look for signs of Vietnam's rarest wildlife. The Con Dao Islands, a 40-minute flight from the city, offer an equally attractive getaway, albeit of a tropical island flavour. A former prison colony under the French and US regimes, Con Dao today boasts largely undiscovered beaches, empty coastal roads and a healthy ecosystem complete with coral reefs and colonies of green sea turtles – one of Vietnam's best places to see them in the wild.

Other fine beaches stretch just east of the gruff oilman's town of Vung Tau. Although lacking the popularity of Mui Ne and Nha Trang further up the coast, there are some sparkling gems here – particularly Long Hai and Ho Tram – for those seeking a quiet beach holiday far from the madding crowd. More popular than HCMC's nearby beaches and forests, however, are the dark, stifling tunnels of Cu Chi, where VC guerrillas once lived, fought and – in many cases – died. Nearby, the fantastical Cao Dai Temple provides a surreal point to learn about Vietnam's uniquely home-grown religion. Both of these sights are extremely popular tour-bus day trips from HCMC.

HIGHLIGHTS

- Bask on lovely beaches, snorkel coral reefs and motorbike empty coastal roads on the **Con Dao Islands** (p395)
- Go hiking or cycling in the lush forests of **Cat Tien National Park** (p392).
- Take in the sun and surf, just a short trip from HCMC, on the sandy beaches of **Long Hai** (p389) and **Ho Tram** (p391)
- Get a taste of subterranean Viet Cong life in the cramped tunnels at **Cu Chi** (p378).
- Witness the colourful spectacle of daily worship services at Tay Ninh's **Cao Dai Great Temple** (p382)

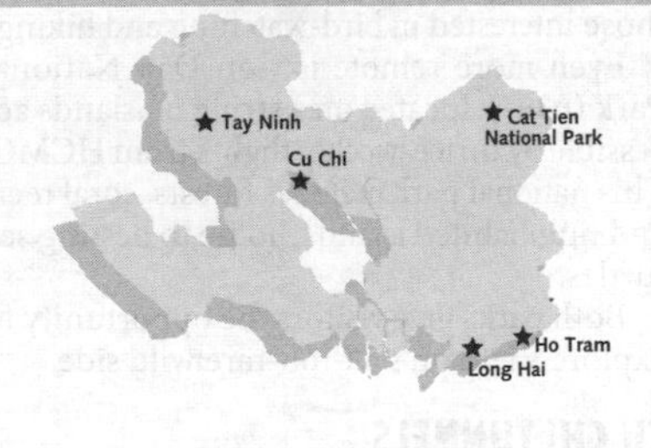

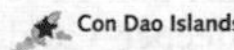

- ELEVATION: 30M
- BEST TIME TO VISIT: DEC-MAR

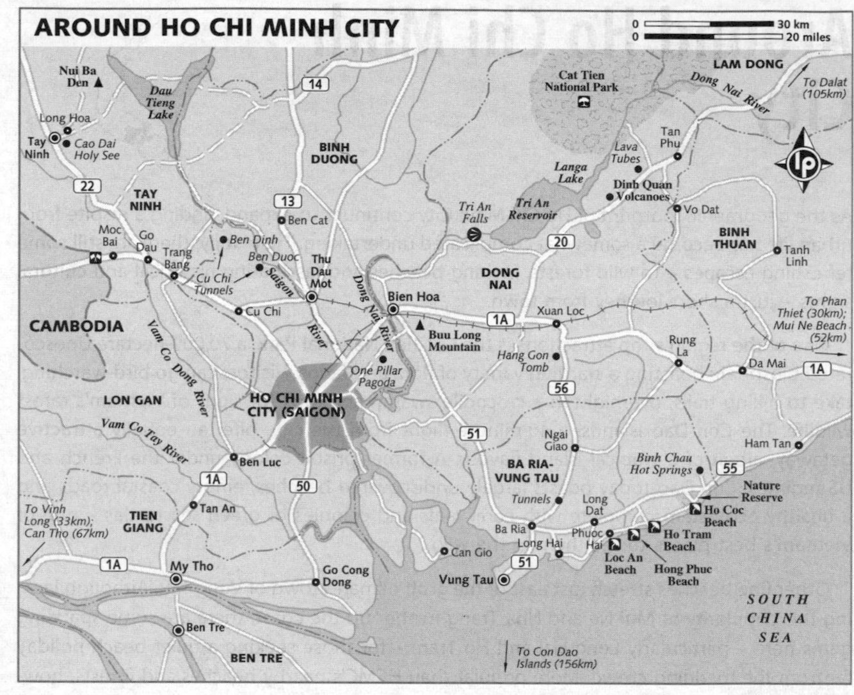

National Parks

Two notable national parks are found in this southern slice of Vietnam. Cat Tien National Park (p392), a few hours from HCMC, makes a lovely detour between HCMC and Dalat for those interested in bird-watching and hiking.

Even more remote is Con Dao National Park (p397), located on a string of islands accessible by thrice-weekly flights from HCMC. This national park includes forests, coral reefs and uninhabited islands, home to nesting sea turtles.

Both parks give visitors the opportunity to explore Vietnam's all-too-rare wild side.

CU CHI TUNNELS

The town of Cu Chi is a district of greater HCMC and has a population of about 200,000 (it had about 80,000 residents during the American War). At first glance there is little evidence here to indicate the intense fighting, bombing and destruction that occurred in Cu Chi during the war. To see what went on, you have to dig deeper – underground.

The tunnel network of Cu Chi became legendary during the 1960s for its role in facilitating Viet Cong (VC) control of a large rural area only 30km to 40km from HCMC. At its height the tunnel system stretched from the South Vietnamese capital to the Cambodian border; in the district of Cu Chi alone there were more than 250km of tunnels. The network, parts of which was several storeys deep, included innumerable trap doors, constructed living areas, storage facilities, weapons factories, field hospitals, command centres and kitchens.

The tunnels made possible communication and coordination between the VC-controlled enclaves, isolated from each other by South Vietnamese and American land and air operations. They also allowed the VC to mount surprise attacks wherever the tunnels went – even within the perimeters of the US military base at Dong Du – and to disappear suddenly into hidden trapdoors without a trace. After ground operations against the tunnels claimed large numbers of US casualties and proved ineffective, the Americans resorted to massive firepower, eventually turning Cu Chi's 420 sq km into what the authors of *The Tunnels of Cu Chi* (Tom Mangold and John Penycate) have called 'the most bombed, shelled, gassed, defoliated and generally devastated area in the history of warfare'.

Cu Chi has become a place of pilgrimage for Vietnamese school children and communist-party cadres. Two sections from this remarkable tunnel network (which are enlarged and upgraded versions of the real thing) are open to the public. One is near the village of Ben Dinh and the other is 15km beyond at Ben Duoc. Most tourists visiting the tunnels end up at Ben Dinh, the favourite of bus tours; those seeking more of a surreal, funhouse atmosphere should head to Ben Duoc.

History

The tunnels of Cu Chi were built over a period of 25 years that began sometime in the late 1940s. They were the improvised response of a poorly equipped peasant army to its enemy's high-tech ordnance, helicopters, artillery, bombers and chemical weapons.

The Viet Minh built the first dugouts and tunnels in the hard, red earth of Cu Chi (ideal for their construction) during the war against the French. The excavations were used mostly for communication between villages and to evade French army sweeps of the area.

When the VC's National Liberation Front (NLF) insurgency began in earnest around 1960, the old Viet Minh tunnels were repaired and new extensions were excavated. Within a few years the tunnel system assumed enormous strategic importance, and most of Cu Chi district and the nearby area came under firm VC control. In addition Cu Chi was used as a base for infiltrating intelligence agents and sabotage teams into Saigon. The stunning attacks in the South Vietnamese capital during the 1968 Tet Offensive were planned and launched from Cu Chi.

BORDER CROSSING: MOC BAI–BAVET

This busy border crossing is the fastest way to get between HCMC and Phnom Penh, crossing via Moc Bai. Numerous traveller cafés in the Pham Ngu Lao (p339) offer transport between the capitals for around US$8, with most buses departing around 8am. Allow about six hours for the trip, including time spent on border formalities. Cambodian visas are issued at the border, though you'll need a passport-sized photo.

In early 1963 the Diem government implemented the botched Strategic Hamlets Program, under which fortified encampments, surrounded by many rows of sharp bamboo spikes, were built to house people who had been 'relocated' from communist-controlled areas. The first strategic hamlet was in Ben Cat district, next to Cu Chi. Not only was the programme carried out with incredible incompetence, alienating the peasantry, but the VC launched a major effort to defeat it. The VC were able to tunnel into the hamlets and control them from within. By the end of 1963 the first showpiece hamlet had been overrun.

The series of setbacks and defeats suffered by the South Vietnamese forces in the Cu Chi area rendered a complete VC victory by the end of 1965 a distinct possibility. In the early months of that year, the guerrillas boldly held a victory parade in the middle of Cu Chi town. VC strength in and around Cu Chi was one of the reasons the Johnson administration decided to involve US troops in the war.

To deal with the threat posed by VC control of an area so near the South Vietnamese capital, one of the USA's first actions was to establish a large base camp in Cu Chi district. Unknowingly, they built it right on top of an existing tunnel network. It took months for the 25th Division to figure out why they kept getting shot at in their tents at night.

The US and Australian troops tried a variety of methods to 'pacify' the area around Cu Chi, which came to be known as the Iron Triangle. They launched large-scale ground operations involving tens of thousands of troops but failed to locate the tunnels. To deny the VC cover and supplies, rice paddies were defoliated, huge swathes of jungle bulldozed, and villages evacuated and razed. The Americans also sprayed chemical defoliants on the area aerially and a few months later ignited the tinder-dry vegetation with gasoline and napalm. But the intense heat interacted with the wet tropical air in such a way as to create cloudbursts that extinguished the fires. The VC remained safe and sound in their tunnels.

Unable to win this battle with chemicals, the US army began sending men down into the tunnels. These 'tunnel rats', who were often involved in underground fire fights, sustained appallingly high casualty rates.

When the Americans began using German shepherd dogs, trained to use their keen sense of smell to locate trapdoors and guerrillas, the VC began washing with American soap, which gave off a scent the canines identified as friendly. Captured US uniforms were put out to confuse the dogs further. Most importantly, the dogs were not able to spot booby traps. So many dogs were killed or maimed that their horrified handlers then refused to send them into the tunnels.

The USA declared Cu Chi a free-strike zone: little authorisation was needed to shoot at anything in the area, random artillery was fired into the area at night, and pilots were told to drop unused bombs and napalm there before returning to base. But the VC stayed put. Finally, in the late 1960s, American B-52s carpet-bombed the whole area, destroying most of the tunnels along with everything else around. The gesture was militarily useless by then because the USA was already on its way out of the war. The tunnels had served their purpose.

The VC guerrillas serving in the tunnels lived in extremely difficult conditions and suffered horrific casualties. Only about 6000 of the 16,000 cadres who fought in the tunnels survived the war. Thousands of civilians in the area were killed. Their tenacity was extraordinary considering the bombings, the pressures of living underground for weeks or months at a time and the deaths of countless friends and comrades.

The villages of Cu Chi have since been presented with numerous honorific awards, decorations and citations by the government, and many have been declared 'heroic villages'. Since 1975 new hamlets have been established and the population of the area has more than doubled; however, chemical defoliants remain in the soil and water, and crop yields are still poor.

The Tunnels of Cu Chi, by Tom Mangold and John Penycate, is a wonderful work documenting the story of the tunnels and the people involved on both sides.

Sights

THE TUNNELS

Over the years the VC developed simple but effective techniques to make their tunnels difficult to detect or disable. Wooden trapdoors were camouflaged with earth and branches; some were booby-trapped. Hidden underwater entrances from rivers were constructed. To cook they used 'Dien Bien Phu kitchens', which exhausted the smoke through vents many metres away from the cooking site. Trapdoors were installed throughout the network to prevent tear gas, smoke or water from moving from one part of the system to another. Some sections were even equipped with electric lighting.

Ben Dinh

This small, renovated section of the **tunnel system** (admission 70,000d) is near the village of Ben Dinh, 50km from HCMC. In one of the classrooms at the visitors centre, a large map shows the extent of the network; the area shown is in the northwestern corner of greater HCMC. The tunnels are marked in red, VC bases in light grey and the river in light blue (the Saigon River is at the top). Fortified villages held by South Vietnamese and US forces are marked in grey, while blue dots represent the American and South Vietnamese military posts that were supposed to ensure the security of nearby villages. The dark blue area in the centre is the base of the US 25th Infantry Division. Most prearranged tours do not take you to this former base, but it is not off limits and you can arrange a visit if you have your own guide and driver.

To the right of the large map are two cross-section diagrams of the tunnels. The bottom diagram is a reproduction of one used by General William Westmoreland, the commander of US forces in Vietnam (1964–68). For once the Americans seemed to have had their intelligence information right (though the tunnels did not pass under rivers, nor did the guerrillas wear headgear underground).

The section of the tunnel system presently open to visitors is a few hundred metres south of the visitors centre. It snakes up and down through various chambers along its 50m length. The tunnels are about 1.2m high and 80cm across, and are unlit. Some travellers find them too claustrophobic for comfort. A knocked-out M-41 tank and a bomb crater are near the exit, which is in a reforested eucalyptus grove.

Be warned that this site tends to get crowded, and you can feel like you're on a tourist conveyor belt most days.

Ben Duoc

Many Vietnamese and the odd foreign visitor make it to the **Ben Duoc tunnels** (admission 70,000d). The tunnels here have been enlarged to accommodate tourists and feature a number of sights within the underground chambers themselves. The emphasis here is more on the fun fair rather than the history of the tunnels. Hence visitors can don guerrilla costumes and gear before scraping through the tunnels in order to feel like a 'real' VC soldier. Inside are bunkers, a hospital and a command centre that played a role in the 1968 Tet Offensive, and the set pieces include tables, chairs, beds, lights, and dummies outfitted in guerrilla gear (aside from your fellow tourists, that is). Although it's amusing, it's not exactly the way the real tunnels once looked – which were cramped and largely barren as per those found at Ben Dinh.

Perhaps more moving than the underground chambers is the small **Ben Duoc temple** built in 1993 in memory of the Vietnamese killed at Cu Chi. It's flanked by a nine-story tower with a flower garden in front.

CU CHI WAR HISTORY MUSEUM

The small **Cu Chi War History Museum** (Nha Truyen Thong Huyen Cu Chi; admission US$1) is not actually at the tunnel sites but just off the main highway in the central area of the town of Cu Chi. Almost all of the explanations are in Vietnamese. There are a few gruesome photos showing civilians who were severely wounded or killed following American bombing raids, and a list of VC guerrillas killed in the Cu Chi area. Overall, it's rather disappointing and doesn't warrant a visit. Most travellers find HCMC's War Remnants Museum (p340) far more edifying.

Tours

An organised tour is the easiest way to visit the Cu Chi tunnels and it's not even remotely expensive.

Most of the cafés on Đ Pham Ngu Lao in HCMC run combined full-day tours to the Cu Chi tunnels and Cao Dai Great Temple (p382) for around US$5. For something a little more interesting, try the half-day boating trip to the tunnels organised by Delta Adventure Tours (p339). It costs around US$9 per person.

Getting There & Around

Cu Chi district covers a large area, parts of which are as close as 30km to central HCMC. The Cu Chi War History Museum is closest to the city, while the Ben Dinh and Ben Duoc tunnels are about 50km and 70km, respectively, from central HCMC by highway. There's a back road that reduces the distance significantly, though it means driving on bumpy dirt roads.

BUS

The buses going to Tay Ninh pass though Cu Chi, but getting from the town of Cu Chi to the tunnels by public transport is impossible – it's 15km, so you'll have to hire a motorbike from Tay Ninh (around US$6 return).

TAXI

Hiring a taxi in HCMC and driving out to Cu Chi is not all that expensive, especially if the cost is shared by several people. The easiest way to do this is to stop by one of the budget travel cafés in Pham Ngu Lao (p339) and arrange a car, or see if you can flag a taxi in that neighbourhood with a driver who will agree to charge you for driving time only. See p376 for details on local taxi companies.

A visit to the Cu Chi tunnel complex can easily be combined with a stop at the headquarters of the Cao Dai sect in Tay Ninh. A taxi for an all-day excursion to both should cost about US$45.

TAY NINH

☎ 066 / pop 42,000

Tay Ninh town, the capital of Tay Ninh province, serves as the headquarters of one of Vietnam's most interesting indigenous religions, Cao Daism. The Cao Dai Great Temple at the sect's Holy See is one of the most striking structures in all of Asia. Built between 1933 and 1955, the temple is a rococo extravaganza combining the conflicting architectural idiosyncrasies of a French church, a Chinese pagoda, Hong Kong's Tiger Balm Gardens and Madame Tussaud's Wax Museum.

Tay Ninh province, northwest of HCMC, is bordered by Cambodia on three sides. The area's dominant geographic feature is Nui Ba Den (Black Lady Mountain), which towers above the surrounding plains. Tay Ninh province's eastern border is formed by the Saigon River. The Vam Co River flows from Cambodia through the western part of the province.

Because of the once-vaunted political and military power of the Cao Dai, this region was the scene of prolonged and heavy fighting during the Franco-Viet Minh War. Tay Ninh province served as a major terminus of the Ho Chi Minh Trail during the American War, and in 1969 the VC captured Tay Ninh town and held it for several days.

During the period of tension between Cambodia and Vietnam in the late 1970s, the Khmer Rouge launched a number of cross-border raids into Tay Ninh province and committed atrocities against civilians. Several cemeteries around Tay Ninh are stark reminders of these events.

Information

Tay Ninh Tourist (☎ 822 376; tanitour@hcm.vnn.vn; 210B Đ 30/4) is located in the Hoa Binh Hotel (opposite). Tay Ninh's **post office** (Đ 30/4) is down the street, but it does not offer internet services.

Sights

CAO DAI HOLY SEE

The Cao Dai Holy See, founded in 1926, is 4km east of Tay Ninh, in the village of Long Hoa.

The complex houses the **Cao Dai Great Temple** (Thanh That Cao Dai), administrative offices, residences for officials and adepts, and a hospital of traditional Vietnamese herbal medicine, which attracts people from all over the south for its treatments. After reunification the government 'borrowed' parts of the complex for its own use (and perhaps to keep an eye on the sect).

Prayers are conducted four times daily in the Great Temple (suspended during Tet). It's worth visiting during prayer sessions – the one at noon is most popular with tour groups from HCMC – but don't disturb the worshippers. Only a few hundred priests participate in weekday prayers, but during festivals several thousand priests, dressed in special white garments, may attend.

The Cao Dai clergy has no objection to your photographing temple objects, but you cannot photograph people without their permission, which is seldom granted. However, you can photograph the prayer sessions from the upstairs balcony, an apparent concession to the troops of tourists who come here every day.

It's important that guests wear modest and respectful attire inside the temple, which means no shorts or sleeveless T-shirts, although sandals are OK since you have to take them off anyway before you enter.

Set above the front portico of the Great Temple is the **divine eye**. Americans often comment that it looks as if it were copied from the back of a US$1 bill. Lay women enter the Great Temple through a door at the base of the tower on the left. Once inside they walk around the outside of the colonnaded hall in a clockwise direction. Men enter on the right and walk around the hall in an anticlockwise direction. Shoes and hats must be removed upon entering the building. The area in the centre of the sanctuary is reserved for Cao Dai priests.

A **mural** in the front entry hall depicts the three signatories of the 'Third Alliance Between God and Man': the Chinese statesman and revolutionary leader Dr Sun Yatsen (1866–1925) holds an ink stone; while the Vietnamese poet Nguyen Binh Khiem (1492–1587) and French poet and author Victor Hugo (1802–85) write 'God and Humanity' and 'Love and Justice' in Chinese and French (Nguyen Binh Khiem writes with a brush; Victor Hugo uses a quill pen). Nearby signs in English, French and German each give a slightly different version of the fundamentals of Cao Daism.

The Great Temple is built over nine levels, representing the nine steps to heaven, with each level marked by a pair of columns. At the far end of the sanctuary, eight plaster columns entwined with multicoloured dragons support a dome representing the heavens – as does the rest of the ceiling. Under the dome is a giant star-speckled blue globe with the 'divine eye' on it.

The largest of the seven chairs in front of the globe is reserved for the Cao Dai pope, a position that has remained unfilled since 1933. The next three chairs are for the three men responsible for the religion's law books. The remaining chairs are for the leaders of the three branches of Cao Daism, represented by the colours yellow, blue and red.

On both sides of the area between the columns are two pulpits similar in design to the *minbar* in mosques. During festivals the pulpits are used by officials to address the assembled worshippers. The upstairs balconies are used if the crowd overflows.

Up near the altar are barely discernible portraits of six figures important to Cao Daism: Sakyamuni (Siddhartha Gautama, the founder of Buddhism), Ly Thai Bach (Li Taibai, a fairy from Chinese mythology), Khuong Tu Nha (Jiang Taigong, a Chinese saint), Laozi (the founder of Taoism), Quan Cong (Guangong, Chinese God of War) and Quan Am (Guanyin, the Goddess of Mercy).

LONG HOA MARKET

Several kilometres south of the Cao Dai Holy See complex is **Long Hoa Market** (5am-6pm). This large market sells meat, food staples, clothing and pretty much everything else you would expect to find in a rural marketplace. Before reunification the Cao Dai sect had the right to collect taxes from the merchants here.

Sleeping & Eating

Anh Dao Hotel (☎ 827 306; 146 Đ 30/4; r 180,000-270,000d) About 500m west of Hoa Binh Hotel, this place is old and rather nondescript, though the rates here also include a decent breakfast.

Hoa Binh Hotel (☎ 821 315; fax 822 345; 210 Đ 30 Thang 4; r 200,000-350,000d;) This is the main place in town, 5km from the Cao Dai Great Temple, where travellers stay if they do spend the night. It's a classic Russian-style concrete slab; rates include breakfast.

Both hotels have in-house restaurants, but there's cheaper and better Vietnamese food right next door to the Hoa Binh Hotel at **Thanh Thuy** (☎ 827 606; Đ 30 Thang 40; mains 35,000-60,000d). You won't find prices on the menu, but the cost is reasonable and portions are large.

If you're heading to Tay Ninh with your own wheels, one of the better restaurants to look for along Hwy 22 is **Kieu** (☎ 850 357; 9/32 Hwy 22; mains 10,000-16,000d), around 5km from Cao Dai Temple towards HCMC. The food is cheap and good, and the brick kilns out the back are interesting to poke around in after lunch.

Getting There & Away

Tay Ninh is on Hwy 22 (Quoc Lo 22), 96km from HCMC. (The road passes through **Trang Bang**, the place where the famous photograph of a severely burnt young girl, screaming and running, was taken by a journalist during a US napalm attack) There are several Cao Dai temples along Hwy 22, including one (which was under construction in 1975) that was heavily damaged by the VC.

BUS

There are buses from HCMC to Tay Ninh that leave from the Tay Ninh bus station (Ben Xe Tay Ninh) in Tan Binh district and Mien Tay bus station in An Lac.

MOTORBIKE

As there's no public transportation to Cu Chi from Tay Ninh, you'll have to hire a motorbike in Tay Ninh. Look for *xe om* drivers in front of the hotels. It will probably cost you around US$6 for a return trip.

TAXI

An easy way to get to Tay Ninh is by chartered taxi, perhaps on a day trip that includes a stop in Cu Chi. An all-day return trip from HCMC to both should cost about US$45.

NUI BA DEN

☎ 066

Fifteen kilometres northeast of Tay Ninh, **Nui Ba Den** (Black Lady Mountain; admission adult/child 8000/4000d) rises 850m above the rice paddies, corn, cassava (manioc) and rubber plantations of the surrounding countryside. Over the centuries Nui Ba Den has served as a shrine for various peoples of the area, including the Khmer, Chams, Vietnamese and Chinese, and there are several interesting **cave temples** on the mountain. The summits of Nui Ba Den are much cooler than the rest of Tay Ninh province, most of which is only a few dozen metres above sea level.

Nui Ba Den was used as a staging area by both the Viet Minh and the VC, and was the scene of fierce fighting during the French and American Wars. At one time there was a US Army firebase and relay station at the summit, which was later, ironically, defoliated and heavily bombed by US aircraft.

The name Black Lady Mountain is derived from the legend of Huong, a young woman who married her true love despite the advances of a wealthy Mandarin. While her husband was away doing military service, she would visit a magical statue of Buddha at the mountain's summit. One day Huong was attacked by kidnappers but, preferring death to dishonour, she threw herself off a cliff. She then reappeared in the visions of a monk who lived on the mountain, and he told her story.

The hike from the base of the mountain to the main temple complex and back takes about 1½ hours. Although steep in parts, it's not a difficult walk – plenty of old people in sandals make the journey to worship at the temple. Around the temple complex a few stands sell snacks and drinks.

If you'd like more exercise, a walk to the summit and back takes about six hours. The fastest, easiest way is via the **chair lift** (one way/return adult 30,000/50,000d, child 15,000/25,000d) that

CAO DAISM

A fascinating fusion of East and West, Cao Daism *(Dai Dao Tam Ky Pho Do)* is a syncretic religion born in 20th-century Vietnam that contains elements of Buddhism, Confucianism, Taoism, native Vietnamese spiritualism, Christianity and Islam – as well as a dash of secular enlightenment thrown in for good measure. The term Cao Dai (meaning high tower or palace) is a euphemism for God. There are an estimated two to three million followers of Cao Daism worldwide.

History

Cao Daism was founded by the mystic Ngo Minh Chieu (also known as Ngo Van Chieu; born 1878), a civil servant who once served as district chief of Phu Quoc Island. He was widely read in Eastern and Western religious works and became active in séances. In 1919 he began receiving revelations in which the tenets of Cao Dai were set forth.

Cao Daism was officially founded as a religion in 1926, and over the next few decades attracted thousands of followers, with the Cao Dai running Tay Ninh province as a virtually independent feudal state. By 1956 the Cao Dai were a serious political force with a 25,000-strong army. Having refused to support the VC during the American War, the sect feared the worst after Reunification. And for good reason: all Cao Dai lands were confiscated by the new communist government and four members of the sect were executed in 1979. Only in 1985, when the Cao Dai had been thoroughly pacified, was the Holy See and some 400 temples returned to their control.

Philosophy

Much of Cao Dai doctrine is drawn from Mahayana Buddhism, mixed with Taoist and Confucian elements (Vietnam's 'Triple Religion'). Cao Dai ethics are based on the Buddhist ideal of 'the good person' but incorporate traditional Vietnamese beliefs as well.

The ultimate goal of the Cao Dai disciple is to escape the cycle of reincarnation. This can only be achieved by refraining from killing, lying, luxurious living, sensuality and stealing, among other things.

The main tenets of Cao Daism are the existence of the soul, the use of mediums to communicate with the spiritual world and belief in one god – though it also incorporates the duality of the Chinese Yin and Yang. In addition to séances, Cao Dai practices include priestly celibacy, vegetarianism and meditative self-cultivation.

According to Cao Daism, history is divided into three major periods of divine revelation. During the first period God's truth was revealed to humanity through Laotse (Laozi) and figures associated with Buddhism, Confucianism and Taoism. The human agents of revelation during the second period were Buddha (Sakyamuni), Mohammed, Confucius, Jesus and Moses. The third and final revelation is the product of the 'Third Alliance Between God and Man', which is where séances play a part. Disciples believe that Cao Daism avoids the failures of the first two periods because spirits of the dead guide the living. Among the contacted spirits who lived as Westerners are Joan of Arc, William Shakespeare, Vladimir Ilyich Lenin and Victor Hugo, who was posthumously named the chief spirit of foreign missionary works owing to his frequent appearance.

All Cao Dai temples observe four daily ceremonies, held at 6am, noon, 6pm and midnight. These rituals, during which dignitaries wear ceremonial dress, include offerings of incense, tea, alcohol, fruit and flowers. All Cao Dai altars have the 'divine eye' above them, which became the religion's official symbol after Ngo Minh Chieu saw it in a vision.

If all this sounds like just what you've been waiting for, you can always join up. Read more on the official Cao Dai site: www.caodai.org.

shuttles the pilgrims up and down the hill. You can also opt to slide down the hill on the mountain's toboggan run.

At the base of the mountain there are lakes and manicured gardens and (as with many such sacred sites in Asia) a mix of religion and tacky amusement park–style attractions: paddle boats for hire, ceramic beaver rubbish bins, and a choo-choo tram car (tickets 2000d) to save the weary a bit of walking.

Very few foreign tourists visit the mountain, but it's a popular place for Vietnamese people. Because of the crowds, visiting on Sunday or during a holiday or festival is a bad idea.

Nui Ba Den appears prominently in a recent memoir published by a former American soldier in *Black Virgin Mountain, A Return to Vietnam* by Larry Heinemann.

Sleeping & Eating

If you get stuck having to overnight at Nui Ba Den, grotty A-frame bungalows and camping options are available at **Nha Nghi Thuy Dong** (☎ 624 204; bungalows 140,000d; A-frame platform tents 75,000d). Bungalows are situated about 500m inside the main entrance gate, on the side of the lake. Each bungalow has a basic squat toilet, and showers are outside. Tent accommodations have shared toilets and cold showers available for 500d. Alternatively, you can shower free of charge at the nearby Trung Pagoda, where the monks will prepare you traditional vegetarian meals with a day's advance notice (the food is free, but a contribution is suggested).

Thuy Dong Restaurant (mains 12,000-25,000d) is attached to the bungalow complex and has nice views of the lake. There are also a few nearby food stalls and kiosks selling cold drinks and souvenirs. Outside the main gate in the parking area, look for the stalls selling locally produced dried fruit and sweets made from coconuts and sugar cane.

Getting There & Away

There is no public transport to Nui Ba Den. If you're not travelling with your own wheels, the easiest way to reach the site is to take a *xe om* from Tay Ninh for around 50,000d.

ONE PILLAR PAGODA

☎ 08

The official name of this interesting pagoda is **Nam Thien Nhat Tru** (Chua Mot Cot Thu Duc; ☎ 896 0780; 1/91 Đ Nguyen Du), but everyone calls it the One Pillar Pagoda of Thu Duc.

The One Pillar Pagoda of Thu Duc is modelled after Hanoi's One Pillar Pagoda, though the two structures are not identical. Hanoi's original pagoda was built in the 11th century, destroyed by the French and rebuilt by the Vietnamese in 1954; HCMC's version was constructed in 1958.

When Vietnam was partitioned in 1954, Buddhist monks and Catholic priests wisely fled south to avoid persecution and continued to practise their religion. One monk from Hanoi who travelled south in 1954 was Thich Tri Dung. Just after his arrival in Saigon, Thich petitioned the South Vietnamese government for permission to construct a replica of Hanoi's famous One Pillar Pagoda. However, President Ngo Dinh Diem was a Catholic with little tolerance for Buddhist clergy and denied permission. Nevertheless, Thich and his supporters raised the funds and built the pagoda in defiance of the president's orders.

At one point the Diem government ordered the monks to tear down the temple, but they refused even though they were threatened with imprisonment for not complying. Faced with significant opposition, the government's dispute with the monks reached a standoff. However, the president's attempts to harass and intimidate the monks in a country that was 90% Buddhist did not go down well and ultimately contributed to Diem's assassination by his own troops in 1963.

During the American War the One Pillar Pagoda of Thu Duc was in possession of an extremely valuable plaque said to weigh 612kg. After liberation the government took it for 'safekeeping' and brought it to Hanoi. However, none of the monks alive in Hanoi today could say just where it is.

The pagoda is in the Thu Duc district, about 15km northeast of central HCMC. Traveller cafés and travel agencies in HCMC (p338) should be able to put together a customised tour to the pagoda or to arrange a car and driver for you.

CAN GIO

☎ 08

Notable for its mangrove forest, Can Gio is a low palm-fringed island some 25km southeast of HCMC. The island, which is at the intersection between the Saigon River and the sea, was created by silt washing downstream. It's hard-packed mud rather than sandy beach, so attracts few visitors and the area remains entirely undeveloped.

The principal attraction here – and it's a minor one – is **Can Gio mangrove forest** (Lam Vien Can Gio; ☎ 874 3069; fax 874 3068; admission 15,000d). Formed by sediment deposits from the Dong Nai and Long Tau Rivers, this forest sounds impressive on paper: its 75,000 hectares contains a high degree of biodiversity with more than 200 species of fauna and 50 species of flora. Infrastructure, however, is lacking, and only mangrove enthusiasts will truly enjoy the trip out. There is also the **Can Gio Museum**, which has displays on the wildlife of the forest, along with exhibits relating to local war history; the park also has a monkey sanctuary, home to at least a hundred simians. Admission to the Can Gio mangrove forest also covers the museum.

CAO DAI TEMPLE

Though much smaller than the Cao Dai Great Temple at Tay Ninh, Can Gio boasts a Cao Dai temple of its own. It's near the market and is easy to find.

CAN GIO MARKET

Can Gio has a large market, which is made very conspicuous by some rather powerful odours. Seafood and salt are definitely the local specialities. The vegetables, rice and fruit are all imported by boat from HCMC.

WAR MEMORIAL & CEMETERY

Adjacent to the local shrimp hatchery is a large and conspicuous cemetery and war memorial (Nghia Trang Liet Si Rung Sac), 2km from Can Gio Market. Like all such sites in Vietnam, the praise for bravery and patriotism goes entirely to the winning side and there is nothing said about the losers. Indeed, all of the former war cemeteries containing remains of South Vietnamese soldiers were bulldozed after liberation – a fact that still causes much bitterness.

CAN GIO BEACH

The southern side of the island faces the sea, creating a beachfront nearly 10km long. Unfortunately a good deal of it is inaccessible because it's been fenced off by shrimp farmers and clam diggers. Nevertheless, there is a point about 4km west of the market where a dirt road leads off the main highway to HCMC, heading towards the beach. The road is easily distinguished by the telephone poles and wires running alongside it. At the beach you'll find a handful of stalls selling food and drinks. The hills of the Vung Tau Peninsula are easily visible on a clear day.

Getting There & Away

Can Gio is about 60km southeast of central HCMC, and the fastest way to make the journey is by car or motorbike (about two hours).

There's a **ferry crossing** (motorbike/car 2000/10,000d) 15km from HCMC at Binh Khanh (Cat Lai), a former US naval base. The road is paved all the way from HCMC to Can Gio. Once you get past the ferry, there is little traffic and the sides of the road are lined with mangrove forests.

BUU LONG MOUNTAIN

Since various tourist pamphlets will tell you that **Buu Long Mountain** (admission 8000d) is the 'Halong Bay of the south', you'd be forgiven for thinking that it must be nothing short of stunningly beautiful. In truth Buu Long Mountain is no Halong Bay, but it's a pretty and peaceful place to make a day trip to escape the crowds of HCMC.

The summit is 60m above the car park, and there are several good walking trails. The top of the mountain is marked by a pagoda, from where you can look down and clearly see **Long An** (Dragon Lake). There is some lovely countryside scenery, good bird-watching and sweeping views of the rural farms along the Dong Nai River.

You can buy cold drinks and noodles at a few refreshment shops, but we recommend trying out the food at the small **vegetarian restaurant** (meals 10,000-20,000d; breakfast & lunch) at the top of the mountain.

Buu Long Mountain is 32km from central HCMC and is best reached by car or motorbike. It's 2km off the main highway after crossing the bridge that marks the border between HCMC municipality and Dong Nai province.

TRI AN FALLS

An 8m-high and 30m-wide cascade on the Song Be (Be River), the Tri An Falls are awesome in the late autumn, when the river's flow is at its greatest. Tri An Falls are in Dong Nai province, 36km from Bien Hoa and 68km northeast of HCMC (via Thu Dau Mot).

Further upstream is **Tri An Reservoir** (Ho Tri An), a large artificial lake fed from the forest highlands around Dalat and created by the Tri An Dam. Completed in the early 1980s with Soviet assistance, the dam and its adjoining hydroelectric station supplies the bulk of HCMC's electric power.

VUNG TAU

☎ 064 / pop 195,400

Vung Tau drones with bass-thumping action on the weekends as visitors from HCMC motor into town; weekdays, however, are blissfully dead. Vung Tau's beaches are easily reached from HCMC, making them a favourite of that city's residents since French colonists first began coming here around 1890.

Known under the French as Cap St Jacques – so-named by Portuguese mariners in honour of their patron saint – Vung Tau is a commercialised beach resort on a peninsula jutting into the South China Sea, about 128km southeast of HCMC (via Bien Hoa). The business of oil-drilling here means the azure horizon is marred by frequent oil tankers, and the population flecked with joy-seeking expats.

The beaches here aren't Vietnam's best, nor is the water pristine due to pollution from oil-drilling, but Vung Tau is an easy, fast beach foray out of HCMC. Beachgoers looking for a tropical-holiday feel might do better making the three-hour trip to beautiful Mui Ne Beach (p300).

Orientation

Vung Tau's peninsula is punctuated by Small Mountain (Nui Nho) to the south and Big Mountain (Nui Lon) in the north. Back Beach (Bai Sau) stretches for kilometres, with a wide, sandy beach and a long strip of guesthouses and hotels. You'll find the downtown action at Front Beach (Bai Truoc), but no beach. If you're looking for a quiet, pebbly beach, head for tranquil Mulberry Beach (Bai Dau), up the northwest coast.

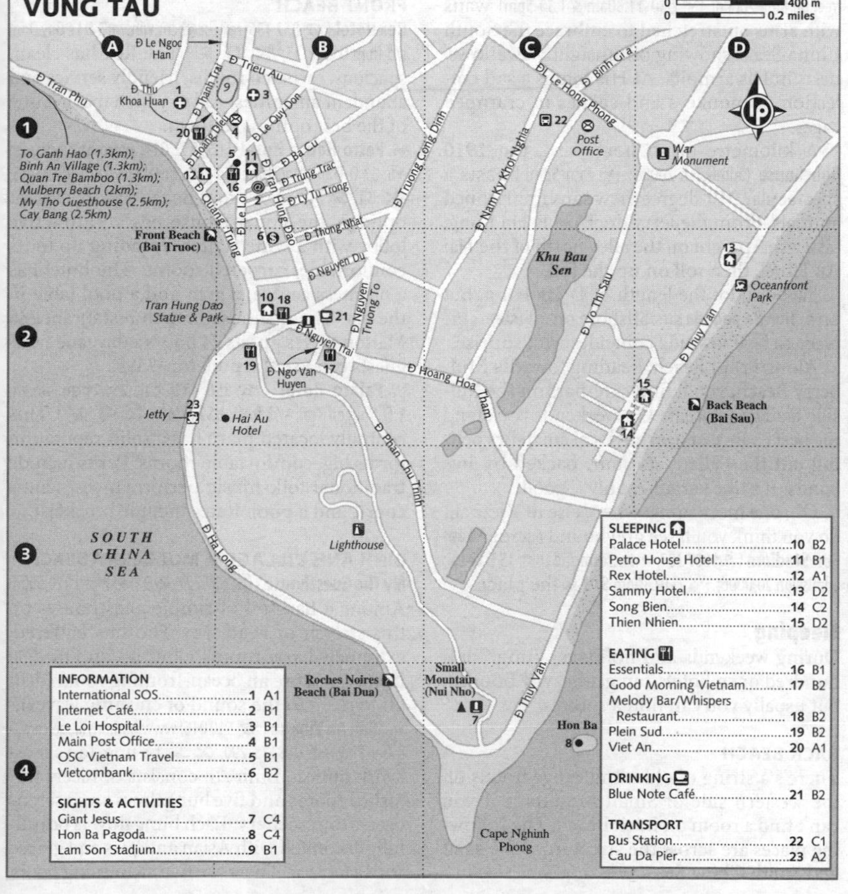

Information

International SOS (☎ 858 776; Đ Le Ngoc Han; consultations US$55-65; 24hr)

Internet Café (4A Đ Ba Cu; per hr 3000d) Fast connections.

Le Loi Hospital (☎ 832 667; 22 Đ Le Loi)

Main post office (8 Đ Hoang Dieu) Located at the ground level of the Petrovietnam Towers building.

OSC Vietnam Travel (☎ 852 008; www.oscvn.com; 9 Đ Le Loi) Vung Tau's biggest travel agency sells a decent city map (20,000d) and offers a host of unique tours, including an old battlefield tour (US$49 per person).

Vietcombank (☎ 852 024; 27-29 Đ Tran Hung Dao) Exchanges cash, travellers cheques and gives credit card advances. You'll also find an ATM at the Rex Hotel at 1 Đ Le Quy Don.

Sights & Activities

Atop Small Mountain, a **giant Jesus** (admission free, parking 2000d; 7.30-11.30am & 1.30-5pm) waits with arms outstretched to embrace the South China Sea – showing off unsightly swallows' nests in His armpits. At His foot is a sad collection of monkeys and snakes in cramped cages.

A kilometre or so northwest, the 1910 **lighthouse** (admission 2000d; 7am-5pm) boasts a spectacular 360-degree view sans imprisoned animals. From the ferry dock on Đ Ha Long, take a sharp right on the alley north of the Hai Au Hotel, then roll on up the hill.

Pagodas dot the length of Đ Ha Long, but prim **Hon Ba pagoda** sits offshore on an islet – *the* place to be if low tide coincides with sunrise.

Along Front Beach, heading towards Mulberry Beach, you'll find café-bars on the hillside facing the ocean. On weekends you stand the best chance of hearing local amateurs belting out the ballads *du jour*, backed by live bands. It's like karaoke, only…good.

Oh, one more thing: where else in Vietnam do you think you'll see greyhound racing? **Lam Son Stadium** (☎ 807 309; www.sesracing.com; 15 Đ Le Loi; admission 20,000d; 7-10.30pm Sat) is the place.

Sleeping

During weekends and holidays, Vung Tau's hundred or so hotels can get heavily booked, but usually you can find a room.

BACK BEACH

There's a string of older midrange hotels on the western side of Small Mountain if you can't find a room on Back Beach. The following places are across the street from the sand and South China Sea.

Thien Nhien (☎ 853 481; 145A Đ Thuy Van; d 100,000-200,000d) Along the main beach drag, this simple, airy guesthouse has tidy rooms, some with balconies, air-con and ocean views.

Song Bien (☎ 523 311; 131A Đ Thuy Van; d 120,000-150,000d) Chinese-style décor brightens this fairly comfortable place; although there are no ocean views, there's a shared terrace on the top floor.

Sammy Hotel (☎ 854 755; sammyhotel@hcm.vnn.vn; 157 Đ Thuy Van; r from US$35) Easily the fanciest place this side of Small Mountain, Sammy has an in-house Chinese restaurant and comfortable rooms with all the trimmings. There's a pool at the oceanfront park across the street. None of the ocean-view rooms have balconies, oddly, though mountain-view rooms do.

FRONT BEACH

Rex Hotel (☎ 852 135; rex.osc@hcm.vnn.vn; 1 Đ Le Quy Don; s/d from US$28/35) The Rex has clean, spacious, carpeted rooms, friendly service and abundant amenities – all of which make it one of the best options in town.

Petro House Hotel (☎ 852 014; petro.htl@hcm.vnn.vn; 63 Đ Tran Hung Dao; s/d with breakfast from US$35/45) One of Front Beach's more elegant options, the Petro House has an attractive lobby with a wide staircase leading up to its comfortable, carpeted rooms. The hotel has a business centre, a gym and a pool table in the bar. The in-house French restaurant Ma Maison serves guests 24 hours a day, and non-guests can use the pool for US$5.

Palace Hotel (☎ 856 411; palacevt@hcm.vnn.vn; 1 Đ Nguyen Trai; s/d from US$40/45) This centrally located place has a solid reputation for its big, comfortable rooms. Perks include traditional folk-music performances, tennis courts and a pool. Rates include breakfast.

BINH ANH VILLAGE & MULBERRY BEACH

My Tho Guesthouse (☎ 551 722; 45 Đ Tran Phu; r 120,000d) Among a handful of simple guesthouses on this stretch of road, My Tho has battered, extremely basic rooms – but it's an OK deal if you can score an ocean-fronting room (drift off to sleep to the sound of crashing waves).

Binh An Village (☎ 510 016; www.binhanvillage.com; 1 Đ Tran Phu; r/ste US$175-290) Vung Tau's most lavish option, Binh An consists of nicely furnished rooms and five bungalows amid serene oceanfront scenery. Each bungalow is beautifully decorated with Asian antiques and graced with a terrace. There are two swimming pools, one ocean-fed and one freshwater, both near the sea's edge. There's also a good open-air restaurant here (set meals US$15 to US$38), which is open for lunch and dinner, with live jazz most weekend nights and à la carte international and Vietnamese cuisine.

Eating & Drinking

The road along Back Beach, Đ Thuy Van, is crammed with *com* shops and seafood restaurants. Most of the nightlife in town is of the oilmen-and-prostitutes variety.

FRONT BEACH

Melodies Bar/Whispers Restaurant (☎ 856 028; 13-15 Đ Nguyen Trai; ⏰ 4pm-midnight) Local expats start their evenings at the downtown BB Bar/Whispers Restaurant with well-prepared Western food and pool tables in a noisy, lively setting.

Plein Sud (☎ 511 570; 152A Đ Ha Long; mains 35,000-150,000d; 💻) Feed your Mediterranean food cravings here. With home-smoked fish and meat, an authentic Italian wood-fired pizza oven and tapas, Plein Sud offers a fixed menu supplemented with rotating specials and freshly baked French bread. There's a lovely terrace lined with banana trees, and a pool table and a bar.

Viet An (☎ 853 735; 1 Đ Hoang Dieu; mains 60,000-90,000d) On a quiet street in town, Viet An has a small, greenery-surrounded patio and prepares nicely spiced halal Indian food.

Good Morning Vietnam (☎ 856 959; 6 Đ Hoang Hoa Tham; pastas 60,000-90,000d; ⏰ breakfast, lunch & dinner) One more outpost in the coastal chain, this pleasant eatery serves up reliably good Italian food. It's an expat favourite.

Essentials (☎ 510 099; 6 Đ Le Quy Don; ⏰ 7.30am-9pm) Imported picnic victuals are available at this tiny shop, from cereals to frozen veal; it also delivers.

Blue Note Café (☎ 532 247; 6 Đ Tran Hung Dao; coffees 6000-8000d; ⏰ breakfast, lunch & dinner) One of a handful of cafés scattered in this neighbourhood, the Blue Note's spacious tree-shaded terrace makes a pleasant stop for a coffee or a drink.

MULBERRY BEACH

Mulberry Beach's main road has several good seafood places down on the water.

Cay Bang (☎ 838 522; 69 Đ Tran Phu; mains 45,000d; ⏰ 11am-10pm) This local favourite, serving fresh seafood, overlooks the water and is a festive place on weekends.

Quan Tre Bamboo (☎ 836 157; 7 Đ Tran Phu; mains 45,000-90,000d; ⏰ lunch & dinner) Go to this place if you're hankering for lobster or a cocktail with a view of the giant Mary with Baby Jesus statue, best enjoyed from the upstairs terrace.

Ganh Hao (☎ 550 909; 3 Đ Tran Phu; mains 50,000-80,000d) The seafood here is superb, and you can enjoy a wide variety of dishes (including a delicious seafood soup) on the terrace overlooking the waves.

Getting There & Away

From Mien Dong bus station in HCMC, air-con minibuses (25,000d, two hours, 128km) leave for Vung Tau throughout the day until around 4.30pm. From Vung Tau's **bus station** (192A Đ Nam Ky Khoi Nghia) to Mulberry Beach or Back Beach, a *xe om* should cost around 10,000d.

Should convenience outweigh cost, catch a **Petro Express hydrofoil** (☎ HCMC 08-821 0650, Vung Tau 816 308) to Vung Tau (120,000d, 90 minutes) at Bach Dang jetty in HCMC. Boats leave roughly two hours starting at 6.30am, but check in HCMC for the latest schedule. In Vung Tau the boat leaves from Cau Da pier, opposite the Hai Au Hotel.

Getting Around

Vung Tau is easily traversed on two wheels. Guesthouses can arrange bicycle hire (per day US$2); motorbikes cost US$5 to US$10 per day. Or just make eye contact with that *cyclo* or *xe om* driver on the corner.

LONG HAI

☎ 064

Those heading south, who also want to escape the mass-tourism soullessness of Vung Tau, could press on to Long Hai, a less-commercialised seaside retreat within a couple of hours' drive of HCMC. The fishing village of Long Hai, 30km northeast of Vung Tau, has a pretty white-sand beach and the area benefits from a microclimate that brings less rain than other parts of the south. Its natural beauty and microclimate are the main reasons why Bao Đai, the last emperor of Vietnam, built a holiday residence here (now the Anoasis Beach Resort; p391).

Long Hai is a peaceful place to visit during the week, but it loses its local character on the weekends when Vietnamese tourists (and the occasional busload of Chinese visitors) pack the sands on weekends. Though there are a couple of low-key resorts in the Long Hai vicinity, western travellers have yet to arrive, so if you're looking for a lively spot with dining and nightlife action, Mui Ne (p304) is probably a better choice.

Sights & Activities

The western end of Long Hai's beach is where fishing boats moor and is therefore none too clean. However, the eastern end is attractive, with a reasonable amount of white sand and palm trees. For even prettier beach, keep heading east.

After the Tet holiday, Long Hai hosts an annual major **fishermen's pilgrimage festival**, where hundreds of boats come from afar to worship at **Mo Co Temple**.

Apart from the beaches, there are several sites in the area well worth exploring. At Minh Dam, 5km from Long Hai, there are **caves** with historical connections to the Franco-Viet Minh and American Wars. Although the caves are little more than spaces between the boulders covering the cliff-face, VC soldiers bunked here off and on between 1948 and 1975; you can still see bullet holes in the rocks from the skirmishes that happened here. Steps hewn into the rock-face lead up to the caves, with spectacular views over the coastal plains at the top.

Nearby there is a **mountain-top temple** with more great panoramic views of the coastline.

Twenty kilometres away at Dia Dao there are **underground tunnels** (similar, but on a smaller scale, to those at Cu Chi) dating from the American War.

If you are heading to/from Hwy 1, north of Long Hai, a less-travelled route is via the **hot springs** at Binh Chau, 60km away from Long Hai. There are also plenty of other beaches to seek out as you make your way north or south along the coastal Rte 55.

You could also treat yourself to a day at **Anoasis Beach Resort** (☎ 868 227; Provincial Rd 44; admission weekday/weekend US$6/10). The tropically landscaped grounds of this luxury resort were once home to another of Emperor Bao Dai's villas. Day passes entitle nonguests to full use of the recreational facilities, which include a swimming pool, tennis courts, billiards and ping-pong tables and a lovely stretch of private beach.

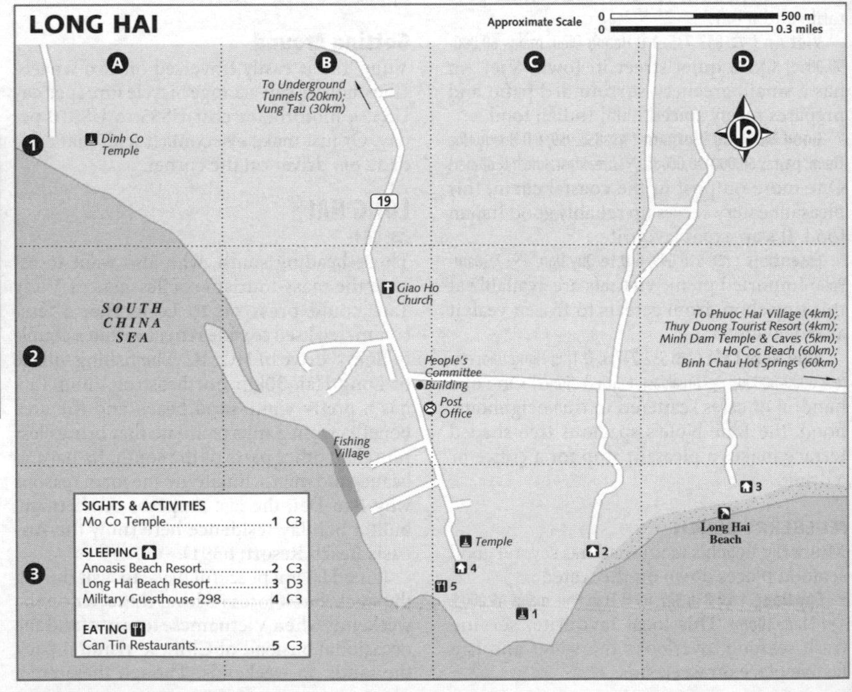

AROUND HO CHI MINH CITY

Sleeping

Military Guesthouse 298 (Doan an Dieu Duong 298; ☎ 868 316; Rte 19; r 150,000-200,000d; ❄) At the dead end of Rte 19, this guesthouse is run by the navy, which may help explain its prime beachfront location. Rooms here are clean and comfortable, with tile floors and hot water; the cheapest rooms are fan only.

Thuy Duong Tourist Resort (☎ 886 215; fax 886 180; bungalow US$20-30, hotel r US$35-60; ❄ 💻) A large complex in Phuoc Hai village, about 4km from Long Hai, this vast resort sprawls out on both sides of the road. Hotel rates include breakfast; bungalow rates don't. Try to avoid the beach bungalows facing the noisy cafés on the beach. Day use of the clean, attractive beach costs 15,000d.

our pick **Anoasis Beach Resort** (☎ 868 227; www.anoasisresort.com.vn; Provincial Rd 44; bungalows with breakfast US$150-300; ❄ 💻 🏊) One of Vietnam's loveliest beachside retreats, this stylish boutique resort is the brainchild of French-Vietnamese helicopter pilot Anoa Dussol-Perran and her husband. Anoasis offers cosy wooden cottages spread out over the landscaped property, and it has a beautiful private beach. Recreational opportunities include cycling, fishing, tennis and, of course, massage. Weekday rates are slightly lower than the weekend rates listed above, with discounts offered for stays of two nights or more.

Long Hai Beach Resort (☎ 661 355; reservation@longhaibeachresortvn.com; Provincial Rd 44; r/bungalow with breakfast from US$105/125; ❄ 💻 🏊) Some 500m east of Anoasis, this new resort has pleasantly furnished rooms and bungalows scattered about a lush complex. The accommodations aren't huge for the money, but all the amenities are on offer – tennis court, pool, gym – and there's a pretty beach just a stroll from your door.

Eating

There's a cluster of thatch-roof beachside restaurants called **Can Tin 1**, **2**, **3** and **4** (mains around 15,000-70,000d; 🕑 7am-7pm) near Military Guesthouse 298. These serve decent Vietnamese mains – including good, simple seafood dishes. Apart from these relaxed places, there aren't many other options in Long Hai.

Getting There & Around

Long Hai is 124km from HCMC and takes about two hours to reach by car. The 30km road between Vung Tau and Long Hai is not served by public transport; a *xe om* ride should cost around 50,000d.

Motorbike-taxi drivers hang around all the likely tourist spots in the area.

LOC AN BEACH

☎ 064

A new road winds along the coast from Long Hai to Binh Chau, crossing through the town of Phuoc Hai before passing by a dune-covered beach and the small **Loc An Resort** (☎ 886 377; www.locanresort.com; d with breakfast 190,000-440,000d; ❄ 🏊). Situated on a lagoon some 50m from the palm-shaded beach, this guesthouse has trim and tidy rooms, and staff are friendly and welcoming. Boats shuttle guests to the beach and back for free. The restaurant has a terrace (mains 40,000d to 60,000d) and serves decent seafood, plus there's a pool table.

At the fork in the road, there's a sign leading to **Thuy Hoang** (☎ 874 223; bungalows 260,000d; ❄), which consists of small A-frame beach bungalows. It has an indoor-outdoor restaurant that serves good locally caught seafood and cold beer.

HO TRAM BEACH

☎ 064

Another 5km east of Loc An, you'll pass by a lovely stretch of sand that's still rather undeveloped. The big draw of this area is the fairly new **Ho Tram Osaka Resort & Spa** (☎ 781 525; www.hotramresort.com; bungalow incl breakfast US$72-160; ❄ 🏊), a peaceful, beautifully landscaped complex sprinkled with attractive bungalows. Each has high ceilings and unique furnishings and layouts (the best are duplexes with beach views). There's also a spa, a beach bar and an open-sided restaurant (mains 80,000d to 120,000d) that's open for breakfast, lunch and dinner, and is well worth visiting if you're passing through the area.

HO COC BEACH

☎ 064

Keep heading along the coastal road, another 12km or so from Ho Tram, and you'll arrive at the remote and beautiful Ho Coc Beach. Golden sands backed by dunes and clear waters, along with the lack of development, make it a draw – particularly on weekdays, when you'll have the beach largely to yourself. As elsewhere along the coast, weekends bring crowds of Vietnamese tourists.

The area around the beach is part of an 11,000-hectare rainforest that was designated a nature reserve in 1975. Most of the larger wildlife was exterminated or else relocated for safety reasons (most of the elephants were sent to Thailand), but plenty of birds and monkeys can be spotted in the forest. Guides for the walking trails can be hired for about 50,000d a day. Inquire at Hang Duong Ho Coc (below).

Sleeping & Eating

There are only a few accommodation choices right at the beach, all of which have decent adjoining restaurants serving good seafood.

Saigon-Ho Coc (☎ 791 036; fax 878 175; bungalows s/d 120,000/160,000d) Also called Khu Du Lich Bien Ho Coc, these beachfront A-frame bamboo bungalows with simple private bathrooms (with cold water) are small and rustic, but are not unpleasant places to bunk.

Hang Duong Ho Coc (☎ 878 145; fax 873 878; bungalows 120,000-200,000d; ❄) About 50m south down the beach from Saigon-Ho Coc, this equally rustic resort has masses of cosy wooden cottages. The rooms have an attached cold-water bathroom, and some have air-con (others are fan only).

Hotel Ven Ven (☎ 791 121; info@kimsabai.com; r 250,000d; ❄) Across the road from the turn-off to the beach bungalows, this attractive newish spot has pleasant, spotless rooms set amid greenery. Although it's not on the beach, Ven Ven is the nicest option in the area, and the sands are just a short stroll away.

Getting There & Away

There's no public transport out here, but some of the budget cafés in HCMC offer appealing day and overnight trips to Ho Coc. **Saigon Tourist** (☎ 08-829 8914; www.saigontourist.net; 49 Đ Le Thanh Ton, HCMC) puts together trips to Ho Coc that include a visit to Binh Chau Hot Springs Resort (below). This also makes for a good (but very long) day trip on a motorbike – which you can also hire in Vung Tau. The new road is in decent shape, and it's a particularly magical ride past sand dunes with lovely ocean views on certain stretches of the road between Ho Tram and Ho Coc.

BINH CHAU HOT SPRINGS

☎ 064

About 150km from HCMC, and 60km northeast of Long Hai, is **Binh Chau Hot Springs** (Suoi Khoang Nong Binh Chau; admission 20,000d) and the **Binh Chau Hot Springs Resort** (☎ 871 131; www.saigonbinhchauecoresort.com; s/d/bungalow incl breakfast from US$25/35/125, camping per person 50,000d).

Chief among the attractions on this 35-hectare site is an outdoor hot-spring-fed swimming pool (admission 30,000d), though visitors wanting the full experience might opt for a soak in a mudbath (admission 120,000d). The pool temperature is around 37°C, and the minerals in the water are said to be beneficial to your bones, muscles and skin, and are also said to improve blood circulation and mental disorders. There's also a spa, with massages available. Also onsite are a golf practice range, tennis court, restaurant and playground.

If you want to stay overnight here, there's a range of accommodation options. The rooms are airy and tidy, with trim furnishings, though the ones at the lower bracket are small. Suites and bungalows provide roomier quarters.

Until about a decade ago there was wildlife in the area, including tigers and elephants, but it seems humans have nearly won the area over. In 1994 six elephants were captured near the springs, but after a few months of keeping them as pets their captors turned them over to the zoo in HCMC. Nowadays the only wildlife you are likely to spot are ceramic lions, cheetahs and panthers, which decorate the marshes around the springs.

The hottest spring reaches 82°C, which is hot enough to boil an egg in 10 to 15 minutes. Vietnamese visitors like to boil eggs in the bamboo baskets set aside for this purpose; you'll find a couple of giant chicken statues decorating the springs where you, too, can boil up a snack for yourself, with raw eggs on sale.

Getting There & Away

The resort is in a compound 6km north of the village of Binh Chau. The road connecting Rte 55 to Binh Chau is a smooth ride, thanks to funds donated by the Australian government in the '90s.

Good highway or not, there's no public transport. You'll need a motorbike or car; if you choose the latter, perhaps you can find some travellers to share the expense.

CAT TIEN NATIONAL PARK

☎ 061 / elevation 700m

One of the outstanding gems of the region, the 72,000-hectare **Cat Tien National Park** (☎/fax 669 228; adult/child 50,000/20,000d; 🕑 7am-10pm)

KIND-HEARTED STRANGERS *Regis St Louis*

Sometimes Vietnam gets a bad rap from travellers. After spending a few days in HCMC or Hanoi, the offers of motorbike and *cyclo* rides, invitations to dine here or come meet beautiful ladies over there can seem a constant stream of tiresome background noise. A few unfortunate events – suffering petty theft, getting grossly overcharged – can even lead to cynicism. 'The Vietnamese are only after my money,' one jaded traveller told me.

Although there are undeniably opportunists in Vietnam – as there are anywhere in the world – these are a small (but unfortunately highly visible) faction. Meanwhile, benevolent, golden-hearted souls go about their days largely invisible to travellers. Sometimes it takes misfortune to bring them out into the open. During research for this book, I had my own minor crisis while motorbiking a lovely but totally empty stretch of road between Vung Tau and Ho Coc, south of HCMC. I was at least 10 km from the nearest town and an hour's ride from my hotel when my bike sputtered and died. It was late in the day and the sun was setting. After a few moments of feeling sorry for myself and some fruitless tinkering with the silent engine, I began pushing the bike.

I covered about 500m when a young couple pulled up next to me and offered help. Although the two spoke little English, the man explained that he would push me – his foot against the back peg of my bike as he drove along, the two of us balanced closely together. He guided me to a shop of his friend, who was unable to fix it, and then he insisted on pushing me the rest of the way to Vung Tau. When we finally arrived, in darkness after a rather gruelling journey, he refused any payment. Instead he invited me out for a drink, and even then he wouldn't let me pay. It was a humbling encounter, meeting such a generous soul who was willing to put himself out for a stranger. It's just one of the reasons why travelling in Vietnam is so rewarding: it's less about seeing the sights than mingling with a truly great people.

comprises an amazingly biodiverse region of lowland tropical rain forest. The hiking, mountain biking and bird-watching are easily the best in Southern Vietnam. Always call ahead for reservations as the park can accommodate only a limited number of visitors.

In the 2nd century AD the Cat Tien area was a religious centre of the Funan empire, and ancient Oc-Eo cultural relics have been discovered in the park. Cat Tien was hit hard by defoliants during the American War, but the large old-growth trees survived and the smaller plants have recovered. Just as importantly, the wildlife has made a comeback and in 2001 Unesco added Cat Tien National Park to its list of biosphere reserves. Since then, infrastructure has improved markedly with decent overnight options. It's worth spending at least two full days here, if possible.

Fauna in the park include 326 bird species, 100 types of mammal, 79 types of reptile, 41amphibian species, plus an incredible array of insects, including 400-odd species of butterfly. Many of these creatures are listed as rare and endangered, including the Javan rhinoceros. Considered one of the rarest mammals in the world, this unusual rhino exists only in Cat Tien (there are believed to be seven or eight living in the park) and on the island of Java, in Indonesia. Leopards are also believed to live in the park, while another unique creature found here is a type of wild ox called a gaur. Rare birds in the park include the orange-necked partridge, green peafowl and Siamese fireback. There is also a healthy population of monkeys. Leeches are a less desirable member of the local fauna so come prepared, especially during the wet season.

Elephants roam the park, but their presence has caused some controversy. In the early 1990s a herd of 10 hungry elephants fell into a bomb crater, created during the American War, just outside of Cat Tien. Local villagers took pity on the elephants and dug out a ramp to rescue them. Tragically, since then 28 villagers have been killed by rampaging elephants. Theoretically, the problem could have been 'solved' by shooting the elephants, but the Vietnamese government wasn't willing to risk the wrath of international environmental groups. However, none of these organisations has come up with the funds for relocating the elephants, some of which were finally removed to zoos. In the longer term such conflicts are likely to be repeated because of the increasing competition between Vietnam's wildlife and its growing population for the same living space.

Cat Tien also boasts a wide range of evergreen, semideciduous and bamboo forests; some 1800 species of plants thrive in the park.

Cat Tien National Park can be explored on foot, by mountain bike, by 4WD and also by boat along the Dong Nai River. There are many well-established hiking trails in the park, though the catch is you'll need to hire a **guide** (per half-/full day 60,000/120,000d), as well as transportation to and from the start of the trail (4WDs can also be rented for 120,000d per hour). Unfortunately, guides don't speak much English.

Highly recommended is an overnight visit to the **Crocodile Swamp** (Bau Sau), which is a 9km drive from the park headquarters and you have to trek the last 4km to the swamp; the walk takes about three hours return. It may be possible for smaller groups (four or less) to spend the night at the ranger's post here. It's a good place to view the wildlife that comes to drink in the swamp. Another evening activity is the **night safari** (160,000d) that the park offers. Wherever you decide to go, be sure to book a guide in advance and take plenty of insect repellent.

The park lies 150km northeast of HCMC and 40km south of Buon Ma Thuot and straddles the border of three provinces – Lam Dong, Dong Nai and Binh Phuoc.

Sleeping & Eating

There are simple, all-wooden shacks as well as comfier, concrete **bungalows** (☎/fax 669 228; shack/bungalow 90,000/160,000d;) near the park headquarters. The facilities here are new and in good condition; a pool and a tennis court are on hand. You can pitch a tent at the park's campsite (20,000d), though you'll need your own gear. There are also several small restaurants near the park entrance, including a simple thatch-roof canteen (mains 12,000d to 24,000d), which opens from 7am to 10pm, and a more modern shinier affair (mains 12,000d to 38,000d) serving heartier fare just down the path. It's open 7am to 8pm.

NATIONAL HIGHWAY 20: ROADSIDE ATTRACTIONS

Langa Lake

The HCMC–Dalat road (Hwy 20) spans this reservoir, which is crossed by a bridge. Lots of floating houses, where families harvest the fish underneath, can be seen here. It's a very scenic spot for photography, and most tourist vehicles on the HCMC–Dalat road make a short pit-stop here.

Volcanic Craters

Near Dinh Quan on Hwy 20 there are three volcanoes – now extinct, but nonetheless very impressive. The craters date from the late Jurassic period, about 150 million years ago. You'll have to do a little walking to see the crater. One is on the left-hand side of the road, about 2km south of Dinh Quan, and another on the right-hand side about 8km beyond Dinh Quan, towards Dalat.

Underground Lava Tubes

A bit beyond the volcanic craters, towards Dalat, are underground lava tubes. These rare caves were formed as the surface lava cooled and solidified, while the hotter underground lava continued to flow, leaving a hollow space. Lava tubes differ sharply in appearance from limestone caves (the latter are formed by underground springs). While limestone caves have abundant stalactites and stalagmites, the walls of lava caves are smooth.

The easiest way to find the lava tubes is to first find the teak forest on Hwy 20 between the Km120 and Km124 markers. The children who live around the forest can point you to the entrance of the lava tubes. However, you are strongly advised *not* to go into the tubes by yourself. It's best to have a guide and, furthermore, inform someone responsible where you are going. You definitely need to take a torch (flashlight).

For more information on the waterfalls and other attractions along Hwy 20, see the Central Highlands chapter (p315).

Getting There & Away

Whichever way you come, you'll be dropped off at the park office, 100m before the ferry across the Dong Nai River to park headquarters. Buy your entrance ticket from the park office, which will include the price of the ferry crossing.

The most common approach to the park is from Hwy 20, which connects Dalat with HCMC. To reach the park, follow the narrow 24km road, which branches west from Hwy 20 at Talai Junction (Nga Ban Talai), 125km north of HCMC and 175km south of Dalat. The road to the park is signposted at the junction, and with your own wheels getting there shouldn't be a hassle.

By bus, take any Dalat-bound service (35,000d, four hours) and tell the driver to let you off at Vuon Quoc Gia Cat Tien. From this junction, you can hire a motorbike (they're always around) to take you the remaining 25km to the park (around 40,000d).

Another approach to Cat Tien National Park is to take a boat across Langa Lake and then go by foot from there. **Dalat Holidays/Phat Tire Ventures** (☎ 063-829 422; www.phattireventures.com) is a reputable ecotour operator in Dalat and is a good place to inquire about this and other access options from the central highlands area (including mountain-biking to the park from Dalat).

Although many travel agencies from HCMC operate tours to the park, we've received mixed reviews from the budget agencies. For a reputable customised birding, bike or hiking tour, contact Sinhbalo Adventures (p338).

CON DAO ISLANDS

☎ 064 / pop 1650

One of the stellar attractions in this region, the Con Dao Archipelago is slowly gaining attention for its startling natural beauty. Con Son, the largest of this chain of 15 islands and islets, is ringed with lovely beaches, coral reefs and scenic bays, and remains partially covered in thick forests. In addition to hiking, diving and exploring empty coastal roads and deserted beaches, there are some excellent wildlife-watching opportunities.

Con Son Island (with a total land area of 20 sq km) is also known by its Europeanised Malay name, Iles Poulo Condore (Pulau Kundur), which means 'Island of the Squashes'. Although it seems something of an island paradise, Con Son was once hell on earth for the thousands of prisoners who languished in confinement during the French and American regimes.

Roughly 80% of the land area in the island chain is part of Con Dao National Park, which protects Vietnam's most important **sea turtle** nesting grounds. For the last decade the World Wildlife Foundation (WWF) has been working with local park rangers on a long-term monitoring program. During nesting season (May to September) the park sets up ranger stations to rescue threatened nests and move them to the safe haven of hatcheries.

Other interesting sea life around Con Dao includes the **dugong**, a rare and seldom-seen marine mammal in the same family as the manatee. Dugongs live as far north as Japan, and as far south as the subtropical coasts of Australia. Their numbers have been on a steady decline, and increasingly efforts are being made to protect these adorable creatures. Major threats include coastal road development, which causes the destruction of shallow-water beds of seagrass, the dugongs' staple diet.

Con Dao is one of those rare places in Vietnam where there are virtually no structures over two storeys, and where the traveller's experience is almost hassle-free. There's even no need to bargain at the local market! Owing to the relatively high cost and the inaccessibility of the islands, mass tourism has thankfully been kept to a minimum.

These days most visitors to Con Son are package-tour groups of former VC soldiers who were imprisoned on the island. The Vietnamese government generously subsidises these jaunts as a show of gratitude for their sacrifice. Foreign tourists are still few and far between, though their numbers are on the rise.

The driest time to visit Con Dao is from November to February, though the seas are calmest from March to July. The rainy season lasts from June to September, but there are also northeast and southwest monsoons in autumn that can bring heavy winds. In November 1997 typhoon Linda did a number here: 300 fishing boats were lost, reefs were wiped out and the forests flattened. September and October are the hottest months, though even then the cool island breezes make Con Dao relatively comfortable when compared with HCMC or Vung Tau.

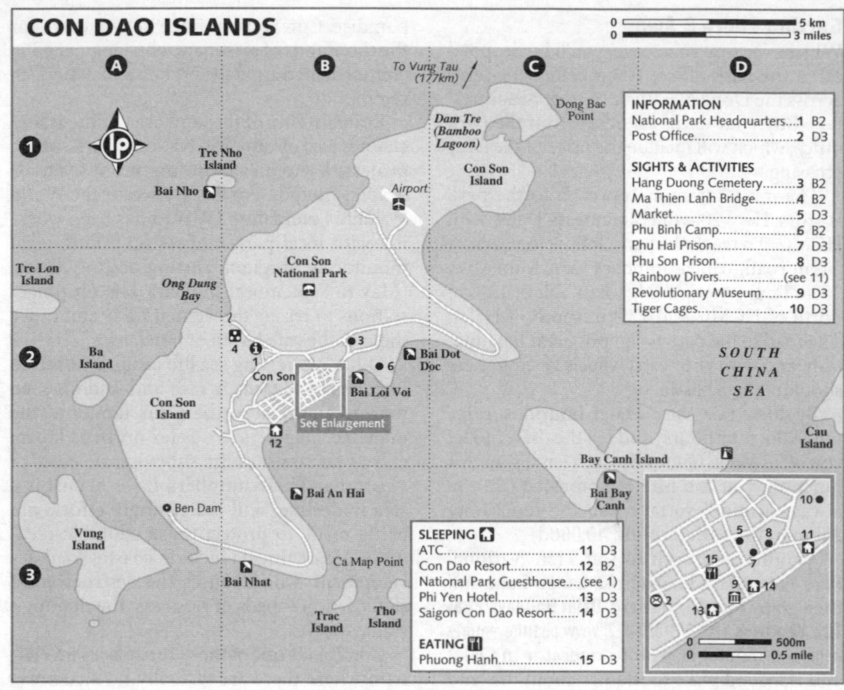

History

Occupied at various times by the Khmer, Malays and Vietnamese, Con Son Island also served as an early base for European commercial ventures in the region. The first recorded European arrival was a ship of Portuguese mariners in 1560. The British East India Company maintained a fortified trading post here from 1702 to 1705 – an experiment that ended when the English on the island were massacred in a revolt by the Macassar soldiers they had recruited on the Indonesian island of Sulawesi.

Con Son Island has a strong political and cultural history, and an all-star line-up of Vietnamese revolutionary heroes (many streets are named after them) were incarcerated here. Under the French, Con Son was used as a major prison for opponents of French colonialism, earning a reputation for the routine mistreatment and torture of prisoners. In 1954 the island was taken over by the South Vietnamese government, which continued to utilise its remoteness to hold opponents of the government (including students) in horrifying conditions. During the American War the South Vietnamese were joined here by US forces.

Information

The **national park headquarters** (☎ 830 150; vqgcdao@hcm.vnn.vn; 29 Đ Vo Thi Sau; 🕑 7-11.30am & 1.30-5pm Mon-Fri, 7.30am-11am & 2-4.30pm Sat) is a good place to get information. Since the military controls access to parts of the national park, stop here first to have staff direct you to possible island excursions and hikes; this office also distributes a free useful handout on hikes around the island. Some hiking trails have interpretive signage in English and Vietnamese. The headquarters also has an exhibition hall with displays on the diversity of local forest and marine life, threats to the local environment, and local conservation activities.

Several slow internet cafés are found in town, including one attached to the **post office** (cnr Đ Tran Phu & Nguyen Thi Minh Khai; per hr 2400d; 🕑 8am-8pm)

PENNILESS IN PARADISE

Before flying out to Con Dao Island, be sure to get ample funds as there are no banks or ATMs on the island.

Sights & Activities

CON DAO NATIONAL PARK

From March to November it's possible to do a beautiful and leisurely two-hour **trek** starting from near the airport runway, but you'll definitely need a local guide to do this (about US$6 for the outing). The walk leads through thick forest and mangroves, and past a hilltop stream to **Bamboo Lagoon** (Dam Tre). This spot is stunning and there's good snorkelling in the bay. You could even consider arranging for a boat to come and pick you up.

A hike that you can do yourself is a 1km walk (about 25 minutes each way) through rain forest to **Ong Dung Bay**. The trail begins a few kilometres north of town. On the road to the trailhead, you'll also pass the ruins of the Ma Thien Lanh Bridge, built by prisoners under the French occupation. The bay itself has only a rocky beach, though there's interesting coral 300m off shore.

Rainbow Divers (☎ 630 023; bin@divevietnam.com) runs an office out of the Phi Yen Hotel, though they're scheduled to move to ATC sometime in 2007. They offer some excellent dives among the coral reefs around the islands. During the dry season (November to May) visibility is good and dives are less likely to be cancelled. This is also a good source of island info (English spoken).

CON SON ISLAND

Con Son town is a sleepy seafront settlement that would make a perfect location for a period film. All three of the town's hotels are on Đ Ton Duc Thang, along a strip of forlorn single-storey French villas (most are abandoned and in disrepair, but nonetheless photogenic). Nearby is the local **market**, which is busiest between 7am and 8am.

The main sights on Con Son Island are a museum, several prisons and a cemetery. If you visit the museum first you can buy a ticket for 35,000d that will get you a guided tour of the museum and prisons – very good value.

The **Revolutionary Museum** (🕒 7-11am & 1.30-5pm Mon-Sat) is next to Saigon Con Dao Hotel and has exhibits on Vietnamese resistance to the French, communist opposition to the Republic of Vietnam, and the treatment of political prisoners (including some gruesome photos of torture). There is also a mock-up of the islands and some curiously embalmed animals – including a monkey smoking a pipe.

Phu Hai Prison, a short walk from the museum, is the largest of the 11 prisons on the island. Built in 1862, the prison houses several enormous detention buildings, one with about 100 shackled and emaciated mannequins that are all too lifelike. Equally eerie are the empty solitary cells with ankle shackles (the decree on the walls in Vietnamese means 'no killing fleas' – prisoners were not allowed to dirty the walls). Nearby is the equally disturbing **Phu Son Prison.**

The notorious **Tiger Cages** were built by the French in the 1940s. From 1957 to 1961 nearly 2000 political prisoners were confined in these tiny cells. Here there are 120 chambers with ceiling bars, where guards could watch down on the prisoners like tigers in a zoo, and another 60 solariums with no roof at all.

Over the course of four decades of war, some 20,000 people were killed on Con Son and 1994 of their graves can be seen at **Hang Duong Cemetery**. Sadly, only 700 of these graves bear the name of the victims. Vietnam's most famous heroine, Vo Thi Sau (1933–1952), was the first woman executed (by a firing squad) on Con Son, on 23 January 1952. Today's pilgrims come to burn incense at her tomb, and make offerings of mirrors and combs (symbolic because she died so young). In the distance behind the cemetery you'll see a huge **monument** symbolising three giant sticks of incense.

Phu Binh Camp is also part of the main tour, though it's outside of town. Built in 1971 by the Americans, this one has 384 chambers and was known as Camp 7 until 1973, when it closed following evidence of torture. After the Paris Agreements in 1973, the name was changed to Phu Binh Camp.

CON SON BEACHES & OTHER ISLANDS

On Con Son there are several good beaches worth finding. Inquire at the hotels about snorkelling gear rental for about 50,000d per day.

Bai Dat Doc is one nice beach with a long stretch of sand. Keep an eye out for dugongs frolicking in the water.

Bai Nhat is small and very nice, though it's exposed only during low tide. **Bai An Hai** looks nice, but there are a good number of fishing boats moored nearby, and a few too many sandflies. **Bai Loi Voi** is OK as well, and shallow, but there can be a fair bit of rubbish and lots of sea shells.

THE RETURN OF THE GREEN SEA TURTLE

Two decades ago the fate of the Green Sea Turtle *(Chelonia mydas)* in Con Dao seemed dire. They were prized for their meat, and their shells had value as souvenirs. To make matters worse, the turtles' numbers were decimated by destructive fishing practices. And yet, today, following a decade of local and foreign initiatives, the turtle has made a remarkable comeback. One of Vietnam's most important sea turtle nesting sites lies scattered around the shores of the Con Dao archipelago. The World Wildlife Foundation (WWF) has helped substantially, as have other international organisations, by setting up conservation stations on the islands of Bay Canh, Tre Lon, Tai and Cau. According to WWF, since 1995 some 300,000 hatchlings have been released into the sea. In 2006, 85% of sea turtle eggs hatched successfully – the highest percentage in Vietnam. Later that year WWF also launched a satellite tracking program (the first of its kind in Vietnam) to give conservation workers a better understanding of migration patterns, as well as key habitats used by the turtles for feeding and mating. Though the population is on the rise, many turtles still die after nesting – often from getting ensnared in fishing nets.

Visitors wishing to see the turtles in their natural habitat can arrange a trip to Bay Canh Island and spend the night at the conversation site. (Turtles only lay their eggs at night, each one producing three to ten nests with an average of 70 eggs.) The best time to see them is during the nesting season, which is from May to September. For information on trips, inquire at Rainbow Divers (p397) or at the Con Dao National Park Headquarters (p396). Tours prices vary from US$30 to US$75.

The best beaches of all are on the smaller islands, such as the beautiful white-sand beach on **Tre Lon**.

Perhaps the best all-round island to visit is **Bay Canh**, which has lovely beaches, old-growth forest, mangroves, coral reefs (good snorkelling at low tide) and sea turtles (seasonal). There is a fantastic two-hour walk to a functioning French-built **lighthouse**.

Sleeping & Eating

Three of the island's five hotels are on the main road facing the bay in town.

Phi Yen Hotel (☎ 830 168; fax 830 428; 34 Đ Ton Duc Thang; s/d 170,000/222,000d; ❄) This basic, friendly minihotel has some rooms with partial sea views. All have air-con and hot water.

ATC (☎ 830 345; atc@fmail.vnn.vn; 8 Đ Ton Duc Thang; bungalow from US$22, villa US$55-75) This friendly guesthouse offers accommodation in eight tidy, brick bungalows, with air-con, hot water and a terrace (several of which overlook the sea). There are also two spacious thatch-roof stilt houses relocated here from Hoa Binh.

Saigon Con Dao Hotel (☎ 830 155; sgtcd@hcm.vnn.vn; 18 Đ Ton Duc Thang; s/d from US$40/50; ❄) Run by Saigon Tourist, this place is 400m south of ATC and offers clean, trim rooms, some with ocean views. It's overpriced for the money, though some visitors end up here on package tours. (Inquire at the Saigon Tourist office, p338, in HCMC if you're looking for a package deal.)

National Park Guesthouse (☎ 830 150; vqgcdao@hcm.vnn.vn; 29 Đ Vo Thi Sau; r 150,000d) A pleasant budget option next to the park headquarters, this friendly place has clean, simple rooms, some with excellent views of the lush mountain. It's 2km north of town.

Con Dao Resort (☎ 830 939; www.condaoresort.com.vn; 8 Đ Nguyen Đuc Thuan; r US$30-35, villa US$40-70; ❄) Con Dao's finest lodging, this place lies about 600m south of town and overlooks a sandy beach rather than the road. Rooms are clean and comfortable and have either beach or mountain views. Buffet breakfast is included. You'll also find here the best restaurant in town (try the excellent prawn salad Con Dao style) with mains from 30,000d to 75,000d.

All of the hotels have restaurants, though if you're looking for something more local in flavour, try **Phuong Hanh** (☎ 830 180; 38C Đ Nguyen Hue; mains around 30,000d), a pleasant indoor-outdoor eatery in the centre of town.

Getting There & Around

AIR

With its newly upgraded airport, Con Son Island offers flights departing every other day from HCMC, operated by Vasco (Vietnam Air Services Company) for US$80 return. The tiny airport is about 15km from the town centre. All of the hotels provide free transport to and from the airport. Although it's advisable to book your hotel ahead and arrange to be met at the airport, you can often show up and grab a seat on one of the hotel shuttle vans that meet the plane – though it would be bad form not to stay at least a night at whatever hotel gives you a free lift.

BOAT

If you want to explore the islands by boat, hire one from the national park office. A 12-person boat costs around 1,200,000d per day.

MOTORBIKE & BICYCLE

Some of the main sites on Con Son, such as the Revolution Museum and Phu Hai Prison, are within walking distance of town, but to get further afield a motorbike is ideal. All of the hotels rent motorbikes for about US$7 to US$10 per day (bicycles cost around US$2 per day). There are good coastal cycling routes (such as from town to Bai Nhat and onto the tiny settlement of Ben Dam), some nice gradual ups and downs and, thankfully, little motor traffic.

Mekong Delta

Vietnam's 'rice basket', the Mekong Delta is a watery landscape of green fields and sleepy villages, everywhere crisscrossed by the brown canals and rivulets fed by the mighty Mekong River. Its inhabitants – stereotyped as friendly and easygoing – have long toiled on the life-sustaining river, with their labours marked by the same cycles governing the waterways.

The delta, which yields enough rice to feed the country with a sizable surplus, was formed by sediment deposited by the Mekong. The process continues today, with silt deposits extending the shoreline by as much as 80m per year. The river is so large that it has two daily tides. Lush with rice paddies and fish farms, this delta plain also nourishes the cultivation of sugarcane, fruit, coconut and shrimp. Although the area is primarily rural, it is one of the most densely populated regions in Vietnam and nearly every hectare is intensively farmed.

The uniquely southern charm with its welcoming introduction to life along the river is the real draw, and visitors can explore quaint riverside towns, sample fruits bartered in the colourful floating markets or dine on home-cooked delicacies before overnighting as a homestay guest. Other highlights include visits to local orchards, flower markets and fish farms. There are also bird sanctuaries, rustic beach getaways like Hon Chong and impressive Khmer pagodas in the regions around Soc Trang and Tra Vinh.

Those seeking an idyllic retreat will find it in Phu Quoc, a forested island dotted with pretty beaches, freshwater springs and empty dirt roads (ideal for motorbike adventures). Good diving and white-sand beauty have led to its growing popularity, with a mix of cheap bungalows and five-star resorts along an uncrowded coastline.

HIGHLIGHTS

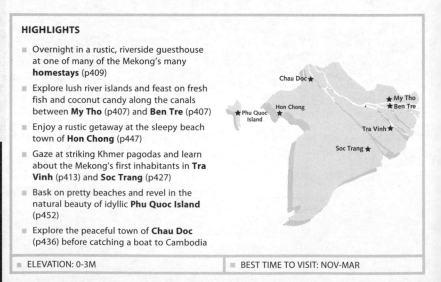

- Overnight in a rustic, riverside guesthouse at one of many of the Mekong's many **homestays** (p409)
- Explore lush river islands and feast on fresh fish and coconut candy along the canals between **My Tho** (p407) and **Ben Tre** (p407)
- Enjoy a rustic getaway at the sleepy beach town of **Hon Chong** (p447)
- Gaze at striking Khmer pagodas and learn about the Mekong's first inhabitants in **Tra Vinh** (p413) and **Soc Trang** (p427)
- Bask on pretty beaches and revel in the natural beauty of idyllic **Phu Quoc Island** (p452)
- Explore the peaceful town of **Chau Doc** (p436) before catching a boat to Cambodia

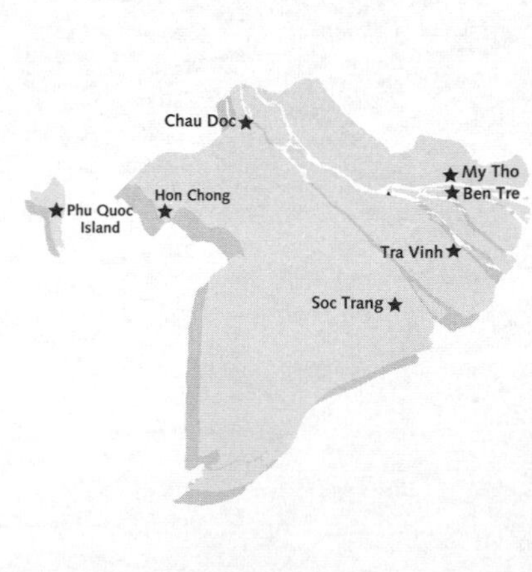

- ELEVATION: 0-3M
- BEST TIME TO VISIT: NOV-MAR

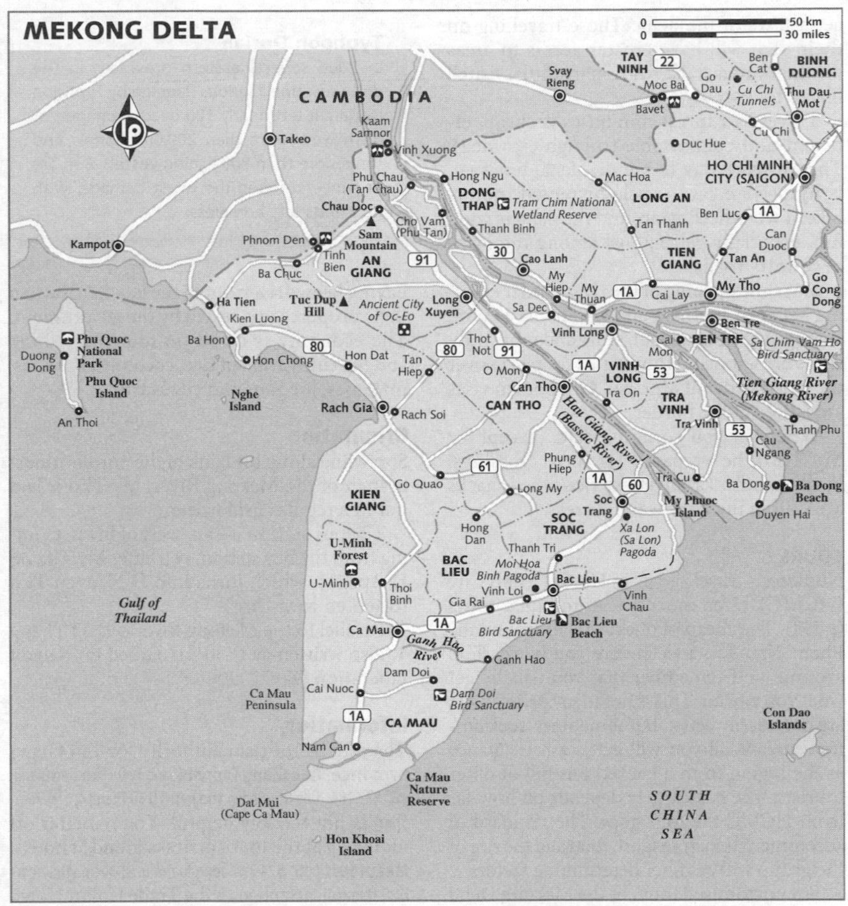

History

The Mekong Delta was once part of the Khmer kingdom, and was the last region of modern-day Vietnam to be annexed and settled by the Vietnamese. Cambodians, mindful that they controlled the area until the 18th century, still call the delta 'Lower Cambodia'. The Khmer Rouge tried to follow up on this claim by raiding Vietnamese villages and massacring the inhabitants. This led the Vietnamese army to invade Cambodia in 1979 and oust the Khmer Rouge from power. Most of the current inhabitants of the Mekong Delta are ethnic Vietnamese, but there are also significant populations of ethnic Chinese and Khmer, as well as a few Chams. For more on the Khmer back story see p415.

When the government introduced collective farming to the delta in 1975, production fell significantly and there were food shortages in Saigon (although farmers in the delta easily grew enough to feed themselves). People from Saigon would head down to the delta to buy sacks of black-market rice, but to prevent 'profiteering' the police set up checkpoints and confiscated rice from anyone carrying more than 10kg. All this ended in 1986 and farmers in this region have since propelled Vietnam forward to become the world's second-largest rice exporter after Thailand.

Getting There & Around

Most travellers head to the Mekong Delta on an organised tour – a cheap and easy way to get a taste of the delta. Those travelling on their own will have greater access to areas off the beaten track, with many little-visited places to discover.

Travel by express minibuses is cheap, efficient and comfortable (though crowded). The ultimate way to see the delta, however, is by private car, bicycle or rented motorbike. Two-wheeling around the delta is good fun, especially getting lost among the maze of country roads!

Since the opening of the river border crossing between Vietnam and Cambodia at Vinh Xuong (near Chau Doc), more and more travellers are choosing this route (see p441) over the land border at Moc Bai. Cambodian visas are issued at the border.

Wherever you go in the delta (except for My Tho), be prepared for ferry crossings. Fruit, soft drinks and sticky rice-based snacks are sold in the ferry waiting areas.

TOURS

Numerous travel agents in Ho Chi Minh City (HCMC) offer inexpensive minibus tours (p338). The cheapest ones are sold around the Pham Ngu Lao area. Before you book, shop around, and remember that you usually get what you pay for. This is not to say pricey tours are necessarily better, but sometimes 'rock bottom' means all you will get is a brief glance at the region from a packed bus full of other tourists. The cost largely depends on how far from HCMC the tour goes. The standard of accommodation, transport, food and the size of the group will be other determining factors.

For customised tours of the Mekong Delta on two or four wheels, HCMC's **Sinhbalo Adventures** (www.sinhbalo.com) cannot be beaten.

MY THO

☎ 073 / pop 180,000

My Tho, the quiet capital city of Tien Giang province, is the traditional gateway to the delta, owing to its proximity to HCMC. Visitors on a whirlwind Vietnam tour often take a day trip here to catch a glimpse of the famous river. In order to visit floating markets, however, you'll need to continue on to Can Tho (p421). The town itself is an important market town, and its quaint but busy waterfront is easily explored on foot.

My Tho was founded in the 1680s by Chinese refugees fleeing Taiwan for political reasons. The Chinese have virtually all gone now, having been driven out in the late 1970s when their property was seized by the government. The economy is based on tourism, fishing and the cultivation of rice, coconuts, bananas, mangoes, longans and citrus fruit.

> **Typhoon Durian**
>
> In 2006 several eastern provinces in the delta sustained serious damage by Typhoon Durian. It left nearly 100 dead, damaged or destroyed more than 200,000 homes and sank more than 800 fishing vessels. Ben Tre province suffered the worst damage, with hundreds left homeless.

Orientation

Sprawling along the bank of the northernmost branch of the Mekong River, My Tho is laid out in a regular grid pattern.

The bus station is 3km west of town. Coming from the bus station, you enter My Tho on Đ Ap Bac, which turns into Đ Nguyen Trai (oriented west–east).

Parallel to the Mekong River is Đ 30 Thang 4 (also written as Đ 30/4), named for Saigon Liberation Day.

Information

The official tourism authority for Ten Giang province, **Tien Giang Tourist** (Cong Ty Du Lich Tien Giang; ☎ 873 184; dulichtg@bdvn.vnd.net; 8 Đ 30 Thang 4; 🕑 7am-5pm) is not terribly helpful. You're better off inquiring at the tourism desks found at hotels. **Mekotours** (☎ 874 324; congdoantourist@hcm.vnn.vn; 61 Đ 30 Thang 4), attached to the Trade Union Hotel, offers a range of excursions including bicycle tours (with an overnight homestay) and boating tours to the floating markets. Most trips are priced at group rates (US$5/10 per person for boating/bicycle excursion), so you'll have to negotiate if you're on your own.

There's an **Incombank ATM** (cnr Đ 30 Thang 4 & Đ Le Loi) near the boat landing. The post office is located at 59 Đ 30 Thang 4; there's an internet café next door.

Sights

CAO DAI TEMPLE

If you missed the one in Tay Ninh (p382), My Tho has its own colourful but smaller **Cao Dai Temple** (Đ Ly Thuong Kiet) that's worth a look. It's west of the town centre between Đ Dong Da and Đ Tran Hung Dao.

MY THO CENTRAL MARKET

This **market** (Đ Trung Trac & Đ Nguyen Hue) is in an area of town that is closed to traffic. The streets are filled with stalls selling everything from fresh food and bulk tobacco to boat propellers. In an attempt to clear these streets, the local government has built a three-storey concrete monstrosity on the riverside, intending to relocate vendors inside. With the high rent and taxes, however, there have been very few takers and the top two floors remain empty.

VINH TRANG PAGODA

The monks at **Vinh Trang Pagoda** (60A Đ Nguyen Trung Truc; admission free; 9-11.30am & 1.30-5pm), a beautiful and well-maintained sanctuary, provide a home for orphans, disabled and other needy children. Donations are always welcome.

The pagoda is about 1km from the city centre. To get there, take the bridge east across the river on Đ Nguyen Trai and after 400m turn left. The entrance to the sanctuary is about 200m from the turn-off, on the right-hand side of the building as you approach it from the ornate gate.

Tours

Boat trips are the highlight of a visit to My Tho. The small wooden vessels can navigate the mighty Mekong (barely), but the target for most trips is cruising past pleasant rural villages through the maze of small canals. Depending on what you book, destinations usually include a coconut-candy workshop, a honeybee farm (try the banana wine!) and an orchid garden.

THE RIVER OF NINE DRAGONS

The Mekong River is one of the world's great rivers and its delta is one of the world's largest. The Mekong originates high in the Tibetan plateau, flowing 4500km through China, between Myanmar and Laos, through Laos, along the Laos–Thailand border, and through Cambodia and Vietnam on its way to the South China Sea. At Phnom Penh (Cambodia), the Mekong River splits into two main branches: the Hau Giang (Lower River, also called the Bassac River), which flows via Chau Doc, Long Xuyen and Can Tho to the sea; and the Tien Giang (Upper River), which splits into several branches at Vinh Long and empties into the sea at five points. The numerous branches of the river explain the Vietnamese name for the Mekong: Song Cuu Long (River of Nine Dragons).

The Mekong's flow begins to rise around the end of May and reaches its highest point in September; it ranges from 1900 to 38,000 cubic metres per second depending on the season. A tributary of the river that empties into the Mekong at Phnom Penh drains Cambodia's Tonlé Sap Lake. When the Mekong is at flood stage, this tributary reverses its flow and drains into Tonlé Sap, thereby somewhat reducing the danger of serious flooding in the Mekong Delta. Unfortunately, deforestation in Cambodia is disturbing this delicate balancing act, resulting in more flooding in Vietnam's portion of the Mekong River basin.

In recent years seasonal flooding has claimed the lives of hundreds and forced tens of thousands of the region's residents to evacuate from their homes. In some areas inhabitants are not able to return to their homes until the waters fully recede several months later. Floods cause millions of dollars worth of damage and have a catastrophic effect on regional rice and coffee crops.

Living on a flood plain presents some technical challenges. Lacking any high ground to escape flooding, many delta residents build their houses on bamboo stilts to avoid the rising waters. Many roads are submerged or turn to muck during floods; all-weather roads have to be built on raised embankments, but this is expensive. The traditional solution has been to build canals and travel by boat. There are thousands of canals in the Mekong Delta – keeping them properly dredged and navigable is a constant but essential chore.

A further challenge is keeping the canals clean. The normal practice of dumping all garbage and sewage directly into the waterways behind the houses that line them is taking its toll. Many of the more populated areas in the Mekong Delta are showing signs of unpleasant waste build-up. The World Wildlife Foundation (WWF) is one organisation that's working with local and provincial governments to improve conservation techniques and sponsoring environmental education and awareness programs. To learn more, contact **WWF Greater Mekong Programme** (www.wwfindochina.org).

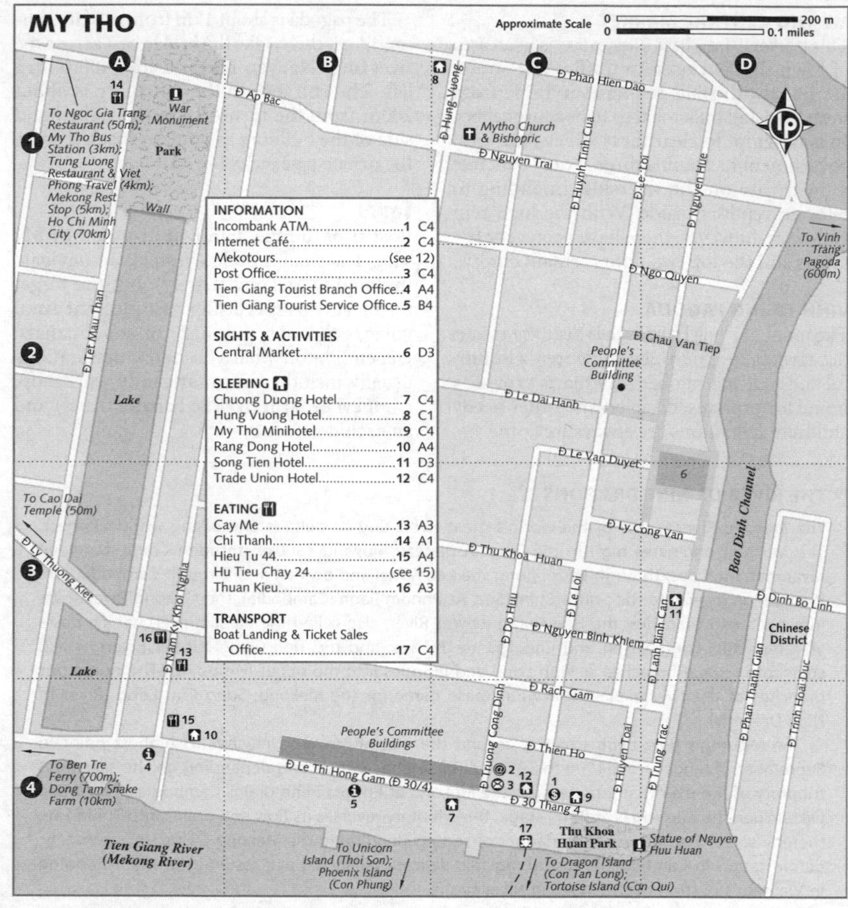

The My Tho People's Committee almost has a monopoly on boat travel, charging around US$25 for a two- to three-hour tour (book at the tourist office). However, private touts operate customised tours cheaper than the 'official' rates (per hour around 50,000d), but they are illegal and there's a small chance your boatman may be fined by the river cops. The best place to look for these freelancers is along the riverfront, but they'll probably find you first.

Inexpensive boat tours can also be booked at the out-of-the-way but friendly **Viet Phong Travel** (☎ 882 522; vietphongtravel@hcm.vnn.vn; 94 Đ Le Thi Hong Gam; 🕓 8am-5pm); it's best to contact its staff at Trung Luong Restaurant (see p406), as its pier office is difficult to find.

Sleeping

BUDGET

Rang Dong Hotel (☎ 874 400; 25 Đ 30 Thang 4; r 130,000-150,000d; ❄) Privately run, this decent, friendly spot remains popular with budget travellers. Third-floor rooms open onto a terrace with river views.

My Tho Minihotel (☎ 872 543; 67 Đ 30 Thang 4; r 100,000-200,000d; ❄) This basic waterfront hotel has simply furnished rooms. Pricier rooms are bigger and have better ventilation. Room No 1 has a river view.

Hung Vuong Hotel (☎ 876 777; 19 Đ Hung Vuong; r 120,000-220,000d; ❄) This popular place has very clean rooms with tall ceilings and simple wood furniture. Some rooms lack natural light.

Song Tien Hotel (☎ 872 009; fax 884 745; 101 Đ Trung Trac; r/ste 160,000/260,000d; ❄) The Song Tien has comfortable rooms with red and white tile floors, TV and fridge. Suites are spacious with polished lacquer furniture. There's also a lift.

Trade Union Hotel (Khach San Cong Doan; ☎ 874 324; congdoantourist@hcm.vnn.vn; 61 Đ 30 Thang 4; r 90,000-210,000d; ❄) This ageing government-run hotel has a mix of rooms from dingy and stifling to clean and roomy – the best are on the upper floor with a shared balcony facing the river.

Chuong Duong annex (☎ 882 264; 1 Đ Truong Cong Dinh; r US$15-30; ❄) This new annexe is up the street from the Chuong Duong Hotel, with a polished feel, but no views.

Chuong Duong Hotel (☎ 870 875; cdhotelmytho@hcm.vnn.vn; 10 Đ 30 Thang 4; r US$25-35; ❄) My Tho's most luxurious accommodation, this place boasts a prime riverside location and respectable in-house restaurant. All rooms overlook the Mekong River.

Other options: overnighting in a bungalow on Unicorn Island (Thoi Son) or in the rarely visited hotel on Phoenix Island (p406);

RICE PRODUCTION

The ancient Indian word for rice, *dhanya* ('sustainer of the human race'), is apt when describing the importance of rice to the Vietnamese.

A Vietnamese fable tells of a time when rice did not need to be harvested. Instead, it would be summoned through prayer and arrive in each home from the heavens in the form of a large ball. One day a man ordered his wife to sweep the floor in preparation for the coming of the rice, but she was still sweeping when the huge ball arrived and struck it by accident, causing it to shatter into many pieces. Since then, the Vietnamese have had to toil to produce rice by hand.

Rural Vietnam today is in many ways similar to what it would have been centuries ago: women in conical hats *(non bai tho)* irrigating fields by hand, farmers stooping to plant the flooded paddies and water buffalo ploughing seedbeds with harrows.

Despite the labour-intensive production process, rice is the single most important crop in Vietnam and involves more than 50% of the working population. While always playing an important role in the Vietnamese economy, its production intensified considerably as a result of economic reforms, known as *doi moi* ('renovation'), in 1986. The reforms helped transform Vietnam from a rice importer to exporter in 1989. Today rice is a substantial part of the country's earnings. In 2006 Vietnam exported around 4.5 million tonnes of rice, earning around US$1.4 billion.

The importance of rice in the diet of the Vietnamese is evident in the many rice dishes available, including rice omelette *(banh xeo),* rice porridge *(chao)* and extremely potent rice wine *(ruou gao),* to name a few. Vietnam's ubiquitous *com pho* (rice-noodle soup) restaurants serve white rice *(com)* with a variety of cooked meat and vegetables, as well as rice-noodle soup *(pho).*

Despite advances in rice production, much of the work is carried out without modern machinery. Fields are ploughed and harrowed with the assistance of water buffaloes, seeds are planted by hand, and when the seedlings reach a certain age they have to be individually uprooted and transplanted to another field to avoid root rot. This painstaking process is mostly undertaken by women. Irrigation is typically carried out by two workers using woven baskets on rope to transfer water from canals to the fields. When the water level is high enough fish can be raised in the paddies.

Rice plants take three to six months to grow, depending on the type and environment. In Vietnam the three major cropping seasons are winter-spring, summer-autumn and the wet season. When ready to harvest, the plants are thigh-high and in about 30cm of water. The grains grow in drooping fronds and are cut by hand, then transported by wheelbarrows to thrashing machines that separate the husk from the plant. Other machines are used to 'dehusk' the rice (for brown rice) or 'polish' it (for white rice). A familiar sight at this stage is brown carpets of rice spread along roads to dry before milling.

In recent rice news (2006), Vietnam, along with Thailand, announced a ban on growing genetically engineered varieties of rice, citing health concerns. The announcement came in the wake of scandals caused by the US and China contaminating the global rice supply with unapproved and illegal genetically engineered rice varieties.

inquire at Tien Giang Tourist (p402). There are also homestay options around Vinh Long (p409).

Eating

RESTAURANTS

Chi Thanh (☎ 873 756; 279 Đ Tet Mau Than; mains 20,000-40,000d; breakfast, lunch & dinner) A tidy spot for delicious Chinese and Vietnamese fare, Chi Thanh has two locations, both with menus in English.

Ngoc Gia Trang (☎ 872 742; 196 Đ Ap Bac; mains 25,000-45,000d; lunch & dinner) This charming, restaurant sits among greenery on the road into My Tho from HCMC. Its pleasant courtyard is a good spot to enjoy traditional dishes. There's an equally attractive café attached.

Mekong Rest Stop (☎ 858 676; Hwy 60; mains around 30,000-40,000d; breakfast, lunch & dinner) About 5km west of town, this airy, thatched-roof restaurant serves an excellent assortment of fresh seafood and traditional dishes amid pleasant water-garden environs.

Trung Luong (☎ 855 441; Hwy 60; set menu 50,000-60,000d; breakfast, lunch & dinner) A few kilometres west of town, Trung Luong is near the gate marking the entry point to My Tho. Here too is a nice garden and nicely prepared dishes (elephant fish is a favourite).

Other good spots:

Cay Me (60 Đ Nam Ky Khoi Nghia; mains 10,000-15,000d; breakfast, lunch & dinner)

Thuan Kieu (☎ 876 636; 47 Đ Nam Ky Khoi Nghia; mains 10,000-20,000d; breakfast, lunch & dinner)

HU TIEU RESTAURANTS

My Tho is known for a special vermicelli soup, *hu tieu my tho*, which is richly garnished with fresh and dried seafood, pork, chicken and fresh herbs. It is served either with broth or dry (with broth on the side) and can also be made vegetarian.

Although *hu tieu* can be found at almost any eatery in town, there's a handful of speciality restaurants. Carnivores will enjoy **Hu Tieu 44** (44 Đ Nam Ky Khoi Nghia; soups 7000d; breakfast, lunch & dinner), while vegetarians should look for **Hu Tieu Chay 24** (24 Đ Nam Ky Khoi Nghia; soups 4000d; breakfast, lunch & dinner).

Getting There & Around

BOAT

The car ferry to Ben Tre province leaves from Ben Pha Rach Mieu station about 1km west of My Tho city centre, near 2/10A Đ Le Thi Hong Gam (the continuation west of Đ 30 Thang 4). The ferry operates between 4am and 10pm and runs at least once an hour (per person/motorbike 1000/5000d). Ten-person trucks shuttle passengers between the ferry terminal and the bus station. A new bridge under construction (due for completion in early 2009) will link My Tho with Ben Tre by road, greatly diminishing travel time between the two towns.

BUS

My Tho is served by buses leaving HCMC from Mien Tay bus station (p372) and from the bus station in Cholon. Buses from Cholon have the added advantage of dropping passengers right in My Tho, as opposed to the bus station outside of town. The trip takes 1½ hours.

The **My Tho bus station** (Ben Xe Khach Tien Giang; 4am-5pm) is several kilometres west of town. To get there from the city centre, take Đ Ap Bac westward and continue on to Hwy 1 (Quoc Lo 1).

Buses to HCMC (18,000d, two hours) leave when full from the early morning until about 5pm. There's also daily bus service to most points in the Mekong Delta.

CAR & MOTORBIKE

The drive from HCMC to My Tho along Hwy 1, by car or motorbike, takes about two hours.

Road distances from My Tho are 16km to Ben Tre, 104km to Can Tho, 70km to HCMC and 66km to Vinh Long.

AROUND MY THO

Phoenix Island

Until his imprisonment by the communists for his antigovernment activities and the consequent dispersion of his flock, the Coconut Monk (Ong Dao Dua; see the boxed text, opposite) led a small community on Phoenix Island (Con Phung), a few kilometres from My Tho. In its heyday the island was dominated by a wildly imagined open-air **sanctuary** (admission 5000d; 8-11.30am & 1.30-6pm). The dragon-enwrapped columns and the multiplatformed tower, with its huge metal globe, must have once been brightly painted, but these days the whole place is faded, rickety and silent. Nevertheless, it's good kitsch – there's even a model of the Apollo rocket set among the Buddhist statues! With some imagination you can picture how it all must have appeared as

THE COCONUT MONK

The Coconut Monk was so named because he once ate only coconuts for three years; others claim he only drank coconut juice and ate fresh young corn. Whatever the story, he was born Nguyen Thanh Nam in 1909, in what is now Ben Tre province. He studied chemistry and physics in France at Lyon, Caen and Rouen from 1928 until 1935, when he returned to Vietnam, got married and had a daughter.

In 1945 the Coconut Monk left his family in order to pursue a monastic life. For three years he sat on a stone slab under a flagpole and meditated day and night. He was repeatedly imprisoned by successive South Vietnamese governments, which were infuriated by his philosophy of achieving reunification through peaceful means. He died in 1990.

Plaques on the 3.5m-high porcelain jar (created in 1972) on Con Phung tell all about the Coconut Monk. He founded a religion, Tinh Do Cu Si, which was a mixture of Buddhism and Christianity. Representations of Jesus and the Buddha appeared together, as did the Virgin Mary and eminent Buddhist women, and the cross and Buddhist symbols. Today only the symbols remain, as the Tinh Do Cu Si community has dissolved from the island.

the Coconut Monk presided over his congregation, flanked by enormous elephant tusks and seated on a richly ornamented throne.

If you really wish to experience the fullness of the island, you can spend the night at the simple **Con Phung Hotel** (☎ 075 822 198; fax 075 894 940; r with/without air-con US$10/7; ❄). Rooms are comfortable, clean and simple, and the best quarters have river views. A restaurant serves decent traditional mains (set menu 50,000d to 80,000d).

Private boat operators can take you to and from the island as part of an organised tour (around 50,000d per hour). You might also keep an eye out for the Coconut Monk's complex as you chug by on the My Tho-Ben Tre ferry.

Dragon Island

Famed for its well-known **longan orchards**, Dragon Island (Con Tan Long) makes for a pleasant stop and stroll. The lush, palm-fringed shores of the island are lined with wooden fishing boats; some of the residents of the island are shipwrights. There is a small restaurant on the island. Dragon Island is a five-minute boat trip (per person 10,000d) from the dock at the southern end of Đ Le Loi.

Other Islands

Two islands in the vicinity, **Tortoise Island** (Con Qui) and **Unicorn Island** (Thoi Son) are worth popular stops for the coconut candy and banana wine workshops. On Tortoise Island is an excellent restaurant, the **Du Lich Xanh Con Qui** (☎ 610 988; set menu 40,000-80,000d; 🕑 lunch). It's a peaceful thatched-roof setting, surrounded by water hyacinths. Although you can visit these islands as part of a package tour from HCMC, you'll have much more freedom if you hire a boat yourself in My Tho. Budget around US$10 to US$14 for a three- or four-hour cruise, making stops along the way.

Dong Tam Snake Farm

Operated by the Vietnamese military for profit and open to the public, the **snake farm** (admission 20,000d; 🕑 7am-5pm) at Dong Tam lies about 10km from My Tho in the direction of Vinh Long. It breeds snakes – mostly pythons and cobras – for eating, for their skins and for producing antivenin. At certain times the keepers feed live animals, including ducks, to the pythons and other snakes. If this bothers you, you may want to forego a visit. A 15-minute video tells the history of the snake farm.

The restaurant here includes cobra on the menu and there's a shop where you can stock up on snake wine and cobratox – a cream made from venom, that's said to be good for treating rheumatism.

You'll need your own transport to get to Dong Tam Snake Farm. Coming from HCMC, continue for 3km beyond the turn-off to My Tho and turn left at the Dong Tam Junction (signposted). From the junction, follow the dirt road for 4km, turn right and continue for 1km until you reach the snake farm.

BEN TRE

☎ 075 / pop 120,000

The picturesque little province of Ben Tre, just south of My Tho, sees little of the tourist traffic of its northern neighbour. Its sleepy

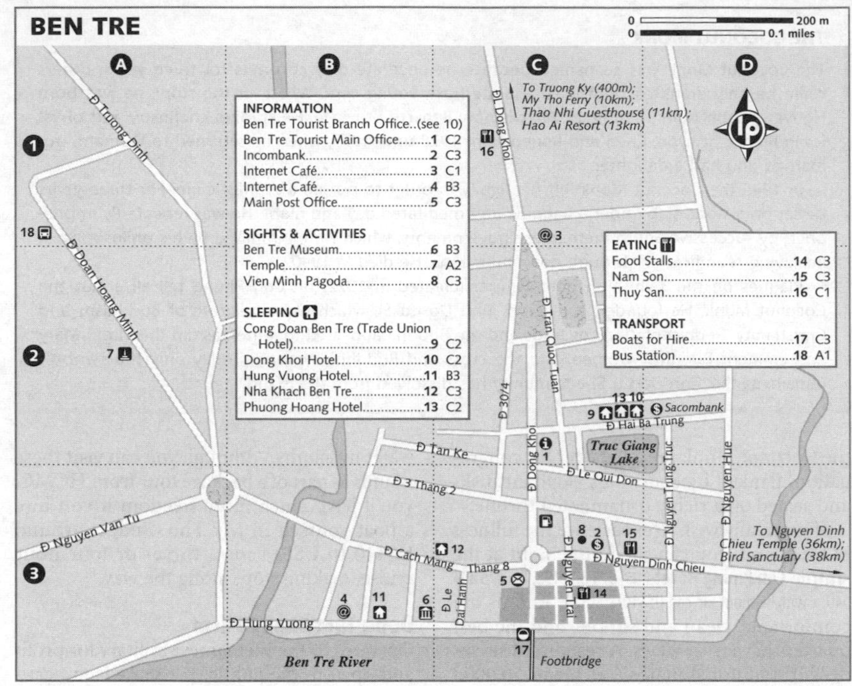

waterfront, lined with ageing villas, and active market nearby makes for a pleasant stroll, and there's good exploring into Ben Tre's rustic settlement across the bridge south of the centre. The town has a tiny lake (Truc Giang), ringed with a few cafés. Ben Tre is also a good place to arrange boat trips (see p410) around the area – particularly those wanting to escape the tour buses.

Ben Tre is famous for *keo dua* (coconut candy). Many local women work in small factories making these sweets, spending their days boiling cauldrons of sticky mixture, before rolling it out and cutting sections off into squares and wrapping them into paper for sale.

Information

The **Ben Tre Tourist Office** (☎ 829 618; ttdhdulichbt@hcm.vnn.vn; cnr Đ Hai Ba Trung & Dong Khoi; 🕐 7-11am & 1-5pm) rents out bikes, boats, canoes and arranges Mekong excursions lasting from four hours (245,000d) to two days (320,000d). You can also hire a 12 passenger speedboat (US$60 per hour). They have a **branch office** (☎ 822 392; dulichbt@hcm.vnn.vn; 3rd fl, 16 Đ Hai Ba Trung; 🕐 7-11am & 1-5pm) inside the Dong Khoi hotel.

Ben Tre has a few **internet cafés** (per hr 4000d), including one on Đ Hung Vuong and another on Đ Tran Quoc Tuan. There's also internet access at the **main post office** (3/1 Đ Dong Khoi; per hr 4000d).

Get cash at **Incombank** (☎ 822 507; 42 Đ Nguyen Dinh Chieu; 🕐 closed weekends).

Sights

In the centre of Ben Tre is the **Vien Minh Pagoda**, which is also the head office of the Buddhist Association of Ben Tre province. Though the history of the pagoda is vague, the local monks say it is over 100 years old. The original structure was made of wood, but it was torn down to make way for the present building. Reconstruction took place from 1951 to 1958 using bricks and concrete.

An interesting feature of Vien Minh Pagoda is a large white statue of Quan The Am Bo Tat (Goddess of Mercy) set in the front courtyard. The Chinese calligraphy that adorns the pagoda was performed by an old monk.

The **Ben Tre Museum** (Bao Tang Ben Tre; Đ Hung Vuong; 🕐 8am-11am & 1-5pm) is set in an ageing but atmospheric old yellow villa. It has the usual assortment of rusty weapons and American

War paraphernalia, along with rousing images of Ho Chi Minh ploughing the fields, talking on the phone and looking in turns kind and tough.

Sleeping

BUDGET

Nha Khach Ben Tre (☎ 822 339; fax 826 205; 5 Đ Cach Mang Thang 8; r with breakfast 80,000-230,000d; ❄) Brought to you by the communist party, this curious place has clean, somewhat stark rooms with tall ceilings, Chinese-inlaid furniture and decent natural lighting. There's an airy café next door.

Thao Nhi Guesthouse (☎ 860 009; thaonhitours@yahoo.com; Hamlet 1, Tan Thach Village; r 80,000-250,000d; ❄) A friendly, rustic place amid abundant greenery, Thao Nhi is 11km north of town, and offers a range of comfortable rooms. The in-house restaurant serves excellent elephant-ear fish, and there's free bike rental; you can also arrange boat trips here. As it's difficult to find, hire a moto-taxi to take you there from the boat dock (arriving from My Tho).

Phuong Hoang Hotel (☎ 821 385; 28 Hai Ba Trung; r 120,000-180,000d; ❄) Should be your last choice in town, with small battered rooms, though 203 and 204 overlook the lake.

Cong Doan Ben Tre (Trade Union Hotel; ☎ 825 082; fax 813 017; 36 Đ Hai Ba Trung; r incl breakfast 130,000-170,000d; ❄) This government-owned place has a range of rooms from airy and decent to utterly depressing. Friendly staff and centrally located.

A NIGHT UPON THE MEKONG

One of the highlights of any Vietnam trip is doing a homestay with some of the friendly Mekong families. Here, you'll get a taste of local customs by sharing a home-cooked meal and possibly a few glasses of rice wine before retiring to your bed or hammock near the river. Although many tourists book through group tours in Saigon, there's no reason you can't do it yourself. The following options all charge around US$10 per night, which includes a night's sleep, dinner and breakfast the next morning. Note that most hosts are unlikely to speak much English, but welcome foreign guests just the same. All of the places listed below are perched along a river or canal. Vinh Long is the best place to arrange for homestays.

Le Thanh Hong (☎ 070 858 612; An Than hamlet, An Binh village, Long Ho district) Located across the Co Chien River from Vinh Long, this place has four small rustic bungalows amid flowers and pretty landscaping. The monkey on a chain is unfortunate. You can also book here through Cuu Long Tourist (p411) in Vinh Long.

Mai Quoc Nam (☎ 070 859 912; fax 859 244; Phuan 1 hamlet, Binh Hoa Phuoc village, Long Ho District) A short boat ride from Vinh Long, Mai Quoc Nam has a modern concrete building in front, but lovely wooden bungalows tucked away in a garden setting in back. You can also arrange boating excursions here.

Nha Co Tran Tuan Kiet (☎ 073 824 498; fax 073 925 051; 22 Phu Hoa hamlet, Dong Hoa Hip village, Cai Be district) This traditional wooden house has beautiful ornate details and a history dating back 150 years – during which it's remained in the same family. The cooking here is excellent (watch and learn while dinner is prepared, then enjoy the feast), and private rooms are available. It's in Cai Be, 25km west of My Tho.

Sau Giao (☎ 070 859 910; Binh Thuan 2 hamlet, Hoa Ninh village, Long Ho district) Located a few kilometres outside of Vinh Long along the river, Sau Giao is a beautiful traditional wooden house (in the same family for four generations) that's set with a bonsai garden in front. They serve excellent cuisine – even if you don't stay here, it's a worthwhile lunch stop (set lunch 60,000d) if you're hiring a boat from Vinh Long. Bicycle hire available (per day US$1).

Song Tien (☎ 070 858 487; An Thanh hamlet, An Binh village, Long Ho District) Across the Co Chien River from Vinh Long, this friendly place offers accommodation in small bungalows with squat toilets. The landscaping here is particularly lush with orange and lemon trees, and the owner and his wife, both former VC soldiers, are known to bust out the mandolin from time to time for a bit of traditional singing for their guests.

Tam Ho (☎ 070 859 859; info@caygiong.com; Binh Thuan 1 hamlet, Hoa Ninh village, Long Ho district) About 1.5km from Vinh Long, Tam Ho is a working orchard run by a friendly, welcoming family – one of the hosts bears a striking resemblance to Ho Chi Minh. Private rooms available.

MIDRANGE

Dong Khoi Hotel (☎ 822 501; dongkhoihotelbtre@vmm.vn; 16 Đ Hai Ba Trung; r 196,000-255,000; ❄) Popular with wedding parties, this hotel with a lift is the best of the three on the lakefront. It has clean, carpeted rooms done in pink and green. There's a decent restaurant (mains 20,000d to 40,000d) with an English menu on the ground floor.

Hung Vuong Hotel (☎ 822 408; 166 Đ Hung Vuong; r US$25-35; ❄) One of Ben Tre's nicest hotels, this riverfront spot has tile floors, polished wood furniture, modern bathrooms with tubs and great river views (from the front rooms). There's a good restaurant as well.

Eating

Nam Son (☎ 822 873; 40 Đ Phan Ngoc Tong; mains 15,000-30,000d; ⏲ lunch & dinner) This place is usually packed with locals feasting on roast chicken and drinking draught beer.

Truong Ky (☎ 813 616; 517 ĐL Dong Khoi; mains 20,000-30,000d; ⏲ lunch & dinner) A trim, multistorey restaurant just outside of town, Truong Ky serves delectable fish and seafood, though there's no English menu.

Thuy San (☎ 833 777; 210B ĐL Dong Khoi; mains 30,000-70,000d) A decent option on the way into town, Thuy San cooks up traditional mains amid faux greenery.

Hao Ai Resort (☎ 610 785; 2nd hamlet, Tan Thach village; ⏲ lunch) A handsome, lushly landscaped restaurant that serves tasty fish plates. Get there by hiring a private boat where the ferry docks from My Tho (around 30,000d).

For ultra-cheap eats, head to the market, which has plenty of **food stalls** (rice plates around 7000d).

Getting There & Away

The My Tho–Ben Tre ferry (motorbike/person 5000/1000d, 15 minutes one way) is the only option between the two towns – though a bridge due for completion in 2009 will provide a road link. Ferries run 24 hours a day, every 20 minutes or so (less frequently between 7pm and 6am). Ferry crossings are much quicker if you're travelling by motorbike (as opposed to car) since there are numerous small boats that can take you across the river.

Public buses stop at the bus station west of the town centre on Đ Doan Hoang Minh. Private minibuses also make the Ben Tre–HCMC run daily. They operate on no fixed schedule, so you'll need to inquire locally. Ask around the market, or by the petrol station on Đ Dong Khoi (where some vans arrive/depart).

Getting Around

Slow boats can be rented at the public pier near the market. Here you can figure on about 30,000d to 50,000d per hour, with a minimum of two hours cruising the local canals. Check with the boat drivers who hang around near the end of the footbridge.

AROUND BEN TRE

Nguyen Dinh Chieu Temple

Dedicated to Nguyen Dinh Chieu, a local scholar, this **temple** (⏲ 7.30-11.30am & 1.30-6.30pm) is in Ba Tri district, which is a 30-minute drive (36km) from Ben Tre. It's a very charming temple, excellent for photography.

Bird Sanctuary

The locals make much of the storks that nest at the local bird sanctuary, **San Chim Vam Ho** (☎ 858 669; admission 10,000d; ⏲ 7-11am & 1-7pm), as a stork sitting on the back of a water buffalo is a quintessential image of the Mekong waterways. The sanctuary is 38km east of Ben Tre town. Ben Tre Tourist has speedboats that can make the round trip in about two hours, or slow boats that take about five hours. Compare the going rates at Ben Tre Tourist with what freelance boat operators charge.

To get there overland, follow Đ Nguyen Dinh Chieu east out of town for 20km to Giong Tram. Turn left onto the windy, rural dirt road leading to Trai Tu K-20 (Prison K-20); you'll reach the prison after travelling 11km (you may see hundreds of prisoners out tilling the fields) – turn right and drive the final 7km to Vam Ho.

VINH LONG

☎ 070 / pop 130,000

A bit more chaotic than other Mekong towns of its size, Vinh Long has noisy, motorbike-filled streets, though its riverfront (and its several restaurants) make for a pleasant escape from the mayhem. Despite the lack of in-town attractions, Vinh Long is the gateway to river islands and some worthwhile sites, including the Cai Be floating market, orchards and homestays – which can be a highlight of a Mekong journey. Vinh Long is the capital of Vinh Long province and situated about midway between My Tho and Can Tho.

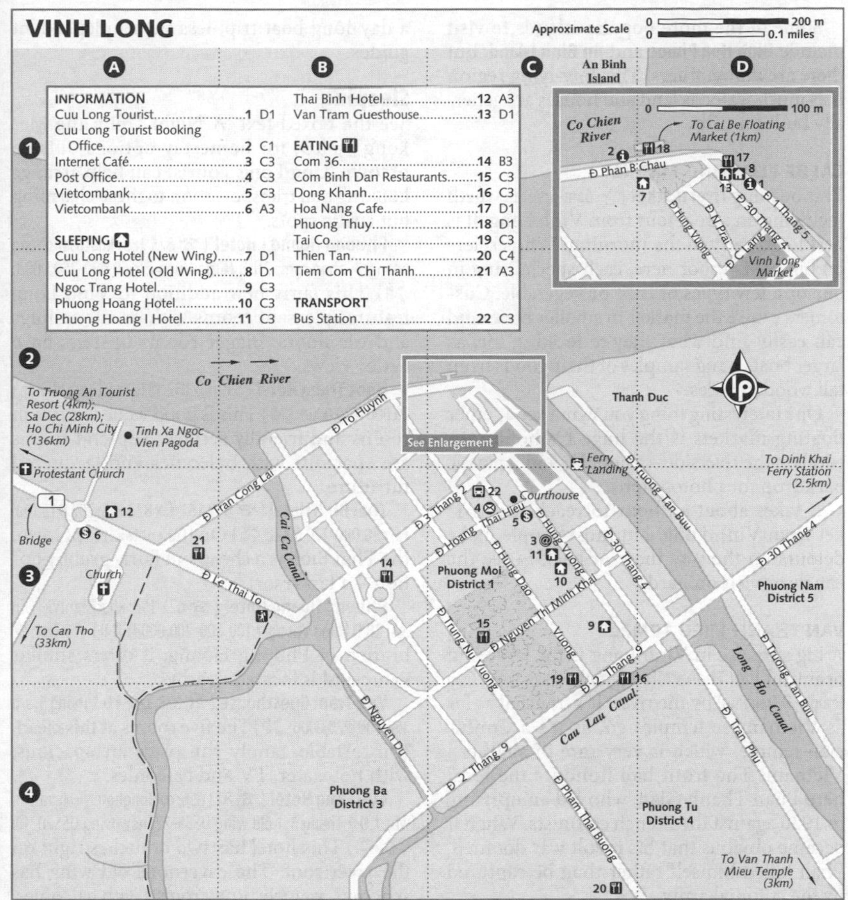

Information

Cuu Long Tourist (☎ 823 616; cuulongtourist1@hcm.vnn.vn; 1 Đ 1 Thang 5; 🕑 7am-5pm) is one of the more capable state-run tour outfits located in the Mekong Delta region. For those interested, it can arrange homestays at an orchard (see p409). It also has a small booking office near the Phuong Thuy restaurant, which can rent out bicycles (per day US$2) and motorbikes (per day US$8).

Next to Phung Hoang Hotel is an **internet café** (2G Đ Hung Vuong; per hr 3000d). **Vietcombank** (☎ 823 109; 143 Đ Le Thai To) has two branches in town and can exchange cash and travellers cheques.

The post office is located on Đ Hoang Thai Hieu.

Sights

MEKONG RIVER ISLANDS

What makes a trip to Vinh Long worthwhile is not the town but the beautiful small islands in the river. The islands are given over to agriculture, especially the growing of tropical fruit, which are shipped to markets in HCMC.

To visit the islands you can charter a boat through Cuu Long Tourist (see left) for around US$10 per person or pay substantially less for a private operator (US$3 to US$4 per hour).

You can also take the public ferry (3000d) to one of the islands and then walk around on your own; however, this isn't as interesting as a boat tour, since you won't cruise the narrow canals.

Some of the more popular islands to visit include **Binh Hoa Phuoc** and **An Binh Island**, but there are many others. This low-lying region is as much water as land and houses are generally built on stilts.

CAI BE FLOATING MARKET

This bustling **river market** (5am-5pm) is worth including on a boat tour from Vinh Long. It is best to go early in the morning. Wholesalers on big boats moor here, each specialising in one or a few types of fruit or vegetable. Customers cruise the market in smaller boats and can easily find what they're looking for, as larger boats hang samples of their goods from tall wooden poles.

One interesting thing you won't see at other floating markets is the huge Catholic cath edral on the riverside – a popular and fantastic backdrop for photographs.

It takes about an hour to reach the market from Vinh Long, but most people make detours on the way there or back to see the canals or visit orchards.

VAN THANH MIEU TEMPLE

A big surprise in Vinh Long is the large and beautiful **Van Thanh Mieu Temple** (Phan Thanh Gian Temple; Đ Tran Phu) by the river. It's unusual as far as Vietnamese temples go, as it's a Confucian temple, which is very rare in southern Vietnam. The front hall honours the local hero Phan Thanh Gian, who led an uprising in 1930 against the French colonists. When it became obvious that his revolt was doomed, Phan killed himself rather than be captured by the colonial army.

The rear hall, built in 1866, has a portrait of Confucius above the altar. The building was designed in the Confucian style and looks like it was lifted straight out of China.

Van Thanh Mieu Temple is 3km southeast of town. Don't confuse it with the much smaller Quoc Cong Pagoda on Đ Tran Phu, which you'll pass along the way.

Tours

Cuu Long Tourist offers a variety of boat tours ranging from three to five hours in length, as well as overnight excursions – though you can also arrange this with local operators. Tour destinations include small canals, fruit orchards, brick kilns, a conical palm hat workshop and the Cai Be Floating Market (above). Plan on about US$25 (per small group) for a day-long boat trip, less with independent guides.

Sleeping

See the boxed text 'A Night Upon the Mekong', p409, for homestay options outside of town. Cuu Long Tourist can help arrange booking and transportation to these charming but rustic spots.

Phuong Hoang I Hotel (825 185; khachsanphunghoang@yahoo.com; 2H Đ Hung Vuong; r 60,000-250,000d;) This fairly new addition to Vinh Long features pleasant rooms with ornate ceilings and tile floors. Bigger rooms upstairs have better views.

Ngoc Trang Hotel (/fax 832 581; 18 Đ Hung Vuong; r 70,000-220,000d;) This is good value with clean rooms and friendly service. Top-end rooms are spacious with balconies and lacquered furniture.

Thai Binh Hotel (827 161; fax 822 213; 202 Đ Le Thai To; r 80,000-120,000d;) On the outskirts of town, the Thai Binh is a cheap but fairly grubby option – a last resort.

Phuong Hoang Hotel (822 156; khachsantvl@vnn.vn; 2R Đ Hung Vuong; r 100,000-200,000d;) Another branch of Phuong Hoang, it offers similar value and is located nearby.

Van Tram Guesthouse (823 820; 4 Đ 1 Thang 5; s/d 150,000-220,000d;) The five rooms at this clean, comfortable, family-run place are spacious, with hot water, TV and balconies.

Cuu Long Hotel (823 656; cuulonghotelvl@hcm.vnn.vn; 1 Đ 1 Thang 5; r old wing US$8-22, new wing US$20-40;) This hotel has two branches right on the riverfront. The cavernous old wing has spacious, vaguely dingy rooms with balconies. New-wing rooms are cleaner and more modern but with less character. All rooms have satellite TV and rates include breakfast.

Truong An Tourist Resort (823 161; r US$25) Midway on the 8km stretch of road between Vinh Long and the My Thuan bridge, this is a quiet place to stay if you don't mind being away from town. There are cottages here, but not much to do except sit by the river and enjoy the park-like surroundings.

Eating

Com 36 (836 290; 36 Đ Hoang Thai Hieu; mains 8000-15,000d; lunch & dinner) A traditional Vietnamese spot with metal tables and a high ceiling. No English menu, but dishes (like pork and stuffed tofu) are displayed behind a glass counter – just point and enjoy.

Tiem Com Chi Thanh (☎ 823 457; 64 Đ Le Thai To; mains 12,000d; ⏰ lunch & dinner) Rice steamed in tiny clay bowls is served with excellent Chinese dishes ranging from tofu and shiitakes to frog to pork intestine.

Tai Co (☎ 824 845; 40A Đ 2 Thang 9; hotpot 30,000d; ⏰ lunch & dinner) *Lau* (hotpot) is the speciality here, but Tai Co also serves good Chinese fare. It's divey but popular.

Dong Khanh (☎ 822 357; 49 Đ 2 Thang 9; mains 30,000-45,000d; ⏰ lunch & dinner) This place serves a tasty variety of dishes, including octopus with mushrooms and fish hotpot (serves two). Red tablecloths and red-backed chairs give it a somewhat classy feel. English menu.

Thien Tan (☎ 824 001; 56/1 Đ Pham Thai Buong; mains 30,000-50,000d; ⏰ lunch & dinner) Specialising in barbecued dishes, this is the best eatery in town. Recommended is the fish cooked in bamboo *(ca loc nuong tre)* and chicken cooked in clay *(ga nuong dat set)*.

Good local point-and-eat **com binh dan restaurants** (rice plates 8000d) line Đ Nguyen Thi Minh Khai. Other good spots:

Hoa Nang Café (Đ 1 Thang 5; mains 10,000-40,000d; ⏰ breakfast, lunch & dinner) Riverfront views to enjoy with your iced coffee.

Phuong Thuy (Đ Phan B Chau; mains 20,000-80,000d; ⏰ lunch & dinner) OK food and fine river views.

Vinh Long Market (Đ 3 Thang 2; ⏰ breakfast, lunch & dinner) Delicious local fruit and meal vendors.

Getting There & Away

BOAT

Cargo boats sometimes take passengers from Vinh Long all the way to Chau Doc (near the Cambodian border); inquire locally if this appeals to you.

BUS

Frequent buses go between Vinh Long and HCMC (three hours, 50,000d), which leave HCMC from Cholon bus station (p372) in District 5, and from Mien Tay bus station (p372). You can also get to Vinh Long by bus from Can Tho (25,000d), My Tho, Tra Vinh, Chau Doc and other points on the Mekong Delta. Vinh Long's bus station is conveniently located smack bang in the middle of town.

CAR & MOTORBIKE

Vinh Long is just off Hwy 1, 66km from My Tho, 33km from Can Tho and 136km from HCMC.

TRA VINH

☎ 074 / pop 96,000

Boasting more than 140 Khmer temples scattered about the province, Tra Vinh is a quiet place for exploring the Mekong's little-touted Khmer connection. The town itself is fairly quiet and sees little tourist traffic, owing to its somewhat isolated location on a peninsula. Getting there is a straight up and back trip, because no car ferries cross the rivers here (motorbikes can be ferried by small boats).

About 300,000 ethnic Khmer live in Tra Vinh province. At first glance they might seem to be an invisible minority since they all speak fluent Vietnamese and there's nothing outwardly distinguishing about their clothing or lifestyle. However, digging a little deeper quickly reveals that Khmer culture is alive and well in this part of Vietnam. Many of its numerous pagodas have schools to teach the Khmer language – many Tra Vinh locals can read and write Khmer at least as well as Vietnamese.

Vietnam's Khmer minority are almost all followers of Theravada Buddhism. If you've visited monasteries in Cambodia, you may have observed that Khmer monks are not involved in growing food and rely on donations from the strictly religious locals. Here in Tra Vinh, Vietnamese guides will proudly point out the monks' rice harvest as one of the accomplishments of liberation. To the Vietnamese government, nonworking monks were seen as parasites. The Khmers don't necessarily see it the same way and continue to donate funds to the monasteries surreptitiously.

Between the ages of 15 and 20, most boys set aside a few months or years to live as monks (they decide themselves on the length of service). Khmer monks are allowed to eat meat, although they cannot kill animals.

There is also a small but active Chinese community in Tra Vinh, one of the few remaining in the Mekong Delta region.

Information

Tra Vinh Tourist (☎ 858 556; tvtourism@hcm.vnn.vn; 64 Đ Le Loi; ⏰ 7.30-11am & 1.30-5pm) is probably the friendliest outfit in the Mekong. The staff can provide regional travel info and book various trips to sites around the province, though the boat trips are the most interesting. A good map (Tra Vinh Yellow map, 12,000d) of the town and province is available here.

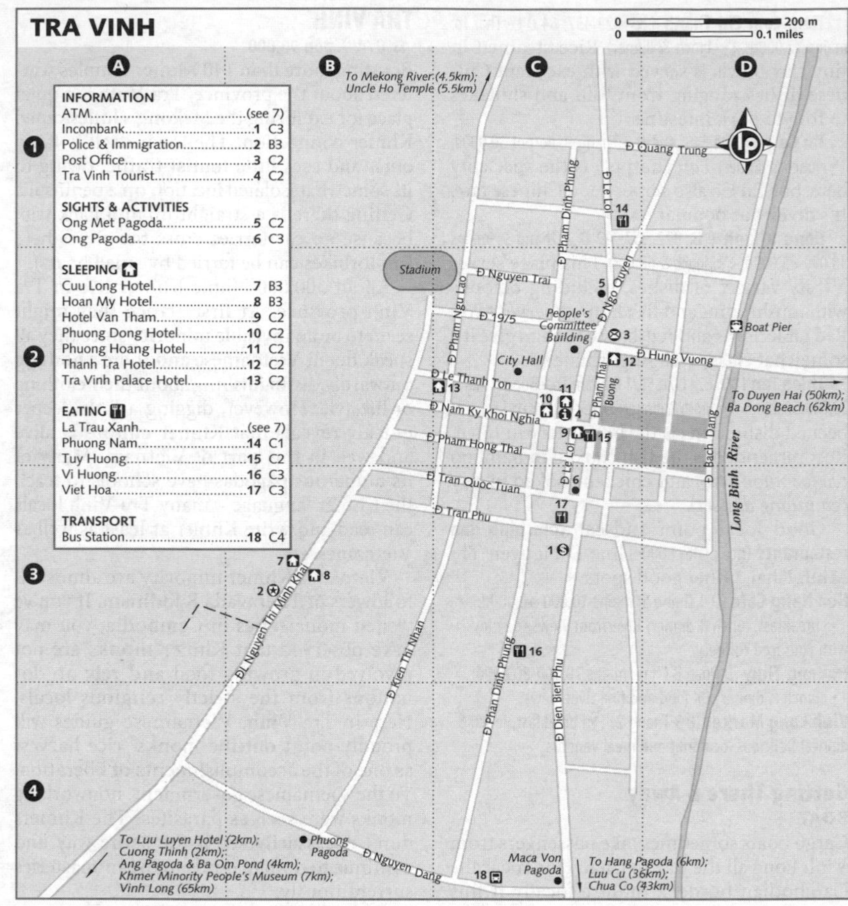

There's an ATM at Cuu Long Hotel. **Incombank** (☎ 863 827; fax 863 886; 15A Đ Dien Bien Phu) exchanges foreign currencies and handles Visa cash advances.

Sights

ONG PAGODA

The very ornate, brightly painted **Ong Pagoda** (Chua Ong & Chua Tau; cnr Đ Pham Thai Buong & Đ Tran Quoc Tuan) is a 100% Chinese pagoda and still a very active place of worship. The red-faced god on the altar is deified general Quan Cong. He is believed to offer protection against war and is based on a historical figure, a soldier of the 3rd century. You can read more about him in the Chinese classic *The Romance of the Three Kingdoms*.

The Ong Pagoda was founded in 1556 by the Fujian Chinese Congregation, but has been rebuilt a number of times. Recent visitors from Taiwan and Hong Kong have contributed money for the pagoda's restoration, which is why it is in such fine shape.

ONG MET PAGODA

The chief reason for visiting the large Khmer **Ong Met Pagoda** (Chua Ong Met) is its accessibility – it's right in the centre of town. The friendly monks will happily show you around.

BA OM POND & ANG PAGODA

Known as Ao Ba Om (Square Lake), this idyllic, square-shaped pond is surrounded by tall trees and makes for a pleasant respite from the city noise. It's a spiritual site for the Khmers and a picnic and drinking spot for local Vietnamese.

More interesting is the nearby Ang Pagoda (Chua An in Vietnamese; Angkor Rek Borei in Khmer), a beautiful and venerable Khmer-style pagoda. Opposite the pagoda entrance is the nicely presented **Khmer Minority People's Museum** (Bao Tang Van Hoa Dan Tac; admission free; 7-11am & 1-5pm Fri-Wed), which displays photos, costumes and other artefacts of traditional Khmer culture.

Ba Om Pond is 7km southwest from Tra Vinh along the highway towards Vinh Long.

HANG PAGODA

This modern Khmer pagoda is also known as the stork pagoda owing to the great white birds that nest in the tall trees here. Although the pagoda itself is modern and painted in soft pastels, the birds are a worthwhile sight if you come at the right time – around dusk during the rainy season. The monks here are particularly friendly and eager to practice their English skills. Chua Hang is located 6km south of town on Đ Dien Bien Phu.

UNCLE HO TEMPLE

The highly unusual (particularly in these southern parts) **Uncle Ho Temple** (Den Tho Bac;

THE PLIGHT OF THE KAMPUCHEA KHMER

Visitors to some Mekong provinces may be surprised to find Khmer towns whose inhabitants speak a different language, follow a different brand of Buddhism and have a vastly different history and culture than their Vietnamese neighbours. Though the Khmer are a minority in the Mekong, they were the first inhabitants here, with an ancestry going back at least 2000 years.

The Kampuchea Krom (meaning 'lower Cambodia') is the unofficial Khmer name for the Mekong Delta region, whose indigenous inhabitants are the Khmer Krom, an ethnic minority living in Southern Vietnam. The Khmer Krom trace their origins back to the 1st century AD, to the founding of Funan, a maritime empire that stretched from the Malay peninsula to the Mekong. Archaeologists believe Funan was a sophisticated society that built canals, traded in precious metals and had a high level of political organisation as well as agricultural know-how. Following the Funan came the Chenla empire (630–802), the mightiest ever in Southeast Asia, and then the Khmer Empire (which saw the creation of Angkor Wat among other great achievements). By the 17th century, however, the empire was in ruins. This was also the time of rising power for their northern rivals, when the Vietnamese empire, under rule from Hue, began expanding south – conquering first the Cham empire before setting their sights on Khmer lands in the Mekong Delta.

According to some historians, there were around 40,000 Khmer families living around Prei Nokor when the Vietnamese arrived in the 1600s. This was an important port of the Khmers that was rechristened in 1698 as Saigon. Waves of Vietnamese settlers populated the city as other colonists continued south. Prior to their arrival there were 700 Khmer temples scattered around South Vietnam. Over the next century the Khmer Krom fought and won a few victories in the region, expelling the intruders, only to lose their gains in new rounds of attacks.

When the French subjugated Indochina in the 19th century, the hope of an independent Kampuchea Krom would be forever destroyed. Although the ethnic Khmer were a majority in Southern Vietnam at that time, the French didn't incorporate the colony with Cambodia but made it a separate protectorate called Cochinchina. When the French were finally driven out in 1954, the delta was incorporated into the state of South Vietnam. Since then, the Vietnamese have adopted a policy of integration and forced assimilation (adopting Vietnamese family names and the Vietnamese language among other things). According to the Khmer Kampuchea-Krom Federation, many atrocities have been committed against the minority in the last four decades, and the Khmer Krom continue to suffer persecution. They report difficult access to Vietnamese health services, religious discrimination (Khmer Krom are Theravada Buddhists, unlike Vietnam's Mahayana Buddhists) and also racial discrimination. The Khmer are the poorest segment of the population. Even their numbers remain a contentious topic. Vietnam reports one million Khmer Krom, which are called 'Nguoi Viet Goc mien' (Vietnamese of Khmer origin) by Vietnamese officials, while KKF claims there are seven million Khmer living in Southern Vietnam. For more information about the ongoing struggles of the Khmer Krom, visit www.khmerkrom.org.

7-11am & 1-5pm) is dedicated, of course, to the late president Ho Chi Minh, and contains a shrine to Ho as well as a small museum displaying photos of his life. The temple was built in 1971, while the war was still in progress, and there's a downed US aircraft on the grounds. The Uncle Ho Temple is at Long Duc commune, 5km north of Tra Vinh town.

Sleeping

BUDGET

Phuong Hoang Hotel (☎ 858 270; 1 Đ Le Thanh Ton; r 50,000-176,000d;) Rooms behind the thin bamboo doors range from dingy to grim. There's no hot water.

Phuong Dong Hotel (☎ 865 486; 1A Đ Pham Dinh Phuong; r 65,000-125,000d;) Another grubby cheapie, with hot water and very basic rooms.

MIDRANGE

Hotel Van Tham (☎ 858 959; 151 Đ Le Loi; r 150,000-180,000d;) Above the market, Hotel Van Tham has clean, light-blue rooms and kind-hearted staff. The worst rooms are small and windowless; the best are spacious with balconies (US$2 spells the difference).

Hoan My Hotel (☎ 862 211; fax 866 600; 105A Đ Nguyen Thi Minh Khai; r 160,000-340,000d;) This tall, slender hotel has a horse painting in the lobby and trim, pleasantly furnished rooms with dark wood furniture, good natural lighting and glass shower stalls.

Tra Vinh Palace Hotel (☎ 864 999; fax 863 005; 3 Đ Le Thanh Ton; r 180,000-280,000d;) Set with a plant-filled courtyard, the Palace features attractive details, making for a pleasant overnight. The best rooms are spacious with tall ceilings, balconies and solid furniture.

Luu Luyen Hotel (☎ 842 306; 16 Đ Nguyen Thi Minh Khai; r 180,000-280,000d, ste 390,000d;) This new hotel has a range of nicely outfitted rooms with a dash of style. A good restaurant is next door. It's located 2km south of downtown on the road to Vinh Long.

Thanh Tra Hotel (☎ 853 621; fax 853 769; 1 Đ Pham Thai Buong; r US$13-27;) This big, central hotel has comfortable and clean rooms and draws occasional tour groups.

Cuu Long Hotel (☎ 862 615; cuulonghoteltravinh@hcm.vnn.vn; 999 Đ Nguyen Thi Minh Khai; r US$17-27, ste US$37;) The three-star Cuu Long has a range of comfortable, bright rooms; the best have balconies, pretty wood furniture and bathrooms with tubs. There's a lift.

Eating

Vi Huong (☎ 865 738; Đ Phan Dinh Phung; mains 10,000d) A cheap place doing simple Vietnamese dishes, including sour soup, fish in a clay pot and pork with rice.

Phuong Nam (☎ 853 511; Đ Chau Van Tiep; mains 12,000-18,000d) The spot for excellent barbecued and clay-pot dishes.

Cuong Thinh (☎ 848 428; 18A Đ Nguyen Thi Minh Khai; mains 15,000-60,000d) This pleasant, open-sided place is popular for its traditional mains and palm-lined ambience. It's 2km south of town on the road to Vinh Long.

Tuy Huong (☎ 858 312; Đ Pham Thai Buong; mains 20,000-30,000d) Serves good Vietnamese and Chinese fare amid simple but not unpleasant ambience.

La Trau Xanh (☎ 862 615; 999 Đ Nguyen Thi Minh Khai; mains 20,000-60,000d) One of the town's best restaurants, La Trau Xanh sits behind the Cuu Long Hotel and offers rich dishes like steamed seabass and shrimp in coconut sauce.

Viet Hoa (☎ 863 046; 80 Đ Tran Phu; mains 30,000d) Run by a friendly Chinese family, Viet Hoa is justly famous in town, serving some of Tra Vinh's best dishes (try the fish kebab or a hotpot to share).

Getting There & Away

Tra Vinh is 65km from Vinh Long and 205km from HCMC. Buses to HCMC depart regularly (60,000d, 4½ hours) from Tra Vinh's intercity bus station on Đ Nguyen Dang, on the south side of town.

AROUND TRA VINH

Chua Co

A Khmer monastery, Chua Co is interesting because the grounds form a bird sanctuary. Several types of stork and ibis arrive here in large numbers before sunset to spend the night. Of course, there are many nests here and you must take care not to disturb them.

Chua Co is 43km from Tra Vinh. Travel 36km to Tra Cu then follow the sandy road for 7km to the monastery.

Luu Cu

Some **ancient ruins** are found at Luu Cu, south of Tra Vinh near the shores of the Hau Giang River. The ruins include brick foundations similar to those found at Cham temples. There have been a series of archaeological digs here and the site is now protected. It's 10km from the town of Tra Cu (36km from Tra Vinh).

Ba Dong Beach

This yellow-sand beach is not bad compared with other 'beaches' in the Mekong Delta, but the main attraction at Ba Dong Beach is the peace and quiet – it sees very few visitors during the week – though weekends can get packed. The big event here – well worth attending if you happen to be in the area – is the **Khmer Ok Om Bok Festival**, featuring colourful boat races. It's held on a weekend in late October early November (ask for details at Tra Vinh Tourist, p413).

Tra Vinh Tourist operates the only accommodation on the beach. The **Ba Dong Beach Resort** (☎ 739 559; badongresort@hcm.vnn.vn; d/bungalow 160,000/22,000d;), opened in 2004, has pleasant bungalows (and simpler rooms) with ocean views and hot-water bathrooms. Rates include breakfast, and there's a seafood restaurant attached. Reserve via Tra Vinh Tourist.

To get here from Tra Vinh, head 50km along the paved road to Duyen Hai and follow the bumpy dirt road for 12km until you reach the beach. About three buses a day make the trip from Tra Vinh to Duyen Hai (15,000d), from which you can hire a moto-taxi (for 10,000d) to take you to the beach.

SA DEC

☎ 067 / pop 108,000

The former capital of Dong Thap province, Sa Dec is a peaceful town of tree-lined streets, fading colonial villas and orchards and flower markets outside of town. It has a small degree of fame as the setting for *The Lover*, a film based on the novel by Marguerite Duras. Two of the classic French villas used in the film can be seen across the river from the market area.

Groups doing a whirlwind tour of the Mekong Delta often make a lunch stop here and drop in on the nurseries.

Information

An **internet café** (☎ 862 010; Đ Hung Vuong) stands next door to the **post office** (cnr Đ Hung Vuong & Quoc Lo 80). There's a **Vietcombank ATM** (251A Đ Nguyen Sinh Sac) at the Bong Hong Hotel . Hwy 80 is known as Đ Nguyen Sinh Sac as it passes through town.

Sights

HUONG TU PAGODA

Of classic Chinese design is the Huong Tu Pagoda (Chua Co Huong Tu), where a bright white statue of Quan The Am Bo Tat standing on a pedestal adorns the grounds. Don't confuse this place with the adjacent **Buu Quang Pagoda**, which is somewhat less glamorous.

NURSERIES

The **nurseries** (vuon hoa; 8-11am & 1-5pm) operate year-round, though they are practically stripped bare of their flowers just before Tet. Note that domestic tourists from HCMC arrive in droves on Sundays – and the nurseries are a major sightseeing attraction around the Tet festival holiday.

There are many small operators here, each with a different speciality. The most famous garden is called the **Tu Ton Rose Garden** (Vuon Hong Tu Ton; 8-11am & 1-5pm), which has over 500 different kinds of rose in 50 different shades and colours.

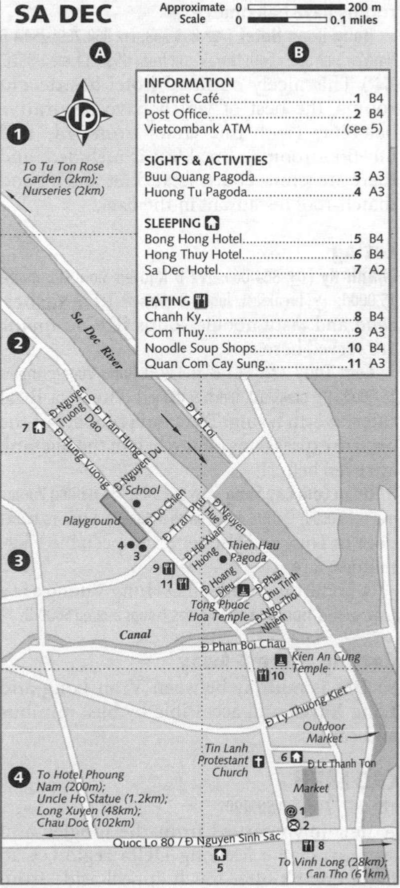

Sleeping

Not many foreigners overnight in Sa Dec, but it's a pleasant, if not very exciting, place to spend an evening.

Hotel Phuong Nam (☎ 867 867; phuongnam384@yahoo.com; 384A Đ Nguyen Sinh Sac; r 80,000-180,000d; ❄) Featuring tidy rooms with wood floors, Phuong Nam is nicely maintained and is a good choice in town.

Sa Dec Hotel (☎ 861 430; fax 862 828; 108/5A Đ Hung Vuong; r with fan/air-con from US$7/10; ❄) The main tourist accommodation in town, this hotel has comfortable rooms with balconies, and bathtubs with hot water. Breakfast included.

Hong Thuy Hotel (☎ 868 963; 58 Đ Le Thanh Ton; r US$7-10; ❄) Overlooking the market, Hong Thuy has trim, mint-coloured rooms with tiled walls and polished wood furniture; some rooms have balconies.

Bong Hong Hotel (☎ 868 288; fax 868 289; 251A Đ Nguyen Sinh Sac; r with fan/air-con from US$8/14, ste US$20; ❄) This nicely outfitted hotel has decent rooms, the best of which have decorative balconies (with fine views from 3rd- and 4th-floor rooms). Breakfast is included, and there are tennis courts next door and a good thatch-roof restaurant in the back.

Eating

Chanh Ky (☎ 864 065; 192 Đ Nguyen Sinh Sac; mains 15,000d; 🕑 breakfast, lunch & dinner) Rice dishes, *chao* and tasty noodle soups like *mi quang* are served here.

Com Thuy (☎ 861 644; 439 Đ Hung Vuong; mains 15,000d; 🕑 breakfast, lunch & dinner) This is a local eatery worth trying. The food is good, but the bizarre expressions on the fish in the big tank are even better!

Quan Com Cay Sung (☎ 861 749; 437 Đ Hung Vuong; mains 15,000d; 🕑 breakfast, lunch & dinner) This is next door to Thuy and also serves respectable Vietnamese fare.

A bit further south on Đ Hung Vuong are a few good **noodle soup shops** (soups around 5000d).

Getting There & Away

Sa Dec is midway between Vinh Long and Long Xuyen and accessible by bus, minibus and car.

CAO LANH

☎ 067 / pop 150,000

A new town carved from the jungles and swamps of the Mekong Delta region, Cao Lanh doesn't offer much appeal aside from its proximity to bird sanctuaries and Rung Tram (Tram Forest) – both major attractions reachable by boat.

Information

Dong Thap Tourist (☎ /fax 855 637; dothatour@hcm.vnn.vn; 2 Đ Doc Binh Kieu) is a friendly, helpful outfit that can arrange boat and other tours of the surrounding area. Expect to pay around US$25 per person for a group of two or three to arrange a boating trip for the day. A boat-station **branch office** (☎ 821 054) handles boat tours from a landing in My Hiep village.

Internet access is available at the **post office** (85 Đ Nguyen Hue; per hr 4000d). Exchange cash at the **Incombank** (☎ 822 030; Đ Nguyen Hue) or the **State Bank of Vietnam** (☎ 852 198; 50 Đ Ly Thuong Kiet).

Sights

DONG THAP MUSEUM

The well-designed **Dong Thap Museum** (admission free; 🕑 7-11.30am & 1.30-5pm) is among the best museums in the Mekong. The 1st floor displays an anthropological history of Dong Thap province, with exhibits of tools, sculpture, models of traditional houses and a few stuffed animals. The 2nd floor is devoted to war history and, of course, to Ho Chi Minh. All interpretive signs are in Vietnamese.

WAR MEMORIAL

Situated on the eastern edge of town off Hwy 30, the War Memorial (Dai Liet Si) is Cao Lanh's most prominent landmark. This socialist-style sculpture features a clamshell-shaped building with a large Vietnamese star alongside a hammer and sickle; concrete statues of victorious peasants and soldiers front the building. The surrounding grounds are decked out with the graves of over 3000 VC who died while fighting in the American War.

NGUYEN SINH SAC GRAVE SITE

Another significant tomb here is that of Nguyen Sinh Sac (1862–1929). Nguyen's main contribution to Vietnamese history was being Ho Chi-Minh's father. His tomb (Lang Cu Nguyen Sinh Sac) occupies 1 hectare about 1km southwest of Cao Lanh.

Although various plaques (in Vietnamese) and tourist pamphlets extol Nguyen Sinh Sac as a great revolutionary, there is little evidence confirming that he was involved in the anti-colonial struggle against the French.

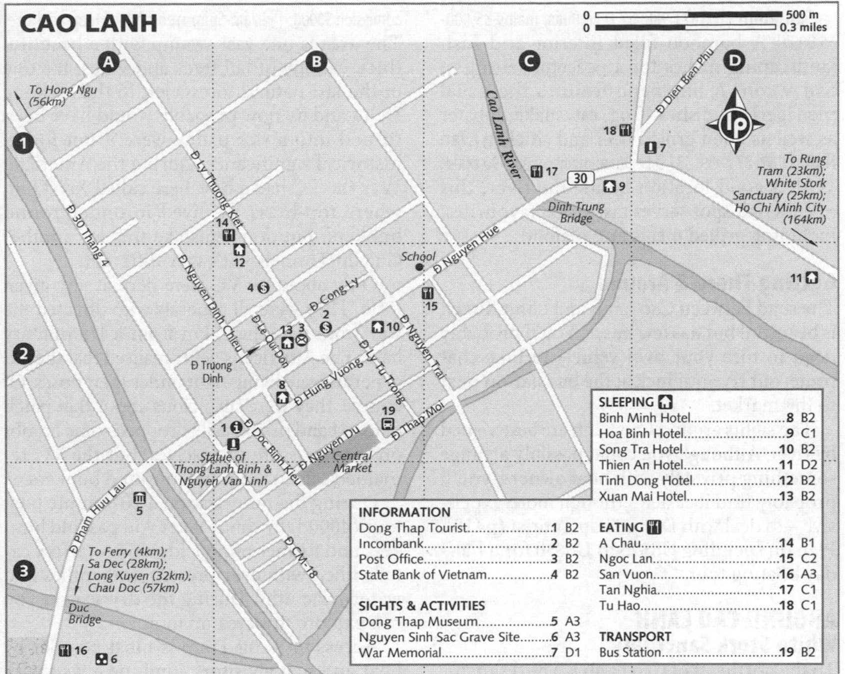

Sleeping

BUDGET

Binh Minh Hotel (☎ 853 423; 157 Đ Hung Vuong; r with fan/air-con 60,000/100,000d; ❄) Owned by a friendly English-speaking school teacher, this is Cao Lanh's cheapest and most basic place to stay, with cold-water bathrooms and bare rooms.

Xuan Mai Hotel (☎ 852 852; fax 856 776; 33 Đ Le Qui Don; r incl breakfast 130,000-150,000d; ❄ 💻) Behind the post office, Xuan Mai has tidy, newly carpeted rooms, all with hot water and bathtubs. For the money, it's the best value in town.

Thien An Hotel (☎ 853 041; 142 Quoc Lo 30; r US$10; ❄) This simple place is fairly priced for its clean, moderately sized rooms. It's about 500m from the War Memorial.

Hoa Binh Hotel (☎ 851 469; fax 851 218; Quoc Lo 30; r US$15-20; ❄) Opposite the War Memorial, this salmon-coloured building has spacious, carpeted rooms with hardwood furniture and sizeable windows.

Song Tra Hotel (☎ 852 624; fax 852 623; 178 Đ Nguyen Hue; r US$14-23; ❄) Recently renovated, the Song Tra has clean rooms with big windows and colourful bedspreads. Rooms in back are quieter. There's a lift.

Tinh Dong Thap Hotel (☎ /fax 872 669; 48 Đ Ly Thuong Kiet; r/ste 200,000/600,000d; ❄) Opened in 2005, this attractive Communist party–run hotel has spotless rooms with polished floors and big windows. Suites, while pricey, are enormous and large enough to accommodate a family or politburo chief.

Eating

Cao Lanh is famous for *chuot dong* (rice-field rats) and it's as good a place as any to sample the local delicacy!

A Chau (☎ 852 202; 42 Đ Ly Thuong Kiet; mains 15,000-40,000d) This place specialises in *banh xeo* (fried pancakes) that you roll up and dip in fish sauce. The *lau de* (goat hotpot) is also flavourful.

Tu Hao (☎ 852 589; Đ Dien Bien Phu; mains 25,000-45,000d) Tu Hao serves all kinds of barbecued food, with decent eel dishes and *cuon banh trang* (fresh spring rolls).

Ngoc Lan (☎ 851 498; 208 Đ Nguyen Hue; mains 20,000-50,000d) You'll find friendly service and home-style cooking at this restaurant on the main road. Enticing options: cuttlefish with ginger and shrimp with cauliflower.

San Vuon (☎ 871 988; 57 Đ Le Duan; mains 35,000-55,000d) A bamboo-filled interior and lush landscaping makes for a peaceful setting at San Vuon. A big menu features the usual menagerie of dishes (frog, rat, snake, lobster as well as good grilled beef and chicken).**Tan Nghia** (☎ 871 989; 331 Đ Le Duan; mains 50,000-90,000d) With a good location beside the river, this open-sided spot serves tasty local favourites, including grilled meats and seafood.

Getting There & Around

The road between Cao Lanh and Long Xuyen is beautiful but has few buses. You'll probably need to hire your own vehicle to take that route, but try your luck at the bus station next to the market.

The sights around Cao Lanh are best visited by river. Although you could possibly arrange something privately with boat owners, you'll probably find it easier – though more expensive – to deal with Dong Thap Tourist (p418). Plan on spending US$25 to US$30 for a half-day boating tour.

AROUND CAO LANH

White Stork Sanctuary

To the northeast of Cao Lanh is a bird sanctuary (Vuon Co Thap Muoi) for white storks. The sanctuary only covers 2 hectares, but the birds seem mostly undisturbed by the nearby farmers.

The storks are accustomed to people and are fairly easy to spot, as they feed in the mangrove and bamboo forests. They live in pairs and don't migrate with the seasons, so you can see them at any time of year.

There are no roads as such to the bird sanctuary, so getting there requires a trip by boat. Dong Thap Tourist (p418) can arrange this, though you may be able to arrange it elsewhere. A speedboat costs US$25 per hour and the ride takes 50 minutes. A slow boat costs US$4 per person (with 20 people) and takes three hours to make the return journey. In the dry season, you have to plan your boat trip according to the two daily tides – at low tide the canals can become impassable.

Many travellers include a trip to White Stork Sanctuary with a visit to Rung Tram (see below).

Rung Tram

Southeast of Cao Lanh and accessible by boat tour is the 52-hectare **Rung Tram** (Tram Forest; admission 5000d; 7am-5pm) near My Hiep village. The area is one vast swamp with a beautiful thick canopy of tall trees and vines. It's one of the last natural forests left in the Mekong Delta and by now probably would have been turned into a rice paddy were it not for its historical significance. During the American War the VC had a base here called Xeo Quit, where top-brass VC lived in underground bunkers. But don't mistake this for another Cu Chi Tunnels – it's very different.

Only about 10 VC were here at any given time. They were all generals who directed the war from here, just 2km from a US military base. The Americans never realised that the VC generals were living right under their noses. Of course, they were suspicious about that patch of forest and periodically dropped some bombs on it to reassure themselves, but the VC remained safe in their underground bunkers.

During the rainy season a 20-minute boat tour (4000d) by canoe takes you past old bunkers and former minefields along narrow canals filled with ever-present dragonflies and water hyacinths. During the dry season you can explore this area on foot.

Access to Rung Tram is most popular by boat and many visitors combine a visit with a trip to White Stork Sanctuary. You can also try hiring a speedboat from Cao Lanh to Rung Tram, which takes around 30 minutes (depending on the tides). It is also possible to reach the forest by road if you are travelling by car or motorbike. From My Hiep, you can also hire a slow boat (seating up to 10 persons) that takes around 40 minutes to make the 2km journey to Rung Tram.

Tram Chim Nature Reserve

Due north of Cao Lanh in Tam Nong (Dong Thap province) is Tram Chim National Wetland Reserve (Tram Chim Tam Nong), which is notable for its **eastern sarus cranes** *(Grus antigone sharpii)*. Over 220 species of bird have been identified within the reserve, but ornithologists will be most interested in the rare red-headed cranes, which grow to over 1.5m high. Seeing these birds, however, requires a considerable commitment (time, effort and money), so it's really for bird enthusiasts only.

The birds nest here from about December to June; from July to November they migrate to Cambodia, so schedule your visit to coordinate with the birds' travel itinerary if you want to see them. Also, the birds are early risers – early morning is the best time to see them, though you might get a glimpse when they return home in the evening. During the day, the birds are engaged in the important business of eating.

Tam Nong is a sleepy town 45km from Cao Lanh. The one-way drive takes about 1½ hours by car; it's also possible to get there by boat. A speedboat takes only one hour, but costs US$25 per hour to rent. A slow boat can be arranged from Dong Thap Tourist (p418). From the guesthouse in Tam Nong it takes another hour by small boat (per hour US$15) to reach the area where the cranes live and another hour to return. Add to this whatever time you spend (perhaps an hour) staring at your feathered friends through binoculars (bring your own), and then the requisite one to four hours to return to Cao Lanh, depending on your mode of transport.

The state-run **guesthouse** (r with fan US$10) in Tam Nong is just before the bridge, heading into town. It has extremely basic rooms; bring your own bug spray. Tam Nong shuts down early – if you want to eat dinner here, make arrangements before 5pm.

CAN THO

☎ 071 / pop 330,000

The largest city in the Mekong, Can Tho is a buzzing town with a lively waterfront and a colourful mix of narrow back streets and wide boulevards that make for some rewarding exploration – especially after a few days spent in the wilds. As the political, economic, cultural and transportation centre of the Mekong Delta, Can Tho hums with activity; while its access to nearby floating markets make it a major draw for tourists, who come here to boat along the myriad canals and rivers leading out of town.

Information

INTERNET ACCESS

Queen (9 Đ Chau Van Liem; per min 100d; 7am-11.30pm) This pleasant internet café serves sandwiches, ice cream and cocktails as well as speedy net access.

MEDICAL SERVICES

Hospital (Khoa Khan Benh; ☎ 820 071; 4 Đ Chau Van Liem)

MONEY

Golf Hotel (2 Đ Hai Ba Trung) Has an ATM.

Sacombank (☎ 810 519; fax 810 523; 13A Đ Phan Dinh Phung) Credit card advances can be done here.

Vietcombank (Ngan Hang Ngoai Thuong Viet Nam; ☎ 820 445; fax 820 694; 7 ĐL Hoa Binh) Has foreign-currency exchange and 24hr ATM.

POST

Post office (2 ĐL Hoa Binh)

TOURIST INFORMATION

Can Tho Tourist (☎ 821 852; fax 822 719; 20 Đ Hai Ba Trung; 7am-5pm & 6-8pm) Staff at this provincial tourism authority are pleasant and helpful; they can speak English and French. Decent city maps are available for 10,000d.

Vietnam Airlines (☎ 824 088) Has a booking desk at the Can Tho Tourist office.

Sights

CAN THO MUSEUM

The enormous, well-presented **Can Tho Museum** (☎ 813 890; 1 ĐL Hoa Binh; admission free; 8-11am & 2-5pm Tue-Thu; 8-11am & 6.30-9pm Sat, Sun & holidays) has exhibits of the history of Can Tho resistance during foreign rule as well as displays on the culture and history of the province. There's a life-size pagoda and ample English signage.

MUNIRANGSYARAM PAGODA

The ornamentation of **Munirangsyaram Pagoda** (36 ĐL Hoa Binh) is typical of Khmer Hinayana Buddhist pagodas: it doesn't have any of the multiple Bodhisattvas and Taoist spirits common in Vietnamese Mahayana pagodas. In the upstairs sanctuary a 1.5m-high representation of Siddhartha Gautama, the historical Buddha, sits serenely under a Bodhi Tree.

Built in 1946, the Munirangsyaram Pagoda serves the Khmer community of Can Tho, which numbers about 2000.

CANTONESE CONGREGATION PAGODA

Occupying a splendid location facing the Can Tho River, this small **Chinese pagoda** (Quan Cong Hoi Quan; Đ Hai Ba Trung) was built by the Cantonese Congregation. The original one was constructed on a different site about 70 years ago. The current pagoda was built with funds donated by overseas Chinese more recently. Can Tho used to have a large ethnic-Chinese population, but most of them fled after the anti-Chinese persecutions (1978–79).

CENTRAL MARKET

Many local farmers and wholesalers arrive at this **market** (Đ Hai Ba Trung) by boat to buy and

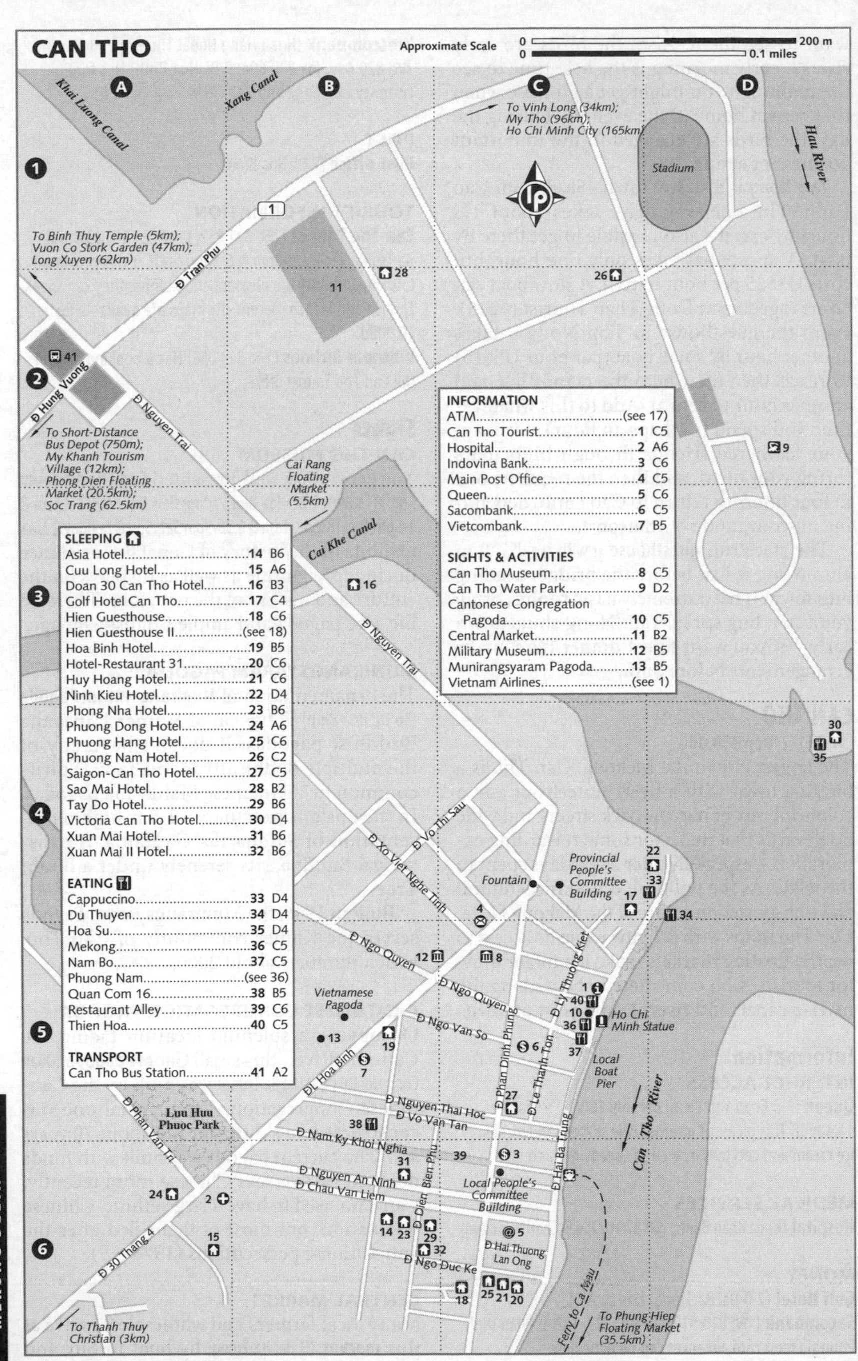
CAN THO
Approximate Scale
0 200 m
0 0.1 miles
A B C D
1 2 3 4 5 6
Khai Luong Canal
Xang Canal
To Vinh Long (34km); My Tho (96km); Ho Chi Minh City (165km)
Stadium
Hau River
To Binh Thuy Temple (5km); Vuon Co Stork Garden (47km); Long Xuyen (62km)
Đ Tran Phu
Đ Hung Vuong
Đ Nguyen Trai
To Short-Distance Bus Depot (750m); My Khanh Tourism Village (12km); Phong Dien Floating Market (20.5km); Soc Trang (62.5km)
Cai Rang Floating Market (5.5km)
Cai Khe Canal
INFORMATION
ATM (see 17)
Can Tho Tourist 1 C5
Hospital 2 A6
Indovina Bank 3 C6
Main Post Office 4 C5
Queen 5 C6
Sacombank 6 C5
Vietcombank 7 B5
SIGHTS & ACTIVITIES
Can Tho Museum 8 C5
Can Tho Water Park 9 D2
Cantonese Congregation Pagoda 10 C5
Central Market 11 B2
Military Museum 12 B5
Munirangsyaram Pagoda 13 B5
Vietnam Airlines (see 1)
SLEEPING
Asia Hotel 14 B6
Cuu Long Hotel 15 A6
Doan 30 Can Tho Hotel 16 B3
Golf Hotel Can Tho 17 C4
Hien Guesthouse 18 C6
Hien Guesthouse II (see 18)
Hoa Binh Hotel 19 B5
Hotel-Restaurant 31 20 C6
Huy Hoang Hotel 21 C6
Ninh Kieu Hotel 22 D4
Phong Nha Hotel 23 B6
Phuong Dong Hotel 24 A6
Phuong Hang Hotel 25 C6
Phuong Nam Hotel 26 C2
Saigon-Can Tho Hotel 27 C5
Sao Mai Hotel 28 B2
Tay Do Hotel 29 B6
Victoria Can Tho Hotel 30 D4
Xuan Mai Hotel 31 B6
Xuan Mai II Hotel 32 B6
EATING
Cappuccino 33 D4
Du Thuyen 34 D4
Hoa Su 35 D4
Mekong 36 C5
Nam Bo 37 C5
Phuong Nam (see 36)
Quan Com 16 38 B5
Restaurant Alley 39 C6
Thien Hoa 40 C5
TRANSPORT
Can Tho Bus Station 41 A2
Đ Vo Thi Sau
Đ Xo Viet Nghe Tinh
Provincial People's Committee Building
Fountain
Đ Ngo Quyen
Đ Ly Thuong Kiet
Vietnamese Pagoda
Ho Chi Minh Statue
Đ Ngo Van So
Đ Phan Dinh Phung
Đ Le Thanh Ton
Local Boat Pier
ĐL Hoa Binh
Can Tho River
Đ Nguyen Thai Hoc
Đ Vo Van Tan
Luu Huu Phuoc Park
Đ Phan Van Tri
Đ Nam Ky Khoi Nghia
Đ Dien Bien Phu
Đ Hai Ba Trung
Đ Nguyen An Ninh
Đ Chau Van Liem
Local People's Committee Building
Đ 30 Thang 4
Đ Hai Thuong Lan Ong
Đ Ngo Duc Ke
Ferry to Ca Mau
To Thanh Thuy Christian (3km)
To Phung Hiep Floating Market (35.5km)

sell. The fruit section, near the intersection of Đ Hai Ba Trung and Đ Ngo Quyen, is particularly colourful and stays open until late evening.

MILITARY MUSEUM

Devoted to all things militaristic, this **museum** (6 ĐL Hoa Binh; admission free; 8-11am & 2-4.30pm Tue, Thu & Fri, 8-11am & 7-9pm Sat) has the usual assortment of American War weaponry and Ho Chi Minh portraits. Missiles and a fighter aircraft sit on the front lawn.

Can Tho for Children

CAN THO WATER PARK

For a bit of glorious chlorinated fun, try the **Can Tho Water Park** (763 343; Cai Khe Ward; water park/pool only 40,000/25,000d; 9am-6pm). Among the attractions are water slides and a wave pool. Children under 1m tall are admitted free.

Tours

The highlight of visiting Can Tho is taking a boat ride through the canals to a floating market. The cost is around 50,000d per hour for a small boat, which can carry two or three passengers. For boat operators (mostly women), just wander by the riverside near the market. You can also book through Can Tho Tourist, but this leaves little room for negotiation.

Larger motorboats can go further afield and it's worth hiring one to make a tour of the Mekong River itself. Check the going rates at Can Tho Tourist then see what's on offer at the pier by the Ninh Kieu Hotel (see right). Prices range from 150,000d for a three-hour tour to 250,000d for a five-hour tour. Negotiation is the name of the game.

For more on the area's floating markets, see p426.

Sleeping

Can Tho boasts the best range of accommodation in the Mekong Delta.

BUDGET

Phong Nha Hotel (821 615; 75 Đ Chau Van Liem; r with fan/air-con from 60,000/120,000d;) It's cheap and basic here, with slatted wood doors and a low-key, family atmosphere. Bathrooms could be cleaner, and it's on a noisy street with many motorbikes.

Hien Guesthouse (812 718; hien_gh@yahoo.com; 118/10 Đ Phan Dinh Phung; r with fan/air-con US$5/8;) A favourite of budget travellers, this friendly, family-run guesthouse is tucked down a narrow alley near the city centre. Small, clean rooms come with floor-level mattresses in the older half of the building.

Hien Guesthouse II (106/3 Đ Phan Dinh Phung; r with fan/air-con US$5/9;) A newer annex, this place has slightly better rooms and there's a shared terrace. Dependable motorbikes are available for around US$5 a day.

Hotel-Restaurant 31 (825 287; 31 Đ Ngo Duc Ke; s/d with fan US$5/8, r with air-con US$10;) Popular with backpackers, this clean hotel has a mix of rooms; the worst are small and cramped; the best (like No 301) are spacious and airy. The restaurant serves good meals (mains 30,000d to 40,000d).

Huy Hoang Hotel (825 833; 35 Đ Ngo Duc Ke; r with fan/air-con from 80,000/120,000d;) This cheapie, bare-bones option has rooms with little or no ventilation, though there are hot-water bathrooms, and the place is clean. Huy Hoang is centrally located and there's a common balcony.

Xuan Mai II Hotel (832 578; 17 Đ Dien Bien Phu; r US$6-12;) A good-value option, this new hotel has spotless rooms with big windows and kind service. The best rooms have bathtubs.

Phuong Hang Hotel (814 978; 41 Đ Ngo Duc Ke; r 120,000d;) This small minihotel has clean quarters with intricately tiled floors. Front rooms have big windows.

Sao Mai Hotel (764 082; fax 764 083; 65 Đ A1, Cai Khe ward; r 150,000-250,000d;) Near the central market, this is one of many new hotels in the neighbourhood. Sao Mai has clean, spacious rooms that are a good value.

Xuan Mai Hotel (811 931; 94 Đ Nguyen An Ninh; r US$12-15;) This friendly new hotel has excellent rooms with polished wood furniture and high ceilings. There's a lift.

Phuong Nam Hotel (/fax 763 949; 118/9/39 Tran Van Kheo; r US$13-22;) Southeast of the main market, this new seven-storey hotel has clean rooms with big bathrooms and wireless access. It's a bit out of the way but it's better value than most waterfront options.

MIDRANGE

Doan 30 Can Tho Hotel (823 623; fax 811 140; 80A Đ Nguyen Trai; r US$10-25;) At the northern end of town on the riverbank, this army-owned place has a dingy lobby, but decent rooms. Some have balconies and river views, as well as huge bathrooms. Rates include a simple breakfast. There's a lift and an outdoor café.

My Khanh Tourism Village (☎ 846 260; www.mykhanh.com; 335 Đ Lo Vong Cung, Phong Dien District; r US$15-35;) Located 12km southwest of Can Tho, this small, lushly landscaped complex has freestanding wood bungalows with attractive furnishings. There's a pool, a decent restaurant, and you can book boating and other excursions.

Cuu Long Hotel (☎ 822 669; cuulongcthotel@hcm.vnn.vn; 52 Đ Quang Trung; r US$16-30;) Rooms at this large hotel are generally light, airy and a bit quieter than those in the centre. Unfortunately, economy rooms are dingy and can't be recommended. Breakfast included. There's a lift.

Phuong Dong Hotel (☎ 812 199; phuongdonghotel@hcm.vnn.vn; 62 Đ 30 Thang 4; r US$19-30;) A newish place with fair, carpeted rooms (some lack windows) that have modern bathrooms. There's a lift and a business centre.

Hoa Binh Hotel (☎ 820 536; hoabinhct@hcm.vnn.vn; 5 ĐL Hoa Binh; r US$20-30, ste US$45;) Rooms have carpeting, IDD phones, wi-fi access and satellite TV. With its elegant wood furniture, it's one of the better deals for this price range, though cheaper rooms lack windows. Breakfast included.

Asia Hotel (Khach San A Chau; ☎ 812 800; asiahotel@hcm.vnn.vn; 91 Đ Chau Van Liem; r US$20-32;) A nicely maintained place with spotless rooms. Deluxe rooms have large balconies; rates include breakfast.

Tay Do Hotel (☎ 827 009; www.taydohotel.vnn.vn; 61 Đ Chau Van Liem; r US$25-30;) Set with a sparkling lobby and abundant amenities (including a sauna and massage services), the Tay Do offers comfortable, carpeted rooms, (deluxe rooms have balconies). Breakfast is included.

Ninh Kieu Hotel (☎ 821 171; fax 821 104; 2 Đ Hai Ba Trung; r new wing US$40-80, old wing US$25-30;) This hotel belongs to the army and occupies a terrific location on the riverfront. Rooms in the new wing are carpeted and have balconies. Old-wing rooms are clean but dated, featuring green colour schemes.

Saigon-Can Tho Hotel (☎ 825 831; www.saigoncantho.com; 55 Đ Phan Dinh Phung; s US$38-50, d US$49-62;) You'll find abundant amenities and a fair selection of carpeted rooms at this three-star place – though only the upper-tier rooms have a window to the outside! All rooms have bathtubs and DSL access, and there's a restaurant, massage service, sauna and karaoke. Rates include breakfast.

TOP END

Golf Hotel Can Tho (☎ 812 210; www.golfhotel.vnn.vn; 2 Đ Hai Ba Trung; r US$60-149, ste US$185-200;) The enormous riverside Golf Hotel is near the Ninh Kieu pier. Tastefully decorated rooms boast incredible views from the upper-floor balconies. Hotel facilities include a health club and a beauty salon; breakfast included.

Victoria Can Tho Hotel (☎ 810 111; Cai Khe Ward; www.victoriahotels-asia.com; r US$161-282;) This lovely place sits right on the riverfront and is Can Tho's *crème de la crème*. Lavish rooms have garden or river views and guests have access to the fine restaurant, open-air bar, tennis courts and swimming pool. Nonguests can use the facilities as long as they order something at the restaurant.

Eating & Drinking

Along the Can Tho River waterfront there are several café-restaurants, most serving Mekong specialities such as fish, frog and turtle, as well as standard backpacker fare.

Other popular eateries line the riverfront strip, across from the giant metallic Uncle Ho statue.

Quan Com 16 (☎ 827 326; 77 Đ Vo Van Tan; mains 15,000; breakfast, lunch & dinner) A very popular traditional eatery serving tasty, inexpensive bites.

Restaurant Alley (Đ Nam Ky Khoi Nghia; mains around 15,000d) This is a good spot to escape the tourist scene on the riverfront. Situated in an alley between Đ Dien Bien Phu and Đ Phan Dinh Phung, there are about a dozen local restaurants scattered on both sides of the street.

Mekong (☎ 821 646; 38 Đ Hai Ba Trung; mains 15,000-25,000d; breakfast, lunch & dinner) Mekong is always packed, for good reason: good Vietnamese food at reasonable prices.

Thien Hoa (☎ 821 942; 26 Đ Hai Ba Trung; mains 15,000-25,000d; breakfast, lunch & dinner) The speciality of the house are delicious Hué-style spring rolls *(dac biet cha gio re)*.

Phuong Nam (☎ 812 077; 48 Đ Hai Ba Trung; mains 25,000d; breakfast, lunch & dinner) As with Mekong, Phuong Nam is a delicious deal.

Nam Bo (☎ 823 908; nambo@hcm.vnn.vn; 50 Đ Hai Ba Trung; mains 25,000-50,000d; lunch & dinner) Housed in a thoughtfully restored, classic French villa, Nam Bo offers excellent European and Vietnamese cuisine in a delightful atmosphere. The view of the local fruit market from the 2nd-storey terrace can't be beaten.

Cappuccino (☎ 825 296; 2 Đ Hai Ba Trung; mains 35,000-70,000d; lunch & dinner) For a break from

THE FRUITS OF VIETNAM

One of the great rewards of travelling through the Mekong is sampling the extraordinary array of fruits available at markets, orchards and street stalls all over the region. A handful of fruits worth seeking include the following:

Buoi (pomelo) – this gargantuan grapefruit has thick skin and sweeter, less acidic fruit than ordinary grapefruit.

Chom Chom (rambutan) – tiny fiery red fruit with hairy skin, and tender sweet white flesh. Most prevalent during the rainy season (May to October).

Đu Đu (papaya) – Vietnam boasts 45 species of papaya; it's great in juices or raw when ripe (orange to red flesh), and used in tangy salads when green.

Dua (pineapple) – another common Mekong fruit, some aren't so sweet. Locals sometimes doctor them up with salt and red chilli powder.

Khe (starfruit) – a five-pointed, shiny skinned fruit that is intensely juicy.

Mang Cau (custard apple) – inside this fruit's bumpy green skin lie black pips surrounded by white flesh – which indeed taste very much like custard.

Mang Cut (mangosteen) – violet, tennis-ball-sized fruit. Cut open to reveal white sour-sweet flesh. Kind of like durian for beginners.

Mit (jackfruit) – giant, blimp-shaped fruit containing chewy yellow segments. It's loaded with vitamins.

Nhan (longan) – this tiny fruit has light brown skin, a translucent juicy white pulp and is used for many purposes in the Mekong (it's even dried and used for kindling).

Oi (guava) – green, edible skin with pink flesh, the guava is loaded with vitamins and is great raw or in juice.

Sau Rieng (durian) – with a memorable odour, this huge spiky fruit has creamy rich interior of a taste somewhat resembling custard; you'll either love it or hate it.

Thanh Long (dragon fruit) – unusual in appearance, dragon fruit is a large red fruit with spiky fronds tipped with green. It has a mild, crisp flesh with numerous edible seeds.

Trai Vai (lychee) – very common, this small, round red spiky fruit has a white fleshy inside, which is particularly sweet.

Xoai (mango) – mangos come in several varieties; the sweetest are large round ones with bright yellow skin. Connoisseurs say the best come from Cao Lanh (p418).

Vu Sua (star apple) – a round, smooth fruit that produces a sweet, milky juice (its name means milk from the breast).

pho, head to this popular Italian restaurant near the riverfront. You'll find a decent selection of pizzas and pastas and delivery is available.

Thanh Thuy Christian (☎ 840 207; 149 Đ 30 Thang 4; mains 40,000-50,000d; 🕑 8am-11pm) This goat-meat speciality restaurant serves tasty curried goat; or if you're feeling adventurous, try the goat-scrotum hotpot. The restaurant is a few kilometres out of town, just beyond the local university. Look for the sign on your left, just beyond the junction with Đ Tran Hoang Na.

Du Thuyen (☎ 810 841; Đ Hai Ba Trung; mains 40,000-75,000d) For a unique dining experience, climb aboard this three-level wooden ship, where you can enjoy the usual standards while floating along the river. Du Thuyen typically sails from 8pm to 9.30pm.

Hoa Su (☎ 820 717; Cai Khe Ward; mains 40,000-85,000d; 🕑 breakfast, lunch & dinner) Overlooking the water, this popular eatery serves seafood and other favourites, to great river views. It's near Victoria Hotel.

So Hom (☎ 815 616; 50 Đ Hai Ba Trung; mains 45,000-70,000d; 🕑 8am-midnight) Inside the former market, this sleek and attractive spot serves a variety of Vietnamese and fusion dishes (shrimp with mango, papaya salad, vegetable tandoori) and the riverside setting is Can Tho's most idyllic spot for a meal or a drink.

Getting There & Away

BUS

There are buses leaving HCMC from Mien Tay bus station (p372; about 65,000d, five hours). Express minibuses make the same trip in about the same time.

The main bus station in Can Tho is about a kilometre north of town at the intersection of Đ Nguyen Trai and Đ Tran Phu. There is another short-haul bus depot about 300m south of the intersection of Đ 30 Thang 4 and Đ Mau Than, which is good for getting to Soc Trang and the Phung Hiep floating market.

CAR & MOTORBIKE

Whether you travel by car or motorbike, the ride from HCMC to Can Tho along Hwy 1 takes about four hours. There is one ferry crossing at Binh Minh (in Can Tho). The Can Tho ferry runs from 4am to 2am.

To get from ĐL Hoa Binh in Can Tho to the ferry crossing, go along Đ Nguyen Trai to the main bus station and turn right onto Đ Tran Phu.

Getting Around

XE LOI

Unique to the Mekong Delta, these makeshift vehicles are the main form of transport around Can Tho. A *xe loi* is essentially a two-wheeled wagon attached to the rear of a motorbike, creating what resembles a motorised *cyclo*, but with four wheels touching the ground rather than two. Fares around town should be about 5000d per person (they can carry two, or sometimes more), a bit higher for trips to outlying areas.

AROUND CAN THO

Perhaps the biggest drawcard of the delta is its colourful **floating markets**, which are on the banks of wide stretches of river. Most market folk begin early to avoid the daytime heat, so try to visit between 6am and 8am. The tides, however, are also a factor as bigger boats must often wait until the water is high enough for them to navigate.

Some of the smaller, rural floating markets are disappearing, largely because of improved roads and access to private and public transport. Many of the larger markets near urban areas, however, are still going strong.

Rural areas of Can Tho province, renowned for their durian, mangosteen and orange orchards, can easily be reached from Can Tho by boat or bicycle.

Cai Rang Floating Market

Just 6km from Can Tho in the direction of Soc Trang is Cai Rang, the biggest floating market in the Mekong Delta. There is a bridge here that serves as a great vantage point for photography. The market is best before 9am, although some vendors hang out until noon, it's less lively by then.

Cai Rang can be seen from the road, but getting there is far more interesting by boat. From the market area in Can Tho it takes about an hour by river, or you can drive to the Cau Dau Sau boat landing (by the Dau Sau Bridge), from where it takes only about 10 minutes to reach the market.

Phong Dien Floating Market

Perhaps the best floating market in the Mekong Delta, Phong Dien has fewer motorised craft and more stand-up rowing boats. It's less crowded than Cai Rang and there are far fewer tourists. The market is at its bustling best between 6am and 8am. It is 20km southwest of Can Tho and most get there by road.

It is theoretically possible to do a whirlwind boat trip here, visiting the small canals on the way and finishing back at the Cai Rang floating market. This journey should take approximately five hours return from Can Tho.

Phung Hiep Floating Market

Until recently, the small town of Phung Hiep was notable for its eerie snake market. In 1998, however, a national law banned the capture and sale of snakes in an effort to control the rapidly multiplying rat population (due to a relative absence of snakes), which had been devastating rice crops. Snake sellers throughout the country are now forced to operate underground.

These days the cages that used to swell with cobras and pythons are empty, and Phung Hiep is now just a regular market. There is a small-scale floating market under the bridge and boats can be hired here for a tour along the river.

Phung Hiep is right on Hwy 1, 35km from Can Tho in the direction of Soc Trang.

Stork Garden

On the road between Can Tho and Long Xuyen, **Vuon Co** (admission 2000d; 5am-6pm) is a 1.3-hectare stork sanctuary. It is a popular stop for group tours coming to view the thousands of resident storks. There is a tall wooden viewing platform. The best times of day to see the birds are around dawn and dusk.

Vuon Co is in the Thot Not district, about 15km southeast of Long Xuyen. Look for a sign in the hamlet of Thoi An: 'Ap Von Hoa'; coming from Can Tho the sign is on the west side of the road, immediately after a small bridge. It is a few kilometres off the main highway – reachable on foot within 30 minutes, or hire a motorbike taxi for about 5000d.

SOC TRANG

☎ 079 / pop 115,000

Soc Trang is the scruffy, workaday capital of Soc Trang province. Khmer people make up about 28% of the population. Although the town itself isn't much, it's a good base for exploring some impressive Khmer temples in the area. Furthermore, there is a colourful annual festival (usually in December) and, if you're in the vicinity at the right time, it's worth your while to catch it.

Soc Trang Tourist (☎ 821 498; www.soctrangtourism.com; 131 Đ Nguyen Chi Thanh; 8-11am & 1.30-5pm) is adjacent to the Phong Lan 2 Hotel. The staff are friendly enough, but speak little English and are not all that accustomed to walk-in tourists.

ATMs are available outside the Khanh Hung Hotel and Que Huong Hotel. The **post office** (☎ 820 051) is at 1 ĐL Tran Hung Dao.

Sights

KH'LEANG PAGODA

Except for the bright orange paint job, this **pagoda** (Chua Kh'leang) looks like it's been transported straight from Cambodia. Originally built from bamboo in 1533, it had a complete rebuild in 1905 (this time using concrete). There are seven religious festivals held here every year that are worth seeing – people come from outlying areas of the province for these events. Even outside of festival times, Khmer people drop in regularly to bring donations and pray.

Several monks reside in the pagoda, which also serves as a base for over 150 student monks who come from around the Mekong Delta to study at Soc Trang's College of Buddhist Education across the street. The monks are friendly and happy to show you around the pagoda and discuss Buddhism.

KHMER MUSEUM

This **museum** (Bao Tang Tinh Soc Trang; ☎ 822 983; 23 Đ Nguyen Chi Thanh; admission free; 7.30-11am & 1.30-4.30pm Mon-Fri) is dedicated to the history and culture of Vietnam's Khmer minority. Indeed,

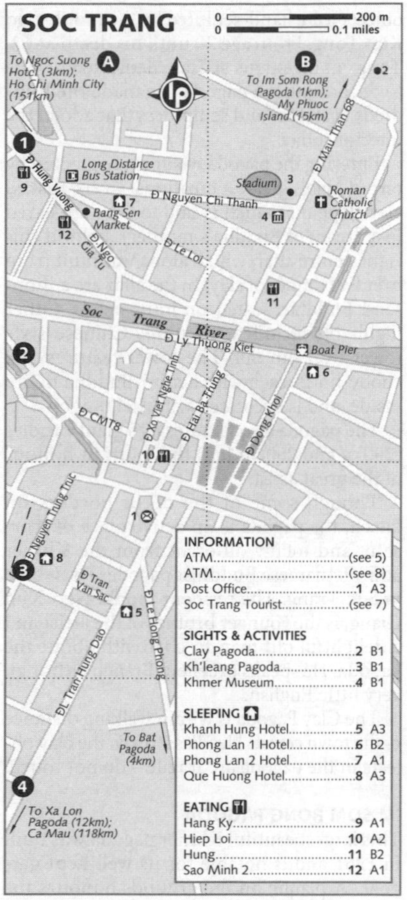

it serves as a sort of cultural centre, and traditional dance and music shows are periodically staged here for larger groups – advance notice is essential.

The Khmer Museum is opposite Kh'leang Pagoda and often appears closed; you may have to rouse someone to let you in.

CLAY PAGODA

Buu Son Tu (Precious Mountain Temple) was founded over 200 years ago by a Chinese family named Ngo. Today the temple is better known as **Chua Dat Set** (163 Đ Mau Than 68), or Clay Pagoda.

Unassuming from the outside, this pagoda is highly unusual in that nearly everything inside is made entirely of clay. These objects were hand-sculpted by the monk Ngo Kim Tong. From age 20 until his death at 62, Tong, an ingenious artisan, dedicated his life to decorating the pagoda. He made the hundreds of statues and sculptures that adorn the interior today.

Entering the pagoda, visitors are greeted by one of Ngo's greatest creations – a six-tusked clay elephant (which is said to have appeared in a dream of Buddha's mother). Behind this is the centre altar, which alone was built from over five tonnes of clay. In the altar are a thousand Buddhas seated on lotus petals. Other highlights include a 13-storey Chinese-style tower over 4m tall. The tower features 208 cubby-holes, each with a mini-Buddha figure inside, and is decorated with 156 dragons.

The pagoda also features two giant candles (200kg and 260cm tall) that burn in honour of the great artist.

Though some of the décor borders on kitsch, the pagoda is an active place of worship, and totally different from the Khmer and Vietnamese Buddhist pagodas elsewhere in Soc Trang. The resident monk, Ngo Kim Giang, is the younger brother of the artist and a delightful old man to chat with about the pagoda. He speaks excellent French although very little English.

The Clay Pagoda is within walking distance of the town centre. Needless to say, the clay objects in the pagoda are fragile – do not touch.

IM SOM RONG PAGODA

This large, beautiful Khmer pagoda was built in 1961 and is notable for its well-kept gardens. A plaque on the grounds honours the man who donated the funds to build the pagoda. There are many monks in residence here, most of whom are very friendly and happy to chat.

Im Som Rong Pagoda is over 1km east of Soc Trang on the road to My Phuoc Island. When you reach the main gate it's a 300m walk along a dirt track to the pagoda itself.

Festivals & Events

OC BOM BOC FESTIVAL

Once a year, the Khmer community turns out for the Oc Bom Boc Festival, with longboat races on the Soc Trang River. This event attracts visitors from all over Vietnam and even Cambodia. First prize is over US$1000, so it's not difficult to see why competition is so fierce.

The races are held according to the lunar calendar on the 15th day of the 10th moon, which roughly means December. The races start at noon, but things get jumping in Soc Trang the evening before. Hotel space is at a premium during the festival and travellers without a prepaid hotel reservation will probably have to sleep in a car or minibus.

Sleeping

Phong Lan 2 Hotel (☎ 821 757; fax 821 757; 133 Đ Nguyen Chi Thanh; r 90,000-130,000; ❄) Though a bit worn, this is still an OK place to stay, with friendly staff and tidy, airy rooms. Rates include breakfast, and there's massage and sauna service.

Khanh Hung Hotel (☎ 821 027; fax 820 099; 15 ĐL Tran Hung Dao; r 110,000-341,000d; ❄) The Khanh Hung boasts a large indoor-outdoor café and trim rooms that range from bare and fan-cooled to air-conditioned and adequately furnished. All rooms have small balconies. There's a lift.

Phong Lan 1 Hotel (☎ 821 619; fax 823 817; 124 Đ Dong Khoi; r with/without hot water 150,000/125,000d; ❄) This riverside hotel is fair value for its clean rooms. As elsewhere, some rooms lack windows, and street-facing rooms may be noisy.

Ngoc Suong Hotel (☎ 613 108; ksngocsuong@hcm.vnn.vn; Km 2127 QL1; r US$20-40, ste US$80; ❄ 🏊) Located 3km outside of town, on the road to Can Tho, this attractive new complex offers light and airy rooms with comfortable furnishings and big windows. There's also a pool and tennis court.

Que Huong Hotel (☎ 616 122; khachsanquehuong@yahoo.com; 128 Đ Nguyen Trung Truc; r 190,000-390,000d; ❄) Run by the People's Committee, this sleek new hotel has comfortable rooms with flat-screen TVs, minifridges, DSL access and sizable windows. There's a good restaurant here, with one of the only English menus in town.

Eating

Most restaurants in Soc Trang do not have English menus, nor are meal prices written anywhere, though no one's likely to gouge you.

Hung (☎ 822 268; 74-76 Đ Mau Than 68; mains 20,000d; 🕑 breakfast, lunch & dinner) One of the best places in town, Hung serves delicious grilled meat and fish and always seems to be busy.

Hang Ky (☎ 612 034; 67 Đ Hung Vuong; mains 20,000-50,000d; 🕑 breakfast, lunch & dinner) Recommended for its good traditional dishes, Hang Ky is a large, airy space that's quite popular (wedding parties included).

Sao Minh 2 (☎ 610 836; 115 Đ Ngo Gia Tu; mains 20,000-50,000d; ⏰ breakfast, lunch & dinner) On the main road into town, Sao Minh 2 is another popular spot, serving tasty *xiu mai* (marinated pork) among other good selections.

Getting There & Away

Long-distance buses stop at the station on Đ Nguyen Chi Thanh, just down the street from Soc Trang Tourist. Buses run between Soc Trang and most Mekong cities, including Can Tho (20,000d) and Ca Mau (40,000d). Regular vans travel to Ho Chi Minh City (80,000d, around six hours).

AROUND SOC TRANG

Bat Pagoda

This is one of the Mekong Delta's most unusual sights and has become a favourite stop-off for both foreign and domestic tourists. The Bat Pagoda (Chua Doi) is a large monastery compound. Upon entering through an archway, you'll almost immediately hear the screeching of the large colony of resident fruit bats. There are thousands of these creatures hanging from the fruit trees. The largest bats weigh about 1kg and have a wingspan of about 1.5m.

Fruit bats make plenty of noise – in the morning the din is incredible (likewise the smell). The bats are not toilet trained, so watch out when standing under a tree, or bring an umbrella. In the evening the bats spread their wings and fly out to invade orchards all over the Mekong Delta, much to the consternation of farmers, who are known to trap the bats and eat them. Inside the monastery the creatures are protected and the bats seem to know this – no doubt this is why they stay.

The best times for visiting are early morning and at least an hour before sunset, when the bats are most active. Around dusk hundreds of bats swoop out of the trees to go foraging.

The monks are very friendly and don't ask for money, though it doesn't hurt to leave a donation. The pagoda is decorated with gilt Buddhas and murals paid for by overseas Vietnamese contributors. In one room there's a life-size statue of the monk who was the former head of the complex. There's also a beautifully painted Khmer longboat here of the type used at the Oc Bom Boc Festival.

Behind the pagoda is an odd tomb painted with the image of a pig. It was erected in memory of a pig with five toenails (usually pigs have only four toenails). It died in 1996, but two other rare pigs with five toenails have survived and are being raised by the monks. These pigs are not for eating – they are pets.

There's a small restaurant just opposite the Bat Pagoda.

The Bat Pagoda is about 4km west of Soc Trang. You can catch a motorbike taxi or easily walk there in under an hour. About 3km out of town towards the pagoda the road splits into two – take the right fork and continue for 1km.

Xa Lon (Sa Lon) Pagoda

This magnificent, classic Khmer pagoda is 12km from Soc Trang, towards Ca Mau, on Hwy 1. The original wooden structure was built over 200 years ago. In 1923 it was completely rebuilt, but proved to be too small. From 1969 to 1985, the present-day large pagoda was slowly built as funds trickled in from donations. The ceramic tiles on the exterior of the pagoda are particularly stunning.

As at other pagodas, the monks lead an austere life. They eat breakfast at 6am and beg for contributions until 11am, when they hold a one-hour worship. They eat again at noon and study in the afternoon – they do not eat dinner.

At present around 25 monks reside here. The pagoda also operates a school for the study of Buddhism and Sanskrit – the language of all original books about Buddhism.

My Phuoc Island

A 15km journey east of Soc Trang brings you to the Hau Giang River. From there it's a short boat ride to My Phuoc Island. It's an isolated spot very suitable for growing fruit. The local government tourist agency likes to bring foreigners here for tours of the orchards. You can do it yourself, though this is a little complicated since you'll need a motorbike to get to the river.

BAC LIEU

☎ 0781 / pop 136,000

The capital of southern Bac Lieu province, Bac Lieu is 280km from HCMC. Of the 800,000 people living in the province, about 8% are of Chinese or Cambodian origin.

The town has a few elegant but forlorn French colonial buildings, like the impressive **Fop House** (now used as a community sports centre), but not much else.

Farming is a difficult occupation in this region because of saltwater intrusion, and the province is better known for its healthy longan orchards. In addition to this, the enterprising locals eke out a living from fishing, oyster collection and shrimp farming, as well as salt production (obtained from evaporating saltwater ponds that form immense salt flats).

Most foreigners use Bac Lieu as a springboard to reach the outstanding bird sanctuary out of town.

Information

The helpful **Bac Lieu tourist office** (☎ 824 272; fax 824 273; 2 Đ Hoang Van Thu; 7-11am & 1-5pm) is next to the Bac Lieu Hotel. Surprisingly, there's often someone on hand who speaks English. Pick up a town map (a rough photocopy) and inquire about trips to the Bird Sanctuary (right) here.

The **post office** (☎ 824 242; 20 Đ Tran Phu) is off the main roundabout downtown; up the same street is **Sacombank** (☎ 932 200; fax 932 201; B2 Đ Tran Phu), which can exchange currency.

Sleeping

In addition to those listed below, there are numerous inexpensive guesthouses that dot the road into town (from Soc Trang), where rooms cost around US$10.

Bac Lieu Guest House (☎ 823 815; 8 Đ Ly Tu Trong; r 130,000;) One of the town's cheapies, this has small, worn rooms that lack natural light. There's a restaurant below.

Bac Lieu Hotel (☎ 822 437; fax 823 655; 4 Đ Hoang Van Thu; r US$16-25;) Near the river, this is a worn but serviceable option with polished tile floors and trim furnishings. Better rooms have balconies and tubs. Next door, a newer Bac Lieu Hotel was under construction in 2006.

Cong Tu Hotel (☎ 953 304; fax 953 111; 13 Đ Dien Bien Phu; r US$16-30;) Just west (50m) of the Bac Lieu Hotel, Cong Tu is a scruffy old colonial gem that's well worn but still popular with Vietnamese. The best rooms have a balcony and are spacious with tall ceilings (but sad carpeting).

Hoang Cung Hotel (☎ 823 362; 1B/5 Đ Tran Phu; r 80,000-200,000d;) About 1km from the roundabout in the direction of Soc Trang (across from the Khmer pagoda gate), this hotel offers clean and comfortable rooms, the best with balconies overlooking a large palm in back.

Eating

Khai Ky (☎ 820 312; 80 Đ Hai Ba Trung; mains 10,000d; breakfast, lunch & dinner) Across the road from the Bac Lieu Hotel, this tiny restaurant serves excellent bowls of noodle soup.

Bac Lieu 2 (☎ 824 951; 89/3 Đ Tran Phu Lo 1; mains 30,000d; breakfast, lunch & dinner) About 700m north of the roundabout (en route to Soc Trang), this is a local favourite serving decent dishes in a clean environment.

Among hotel restaurants, the best is at the **Cong Tu Hotel** (Đ Dien Bien Phu; mains 20,000-60,000d; breakfast, lunch & dinner), with traditional mains and a pleasant outdoor setting.

Getting There & Around

The bus station is on the main road into town, 1 km west of the centre. From here you can catch regular buses to Ho Chi Minh City (80,000d), Ca Mau (25,000d) and Soc Trang (25,000d).

For trips to outlying areas (including the Bird Sanctuary), you can arrange a taxi through the Bac Lieu tourist office or by calling ☎ 922 922. Rates are 40,000d for the first 2 km, and 6500d for every kilometre thereafter.

AROUND BAC LIEU

Bac Lieu Bird Sanctuary

Five kilometres south of town, **Bac Lieu Bird Sanctuary** (Vuon Chim Bac Lieu; ☎ 835 991; admission 40,000d; 7.30am-5pm) is notable for its 50-odd species of bird, including a large population of graceful white herons. This is one of the most interesting sights in the Mekong Delta and is surprisingly popular with Vietnamese tourists. Foreign visitors are rare, probably because Bac Lieu is so out-of-the-way.

Whether or not you see any birds depends on what time of year you visit. Bird populations are at their peak in the rainy season – approximately May to October. The birds hang around to nest until about January, then fly off in search of greener pastures. There are basically no birds here from February until the rainy season begins again.

The drive is only 5km but the road is in bad shape. The rest of the trek is through dense (and often muddy) jungle. Bring plenty of repellent, good shoes, water and binoculars.

Pay the admission fee when you reach the entrance of the bird sanctuary. You can (and should) hire a guide here – you'll probably get lost without one. The guides aren't supposed to take any money, so tip them (US$2 is enough) discreetly; most guides do not speak English. Transport and guides can also be arranged at the Bac Lieu tourist office (see opposite), but hiring a guide there will cost you around US$10 for the day.

Bac Lieu Beach

The same road leading to the Bac Lieu Bird Sanctuary terminates 10km from Bac Lieu at this beach (Bai Bien Bac Lieu). Don't expect white sand – it's all hard-packed Mekong Delta mud. Quite a few shellfish and other slimy things crawl around where the muck meets the sea. Tide pool enthusiasts might be impressed. Locals may be willing to take you for a walk on the tidal flats where they harvest oysters. There's a simple restaurant on the beach for local seafood dishes; another restaurant is scheduled to open there in 2007.

Moi Hoa Binh Pagoda

This Khmer pagoda (Chua Moi Hoa Binh or Se Rey Vongsa) is 13km south of Bac Lieu along Hwy 1 (look to your left while driving to Ca Mau).

The pagoda is uniquely designed and chances are good that the monastery's enormous tower will catch your eye even if you're not looking for it. As pagodas in Vietnam go, it's relatively new, having first been built in 1952. The tower was added in 1990 and is used to store the bones of the deceased. There is a large and impressive meeting hall in front of the tower.

Most Khmer people in the area head for monastery schools in Soc Trang in order to receive a Khmer education. Apart from the small contingent of student monks, very few students study at the Moi Hoa Binh Pagoda.

CA MAU

☎ 0780 / pop 176,000

Built on the swampy shores of the Ganh Hao River, Ca Mau is the capital and largest city in Ca Mau province, which was devastated by Typhoon Linda in 1997. It occupies the southern tip of the Mekong Delta – a wasteland for centuries, the area was first cultivated in the late 17th century. The population of Ca Mau includes many ethnic Khmers.

Owing to the boggy terrain, this area has the lowest population density in southern Vietnam. Ca Mau lies in the middle of Vietnam's largest swamp and is known for its powerful mosquitoes.

Ca Mau has developed rapidly in recent years, but the actual town itself is rather dull. The main attractions here are the nearby swamps and forests, which can be easily explored by boat. Bird-watchers and aspiring botanists are reportedly enthralled with the area for its stork-sighting opportunities and swamp ecology. Consult Ca Mau Tourist before undertaking trips to these outlying attractions.

Information

Interesting boat trips – two days and two nights to Nam Can, Dat Mui (Cape Ca Mau), the Da Bac Islands and the U-Minh Forest – can be organised at **Ca Mau Tourist** (Cong Ty Du Lich Minh Hai; ☎ 831 238; 3-5 Đ Ly Bon; 8-11am & 1-5pm). Other services available here include foreign-currency exchange, car and boat rentals and visa extensions.

Near the post office, **Incombank** (☎ 838 677; icbcamau@hcm.vnn.vn; 94 Đ Ly Thuong Kiet) offers foreign-currency exchange and cash advances. There's an ATM located inside the Anh Nguyet Hotel.

In an emergency, seek medical help at **Ca Mau Hospital** (Benh Vien Ca Mau; ☎ 831 015; Đ Ly Thuong Kiet).

Sights

CA MAU MARKET

This is a wholesale **market** (6am-6pm) and not really a place for people to shop. The animal life on display – such as fish and turtles – is cleaned, packed into crates, frozen and sent to HCMC by truck. It's an interesting place to wander around – it certainly bears little resemblance to the supermarkets at home. However, animal rights advocates will not be pleased.

There's also a **floating market** (6am–mid-afternoon) here.

CAO DAI TEMPLE

Though not as large as the one in Tay Ninh (p381), the **Cao Dai Temple** (Đ Phan Ngoc Hien) is still an impressive place and it's staffed by friendly monks. The temple was built in 1966 and seems to be fairly active.

Sleeping

BUDGET

Than Son Hotel (☎ 815 825; 23 Đ Phan Ngoc Hien; r 80,000-230,000d;) This slender five-storey hotel has clean, nicely maintained rooms with decent-sized windows.

Ca Mau Hotel (☎ 831 165; fax 835 075; 20 Đ Phan Ngoc Hien; r 120,000-220,000d; ❄) Small, trim, well-outfitted rooms here have bathrooms with tubs. Rates include breakfast.

Quoc Nam Hotel (☎ 827 281; 23 Đ Phan Boi Chau; r 120,000-250,000d; ❄) This is a friendly, low-key affair with clean, simple, pleasant rooms – some brighter than others. Its top-floor restaurant overlooks the market.

Ca Mau Trade Union Hotel (☎ 825 037; fax 830 873; 9 Đ Luu Tan Tai; r 130,000-300,000d; ❄) Almost opposite the Cao Dai Temple, this hotel has a range of rooms from small, dingy and dark to spacious, bright and clean.

Song Ngoc Hotel (☎ 817 303; 2B Đ Hung Vuong; r 150,000-250,000d; ❄) Situated on a busy road, Song Ngoc is a newish place with small, clean rooms with kitschy bedspreads. There's a lift.

MIDRANGE

Phuong Nam Hotel (☎ 831 752; fax 834 402; 91 Đ Phan Dinh Phung; r/ste 170,000/240,000d; ❄) Another good-value place, Phuong Nam is clean and pleasantly furnished. Some rooms have balconies.

Quoc Te Hotel (International Hotel; ☎ 826 745; ksquocte@hcm.vnn.vn; 179 Đ Phan Ngoc Hien; r 200,000-700,000d; ❄) Boasting a lift, a restaurant and massage service, the Quoc Te is a solid midrange choice. The priciest rooms have big views of the city; breakfast buffet is included.

Anh Nguyet Hotel (☎ 567 666; anhnguyethotel@yahoo.com; 207 Đ Phan Ngoc Hien; r US$19-69; ❄ 💻) This top midrange option has comfortable, carpeted rooms with trim furnishings, colourful bedspreads and big windows.

Eating

Ca Mau's speciality is shrimp, which are raised in ponds and mangrove forests. Oddly, Ca Mau's best restaurants are in a row on the north end of town.

Pho Xua (☎ 829 830; 126 Đ Phan Ngoc Hien; mains 40,000-50,000d) Featuring many shrimp and fish dishes, Pho Xua is a snazzy place with lush landscaping.

Thanh Truc (☎ 820 021; 126 Đ Phan Ngoc Hien; mains 45,000d) Next door to Pho Xua, this is a good place for hot pot and grilled meat dishes.

There is a cluster of small, cheap roadside restaurants on Đ Ly Bon, at the entrance to the street market. The friendly outdoor restaurant in the Ca Mau Trade Union Hotel is also a good bet.

Getting There & Away

BOAT

Ca Mau has several piers, where you can catch boats around the region. Three to four hydrofoils a day travel between Ca Mau and Rach Gia (the boat docks in Rach Soi, about 10km from Rach Gia). This departs from Ferry Pier Can Ganh Hao daily between 7.30am and 1pm (90,000d, three hours). This pier is also where you can catch a speedboat south to Nam Can (one daily, one hour, 40,000d). Ferry Pier B also has departures to Nam Can (one daily, one hour, 40,000d).

Boats to Can Tho (three daily, three to four hours, 97,000d), with a stop in Phung Hiep, depart from Cong Ca Mau pier (Đ Quang Trung), 3km east of town.

Also popular are the (slow) boats to U-Minh Forest (opposite). These depart from Ferry Pier A (two hours, 25,000d). For a guided tour, it's best to inquire at the tourist office.

BUS

The buses from HCMC to Ca Mau leave from Mien Tay bus station (p372). The trip takes 11 hours by regular bus and eight hours by express bus (around 115,000d). There are several daily express buses to HCMC leaving between 5am and 10.30am. Regular daily buses also connect to other towns in the region, including Bac Lieu (24,000d) and Can Tho (60,000d).

The Ca Mau bus station is 2.5km from the centre of town, along Hwy 1 towards HCMC.

CAR & MOTORBIKE

Ca Mau is the end of the line for Hwy 1; it's the southernmost point in Vietnam that's accessible by car and bus. Drivers who boldly attempt to drive on the 'highway' south of Ca Mau will soon find their vehicles sinking into a quagmire of mud and mangroves.

Ca Mau is 178km from Can Tho (three hours) and 347km from HCMC (eight hours).

Getting Around

There are plenty of water taxis along the canal at the back of Ca Mau Market. For longer trips upriver, larger longboats collect at the cluster of jetties just outside the market area. You can either join the throngs of passengers going downriver or hire the whole boat for about 50,000d an hour.

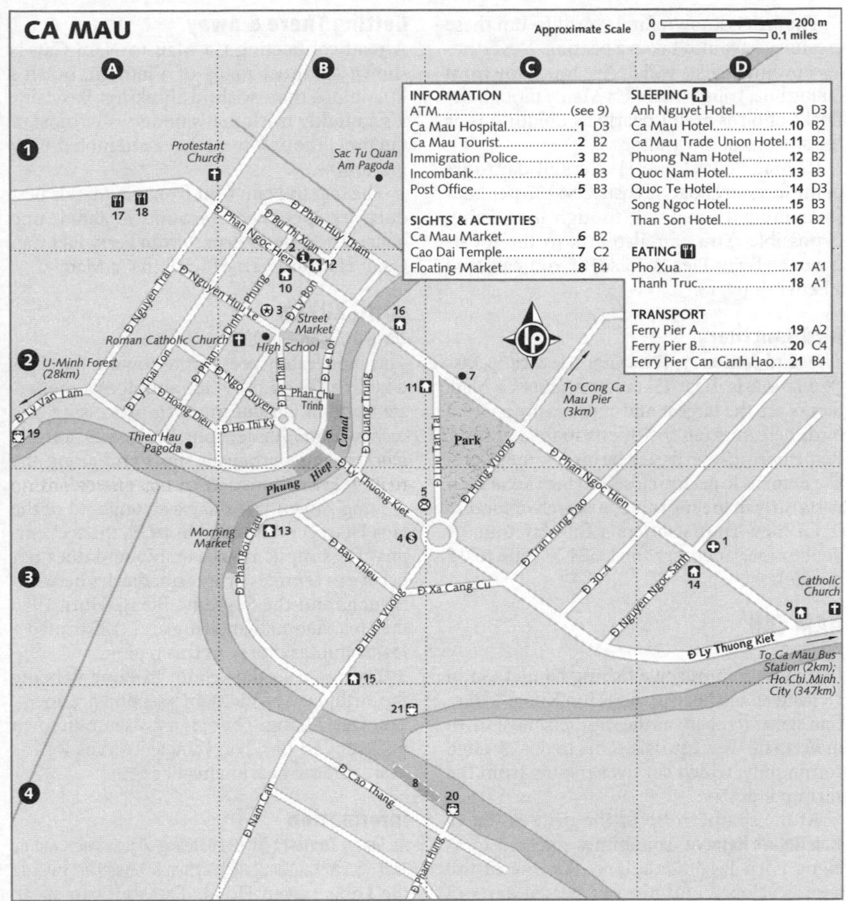

AROUND CA MAU

U-Minh Forest

The town of Ca Mau borders the U-Minh Forest, a huge mangrove forest covering 1000 sq km of Ca Mau and Kien Giang provinces. Local people use certain species of mangrove as a source of timber, charcoal, thatch and tannin. When the mangroves flower, bees feed on the blossoms, providing both honey and wax. The area is an important habitat for waterfowl.

The U-Minh Forest, which is the largest mangrove forest in the world outside of the Amazon basin, was a favourite hideout for the VC during the American War. US patrol boats were frequently ambushed here and the VC regularly planted mines in the canals. The Americans responded with chemical defoliation, which made their enemy more visible while doing enormous damage to the forests. Replanting efforts at first failed because the soil was so toxic, but gradually the heavy rainfall has washed the dioxin out to sea and the forest is returning. Many eucalyptus trees have also been planted here because they have proved to be relatively resistant to dioxin.

Unfortunately the mangrove forests are being further damaged by clearing for shrimp-farming ponds, charcoal production and woodchipping. The government has tried to limit these activities, but the conflict between nature and humans continues. The conflict will probably get worse before it gets better, because Vietnam's population is still growing rapidly.

The area is known for its birdlife, but these creatures have also taken a beating. Nevertheless, ornithologists will derive much joy from taking boat trips around Ca Mau – though the flocks of birds aren't nearly as ubiquitous as the swarms of mosquitoes.

Ca Mau Tourist (p431) offers all-day tours of the forest by boat. It costs US$135 per boat (maximum 10 people), though bargaining is possible. You can also talk to the locals down at Ferry Pier A to see if you can find a better deal.

Bird Sanctuary

The **Bird Sanctuary** (Vuon Chim; admission 50,000d; dawn-dusk) is about 45km southeast of Ca Mau. Storks are the largest and most easily spotted birds here, making their nests in the tall trees. Remember that birds will be birds – they don't like humans to get too close and they leave their nests early in the morning in search of food.

Ca Mau Tourist offers a full-day tour by boat to the sanctuary for US$120 (one to 10 people).

NAM CAN

☎ 0780

Except for a minuscule fishing hamlet (Tran De) and an offshore island (Hon Khoai), Nam Can stakes its claim as the southernmost town in Vietnam. Few tourists come to this isolated community, which survives mainly from the shrimp industry.

At the southern tip of the delta is the **Ca Mau Nature Reserve**, sometimes referred to as Ngoc Hien Bird Sanctuary. It's one of the least developed and most protected parts of the Mekong Delta region. Shrimp farming is prohibited here. Access is by boat.

At the southern end of the reserve is the tiny fishing village of Tran De. A public ferry connects Tran De to Nam Can. If you are obsessed with reaching Vietnam's southern tip, take a boat from Tran De to Hon Khoai Island.

If you're looking to visit another remote spot, you can hire a boat to take you to Dat Mui (Cape Ca Mau), the southwestern tip of Vietnam. However, few people find this worthwhile.

Sleeping

Cam Ha Hotel (☎ 877 235; r US$15;) This is the only decent accommodation option in Nam Can, so you'll have little choice unless you plan on camping.

Getting There & Away

A road connecting Ca Mau to Nam Can is shown on most maps of Vietnam, but it's little more than wishful thinking. Basically, it's a muddy track that's underwater most of the time, though some have attempted it by motorbike.

The trip to Nam Can from Ca Mau is best done by speedboat (around 40,000d, one hour). These boats depart from Ferry Pier Can Ganh Hao and Ferry Pier B in Ca Mau.

LONG XUYEN

☎ 076 / pop 240,000

This moderately prosperous town is the capital of An Giang province and does a moderate trade in agriculture, fish processing and cashew nuts. Aside from a few sites, a lively market, and perhaps a short trip along the river, there's little to detain travellers here.

Long Xuyen was once a stronghold of the Hoa Hao sect. Founded in 1939, the sect emphasises simplicity in worship and does not believe in temples or intermediaries between humans and the Supreme Being. Until 1956 the Hoa Hao had an army and constituted a major military force in this region.

The town's other claim to fame is being the birthplace of Vietnam's second president, Ton Duc Thang. There is a museum in town dedicated to Bac Ton (Uncle Ton) as well as a large statue bearing his likeness.

Information

An Giang Tourist (☎ 841 036; angiangtour@hcm.vnn.vn; 17 Đ Nguyen Van Cung; 7-11am & 1-5pm) is beside the Long Xuyen Hotel. The staff can speak some English but aren't terribly helpful. They should be able to put you in touch with a guide to Oc-Eo (p436).

Vietcombank (☎ 841 075; 1 Đ Hung Vuong; closed weekends) gives cash advances on credit cards and also exchanges travellers cheques. There's also an **Incombank** (☎ 841 704; 20-22 Ngo Gia Tu) near the post office. Get online at the **internet café** (81 Nguyen Hue).

Sights

LONG XUYEN CATHOLIC CHURCH

One of the largest churches in the Mekong Delta, **Long Xuyen Catholic Church** (7.30am-5.30pm) is an impressive modern structure that boasts a 50m-high bell tower. It was constructed between 1966 and 1973 and can seat 1000 worshippers.

AN GIANG MUSEUM

This sleepy little **museum** (Bao Tang An Giang; ☎ 841 251; 77 Đ Thoai Ngoc Hau; admission free; ⏰ 7.30-10.30am Tue, Thu, Sat & Sun, plus 2-4.30pm Sat & Sun) is a proud highlight of An Giang province and features photographs and personal effects of the former president, Ton Duc Thang. There are also some artefacts from the Oc-Eo site near Long Xuyen (see p436) and displays that detail the history of this region from the 1930s to the present day.

CHO MOI DISTRICT

Across the river from Long Xuyen, **Cho Moi district** is known for its rich groves of fruit such as bananas, durians, guava, jackfruit, longans, mangoes, mangosteens and plums.

Cho Moi district can be reached by boat from the ferry terminal at the foot of Đ Nguyen Hue.

LONG XUYEN CROCODILE FARM

For a close-up view of the reptile that once ruled the Mekong, this **farm** (☎ 831 298; longxuyencrocodilefarm@yahoo.com; 44/1A Đ Tran Hung Dao; admission 5000d; ⏰ 7am-6pm) is home to thousands of crocodiles, ranging in size from 10cm to 4m. The meat and skin of these animals is largely exported, though some Vietnamese drop-in for fresh or frozen crocodile meat (50,000d to 140,000d per kg). The farm lies 8km south of town on the road to Can Tho.

Sleeping

Thai Binh Hotel II (☎ 847 078; fax 846 451; 4 Đ Nguyen Hue A; r 70,000-220,000d; ❄) The cheapest rooms are stifling at this older, privately run place, but the air-con quarters are spacious and airy with balconies. Friendly staff are a bonus.

Long Xuyen Hotel (☎ 841 927; longxuyenhotel@hcm.vnn.vn; 19 Đ Nguyen Van Cung; r 140,000-270,000d; ❄) This ageing classic has rooms in fair shape with shared balconies and baths with hot water.

Dong Xuyen Hotel (☎ 942 260; dongxuyenag@hcm.vnn.vn; Đ 9A Luong Van Cu; d 300,000-500,000d, ste 600,000d; ❄) Long Xuyen's fanciest digs are located right in the centre of town. Well-appointed rooms (satellite TV, minibar etc) are matched by facilities and services like massage and steam bath. Even the staff sparkle with friendliness and good English skills.

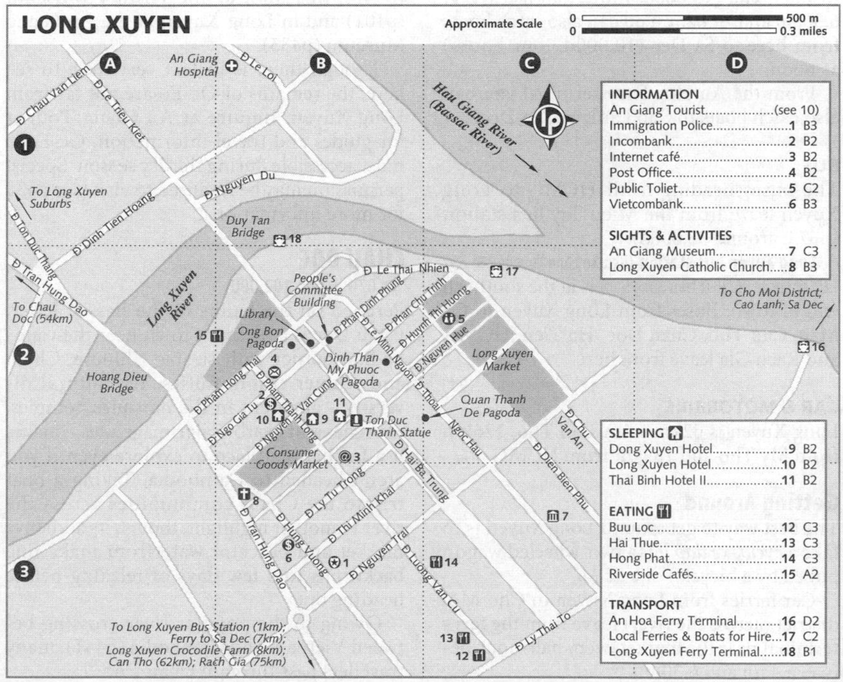

Eating

Besides the hotel restaurants, it's slim pickings for decent eating spots in Long Xuyen.

Hai Thue (☎ 845 573; 245/3 Đ Luong Van Cu; mains 15,000d; breakfast, lunch & dinner) A popular choice serving up excellent and cheap Vietnamese food.

Buu Loc (☎ 844 401; 246/3 Đ Luong Van Cu; mains 15,000d; breakfast, lunch & dinner) There's no English menu, but this is another top local place for satisfying, inexpensive meals.

Hong Phat (☎ 842 359; 242/4 Đ Luong Van Cu; mains 15,000-30,000d; breakfast, lunch & dinner) A good, value place for its simple seafood dishes.

There's good coffee and a happening scene at the **riverside cafés** (coffee 4000d) on Đ Pham Hong Thai.

Getting There & Away

BOAT

To get to the Long Xuyen ferry dock from Đ Pham Hong Thai, you'll need to cross Duy Tan Bridge and turn right. Passenger ferries leave from here to Cho Vam, Dong Tien, Hong Ngu, Kien Luong, Lai Vung, Rach Gia, Sa Dec and Phu Chau (Tan Chau). Boats to Rach Gia (15,000d, nine hours) leave at 6.30am and/or 8am. You can also catch boats from here to Sa Dec (10,000d, four hours) at noon.

From the An Hoa ferry terminal you can also catch boats to Cao Lanh and Sa Dec.

BUS

The buses heading from HCMC to Long Xuyen leave from the Mien Tay bus station (p372; around 35,000d).

Long Xuyen bus station (Ben Xe Long Xuyen; ☎ 852 125; opposite 96/3B Đ Tran Hung Dao) is at the southern end of town. Buses from Long Xuyen to Ca Mau, Can Tho, Chau Doc, Ha Tien, HCMC and Rach Gia leave from here.

CAR & MOTORBIKE

Long Xuyen is 62km from Can Tho, 126km from My Tho and 189km from HCMC.

Getting Around

The best way to get around Long Xuyen is to take a *cyclo, xe dap loi* (a two-wheeled wagon pulled by a bicycle) or a *xe loi*.

Car ferries from Long Xuyen to Cho Moi district (across the river) leave from the ferry terminal near the market every half-hour between 4am and 6.30pm.

AROUND LONG XUYEN

Ancient City of Oc-Eo

During the 1st to 6th centuries AD, when southern Vietnam, much of southern Cambodia and the Malay peninsula were ruled by Funan, the Indian-influenced empire, Oc-Eo was a major trading city. Much of what is known about the Funan empire, which reached its height during the 5th century AD, comes from contemporary Chinese sources and the excavations at Oc-Eo. The excavations have uncovered evidence of contact between Oc-Eo and what is now Thailand, Malaysia and Indonesia, as well as Persia and the Roman Empire.

An elaborate system of canals around Oc-Eo was once used for both irrigation and transportation, prompting Chinese travellers of the time to write about 'sailing across Funan' on their way to the Malay peninsula. Most of the buildings of Oc-Eo were built on piles and pieces of these structures indicate the high degree of refinement achieved by Funanese civilisation. Artefacts found at Oc-Eo are on display in HCMC at the History Museum (p341) and Fine Arts Museum (p342), in Hanoi at the History Museum (p101) and in Long Xuyen at the An Giang Museum (p435).

Though there is in fact very little to see here, the remains of Oc-Eo are not far from Long Xuyen. Inquire at An Giang Tourist for guides and travel information. Oc-Eo is most accessible during the dry season. Special permission may be required to visit (see p434 for more information).

CHAU DOC

☎ 076 / pop 102,000

Perched on the banks of the Bassac River, Chau Doc is a pleasant town near the Cambodian border with sizable Chinese, Cham and Khmer communities. Its cultural diversity – apparent in the mosques, temples, churches and nearby pilgrimage sites – makes it a fascinating place to explore even if you aren't headed to Cambodia. Taking a boat trip to the Cham communities across the river is another highlight, though its addictive market and peaceful waterfront make fine backdrops to a few days of relaxing before heading out.

Owing to the popular river crossing between Vietnam and Cambodia (p441), many travellers pass through Chau Doc.

Information

There's **internet service** (per hr 4000d; 7am-9pm) in the courtyard of Chau Doc's main **post office** (☎ 869 200; 2 Đ Le Loi). Foreign currency can be exchanged at **Incombank** (☎ 866 497; 68-70 Đ Nguyen Huu Canh).

Though not officially a tourist office, there's a travel information desk at Vinh Phuoc Hotel (right) where objective, pressure-free travel advice is dispensed. Tours and onward travel arrangements are sold at reasonable prices. Check here first for up-to-date reports on hydrofoils to Phu Quoc Island, border crossing information, slow cargo boats and bus schedules.

Other agencies where you can buy boat transport to Phnom Penh and book half- and full-day boating trips on the Mekong include **Mekong Tours** (☎ 868 222; www.mekongvietnam.com; 14 Đ Nguyen Huu Canh) and **Delta Adventure** (☎ 563 810; 53 Đ Le Loi).

Sights

CHAU PHU TEMPLE

In 1926 the **Chau Phu Temple** (Dinh Than Chau Phu; cnr Đ Nguyen Van Thoai & Đ Gia Long) was built to worship the Nguyen dynasty official Thoai Ngoc Hau, who is buried at Sam Mountain (p440). The structure is decorated with both Vietnamese and Chinese motifs. Inside are funeral tablets bearing the names of the deceased and some biographical information about them.

MOSQUES

Domed and arched **Chau Giang Mosque**, in the hamlet of Chau Giang, serves the local Cham Muslims. To get there, take the car ferry from Chau Giang ferry landing in Chau Doc across the Hau Giang River. From the ferry landing, walk away from the river for 30m, turn left and walk 50m.

The **Mubarak Mosque** (Thanh Duong Hoi Giao), where children study the Koran in Arabic script, is also on the river bank opposite Chau Doc. Visitors are permitted, but you should avoid entering during the calls to prayer (five times daily) unless you are a Muslim.

There are other small mosques in the Chau Doc area. They are accessible by boat, but you'll need a local guide to find them all.

FLOATING HOUSES

These houses, whose floats consist of empty metal drums, are both a place to live and a livelihood for their residents. Under each house, fish are raised in suspended metal nets: the fish flourish in their natural river habitat; the family can feed them whatever scraps are handy; and catching the fish requires less exertion than fishing. You can find these houses floating around Chau Doc and get a close-up by hiring a boat (but please be respectful of their privacy). To learn more about the workings of these fish cages, see p440.

Sleeping

BUDGET

Vinh Phuoc Hotel (☎ 866 242; 12 Đ Quang Trung; r US$6-15; ❄) A good budget deal, this place is run by an amiable Brit who is an excellent source of local travel information. There's a good in-house restaurant serving Vietnamese and Western food (mains around 30,000d).

Ngoc Phu Hotel (☎ 866 484; 17 Đ Doc Phu Thu; r 90,000-150,000d; ❄) Even the fan rooms at this large, liveable place have hot water, TV and fridge. The staff here are particularly cheery and helpful. Under renovation at the time of writing, Ngoc Phu may raise rates in coming years.

Thuan Loi Hotel (☎ 866 134; hotelthuanloi@hcm.vnn.vn; 18 Đ Tran Hung Dao; r 100,000-190,000d; ❄) Overlooking the riverside, this pleasant place with communal terrace has friendly staff and a relaxed atmosphere. Fan rooms are very basic, with cold-water bathrooms. Air-conditioned rooms are bright and airy.

Delta Adventure Inn (Nha Khach Long Chau; ☎ 861 249; deltaadventureinn@hotmail.com; r 120,000-240,000d; ❄) This cosy terracotta-tiled compound sits amid the rice paddies about 4km from Chau Doc. The views of Sam Mountain are lovely from the island café-restaurant on the grounds.

Hoa Mai Hotel (☎ 867 608; 24/4 Đ Khom Chau Thoi 2; r US$10; ❄) This newish place has an elegant façade and clean, spacious rooms opening onto a shared balcony. It's in a quiet setting southwest of the centre.

Song Sao Hotel (☎ 561 777; songsaohotel@yahoo.com; 12-13 Đ Nguyen Huu Canh; r US$11-16; ❄) Song Sao has simple, tidy rooms with wood furniture. Some are small and lack natural light; others have balconies.

Trung Nguyen Hotel (☎ 866 158; trunghotel@yahoo.com; 86 Đ Bach Dang; r US$12-17; ❄) This handsome, polished place has bright and airy rooms, each with a balcony. There's friendly, helpful management, and breakfast is included.

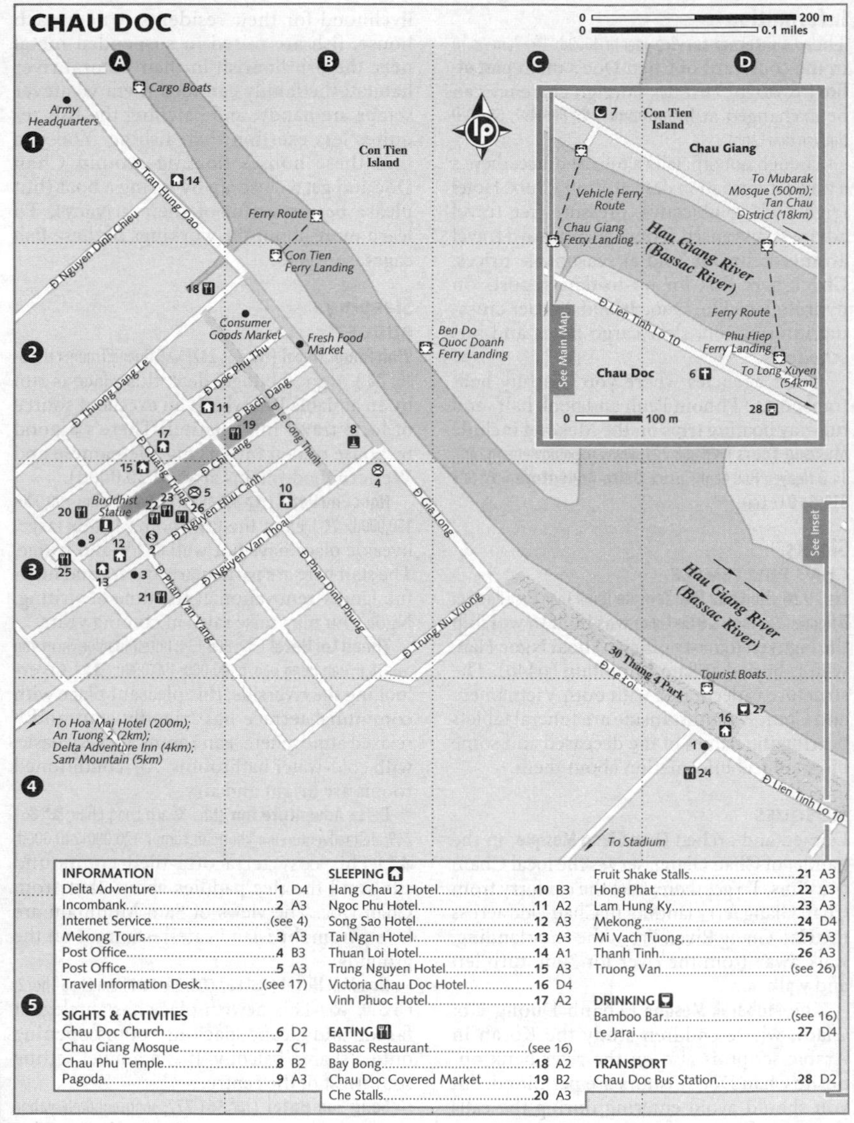

Tai Ngan Hotel (☎ 866 435; tainganfood@yahoo.com; 11 Đ Nguyen Huu Canh; r 150,000-180,000d; ❄) A good-value hotel for most of the rooms. The best are spacious and have a balcony overlooking the plaza.

Hang Chau 2 Hotel (☎ 868 891; hangchau2agg@hcm.vnn.vn; 10 Đ Nguyen Van Thoai; r 150,000-280,000d; ❄) Spacious, comfortably furnished rooms have nice touches – balconies or leather armchairs, while the 'VIP' room has wood floors.

TOP END

Victoria Chau Doc Hotel (☎ 865 010; www.victoria hotels-asia.com; 32 Đ Le Loi; r US$115-196; internet rates US$92-144; ❄ 💻 🏊) Perched on the riverside, the Victoria is the swishest place in town. All rooms have wood floors, bathtubs and gorgeous decor. The hotel's Bassac Restaurant is superb and the top-floor massage salon offers the best river views around.

Eating

RESTAURANTS

Chau Doc has some excellent restaurants on offer.

Bay Bong (☎ 867 271; 22 Đ Thuong Dang Le; mains 35,000-45,000d; ⏰ lunch & dinner) This place specialises in hotpots and soups, as well as fresh fish dishes. Try the *ca kho to* (stewed fish in a clay pot) or *canh chua* (sweet-and-sour soup).

Mekong (☎ 867 381; 41 Đ Le Loi; mains 35,000-45,000d; ⏰ lunch & dinner) Just across the road from the Victoria Chau Doc Hotel, Mekong is a popular spot for inexpensive meals. You can dine outdoors in front of an ageing villa.

Bassac Restaurant (☎ 865 010; 32 Đ Le Loi; mains US$8-14; ⏰ 6-11am & 6-11pm) Sophisticated dining is paired with a relaxed colonial ambience at Bassac, located inside the Victoria Chau Doc Hotel. It also has good snack food served at the hotel's poolside Bamboo Bar.

Lam Hung Ky (☎ 866 745; 71 Đ Chi Lang; mains 40,000d; ⏰ breakfast, lunch & dinner) This joint serves up good Chinese and Vietnamese food, with misleadingly unappetising menu items like 'instant boiled assorted meats'.

Hong Phat (☎ 866 950; 77 Đ Chi Lang; mains 40,000d; ⏰ breakfast, lunch & dinner) Similar in standard and fare to Lam Hung Ky.

Other options:

Mi Vach Tuong (Đ Thu Khoa Nghia; noodles 7000d; ⏰ breakfast & dinner) Beside the local basketball court, this simple spot is a good choice for noodle soups.

Thanh Tinh (☎ 865 064; 13 Đ Quang Trung; mains 15,000d; ⏰ breakfast, lunch & dinner) Great vegetarian food at the well-known place whose name means 'to calm the body down'.

Truong Van (☎ 866 567; 15 Đ Quang Trung; mains 15,000d; ⏰ breakfast, lunch & dinner) Good Vietnamese food at decent prices.

QUICK EATS

To sample the best *sinh to* (fruit shakes) in town, look out for the stalls on the corner of Đ Phan Van Vang and Đ Nguyen Van Thoai.

At night, you can also try a variety of cool dessert *che* (dessert soups) at che stalls on Đ Bach Dang, next to the pagoda.

The **Chau Doc Covered Market** (Đ Bach Dang) has excellent Vietnamese food (plates 4000d to 10,000d).

Drinking & Entertainment

Chau Doc is a fairly sleepy town and tends to shut down early.

Le Jarai (32 Đ Le Loi; ⏰ 4-11pm most nights) Moored on the river behind the Victoria Hotel, this (nonsailing) boat makes a pleasant setting for a cocktail.

Gio Dong (Map p442; ☎ 563 310; QL 91 Quoc Lo) An attractive waterside spot 2km out of town on the way to Sam Mountain, Gio Drong is an idyllic spot for a drink and is popular with couples.

A dance hall that's popular with the locals, **An Tuong 2** (admission 20,000d; ⏰ 8-11pm, closed Mon & Wed), is nearby. The entry fee includes one drink.

The inviting Lobby Bar in the Victoria Chau Doc Hotel has tropical French-colonial allure, a large drink menu and a pool table.

Getting There & Away

BOAT

No-frills cargo boats run twice weekly between Chau Doc and Ha Tien via the Vinh Te Canal (150,000d, eight to 12 hours), which straddles the Cambodian border; it's an interesting 95km trip. Departures are at 5am from a tiny pier (near 60 Đ Trung Hung Dao).

Cargo boats also travel to/from Vinh Long. For information on travelling into Cambodia see p441 and p445.

BUS

The buses from HCMC to Chau Doc leave from the Mien Tay bus station (p372); the express bus can make the run in six hours and costs around 84,000d.

The Chau Doc bus station (Ben Xe Chau Doc) is east of town towards Long Xuyen. Buses from Chau Doc leave here for Rach Gia (40,000d, four hours), Ca Mau, Can Tho, Ha Tien, Long Xuyen, My Tho, HCMC, Soc Trang and Tra Vinh.

CAR & MOTORBIKE

By road, Chau Doc is approximately 117km from Can Tho, 181km from My Tho and 245km from HCMC.

The Chau Doc–Ha Tien road is 100km in length and is in miserable shape, but improvements were underway at research time. As you approach Ha Tien, the land turns into a mangrove forest that is infertile and almost uninhabited.

This area is considered reasonably safe during the day, but it's not advisable to be out

FISH FARMING & BIO-FUEL

Fish farming constitutes around 20% of Vietnam's total seafood output and is widely practised in An Giang province, in the region near the Cambodian border. The highest concentration of 'floating houses' with fish cages can be observed on the banks of the Bassac River in Chau Doc, near its confluence with the mighty Mekong.

The fish farmed here are two members of the Asian catfish family, basa (*Pangasius bocourti*) and tra (*P hypophthalmus*). It is interesting to note that even with two tides a day here, there is no salt water in the river. Around 18,000 tonnes of fish are exported annually, primarily to European and American markets (as well as Australia and Japan), in the form of frozen white fish fillets.

The two-step production cycle starts with capturing fish eggs from the wild, followed by raising the fish to a marketable size – usually about 1kg. Fish are fed on a kind of dough made by the farmers from cereal, vegetables and fish scraps. The largest cage measures 2000 cubic metres and can produce up to 400 tonnes of raw fish in each 10-month production cycle.

One of the more interesting developments affecting fish-farming was announced in 2006, when Saigon Petrol and An Giang Fisheries Import-Export Company (Agifish) agreed to set up a joint venture to produce bio-fuel from the fat of the tra and basa catfish. Some 400,000 tonnes of the two fish are consumed annually in the Mekong River provinces, and if some of its by-products could be utilised the effects would be groundbreaking. One kilogram of fish fat can yield 1L of bio-diesel fuel, according to one project specialist, meaning some 60,000 tonnes of bio-diesel fuel could be made yearly if all the tra and basa fat could be utilised from the processing plants in the region. Agifish, which sets its initial projections at producing 10,000 tonnes a year, claims the bio-fuel will be more efficient than diesel, that it's nontoxic and will generate far less exhaust. After the factory is up and running (it's slated to be built near Can Tho), Agifish claims it will be a boon to the local economy, to local fish farmers who will earn more money, and even to the environment. Those who've gotten a whiff of *nuoc mam* (fish sauce) and thought, 'you can power a dump truck on this stuff' aren't far off the mark.

here after dark due to the risk of robbery in this remote, unlit area.

The drive takes about three hours, and it's possible to visit Ba Chuc and Tup Duc en route. If you don't plan to drive yourself, *xe om* drivers typically charge about US$15.

Getting Around

Xe loi can be hired around town for a few thousand dong.

Boats to Chau Giang district (across the Hau Giang River) leave from two docks: vehicle ferries depart from Chau Giang ferry landing (Ben Pha Chau Giang), opposite 419 Đ Le Loi; smaller, more frequent boats leave from Phu Hiep ferry landing (Ben Pha FB Phu Hiep), a little further south.

Vehicle ferries to Con Tien Island depart from the Con Tien ferry landing (Ben Pha Con Tien) at the river end of Đ Thuong Dang Le; you can catch boats to Chau Giang and Phu Chau (Tan Chau) from the Ben Do Quoc Doanh ferry landing on Đ Gia Long, opposite the post office.

Private boats (30,000d for a few hours), which are rowed standing up, can be hired from either of these spots, and are highly recommended for seeing the floating houses and visiting nearby Cham minority villages and mosques. Motorboats (50,000d per hour) can be hired in the same area.

Prices for all of the public ferries (per person 500d, motorbike or bicycle 1000d) double at night; bicycles or motorbikes require their own ticket.

AROUND CHAU DOC

Phu Chau (Tan Chau) District

Traditional silk making has brought fame to Phu Chau (Tan Chau) district across southern Vietnam. The **market** in Phu Chau has a selection of competitively priced Thai and Cambodian goods.

To get to Phu Chau district from Chau Doc, take a boat across the Hau Giang River from the Phu Hiep ferry landing, then catch a ride on the back of a *xe om* (about 15,000d) for the 18km trip to Phu Chau district.

Sam Mountain

There are dozens of pagodas and temples, many of them set in caves, around Sam Mountain (Nui Sam), which is about 6km southwest of Chau Doc via Đ Bao Ho Thoai. The Chinese influence is obvious and Sam Mountain is a favourite spot for ethnic Chinese (both pilgrims from Vietnam and abroad).

Climbing the peak is a highlight of a visit to Sam Mountain. The views from the top are excellent (weather permitting) and you can gaze over Cambodia. There's a military outpost on the summit, a legacy of the days when the Khmer Rouge made cross-border raids and massacred Vietnamese civilians.

Walking down is easier than walking up, so if you want to cheat, have a motorbike take you to the summit. The road to the top is on the east side of the mountain. You can walk down along a peaceful, traffic-free trail on the north side, which will bring you to the main temple area. The summit road has been decorated with amusement-park ceramic dinosaurs and the like. But there are also some small shrines and pavilions, which add a bit of charm and also remind you that this is indeed Vietnam and not Disneyland.

TAY AN PAGODA

This pagoda (Chua Tay An) is renowned for the fine carving of its hundreds of religious figures, most of which are made of wood. Aspects of the building's architecture reflect Hindu and Islamic influences. The first chief monk of Tay An Pagoda (founded in 1847) came from Giac Lam Pagoda in Saigon. Tay An was last rebuilt in 1958.

The main gate is of traditional Vietnamese design. Above the roof are figures of lions and two dragons fighting for possession of pearls, chrysanthemums, apricot trees and lotus blossoms. Nearby is a statue of Quan Am Thi Kinh, the Guardian Spirit of Mother and Child.

In front of the pagoda are statues of a black elephant with two tusks and a white elephant with six tusks. Around the pagoda are monks' tombs. Inside are Buddha statues adorned with psychedelic disco lights.

TEMPLE OF LADY XU

Founded in the 1820s, the **Temple of Lady Xu** (Mieu Ba Chua Xu) faces Sam Mountain, not far from Tay An Pagoda. The first building here was made of bamboo and leaves; the last reconstruction took place in 1972.

According to legend, the statue of Lady Xu used to stand at the summit of Sam Mountain. In the early 19th century Siamese troops invaded the area and, impressed with the statue, decided to take it back to Thailand. But as they carried the statue down the hill, it became heavier and heavier, and they were forced to abandon it by the side of the path.

BORDER CROSSING: VINH XUONG–KAAM SAMNOR

One of the most enjoyable ways of entering Cambodia is via this crossing located just west of Chau Doc along the Mekong River. If coming from Cambodia, get a visa. If exiting, Cambodian visas are available on arrival, but minor overcharging is common.

Numerous agencies in Chau Doc sell boat tickets taking you from Chau Doc to Phnom Penh via the Vinh Xuong border. Slow boats for the trip cost around US$8 to US$10 and take eight hours (leaving around 8am and arriving in Phnom Penh at 4pm).

There are several companies offering faster boats between Chau Doc and Phnom Penh. **Hang Chau** (Phnom Penh; ☎ 012-883 542) departs Chau Doc at 7am and Phnom Penh at 12 noon and costs US$15. The more upmarket **Blue Cruiser** (Phnom Penh; ☎ 023 990 441; Chau Doc ☎ 091-401622) pulls out at 8.30am and at 1.30pm respectively, costing US$35. It takes about four hours including a slow border check. More expensive again is the **Victoria Hotels express boat** (www.victoriahotels-asia.com), which runs from the Victoria Chau Doc Hotel to Phnom Penh. At US$75 per person, it tends to be exclusive to Victoria hotel guests.

Some adventurous travellers like to plot their own course. Catch a minibus from Chau Doc to the border at Vinh Xuong (US$1, one hour). The border posts here are some way apart so hire a moto (US$1) to carry you from building to building to deal with the lengthy bureaucracy. There are separate offices for immigration and customs on both sides of the border, so it can end up taking as much as an hour. Luggage has to be x-rayed on the Vietnamese side of the border. Once officially in Cambodia at Kaam Samnor, arrange a speedboat to Neak Luong (US$2.50 per person, US$15 for the boat, one hour). Once in Neak Luong, change to a local bus (4500r, regular departures) to Phnom Penh, which will terminate at the Central Market.

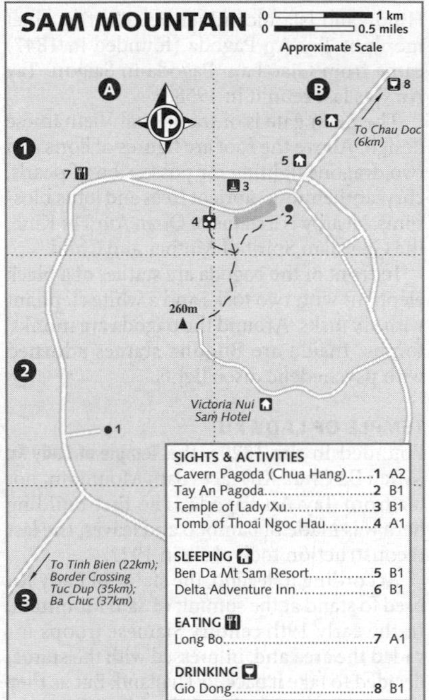

One day some villagers who were cutting wood came upon the statue and decided to bring it back to their village in order to build a temple for it; but it weighed too much for them to budge. Suddenly, there appeared a girl who, possessed by a spirit, declared herself to be Lady Xu. She announced to them that 40 virgins were to be brought and that they would be able to transport the statue down the mountainside. The 40 virgins were then summoned and carried the statue down the slope, but when they reached the plain, it became too heavy and they had to set it down. The people concluded that the site where the virgins halted had been selected by Lady Xu for the temple construction and it's here that the Temple of Lady Xu stands to this day.

Offerings of roast whole pigs are frequently made here, providing an interesting photo opportunity. The temple's most important festival is held from the 23rd to the 26th day of the fourth lunar month. During this time, pilgrims flock here, sleeping on mats in the large rooms of the two-storey resthouse next to the temple.

TOMB OF THOAI NGOC HAU

A high-ranking official, Thoai Ngoc Hau (1761–1829) served the Nguyen Lords and, later, the Nguyen dynasty. In early 1829, Thoai Ngoc Hau ordered that a tomb be constructed for himself at the foot of Sam Mountain. The site he chose is not far from Tay An Pagoda.

The steps are made of red 'beehive' stone *(da ong)* brought from the southeastern part of Vietnam. In the middle of the platform is the tomb of Thoai Ngoc Hau and those of his wives, Chau Thi Te and Truong Thi Miet. Nearby are several dozen other tombs where his officials are buried.

CAVERN PAGODA

The Cavern Pagoda (Chua Hang, also known as Phuoc Dien Tu) is about halfway up the western side of Sam Mountain. The lower part of the pagoda includes monks' quarters and two hexagonal tombs in which the founder of the pagoda, a female tailor named Le Thi Tho, and a former head monk, Thich Hue Thien, are buried.

The upper section has two parts: the main sanctuary, in which there are statues of A Di Da (the Buddha of the Past) and Thich Ca Buddha (Sakyamuni, the Historical Buddha); and the cavern. At the back of the cave behind the sanctuary building is a shrine dedicated to Quan The Am Bo Tat.

According to legend, Le Thi Tho came from Tay An Pagoda to this site half a century ago to lead a quiet, meditative life. When she arrived, she found two enormous snakes, one white and the other dark green. Le Thi Tho soon converted the snakes, which thereafter led pious lives. Upon her death, the snakes disappeared.

Sleeping & Eating

For details on the Delta Adventure Inn between Chau Doc and Sam Mountain, see p437.

Ben Da Mt Sam Resort (☎ 076-861745; bendanuisam@hcm.vnn.vn; Quoc Lo 91; r 217,000-350,000d; ❄) This large complex has pleasant, attractive rooms, some of which overlook a lily-filled water garden. You'll find the standard amenities, plus steam bath, massage and sauna. Breakfast is included and there's an outdoor restaurant.

Long Bo (☎ 076-861 479; Khom Vinh Tay1; mains 60,000d) Well worth the trek out here, this excellent grilled-meat restaurant is among

Chau Doc's gems. A favourite dish is *bo lui xa,* which is beef wrapped around lemongrass. You cook it yourself on the hot coals brought to your table. It's 1km west of Lady Xu Temple.

BA CHUC

Close to the Cambodian border, just inside Vietnam, is Ba Chuc, otherwise known as the Bone Pagoda. The pagoda stands as a grisly reminder of the horrors perpetrated by the Khmer Rouge. Between 1975 and 1978 Khmer Rouge guerrillas regularly crossed the border into Vietnam and slaughtered civilians. And this is to say nothing of the million or so Cambodians who were also killed.

Between 12 April and 30 April 1978, the Khmer Rouge killed 3157 people at Ba Chuc. Only two people are known to have survived. Many of the victims were tortured to death. The Vietnamese government might have had other motives for invading Cambodia at the end of 1978, but certainly outrage at the Ba Chuc massacre was a major reason.

Two other notable pagodas at Ba Chuc are Chua Tam Buu and Chua Phi Lai. The Bone Pagoda has a common tomb housing the skulls and bones of over 1100 victims. This resembles Cambodia's Choeung Ek killing fields, where thousands of skulls of Khmer Rouge victims are on display. Near the skull collection is a temple that displays gruesome photos taken shortly after the massacre. The display is both fascinating and horrifying and you will need a strong stomach in order to visit.

To reach Ba Chuc follow the road that runs along the canal from Chau Doc to Ha Tien. Turn off this main road onto Hwy 3T and follow it for 4km.

TUC DUP HILL

elevation 216m

Because of its network of connecting caves, Tuc Dup Hill served as a strategic base of operations during the American War. *Tuc dup* is Khmer for 'water runs at night' and it is also known locally as 'Two Million Dollar Hill', in reference to the amount of money the Americans sank into securing it. Tuc Dup is 35km from Chau Doc and 64km from Long Xuyen.

This is a place of historical interest but there isn't much to see. It's worth a trip if you're visiting Ba Chuc.

HA TIEN

☎ 077 / pop 93,000

Lying just 8km from the Cambodian border, Ha Tien is on the Gulf of Thailand and has a vastly different feel from other delta settlements. All around the area are lovely, towering limestone formations, which support a network of caves, some of which have been turned into temples. Plantations of pepper trees cling to the hillsides. On a clear day, Phu Quoc Island (p452) is easily visible to the west. The town itself has a sleepy charm, with crumbling colonial villas and a colourful riverside market. It sees only a handful of visitors, who come to explore the unique sights out of town.

Ha Tien was a province of Cambodia until 1708. In the face of attacks by the Thais, the Khmer-appointed governor, a Chinese immigrant named Mac Cuu, turned to the Vietnamese for protection and assistance. Mac Cuu thereafter governed this area as a fiefdom under the protection of the Nguyen Lords. He was succeeded as ruler by his son, Mac Thien Tu. During the 18th century the area was invaded and pillaged several times by the Thais. Rach Gia and the southern tip of the Mekong Delta came under direct Nguyen rule in 1798.

During the Khmer Rouge regime, Cambodian forces repeatedly attacked the Vietnamese territory and massacred thousands of civilians here. The entire populations of Ha Tien and nearby villages (in fact, tens of thousands of people) fled their homes. Also during this period, areas north of Ha Tien (along the Cambodian border) were sown with mines and booby traps, which have yet to be cleared.

Though the government has designated Ha Tien a 'frontier economic zone', the border crossing here is not yet open to tourists. This may change in upcoming years. Check with travel agencies in Ha Tien.

Information

The **post office** (☎ 852 190; 3 Đ To Chau; 🕑 7am-10pm) also has internet access for 4000d per hour.

There's an **Agricultural Bank** (Ngan Hang Nong Nhiep; ☎ 852 055; fax 851 888; 37 Đ Lam Son) near the market area.

Sights

MAC CUU FAMILY TOMBS

On a low ridge not far from town are the Mac Cuu Family Tombs (Lang Mac Cuu). They are known locally as Nui Lang, the Hill of the

Tombs. Several dozen relatives of Mac Cuu are buried here in traditional Chinese tombs decorated with figures of dragons, phoenixes, lions and guardians.

The largest tomb is that of Mac Cuu himself; it was constructed in 1809 on the orders of Emperor Gia Long and is decorated with finely carved figures of Thanh Long (Green Dragon) and Bach Ho (White Tiger). The tomb of Mac Cuu's first wife is flanked by dragons and phoenixes. At the bottom of the ridge is a shrine dedicated to the Mac family.

TAM BAO PAGODA

Founded by Mac Cuu in 1730 is the **Tam Bao Pagoda** (Sac Tu Tam Bao Tu; 328 Đ Phuong Thanh; prayers

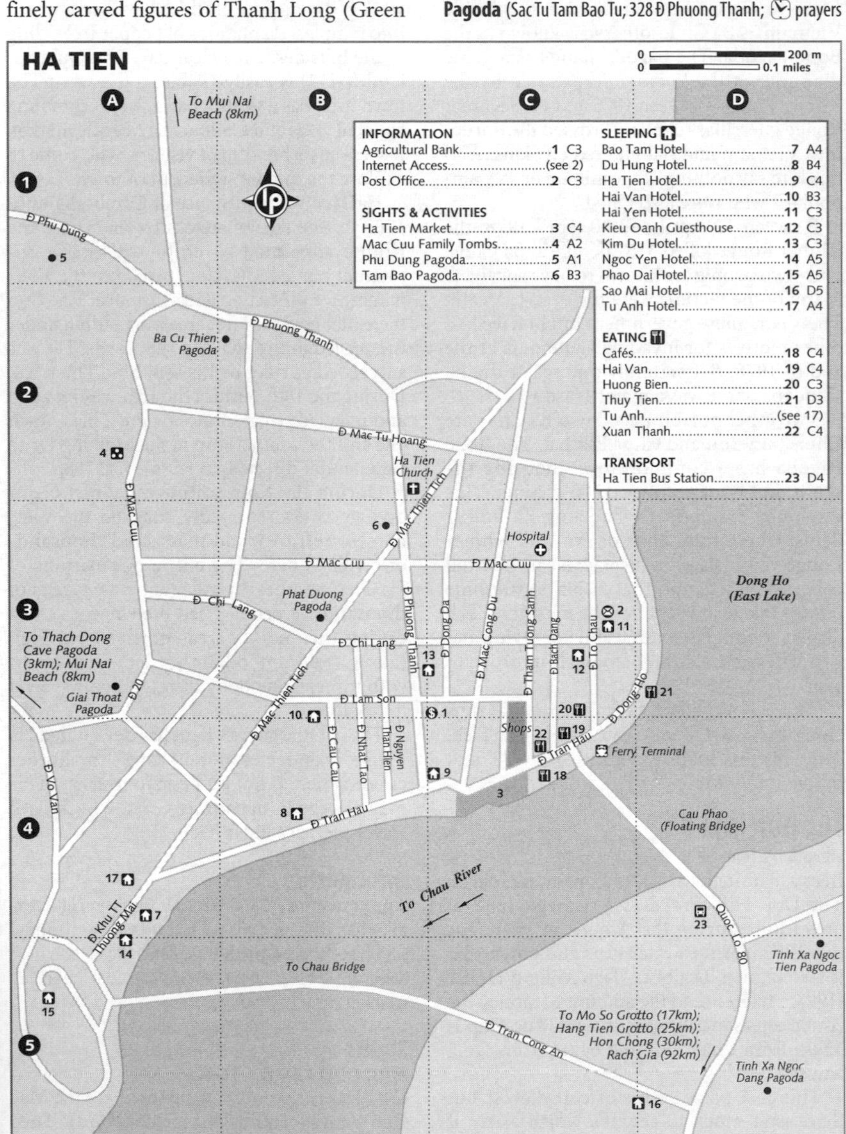

8-9am & 2-3pm). It is now home to several Buddhist nuns. In front of the pagoda is a statue of Quan The Am Bo Tat standing on a lotus blossom in the middle of a pond. Inside the sanctuary, the largest statue on the dais is of A Di Da, the Buddha of the Past. It is made of bronze, but has been painted. Outside the building are the tombs of 16 monks.

Near Tam Bao Pagoda is a section of the city wall dating from the early 18th century.

PHU DUNG PAGODA

This **pagoda** (Phu Cu Am Tu; prayers 4-5am & 7-8pm) was founded in the mid-18th century by Mac Thien Tich's wife, Nguyen Thi Xuan. It is now home to one monk.

In the middle of the main hall is a statue of nine dragons embracing a newly born Thich Ca Buddha. The most interesting statue on the main dais is a bronze Thich Ca Buddha from China. On the hillside behind the main hall are the tombs of Nguyen Thi Xuan and one of her female servants; nearby are four monks' tombs.

Behind the main hall is a small temple, Dien Ngoc Hoang, dedicated to the Taoist Jade Emperor. The figures inside are of Ngoc Hoang flanked by Nam Tao, the Taoist God of the Southern Polar Star and the God of Happiness (on the right); and Bac Dao, the Taoist God of the Northern Polar Star and the God of Longevity (on the left). The statues are made of papier-mâché moulded over bamboo frames.

To get to Phu Dung Pagoda, turn off Đ Phuong Thanh at No 374.

THACH DONG CAVE PAGODA

Also known as Chua Thanh Van, this is a subterranean Buddhist temple 4km from town.

To the left of the entrance is the Stele of Hatred (Bia Cam Thu), which commemorates the massacre by the Khmer Rouge of 130 people here on 14 March 1978.

Several of the chambers contain funerary tablets and altars to Ngoc Hoang, Quan The Am Bo Tat and the two Buddhist monks who founded the temples of this pagoda. The wind here creates extraordinary sounds as it blows through the grotto's passageways. Openings in several branches of the cave afford views of nearby Cambodia.

DONG HO

The name translates as East Lake, but Dong Ho is not a lake but an inlet of the sea. The 'lake' is just east of Ha Tien, and is bounded to the east by a chain of granite hills known as the Ngu Ho (Five Tigers) and to the west by the To Chan hills. Dong Ho is said to be most beautiful on nights when there is a full or almost-full moon. According to legend, on such nights fairies dance here.

HA TIEN MARKET

Ha Tien has an excellent market along the To Chau River. It's well worth your while to stop here – many of the goods are from Thailand and Cambodia, and prices are lower than in HCMC. Cigarette smuggling is particularly big business.

BORDER CROSSING: TINH BIEN–PHNOM DEN

This little-used border crossing is less convenient for Phnom Penh–bound travellers, but may be of interest if you're in a hurry to reach Cambodia's south coast. The border is in a remote area with little in the way of transport getting you there and away. You'll need to arrange a visa before heading to Tinh Bien, as visas are not currently issued at the border. Take care of this at the Cambodian consulate in HCMC (p467).

Sleeping

BUDGET

Phao Dai Hotel (☎ 851 849; r 80,000-200,000d;) On a hill in the far southwest of town, the Phao Dai is a relatively quiet place. Air-con rooms have ocean views, and the best rooms open onto shared terraces. Facilities include massage, a karaoke bar and a restaurant.

Ngoc Yen Hotel (☎ 952 953; fax 952 955; 12 Đ Khu Trung Tam Thuong Mai; r 120,000-220,000d;) This is good value with its newish feel and clean, modern rooms set with polished wood furniture. Some windows open only onto the corridor.

Bao Tam Hotel (☎ 952 944; fax 952 945; 23 Đ Khu Trung Tam Thuong Mai; r 140,000-170,000d;) This friendly, new spot has tidy, nicely outfitted rooms with green tile floors. Upper-storey rooms have balconies. As elsewhere some rooms lack windows.

Tu Anh Hotel (☎ 852 622; fax 951 703; 170 Đ Mac Thien Tich; r 150,000-250,000d;) With windows and air-conditioning in every room, Tu Anh is one of Ha Tien's best newcomers. It has clean and polished rooms and friendly service.

Other budget choices:

Kieu Oanh Guesthouse (852 748; 20 Đ To Chau; r 50,000-80,000d;) A friendly, family-run place with battered rooms. Cold-water bathrooms.

Sao Mai Hotel (852 740; Đ Tran Cong An; r 80,000-150,000d;) A nice, clean place south of the floating bridge. Ocean views from top-floor rooms.

MIDRANGE

Hai Van Hotel (852 001; fax 851 685; 55 Đ Lam Son; r 70,000-220,000d;) Hai Van offers a range of rooms from cheap and basic fan-cooled rooms (with cold-water bathrooms) to comfortably set rooms in the new wing with balconies. There's a lift.

Kim Du Hotel (851 929; fax 852 119; 14 Đ Phuong Thanh; r 120,000-200,000d;) Rooms at this decent but ageing option have big windows and are in OK shape. The in-house restaurant is good. It has a lift.

Du Hung Hotel (951 555; fax 852 267; 17A Đ Tran Hau; r 180,000-250,000d;) Another new, good-value option with clean rooms and dark wood furniture. Lift available.

Hai Yen Hotel (851 580; fax 851 889; 15 Đ To Chau; r 200,000-350,000d;) Offers spotless rooms with colourful bedspreads and decorative ceilings. Some rooms lack windows; others (like room 517) have fine river views.

Ha Tien Hotel (952 093; fax 951 102; 36 Đ Tran Hau; r 300,000-400,000d;) Ha Tien's finest hotel has comfortable, carpeted rooms with dark wood furniture, though some rooms lack windows. An inviting, open-sided restaurant fronts the place.

Eating & Drinking

Ha Tien's speciality is an unusual variety of coconut that can only be found in Cambodia and this part of Vietnam. These coconuts contain no milk, but the delicate flesh is delicious. Restaurants all around the Ha Tien area serve the coconut flesh in a glass with ice and sugar.

Hai Van (850 344; 4 Đ Tran Hau; mains 10,000-15,000d; breakfast, lunch & dinner) Dishes up good Vietnamese, Chinese and Western meals.

Xuan Thanh (852 197; 20 Đ Tran Hau; mains 15,000-40,000d; lunch & dinner) Set with chrome chairs opposite the market, this cheery place serves tasty plates of fish, shrimp and other Vietnamese fair.

Tu Anh (852 622; 170 Đ Mac Thien Tich; mains 20,000-40,000d; breakfast, lunch & dinner) The restaurant of this decent hotel also serves excellent dishes, including delicious seafood with noodles.

Huong Bien (852 072; 974 Đ To Chau; mains 20,000-30,000d) Another excellent eatery.

Thuy Tien (851 828; Đ Dong Ho; coffee 3000d) For an iced coffee against the lakeside scenery, stop by this low-key café.

For livelier backdrop try the cafés along the waterfront.

Getting There & Away

BOAT

Passenger ferries dock at the ferry terminal, which is not far from the To Chau Hotel near the floating bridge. Daily ferries depart to Phu Quoc (55,000d, 8.30am), but these are worn, wooden boats that may not be seaworthy. It's wise to take a more reliable hydrofoil from Rach Gia.

BUS

Buses from HCMC to Ha Tien leave three times daily from the Mien Tay bus station (p372); the trip (around 110,000d) takes eight to 10 hours.

Ha Tien bus station (Ben Xe Ha Tien) is on the other side of the floating toll bridge from the centre of town. Buses leave from here to HCMC, Can Tho (67,000d, five hours, three daily), Chau Doc (41,000d, four hours, four daily) and Rach Gia (22,000d, two hours, frequent) among other destinations.

CAR & MOTORBIKE

Ha Tien is 92km from Rach Gia, 95km from Chau Doc, 206km from Can Tho and 338km from HCMC.

AROUND HA TIEN

There are many other islands off the coast between Rach Gia and the Cambodian border. Some locals make a living gathering swiftlet nests (the most important ingredient of that famous Chinese delicacy, bird's-nest soup), on the islands' rocky cliffs.

Beaches

The beaches in this part of Vietnam face the Gulf of Thailand. The water is incredibly warm and calm here, like a placid lake. The beaches are OK for bathing and diving but hopeless for surfing.

Mui Nai (Stag's Head Peninsula) is 8km west of Ha Tien; it supposedly resembles the head of a stag with its mouth pointing upward. On top is a lighthouse and there are sand beaches on both sides of the peninsula. Mui Nai is accessible by road from both Ha Tien and from Thach Dong Cave Pagoda (admission person/car 2000/10,000d).

There are simple restaurants overlooking the beach, and several guesthouses in the area, including **Kim Ngan** (☎ 077-951 661; r 150,000-200,000d; ❄), a basic place with clean rooms just steps from the beach (no view).

There's no public transport to the beach. A moto-taxi there should set you back around 10,000d.

No Beach (Bai No), lined with coconut palms, and shady **Bang Beach** (Bai Bang) are several kilometres west of Ha Tien and can be reached from the road to Mui Nai Beach.

Mo So Grotto

About 17km towards Rach Gia from Ha Tien, and 3km from the road, Mo So Grotto consists of three large rooms and a labyrinth of tunnels. Sadly, the local Morning Star cement factory has carted away a substantial amount of limestone and managed to cause irreparable damage to the grotto. The cave is accessible on foot during the dry season and by small boat during the wet season. Visitors should take torches (flashlights) and a local guide.

Hang Tien Grotto

About 25km towards Rach Gia from Ha Tien, Hang Tien Grotto served as a hideout for Nguyen Anh (later Emperor Gia Long) in 1784, when he was being pursued by the Tay Son Rebels. His fighters found zinc coins buried here, a discovery that gave the cave its name, Coin Grotto. Hang Tien Grotto is accessible by boat (20,000d) from the ferry terminal in Ha Tien. The trip takes about an hour.

Hon Giang Island

About 15km from Ha Tien and accessible by small boat, Hon Giang Island has a lovely, secluded beach.

HON CHONG

☎ 077

This small and secluded village beach resort has the most scenic stretch of coastline on the Mekong Delta mainland. It's a peaceful place most of the year and sees few foreign travellers. The big attractions here are Chua Hang Grotto, Duong Beach and Nghe Island. Though they are a far cry from the stunning 3000-plus islands and grottoes of Halong Bay, the stone formations here are indeed photogenic. Aside from the three gargantuan cement factories that spew out smoke along the road from Ha Tien, the coastal drive there boasts some beautiful landscape.

Hon Chong lies along both sides of the road from Ba Hon, curving along the coast. Rustic and midrange hotels dot the road, which terminates at Chua Hang Grotto and the temple there.

Chua Hang Grotto

Chua Hang Grotto is entered through a Buddhist temple set against the base of a hill. The temple is called **Hai Son Tu** (Sea Mountain Temple; admission 2000d). Visitors light incense and offer prayers here before entering the grotto itself, whose entrance is located behind the altar. Inside is a statue of Quan The Am Bo Tat.

Duong Beach

Running north from Chua Hang Grotto, this beach (Bai Duong) is named for its long-needled pine trees *(duong)*. The southern area can get busy with Vietnamese tourists – and their beloved karaoke – but otherwise the 3km stretch of coast is quite tranquil.

Although this is easily the prettiest beach in the Mekong Delta, don't expect any white sand. The waters around the delta contain heavy concentrations of silt (and cement dust), so the beach sand tends to be hard while in the water it's muddy. Still, the water is reasonably clear here and this is the only beach south of HCMC (excluding those on Phu Quoc Island) that looks appealing to swimmers. The beach is known for its spectacular sunsets.

From the busy southern end of the beach (near Chua Hang Grotto), you can see remnants of **Father and Son Isle** (Hon Phu Tu) several hundred metres offshore; it was said to be shaped like a father embracing his son – though the father was washed away in 2006. Boats can be hired at the shore to row out for a closer look.

Nghe Island

This is the most beautiful island in the area and is a favourite pilgrimage spot for Buddhists. The island contains a **cave temple** (Chua Hang) next to a large statue of Quan The Am Bo Tat, which faces the sea. The area where you'll find the cave temple and statue is called Doc Lau Chuong.

Finding a boat to the island is not too difficult, though it is much cheaper if you round up a group. Inquire at the Hon Trem Guesthouse (below). You can also rent a speed boat for the day for 900,000d from the Tan Phat restaurant (right). The boat seats up to 20, and the captain can take you on a tour of four islands in the area. Tourists are not permitted to stay on the island.

Sleeping

The hotels are completely booked when Buddhists arrive to worship 15 days before and one month after Tet. Another worship deluge occurs in March and April. The following hotels are listed in order, as you approach them on the main (and only) road into town.

Green Hill Guesthouse (☎ 854 369; 905 Hon Chong; d US$14-20;) This lovely villa on the hill is the first place you'll see upon arriving in Hon Chong. Perched on a knoll overlooking Duong Beach, this friendly, family-run guesthouse has comfortable, spacious rooms. The 2nd-storey balcony, festooned with orchids and bougainvillea, has great views. Try booking the top-floor room, with its neat conical ceiling and private terrace.

An Hai Son Resort (☎ 759 226; anhaison@hcm.vnn.vn; Bai Gieng Hamlet; r 240,000-300,000d;) Some 500m from Green Hill Guesthouse, this resort has clean, pleasantly furnished rooms amid a nicely landscaped setting. Villa rooms are smaller, cheaper and nicer, with stylish furniture. Rooms on the 2nd storey have sea views. There's a tennis court and massage services; breakfast included.

My Lan Hotel (☎ 759 044; mylanhotel@vnn.vn; r 150,000-210,000d;) Another 150m from An Hai, this hotel has a range of rooms, some so white as to be on the clinical side, while others are roomy with decent windows and even shower curtains in the bathrooms!

Diem My Hotel (☎ 759 216; 1022 Hamlet 3; r 60,000-160,000d;) About 200m further, Diem My is one of Hong Chong's cheapest options. Expect basic rooms, light pink walls and a somewhat musty smell. The bathrooms are cold-water only.

Binh An Hotel (☎ 854 332; fax 854 533; 1030 Hamlet 3; r 80,000-200,000d;) Up the road (another 200m), Binh An is a fine but ageing place with gardens. The old-wing fan rooms are grotty but cheap; new-wing rooms are nicer with air-con.

Hon Trem Guesthouse (☎ 854 331; contact@hontremresort.com; r/bungalow 400,000/450,000d;) Hong Chong's best overnight is found 300m past Binh An. This recently overhauled guesthouse has attractive, light and airy bungalows with artwork on the walls, private terraces and sizable bathtubs. Guesthouse rooms are handsomely designed but lack the fine views. There's also a good seafood restaurant (mains 60,000d to 90,000d) overlooking the water, and you can book spa services and boat tours here. Breakfast included.

Huong Bien Guesthouse (☎ 854 537; Hamlet 3; r 150,000d;) The last place in town before reaching the Chua Hang Grotto, this guesthouse has trim rooms with green tile floors, small windows and cold-water bathrooms. It's run by a friendly young family. Across the street are a few basic restaurants.

Eating

Tan Phat (☎ 759 943; Hamlet 3; mains 30,000-60,000d;) Just outside of Hon Chong (400m from Green Hill Guesthouse) on the road to Ha Tien, this excellent restaurant serves filling seafood dishes, which you can enjoy on the back deck above the water.

Hong Ngoc (coconuts around 3000d), just near the entrance gate to the Chua Hang Grotto, is a good place to sample delicious Ha Tien coconuts.

Aside from special orders prepared at your hotel, there are **thatch-roof restaurants** (mains 10,0000-40,000d) along the beach and **food stalls** (mains around 10,000d) near the entrance of Chua Hang Grotto. For only a few dollars, you can point to one of the live chickens, which will be summarily executed and barbecued for you.

Getting There & Away

Chua Hang Grotto and Duong Beach are 32km from Ha Tien towards Rach Gia. The access road branches off the Rach Gia–Ha Tien highway at the small town of Ba Hon, which is just west of the cement factory at Kien Luong. Buses can drop you off at Ba Hon, from where you can hire a motorbike to get around.

There's also a direct bus service from Rach Gia to Hon Chong (25,000d, 2½ hours, three daily). It departs from the **Ben Xe Ha Tien bus station** (Đ 30 Thang 4) in Rach Gia and in Hon Chong from outside the Huong Bien Guesthouse.

RACH GIA

☎ 077 / pop 180,000

The prosperous capital of Kien Giang province, Rach Gia is a booming port city on the

Gulf of Thailand. The population includes significant numbers of both ethnic Chinese and ethnic Khmers. Most travellers give the chaotic centre short shrift, heading straight to the port for boats to Phu Quoc Island. Those who linger, however, might be charmed by the quaint waterfront and sleepy nearby streets, which provide great opportunities for both pleasant strolls and some decent seafood.

With its easy access to the sea and the proximity of Cambodia and Thailand, fishing, agriculture and smuggling are profitable trades in this province. The area was once famous for supplying the large feathers used to make ceremonial fans for the Imperial Court.

Information

The provincial tourism authority is **Kien Giang Tourist** (Du Lich Lu Hanh Kien Giang; ☎ 862 081; dlluhanhkg@hcm.vnn.vn; 5 Đ Le Loi; ⏰ 7am-5pm).

Vietcombank (☎ 863 178; fax 866 243; 2 Đ Mac Cuu) has a 24-hour ATM. On the road towards Long Xuyen, **Rach Gia Internet Café** (152 Đ Nguyen Trung Truc) has a pretty fast connection. The **post office** (☎ 873008; 2 Đ Mau Than) is centrally located near the river.

Sights

RACH GIA MUSEUM

The **Rach Gia Museum** (☎ 863 727; 21 Đ Nguyen Van Troi; admission free; ⏰ 7-11am Mon-Fri plus 1-5pm Mon-Wed) was recently restored and is worth a visit to see the Oc-Eo artefacts and pottery.

NGUYEN TRUNG TRUC TEMPLE

This **temple** (18 Đ Nguyen Cong Tru) is dedicated to Nguyen Trung Truc, a leader of the resistance campaign of the 1860s against the newly arrived French. Among other exploits, he led the raid that resulted in the burning of the French warship *Espérance*. Despite repeated attempts to capture him, Nguyen Trung Truc continued to fight until 1868, when the French took his mother and a number of civilians hostage and threatened to kill them if he did not surrender. Nguyen Trung Truc turned himself in and was executed by the French in the marketplace of Rach Gia on 27 October 1868.

The first temple structure was a simple building with a thatched roof; over the years it has been enlarged and rebuilt several times. The last reconstruction took place between 1964 and 1970. In the centre of the main hall is a portrait of Nguyen Trung Truc on an altar.

PHAT LON PAGODA

This large Cambodian Hinayana Buddhist pagoda, whose name means Big Buddha, was founded about two centuries ago. Though all of the three dozen monks who live here are ethnic Khmers, ethnic Vietnamese also frequent the pagoda.

Inside the sanctuary *(vihara)*, figures of the Thich Ca Buddha wear Cambodian- and Thai-style pointed hats. Around the exterior of the main hall are eight small altars.

The two towers near the main entrance are used to cremate the bodies of deceased monks. Near the pagoda are the tombs of about two dozen monks.

Prayers are held here daily from 4am to 6am and 5pm to 7pm. The pagoda, off Đ Quang Trung, is officially open during the seventh, eighth and ninth lunar months (summer season), but guests are welcome all year round.

PHO MINH PAGODA

Only a handful of Buddhist nuns live at **Pho Minh Pagoda** (cnr Đ Co Bac & Đ Nguyen Van Cu; prayers 3.30-4.30am & 6.30-7.30pm). This small pagoda was built in 1967 and contains a large Thai-style Thich Ca Buddha that was donated by a Buddhist organisation based in Thailand. Near the Thai-style Buddha there is a Vietnamese-style Thich Ca Buddha. The nuns living here reside in a building located behind the main hall. The pagoda is open to visitors and prayers are held daily.

TAM BAO PAGODA

This **pagoda** (prayers 4.30-5.30am & 5.30-6.30pm), which dates from the early 19th century, is near the corner of Đ Thich Thien An and Đ Ngo Quyen; it was last rebuilt in 1913. The garden contains numerous trees sculpted as dragons, deer and other animals.

CAO DAI TEMPLE

This small **Cao Dai Temple** (189 Đ Nguyen Trung Truc) was constructed in 1969 and is worth a peek if you missed the Great Temple in Tay Ninh.

Sleeping

Phuong Hong Hotel (866 138; 5 Đ Tu Do; r 80,000-180,000d;) Although the rooms are small, this family-run spot is clean and friendly, and the quarters are nicely maintained. Some bathrooms are cold-water only.

Hung Tai Hotel (877 508; 30/4 Đ Le Than Thon; r 120,000-250,000d;) A fair range of rooms are on offer here, from windowless cells to bright and airy, green-hued quarters. Most rooms lack hot water.

Nhat Quang Hotel (863 433; 16 Đ Tu Do; r 130,000-160,000d;) Although the walls are thin and the rooms smallish, this is a friendly place on a pleasant street near the river mouth.

Hong Yen Hotel (879 095; fax 863 789; 259 Đ Mac Cuu; r 150,000/250,000d;) Modern, comfortable rooms are good value. Some rooms have balconies.

Hong Nam Hotel (873 090; fax 873 424; Đ Ly Thai To; r 150,000-250,000d;) This minihotel offers sparkly, spacious rooms decked out with all the modern comforts. It's near the Rach Gia Trade Centre. Some have balconies.

Hoang Cung Hotel (872 655; fax 872 656; 26 Đ Le Thanh Ton; r 150,000-250,000d) Similar in standard and near the Hong Nam, the pricier rooms at this place have stuffed armchairs, bathtubs and funky bas-reliefs gracing the bedroom walls.

Kim Co Hotel (879 610; fax 879 611; 141 Đ Nguyen Hung Son; r 160,000/200,000d;) This friendly place has colourful rooms (mint walls, orange curtains) and tubs in some bathrooms. Most rooms lack windows.

Gia Thao Hotel (878 576; fax 868 091; 164 Đ Tran Phu; r 160,000-300,000;) This well-located hotel has clean, nicely maintained rooms with polished floors. The best rooms have balconies; the worst lack windows.

Hoang Gia 2 Hotel (920 980; tuananggia@vnn.vn; 31 Đ Le Than Thon; r 180,000-250,000d;) Set with nice wood furnishings and bathtubs, the rooms here are in good shape, though some could use more light. There's a lift.

Tan Hoang Phuc Hotel (☎/fax 878 855; 173 Đ Nguyen Trung Truc; r 180,000-200,000d;) A bit out of the way, Tan Hoang Phuc is excellent value for its clean and sizable rooms with attractive furnishings and big windows.

Palace Hotel (☎ 866 146; fax 867 423; 243 Đ Tran Phu; r US$10-20;) Surprisingly, the cheapest rooms on the top floor are the ones with balconies. This place is clean, but some rooms lack windows.

Eating

Rach Gia is known for its seafood, dried cuttlefish, dried fish slices *(ca thieu)*, fish sauce and black pepper.

Ao Dai Moi (☎ 866 295; 26 Đ Ly Tu Trong; soups 8,000d; breakfast) The name means 'new *ao dai*' and Ao Dai Moi is run by a local tailor. The simple place has very good *pho* and won ton soup in the morning.

Than Binh (☎ 874 780; 2 Đ Nguyen Thai Hoc; mains 10,000-15,000d; breakfast, lunch & dinner) Near Hai Au, this is another popular spot with an enticing assortment of fresh-cooked dishes displayed on a long counter.

Tinh Tam (☎ 861 452; 22 Đ Ly Tu Trong; mains 10,000-20,000d; 7-10am; breakfast, lunch & dinner) This friendly, clean, minimalist place serves good vegetarian fare for breakfast only.

Nam Long (☎ 862 268; 100 Đ Nguyen Hung Son; mains 15,000d; breakfast, lunch & dinner) A hole-in-the-wall spot delivering cheap plates of batter-fried shrimp and fried noodles.

Tan Hung Phat (☎ 867 599; 118 Đ Nguyen Hung Son; mains 15,000-30,000d; breakfast, lunch & dinner) This friendly newish place has a good selection of fish and seafood dishes. Blue tablecloths lend a homey vibe.

Valentine (☎ 920 852; 35 Đ Hung Vuong; mains 15,000-40,000d; breakfast, lunch & dinner) This is a cosy spot for coffee or a meal, with faux brickwork and pink, heart-covered columns. If all the frippery makes you giddy, head upstairs for karaoke.

Tay Ho (☎ 863 031; 6 Đ Nguyen Du; meals 15,000-50,000d; breakfast, lunch & dinner) Serves excellent Chinese and Vietnamese dishes at reasonable prices.

Quan F28 (☎ 867 334; 28 Đ Le Than Thon; mains 30,000-50,000d; lunch & dinner) With pavement seating and a popular night-time buzz, Quan F28 is the place to go for molluscs – crab, shrimp, snails, blood cockles and the like.

Hai Au (☎ 863 740; 2 Đ Nguyen Trung Truc; mains 40,000-80,000d; breakfast, lunch & dinner) Popular Hai Au serves decent Vietnamese standards, though its sunny terrace overlooking the Cai Lon River is the real draw.

Cheap, tasty Vietnamese food is sold from food stalls along Đ Hung Vuong between Đ Bach Dang and Đ Le Hong Phong.

Vinh Thanh Van Market, Rach Gia's main market area, stretches east of Đ Tran Phu along Đ Nguyen Thoai Hau, Đ Trinh Hoai Duc and Đ Thu Khoa Nghia.

Getting There & Away

AIR

Vietnam Airlines flies between HCMC and Rach Gia twice weekly; see p485 for more details. The same flight carries on to Phu Quoc Island (p458).

BOAT

At the western end of Đ Nguyen Cong Tru is Rach Gia Park, where you catch the ferries across to Phu Quoc Island.

Mui Voi ferry terminal (*mui* means nose and *voi* means elephant – so named because of the shape of the island) is at the northeastern end of Đ Nguyen Thoai Hau.

Approximately three boats daily leave for Ca Mau (80,000d, three to five hours) from the **Rach Meo ferry terminal** (☎ 811 306; 747 Đ Ngo Quyen), about 2km south of town.

BUS

Buses from HCMC to Rach Gia leave from the Mien Tay bus station (p372); the express bus takes six to seven hours (around 90,000d). Night buses leave Rach Gia for HCMC between 7pm and 11pm.

The **Central bus station** (Đ Nguyen Binh Khiem) is in town, near the Rach Gia New Trade Center, and has daily express services to Can Tho (40,000d, three hours, every two hours), Ha Tien (22,000d, three hours, hourly), Long Xuyen, Sa Dec and HCMC. You can catch buses to Hon Chong (25,000d, 2½ hours, three daily).

There's also a bigger **Rach Gia bus station** (Ben Xe Rach Soi; 78 Đ Nguyen Trung Truc), 7km south of the city (towards Long Xuyen and Can Tho). Buses link Rach Gia with Can Tho, Dong Thap, Ha Tien, Long Xuyen and HCMC.

CAR & MOTORBIKE

Rach Gia is 92km from Ha Tien, 125km from Can Tho and 248km from HCMC.

PHU QUOC ISLAND

☎ 077 / pop 85,000

One of Vietnam's star attractions, mountainous and forested Phu Quoc is a splendid tropical getaway set with beautiful white-sand beaches and quaint fishing villages. Adventure comes in many forms here – from motorbiking the empty dirt roads circling the island to sea kayaking its quiet inlets, scuba diving the coral reefs or simply having a bang-up seafood meal followed by a cocktail on the beach. Once a sleepy, backpackers' retreat, Phu Quoc has ramped up tourism significantly, and visitors can now choose between five-star resorts and rustic family-run bungalows. Plans are underway for developing the island even more heavily – a la Phuket style. If package tourism isn't your bag, get there now before this happens.

The tear-shaped island lies in the Gulf of Thailand, 45km west of Ha Tien and 15km south of the coast of Cambodia. At 48km long (with an area of 1320 sq km), Phu Quoc is Vietnam's largest island and its most politically contentious: Phu Quoc is claimed by Cambodia; its Khmer name is Ko Tral – which is why the Vietnamese have built a substantial military base covering much of the northern end of the island (thankfully, the military presence is fairly invisible).

Phu Quoc Island served as a base for the French missionary Pigneau de Behaine during the 1760s and 1780s. Prince Nguyen Anh, who later became Emperor Gia Long, was sheltered here by Behaine when he was being hunted by the Tay Son Rebels.

Phu Quoc is not really part of the Mekong Delta and doesn't share the delta's extraordinary ability to produce rice. The most valuable crop is black pepper, but the islanders here have traditionally earned their living from the sea. Phu Quoc is also famous in Vietnam for its production of high-quality fish sauce *(nuoc mam)*.

The island has some unusual hunting dogs, which have ridgebacks, curly tails and blue tongues and are said to be able to pick up their masters' scent from over 1km away (the *nuoc mam* their masters eat certainly helps). Unfortunately, the dogs have decimated much of the island's wildlife.

Despite the impending development (of a new international airport, a golf course and a casino), much of this island is still protected since becoming a national park in 2001. **Phu Quoc National Park** covers close to 70% of the island, an area of 31,422 hectares.

Phu Quoc's rainy season is from July to November. The peak season for tourism is midwinter, when the sky is blue and the sea is calm; however, when it's not raining it's stinking hot. Bring sunglasses and plenty of sunblock. Take plenty of water when setting out to explore the island.

Orientation

The main shipping port is **An Thoi** at the southern tip of Phu Quoc Island. This town is not blessed with scenic sights, though the market here is definitely worth a peek. This is the embarkation point for Rach Gia (p451), or for day trips to the An Thoi Islands (below).

The island's chief fishing port is Duong Dong, on the central west coast. The airport and most of the hotels are here.

The town is not that exciting, though the markets are mildly interesting. The bridge nearby forms a good vantage point to photograph the island's fishing fleet – you'll notice that this tiny harbour is anything but clean.

Information

The post office (Map p455) is in downtown Duong Dong.

Internet access is available in the big hotels (try La Veranda, Sasco Blue Lagoon or Saigon Phu Quoc). In Duong Dong, there are several internet cafés including **Net Café** (Map p455; 5 Đ Nguyen Dinh Chieu; per hr 10,000d; 🕑 7am-10pm).

Flights back to HCMC can be booked through the Vietnam Airlines office in front of **Saigon-Phu Quoc Resort** (Map p453; 1 Đ Tran Hung Dao). This is also where you'll find a useful ATM.

There's a **pharmacy** (Nha Thuoc Khai Hoan; ☎ 993 756) on Đ Ngo Quyen near the market.

Sights & Activities

BEACHES

Bai Dai & Bai Thom

These are both remote beaches: Bai Dai (Map p453) is in the far northwest and Bai Thom (Map p453) is on the northeastern coast. A new road to Bai Dai cuts down on motorbike time and red dust in your face. You can rest assured that neither beach will be crowded.

Both are in military areas, but Bai Dai is open to the public and has a couple of restaurants. The military usually opens Bai Thom to

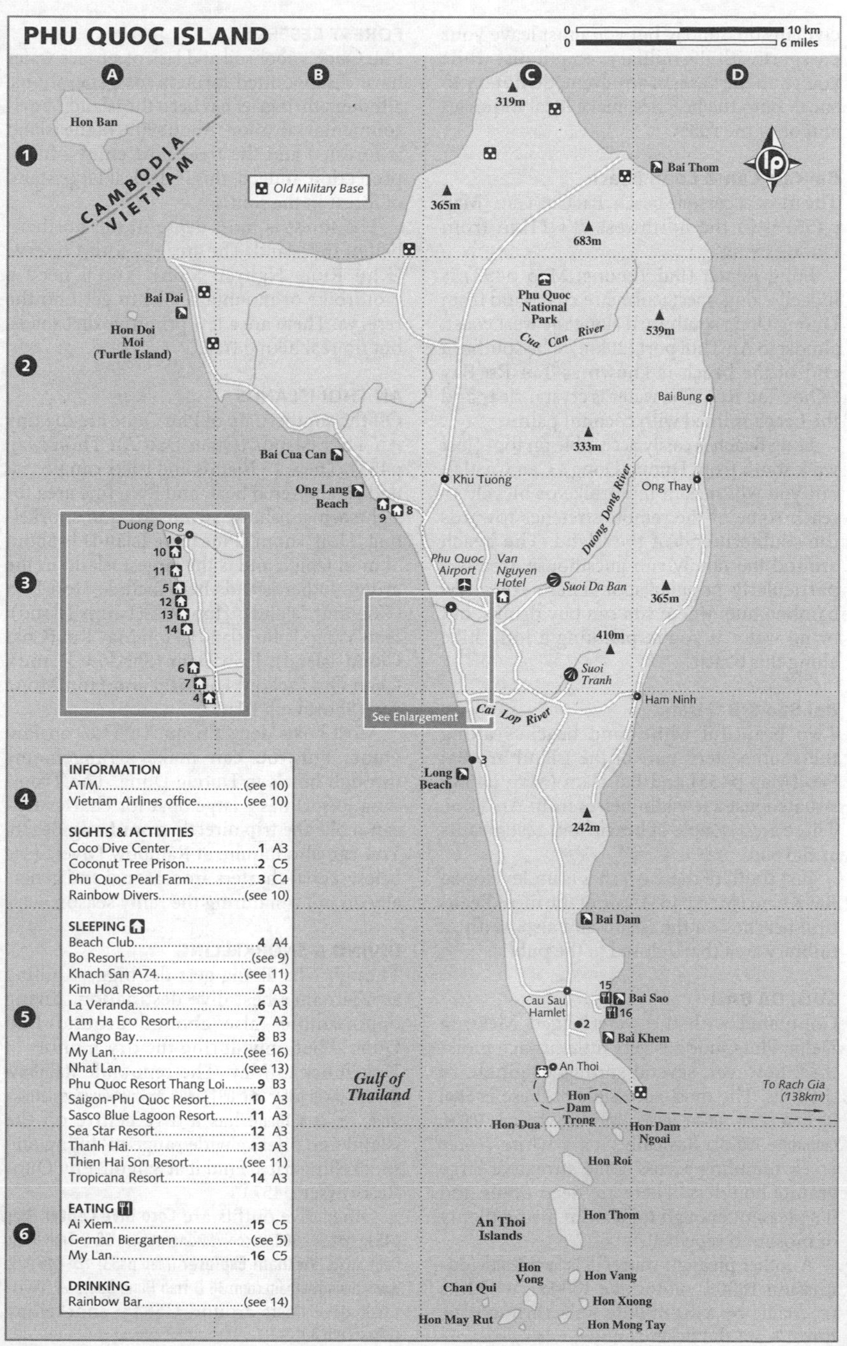
PHU QUOC ISLAND
0 10 km
0 6 miles
Hon Ban
CAMBODIA
VIETNAM
Old Military Base
319m
365m
683m
Bai Thom
Bai Dai
Hon Doi Moi (Turtle Island)
Phu Quoc National Park
Cua Can River
539m
Bai Bung
333m
Bai Cua Can
Ong Lang Beach
Khu Tuong
Duong Dong River
Ong Thay
Duong Dong
Phu Quoc Airport
Van Nguyen Hotel
Suoi Da Ban
365m
410m
Suoi Tranh
Ham Ninh
See Enlargement
Cai Lop River
Long Beach
242m
Bai Dam
Cau Sau Hamlet
Bai Sao
Bai Khem
An Thoi
Gulf of Thailand
To Rach Gia (138km)
Hon Dam Trong
Hon Dua
Hon Dam Ngoai
Hon Roi
Hon Thom
An Thoi Islands
Hon Vong
Hon Vang
Chan Qui
Hon Xuong
Hon May Rut
Hon Mong Tay
INFORMATION
ATM (see 10)
Vietnam Airlines office (see 10)
SIGHTS & ACTIVITIES
Coco Dive Center 1 A3
Coconut Tree Prison 2 C5
Phu Quoc Pearl Farm 3 C4
Rainbow Divers (see 10)
SLEEPING
Beach Club 4 A4
Bo Resort (see 9)
Khach San A74 (see 11)
Kim Hoa Resort 5 A3
La Veranda 6 A3
Lam Ha Eco Resort 7 A3
Mango Bay 8 B3
My Lan (see 16)
Nhat Lan (see 13)
Phu Quoc Resort Thang Loi 9 B3
Saigon-Phu Quoc Resort 10 A3
Sasco Blue Lagoon Resort 11 A3
Sea Star Resort 12 A3
Thanh Hai 13 A3
Thien Hai Son Resort (see 11)
Tropicana Resort 14 A3
EATING
Ai Xiem 15 C5
German Biergarten (see 5)
My Lan 16 C5
DRINKING
Rainbow Bar (see 14)

civilians on Sunday but you must leave your passport with the military receptionist while you're on the base. In any event, do not try to sneak onto the beaches: make local inquiries and obey the rules.

Bai Cua Can & Long Beach

The most accessible beach, Bai Cua Can (Map p453) is in the northwest. It's 11km from Duong Dong.

Long Beach (Bai Truong; Map p453) is indeed a long, spectacular stretch of sand from Duong Dong southward along the west coast, almost to An Thoi port (20km). The southern end of the beach is known as Tau Ru Bay (Khoe Tau Ru). The water is crystal clear and the beach is lined with coconut palms.

Long Beach is easily accessible on foot (just walk south from Duong Dong's Cau Castle), but you will need a motorbike or bicycle to reach some of the remote stretches towards the southern end of the island. The beach around the family-run guesthouse area is a particularly popular spot. There are a few bamboo huts where you can buy drinks, but bring water if you're planning a long hike along this beach.

Bai Sao & Bai Dam

Two beautiful white-sand beaches along the southeastern part of the island are Bai Sao (Map p453) and Bai Dam (Map p453), situated just a few kilometres from An Thoi. There are a couple of beachfront restaurants at Bai Sao.

Just south of these beaches is undeveloped Bai Khem (Map p453), one of the most beautiful beaches on the island and also, sadly, a military area that's closed to the public.

SUOI DA BAN

Compared with the waterlogged Mekong Delta, Phu Quoc has very little surface moisture; however, several springs originate in the hills. The most accessible of these is **Suoi Da Ban** (Stony Surface Spring; Map p453; admission 1000d, motorbike 1000d). Basically, it's a white-water creek tumbling across some attractive large granite boulders. There are deep pools and it's pleasant enough for a swim. Bring plenty of mosquito repellent.

Another pleasant waterfall is **Suoi Tranh** (admission 1000d, motorbike 1000d), which is reachable by a 10-minute walk through the forest from the ticket counter.

FOREST RESERVE

Phu Quoc's poor soil and lack of surface water have disappointed farmers for generations, although their grief has been the island's environmental salvation. About 90% of the island is forested and the trees now enjoy official protection. Indeed, this is the last large stand of forest in the south.

The forest is most dense in the northern half of the island. The area is a forest reserve (Khu Rung Nguyen Sinh). You'll need a motorbike or mountain bike to get into the reserve. There are a few primitive dirt roads, but no real hiking trails.

AN THOI ISLANDS

Off the southern tip of Phu Quoc are the tiny An Thoi Islands (Quan Dao An Thoi; Map p453). These 15 islands and islets can be visited by chartered boat, and it's a fine area for sightseeing, fishing, swimming and snorkelling. Hon Thom (Pineapple Island) is about 3km in length and is the largest island in the group. Other islands here include Hon Dua (Coconut Island), Hon Roi (Lamp Island), Hon Vang (Echo Island), Hon May Rut (Cold Cloud Island), Hon Dam (Shadow Island), Chan Qui (Yellow Tortoise) and Hon Mong Tay (Short Gun Island).

Most boats depart from An Thoi on Phu Quoc, but you can make arrangements through hotels in Duong Dong. The Tropicana Resort has a large boat for charter that can make the trip directly from Long Beach. You can also inquire at Rainbow Divers (see below). Boat charters are seasonal and generally do not run during the rainy season.

DIVING & SNORKELLING

Though Nha Trang gets the biggest billing as Vietnam's best dive destination, diving opportunities also abound around Phu Quoc – but only during the dry months of November to May. The reputable **Rainbow Divers** (Map p455; ☎ 0913-400 964; www.divevietnam.com; 🕑 7am-10pm) has a dive centre on the island and offers a wide range of diving and snorkelling trips. Find it at Saigon-Phu Quoc Resort (see p457).

Other dive outfits are **Coco Dive Center** (Map p453; ☎ 982 100; cocodive@dng.vnn.vn; 58 Đ Tran Hung Dao) and **Vietnam Explorer** (Map p453; ☎ 846 372; www.divingvietnam.com; 36 Đ Tran Hung Dao). A two-tank dive costs around US$45; snorkelling trips run US$20.

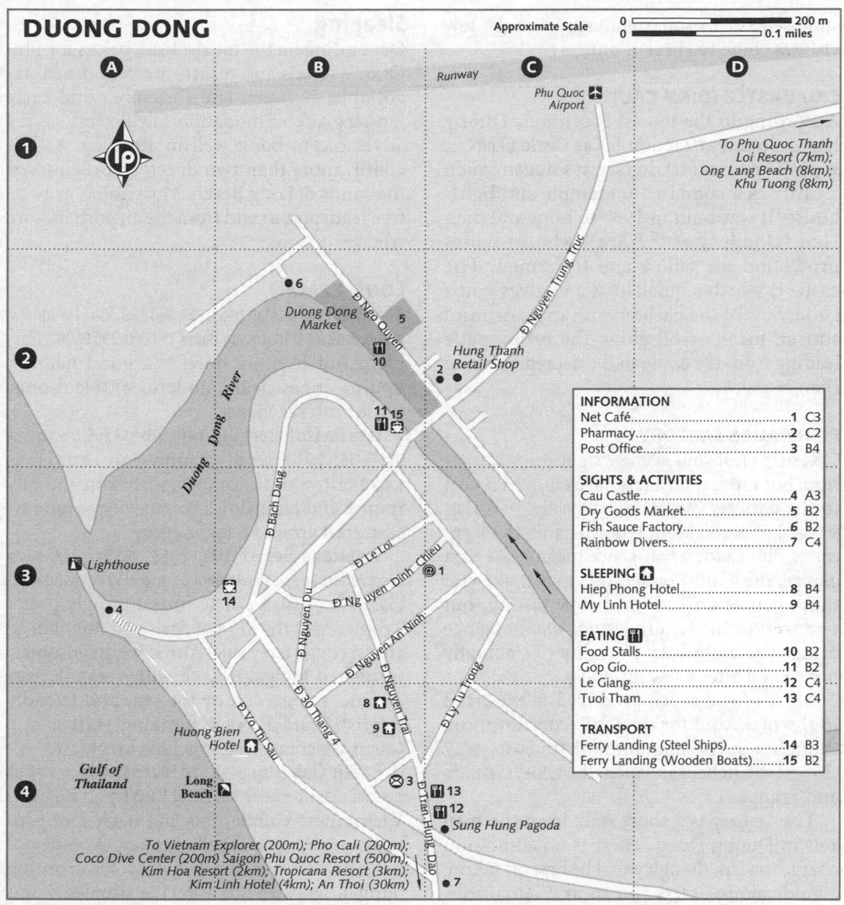

KAYAKING

There are several places to rent kayaks along Bai Sao beach, and its protected, fairly calm waters make for a smooth ride. In addition to locals who hire out boats, you can ask at either restaurant along the beach: **My Lan** (Map p453; ☎ 990 779) and **Ai Xiem** (Map p453; ☎ 990 510). You can expect to pay around 60,000d per hour.

PHU QUOC PEARL FARM

On an isolated stretch of Long Beach, **Phu Quoc Pearls** (Map p453; ☎ 980 585; www.treasuresfromthedeep.com; 8am-5pm) is a requisite stop if you're shopping for pearls. A small shop sells pearl necklaces and earrings, and wall panels describe (in English) how the oysters yield their goods. There's a tiny café on site. Avid pearl hunters can find cheaper wares at kiosks in the village of Ham Ninh.

COCONUT TREE PRISON

Being an island and an economically marginal area of Vietnam, Phu Quoc was useful to the French colonial administration – chiefly as a prison. The Americans took over where the French left off and as a consequence Phu Quoc was used to house about 40,000 VC prisoners.

The island's main penal colony was known as the Coconut Tree Prison (Nha Lao Cay Dua; Map p453) and is near An Thoi town. Though it's considered an historic site, plans to open a museum here have been stalled. It's still used as a prison, so not surprisingly, few visitors come to check it out.

CAU CASTLE (DINH CAU)

According to the tourist brochures, Duong Dong's main attraction is **Cau Castle** (Dinh Cau; Map p455; admission free). In fact, it's not so much a castle as a combination temple and lighthouse. It was built in 1937 to honour Thien Hau (Goddess of the Sea), who provides protection for sailors and fishermen. The castle is worth a quick look and gives you a good view of the harbour entrance. Around sunset, locals stroll along the promenade leading from the castle to the decrepit Huong Bien Hotel.

FISH SAUCE FACTORY

OK, so it's not your average sightseeing attraction, but more than a few have enjoyed a visit to the **distillery** (Map p455; admission free; 8-11am & 1-5pm) of Nuoc Mam Hung Thanh, the largest of Phu Quoc's fish-sauce makers. At first glance, the giant wooden vats may make you think you've arrived for a wine tasting, but one sniff of the festering *nuoc mam* essence brings you right back to reality (it's actually not so bad after a few minutes).

Most of the sauce produced is exported to the mainland for domestic consumption, though a surprising amount finds its way abroad to kitchens in Japan, the USA, Canada and France.

The factory is a short walk from the **markets** in Duong Dong. There is no admission charge to visit, though you'd be best off taking a guide along unless you speak Vietnamese. Keep in mind that although *nuoc mam* makes a wonderful gift for your distant relatives, you may not be able to take it out of the country. Vietnam Airlines, among other carriers, has banned it from its planes.

Tours

Your best bet for booking tours is through your hotel, as there's no local tourism authority in Duong Dong. Most travellers get around the island by hired motorbike. There are a handful of English-speaking motorbike guides on the island, the most notorious of whom is **Tony** (091 319 7334). Raised by a US military family, Tony speaks a distinctive breed of Al Pacino English that could easily land him a role in the next *Sopranos* episode.

Sleeping

Depending on the tourist load, prices for Phu Quoc's hotels and resorts are very much negotiable. Between late December and early January, accommodation fills up fast, so it's advisable to book well in advance. At last count, more than two dozen resorts littered the sands of Long Beach. Most hotels provide free transport to and from the airport; inquire when you book.

LONG BEACH

Khach San A74 (Map p453; 980 899; ksa74phuquoc@yahoo.com; 72 Đ Tran Hung Dao; r 150,000-250,000d) This plain but friendly hotel is a good fallback option. It has clean, modern, sizable rooms, some with sea views.

Lam Ha Eco Resort (Map p453; 847 369; r/bungalow US$12/15;) Friendly, family-run Lam Ha is excellent value for money, with trim and tidy rooms and bungalows (some with verandas) scattered around a lush setting.

Tropicana Resort (Map p453; 847 127; www.reservation@tropicanavietnam.com; d US$15, bungalows US$35-70;) The unassumingly pretty Tropicana is the kind of oasis you might need after a rough ferry ride. Attractive, handsomely furnished bungalows, all with veranda, face around the garden or the sea, and friendly English- and French-speaking staff give a warm welcome. Rates include breakfast.

Beach Club (Map p453 980 998; www.beachclubvietnam.com; r/bungalow US$15/20) Run by an English-Vietnamese couple, this laid-back spot provides great value for the money. Accommodations are in rustic but cosy sea-fronting bungalows (with hot water) or simpler rooms (with cold water). The owner is a great source of local info. There's a pleasant beachside restaurant.

Sea Star Resort (Map p453; 982 161; www.seastarresort.com; r US$20, bungalow US$30-38;) New in 2005, this resort features pleasant, modern, yellow bungalows, all with individual porches; the best are just a few feet from the sea. Rooms are simple, clean and tidy.

Kim Hoa Resort (Map p453; 848 969; kimhoapqresort@hcm.vnn.vn; r US$22-32, bungalow US$22-35;) This popular guesthouse has wooden-sided bungalows (some overlooking the ocean) and rooms opening onto a garden. Accommodations are clean and nicely outfitted.

Thien Hai Son Resort (Map p453; 983 044; www.phuquocthienhaison.com; 68 Đ Tran Hung Dao; r US$32-35, bungalow US$42-44;) This green-hued complex has comfortable, airy rooms and trim, tidy bungalows, some with sea views. There are massage services, a tennis court and a pool. Breakfast included.

Sasco Blue Lagoon Resort (Map p453; ☎ 994 499; www.sasco-bluelagoon-resort.com; s/d from US$80/100, bungalow US$100-140;) New in 2006, this high-end resort offers trim, attractively furnished rooms and bungalows – all with balconies. Spa services available.

Saigon-Phu Quoc Resort (Map p453; ☎ 846 510; www.vietnamphuquoc.com; 1 Đ Tran Hung Dao; r US$95-190;) Attractive rooms here are in villa-type houses, and have good views overlooking the beach. Rates include buffet breakfast; book through the website for significant deals.

Down a narrow road to the beach, 1km south of Tropicana, is a string of family-run bungalows and guesthouses as well as a few high-end options:

Thanh Hai (Map p453; ☎ 847 482; thanhhai99926@yahoo.com; r/bungalow from US$4/6;) One of the best deals on the island, this peaceful, family-run spot in the woods has clean and simple rooms and bungalows.

Nhat Lan (Map p453; ☎ 847 663; nhatlan98@yahoo.com; bungalow US$8) Run by a kind family, Nhat Lan has comfortable concrete bungalows with thatch-roofs; there are hammocks for relaxing and a pleasant restaurant.

La Veranda (Map p453; ☎ 982 988; www.laverandaresort.com; r/villa from US$140/210;) Phu Quoc's fanciest resort, La Veranda has airy, stylish rooms with all the creature comforts and top-notch service. There's also a spa and the island's best restaurant (mains US$12 to US$15).

ONG LANG BEACH

Although it is rockier and less beautiful than Long Beach, Ong Lang Beach, 7km north of Duong Dong near the hamlet of Ong Lang, is unquestionably less crowded and quieter.

Phu Quoc Resort Thang Loi (Map p453; ☎ 985 002; www.phu-quoc.de; bungalows US$15-30) A lovely resort, the Thang Loi has 12 wooden bungalows in a vast open garden setting, under the shade of cashew nut, palm and mango trees. The staff are friendly and the restaurant is cosy. Room rates vary depending on the size. Email ahead for reservations.

Mango Bay (Map p453; ☎ 0903-382 207; www.mangobayphuquoc.com; bungalows US$25-50) This attractive, relaxed resort offers stylish rooms and bungalows, all with terraces. It's also an eco-friendly resort that uses solar- panels and organic and recycled building materials.

Bo Resort (Map p453; ☎ 0913-640 520; www.boresort.com; bungalows US$30-65) Recommended by travellers, this resort with a good restaurant is run by a French-Vietnamese couple.

BAI SAO

My Lan (Map p453; ☎ 990 779; bungalow US$15) Currently the only place to stay on this lovely beach, My Lan rents small, rustic but charming bungalows, each with wood floors, a thatch roof and a cold-water shower and toilet out back. There's a decent restaurant where you can eat fresh seafood and dig your feet into the sand.

DUONG DONG

Most travellers prefer to stay at the beach, though there are options if Duong Dong town steals your heart.

Hiep Phong Hotel (Map p455; ☎ 847 342; 17 Nguyen Trai; r 100,000d;) A friendly family-run spot offering clean, tidy rooms with air-conditioning and hot water bathrooms.

My Linh Hotel (Map p455; ☎ 848 674; 9 Nguyen Trai; r with fan/air-con 100,000/130,000d;) A few doors down from Hiep Phong, this minihotel is similar value with new rooms and English-speaking owners.

AN THOI

Although few travellers care to stay in workaday An Thoi (Map p453), there are some decent options.

Huyn Tham (☎ 990 505; Khu Pho 1; r with fan/air-con 100,000/150,000d;) One of several sparklingly new minihotels on the main road into town, Huyn Tham has clean, comfortable rooms, some with views over the water. It's 150m from the ferry pier.

Eating

Tuoi Tham (Map p455; ☎ 846 368; Đ Tran Hung Dao) A popular local place with good food (mains around 10,000d to 30,000d) and welcoming atmosphere on the way from Duong Dong to Long Beach. Outdoor seating.

Le Giang (Map p455; ☎ 846 444; 289 Đ Tran Hung Dao; lunch & dinner) This is very similar to Tuoi Tham in terms of popularity, atmosphere, location and prices. Outdoor seating.

Pho Cali (Map p453; ☎ 994 177; 39 Đ Tran Hung Dao; mains 15,000-20,000d; lunch & dinner) This inviting noodle shop serves tasty bowls of *pho* and hot spring rolls. The English-speaking owner is a good source of island info.

Gop Gio (Map p455; ☎ 847 057; 78 Đ Tran Hung Dao; mains 30,000-50,000d; ⏰ lunch & dinner) On the main road into Duong Dong, this casual indoor-outdoor eatery has excellent seafood, with fresh, tasty dishes like shrimp with mango and steamed grouper with ginger.

German Biergarten (Map p453; 50 Đ Tran Hung Dao; mains 30,000-80,000d; ⏰ lunch & dinner) A favourite meeting spot of local expats, this place serves Bockwurst, pork chops, beef goulash and other Teutonic hits, along with German beer in bottles. There's bench-style seating and Johnny Cash singing overhead.

Ai Xiem (Map p453; ☎ 990 510; Bai Sao; mains 40,000-60,000d; ⏰ lunch & dinner) Located on the lovely white sands of Bai Sao beach, this is a great, low-key place for fresh seafood (including barbecue fish and fish cooked in clay pot). Tables are on the sands, a few metres from lapping waves. To get here, follow the paved road a few kilometres north of An Thoi and look for the 'My Lan' sign on the right, which leads down a rugged dirt track to the beach.

My Lan (Map p453; ☎ 990 779; Bai Sao; mains 40,000-60,000d; ⏰ lunch & dinner) About 400m south of Ai Xiem, My Lan offers equally good seafood and the same beachside allure.

For atmosphere and fine food, check out the seafront terrace restaurants at the Tropicana Resort (p456) and the Kim Hoa Resort (p456). La Veranda (p457) serves excellent dishes in a marvellous setting.

For something a bit more local, try the restaurants in the fishing village of Ham Ninh. There are several along the pier (end of the road), including **Kim Cuong I** (Map p453; ☎ 849 978; Ham Ninh; mains 30,000-40,000d).

There are heaps of cheap food stalls (Map p455) all around the market area in Duong Dong.

Drinking

Run by the same great crew who made this erstwhile Nha Trang institution a legendary good time, the friendly Rainbow Bar (Map p453) is located right on the beach, just south (150m) of Tropicana Resort.

Getting There & Away

AIR

Vietnam Airlines has four flights daily between HCMC and Duong Dong, Phu Quoc's main town.

A popular round trip between HCMC and Phu Quoc is to travel overland through the Mekong Delta, taking a ferry to the island from Rach Gia and, when you're finally tanned and rested, taking the short one-hour flight (US$35) back to HCMC.

BOAT

Numerous companies operate speedy hydrofoils that sail between Rach Gia and Phu Quoc. Boats leave the mainland daily between 7am and 8.30am, and return from Phu Quoc between 12.30pm and 1.30pm. Ticket prices for the 2½-hour journey range from 150,000 to 200,000d for adults, and 70,000 to 90,000d for children. Tickets must be purchased in advance – though you can usually find a seat by booking as little as 30 minutes ahead. There are no fast boats going between Ha Tien and Phu Quoc, though dodgy wooden market boats also make the journey (p446).

Hydrofoil companies include **Super Dong** (Rach Gia ☎ 077-878 475, Phu Quoc 077-980 111), **Duong Dong Express** (Rach Gia ☎ 077-879 765, Phu Quoc 077-990 747) and **Hai Au** (Rach Gia ☎ 077-879 455, Phu Quoc 077-990 555). All have offices by the dock in Rach Gia and in Phu Quoc – both by the An Thoi dock and in Duong Dong. Most travel agents can book passage.

All passenger ferries departing and arriving at Phu Quoc use the port of An Thoi on the southern tip of the island.

Getting Around

TO/FROM THE AIRPORT

Phu Quoc's airport is almost in central Duong Dong. The motorbike drivers at the airport will charge you about US$1 to most hotels in Phu Quoc, but are notorious for trying to cart people off to where they can collect a commission. If you know where you want to go, tell them you've already got a reservation.

BICYCLE

If you can ride a bicycle in the tropical heat over these dusty, bumpy roads, more power to you. Bicycle rentals are available through most hotels for about US$1 per day.

BUS

There is a skeletal bus service between An Thoi and Duong Dong. Buses run perhaps once every hour or two. A bus (tickets 10,000d) waits for the ferry at An Thoi to take passengers to Duong Dong.

MOTORBIKE

You won't have to look for the motorbike taxis – they'll find you. Some polite bargaining may be necessary. For short runs within the town, 5000d should be sufficient. Otherwise, figure on around 10,000d for about 5km. From Duong Dong to An Thoi will cost you 30,000d.

Motorbikes can be hired from most hotels and bungalows for around US$7 per day – though some of these bikes are fairly dodgy: inspect thoroughly before setting out. For pricier but very reliable motorbikes inquire at **Pho Cali** (Map p453; ☎ 994 177; 39 Đ Tran Hung Dao; per day from 250,000d).

Directory

CONTENTS

ACCOMMODATION

Vietnam has something for everyone – from dives to the divine – and we cover them all. Most hotels in Vietnam quote prices in a mix of Vietnamese dong and US dollars. In the provinces the lower dong price is usually reserved for locals, while foreigners pay the higher dollar price. Prices are quoted in dong or dollars throughout this book based on the preferred currency of the particular property.

When it comes to budget, we are talking about guesthouses or hotels where the majority of rooms cost less than US$20. These are usually family-run guesthouses, mini-hotels or, usually the least-appealing option, government-run guesthouses that time forgot. Budget rooms generally come well equipped for the money, so don't be surprised to find air-con, hot water and a TV for 10 bucks or less.

Moving on to midrange, we are referring to rooms in the US$20 to US$75 range, which buys some pretty tasty extras in Vietnam. At the lower end of this bracket, many of the hotels are similar to budget hotels but with bigger rooms or balconies. Flash a bit more cash and three-star touches are available, like access to a swimming pool and a hairdryer hidden away somewhere.

At the top end are a host of international-standard hotels and resorts that charge from US$75 a room to US$750 a suite. Some of these are fairly faceless business hotels, while others ooze opulence or resonate with history. There are some real bargains when compared with the Hong Kongs and Singapores of this world, so if you fancy indulging yourself, Vietnam is a good place to do it. Most hotels at the top end levy a tax of 10% and a service charge of 5%, displayed as ++ ('plus plus') on the bill.

Be aware that some budget and midrange hotels also apply the 10% tax. Check carefully before taking the room to avoid any unpleasant shocks on departure.

Accommodation options are limited in off-the-beaten track destinations in the far north and the central highlands. Usually there will just be a few guesthouses and basic hotels. However, in major towns and along the coastal strip, there is now an excellent range of rooms, including some of the world's biggest names, like Sofitel and Six Senses.

BOOK ACCOMMODATION ONLINE

For more accommodation reviews and recommendations by Lonely Planet authors, check out the online booking service at www.lonelyplanet.com. You'll find the true, insider lowdown on the best places to stay. Reviews are thorough and independent. Best of all, you can book online.

PRACTICALITIES

Electricity The usual voltage is 220V, 50 cycles, but sometimes you encounter 110V, also at 50 cycles, just to confuse things. Electrical sockets are usually two-pin.

Laundry Most guesthouses and hotels have cheap laundry services, but check it has a dryer if the weather is bad. There are dry-cleaning outlets in every town. Washing powder is cheap and readily available.

Newspapers & Magazines *Vietnam News* and the *Saigon Times* are popular English-language dailies. Good magazines include the *Vietnam Economic Times,* plus its listings mag, the *Guide*, and the *Vietnam Investment Review*.

Radio & TV *Voice of Vietnam* hogs the airwaves all day and is pumped through loudspeakers in many smaller towns. There are several TV channels and a steady diet of satellite stuff.

Weights & Measures The Vietnamese use the metric system for everything except precious metals and gems, where they follow the Chinese system.

Peak tourist demand for hotel rooms comes at Christmas and New Year, when prices may rise by as much as 25%. There is also a surge in many cities during Tet, when half of Vietnam is on the move. Try and make a reservation at these times so as not to get caught out. During quiet periods it is often possible to negotiate a discount, either by email in advance or over the counter on arrival, as there will now be a surplus of hotel beds in many destinations.

Passports are almost always requested on arrival at a hotel. It is not absolutely essential to hand over your actual passport, but at the very least you need to hand over a photocopy of the passport details, visa and departure card.

Accommodation prices listed are high-season prices for rooms with attached bathroom, unless stated otherwise. An icon is included if air-con is available; otherwise, assume that a fan will be provided.

Camping

Perhaps because so many Vietnamese spent much of the war years living in tents, as either soldiers or refugees, camping is not yet the popular pastime it is in the West.

Some innovative private travel agencies in Ho Chi Minh City (HCMC) and Hanoi offer organised camping trips to national parks, plus camping out in beauty spots like Halong Bay (p136). See Travel Agencies in Hanoi (p91) and HCMC (p338).

Guesthouses & Hotels

Many of the large hotels *(khach san)* and guesthouses *(nha khach* or *nha nghi)* are government-owned or joint ventures. There has also been a mushrooming of minihotels – small, smart private hotels that represent good value for money. The international hotel chains are now well represented in Hanoi and HCMC.

There is considerable confusion over the terms 'singles', 'doubles', 'double occupancy' and 'twins', so let's set the record straight here. A single contains one bed, even if two people sleep in it. If there are two beds in the room, that is a twin, even if only one person occupies it. If two people stay in the same room, that is double occupancy. In some hotels 'doubles' means twin beds, while in others it means double occupancy.

While many of the newer hotels have lifts, older hotels often don't and the cheapest rooms are at the end of several flights of stairs. It's a win-win situation: cheaper rooms, a bit of exercise and better views! Bear in mind

HOTELS FROM HELL

It is hardly unique to Vietnam, but there are quite a lot of hotel scams in Vietnam. They are mostly, although not exclusively, happening in Hanoi, although keep the radar up in most of the major cities. Copycat hotels, dodgy taxi drivers, persistent touts, all this is possible and more. Overcharging is a concern, as is constant harassment to book a tour. However, most guesthouse and hotel operators are decent folk and honest in their dealings with tourists. Don't let the minority ruin your Vietnam experience. For more on horror hotels in Hanoi, see p124.

that power outages are possible in some towns and this can mean 10 flights of stairs just to get to your room in a tall, skinny Saigon-style skyscraper.

Many hotels post a small sign warning guests not to leave cameras, passports and other valuables in the room. Most places have a safety deposit system of some kind, but if leaving cash (not recommended) or travellers cheques, be sure to seal the loot in an envelope and have it counter-signed by staff. However, many readers have been stung when leaving cash at cheaper hotels, so proceed with caution.

Homestays

Homestays are a popular option in parts of Vietnam, but some local governments are more flexible than others about the concept. Homestays were pioneered in the Mekong Delta (p409), where it has long been possible to stay with local families. At the opposite end of the map, there are also homestays on the island of Cat Ba (p145).

Many people like to stay with ethnic minority families in the far north of Vietnam. Mai Chau (p165) was the first place to offer the chance to stay with the hospitable White Thai families. Sapa (p172) is the number one destination to meet the hill tribes in Vietnam and it is possible to undertake two- or three-day treks with an overnight in a H'mong or Dzao village. If you are serious about homestays throughout the north, consider contacting one of the travel agencies (p91) or motorbike touring companies (p107) who can help organise things. Vietnam is not the sort of country where you can just drop-in and hope things work out, as there are strict rules about registering foreigners who stay overnight with a Vietnamese family.

Resorts

Resorts have really taken off in the last few years, particularly along the beautiful coastline. Top beach spots such as China Beach, Nha Trang and Mui Ne all have a range of sumptuous places for a spot of pampering. Up-and-coming destinations such as Phu Quoc Island are fast catching up. There are also a number of ecoresorts in the mountains of the north and the far flung corners of Bai Tu Long Bay, a trend that looks set to continue.

ACTIVITIES

If you are looking for action, Vietnam can increasingly deliver. Biking and hiking are taking off up and down the country, while offshore there is kayaking and surfing above the water and diving and snorkelling beneath. If it all sounds like too much hard work, rent a motorbike and let the engine take the strain.

Cycling

For distances near and far, cycling is an excellent way to experience Vietnam. A bicycle can be rented in most tourist centres from as little as US$1 a day.

The flatlands of the Mekong Delta region are an ideal place for a long-distance ride through the back roads. The entire coastal route along Hwy 1 is an alluring achievement, but the insane traffic makes it tough going and dangerous. A better option is the newer inland route, Hwy 14, also known as the Ho Chi Minh Trail (not to be confused with the original wartime trail), which offers stunning scenery and little traffic.

North of the old Demilitarised Zone (DMZ), cycling is a bad idea in the winter months, particularly if heading from the south to the north, thanks to the massive monsoon winds, which blow from the north. There are some incredible, and incredibly challenging, rides through the Tonkinese Alps (Hoang Lien Mountains) of the north, but the opportunity to get up close and personal with the minority peoples of the region makes it more than worth the while.

For some laughs, as well as the lowdown on cycling in Vietnam, visit the website www.mrpumpy.net.

Diving & Snorkelling

The most popular scuba-diving area in Vietnam is around Nha Trang (p281). There are several reputable dive operators here, whose equipment and training is up to international standards. It is also possible to hire snorkelling gear and scuba equipment at several beach resorts along the coast, including Cua Dai Beach (p239), Ca Na (p299) and China Beach (p237). Phu Quoc Island (p452) has the potential to be the next big thing in underwater exploration and dive operators are starting to spread the word.

Golf

Mark Twain once said that playing golf was 'a waste of a good walk' and apparently Ho Chi Minh agreed with him. Times have changed and government officials can often be seen fraternising on the fairways.

All over East Asia playing golf wins considerable points in the 'face game', even if you never hit a ball. For maximum snob valuc you need to join a country club, and in Vietnam memberships start at around US$10,000. Most golf clubs will allow you to pay a guest fee.

The best golf courses in Vietnam are located in Dalat (p307) and Phan Thiet (p304), but there are also plenty of courses in and around Hanoi and HCMC.

For information about golf package deals visit www.vietnamgolfresorts.com.

Kayaking

Kayaking has taken off around Halong Bay in the past few years, following in the footsteps of Krabi in Thailand. Several companies offer kayaking itineraries around the majestic limestone pinnacles, including overnights on islands in the bay. Even the standard Halong Bay tours now include the option of kayaking through the karsts for those that want the experience without the effort.

Motorbiking

Motorbiking through Vietnam's 'deep north' is unforgettable. For those seeking true adventure there is no better way to go. If you are not confident riding a motorbike, it's comparatively cheap to hire someone to drive it for you. 4WD trips in the north are also highly recommended, though the mobility of two wheels is unrivalled. Motorbikes can traverse trails that even the hardiest 4WD cannot follow. Just remember to watch the road when the scenery is sublime!

Rock Climbing

Well, it's still early days, but with the sheer range of limestone karsts found up and down the country, it is only a matter of time before the word gets out. For now, it is Halong Bay (p136) that is emerging as the premier spot, but in time Ninh Binh (p186) and Phong Nha (p195) could offer some competition.

Surfing, Kitesurfing & Windsurfing

Surfing and windsurfing have only recently arrived on the scene, but these are quickly catching on in popularity. The best place to practice these pursuits is at Mui Ne Beach (p300), but experienced surfers head for China Beach in Danang (p229). Kite surfing is now one of Mui Ne's biggest draws for thrillseekers.

Trekking

Vietnam offers excellent trekking opportunities, notably in its growing array of national parks and nature reserves. There are ample opportunities to hike to minority villages in the northwest, northeast and central highlands regions. Anything is possible, from half-day hikes to an assault on Fansipan, Vietnam's highest mountain. The best bases from which to arrange treks are Sapa (p172), Bac Ha (p180) and Cat Ba (p143), all in northern Vietnam; Bach Ma National Park (p225) in central Vietnam; and Cat Tien (p392) and Yok Don (p323) National Parks in the south. Tour operators in Hanoi and HCMC offer a variety of programmes featuring hiking and trekking.

Bear in mind that it may be necessary to arrange special permits, especially if you plan to spend the night in remote mountain villages where there are no hotels.

BUSINESS HOURS

Vietnamese people rise early and consider sleeping in to be a sure indication of illness. Offices, museums and many shops open between 7am and 8am and close between 4pm and 5pm. Post offices keep longer hours and are generally open from 6.30am to 9pm. Banks are generally open from 8am to 11.30am and 1pm to 4pm during the week and 8am to 11.30am on Saturday.

Most government offices are open on Saturday until noon but are closed on Sunday. Most museums are closed on Monday while temples and pagodas are usually open every day from around 5am to 9pm.

Many of the small privately owned shops, restaurants and street stalls stay open seven days a week, often until late at night.

Lunch is taken very seriously and virtually everything shuts down between noon and 1.30pm. Government workers tend to take longer breaks, so figure on getting nothing done between 11.30am and 2pm.

CHILDREN

Children get to have a good time in Vietnam, mainly because of the overwhelming amount of attention they attract and the fact that almost everybody wants to play with them! However, this attention can sometimes be overwhelming, particularly for blond-haired, blue-eyed babes. Cheek pinching, or worse still (if rare), groin grabbing, are distinct possibilities, so keep close. For the full picture on surviving and thriving on the road, check out Lonely Planet's *Travel with Children* by Cathy Lanigan, with a rundown on health precautions for kids and advice on travel during pregnancy.

Practicalities

When it comes to feeding and caring for babies, almost anything and everything is available in the major cities of Vietnam, but supplies dry up quickly in the countryside. Cot beds are available in international-standard midrange and top-end hotels, but not elsewhere. There are no safety seats in rented cars or taxis, but some Western restaurants can usually find a highchair when it comes to eating.

Breastfeeding in public is quite common in Vietnam, so there is no need to worry about crossing a cultural boundary. But there are few facilities for changing babies other than the usual bathrooms. You'll need to pack a baby bag everywhere you go. For kiddies who are too young to handle chopsticks, most restaurants also have cutlery.

Sights & Activities

There is plenty to do in big cities to keep kids interested, though in most smaller towns and rural areas you will probably encounter the boredom factor. The zoos, parks and some of the best ice-cream shops in the region are usually winners. Children visiting the south should not miss HCMC's water parks (p355), while Hanoi's two musts are the circus (p118) and a water-puppet performance (p119).

Nature lovers with children can hike in one of Vietnam's expansive national parks or nature reserves. Cuc Phuong National Park (p190) is home to the excellent Endangered Primate Rescue Centre, where endangered species of monkeys are protected and bred. This is a great place to see gibbons gallivanting about their safe houses and to learn about the plight of our furry friends.

With such a long coast, there are some great beaches for young children to enjoy, but pay close attention to any playtime in the sea, as there are some big riptides at many of the most popular beaches. Note that these rips are not marked by flags.

CLIMATE CHARTS

The climate of Vietnam varies considerably from region to region. Although the entire country lies in the tropics and subtropics, local conditions vary from frosty winters in the far northern hills to year-round, subequatorial warmth in the Mekong Delta.

For more climatic kudos, take a look at the When to Go information (p18).

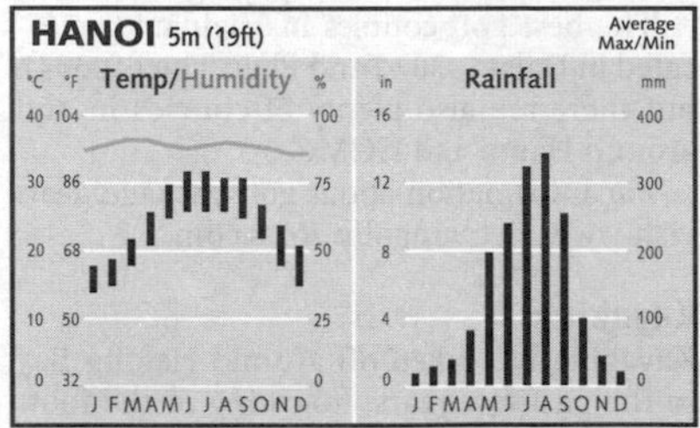

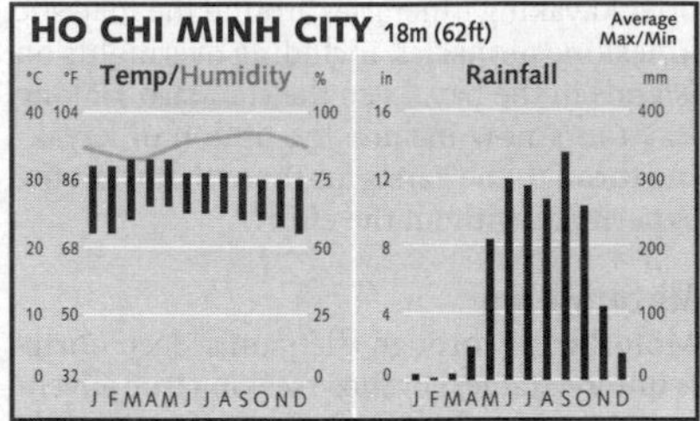

COURSES

Cooking

For the full story on cooking courses, check out the Food & Drink chapter (p52).

Language

There are Vietnamese language courses offered in HCMC, Hanoi and elsewhere. To qualify for student-visa status you need to enrol at a bona fide university, as opposed to a private language centre or with a tutor. Lessons usually last for two hours per day, and cost from US$3 (university) to US$10 (private) per hour.

It is important to decide on whether to study Vietnamese in Hanoi or HCMC, as the northern and southern dialects are quite different. Many have been dismayed to discover that if they studied in one city they could not communicate clearly in the other. For more details, see under Language Courses in Hanoi (p107) and Ho Chi Minh City (p355).

CUSTOMS

Enter Vietnam by air and the whole procedure only takes a few minutes. If you enter overland expect a bit more attention.

Duty free allowances are the standard 200 cigarettes and a bottle of booze variety. Visitors can bring unlimited foreign currency into Vietnam, but large sums (US$7000 and greater) must be declared upon arrival.

DANGERS & ANNOYANCES

Beggar Fatigue

Just as you're about to dig into the scrumptious Vietnamese meal you've ordered, you feel a tug on your shirt sleeve. This latest 'annoyance' is a bony, eight-year-old boy holding his three-year-old sister in his arms. The little girl has a distended stomach and her hungry eyes are fixed on your full plate.

This is the face of poverty. How do you deal with these situations? If you're like most of us, not very well. Taking the matter into your own hands by giving out money or gifts to people on the streets can cause more damage than good. The more people are given hand-outs, the more reliant and attracted to life on the streets they become. When money is tight, people recognise that life on the streets is no longer so fruitful. This will hopefully discourage parents and 'pimps' forcing children and beggars onto the streets.

One way to contribute and help improve the situation is to invest just a few hours to find out about local organisations that work with disadvantaged people; these groups are far more likely to make sure contributions are used in the most effective way possible to help those who need it.

However, if you want to do something on the spot, at least avoid giving money or anything that can be sold. The elderly and the young are easily controlled and are ideal begging tools. If you are going to give something directly to a beggar, it's better to give food than money; take them to a market or stall and buy them a nutritious meal or some fruit to be sure they are the only beneficiaries.

> **GOVERNMENT TRAVEL ADVICE**
>
> The following government websites offer travel advisories and information on current hot spots.
>
> **Australian Department of Foreign Affairs** (☎ 1300 139 281; www.smarttraveller.gov.au)
>
> **British Foreign Office** (☎ 0845-850-2829; www.fco.gov.uk/countryadvice)
>
> **Canadian Department of Foreign Affairs** (☎ 800-267 6788; www.dfait-maeci.gc.ca)
>
> **US State Department** (☎ 888-407 4747; http://travel.state.gov)

Noise

Remember Spinal Tap? The soundtrack of Vietnam is permanently cranked up to 11! Not just any noise, but a whole lot of noises that just never seem to stop. At night there is most often a competing cacophony from motorbikes, discos, cafés, video arcades, karaoke lounges and restaurants; if your hotel is near any or all of these, it may be difficult to sleep.

Fortunately most noise subsides around 10pm or 11pm, as few places stay open much later than that. Unfortunately, however, Vietnamese are up and about from around 5am onwards. This not only means that traffic noise starts early, but you may be woken up by the crackle of loud speakers as the Voice of Vietnam cranks into life at 5am in small towns and villages. It's worth trying to get a room at the back of a hotel.

One last thing…don't forget the earplugs!

Prostitution

Karaoke clubs and massage parlours are ubiquitous throughout Vietnam. Sometimes this may mean an 'orchestra without instruments', or a healthy massage to ease a stiff body. However, more often than not, both of these terms are euphemisms for some sort of prostitution. There may be some singing or a bit of shoulder tweaking going on, but ultimately it is just a polite introduction to something naughtier. Legitimate karaoke and legitimate massage do exist in the bigger cities, but as a general rule of thumb, if the place looks small and sleazy, it most probably is.

Scams

Con artists and thieves are always seeking new tricks to separate naive tourists from their money and are becoming more savvy in their ways. We can't warn you about every trick you might encounter, so maintain a healthy scepticism and be prepared to argue when unnecessary demands are made for your money.

Beware of a motorbike-rental scam that some travellers have encountered in HCMC. Rent a motorbike and the owner supplies an excellent lock, insisting you use it. What he doesn't tell you is that he has another key and that somebody will follow you and 'steal' the bike at the first opportunity. You then have to pay for a new bike, as per the signed contract.

More common is when your motorbike won't start after you parked it in a 'safe' area with a guard. But yes, the guard knows somebody who can repair your bike. The mechanic shows up and quickly reinstalls the parts they removed earlier and the bike works again. That will be US$10, please.

Beware of massage boys who, after a price has been agreed upon, try to extort money from you afterwards by threatening to set the police on you (these threats are generally empty ones).

The most common scam most visitors encounter is the oldest in the book. The hotel of choice is 'closed' or 'full', but the helpful taxi driver will take you somewhere else. This has been perfected in Hanoi, where there are often several hotels with the same name in the same area. Book by telephone or email in advance and stop the scammers in their tracks.

Despite an array of scams, however, it is important to keep in mind the Vietnamese are not always out to get you. One concerning trend we're noticing in Vietnam, relative to neighbouring countries such as Cambodia and Laos, is a general lack of trust in the locals on the part of foreigners. Try to differentiate between who is good and bad and do not close yourself off to every person you encounter.

Sea Creatures

If you plan to spend your time swimming, snorkelling and scuba diving, familiarise yourself with the various hazards. The list of dangerous creatures that are found in seas off Vietnam is extensive and includes sharks, jellyfish, stonefish, scorpion fish, sea snakes and stingrays. However, there is little cause for alarm as most of these creatures avoid humans, or humans avoid them, so the number of people injured or killed is very small.

Jellyfish tend to travel in groups, so as long as you look before you leap into the sea, avoiding them should not be too hard. Stonefish, scorpion fish and stingrays tend to hang out in shallow water along the ocean floor and can be very difficult to see. One way to protect against these nasties is to wear enclosed shoes in the sea.

PLANET OF THE FAKES

You'll probably notice a lot of cut-price Lonely Planet *Vietnam* titles available as you travel around the country. Don't be deceived. These are pirate copies, churned out on local photocopiers. Sometimes the copies are very good, sometimes awful. The only certain way to tell is price. If it's cheap, it's a copy. Look at the print in this copy... if it is faded and the photos are washed out, then this book will self-destruct in five seconds.

Theft

The Vietnamese are convinced that their cities are full of criminals. Street crime is commonplace in HCMC and Nha Trang, and on the rise in Hanoi, so it doesn't hurt to keep the antennae up wherever you are.

HCMC is the place to really keep your wits about you. Don't have anything dangling from your body that you are not ready to part with, including bags and jewellery, which might tempt a robber. Keep an eye out for drive-by thieves on motorbikes – they specialise in snatching handbags and cameras from tourists on foot and taking *cyclos* in the city.

Pickpocketing, which often involves kids, women with babies and newspaper vendors, is also a serious problem, especially in the tourist areas of HCMC. Many of the street kids, adorable as they may be, are very skilled at liberating people from their wallets.

Avoid putting things down while you're eating, or at least take the precaution of fastening these items to your seat with a strap or chain. Remember, any luggage that you leave unattended for even a moment may grow legs and vanish.

There are also 'taxi girls' (sometimes transvestites) who approach Western men, give them a big hug, often more, and ask if they'd like 'a good time'. Then they suddenly change their mind and depart, along with a mobile phone and wallet.

We have also had reports of people being drugged and robbed on long-distance buses. It usually starts with a friendly passenger offering a free Coke, which turns out to be a chloral-hydrate cocktail. You wake up hours later to find your valuables and new-found 'friend' gone.

Despite all this, don't be overly paranoid. Although crime certainly exists and you need to be aware of it, theft in Vietnam does not seem to be any worse than what you'd expect anywhere else. Don't assume that everyone's a thief – most Vietnamese are poor, but honest.

Undetonated Explosives

For more than three decades four armies expended untold energy and resources mining, booby-trapping, rocketing, strafing, mortaring and bombarding wide areas of Vietnam. When the fighting stopped most of this ordnance remained exactly where it had landed or been laid; American estimates at the end of the war placed the quantity of unexploded ordnance at 150,000 tonnes.

Since 1975 more than 40,000 Vietnamese have been maimed or killed by this leftover ordnance. While cities, cultivated areas and well-travelled rural roads and paths are safe for travel, straying from these areas could land you in the middle of a minefield that is completely unmarked.

Never touch any rockets, artillery shells, mortars, mines or other relics of war you may come across. Such objects can remain lethal for decades. And don't climb inside bomb craters – you never know what un-detonated explosive device is at the bottom.

You can learn more about the issue of landmines from the Nobel Peace Prize–winning **International Campaign to Ban Landmines** (ICBL; www.icbl.org), or see the boxed text, p203.

DISCOUNT CARDS

Senior Cards

There are no 'senior citizen' discounts for pensioners, as all foreigners who can afford to fly to Vietnam are considered rich enough to pay the full whack.

Student & Youth Cards

Ditto for student cards. Carry one if you are travelling through the region, but it will gather dust in your wallet while you are in Vietnam.

EMBASSIES & CONSULATES

Vietnamese Embassies & Consulates

The following are Vietnamese diplomatic representations abroad:

Australia Canberra (☎ 02-6286 6059; www.vietnamembassy.org.au; 6 Timbarra Cres, O'Malley, ACT 2606); Sydney (☎ 02-9327 2539; tlssyd@auco.net.au; 489 New South Head Rd, Double Bay, NSW 2028)

Cambodia Phnom Penh (☎ 023-362531; 436 Monivong Blvd)

Canada Ottawa (☎ 613-236 1398; www.vietnamembassy-canada.ca; 470 Wilbrod St, ON K1N 6M8)

China Beijing (☎ 010-6532 1125; vnaemba@mailhost.cinet.co.cn; 32 Guanghua Lu, 100600); Guangzhou (☎ 020-8652 7908; Jin Yanf Hotel, 92 Huanshi Western Rd)

France Paris (☎ 01 44 14 6400; 62-66 Rue Boileau, 75016)

Germany Berlin (☎ 030-509 8262; Konigswinter St 28, D-10318)

Hong Kong Wan Chai (☎ 22-591 4510; 15th fl, Great Smart Tower, 230 Wan Chai Rd)

Italy Rome (☎ 06-6616 0726; 156 Via di Bravetta, 00164)

Japan Tokyo (☎ 03-3466 3311; 50-11 Moto Yoyogi-Cho, Shibuya-ku, 151); Osaka (☎ 06-263 1600; 10th fl, Estate Bakurocho Bldg, 1-4-10 Bakurocho, Chuo-ku)

Laos Vientiane (☎ 21-413 409; That Luang Rd); Savannakhet (☎ 41-212 239; 418 Sisavang Vong)

Philippines Metro Manila (☎ 2-525 2837; 670 Pablo Ocampo, Makati City)

Thailand Bangkok (☎ 2-251 7202; 83/1 Wireless Rd 10500)

UK London (☎ 020-7937 1912; www.vietnamembassy.org.uk/consular.html; 12-14 Victoria Rd, W8 5RD)

USA Washington (☎ 202-861 0737; www.vietnamembassy-usa.org; 1233 20th St NW, Ste 400, DC 20036); San Francisco (☎ 415-922 1707; www.vietnamconsulate-sf.org; 1700 California St, Ste 430, CA 94109)

Embassies & Consulates in Vietnam

With the exception of those for Cambodia, China and Laos, Hanoi's embassies and HCMC's consulates do very little visa business for non-Vietnamese.

It's important to realise what your country's embassy can and can't do to help if you get into trouble. Generally speaking, it won't be much help if the trouble you're in is remotely your own fault. Remember that you are bound by the laws of the country you are in. Your embassy won't be sympathetic if you end up in jail after committing a crime, even if such actions are legal in your own country.

In genuine emergencies you might get some assistance, but only if other channels have been exhausted. If you have all your money and documents stolen, it might assist with getting a new passport, but a loan for onward travel is out of the question.

The following are some of the embassies and consulates found in Vietnam.

Australia (www.ausinvn.com) Hanoi (Map pp88-9; ☎ 831 7755; 8 Duong Dao Tan, Ba Dinh District); HCMC (Map p350; ☎ 829 6035; 5th fl, 5B Đ Ton Duc Thang)

Cambodia Hanoi (Map pp92-3; ☎ 825 3788; 71A Pho Tran Hung Dao); HCMC (Map p336; ☎ 827 7696; cambocg@hcm.vnn.vn; 41 Đ Phung Khac Khoan)

Canada (www.dfait-maeci.gc.ca/vietnam) Hanoi (Map pp92-3; ☎ 823 5500; 31 Đ Hung Vuong); HCMC (Map p350; ☎ 827 9899; 10th fl, 235 Đ Dong Khoi)
China Hanoi (Map pp92-3; ☎ 845 3736; Pho Hoang Dieu); HCMC (Map p336; ☎ 829 2457; chinaconsul_hcm_vn@mfa.gov.cn; 39 Đ Nguyen Thi Minh Khai)
France Hanoi (Map pp92-3; ☎ 943 7719; Pho Tran Hung Dao); HCMC (Map p336; ☎ 829 7231; 27 Đ Nguyen Thi Minh Khai)
Germany Hanoi (Map pp92-3; ☎ 845 3836; 29 Đ Tran Phu); HCMC (Map p336; ☎ 822 4385; 126 Đ Nguyen Dinh Chieu)
Japan Hanoi (Map pp88-9; ☎ 846 3000; 27 Pho Lieu Giai, Ba Dinh District); HCMC (Map p350; ☎ 822 5314; 13-17 ĐL Nguyen Hue)
Laos Hanoi (Map pp92-3; ☎ 825 4576; 22 Pho Tran Binh Trong); HCMC (Map p350; ☎ 829 7667; 93 Đ Pasteur); Danang (Map p230; 16 Đ Tran Qui Cap)
Netherlands HCMC (Map p336; ☎ 823 5932; hcm-ca@minbuza.nl; 29 ĐL Le Duan)
New Zealand Hanoi (Map p350; ☎ 824 1481; nzembhan@fpt.vn; Level 5, 63 Pho Ly Thai To); HCMC (Map p336; ☎ 822 6907; Ste 909, 235 Đ Dong Khoi)
Philippines Hanoi (Map pp92-3; ☎ 825 7948; 27B Pho Tran Hung Dao)
Singapore Hanoi (Map pp92-3; ☎ 823 3965; 41-43 Đ Tran Phu)
Sweden Hanoi (Map pp88-9; ☎ 726 0400; 2 Đ Nui Truc)
Thailand Hanoi (Map pp92-3; ☎ 823 5092; 63-65 Pho Hoang Dieu); HCMC (Map p336; ☎ 932 7637; 77 Đ Tran Quoc Thao)
UK (www.uk-vietnam.org) Hanoi (Map p96; ☎ 936 0500; Central Bldg, 31 Pho Hai Ba Trung); HCMC (Map p336; ☎ 829 8433; 25 ĐL Le Duan)
US (http://usembassy.state.gov/vietnam) Hanoi (Map pp88-9; ☎ 772 1500; 7 Pho Lang Ha, Ba Dinh District); HCMC (Map p336; ☎ 822 9433; 4 ĐL Le Duan)

FESTIVALS & EVENTS

Major religious festivals in Vietnam have lunar dates; check against any Vietnamese calendar for the Gregorian dates. If you know when Tet kicks off, simply count from there.

Special prayers are held at Vietnamese and Chinese pagodas when the moon is full or a thin sliver. Many Buddhists eat only vegetarian food on these days, which, according to the Chinese lunar calendar, fall on the 14th and 15th days of the month and from the last day of the month to the first day of the next month.

Tet (Tet Nguyen Dan) The Big One! The Vietnamese Lunar New Year is Christmas, New Year and birthdays all rolled into one. Lasting from the first to seventh days of the first moon, the Tet Festival falls in late January or early February. See p64 for more on Tet.
Holiday of the Dead (Thanh Minh) It's time to honour the ancestors with a visit to graves of deceased relatives. Fifth day of the third moon.
Buddha's Birth, Enlightenment and Death A big celebration at Buddhist temples and pagodas with lively processions. Eighth day of the fourth moon.
Summer Solstice Day (Tiet Doan Ngo) Keep the epidemics at bay with offerings to the spirits, ghosts and the God of Death. Fifth day of the fifth moon.
Wandering Souls Day (Trung Nguyen) Second in the pecking order to Tet, offerings are made for the wandering souls of the forgotten dead. Fifteenth day of the seventh moon.
Mid-Autumn Festival (Trung Thu) A fine time for foodies with moon cakes of sticky rice filled with lotus seeds, watermelon seeds, peanuts, the yolks of duck eggs, raisins and other treats. Fifteenth day of the eighth moon.
Confucius' Birthday Happy birthday to China's leading philosophical export. Twenty-eighth day of the ninth moon.
Christmas Day (Giang Sinh) Needs no introduction, this is not a national holiday, but is celebrated throughout Vietnam, particularly by the sizable Catholic population.

FOOD

Vietnamese cuisine has become a favourite throughout the Western world and a journey through Vietnam is a gastronomic treat. For the full story on Vietnamese cuisine, see the Food & Drink chapter (p45).

GAY & LESBIAN TRAVELLERS

Vietnam is a relatively hassle-free place for homosexuals. There are no official laws on same-sex relationships in Vietnam, nor much in the way of individual harassment.

That said, the government is notorious for clamping down on gay venues, and places that are covered in the mass media are 'coincidentally' closed down days later. Most gay venues keep a fairly low profile. There is, however, a healthy gay scene in Hanoi and HCMC, evidenced by unabashed cruising around certain lakes in Hanoi (p116) and the thriving café scene in HCMC (p369).

Homosexuality is still far from accepted in the wider community, though the lack of any laws keeps things fairly safe. Major headlines were made in 1997 with Vietnam's first gay marriage, and again in 1998 at the country's first lesbian wedding, in the Mekong Delta. However, displaying peculiar double standards, two weeks later government officials broke up the marriage of the women and the couple signed an agreement promising not to live together again.

With the vast number of same-sex travel partners – gay or otherwise – checking into hotels throughout Vietnam, there is little scrutiny over how travelling foreigners are related. However, it would be prudent not to flaunt your sexuality. As with heterosexual couples, passionate public displays of affection are considered a basic no-no.

Utopia (www.utopia-asia.com) features gay travel information and contacts, including detailed sections on the legality of homosexuality in Vietnam and some local gay terminology.

HOLIDAYS

Politics affects everything, including public holidays. After a 15-year lapse, religious holidays were re-established in 1990. The following are public holidays in Vietnam:

New Year's Day (Tet Duong Lich) 1 January

Anniversary of the Founding of the Vietnamese Communist Party (Thanh Lap Dang CSVN) 3 February – the date the party was founded in 1930.

Liberation Day (Saigon Giai Phong) 30 April – the date on which Saigon surrendered is commemorated nationwide as Liberation Day.

International Workers' Day (Quoc Te Lao Dong) 1 May

Ho Chi Minh's Birthday (Sinh Nhat Bac Ho) 19 May

Buddha's Birthday (Phat Dan) Eighth day of the fourth moon (usually June).

National Day (Quoc Khanh) 2 September – commemorates the Declaration of Independence by Ho Chi Minh in 1945.

INSURANCE

Insurance is a *must* for Vietnam, as the cost of major medical treatment is prohibitive. Although you may have medical insurance in your own country, it is probably not valid while you are in Vietnam. A travel insurance policy to cover theft, loss and medical problems is the best bet.

There is a wide variety of policies available, so check the small print. Some insurance policies specifically exclude such 'dangerous activities' as riding motorbikes, diving and even trekking. Check that the policy covers an emergency evacuation in the event of serious injury.

INTERNET ACCESS

Today the internet is widely available throughout towns and cities in Vietnam. There is everything from trendy cybercafés to computer terminals in the lobbies of hotels and guesthouses, plus public internet access in many Vietnamese post offices. Many of the budget and midrange hotels in major cities offer free internet in the lobby. Some even offer free access in the room for those travelling with a laptop.

The cost of internet access generally ranges from 3000d to 20,000d per hour, depending on where you are and what the competition is like. Printing usually costs around 1000d per page and scanning about 2000d a page.

Wi-fi access is spreading fast. Hanoi, HCMC and other big towns have plenty of cafés and bars offering free access. Many of the leading hotels also offer wi-fi, but in keeping with the five-star tradition, it is not a free service.

For laptop travellers with older machines, check out the prepaid internet-access cards that can provide you with nationwide dial up to the net. FPT is one of Vietnam's largest ISPs, and its internet card is sold in most cities.

Remember that the power supply voltage will vary from that at home. The best investment is a universal AC adapter, which will enable you to plug it in anywhere without frying the innards of your equipment. For more information on travelling with a portable computer, see www.teleadapt.com.

LAUNDRY

It is easy to get your laundry done at guesthouses and cheaper hotels for just a few US dollars. There have, however, been a number of reports of gross overcharging at certain hotels, so make sure you check the price beforehand.

Budget hotels do not have clothes dryers, as they rely on the sunshine – so allow at least a day and a half for washing and drying, especially during the wet season. You can also elect to wash your own clothes as washing powder is cheap and readily available.

LEGAL MATTERS

Civil Law

On paper it looks good, but in practice the rule of law in Vietnam is a fickle beast. Local officials interpret the law any way it suits them, often against the wishes of Hanoi. There is no independent judiciary. Not surprisingly, most legal disputes are settled out of court. In general, you can accomplish more with a carton of cigarettes and a bottle of good cognac than you can with a lawyer.

Drugs

The drug trade has made a comeback in Vietnam. The country has a very serious problem with heroin these days and the authorities are clamping down hard.

Marijuana and, in the northwest, opium are readily available, but giving in to this temptation is a risk. There are many plain-clothes police in Vietnam and, if arrested, the result might be a large fine and/or a long prison term.

Police

Vietnamese police are the best that money can buy. Police corruption is an everyday reality and has been acknowledged in official newspapers. If something does go wrong, or if something is stolen, the police can't do much more than prepare an insurance report for a fee (no fixed cost).

Hanoi has warned all provincial governments that any police caught shaking down foreign tourists will be fired and arrested. The crackdown has dented the enthusiasm of the police to confront foreigners directly with demands for bribes, but it still happens in more out-of-the-way places.

MAPS

Most bookshops in Vietnam stock a good range of maps. A must for its detailed road maps of every province is the *Viet Nam Administrative Atlas,* published by Ban Do. It is perfect for cyclists or motorbikers looking for roads less travelled and costs 68,000d in softback.

Ban Do also publishes reasonable tourist maps of HCMC, Hanoi, Danang, Hué and a few other cities. Unfortunately, maps of smaller towns are practically nonexistent. Most of the listings mags produced in Vietnam have city maps of Hanoi and HCMC, and there are some good hand-drawn 3D maps of Hanoi, Hué and Sapa available from Covit, a local publisher.

Vietnamese street names are preceded with the words Pho, Duong and Dai Lo – on the maps and in the text in this book, they appear respectively as P, Đ and ĐL.

MONEY

The first currency of Vietnam is the dong, which is abbreviated to 'd'. Banknotes come in denominations of 500d, 1000d, 2000d, 5000d, 10,000d, 20,000d, 50,000d, 100,000d, 200,000d and 500,000d. Now that Ho Chi Minh has been canonised (against his wishes), his picture is on *every* banknote. Coins are also in circulation, although they are more common in the cities, including 500d, 1000d and 5000d. The second currency is the US dollar and that needs no introduction.

The dong has experienced its ups and downs. The late 1990s Asian economic crisis, which wreaked severe havoc on the regional currencies, caused the dong to lose about 15% of its US-dollar value. Since then the dong has stabilised at around 16,000d to the US dollar.

Where prices are quoted in dong, we quote them in this book in dong. Likewise, when prices are quoted in dollars, we follow suit. While this may seem inconsistent, this is the way it's done in Vietnam and the sooner you get used to thinking comparatively in dong and dollars, the easier your travels will be.

For a smattering of exchange rates at the time of going to print, see the Quick Reference section on the inside front cover of this book.

ATMs

It used to be just a couple of foreign banks in Hanoi and HCMC that offered ATMs, but Vietnamese banks have now got into this game in a big way. Vietcombank has the best network in the country, including most of the major tourist destinations and all the big cities. Every branch stocks a useful leaflet with a list of their nationwide ATMs. Withdrawals are issued in dong, and there is a single withdrawal limit of 2,000,000d (about US$125). However, you can do multiple withdrawals until you hit your own account limit. ANZ offers 4,000,000d withdrawals per transaction. Most banks charge 20,000d per transaction. Cash advances for larger amounts of dong, as well as US dollars, can be arranged over the counter during office hours.

Black Market

The black market is Vietnam's unofficial banking system that is almost everywhere and operates quite openly. Private individuals and some shops and restaurants will exchange US dollars for dong and vice versa. While the practice is technically illegal, law enforcement is virtually nonexistent. Ironically, black market exchange rates are usually *worse* than the official exchange rates, so the only advantage is the convenience of changing money when and where you like.

If people approach you on the street with offers to change money at rates better than the official one, you can rest assured that you are being set up for a rip-off. Fake notes or too few notes, they will get you somehow. Don't even think about trying it! Remember, if an offer seems too good to be true, that's because it probably is.

Cash

Most major currencies can be exchanged at leading banks in Vietnam, but away from the tourist centres the US dollar remains king. Vietcombank is the most organised of the local banks for changing cash and can deal with euros, pounds and pretty much anything else you are packing. The US dollar exchange rate worsens the further you get from the tourist trail, so stock up on dong if you are heading into remote areas. In small towns it can be difficult to get change for the larger notes, so keep a stack of smaller bills handy. Changing US$100 will make you an instant millionaire!

It's a good idea to check that any big dollar bills you take do not have any small tears or look too tatty, as no-one will want to touch them in Vietnam.

You cannot legally take the dong out of Vietnam but you can reconvert reasonable amounts of it into US$ dollars on departure.

Credit Cards

Visa, MasterCard and JCB cards are now widely acceptable in all major cities and many tourist centres. However, a 3% commission charge on every transaction is pretty common; check first, as some charge higher commissions than others. Some merchants also accept Amex, but the surcharge is typically 4%. Better hotels and restaurants do not usually slap on an additional charge.

Getting a cash advance from Visa, Master Card and JCB is possible at Vietcombank in most cities, as well as at some foreign banks in HCMC and Hanoi. Banks generally charge a 3% commission for this service. This is handy if you want to get out large sums, as the ATMs have low daily limits.

Tipping

Tipping is not expected in Vietnam, but it is enormously appreciated. For a person who earns US$100 per month, a US$1 tip is significant. Upmarket hotels and some restaurants may levy a 5% service charge, but this may not make it to the staff. If you stay a couple of days in the same hotel, try and remember to tip the staff who clean your room.

You should also consider tipping drivers and guides – after all, the time they spend on the road with you means time away from home and family. Typically, travellers on minibus tours will pool together to collect a communal tip to be split between the guide and driver.

It is considered proper to make a small donation at the end of a visit to a pagoda, especially if a monk has shown you around; most pagodas have contribution boxes for this purpose.

Travellers Cheques

It is wise not to rely entirely on travellers cheques by keeping a reasonable stash of US dollars to hand. Travellers cheques can only be exchanged at authorised foreign-exchange banks, but these aren't found throughout Vietnam. Strangely, there are no banks at most of the land border crossings. The only way to change money at these places is on the black market.

If you only have travellers cheques, stock up on US dollars at a bank, which will usually charge anywhere from 0.5% to 2% commission to change them into cash. Vietcombank charges no commission for exchanging Amex travellers cheques; a reasonable 0.5% for other types.

If your travellers cheques are in currencies other than US dollars, they may be useless beyond the major cities. Hefty commissions are the norm if they can be exchanged at all.

PHOTOGRAPHY & VIDEO

Memory cards are pretty cheap in Vietnam, pretty fortunate given the visual feast awaiting even the amateur photographer. Most internet cafés can also burn photos on to a CD or DVD to free up storage space. It's worthwhile bringing the attachment for viewing your files on televisions, as many hotels come equipped with televisions.

Colour print film is widely available and prices are pretty reasonable at about US$2.50 for a roll of 36 print film. Slide film can be bought in Hanoi and HCMC, but don't count on it elsewhere. Supplies of black-and-white film are rapidly disappearing, so bring your own.

Photo-processing shops are located all over Vietnam and developing costs are about US$4 per roll depending on the print size selected. The quality is generally very good. Processing slide film is best saved for somewhere else. Printing digital shots is pretty cheap and works out at between 1000d and 2000d a photo.

Cameras are a reasonable price in Vietnam but the selection is limited. All other camera supplies are readily accessible in major towns, but soon dry up in remote areas.

The Vietnamese police usually don't care what you photograph, but on occasion they get pernickety. Obviously, don't photograph sensitive sites such as airports and border checkpoints. Don't even think of trying to get a snapshot of Ho Chi Minh in his glass sarcophagus!

Photographing anyone, particularly hill-tribe people, demands patience and the utmost respect for local customs (see p77). Photograph with discretion and manners. It's always polite to ask first and if the person says no, don't take the photo. If you promise to send a copy of the photo, make sure you do. For endless tips on better travel photography, pick up a copy of Lonely Planet's *Travel Photography*.

POST

Every city, town, village and rural subdistrict in Vietnam has some sort of post office *(buu dien)*. Post offices all over the country keep long hours, from about 6.30am to 9pm including weekends and public holidays (even Tet).

Vietnam has a pretty reliable post service these days. Gone are the days of your stamps being steamed off and your postcards being delivered to the rubbish bin. International postal rates are similar to those in European countries. Postcards cost from 7000d to 10,000d depending on the destination.

Items mailed from anywhere other than large towns and cities might take a month to arrive at their international destination. Airmail service from HCMC and Hanoi takes approximately five to 10 days to get to most Western countries. Express-mail service (EMS), available in the larger cities, is twice as fast as regular airmail and everything is registered.

Private couriers such as FedEx, DHL and UPS are reliable for transporting small parcels or documents.

Poste restante works well in post offices in Hanoi and HCMC. Foreigners must pay a small service charge for each letter received through the poste restante.

Receiving even a small package from abroad can cause a headache and large ones will produce a migraine. If the parcel contains books, documents, CDs, DVDs or dangerous goods it's possible that a lengthy inspection will be required, which could take anywhere from a few days to a few weeks.

SHOPPING

Vietnam has some fantastic shopping opportunities so it is well worth setting aside half a day or more to properly peruse. Hotspots include Hanoi, Hoi An and HCMC, each of which has a tempting selection of everything from avant-garde art to sumptuous silk suits. Some of the best buys on the block include gorgeous glazed pottery, classic lanterns, 'almost' antiques, embroidered tablecloths, fine furnishings, and lavish silk and linen creations in designer boutiques.

Art & Antiques

There are several good shops to hunt for art and antiques, but Vietnam has strict regulations on the export of real antiques, so be sure the items are allowed out of the country. Most reputable shops can provide the necessary paperwork.

Both traditional and modern paintings are a popular item. Cheaper mass-produced stuff is touted in souvenir shops and by street vendors. More sophisticated works are displayed in art galleries, with paintings from US$50 to US$500, but some of the hottest Vietnamese artists now fetch up to 10 times that. It's important to know that there are forgeries around – just because you spot a painting by a 'famous Vietnamese artist' does not mean that it's an original.

A Vietnamese speciality is the 'instant antique', such as a teapot or ceramic dinner plate, with a price tag of around US$2. Of course, it's OK to buy fake antiques as long as you aren't paying genuine prices.

Clothing

Forget the rubber sandals and pith helmets, Vietnam is emerging as a regional design centre and there are some extravagant creations in the boutiques of Hanoi and HCMC. Beautiful silk dresses cost a fraction of what they would at home, and men can get in on the action with some flamboyant shirts or sharp suits.

Ao dai (*ow*-zai in the north, *ow*-yai in the south) is the national dress for Vietnamese women and is a popular item to take home. Ready-made *ao dai* cost from US$15 to US$30, but custom numbers can cost a lot more but may be required due to sizing differentiation. There are *ao dai* tailors nationwide, but those in the tourist centres are more familiar with foreigners.

These days more and more hill-tribe gear is winding its way to shops in Hanoi and HCMC. It is brightly patterned stuff, but you may need to set the dyes yourself (try to soak the clothes in some salty water overnight) so those colours don't bleed all over the rest of your clothes. Alternatively, put it in a plastic bag and wait until you get home.

Women all over the country wear conical hats to keep the sun off their faces, though they also function as umbrellas in the rain. The best-quality conical hats are produced in the Hué area.

T-shirts are ever popular items with travellers. A printed shirt starts from 20,000d while an embroidered design will cost about 50,000d.

Handicrafts

Hot items on the tourist market include lacquerware, boxes and wooden screens with mother-of-pearl inlay, ceramics (check out the elephants), colourful embroidery, silk greeting cards, wood-block prints, oil paintings, watercolours, blinds made of hanging bamboo beads, reed mats, carpets, jewellery and leatherwork.

War Souvenirs

In places frequented by tourists, it's easy to buy what looks like equipment left over from the American War. However, almost all of these items are reproductions and your chances of finding anything original are slim.

The fake Zippo lighters engraved with platoon philosophy are still one of the hottest-selling items. You can pay extra to get one that's been beat up to look like a war relic, or just buy a brand-new shiny one for less.

Bargaining

Some bargaining is essential in most tourist transactions. Remember that in Asia 'saving face' is important, so bargaining should be good-natured. Smile and don't get angry or argue. In some cases you will be able to get a 50% discount or more, at other times this may only be 10%. And once the money is accepted, the deal is done. Don't waste time getting stressed if you find out someone else got it for less, it is about paying the price that is right for you, not always the 'right' price.

TELEPHONE & FAX

For the all-important numbers like emergency services and the international access code, check out the Quick Reference section on the inside cover of this book.

Every city has a **general information service** (☎ 1080) that provides everything from phone numbers and train and air timetables to exchange rates and the latest football scores. It even provides marriage counselling or bedtime lullabies for your child – no kidding! You can usually be connected to an operator who speaks English or French.

Domestic Calls

Phone numbers in Hanoi, HCMC and Haiphong have seven digits. Elsewhere around the country phone numbers have six digits. Telephone area codes are assigned according to the province.

Local calls can usually be made from any hotel or restaurant phone and are often free. Confirm this with the hotel so you don't receive any unpleasant surprises when you check out. Domestic long-distance calls are reasonably priced and cheaper if you dial direct. Save up to 20% by calling between 10pm and 5am.

International Calls

Charges for international calls from Vietnam have dropped significantly in the past few years. With the introduction of Voice Over Internet Protocol (VOIP), international phone calls to most countries cost a flat rate of just US$0.50 per minute. The service is easy to use from any phone in the country; just dial ☎ 17100, the country code and the number.

International and domestic long-distance calls can be made at hotels, but it's expensive at the smarter places. However, many of the cheaper hotels and guesthouses now operate VOIP services which are very cheap. Another option is to make these calls from the post office, which have handy displays telling you the cost of the call.

Reverse charges or collect calls are possible to most, but not all, Western countries including Australia, Canada, France, Japan, New Zealand, the UK and the USA.

Mobile (Cellular) Phones

Vietnam is putting a lot of money into its cellular network. Vietnam uses GSM 900/1800, which is compatible with most of Asia, Europe and Australia but not with North America.

If your phone has roaming, it is easy enough, if expensive, to make calls in Vietnam. Another option is to buy a SIM card with a local number to use in Vietnam.

There are at least six mobile phone companies battling it out in the local market with gimmicks galore to attract new customers. All these companies have offices and branches nationwide.

Be aware that mobile-phone numbers in Vietnam start with the prefix ☎ 09 and cost more to call than a local number.

Fax

Most post offices and hotels offer fax services. Hotels charge considerably more than the post office.

TIME

Vietnam is seven hours ahead of Greenwich Mean Time/Universal Time Coordinated (GMT/UTC). Because of its proximity to the equator, Vietnam does not have daylight-saving or summer time. When it's noon in Vietnam it is 9pm the previous day in Vancouver, midnight in New York, 5am in London and 3pm in Sydney.

TOILETS

The issue of toilets and what to do with used toilet paper causes some concern. In general, if there's a wastepaper basket next to the toilet, that is where the toilet paper goes, as many sewage systems cannot handle toilet paper.

Toilet paper is seldom provided in the toilets at bus and train stations or in other public buildings. You'd be wise to keep a stash of your own with you at all times while on the move.

Another thing to be mentally prepared for is squat toilets. For the uninitiated, a squat toilet has no seat for you to sit on while reading this guidebook; it's a hole in the floor. The only way to flush it is to fill the conveniently placed bucket with water and pour it into the hole. Most hotels will have Western-style loos, but squats are the norm in older hotels and public places.

The scarcity of public toilets is more of a problem for women than for men. Vietnamese men often urinate in public. Women might find road-side toilet stops easier if wearing a sarong.

TOURIST INFORMATION

Tourist offices in Vietnam have a different philosophy from the majority of tourist offices worldwide. These government-owned enterprises are really travel agencies whose primary interests are booking tours and turning a profit. Don't come here hoping for freebies.

Vietnam Tourism and Saigon Tourist are old examples of this genre, but nowadays every province has at least one such organisation. Travel cafés, budget agencies and your fellow travellers are a much better source of information than any of the so-called 'tourist offices'.

TRAVELLERS WITH DISABILITIES

Vietnam is not the easiest of places for disabled travellers, despite the fact that many Vietnamese are disabled as a result of war injuries. Tactical problems include the chaotic traffic, a lack of pedestrian footpaths, a lack of lifts in smaller hotels and the ubiquitous squat toilets.

That said, with some careful planning it is possible to have a relatively stress-free trip to Vietnam. Find a reliable company to make the travel arrangements and don't be afraid to double-check things with hotels and restaurants yourself. In the major cities many hotels have lifts and disabled access is improving. Bus and train travel is not really geared up for disabled travellers, but rent a private vehicle with a driver and almost anywhere becomes instantly accessible. As long as you are not too proud about how you get in and out of a boat or up some stairs, anything is possible, as the Vietnamese are always willing to help.

You might try contacting the following organisations:

Accessible Journeys (☎ 610-521 0339; www.disabilitytravel.com)

Mobility International USA (☎ 54-1343 1284; www.miusa.org)

Royal Association for Disability and Rehabilitation (Radar; ☎ 020-7250 3222; www.radar.org.uk)

Society for Accessible Travel & Hospitality (SATH; ☎ 212-447 7284; www.sath.org)

Lonely Planet's **Thorn Tree** (www.lonelyplanet.com) is a good place to seek the advice of other travellers.

VISAS

Tourist visas allow visitors to enter and exit Vietnam at Hanoi, HCMC and Danang airports or at any of its twelve land borders, three each with Cambodia and China, and six with Laos.

Tourist visas are valid for a single 30-day stay. The government often talks about issuing visas on arrival to certain favoured nationalities, but as yet this sensible scheme has failed to materialise. Arranging the paperwork for a Vietnamese visa has become fairly straightforward, but it remains expensive and unnecessarily time-consuming. Processing a tourist-visa application typically takes four or five working days in countries in the West.

It is possible to arrange a visa on arrival through a Vietnamese travel agent. They will need passport details in advance and will send a confirmation for the visa to be issued at your airport of arrival.

In Asia the best place to pick up a Vietnamese visa is Cambodia, where it costs around US$30 and can be arranged the same day. Bangkok is also a popular place as many agents offer cheap packages with an air ticket and visa thrown in.

If you plan to spend more than a month in Vietnam, or if you plan to exit Vietnam and enter again from Cambodia or Laos, arrange a three-month multiple-entry visa. These cost around US$95 in Cambodia, but are not available from all Vietnamese embassies.

In our experience personal appearance influences the reception you receive from airport immigration – if you wear shorts or scruffy clothing, look dirty or unshaven, you can expect problems. Try your best to look 'respectable'.

Business Visas

Business visas are usually valid for three or six months, allow multiple entries and the right to work. Getting a business visa has now become cheap and easy, although prices are about double those of a tourist visa. It is generally easier to apply for a business visa once in Vietnam, after having arrived on a tourist visa.

Student Visas

A student visa is usually arranged after your arrival. It's acceptable to enter Vietnam on a tourist visa, enrol in a Vietnamese language course and then apply at the immigration police for a change in status. In reality, the easiest way to do it is to contact a travel company and have them help you make the application.

Visa Extensions

If you've got the dollars, they've got the rubber stamp. Tourist-visa extensions cost as little US$10, but it is easier to pay more and sort this out through a travel agency. Getting the stamp yourself can be a bureaucratic nightmare. The procedure takes two or three days and you can only extend one time for 30 days.

In theory you should be able to extend your visa in any provincial capital. In practice it goes smoothest in major cities, such as HCMC, Hanoi, Danang and Hué, which cater to mass tourism.

Re-Entry Visas

It's possible to enter Cambodia, Laos or any other country from Vietnam and then re-enter without having to apply for another visa. However, you must apply for a re-entry visa *before* you leave Vietnam. If you do not have a re-entry visa, you will have to go through the whole Vietnamese visa nonsense again.

Re-entry visas are easiest to arrange in Hanoi or HCMC, but you will almost certainly have to ask a travel agent to do the paperwork for you. Travel agents charge about US$25 for this service and can complete the procedure in a day or two.

VOLUNTEERING

There are fewer opportunities for volunteering than one might imagine in a country such as Vietnam. This is partly due to the sheer number of professional development workers based here, and the fact that development is a pretty lucrative industry these days.

For information on volunteer work opportunities, chase up the full list of non- government organisations (NGOs) at the **NGO Resource Centre** (☎ 04-832 8570; www.ngocentre.org.vn; Hotel La Thanh, 218 Pho Doi Can, Hanoi), which keeps a database of all of the NGOs assisting Vietnam.

Try contacting the following organisations if you want to help in some way:

15 May School (www.15mayschool.org) A school in HCMC for disadvantaged children, which provides free education and vocational training.
Street Voices (www.streetvoices.com.au) Donate your skills, time or money to help give street children career opportunities. Street Voices' primary project is KOTO Restaurant (p111); check its website to see what you can do to help in Vietnam or Australia.

The other avenue is professional volunteering through an organisation back home that offers one- or two-year placements in Cambodia. One of the largest is **Voluntary Service Overseas** (VSO; www.vso.org.uk) in the UK, but other countries have their own organisations, including **Australian Volunteers International** (AVI; www.australianvolunteers.com) and **Volunteer Service Abroad** (VSA; www.vsa.org.nz). The UN also operates its own volunteer programme; details are available at www.unv.org. Other general volunteer sites with links all over the place include www.worldvolunteerweb.com, www.volunteerabroad.com and www.idealist.org.

WOMEN TRAVELLERS

Like Thailand and other predominantly Buddhist countries, Vietnam is relatively free of serious hassles for Western women. But it is a different story for some Asian women, particularly those who are young. It's not uncommon for an Asian woman accompanied by a Western male to be stereotyped as a Vietnamese prostitute. The fact that the couple could be married, or friends, doesn't seem to occur to everyone, or that the woman may not be Vietnamese at all. Asian women travelling in Vietnam with a Western male companion have occasionally reported verbal abuse.

However, there's no need to be overly paranoid, as locals are becoming more accustomed to seeing Asian women. Things have improved as more Vietnamese people are exposed to foreign visitors.

Sanitary napkins are available in larger cities, though tampons are harder to find.

WORK

Vietnam's opening up to capitalist countries has suddenly created all sorts of work opportunities for Westerners. The best-paid Westerners living in Vietnam are those working for international organisations or foreign companies, but most of these jobs are secured before arrival in the country.

Foreigners who look like Rambo have occasionally been approached by Vietnamese talent scouts wanting to recruit them to work as extras in war movies, but for most travellers the main work opportunities are teaching a foreign language.

English is by far the most popular foreign language with Vietnamese students, but some students also want to learn French. There is also a limited demand for teachers of Japanese, German, Spanish and Korean.

Government-run universities in Vietnam hire some foreign teachers. Pay is generally around US$5 to US$10 per hour, but benefits such as free housing and unlimited visa renewals are usually thrown in.

There is also a budding free market in private language centres and home tutoring; this is where most newly arrived foreigners seek work. Pay in the private sector is slightly better, at about US$6 to US$15 per hour, but these private schools won't offer the same extras as a government-run school. Private tutoring usually pays even better, at around US$10 to US$20 per hour.

Finding teaching jobs is quite easy in places such as HCMC and Hanoi, and is sometimes possible in towns that have universities. Pay in the smaller towns tends to be lower and work opportunities fewer.

Looking for employment is a matter of asking around – jobs are rarely advertised. The longer you stay, the easier it is to find work – travellers hoping to land a quick job and depart two months later will be disappointed. Check out the website www.livinginvietnam.com for job opportunities.

Transport

CONTENTS

GETTING THERE & AWAY

ENTERING VIETNAM

It's possible to enter Vietnam by train, plane, automobile and other forms of transport. Air is popular for those holidaying in Vietnam, while bus is the most common route for those travelling extensively in the region. Anyone planning on arriving from China should consider the spectacular train ride from Kunming in China's Yunnan province to Hanoi (although there are currently no trains on the Chinese side: check for updates). Entering from Cambodia, the boat ride down the Mekong River from Phnom Penh to Chau Doc is memorable.

Formalities at Vietnam's international airports are generally smoother than at land borders, as the volume of traffic is greater. That said, crossing overland from Cambodia and China is now relatively stress-free. Crossing the border between Vietnam and Laos remains somewhat stressful.

Passport

There are no 'suspect' stamps that will prevent foreigners from visiting Vietnam, but some Vietnamese who live overseas may be given a harder time by immigration and customs than non-Vietnamese visitors. Arranging a visa remains essential before arrival in Vietnam, but these are easy to obtain from embassies worldwide or through Vietnamese travel agents in advance (see p490).

AIR

Airports & Airlines

There are three international airports in Vietnam. **Tan Son Nhat airport** (SGN; ☎ 08-844 6665) serves Ho Chi Minh City (HCMC) and is Vietnam's busiest international air hub. Hanoi's **Noi Bai airport** (HAN; ☎ 04-886 5047) is the destination of choice for those concentrating on northern Vietnam, while a handful of international flights also serve **Danang airport** (DAD; ☎ 0511-830 339), a useful gateway to the charms of central Vietnam.

Vietnam Airlines (www.vietnamair.com.vn) Hanoi (☎ 04-943 9660) HCMC (☎ 08-832 0320) is the state-owned flag carrier, and the majority of flights into and out of Vietnam are joint operations between Vietnam Airlines and foreign airlines.

Vietnam Airlines has a modern fleet of Airbuses and Boeings and the level of service on its international flights is starting to catch up with its bigger rivals. However, on the domestic front, cancellations and late flights are still possible.

Many international flights leaving Hanoi connect through HCMC, but it's a headache. Passengers have to pay a domestic departure tax, fly to HCMC, claim their bags, check in again, and pay an international departure tax before boarding the international flight.

THINGS CHANGE...

The information in this chapter is particularly vulnerable to change. Check directly with the airline or a travel agent to make sure you understand how a fare (and ticket you may buy) works and be aware of the security requirements for international travel. Shop carefully. The details given in this chapter should be regarded as pointers and are not a substitute for your own careful, up-to-date research.

CLIMATE CHANGE & TRAVEL

Climate change is a serious threat to the ecosystems that humans rely upon, and air travel is the fastest-growing contributor to the problem. Lonely Planet regards travel, overall, as a global benefit, but believes we all have a responsibility to limit our personal impact on global warming.

Flying & Climate Change

Pretty much every form of motorised travel generates CO_2 (the main cause of human-induced climate change) but planes are far and away the worst offenders, not just because of the sheer distances they allow us to travel, but because they release greenhouse gases high into the atmosphere. The statistics are frightening: two people taking a return flight between Europe and the US will contribute as much to climate change as an average household's gas and electricity consumption over a whole year.

Carbon Offset Schemes

Climatecare.org and other websites use 'carbon calculators' that allow travellers to offset the level of greenhouse gases they are responsible for with financial contributions to sustainable travel schemes that reduce global warming – including projects in India, Honduras, Kazakhstan and Uganda.

Lonely Planet, together with Rough Guides and other concerned partners in the travel industry, support the carbon offset scheme run by climatecare.org. Lonely Planet offsets all of its staff and author travel. For more information check out our website: www.lonelyplanet.com.

AIRLINES FLYING TO & FROM VIETNAM

All phone numbers are in Hanoi (area code 04) unless otherwise stated.

Aeroflot (airline code SU; ☎ 771 8742; www.aeroflot.com; hub Moscow)
Air Asia (airline code AK; www.airasia.com; hub Kuala Lumpur)
Air France (airline code AF; ☎ 825 3484; www.airfrance.fr; hub Paris)
Asiana Airlines (airline code OZ; ☎ 831 5141; www.us.flyasiana.com; hub Seoul)
Cathay Pacific (airline code CX; ☎ 826 7298; www.cathaypacific.com; hub Hong Kong)
China Airlines (airline code CI; ☎ 824 2688; www.china-airlines.com; hub Taipei)
China Southern Airlines (airline code CZ; ☎ 771 6611; www.cs-air.com; hub Guangzhou)
Japan Airlines (airline code JL; ☎ 826 6693; www.jal.co.jp; hub Tokyo)
Jetstar Asia (airline code 3K; www.jetstarasia.com; hub Singapore)
Korean Air (airline code KE; ☎ in HCMC 08-824 2878; www.koreanair.com; hub Seoul)
Lao Airlines (airline code QV; ☎ 822 9951; www.laoairlines.com; hub Vientiane)
Lufthansa (airline code LH; ☎ in HCMC 08-829 8529; www.lufthansa.com; hub Frankfurt)
Malaysia Airlines (airline code MY; ☎ 826 8820; www.malaysiaairlines.com; hub Kuala Lumpur)
Philippine Airlines (airline code PR; ☎ in HCMC 08-822 2241; www.philippineair.com; hub Manila)
Qantas (airline code QF; ☎ 933 3025; www.qantas.com.au; hubs Sydney & Melbourne)
Singapore Airlines (airline code SQ; ☎ 826 8888; www.singaporeair.com; hub Singapore)
Thai Airways (airline code TG; ☎ 826 6893; www.thaiair.com; hub Bangkok)
Tiger Airways (airline code TR; www.tigerairways.com; hub Singapore)
United Airlines (airline code UA; ☎ in HCMC 08-823 1833; www.unitedairlines.com; hub Seattle)

Tickets

Shop around and it is possible to find a good deal to Vietnam. If there are no obvious bargains to Hanoi or HCMC, then consider buying a discounted ticket to Bangkok or Hong Kong and picking up a flight or travelling overland from Thailand on to Vietnam.

Discounted flights are available into Vietnam, but Vietnam Airlines will not allow foreign carriers to sell cheap outbound tickets from Vietnam. A ticket from Bangkok to Hanoi or HCMC costs almost half the price of a Vietnam Airlines' flight, if it's purchased

DEPARTURE TAX

There is an international departure tax of US$14 from the main airports at Hanoi, HCMC and Danang.

in Bangkok. This also means that for anyone planning to purchase a long-haul flight in the region, Vietnam is not the place to do it with Bangkok just a short hop away.

It's hard to get reservations for flights to/from Vietnam during holidays, especially Tet, which falls between late January and mid-February. If you will be in Vietnam during Tet, make reservations well in advance or you may find yourself marooned in a regional airport along the way. The chaos begins a week before Tet and can last for about two weeks after it.

Be aware that Vietnam is not the only country to celebrate the Lunar New Year, as it falls at the same time as Chinese New Year. Many people hit the road at this time, resulting in overbooked airlines, trains and hotels all over Asia.

Asia

Although many Asian countries now offer competitive deals, Bangkok, Singapore and Hong Kong are still the best places to shop around for discount tickets.

CAMBODIA

Vietnam Airlines currently has a monopoly on the Phnom Penh to HCMC route, with several flights a day. There are no direct flights from Phnom Penh to Hanoi, only via HCMC or Vientiane. Vietnam Airlines also offers numerous services daily between Siem Reap and HCMC and a couple of more expensive flights direct to Hanoi. A good agent is **Hanuman Tourism** (☎ 855-23 218356; www.hanumantourism.com; 12 St 310, Phnom Penh).

CHINA

Vietnam Airlines now offers links from Hanoi to several major cities in China, including Beijing, Guangzhou and Kunming. These routes are shared with Air China, China Southern Airlines and China Yunnan Airlines, respectively. The only direct flights between HCMC and mainland China are to Beijing and Guangzhou.

HONG KONG

Vietnam Airlines and Cathay Pacific jointly operate daily services between Hong Kong and both Hanoi and HCMC. The open-jaw option is a popular deal, allowing you to fly into one and out of the other.

Reliable travel agents in Hong Kong:

Four Seas Tours (☎ 2200 7760; www.fourseastravel.com)
STA Travel (☎ 2736 1618; www.statravel.com.hk)

JAPAN

ANA, Japan Airlines and Vietnam Airlines connect Hanoi and HCMC with Osaka and Tokyo. Cheaper indirect flights are available via other Asian capitals.

Recommended travel agents in Japan:

No 1 Travel (☎ 03-3205 6073; www.no1-travel.com)
STA Travel (☎ 03-5391 2922; www.statravel.co.jp)

LAOS

Both Lao Airlines and Vietnam Airlines operate daily flights between Vientiane and Hanoi or HCMC. There are also now several flights a week between Luang Prabang and Hanoi.

MALAYSIA

Malaysia Airlines and Vietnam Airlines have daily connections between Kuala Lumpur and both Hanoi and HCMC, but Air Asia is gaining favour thanks to low fares.

SINGAPORE

Singapore Airlines and Vietnam Airlines have daily flights from Singapore to both Hanoi and HCMC. Jetstar Asia and Tiger Airways are cheaper budget carriers and e-tickets can be booked via their websites. For reliable fares from Singapore to Vietnam, contact **STA Travel** (☎ 6737 7188; www.statravel.com.sg).

SOUTH KOREA

Asiana Airlines, Korean Air and Vietnam Airlines all fly the Seoul–HCMC route, so there's at least one flight offered per day. There are also several direct Seoul–Hanoi flights per week.

A good agent for ticketing in Seoul is **Joy Travel Service** (☎ 02-776 9871).

TAIWAN

Airlines flying from Taipei include China Airlines, Eva Air and Vietnam Airlines.

A long-running discount travel agent with a good reputation is **Jenny Su Travel** (☎ 02-2594 7733; jennysu@tpe.atti.net.tw).

THAILAND

Bangkok is still the most popular gateway to Vietnam. Air France, Thai Airways and Vietnam Airlines offer daily connections from Bangkok to Hanoi and HCMC. Air Asia is a cheaper option to both Hanoi and HCMC.

One popular choice is an open-jaw ticket that involves a flight to either HCMC or Hanoi, an overland journey to the other city, and a flight back to Bangkok.

Khao San Rd in Bangkok is the budget-travellers headquarters. If some of the agents there look too fly-by-night, try **STA Travel** (☎ 0 2236 0262; www.statravel.co.th).

Australia

Fares between Australia and Asia are relatively expensive considering the distances involved. Most of the cheaper flights between Australia and Vietnam involve stopovers at Kuala Lumpur, Bangkok or Singapore, but Qantas and Vietnam Airlines have services linking Brisbane, Melbourne, Perth and Sydney with either Hanoi or HCMC.

The following are good places to pick up tickets in Australia:

Flight Centre (☎ 133 133; www.flightcentre.com.au)
STA Travel (☎ 1300 733 035; www.statravel.com.au)

Canada

Discount tickets from Canada tend to cost about 10% more than those sold in the USA. For the lowdown on cheap fares, contact **Travel Cuts** (☎ 800-667 2887; www.travelcuts.com), with offices across the country.

Continental Europe

Although London is the discount-travel capital of Europe, major airlines and big travel agents usually have offers from all the major cities on the continent.

Recommended agents with branches across France:

Nouvelles Frontières (☎ 08 25 00 07 47; www.nouvelles-frontieres.fr)
OTU Voyages (www.otu.fr) This agency specialises in student and youth travel.
Voyageurs du Monde (☎ 01 40 15 11 15; www.vdm.com)

Reliable agencies in Germany:

Just Travel (☎ 089-747 33 30; www.justtravel.de)
STA Travel (☎ 0180-545 64 22; www.statravel.de)

From other countries in Europe, try the following agencies in Italy, Netherlands and Spain.

Airfair (☎ 0206-20 51 21; www.airfair.nl; Netherlands)
Barcelo Viajes (☎ 902 11 62 26; www.barceloviajes.com; Spain)
CTS Viaggi (☎ 064 62 04 31; www.cts.it; Italy)
NBBS Reizen (☎ 0206-20 50 71; www.nbbs.nl; Netherlands)
Nouvelles Frontières (☎ 902 17 09 79; www.nouvelles-frontieres.es; Spain)

New Zealand

The best way to get from New Zealand to Vietnam is to use one of the leading Asian carriers like Malaysian, Singapore or Thai. Good agencies to start shopping around for tickets:

Flight Centre (☎ 0800 243 544; www.flightcentre.co.nz)
STA Travel (☎ 0508 782 872; www.statravel.co.nz)

UK & Ireland

From London there are some great fares to Asia, although prices to Vietnam are not as cheap as to Bangkok or Hong Kong. There are oodles of agencies in the UK. Some of the best bets:

Flightbookers (☎ 087-0010 7000; www.ebookers.com)
North-South Travel (☎ 01245-608291; www.northsouthtravel.co.uk) North-South Travel donates part of its profit to projects in the developing world.
STA Travel (☎ 087-0160 0599; www.statravel.co.uk)
Trailfinders (☎ 084-5050 5891; www.trailfinders.co.uk)
Travel Bag (☎ 087-0890 1456; www.travelbag.co.uk)

USA

Discount travel agents in the USA are known as consolidators. San Francisco is the ticket-consolidator capital of America, although some good deals can be found in Los Angeles, New York and other big cities.

Useful online options in the USA:

- www.cheaptickets.com
- www.itn.net
- www.lowestfare.com
- www.sta.com
- www.travelocity.com

LAND

Vietnam shares land borders with Cambodia, China and Laos and there are several border crossings open to foreigners with each neighbour, a big improvement on a decade ago.

Border Crossings

It is essential to have a Vietnam visa before rocking up to the border, as they are not issued at land crossings. There are currently twelve international land borders: three each with Cambodia and China and six with Laos. We list the Vietnam side of the border first in the following country coverage. More are set

BORDER CROSSINGS

Country	Border Crossing	Connecting	Visa on Arrival
Cambodia	Moc Bai/Bavet	HCMC/Phnom Penh	Cambodia (Y)/Vietnam (N)
	Vinh Xuong/Kaam Samnor	Chau Doc/Phnom Penh	Cambodia (Y)/Vietnam (N)
	Tinh Bien/Phnom Den	Chau Doc/Takeo	Cambodia (N)/Vietnam (N)
China	Youyi Guan/Huu Nghi Quan (Friendship Gate)	Hanoi/Nanning	China (N)/Vietnam (N)
	Lao Cai/Hekou	Hanoi/Kunming	China (N)/Vietnam (N)
	Mong Cai/Dongxing	Mong Cai/Dongxing	China (N)/Vietnam (N)
Laos	Lao Bao/Dansavanh	Dong Ha/Savannakhet	Laos (Y)/Vietnam (N)
	Bo Y/Attapeu	Pleiku/Attapeu	Laos (N)/Vietnam (N)
	Cha Lo/Na Phao	Dong Hoi/Tha Kaek	Laos (N)/Vietnam (N)
	Nam Can/Nong Haet	Vinh/Phonsovan	Laos (Y)/Vietnam (N)
	Cau Treo/Nam Phao	Vinh/Tha Kaek	Laos (Y)/Vietnam (N)
	Na Meo/Nam Xoi	Thanh Hoa/Sam Neua	Laos (N)/Vietnam (N)

to open during the lifetime of this book, so ask around in Hanoi or HCMC for the latest information.

There are few legal money-changing facilities on the Vietnamese side of these crossings, so be sure to have some small-denomination US dollars handy. The black market is also an option for local currencies – Vietnamese dong, Chinese renminbi, Lao kip and Cambodian riel. Remember that black marketeers have a well-deserved reputation for shortchanging and outright theft.

Vietnamese police at the land-border crossings, especially the Lao borders, have a bad reputation for petty extortion. Most travellers find that it's much easier to exit Vietnam overland than it is to enter. Travellers at the border crossings are occasionally asked for an 'immigration fee' of some kind, although this is less common than it used to be.

CAMBODIA

The Moc Bai–Bavet border is the traditional favourite for a cheap and quick way between HCMC and Phnom Penh. For those willing to take their time, it is much nicer to meander through the Mekong Delta and travel by river between Chau Doc and Phnom Penh. One-month Cambodian visas are issued on arrival at Bavet and Kaam Samnor for US$20, but they are not currently available at Phnom Den. Overcharging is common at Kaam Samnor.

Moc Bai–Bavet

The most popular border crossing between Cambodia and Vietnam is Moc Bai (p373), which connects Vietnam's Tay Ninh province with Cambodia's Svay Rieng province. There are several buses daily between Phnom Penh and HCMC (via Moc Bai), usually departing around 8am, taking about six hours and costing as little as US$8.

Vinh Xuong–Kaam Samnor

A more pleasurable alternative to the Moc Bai crossing is the Vinh Xuong–Kaam Samnor border (p441) near Chau Doc. This offers the advantage of a leisurely look at the Mekong Delta without the bother of backtracking to HCMC.

There are two companies that offer luxury boat cruises between HCMC and Siem Reap via this border: the international player **Pandaw Cruises** (www.pandaw.com) and Cambodian company **Toum Teav Cruises** (www.cfmekong.com). Pandaw is an expensive option favoured by high-end tour companies, while Toum Teav is smaller and is well regarded for the personal service and excellent food.

Tinh Bien–Phnom Den

This border crossing point (p445) sees little traffic, as most visitors in Chau Doc tend to use the river crossing direct to Phnom Penh. It's relatively remote but the roads are in better shape than they used to be, so this crossing may start to see a trickle of travellers or cyclists.

CHINA

There are currently three border checkpoints where foreigners are permitted to cross between Vietnam and China: Huu Nghi Quan (the Friendship Pass), Lao Cai and Mong Cai.

TRANSPORT

It is necessary to arrange a Chinese visa in advance (US$30 for three months, add US$30 for same-day service) through the embassy in Hanoi (p468; 8.30am to 11am for visas).

The Vietnam–China border-crossing hours vary a little but are generally between 7am to 5pm (Vietnam time). Set your watch when you cross the border as the time in China is one hour ahead. Cross-border trade rumbles on all night, but foreigners can only cross during standard hours.

Youyi Guan–Huu Nghi Quan (Friendship Gate)

The busiest border crossing (p154) between Vietnam and China is located at the Vietnamese town of Dong Dang, 164km northeast of Hanoi. It connects Hanoi with Nanning and is on the overland route to Yuanshou and Hong Kong. Dong Dang is an obscure town, about 18km north of bustling Lang Son.

There is a twice-weekly international train between Beijing and Hanoi, departing on Tuesday and Friday at 6.30pm, that stops at Huu Nghi Quan (Friendship Pass). You can board or get off at numerous stations in China. The entire Hanoi–Beijing run is about 2951km and takes approximately 48 hours, including a three-hour delay (if you are lucky) at the border checkpoint.

Train tickets to China are more expensive in Hanoi, so some travellers prefer to buy a ticket to Dong Dang, cross the border and then buy another ticket on the Chinese side. While this plan involves a motorbike to the border and a bus or taxi on to Pingxiang, it helps avoid the three-hour delay while the international train is given the once over at the border checkpoint.

Lao Cai–Hekou

There's a 762km railway linking Hanoi with Kunming in China's Yunnan province. The border town on the Vietnamese side of this border crossing (p180) is Lao Cai, 294km from Hanoi. On the Chinese side, the border town is Hekou, 468km south of Kunming.

There are currently no trains on the Chinese side. You will need to leave the train on the Vietnamese side, cross into Hekou and arrange a bus (Y119; 12 hours) from there. There are several train services a day from Hanoi to Lao Cai, so it is easy to combine a stop at Sapa (p172) by bus before returning to Lao Cai when crossing this way.

> **CHINA GUIDEBOOKS CONFISCATED**
>
> Travellers entering China by road or rail from Vietnam report that Lonely Planet *China* guidebooks have been confiscated by border officials. The guidebook's maps show Taiwan as a separate country, and this is a sensitive issue. If you are carrying a copy of Lonely Planet's *China* guide, consider putting a cover on the book to make it less recognisable and, just to be safe, copy down any crucial details you might need while in China.

Mong Cai–Dongxing

Vietnam's third (but seldom-used) border crossing (p150) to China can be found at Mong Cai in the northeast of the country, opposite the Chinese city of Dongxing. It might be useful for anyone planning to travel between Halong Bay and Hainan Island, but otherwise it is well out of the way.

LAOS

There are six overland crossings and counting between Laos and Vietnam. Thirty-day Lao visas are now available at the busier borders, but not currently at Nam Xoi, Na Phao and the Attapeu border. We have received scores of letters complaining about immigration and local-transport hassles on the Vietnamese side of these borders. In fact, these border crossings are probably second only to Hanoi hotel scams in the volume of email they generate. Lies about journey times are common: yes, it really does take almost 24 hours to get from Hanoi to Vientiane and not 12. Worse are the devious drivers who stop the bus in the middle of nowhere and renegotiate the price. Transport links on both sides of the border can be very hit and miss, so don't use the more remote borders unless you have plenty of time, and patience, to play with.

Keep your ears open for news on the Tay Trang–Sop Hun border (see p171) near Dien Bien Phu (northwestern Vietnam) opening up to foreigners. This has been rumoured for years, but it might just happen this time.

Lao Bao–Dansavanh

Known as Lao Bao–Dansavanh (p210), this is the most popular border crossing between Laos and Vietnam and is usually the most hassle-free. The border town of Lao Bao is on

Hwy 9, 80km west of Dong Ha. Just across the border is the southern Lao province of Savannakhet; the first town you come to is Sepon. There is an international service from Hué to Savannakhet (US$15, nine hours, departing at 6am every second day) that passes through Dong Ha (US$12, 7½ hours, around 8am). Coming in the other direction there are daily buses from Savannakhet at 10pm.

Cau Treo–Nam Phao

Vietnam's Hwy 8 hits Laos at the Keo Nua Pass (734m), known as Cau Treo (p196) in Vietnamese, Kaew Neua in Lao.

The nearest Vietnamese city of any importance is Vinh, 96km east of the border. On the Lao side it's about 200km from the border to Tha Khaek. Most people use this border when travelling on the direct buses between Hanoi and Vientiane, but this is no picnic. In fact it's a set menu from hell. The journey takes about 24 hours and the buses get progressively more dangerous and overcrowded. The bus hardly stops for bathrooms or meals, but stops randomly when the driver fancies a sleep. Invariably the bus arrives at the border at an ungodly hour. Almost everyone ends up wishing they had flown! If you are a sucker for punishment, travel agents and guesthouses in Hanoi and Vientiane can help set you up, literally, for somewhere in the region of US$20 to US$25.

Nam Can–Nong Haet

The Nam Can–Nong Haet border (p195) links Vinh with Phonsovan and the Plain of Jars. On Tuesdays, Thursdays and Sundays it's possible to catch a bus at 6am from Vinh to Phonsavan (US$12, 11 hours, bookings Mr Lam ☎ 038-383 5782).

Cha Lo–Na Phao

There is a border at Cha Lo–Na Phao (p198) that links Dong Hoi and Tha Khaek, but very few travellers have used it until now. Two buses a week run between these two cities each week.

Na Meo–Nam Xoi

Arguably the most remote of remote borders is the Na Meo–Nam Xoi (p192) which connects Thanh Hoa, a transit town 153km south of Hanoi, with the town of Sam Neua and the famous Pathet Lao caves of Vieng Xai. This involves several changes of transport and a lot of overcharging. Some hardy travellers who have come this way have taken a full four days to get from Luang Prabang to Hanoi. Check out the box details if you dare (p481).

Bo Y–Attapeu

This is a new crossing (p276) that links Kon Tum and Quy Nhon with Attapeu and Pakse. The road and border only opened in mid-2006 and at the time of writing the crossing had still to be given a name. Transport is still sorting itself out but three Vietnamese-run buses link Attapeu and Pleiku (US$10, 12 hours), departing Attapeu at 9am Monday, Wednesday and Friday, coming the other way Tuesday, Thursday and Saturday. There are direct buses from Quy Nhon to Pakse (250,000d, 12 hours, four per week), but Lao visas are not available at this border.

Bus

It is possible to cross into Vietnam by bus from Cambodia or Laos. The most popular way from Cambodia is a cheap tourist shuttle via the Bavet–Moc Bai border crossing. From Laos, most travellers take the nightmare bus from Vientiane to Hanoi via the Cau Treo crossing or the easier route from Savannakhet in southern Laos to Hué in central Vietnam via the Lao Bao border crossing.

Car & Motorbike

It is theoretically possible to travel in and out of Vietnam by car or motorbike, but only through borders shared with Cambodia and Laos. However, in reality the bureaucracy makes this a real headache. It is generally easy enough to take a Vietnamese motorbike into Cambodia or Laos, but very difficult in the other direction. It is currently not possible to take any sort of vehicle into China from Vietnam.

Drivers of cars and riders of motorbikes will need the vehicle's registration papers, liability insurance and an International Driving Permit, in addition to a domestic licence. Most important is a *carnet de passage en douane*, which is effectively a passport for the vehicle and acts as a temporary waiver of import duty.

Train

Several international trains link China and Vietnam. The most scenic stretch of railway is between Hanoi and Kunming via Lao Cai, but the mammoth journey from Hanoi to Beijing via Lang Son is also a possibility. There are no railway lines linking Vietnam to Cambodia or Laos.

RIVER

There is a river border crossing between Cambodia and Vietnam on the banks of the Mekong. Regular fast boats ply the route between Phnom Penh in Cambodia and Chau Doc in Vietnam, with a change at the Vinh Xuong–Kaam Samnor border. There are also two river boats running all the way to the temples of Angkor at Siem Reap in Cambodia.

TOURS

Package tours to Vietnam are offered by travel agencies worldwide. Nearly all these tours follow one of a dozen or so set itineraries. Tours come in every shape and size from budget trips to ultimate indulgences. Tours booked outside Vietnam are not bad value when you tally everything up (flights, hotels, transport), but then again it's a cheap country for travelling.

It's easy enough to fly into Vietnam and make the travel arrangements after arrival (see p490). The main saving through booking before arrival is time, and if time is more precious than money, a pre-booked package tour is probably right for you.

Almost any good travel agency can book you on a standard mad-dash minibus tour around Vietnam. More noteworthy are the adventure tours arranged for people with a particular passion. These include speciality tours for cyclists, trekkers, bird-watchers, war veterans, culture vultures and gourmet travellers.

For a rewarding trip to Vietnam, consider contacting the following outfits:

Australia

Adventure World (☎ 02-8913 0755; www.adventureworld.com.au) Adventure tours to Vietnam, as well as Cambodia and Laos.
Griswalds Vietnamese Vacations (☎ 02-9564 5040; www.vietnamvacations.com.au) Popular Australian company offering affordable adventures.
Intrepid Travel (☎ 1300 360 667; www.intrepidtravel.com.au) Small group tours for all budgets with an environmental, social and cultural edge.
Peregrine (☎ 02-9290 2770; www.peregrine.net.au) Small-group and tailor-made tours supporting responsible tourism.
Wide Eyed Tours (☎ 02-9290 2770; www.wideeyedtours.com) Set up by former Intrepid tour leaders, this company offers tours all over Vietnam and has an office in the Old Quarter of Hanoi.

France

Compagnie des Indes & Orients (☎ 01 53 63 33 40; www.compagniesdumonde.com)
Intermedes (☎ 01 45 61 90 90; www.intermedes.com)
La Route des Indes (☎ 01 42 60 60 90; www.laroutedesindes.com)

New Zealand

Adventure World (☎ 09-524 5118; www.adventureworld.co.nz) A wide range of adventure tours covering the country.
Pacific Cycle Tours (☎ 03-972 9913; www.bike-nz.com) Mountain bike tours through Vietnam, plus hiking trips to off-the-beaten-path destinations.

UK

Audley Travel (☎ 01604-234855; www.audleytravel.com) Popular tailor-made specialist covering all of Vietnam
Cox & Kings (☎ 020-7873 5000; www.coxandkings.co.uk) Well-established high-end company, strong on cultural tours.
Exodus (☎ 020-8675 5550; www.exodus.co.uk) Popular adventure company with affordable overland trips.
Hands Up Holidays (☎ 0776-501 3631; www.handsupholidays.com) A new company bringing guests close to the people of Vietnam through its responsible holidays with a spot of volunteering.
Mekong Travel (☎ 01494-674456; www.mekong-travel.com) Mekong region specialist with in-depth knowledge of Vietnam.
Selective Asia (☎ 0845-370 3344; www.selectiveasia.com) New company that cherry-picks the best trips from leading local agents.
Symbiosis (☎ 020-7924 5906; www.symbiosis-travel.com) Small bespoke travel company with an emphasis on cycling and diving.
Wild Frontiers (☎ 020-7376 3968; www.wildfrontiers.co.uk) Adventure specialist with themed tours like Apocalypse Now.

USA

Asia Transpacific Journeys (☎ 800-642 2742; www.asiatranspacific.com) Group tours and tailor-made across the Asia-Pacific region.
Distant Horizons (☎ 800-333 1240; www.distant-horizons.com) Educational tours for discerning travellers.
Geographic Expeditions (☎ 800-777 8183; www.geoex.com) Well-established high-end adventure travel company.
Global Adrenaline (☎ 800-825 1680; www.globaladrenaline.com) Luxury adventures for the experienced traveller.

TRANSPORT

GETTING AROUND

AIR

Airlines in Vietnam

Vietnam Airlines (www.vietnamairlines.com.vn) has a monopoly on domestic flights, as it owns the only rival, **Pacific Airlines** (www.pacificairlines.com.vn), which flies the Hanoi–HCMC route and the HCMC–Danang route.

Most travel agents do not charge any more than when you book directly with the airline, as they receive a commission. A passport is required to make a booking on all domestic flights.

Vietnam Airlines has come a long way and many (but not all) branch offices accept credit cards for ticket purchases. The airline has retired its ancient Soviet-built fleet (thank heavens!) and purchased new Western-made aircraft.

> **DEPARTURE TAX**
>
> Domestic departure tax is 25,000d, but is included when you buy the ticket.

See the Air Routes map, below, for routes available within Vietnam.

BICYCLE

A great way to get around Vietnam's towns and cities is to do as the locals do and ride a bicycle. During rush hours, urban thoroughfares approach gridlock, as rushing streams of cyclists force their way through intersections without the benefit of traffic lights. In the countryside, Westerners on bicycles are often greeted enthusiastically by locals who don't see many foreigners pedalling around.

Long-distance cycling is popular in Vietnam. Much of the country is flat or only moderately hilly, and the major roads are in good shape. Safety, however, is a considerable concern. Bicycles can be transported around the country on the top of buses or in train baggage compartments. Lonely Planet's *Cycling Vietnam, Laos & Cambodia* gives the lowdown on cycling through Vietnam.

Decent bikes can be bought at a few speciality shops in Hanoi and HCMC, but it's better to bring your own if you plan on cycling over

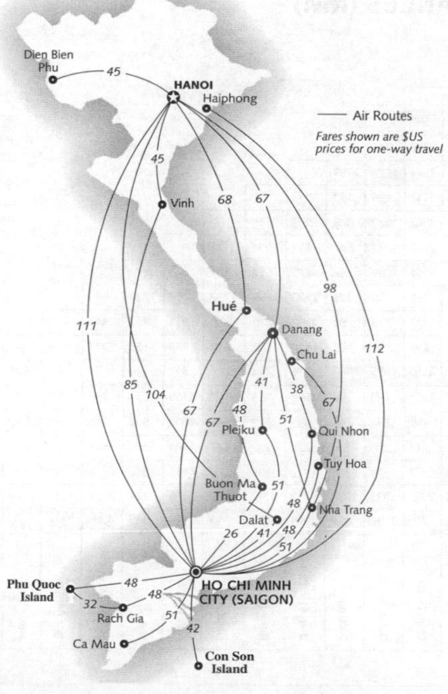

long distances. Mountain bikes are preferable, as large potholes or unsealed roads are rough on the rims. Basic cycling safety equipment and authentic spare parts are also in short supply, so bring all this from home. A bell or horn is mandatory – the louder the better.

Hotels and some travel agencies rent bicycles for about US$1 to US$5 per day and it is a great way to explore some of the smaller cities like Hué or Nha Trang. There are innumerable bicycle-repair stands along the side of the roads in every city and town in Vietnam.

Groups of foreign cyclists touring Vietnam are a common sight these days, and there are several tour companies that specialise in bicycling trips.

BOAT

Vietnam has an enormous number of rivers that are at least partly navigable, but the most important by far is the Mekong River and its tributaries. Scenic day trips by boat are possible on rivers in Hoi An, Danang, Hué, Tam Coc and even HCMC, but only in the Mekong Delta are boats used as a practical means of transport.

Boat trips are also possible on the sea. Cruising the islands of Halong Bay is a must for all visitors to north Vietnam. In the south, a trip to the islands off the coast of Nha Trang is popular.

In some parts of Vietnam, particularly the Mekong Delta, there are frequent ferry crossings. Don't stand between parked vehicles on the ferry as they can roll and you could wind up as the meat in the sandwich.

BUS

Vietnam has an extensive network of dirt-cheap buses that reach the far-flung corners of the country. Until recently, few foreign travellers used them because of safety concerns and overcharging, but the situation has improved dramatically with modern buses and fixed-price ticket offices at most bus stations.

Bus fleets are being upgraded as fast as the roads, so the old French, American and Russian buses from the '50s, '60s and '70s are becoming increasingly rare. On most popular routes, modern Korean buses are the flavour of the day. Most of these offer air-con and comfortable seats, but on the flipside most

ROAD DISTANCES (KM)

	Can Tho	Chau Doc	Dalat	Danang	Dien Bien Phu	Dong Ha	Haiphong	Halong City	Hanoi	Ho Chi Minh City	Hoi An	Hue	Lang Son	Kon Tum	Mui Ne	Nha Trang	Qui Nhon	Sapa
Can Tho	---																	
Chau Doc	116	---																
Dalat	477	593	---															
Danang	1141	1257	746	---														
Dien Bien Phu	2418	2534	1979	1233	---													
Dong Ha	1331	1447	936	190	1043	---												
Haiphong	1971	2087	1532	826	573	636	---											
Halong City	2026	2142	1587	881	691	691	55	---										
Hanoi	1948	2064	1509	763	470	617	103	165	---									
Ho Chi Minh City	169	285	308	972	2180	1169	1733	1788	1710	---								
Hoi An	1111	1227	716	30	1263	220	856	911	793	942	---							
Hué	1229	1445	854	108	1128	72	718	773	658	1097	138	---						
Lang Son	2094	2210	1655	909	616	763	249	311	146	1856	939	804	---					
Kon Tum	1053	1169	641	274	1507	464	1100	1155	1037	896	258	380	1183	---				
Mui Ne	379	495	257	762	1995	952	1548	1603	1525	210	732	870	1671	646	---			
Nha Trang	617	733	205	541	1774	731	1327	1383	1304	448	511	649	1450	436	238	---		
Qui Nhon	855	971	453	303	1536	493	1089	1144	1066	686	273	411	1212	198	979	470	---	
Sapa	2271	2388	1833	1087	253	897	427	489	324	2034	1117	979	470	1361	1849	1628	1390	---
Vinh	1629	1745	1190	484	789	294	342	397	319	1391	514	376	465	758	1206	985	747	643

of them are equipped with TVs and dreaded karaoke machines. You can ignore the crazy kung fu videos by closing your eyes (or wearing a blindfold), but you'd need to be deaf to sleep through the karaoke sessions – ear plugs are recommended!

Figuring out the bus system is not always that simple. Many cities have several bus stations, and responsibilities are divided according to the location of the destination (whether it is north or south of the city) and the type of service being offered (local or long distance, express or nonexpress).

Short-distance buses, mostly minibuses, depart when full (ie jam-packed with people and luggage). They often operate throughout the day, but don't count on many leaving after about 4pm.

Nonexpress buses and minibuses drop off and pick up as many passengers as possible along the route, so try to avoid these. The frequent stops make for a slow journey.

Express buses make a beeline from place to place. This is the deluxe class and you can usually be certain of there being enough space to sit comfortably. Such luxury comes at a price, but it's very cheap by Western standards.

It is also perfectly feasible (and highly recommended) to kick in with some fellow travellers and charter your own minibus.

If possible, try to travel during daylight hours only. Many drivers refuse to drive after dark because the unlit highways are teeming with bicycles and pedestrians who seem oblivious to the traffic. However, if you like living dangerously, there are some overnight buses.

Be aware that luggage is easily pilfered at toilet stops unless someone is looking after it. Bound to the rooftop, it should be safe from swift hands, but try to keep the bags in sight. A distinct disadvantage of having your gear on top is that it will be exposed to constant dust and sometimes heavy rain. You may want to consider putting your luggage in waterproof liners, if you can.

No matter how honest your fellow passengers might seem, never accept drinks from them, as there is a chance you may be drugged and robbed.

Reservations & Costs

Reservations aren't required for most of the frequent, popular services between towns and cities, but it doesn't hurt to purchase the ticket the day before if you're set on a specific departure time. Most major bus stations now have ticket offices with official prices clearly displayed. Always buy a ticket from the office, as bus drivers are notorious overchargers.

Costs are negligible, though on rural runs foreigners are typically charged anywhere from twice to 10 times the going rate. If you have to battle it out with the bus driver, it is helpful to determine the cost of the ticket for locals before starting negotiations. As a benchmark, a typical 100km ride is between US$2 and US$3.

Open Tours

In backpacker haunts throughout Vietnam, you'll see lots of signs advertising 'Open Tour', 'Open Date Ticket' or 'Open Ticket'. This is a bus service catering mostly to foreign budget travellers, not to Vietnamese. These air-con buses run between HCMC and Hanoi and people can hop on and hop off the bus at any major city along the route.

Competition has driven the price of these tours so low that it would practically only be cheaper if you walked. Sample prices from HCMC are as follows:

Route	Price
Ho Chi Minh City–Dalat	US$5
Ho Chi Minh City–Mui Ne	US$6
Ho Chi Minh City–Nha Trang	US$6
Ho Chi Minh City–Hoi An	US$13
Ho Chi Minh City–Hué	US$15
Ho Chi Minh City–Hanoi	US$23

In some ways they should raise the cost of the tickets and, by actually making money on the bus fare, allow passengers some freedom of choice on arrival at a destination. Unfortunately, they depend on kickbacks from a very elaborate and well-established network of sister hotels and restaurants along the way, making the whole experience feel like you are part of the herd.

As cheap and popular as it is, the open-tour deal is not the ideal way to experience Vietnam. Once you've bought the ticket, you're stuck with it. It really isolates visitors from Vietnam, as few locals travel this way. Buying shorter point-to-point tickets on the open-tour buses costs a bit more but you achieve more flexibility, including the chance to take a train, rent a motorbike or simply change plans.

Nevertheless, cheap open-tour tickets are a temptation and many people go for them. A couple of shorter routes to try are HCMC–Dalat and HCMC–Mui Ne Beach, two places that are not serviced by train.

If you are set on open-tour tickets, look for them at budget cafés in HCMC and Hanoi. From the original Sinh Café concept a decade ago, there are now lots of companies in on this game. Buses vary in size and standard, so a good rule of thumb is to turn up and check out the bus before committing to a company. Sinh Café still has some of the best buses, closely followed by Hanh Café.

CAR & MOTORBIKE

The relative affordability of vehicle hire makes the latter a popular option. Having your own set of wheels gives you maximum flexibility to visit remote regions and stop when and where you please.

Driving Licence

In order to drive a car in Vietnam, you need a Vietnamese licence and an International Driving Permit, usually issued by your automobile association back home. When it comes to renting motorbikes, it's a case of no licence required.

Fuel & Spare Parts

Fuel is pretty cheap in Vietnam, at around 10,000d a litre. Fuel is readily available throughout the country, but prices rise in rural areas. Even the most isolated communities usually have someone selling petrol out of Fanta or Johnnie Walker bottles. Some sellers mix this fuel with kerosene to make a quick profit – use it sparingly, in emergencies only.

When it comes to spare parts, Vietnam is awash with Japanese motorbikes, so it is easy to get parts for Hondas, Yamahas or Suzukis, but finding a part for a Harley or a Ducati is another matter. Likewise for cars, spares for Japanese cars are easy to come by, as are spares for international brands manufactured in Vietnam like Ford and Mercedes. But if you are driving something obscure, whether with two wheels or four, bring substantial spares.

Hire

The major considerations are safety, the mechanical condition of the vehicle, reliability of the rental agency and your budget. Don't think about driving a car yourself in Vietnam (a motorbike is challenging enough) and moreover, hire charges for the car include a driver.

CAR & MINIBUS

Self-drive rental cars have yet to make their debut in Vietnam, which is a blessing in disguise given traffic conditions, but cars with drivers are popular and plentiful. Renting a vehicle with a driver and guide is a realistic option even for budget travellers, providing you have friends to share the cost.

Hanoi and HCMC have an especially wide selection of travel agencies that rent vehicles. For sightseeing trips around HCMC or Hanoi, a car with driver can also be rented by the day. It costs about US$25 to US$50 per day, depending on the car.

Renting a minibus (van) is good value for larger groups, as they hold between eight and 15 passengers. They are also a smart option for small groups planning to travel long distances at night, as everyone can stretch out.

For the really bad roads of northwestern Vietnam, the only reasonably safe vehicle is a 4WD. Without one, the muddy mountain roads can be deadly. In Vietnam, 4WDs come in different flavours – the cheapest (and least comfortable) are Russian made, while more cushy Korean and Japanese vehicles with air-con are about twice the price. Expect to pay about US$80 to US$100 a day for a decent 4WD in the far north of Vietnam.

MOTORBIKE

Motorbikes can be rented from cafés, hotels, motorbike shops and travel agencies. If you don't fancy self-drive, there are plenty of local drivers willing to act as a chauffeur and guide for around US$6 to US$10 per day.

Renting a 100cc moped is cheap from around US$5 per day, usually with unlimited mileage. To tackle the mountains of the north, it is best to go with a Minsk. The 'mule of the mountains', these sturdy Russian steeds don't look up to much, but they are designed to get you through, or over, anything. They are available for rent from specialist shops in Hanoi (see p122). For the ultimate experience in mountains of the north, consider joining a motorbike tour to discover the secret backroads; see p491 for more on motorbike touring companies.

Most places will ask to keep your passport until you return the bike. Try and sign some sort of agreement – preferably in a language you understand – clearly stating what you are renting, how much it costs, the extent of compensation and so on. For more information, see p465.

Insurance

If you are travelling in a tourist vehicle with a driver, then it is almost guaranteed to be insured. When it comes to motorbikes, many rental bikes are not insured and you will have to sign a contract agreeing to a valuation for the bike if it is stolen. Make sure you have a strong lock and always leave it in guarded parking where available.

Do not even consider renting a motorbike if you are daft enough to be travelling in Vietnam without insurance. The cost of treating serious injuries can be bankrupting for budget travellers.

Road Conditions & Hazards

Road safety is definitely not one of Vietnam's strong points. The intercity road network of two-lane highways is becoming more and more dangerous. High-speed, head-on collisions between buses, trucks and other smaller vehicles (such as motorbikes and bicycles) have become a sickeningly familiar sight on the major highways. Vietnam does not have an efficient emergency-rescue system, so if something happens on the road, it could be some time until even rudimentary medical treatment. Locals might help in extreme circumstances, but in most cases it will be up to you or your guide to get you to the hospital or clinic.

In general, the major highways are hard surfaced and reasonably well maintained, but seasonal flooding can be a problem. A big typhoon can create potholes the size of bomb craters. In remote areas, roads are not surfaced and transform themselves into a sea of mud when the weather turns bad – such roads are best tackled with a 4WD vehicle or motorbike. Mountain roads are particularly dangerous: landslides, falling rocks and runaway vehicles can add an unwelcome edge to your journey. The occasional roadside shrine often indicates where a bus has plunged into the abyss.

For motorbikers, serious sunburn is a major risk and well worth preventing. The cooling breeze prevents you from realising how badly you are burning until it's too late. Cover up exposed skin or wear sunscreen. Bikers also must consider the opposite problem – occasional heavy rains. A rainsuit or poncho is essential, especially during the monsoon season.

Road Rules

Basically, there aren't many, arguably any. Size matters and the biggest vehicle wins by default. Be particularly careful about children on the road. It's common to find kids playing hopscotch in the middle of a major highway. Livestock on the road is also a menace; hit a cow on a motorbike and you'll both be hamburger.

Although the police frequently stop drivers and fine them for all sorts of real and imagined offences, speeding is the flavour of the month. New speed limits are surprisingly slow, probably a way to ensure more revenue from fines. In cities, there is a rule that you cannot turn right on a red light. It's easy to run afoul of this law in Vietnam and the police will fine you for this offence.

Honking at all pedestrians and bicycles (to warn them of your approach) is considered a basic element of safe driving – larger trucks and buses might as well have a dynamo-driven horn.

There is no national seat-belt law and the locals often laugh at foreigners who insist on using seat belts. Helmets are now required for motorbike riders on national highways and, although this is not always enforced, it's wise to make it a personal rule. Decent helmets are available in HCMC and Hanoi for around US$20.

Legally a motorbike can carry only two people, but we've seen up to seven on one vehicle…plus luggage! This law is enforced in major cities, but ignored in rural areas.

HITCHING

Hitching is never entirely safe in any country in the world, and we don't recommend it. Travellers who decide to hitch should understand that they are taking a potentially serious risk. People who do choose to hitch will be safer if they travel in pairs and let someone know where they are planning to go.

LOCAL TRANSPORT

Bus

The bus systems in Hanoi and HCMC have improved immeasurably in the past few years. Get your hands on a bus map and it is now possible to navigate the suburbs cheaply and efficiently. Some of the most popular sights in Hanoi and HCMC are accessible by public transport, making for a cheap visit. However, many travellers prefer other fast and economical options, such as meter taxis, *cyclos* and motorbike taxis.

Cyclo

The *cyclo* (*xich*-lo), from the French *cyclo-pousse*, offers cheap and environmentally friendly transportation around Vietnam's sprawling cities.

Groups of *cyclo* drivers always hang out near major hotels and markets, and many speak at least broken English. To make sure the driver understands where you want to go, it's useful to bring a city map. Bargaining is imperative. Settle on a fare before going anywhere or you're likely to get stiffed.

As a basic rule, short rides around town should cost about 10,000d. For a longer ride or a night ride, expect to pay double that or more. It pays to have the exact change when taking a *cyclo*, as drivers may claim they don't have change. *Cyclos* are cheaper by time rather than distance. A typical price is US$1 to US$2 per hour.

There have been many stories of travellers being mugged by their *cyclo* drivers in HCMC so, as a general rule of thumb, hire *cyclos* only during the day. When leaving a bar late at night, take a meter taxi.

Taxi

Western-style taxis with meters, found in most major cities, are very, very cheap by international standards and a safe way to travel around at night. Average tariffs are about 10,000d per kilometre. However, there are many dodgy taxis roaming the streets of Hanoi and HCMC and the meters are clocked to run at two or three times the normal pace. Only travel with reputable or recommended companies. See the Getting Around sections in Hanoi and HCMC for listings.

Xe Om

The *xe om* (*zay*-ohm) is a motorbike that carries one passenger, like a two-wheeled taxi. *Xe* means motorbike, and *om* means hug (or hold), so you get the picture. Getting around by *xe om* is easy, as long as you don't have a lot of luggage.

Fares are comparable with those for a *cyclo*, but negotiate the price beforehand. There are plenty of *xe om* drivers hanging around street corners, markets, hotels and bus stations. They will find you before you find them…

TOURS

We are drowning in letters complaining about the quality of bottom-end budget tours being peddled in HCMC and Hanoi. Some are better than others, but remember the old adage that 'you get what you pay for'. Tour-operator gimmicks like 'one free beer' or '10 minutes of internet' are not a promising sign.

Renting a car with a driver and guide gives you the chance to design a tailor-made itinerary for you and your companions. Seeing the country this way is almost like independent travel, except that it's more comfortable, less time-consuming and allows for stops anywhere, or everywhere, along the way.

The cost varies considerably. At the high end are tours booked through government travel agencies and upmarket tour companies, while budget and midrange companies can usually arrange something just as enjoyable at a cheaper price.

The price typically includes accommodation, a guide, a driver and a car. The cost of the car depends largely on the type of vehicle.

Once you've settled on an itinerary, get a copy from the travel agency. If you find that your guide is making it up as they go along, ignoring the agreed itinerary, that piece of paper is your most effective leverage.

A good guide can be your translator and travelling companion, and can usually save you as much money along the way as they cost you. A bad guide can ruin your trip. If possible, you should meet your guide before starting out – make sure that this is someone you can travel with.

Travelling with a freelance guide, you are usually responsible for their travel expenses, but if you pay for a package through a company, any expenses for the guide and driver should be included.

For trips in and around big cities like HCMC and Hanoi, you'll often find women working as guides. However, it seems relatively few women are employed as guides on long-distance trips.

The following are Vietnam-based travel agencies who offer premium tours throughout Vietnam and Indochina:

Buffalo Tours (Map p96; ☎ 04-828 0702; www.buffalotours.com; 11 Pho Hang Muoi, Hanoi)

THE REUNIFICATION EXPRESS

Construction of the 1726km-long Hanoi–Saigon railway, the Transindochinois, began in 1899 and was completed in 1936. In the late 1930s the trip from Hanoi to Saigon took 40 hours and 20 minutes at an average speed of 43km/h. During WWII the Japanese made extensive use of the rail system, resulting in Viet Minh sabotage on the ground and US bombing from the air. After WWII efforts were made to repair the Transindochinois, major parts of which were either damaged or had become overgrown.

During the Franco-Viet Minh War, the Viet Minh engaged in sabotage against the rail system. At night the Viet Minh made off with rails to create a 300km network of tracks (between Ninh Hoa and Danang) in an area wholly under their control – the French quickly responded with their own sabotage.

In the late 1950s the South, with US funding, reconstructed the track between Saigon and Hué, a distance of 1041km. But between 1961 and 1964 alone, 795 Viet Cong attacks were launched on the rail system, forcing the abandonment of large sections of track (including the Dalat spur).

By 1960 the North had repaired 1000km of track, mostly between Hanoi and China. During the US air war against the North, the northern rail network was repeatedly bombed. Even now clusters of bomb craters can be seen around virtually every rail bridge and train station in the north.

After reunification the government immediately set about re-establishing the Hanoi–Ho Chi Minh City (HCMC) rail link as a symbol of Vietnamese unity. By the time the *Reunification Express* trains were inaugurated on 31 December 1976, 1334 bridges, 27 tunnels, 158 stations and 1370 shunts (switches) had been repaired.

Today the *Reunification Express* chugs along slightly faster than the trains did in the 1930s, at an average of 50km/h.

Destination Asia (☎ 08-844 8071; www.destination-asia.com; 143 Đ Nguyen Van Troi, Phu Nhuan district, HCMC)
Exotissimo (☎ 04-828 2150; www.exotissimo.com; 26 Tran Nhat Duat, Hanoi)
Sinhbalo Adventures (Map p357; ☎ 08-837 6766; www.sinhbalo.com; 283/20 Đ Pham Ngu Lao, District 1, HCMC)
Sisters Tours (☎ 04-562 2733; www.sisterstoursvietnam.com; 37 Đ Thai Thinh, Hanoi)
Tonkin Travel (☎ 08-747 3239; www.tonkintravel.com; 8, 34A Đ Tran Phu, Hanoi)

For a list of recommended budget and midrange operators running tours of northern Vietnam out of Hanoi, see p91.

Motorbike Tours

Specialised motorbike tours through Vietnam are growing in popularity. It is a great way to get off the trail and explore the mountainous regions of the north and centre of the country. Two-wheels can reach the parts that four-wheels sometimes can't, traversing small trails and traffic-free backroads. A little experience helps, but many of leading companies also offer tuition for first-timers. Mounting a Minsk to take on the peaks of the north is one of Vietnam's defining moments and should not be missed.

Foreign guides charge considerably more than local Vietnamese guides. Based on a group of four people, you can expect to pay around US$100 per day per person for an all-inclusive tour providing motorbike rental, petrol, guide, food and accommodation. Some of the best companies running trips in the north include the following:

Explore Indochina (☎ 0913-524 658; www.exploreindochina.com) Run by Digby, Dan and Thuan, these guys have biked all over the country and can take you to the parts others cannot reach. You can usually find them at Highway 4 (Map pp88-9), a bar on Pho Hang Tre. Prices are around US$135 per day.
Free Wheelin Tours (☎ 04-747 0545; www.freewheelin-tours.com) Run by Fredo (Binh in Vietnamese), who speaks French, English and Vietnamese, this company has its own homestays in the northeast, plus 4WD trips. Prices start from just US$70 per day with a group of four. It's located opposite Cuong Minsk on Luong Ngoc Quyen
Voyage Vietnam (☎ 04-926 2373; www.voyagevietnam.net) A newer, locally run outfit, this company is quickly earning itself a good reputation. Prices start from around US$60 per day.

For more on the Easy Riders operating out of Dalat, see p310. There are a host of other motorbike and bicycle day trips covered under individual towns throughout this book.

TRAIN

The 2600km Vietnamese railway system, operated by **Vietnam Railways** (Duong Sat Viet Nam; ☎ 04-747 0308; www.vr.com.vn), runs along the coast between HCMC and Hanoi, and links the capital with Hai Phong and northern towns. While sometimes even slower than buses, trains offer a more relaxing way to get around and more room than the jam-packed buses. The trains are also considered safer than the country's kamikaze bus fleet.

Vietnam's railway authority has been rapidly upgrading trains and facilities – with air-con sleeping berths and dining cars available now on express trains – and lowering the price for foreigners. Foreigners and Vietnamese are now charged the same price, a big change from a few years ago when foreigners were charged 400% more.

The quickest train journey between Hanoi and HCMC takes 30 hours. The slowest express train on this route takes 41 hours. There are also local trains that only cover short routes, but these can crawl along at 15km/h, as there is only one track with many passing points and local trains have the lowest priority. Vietnam is planning a massive overhaul of its rail network in the next decade, including the introduction of high-speed trains. Hoorah!

Petty crime is a problem on Vietnamese trains. While there doesn't seem to be organised pack-napping gangs, such as those in India, thieves have become proficient at grabbing packs through the windows as trains pull out of stations. Always keep your bag nearby and lock or tie it to something, especially at night.

Another hazard is children throwing rocks at the train. Passengers have been severely injured this way and many conductors insist that you keep down the metal window shield. Unfortunately, however, these shields also obstruct the view.

Bicycles and motorbikes must travel in the freight car. Just make sure that the train you are on has a freight car (most have) or your bike will arrive later than you do.

Eating is easy, as there are vendors at every station who board the train and practically stuff food, drinks and cigarettes into your pockets. The food supplied by the railway company, included in the ticket price on some long journeys, isn't Michelin-starred. It's a good idea to stock up on your favourite munchies before taking a long trip.

Odd-numbered trains travel south and even-numbered ones travel north. The fastest train service is provided by the *Reunification Express*, which runs between HCMC and Hanoi, making only a few short stops en route. If you want to stop at some obscure point between the major towns, use one of the slower local trains or catch a bus.

Aside from the main HCMC–Hanoi run, three rail-spur lines link Hanoi with the other parts of northern Vietnam. One runs east to the port city of Hai Phong. A second heads northeast to Lang Son, crosses the border and continues to Nanning, China. A third goes northwest to Lao Cai and on to Kunming, China.

Several *Reunification Express* trains depart from HCMC's Saigon station between 9am and 10.30pm every day. In the other direction, there are departures from Hanoi between 5am and 6.40pm daily.

The train schedules change frequently. The timetables for all trains are posted on the Vietnam Railway website and at major stations. Another excellent resource is the

REUNIFICATION EXPRESS FARES FROM HANOI

Hanoi–HCMC (S1 Express Train); 33 hours

Station	Soft seat air-con	Bottom hard air-con (6 berth)	Bottom soft air-con (4 berth)
Vinh	113,000d	168,000d	180,000d
Dong Hoi	196,000d	290,000d	310,000d
Hué	260,000d	417,000d	445,000d
Danang	297,000d	462,000d	478,000d
Nha Trang	513,000d	834,000d	890,000d
HCMC	612,000d	905,000d	965,000d

Man in Seat Sixty-One (www.seat61.com/vietnam.htm), the top international train website. Most travel agents and some hotels keep a copy of the latest schedule on hand. In HCMC call or visit the **Saigon Railways Tourist Service** (☎ 08-836 7640; 275C Đ Pham Ngu Lao, District 1) in the Pham Ngu Lao area.

It's important to realise that the train schedule is 'bare-bones' during the Tet festival. The *Reunification Express* is suspended for nine days, beginning four days before Tet and continuing for four days afterwards.

Classes

There are four main classes of train travel in Vietnam: hard seat, soft seat, hard sleeper and soft sleeper. The latter three are also split into air-con and nonair-con options; presently, air-con is only available on the faster express trains. Since it's all that many Vietnamese can afford, hard-seat class is usually packed. Hard seat is tolerable for day travel, but overnight it is worse than the bus. Soft-seat carriages have vinyl-covered seats rather than the uncomfortable hard benches.

A hard sleeper has three tiers of beds (six beds per compartment). Because of limited head room and the climb, the upper berth is cheapest, followed by the middle berth and finally the lower berth. There is no door to separate the compartment from the corridor. Soft sleeper has two tiers (four beds per compartment) and all bunks are priced the same. These compartments have a door.

Costs

Ticket prices vary depending on the train, and the fastest trains are naturally the most expensive. See the table, p492, for some sample fares from Hanoi to stations south. For all the details on trains from Hanoi to Haiphong (p136), Lao Cai (p180) and Lang Son (p154), see the relevant sections.

Reservations

The supply of train seats is frequently insufficient to meet demand. Reservations for all trips should be made at least one day in advance. For sleeping berths, it is wise to book several days before the date of departure. You'll need to bring your passport when buying train tickets.

Many travel agencies, hotels and cafés sell train tickets for a small commission, and this can save considerable time and trouble. It's a good idea to make reservations for onward travel as soon as you arrive in a city.

WALKING

If you don't want to wind up like a bug on a windshield, pay close attention to a few pedestrian survival rules when crossing the street, especially on the streets of motorbike-crazed HCMC and Hanoi. Foreigners frequently make the mistake of thinking that the best way to cross a busy street in Vietnam is to run quickly across it. This does not always work in practice, and could get you creamed. Most Vietnamese cross the street slowly – very slowly – giving the motorbike drivers sufficient time to judge their position so they can pass on either side. They won't stop or even slow down, but they will try to avoid hitting you. Just don't make any sudden moves. Good luck!

Health Dr Trish Batchelor

CONTENTS

Health issues and the quality of medical facilities vary enormously depending on where and how you travel in Vietnam. Many of the major cities are now very well developed, although travel to rural areas can expose you to a variety of health risks and inadequate medical care.

Travellers tend to worry about contracting infectious diseases when in the tropics, but infections are a rare cause of serious illness or death in travellers. Pre-existing medical conditions such as heart disease, and accidental injury (especially traffic accidents), account for most life-threatening problems.

Becoming ill in some way, however, is a relatively common thing. Fortunately most common illnesses can either be prevented with some common-sense behaviour or be treated easily with a well-stocked traveller's medical kit.

The following advice is a general guide only and does not replace the advice of a doctor trained in tropical medicine.

BEFORE YOU GO

Pack medications in their original, clearly labelled, containers. A signed and dated letter from your physician describing your medical conditions and medications, including generic names, is also a good idea. If carrying syringes or needles, be sure to have a physician's letter documenting their medical necessity. If you have a heart condition bring a copy of your ECG taken just prior to travelling.

If you happen to take any regular medication bring double your needs in case of loss or theft. In most Southeast Asian countries you can buy many medications over the counter without a doctor's prescription, but it can be difficult to find some of the newer drugs, particularly the latest antidepressant drugs, blood pressure medications and contraceptive pills.

HEALTH ADVISORIES

It's usually a good idea to consult your government's travel-health website before departure, if one is available:

Australia (www.dfat.gov.au/travel)
Canada (www.travelhealth.gc.ca)
New Zealand (www.mfat.govt.nz/travel)
UK (http://www.dh.gov.uk/Policyandguidance/Healthadvicefortravellers/fs/en)
US (www.cdc.gov/travel)

INSURANCE

Even if you are fit and healthy, don't travel without health insurance – accidents do happen. Declare any existing medical conditions you have – the insurance company *will* check if your problem is pre-existing and will not cover you if it is undeclared. You may require extra cover for adventure activities such as rock climbing. If your health insurance doesn't cover you for medical expenses abroad, consider getting extra insurance – check **LonelyPlanet.com** (www.lonelyplanet.com) for more information. If you're uninsured, emergency evacuation is expensive; bills of over US$100,000 are not uncommon.

You should find out in advance if your insurance plan will make payments directly to providers or if they reimburse you later for overseas health expenditures. (Note that in many countries doctors expect payment in cash.) Some policies offer lower and higher medical-expense options; the higher ones are chiefly for countries that have extremely high medical costs, such as the USA.

You may prefer a policy that pays doctors or hospitals directly rather than you having to pay on the spot and claim later. If you have to claim later, make sure you keep all documentation. Some policies ask you to call back (reverse charges) to a centre in your home country where an immediate assessment of your problem is made.

VACCINATIONS

The only vaccine required by international regulations is yellow fever. Proof of vaccination will only be required if you have visited a country in the yellow-fever zone within the six days prior to entering Vietnam. If you are travelling to Vietnam from Africa or South America you should check to see if you require proof of vaccination.

Specialised travel-medicine clinics are your best source of information; they stock all available vaccines and will be able to give specific recommendations for you and your trip. The doctors will take into account factors such as past vaccination history, the length of your trip, activities you may be undertaking, and underlying medical conditions, such as pregnancy.

Most vaccines don't produce immunity until at least two weeks after they're given, so visit a doctor four to eight weeks before departure. Ask your doctor for an International Certificate of Vaccination (otherwise known as the yellow booklet), which will list all the vaccinations you've received. In the US, the yellow booklet is no longer issued, but it is highly unlikely the Vietnam authorities will ask for proof of vaccinations (unless you have recently been in a yellow-fever affected country).

For info on current immunisation recommendations for Vietnam, contact the international team of doctors at the **Family Medical Practice** (www.doctorkot.com) in Hanoi (p90) and HCMC (p337). They can provide the latest information on vaccinations, malaria and dengue-fever status, and offer general medical advice regarding Vietnam.

See the boxed text, p496, for possible vaccinations you may require.

MEDICAL CHECKLIST

Recommended items for a personal medical kit:

- antibacterial cream, eg Muciprocin
- antibiotics for skin infections, eg Amoxicillin/Clavulanate or Cephalexin
- antibiotics for diarrhoea, eg Norfloxacin or Ciprofloxacin; Azithromycin for bacterial diarrhoea; and Tinidazole for giardiasis or amoebic dysentery
- antifungal cream, eg Clotrimazole
- antihistamines for allergies, eg Cetrizine for daytime and Promethazine for night
- anti-inflammatories, eg Ibuprofen
- antinausea medication, eg Prochlorperazine
- antiseptic for cuts and scrapes, eg Betadine
- antispasmodic for stomach cramps, eg Buscopa
- contraceptives
- decongestant for colds and flus, eg Pseudoephedrine
- DEET-based insect repellent
- diarrhoea 'stopper', eg Loperamide
- first-aid items such as scissors, plasters (Band Aids), bandages, gauze, thermometer (electronic, not mercury), sterile needles and syringes, safety pins and tweezers
- indigestion medication, eg Quick Eze or Mylanta
- iodine tablets (unless you are pregnant or have a thyroid problem) to purify water
- laxatives, eg Coloxyl
- migraine medication (your personal brand), if a migraine sufferer
- oral-rehydration solution for diarrhoea, eg Gastrolyte
- paracetamol for pain
- permethrin (to impregnate clothing and mosquito nets) for repelling insects
- steroid cream for allergic/itchy rashes, eg 1% to 2% hydrocortisone
- sunscreen and hat
- throat lozenges
- thrush (vaginal yeast infection) treatment, eg Clotrimazole pessaries or Diflucan tablet
- urine alkalisation agent, eg Ural, if you're prone to urinary tract infections.

INTERNET RESOURCES

There is a wealth of travel health advice on the Internet. For further information, **LonelyPlanet.com** (www.lonelyplanet.com) is a good place to start. The **World Health Organization** (WHO; www.who.int/ith/) publishes a superb book called

RECOMMENDED VACCINATIONS

The World Health Organization (WHO) recommends the following vaccinations for travellers to Southeast Asia:

- Adult diphtheria and tetanus – single booster recommended if you've had none in the previous 10 years. Side effects include a sore arm and fever.
- Hepatitis A – provides almost 100% protection for up to a year; a booster after 12 months provides at least another 20 years' protection. Mild side effects such as headache and a sore arm occur for between 5% and 10% of people.
- Hepatitis B – now considered routine for most travellers. Given as three shots over six months. A rapid schedule is also available, as is a combined vaccination with Hepatitis A. Side effects are mild and uncommon, usually a headache and sore arm. Lifetime protection occurs in 95% of people.
- Measles, mumps and rubella – two doses of MMR required unless you have had the diseases. Occasionally a rash and flulike illness can develop a week after receiving the vaccine. Many young adults require a booster.
- Polio – in 2002, no countries in Southeast Asia reported a single case of polio. Only one booster is required as an adult for lifetime protection. Inactivated polio vaccine is safe during pregnancy.
- Typhoid – recommended unless your trip is less than a week and only to developed cities. The vaccine offers around 70% protection, lasts for two or three years and comes as a single shot. Tablets are also available; however, the injection is usually recommended as it has fewer side effects. Sore arm and fever may occur.
- Varicella – if you haven't had chickenpox, discuss this vaccination with your doctor.

Long-term Travellers

These vaccinations are recommended for people travelling more than one month, or those at special risk:

- Japanese B Encephalitis – three injections in all. A booster is recommended after two years. A sore arm and headache are the most common side effects reported. Rarely, an allergic reaction comprising hives and swelling can occur up to 10 days after any of the three doses.
- Meningitis – single injection. There are two types of vaccination: the quadrivalent vaccine gives two to three years protection; meningitis group C vaccine gives around 10 years protection. Recommended for long-term travellers aged under 25.
- Rabies – three injections in all. A booster after one year will provide 10 years of protection. Side effects are rare – occasionally a headache and sore arm.
- Tuberculosis – adult long-term travellers are usually recommended to have a TB skin test before and after travel, rather than vaccination. Note that only one vaccine is given in a lifetime.

International Travel & Health, which is revised annually and is available free on line. Another website of general interest is **MD Travel Health** (www.mdtravelhealth.com), which provides complete travel health recommendations for every country and is updated daily. The **Centers for Disease Control and Prevention** (CDC; www.cdc.gov) website also has good general information.

FURTHER READING

Lonely Planet's *Healthy Travel – Asia & India* is a handy pocket-size book that is packed with useful information including pretrip planning, emergency first aid, immunisation and disease information and what to do if you get sick on the road.

Other good recommended references include *Traveller's Health* by Dr Richard Dawood as well as *Travelling Well* by Dr Deborah Mills – check out the website (www.travelling well.com.au).

IN TRANSIT

DEEP VEIN THROMBOSIS (DVT)

Deep vein thrombosis (DVT) occurs when blood clots form in the legs during plane flights, chiefly because of prolonged immobility. The longer the flight, the greater the risk. Though most blood clots are reabsorbed uneventfully, some may break off and travel through the blood vessels to the lungs, where they may cause life-threatening complications.

The chief symptom of DVT is swelling or pain of the foot, ankle or calf, usually on just one side. When a blood clot travels to the lungs, it may cause chest pain and difficulty in breathing. Travellers with any of these symptoms should immediately seek medical attention.

To prevent the development of DVT on long flights you should walk about the cabin, stretch your legs and contract the leg muscles while sitting, drink plenty of fluids, and avoid alcohol. Also, try to avoid tobacco before and after flights.

JET LAG & MOTION SICKNESS

Jet lag is common when crossing more than five time zones; it results in insomnia, fatigue, malaise or nausea. To avoid jet lag try drinking plenty of fluids (nonalcoholic) and eating light meals. Upon arrival, seek exposure to natural sunlight and readjust your schedule (for meals, sleep etc) as soon as possible.

Antihistamines such as dimenhydrinate (Dramamine) and meclizine (Antivert, Bonine) are usually the first choice for treating motion sickness. Their main side effect is drowsiness. A herbal alternative is ginger, which works like a charm for some people.

IN VIETNAM

AVAILABILITY OF HEALTH CARE

The significant improvement in Vietnam's economy has brought with it some major advances in public health. Rural areas can still pose a problem when it comes to finding good health care, however; although foreigners with hard cash will receive the best treatment available, even bars of gold cannot buy blood tests or X-rays when the local clinic doesn't even have a thermometer or any aspirin. If you become seriously ill in rural Vietnam, get to Ho Chi Minh City (HCMC) or Hanoi as quickly as you can. If you need any type of surgery or other extensive treatment, don't hesitate to fly to Bangkok, Hong Kong or another renowned medical centre as soon as possible.

Government hospitals in Vietnam are overcrowded and basic. In order to treat foreigners, a facility needs to obtain a special license and so far only a few have been provided. The private clinics in Hanoi and HCMC should be your first port of call. They are familiar with the local resources and can organise evacuations if necessary. The contact details of the best medical facilities in Vietnam are listed in the Hanoi (p90) and HCMC (p337) chapters. These are the only cities where you are likely to find health facilities that come close to meeting the standard of developed countries.

Self-treatment may be appropriate if your problem is minor (eg travellers' diarrhoea), you are carrying the appropriate medication and you cannot attend a recommended clinic. If you think you may have a serious disease, especially malaria, do not waste time – travel to the nearest quality facility to receive attention. It is always better to be assessed by a doctor than to rely on self-treatment.

Buying medication over the counter is not recommended, as fake medications and poorly stored or out-of-date drugs are common. Check the expiry dates on any medicines you buy. If you need special medication then take it with you.

INFECTIOUS DISEASES

Dengue

This mosquito-borne disease is becoming increasingly problematic throughout Southeast Asia, especially in the cities. As there is no vaccine available it can only be prevented by avoiding mosquito bites. The mosquito that carries dengue bites day and night, so use insect avoidance measures at all times. Symptoms include high fever, severe headache and body ache (dengue was once known as 'breakbone fever'). Some people develop a rash and experience diarrhoea. There is no specific treatment, just rest and paracetamol – do not take aspirin as it increases the likelihood of haemorrhaging. See a doctor to be diagnosed and monitored.

Filariasis

This is a mosquito-borne disease that is very common in the local population, yet very rare in travellers. Mosquito-avoidance measures are the best way to prevent this disease.

Hepatitis A

A problem throughout the region, this food- and water-borne virus infects the liver, causing jaundice (yellow skin and eyes), nausea and lethargy. There is no specific treatment for hepatitis A, you just need to allow time for the liver to heal. All travellers to Vietnam should be vaccinated against hepatitis A.

Hepatitis B

The only sexually transmitted disease that can be prevented by vaccination, hepatitis B is spread by body fluids, including sexual contact. In some parts of Southeast Asia up to 20% of the population are carriers of hepatitis B, and usually are unaware of this. The long-term consequences can include liver cancer and cirrhosis.

Hepatitis E

Hepatitis E is transmitted through contaminated food and water and has similar symptoms to hepatitis A, but is far less common. It is a severe problem in pregnant women and can result in the death of both mother and baby. There is currently no vaccine, and prevention is by following safe eating and drinking guidelines.

HIV

The official figures on the number of people with HIV/AIDS in Vietnam are vague, but they are on the rise. Health-education messages relating to HIV/AIDS can be seen all over the countryside, however the official line is that infection is largely limited to sex workers and drug users. Condoms are widely available throughout Vietnam.

Influenza

Present year-round in the tropics, influenza (flu) symptoms include high fever, muscle aches, runny nose, cough and sore throat. It can be very severe in people over the age of 65 or in those with underlying medical conditions such as heart disease or diabetes; vaccination is recommended for these individuals. There is no specific treatment, just rest and paracetamol.

Japanese B Encephalitis

While a rare disease in travellers, at least 50,000 locals are infected with Japanese B Encephalitis each year in Southeast Asia. This viral disease is transmitted by mosquitoes. Most cases occur in rural areas and vaccination is recommended for travellers spending more than one month outside of cities. There is no treatment, and a third of infected people will die while another third will suffer permanent brain damage.

Malaria

For such a serious and potentially deadly disease, there is an enormous amount of misinformation concerning malaria. You must get expert advice as to whether your trip actually puts you at risk. Many parts of Vietnam, particularly city and resort areas, have minimal to no risk of malaria, and the risk of side effects from the tablets may outweigh the risk of getting the disease. For most rural areas, however, the risk of contracting the disease far outweighs the risk of any tablet side effects. Travellers to isolated areas in high-risk regions such as Ca Mau (p431) and Bac Lieu (p429) provinces, and the rural south, may like to carry a treatment dose of medication for use if symptoms occur. Remember that malaria can be fatal. Before you travel, seek medical advice on the right medication and dosage for you.

Malaria is caused by a parasite transmitted by the bite of an infected mosquito. The most important symptom of malaria is fever, but general symptoms such as headache, diarrhoea, cough, or chills may also occur. Diagnosis can only be made by taking a blood sample.

Two strategies should be combined to prevent malaria – mosquito avoidance, and antimalarial medications. Most people who catch malaria are taking inadequate or no antimalarial medication.

Travellers are advised to prevent mosquito bites by taking these steps:

- Choose accommodation with screens and fans (if not air-conditioned).
- Impregnate clothing with Permethrin in high-risk areas.
- Sleep under a mosquito net impregnated with Permethrin.
- Spray your room with insect repellent before going out for your evening meal.
- Use a DEET-containing insect repellent on exposed skin. Wash this off at

HEALTH

night, as long as you are sleeping under a mosquito net. Natural repellents such as Citronella can be effective, but must be applied more frequently than products containing DEET.
- Use mosquito coils.
- Wear long sleeves and trousers in light colours.

MALARIA MEDICATION

There are a variety of medications available. The effectiveness of the Chloroquine and Paludrine combination is now limited in most of Southeast Asia. Common side effects include nausea (40% of people) and mouth ulcers. It is generally not recommended.

Lariam (Mefloquine) has received a lot of bad press, some of it justified, some not. This weekly tablet suits many people. Serious side effects are rare but include depression, anxiety, psychosis and seizures. Anyone with a history of depression, anxiety, other psychological disorder or epilepsy should not take Lariam. It is considered safe in the second and third trimesters of pregnancy. It is around 90% effective in most parts of Southeast Asia, but there is significant resistance in parts of northern Thailand, Laos and Cambodia. Tablets must be taken for four weeks after leaving the risk area.

Doxycycline, taken as a daily tablet, is a broad-spectrum antibiotic that has the added benefit of helping to prevent a variety of tropical diseases, including leptospirosis, tick-borne disease, typhus and melioidosis. The potential side effects include photosensitivity (a tendency to sunburn), thrush in women, indigestion, heartburn, nausea and interference with the contraceptive pill. More serious side effects include ulceration of the oesophagus – you can help prevent this by taking your tablet with a meal and a large glass of water, and never lying down within half an hour of taking it. It must be taken for four weeks after leaving the risk area.

Malarone is a new drug combining Atovaquone and Proguanil. Side effects are uncommon and mild, most commonly nausea and headaches. It is the best tablet for scuba divers and for those on short trips to high-risk areas. It must be taken for one week after leaving the risk area.

Derivatives of Artesunate are not suitable as a preventive medication. They are useful treatments under medical supervision.

SCORCHED OEUF POLICY

There have been periodic outbreaks of avian influenza or bird flu in Vietnam in the past few years. Dozens people have died and the threat of human-to-human transmission remains very real. Now the H5-N1 strain has now gone global, Vietnam is no longer in the spotlight. However, when outbreaks occur, eggs and poultry are usually banished from the menu in many hotels and restaurants. Even where eggs are available, we recommend a scorched oeuf policy. Ensure they are well cooked in whatever shape or form they come. No runny omelettes, no sunny side up. Don't take risks or you might end up with egg on your face.

A final option is to take no preventive medication but to have a supply of emergency medication should you develop the symptoms of malaria. This is less than ideal, and you'll need to get to a good medical facility within 24 hours of developing a fever. If you choose this option the most effective and safest treatment is Malarone (four tablets once daily for three days). Other options include Mefloquine and Quinine but the side effects of these drugs at treatment doses make them less desirable. Fansidar is no longer recommended.

Measles

Measles remains a problem in some parts of Vietnam. This highly contagious bacterial infection is spread via coughing and sneezing. Many people born before 1966 are immune as they had the disease in childhood. Measles starts with a high fever and rash and can be complicated by pneumonia and brain disease. There is no specific treatment.

Rabies

This uniformly fatal disease is spread by the bite or lick of an infected animal – most commonly a dog or monkey. Seek medical advice immediately after any animal bite and commence post-exposure treatment. Having a pretravel vaccination means the postbite treatment is greatly simplified. If an animal bites you, gently wash the wound with soap and water, and apply iodine-based antiseptic. If you are not vaccinated you will need to receive rabies immunoglobulin as soon as possible.

Schistosomiasis

Schistosomiasis (also called bilharzia) is a tiny parasite that enters your skin after you've been swimming in contaminated water – travellers usually only get a light infection and hence have no symptoms. If you are concerned, you can be tested three months after exposure. On rare occasions, travellers may develop 'Katayama fever' – this occurs some weeks after exposure, as the parasite passes through the lungs and causes an allergic reaction – symptoms are coughing and fever. Schistosomiasis is easily treated with medications.

STDs

Sexually transmitted diseases include herpes, warts, syphilis, gonorrhoea and chlamydia. People carrying these diseases often have no signs of infection. Condoms will prevent gonorrhoea and chlamydia but not warts or herpes. If after a sexual encounter you develop any rash, lumps, discharge or pain when passing urine seek immediate medical attention. If you have been sexually active during your travels have an STD check on your return home.

While abstinence from sexual contact is the only 100% effective prevention, using condoms is also effective. Condoms are widely available throughout Vietnam; when purchasing, ensure the package hasn't been stored in the sun as the rubber could have deteriorated.

Tuberculosis

Tuberculosis (TB) is rare in short-term travellers. Medical and aid workers, and long-term travellers who have significant contact with the local population should take precautions, however. Vaccination is usually only given to children under the age of five, but adults at risk are recommended pre- and post-travel TB testing. The main symptoms are fever, cough, weight loss, night sweats and tiredness.

Typhoid

This serious bacterial infection is spread via food and water. It gives a high, slowly progressive fever and headache, and may be accompanied by a dry cough and stomach pain. It is diagnosed by blood tests and treated with antibiotics. Vaccination is recommended for all travellers spending more than a week in Southeast Asia, or travelling outside of the major cities. Be aware that vaccination is not 100% effective so you must still be careful with what you eat and drink.

Typhus

Murine typhus is spread by the bite of a flea whereas scrub typhus is spread via a mite. These diseases are rare in travellers. Symptoms include fever, muscle pains and a rash. You can avoid these diseases by following general insect-avoidance measures. Doxycycline will also prevent them.

TRAVELLERS' DIARRHOEA

Travellers' diarrhoea is by far the most common problem affecting travellers – between 30% and 50% of people will suffer from it within two weeks of starting their trip. In over 80% of cases, travellers' diarrhoea is caused by a bacteria (there are numerous potential culprits), and therefore responds promptly to treatment with antibiotics. Treatment with antibiotics will depend on your situation –

DRINKING WATER

The number one rule is *be careful of the water*. Ice can be particularly risky; if you don't know for certain that the water is safe, assume the worst. However, a lot of the ice in Vietnam comes from factories introduced by the French, so it is as safe as the bottled water. Following these rules will help you avoid water-borne diseases.

- Never drink tap water.
- Bottled water is generally safe – check the seal is intact at purchase.
- Boiling water is the most efficient method of purifying it.
- The best chemical purifier is iodine. It should not be used by pregnant women or those people who suffer with thyroid problems.
- Water filters should filter out viruses. Ensure your filter has a chemical barrier such as iodine and a small pore size, ie less than four microns.

how sick you are, how quickly you need to get better, where you are and so on.

Travellers' diarrhoea is defined as the passage of more than three watery bowel-actions within 24 hours, plus at least one other symptom such as fever, cramps, nausea, vomiting or feeling generally unwell.

Treatment consists of staying well-hydrated. Rehydration solutions like Gastrolyte are the best for this. Antibiotics such as Norfloxacin, Ciprofloxacin or Azithromycin will kill the bacteria quickly.

Loperamide is just a 'stopper' and doesn't get to the cause of the problem. It can be helpful, for example if you have to go on a long bus ride. Don't take Loperamide if you have a fever, or blood in your stools. Seek medical attention quickly if you do not respond to an appropriate antibiotic.

Amoebic Dysentery

Amoebic dysentery is very rare in travellers but is often misdiagnosed by poor-quality labs in Southeast Asia. Symptoms are similar to bacterial diarrhoea, ie fever, bloody diarrhoea and generally feeling unwell. You should always seek reliable medical care if you have blood in your diarrhoea. Treatment involves two drugs: Tinidazole or Metroniadzole to kill the parasite in your gut and then a second drug to kill the cysts. If left untreated complications such as liver or gut abscesses can occur.

Giardiasis

Giardia lamblia is a parasite that is relatively common in travellers. Symptoms include nausea, bloating, excess gas, fatigue and intermittent diarrhoea. 'Eggy' burps are often attributed solely to giardiasis, but work in Nepal has shown that they are not specific to this infection. The parasite will eventually go away if left untreated but this can take months. The treatment of choice is Tinidazole, with Metronidazole being a second-line option.

ENVIRONMENTAL HAZARDS

Air Pollution

Air pollution, particularly vehicle pollution, is an increasing problem in most of Vietnam's major cities. If you have severe respiratory problems speak with your doctor before travelling to any heavily polluted urban centres.

This pollution also causes minor respiratory problems such as sinusitis, dry throat and irritated eyes. If troubled by the pollution leave the city for a few days and get some fresh air.

Food

Eating in restaurants is the biggest risk factor for contracting travellers' diarrhoea. Ways to avoid it include eating only freshly cooked food, and avoiding shellfish and food that has been sitting around in buffets. Peel all fruit, cook vegetables, and soak salads in iodine water for at least 20 minutes. Eat in busy restaurants with a high turnover of customers.

Heat

Many parts of Southeast Asia are hot and humid throughout the year. For most people it takes at least two weeks to adapt to the hot climate. Swelling of the feet and ankles is common, as are muscle cramps caused by excessive sweating. Prevent these by avoiding dehydration and excessive activity in the heat. Take it easy when you first arrive. Don't eat salt tablets (they aggravate the gut) but do drink rehydration solution and eat salty food. Treat cramps by stopping activity, resting, rehydrating with double-strength rehydration solution and gently stretching.

Dehydration is the main contributor to heat exhaustion. Symptoms include feeling weak, headache, irritability, nausea or vomiting, sweaty skin, a fast, weak pulse and a normal or slightly elevated body temperature. Treatment involves getting out of the heat and/or sun, fanning the victim and applying cool wet cloths to the skin, laying the victim flat with their legs raised and rehydrating with water containing a quarter of a teaspoon of salt per litre. Recovery is usually rapid, though it is common to feel weak for some days afterwards.

Heatstroke is a serious medical emergency. Symptoms come on suddenly and include weakness, nausea, a hot dry body with a body temperature of over 41°C, dizziness, confusion, loss of coordination, seizures and eventually collapse and loss of consciousness. Seek medical help and commence cooling by getting the person out of the heat, removing their clothes, fanning them and applying cool wet cloths or ice to their body, especially to the groin and armpits.

Prickly heat is a common skin rash in the tropics, caused by sweat being trapped under the skin. The result is an itchy rash of tiny lumps. Treat by moving out of the heat and into an air-conditioned area for a few hours and by having cool showers. Creams and ointments clog the skin so they should be avoided. Locally bought prickly heat powder can be helpful.

Tropical fatigue is common in long-term expats based in the tropics. It's rarely due to disease and is caused by the climate, inadequate mental rest, excessive alcohol intake and the demands of daily work in a different culture.

Insect Bites & Stings

Bedbugs don't carry disease but their bites are very itchy. They live in the cracks of furniture and walls and then migrate to the bed at night to feed on you. You can treat the itch with an antihistamine. You can try to prevent or minimise their bite by using your own sheet sleeping bag cover. Lice inhabit various parts of your body but most commonly your head and pubic area. Transmission is via close contact with an infected person, although body lice can come from contaminated bedclothes. They can be difficult to treat and you may need numerous applications of an antilice shampoo such as Permethrin, or in the case of body lice, with medicated creams or ointments. Pubic lice are usually contracted from sexual contact.

Ticks are contracted during walks in rural areas. They are commonly found behind the ears, on the belly and in armpits. If you have had a tick bite and experience symptoms such as a rash (at the site of the bite or elsewhere), fever or muscle aches you should see a doctor. Doxycycline prevents tick-borne diseases.

Leeches are found in humid forest areas. They do not transmit any disease but their bites are often intensely itchy for weeks afterwards and can easily become infected. Apply an iodine-based antiseptic to any leech bite to help prevent infection.

Bee and wasp stings mainly cause problems for people who are allergic to them. Anyone with a serious bee or wasp allergy should carry an injection of adrenaline (eg an Epipen) for emergency treatment. For others pain is the main problem – apply ice to the sting and take painkillers.

Most jellyfish in Vietnamese waters are not dangerous, just irritating. First aid for jellyfish stings involves pouring vinegar onto the affected area to neutralise the poison. Do not rub sand or water onto the stings. Take painkillers, and anyone who feels ill in any way after being stung should seek medical advice. Take local advice if there are dangerous jellyfish around and keep out of the water.

Parasites

Numerous parasites are common in local populations in Vietnam; however, most of these are rare in travellers. The two rules to follow if you wish to avoid parasitic infections are to wear shoes and to avoid eating raw food, especially fish, pork and vegetables. A number of parasites are transmitted via the skin by walking barefoot including strongyloides, hookworm and cutaneous larva migrans.

Skin Problems

Fungal rashes are common in humid climates. There are two common fungal rashes that affect travellers. The first occurs in moist areas that get less air such as the groin, armpits and between the toes. It starts as a red patch that slowly spreads and is usually itchy. Treatment involves keeping the skin dry, avoiding chafing and using an antifungal cream such as Clotrimazole or Lamisil. *Tinea versicolor* is also common – this fungus causes small, light-coloured patches, most commonly on the back, chest and shoulders. Consult a doctor.

Cuts and scratches become easily infected in humid climates. Take meticulous care of any cuts and scratches to prevent complications such as abscesses. Immediately wash all wounds in clean water and apply antiseptic. If you develop signs of infection (increasing pain and redness) see a doctor. Divers and surfers should be particularly careful with coral cuts as they become easily infected.

Snakes

Vietnam is home to many species of both poisonous and harmless snakes. Assume all snakes are poisonous and never try to catch one. Always wear boots and long pants if walking in an area that may have snakes. First-aid in the event of a snakebite involves pressure immobilisation via an elastic bandage firmly wrapped around the affected limb, starting at the bite site and working up towards the chest. The bandage should not be so tight that the circulation is cut off, and the fingers or toes should be kept free so the circulation can be checked. Immobilise the limb with a splint and carry the victim to medical attention. Do not use tourniquets or try to suck the venom out. Antivenom is available only in major cities.

Sunburn

Even on a cloudy day sunburn can occur rapidly. Always use a strong sunscreen (at least factor 30), making sure to reapply after a swim, and always wear a wide-brimmed hat and sunglasses outdoors. Avoid lying in the sun during the hottest part of the day (from 10am to 2pm). If you become sunburnt stay out of the sun until you have recovered, apply cool compresses and take painkillers for the discomfort. One percent hydrocortisone cream applied twice daily is also helpful.

WOMEN'S HEALTH

Pregnant women should receive specialised advice before travelling. The ideal time to travel is in the second trimester (between 16 and 28 weeks), during which the risk of pregnancy-related problems is at its lowest and pregnant women generally feel at their best. During the first trimester there is a risk of miscarriage and in the third trimester complications such as premature labour and high blood pressure are possible. It's wise to travel with a companion.

Always carry a list of quality medical facilities available at your destination and ensure you continue your standard antenatal care at these facilities. Avoid rural travel in areas with poor transportation and medical facilities. Most of all, ensure travel insurance covers all pregnancy-related possibilities, including premature labour.

Malaria is a high-risk disease in pregnancy. WHO recommends that pregnant women do *not* travel to areas that have Chloroquine-resistant malaria. None of the more effective antimalarial drugs are completely safe in pregnancy.

Travellers' diarrhoea can quickly lead to dehydration and result in inadequate blood flow to the placenta. Many of the drugs used to treat various diarrhoea bugs are not recommended in pregnancy. Azithromycin is considered safe.

In the urban areas of Vietnam, supplies of sanitary products are readily available. Birth control options may be limited so bring adequate supplies of contraception. Heat, humidity and antibiotics can all contribute to thrush. Treatment is with antifungal creams and pessaries such as Clotrimazole. A practical alternative is a single tablet of Fluconazole (Diflucan). Urinary tract infections can be precipitated by dehydration or long bus journeys without toilet stops; bring suitable antibiotics.

TRADITIONAL MEDICINE

A number of traditional medical treatments are practised in Vietnam. Herbal medicine, much of it imported from China, is widely available and sometimes very effective. As with Western medicine, self-diagnosis is not advisable – see a doctor. Traditional Chinese doctors are found wherever a large Chinese community exists, including HCMC, Hanoi and Hoi An.

If you visit traditional Chinese doctors, you might be surprised by what they discover about your body. For example, the doctor will almost certainly take your pulse and then may perhaps tell you that you have a 'slippery' or 'thready' pulse. They have identified more than 30 different kinds of pulse. A pulse could be empty, prison, leisurely, bowstring, irregular or even regularly irregular. The doctor may then examine your tongue to see if it is slippery, dry, pale, greasy, has a thick coating or possibly no coating at all. The doctor, having discovered your ailment, such as wet heat, as evidenced by a slippery pulse and a red greasy tongue, will prescribe the proper herbs for your condition.

Once you have a diagnosis you may be treated by moxibustion, a traditional treatment whereby various types of herbs, rolled into what looks like a ball of fluffy cotton, are held near the skin and ignited. A slight variation of this method is to place the herb on a slice of ginger and then ignite it. The idea is to apply the maximum amount of heat possible without burning the patient. This heat treatment is supposed to be very good for diseases such as arthritis.

It is common to see Vietnamese people with long bands of red welts on their necks, foreheads and backs. Don't worry, this is not some kind of hideous skin disease, but rather a treatment known as *cao gio*, literally 'scrape wind'. In traditional Vietnamese folk medicine, many illnesses are attributed to 'poisonous wind', which can be released by applying eucalyptus oil or tiger balm and scraping the skin with a spoon or coin, thus raising the welts. The results aren't pretty, but the locals say this treatment is good for the common cold, fatigue, headaches and other ailments. Whether the cure hurts less than the disease is something one can only judge from experience.

Another technique to battle bad breezes is called *giac hoi*. This one employs suction cups, typically made of bamboo or glass, which are placed on the patient's skin. A burning piece of alcohol-soaked cotton is briefly put inside the cup to drive out the air before it is applied. As the cup cools, a partial vacuum is produced, leaving a nasty-looking but harmless red circular mark on the skin, which goes away in a few days. Looks pretty weird on the forehead though!

There is some solid evidence attesting to the efficacy of acupuncture. Some major surgical operations have been performed using acupuncture as the only anaesthetic (this works best on the head). In this case, a small electric current (from batteries) is passed through the needles.

If done properly the practice doesn't hurt. Knowing where to insert the needle is crucial. Acupuncturists have identified more than 2000 insertion points, but only about 150 are commonly used. The exact mechanism by which it works is not fully understood. Practitioners talk of energy channels or meridians that connect the needle insertion point to the particular organ, gland or joint being treated. The acupuncture point is sometimes quite far from the area of the body being treated.

Nonsterile acupuncture needles pose a genuine health risk in this era of AIDS. You would be wise to purchase your own acupuncture needles if you plan on having this treatment in Vietnam.

Language

CONTENTS

LANGUAGES IN VIETNAM

Vietnamese is the official language of Vietnam, and it is spoken throughout the country. There are dialectical differences between the north, central and southern regions. There are also dozens of different languages spoken by the various ethnic minorities, particularly in the central highlands and in the far north of the country. Khmer, the Cambodian language, is spoken in parts of the Mekong Delta, and Lao and various Chinese dialects are evident in areas bordering Laos and China.

The Vietnamese people's knowledge of foreign languages reflects their country's relationship with foreign powers – cordial or otherwise – in recent history.

Much of Vietnam's elder generation still speak French, while many middle-aged Vietnamese speak Russian and other Eastern European languages – many of these people spent time in countries like Russia, Bulgaria and the former East Germany during the Cold War (at least until it thawed in the late 1980s). Today, however, Vietnam's youth has fully embraced the English language. A fair number of young people also study Japanese, French and other Western European languages.

The most widely spoken foreign languages in Vietnam are Chinese (Cantonese and Mandarin), English and French, more or less in that order. People in their 50s and older (who grew up during the colonial period) are much more likely to understand some French than southerners of the successive generation, for whom English was indispensable for professional and commercial contacts with the Americans. Some southern Vietnamese men – former combat interpreters – speak a quaint form of English peppered with all sorts of charming southern-American expressions such as 'y'all come back' and 'it ain't worth didley squat', pronounced with a perceptible drawl. Apparently, they worked with Americans from the deep south, carefully studied their pronunciation and diligently learned every nuance.

Many of the Vietnamese who can speak English – especially former South Vietnamese soldiers and officials – learned it while working with the Americans during the war. After reunification, almost all of them spent periods of time ranging from a few months to 15 years in 're-education camps'. Many of these former South Vietnamese soldiers and officials will be delighted to renew contact with Americans, with whose compatriots they spent so much time, often in very difficult circumstances, more than half a lifetime ago.

These days almost everyone has a desire to learn English. If you're looking to make contacts with English students, the best place is at the basic food stalls in university areas.

Spoken Chinese (both Cantonese and Mandarin) is making a definite comeback after years of being supressed. The large number of free-spending tourists and investors from Taiwan and Hong Kong provide the chief motivation for studying Chinese. In addition, cross-border trade with mainland China has been increasing rapidly and those who are able to speak Chinese are well positioned to profit from it.

After reunification, the teaching of Russian was stressed all over the country. With the collapse of the USSR in 1991, all interest in studying Russian ground to a screeching halt. Most Vietnamese who bothered to learn the language have either forgotten it or are in the process of forgetting it.

VIETNAMESE

The Vietnamese language *(Kinh)* is a fusion of Mon-Khmer, Tai and Chinese elements. Vietnamese derived a significant percentage of its basic words from the nontonal Mon-Khmer languages. From the Tai languages came certain grammatical elements and tonality. Chinese gave Vietnamese most of its literary, technical and governmental vocabulary, as well as its traditional writing system.

The following list of words and phrases will help get you started. If you'd like a more comprehensive guide to the language, pick up a copy of Lonely Planet's pocket-sized *Vietnamese Phrasebook*.

The variation in vocabulary between the Vietnamese of the north and that of the south is indicated in this chapter by (N) and (S) respectively.

WRITTEN VIETNAMESE

For centuries, the Vietnamese language was written in standard Chinese characters *(chữ nho)*. Around the 13th century, the Vietnamese devised their own writing system called *chữ nôm* (or just *nôm*), which was created by combining two Chinese words or by using single Chinese characters for their phonetic value. Both writing systems were in use until the 20th century – official business and scholarship was conducted in *chữ nho*, while *chữ nôm* was used for popular literature. The Latin-based *quốc ngữ* script, widely used since WWI, was developed in the 17th century by Alexandre de Rhodes (see the boxed text, right). *Quốc ngữ* served to undermine the position of Mandarin officials, whose power was based on traditional scholarship in *chữ nho* and *chữ nôm*, scripts that were largely inaccessible to the masses.

The Vietnamese treat every syllable as an independent word, so 'Saigon' is spelt 'Sai Gon' and 'Vietnam' is written as 'Viet Nam'. Foreigners aren't too comfortable with this system – we prefer to read 'London' rather than 'Lon Don'. This leads to the notion that Vietnamese is a 'monosyllabic language', where every syllable represents an independent word. This idea appears to hark back to the Chinese writing system, where every syllable is represented by an independent character and each character is treated as a meaningful word in its own right. In reality, Vietnamese appears to be polysyllabic, like English. However, writing systems do influence people's perceptions of their own language, so the Vietnamese themselves will insist that their language is monosyllabic – it's a debate probably not worth pursuing.

ALEXANDRE DE RHODES

One of the most illustrious of the early missionaries was the brilliant French Jesuit scholar Alexandre de Rhodes (1591–1660). De Rhodes first preached in Vietnamese only six months after arriving in the country in 1627, and he is most recognised for his work in devising *quốc ngữ*, the Latin-based phonetic alphabet in which Vietnamese is written to this day. By replacing Chinese characters with *quốc ngữ*, de Rhodes facilitated the propagation of the gospel to a wide audience.

Over the course of his long career, de Rhodes travelled back and forth between Hanoi, Macau, Rome and Paris, seeking support and funding for his missionary activities and battling both Portuguese colonial opposition and the intractable Vatican bureaucracy. In 1645 he was sentenced to death for illegally entering Vietnam to proselytise, but was expelled instead; two of the priests with him were beheaded.

For his contributions, de Rhodes gained the highest respect from the Vietnamese (in the south, anyway), who called him *cha caả* (father). A memorial statue of de Rhodes stands in central Saigon.

PRONUNCIATION

Most of the names of the letters of the *quốc ngữ* alphabet are pronounced like the letters of the French alphabet. Dictionaries are alphabetised as in English except that each vowel/tone combination is treated as a different letter.

Most of the consonants of the Romanised Vietnamese alphabet are pronounced more or less as they are in English with a few exceptions. Vietnamese doesn't use the English letters 'f', 'j', 'w' and 'z'.

To help you make sense of what is (for non-Vietnamese) a very tricky writing system, the words and phrases in this language guide include pronunciations that use a written form more familiar to English speakers. The same symbols as *quốc ngữ* are used for marking the tones.

For example, Vietnamese **d** and **gi-** are represented with 'z', **đ** with 'd', **ph-** with 'f', **x** with 's', **-ng** with 'm', **-nh** with 'ny' etc.

SYMBOL & PRONUNCIATION

c, k	**ğ**	an unaspirated 'k'
đ	**đ**	(with crossbar) as in 'do'
d	**z/y**	(without crossbar) as the 'z' in 'zoo' (N); as the 'y' in 'yes' (S)
gi-	**z/y**	as a 'z' (N); as a 'y' (S)
kh-	**ch**	as the 'ch' in German *buch*
ng-	**ng**	as the '-nga-' sound in 'long ago'
nh-	**ny**	as the 'ny' in 'canyon'
ph-	**f**	as in 'farm'
r	**z/r**	as 'z' (N); as 'r' (S)
s	**s/sh**	as 's' (N); as 'sh' (S)
tr-	**ch/tr**	as 'ch' (N); as 'tr' (S)
th-	**t**	a strongly aspirated 't'
x	**s**	like an 's'
-ch	**k**	like a 'k'
-ng	**ng**	as the 'ng' in 'long' but with the lips closed; sounds like English 'm'
-nh	**ng**	as in 'singing'

TONES

The hardest part of studying Vietnamese for Westerners is learning to differentiate between the tones. There are six tones in spoken Vietnamese. Thus, every syllable in Vietnamese can be pronounced six different ways. For example, depending on the tones, the word *ma* can be read to mean 'phantom', 'but', 'mother', 'rice seedling', 'tomb' or 'horse'.

The six tones of spoken Vietnamese are represented by five diacritical marks in the written language (the first tone is left unmarked). These should not be confused with the four other diacritical marks that are used to indicate special consonants and vowels.

The following examples show the six different tone representations:

ma (ghost): middle of the vocal range
mà (which): begins low & falls lower
mả (tomb): begins low, dips and then rises to higher pitch
mã (horse): begins high, dips slightly, then rises sharply
mạ (rice seedling): begins low, falls to a lower level, then stops
má (mother): begins high and rises sharply

A visual representation looks something like this:

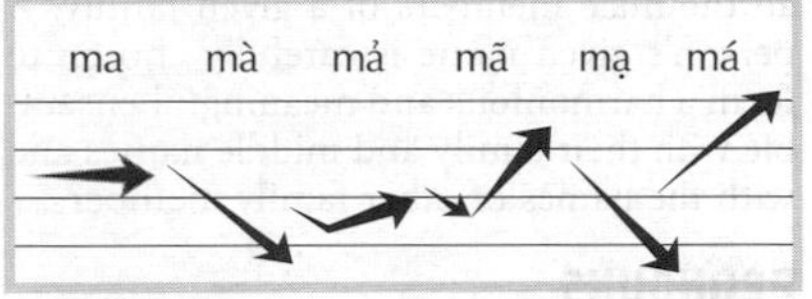

GRAMMAR

Vietnamese grammar is fairly straightforward, with a wide variety of possible sentence structures. Nouns have no masculine, feminine or plural forms and verbs have only one form regardless of gender, person or tense. Instead, tool words and classifiers are used to show a word's relationship to its neighbours. For example, in the expression *con mèo (của) tôi* (my cat), *con* is the classifier, *mèo* is the noun, *của* means 'of/belong to' (and can be omitted), and *tôi* is the personal pronoun 'I'.

PROPER NAMES

Most Vietnamese names consist of a family name, a middle name and a given name, in that order. Thus, if Henry David Thoreau had been Vietnamese, he would have been named Thoreau David Henry and would have been addressed as Mr Henry – people are called by their given name, but to do this without using the title Mr, Mrs or Miss is considered as expressing either great intimacy or arrogance of the sort a superior would use with his or her inferior.

In Vietnamese, Mr is *Ông* if the man is of your grandparents' generation, *Bác* if he is of your parents' age, *Chú* if he is younger than your parents and *Anh* if he is in his teens or early 20s. Mrs is *Bà* if the woman is of your grandparents' age and *Bác* if she is of your parents' generation or younger. Miss is *Chị* or *Em* unless the woman is very young, in which case *Cô* might be more appropriate. Other titles of respect are *Thầy* (Buddhist monk or male teacher), *Bà* (Buddhist nun), *Cha* (Catholic priest) and *Cô* (Catholic nun).

There are 300 or so family names in use in Vietnam, the most common of which is Nguyen (which is pronounced something like 'nwee-en'). About half of all Vietnamese have the surname Nguyen! When women marry, they usually (but not always) take their husband's family name. The middle name may be purely ornamental, may indicate the sex of its bearer or may be used by all the male members of a given family. A person's given name is carefully chosen to form a harmonious and meaningful ensemble with their family and middle names and with the names of other family members.

PRONOUNS

I
tôi — doy

you
ông — awm (to an older man)
bà — baà (to an older woman)
anh — aang (to a man your own age)
cô — ğaw (to a woman your own age)

he
anh ấy — ang áy

she
cô ấy — ğó áy

we
chúng tôi — júm doy

they
họ — họ

ACCOMMODATION

Where is there a (cheap) ...?
đâu có ... (rẻ tiền)? — đoh ğó ... (zả đee·ùhn)?

camping ground
nơi cắm trại — ner·ee ğúhm chại

hotel
khách sạn — kaák saạn

guesthouse
nhà khách — nyaà kaák

What is the address?
Địa chỉ là gì?
đee·ụh cheẻ laà zeè?

Could you write the address down, please?
Bạn có thể viết giùm địa chỉ được không?
baạn ğó tẻ vee·úht zòom đee·ụh jeẻ đuhr·ẹrk kawm?

I need to leave at ... o'clock (tomorrow morning).
Tôi phải đi lúc ... giờ (sáng mai).
doy faí đee lúp ... zèr (saáng mai)

How much does a room cost?
Giá một phòng là bao nhiêu?
zaá mạwt fòm laà bow nyee·oo?

I'd like (a) ...
Tôi muốn ... — doy moo·úhn ...

bed
cái giường — ğaí zuhr·èrng

single room
phòng đơn — fòm dern

double-bed
giường đôi — zuhr·èrng đoy

room
phòng — fòm

room with two beds
phòng gồm hai giường ngủ — fòm gàwm hai zuhr·èrng ngoỏ

room with a bathroom
phòng có phòng tắm — fòm ğó fòm dúhm

to share a dorm
ở chung phòng nội trú — ẻr jum fòm nọy choó

air-conditioning
máy lạnh — máy laạng

bathroom
phòng tắm — fòm dúhm

blanket
mền — mèn

fan
quạt máy — gwaạt máy

hot water
nước nóng — nuhr·érk nóm

laundry
giặt ủi — zụht oỏ·ee

mosquito net
màng — maàng

reception
tiếp tân — dee·úhp duhn

room
phòng — fòm

room key
chìa khóa phòng — chee·aà kwaá fòm

1st-class room
phòng loại 1 — fòm lwaị mạwt

MAKING A RESERVATION
(for written and phone inquiries)

To ...
Đến ... — đén ...
From ...
Từ ... — dùhr ...
Date
ngày tháng — ngày taáng
I'd like to book ...
Làm ơn cho tôi đặt trước một ... — laàm ern jo doy đụht truhr·érk mạwt ...
in the name of ...
tên là ... — den laà ...
from ... (date)
Từ ... — dùhr ...
until ...
Đến ... — đén ...
credit card
thẻ tín dụng — tả dín zoọm
number
số — sáw
expiry date
hết hàng — hét haàng

2nd-class room
phòng loại 2 — fòm lwại hai
sheet
ra trãi giường — zaa chaĩ zuhr·èrng
toilet
nhà vệ sinh — nyaà vẹ sing
toilet paper
giấy vệ sinh — záy vẹ sing
towel
khăn tắm — kúhn dúhm

How much is it ...?
Giá bao nhiêu ...? — zaá bow nyee·oo ...?
per night
một đêm — mạwt đem
per person
một người — mạwt nguhr·eè

May I see it?
Tôi có thể xem phòng được không?
doy ğó tẻ sam fòm đuhr·ẹrk kawm?
Where is the bathroom?
Phòng tắm ở đâu?
fòm dúhm ẻr đoh?
Where is the toilet?
Nhà vệ sinh ở đâu?
nyaà vẹ sing ẻr đoh?
I'm leaving today.
Hôm nay tôi rời đay.
hawm nay doy zer·eè đay
We're leaving tomorrow.
Ngày mai chúng tôi rời đay.
ngày mai júm doy zer·eè đay

CONVERSATION & ESSENTIALS

Hello.
Xin chào. — sin jòw
Goodbye.
Tạm biệt. — daạm bee·ụht
Yes.
Vâng. (N)/*Dạ.* (S) — vuhng/yạ
No.
Không. — kawm
Please.
Làm ơn. — laàm ern
Thank you.
Cảm ơn. — ğaảm ern
You're welcome.
Không có chi. — kawm ğó jee
Excuse me. (often used before questions)
Xin lỗi. — sin lõy
Sorry.
Xin lỗi. — sin lõy
How are you?
Có khỏe không? — ğáw kwả kawm?
Fine, thank you.
Khỏe, cám ơn. — kwả ğaảm ern
Good night.
Chúc ngủ ngon. — júp ngoỏ ngon
What's your name?
Tên là gì? — den laà zeè?
My name is ...
Tên tôi là ... — den doy laà ...
Where are you from?
Bạn từ đâu đến? — baạn dùhr đoh đén?
I'm from ...
Tôi đến từ ... — doy đén tùhr ...
I like ...
Tôi thích ... — doy tík
I don't like ...
Tôi không thích ... — doy kawm tík
I want ...
Tôi muốn ... — doy moo·úhn ...
I don't want ...
Tôi không muốn ... — doy kawm moo·úhn ...

DIRECTIONS

Where is ...?
ở đâu ...? — ẻr đoh ...?
Go straight ahead.
Thẳng tới trước. — tủhng der·eé chuhr·érk
Turn left.
Sang trái. — saang chaí
Turn right.
Sang phải. — saang fai

SIGNS

Lối Vào	Entrance
Lối Ra	Exit
Hướng Dẫn	Information
Mở	Open
Đóng	Closed
Cấm	Prohibited
Cảnh Sát/Công An	Police
Nhà Vệ Sinh	Toilets/WC
Đàn Ông	Men
Phụ Nữ	Women

at the corner
ở góc đường ér góp đuhr·èrng
at the traffic lights
tại đèn giao thông dại đèn zow tawm
behind
đằng sau dùhng sow
in front of
đằng trước đùng chuhr·érk
far
xa saa
near (to)
gần gùhn
opposite
đối diện đóy zee·ụhn
north
bắc búhk
south
nam naam
east
đông đawm
west
tây day

beach
bãi biển baĩ beẻ·uhn
boulevard
đại lộ đại lạw
bridge
cầu ğóh
island
đảo đỏw
main square
quảng trường chính gwaảng chuhr·èrng jíng
market
chợ trường jẹr chuhr·èrng
mountain
núi noo·eé
quay
bến tàu bén dòh
river
sông sawm
sea
biển beẻ·uhn
square (in a city)
công viên ğawm vee·uhn
street
phố/đường (N/S) fáw/đuhr·èrng
temple
chùa joo·ùh

HEALTH

I'm sick.
Tôi bị đau.
doy beẹ đoh
It hurts here.
Chỗ bị đau ở đây.
jãw beẹ đoh ér đay
Please take me to the hospital.
Làm ơn đưa tôi bệnh viện.
laàm ern đuhr·uh doy bẹn vee·ụhn

dentist
nha sĩ nyaa seẽ
doctor
bác sĩ baák seẽ
pharmacy
nhà thuốc tây nyaà too·úhk day

I'm ...
Tôi bị ... doy beẹ ...
asthmatic
suyễn sweẽ·uhn
diabetic
bệnh đái đường bẹn đái đuhr·èrng
epileptic
động kinh đạwm ğing

I'm allergic to ...
Tôi bị dị ứng với ... doy beẹ zeẹ úhrng ver·eé ...
antibiotics
thuốc kháng sinh too·úhk kaáng sing
aspirin
thuốc giảm đau too·úhk zaảm đoh
penicillin
thuốc pênicilin too·úhk pe·nee·see·lin
bees
con ong ğon om
peanuts
đậu phọng đọh fọm

backache
đau lưng đoh luhrng
diarrhoea
tiêu chảy dee·oo jảy
dizziness
chóng mặt jóm mụht

LANGUAGE

EMERGENCIES

Help!
Cứu tôi! ğuhr·oó doy!
There's been an accident!
Có tai nạn! ğó dai naạn!
I'm lost.
Tôi bị lạc đường. doi beẹ laạk đuhr·èrng
Leave me alone!
Thôi! toy!
Thief!
Ăn cắp! uhn ğúhp!
Pickpocket!
Móc túi! móp doo·eé
Please call ...
Làm ơn gọi ... laàm ern gọy ...
an ambulance
xe cứu thương sa ğúuhr·oó tuhr·erng
a doctor
bác sĩ baák seẽ
the police
công an ğawm aan

fever
bệnh sốt bẹn sáwt
headache
nhức đầu nyúhrk đoh
malaria
sốt rét sáwt zét
nausea
buồn nôn boo·ùhn nawn
stomachache
đau bụng đoh bụm
toothache
nhức răng nyúhrk zuhng
vomiting
ói óy
antiseptic
thuốc khử trùng too·úhk kủhr chùm
condoms
bao dương vật bow zuhr·erng vụht
contraceptive
cách ngừa thai ğaák nguhr·ùh tai
insect repellent
thuốc chống muỗi too·úhk jáwm moõ·ee
medicine
y thuốc ee too·úhk
mosquito coils
hương đốt chống muỗi (N) huhr·erng đért jáwm moõ·ee
nhang chống muỗi (S) nyaang jáwm moõ·ee
sanitary pads
băng vệ sinh buhng vẹ sing
sunblock cream
kem chống nắng ğam jáwm núhng
tampons
ống băng vệ sinh áwm buhng vẹ sing

LANGUAGE DIFFICULTIES

Do you speak English?
Bạn có nói được tiếng Anh không?
Baạn ğó nóy đuhr·ẹrk díng aang kawm?
Does anyone here speak English?
Có ai biết nói tiếng Anh không?
ğó ai bee·úht nóy díng aang kawm?
What does that mean?
Nghĩa là gì?
ngee·ũh laà zeè?
I (don't) understand.
Tôi (không) hiểu.
doy (kawm) heẻ·oo
Could you write it down, please?
Xin viết ra giùm tôi.
sin vee·úht zaa zùm doy
Can you show me (on the map)?
Xin chỉ giùm (trên bản đồ này).
sin jeẻ zùm (chen baản dàw này)

NUMBERS

1	*một*	mạwt
2	*hai*	hai
3	*ba*	baa
4	*bốn*	báwn
5	*năm*	nuhm
6	*sáu*	sóh
7	*bảy*	bảy
8	*tám*	dúhm
9	*chín*	jín
10	*mười*	muhr·eè
11	*mười một*	muhr·eè mọt
19	*mười chín*	muhr·eè jín
20	*hai mươi*	hai muhr·ee
21	*hai mươi mốt*	hai muhr·ee máwt
22	*hai mươi hai*	hai muhr·ee hai
30	*ba mươi*	ba muhr·ee
90	*chín mươi*	jín muhr·ee
100	*một trăm*	mạwt chuhm
200	*hai trăm*	hai chuhm
900	*chín trăm*	jín chuhm
1000	*một nghìn* (N)	mạwt ngyìn
	một ngàn (S)	mọt ngaàn
10,000	*mười nghìn* (N)	muhr·eè ngyìn
	mười ngàn (S)	muhr·eè ngaàn
1,000,000	*một triệu*	mạwt chee·ọọ
2,000,000	*hai triệu*	hai chee·ọọ
first	*thứ nhất*	túhr nyúht
second	*thứ hai*	túhr hai

PAPERWORK

name
tên den
nationality
quốc gia gwáwk zaa
address
địa chỉ đee·uh jeẻ
date/place of birth
ngày/nơi sinh ngày/ner·ee sing
sex/gender
giới tính zer·eé díng
passport (number)
(số) hộ chiếu (sáw) hạw jee·oó
visa
thị thực teẹ tụhrk

QUESTION WORDS

Who?
Ái? aí?
What?
Cái gì? ğaí zeè?
What is it?
Cái này là cái gì? ğaí này laà ğaí zeè?
When?
Khi nào? kee nòw?
Where?
Ở đâu? ẻr đoh?
Which?
Cái nào? ğaí nòw?
Why?
Tại sao? taị sow?
How?
Làm sao? laàm sow?

SHOPPING & SERVICES

I'd like to buy ...
Tôi muốn mua ...
doy moo·úhn moo·uh ...
How much is this?
Cái này giá bao nhiêu?
ğaí này zaá bow nyee·oo?
I want to pay in dong.
Tôi muốn trả bằng tiền Việt Nam.
doy moo·úhn chả bùhng đee·ùhn vee·ụht naam
I don't like it.
Tôi không thích nó.
doy kawm tík nó
May I look at it?
Tôi có thể xem được không?
doy ğó tẻ sam đuhr·ẹrk kawm?
I'm just looking.
Tôi chỉ ngắm xem.
doy jeẻ ngúhm sam
It's cheap.
Cái này rẻ.
ğaí này zả
It's too expensive.
Cái này quá mắc.
ğaí này gwaá múhk
I'll take it.
Tôi lấy cái này.
doy láy ğaí này

Do you accept ...?
Bạn có nhận ... không?
baạn kó nyụhn ... kawm?
credit cards
thẻ tín dụng tả dín zụm
travellers cheques
xét du lịch sát zoo lịk

more *nhiều hơn* nyee·oò hern
less *ít hơn* ít hern
smaller *nhỏ hơn* nyỏ hern
bigger *lớn hơn* lérn hern

I'm looking for ...
Tôi tìm ...
doy dìm ...
a bank
ngân hàng nguhn haàng
the church
nhà thờ nyaà tèr
the city centre
trung tâm thành phố chum duhm taàng fáw
the ... embassy
sự quan ... sụr gwaan ...
the hospital
nhà thương nyaà tuhr·erng
my hotel
khách sạn của tôi kaák saạn ğoỏ·uh doy
the market
chợ jẹr
the museum
viện bảo tàng vee·ụhn bỏw daàng
the police
cảnh sát ğaảng saát
the post office
bưu điện buhr·oo đee·ụhn
a public phone
phòng điện thoại fòm đee·ụhn twaị
a restaurant
nhà hàng nyaà haàng
a public toilet
phòng vệ sinh fòm vẹ sing
tourist office
văn phòng hướng dẫn du lịch vuhn fòm huhr·érng zũhn zoo lịk

TIME & DATES

What time is it?
Mấy giờ rồi? máy zèr zòy?
It's (8) o'clock.
Bây giờ là (tám) giờ. bay zèr laà (dúhm) zèr
When?
Khi nào? kee nòw?
now
bây giờ bay zèr
in the morning
sáng saáng
in the afternoon
chiều jee·oò
in the evening
tối dóy
today
hôm nay hawm nay
tomorrow
ngày mai ngày mai

Monday	*thứ hai*	túhr hai
Tuesday	*thứ ba*	túhr baa
Wednesday	*thứ tư*	túhr duhr
Thursday	*thứ năm*	túhr nuhm
Friday	*thứ sáu*	túhr sóh
Saturday	*thứ bảy*	túhr bảy
Sunday	*chủ nhật*	jỏo nhuht

January	*tháng giêng*	taáng zee·uhng
February	*tháng hai*	taáng hai
March	*tháng ba*	taáng baa
April	*tháng tư*	taáng tuhr
May	*tháng năm*	taáng nuhm
June	*tháng sáu*	taáng sóh
July	*tháng bảy*	taáng bảy
August	*tháng tám*	taáng dúhm
September	*tháng chín*	taáng jín
October	*tháng mười*	taáng muhr·eè
November	*tháng mười một*	taáng muhr·eè mạwt
December	*tháng mười hai*	taáng muhr·eè hai

TRANSPORT

Public Transport

What time does the (first)... leave/arrive?
Chuyến ... (sớm nhất) chạy lúc mấy giờ?
jwee·úhn ... (sérm nyúht) jạy lúp máy zèr?
boat
tàu/thuyền dòw/twee·ùhn
bus
xe buýt sa beét
plane
máy bay máy bay
train
xe lửa sa lủhr·uh

I'd like a ... ticket.
Tôi muốn vé ...
doy moo·úhn vá ...
one way
đi một chiều đee mạt jee·oò
return
khứ hồi kúhr haw·eè
1st class
hạng nhất haạng nyúht
2nd class
hạng nhì haạng nyeè

I want to go to ...
Tôi muốn đi ...
doy moo·úhn đee ...
How long does the trip take?
Chuyến đi sẽ mất bao lâu?
jwee·úhn đee sã múht bow loh?
What time does it arrive?
Mấy giờ đến?
máy zèr đén?
The train has been cancelled.
Chuyến xe lửa bị hủy bỏ.
jwee·úhn sa lủhr·uh beẹ hweẻ bỏ

the first
đầu tiên đòw dee·uhn
the last
cuối cùng goo·eé gùm
bus station
bến xe bén sa
ticket office
phòng bán vé fòm baán vá
timetable
thời biểu ter·eè beé·oo
sleeping berth
giường ngủ zùhr·erng ngoỏ
railway station
ga xe lửa gaa sa lủhr·uh

Private Transport

I'd like to hire a ...
Tôi muốn thuê ...(N) doy moo·úhn twe ...
Tôi muốn mướn ...(S) doy moo·úhn muhr·érn ...
car
xe hơi sa her·ee
motorbike
xe moto sa mo·to
bicycle
xe đạp sa đạp
cyclo (pedicab)
xe xích lô sa sík law

LANGUAGE

Is this the road to ...?
Con đường nầy có dẫn đến ...?
ğon đuhr·èrng này ğó zũhn đén ...?
How many kilometres to ...?
... cách đây bao nhiêu ki-lô-mét?
... ğaák đay bow nyee·oo kee·law·mét?
Where's a service station?
Trạm xăng ở đâu?
chaạm suhng ẻr doh?
Please fill it up.
Làm ơn đổ đầy bình.
laàm ern đỏ đày bìng
I'd like ... litres.
Tôi muốn ... lít.
doy moo·úhn ... léet

diesel
dầu diesel zòh dee·sel
leaded petrol
dầu xăng có chì zòh suhng ğó jeè
unleaded petrol
dầu xăng zòh suhng
highway
xa lộ saa lạw
National Highway 1
Quốc Lộ 1 gwáwk lạw mạwt
map
bản đồ baản đàw

(How long) Can I park here?
Chúng tôi có thể đậu xe được (bao lâu)?
júm doy ğó tẻ dọh sa đuhr·ẹrk (bow loh)?
Where do I pay?
Trả tiền ở đâu?
chaả dee·ùhn ẻr đoh?
I need a mechanic.
Chúng tôi cần thợ sửa xe.
júm doy ğùhn tẹr sůhr·uh sa
The car/motorbike has broken down (at ...)
Xe bị hư (tại ...).
sa beẹ huhr (daị ...)
The car/motorbike won't start.
(Xe hơi/Xe moto) không đề được.
(sa her·ee/sa mo·to) kawm đè đuhr·ẹrk
I have a flat tyre.
Bánh xe tôi bị xì.
baáng sa doy beẹ seè
I've run out of petrol.
Tôi bị hết dầu/xăng.
doy beẹ hét zòh/suhng

TRAVEL WITH CHILDREN

Is there a/an ...?
Ở đây có ...? ẻr đay ğó ...?
I need a/an ...
Tôi cần ... doy ğùhn ...
baby change room
phòng thay quần áo fòm tay gwùhn ów
cho em bé jo am bá
car baby seat
ghế ngồi trong xe gé ngòy chom sa
cho em bé jo am bá
child-minding service
dịch vụ giữ trẻ em zịk voọ zũhr chả am
children's menu
thực đơn cho trẻ em tụhrk đern jo chả am
disposable nappies/diapers
tã lót daã lót
(English-speaking) babysitter
người giữ trẻ em nguhr·eè zũhr chả am
nói tiếng Anh nóy díng aang
highchair
ghế cao cho em bé gé kow jo am bá
potty
bô cho trẻ em bo jo chả am
stroller
xe đẩy cho em bé sa đay jo am bá

Do you mind if I breastfeed here?
Xin lỗi tôi có thể cho con tôi bú ở đây không?
sin lõy doy ğó tẻ jo ğon doy bóo ér đay kawm?
Are children allowed?
Trẻ em có được phép vào không?
chả am ğó đuhr·ẹrk fáp vòw kawm?

HILL TRIBE LANGUAGES

The task of neatly classifying the different hill tribe groups of Vietnam is not an easy one. Ethnologists typically classify the Montagnards by linguistic distinction and commonly refer to three main groups (which further splinter into vast and quite complex sub-groupings). The Austro-Asian family includes the Viet-Muong, Mon-Khmer, Tay-Tai and Meo-Dzao language groups; the Austronesian family includes Malayo-Polynesian languages; and the Sino-Tibetan family encompasses the Chinese and Tibeto-Burmese language groups. In addition, within a single spoken language there are often myriad dialectical variations.

The following words and phrases should prove useful when visiting members of the larger Vietnamese hill tribes. If you're planning on spending a lot of time within hill tribe areas, consider taking Lonely Planet's *Hill Tribes Phrasebook* with you. For more information on hill tribes and the areas they inhabit see p72.

TAY

Also known as the Ngan, Pa Di, Phen, Thu Lao and Tho, the Tay belong to the Tay-Thai language group.

Hello. *Pá prama.*
Goodbye. *Pá paynó.*
Yes. *Mi.*
No. *Boomi.*
Thank you. *Đay fon.*
What's your name? *Ten múng le xãng ma?*
Where are you from? *Mu'ng du' te là ma?*
How much is this? *Ău ni ki lai tiên?*

H'MONG

The H'mong are also known as Meo, Mieu, Mong Do (White H'mong), Mong Du (Black H'mong), Mong Lenh (Flower H'mong), Mong Si (Red H'mong). They belong to the H'mong-Dzao language group, but their spoken language resembles Mandarin Chinese.

Hello. *Ti nấu/Caó cu.*
Goodbye. *Caó mun'g chè.*
Yes. *Có mua.*
No. *Chúi muá.*
Thank you. *Ô chờ.*
What's your name? *Caó be hua chan'g?*
Where are you from? *Caó nhao từ tuả?*
How much is this? *Pổ chố chá?*

DZAO

Also known as Coc Mun, Coc Ngang, Dai Ban, Diu Mien, Dong, Kim Mien, lan Ten, Lu Gang, Tieu Ban, Trai and Xa, this tribe belongs to the Mong Dzao language group.

Hello. *Puang tọi.*
Goodbye. *Puang tọi.*
Yes. *Mái.*
No. *Mái mái.*
Thank you. *Tỡ dun.*
What's your name? *Mang nhi búa chiên nay?*
Where are you from? *May hải đo?*
How much is this? *Pchiả nhăng?*

Also available from Lonely Planet:
Vietnamese Phrasebook and *Hill Tribes Phrasebook*

Glossary

For food and drink terms, see Eat Your Words on p53. For information on the Vietnamese language, and pronunciation, see the Language chapter (p505).

A Di Da – Buddha of the Past
Agent Orange – toxic, carcinogenic chemical herbicide used extensively during the American War
am duong – Vietnamese equivalent of Yin and Yang
Amerasians – children borne of unions between Asian women and US servicemen during the American War
American War – Vietnamese name for what is also known as the 'Vietnam War'
Annam – old Chinese name for Vietnam, meaning 'Pacified South'
Annamites – term with derogatory overtones used by the French to describe the Vietnamese
ao dai – Vietnamese national dress worn by women
apsaras – heavenly maidens
arhat – anyone who has attained nirvana
ARVN – Army of the Republic of Vietnam (former South Vietnamese army)

ba mu – midwife. There are 12 'midwives', each of whom teaches newborns a different skill necessary for the first year of life: smiling, sucking, lying on their stomachs and so forth
Ba Tay – a term used to refer to Western women, meaning 'Mrs Westerner'
ban – mountainous village
bang – congregation (in the Chinese community)
bar om – literally 'holding' bars associated with the sex industry; also known as 'karaoke om'
Black Flags – a semi-autonomous army of Chinese, Vietnamese and hill-tribe troops
bo de – Bodhi tree, or pipal tree
bonze – Vietnamese Buddhist monk
buu dien – post office

cai luong – Vietnamese modern theatre
Cao Daism – indigenous Vietnamese religion
cay son – tree from whose resin lacquer is made
Cham – ethnic minority descended from the people of *Champa*
cham cui – acupuncture
Champa – Hindu kingdom dating from the late 2nd century AD
Charlie – nickname for the Viet Cong, used by US soldiers
chua – pagoda
chu nho – standard Chinese characters (script)
Cochinchina – the southern part of Vietnam during the French-colonial era
com pho – rice and rice-noodle soup; common sign on restaurants
cong – gong
corbeille à bec – wooden staff with a crayon attached for writing messages from spirits
cowboys – motorbike-riding thieves
crachin – fine drizzle
crémaillère – cog railway
cu ly – fern stems used to stop bleeding; also known as *kim mao cau tich*
cyclo – pedicab or bicycle rickshaw

Dai The Chi Bo Tat – an assistant of *A Di Da*
dan bau – single-stringed zither that generates an astounding magnitude of tones
dan tranh – 16-stringed zither
danh de – illegal numbers game
den – temple
Di Lac Buddha – Buddha of the Future
dikpalaka – gods of the directions of the compass
dinh – communal meeting hall
DMZ – the misnamed Demilitarised Zone, a strip of land that once separated North and South Vietnam
doi moi – economic restructuring or reform, started in Vietnam in 1986
dong – natural caves; also Vietnamese currency
dong chi – comrade
do son – drums
DRV – Democratic Republic of Vietnam (the old North Vietnam)

ecocide – term used to describe the devastating effects of the herbicides sprayed over Vietnam during the American War

feng shui – see *phong thuy*
flechette – experimental US weapon; an artillery shell containing thousands of darts
fu – talisman
Funan – see *Oc-Eo*

garuda – Sanskrit term for griffin-like sky beings who feed on *naga*
ghe – long, narrow rowboat
giay phep di lai – internal travel permit
gom – ceramics

hai dang – lighthouse
han viet – Sino-Vietnamese literature

hat boi – classical theatre in the south
hat cheo – Vietnamese popular theatre
hat tuong – classical theatre in the north
hieu – filial piety
ho ca – aquarium
Ho Chi Minh Trail – route used by the North Vietnamese Army and Viet Cong to move supplies to guerrillas in the South
ho khau – residence permit needed for everything (eg school, employment, land ownership, vehicle registration, home and business ownership)
Hoa – ethnic-Chinese, one of the largest single minority groups in Vietnam
hoi – 60-year period (used in calendars)
hoi quan – Chinese congregational assembly halls
Honda Dream – most popular model of Honda motor-scooter sold in Vietnam
Honda om – motorbike taxi, also called *xe om*
huong – perfume
huyen – rural district

Indochina – Vietnam, Cambodia and Laos. The name derives from Indian and Chinese influences.

kala-makara – sea-monster god
kalan – a religious sanctuary
ken doi – musical instrument made from two seven-holed bamboo flutes
khach san – hotel
Khmer – ethnic-Cambodians
Khong Tu – Confucius
kich noi – spoken drama
kim mao cau tich – fern used to stop bleeding in traditional Chinese medicine; also known as *cu ly*
Kinh – Vietnamese language
Kuomintang – Chinese Nationalist Party, also known as KMT. The KMT controlled China between 1925 and 1949 until defeated by the communists.
ky – 12-year cycle (used in calendars)

lang – hereditary noble family who rules the communal land and collects the benefits of labour and tax through its use by locals
lang tam – tombs
li xi – lucky money distributed during the Vietnamese Lunar New Year
liberation – 1975 takeover of the South by the North; what most foreigners call 'reunification'
Lien Xo – literally, Soviet Union; used to call attention to a foreigner
linga – stylised phallus which represents the Hindu god Shiva

MAAG – Military Assistance Advisory Group, set up to instruct troops receiving US weapons on how to use them
mai son – lacquer
mandapa – meditation hall
mang dang – bitter bamboo-shoot soup
manushi-buddha – Buddha who appeared in human form
mat cua – 'door eyes', supposed to protect the residents of a house from harm
MIA – missing in action
mihrab – niche in a mosque wall indicating the direction of Mecca
minbar – feature of mosques
moi – derogatory word meaning 'savages', mostly used by ethnic-Vietnamese to describe hill-tribe people
Montagnards – term meaning highlanders or mountain people, used to refer to the ethnic minorities who inhabit remote areas of Vietnam
muong – large village unit made up of *quel* (small stilt-houses)

naga – Sanskrit term for a mythical serpent being with divine powers; often depicted forming a kind of shelter over the Buddha
nam phai – for men
napalm – jellied petrol (gasoline) dropped and lit from aircraft; used by US forces with devastating effect during the *American War*
NGO – nongovernment organisation
nha hang – restaurant
nha khach – hotel; guesthouse
nha nghi – guesthouse
nha rong – large stilt house, used by hill tribes as a kind of community centre
nha tro – dormitory
NLF – National Liberation Front; official name for the VC
nom – Vietnamese script, used between the 10th and early 20th centuries
nu phai – for women
nui – mountain
nuoc mam – fish sauce, added to almost every main dish in Vietnam
NVA – North Vietnamese Army

Oc-Eo – Indianised kingdom (also called Funan) in southern Vietnam between the 1st and 6th centuries
Ong Bon – Guardian Spirit of Happiness and Virtue
Ong Tay – a term used to refer to Western men, meaning 'Mr Westerner'
Orderly Departure Program (ODP) – carried out under the auspices of the United Nations High Commissioner for Refugees (UNHCR), designed to allow orderly resettlement of Vietnamese political refugees
OSS – US Office of Strategic Services; the predecessor of the CIA

pagoda – traditionally an eight-sided Buddhist tower, but in Vietnam the word is commonly used to denote a temple

Phoenix Program – also known as Operation Phoenix; a controversial program run by the CIA, aimed at eliminating VC cadres by assassination, capture or defection
phong thuy – literally, 'wind and water'; used to describe geomancy. Also known by its Chinese name, feng shui.
piastre – the local currency in the days of French Indochina
pneumatographie – Cao Dai ritual in which a blank slip of paper is sealed in an envelope and hung above an altar. When it is taken down, there is a message on the paper.
Politburo – Political Bureau; about a dozen members overseeing the Party's day-to-day functioning with the power to issue directives to the government
POW – prisoner of war
PRG – Provisional Revolutionary Government, the temporary Communist government set up by the *VC* in the South. It existed from 1969 to 1976.

quan – urban district
Quan Cong – Chinese God of War
quan lai – mandarins
Quan The Am Bo Tat – Goddess of Mercy
quel – small stilt-house hamlets
quoc am – modern Vietnamese literature
quoc ngu – Latin-based phonetic alphabet in which Vietnamese is written

rap – cinema
Revolutionary Youth League – first Marxist group in Vietnam and predecessor of the Communist Party
roi can – conventional puppetry
roi nuoc – water puppetry
rong – see *nha rong*
RVN – Republic of Vietnam (the old South Vietnam)

salangane – swiftlet
sao – wooden flute
sao la – antelopelike creature
shakti – feminine manifestation of Shiva
social evils – campaign to prevent evil ideas from the West 'polluting' Vietnamese society
song – river
SRV – Socialist Republic of Vietnam (Vietnam's official name)
Strategic Hamlets Program – programme (by South Vietnam and the USA) of forcibly moving peasants into fortified villages to deny the *VC* bases of support
sung – fig tree

Tam Giao – literally, 'triple religion'; Confucianism, Taoism and Buddhism fused over time with popular Chinese beliefs and ancient Vietnamese animism
Tao – the Way; the essence of which all things are made
Tet – Vietnamese Lunar New Year
thai cuc quyen – Vietnamese for t'ai chi
Thich Ca Buddha – the historical Buddha Sakyamuni, whose real name was Siddhartha Gautama
Thien Hau Thanh Mau – Goddess of the Sea and Protector of Fishermen and Sailors
thong nhat – reunification, also a common term for the *Reunification Express* train
thung chai – gigantic round wicket baskets sealed with pitch; used as rowboats
thuoc bac – Chinese medicine
to rung – large bamboo xylophone
toc hanh – express bus
Tonkin – the northern part of Vietnam during the French-colonial era; also the name of a body of water in the north (Tonkin Gulf)
trong com – cylindrical drums
truyen khau – traditional oral literature
tu sat – dominoes

UNHCR – UN High Commissioner for Refugees

VC – Viet Cong or Vietnamese Communists
Viet Kieu – overseas Vietnamese
Viet Minh – League for the Independence of Vietnam, a nationalistic movement that fought the Japanese and French but later became Communist-dominated
VNQDD – Viet Nam Quoc Dan Dang; largely middle-class nationalist party
vo binh dinh – traditional martial art performed with a bamboo stick

xang – petrol
xe dap loi – wagon pulled by a bicycle
xe Honda loi – wagon pulled by a motorbike
xe lam – tiny three-wheeled trucks used for short-haul passenger and freight transport
xe loi – wagon pulled by a motorbike in the Mekong Delta region
xeo – rice wine
xe om – motorbike taxi, also called *Honda om*
xich lo – *cyclo*, from the French *cyclo-pousse*
xo so – state lottery

yang – genie

Behind the Scenes

THIS BOOK

This is the 9th edition of *Vietnam*. Nick Ray was the coordinating author and he was skilfully assisted by Peter Dragicevich and Regis St Louis. Nick, Peter and Regis worked with text from *Vietnam 8* that was prepared by Nick Ray and Wendy Yanagihara. *Vietnam 7* was researched by Mason Florence and Virginia Jealous. The Food & Drink chapter was written by Nick, with text from *World Food Vietnam* by Richard Sterling. Austin Bush supplied wonderful images for the Food & Drink colour chapter.

This guidebook was commissioned in Lonely Planet's Melbourne office, and produced by the following:

Commissioning Editor Kalya Ryan
Coordinating Editors Jeanette Wall, Justin Flynn
Coordinating Cartographer Anthony Phelan
Coordinating Layout Designer Jim Hsu
Managing Editor Suzannah Shwer
Managing Cartographer Julie Sheridan
Assisting Editors Peter Cruttenden, Andrea Dobbin, Emma Gilmour, Gina Tsarouhas
Assisting Cartographers Ross Butler, Owen Eszeki, Tony Fankhauser, Andy Rojas
Cover Designer Liz Lindsay
Language Content Coordinator Quentin Frayne
Project Manager Chris Love

Thanks to David Burnett, Sally Darmody, Ben Handicott, Nicole Hansen, David Kemp, Craig Kilburn, Yvonne Kirk, Chi Van Nguyen, Darren O'Connell, Stephanie Pearson, Averil Robertson, Sarah Sloane, Celia Wood

THANKS FROM THE AUTHORS

NICK RAY

So many people have been instrumental in helping to put this book together. First thanks to my wonderful wife, Kulikar Sotho, who has joined me on many a trip to Vietnam, sharing saddles and sore backsides the length and breadth of the country. Thanks also to our wonderful young son Mr J for coming up to Hanoi and Halong Bay to explore. Thanks to Mum and Dad for the support and encouragement that carried me to faraway lands from a young age.

Many people in Hanoi and the north were very helpful along the way. In no particular order, many thanks to Vinh, Linh, Thanh, Dida, Tim, Digby, Dan, Marcus, Travis, Mike, Kurt, Ronan, Khanh, Fredo, Linh, Huong and Thuan.

A big thanks also to Le Van Sinh for all the effort he put into early editions of this book and a major thanks to Mason Florence for all his good work on several incarnations of this book. Thanks to my co-authors Peter and Regis for all their work in other parts of Vietnam. And a big thanks to the in-house team at Lonely Planet who carry this from conception to reality. Finally, thanks to all the readers who have written in: you're all part of the big picture.

PETER DRAGICEVICH

Many thanks to the travellers who generously swapped their stories on the road – Cherie Earles, Mark Forrest, Laryssa Nyrvana, Guy Fixsen, Romy Colleran, Maria Franke, Ben Whitburn, Elmer Jacobs, Valesca Meist, Jason Bryce, Jo Schmidt, Cameron Mellor, Vanessa Lefort, Chris Connaughton and the crazy London karaoke crew (Lee, Michelle, Lauren, Nikki and Catherine). Extra special thanks to Ross Bernays, Bui Thi Khanh Chieu, Ms Binh, Kimmy Le, Long Thanh and Barbara Dawson for their insider's insight. Lots of love to my generous benefactors Ben Preston, Adrienne Wong Preston, Tania Wong and Bob Dragicevich, and Braith Bamkin for the travel tips.

REGIS ST LOUIS

Many kind locals helped with recommendations and tips on Saigon and the Mekong Delta. I'd especially like to thank Sinh for his considerable expertise and guidance; Nghi and Si, who proved invaluable guides and fun travelling companions in the Mekong; and Thinh, for his kindness at seeing me back to Vung Tau when my motorbike died. Heartfelt congratulations go to Linh, who invited me to his wedding party. I also enjoyed drinks and Vietnam talk with Nick Ray, Robert Reid, David Relin and others in Hanoi, Saigon and southern parts of Vietnam. Many thanks to Cassandra for her continued support.

OUR READERS

Many thanks to the travellers who used the last edition and wrote to us with helpful hints, useful advice and interesting anecdotes:

A Benjamin Abbott, Lachlan Abbott, Michale Ae, Nick Ainsworth, Beck Alan, Patricia Alberth, Kimberley Aldrich, Wolf & Nancy

Ametsbichler, Jerome Amin, Kelly Andrews, Ray Anastas, Angelina Andreoni, Sean Arnold, Marie Arsenin, Bettina Augeneder, Ismail Azizlerli **B** Matt Bailey, Linda Baird, Germaine Bakker, Robert Baldwin, Jill Ballantine, Paul Barker, Hilary Barker, Peter Barry, Gil Barzilay, Lara Baxter, Keith Baybayan, Angeal Bayley, Jeff Beard, Iain Beat, Severine Beaudoin, Severine Beaudoin, R Beck, Julianne Becker, Rob Bell, Robert Bennett, Richard Benton, Emily Besley, Har Beurskens, Jay Bharadia, Aldo Biondi, Clint & Carly Blackbourn, Jarni Blakkarly, Christel Bockting, Avril Boland, Brian Bongers, Gijs Boot, Alexander Bort, Roni Bossin, M Bowman, K Braat, Beau Bracken, Bernadette Brady, Victor Braun, Adam Bray, Sofie Bredberg, Emmett Breen, Margaret Brennan, Marcus Bridle, Suzanne Brierley, Victoria Brookes, N Brookes, Anna Brooks, Wendy Brown, Claudia Brune, Dam Bui, Bjorn Bulen, Michael Bulow, Kim Bulsink, Sue Buparai, Jayne Burke, Richard Burrows, Joanna Bushill **C** Jennie Caddick, Sharon Calder, Carrie Callagher, Thomas Cambier, Ken Campbell, Anna Canton, Mike Carden, Jack Carmenta, Kylie Carter, Richard Cassidy, Laurel Cavenagh, Berthouly Cecile, Graham Challender, Lorelle Champion, Cherilene Chan, Dave Chandler, Elise Chandler, Peter Chang, Selina Chu, Lefran Ciofalo, Samantha Claasen, Lauras Claire, Robyn Clarke, Nina Codling, Fiona Cole, Michael Collin, Gregory Collins, Alexandra Condellis, Matthew Condie, Mary & Jez Cowley, Patrick Cowsill, Annette & Paul Crabtree, Eddy Crescent, James Cryan, Judi Cunliffe, William Cunynghame, Jesse Czaja **D** Danny Dang, Amit Dankwerth, Ross Davidson, Neil Davidson, John Davies, Matthew Davis, Neil Davis, Robin Day, Joy Day, Katy Day, Cynthia Day, Hugo De Baaij, Rudolf De Blij, Irene De Both, Royce De Melo, Klaus Deaskowitsch, Jeroen Decuyper, Brecht Dejong, Andrea & Jurrian Dekkers, Antoine Delaplace, Eleanor Demuth, Johan & Maya Despeghel, Robert Devlin, Caroline Dherbey, Niels Dieleman, Aaron Dingle, Peter Divine, Maggi Domone, Micheline Don, Stephan Dorrenberg, Saloni Dosoruth, Heather Douglas, Eric & Laurence Ducher, Joshuah Duchesne, Gertjan Duiker, Olivia Dunne, Trinh Duong, Hung Duong, Julie Duvivier, Andrew Duy, Daphne Dyce **E** Hannah Evans, Charlie Earl, Alfonso Echazarra, Mary Edgerton, Wendy Edmonds, Danielle Efford, Tracey Egan, Mike Eglesfield, Peter Elgaard, Brendan Elliot, Phil Elliott, Dianne Ellmers, William Evans **F** Paddy Fahy, Philipp Farenholtz, Mark Fay, David Fenig, Sue Fenn, Karianne Fieldus, Bernd Finkenwirth, Brian Finnegan, Andy Fish, Petra Fleck, Matthias Fleischer, Wilbert & Liesbeth Florack, Jana Fluegge, Rob Flynn, Paul Foey, Esther Folkers, Alison Foulis, Emma Freeman, Vanessa Fries, Ying Fu **G** Andy Gallop, Peter Garratt, Steve Garvey, Maria Gay, Eitan Geft, Michael Geluardi, May Gent, Daniel Gerster, Sue Gibbins, Ani Gibson, Christine Gibson, Anna Giertz, Sibeal Ginnea, Danielle Glover, Gunter Glockle, Peter & Andrea Gnepf, Michael Golden, Emilie Goldstein, Gema Gonzalez, Patricia Gonzalez Anton-Pacheco, Darrell Gorsuch, Justin Goulding, G Gowens, Eileen Grant, Michelle Grant, Brian Grant, Nic Greaves, Mark Green, Sally Greenberg, Oliver Gressieker, Kevin Griffith, Malou Gronloh, Beate Gross, Coralyn Gunton, Fernando Gurtubay, Lianne Gutcher, Phil Gwynne **H** Le Hong Ha, Rupert Haag, Jackie Hadel, Bernadette Hadley, Judith Ham, Barry Hameister, Sonja Hanchar, Tom Hannan, Ozi Harari, Kelly Hardwick, Mark Harman, Spike Harms, Carolyn Harrington, Kristen Harvey, Chris Hastings, Karen Hastings, Knut Per Hasund, Amanda Hatzistamatis, Elo Haugas, Mark Havery, Regan Hawkins, Maggie Hayes, Sarah & Jonathan Haynes, John Hazen, Mark Heald, Tricia Heard, Lee Heath, Cameron Heath, Dan Hellier, Eva Helmig, Michelle Heming, Tim Hendley, Megan Henry, Jasper Hermans, Colin Hewens, Wendy Heywood, Pete Hiam, Grahame Hill, Peter Hill, Roland Hiltmann, Sonja Hippold, Bill Hoad, Terry Hogan, Spencer Hogg, Margaret Holding, Elvira Honey, Azam Hossain, Andrew Houston, J Houtman, Denis Howe, Tom Hughes, Simone Huigen, Ton-Tijn Hulleman, Lyn Hulston, Ray Hunt, Austin & Isabel Hutcheon **I** Suzanne Ijsselmuiden, Susan Ingram, Yiannis Ioannou **J** Ralpha Jacobson, Julian James, Arif Janmohamed, Maurice Jeukens, Morten & Per Joergensen, Anna-Karin Johansson, Amy Johnson, Eric Johnson, Bruce Johnston, Peter Jones, David Jones, Christine Ju, David & Wendy Justice **K** Ton & Irene Kaarsgaren, Gerard & Jeanette Kamberg, Peter Kastan, Judith Katzeff, Fred Kauffmann, Mary Kavanagh, Stephanie Kays, Eimear Keane, Hugo Kearney, Mike Kehoe, Melanie Kelleher, Jonathan Kelly, Justin Kempe, Simon Kennedy, Gary Kepler, Jorg Kerbus, Yafa Kfir, Paul Khoo, Ori Kidron, Uwe Killer, Peter & Sheereen Kindler, June King, Adam King, Lisa Klavans, Henk Klijn, Frans Knapen, Silvia Knaus, Pat Knox, Allan Jones, Laura Koenders, Magdalena Korb, Marijke Kors, Jochem Kramer, Manfred Krautter, Lars Kroon, Rob Krutzen **L** Marcus L'Estrange, Robert La Bua, Kim Lan, Susanne Lang, Therese Lanthier-Wallace, Jill Lapato, Mariëlle Lapidaire, Susan Larson, Monica Larsson, Paul Laverty, David Lawson, Loan Le, Verne

THE LONELY PLANET STORY

The story begins with a classic travel adventure: Tony and Maureen Wheeler's 1972 journey across Europe and Asia to Australia. There was no useful information about the overland trail then, so Tony and Maureen published the first Lonely Planet guidebook to meet a growing need.

From a kitchen table, Lonely Planet has grown to become the largest independent travel publisher in the world, with offices in Melbourne (Australia), Oakland (USA) and London (UK). Today Lonely Planet guidebooks cover the globe. There is an ever-growing list of books and information in a variety of media. Some things haven't changed. The main aim is still to make it possible for adventurous individuals to get out there – to explore and better understand the world.

At Lonely Planet we believe individuals can make a positive contribution to the countries they visit – if they respect their host communities and spend their money wisely. Every year 5% of company profit is donated to charities around the world.

SEND US YOUR FEEDBACK

We love to hear from travellers – your comments keep us on our toes and help make our books better. Our well-travelled team reads every word on what you loved or loathed about this book. Although we cannot reply individually to postal submissions, we always guarantee that your feedback goes straight to the appropriate authors, in time for the next edition. Each person who sends us information is thanked in the next edition – and the most useful submissions are rewarded with a free book.

To send us your updates – and find out about Lonely Planet events, newsletters and travel news – visit our award-winning website: **www.lonelyplanet.com/contact**.

Note: we may edit, reproduce and incorporate your comments in Lonely Planet products such as guidebooks, websites and digital products, so let us know if you don't want your comments reproduced or your name acknowledged. For a copy of our privacy policy visit www.lonelyplanet.com/privacy.

Lee, Less Lee, Nancia Leggett, Kathryn Leslie, Nicole Lester, Kenneth Levine, Dianne Lewis, Nathaniel Liberge, Teeng Lim, Cassie Lim, Elisabeth Lin, Anna Lincoln, Bruce Lindsay, Amanda Lo, Charles Locher, Tim & Melissa Locke, David Lofting, Liam Long, Shep & Hiep Lowman, Katherine Luke, Iris Lumetzberger, Martin Lutterjohann, Florian Lutz, Lynley Lysons **M** Alain Macchi, Adrienne Macdonald, Jonathan Mackay, Violeta Madireddi, Benjamin Mahr, Ryan Mai, Cedric Maizieres, Anna Malczyk, Rattan Mangharam, Grant Marjoribanks, Jeremie Martin, Matthew Martin, Warren Mascoll, Oliver Matthews, Trevor Mazzucchelli, Deirdre Mc Grane, Joel Mcconvey, Melanie Mcconville, Brock Mccurdy, Kelly Mcdonald, Raeleen Mckenzie, Dick Mckenzie, Debbie Mclean, Philip Mccluskey, Deann Mcglinchey, Robert Mcguigan, Maureen Mcinroy, Peter Mclay, Benita Meagher, Diane Meissirel, Alexandra Meixner, Noeme Mennes, Jessica Metherell, Cynthia Meurling, Jeong Mi Gyeong, Jeong Mi Gyeong, Mike Milasincic, Andrew Mills, Denise Mitchell, Louis Montana, Hayley Moore, James Moore, Kathy Moore, Mary Moses, Laurissa Muehlich, Daniel Mueller, Christopher Munro, Ezra Murad, Richard Muraszko, Beth Murphy, Patricio Musalem **N** Alexander Naess, David Napier, Marc Nelissen, Telly Ng, Angela Ngan, Kim Ngo, Tammy Nguyen, V Nguyen, Billy Nguyen, Marchand Nicolas, J Nicole, Jason Noble, Tak Nomura, Karolina Norman, Daniel Norton, Hannah Norwood **O** Frank O'Brien, Kerry O'Connor, Greg O'Hern, James Offer, Dax Oliver, Roy Oltmans, Marieke Prommenschenckel, Cathrine Opedal, Uta Orlamünde, Peter Ormond, Stacy Orr, Thomas Osborn **P** Marion Pack, Rorgani Padayachy, George Palmer, Albert Pannell, Riki Parata, Jasmine Pariera, Pedro Pastrano, Pedro Pastrano, Sonia & Dustin Paz, Matthew Peak, Martijn Peereboom, Edward Pennant-Rea, Fiona Pepper, Gemma Perkins, Tom Peters, Anh Pham, Jeffrey Phillips, Robyn Phillips, Paul Phillips, Charles Philpott, Carolyn Picard, Denise Piché, Jodie Pidcock, Isabella Pietrzak, Mikko Planasch, Sue Pola, Mandy Polley, Nicola Poretti, Jane Poulsen, Dean Pratley, Darren Price, Steve Price-Thomas, Ross Pringle, Jamie Proffitt, Vaclav Pscolka **Q** Anne-Marie Quinn, Alby Quinn **R** Andreas Raemisch, Fleur Rake, Alan Ramsdale, Yvonne Rasmussen, Aare Raudsepp, Kate Raynor, Sheilah Rechtschaffer, Ali Rehn, Gordon Reid, David Restall, Jurrian Reurings, Jan Rich, Marlise Richter, Aimee Rizzardo, Alexa Roberts, Heather Roberts, Claire Roche, Rachel Rokach, Gert Roschinski, Kate Rosen, Dana Ross, Dylan Roux, Patrick Rouzé, Steve Roylance, Jenny Rubie, Tomasz Rutkowski **S** Philipp Sadowski, Adrian Sager, Georgia Salpa, Aurelie Salvaire, John Sampson, Kyrin Sandles, Michelle Saville, Scott Schmidt, Sandra Schmitt, Mo Schofield, Ron Scholte, Eric Schopmeyer, Christian Schulz, Paulina Sculli, Mark Secker, Jennifer Segal, Lee Seldon, Patricia Senner, Olly Seviour, Adam Shamoon, Larry Shapiro, Deborah Shepley, Amy Sheppey, Zac Sim, Brett Simchowitz, Chelise Simmons, Reto Sinniger, Megan Sinnott, Rebecca Sizer, Katarina Sjostedt, Maryann Skudar, Gemma Small, Alexander Smeets, Patricia Smiley, Heidi Smith, Sharon Smith, Lauren Smith, Denise Smith, Michael Smith, Scot Smyth, Soeren Soenderby, Kathrin Sonderegger, Ariane St-Louis, Georgina Staley, Kelly Stevenson, Chandler Stewart, John Stockton, Tommy Storm, Daniele Stracca, Ernest Strohmeyer, Jay Strouch, Tunya Struzina, Michael Stubbs, Wendy Suen, Ezra Sumner, Murugesan & Sharmini Suppayyan, Tanya Surridge, Chris Swanicke **T** Hagit Taiber, Tracy Takahashi, Liad Tal, Ka Tam, Kar Tan, Georgia Tarjan, Kristine Tay, Karen Taylor, Gabriel Teoman, Nguyen Thang, Xuan Thanh, Tran Thanh, Michael Thomas, Hans Thorne, Felix Timischl, Daniel Tinsley, Michelle Tobin, Joshua Tokita, David Tomney, Duong Tong, David Toscano, Emerick Toth, Marni Triggs, Lorenzo Trimp, Carley Tucker **U** Maxine Underdown **V** Ronny Van Eenooge, Kristien Van Hese, Wim Van Kuijk, Katleen Verloo, Marcus Vey, Oscar Viberg, Jerome Vincent **W** Xiaojia Wang, Michael Walker, Kevin Wallace, Steve Waller, Michael Waller, Sheryl Walpole, Arthur Walsh, Timothy Waters, Tyler Watts, Donald Webb, Urs Weidermann, Almut Weissbrich, Penny Weitnauer, Sabine Welte, John Westbury, Sara Wick, Manuela Wieser, Sarah Wilcox, Alison Williams, Bruce Williams, Don Williams, Laurence & Hugues Williamson, Greg Winkler, Angelika Winner, Rohan Wittmer, Sue Wooles, Glenn Wortel, Chris Wragg, Ron Wren, James Wright, Pat Wright, Rowan Wyborn **Y** Tianxiong Ye, Robert Young, Patrick Young **Z** Tamara Zeier, George Zych

ACKNOWLEDGMENTS

Many thanks to the following for the use of their content:

Globe on title page ©Mountain High Maps 1993 Digital Wisdom, Inc.

Index

000 Map pages
000 Photograph pages

INDEX

000 Map pages
000 Photograph pages

INDEX

12am
1am
2am
3am
4am
5am
6am
7am
8am
9am
10am
11am
12pm
International Date Line
Mon
Sun
ARCTIC OCEAN
Queen Elizabeth Is (Can)
Ellesmere Is (Can)
9am
Greenland (Denmark)
GREENLAND SEA
11am
NORWEGIAN SEA
BAFFIN BAY
CHUKCHI SEA
BEAUFORT SEA
Banks Is (Can)
Victoria Is (Can)
Baffin Is (Can)
Iceland
NORTH SEA
Russia
Alaska (US)
5am
4am
3am
BERING SEA
GULF OF ALASKA
2am
HUDSON BAY
Canada
6am
LABRADOR SEA
8am
8.30am
7am
United Kingdom
Ireland
NORTH ATLANTIC OCEAN
United States
Azores (Port)
Portugal
Spain
Bermuda (UK)
Morocco
NORTH PACIFIC OCEAN
1am
Midway Is (US)
Canary Is (Sp)
Mexico
GULF OF MEXICO
The Bahamas
Cuba
Haiti
Hawaii (US)
CARIBBEAN SEA
Eastern Caribbean Islands
Mauritania
Mali
12pm
Cape Verde
Guatemala
Nicaragua
Senegal
Burkina Faso
Guinea
Panama
Venezuela
Guyana
Liberia
Ghana
Colombia
Suriname
Galapagos Is (Ecuador)
GULF OF GUINEA
EQUATOR
Kiribati
Ecuador
Samoa
2.30am
8am
Ascension (UK)
Peru
7am
Brazil
9am
Tahiti
French Polynesia (Fr)
Tonga
12am
Cook Is (NZ)
2am
Bolivia
Pitcairn Is (UK)
3.30am
Easter Is (Chile)
SOUTH ATLANTIC OCEAN
1am
Paraguay
Chile
Uruguay
New Zealand
Argentina
Tristan da Cunha (UK)
12.45am
Chatham Is (NZ)
SOUTH PACIFIC OCEAN
Gough Is (UK)
Falkland Is (UK)
South Georgia & South Sandwich Is (UK)
Bouvet Is (Norway)

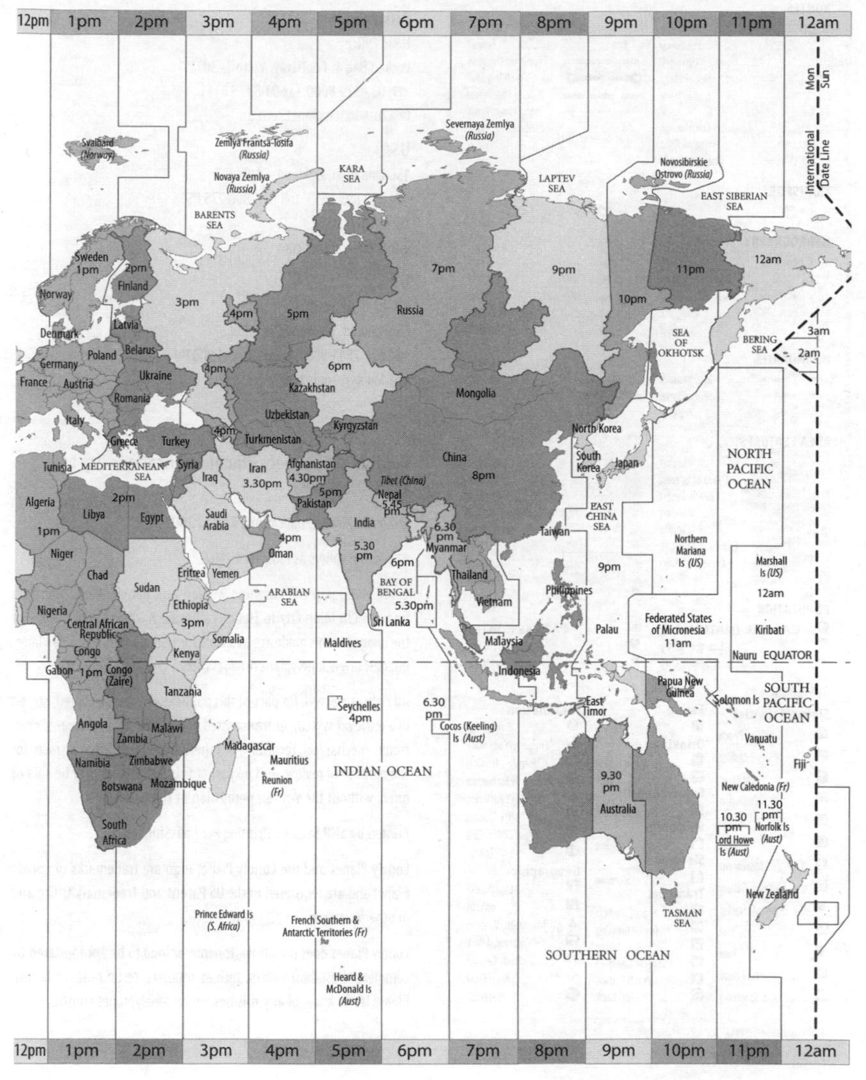
12pm
1pm
2pm
3pm
4pm
5pm
6pm
7pm
8pm
9pm
10pm
11pm
12am
Mon
Sun
International Date Line
Svalbard (Norway)
Zemlya Frantsa-Iosifa (Russia)
Severnaya Zemlya (Russia)
Novaya Zemlya (Russia)
KARA SEA
LAPTEV SEA
Novosibirskie Ostrovo (Russia)
EAST SIBERIAN SEA
BARENTS SEA
Sweden 1pm
2pm
Finland
Norway
3pm
4pm
5pm
7pm
Russia
9pm
10pm
11pm
12am
Denmark
Latvia
Poland
Belarus
Germany
Ukraine
France
Austria
Romania
Italy
Greece
Turkey
4pm
6pm
Kazakhstan
Uzbekistan
Turkmenistan
Kyrgyzstan
Mongolia
SEA OF OKHOTSK
BERING SEA
3am
2am
North Korea
South Korea
Japan
NORTH PACIFIC OCEAN
Tunisia
MEDITERRANEAN SEA
Syria
Iraq
Iran 3.30pm
Afghanistan 4.30pm
5pm
Pakistan
Tibet (China)
China
8pm
Nepal 5.45 pm
Algeria
2pm
Libya
Egypt
Saudi Arabia
India
EAST CHINA SEA
Taiwan
1pm
Niger
Chad
4pm
Oman
5.30 pm
6.30 pm
Myanmar
Northern Mariana Is (US)
Marshall Is (US)
Eritrea
Yemen
Sudan
6pm
Thailand
9pm
12am
ARABIAN SEA
BAY OF BENGAL
Philippines
Nigeria
Ethiopia
3pm
5.30pm
Vietnam
Central African Republic
Sri Lanka
Somalia
Federated States of Micronesia 11am
Palau
Kiribati
Congo
Maldives
Malaysia
Kenya
Nauru
EQUATOR
Gabon
1pm
Congo (Zaire)
Indonesia
Papua New Guinea
Tanzania
SOUTH PACIFIC OCEAN
Solomon Is
Seychelles 4pm
6.30 pm
East Timor
Angola
Malawi
Cocos (Keeling) Is (Aust)
Zambia
Vanuatu
Madagascar
Namibia
Zimbabwe
Mauritius
Fiji
INDIAN OCEAN
Mozambique
Reunion (Fr)
9.30 pm
Botswana
Australia
New Caledonia (Fr)
11.30 pm
10.30 pm
Norfolk Is (Aust)
South Africa
Lord Howe Is (Aust)
New Zealand
Prince Edward Is (S. Africa)
French Southern & Antarctic Territories (Fr)
TASMAN SEA
SOUTHERN OCEAN
Heard & McDonald Is (Aust)

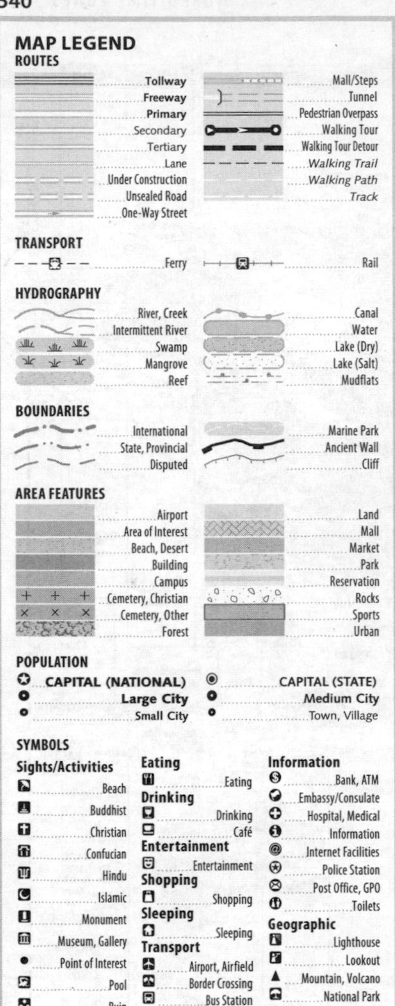

LONELY PLANET OFFICES

Australia
Head Office
Locked Bag 1, Footscray, Victoria 3011
☎ 03 8379 8000, fax 03 8379 8111
talk2us@lonelyplanet.com.au

USA
150 Linden St, Oakland, CA 94607
☎ 510 893 8555, toll free 800 275 8555
fax 510 893 8572
info@lonelyplanet.com

UK
72–82 Rosebery Ave,
Clerkenwell, London EC1R 4RW
☎ 020 7841 9000, fax 020 7841 9001
go@lonelyplanet.co.uk

Published by Lonely Planet Publications Pty Ltd
ABN 36 005 607 983

Cover photograph: A laughing woman and her child ride the train from Ho Chi Minh City to Hanoi, Catherine Karnow/Corbis. Many of the images in this guide are available for licensing from Lonely Planet Images: www.lonelyplanetimages.com.

Printed by SNP Security Printing Pte Ltd, Singapore